GARDNER'S

ART

THROUGH THE

AGES

GARDNER'S
ART
through the
AGES

A GLOBAL HISTORY

VOLUME II

FIFTEENTH EDITION

FRED S. KLEINER

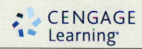

CENGAGE
Learning®

Australia • Brazil • Mexico • Singapore • United Kingdom • United States

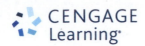

**Gardner's Art through the Ages:
A Global History, Fifteenth Edition, Volume II**
Fred S. Kleiner

Product Director: Monica Eckman

Product Manager: Sharon Adams Poore

Content Developer: Rachel Harbour

Associate Content Developer: Erika Hayden

Product Assistant: Rachael Bailey

Media Developer: Chad Kirchner

Marketing Manager: Jillian Borden

Senior Content Project Manager: Lianne Ames

Senior Art Director: Cate Rickard Barr

Manufacturing Planner: Sandee Milewski

IP Analyst: Jessica Elias

IP Project Manager: Farah Fard

Production Service and Layout: Dovetail
    Publishing Services

Compositor: Cenveo® Publisher Services

Text Designer: Frances Baca

Cover Designer: Mark Fox, Design is Play

Cover Image: Photography © 2011 Museum of
    Fine Arts, Boston, 99.22

© 2016, 2013, 2009 Cengage Learning

WCN: 01-100-101

For product information and technology assistance, contact us at
Cengage Learning Customer & Sales Support, 1-800-354-9706

For permission to use material from this text or product,
submit all requests online at **www.cengage.com/permissions**.
Further permissions questions can be emailed to
permissionrequest@cengage.com.

Library of Congress Control Number: 2014943688

Volume II:
ISBN: 978-1-285-83939-4

Cengage Learning
20 Channel Center Street
Boston, MA 02210
USA

Cengage Learning is a leading provider of customized learning solutions with office locations around the globe, including Singapore, the United Kingdom, Australia, Mexico, Brazil, and Japan. Locate your local office at **www.cengage.com/global**.

Cengage Learning products are represented in Canada by Nelson Education, Ltd.

To learn more about Cengage Learning Solutions, visit **www.cengage.com**.

Purchase any of our products at your local college store or at our preferred online store **www.cengagebrain.com**.

Printed in the United States of America
Print Number: 01   Print Year: 2014

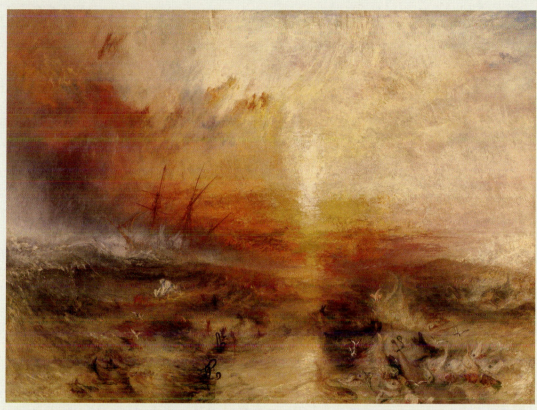

JOSEPH MALLORD WILLIAM TURNER, *The Slave Ship* (*Slavers Throwing Overboard the Dead and Dying, Typhoon Coming On*), 1840. Oil on canvas, 2' 11$\frac{1}{4}$" × 4'. Museum of Fine Arts, Boston (Henry Lillie Pierce Fund).

The first painters, who covered the walls and ceilings of the caves of France and Spain beginning around 30,000 years ago, chose animals and occasionally humans as their exclusive subjects. The first landscapes appeared many thousands of years later, but soon became staples of most, but by no means all, artistic cultures worldwide.

The Slave Ship, by the British painter Joseph Mallord William Turner (1775–1851), is one of the finest examples of landscape (or, more precisely, seascape) painting, but it is also a work of social commentary. It records the decision by the captain of the slave ship *Zong* to throw 50 sick and dying slaves overboard when he realized that his insurance would reimburse him for slaves lost at sea but not for those who died en route. Turner's frenzied emotional depiction of the dumping of the slaves into the sea matches the deed's barbaric nature. His great innovation as a painter was to release color from any defining outlines so as to express both the forces of nature and the painter's emotional response to them. In his works, color and brushstrokes themselves become almost the subject of the paintings, an important step on the road to completely abstract artworks during the following century.

Turner's intensely personal approach to painting characterizes the art of the modern era in general, but it is not typical of many periods of the history of art, when artists toiled in anonymity to fulfill the wishes of their patrons, whether Egyptian pharaohs, Roman emperors, or medieval monks. *Art through the Ages* surveys the art of all periods from prehistory to the present, and worldwide, and examines how artworks of all kinds have always reflected the historical contexts in which they were created.

Brief Contents

Contents

Preface

I take great pleasure in introducing the extensively revised and expanded 15th edition of *Gardner's Art through the Ages: A Global History*, which, like the 14th edition, is a hybrid art history textbook—the first, and still the only, introductory survey of the history of art of its kind. This innovative new kind of "Gardner" retains all of the best features of traditional books on paper while harnessing 21st-century technology to significantly increase the number of works examined—without substantially increasing the size of the text or abbreviating the discussion of each work.

When Helen Gardner published the first edition of *Art through the Ages* in 1926, she could not have imagined that nearly a century later, instructors all over the world would still be using her textbook (available even in Mandarin Chinese) in their classrooms. Indeed, if she were alive today, she would not recognize the book that, even in its traditional form, long ago became—and remains—the world's most widely read introduction to the history of art and architecture. I hope that instructors and students alike will agree that this new edition lives up to the venerable Gardner tradition and even exceeds their high expectations.

The 15th edition follows the 14th in incorporating an innovative new online component that includes, in addition to a host of other features (enumerated below), *bonus essays* and *bonus images* (with zoom capability) of more than 300 additional important works of all eras, from prehistory to the present and worldwide. The printed and online components of the hybrid 15th edition are very closely integrated. For example, every one of the more than 300 bonus essays is cited in the text of the traditional book, and a thumbnail image of each work, with abbreviated caption, is inset into the text column where the work is mentioned. The integration extends also to the maps, index, glossary, and chapter summaries, which seamlessly merge the printed and online information.

KEY FEATURES OF THE 15TH EDITION

In this new edition, in addition to revising the text of every chapter to incorporate the latest research and methodological developments, I have added several important features while retaining the basic format and scope of the previous edition. Once again, the hybrid Gardner boasts roughly 1,700 photographs, plans, and drawings, nearly all in color and reproduced according to the highest standards of clarity and color fidelity. Included in this count are updated and revised maps along with hundreds of new images, among them a new series of superb photos taken by Jonathan Poore exclusively for *Art through the Ages* during three photographic campaigns in Germany and Rome in 2012–2014 (following similar forays into France and Tuscany in 2011–2013). The online component also includes custom videos made at architectural sites. This extraordinary new archive of visual material ranges from ancient temples in Rome; to medieval, Renaissance, and Baroque churches in France, Germany, and

Italy; to such modernist masterpieces as the Notre-Dame-du-Haut in Ronchamp, France, and the Guggenheim Museum in New York. The 15th edition also features an expanded number of the highly acclaimed architectural drawings of John Burge. Together, these exclusive photographs, videos, and drawings provide readers with a visual feast unavailable anywhere else.

Once again, a scale accompanies the photograph of every painting, statue, or other artwork discussed—another unique feature of the Gardner text. The scales provide students with a quick and effective way to visualize how big or small a given artwork is and its relative size compared with other objects in the same chapter and throughout the book—especially important given that the illustrated works vary in size from tiny to colossal.

Also retained in this edition are the Quick-Review Captions (brief synopses of the most significant aspects of each artwork or building illustrated) that students have found invaluable when preparing for examinations. These extended captions accompany not only every image in the printed book but also all the digital images in the online supplement. Each chapter also again ends with the highly popular full-page feature called *The Big Picture*, which sets forth in bullet-point format the most important characteristics of each period or artistic movement discussed in the chapter. Also retained from the 14th edition are the timeline summarizing the major artistic and architectural developments during the era treated (again in bullet-point format for easy review) and a chapter-opening essay called *Framing the Era*, which discusses a characteristic painting, sculpture, or building and is illustrated by four photographs.

Another pedagogical tool not found in any other introductory art history textbook is the *Before 1300* section that appears at the beginning of the second volume of the paperbound version of the book and at the beginning of Book D of the backpack edition. Because many students taking the second half of a survey course will not have access to Volume I or to Books A, B, and C, I have provided a special (expanded) set of concise primers on architectural terminology and construction methods in the ancient and medieval worlds, and on mythology and religion—information that is essential for understanding the history of art after 1300, both in the West and the East. The subjects of these special boxes are Greco-Roman Temple Design and the Classical Orders; Arches and Vaults; Basilican Churches; Central-Plan Churches; the Gods and Goddesses of Mount Olympus; the Life of Jesus in Art; Early Christian Saints and Their Attributes; Buddhism and Buddhist Iconography; and Hinduism and Hindu Iconography.

Boxed essays once again appear throughout the book as well. These essays fall under six broad categories, two of which are new to the 15th edition:

Architectural Basics boxes provide students with a sound foundation for the understanding of architecture. These discussions are concise explanations, with drawings and diagrams, of the major aspects of design and construction. The information included is essential to an understanding of architectural technology and terminology.

Materials and Techniques essays explain the various media that artists employed from prehistoric to modern times. Because materials and techniques often influence the character of artworks, these discussions contain essential information on why many monuments appear as they do.

Religion and Mythology boxes introduce students to the principal elements of the world's great religions, past and present, and to the representation of religious and mythological themes in painting and sculpture of all periods and places. These discussions of belief systems and iconography give readers a richer understanding of some of the greatest artworks ever created.

Art and Society essays treat the historical, social, political, cultural, and religious context of art and architecture. In some instances, specific monuments are the basis for a discussion of broader themes.

Written Sources present and discuss key historical documents illuminating important monuments of art and architecture throughout the world. The passages quoted permit voices from the past to speak directly to the reader, providing vivid and unique insights into the creation of artworks in all media.

In the *Artists on Art* boxes, artists and architects throughout history discuss both their theories and individual works.

New to the 15th edition are *The Patron's Voice* boxed essays, which underscore the important roles played by the individuals and groups who paid for the artworks and buildings in determining the character of those monuments. Also new are boxes designed to make students think critically about the decisions that went into the making of every painting, sculpture, and building from the Old Stone Age to the present. Called *Problems and Solutions*, these essays address questions of how and why various forms developed; the problems that painters, sculptors, and architects confronted; and the solutions they used to resolve them.

Other noteworthy features retained from the 14th edition are the extensive (updated) bibliography of books in English; a glossary containing definitions of and page references for italicized terms introduced in both the printed and online texts; and a complete museum index, now housed online only, listing all illustrated artworks by their present location. The host of state-of-the-art online resources accompanying the 15th edition are enumerated on page xx).

ACKNOWLEDGMENTS

A work as extensive as a global history of art could not be undertaken or completed without the counsel of experts in all areas of world art. As with previous editions, Cengage Learning has enlisted more than a hundred art historians to review every chapter of *Art through the Ages* in order to ensure that the text lives up to the Gardner reputation for accuracy as well as readability. I take great pleasure in acknowledging here the important contributions to the 15th edition made by the following: Patricia Albers, San Jose State University; Kirk Ambrose, University of Colorado Boulder; Jenny Kirsten Ataoguz, Indiana University–Purdue University Fort Wayne; Paul Bahn, Hull; Denise Amy Baxter, University of North Texas; Nicole Bensoussan, University of Michigan-Dearborn; Amy R. Bloch, University at Albany, State University of New York; Susan H. Caldwell, The University of Oklahoma; David C. Cateforis, The University of Kansas; Thomas B. F. Cummins, Harvard University; Joyce De Vries, Auburn University; Verena Drake, Hotchkiss School; Jerome Feldman, Hawai'i Pacific University; Maria Gindhart, Georgia State University; Annabeth Headrick, University of Denver;

Shannen Hill, University of Maryland; Angela K. Ho, George Mason University; Julie Hochstrasser, The University of Iowa; Hiroko Johnson, San Diego State University; Julie Johnson, The University of Texas at San Antonio; Paul H.D. Kaplan, Purchase College, State University of New York; Rob Leith, Buckingham Browne & Nichols School; Brenda Longfellow, The University of Iowa; Susan McCombs, Michigan State University; Jennifer Ann McLerran, Northern Arizona University; Patrick R. McNaughton, Indiana University Bloomington; Mary Miller, Yale University; Erin Morris, Estrella Mountain Community College; Nicolas Morrissey, The University of Georgia; Basil Moutsatsos, St. Petersburg College–Seminole; Johanna D. Movassat, San Jose State University; Micheline Nilsen, Indiana University South Bend; Catherine Pagani, The University of Alabama; Allison Lee Palmer, The University of Oklahoma; William H. Peck, University of Michigan–Dearborn; Lauren Peterson, University of Delaware; Holly Pittman, University of Pennsylvania; Romita Ray, Syracuse University; Wendy Wassyng Roworth, The University of Rhode Island; Andrea Rusnock, Indiana University South Bend; Bridget Sandhoff, University of Nebraska Omaha; James M. Saslow, Queens College, City University of New York; Anne Rudolph Stanton, University of Missouri; Achim Timmermann, University of Michigan; David Turley, Weber State University; Lee Ann Turner, Boise State University; Marjorie S. Venit, University of Maryland; Shirley Tokash Verrico, Genesee Community College; Louis A. Waldman, The University of Texas at Austin; Ying Wang, University of Wisconsin-Milwaukee; Gregory H. Williams, Boston University; and Benjamin C. Withers, University of Kentucky.

I am especially indebted to the following for creating the instructor and student materials for the 15th edition: Ivy Cooper, Southern Illinois University Edwardsville; Patricia D. Cosper (retired), The University of Alabama at Birmingham; Anne McClanan, Portland State University; Amy M. Morris, The University of Nebraska Omaha; Erika Schneider, Framingham State University; and Camille Serchuk, Southern Connecticut State University. I also thank the more than 150 instructors and students who participated in surveys, focus groups, design sprints, and advisory boards to help us better understand readers' needs in our print and digital products.

I am also happy to have this opportunity to express my gratitude to the extraordinary group of people at Cengage Learning involved with the editing, production, and distribution of *Art through the Ages*. Some of them I have now worked with on various projects for nearly two decades and feel privileged to count among my friends. The success of the Gardner series in all of its various permutations depends in no small part on the expertise and unflagging commitment of these dedicated professionals, especially Sharon Adams Poore, product manager (as well as videographer extraordinaire); Rachel Harbour, content developer; Lianne Ames, senior content project manager; Chad Kirchner, media developer; Erika Hayden, associate content developer; Elizabeth Newell, associate media developer; Rachael Bailey, senior product assistant; Cate Barr, senior art director; Jillian Borden, marketing manager; and the incomparable group of local sales representatives who have passed on to me the welcome advice offered by the hundreds of instructors they speak to daily during their visits to college campuses throughout North America.

I am also deeply grateful to the following out-of-house contributors to the 15th edition: the incomparable quarterback of the entire production process, Joan Keyes, Dovetail Publishing Services; Helen Triller-Yambert, developmental editor; Michele Jones, copy editor; Susan Gall, proofreader; Mark Fox, Design is Play, cover designer; Frances Baca, text designer; PreMediaGlobal, photo researchers; Cenveo Publisher Services; Jay and John Crowley, Jay's Publishing Services;

Mary Ann Lidrbauch, art log preparer; and, of course, Jonathan Poore and John Burge, for their superb photos and architectural drawings.

I also owe thanks to two individuals not currently associated with this book but who loomed large in my life for many years: Clark Baxter, who retired in 2013 at the end of a long and distinguished career, from whom I learned much about textbook publishing and whose continuing friendship I value highly; and former coauthor and long-time friend and colleague, Christin J. Mamiya of the University of Nebraska–Lincoln, with whom I have had innumerable conversations not only about *Art through the Ages* but the history of art in general. Her thinking continues to influence my own, especially with regard to the later chapters on the history of Western art. I conclude this long (but no doubt incomplete) list of acknowledgments with an expression of gratitude to my colleagues at Boston University and to the thousands of students and the scores of teaching fellows in my art history courses since I began teaching in 1975, especially my research assistant, Angelica Bradley. From them I have learned much that has helped determine the form and content of *Art through the Ages* and made it a much better book than it otherwise might have been.

Fred S. Kleiner

CHAPTER-BY-CHAPTER CHANGES IN THE 15TH EDITION

The 15th edition is extensively revised and expanded, as detailed below. Each chapter contains a revised Big Picture feature, and all maps in the text are new to this edition. Instructors will find a very helpful figure number transition guide in the online instructor companion site.

Introduction: What Is Art History? Added 18th-century Benin Altar to the Hand and details of Claude Lorrain's *Embarkation of the Queen of Sheba.*

14: Late Medieval Italy. Expanded discussions of Nicola and Giovanni Pisano, Pietro Cavallini, and Orvieto Cathedral. Addition of Pisa Cathedral pulpit. New photographs of Giovanni Pisano's *Nativity,* Pietro Cavallini's *Last Judgment,* Giotto's *Entry into Jerusalem,* and the Doge's Palace in Venice.

20: Late Medieval and Early Renaissance Northern Europe. New Framing the Era essay "Rogier van der Weyden and Saint Luke." New Problems and Solutions box "How to Illustrate Printed Books." Revised Materials and Techniques box "Engraving and Etching." New in-text discussion of the *Hours of Mary of Burgundy.* New photograph of Riemenschneider's *Creglingen Altarpiece.*

21: The Renaissance in Quattrocento Italy. New Framing the Era essay "The Medici, Botticelli, and Classical Antiquity." New Problems and Solutions box "Linear Perspective." New Artists on Art boxes "The *Commentarii* of Lorenzo Ghiberti" and "Leon Battista Alberti's *On the Art of Building.*" New section on Venice, with discussions of the Ca d'Oro, Giovanni Bellini's early work, and a new Written Sources box "The Tomb of Doge Pietro Mocenigo." New photographs of Donatello's *Gattamelata,* Brunelleschi's dome of Florence Cathedral, the Ca d'Oro and the tomb of Pietro Mocenigo in Venice, and the restored *Saint James Led to Martyrdom* by Mantegna.

22: Renaissance and Mannerism in Cinquecento Italy. Revised discussion of Mannerism. New Written Sources box "Giorgio Vasari's *Lives.*" New Problems and Solutions boxes "How to Impress a Pope" and "Rethinking the Basilican Church." New Patron's Voice box "Federigo Gonzaga, Giulio Romano, and the Palazzo del Tè."

New photographs of Bramante's Tempietto, the Palazzo Farnese, and the exterior and interior of Il Gesù in Rome, and of the interior of San Giorgio Maggiore in Venice.

23: High Renaissance and Mannerism in Northern Europe and Spain. Major reorganization of the material discussed, with a new sequence of regions and also of individual artists. New Framing the Era essay "Albrecht Dürer, Melancholic Genius." New Art and Society box "Witchcraft, Disease, Plague, and Death." New Patron's Voice box "Francis I, Royal Art Patron and Collector." New photographs of Holbein's *French Ambassadors,* Bosch's *Garden of Earthly Delights,* and the Colegio de San Gregorio in Valladolid, Spain.

24: The Baroque in Italy and Spain. New Problems and Solutions boxes "Completing Saint Peter's," "Rethinking the Church Facade," and "How to Make a Ceiling Disappear." New Patron's Voice box "Velázquez and Philip IV." New in-text discussion of Caravaggio's *Musicians* and brief discussion of Elisabetta Sirani. Reorganized and expanded treatment of Spanish Baroque art and architecture, including colonial Latin America, with the addition of Metropolitan Cathedral in Mexico City and the Church of the Society of Jesus in Cuzco, Peru. New photographs of Bernini's Four Rivers Fountain; the facade of Santa Susanna; Saint Peter's (facade and aerial view); the exterior and interior of Borromini's San Carlo alle Quattro Fontane and the facade and dome of Sant'Ivo alla Sapienza; Gaulli's *Triumph in the Name of Jesus*; and Pozzo's *Glorification of Saint Ignatius.*

25: The Baroque in Northern Europe. New Framing the Era essay "The Art of Painting in a Dutch Home." New Problems and Solutions box "Frans Hals's Group Portraits." New Materials and Techniques box "Rembrandt's Use of Light and Shade." New Art and Society box "The Sun King's Palace at Versailles." New photographs of Girardon's *Apollo Attended by the Nymphs of Thetis* and the Baths of Apollo at Versailles (with new bonus essay).

26: Rococo to Neoclassicism: The 18th Century in Europe and America. New Framing the Era essay "Angelica Kauffman, the Enlightenment, and Neoclassicism." New Art and Society boxes "Poussinistes and Rubénistes," "Joseph Wright of Derby and the Industrial Revolution," and "Vigée-Lebrun, Labille-Guiard, and the French Royal Academy." New Problems and Solutions box "Grand Manner Portraiture." New Written Sources box "Winckelmann and the History of Classical Art." New Patron's Voice box "Thomas Jefferson, Patron and Practitioner." New discussion of the portraits of Pompeo Batoni. New photographs of the exterior and interior of Vierzehnheiligen.

27: Romanticism, Realism, Photography: Europe and America, 1800 to 1870. New Framing the Era essay "The Horror—and Romance—of Death at Sea." New Patron's Voice box "The Coronation of Napoleon." New Written Sources box "Friedrich's *Wanderer above a Sea of Mist.*" New Artists on Art boxes "John Constable on Landscape Painting" and "Thomas Cole on the American Landscape." New Art and Society box "Edmonia Lewis, an African American Sculptor in Rome." New Problems and Solutions boxes "The First Public Art Museum" and "Prefabricated Architecture." New bonus essays on the Arc de Triomphe in Paris and the Brandenburg Gate in Berlin. New photographs of Daumier's *Rue Transnonain*; the Altes Museum in Berlin; the Houses of Parliament in London; and the Brooklyn Bridge.

28: Impressionism, Post-Impressionism, Symbolism: Europe and America, 1870 to 1900. Major rewriting of the sections on Impressionism, Post-Impressionism, and Symbolism. New Framing the Era essay "Modernism at the Folies-Bergère." New Problems and Solutions boxes "Painting Impressions of Light and Color," "Making Impressionism Solid and Enduring," "Painting Psychic Life," and "The First Skyscrapers." New Art and Society boxes "Women Impressionists" and "The Arts and Crafts Movement." New Written Sources box "Albert Aurier on Symbolism." Added Camille Claudel's *The Waltz*. New photograph of the Eiffel Tower in Paris and of Casa Milá in Barcelona.

29: Modernism in Europe and America, 1900 to 1945. New Framing the Era essay "Picasso Disrupts the Western Pictorial Tradition." New Problems and Solutions boxes "Delaunay, Orphism, and the Representation of Modern Life" and "Léger, the Machine Aesthetic, and the Representation of Modern Life." New Art and Society boxes "The Harlem Renaissance" and "Jacob Lawrence's *Migration of the Negro*." New Written Sources box "André Breton's *First Surrealist Manifesto*." New Artists on Art boxes "Alfred Stieglitz on 'Straight Photography,'" "Frank Lloyd Wright on Organic Architecture," "Piet Mondrian on Neoplasticism," and "Grant Wood's *Revolt against the City*." New Patron's Voice box "The Museum of Modern Art as Collector and Patron." Added Adolf Loos's Villa Müller in Prague. New photographs of Rietveld's Schröder House in Utrecht and of the Bauhaus Shop Block in Dessau.

30: Modernism and Postmodernism in Europe and America, 1945 to 1980. New Framing the Era essay "After Modernism: Postmodern Architecture." New Artists on Art box "Jena Dubuffet on Crude Art." New Written Sources box "Greenbergian Formalism." New or expanded Artists on Art boxes "Helen Frankenthaler on Color-Field Painting," "Roy Lichtenstein on Pop Art and Comic Books," "James Rosenquist on *F-111*," and "Judy Chicago on *The Dinner Party*." New Problems and Solutions boxes "Robert Venturi and Postmodernist Complexity and Contradiction" and "Rethinking 'Art': Conceptual Art." Added discussions of Gerhard Richter, James Rosenquist, and Pier Luigi Nervi, with new photographs of *Townscape Paris, F-111*, and the Palazzetto dello Sport, Rome, as well as new photographs of the interior of Saarinen's TWA terminal and Graves's Portland Building.

31: Contemporary Art Worldwide. Major reorganization and expansion with the addition of Sandow Birk's *Death of Manuel*, Martha Rosler's *Gladiators*, Fernando Botero's *Abu Ghraib 46*, Zhang Xiaogang's *Big Family No. 2*, Helen Oji's *Mount St. Helens*, Elizabeth Murray's *Can You Hear Me?*, Yayoi Kusama's abstract canvases, El Anatsui's *Bleeding Takari II*, Anish Kapoor's *Cloud Gate*, Do-Ho Suh's *Bridging Home*, Zaha Hadid's Signature Towers project in Dubai, and Norman Foster's Gherkin in London. New Artists on Art boxes "Shirin Neshat on Iran after the Revolution" and "Leon Golub on *Mercenaries*." New Problems and Solutions boxes "Rethinking the Shape of Painting" and "Norman Foster, the Gherkin, and Green Architectural Design." New photographs of Christo and Jeanne-Claude's *Surrounded Islands*, Stirling's Neue Staatsgalerie and Behnisch's Hysolar Institute in Stuttgart, and Gehry's Guggenheim Museo in Bilbao.

32: South and Southeast Asia, 1200 to 1980. New Patron's Voice box "The Qutb Minar and the Triumph of Islam." Expanded discussion of the Taj Mahal, including new Written Sources box "Abd al-Hamid Lahori on the Taj Mahal." New Problems and Solutions box "Victoria Terminus as Cathedral of Modernization." New bonus essay on Tagore's *Bharat Mata*. New photographs of the pietra dura stonework of the Taj Mahal and of the sculptures of one of the gopuras of the Great Temple at Madurai.

33: China and Korea, 1279 to 1980. Revised Framing the Era essay "The Forbidden City." New Problems and Solutions box "Planning an Unplanned Garden." New photographs of the Yuan *David Vases*, the throne room in Beijing's Forbidden City, the Wangshi and Liu gardens at Suzhou, and Ye Yushan's *Rent Collection Courtyard*. Added Shitao's *Riding the Clouds*.

34: Japan, 1333 to 1980. New Framing the Era essay "The Floating World of Edo." New Written Sources box on Sesshu Toyo. New in-text discussion of the Ryoanji rock garden and of Himeji Castle. New bonus essay on the kokedara garden of Saihoji. New example of a tea ceremony Kogan and of a ceramic work by Hamada Shoji.

35: Native American Cultures, 1300 to 1980. New Framing the Era essay "Tlaltecuhtli, the Aztec Earth Goddess." New Problems and Solutions box "Inka Record-Keeping and the Khipu." New Art and Society box "Kwakwaka'wakw Transformation Masks." Added the *Codex Murúa*. Expanded discussion of Navajo textiles.

36: Oceania before 1980. New discussions of Abelam tamberans and of New Ireland uli figures. New photographs of the Te Hau-ki-Turanga meetinghouse at Poverty Bay, Asmat bisj poles from Omadesep village, and a row of moai on Easter Island.

37: Africa, 1800 to 1980. Reorganized thematically and extensively revised and expanded with new discussions of Bamana Ci Wara headdresses, Baga d'mba masks, and Dan figural spoons. Revised Framing the Era essay "Honoring Chiefs and Ancestors."

ABOUT THE AUTHOR
Fred S. Kleiner

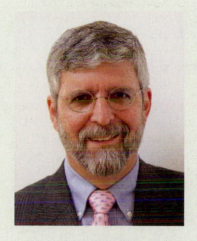

FRED S. KLEINER (Ph.D., Columbia University) has been the author or coauthor of *Gardner's Art through the Ages* beginning with the 10th edition in 1995. He has also published more than a hundred books, articles, and reviews on Greek and Roman art and architecture, including *A History of Roman Art,* also published by Cengage Learning. Both *Art through the Ages* and the book on Roman art have been awarded Texty prizes as the outstanding college textbook of the year in the humanities and social sciences, in 2001 and 2007, respectively. Professor Kleiner has taught the art history survey course since 1975, first at the University of Virginia and, since 1978, at Boston University, where he is currently professor of the history of art and architecture and classical archaeology and has served as department chair for five terms, most recently from 2005 to 2014. From 1985 to 1998, he was editor-in-chief of the *American Journal of Archaeology.*

Long acclaimed for his inspiring lectures and devotion to students, Professor Kleiner won Boston University's Metcalf Award for Excellence in Teaching as well as the College Prize for Undergraduate Advising in the Humanities in 2002, and he is a two-time winner of the Distinguished Teaching Prize in the College of Arts & Sciences Honors Program. In 2007, he was elected a Fellow of the Society of Antiquaries of London, and, in 2009, in recognition of lifetime achievement in publication and teaching, a Fellow of the Text and Academic Authors Association.

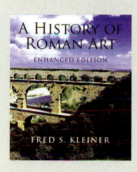

Also by Fred Kleiner: *A History of Roman Art, Enhanced Edition* (Wadsworth/Cengage Learning 2010; ISBN 9780495909873), winner of the 2007 Texty Prize for a new college textbook in the humanities and social sciences. In this authoritative and lavishly illustrated volume, Professor Kleiner traces the development of Roman art and architecture from Romulus's foundation of Rome in the eighth century BCE to the death of Constantine in the fourth century CE, with special chapters devoted to Pompeii and Herculaneum, Ostia, funerary and provincial art and architecture, and the earliest Christian art. The enhanced edition also includes a new introductory chapter on the art and architecture of the Etruscans and of the Greeks of South Italy and Sicily.

Resources

FOR FACULTY

Instructor Companion Site

Access the Instructor Companion Site to find resources to help you teach your course and engage your students. Here you will find the Instructor's Manual; Cognero computerized testing; and Microsoft PowerPoint slides with lecture outlines and images that can be used as offered or customized by importing personal lecture slides or other material.

Digital Image Library

Display digital images in the classroom with this powerful tool. This one-stop lecture and class presentation resource makes it easy to assemble, edit, and present customized lectures for your course. Available on Flashdrive, the Digital Image Library provides high-resolutions images (maps, diagrams, and the fine art images from the text) for lecture presentations and allows you to easily add your own images to supplement those provided. A zoom feature allows you to magnify selected portions of an image for more detailed display in class, or you can display images side-by-side for comparison.

Google Earth™

Take your students on a virtual tour of art through the ages! Resources for the 15th edition include Google Earth™ coordinates for all works, monuments, and sites discussed in the text, encouraging students to make geographical connections between places and sites. Use these coordinates to start your lectures with a virtual journey to locations all over the globe, or take aerial screenshots of important sites to incorporate in your lecture materials.

FOR STUDENTS

MindTap for *Art through the Ages*

MindTap for *Gardner's Art through the Ages: A Global History*, 15th edition, helps you engage with your course content and achieve greater comprehension. Highly personalized and fully online, the MindTap learning platform presents authoritative Cengage Learning content, assignments, and services offering you a tailored presentation of course curriculum created by your instructor.

MindTap guides you through the course curriculum via an innovative Learning Path Navigator where you will complete reading assignments, annotate your readings, complete homework, and engage with quizzes and assessments. Concepts are brought to life with: zoomable versions of close to 1,500 images; videos to reinforce concepts and expand knowledge of particular works or art trends; numerous study tools, including image flashcards; a glossary complete with an audio pronunciation guide; Google Earth™ coordinate links for all works, monuments, and sites discussed in the text; and much more! Additional features, such as the ability to synchronize your eBook notes with your personal EverNote account, provide added convenience to help you take your learning further, faster.

Slide Guides

The Slide Guide is a lecture companion that allows you to take notes alongside representations of the art images shown in class. This handy resource includes reproductions of the images from the book, with full captions and space for note-taking.

Before 1300

Students enrolled in the second semester of a yearlong introductory survey of the history of art may not have access to paperback Volume I (or backpack Books A, B, and C). Therefore, Volume II and Book D of *Art through the Ages: A Global History* open with a special set of concise primers on Greco-Roman and medieval architectural terminology and construction methods and on Greco-Roman, Christian, Buddhist, and Hindu iconography—information that is essential for understanding the history of art and architecture after 1300 both in the West and the East.

Contents

ARCHITECTURAL BASICS

Greco-Roman Temple Design and the Classical Orders

The gable-roofed columnar stone temples of the Greeks and Romans have had more influence on the later history of architecture in the Western world than any other building type ever devised. Many of the elements of classical temple architecture are present in buildings from the Renaissance to the present day.

The basic design principles of Greek and Roman temples and the most important components of the classical orders can be summarized as follows.

■ **Temple design** The core of a Greco-Roman temple was the *cella,* a room with no windows that usually housed the statue of the god or goddess to whom the shrine was dedicated. Generally, only the priests, priestesses, and chosen few would enter the cella. Worshipers gathered in front of the building, where sacrifices occurred at open-air altars. In most Greek temples, for example, the temple erected in honor of Hera or Apollo at Paestum, a *colonnade* was erected all around the cella to form a *peristyle.*

In contrast, Roman temples, for example, the Temple of Portunus in Rome, usually have freestanding columns only in a porch at the front of the building. Sometimes, as in the Portunus temple, *engaged* (attached) half-columns adorn three sides of the cella to give the building the appearance of a *peripteral* temple. Architectural historians call this a *pseudoperipteral* design. The Greeks and Romans also built round temples (called *tholos* temples), a building type that also had a long afterlife in Western architecture.

■ **Classical orders** The Greeks developed two basic architectural orders, or design systems: the *Doric* and the *Ionic.* The forms of the columns and *entablature* (superstructure) generally differentiate the orders. Classical columns have two or three parts, depending on the order: the shaft, which is usually marked with vertical channels (*flutes*); the *capital*; and, in the Ionic order, the *base.* The Doric capital consists of a round *echinus* beneath a square abacus block. Spiral *volutes* constitute the distinctive feature of the Ionic capital. Classical entablatures have three parts: the *architrave,* the *frieze,* and the triangular *pediment* of the gabled roof, framed by the *cornice.* In the Doric order, the frieze is subdivided into *triglyphs* and *metopes,* whereas in the Ionic, the frieze is left open.

The *Corinthian capital,* a later Greek invention very popular in Roman times, is more ornate than either the Doric or Ionic. It consists of a double row of acanthus leaves, from which tendrils and flowers emerge. Although this capital often is cited as the distinguishing element of the Corinthian order, in strict terms no Corinthian order exists. Architects simply substituted the new capital type for the volute capital in the Ionic order, as in the Roman temple probably dedicated to Vesta at Tivoli.

Sculpture played a major role on the exterior of classical temples, partly to embellish the deity's shrine and partly to tell something about the deity to those gathered outside. Sculptural ornament was concentrated on the upper part of the building, in the pediment and frieze.

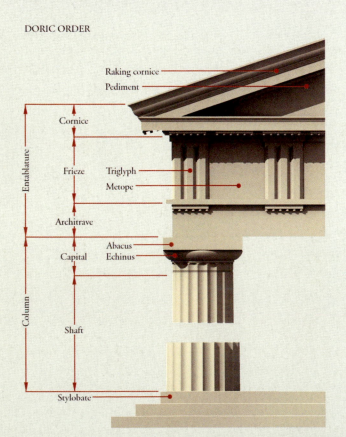

DORIC ORDER

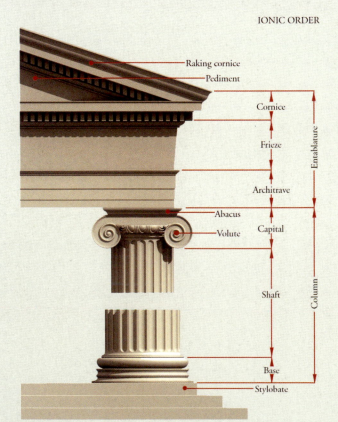

IONIC ORDER

Doric and Ionic orders

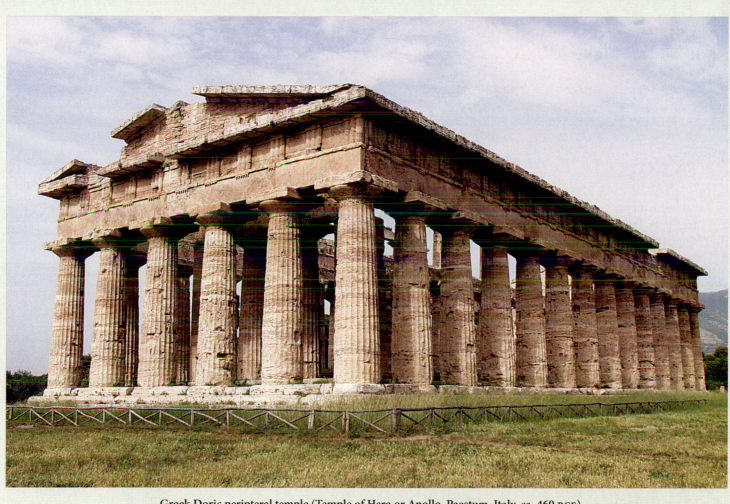

Greek Doric peripteral temple (Temple of Hera or Apollo, Paestum, Italy, ca. 460 BCE)

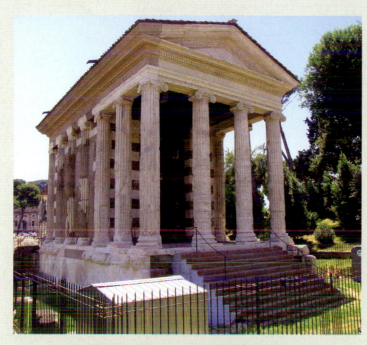

Roman Ionic pseudoperipteral temple
(Temple of Portunus, Rome, Italy, ca. 75 BCE)

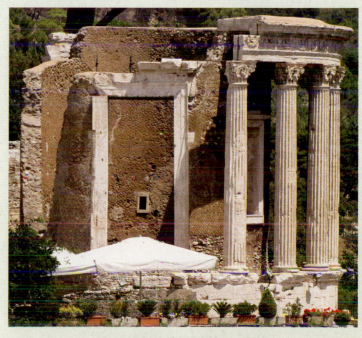

Roman Corinthian tholos temple
(Temple of Vesta, Tivoli, Italy, early first century BCE)

ARCHITECTURAL BASICS
Arches and Vaults

Although earlier architects used both arches and vaults, the Romans employed them more extensively and effectively than any other ancient civilization. The Roman forms became staples of architectural design from the Middle Ages until today.

- **Arch** The arch is one of several ways of spanning a passageway. The Romans preferred it to the *post-and-lintel* (column-and-architrave) system used in the Greek orders. Builders construct arches using wedge-shaped stone blocks called *voussoirs.* The central voussoir is the arch's *keystone.*
- **Barrel vault** Also called the *tunnel vault,* the barrel vault is an extension of a simple arch, creating a semicylindrical ceiling over parallel walls.
- **Groin vault** The groin vault, or *cross vault,* is formed by the intersection at right angles of two barrel vaults of equal size. When a series of groin vaults covers an interior hall, the open lateral arches of the vaults function as windows admitting light to the building.
- **Dome** The hemispherical dome may be described as a round arch rotated around the full circumference of a circle, usually resting on a cylindrical *drum.* The Romans normally constructed domes using *concrete,* a mix of lime mortar, volcanic sand, water, and small stones, instead of with large stone blocks. Concrete dries to form a solid mass of great strength, which enabled the Romans to puncture the apex of a concrete dome with an *oculus* (eye), so that much-needed light could reach the interior of the building.

Barrel vaults, as noted, resemble tunnels, and groin vaults are usually found in a series covering a similar *longitudinally* oriented interior space. Domes, in contrast, crown *centrally* planned buildings, so named because the structure's parts are of equal or almost equal dimensions around the center.

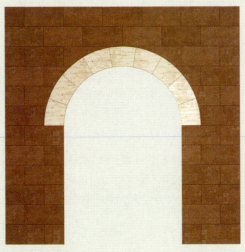

Arch

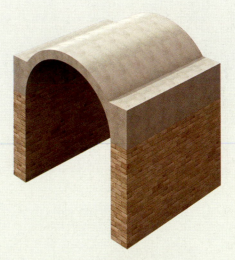

Barrel vault

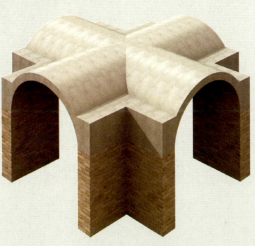

Groin vault

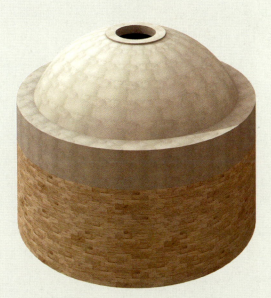

Hemispherical dome with oculus

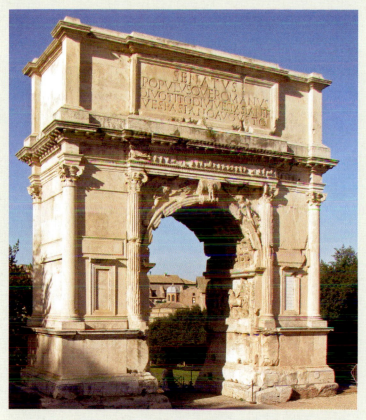

Roman arch (Arch of Titus, Rome, Italy, ca. 81)

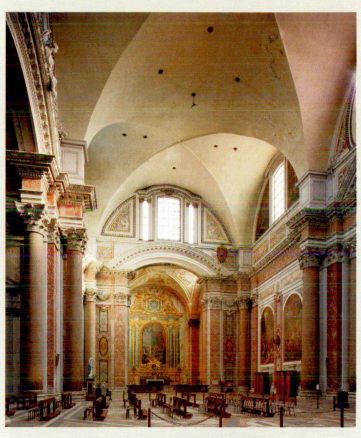

Roman hall with groin vaults (Baths of Diocletian, now
Santa Maria degli Angeli, Rome, Italy, ca. 298–306)

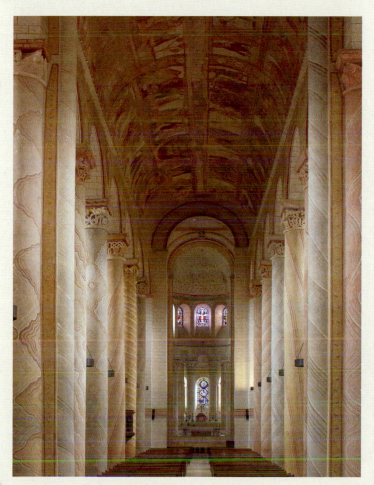

Medieval barrel-vaulted church
(Saint-Savin, Saint-Savin-sur-Gartempe, France, ca. 1100)

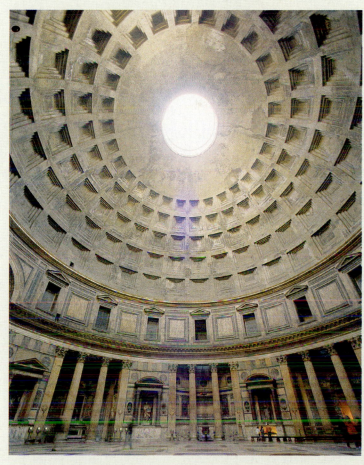

Roman dome with oculus (Pantheon, Rome, Italy, 118–125)

ARCHITECTURAL BASICS

Basilican Churches

Church design during the Middle Ages set the stage for ecclesiastical architecture from the Renaissance to the present. Both the longitudinal- and central-plan building types of antiquity had a long postclassical history.

In Western Christendom, the typical medieval church had a *basilican* plan, which evolved from the Roman columnar hall, or *basilica*. The great European *cathedrals* of the Gothic age, which were the immediate predecessors of the churches of the Renaissance and Baroque eras, shared many elements with the earliest basilican churches constructed during the fourth century, including a wide central *nave* flanked by *aisles* and ending in an *apse*. Some basilican churches also have a *transept*, an area perpendicular to the nave. The nave and transept intersect at the *crossing*. Gothic churches, however, have many additional features. The key components of Gothic design are labeled in the drawing of a typical French Gothic cathedral, which can be compared to the interior view of Amiens Cathedral and the plan of Chartres Cathedral.

Gothic architects frequently extended the aisles around the apse to form an *ambulatory*, onto which opened *radiating chapels* housing sacred relics. Groin vaults formed the ceiling of the nave, aisles, ambulatory, and transept alike, replacing the timber roof of the typical Early Christian basilica. These vaults rested on *diagonal* and *transverse ribs* in the form of *pointed arches*. On the exterior, *flying buttresses* held the nave vaults in place. These masonry struts transferred the thrust of the nave vaults across the roofs of the aisles to tall *piers* frequently capped by pointed ornamental *pinnacles*. This structural system made it possible to open up the walls above the *nave arcade* with huge *stained-glass* windows in the nave *clerestory*.

In the later Middle Ages, especially in the great cathedrals of the Gothic age, church *facades* featured extensive sculptural ornamentation, primarily in the portals beneath the stained-glass *rose windows* (circular windows with *tracery* resembling floral petals). The major sculpted areas were the *tympanum* above the doorway (akin to a Greco-Roman temple pediment), the *trumeau* (central post), and the *jambs*.

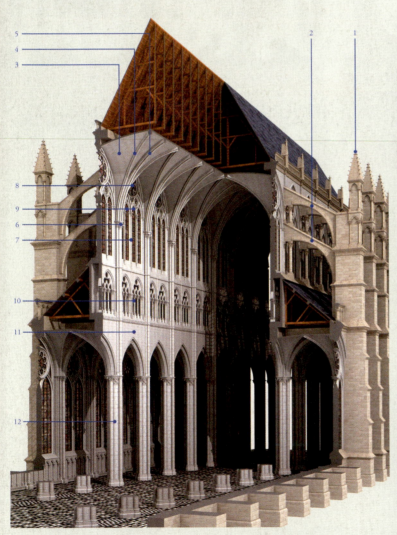

Cutaway view of a typical French Gothic cathedral
(1) pinnacle, (2) flying buttress, (3) vaulting web, (4) diagonal rib,
(5) transverse rib, (6) springing, (7) clerestory, (8) oculus, (9) lancet,
(10) triforium, (11) nave arcade, (12) compound pier with responds

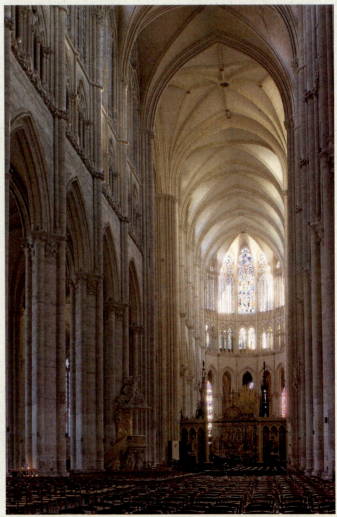

Nave of Amiens Cathedral, France, begun 1220

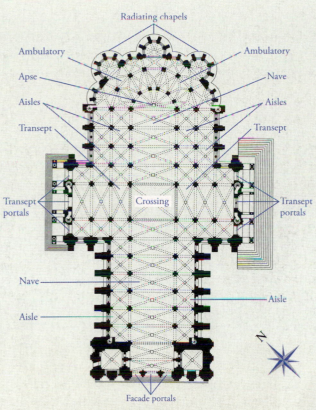

Plan of Chartres Cathedral, Chartres, France, rebuilt after 1194

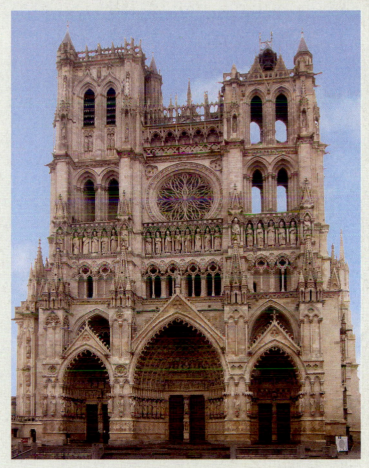

West facade of Amiens Cathedral, Amiens, France, begun 1220

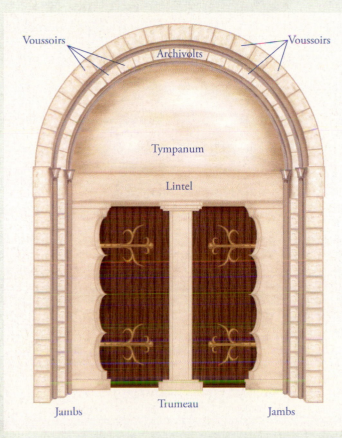

Diagram of medieval portal sculpture

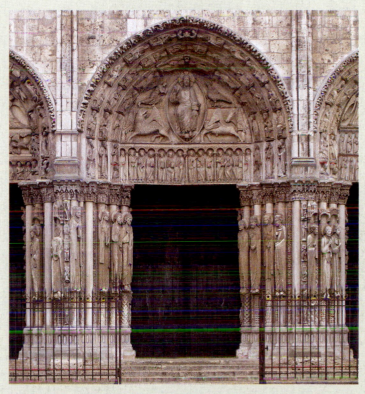

Central portal, west facade, Chartres Cathedral, ca. 1145–1155

ARCHITECTURAL BASICS
Central-Plan Churches

The domed central plan of classical antiquity dominated the architecture of the Byzantine Empire but with important modifications. Because the dome covered the crossing of a Byzantine church, architects had to find a way to erect domes on square bases instead of on the circular bases (cylindrical drums) of Roman buildings. The solution was *pendentive* construction in which the dome rests on what is in effect a second, larger dome. The top portion and four segments around the rim of the larger dome are omitted, creating four curved triangles, or pendentives. The pendentives join to form a ring and four arches whose planes bound a square. The first use of pendentives on a grand scale occurred in the sixth-century church of Hagia Sophia (Holy Wisdom) in Constantinople.

The interiors of Byzantine churches differed from those of basilican churches in the West not only in plan and the use of domes but also in the manner in which they were adorned. The original *mosaic* decoration of Hagia Sophia is lost, but at Saint Mark's in Venice, some 40,000 square feet of mosaics cover all the walls, arches, vaults, and domes.

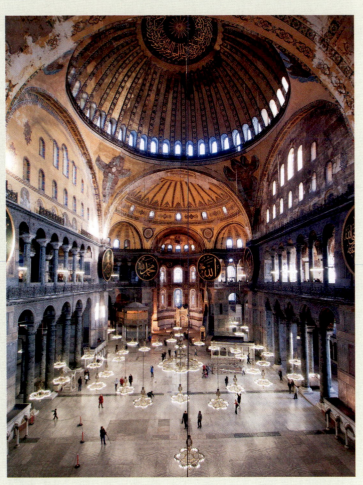

Hagia Sophia, Constantinople (Istanbul), Turkey, 532–537

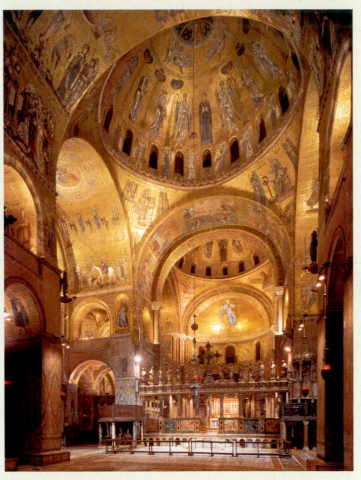

Saint Mark's, Venice, Italy, begun 1063

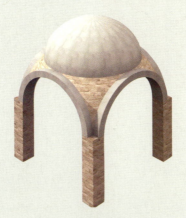

Dome on pendentives

RELIGION AND MYTHOLOGY
The Gods and Goddesses of Mount Olympus

The chief deities of the Greeks ruled the world from their home on Mount Olympus, Greece's highest peak. They figure prominently not only in Greek, Etruscan, and Roman art but also in art from the Renaissance to the present.

The 12 Olympian gods (and their Roman equivalents) were:

- **Zeus (Jupiter)** King of the gods, Zeus ruled the sky and allotted the sea to his brother Poseidon and the Underworld to his other brother, Hades. His weapon was the thunderbolt. Jupiter was also the chief god of the Romans.
- **Hera (Juno)** Wife and sister of Zeus, Hera was the goddess of marriage.
- **Poseidon (Neptune)** Poseidon was lord of the sea. He controlled waves, storms, and earthquakes with his three-pronged pitchfork (*trident*).
- **Hestia (Vesta)** Sister of Zeus, Poseidon, and Hera, Hestia was goddess of the hearth.
- **Demeter (Ceres)** Third sister of Zeus, Demeter was the goddess of grain and agriculture.
- **Ares (Mars)** God of war, Ares was the son of Zeus and Hera and the lover of Aphrodite. His Roman counterpart, Mars, was the father of the twin founders of Rome, Romulus and Remus.
- **Athena (Minerva)** Goddess of wisdom and warfare, Athena was a virgin born from the head of her father, Zeus.

- **Hephaistos (Vulcan)** God of fire and of metalworking, Hephaistos was the son of Zeus and Hera. Born lame and, uncharacteristically for a god, ugly, he married Aphrodite, who was unfaithful to him.
- **Apollo (Apollo)** God of light and music and son of Zeus, the young, beautiful Apollo was an expert archer, sometimes identified with the sun (**Helios/Sol**).
- **Artemis (Diana)** Sister of Apollo, Artemis was goddess of the hunt. She was occasionally equated with the moon (**Selene/Luna**).
- **Aphrodite (Venus)** Daughter of Zeus and a *nymph* (goddess of springs and woods), Aphrodite was the goddess of love and beauty.
- **Hermes (Mercury)** Son of Zeus and another nymph, Hermes was the fleet-footed messenger of the gods and possessed winged sandals. He carried the *caduceus*, a magical herald's rod.

Other important Greek gods and goddesses were:

- **Hades (Pluto)** Lord of the Underworld and god of the dead. Although the brother of Zeus and Poseidon, Hades never resided on Mount Olympus.
- **Dionysos (Bacchus)** God of wine, another of Zeus's sons.
- **Eros (Amor** or **Cupid)** The winged child-god of love, son of Aphrodite and Ares.
- **Asklepios (Aesculapius)** God of healing, son of Apollo. His serpent-entwined staff is the emblem of modern medicine.

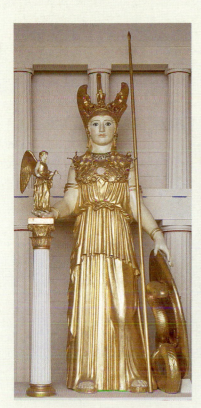

Athena, by Phidias, ca. 438 BCE

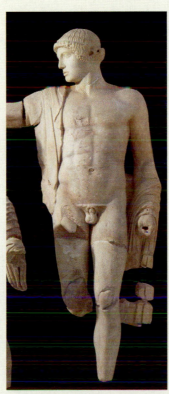

Apollo, from Olympia, ca. 470–456 BCE

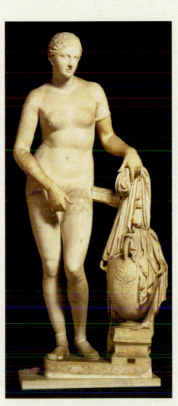

Aphrodite, by Praxiteles, ca. 350–340 BCE

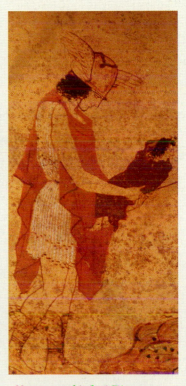

Hermes and infant Dionysos, by the Phiale Painter, ca. 440–435 BCE

RELIGION AND MYTHOLOGY
The Life of Jesus in Art

Christians believe that Jesus of Nazareth is the son of God, the *Messiah* (Savior, Christ) of the Jews prophesied in Hebrew scripture. His life—his miraculous birth from the womb of a virgin mother, his preaching and miracle working, his execution by the Romans and subsequent ascent to Heaven—has been the subject of countless artworks from Roman times through the present day.

INCARNATION AND CHILDHOOD

The first "cycle" of the life of Jesus consists of the events of his conception (incarnation), birth, infancy, and childhood.

- **Annunciation to Mary** The archangel Gabriel announces to the Virgin Mary that she will miraculously conceive and give birth to God's son, Jesus.
- **Visitation** The pregnant Mary visits her cousin Elizabeth, who is pregnant with John the Baptist. Elizabeth is the first to recognize that the baby Mary is bearing is the Son of God.
- **Nativity**, **Annunciation to the Shepherds**, and **Adoration of the Shepherds** Jesus is born at night in Bethlehem and placed in a basket. Mary and her husband, Joseph, marvel at the newborn, while an angel announces the birth of the Savior to shepherds in the field, who rush to adore the infant Jesus.
- **Adoration of the Magi** A bright star alerts three wise men (*magi*) in the East that the King of the Jews has been born. They travel 12 days to present precious gifts to the infant Jesus.
- **Presentation in the Temple** In accordance with Jewish tradition, Mary and Joseph bring their firstborn son to the temple in Jerusalem, where the aged Simeon recognizes Jesus as the prophesied savior of humankind.

- **Massacre of the Innocents** and **Flight into Egypt** King Herod, fearful that a rival king has been born, orders the massacre of all infants, but the holy family escapes to Egypt.
- **Dispute in the Temple** Joseph and Mary travel to Jerusalem for the feast of Passover. Jesus, only a boy, debates the astonished Jewish scholars in the temple, foretelling his ministry.

PUBLIC MINISTRY

The public-ministry cycle comprises the teachings of Jesus and the miracles he performed.

- **Baptism** Jesus's public ministry begins with his baptism at age 30 by John the Baptist in the Jordan River. God's voice is heard proclaiming Jesus as his son.
- **Calling of Matthew** Jesus summons Matthew, a tax collector, to follow him, and Matthew becomes one of his 12 disciples, or *apostles* (from the Greek for "messenger").
- **Miracles** Jesus performs many miracles, revealing his divine nature. These include acts of healing and raising the dead, turning water into wine, walking on water and calming storms, and creating wondrous quantities of food.
- **Delivery of the Keys to Peter** Jesus chooses the fisherman Peter (whose name means "rock") as his successor. He declares that Peter is the rock on which his church will be built and symbolically delivers to Peter the keys to the kingdom of Heaven.
- **Transfiguration** Jesus scales a mountain and, in the presence of Peter and two other disciples, is transformed into radiant light. God, speaking from a cloud, discloses that Jesus is his son.
- **Cleansing of the Temple** Jesus returns to Jerusalem, where he finds money changers and merchants conducting business in the temple. He rebukes them and drives them out.

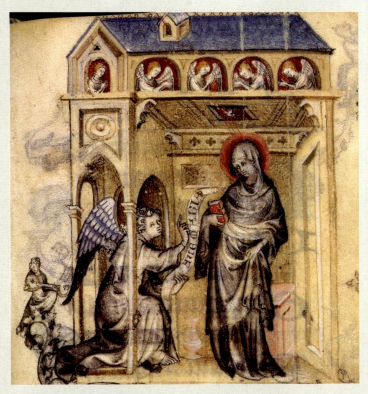

Annunciation, by Jean Pucelle, ca. 1325–1328

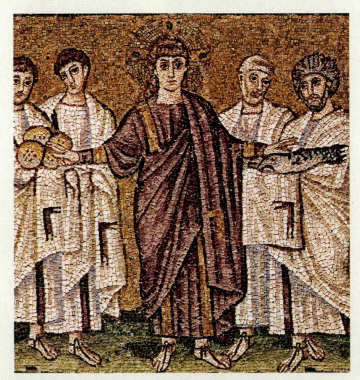

Miracle of Loaves and Fishes, Sant'Apollinare Nuovo, Ravenna, Italy, ca. 504

PASSION

The passion (Latin *passio*, "suffering") cycle includes the events leading to Jesus's trial, death, resurrection, and ascent to Heaven.

- **Entry into Jerusalem** On the Sunday before his crucifixion (Palm Sunday), Jesus rides into Jerusalem on a donkey.
- **Last Supper** In Jerusalem, Jesus celebrates Passover with his disciples. During this last supper, Jesus foretells his imminent betrayal, arrest, and death and invites the disciples to remember him when they eat bread (symbol of his body) and drink wine (his blood). This ritual became the celebration of *Mass* (*Eucharist*).
- **Agony in the Garden** Jesus goes to the Mount of Olives in the Garden of Gethsemane, where he struggles to overcome his human fear of death by praying for divine strength.
- **Betrayal** and **Arrest** The disciple Judas Iscariot betrays Jesus to the Jewish authorities for 30 pieces of silver. Judas identifies Jesus to the soldiers by kissing him, and Jesus is arrested.
- **Trials of Jesus** The soldiers bring Jesus before Caiaphas, the Jewish high priest, who interrogates Jesus about his claim to be the Messiah. Jesus is then brought before the Roman governor of Judaea, Pontius Pilate, on the charge of treason because he had proclaimed himself king of the Jews. Pilate asks the crowd to choose between freeing Jesus or Barabbas, a murderer. The people choose Barabbas, and the judge condemns Jesus to death.
- **Flagellation** The Roman soldiers who hold Jesus captive whip (flagellate) him and mock him by dressing him as king of the Jews and placing a crown of thorns on his head.
- **Carrying of the Cross, Raising of the Cross**, and **Crucifixion** The Romans force Jesus to carry the cross on which he will be crucified from Jerusalem to Mount Calvary. Soldiers erect the cross and nail Jesus's hands and feet to it. Jesus's mother, John the Evangelist, and Mary Magdalene mourn at the foot of the cross, while the soldiers torment Jesus. One of them stabs Jesus in the side with a spear. After suffering great pain, Jesus dies on Good Friday.
- **Deposition**, **Lamentation**, and **Entombment** Two disciples, Joseph of Arimathea and Nicodemus, remove Jesus's body from the cross (deposition) and take him to his tomb. Joseph, Nicodemus, the Virgin Mary, John the Evangelist, and Mary Magdalene mourn over the dead Jesus (lamentation). (When in art the isolated figure of the Virgin Mary cradles her dead son in her lap, it is called a *Pietà*—Italian for "pity.") Then his followers lower Jesus into a sarcophagus in the tomb (entombment).
- **Resurrection** and **Three Marys at the Tomb** On the third day (Easter Sunday), Christ rises from the dead and leaves the tomb. The Virgin Mary, Mary Magdalene, and Mary, the mother of James, visit the tomb but find it empty. An angel informs them that Jesus has been resurrected.
- **Noli Me Tangere**, **Supper at Emmaus**, and **Doubting of Thomas** During the 40 days between Christ's resurrection and his ascent to Heaven, he appears on several occasions to his followers. Christ warns Mary Magdalene, weeping at his tomb, with the words "Don't touch me" (*Noli me tangere* in Latin). At Emmaus he eats supper with two astonished disciples. Later, Christ invites Thomas, who cannot believe Christ has risen, to touch the wound in his side inflicted at his crucifixion.
- **Ascension** On the 40th day, on the Mount of Olives, with his mother and apostles as witnesses, Christ gloriously ascends to Heaven in a cloud.

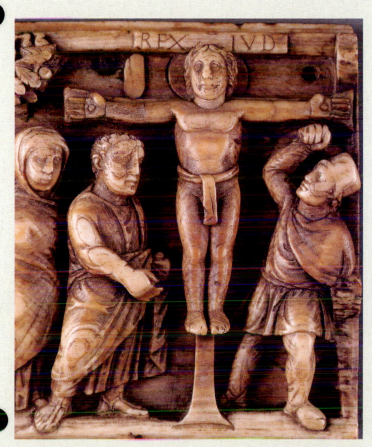

Crucifixion, ivory plaque, Italy, early fifth century

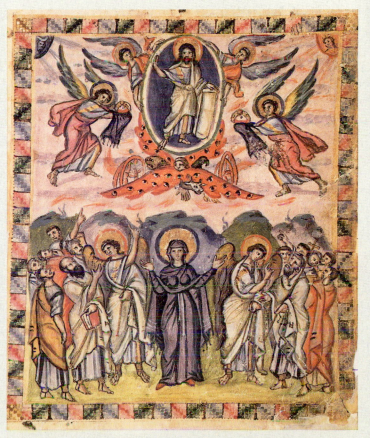

Ascension of Christ, Rabbula Gospels, 586

RELIGION AND MYTHOLOGY
Early Christian Saints and Their Attributes

A distinctive feature of Christianity is the veneration accorded to *saints* (from the Latin word for "holy"—*sanctus*), a practice dating to the second century. Most of the earliest Christian saints were *martyrs* who died for their faith at the hands of the Roman authorities, often after suffering cruel torture. During the first millennium of the Church, the designation of sainthood, or *canonization*, was an informal process, but in the late 12th century, Pope Alexander III (r. 1159–1181) ruled that only the papacy could designate individuals as saints, and only after a protracted review of the life, character, deeds, and miracles of the person under consideration. A preliminary stage is *beatification*, the official determination that a deceased individual is a *beatus* (blessed person).

In Christian art, saints almost always have *halos* around their heads. To distinguish individual saints, artists commonly depicted them with one or more characteristic *attributes*—often the means of their martyrdom, although saintly attributes take a wide variety of forms.

The most important saints during the early centuries of Christianity were contemporaries of Jesus. They may be classified in three general categories.

FAMILY OF JESUS AND MARY

- **Anne** The parents of the Virgin Mary were Anne and Joachim, a childless couple after 20 years of marriage. Angels separately announced to them that Anne would give birth.

- **Elizabeth** A cousin of Anne, Elizabeth was also an elderly barren woman. The angel Gabriel announced to her husband, the priest Zacharias, that she would give birth to a son named John. Six months later, Gabriel informed Mary that she would become the mother of the son of God (*Annunciation*), whereupon Mary visited Elizabeth (*Visitation*), and in Elizabeth's womb the future John the Baptist leaped for joy at the approach of the Mother of God.

- **Joseph** Although a modest craftsman, Joseph was a descendant of King David. An elderly widower, he was chosen among several suitors to wed the much younger Mary when his staff miraculously blossomed. Joseph's principal attributes are the flowering staff and carpentry tools.

- **John the Baptist** Elizabeth's son, John, became a preacher who promoted baptism as a means of cleansing Jews of their sins in preparation for the Messiah. John most often appears in art as a bearded hermit baptizing a much younger Jesus in the Jordan River, even though John was only six months older. His attribute is a lamb.

APOSTLES

During the course of his ministry, Jesus called 12 men to be his *apostles*, or messengers, to spread the news of the coming of the son of God. All 12 apostles were present at the *Last Supper*. After Judas's betrayal and suicide, the remaining 11 witnessed Jesus's *Ascension* and chose

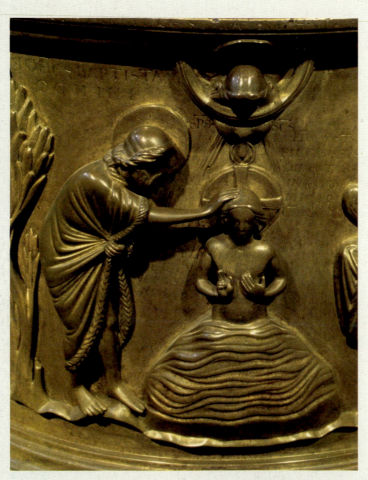

John the Baptist baptizing Jesus, Liège, Belgium, 1118

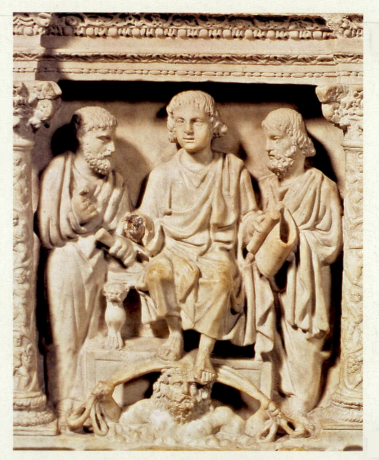

Christ between Saints Peter and Paul,
Sarcophagus of Junius Bassus, ca. 359

another follower of Jesus to replace Judas. At the *Pentecost*, the Holy Spirit assigned the 12 apostles the mission of spreading the Gospel throughout the world. All but John the Evangelist eventually suffered martyrdom. Four of the apostles figure prominently in the history of art.

- **Peter** The "prince of apostles," Peter was a fisherman whom Jesus designated as the rock on which he would found his Church. The Savior presented the apostle with the keys to the kingdom of Heaven. Peter was the first bishop of Rome and the head of the long line of popes. He was crucified upside down because he insisted that he was unworthy to die as Jesus did. Peter's chief attributes are the keys.
- **John the Evangelist** Another fisherman, John was the youngest apostle and "the disciple whom Jesus loved." He was one of two apostles who became *evangelists*—those who recorded Jesus's life in the Gospels. John also wrote the Book of Revelation. His attribute is an eagle.
- **Matthew** The second evangelist among the apostles, Matthew was a Jewish tax collector. Different accounts say that he was either stabbed to death or beheaded while saying Mass. Matthew appears most frequently in art as a seated robed figure writing his Gospel. His attribute is a winged man.
- **James** The brother of John the Evangelist and also a fisherman, James was the first apostle to be martyred—by beheading. According to tradition, before his martyrdom he preached the Gospel in Spain. James's attribute is a scallop shell, the emblem of pilgrims to his shrine at Santiago de Compostela.

OTHER EARLY SAINTS

Several other saints who died before Constantine ended the persecution of Christians have also frequently been the subjects of artworks:

- **Paul** Born a Jew named Saul, Paul fervently opposed Christian teaching until Christ spoke to him in a blinding burst of light. Paul became the "Apostle to the Gentiles," preaching the Gospel to non-Jews as well as Jews. His *Epistles* are the foundation of Christian theology. In Early Christian art, he holds a scroll and often appears with Peter flanking Christ, although, unlike the original apostles, Paul never met Jesus. In later representations he may hold the sword of his martyrdom.
- **Mark** One of the two evangelists who were not apostles, Mark accompanied Paul on his earliest missionary journey and became the first bishop of Alexandria, where he was martyred by being dragged with a rope around his neck. The Venetians acquired Mark's remains in 828. The saint's attribute—a lion—is the emblem of Venice to this day.
- **Luke** A Gentile physician in addition to being a Gospel author, Luke painted a portrait of Mary and the infant Jesus, and consequently became the patron saint of artists as well as doctors. His attribute is an ox.
- **Mary Magdalene** Born in Magdala on the Sea of Galilee, Mary Magdalene washed Jesus's feet with her tears and dried them with her hair. She was the first to discover Christ's empty tomb and to encounter the resurrected Savior. Mary's major attribute is her long hair.

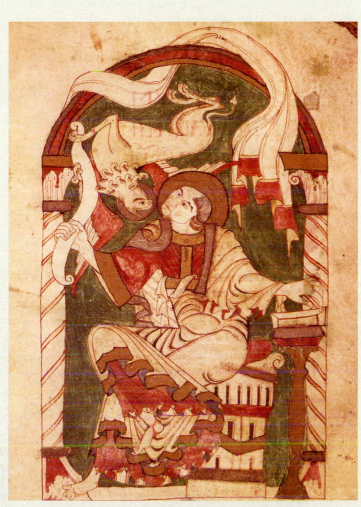

Mark, with his lion, writing his Gospel, *Corbie Gospels*, ca. 1120

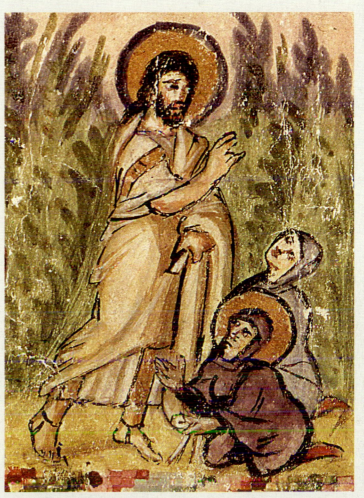

Mary Magdalene and the resurrected Christ, *Rabbula Gospels*, 586

RELIGION AND MYTHOLOGY
Buddhism and Buddhist Iconography

The Buddha (Enlightened One) was born around 563 BCE as Prince Siddhartha Gautama. When he was 29, he renounced his opulent life and became a wandering ascetic searching for knowledge through meditation. Six years later, he achieved complete enlightenment, or buddhahood, while meditating beneath a pipal tree (the Bodhi tree) at Bodh Gaya (place of enlightenment) in eastern India. The Buddha preached his first sermon in the Deer Park at Sarnath. There he set into motion the Wheel (*chakra*) of the Law (*dharma*) and expounded the Four Noble Truths: (1) life is suffering; (2) the cause of suffering is desire; (3) one can overcome and extinguish desire; (4) the way to conquer desire and end suffering is to follow the Buddha's Eightfold Path of right understanding, right thought, right speech, right action, right livelihood, right effort, right mindfulness, and right concentration. The Buddha's path leads to *nirvana*, the cessation of the endless cycle of painful life, death, and rebirth. The Buddha continued to preach until his death at age 80 at Kushinagara.

The earliest form of Buddhism is called Theravada (Path of the Elders) Buddhism. The second major school of Buddhist thought, Mahayana (Great Path) Buddhism, emerged around the beginning of the Christian era. Mahayana Buddhists refer to Theravada Buddhism as Hinayana (Lesser Path) Buddhism and believe in a larger goal than nirvana for an individual—namely, buddhahood for all. Mahayana Buddhists also revere *bodhisattvas* (Buddhas-to-be), exemplars of compassion who restrain themselves at the threshold of nirvana to aid others in earning merit and achieving buddhahood. A third important Buddhist sect, especially popular in East Asia, venerates the Amitabha Buddha (Amida in Japanese), the Buddha of Infinite Light and Life. The devotees of this Buddha hope to be reborn in the Pure Land Paradise of the West, where the Amitabha resides and can grant them salvation.

The earliest (first century CE) known depictions of the Buddha in human form show him as a robed monk. Artists distinguished the Enlightened One from monks and bodhisattvas by *lakshanas*, body attributes indicating the Buddha's suprahuman nature. These distinguishing marks include an *urna*, or curl of hair between the eyebrows; an *ushnisha*, or cranial bump; and, less frequently, palms of hands and soles of feet imprinted with a wheel. The Buddha is also recognizable by his elongated ears, the result of wearing heavy royal jewelry in his youth.

Representations of the Buddha also feature a repertory of mudras, or hand gestures. These include the *dhyana* (meditation) mudra, with the right hand over the left, palms upward; the *bhumisparsha* (earth-touching) mudra, right hand down reaching to the ground, calling the earth to witness the Buddha's enlightenment; the *dharmachakra* (Wheel of the Law, or teaching) mudra, a two-handed gesture with right thumb and index finger forming a circle; and the *abhaya* (do not fear) mudra, right hand up, palm outward, a gesture of protection or blessing.

Episodes from the Buddha's life are among the most popular subjects in all Buddhist artistic traditions. Four of the most important events are his birth at Lumbini from the side of his mother; his achievement of buddhahood while meditating beneath the Bodhi tree; his first sermon at Sarnath; and his attainment of nirvana when he died (*parinirvana*) at Kushinagara.

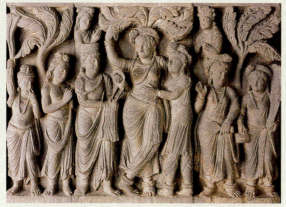

a

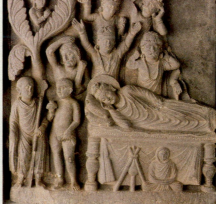

b

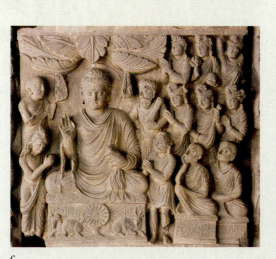

c

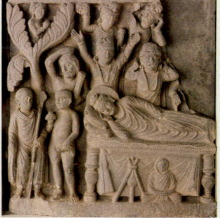

d

Life and death of the Buddha, from Gandhara, second century. (a) Birth at Lumbini, (b) enlightenment at Bodh Gaya, (c) first sermon at Sarnath, (d) death at Kushinagara (parinirvana)

RELIGION AND MYTHOLOGY
Hinduism and Hindu Iconography

Unlike Buddhism (and Christianity, Islam, and other religions), Hinduism recognizes no founder or great prophet. Hindism also has no simple definition, but means "the religion of the Indians." The practices and beliefs of Hindus vary tremendously, but ritual sacrifice is central to Hinduism. The goal of sacrifice is to please a deity in order to achieve release (*moksha,* liberation) from the endless cycle of birth, death, and rebirth (*samsara*) and become one with the universal spirit.

Not only is Hinduism a religion of many gods, but the Hindu deities also have various natures and take many forms. This multiplicity suggests the all-pervasive nature of the Hindu gods. The three most important deities are the gods Shiva and Vishnu and the goddess Devi. Each of the three major sects of Hinduism today considers one of these three to be supreme—Shiva in Shaivism, Vishnu in Vaishnavism, and Devi in Shaktism. (*Shakti* is the female creative force.)

■   **Shiva** is the Destroyer, but, consistent with the multiplicity of Hindu belief, he is also a regenerative force and, in the latter role, can be represented in the form of a *linga* (a phallus or cosmic pillar). When Shiva appears in human form in Hindu art, he frequently has multiple limbs and heads, signs of his suprahuman nature, and matted locks piled atop his head, crowned by a crescent moon. Sometimes he wears a serpent scarf and has a third eye on his forehead (the emblem of his all-seeing nature). Shiva rides the bull **Nandi** and often carries a trident.

■   **Vishnu** is the Preserver of the Universe. Artists frequently portray him with four arms holding various attributes, including a conch-shell trumpet and discus, sometimes sleeping on the serpent Ananta floating on the waters of the cosmic sea as he dreams the universe into reality. When the evil forces in the world become too strong, he descends to earth to restore balance and assumes different forms (*avatars,* or incarnations), including a boar, fish, and tortoise, as well as **Krishna**, the divine lover, and even the Buddha himself.

■   **Devi** is the Great Goddess who takes many forms and has many names. Hindus worship her alone or as a consort of male gods (**Parvati** or **Uma**, wife of Shiva; **Lakshmi**, wife of Vishnu), as well as **Radha**, lover of Krishna. She has both benign and horrific forms. She creates and destroys. In one manifestation, she is **Durga**, a multiarmed goddess who often rides a lion. Her son is the elephant-headed **Ganesha**.

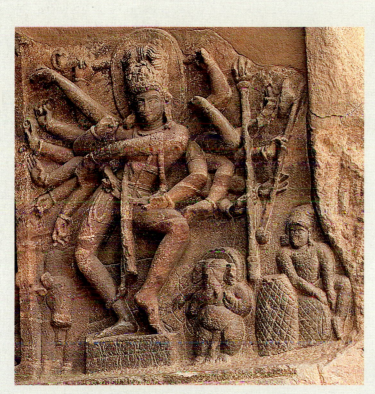

Dancing Shiva with Ganesha, Badami, India, late sixth century

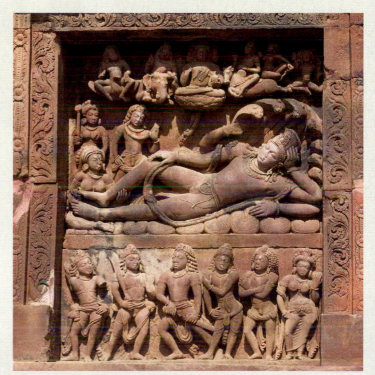

Vishnu Asleep on the Serpent Ananta, Deogarh, India, early sixth century

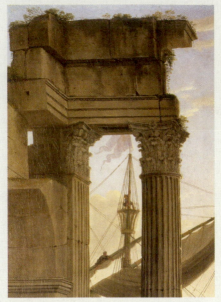

▲ **I-1a** Among the questions art historians ask is why artists chose the subjects they represented. Why would a 17th-century French painter set a biblical story in a contemporary harbor with a Roman ruin?

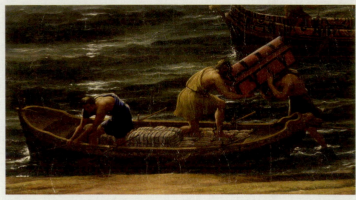

▲ **I-1b** Why is the small boat in the foreground much larger than the sailing ship in the distance? What devices did Western artists develop to produce the illusion of deep space in a two-dimensional painting?

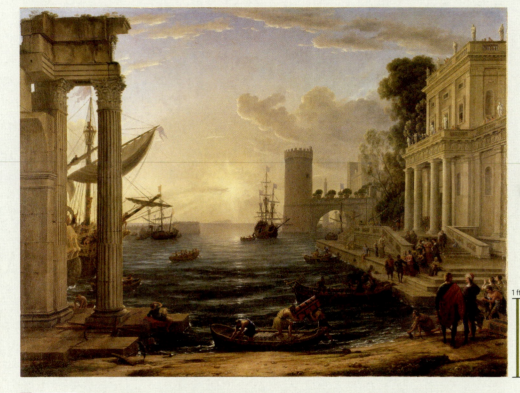

I-1 CLAUDE LORRAIN, *Embarkation of the Queen of Sheba,* 1648. Oil on canvas, 4' 10" × 6' 4". National Gallery, London.

1 ft.

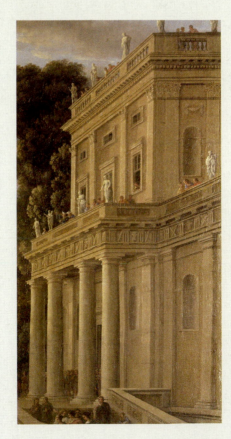

◄ **I-1c** Why does the large port building at the right edge of this painting seem normal to the eye when the top and bottom of the structure are not parallel horizontal lines, as they are in a real building?

What Is Art History?

What is art history? Except when referring to the modern academic discipline, people do not often juxtapose the words *art* and *history*. They tend to think of history as the record and interpretation of past human events, particularly social and political events. In contrast, most think of art, quite correctly, as part of the present—as something people can see and touch. Of course, people cannot see or touch history's vanished human events, but a visible, tangible artwork is a kind of persisting event. One or more artists made it at a certain time and in a specific place, even if no one now knows who, when, where, or why. Although created in the past, an artwork continues to exist in the present, long surviving its times. The first painters and sculptors died 30,000 years ago, but their works remain, some of them exhibited in glass cases in museums built only a few years ago.

Modern museum visitors can admire these objects from the remote past and countless others produced over the millennia—whether a large painting on canvas by a 17th-century French artist (FIG. I-1), a wood portrait from an ancient Egyptian tomb (FIG. I-14), an illustrated book by a medieval German monk (FIG. I-8), or an 18th-century bronze altar glorifying an African king (FIG. I-15)—without any knowledge of the circumstances leading to the creation of those works. The beauty or sheer size of an object can impress people, the artist's virtuosity in the handling of ordinary or costly materials can dazzle them, or the subject depicted can move them emotionally. Viewers can react to what they see, interpret the work in the light of their own experience, and judge it a success or a failure. These are all valid responses to a work of art. But the enjoyment and appreciation of artworks in museum settings are relatively recent phenomena, as is the creation of artworks solely for museum-going audiences to view.

Today, it is common for artists to work in private studios and to create paintings, sculptures, and other objects to be offered for sale by commercial art galleries. This is what American artist CLYFFORD STILL (1904–1980) did when he created his series of paintings (FIG. I-2) of pure color titled simply with the year of their creation. Usually, someone the artist has never met will purchase the artwork and display it in a setting that the artist has never seen. This practice is not a new phenomenon in the history of art—an ancient potter decorating a vase for sale at a village market stall probably did not know who would buy the pot or where it would be housed—but it is not at all typical. In fact, it is exceptional. Throughout history, most artists created paintings, sculptures, and other objects for specific patrons and settings and to fulfill a specific purpose, even if today no one knows the original contexts of those artworks. Museum visitors can appreciate the visual and tactile qualities of these objects, but they cannot understand why they were made or why they appear as they do without knowing the circumstances of their creation. Art *appreciation* does not require knowledge of the historical context of an artwork (or a building). Art *history* does.

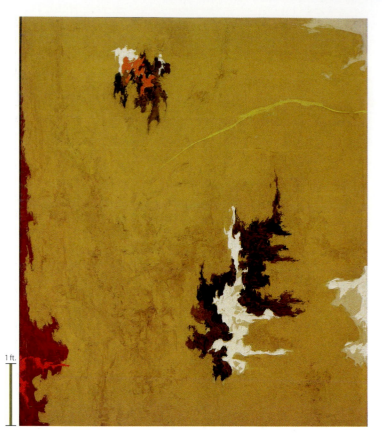

1 ft.

I-2 Clyfford Still, *1948-C,* 1948. Oil on canvas, 6' 8⅞" × 5' 8¾". Hirshhorn Museum and Sculpture Garden, Smithsonian Institution, Washington, D.C. (purchased with funds of Joseph H. Hirshhorn, 1992).

Clyfford Still painted this abstract composition without knowing who would purchase it or where it would be displayed, but throughout history, most artists created works for specific patrons and settings.

Thus a central aim of art history is to determine the original context of artworks. Art historians seek to achieve a full understanding not only of why these "persisting events" of human history look the way they do but also of why the artistic events happened at all. What unique set of circumstances gave rise to the construction of a particular building or led an individual patron to commission a certain artist to fashion a singular artwork for a specific place? The study of history is therefore vital to art history. And art history is often indispensable for a thorough understanding of history. In ways that other historical documents may not, art objects and buildings can shed light on the peoples who made them and on the times of their creation. Furthermore, artists and architects can affect history by reinforcing or challenging cultural values and practices through the objects they create and the structures they build. Although the two disciplines are not the same, the history of art and architecture is inseparable from the study of history.

The following pages introduce some of the distinctive subjects that art historians address and the kinds of questions they ask, and explain some of the basic terminology they use when answering these questions. Readers armed with this arsenal of questions and terms will be ready to explore the multifaceted world of art through the ages.

ART HISTORY IN THE 21ST CENTURY

Art historians study the visual and tangible objects that humans make and the structures that they build. Scholars traditionally have classified these works as architecture, sculpture, the pictorial arts (painting, drawing, printmaking, and photography), and the craft arts, or arts of design. The craft arts comprise utilitarian objects, such as ceramics, metalwork, textiles, jewelry, and similar accessories of ordinary living—but the fact that these objects were used does not mean that they are not works of art. In fact, in some times and places, these so-called minor arts were the most prestigious artworks of all. Artists of every age have blurred the boundaries among these categories, but this is especially true today, when multimedia works abound.

Beginning with the earliest Greco-Roman art critics, scholars have studied objects that their makers consciously manufactured as "art" and to which the artists assigned formal titles. But today's art historians also study a multitude of objects that their creators and owners almost certainly did not consider to be "works of art." Few ancient Romans, for example, would have regarded a coin bearing their emperor's portrait as anything but money. Today, an art museum may exhibit that coin in a locked case in a climate-controlled room, and scholars may subject it to the same kind of art historical analysis as a portrait by an acclaimed Renaissance or modern sculptor or painter.

The range of objects that art historians study is constantly expanding and now includes, for example, computer-generated images, whereas in the past almost anything produced using a machine would not have been regarded as art. Most people still consider the performing arts—music, drama, and dance—as outside art history's realm because these arts are fleeting, impermanent media. But during the past few decades, even this distinction between "fine art" and "performance art" has become blurred. Art historians, however, generally ask the same kinds of questions about what they study, whether they employ a restrictive or expansive definition of art.

The Questions Art Historians Ask

HOW OLD IS IT? Before art historians can write a history of art, they must be sure they know the date of each work they study. Thus an indispensable subject of art historical inquiry is *chronology,* the dating of art objects and buildings. If researchers cannot determine a monument's age, they cannot place the work in its historical context. Art historians have developed many ways to establish, or at least approximate, the date of an artwork.

Physical evidence often reliably indicates an object's age. The material used for a statue or painting—bronze, plastic, or oil-based pigment, to name only a few—may not have been invented before a certain time, indicating the earliest possible date (the *terminus post quem*: Latin, "point after which") someone could have fashioned the work. Or artists may have ceased using certain materials—such as specific kinds of inks and papers for drawings—at a known time, providing the latest possible date (the *terminus ante quem*: Latin, "point before which") for objects made of those materials. Sometimes the material (or the manufacturing technique) of an object or a building can establish a very precise date of production or construction. The study of tree rings, for instance, usually can determine within a narrow range the date of a wood statue or a timber roof beam.

Documentary evidence can help pinpoint the date of an object or building when a dated written document mentions the work. For example, official records may note when church officials commissioned a new altarpiece—and how much they paid to which artist.

Internal evidence can play a significant role in dating an artwork. A painter might have depicted an identifiable person or a kind of hairstyle, clothing, or furniture fashionable only at a certain time. If so, the art historian can assign a more accurate date to that painting.

Stylistic evidence is also very important. The analysis of *style*—an artist's distinctive manner of producing an object—is the art historian's special sphere. Unfortunately, because it is a subjective assessment, an artwork's style is by far the most unreliable chronological criterion. Still, art historians find stylistic evidence a very useful tool for establishing chronology.

WHAT IS ITS STYLE? Defining artistic style is one of the key elements of art historical inquiry, although the analysis of artworks solely in terms of style no longer dominates the field the way it once did. Art historians speak of several different kinds of artistic styles.

Period style refers to the characteristic artistic manner of a specific era or span of years, usually within a distinct culture, such as "Archaic Greek" or "High Renaissance." But many periods do not display any stylistic unity at all. How would someone define the artistic style of the second decade of the new millennium in North America? Far too many crosscurrents exist in contemporary art for anyone to describe a period style of the early 21st century—even in a single city such as New York.

Regional style is the term that art historians use to describe variations in style tied to geography. Like an object's date, its *provenance,* or place of origin, can significantly determine its character. Very often two artworks from the same place made centuries apart are more similar than contemporaneous works from two different regions. To cite one example, usually only an expert can distinguish between an Egyptian statue carved in 2500 BCE and one made in 500 BCE. But no one would mistake an Egyptian statue of 500 BCE for one of the same date made in Greece or Mexico.

Considerable variations in a given area's style are possible, however, even during a single historical period. In late medieval Europe, French architecture differed significantly from Italian architecture. The interiors of Beauvais Cathedral (FIG. I-3) and the church of Santa Croce (Holy Cross, FIG. I-4) in Florence typify the architectural styles of France and Italy, respectively, at the end of the 13th century. The rebuilding of the east end of Beauvais Cathedral began in 1284. Construction commenced on Santa Croce only 10 years later. Both structures employ the *pointed arch* characteristic of this era, yet the two churches differ strikingly. The French church has towering stone ceilings and large expanses of colored-glass windows, whereas the Italian building has a low timber roof and small,

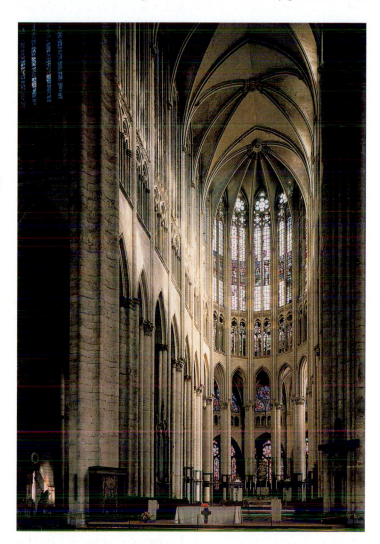

I-3 Choir of Beauvais Cathedral (looking east), Beauvais, France, rebuilt after 1284.

The style of an object or building often varies from region to region. This cathedral has towering stone vaults and large stained-glass windows typical of 13th-century French architecture.

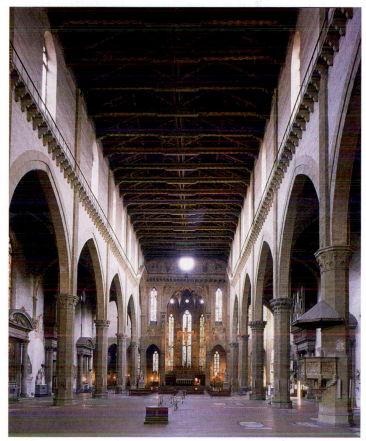

I-4 Interior of Santa Croce (looking east), Florence, Italy, begun 1294.

In contrast to Beauvais Cathedral (FIG. I-3), this contemporaneous Florentine church conforms to the quite different regional style of Italy. The building has a low timber roof and small windows.

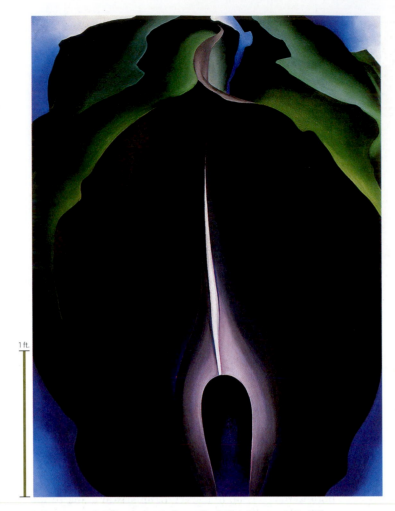

1 ft.

I-5 GEORGIA O'KEEFFE, *Jack-in-the-Pulpit No. 4,* 1930. Oil on canvas, 3' 4" × 2' 6". National Gallery of Art, Washington, D.C. (Alfred Stieglitz Collection, bequest of Georgia O'Keeffe).

O'Keeffe's paintings feature close-up views of petals and leaves in which the organic forms become powerful abstract compositions. This approach to painting typifies the artist's distinctive personal style.

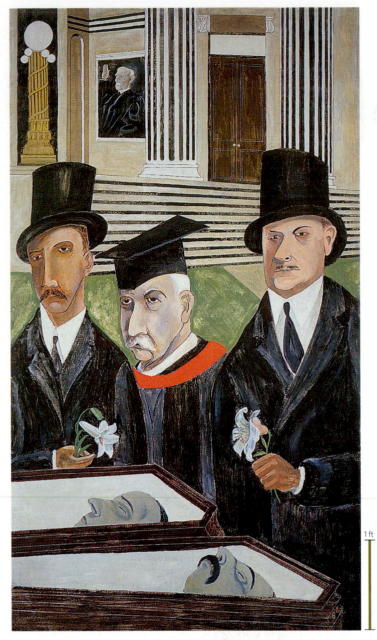

1 ft

I-6 BEN SHAHN, *The Passion of Sacco and Vanzetti,* 1931–1932. Tempera on canvas, 7' $\frac{1}{2}$" × 4'. Whitney Museum of American Art, New York (gift of Edith and Milton Lowenthal in memory of Juliana Force).

O'Keeffe's contemporary, Shahn developed a style markedly different from hers. His paintings are often social commentaries on recent events and incorporate readily identifiable people.

widely separated clear windows. Because the two contemporaneous churches served similar purposes, regional style mainly explains their differing appearance.

Personal style, the distinctive manner of individual artists or architects, often decisively explains stylistic discrepancies among paintings, sculptures, and buildings of the same time and place. For example, in 1930, the American painter GEORGIA O'KEEFFE (1887–1986) produced a series of paintings of flowering plants. One of them—*Jack-in-the-Pulpit No. 4* (FIG. I-5)—is a sharply focused close-up view of petals and leaves. O'Keeffe captured the growing plant's slow, controlled motion while converting the plant into a powerful abstract composition of lines, forms, and colors (see the discussion of art historical vocabulary in the next section). Only a year later, another American artist, BEN SHAHN (1898–1969), painted *The Passion of Sacco and Vanzetti* (FIG. I-6), a stinging commentary on social injustice inspired by the trial and execution of two Italian anarchists, Nicola Sacco and Bartolomeo Vanzetti. Many people believed that Sacco and Vanzetti had been unjustly convicted of killing two men in a robbery in 1920. Shahn's painting compresses time in a symbolic representation of the trial and its aftermath. The two executed men lie in their coffins. Presiding over them are the three members of the commission (headed by a college president wearing

academic cap and gown) who declared that the original trial was fair and cleared the way for the executions. Behind, on the wall of a stately government building, hangs the framed portrait of the judge who pronounced the initial sentence. Personal style, not period or regional style, sets Shahn's canvas apart from O'Keeffe's. The contrast is extreme here because of the very different subjects that the artists chose. But even when two artists depict the same subject, the results can vary widely. The *way* O'Keeffe painted flowers and the *way* Shahn painted faces are distinctive and unlike the styles of their contemporaries. (See the "Who Made It?" discussion on page 6.)

The different kinds of artistic styles are not mutually exclusive. For example, an artist's personal style may change dramatically during a long career. Art historians then must distinguish among

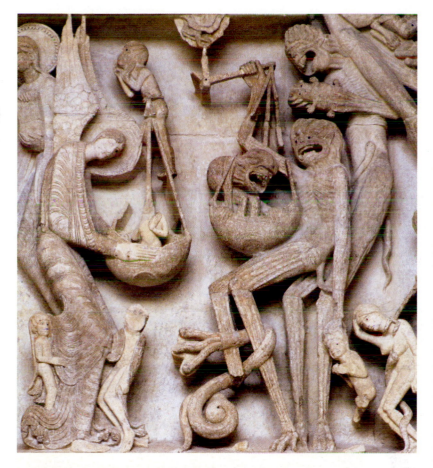

I-7 GISLEBERTUS, weighing of souls, detail of *Last Judgment* (FIG. 12-15), west tympanum of Saint-Lazare, Autun, France, ca. 1120–1135.

In this high relief portraying the weighing of souls on judgment day, Gislebertus used disproportion and distortion to dehumanize the devilish figure yanking on the scales of justice.

the different period styles of a particular artist, such as the "Rose Period" and the "Cubist Period" of the prolific 20th-century artist Pablo Picasso.

WHAT IS ITS SUBJECT? Another major concern of art historians is, of course, subject matter, encompassing the story, or narrative; the scene presented; the action's time and place; the persons involved; and the environment and its details. Some artworks, such as modern abstract paintings (FIG. I-2), have no subject, not even a setting. The "subject" is the artwork itself—its colors, textures, composition, and size. But when artists represent people, places, or actions, viewers must identify these features to achieve complete understanding of the work. Art historians traditionally separate pictorial subjects into various categories, such as religious, historical, mythological, *genre* (daily life), portraiture, *landscape* (a depiction of a place), *still life* (an arrangement of inanimate objects), and their numerous subdivisions and combinations.

Iconography—literally, the "writing of images"—refers both to the content, or subject, of an artwork, and to the study of content in art. By extension, it also includes the study of *symbols,* images that stand for other images or encapsulate ideas. In Christian art, two intersecting lines of unequal length or a simple geometric cross can serve as an emblem of the religion as a whole, symbolizing the cross of Jesus Christ's crucifixion. A symbol also can be a familiar object that an artist has imbued with greater meaning. A balance or scale, for example, may symbolize justice or the weighing of souls on judgment day (FIG. I-7).

Artists may depict figures with unique *attributes* identifying them. In Christian art, for example, each of the authors of the biblical gospel books, the four evangelists (FIG. I-8), has a distinctive attribute. People can recognize Saint Matthew by the winged man associated with him, John by his eagle, Mark by his lion, and Luke by his ox.

Throughout the history of art, artists have used *personifications*—abstract ideas codified in human form. Because of the fame of the colossal statue set up in New York City's harbor in 1886, people everywhere visualize Liberty as a robed woman wearing a rayed crown and holding a torch. Four different personifications appear in *The Four Horsemen*

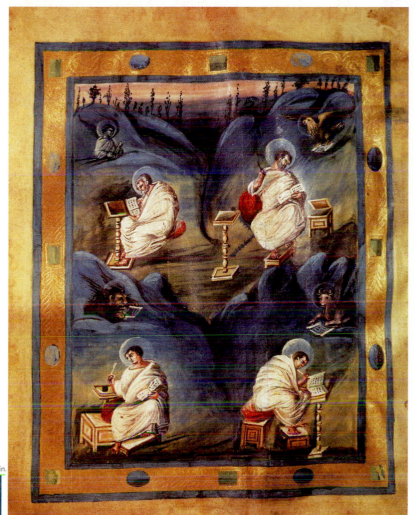

I-8 The four evangelists, folio 14 verso of the *Aachen Gospels,* ca. 810. Ink and tempera on vellum, $1' \times 9\frac{1}{2}''$. Domschatzkammer, Aachen.

Artists depict figures with attributes in order to identify them for viewers. The authors of the four gospels have distinctive attributes—winged man (Matthew), eagle (John), lion (Mark), and ox (Luke).

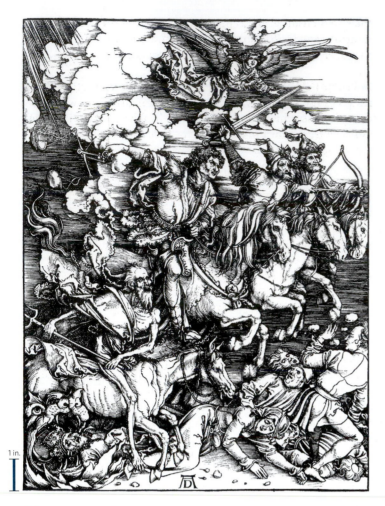

1 in.

I-9 ALBRECHT DÜRER, *The Four Horsemen of the Apocalypse,* ca. 1498. Woodcut, 1' 3$\frac{1}{4}$" × 11". Metropolitan Museum of Art, New York (gift of Junius S. Morgan, 1919).

Personifications are abstract ideas codified in human form. Here, Albrecht Dürer represented Death, Famine, War, and Pestilence as four men on charging horses, each one carrying an identifying attribute.

of the Apocalypse (FIG. I-9) by German artist ALBRECHT DÜRER (1471–1528). The late-15th-century print is a terrifying depiction of the fateful day at the end of time when, according to the Bible's last book, Death, Famine, War, and Pestilence will annihilate the human race. Dürer personified Death as an emaciated old man with a pitchfork. Famine swings the scales for weighing human souls (compare FIG. I-7). War wields a sword, and Pestilence draws a bow.

Even without considering style and without knowing a work's maker, informed viewers can determine much about the work's period and provenance by iconographical and subject analysis alone. In *The Passion of Sacco and Vanzetti* (FIG. I-6), for example, the two coffins, the trio headed by an academic, and the robed judge in the background are all pictorial clues revealing the painting's subject. The work's date must be after the trial and execution, probably while the event was still newsworthy. And because the two men's deaths caused the greatest outrage in the United States, the painter–social critic was probably an American.

WHO MADE IT? If Ben Shahn had not signed his painting of Sacco and Vanzetti, an art historian could still assign, or *attribute* (make an *attribution* of), the work to him based on knowledge of the

artist's personal style. Although signing (and dating) works is quite common (but by no means universal) today, in the history of art, countless works exist whose artists remain unknown. Because personal style can play a major role in determining the character of an artwork, art historians often try to attribute anonymous works to known artists. Sometimes they assemble a group of works all thought to be by the same person, even though none of the objects in the group is the known work of an artist with a recorded name. Art historians thus reconstruct the careers of artists such as "the Achilles Painter," the anonymous ancient Greek artist whose masterwork is a depiction of the hero Achilles. Scholars base their attributions on internal evidence, such as the distinctive way an artist draws or carves drapery folds, earlobes, or flowers. It requires a keen, highly trained eye and long experience to become a *connoisseur,* an expert in assigning artworks to "the hand" of one artist rather than another. Attribution is subjective, of course, and ever open to doubt. For example, scholars continue to debate attributions to the famous 17th-century Dutch painter Rembrandt van Rijn.

Sometimes a group of artists works in the same style at the same time and place. Art historians designate such a group as a *school.* "School" does not mean an educational institution or art academy. The term connotes only shared chronology, style, and geography. Art historians speak, for example, of the Dutch school of the 17th century and, within it, of subschools such as those of the cities of Haarlem, Utrecht, and Leyden.

WHO PAID FOR IT? The interest that many art historians show in attribution reflects their conviction that the identity of an artwork's maker is the major reason the object looks the way it does. For them, personal style is of paramount importance. But in many times and places, artists had little to say about what form their work would take. They toiled in obscurity, doing the bidding of their *patrons,* those who paid them to make individual works or employed them on a continuing basis. The role of patrons in dictating the content and shaping the form of artworks is also an important subject of art historical inquiry, more so today than at any time in the past.

In the art of portraiture, to name only one category of painting and sculpture, the patron has often played a dominant role in deciding how the artist represented the subject, whether that person was the patron or another individual, such as a spouse, son, or mother. Many Egyptian pharaohs and some Roman emperors, for example, insisted that artists depict them with unlined faces and perfect youthful bodies no matter how old they were when portrayed. In these cases, the state employed the sculptors and painters, and the artists had no choice but to portray their patrons in the officially approved manner. This is why Augustus, who lived to age 76, looks so young in his portraits (FIG. I-10). Although Roman emperor for more than 40 years, Augustus demanded that artists always represent him as a young, godlike head of state.

All modes of artistic production reveal the impact of patronage. Learned monks provided the themes for the sculptural decoration of medieval church portals (FIG. I-7). Renaissance princes and popes dictated the subject, size, and materials of artworks destined for display in buildings also constructed according to their specifications. An art historian could make a very long list of commissioned works, and it would indicate that patrons have had diverse tastes and needs throughout history and consequently have demanded different kinds of art. Whenever a patron contracts with an artist or architect to paint, sculpt, or build in a prescribed manner, personal style often becomes a very minor factor in the ultimate

their color, texture, and other qualities. *Composition* refers to how an artist *composes* (organizes) forms in an artwork, either by placing shapes on a flat surface or by arranging forms in space.

MATERIAL AND TECHNIQUE To create art forms, artists shape materials (pigment, clay, marble, gold, and many more) with tools (pens, brushes, chisels, and so forth). Each of the materials and tools available has its own potentialities and limitations. Part of all artists' creative activity is to select the *medium* and instrument most suitable to the purpose—or to develop new media and tools, such as bronze and concrete in antiquity and cameras and computers in modern times. The processes that artists employ, such as applying paint to canvas with a brush, and the distinctive, personal ways that they handle materials constitute their *technique.* Form, material, and technique interrelate and are central to analyzing any work of art.

LINE Among the most important elements defining an artwork's shape or form is *line.* A line can be understood as the path of a point moving in space, an invisible line of sight. More commonly, however, artists and architects make a line visible by drawing (or chiseling) it on a *plane,* a flat surface. A line may be very thin, wirelike, and delicate. It may be thick and heavy. Or it may alternate quickly from broad to narrow, the strokes jagged or the outline broken. When a continuous line defines an object's outer shape, art historians call it a *contour line.* All of these line qualities are present in Dürer's *Four Horsemen of the Apocalypse* (FIG. I-9). Contour lines define the basic shapes of clouds, human and animal limbs, and weapons. Within the forms, series of short broken lines create shadows and textures. An overall pattern of long parallel strokes suggests the dark sky on the frightening day when the world is about to end.

COLOR Light reveals all colors. Light in the world of the painter and other artists differs from natural light. Natural light, or sunlight, is whole or *additive light.* As the sum of all the wavelengths composing the visible *spectrum,* it may be disassembled or fragmented into the individual colors of the spectral band. The painter's light in art—the light reflected from pigments and objects—is *subtractive light.* Paint pigments produce their individual colors by reflecting a segment of the spectrum while absorbing all the rest. Green pigment, for example, subtracts or absorbs all the light in the spectrum except that seen as green.

Hue is the property giving a color its name. Although the spectrum colors merge into each other, artists usually conceive of their hues as distinct from one another. Color has two basic variables—the apparent amount of light reflected and the apparent purity. A change in one must produce a change in the other. Some terms for these variables are *value* or *tonality* (the degree of lightness or darkness) and *intensity* or *saturation* (the purity of a color, its brightness or dullness).

Artists call the three basic colors—red, yellow, and blue—the *primary colors.* The *secondary colors* result from mixing pairs of primaries: orange (red and yellow), purple (red and blue), and green (yellow and blue). *Complementary colors* represent the pairing of a primary color and the secondary color created from mixing the two other primary colors—red and green, yellow and purple, and blue and orange. They "complement," or complete, each other, one absorbing the colors that the other reflects.

Artists can manipulate the appearance of colors, however. One artist who made a systematic investigation of the formal aspects of art, especially color, was JOSEPH ALBERS (1888–1976), a German-born

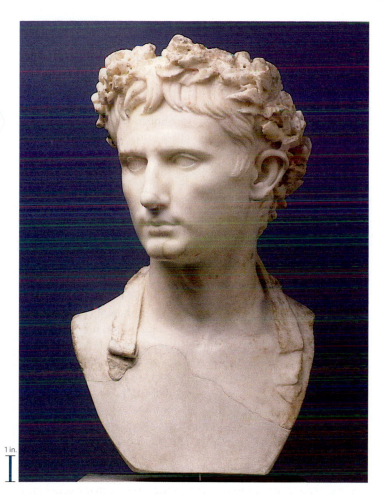

1 in.

I-10 Bust of Augustus wearing the corona civica, early first century CE. Marble, 1' 5" high. Glyptothek, Munich.

Patrons frequently dictate the form that their portraits will take. Emperor Augustus demanded that he always be portrayed as a young, godlike head of state even though he lived to age 76.

appearance of the painting, statue, or building. In these cases, the identity of the patron reveals more to art historians than does the identity of the artist or school. The portrait of Augustus illustrated here (FIG. I-10)—showing the emperor wearing a *corona civica,* or civic crown—was the work of a virtuoso sculptor, a master wielder of hammer and chisel. But scores of similar portraits of this Roman emperor also exist today. They differ in quality but not in kind from this one. The patron, not the artist, determined the character of these artworks. Augustus's public image never varied.

The Words Art Historians Use

As in all fields of study, art history has its own specialized vocabulary consisting of hundreds of words, but certain basic terms are indispensable for describing artworks and buildings of any time and place. They make up the essential vocabulary of *formal analysis,* the visual analysis of artistic form. Definitions and discussions of the most important art historical terms follow.

FORM AND COMPOSITION *Form* refers to an object's shape and structure, either in two dimensions (for example, a figure painted on a wood panel) or in three dimensions (such as a statue carved from a marble block). Two forms may take the same shape but differ in

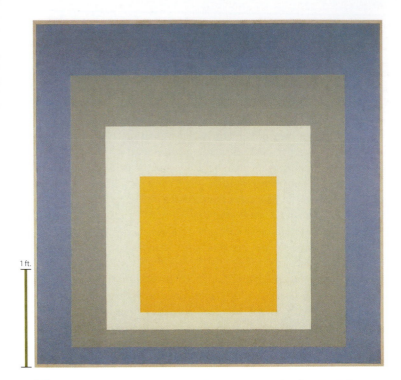

1 ft.

I-11 JOSEF ALBERS, *Homage to the Square: "Ascending,"* 1953. Oil on composition board, 3' 7½" × 3' 7½". Whitney Museum of American Art, New York.

Albers created hundreds of paintings using the same composition but employing variations in hue, saturation, and value in order to reveal the relativity and instability of color perception.

artist who emigrated to the United States in 1933. In connection with his studies, Albers created the series *Homage to the Square*—hundreds of paintings, most of which are color variations on the same composition of concentric squares, as in the illustrated example (FIG. I-11). The series reflected Albers's belief that art originates in "the discrepancy between physical fact and psychic effect."[1] Because the composition in most of these paintings remains constant, the works succeed in revealing the relativity and instability of color perception. Albers varied the hue, saturation, and value of each square in the paintings in this series. As a result, the sizes of the squares from painting to painting appear to vary (although they remain the same), and the sensations emanating from the paintings range from clashing dissonance to delicate serenity. Albers explained his motivation for focusing on color juxtapositions:

> They [the colors] are juxtaposed for various and changing visual effects. . . . Such action, reaction, interaction . . . is sought in order to make obvious how colors influence and change each other; that the same color, for instance—with different grounds or neighbors—looks different. . . . Such color deceptions prove that we see colors almost never unrelated to each other.[2]

TEXTURE The term *texture* refers to the quality of a surface, such as rough or shiny. Art historians distinguish between true texture—that is, the tactile quality of the surface—and represented texture, as when painters depict an object as having a certain texture even though the pigment is the true texture. Sometimes artists combine different materials of different textures on a single surface, juxtaposing paint with pieces of wood, newspaper, fabric, and so forth. Art historians refer to this mixed-media technique as *collage*. Texture

is, of course, a key determinant of any sculpture's character. People's first impulse is usually to handle a work of sculpture—even though museum signs often warn "Do not touch!" Sculptors plan for this natural human response, using surfaces varying in texture from rugged coarseness to polished smoothness. Textures are often intrinsic to a material, influencing the type of stone, wood, plastic, clay, or metal that a sculptor selects.

SPACE, MASS, AND VOLUME *Space* is the bounded or boundless "container" of objects. For art historians, space can be the real three-dimensional space occupied by a statue or a vase or contained within a room or courtyard. Or space can be *illusionistic,* as when painters depict an image (or illusion) of the three-dimensional spatial world on a two-dimensional surface.

Mass and *volume* describe three-dimensional objects and space. In both architecture and sculpture, mass is the bulk, density, and weight of matter in space. Yet the mass need not be solid. It can be the exterior form of enclosed space. Mass can apply to a solid Egyptian pyramid or stone statue; to a church, synagogue, or mosque (architectural shells enclosing sometimes vast spaces); and to a hollow metal statue or baked clay pot. Volume is the space that mass organizes, divides, or encloses. It may be a building's interior spaces, the intervals between a structure's masses, or the amount of space occupied by a three-dimensional object such as a statue, pot, or chair. Volume and mass describe both the exterior and interior forms of a work of art—the forms of the matter of which it is composed and the spaces immediately around the work and interacting with it.

PERSPECTIVE AND FORESHORTENING *Perspective* is one of the most important pictorial devices for organizing forms in space. Throughout history, artists have used various types of perspective to create an illusion of depth or space on a two-dimensional surface. The French painter CLAUDE LORRAIN (1600–1682) employed several perspective devices in *Embarkation of the Queen of Sheba* (FIG. I-1), a painting of a biblical episode set in a 17th-century European harbor with an ancient Roman ruin in the left foreground—an irrationally anachronistic combination that the art historian can explain only in the context of the cultural values of the artist's time and place. In Claude's painting, the figures and boats on the shoreline are much larger than those in the distance, because decreasing the size of an object makes it appear farther away. The top and bottom of the port building at the painting's right side are not parallel horizontal lines, as they are in a real building. Instead, the lines converge beyond the structure, leading the viewer's eye toward the hazy, indistinct sun on the horizon. These three perspective devices—the reduction of figure size, the convergence of diagonal lines, and the blurring of distant forms—have been familiar features of Western art since they were first employed by the ancient Greeks. It is important to state, however, that all kinds of perspective are only pictorial conventions, even when one or more types of perspective may be so common in a given culture that people accept them as "natural" or as "true" means of representing the natural world.

These perspective conventions are by no means universal. In *Waves at Matsushima* (FIG. I-12), a Japanese seascape painting on a six-part folding screen, OGATA KORIN (1658–1716) ignored these Western "tricks" for representing deep space on a flat surface. A Western viewer might interpret the left half of Korin's composition as depicting the distant horizon, as in the French painting, but the sky is an unnatural gold, and the clouds that fill that unnaturally colored sky are almost indistinguishable from the waves below.

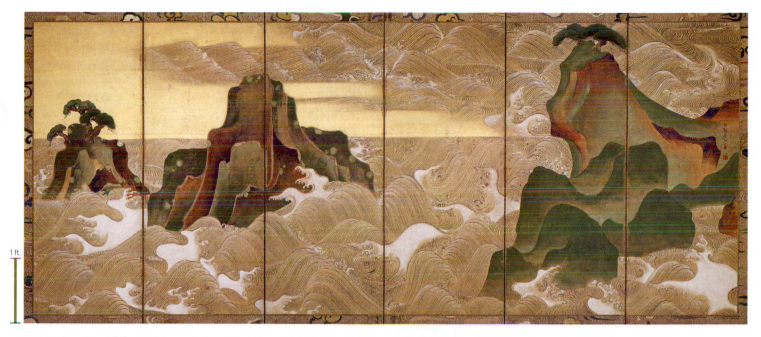

1 ft.

I-12 OGATA KORIN, *Waves at Matsushima,* Edo period, ca. 1700–1716. Six-panel folding screen, ink, color, and gold leaf on paper, 4' 11 $\frac{1}{8}$" × 12' $\frac{7}{8}$". Museum of Fine Arts, Boston (Fenollosa-Weld Collection).

Asian artists rarely employed Western perspective (FIG. I-1). Korin was more concerned with creating an intriguing composition of shapes on a surface than with locating boulders, waves, and clouds in space.

The rocky outcroppings decrease in size with distance, but all are in sharp focus, and there are no shadows. The Japanese artist was less concerned with locating the boulders and waves and clouds in space than with composing shapes on a surface, playing the swelling curves of waves and clouds against the jagged contours of the rocks. Neither the French nor the Japanese painting can be said to project "correctly" what viewers "in fact" see. One painting is not a "better" picture of the world than the other. The European and Asian artists simply approached the problem of picture making differently.

Artists also represent single figures in space in varying ways. When Flemish artist PETER PAUL RUBENS (1577–1640) painted *Lion*

Hunt (FIG. I-13), he used *foreshortening* for all the hunters and animals—that is, he represented their bodies at angles to the picture plane. When in life one views a figure at an angle, the body appears to contract as it extends back in space. Foreshortening is a kind of perspective. It produces the illusion that one part of the body is farther away than another, even though all the painted forms are on the same plane. Especially noteworthy in *Lion Hunt* are the gray horse at the left, seen from behind with the bottom of its left rear hoof facing viewers and most of its head hidden by its rider's shield, and the fallen hunter at the painting's lower right corner, whose barely visible legs and feet recede into the distance.

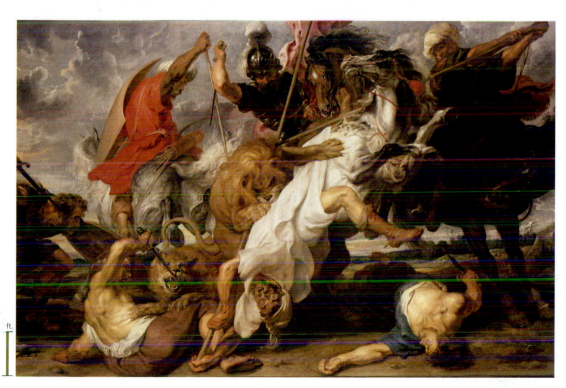

ft.

I-13 PETER PAUL RUBENS, *Lion Hunt,* 1617–1618. Oil on canvas, 8' 2" × 12' 5". Alte Pinakothek, Munich.

Foreshortening—the representation of a figure or object at an angle to the picture plane—is a common device in Western art for creating the illusion of depth. Foreshortening is a type of perspective.

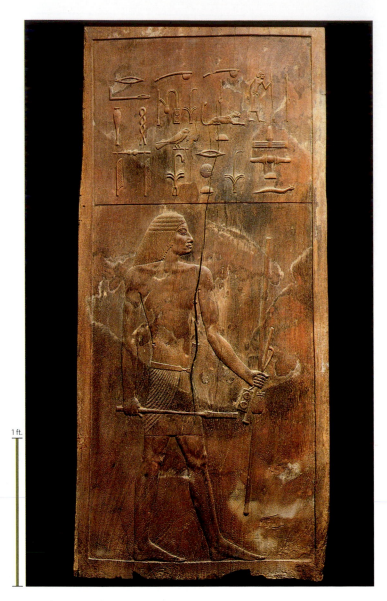

I-14 Hesire, relief from his tomb at Saqqara, Egypt, Dynasty III, ca. 2650 BCE. Wood, 3' 9" high. Egyptian Museum, Cairo.

Egyptian artists combined frontal and profile views to give a precise picture of the parts of the human body, as opposed to depicting how an individual body appears from a specific viewpoint.

The artist who carved the portrait of the ancient Egyptian official Hesire (FIG. I-14) for display in Hesire's tomb did not employ foreshortening. That artist's purpose was to present the various human body parts as clearly as possible, without overlapping. The lower part of Hesire's body is in profile to give the most complete view of the legs, with both the heel and toes of each foot visible. The frontal torso, however, allows viewers to see its full shape, including both shoulders, equal in size, as in nature. (Compare the shoulders of the hunter on the gray horse or those of the fallen hunter in *Lion Hunt*'s left foreground.) The result—an "unnatural" 90-degree twist at the waist—provides a precise picture of human body parts, if not an accurate picture of how a standing human figure really looks. Rubens and the Egyptian sculptor used very different means of depicting forms in space. Once again, neither is the "correct" manner.

PROPORTION AND SCALE *Proportion* concerns the relationships (in terms of size) of the parts of persons, buildings, or objects. People can judge "correct proportions" intuitively ("that statue's head

seems the right size for the body"). Or proportion can be a mathematical relationship between the size of one part of an artwork or building and the other parts within the work. Proportion in art implies using a *module,* or basic unit of measure. When an artist or architect uses a formal system of proportions, all parts of a building, body, or other entity will be fractions or multiples of the module. A module might be the diameter of a *column,* the height of a human head, or any other component whose dimensions can be multiplied or divided to determine the size of the work's other parts.

In certain times and places, artists have devised *canons,* or systems, of "correct" or "ideal" proportions for representing human figures, constituent parts of buildings, and so forth. In ancient Greece, many sculptors formulated canons of proportions so strict and all-encompassing that they calculated the size of every body part in advance, even the fingers and toes, according to mathematical ratios.

Proportional systems can differ sharply from period to period, culture to culture, and artist to artist. Part of the task that art history students face is to perceive and adjust to these differences. In fact, many artists have used disproportion and distortion deliberately for expressive effect. In the medieval French depiction of the weighing of souls on judgment day (FIG. I-7), the devilish figure yanking down on the scale has distorted facial features and stretched, lined limbs with animal-like paws for feet. Disproportion and distortion make him appear "inhuman," precisely as the sculptor intended.

In other cases, artists have used disproportion to focus attention on one body part (often the head) or to single out a group

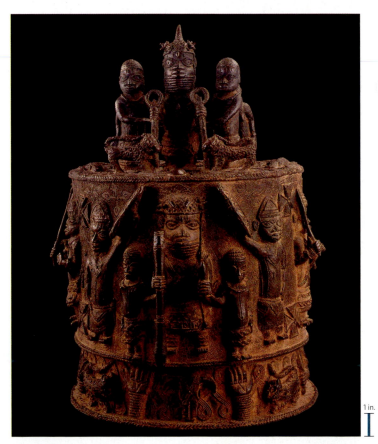

I-15 Altar to the Hand (ikegobo), from Benin, Nigeria, ca. 1735–1750. Bronze, 1' 5½" high. British Museum, London (gift of Sir William Ingram).

One of the Benin king's praise names is Great Head, and on this cast-bronze royal altar, the artist represented him larger than all other figures and with a disproportionately large head.

member (usually the leader). These intentional "unnatural" discrepancies in proportion constitute what art historians call *hierarchy of scale*, the enlarging of elements considered the most important. On the bronze altar from Benin, Nigeria, illustrated here (FIG. I-15), the sculptor varied the size of each figure according to the person's social status. Largest, and therefore most important, is the Benin king, depicted twice, each time flanked by two smaller attendant figures and shown wearing a multistrand coral necklace emblematic of his high office. The king's head is also disproportionately large compared to his body, consistent with one of the Benin ruler's praise names: Great Head.

One problem that students of art history—and professional art historians too—confront when studying illustrations in art history books is that although the relative sizes of figures and objects in a painting or sculpture are easy to discern, it is impossible to determine the absolute size of the work reproduced because they all are printed at approximately the same size on the page. Readers of *Art through the Ages* can learn the exact size of all artworks from the dimensions given in the captions and, more intuitively, from the scales positioned at the lower left or right corner of each illustration.

CARVING AND CASTING Sculptural technique falls into two basic categories, *subtractive* and *additive*. *Carving* is a subtractive technique. The final form is a reduction of the original mass of a block of stone, a piece of wood, or another material. Wood statues were once

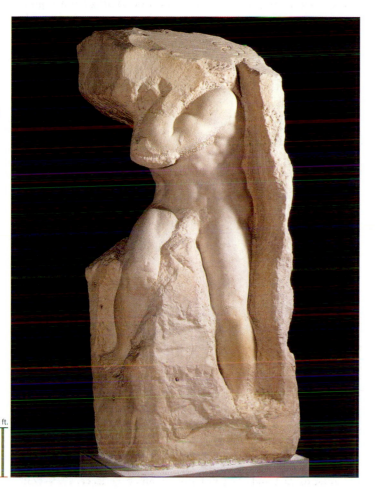

1 ft.

I-16 MICHELANGELO BUONARROTI, unfinished statue, 1527–1528. Marble, 8' 7 1/2" high. Galleria dell'Accademia, Florence.

Carving a freestanding figure from stone or wood is a subtractive process. Michelangelo thought of sculpture as a process of "liberating" the statue contained within the block of marble.

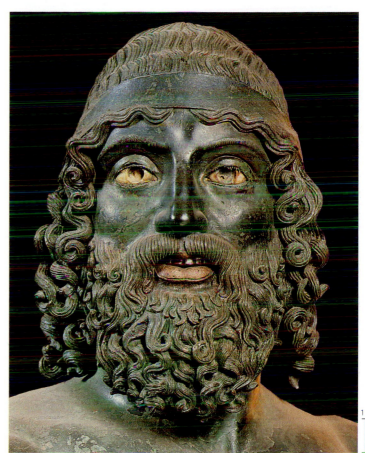

1 in.

I-17 Head of a warrior, detail of a statue (FIG. 5-36) from the sea off Riace, Italy, ca. 460–450 BCE. Bronze, full statue 6' 6" high. Museo Archeologico Nazionale, Reggio Calabria.

The sculptor of this life-size statue of a bearded Greek warrior cast the head, limbs, torso, hands, and feet in separate molds, then welded the pieces together and added the eyes in a different material.

tree trunks, and stone statues began as blocks pried from mountains. The unfinished marble statue illustrated here (FIG. I-16) by renowned Italian artist MICHELANGELO BUONARROTI (1475–1564) clearly reveals the original shape of the stone block. Michelangelo thought of sculpture as a process of "liberating" the statue within the block. All sculptors of stone or wood cut away (subtract) "excess material." When they finish, they "leave behind" the statue—in this example, a twisting nude male form whose head Michelangelo never freed from the stone block.

In additive sculpture, the artist builds up the forms, usually in clay around a framework, or *armature*. Or a sculptor may fashion a *mold,* a hollow form for shaping, or *casting,* a fluid substance such as bronze or plaster. The ancient Greek sculptor who made the bronze statue of a warrior found in the sea near Riace, Italy, cast the head (FIG. I-17) as well as the limbs, torso, hands, and feet (FIG. 5-36) in separate molds and then *welded* them together (joined them by heating). Finally, the artist added features, such as the pupils of the eyes (now missing), in other materials. The warrior's teeth are silver, and his lower lip is copper.

RELIEF SCULPTURE *Statues* and *busts* (head, shoulders, and chest) that exist independent of any architectural frame or setting and that viewers can walk around are *freestanding sculptures,* or *sculptures in the round,* whether the artist produced the piece by carving (FIG. I-10) or casting (FIG. I-17). In *relief sculpture,* the subjects project from the background but remain part of it. In *high-relief* sculpture, the images project boldly. In some cases, such as the medieval weighing-of-souls scene (FIG. I-7), the *relief* is so high that not only do the forms cast shadows on the background, but some parts are even in the round, which explains why some pieces— for example, the arms of the scales—broke off centuries ago. In *low-relief*, or *bas-relief*, sculpture, such as the portrait of Hesire (FIG. I-14), the projection is slight. Artists can produce relief sculptures, as they do sculptures in the round, either by carving or casting. The altar from Benin (FIG. I-15) is an example of bronze-casting in high relief (for the figures on the cylindrical altar) as well as in the round (for the king and his two attendants on the top).

ARCHITECTURAL DRAWINGS Buildings are groupings of enclosed spaces and enclosing masses. People experience architecture both visually and by moving through and around it, so they perceive architectural space and mass together. These spaces and masses can be represented graphically in several ways, including as plans, sections, elevations, and cutaway drawings.

A *plan,* essentially a map of a floor, shows the placement of a structure's masses and, therefore, the spaces they circumscribe and enclose. A *section,* a kind of vertical plan, depicts the placement of the masses as if someone cut through the building along a plane. Drawings showing a theoretical slice across a structure's width are *lateral sections.* Those cutting through a building's length are *longitudinal sections.* Illustrated here are the plan and lateral section of Beauvais Cathedral (FIG. I-18), which readers can compare with the photograph of the church's *choir* (FIG. I-3). The plan shows the choir's shape and the location of the *piers* dividing the *aisles* and supporting the *vaults* above, as well as the pattern of the crisscrossing vault *ribs.* The lateral section shows not only the interior of the choir with its vaults and tall *stained-glass* windows but also the structure of the roof and the form of the exterior *flying buttresses* holding the vaults in place.

Other types of architectural drawings appear throughout this book. An *elevation* drawing is a head-on view of an external or internal wall. A *cutaway* combines in a single drawing an exterior view with an interior view of part of a building.

This overview of the art historian's vocabulary is not exhaustive, nor have artists used only painting, drawing, sculpture, and architecture as media over the millennia. Ceramics, jewelry, textiles, photography, and computer graphics are just some of the numerous other arts. All of them involve highly specialized techniques described in distinct vocabularies. As in this introductory chapter, new terms are in *italics* when they first appear. The comprehensive Glossary at the end of the book contains definitions of all italicized terms.

Art History and Other Disciplines

By its very nature, the work of art historians intersects with the work of others in many fields of knowledge, not only in the humanities but also in the social and natural sciences. Today, art historians must go beyond the boundaries of what the public and even professional art historians of previous generations traditionally considered the specialized discipline of art history. In short, art historical research in the 21st century is typically interdisciplinary in nature. To cite one example, in an effort to unlock the secrets of a particular statue, an art historian might conduct archival research hoping to uncover new documents shedding light on who paid for the work and why, who made it and when, where it originally stood, how people of the time viewed it, and a host of other questions. Realizing, however, that the authors of the written documents often were not objective recorders of fact but observers with their own biases and agendas, the art historian may also use methodologies developed in such fields as literary criticism, philosophy, sociology, and gender studies to weigh the evidence that the documents provide.

At other times, rather than attempting to master many disciplines at once, art historians band together with other specialists in multidisciplinary inquiries. Art historians might call in chemists to date an artwork based on the composition of the materials used, or might

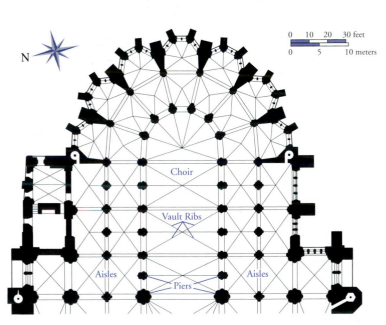

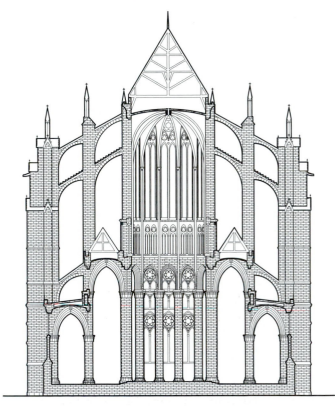

I-18 Plan (*left*) and lateral section (*right*) of Beauvais Cathedral, Beauvais, France, rebuilt after 1284.

Architectural drawings are indispensable aids for the analysis of buildings. Plans are maps of floors, recording the structure's masses. Sections are vertical "slices" across a building's width or length.

ask geologists to determine which quarry furnished the stone for a particular statue. X-ray technicians might be enlisted in an attempt to establish whether a painting is a forgery. Of course, art historians often reciprocate by contributing their expertise to the solution of problems in other disciplines. A historian, for example, might ask an art historian to determine—based on style, material, iconography, and other criteria—if any of the portraits of a certain king date after his death. Such information would help establish the ruler's continuing prestige during the reigns of his successors. Some portraits of Augustus (FIG. I-10), the founder of the Roman Empire, postdate his death by decades, even centuries, as do the portraits of several deceased U.S. presidents on coins and paper currency produced today.

DIFFERENT WAYS OF SEEING

The history of art can be a history of artists and their works, of styles and stylistic change, of materials and techniques, of images and themes and their meanings, and of contexts and cultures and patrons. The best art historians analyze artworks from many viewpoints. But no art historian (or scholar in any other field), no matter how broad-minded in approach and no matter how experienced, can be truly objective. Like the artists who made the works illustrated and discussed in this book, art historians are members of a society, participants in its culture. How can scholars (and museum visitors and travelers to foreign locales) comprehend cultures unlike their own? They can try to reconstruct the original cultural contexts of artworks, but they are limited by their distance from the thought patterns of the cultures they study and by the obstructions to understanding—the assumptions, presuppositions, and prejudices peculiar to their own culture—that their own thought patterns raise. Art historians may reconstruct a distorted picture of the past because of culture-bound blindness.

A single instance underscores how differently people of diverse cultures view the world and how various ways of seeing can result in sharp differences in how artists depict the world. Illustrated here are two contemporaneous portraits of a 19th-century Maori chieftain (FIG. I-19)—one by an Englishman, JOHN SYLVESTER (active early 19th century), and the other by the New Zealand chieftain himself, TE PEHI KUPE (d. 1829). Both reproduce the chieftain's facial *tattoo*. The European artist (FIG. I-19, *left*) included the head and shoulders and downplayed the tattooing. The tattoo pattern is one aspect of the likeness among many, no more or less important than the chieftain's European attire. Sylvester also recorded his subject's momentary glance toward the right and the play of light on his hair, fleeting aspects having nothing to do with the figure's identity.

In contrast, Te Pehi Kupe's self-portrait (FIG. I-19, *right*)—made during a trip to Liverpool, England, to obtain European arms to take back to New Zealand—is not a picture of a man situated in space and bathed in light. Rather, it is the chieftain's statement of the supreme importance of the tattoo design announcing his rank among his people. Remarkably, Te Pehi Kupe created the tattoo patterns from memory, without the aid of a mirror. The splendidly composed insignia, presented as a flat design separated from the body and even from the head, is Te Pehi Kupe's image of himself. Only by understanding the cultural context of each portrait can art historians hope to understand why either representation appears as it does.

As noted at the outset, the study of the context of artworks and buildings is one of the central concerns of art historians. *Art through the Ages* seeks to present a history of art and architecture that will help readers understand not only the subjects, styles, and techniques of paintings, sculptures, buildings, and other art forms created in all parts of the world during 30 millennia but also their cultural and historical contexts. That story now begins.

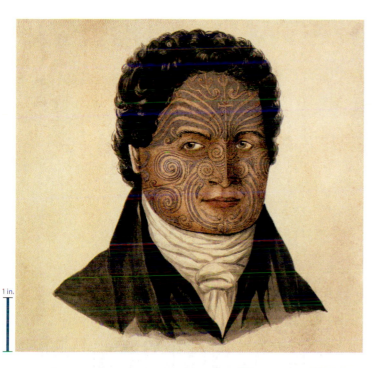

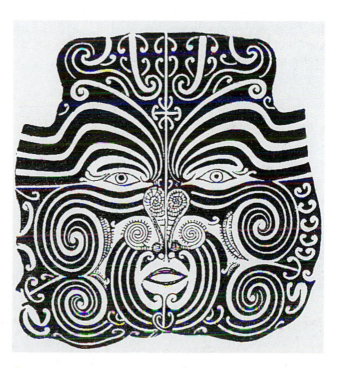

1 in.

I-19 *Left:* JOHN HENRY SYLVESTER, *Portrait of Te Pehi Kupe*, 1826. Watercolor, 8 ¼" × 6 ¼". National Library of Australia, Canberra (Rex Nan Kivell Collection). *Right:* TE PEHI KUPE, *Self-Portrait*, 1826. From Leo Frobenius, *The Childhood of Man: A Popular Account of the Lives, Customs and Thoughts of the Primitive Races* (Philadelphia: J. B. Lippincott, 1909), 35, fig. 28.

These strikingly different portraits of the same Maori chief reveal the different ways of seeing by a European artist and an Oceanic one. Understanding the cultural context of artworks is vital to art history.

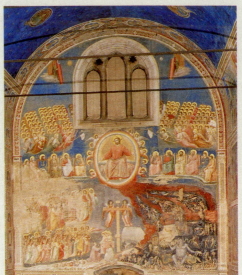

▲ **14-1a** Giotto's vision of the Last Judgment fills the west wall above the entrance to the Arena Chapel. The Paduan banker Enrico Scrovegni built the chapel to atone for the moneylender's sin of usury.

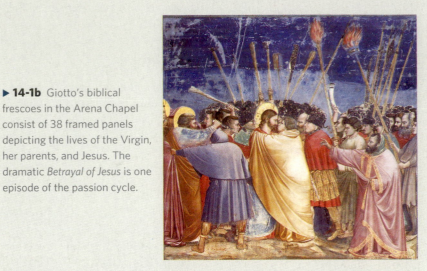

▶ **14-1b** Giotto's biblical frescoes in the Arena Chapel consist of 38 framed panels depicting the lives of the Virgin, her parents, and Jesus. The dramatic *Betrayal of Jesus* is one episode of the passion cycle.

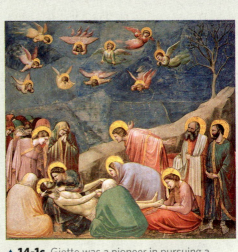

▲ **14-1c** Giotto was a pioneer in pursuing a naturalistic approach to representing figures in space. In *Lamentation,* set in a landscape, he revived the classical tradition of depicting some figures from the rear.

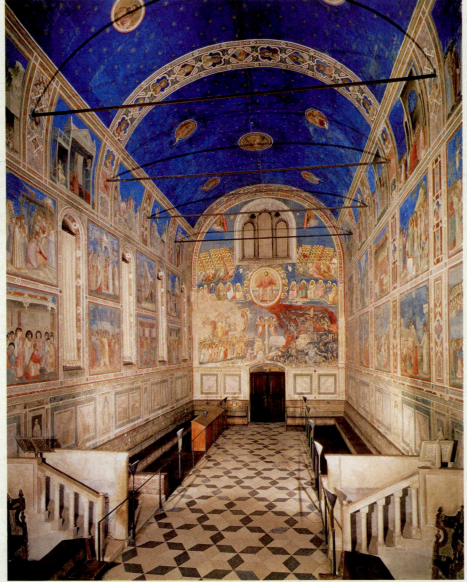

14-1   GIOTTO DI BONDONE, interior of the Arena Chapel (Cappella Scrovegni; looking west), Padua, Italy, 1305–1306.

Late Medieval Italy

LATE MEDIEVAL OR PROTO-RENAISSANCE?

Art historians debate whether the art of Italy between 1200 and 1400 is the last phase of medieval art or the beginning of the rebirth, or *Renaissance,* of Greco-Roman *naturalism.* All agree, however, that these two centuries mark a major turning point in the history of Western art and that the pivotal figure of this age was the Florentine painter GIOTTO DI BONDONE (ca. 1266–1337). Giotto's masterwork is the fresco cycle of the Arena Chapel (FIG. **14-1**) in Padua, which takes its name from an adjacent ancient Roman arena (*amphitheater*). A banker, Enrico Scrovegni, built the chapel on a site adjacent to his palace and consecrated it in 1305, in the hope that the chapel would atone for the moneylender's sin of usury.

In 38 framed panels, Giotto presented, in the top level, the lives of the Virgin and her parents, Joachim and Anna; in the middle zone, the life and mission of Jesus; and, in the lowest level, the Savior's passion and resurrection. The climactic *Last Judgment* covers most of the west wall, where Scrovegni appears among the saved, kneeling as he presents his chapel to the Virgin.

The *Entry into Jerusalem, Betrayal of Jesus,* and *Lamentation* panels reveal the essentials of Giotto's style. In contrast to the common practice of his day, Giotto set his goal as emulating the appearance of the natural world—the approach championed by the ancient Greeks and Romans but largely abandoned in the Middle Ages in favor of representing spiritual rather than physical reality. Subtly scaled to the chapel's space, Giotto's stately and slow-moving half-life-size figures act out the religious dramas convincingly and with great restraint. The biblical actors are sculpturesque, simple, and weighty, often *foreshortened* (seen from an angle) and modeled with light and shading in the ancient manner. They convey individual emotions through their postures and gestures. Giotto's naturalism displaced the *Byzantine* style (see Chapter 9) in Italy, inaugurating an age some scholars call "early scientific." By stressing the preeminence of sight for gaining knowledge of the world, Giotto and his successors contributed to the foundation of empirical science. Praised in his own and later times for his fidelity to nature, Giotto was more than a mere imitator of it. He showed his generation a new way of seeing. With Giotto, European painters turned away from representing the spiritual world—the focus of medieval artists both in the Latin West and Byzantium—and once again made recording the visible world a central, if not the sole, aim of their art.

DUECENTO (13TH CENTURY)

When the Italian humanists of the 16th century condemned the art of the late Middle Ages in northern Europe as "Gothic" (see page 374), they did so by comparing it with the contemporaneous art of Italy (MAP 14-1), which consciously revived the *classical** art of antiquity. Italian artists and scholars regarded medieval artworks as distortions of the noble art of the Greeks and Romans. Interest in the art of classical antiquity was not entirely absent during the medieval period, however, even in France, the origin and center of the Gothic style. For example, on the west front of Reims Cathedral, the 13th-century statues of Christian *saints* and angels (FIG. 13-24) reveal the unmistakable influence of ancient Roman art on French sculptors. However, the classical revival that took root in Italy during the 13th and 14th centuries was much more pervasive and longer lasting.

Sculpture

Italian admiration for classical art surfaced early on at the court of Frederick II, King of Sicily (r. 1197–1250) and Holy Roman Emperor (r. 1220–1250). Frederick's nostalgia for Rome's past grandeur fostered a revival of classical sculpture in Sicily and southern Italy during the 13th century (the *Duecento,* the 1200s) not unlike the classical *renovatio* (renewal) that Charlemagne encouraged in Germany and France four centuries earlier (see page 322).

NICOLA PISANO The sculptor Nicola d'Apulia (Nicholas of Apulia), better known as NICOLA PISANO (active ca. 1258–1278) after his adopted city (see "Italian Artists' Names," page 413), received his early training in southern Italy during Frederick's rule. In 1250, Nicola traveled northward and eventually settled in Pisa. Then at the height of its political and economic power, the maritime city was a magnet for artists seeking lucrative commissions. Nicola specialized in carving marble reliefs and may have been the inventor of a new kind of church furniture—the monumental stone *pulpit*

* In *Art through the Ages,* the adjective "Classical," with uppercase *C,* refers specifically to the Classical period of ancient Greece, 480–323 BCE. Lowercase "classical" refers to Greco-Roman antiquity in general—that is, the period treated in Chapters 5, 6, and 7.

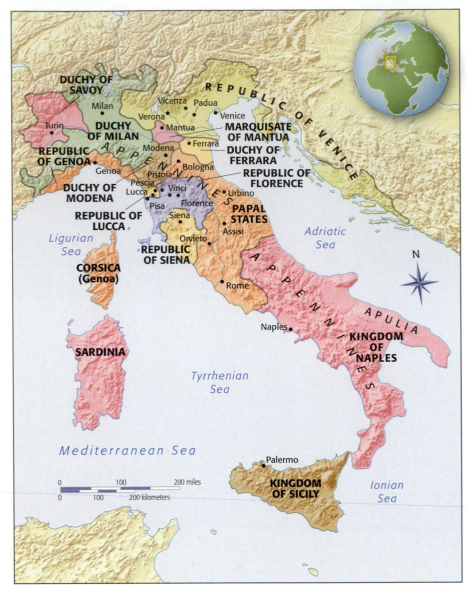

MAP 14-1 Italy around 1400.

(raised platform from which priests delivered sermons) with supports in the form of freestanding statues and wraparound narrative reliefs depicting biblical themes.

Nicola fashioned the first such pulpit (FIG. 14-2) in 1260 for Pisa's century-old baptistery (FIG. 12-29, *left*). Some elements of the pulpit's design carried on medieval traditions—for example, the *trefoil* (triple-curved) *arches* and the lions supporting some of the *columns*—but Nicola also incorporated classical elements. The large *capitals* with two rows of thick overlapping leaves crowning the columns are a Gothic variation of the *Corinthian capital*

LATE MEDIEVAL ITALY

1200-1300
Duecento

- Bonaventura Berlinghieri and Cimabue are the leading painters working in the Italo-Byzantine style, or *maniera greca*
- Nicola and Giovanni Pisano, father and son, represent two contrasting sculptural styles, the classical and the Gothic respectively
- Pietro Cavallini's fresco cycles in Rome and those in San Francesco at Assisi foreshadow the revolutionary art of Giotto

1300-1400
Trecento

- In Florence, Giotto, considered the first Renaissance artist, pioneers a naturalistic approach to painting
- In Siena, Duccio softens the maniera greca and humanizes religious subject matter
- Secular themes emerge as important subjects in civic commissions, as in the frescoes of Siena's Palazzo Pubblico
- Florence, Siena, and Orvieto build new cathedrals that are stylistically closer to Early Christian basilicas than to French Gothic cathedrals

Italian Artists' Names

In contemporary societies, people have become accustomed to a standardized method of identifying individuals, in part because of the proliferation of official documents such as driver's licenses, passports, and student identification cards. Modern names consist of given names (names selected by the parents) and family names, although the order of the two (or more) names varies from country to country. In China, for example, the family name precedes the given name.

This kind of regularity in names was not, however, the norm in premodern Italy. Many individuals were known by their place of birth or adopted hometown. Nicola Pisano (FIGS. 14-2 and 14-3) was "Nicholas the Pisan," Giulio Romano was "Julius the Roman," and Domenico Veneziano was "Dominic the Venetian." Leonardo da Vinci ("Leonard from Vinci") hailed from the small town of Vinci, near Florence (MAP 14-1). Art historians therefore refer to these artists by their given names, not the names of their towns. (The title of Dan Brown's best-selling novel should have been *The Leonardo Code*, not *The Da Vinci Code*.)

Nicknames were also common. Giorgione was "Big George." People usually referred to Tommaso di Cristoforo Fini as Masolino ("Little Thomas") to distinguish him from his more famous pupil Masaccio ("Brutish Thomas"). Guido di Pietro was called Fra Angelico ("Angelic Friar"). Cenni di Pepo is remembered as Cimabue (FIG. 14-6), which means "bull's head."

The format of names was also impermanent and could be changed at will. This flexibility has resulted in significant challenges for historians, who often must deal with archival documents and other records referring to the same artist by different names.

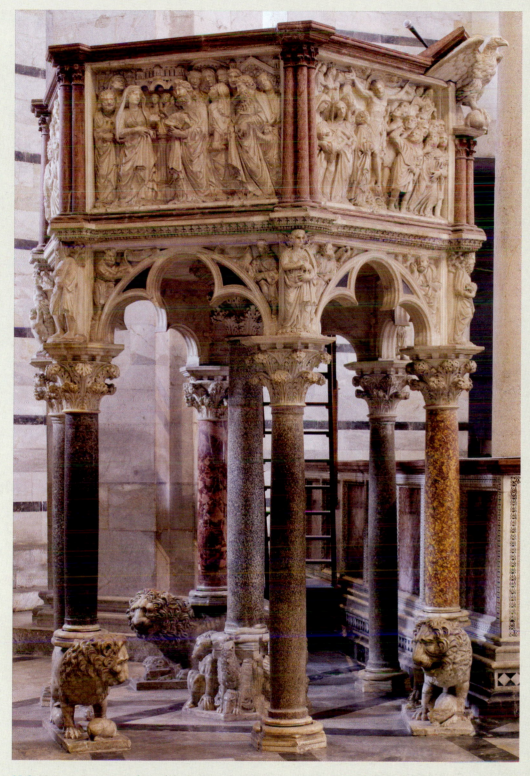

14-2 Nicola Pisano, pulpit of the baptistery, Pisa, Italy, 1259–1260. Marble, 15' high.

The Pisa baptistery pulpit by Nicola Pisano (Nicholas of Pisa) retains many medieval features—for example, trefoil arches—but many of the figures derive from ancient Roman relief sculptures.

(FIG. 5-73). The arches are round, as in Roman architecture, rather than pointed (*ogival*), as in Gothic buildings. Also, each of the large rectangular relief panels resembles the sculptured front of a Roman *sarcophagus* (coffin; for example, FIG. 7-68).

The densely packed large-scale figures of the individual panels also seem to derive from the compositions found on Roman sarcophagi. One of the six panels of the baptistery pulpit depicts scenes from the infancy cycle of Christ (see "The Life of Jesus in Art,"

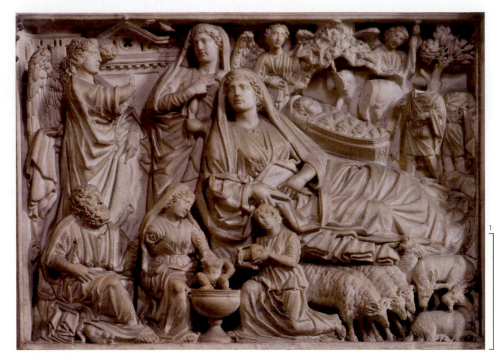

14-3 NICOLA PISANO, *Annunciation, Nativity, and Adoration of the Shepherds,* relief panel on the pulpit of the baptistery, Pisa, Italy, 1259–1260. Marble, 2' 10" × 3' 9".

Classical sculptures inspired the faces, beards, coiffures, and draperies, as well as the bulk and weight of Nicola's figures. The *Nativity* Madonna resembles lid figures on Roman sarcophagi.

1 ft.

pages 240–241), including *Annunciation* (FIG. **14-3**, top left), *Nativity* (center and lower half), and *Adoration of the Shepherds* (top right). Mary appears twice, and her size varies. The focus of the composition is the reclining Virgin of the *Nativity* episode, whose posture and drapery are reminiscent of those of the lid figures on Etruscan (FIG. 6-6) and Roman (FIG. 7-59) sarcophagi. The face types, beards, and coiffures, as well as the bulk and weight of Nicola's figures, also reveal the influence of classical relief sculpture. Art historians have even been able to pinpoint the models of some of the pulpit figures, including the reclining Mary, in Roman sculptures in Pisa.

GIOVANNI PISANO Nicola's son, GIOVANNI PISANO (ca. 1250–1320), likewise became a sought-after sculptor of church pulpits. His career extended into the early 14th century, when he carved (singlehand-edly, according to an inscription) the marble pulpit in Pisa's cathedral (FIG. 12-29, *center*). The pulpit is the largest known example of the type. It boasts nine curved narrative panels, including, in addition to the subjects Giovanni's father represented, scenes from the life of John the Baptist. The panel of the *Nativity* and related scenes (FIG. **14-4**) offers a striking contrast to Nicola's quiet, dignified presenta-tion of the religious narrative. The younger sculptor arranged the figures loosely and dynamically. They twist and bend in excited animation, and the deep spaces between them suggest their motion. In *Annunciation* (top left), the Virgin shrinks from the angel's sudden appearance in a pos-ture of alarm touched with humility. The same spasm of apprehension contracts her supple body as she reclines in *Nativity* (left center). The drama's principals share in a peculiar ner-vous agitation, as if spiritual passion suddenly moves all of them. Only the shepherds and the sheep (right) do not yet share in the miracu-lous event. The swiftly turning, slender and sinuous figures and the general emotionalism

of the scene are features not found in Nicola Pisano's interpretation. The father worked in the classical tradition, the son in a style derived from French Gothic. These styles were two of the three most impor-tant ingredients in the formation of the distinctive and original art of 14th-century Italy.

Painting and Architecture

The third major stylistic element in late medieval Italian art was the Byzantine tradition (see Chapter 9). Throughout the Middle Ages, the Byzantine style dominated Italian painting, but its influence was especially strong after the fall of Constantinople in 1204, which pre-cipitated a migration of Byzantine artists to Italy.

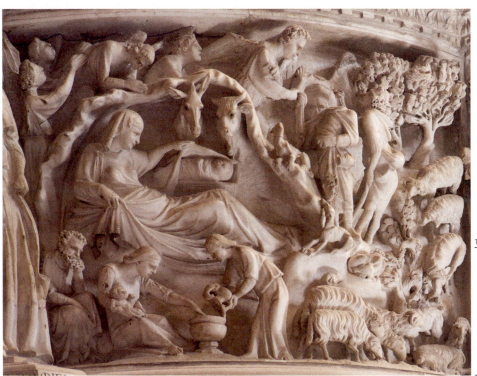

14-4 GIOVANNI PISANO, *Annunciation, Nativity, and Adoration of the Shepherds,* relief panel on the pulpit of the cathedral, Pisa, Italy, 1302–1310. Marble, 2' 10⅜" × 3' 7".

The French Gothic style had a greater influence on Giovanni Pisano, Nicola's son. Giovanni arranged his figures loosely and dynamically. They display a nervous agitation, as if moved by spiritual passion.

1 ft.

RELIGION AND MYTHOLOGY
The Great Schism, Mendicant Orders, and Confraternities

In 1305, the College of Cardinals (the collective body of all cardinals) elected a French pope, Clement V (r. 1305–1314), who settled in Avignon. Subsequent French popes remained in Avignon, despite their announced intentions to return to Rome. Understandably, the Italians, who saw Rome as the rightful capital of the universal Church, resented the Avignon papacy. The conflict between the French and the Italians resulted in the election in 1378 of two popes—Clement VII, who resided in Avignon (and who does not appear in the Catholic Church's official list of popes), and Urban VI (r. 1378–1389), who remained in Rome. Thus began what became known as the Great Schism. After 40 years, Holy Roman Emperor Sigismund (r. 1410–1437) convened a council that resolved this crisis by electing a new Roman pope, Martin V (r. 1417–1431), who was acceptable to all.

The pope's absence from Italy during much of the 14th century contributed to an increase in prominence of *monastic orders*. The Augustinians, Carmelites, and Servites became very active, ensuring a constant religious presence in the daily life of Italians, but the largest and most influential monastic orders were the *mendicants* (begging friars)—the Franciscans, founded by Francis of Assisi (ca. 1181–1226; FIGS. 14-5 and 14-5A), and the Dominicans, founded by the Spaniard Dominic de Guzman (ca. 1170–1221). As did other monks, the mendicant friars renounced all worldly goods and committed themselves to spreading God's word, performing good deeds, and ministering to the sick and dying. But unlike the many monks who resided in rural and often isolated monasteries, the mendicants lived in the heart of cities and preached to large urban crowds. The Dominicans, in particular, contributed significantly to establishing urban educational institutions. The Franciscans and Dominicans became very popular in Italy because of their concern for the poor and the personal relationship with God that they encouraged common people to cultivate.

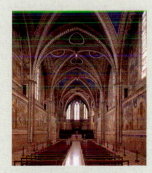
14-5A San Francesco, Assisi, 1228–1253.

Although both mendicant orders worked for the glory of God, a degree of rivalry nevertheless existed between the two. For example, in Florence they established their churches on opposite sides of the city—Santa Croce (FIG. I-4), the Franciscan church, on the eastern side, and the Dominicans' Santa Maria Novella (FIG. 14-5B) on the western (MAP 21-1).

Confraternities, organizations consisting of laypersons who dedicated themselves to strict religious observance, also grew in popularity during the 14th and 15th centuries. The mission of confraternities included tending the sick, burying the dead, singing hymns, and performing other good works. The confraternities as well as the mendicant orders continued to play an important role in Italian religious life through the 16th century. The numerous artworks and monastic churches they commissioned have ensured their enduring legacy.

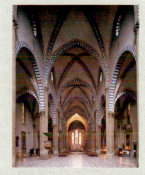
14-5B Santa Maria Novella, Florence, begun ca. 1246.

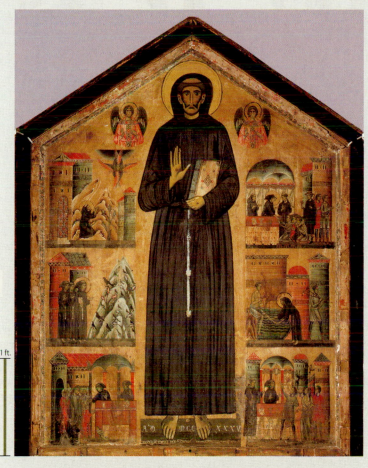

14-5 BONAVENTURA BERLINGHIERI, *Saint Francis Altarpiece,* San Francesco, Pescia, Italy, 1235. Tempera on wood, 5′ × 3′.

Berlinghieri painted this altarpiece in the Italo-Byzantine style, or maniera greca, for the mendicant (begging) order of Franciscans. It is the earliest securely dated portrayal of Saint Francis of Assisi.

BONAVENTURA BERLINGHIERI One of the leading painters working in the Italo-Byzantine style, or *maniera greca* (Greek style), was BONAVENTURA BERLINGHIERI (active ca. 1235–1244) of Lucca. His most famous work is the *Saint Francis Altarpiece* (FIG. 14-5) in the church of San Francesco (Saint Francis) in Pescia. Painted in 1235 using *tempera* on wood panel (see "Tempera and Oil Painting," page 559), the *altarpiece* honors Saint Francis of Assisi, whose most important shrine (FIG. 14-5A) was at Assisi itself. The Pescia altarpiece highlights the increasingly prominent role of religious orders in late medieval Italy (see "The Great Schism, Mendicant Orders, and Confraternities," above). Saint Francis's Franciscan order worked diligently to impress on the public the saint's valuable example and to demonstrate the order's commitment to teaching and to alleviating suffering. Berlinghieri's altarpiece, painted only nine years after Francis's death, is the earliest securely dated representation of the saint.

Berlinghieri depicted Francis wearing the costume later adopted by all Franciscan monks: a coarse clerical robe tied at the waist with a rope. The saint displays the *stigmata*—marks resembling Christ's wounds—that miraculously appeared on his hands and feet. Flanking Francis are two angels, whose frontal poses, prominent *halos,* and lack of modeling reveal the Byzantine roots of Berlinghieri's style. So, too, does the use of *gold leaf* (gold beaten into tissue-paper-thin sheets, then applied to surfaces), which emphasizes the image's flatness and otherworldly, spiritual nature. Appropriately, Berlinghieri's panel focuses on the aspects of the saint's life that the Franciscans wanted to promote, thereby making visible (and thus more credible) the legendary life of this holy man. Saint Francis believed that he could get closer to God by rejecting worldly goods, and to achieve this he stripped himself bare in a public square and committed himself to a strict life of fasting, prayer, and meditation. His followers considered the appearance of stigmata on Francis's hands and feet (clearly visible in the saint's frontal image, which resembles a Byzantine *icon;* compare FIG. 9-16) as God's blessing, and viewed Francis as a second Christ. Fittingly, four of the six narrative scenes along the sides of the panel depict miraculous healings, connecting Saint Francis even more emphatically to Christ. The narrative scenes provide an active contrast to the stiff formality of the large central image of Francis. At the upper left, taking pride of place at the saint's right, Francis receives the stigmata. Directly below, the saint preaches to the birds, a subject that also figures prominently in the fresco program (FIG. 14-5C) of San Francesco at Assisi, the work of a painter art historians call the SAINT FRANCIS MASTER. These and the scenes depicting Francis's

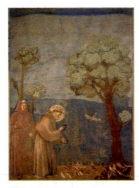

14-5C ST. FRANCIS MASTER, *Francis Preaching to the Birds,* ca. 1290–1300.

miracle cures strongly suggest that Berlinghieri's source was one or more Byzantine *illuminated manuscripts* (compare FIGS. 9-17B, 9-18, and 9-18A) with biblical narrative scenes.

CIMABUE One of the first artists to break from the Italo-Byzantine style that dominated 13th-century Italian painting was Cenni di Pepo, better known as CIMABUE (ca. 1240–1302). Cimabue challenged some of the major conventions of late medieval art in pursuit of a closer approximation of the appearance of the natural world—the core of the classical naturalistic tradition. He painted *Madonna Enthroned with Angels and Prophets* (FIG. 14-6) for Santa Trinità (Holy Trinity) in Florence, the Benedictine church near the Arno River built between 1258 and 1280. The composition and the gold background reveal the painter's reliance on Byzantine models (compare FIG. 9-19). Cimabue also used the gold embellishments common to Byzantine art for the folds of the Madonna's robe, but they are no longer merely decorative patterns. In his panel, they enhance the three-dimensionality of the drapery. Furthermore, Cimabue constructed a deeper space for the Madonna and the surrounding figures to inhabit than was common in Byzantine art. The Virgin's throne, for example, is a massive structure that Cimabue convincingly depicted as receding into space. The overlapping bodies of the angels on each side of the throne and the half-length prophets who look outward or upward from beneath it reinforce the sense of depth.

PIETRO CAVALLINI The authors of the most important Renaissance commentaries on Italian art of the 13th and 14th centuries

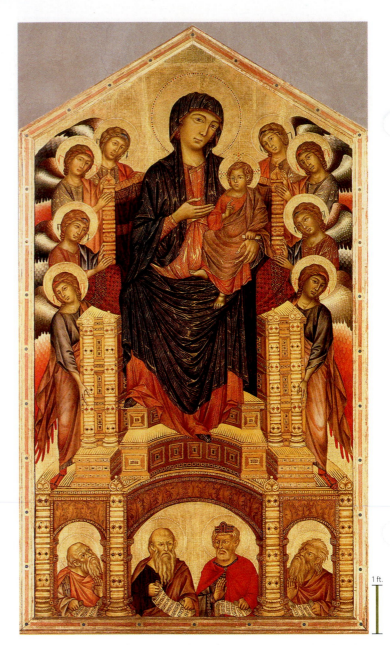

1 ft.

14-6 CIMABUE, *Madonna Enthroned with Angels and Prophets,* from Santa Trinità, Florence, ca. 1280–1290. Tempera and gold leaf on wood, 12' 7" × 7' 4". Galleria degli Uffizi, Florence.

Cimabue was one of the first artists to break away from the maniera greca. Although he relied on Byzantine models, Cimabue depicted the Madonna's massive throne as receding into space.

were all Florentines, and civic pride doubtless played a role in attributing the reorientation of the art of painting to Florentine artists, especially Giotto (FIG. 14-1). Giorgio Vasari (1511–1574), the "father of art history" (see "Vasari's *Lives,*" page 636), lauded Giotto as the first to make a definitive break from the maniera greca of late medieval painting and to return to the naturalism of the ancients. But the stylistic revolution that Giotto represents was not solely his creation. Other artists paved the way for the Florentine master in the mural program (FIGS. 14-5A and 14-5C) of San Francesco at Assisi and in the churches of Rome.

The leading Roman painter at the end of the 13th century was Pietro dei Cerroni, known as PIETRO CAVALLINI (ca. 1240–ca. 1340), or "Little Horse" (see "Italian Artists' Names," page 413),

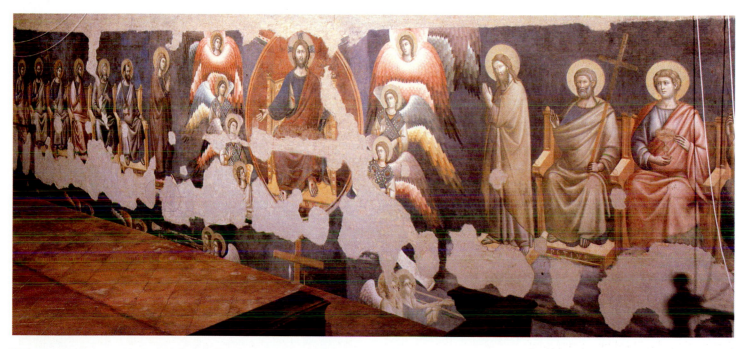

14-7 PIETRO CAVALLINI, *Last Judgment,* fresco on the west wall of the nave of Santa Cecilia in Trastevere, Rome, Italy, ca. 1290–1295.

A pioneer in the representation of fully modeled figures seen in perspective with light illuminating their faces and garments, Pietro Cavallini of Rome may have influenced Giotto di Bondone (FIG. 14-1).

who his son said lived to age 100. Cavallini enjoyed the patronage of Pope Nicholas III (r. 1277–1280), who commissioned him to restore the Early Christian frescoes in San Paolo fuori le mura (Saint Paul's Outside the Walls) in Rome. Cavallini's careful study and emulation of those Late Antique paintings must have profoundly influenced his later work, which unfortunately survives only in fragments.

Around 1290, Cavallini received two important commissions for churches in Trastevere, on the western bank of the Tiber near the Vatican. He produced mosaics depicting the life of the Virgin for Santa Maria in Trastevere, and painted a fresco cycle of Old and New Testament scenes in Santa Cecilia in Trastevere, of which only part of his *Last Judgment* (FIG. **14-7**) survives, but what remains confirms his stature as an innovative artist of the highest order. Christ appears at the center with the Virgin Mary to his right, John the Baptist to his left, and six enthroned *apostles* to each side (see "Early Christian Saints," pages 236–237). Below the Savior is an altar with the instruments of his martyrdom (cross, nails, Longinus's spear, and so on). At each side of the altar, angels (at the left, the Savior's right side) present to Christ those about to be saved, while the agents of the Devil (on his left) claim the damned. The theme is familiar from Romanesque portal sculpture (FIG. 12-15), but here it appears inside the church on the entrance (west) wall as the culmination of the biblical cycle painted on the nave walls. Cavallini's apostles sit on deep thrones seen in *perspective* (the illusionistic depiction on a two-dimensional surface of three-dimensional objects in space). Both the disciples and their thrones face inward toward Christ, uniting both sides of the composition with the central figure. The apostles' garments have deep folds that catch the light. Light also illuminates the figures' faces. Cavallini used light effectively to create volume and mass, a radical departure from the maniera greca, but the light does not come from a uniform source, and the apostles appear against a neutral dark background.

Cavallini has not received the recognition he deserves because his extant works are few and poorly preserved and because of the

enduring influence of Vasari's artist biographies, but he was a pioneering figure in the creation of the Renaissance style in Italy.

TRECENTO (14TH CENTURY)

In the 14th century (the *Trecento,* or 1300s), Italy consisted of numerous independent *city-states,* each corresponding to a geographic region centered on a major city (MAP 14-1). Most of the city-states, such as Venice, Florence, Lucca, and Siena, were republics—constitutional oligarchies governed by executive bodies, advisory councils, and special commissions. Other powerful 14th-century states included the Papal States, the Kingdom of Naples, and the duchies of Milan, Modena, Ferrara, and Savoy. As their names indicate, these states were politically distinct from the republics, but all the states shared in the prosperity of the period. The sources of wealth varied from state to state. Italy's port cities expanded maritime trade, whereas the economies of other cities depended on banking or the manufacture of arms or textiles.

The outbreak of the Black Death (bubonic plague) in the late 1340s threatened this prosperity, however. Originating in China, the Black Death swept across Europe. The most devastating natural disaster in European history, the Black Death eliminated between 25 and 50 percent of the Continent's population in about five years. The plague devastated Italy's inhabitants. In large Italian cities, where people lived in relatively close proximity, the death tolls climbed as high as 50 to 60 percent of the population. The Black Death also had a significant effect on art. It stimulated religious bequests and encouraged the commissioning of devotional images. The focus on sickness and death also led to a burgeoning in hospital construction.

Another significant development in 14th-century Italy was the blossoming of a vernacular literature (written in the commonly spoken language instead of Latin), which dramatically affected Italy's intellectual and cultural life. Latin remained the official language of Church liturgy and state documents. However, the creation of an Italian vernacular literature (based on the Tuscan dialect common in Florence) expanded the audience for philosophical and intellectual concepts because of its greater accessibility. Dante Alighieri (1265–1321, author of *The Divine Comedy*), the poet and scholar Francesco Petrarch (1304–1374), and Giovanni Boccaccio (1313–1375, author of *Decameron*) were most responsible for establishing this vernacular literature.

RENAISSANCE HUMANISM The development of easily accessible literature was one important sign that the essentially religious view that had dominated Europe during the Middle Ages was about to change dramatically in what historians call the *Renaissance.* Although religion continued to occupy a primary position in the lives of Europeans, a growing concern with the natural world, the individual, and humanity's worldly existence characterized the Renaissance period—the 14th through 16th centuries. The word *renaissance* in French and English (*rinascità* in Italian) refers to a "rebirth" of art and culture. A revived interest in classical cultures—indeed, the veneration of classical antiquity as a model—was central to this rebirth. The notion that the Renaissance represented the restoration of the glorious past of Greece and Rome gave rise to the concept of the "Middle Ages" as the era falling between antiquity and the Renaissance. The transition from the medieval to the Renaissance, though dramatic, did not come about abruptly, however. In fact, much that is medieval persisted in the Renaissance and in later periods.

Fundamental to the development of the Italian Renaissance was *humanism,* which emerged during the 14th century and became a central component of Italian art and culture in the 15th and 16th centuries. Humanism was more a code of civil conduct, a theory of education, and a scholarly discipline than a philosophical system. The chief concerns of Italian humanists, as their name suggests, were human values and interests as distinct from—but not opposed to—religion's otherworldly values. Humanists pointed to classical cultures as particularly praiseworthy. This enthusiasm for antiquity involved study of Latin literature, especially the elegant Latin of Cicero (106–43 BCE) and the Augustan age (27 BCE–14 CE), and a conscious emulation of what proponents believed were the Roman civic virtues. These included self-sacrificing service to the state, participation in government, defense of state institutions (especially the administration of justice), and stoic indifference to personal misfortune in the performance of duty. With the help of a new interest in and knowledge of Greek, the humanists of the late 14th and 15th centuries recovered a large part of Greek as well as Roman literature and philosophy that had been lost, left unnoticed, or cast aside in the Middle Ages. Indeed, classical cultures provided humanists with a model for living in this world, a model primarily of human focus derived not from an authoritative and traditional religious dogma but from reason.

Ideally, humanists sought no material reward for services rendered. The sole reward for heroes of civic virtue was fame, just as the reward for leaders of the holy life was sainthood. For the educated, the lives of heroes and heroines of the past became models of conduct as important as the lives of the saints. Petrarch wrote a book on illustrious men, and his colleague Boccaccio complemented it with 106 biographies of famous women—from Eve to Joanna, queen of Naples (r. 1343–1382). Both Petrarch and Boccaccio were renowned in their own day as poets, scholars, and men of letters—their achievements equivalent in honor to those of the heroes of civic virtue. In 1341 in Rome, Petrarch received the laurel wreath crown, the ancient symbol of victory and merit (compare FIGS. I-10, 7-69, and 7-79, *left*). The humanist cult of fame emphasized the importance of creative individuals and their role in contributing to the renown of the city-state and of all Italy.

Giotto

Celebrated in his own day as the first Renaissance painter, Giotto di Bondone (FIG. 14-1) is a towering figure in the history of art. Scholars still debate the sources of the Florentine painter's style, but one formative influence must have been Cimabue, whom Vasari identified as Giotto's teacher, while noting that the pupil eclipsed his master by abandoning the "crude maniera greca" (see "Vasari's *Lives,*" page 636). The 13th-century *murals* of San Francesco at Assisi (FIGS. 14-5A and 14-5C) and those of Pietro Cavallini in Rome (FIG. 14-7) may also have influenced Giotto—although some scholars believe that the young Giotto himself was one of the leading painters of the Assisi church. French Gothic sculpture (which Giotto may have seen but which was certainly familiar to him from the work of Giovanni Pisano, who had spent time in Paris) and ancient Roman art probably also contributed to Giotto's artistic education. Yet no mere synthesis of these varied influences could have produced the significant shift in artistic approach that has led some scholars to describe Giotto as the father of Western pictorial art.

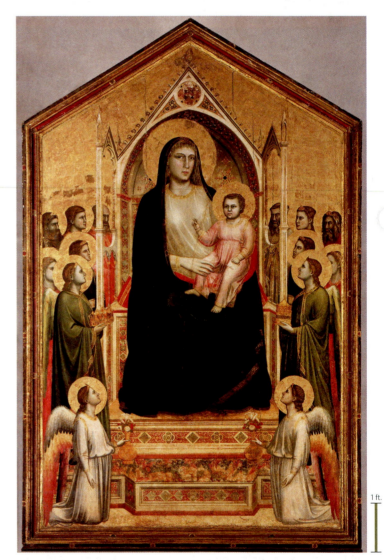

1 ft.

14-8 GIOTTO DI BONDONE, *Madonna Enthroned (Ognissanti Madonna),* from the Chiesa di Ognissanti (All Saints' Church), Florence, ca. 1310. Tempera and gold leaf on wood, 10′ 8″ × 6′ 8″. Galleria degli Uffizi, Florence.

Giotto displaced the Byzantine style in Italian painting and revived classical naturalism. His figures have substance, dimensionality, and bulk, and create the illusion that they could throw shadows.

MATERIALS AND TECHNIQUES
Fresco Painting

Fresco painting has a long history, particularly in the Mediterranean region, where the Minoans (FIGS. 4-7 to 4-10) used it as early as the 17th century BCE. *Fresco* (Italian for "fresh") is a mural-painting technique involving the application of permanent limeproof pigments, diluted in water, on freshly laid lime plaster. Because the surface of the wall absorbs the pigments as the plaster dries, fresco is one of the most durable painting techniques. The stable condition of the ancient Minoan frescoes, as well as those found at Pompeii and other Roman sites (FIGS. 7-17 to 7-26), in San Francesco (FIGS. 14-5A and 14-5C) at Assisi, and in the Arena Chapel (FIGS. 14-1 and 14-9, 14-9A, and 14-9B) at Padua, testify to the longevity of this painting method. The colors have remained vivid (although dirt and soot have necessitated cleaning—most famously in the Vatican's Sistine Chapel; FIG. 22-18B) because of the chemically inert pigments the artists used.

This *buon fresco* ("true" fresco) process is time-consuming and demanding and requires several layers of plaster. Although buon fresco methods vary, generally the artist (or, more precisely, an apprentice in the master's workshop) prepares the wall with a rough layer of lime plaster called the *arriccio* (brown coat). The artist then transfers the composition to the wall, usually by drawing directly on the arriccio with a burnt-orange pigment called *sinopia* (most popular during the 14th century), or by transferring a *cartoon* (a full-size preparatory drawing). Cartoons increased in usage in the 15th and 16th centuries, largely replacing sinopia underdrawings. Finally, the painter lays the *intonaco* (painting coat) smoothly over the drawing in sections (called *giornate*—Italian for "days") only as large as the artist expects to complete in that session. (It is easy to distinguish the various giornate in Giotto's *Lamentation* [FIG. 14-9].) The buon fresco painter must apply the colors quickly, because once the plaster is dry, it will no longer absorb the pigment. Any unpainted areas of the intonaco after a session must be cut away so that fresh plaster can be applied for the next giornata.

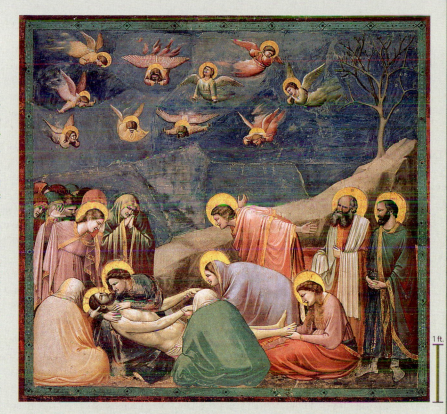

14-9 GIOTTO DI BONDONE, *Lamentation*, Arena Chapel (Cappella Scrovegni; FIG. 14-1), Padua, Italy, ca. 1305. Fresco, 6' 6¾" × 6' ¾".

Giotto painted *Lamentation* in several sections, each corresponding to one painting session, or giornata. Artists employing the buon fresco technique must complete each section before the plaster dries.

In addition to the buon fresco technique, artists used *fresco secco* (dry fresco). Fresco secco involves painting on dried lime plaster, the method the ancient Egyptians employed (FIGS. 3-28 and 3-29). Although the finished product visually approximates buon fresco, the plaster wall does not absorb the pigments, which simply adhere to the surface, so fresco secco is not as permanent as buon fresco.

In areas of high humidity, such as Venice, fresco was less appropriate because moisture is an obstacle to the drying process. Over the centuries, fresco became less popular, although it did experience a revival in the 1930s with the Mexican muralists (FIGS. 29-74 and 29-75).

MADONNA ENTHRONED On nearly the same great scale as Cimabue's enthroned Madonna (FIG. 14-6) is Giotto's panel (FIG. 14-8) depicting the same subject, painted for the high altar of Florence's Church of the Ognissanti (All Saints). Although still portrayed against the traditional gold background, Giotto's Madonna sits on her Gothic throne with the unshakable stability of an ancient marble goddess (compare FIG. 7-30). Giotto replaced Cimabue's slender Virgin, fragile beneath the thin ripplings of her drapery, with a weighty, queenly mother. In Giotto's painting, the Madonna's body is not lost—indeed, it is asserted. Giotto even showed Mary's breasts pressing through the thin fabric of her white undergarment. Gold highlights have disappeared from her heavy robe. Giotto aimed instead to construct a figure with substance, dimensionality, and bulk—qualities suppressed in favor of a spiritual immateriality in Byzantine and Italo-Byzantine art. The different approaches of teacher and pupil can also be seen in the angels flanking the Madon-

na's throne. Cimabue stacked his angels to fill the full height of the panel. Giotto's angels stand on a common level, leaving a large blank area above the heads of the background figures. Works painted in the new style portray statuesque figures projecting into the light and creating the illusion that they could throw shadows. Giotto's *Madonna Enthroned* marks the end of medieval painting in Italy and the beginning of a new naturalistic approach to art.

ARENA CHAPEL Projecting on a flat surface the illusion of solid bodies moving through space presents a double challenge. Constructing the illusion of a weighty, three-dimensional body also requires constructing the illusion of a space sufficiently ample to contain that body. In his *fresco* cycles (see "Fresco Painting," above), Giotto constantly strove to reconcile these two aspects of *illusionistic* painting. His murals in Enrico Scrovegni's Arena Chapel (FIGS. 14-1 and 14-9) at Padua show his art at its finest. (Some

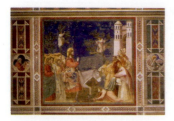

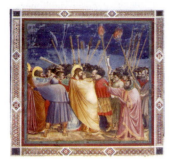

14-9A Giotto, *Entry into Jerusalem*, ca. 1305.

14-9B Giotto, *Betrayal of Jesus*, ca. 1305.

scholars have suggested that Giotto may also have been the chapel's architect, because its design so perfectly suits its interior decoration. The rectangular hall has only six windows, all in the south wall, which provide ample illumination for the frescoes that fill the almost unbroken surfaces of the other walls.) In 38 framed scenes (FIGS. 14-9, **14-9A,** and **14-9B**), Giotto presented one of the most impressive and complete Christian pictorial cycles ever rendered. The narrative unfolds on the north and south walls in three zones, reading from top to bottom. Below, imitation marble veneer—reminiscent of ancient Roman *revetment* (FIG. 7-51), which Giotto may have seen—alternates with personified Virtues and Vices painted in *grisaille* (monochrome grays, often used for modeling in paintings) to resemble sculpture. On the west wall above the chapel's entrance is Giotto's dramatic *Last Judgment,* the culminating scene also of Cavallini's late-13th-century fresco cycle (FIG. 14-7) in Santa Cecilia in Trastevere in Rome. In fact, Giotto's enthroned apostles are strikingly similar to Cavallini's. The chapel's vaulted ceiling is blue, an azure sky dotted with golden stars symbolic of Heaven. Medallions bearing images of Christ, Mary, and various prophets also appear on the vault. Giotto painted the same blue in the backgrounds of the narrative panels on the walls below. The color thereby functions as a unifying agent for the entire decorative scheme.

LAMENTATION The panel in the lowest zone of the north wall, *Lamentation* (FIG. 14-9), illustrates particularly well the revolutionary nature of Giotto's style. In the presence of boldly foreshortened angels, seen head-on with their bodies receding into the background and darting about in hysterical grief, a congregation mourns over the dead Savior just before his entombment. Mary cradles her son's body. Mary Magdalene looks solemnly at the wounds in Christ's feet. Saint John the Evangelist throws his arms back dramatically. Giotto arranged a shallow stage for the figures, bounded by a thick diagonal rock incline defining a horizontal ledge in the foreground. Though narrow, the ledge provides firm visual support for the figures. The rocky setting recalls the landscape of a 12th-century Byzantine mural (FIG. 9-30) at Nerezi in Macedonia. Here, the steep slope leads the viewer's eye toward the picture's dramatic focal point at the lower left.

The postures and gestures of Giotto's figures convey a broad spectrum of grief. They range from Mary's almost fierce despair to the passionate outbursts of Mary Magdalene and John to the philosophical resignation of the two disciples at the right and the mute sorrow of the two hooded mourners in the foreground. In *Lamentation,* a single event provokes a host of individual responses in figures that are convincing presences both physically and psychologically. Painters before Giotto rarely attempted, let alone achieved, this combination of naturalistic representation, compositional complexity, and emotional resonance.

The formal design of the *Lamentation* fresco—the way Giotto grouped the figures within the constructed space—is worth close

study. Each group has its own definition, and each contributes to the rhythmic order of the composition. The strong diagonal of the rocky ledge, with its single dead tree (the tree of knowledge of good and evil, which withered after Adam and Eve's original sin), concentrates the viewer's attention on the heads of Christ and his mother, which Giotto positioned dynamically off center. The massive bulk of the seated mourner in the painting's left corner arrests and contains all movement beyond Mary and her dead son. The seated mourner to the right establishes a relation with the center figures, who, by gazes and gestures, draw the viewer's attention back to Christ's head. Figures seen from the back, which are frequent in Giotto's compositions (compare FIG. 14-9B), represent an innovation in the movement away from the Italo-Byzantine style. These figures emphasize the foreground, aiding the visual placement of the intermediate figures farther back in space. This device, the very contradiction of Byzantine frontality, in effect puts viewers behind the "observer figures," who, facing the action as spectators, reinforce the sense of stagecraft as a model for painting. Also markedly different from the maniera greca is Giotto's habit of painting incomplete figures cut off by the composition's frame, a feature also of his Ognissanti Madonna (FIG. 14-8).

Giotto's new devices for depicting spatial depth and body mass could not, of course, have been possible without his management of light and shade. He shaded his figures to indicate both the direction of the light illuminating their bodies and the shadows (the diminished light), thereby giving the figures volume. In *Lamentation*, light falls upon the upper surfaces of the figures (especially the two central bending figures) and passes down to dark in their garments, separating the volumes one from the other and pushing one to the fore, the other to the rear. The graded continuum of light and shade, directed by an even, neutral light from a single steady source—not shown in the picture—was the first step toward the development of *chiaroscuro* (the use of contrasts of dark and light to produce modeling) in later Renaissance painting (see page 627).

The stagelike settings (FIGS. 14-9A and 14-9B) made possible by Giotto's innovations in perspective and lighting suited perfectly the dramatic narrative that the Franciscans emphasized then as a principal method for educating the faithful in their religion. In this new age of humanism, the old stylized presentations of the holy mysteries had evolved into *mystery plays.* Actors extended the drama of the Mass into one- and two-act tableaus and scenes and then into simple narratives offered at church portals and in city squares. (Eventually, confraternities also presented more elaborate religious dramas called *sacre rappresentazioni*—holy representations.) The great increase in popular sermons to huge city audiences prompted a public taste for narrative, recited as dramatically as possible. The arts of illusionistic painting, of drama, and of sermon rhetoric with all their theatrical flourishes developed simultaneously and were mutually influential. Giotto's art masterfully synthesized dramatic narrative, holy lesson, and truth to human experience in a visual idiom of his own invention, accessible to all. Not surprisingly, Giotto's frescoes served as textbooks for generations of Renaissance painters.

Siena

Among 14th-century Italian city-states, the Republics of Siena and Florence were the most powerful. Both were urban centers of bankers and merchants with widespread international contacts and large sums available for the commissioning of artworks (see "Artists' Guilds, Artistic Commissions, and Artists' Contracts," page 422).

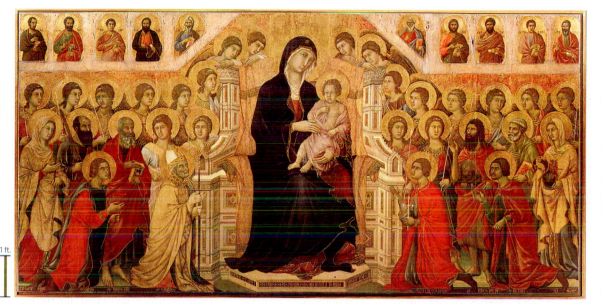

1 ft.

DUCCIO The works of DUCCIO DI BUONINSEGNA (active ca. 1278–1318) are the supreme examples of 14th-century Sienese art. His most famous commission, the immense altarpiece called the *Maestà* (*Virgin Enthroned in Majesty;* FIG. 14-10), replaced a much smaller painting of the Virgin Mary on the high altar of Siena Cathedral (FIG. 14-13A). The Sienese believed that the Virgin had brought them victory over the Florentines at the battle of Monteperti in 1260, and she was the focus of the religious life of the republic. Duccio and his assistants began work on the prestigious commission in 1308 and completed the altarpiece in 1311, causing the entire city to celebrate. Shops closed, and the bishop led a great procession of priests, civic officials, and the populace at large in carrying the altarpiece from Duccio's studio outside the city gate

through the *Campo* (literally "field"—Siena's main *piazza,* or plaza), past the town hall (FIG. 14-16), and up to its home on Siena's highest hill. So great was Duccio's stature that the church's officials permitted him to include his name in the dedicatory inscription on the front of the altarpiece on the Virgin's footstool: "Holy Mother of God, be the cause of peace for Siena and of life for Duccio, because he painted you thus."

As originally executed, Duccio's *Maestà* consisted of the seven-foot-high central panel (FIG. 14-10) with the dedicatory inscription, surmounted by seven *pinnacles* above, and a *predella,* or raised shelf, of panels at the base, altogether some 13 feet high. Painted in tempera front and back (FIG. 14-11), the work unfortunately can no longer be seen in its entirety, because of its dismantling in

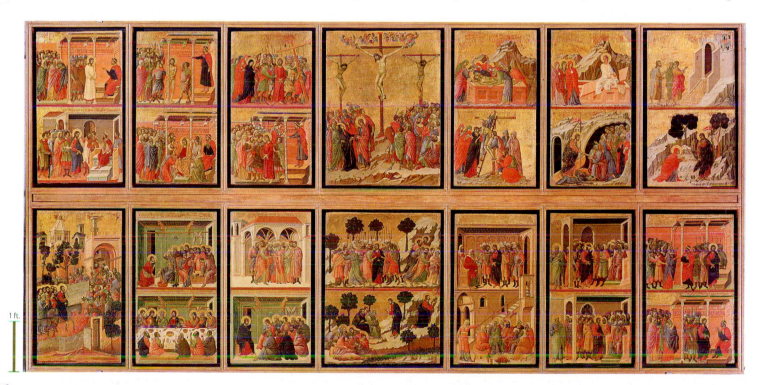

1 ft.

14-11 DUCCIO DI BUONINSEGNA, *Life of Jesus,* 14 panels from the back of the *Maestà* altarpiece (FIG. 14-10), from Siena Cathedral, Siena, Italy, 1308–1311. Tempera and gold leaf on wood, 7' × 13'. Museo dell'Opera del Duomo, Siena.

On the back of the *Maestà* altarpiece, Duccio painted Jesus's passion in 24 scenes on 14 panels, beginning with *Entry into Jerusalem* (FIG. 14-11A), at the lower left, through *Noli me tangere,* at top right.

THE PATRON'S VOICE
Artists' Guilds, Artistic Commissions, and Artists' Contracts

The structured organization of economic activity during the 14th century, when Italy had established a thriving international trade and held a commanding position in the Mediterranean world, extended to many trades and professions. *Guilds* (associations of master craftspeople, apprentices, and tradespeople), which had emerged during the 12th century, became prominent. These associations not only protected members' common economic interests against external pressures, such as taxation, but also provided them with the means to regulate their internal operations (for example, training apprentices and assuring high-quality work).

Because of today's international open art market, the notion of an "artists' union" may seem strange. The general public tends to think of art as the creative expression of an individual artist. However, artists did not always enjoy this degree of freedom. Historically, they rarely undertook projects without receiving a specific commission. The patron contracting for the artist's services could be a civic group, religious institution, private individual, or even the artists' guild itself. Guilds, although primarily business organizations, also contributed to their city's religious and artistic life by subsidizing the building and decoration of numerous churches and hospitals. For example, the wool manufacturers' guild oversaw the start of Florence Cathedral (FIGS. 14-19 and 14-19A) in 1296, and the wool merchants' guild supervised the completion of its dome (FIG. 21-29A). The guild of silk manufacturers and goldsmiths provided the funds to build Florence's foundling hospital, the Ospedale degli Innocenti (FIG. 21-30).

Monastic orders, confraternities, and the Vatican were also major art patrons. In addition, wealthy families and individuals—for example, the Paduan banker Enrico Scrovegni (FIG. 14-1)—commissioned artworks for a wide variety of reasons. Besides the aesthetic pleasure these patrons derived from art, the images often also served as testaments to the patron's piety, wealth, and stature. (In Scrovegni's case, he hoped that building the Arena Chapel and decorating it with biblical frescoes would outweigh his sins as a moneylender and earn him a place in Heaven.) Because artworks during this period were the product of service contracts, a patron's needs or wishes played a crucial role in the final form of any painting, sculpture, or building.

Some early contracts between patrons and artists still exist. Patrons normally asked artists to submit drawings or models for approval, and they expected the artists they hired to adhere closely to the approved designs. The contracts usually stipulated certain conditions, such as the insistence on the artist's own hand in the production of the work, the quality of pigment and amount of gold or other costly materials to be used, completion date, payment terms, and penalties for failure to meet the contract's terms.

A few extant 13th- and 14th-century painting contracts are especially illuminating. Although they may specify the subject to be represented, these binding legal documents always focus on the financial aspects of the commission and the responsibilities of the painter to the patron (and vice versa). In a contract dated November 1, 1301, between Cimabue (FIG. 14-6) and another artist and the Hospital of Santa Chiara in Pisa, the artists agree to supply an altarpiece

> with colonnettes, tabernacles, and predella, painted with histories of the divine majesty of the Blessed Virgin Mary, of the apostles, of the angels, and with other figures and pictures, as shall be seen fit and shall please the said master of or other legitimate persons for the hospital.*

Other terms of the Santa Chiara contract specify the size of the panel and require the artists to use gold and silver gilding for parts of the altarpiece.

The contract for an altarpiece's frame was usually a separate document, because it necessitated employing the services of a master carpenter. For example, on April 15, 1285, the leading painter of Siena, Duccio di Buoninsegna (FIGS. 14-10, 14-11, 14-11A, and 14-12), signed a contract with the rectors of the Confraternity of the Laudesi, the lay group associated with the Dominican church of Santa Maria Novella (FIG. 14-5B) in Florence. The contract specified only that Duccio was to provide the painting, not its frame—and it imposed conditions that the painter had to meet if he was to be paid.

> [The rectors] promise . . . to pay the same Duccio . . . as the payment and price of the painting of the said panel that is to be painted and done by him in the way described below . . . 150 lire of the small florins. . . . [Duccio, in turn, promises] to paint and embellish the panel with the image of the blessed Virgin Mary and of her omnipotent Son and other figures, according to the wishes and pleasure of the lessors, and to gild [the panel] and do everything that will enhance the beauty of the panel, his being all the expenses and the costs. . . . If the said panel is not beautifully painted and it is not embellished according to the wishes and desires of the same lessors, they are in no way bound to pay him the price or any part of it.†

Sometimes patrons furnished the materials and paid artists by the day instead of a fixed amount. That was the arrangement Duccio made on October 9, 1308, when he agreed to paint the *Maestà* (FIG. 14-10) for the high altar of Siena Cathedral.

> Duccio has promised to paint and make the said panel as well as he can and knows how, and he further agreed not to accept or receive any other work until the said panel is done and completed. . . . [The church officials promise] to pay the said Duccio sixteen solidi of the Sienese denari as his salary for the said work and labor for each day that the said Duccio works with his own hands on the said panel . . . [and] to provide and give everything that will be necessary for working on the said panel so that the said Duccio need contribute nothing to the work save his person and his effort.§

In all cases, the artists worked for their patrons and could count on being compensated for their talents and efforts only if the work they delivered met the standards of those who ordered it.

*Translated by John White, *Duccio: Tuscan Art and the Medieval Workshop* (London: Thames & Hudson, 1979), 34.
†Translated by James H. Stubblebine, *Duccio di Buoninsegna and His School* (Princeton, N.J.: Princeton University Press, 1979), 1: 192.
§Stubblebine, *Duccio,* 1: 201.

subsequent centuries. Many of Duccio's panels are on display today as single masterpieces, scattered among the world's museums.

The main panel on the front of the altarpiece represents the Virgin enthroned as queen of Heaven amid choruses of angels and saints. Duccio derived the composition's formality and symmetry, along with the figures and facial types of the principal angels and saints, from Byzantine tradition. But the artist relaxed the strict frontality and rigidity of the figures. They turn to each other in quiet conversation. Further, Duccio individualized the faces of the four patron saints of Siena (Ansanus, Savinus, Crescentius, and Victor) kneeling in the foreground, who perform their ceremonial gestures without stiffness. Similarly, he softened the usual Byzantine hard body outlines and drapery patterning. The folds of the garments, particularly those of the female saints at both ends of the panel, fall and curve loosely. This is a feature familiar in French Gothic works (FIG. 13-37) and is a mark of the artistic dialogue between Italy and northern Europe in the 14th century.

Despite these changes revealing Duccio's interest in the new naturalism, he respected the age-old requirement that as an altarpiece, his *Maestà* would be the focus of worship in Siena's largest and most important church, its *cathedral,* the seat of the bishop of Siena. Duccio knew that the altarpiece should be an object holy in itself—a work of splendor to the eyes, precious in its message and its materials—and recognized how the function of the artwork limited experimentation in depicting narrative action and producing illusionistic effects (such as Giotto's) by modeling forms and adjusting their placement in pictorial space.

Instead, the queen of Heaven panel is a miracle of color composition and texture manipulation, unfortunately not fully revealed in photographs. Close inspection of the original reveals what the Sienese artist learned from other sources. In the 13th and 14th centuries, Italy was the distribution center for the great silk trade from China and the Middle East (see "Silk and the Silk Road," page 467). After processing the silk in city-states such as Lucca and Florence, the Italians exported the precious fabric throughout Europe to satisfy an immense market for elegant dress. (Dante, Petrarch, and many other humanists decried the appetite for luxury in costume,

which to them represented a decline in civic and moral virtue.) People throughout Europe (Duccio and other artists among them) prized fabrics from China, Persia, Byzantium, and the Islamic world. In his depiction of the enthroned Virgin among saints, Duccio created the glistening and shimmering effects of textiles, adapting the motifs and design patterns of exotic materials. Complementing the sumptuous fabrics and the (lost) gilded wood frame are the halos of the holy figures, which feature tooled decorative designs in gold leaf (*punchwork*). But, as did Giotto in his *Ognissanti Madonna* (FIG. 14-8), Duccio eliminated almost all the gold patterning of the figures' garments in favor of creating three-dimensional volume. Traces remain only in the Virgin's red dress.

In contrast to the main panel, the predella and the back (FIG. 14-11) of the *Maestà* present an extensive series of narrative panels of different sizes and shapes, beginning with the annunciation of Jesus's birth to Mary and culminating with the Savior's resurrection and other episodes following his crucifixion (see "The Life of Jesus in Art," pages 240–241). The section reproduced here, consisting of 24 scenes in 14 panels, relates the events of Christ's passion. The largest scene, at top center, is the *Crucifixion*—highly appropriate for an altarpiece where the Sienese bishop celebrated Mass, the ritual reenactment of the Savior's sacrifice. Duccio drew the details of his scenes from the accounts in all four Gospels. The viewer reads the pictorial story in zigzag fashion, beginning with *Entry into Jerusalem* (FIG. 14-11A) at the lower left. The narrative ends with Christ's appearance to Mary Magdalene (*Noli me tangere*) at the top right. Duccio consistently dressed Jesus in blue robes in most of the panels, but beginning with *Transfiguration*, the Savior's garment is gilded.

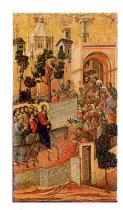

⬀**14-11A** Duccio, *Entry into Jerusalem*, 1308–1311.

On the front panel, Duccio showed himself as the great master of the traditional altarpiece. However, in the small accompanying panels, front and back, he allowed himself greater latitude for experimentation. (Worshipers could always view both sides of the *Maestà* because the high altar stood at the center of the sanctuary.) The New Testament scenes on the back of the altarpiece reveal Duccio's powers as a narrative painter. In *Betrayal of Jesus* (FIG. **14-12**; compare FIG. 14-9B), for example, the artist

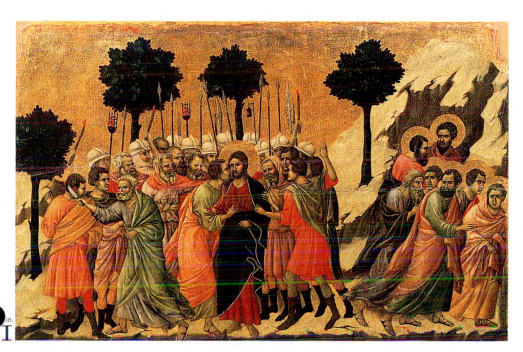

14-12 DUCCIO DI BUONINSEGNA, *Betrayal of Jesus*, panel on the back (FIG. 14-11) of the *Maestà* altarpiece (FIG. 14-10), from Siena Cathedral, Siena, Italy, 1308–1311. Tempera and gold leaf on wood, 1' 10$\frac{1}{2}$" × 3' 4". Museo dell'Opera del Duomo, Siena.

In this dramatic depiction of Judas's betrayal of Jesus, the actors display a variety of individual emotions. Duccio here took a decisive step toward the humanization of religious subject matter.

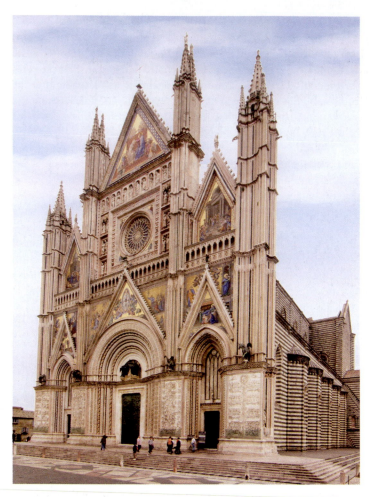

14-13 LORENZO MAITANI, Orvieto Cathedral (looking northeast), Orvieto, Italy, begun 1310.

The pointed gables over the doorways, the rose window, and the large pinnacles derive from French Gothic architecture, but the facade of Orvieto Cathedral masks a traditional timber-roofed basilica.

represented several episodes of the event—the betrayal of Jesus by Judas's false kiss, the disciples fleeing in terror, and Peter cutting off the ear of the high priest's servant. Although the background, with its golden sky and rock formations, remains traditional, the style of the figures before it has changed radically. The bodies are not the flat frontal shapes of Italo-Byzantine art. Duccio imbued them with mass, modeled them with a range of tonalities from light to dark, and arranged their draperies around them convincingly. Even more novel and striking is the way the figures seem to react to the central event. Through posture, gesture, and even facial expression, they display a variety of emotions. Duccio carefully differentiated among the anger of Peter, the malice of Judas (echoed in the faces of the throng about Jesus), and the apprehension and timidity of the fleeing disciples. These figures are actors in a religious drama that the artist interpreted in terms of thoroughly human actions and reactions. In this and the other narrative panels—for example, *Entry into Jerusalem* (FIG. 14-11A), a theme treated also by Giotto in the Arena Chapel (FIG. 14-9A)—Duccio took a decisive step toward the humanization of religious subject matter.

ORVIETO CATHEDRAL While Duccio was working on the *Maestà* altarpiece for Siena's most important church, a Sienese architect, LORENZO MAITANI, received the commission to design Orvieto's

Cathedral (FIG. 14-13). The Orvieto *facade*, like the earlier facade of Siena Cathedral (FIG. 14-13A), begun by Giovanni Pisano (FIG. 14-4), highlights the appeal of the vocabulary of French Gothic art and architecture in Italy at the end of the 13th and beginning of the 14th century. Characteristically French are the pointed gables over Orvieto Cathedral's three

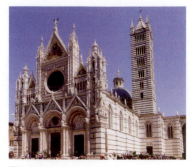

14-13A Siena Cathedral, begun ca. 1226.

doorways, the *rose window* and statues in niches in the *kings' gallery* of the upper zone, and the four large *pinnacles* dividing the facade into three *bays* (see "Building a High Gothic Cathedral," page 381, for the architectural terminology). The outer pinnacles serve as miniature substitutes for the tall northern European west-front towers. Adorning the four piers flanking the three portals are elaborate reliefs representing, from left to right, Old Testament scenes, the Tree of Jesse, New Testament scenes, and the Last Judgment. The individual episodes of the stories fill the spaces between tree branches. Both compositionally and iconographically, the Orvieto reliefs derive from the French Late Gothic tradition.

Maitani's facade, however, is a Gothic overlay masking a marble-revetted *basilican* structure in the Tuscan *Romanesque* tradition, as the three-quarter view of the cathedral in FIG. 14-13 reveals. Few Italian architects fully embraced the Gothic style. The Orvieto facade resembles a great altar screen. Its single plane may be covered with carefully placed Gothic carved and painted decoration, but in principle, Orvieto Cathedral belongs with Pisa Cathedral (FIG. 12-29) and other earlier Italian buildings, rather than with the French cathedrals at Amiens (FIG. 13-22) and Reims (FIG. 13-1). Inside, the Orvieto church has a timber-roofed *nave* with a two-story *elevation* (columnar *arcade* and *clerestory*) in the Early Christian manner. Both the *chancel arch* framing the *apse* and the nave arcade's arches are round as opposed to pointed.

SIMONE MARTINI Duccio's successors in the Sienese school also produced innovative works. SIMONE MARTINI (ca. 1285–1344) was a pupil of Duccio's and may have assisted him in painting the *Maestà* altarpiece. Martini was a close friend of Petrarch's, and the poet praised him highly for his portrait of "Laura" (the woman to whom Petrarch dedicated his sonnets). Martini worked for the French kings in Naples and Sicily and, in his last years, produced paintings for the papal court at Avignon, where he came in contact with French painters. By adapting the elegant and luxuriant patterns of the Gothic style to Sienese art and, in turn, by acquainting painters north of the Alps with the Sienese style, Martini was instrumental in creating the so-called *International Gothic* style. This new style swept Europe during the late 14th and early 15th centuries because it appealed to the aristocratic taste for brilliant colors, lavish costumes, intricate ornamentation, and themes involving splendid processions (compare FIG. 21-17).

The Saint Ansanus altarpiece (FIG. 14-14) Martini created for Siena Cathedral (FIG. 14-13A) features radiant colors, fluttering lines, and weightless elongated figures in a spaceless setting—all hallmarks of the artist's style. The complex etiquette of the European chivalric courts probably inspired Martini's presentation of the annunciation. The angel Gabriel has just alighted, the breeze of his passage lifting his mantle, his iridescent wings still beating.

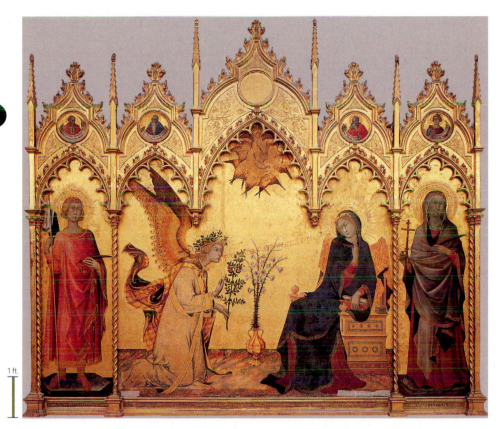

14-14 SIMONE MARTINI and LIPPO MEMMI, *Annunciation*, from the altar of Saint Ansanus, Siena Cathedral, Siena, Italy, 1333 (frame reconstructed in the 19th century). Tempera and gold leaf on wood, center panel 10' 1" × 8' 8¾". Galleria degli Uffizi, Florence.

A pupil of Duccio's, Simone Martini was instrumental in the creation of the International Gothic style. Its hallmarks are radiant colors, flowing lines, and weightless figures in golden, spaceless settings.

of the Virgin's purity. Despite Mary's modesty and diffidence and the tremendous import of the angel's message, the scene subordinates drama to court ritual, and structural experimentation to surface splendor. The intricate *tracery* of the richly tooled (reconstructed) French Gothic–inspired frame and the elaborate punchwork halos (by then a characteristic feature of Sienese panel painting) enhance the tactile magnificence of the altarpiece.

Simone Martini and his student and assistant, LIPPO MEMMI (active ca. 1317–1350), signed the *Annunciation* panel and dated it (1333). The latter's contribution to the altarpiece is still a matter of debate, but most art historians believe that he painted the two lateral saints (Ansanus at left, Margaret at right). These figures, which are reminiscent of the jamb statues of Gothic church portals, have greater solidity and lack the linear elegance of Martini's central pair. Given the nature of medieval and Renaissance workshop practices, it is often difficult to distinguish the master's hand from those of assistants, especially if the master corrected or redid part of the pupil's work (see "Artistic Training in Renaissance Italy," page 426).

The gold of his sumptuous gown signals that he has descended from Heaven to deliver his message. The Virgin, putting down her book of devotions, shrinks demurely from Gabriel's reverent bow—an appropriate act in the presence of royalty. Mary draws about her the deep-blue, golden-hemmed mantle, colors befitting the queen of Heaven. Between the two figures is a vase of white lilies, symbolic

PIETRO LORENZETTI Another of Duccio's students, PIETRO LORENZETTI (ca. 1280–1348), contributed significantly to the general experiments in pictorial realism taking place in 14th-century Italy. Surpassing even his renowned master, Lorenzetti achieved a remarkable degree of spatial illusionism in his *Birth of the Virgin* (FIG. **14-15**), a large *triptych* (three-part panel painting) created for the altar of Saint Savinus in Siena Cathedral (FIG. 14-13A). Lorenzetti painted the timber architectural members dividing the altarpiece into three sections as though they extended back into the painted space. Viewers seem to look through the frame (added later) into a boxlike stage, where the event takes place. That one of the vertical members cuts across a figure, blocking part of it from view, strengthens the illusion. In subsequent centuries, artists exploited this use of

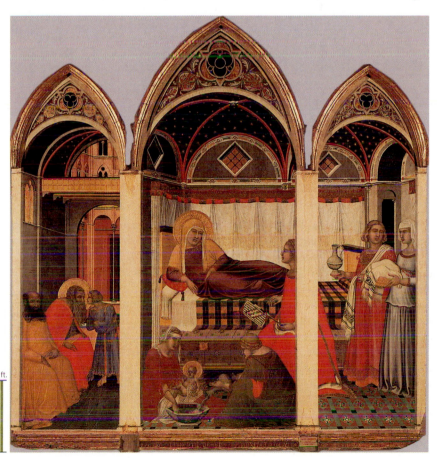

14-15 PIETRO LORENZETTI, *Birth of the Virgin*, from the altar of Saint Savinus, Siena Cathedral, Siena, Italy, 1342. Tempera on wood, 6' 1" × 5' 11". Museo dell'Opera del Duomo, Siena.

In this triptych, Pietro Lorenzetti revived the pictorial illusionism of ancient Roman murals and painted the architectural members dividing the panel as if they extended back into the painted space.

Artistic Training in Renaissance Italy

In Italy during the 14th through 16th centuries, training to become a professional artist capable of earning membership in the appropriate guild was a laborious and lengthy process. Aspiring artists started their training at an early age, anytime from 7 to 15 years old. Their fathers would negotiate an arrangement with a master artist whereby each youth lived with that master for a specified number of years, usually five or six. During that time, the boys served as apprentices to the master of the workshop, learning the trade. (This living arrangement served as a major obstacle for women who wished to become professional artists, because it was inappropriate for young girls to live in a male master's household.) The guilds supervised this rigorous training. They wanted not only to ensure their professional reputations by admitting only the most talented members but also to control the number of artists (and thereby limit competition). Toward this end, they frequently tried to regulate the number of apprentices working under a single master.

The skills that apprentices learned varied with the type of studio they joined. Those apprenticed to painters learned to grind pigments, draw, prepare wood panels for painting, gild, and lay plaster for fresco. Sculptors in training learned to manipulate different materials—wood, stone, *terracotta* (baked clay), or bronze—although many sculpture workshops specialized in only one or two of these materials. For stone carving, apprentices learned their craft by blocking out the master's designs for statues. As their skills developed, apprentices took on increasingly difficult tasks.

Cennino Cennini (ca. 1370–1440) explained the value of this apprenticeship system and, in particular, the advantages for young artists in studying and copying the works of older masters, in an influential book he published in 1400, *Il libro dell'arte* (*The Handbook of Art*):

> Having first practiced drawing for a while, . . . take pains and pleasure in constantly copying the best things which you can find done by the hand of great masters. And if you are in a place where many good masters have been, so much the better for you. But I give you this advice: take care to select the best one every time, and the one who has the greatest reputation. And, as you go on from day to day, it will be against nature if you do not get some grasp of his style and of his spirit. For if you undertake to copy after one master today and after another one tomorrow, you will not acquire the style of either one or the other, and you will inevitably, through enthusiasm, become capricious, because each style will be distracting your mind. You will try to work in this man's way today, and in the other's tomorrow, and so you will not get either of them right. If you follow the course of one man through constant practice, your intelligence would have to be crude indeed for you not to get some nourishment from it. Then you will find, if nature has granted you any imagination at all, that you will eventually acquire a style individual to yourself, and it cannot help being good; because your hand and your mind, being always accustomed to gather flowers, would ill know how to pluck thorns.*

After completing their apprenticeships, artists entered the appropriate guilds. For example, painters, who ground pigments, joined the guild of apothecaries. Sculptors were members of the guild of stoneworkers, and goldsmiths entered the silk guild, because metalworkers often stretched gold into threads wound around silk for weaving. Guild membership served as certification of the artists' competence, but did not mean that they were ready to open their own studios. New guild-certified artists usually served as assistants to master artists, because until they established their reputations, they could not expect to receive many commissions, and the cost of establishing their own workshops was high. In any case, this arrangement was not permanent, and workshops were not necessarily static enterprises. Although well-established and respected studios existed, workshops could be organized around individual masters (with no set studio locations) or organized for a specific project, especially an extensive decoration program.

Generally, assistants to painters were responsible for gilding frames and backgrounds, completing decorative work, and, occasionally, rendering architectural settings. Artists regarded figures, especially those central to the represented subject, as the most important and difficult parts of a painting, and the master reserved these for himself. Sometimes assistants painted secondary or marginal figures but only under the master's close supervision. That was probably the case with Simone Martini's *Annunciation* altarpiece (FIG. 14-14), in which the master painted the Virgin and angel, and the flanking saints are probably the work of his assistant, Lippo Memmi.

*Translated by Daniel V. Thompson Jr., *Cennino Cennini, The Craftsman's Handbook (Il Libro dell'Arte)* (New York: Dover Publications, 1960; reprint of 1933 ed.), 14–15.

---

architectural elements to enhance the illusion of painted figures acting out a drama a mere few feet away. This kind of pictorial illusionism characterized ancient Roman mural painting (FIGS. 7-18 and 7-19, *right*), but had not been practiced in Italy for a thousand years.

The setting for *Birth of the Virgin* also represented a marked step in the advance of worldly realism. Unlike in other altarpieces of this era, the figures in Lorenzetti's painting are not seen against an otherworldly gold background. Instead, the Sienese master painted a detailed interior of an upper-class Italian home of the period, complete with floor tiles and fabrics whose receding lines enhance the sense of depth. Lorenzetti removed the front walls of the house to enable the viewer to peer inside, where Saint Anne (see "Early Christian Saints," page 236) props herself up wearily as the midwives wash the newborn Virgin and the women bring gifts. Anne, like Nicola Pisano's *Nativity Virgin* (FIG. 14-3), resembles a reclining figure on the lid of a Roman sarcophagus (FIG. 7-59). At the left, in a side chamber, Joachim eagerly awaits news of the delivery. Lorenzetti's altarpiece is as noteworthy for the painter's careful inspection and recording of details of the everyday world as for his innovations in spatial illusionism.

PALAZZO PUBBLICO Not all Sienese painting of the early 14th century was religious in character. One of the most important fresco cycles of the period (discussed next) was a civic commission for Siena's *Palazzo Pubblico* ("public palace" or city hall; FIG. 14-16). Siena was a proud commercial and political rival of Florence. The secular center of the community, the civic meeting hall in the main square (the Campo), was almost as great an object of civic pride as the city's cathedral (FIG. 14-13A). The Palazzo Pubblico has a slightly concave facade (to conform to the irregular shape of the Campo) and a gigantic tower visible from miles around (compare FIGS. 13-29 and

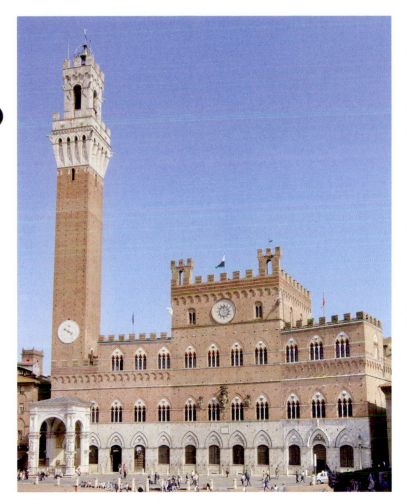

14-16 Palazzo Pubblico (looking east), Siena, Italy, 1288–1309.

Siena's Palazzo Pubblico has a concave facade and a gigantic tower visible for miles around. The tower served as both a defensive lookout over the countryside and a symbol of the city-state's power.

14-19B). The imposing building and tower must have earned the admiration of Siena's citizens as well as of visitors to the city, inspiring in them respect for the republic's power and success. The tower served as a lookout over the city and the countryside around it and as a bell tower (*campanile*) for ringing signals of all kinds to the populace. Siena, like other Italian city-states, had to defend itself against neighboring cities and often against kings and emperors. In addition, it had to secure itself against internal upheavals common in the history of the Italian city-republics. Class struggle, feuds among rich and powerful families, and even uprisings of the whole populace against the city governors (known as "the Nine" in Siena) were constant threats in medieval Italy. The heavy walls and *battlements* (fortified *parapets*) of the Sienese town hall eloquently express how frequently the city governors needed to defend themselves against their own citizens. The Palazzo Pubblico tower, out of reach of most missiles, incorporates *machicolated galleries* (galleries with holes in their floors to enable defenders to dump stones or hot liquids on attackers below) built out on *corbels* (projecting supporting architectural members) for defense of the tower's base.

AMBROGIO LORENZETTI The painter entrusted with the major fresco program in the Palazzo Pubblico was Pietro Lorenzetti's younger brother, AMBROGIO LORENZETTI (ca. 1290–1348). In the frescoes Ambrogio produced for the Sala della Pace (Hall of Peace; FIG. **14-16A**), he elaborated his brother's advances in illusionistic representation in spectacular fashion while giving visual form to Sienese civic concerns in a series of allegorical paintings: *Allegory of Good Government, Bad Government and the Effects of Bad*

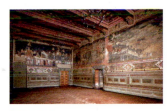

14-16A Sala della Pace, Siena, 1338–1339.

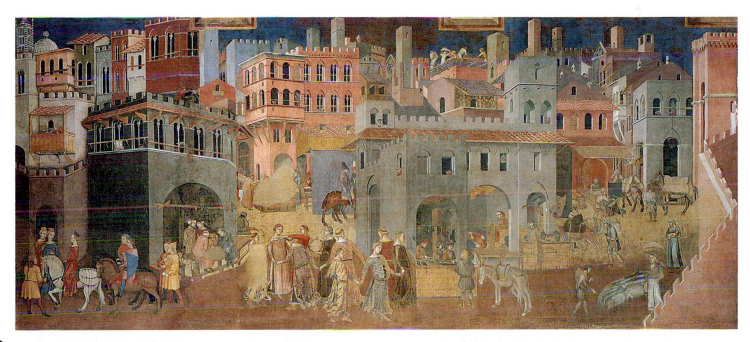

14-17 AMBROGIO LORENZETTI, *Peaceful City*, detail from *Effects of Good Government in the City and in the Country*, east wall of the Sala della Pace (FIG. 14-16A) in the Palazzo Pubblico (FIG. 14-16), Siena, Italy, 1338–1339. Fresco.

In the Hall of Peace of Siena's city hall, Ambrogio Lorenzetti painted an illusionistic panorama of a bustling 14th-century city. The fresco is an allegory of good government in the Sienese republic.

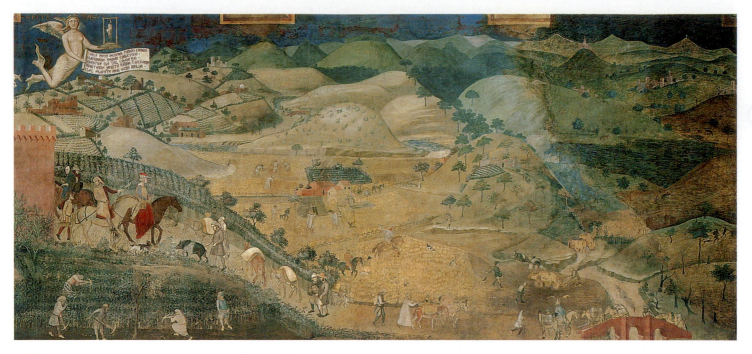

14-18 AMBROGIO LORENZETTI, *Peaceful Country*, detail from *Effects of Good Government in the City and in the Country*, east wall of the Sala della Pace (FIG. 14-16A) in the Palazzo Pubblico (FIG. 14-16), Siena, Italy, 1338–1339. Fresco.

This sweeping view of the countryside is one of the first instances of pure landscape painting in Western art since antiquity. The winged figure of Security promises safety to all who live under Sienese law.

Government in the City and *Effects of Good Government in the City and in the Country*. The turbulent politics of the Italian cities—the violent party struggles, the overthrow and reinstatement of governments—called for solemn reminders of fair and just administration, and the city hall was just the place to display murals contrasting good and bad government. Indeed, the Sienese leaders who commissioned this fresco series had undertaken the "ordering and reformation of the whole city and countryside of Siena."

In *Effects of Good Government in the City and in the Country*, Ambrogio depicted the urban and rural effects of good government. *Peaceful City* (FIG. 14-17) is a panoramic view of Siena, with its clustering palaces, markets, towers, churches, streets, and walls, reminiscent of the townscapes of ancient Roman murals (FIG. 7-19, *left*). The city's traffic moves peacefully, guild members ply their trades and crafts, and radiant maidens, clustered hand in hand, perform a graceful circling dance. Dances were regular features of festive springtime rituals. Here, dancing also serves as a metaphor for a peaceful commonwealth. The artist fondly observed the life of his city, and its architecture gave him an opportunity to apply Sienese artists' rapidly growing knowledge of perspective.

In *Peaceful Country* (FIG. 14-18), Ambrogio's representation of the countryside beyond Siena's walls, the painter presented a bird's-eye view of the undulating Tuscan terrain—its villas, castles, plowed farmlands, and peasants going about their occupations at different seasons of the year. Although it is an allegory, not a snapshot of the Tuscan countryside on a specific day, Lorenzetti's *Peaceful Country*, like his *Good Government in the City*, has the character of a portrait of a specific place and environment. *Peaceful Country* is one of the first examples of a pure *landscape* in Western art since antiquity (FIG. 7-20).

A *personification* of Security hovers above the hills and fields, unfurling a scroll promising safety to all who live under the rule of

law—that is, the law administered by the Nine, who met in this room to oversee Sienese affairs. The Nine had the power to enforce their laws by imposing penalties, including even capital punishment. As a warning to those who might defy the Nine, Security carries a model of a gallows with a hanged criminal.

The Nine, however, could not protect Siena's citizens from the plague sweeping through Europe in the mid-14th century. The Black Death (see page 417) killed thousands of Sienese and may have ended the careers of the Lorenzetti brothers. They disappear from historical records in 1348.

Florence

Like Siena, the Republic of Florence was a dominant city-state during the 14th century. The historian Giovanni Villani (ca. 1270–1348), for example, described Florence as "the daughter and the creature of Rome," suggesting a preeminence inherited from the Roman Empire. Florentines were fiercely proud of what they perceived as their economic and cultural superiority. Florence controlled the textile industry in Italy, and the republic's gold *florin* was the standard coin of exchange everywhere in Europe.

SANTA MARIA DEL FIORE Florentines translated their pride in their predominance into such landmark buildings as Santa Maria del Fiore (Saint Mary of the Flower; FIGS. 14-19 and 14-19A), Florence's cathedral, the site of the most important religious observances in the city. ARNOLFO DI CAMBIO (ca. 1245–1302) began work on the cathedral (*Duomo* in Italian) in

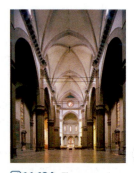

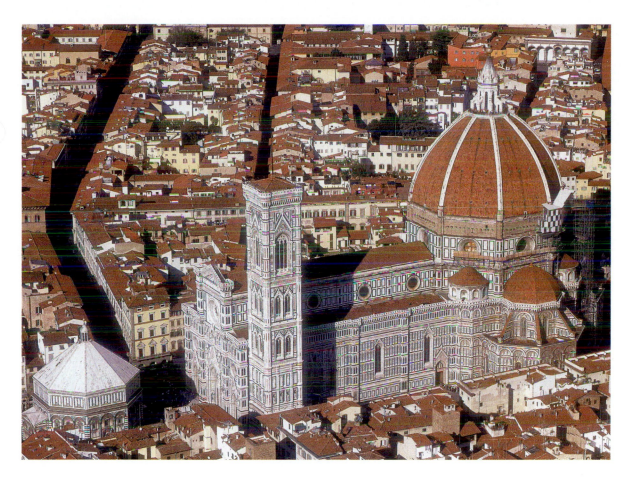

14-19 ARNOLFO DI CAMBIO and others, aerial view of Santa Maria del Fiore (and the Baptistery of San Giovanni; looking northeast), Florence, Italy, begun 1296. Campanile designed by GIOTTO DI BONDONE, 1334.

The Florentine Duomo's marble revetment carries on the Tuscan Romanesque architectural tradition, linking this basilican church more closely to Early Christian Italy than to Gothic France.

1296, three years before he received the commission to build the city's town hall, the Palazzo della Signoria (FIG. **14-19B**). Intended as the "most beautiful and honorable church in Tuscany," the cathedral reveals the competitiveness Florentines felt with cities such as Siena (FIG. 14-13A) and Pisa (FIG. 12-29). Church authorities planned for the Duomo to hold the city's entire population, and although its capacity is only about 30,000 (Florence's population at the time was slightly less than 100,000), the building seemed so large that even the noted architect Leon Battista Alberti (see page 608) commented that it seemed to cover "all of Tuscany with its shade." The builders ornamented the cathedral's surfaces, in the old Tuscan fashion, with marble geometric designs, matching the revetment to that of the facing 11th-century Romanesque baptistery of San Giovanni (FIGS. 12-30 and 14-19, *left*).

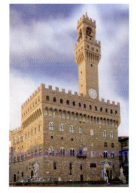

🔗 **14-19B** Palazzo della Signoria, Florence, 1299–1310.

The vast gulf separating Santa Maria del Fiore from its northern European counterparts becomes evident in a comparison between the Florentine church and the High Gothic cathedrals of Amiens (FIG. 13-22), Reims (FIG. 13-1), and Cologne (FIG. 13-51A). Gothic architects' emphatic stress on the vertical produced an awe-inspiring upward rush of unmatched vigor and intensity. The French and German buildings express organic growth shooting heavenward, as the pierced, translucent stone tracery of the spires merges with the atmosphere. Florence Cathedral, in contrast, clings to the ground and has no aspirations to flight. All emphasis is on the horizontal elements of the design, and the building rests firmly and massively on the ground. The clearly defined simple geometric volumes of the cathedral show no tendency to merge either into each other or into the sky.

Giotto di Bondone designed the Duomo's campanile in 1334. In keeping with Italian tradition (FIGS. 12-23A, 12-29, and 12-29A), it stands apart from the church. In fact, it is essentially self-sufficient and could stand anywhere else in the city without looking out of place. The same cannot be said of the bell towers of Amiens, Reims, and Cologne cathedrals. They are essential elements of the structures behind them, and it would be unthinkable to detach one of them and place it somewhere else. No individual element of Gothic churches seems capable of an independent existence. One form merges into the next in a series of rising movements pulling the eye upward and never permitting it to rest until it reaches the sky. The Florentine campanile is entirely different. Neatly subdivided into cubic sections, Giotto's tower is the sum of its component parts. Not only could this tower be removed from the building without adverse effects, but also each of the parts—cleanly separated from each other by continuous moldings—seems capable of existing independently as an object of considerable aesthetic appeal. This compartmentalization is reminiscent of the Romanesque style, but it also forecasts the ideals of Renaissance architecture. Artists hoped to express structure in the clear, logical relationships of the component parts and to produce self-sufficient works that could exist in complete independence. Compared with northern European towers, Giotto's campanile has a cool and rational quality more appealing to the intellect than to the emotions.

The facade of Florence Cathedral was not completed until the 19th century, and then in a form much altered from its original

14-20 ANDREA PISANO, south doors of the Baptistery of San Giovanni (FIG. 12-30), Florence, Italy, 1330–1336. Gilded bronze, doors 16' × 9' 2"; individual panels 1' 7$\frac{1}{4}$" × 1' 5".

Andrea Pisano's bronze doors have 28 panels with figural reliefs in French Gothic quatrefoil frames. The lower eight depict Christian virtues. The rest represent the life of John the Baptist.

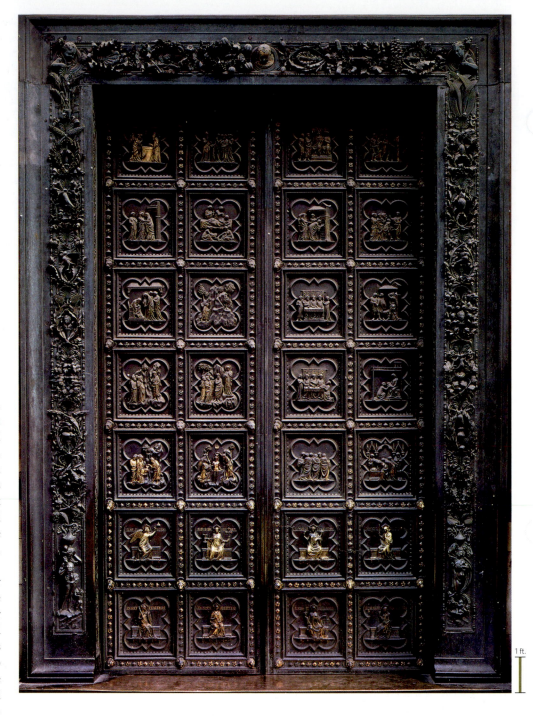

1 ft.

design. In fact, until the 17th century, Italian builders exhibited little concern for the facades of their churches, and dozens remain unfinished to this day. One reason for this may be that Italian architects did not conceive the facades as integral parts of the structures but rather, as in the case of Orvieto Cathedral (FIG. 14-13), as screens that could be added to the church exterior at any time.

ANDREA PISANO A generation after work began on Santa Maria del Fiore, the Florentines decided also to beautify their 11th-century baptistery (FIGS. 12-30 and 14-19, *left*) with a set of bronze doors (FIG. **14-20**) for the south entrance to the building. The sponsors were the members of Florence's guild of wool importers, who competed for business and prestige with the wool manufacturers' association, an important sponsor of the cathedral building campaign. The wool importers' guild hired ANDREA PISANO (ca. 1290–1348), a native of Pontedera in the territory of Pisa—unrelated to Nicola and Giovanni Pisano (see "Italian Artists' Names," page 413)—to create the doors. Andrea designed 28 bronze panels for the doors, each cast separately, of which 20 depict episodes from the life of John the Baptist, to whom the baptistery was dedicated. Eight panels (at the bottom) represent personified Christian virtues. The *quatrefoil* (four-lobed, cloverlike) frames are of the type used earlier for reliefs flanking the doorways of Amiens Cathedral (FIG. 13-22), suggesting that French Gothic sculpture was one source of Andrea's style. The gilded figures stand on projecting ledges in each quatrefoil. Their proportions and flowing robes also reveal a debt to French sculpture, but the compositions, both in general conception (small groups of figures in stagelike settings)

and in some details, owe a great deal to Giotto, for whom Andrea had earlier executed reliefs for the cathedral's campanile, perhaps according to Giotto's designs.

The wool importers' patronage of the baptistery did not end with this project. In the following century, the guild paid for the even more prestigious east doors (FIG. 21-10), directly across from the cathedral's west facade, and also for a statue of John the Baptist on the facade of Or San Michele. The latter was a multipurpose building housing a 14th-century tabernacle (FIG. **14-20A**) by ANDREA ORCAGNA (active ca. 1343–1368) featuring the painting *Madonna and Child Enthroned with Saints* by BERNARDO DADDI (active ca. 1312–1348).

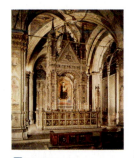

14-20A ORCAGNA, Or San Michele tabernacle, 1355–1359.

Pisa

Siena and Florence were inland centers of commerce. Pisa was one of Italy's port cities, which, with Genoa and Venice, controlled the rapidly growing maritime avenues connecting western Europe with the lands of Islam, with Byzantium and Russia, and with China. As prosperous as Pisa was as a major shipping power, however, it was not immune from the disruption that the Black Death wreaked across all of Italy and Europe in the late 1340s. Concern with death, a significant theme in art even before the onset of the plague, became more prominent in the years after midcentury.

CAMPOSANTO *Triumph of Death* (FIGS. 14-21 and 14-22) is a tour de force of death imagery. The creator of this large-scale fresco measuring more than 18 by 49 feet remains disputed. Some art historians attribute the work to FRANCESCO TRAINI (active ca. 1321–1363), while others argue for BUONAMICO BUFFALMACCO (active

ca. 1315–1336). Painted on one wall of the Camposanto (Holy Field), the enclosed burial ground adjacent to Pisa's cathedral (FIG. 12-29), the immense fresco captures the horrors of death and forces viewers to confront their mortality. The painter rendered each scene with naturalism and emotive power. In the left foreground (FIG. 14-21), stylish young aristocrats mounted on fine horses encounter three coffin-encased corpses in differing stages of decomposition. As the horror of the confrontation with death strikes them, the ladies turn away with delicate disgust, while a gentleman holds his nose. (The animals, horses and dogs, sniff excitedly.) At the far left, Marcarius, an early hermit saint, unrolls a scroll bearing an inscription commenting on the folly of pleasure and the inevitability of death. On the far right (FIG. 14-22), ladies and gentlemen ignore dreadful realities, occupying themselves in an orange grove with music and amusements while all around them angels and demons reminiscent of the grieving angels of Giotto's *Lamentation* (FIG. 14-9) struggle for the souls of the corpses heaped in the foreground.

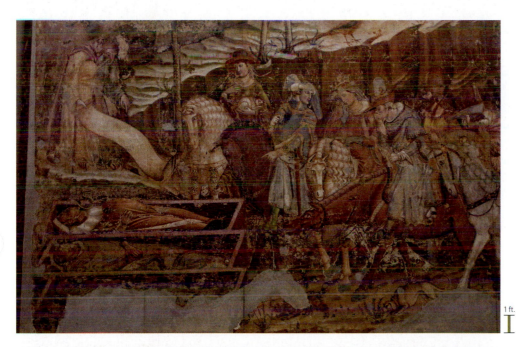

14-21 FRANCESCO TRAINI or BUONAMICO BUFFALMACCO, riders discover three corpses, detail of *Triumph of Death*, Camposanto, Pisa, Italy, 1330s. Full fresco, 18' 6" × 49' 2".

Befitting its location on a wall in Pisa's Camposanto, the enclosed burial ground adjacent to the cathedral, this fresco captures the horrors of death and forces viewers to confront their mortality.

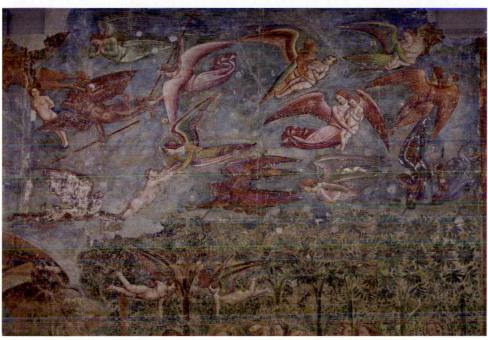

14-22 FRANCESCO TRAINI or BUONAMICO BUFFALMACCO, angels and demons vie for souls, detail of *Triumph of Death*, Camposanto, Pisa, Italy, 1330s. Full fresco, 18' 6" × 49' 2".

Above a scene of the good life of music and feasting in an orange grove, angels and demons struggle for the souls of the corpses in this dramatic vision of the triumph of death in Pisa's major cemetery.

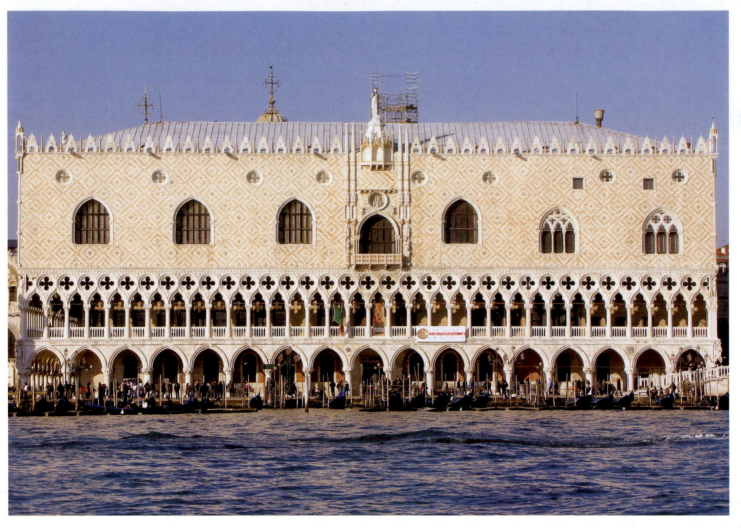

14-23 Doge's Palace (looking north), Venice, Italy, begun ca. 1340–1345; expanded and remodeled, 1424–1438.

The delicate patterning in cream- and rose-colored marbles, the pointed and ogee arches, and the quatrefoil medallions of the Doge's Palace constitute a Venetian variation of northern Gothic architecture.

In addition to these direct and straightforward scenes, the mural contains details conveying more subtle messages. For example, the painter depicted those who appear unprepared for death—and thus unlikely to achieve salvation—as wealthy and reveling in luxury. Given that the Dominicans—an order committed to a life of poverty (see "Mendicant Orders," page 415)—played a role in designing this fresco program, this imagery surely was a warning against greed and lust.

Venice

One of the wealthiest cities of late medieval Italy—and of Europe—was Venice, renowned for its streets of water. Situated on a lagoon on the northeastern coast of Italy, Venice was secure from land attack and could rely on a powerful navy for protection against invasion from the sea. Internally, Venice was a tight corporation of ruling families that, for centuries, provided stable rule and fostered economic growth.

DOGE'S PALACE The Venetian republic's seat of government was the Doge's (Duke's) Palace (FIG. **14-23**), situated on the Grand Canal

adjacent to Venice's most important church, San Marco (Saint Mark's; FIG. 9-27). Begun around 1340 to 1345 and significantly remodeled after 1424, Venice's ducal palace was the most ornate public building in medieval Italy. In a stately march, the first level's short and heavy columns support rather severe *pointed arches* that look strong enough to carry the weight of the upper structure. Their rhythm doubles in the upper arcades, where more slender columns carry *ogee arches* (made up of double-curving lines), which terminate in flamelike tips between medallions pierced with quatrefoils. Each story is taller than the one beneath it, the topmost as high as the two lower arcades combined. Yet the building does not look top-heavy. This is due in part to the complete absence of articulation in the top story and in part to the walls' delicate patterning, in cream- and rose-colored marbles, which makes them appear paper thin. The palace in which Venice's *doges* conducted state business represents a delightful and charming variant of Late Gothic architecture. Colorful, decorative, light and airy in appearance, their Venetian palace is ideally suited to the unique Italian city that floats between water and air.

LATE MEDIEVAL ITALY

Duecento (13th Century)

- Diversity of style characterizes the art of 13th-century Italy, with some artists working in the *maniera greca*, or Italo-Byzantine style, some in the mode of Gothic France, and others in the newly revived classical naturalistic tradition.

- The leading painters working in the Italo-Byzantine style were Bonaventura Berlinghieri and Cimabue, whose most famous pupil was Giotto di Bondone. Both drew inspiration from Byzantine icons and illuminated manuscripts. Berlinghieri's *Saint Francis Altarpiece* is the earliest dated portrayal of Saint Francis of Assisi, who died in 1226.

- Trained in southern Italy in the court style of Frederick II (r. 1197–1250), Nicola Pisano was a master sculptor who settled in Pisa and carved pulpits incorporating marble panels that, both stylistically and in individual motifs, derive from ancient Roman sculptures. Nicola's son, Giovanni Pisano, whose career extended into the 14th century, also was a sculptor of church pulpits, but his work more closely reflects French Gothic sculpture.

- At the end of the 13th century, in Rome and Assisi, Pietro Cavallini and other fresco painters created mural programs foreshadowing the revolutionary art of Giotto.

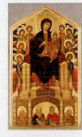

Cimabue, *Madonna Enthroned*, ca. 1280–1290

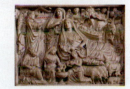

Nicola Pisano, Pisa Baptistery pulpit, 1259–1260

Trecento (14th Century)

- During the 14th century, Italy suffered the most devastating natural disaster in European history—the Black Death—but it was also the time when Renaissance humanism took root. Although religion continued to occupy a primary position in Italian life, scholars and artists became increasingly concerned with the natural world.

- Art historians from Giorgio Vasari in the 16th century to today regard Giotto di Bondone of Florence as the first Renaissance painter. His masterpiece is the extensive series of frescoes adorning the interior of the Arena Chapel in Padua, where he established himself as a pioneer in pursuing a naturalistic approach to representation, which was at the core of the classical tradition in art. The Renaissance marked the rebirth of classical values in art and society.

- The greatest master of the Sienese school of painting was Duccio di Buoninsegna, whose *Maestà* retains many elements of the maniera greca. However, Duccio relaxed the frontality and rigidity of his figures, and in the *Maestà*'s narrative scenes took a decisive step toward humanizing religious subject matter by depicting actors displaying individual emotions.

- Secular themes also came to the fore in 14th-century Italy, most notably in Ambrogio Lorenzetti's frescoes for Siena's Palazzo Pubblico. His representations of the city and its surrounding countryside are among the first landscapes in Western art since antiquity.

- The prosperity of the 14th century led to many major building campaigns, both religious and secular, including new cathedrals in Florence, Siena, and Orvieto, and new administrative palaces in Florence, Siena, and Venice.

- The 14th-century architecture of Italy underscores the regional character of late medieval art. Orvieto Cathedral's facade, for example, incorporates many elements of the French Gothic vocabulary, but it is a screen masking a timber-roofed structure in the Early Christian tradition with round arches in the nave arcade.

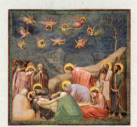

Giotto, *Lamentation*, ca. 1305

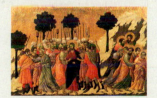

Duccio, *Betrayal of Jesus*, 1308–1311

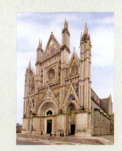

Orvieto Cathedral, begun 1310

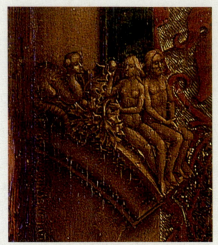

◀ **20-1a** Many details have symbolic meaning. The armrest depicting Adam, Eve, and the serpent reminded viewers that Mary is the new Eve and Christ the new Adam who will redeem humanity from original sin.

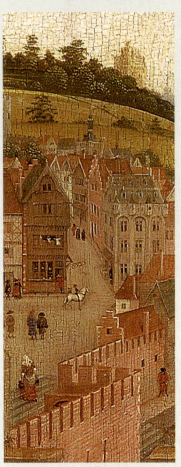

▲ **20-1b** The Virgin Mary has invited Saint Luke to paint her portrait in her elegant home—the type that wealthy 15th-century Flemish merchants owned. In the background is a view of a typical Flemish town.

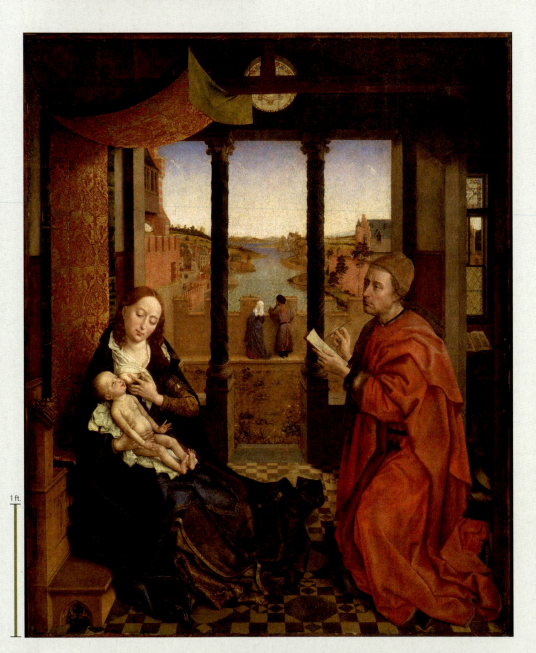

1 ft.

20-1 ROGIER VAN DER WEYDEN, *Saint Luke Drawing the Virgin*, ca. 1435–1440. Oil and tempera on wood, 4′ 6$\frac{1}{8}$″ × 3′ 7$\frac{5}{8}$″. Museum of Fine Arts, Boston (gift of Mr. and Mrs. Henry Lee Higginson).

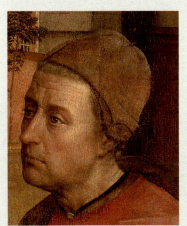

▲ **20-1c** Probably commissioned by the painters' guild in Brussels, *Saint Luke* honors the first Christian artist and the profession of painting. Saint Luke may be a self-portrait of Rogier van der Weyden.

Late Medieval and Early Renaissance Northern Europe

ROGIER VAN DER WEYDEN AND SAINT LUKE

In the 15th-century, Flanders—a region corresponding to what is today Belgium, the Netherlands, Luxembourg, and part of northern France (MAP 20-1)—enjoyed widespread prosperity. Successful merchants and craft guilds joined the clergy and royalty in commissioning artists to produce works for both public and private venues. Especially popular were paintings prepared using the recently perfected medium of oil-based pigments, which soon became the favored painting medium throughout Europe (see "Tempera and Oil Painting," page 559).

One of the early masters of oil painting was ROGIER VAN DER WEYDEN (ca. 1400–1464) of Tournai in present-day Belgium. Rogier made Brussels his home in 1435 and soon thereafter painted *Saint Luke Drawing the Virgin* (FIG. 20-1), probably for the city's artists' *guild*, the Guild of Saint Luke. Luke was the patron saint of artists because legend said that he had painted a portrait of the Virgin Mary (see "Early Christian Saints," page 237). Rogier's subject was therefore perfectly suited for the headquarters of a painters' guild. It shows Luke (his identifying attribute, the ox, is at the right; see "The Four Evangelists," page 318) at work in the kind of private residence that wealthy Flemish merchants of this era owned. Mary has miraculously appeared before Luke and invited him to paint her portrait as she nurses her son. The saint begins the process by making a preliminary drawing using a *silverpoint* (a sharp *stylus* that creates a fine line), the same instrument Rogier himself would have used when he began this commission. The painting thus not only honors Luke but also pays tribute to the profession of painting in Flanders (see "The Artist's Profession in Flanders," page 566) by documenting the preparatory work required before artists can begin painting the figures and setting.

The subject also draws attention to the venerable history of portrait painting. A rare genre during the Middle Ages, portraiture became a major source of income for Flemish artists, and Rogier was one of the best portrait painters (FIG. 20-8A) in Flanders. In fact, many scholars believe that Rogier's Saint Luke is a self-portrait, identifying the painter with the first Christian artist and underscoring the holy nature of painting. *Saint Luke Drawing the Virgin* is also emblematic of 15th-century Flemish painting in aiming to record every detail of a scene with loving fidelity to optical appearance, seen here in the rich fabrics, the patterned floor, and the landscape visible through the window. Also characteristic of Flemish art is the imbuing of many of the painting's details with symbolic significance. For example, the carved armrest of the Virgin's bench depicts Adam, Eve, and the serpent, reminding the viewer that Mary is the new Eve and Christ the new Adam who will redeem humanity from Adam and Eve's original sin.

NORTHERN EUROPE IN THE 15TH CENTURY

As the 15th century opened, Rome and Avignon were still the official seats of two competing popes (see "The Great Schism," page 415), and the Hundred Years' War (1337–1453) between France and England still raged. The general European movement toward centralized royal governments, begun in the 12th century, continued apace, but the corresponding waning of *feudalism* brought social turmoil. Nonetheless, despite widespread conflict and unrest, a new economic system emerged—the early stage of European capitalism. In response to the financial requirements of trade, new credit and exchange systems created an economic network of enterprising European cities. Trade in money accompanied trade in commodities, and the former financed industry. Both were in the hands of international banking companies, such as those of Jacques Coeur in Bourges (see page 393) and the Medici in Florence (see page 581). In 1460, Flemish entrepreneurs established the first international commercial stock exchange in Antwerp. In fact, the French word for stock market (*bourse*) comes from the name of the van der Beurse family of Bruges, the wealthiest city in 15th-century Flanders.

Art also thrived in northern Europe during this time, under royal, ducal, church, and private patronage. Two developments in particular were of special significance: the adoption by Rogier van der Weyden (FIG. 20-1) and his contemporaries of oil-based pigment as the preferred medium for painting, and the blossoming of printmaking as a major art form, which followed the invention of moveable type. These new media had a dramatic influence on artistic production both north and south of the Alps.

BURGUNDY AND FLANDERS

In the 15th century, Flanders was not an independent state but a region under the control of the duke of Burgundy, the ruler of the fertile east-central region of France still famous for its wines (MAP 20-1). Duke Philip the Bold (r. 1363–1404) was one of four sons of King John II (r. 1350–1364) of France. In 1369, Philip married Margaret de Mâle, the daughter of the count of Flanders, and

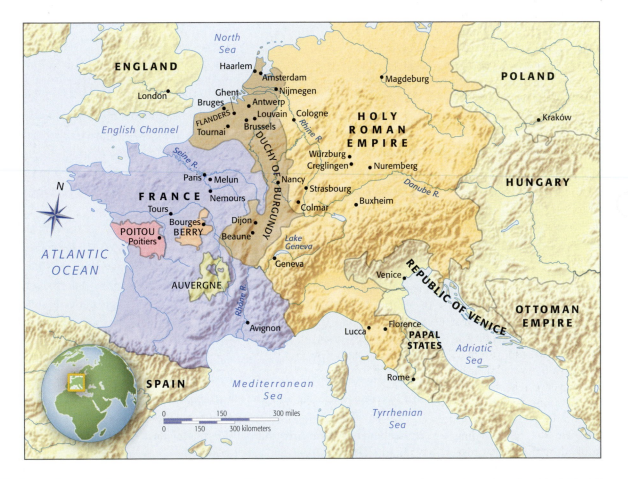

MAP 20-1 France, the duchy of Burgundy, and the Holy Roman Empire in 1477.

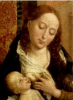

LATE MEDIEVAL AND EARLY RENAISSANCE NORTHERN EUROPE

1395–1425
- Claus Sluter carves life-size statues of biblical figures with portraitlike features for Philip the Bold, duke of Burgundy
- The Limbourg brothers expand the illusionistic capabilities of manuscript illumination for Jean, duke of Berry

1425–1450
- In Flanders, Robert Campin, Jan van Eyck, and Rogier van der Weyden use oil paints to record the exact surface appearance of objects, fabrics, and faces
- Flemish painters establish portraiture as a major art form
- German graphic artists pioneer woodcut printing, making art affordable to the masses

1450–1475
- The second generation of Flemish master painters—Petrus Christus, Dieric Bouts, and Hugo van der Goes—continues to use oil paints for altarpieces featuring naturalistic representations of religious themes
- In Germany, Johannes Gutenberg invents moveable type and prints the first Bibles on a letterpress

1475–1500
- In Flanders, Hans Memling specializes in paintings of the Madonna and Child and portraits of wealthy merchants
- The Late Gothic style lingers in Germany in the large wood altarpieces carved by Veit Stoss and Tilman Riemenschneider
- Martin Schongauer becomes the first northern European master of metal engraving

acquired territory in the Netherlands. Thereafter, the major source of Burgundian wealth was Bruges, the city that made Burgundy a powerful rival of France, which then, as in the Gothic age, was a much smaller kingdom geographically than the modern nation-state. Bruges initially derived its wealth from the wool trade, but soon expanded into banking, becoming the financial clearinghouse for all of northern Europe. Indeed, Bruges so dominated Flanders that the duke of Burgundy eventually chose to make the city his capital and moved his court there from Dijon.

Due to the expanded territory and the prosperity of the duchy of Burgundy, Philip the Bold and his successors were probably the most powerful northern European rulers during the first three quarters of the 15th century. Although members of the French royal family, they usually supported England during the Hundred Years' War because they relied on English raw materials for their wool industry. At times, the dukes of Burgundy controlled much of northern France, including Paris, the seat of the French monarchy. At the height of Burgundian power, the ducal lands stretched from the Rhône River to the North Sea.

Chartreuse de Champmol

The great wealth that the dukes of Burgundy acquired enabled them to become major patrons of the arts. The dukes fully appreciated that artworks could support their dynastic and political goals as well as adorn their castles and townhouses. Philip the Bold's grandest artistic enterprise was the Chartreuse de Champmol, near Dijon. A *chartreuse* ("charter house" in English) is a Carthusian monastery. The Carthusian order, founded by Saint Bruno (ca. 1030–1101) in the late 11th century at Chartreuse, near Grenoble in southeastern France, consisted of monks who devoted their lives to solitary living and prayer. Unlike monastic orders that earned income from farming and other work, the Carthusians generated no revenues. Philip's generous endowment at Champmol was therefore the sole funding for an ambitious artistic program inspired by the French royal abbey at Saint-Denis (FIGS. 13-1A and 13-2), the burial site of the French kings. The duke's choice for architect was DROUET DE DAMMARTIN, who had worked for his brother, King Charles V (r. 1364–1380), on the Louvre (FIG. 20-16), the French royal palace in Paris. In 1372, Philip appointed as chief sculptor the Netherlandish master Jean de Marville (d. 1389), who had also worked for Charles V, but at Rouen Cathedral. Philip intended the Dijon chartreuse to become a ducal *mausoleum* and

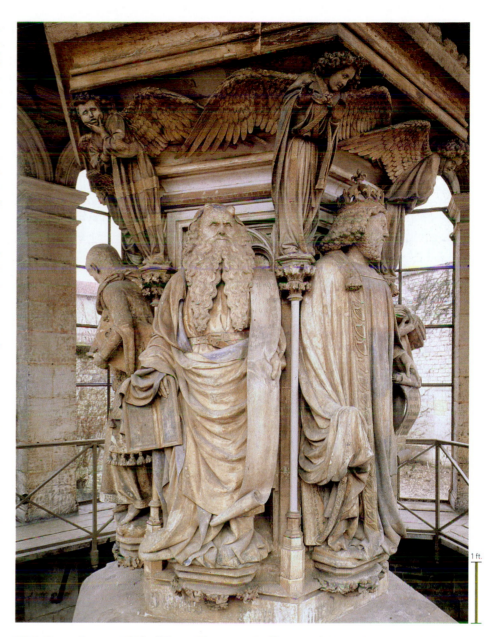

20-2 CLAUS SLUTER, *Well of Moses*, Chartreuse de Champmol, Dijon, France, 1396–1406. Asnières limestone, painted and gilded by JEAN MALOUEL, Moses 6' high.

The *Well of Moses*, a symbolic fountain of life made for the duke of Burgundy, originally supported a crucifixion group. Sluter's figures recall French Gothic jamb statues but are far more realistic.

serve both as a means of securing salvation in perpetuity for the Burgundian dukes (the monks prayed continuously for the souls of the ducal family) and as a dynastic symbol of Burgundian power.

CLAUS SLUTER In 1389, following the death of Jean de Marville, Philip the Bold placed the Netherlandish sculptor CLAUS SLUTER (ca. 1360–1406) of Haarlem in charge of the sculptural program (FIGS. 20-2 and 20-2A). Sluter had joined the Chartreuse de Champmol sculpture workshop as Jean's assistant in 1385. For the portal (FIG. 20-2A) of the monastery's chapel, Sluter's workshop produced statues of the duke and his wife kneeling before the Virgin and Child. For the cloister, Sluter designed a large sculptural fountain located in a well (FIG. 20-2). The well served as a water source for the monastery, but water probably did not spout from the fountain because the Carthusian commitment to silence and prayer would have precluded anything producing sound.

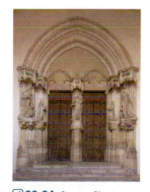

⏷ 20-2A SLUTER, Chartreuse de Champmol portal, 1390–1393.

Sluter's *Well of Moses* features statues of Moses and five other prophets (David, Daniel, Isaiah, Jeremiah, and Zachariah) ringing a base that once supported a 25-foot-tall group of Christ on the cross, the Virgin Mary, John the Evangelist, and Mary Magdalene. The Carthusians called the *Well of Moses* a *fons vitae,* a fountain of everlasting life. The blood of the crucified Christ symbolically flowed down over the grieving angels and Old Testament prophets, spilling into the well below, washing over Christ's prophetic predecessors and redeeming anyone who would drink water from the well. Whereas the models for the Dijon chapel statues were the sculptured portals of French Gothic cathedrals, the inspiration for the *Well of Moses* may have come in part from contemporaneous *mystery plays* in which actors portraying prophets frequently delivered commentaries on events in Christ's life.

The six prophets have almost portraitlike features and distinct individual personalities and costumes. For example, David is an elegantly garbed Gothic king and Moses an elderly horned prophet (compare FIG. 12-38) with a waist-length beard. Sluter intensely studied the natural appearance of faces and fabrics in order to sculpt the biblical figures in minute detail. Heavy draperies with voluminous folds swathe the life-size statues. Sluter succeeded in making their difficult, complex surfaces seem remarkably naturalistic. He enhanced this effect by skillfully differentiating textures, from coarse drapery to smooth flesh and silky hair. Originally, paint, much of which has flaked off, further augmented the naturalism of the figures. (The painter was JEAN MALOUEL [ca. 1365–1415], another Netherlandish master.) This fascination with the specific and tangible in the visible world became one of the chief characteristics of 15th-century Flemish art.

MELCHIOR BROEDERLAM Philip the Bold also commissioned a major altarpiece for the main altar in the chapel of the Chartreuse. A collaborative project between two Flemish artists, this altarpiece consisted of a large sculptured shrine by Jacques de Baerze (active ca. 1384–1399) and a pair of painted exterior panels (FIG. **20-3**) by MELCHIOR BROEDERLAM (active ca. 1387–1409).

Altarpieces were a major art form north of the Alps in the late 14th and 15th centuries. From their position behind the altar, they served as backdrops for the *Mass.* The Mass represents a ritual celebration of the Holy *Eucharist.* At the last supper, Christ commanded his apostles to repeat in memory of him the communion credo that he is tendering them his body to eat and his blood to drink, as reenacted in the Eucharist (see "The Life of Jesus in Art," page 241). This act serves as the nucleus of the Mass, which involves this reenactment as well as prayer and contemplation of the word of God. Because the Mass involves not only a memorial rite but Christian doctrine as well, art has traditionally played an important role in giving visual form to complex theological concepts for the faithful. Like the narrative reliefs in medieval church portals, these altarpieces had an important teaching function, especially for the illiterate. By reinforcing Church doctrines, they also stimulated devotion.

Given their placement in churches as backdrops to the Mass, it is not surprising that many altarpieces depict scenes directly related to Christ's sacrifice. The Champmol altarpiece, or *retable,* for example, features sculpted passion scenes on the interior. These altarpieces most often took the form of *polyptychs*—hinged multipaneled paintings or multiple carved relief panels. The hinges enabled the clergy to close the polyptych's side wings over the central panel(s). Artists decorated both the exterior and interior of the altarpieces. This multi-image format provided the opportunity to construct narratives through a sequence of images, somewhat as in manuscript illustration.

Although concrete information is lacking about when the clergy opened and closed the altarpieces, the wings probably normally remained closed but were opened on Sundays and feast days. On this schedule, viewers could have seen both the interior and exterior—diverse imagery at various times according to the liturgical calendar.

On the painted wings (FIG. 20-3) of the *Retable de Champmol* are *Annunciation* and *Visitation* (on the left panel) and *Presentation in the Temple* and *Flight into Egypt* (on the right; see "The Life of Jesus in Art," page 240). Dealing with Christ's birth and infancy, Broederlam's painted images on the altarpiece's exterior set the stage for de Baerze's interior sculpted passion scenes (not illustrated). The exterior panels are an unusual combination of different styles, locales, and religious symbolism. The two paintings include both landscape and interior scenes. Broederlam depicted the buildings in both *Romanesque* and *Gothic* styles. Scholars have suggested that the juxtaposition of different architectural styles in the left panel is symbolic. The *rotunda* (round building, usually with a dome, a common antique type) refers to the Old Testament, whereas the "modern" Gothic porch with its *lancet* windows and *tracery* relates to the New Testament. In the right panel, a statue of a Greco-Roman god falls from the top of a column as the holy family approaches. These and other details symbolically announce the coming of the new order under Christ.

Stylistically, Broederlam's panels are a mixture of three-dimensional rendition of the landscape and buildings with a solid gold background and flat golden halos for the holy figures, regardless of the positions of their heads. Despite these lingering medieval pictorial conventions, the altarpiece is an early example of many of the artistic developments that preoccupied European artists throughout the 15th century, especially the illusionistic depiction of three-dimensional objects and the naturalistic representation of landscape.

OIL PAINTING The *Retable de Champmol* also foreshadowed another significant development in 15th-century art—the widespread adoption of *oil paints,* which Broederlam mixed with *tempera* in this early example (see "Tempera and Oil Painting," page 559). Oil paints facilitated the exactitude in rendering details so characteristic of northern European painting. Although the Italian biographer Giorgio Vasari (see "Giorgio Vasari's *Lives,*" page 636) and other 16th-century commentators credited the Flemish master Jan van Eyck (FIGS. 20-5 to 20-8) with the invention of oil painting, recent evidence has revealed that oil paints had been known for some time, well before Melchior Broederlam liberally used oils for Philip the Bold's Dijon altarpiece. Flemish painters built up their pictures by superimposing translucent paint layers on a layer of underpainting, which in turn had been built up from a carefully planned drawing (compare Saint Luke at work in FIG. 20-1) made on a panel prepared with a white ground. With the oil medium, artists could create richer colors than previously possible, giving their paintings an intense tonality, the illusion of glowing light, and glistening surfaces. These traits differed significantly from the high-keyed color, sharp light, and rather *matte* (dull) surface of tempera. The brilliant and versatile oil medium suited perfectly the formal intentions of the generation of Flemish painters after Broederlam, who aimed for sharply focused clarity of detail in their representation of objects ranging in scale from large to almost invisible.

Master of Flémalle

One of the greatest Flemish painters of the generation after Melchior Broederlam was the man known as the MASTER OF FLÉMALLE, whom most art historians identify as ROBERT CAMPIN

MATERIALS AND TECHNIQUES
Tempera and Oil Painting

The generic words *paint* and *pigment* encompass a wide range of substances that artists have used through the ages. Fresco aside (see "Fresco Painting," page 419), during the 14th century, egg *tempera* was the material of choice for most painters, both in Italy and northern Europe. Tempera consists of egg combined with a wet paste of ground pigment. In his influential 1437 guidebook *Il libro dell'arte* (*The Handbook of Art*; see page 426), Cennino Cennini (ca. 1370–ca. 1440) noted that artists mixed only the egg yolk with the ground pigment, but analyses of paintings from this period have revealed that some artists chose to use the entire egg. Images painted with tempera have a velvety sheen. Artists usually applied tempera to the painting surface with a light touch because thick application of the pigment mixture would result in premature cracking and flaking.

Some artists used oil paints (powdered pigments mixed with linseed oil) as far back as the eighth century, but not until the early 1400s did oil painting become widespread. Melchior Broederlam (FIG. 20-3) and other Flemish artists were among the first to employ oils extensively (often mixing them with tempera, as Broederlam did), and Italian painters quickly followed suit. The discovery of better drying components in the early 15th century enhanced the setting capabilities of oils. Rather than apply these oils in the light, flecked brushstrokes that the tempera technique encouraged, artists laid down the oils in transparent layers, or *glazes*, over opaque or semiopaque underlayers. In this manner, painters could build up deep tones through repeated *glazing*. Unlike works in tempera, whose surface dries quickly due to water evaporation, oils dry more uniformly and slowly, giving the artist time to rework areas. This flexibility must have been particularly appealing to artists who worked very deliberately, such as Rogier van der Weyden (FIGS. 20-1, 20-9, and 20-9A), Robert Campin (FIG. 20-4), Jan van Eyck (FIGS. 20-5 to 20-8), and the other Flemish masters discussed in this chapter, as well as the Italian Leonardo da Vinci (FIGS. 22-2 and 22-5). Leonardo also preferred oil paint because its gradual drying process and consistency enabled him to blend the pigments, thereby creating the impressive *sfumato* (smoky) effect that contributed to his fame. Moreover, while drying, oil paints smooth out, erasing any trace of the brush that applied the paint. Oil paints also reflect natural light, giving the surface a glow and creating a rich visual effect unlike the duller sheen of the more light-absorbent tempera medium.

Both tempera and oils can be applied to various surfaces. Through the early 16th century, wood panels served as the foundation for most paintings. Italians painted on poplar. Northern European artists used oak, lime, beech, chestnut, cherry, pine, and silver fir. Local availability of these timbers determined the choice of wood. Linen canvas became increasingly popular in the late 16th century. Although evidence suggests that artists did not intend permanency for their early images on canvas, the material proved particularly useful in areas such as Venice where high humidity warped wood panels and made fresco unfeasible. Furthermore, until artists began to use wood bars to stretch the canvas to form a taut surface, canvas paintings could be rolled and were lighter and more compact and therefore more easily portable than wood panels.

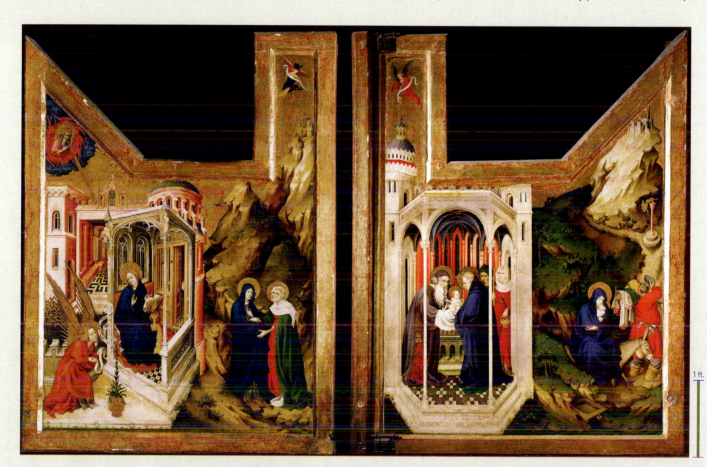

20-3 MELCHIOR BROEDERLAM, *Retable de Champmol*, from the chapel of the Chartreuse de Champmol, Dijon, France, installed 1399. Oil and tempera on wood, each wing 5' 5¾" × 4' 1¼". Musée des Beaux-Arts, Dijon.

This early example of oil painting attempts to represent the three-dimensional world on a two-dimensional surface, but the gold background and flat halos recall medieval pictorial conventions.

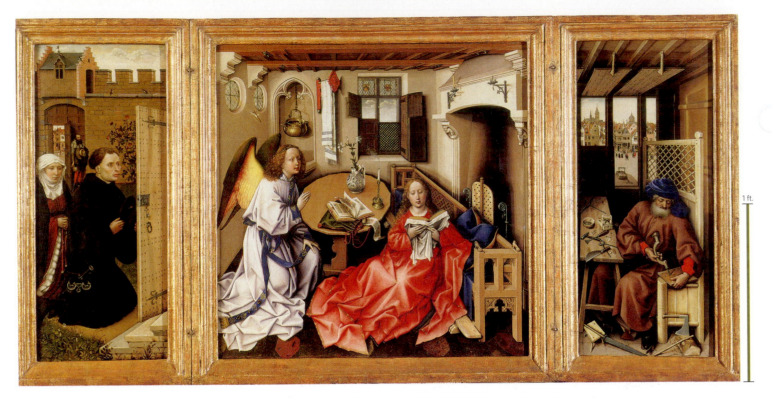

20-4 ROBERT CAMPIN (MASTER OF FLÉMALLE), *Mérode Altarpiece* (open), ca. 1425–1428. Oil on wood, center panel 2' 1⅜" × 2' ⅞", each wing 2' 1⅜" × 10⅞". Metropolitan Museum of Art, New York (The Cloisters Collection, 1956).

Campin was the leading painter of Tournai and an early master of oil painting. In the *Mérode Altarpiece,* he set the Annunciation in a Flemish merchant's home in which many objects have symbolic significance.

(ca. 1375–1444), the leading painter of Tournai. His most famous work is the *Mérode Altarpiece* (FIG. 20-4), one of the many small altarpieces of this period produced for private patrons and intended for household prayer. Perhaps the most striking feature of these private devotional images is the integration of religious and secular concerns. For example, artists often presented biblical scenes as taking place in a house (compare FIG. 20-1). Religion was such an integral part of Flemish life that separating the sacred from the secular was almost impossible—and undesirable. Furthermore, the presentation in religious art of familiar settings and objects no doubt strengthened the direct bond that the patron or viewer felt with biblical figures.

Annunciation, the popular theme prophesied in Isaiah 7:14, occupies the Mérode triptych's central panel. Unseen by the Virgin, a tiny figure of Christ carrying the cross of his martyrdom and of human salvation enters the room on a ray of light, a potent symbol of the incarnation and a foreshadowing of what lies ahead for the future Mother of God and her son. The archangel Gabriel approaches Mary, who sits reading inside a well-kept Flemish home. Through the window in the background of the right wing, the viewer sees a local cityscape, as in Rogier van der Weyden's *Saint Luke* (FIG. 20-1). The depicted accessories, furniture, and utensils confirm the locale as Flanders. However, the objects represented are not merely decorative. They also function as religious symbols.

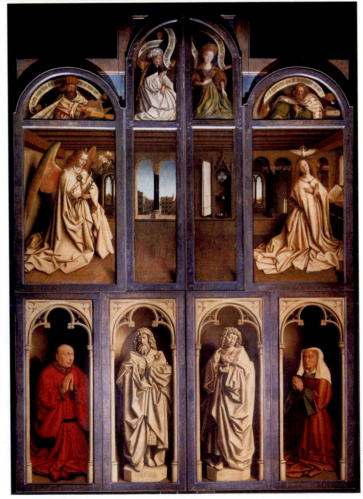

20-5 HUBERT and JAN VAN EYCK, *Ghent Altarpiece* (closed), Saint Bavo Cathedral, Ghent, Belgium, ca. 1423–1432. Oil on wood, 11' 5" × 7' 6".

Monumental painted altarpieces were popular in Flemish churches. Artists decorated both the interiors and exteriors of these polyptychs, which often, as here, included donor portraits.

The book, extinguished candle, and lilies on the table; the copper basin in the corner niche; the towels, fire screen, and bench all symbolize, in different ways, the Virgin's purity and her divine mission.

In the right panel, Joseph, apparently unaware of the angel's arrival, has constructed two mousetraps, symbolic of the theological concept that Christ is bait set in the trap of the world to catch the Devil. The ax, saw, and rod that Campin painted in the foreground of Joseph's workshop not only are tools of the carpenter's trade but also are mentioned in Isaiah 10:15. In the left panel, the closed garden is symbolic of Mary's purity, and the flowers Campin included relate to Mary's virtues, especially humility.

The altarpiece's donor, Peter Inghelbrecht, a wealthy merchant, and his wife, Margarete Scrynmakers, kneel in the garden and witness the momentous event through an open door. *Donor portraits*—portraits of the individual(s) who commissioned (or "donated") the work—became very popular in the 15th century. In this instance, in addition to asking to be represented in their altarpiece, the Inghelbrechts probably specified the subject. Inghelbrecht

means "angel bringer," descriptive of the Annunciation theme of the central panel. Scrynmakers means "cabinet- or shrine-makers," and probably inspired the workshop scene in the right panel.

Jan van Eyck

The first Netherlandish painter to achieve international fame was JAN VAN EYCK (ca. 1395–1441), who in 1425 became the court painter of Philip the Good, duke of Burgundy (r. 1419–1467). In 1431, he moved his studio to Bruges, where the duke maintained his official residence.

GHENT ALTARPIECE The year Jan arrived in Bruges, he set out to complete the *Ghent Altarpiece* (FIGS. **20-5** and **20-6**), which, according to the dedicatory inscription, his older brother HUBERT VAN EYCK (ca. 1385–1426) had begun. Given Jan's stature today, it is noteworthy that the inscription describes Hubert as an artist "than whom there was no greater" and Jan as "his brother, second in art." The nearly 12-foot-tall Ghent retable is one of the largest of the 15th century. Jodocus Vyd (d. 1439), diplomat-retainer of Philip the Good, and his wife, Elisabeth Borluut (d. 1443), commissioned the polyptych as the centerpiece of the chapel that Vyd built in the Ghent church originally dedicated to Saint John the Baptist (since 1540, Saint Bavo Cathedral). Vyd's largesse and the political and social connections that the *Ghent Altarpiece* revealed to its audience contributed to Vyd's appointment as the city's *burgomeister* (chief

20-6 HUBERT and JAN VAN EYCK, *Ghent Altarpiece* (open), Saint Bavo Cathedral, Ghent, Belgium, ca. 1423–1432. Oil on wood, 11' 5" × 15' 1".

In this sumptuous painting of salvation from the original sin of Adam and Eve, God the Father presides in majesty. The van Eyck brothers used oil paints to render every detail with loving fidelity to appearance.

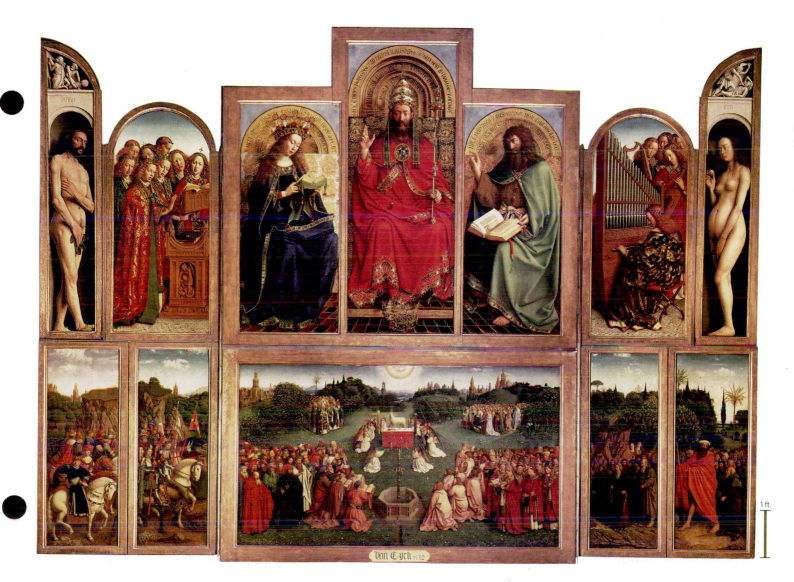

magistrate; mayor) shortly after the unveiling of the work. Two of the exterior panels (FIG. 20-5) depict the donors. The husband and wife, in paired niches with Gothic tracery, kneel with their hands clasped in prayer. They gaze piously at two illusionistically rendered stone statues that reflect the innovative style of Claus Sluter (FIGS. 20-2 and 20-2A). The sculptures represent Ghent's patron saints, John the Baptist and John the Evangelist (who was probably also Vyd's patron saint). The Annunciation appears on the upper register, with a careful representation of a Flemish town outside the painted window of the center panel (compare FIGS. 20-1 and 20-4). In the uppermost arched panels, Jan depicted the Old Testament prophets Zachariah and Micah, along with *sibyls,* Greco-Roman mythological female prophets whose writings the Church interpreted as prophecies of Christ.

When open (FIG. 20-6), the altarpiece reveals a sumptuous, superbly colored painting of human redemption through Christ. In the upper register, God the Father—wearing the pope's triple tiara, with a worldly crown at his feet and resplendent in a deep-scarlet mantle—presides in majesty. To God's right is the Virgin, represented, as in the Gothic age and in a small Jan van Eyck *diptych* (two-paneled painting; FIG. 20-6A), as the queen of Heaven, with a crown of 12 stars upon her head. John the Baptist sits to God's left. To either side is a choir of angels, with an angel playing an organ on the right. Adam and Eve appear in the far panels. The inscriptions in the arches above Mary and Saint John extol the Virgin's virtue and purity and Saint John's greatness as the forerunner of Christ (see "Early Christian Saints," page 236). The inscription above the Lord's head translates as "This is God, all-powerful in his divine majesty; of all the best, by the gentleness of his goodness; the most liberal giver, because of his infinite generosity." The step behind the crown at the Lord's feet bears the inscription, "On his head, life without death. On his brow, youth without age. On his right, joy without sadness. On his left, security without fear." The entire altarpiece amplifies the central theme of salvation. Even though humans, personified by Adam and Eve, are sinful, they will be saved because God, in his infinite love, will sacrifice his own son for their sake.

The panels of the lower register extend the symbolism of the upper. In the center panel, saints arrive from the four corners of the earth through an opulent, flower-spangled landscape. They proceed toward the altar of the lamb and the octagonal fountain of life (compare FIG. 20-2). The book of Revelation passage that recounts the adoration of the Lamb is the main reading on All Saints' Day (November 1). The Lamb symbolizes the sacrificed son of God, whose heart bleeds into a chalice, while into the fountain spills the "pure river of water of life, clear as crystal, proceeding out of the throne of God and of the Lamb" (Rev. 22:1). On the right, the 12 apostles and a group of martyrs in red robes advance. On the left appear prophets. In the right background come the virgin martyrs, and in the left background the holy confessors approach. On the lower wings, hermits, pilgrims, knights, and judges enter from left and right. They symbolize the four cardinal virtues: Temperance, Prudence, Fortitude, and Justice, respectively. The altarpiece celebrates the whole

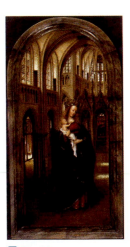

20-6A VAN EYCK, *Madonna in a Church,* ca. 1430–1440.

Christian cycle from the fall of man to the redemption, presenting the Church triumphant in heavenly Jerusalem.

Jan used oil paints to render the entire altarpiece in a shimmering splendor of color that defies reproduction. No small detail escaped the painter. With pristine specificity, he revealed the beauty of the most insignificant object. He depicted the soft texture of hair, the glitter of gold in the heavy brocades, the luster of pearls, and the flashing of gems, all with loving fidelity to appearance. This kind of meticulous attention to recording the exact surface appearance of humans, animals, objects, and landscapes, already evident in the *Mérode Altarpiece* (FIG. 20-4), became a hallmark of Flemish panel painting in the 15th century.

GIOVANNI ARNOLFINI Emerging capitalism led to prosperity in Europe's booming urban centers and fueled in turn the growing bourgeois market for art objects, particularly in Bruges, Antwerp, and, later, Amsterdam. The increased wealth of the merchant class contributed to an expanded market for secular art in addition to religious artworks. It is noteworthy, for example, that both the *Mérode Altarpiece* and the *Ghent Altarpiece*—certainly to be categorized as "religious art"—include painted portraits of their donors. These paintings marked a significant revival of portraiture, a genre that had languished since antiquity. Private commissions for portraits as independent artworks began to multiply as both artists and patrons became interested in the reality (both physical and psychological) that portraits could reveal.

In the 15th century, Flemish patrons eagerly embraced the opportunity to have their likenesses painted. The elite wanted to memorialize themselves in their dynastic lines and to establish their identities, ranks, and stations with images far more concrete than heraldic coats of arms. Portraits also served to represent state officials at events that they could not attend. Sometimes, royalty, nobility, and the very rich would send artists to paint the likeness of a prospective bride or groom. For example, when young King Charles VI (r. 1380–1422) of France sought a bride, he dispatched a painter to three different royal courts to make portraits of the candidates. But prosperous merchants also commissioned portraits for their homes.

An early example of secular portraiture is Jan van Eyck's oil painting *Giovanni Arnolfini and His Wife* (FIG. 20-7). Jan depicted the Lucca financier (who had established himself in Bruges as an agent of the Medici family) in his home. Arnolfini holds the hand of his second wife, whose name is not known. That much is certain, but the purpose and meaning of the double portrait remain the subject of considerable debate. According to the traditional interpretation of the painting, Jan recorded the couple taking their marriage vows. As in the *Mérode Altarpiece* (FIG. 20-4), almost every object portrayed carries meaning. For example, the little dog symbolizes fidelity (the common canine name *Fido* originated from the Latin *fidere,* "to trust"). The *finial* (crowning ornament) of the marriage bed at the right is a tiny statue of Saint Margaret, patron saint of childbirth. (The bride is not yet pregnant, although the fashionable costume she wears makes her appear so.) From the finial hangs a whisk broom, symbolic of domestic care. Indeed, even the placement of the two figures in the room is meaningful. The woman stands near the bed and well into the room, whereas the man stands near the open window, symbolic of the outside world.

Many art historians, however, dispute this interpretation because, among other things, the room in which Arnolfini and his wife stand is a public reception area, not a bedchamber. One scholar

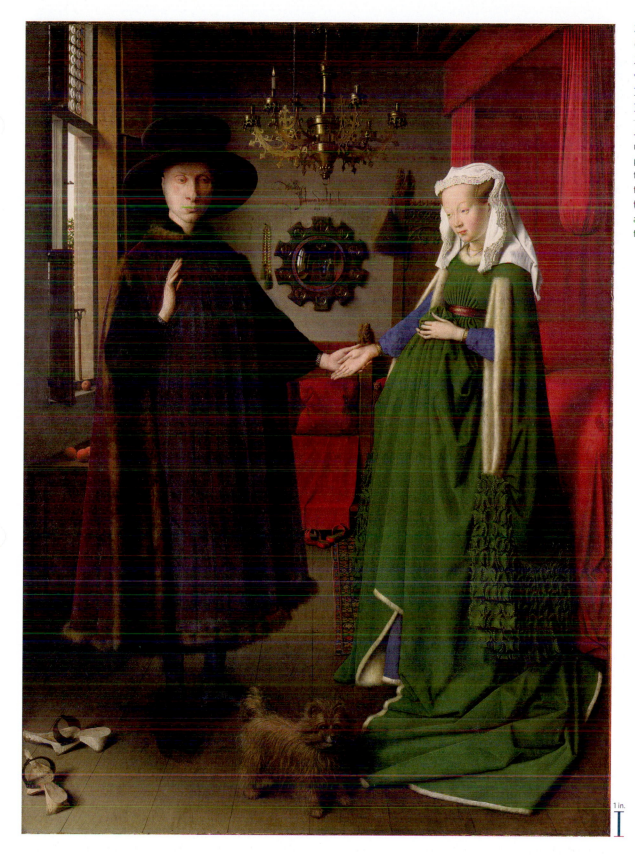

20-7 Jan van Eyck, *Giovanni Arnolfini and His Wife,* 1434. Oil on wood, 2' 9" × 1' 10½". National Gallery, London.

Jan van Eyck played a major role in establishing portraiture as an important Flemish art form. In this portrait of an Italian financier and his wife, he also portrayed himself in the mirror.

1 in.

has suggested that Arnolfini is conferring legal privileges on his wife to conduct business in his absence. In either case, an important aspect of the painting is that the artist functions as a witness to whatever event is taking place. In the background, between the two figures, is a convex mirror (complete with its spatial distortion, brilliantly recorded), in which Jan depicted not only the principals, Arnolfini and his wife, but also two persons who look into the room through the door. (Arnolfini's raised right hand may be a gesture of greeting to the two men.) One of these must be the artist himself, as the elegant inscription above the mirror, *Johannes de Eyck fuit hic* ("Jan van Eyck was here"), announces that he was present. The self-portrait also underscores the painter's self-consciousness as a professional artist whose role deserves to be recorded and remembered.

MATERIALS AND TECHNIQUES
Framed Paintings

Until the mid-20th century, when painters began simply to affix canvas to wood *stretcher bars* to provide a taut painting surface devoid of ornamentation, artists considered the frame an integral part of the painting. Frames served a number of functions, some visual, others conceptual. For paintings such as large-scale altarpieces that were part of a larger environment, frames often served to integrate the painting with its surroundings. Frames could also be used to reinforce the illusionistic nature of the painted image. For example, the Italian painter Giovanni Bellini, in his *San Zaccaria Altarpiece* (FIG. 22-32), duplicated the carved *pilasters* of the architectural frame in the painting itself, thereby enhancing the illusion of space and giving the painted figures an enhanced physical presence. In the *Ghent Altarpiece,* the frame seems to cast shadows on the floor between the angel and Mary in the *Annunciation* (FIG. 20-5, *top*). More commonly, artists used frames specifically to distance the viewer from the (often otherworldly) scene by calling attention to the separation of the image from the viewer's space.

Most 15th- and 16th-century paintings included elaborate frames that the artists themselves helped design and construct. Extant contracts reveal that the frame could account for as much as half of the cost of an altarpiece. Frequently, the commissions called for painted or gilded frames, adding to the expense. For small works, artists sometimes affixed the frames to the panels before painting, so that the frame was a point of reference as they worked. Occasionally, a single piece of wood served as both panel and frame, and the artist (or, in practice, an assistant) carved the painting surface from the wood, leaving the edges as a frame. Larger images with elaborate frames, such as altarpieces, required the services of a professional woodcarver or stonemason. The painter worked closely with the individual constructing the frame to ensure its appropriateness for the image(s) produced.

Unfortunately, over time, many frames have been removed from their paintings. For instance, in 1566 church officials dismantled the *Ghent Altarpiece* and detached its elaborately carved frame in order to protect the sacred work from Protestant *iconoclasts* (see page 682). As ill luck would have it, when the panels were reinstalled in 1587, no one could find the frame. Sadly, the absence of many of the original frames of old paintings deprives viewers today of the painter's complete artistic vision. Conversely, when the original frames

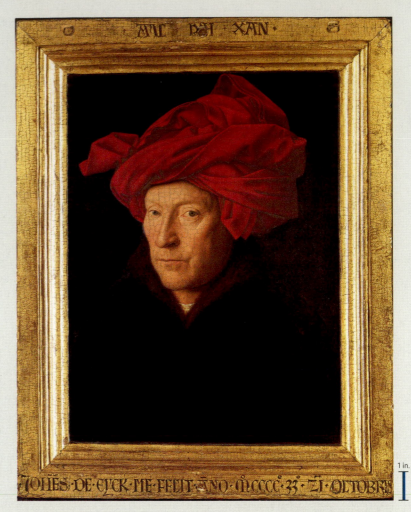

20-8 JAN VAN EYCK, *Man in a Red Turban*, 1433. Oil on wood, 1' 1$\frac{1}{8}$" × 10$\frac{1}{4}$". National Gallery, London.

Man in a Red Turban is the first known Western painted portrait in a thousand years in which the sitter looks directly at the viewer. The inscribed frame suggests that it is a self-portrait of Jan van Eyck.

exist, they sometimes provide essential information, such as the subject, name of the painter, and date. For example, the inscriptions on the frame of Jan van Eyck's *Man in a Red Turban* (FIG. 20-8) state that he painted it on October 21, 1433, and the inclusion of "As I can" and omission of the sitter's name suggest that the painting is a self-portrait.

MAN IN A RED TURBAN Whatever the intended meaning of *Giovanni Arnolfini and His Wife*, the painting is representative of the emergence of secular portraiture in 15th-century Flanders. In *Man in a Red Turban* (FIG. **20-8**), the man Jan van Eyck portrayed looks directly at the viewer. This is the first known Western painted portrait in a thousand years where the sitter does so. The level, composed gaze, directed from a true three-quarter head pose, must have impressed observers deeply. The painter created the illusion that from whatever angle a viewer observes the face, the eyes return that gaze. Jan, with his considerable observational skill and controlled painting style, injected a heightened sense of specificity into this portrait by including beard stubble, veins in the bloodshot left eye, and weathered, aged skin. Although a definitive identification of the

sitter has yet to be made, most art historians consider *Man in a Red Turban* a self-portrait, which Jan painted by looking at his image in a mirror (as he depicted himself in the mirror in the Arnolfinis' home; FIG. 20-7). The inscriptions on the frame (see "Framed Paintings," above) reinforce this identification. Across the top, Jan wrote "As I can" in Flemish using Greek letters. One suggestion is that this portrait was a demonstration piece intended for prospective clients, who could compare the painting with the painter and judge what he "could do" in terms of recording a faithful likeness. Across the bottom appear the date and a statement in Latin: "Jan van Eyck made me." The use of both Greek and Latin suggests that the artist viewed himself as both a learned man and a worthy successor to the fabled painters of antiquity.

Rogier van der Weyden

When Jan van Eyck received the commission for the *Ghent Altarpiece*, Rogier van der Weyden (FIG. 20-1) was an assistant in the workshop of Robert Campin (FIG. 20-4), but the younger Tournai painter's fame eventually rivaled Jan's. Rogier quickly became renowned for his portraits (FIG. 20-8A) and his dynamic compositions stressing human action and drama. He concentrated on Christian themes, especially those episodes in the life of Jesus that elicited powerful emotions—for example, the crucifixion and *Pietà* (the Virgin Mary cradling the dead body of her son)—moving observers deeply by vividly portraying the sufferings of Christ.

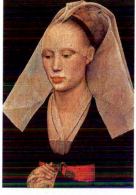

20-8A VAN DER WEYDEN, *Portrait of a Lady*, ca. 1460.

DEPOSITION One of Rogier's early masterworks is *Deposition* (FIG. 20-9), the center panel of a triptych commissioned by the archers' guild of Louvain for the church of Notre-Dame hors-les-murs (Church of Our Lady—the Virgin—outside the [town] walls). Rogier acknowledged the patrons of this large painting by incorporating the crossbow (the guild's symbol) into the decorative tracery in the corners. Instead of creating a deep landscape setting, as Jan van Eyck might have, Rogier compressed the figures and action onto a shallow stage with a golden back wall, imitating the large sculptured shrines so popular in the 15th century, especially in the Holy Roman Empire (FIGS. 20-20 and 20-21). The device admirably served his purpose of expressing maximum action within a limited space, but the setting of the crucifixion in a box is unrealistic, as is the size of the cross, the arms of which are not wide enough for Jesus's hands to have been nailed to them. The painting, with the artist's crisp drawing and precise modeling of forms, resembles a stratified relief carving, and the viewer may wonder if this is a painting of the biblical event or a painting of a shrine representing the event. In

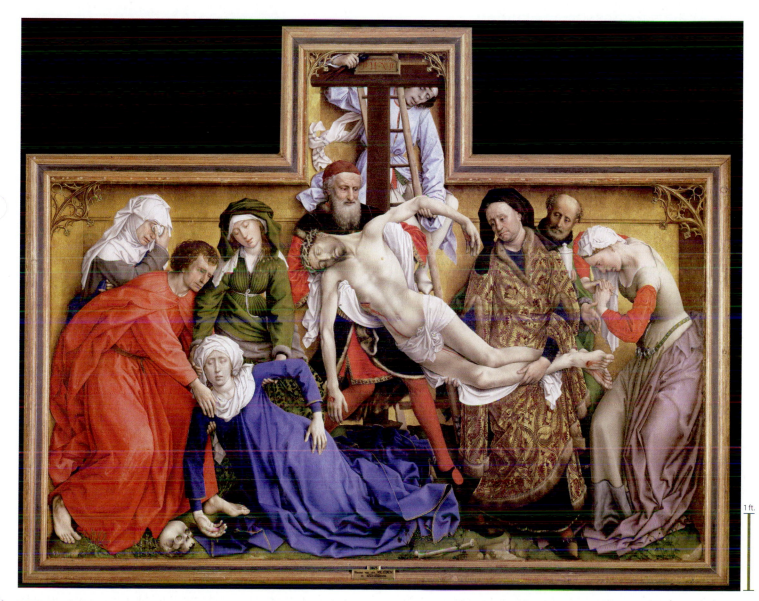

1 ft.

20-9 ROGIER VAN DER WEYDEN, *Deposition*, center panel of a triptych from Notre-Dame hors-les-murs, Louvain, Belgium, ca. 1435–1442. Oil on wood, 7' 2⅝" × 8' 7⅛". Museo del Prado, Madrid.

Deposition resembles a relief carving in which the biblical figures act out a drama of passionate sorrow as if on a shallow theatrical stage. The painting makes an unforgettable emotional impression.

any case, a series of lateral undulating movements gives the group a compositional unity, a formal cohesion that Rogier strengthened by depicting the sorrowful anguish many of the figures share. Present are the Virgin, several of her half-sisters, Joseph of Arimathea, Nicodemus, Saint John the Evangelist, and Mary Magdalene. The similar poses of Christ and his mother further unify the composition and reflect the belief that Mary suffered the same pain at the crucifixion as her son. Their echoing postures also resemble the shape of a crossbow.

Rogier's extraordinary ability to represent flesh and fabric rivaled the skill of Jan van Eyck, and few painters, not even Jan, have equaled the Tournai master in rendering passionate sorrow as it vibrates through a figure or distorts a tearstained face. Rogier's

depictions of the agony of loss in *Deposition* and of the terror of the damned in *Last Judgment* (FIG. 20-9A) are among the most moving and unforgettable images in religious art. It was

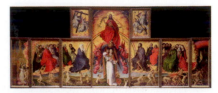

🔼 **20-9A** Van der Weyden, *Last Judgment Altarpiece*, ca. 1443–1451.

probably Rogier whom Michelangelo had in mind when, according to the Portuguese painter Francisco de Hollanda (1517–1584), the Italian master observed, "Flemish painting [will] please the devout better than any painting of Italy, which will never cause him to shed a tear, whereas that of Flanders will cause him to shed many."[1]

ART AND SOCIETY

The Artist's Profession in Flanders

As in Italy (see "Artistic Training," page 426), guilds controlled artistic production in Flanders. To pursue a craft, individuals had to belong to the guild controlling that craft. Painters, for example, sought admission to the Guild of Saint Luke, the patron saint of painters because Luke made a portrait of the Virgin Mary (FIG. 20-1). The patron saint of the metalworkers' guild was Saint Eligius (FIG. 20-10), who was a goldsmith before devoting himself to the Church and eventually becoming bishop of Tournai.

The path to eventual membership in the guild began, for men, at an early age, when the father apprenticed his son in boyhood to a master, with whom the young aspiring painter lived. The master taught the fundamentals of his craft—how to make implements, prepare panels with *gesso* (plaster mixed with a binding material), and mix colors, oils, and varnishes. Once the youth mastered these procedures and learned to work in the master's traditional manner, he usually spent several years working as a journeyman in various cities, observing and absorbing ideas from other masters. He then was eligible to become a master and could apply for admission to the guild. Fees could be very high, especially if an artist was not a citizen of the same city. Sometimes, an artist seeking admission to a guild would marry the widow of a member. (A woman could inherit her husband's workshop but could not run it.) Guild membership was essential for establishing an artist's reputation and for obtaining commissions. The guild inspected paintings to evaluate workmanship and ensure that its members used quality materials. It also secured adequate payment for its artists' labor.

Women had many fewer opportunities than men to train as artists, in large part because of social and moral constraints that forbade women to reside as apprentices in the homes of male masters. Moreover, from the 16th century, when academic training courses supplemented and then replaced guild training, until the 20th century, women would not as a rule expect or be permitted instruction in figure painting, because it involved dissection of cadavers and study of the nude male model. Flemish women interested in pursuing art as a career—for example, Caterina van Hemessen (FIG. 23-16)—most often received tutoring from fathers and husbands who were professionals and whom the women assisted in all the technical

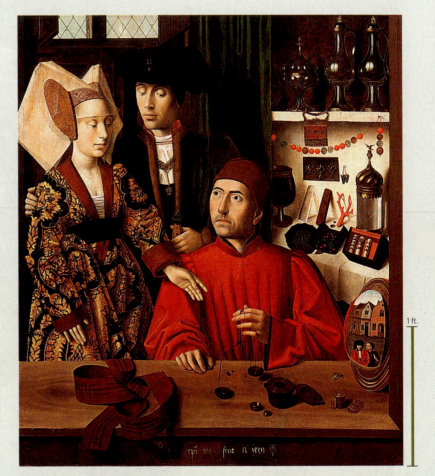

1 ft.

20-10 Petrus Christus, *A Goldsmith in His Shop,* 1449. Oil on wood, 3′ 3″ × 2′ 10″. Metropolitan Museum of Art, New York (Robert Lehman Collection, 1975).

Once thought to depict Eligius, the patron saint of goldsmiths, Christus's painting, made for the Bruges goldsmiths' guild, is more likely a genre scene of a couple shopping for a wedding ring.

procedures of the craft. Despite these obstacles, membership records of the art guilds of Bruges and other cities reveal that a substantial number of Flemish women were able to establish themselves as artists during the 15th century. That they succeeded in negotiating the difficult path to acceptance as professionals is a testament to both their tenacity and their artistic skill.

Later Flemish Painters

Robert Campin, Jan van Eyck, and Rogier van der Weyden were the leading figures of the first generation of "Northern Renaissance" painters. (Art historians usually transfer to northern Europe, with less validity than in its original usage, the term "Renaissance," coined to describe the conscious revival of classical art in Italy.) The second generation of Flemish masters, active during the latter half of the 15th century, had much in common with their illustrious predecessors, especially a preference for using oil paints to create naturalistic representations, often, although not always, of traditional Christian subjects for installation in churches.

PETRUS CHRISTUS One work of uncertain Christian content is *A Goldsmith in His Shop* (FIG. 20-10) by PETRUS CHRISTUS (ca. 1410–1472), who settled in Bruges in 1444. According to the traditional interpretation, *A Goldsmith in His Shop* portrays Saint Eligius (who was initially a master goldsmith before committing his life to God) sitting in his stall, showing an elegantly attired couple a selection of rings. The bride's betrothal girdle lies on the table as a symbol of chastity, and the woman reaches for the ring the goldsmith weighs. The artist's inclusion of a crystal container for Eucharistic wafers (on the lower shelf to the right of Saint Eligius) and the scales (a reference to the Last Judgment) supports a religious interpretation of this painting and continues the Flemish tradition of imbuing everyday objects with symbolic significance. A halo once encircled the goldsmith's head, seemingly confirming the religious nature of

this scene. Scientists have determined, however, that the halo was a later addition by another artist, and restorers have removed it.

Most scholars now think that the painting, although not devoid of religious content, should be seen as a vocational painting of the type often produced for installation in Flemish guild chapels. Although the couple's presence suggests a marriage portrait, the patrons were probably not the couple portrayed but rather the goldsmiths' guild in Bruges. Saint Eligius was the patron saint of gold- and silversmiths, blacksmiths, and metalworkers, all of whom shared a chapel in a building adjacent to their meetinghouse. The reconsecration of this chapel took place in 1449, the same date as the Christus painting. Therefore, it seems probable that the artist painted *A Goldsmith in His Shop*, which illustrates an economic transaction and focuses on the goldsmith's profession, specifically for the guild chapel. A guild chapel is also the likely setting of Rogier van der Weyden's *Saint Luke Drawing the Virgin* (FIG. 20-1). As noted, in the 15th century, in addition to their primary function as "trade unions," guilds played an increasingly important role in community life and often became major patrons of art in their cities (see "The Artist's Profession in Flanders," page 566).

Christus went to great lengths to produce a historically credible image. For example, the variety of objects depicted in the painting serves as advertisement for the goldsmiths' guild. Included are the goldsmiths' raw materials (precious stones, beads, crystal, coral, and seed pearls) scattered among finished products (rings, buckles, and brooches). The pewter vessels on the upper shelves are donation pitchers, which town leaders gave to distinguished guests. All these meticulously painted objects not only attest to the centrality and importance of goldsmiths to both the secular and sacred communities but also enhance the naturalism of the painting. The convex mirror in the foreground showing another couple and a street with houses serves to extend the painting's space into the viewer's space, further creating the illusion of reality, as in Jan van Eyck's Arnolfini portrait (FIG. 20-7).

DIERIC BOUTS In *Last Supper* (FIG. 20-11), DIERIC BOUTS (ca. 1415–1475) of Haarlem chose a different means of suggesting spatial recession. The painting is the central panel of the *Altarpiece of the Holy Sacrament,* which the Confraternity of the Holy Sacrament in Louvain commissioned in 1464. Four years later, Bouts became the city's official painter and was asked to produce a series of panels—including *Wrongful Beheading of the Count* (FIG. 20-11A) and *Justice of Otto III* (FIG. 20-11B)—for Louvain's town hall. Bouts's *Last Supper* is one of the earliest Northern Renaissance paintings to employ *linear perspective* and a *vanishing point* to create the illusion of depth. All of the central room's *orthogonals* (converging diagonal lines imagined to be behind and perpendicular to the picture plane) lead to the vanishing point in the center of the mantelpiece above Jesus's head. The small side room, however, has its own vanishing point, and neither it nor the vanishing point of the main room falls on the horizon of the landscape (the *horizon*

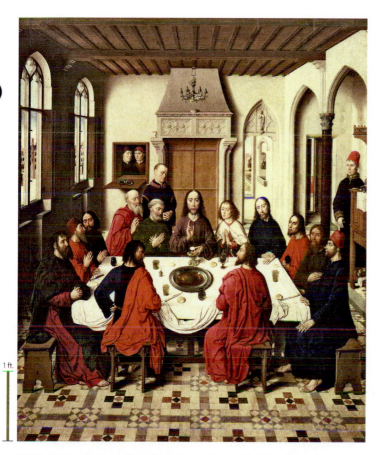

20-11 DIERIC BOUTS, *Last Supper,* center panel of the *Altarpiece of the Holy Sacrament,* Saint Peter's, Louvain, Belgium, 1464–1468. Oil on wood, 6' × 5'.

One of the earliest Northern Renaissance paintings to employ Italian linear perspective, this *Last Supper* includes four servants in Flemish attire—portraits of the altarpiece's patrons.

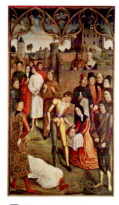

🔗 **20-11A** BOUTS, *Beheading of the Count,* ca. 1473–1481.

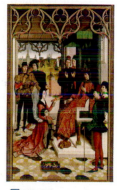

🔗 **20-11B** BOUTS, *Justice of Otto III,* ca. 1470–1473.

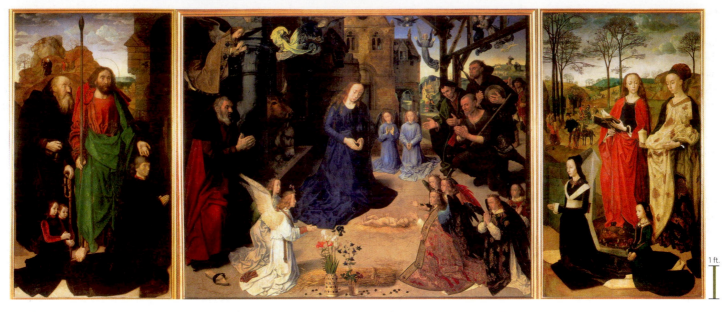

20-12 HUGO VAN DER GOES, *Adoration of the Shepherds* (*Portinari Altarpiece,* open), from Sant'Egidio, Florence, Italy, ca. 1473–1478. Tempera and oil on wood, center panel 8' 3½" × 10', each wing 8' 3½" × 4' 7½". Galleria degli Uffizi, Florence.

This altarpiece is a rare instance of the awarding of a major commission in Italy to a Flemish painter. The Florentines admired Hugo's realistic details and brilliant portrayal of human character.

line) seen through the windows, as in Italian Renaissance paintings composed according to the strict rules of linear perspective (see "Linear Perspective," page 587).

In *Last Supper,* Bouts did not depict the biblical narrative itself but instead presented Jesus in the role of a priest performing the liturgical ritual of the consecration of the Eucharistic wafer. By divid-

ing the apostles into two asymmetrical groups with no one sitting at the middle of the near side of the table, Bouts focused attention on the Savior and the food platter and wine chalice at the table's center. Bouts's *Last Supper* contrasts strongly with other depictions of the same subject, which often represented Jesus's prediction of Judas's betrayal or his comforting of John. The Confraternity of the

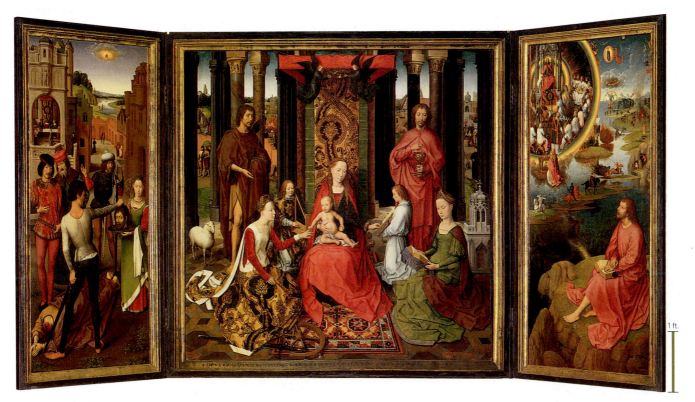

20-13 HANS MEMLING, *Virgin with Saints and Angels,* center panel of the *Saint John Altarpiece,* Hospitaal Sint Jan, Bruges, Belgium, 1479. Oil on wood, center panel 5' 7¾" × 5' 7¾", each wing 5' 7¾" × 2' 7⅛".

Memling specialized in images of the Madonna. His *Saint John Altarpiece* exudes an opulence that results from the sparkling and luminous colors and the realistic depiction of rich tapestries and brocades.

Holy Sacrament dedicated itself to the worship of the Eucharist, and the smaller panels on the altarpiece's wings depict Old Testament *prefigurations* of the Eucharist. Bouts also added four servants (two looking through the windowlike opening in the rear wall and two standing) not mentioned in the biblical account, all dressed in Flemish attire. These are portraits of the four members of the confraternity who contracted Bouts to paint the altarpiece, continuing the Flemish tradition of inserting into representations of biblical events portraits of the painting's patrons, first noted in the *Mérode Altarpiece* (FIG. 20-4).

HUGO VAN DER GOES By the mid-15th century, Flemish art had achieved renown throughout Europe. The *Portinari Altarpiece* (FIG. 20-12), for example, is a large-scale Flemish work in a family chapel in Florence, Italy. The artist who received the commission was HUGO VAN DER GOES (ca. 1440–1482), who joined the painters' guild of Ghent as a master in 1467 and served as the guild's dean from 1473 to 1475. Hugo painted the triptych in Flanders for Tommaso Portinari, an Italian shipowner and agent in Bruges for the powerful Medici bank of Florence. The altarpiece was Portinari's gift to the church of Sant'Egidio, and he appears on the wings with his family and their patron saints. The main panel, *Adoration of the Shepherds*, depicts a subject based on the 14th-century vision of a Swedish saint in which Mary, instead of cradling her newborn son, kneels solemnly to join Joseph, the angels, and the shepherds in adoring the infant Savior, who lies on the ground and glows with divine light. In order to situate the main actors at the center of the panel, Hugo tilted the ground, a compositional device he may have derived from the tilted stage floors of 15th-century mystery plays. Three shepherds enter from the right rear. Hugo represented them in attitudes of wonder, piety, and gaping curiosity. Their lined faces, work-worn hands, and uncouth dress and manner seem immediately familiar.

The architecture and a continuous wintry northern European landscape unify the three panels. Symbols surface throughout the altarpiece. Iris and columbine flowers are emblems of the sorrows of the Virgin. The angels represent the 15 joys of Mary. A sheaf of wheat stands for Bethlehem (the "house of bread" in Hebrew), a reference to the Eucharist. The harp of David, emblazoned over the building's portal in the middle distance (just to the right of the Virgin's head), signifies the ancestry of Christ. To stress the meaning and significance of the illustrated event, Hugo revived medieval pictorial devices. Small scenes shown in the background of the altarpiece represent (from left to right) the journey of Mary and Joseph to Bethlehem, the annunciation to the shepherds, and the arrival of the magi. Hugo's variation in the scale of his figures to differentiate them by their importance to the central event also reflects older traditions. Still, he put a vigorous, penetrating realism to work in a new direction, characterizing human beings according to their social level while showing their common humanity.

After Portinari placed the altarpiece in his family's chapel in the Florentine church of Sant'Egidio, it created a considerable stir among Italian artists. Although the painting may have seemed unstructured to them, Hugo's masterful technique and what the Florentines deemed incredible realism in representing drapery, flowers, animals, and, above all, human character and emotion made a deep impression on them. At least one Florentine artist, Domenico Ghirlandaio (FIGS. 21-26 and 21-27), paid tribute to the Flemish master by using Hugo's most striking motif, the adoring shepherds, in one of his own *Nativity* paintings.

HANS MEMLING Hugo's contemporary, HANS MEMLING (ca. 1430–1494), may have trained as a painter in Rogier van der Weyden's studio. He became a citizen of Bruges in 1465 and received numerous commissions from the city's wealthy merchants, Flemish and foreign alike. He specialized in portraits of his patrons (one of whom was Tommaso Portinari; FIG. 20-14A) and images of the Madonna. Memling's many paintings of the Virgin portray young, slight, pretty princesses, each holding a doll-like infant Jesus. The center panel of the *Saint John Altarpiece* is *Virgin with Saints and Angels* (FIG. 20-13). The patrons of this altarpiece—two brothers and two sisters of the order of the Hospital of Saint John in Bruges—appear on the exterior side panels (not illustrated). In the main panel, two angels, one playing a musical instrument and the other holding a book, flank the Virgin. To the sides of Mary's throne stand Saints John the Baptist on the left and John the Evangelist on the right. Seated in the foreground are Saints Catherine and Barbara. This gathering celebrates the *mystic marriage* of Saint Catherine of Alexandria, one of many virgin saints believed to have entered into a spiritual marriage with Christ. As one of the most revered virgins of Christ, Saint Catherine provided a model of devotion that resonated with women viewers (especially nuns). The altarpiece exudes an opulence that results from the rich colors, the meticulously depicted tapestries and brocades, and the serenity of the figures. The composition is balanced and serene, the color sparkling and luminous, and the execution of the highest technical quality.

Memling combined portraiture and Madonna imagery again in a much less ambitious—and more typical—work (FIG. 20-14) he painted for Martin van Nieuwenhove (1464–1500). The smaller scale of the private commission and its

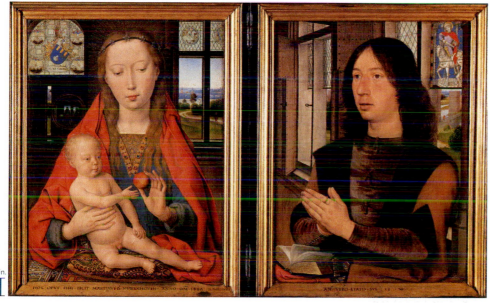

20-14 HANS MEMLING, *Diptych of Martin van Nieuwenhove*, 1487. Oil on wood, each panel 1' 5 3/8" × 1' 1". Memlingmuseum, Bruges.

In this diptych, the Virgin and Child pay a visit to the home of 23-year-old Martin van Nieuwenhove. A round convex mirror reflects the three figures and unites the two halves of the diptych spatially.

much more intimate character underscore the different approaches the same painter regularly took when producing artworks for different kinds of patrons and for public versus private settings. Martin van Nieuwenhove was the scion of an important Bruges family that held various posts in the civic government. He himself served as burgomeister of Bruges in 1497. The painting takes the form of a diptych, with the patron portrayed on the right wing praying to the Madonna and Child on the left wing. According to inscriptions on the frames, van Nieuwenhove commissioned the work in 1487 when he was 23 years old. He died only 13 years later, 3 years after becoming mayor.

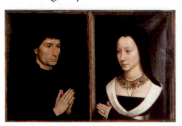

⚹ **20-14A** MEMLING, *Tommaso Portinari and Maria Baroncelli*, ca. 1470.

The format of the van Nieuwenhove diptych follows the pattern that Memling used earlier for his wedding triptych *Tommaso Portinari and Maria Baroncelli* (FIG. **20-14A**) but with only a single (male) portrait. (The lost central section of the Portinari triptych probably closely resembled the van Nieuwenhove Madonna and Child.) Memling's portrayals of Mary and Jesus consistently feature a tender characterization of the young Virgin and her nude infant son. Here, however, Memling set both the Madonna and her patron in the interior of a well-appointed Flemish home featuring stained-glass windows. The window to the left of the Virgin's head bears van Nieuwenhove's coat of arms. The window behind the donor depicts his patron saint, Martin of Tours. These precisely recorded details identify the home as van Nieuwenhove's (the Minnewater Bridge in Bruges is visible through the open window), and the Madonna and Child have honored him by coming to his private residence. Even Saint Luke had to go to the Virgin's home to paint her portrait (FIG. 20-1), but the conceit is a familiar one in Flemish painting. An early example is the Annunciation taking place in the home of Peter Inghelbrecht in Robert Campin's *Mérode Altarpiece* (FIG. 20-4). In the Memling portrait diptych, the Christ Child sits on the same ledge as the donor's open prayer book. Also uniting the two wings of the diptych is the round convex mirror behind the Virgin's right shoulder in which the viewer sees the reflection of the Virgin and van Nieuwenhove as well as the rest of the room (compare FIGS. 20-7 and 20-10).

FRANCE

In contrast to the prosperity and peace that Flanders enjoyed during the 15th century, in France the Hundred Years' War crippled economic enterprise and prevented political stability. The anarchy of war and the weakness of the kings gave rise to a group of duchies, each with significant power and the resources to commission major artworks. The strongest and wealthiest of these has already been examined—the duchy of Burgundy, which controlled Flanders. But the dukes of Berry, Bourbon, and Nemours as well as members of the French royal court were also important art patrons.

Manuscript Painting

During the 15th century, French artists built on the achievements of Gothic painters (see page 395) and produced exquisitely refined illuminated manuscripts. Among the most significant developments in French manuscript painting was a new conception and presentation of space. Paintings in manuscripts took on more pronounced char-

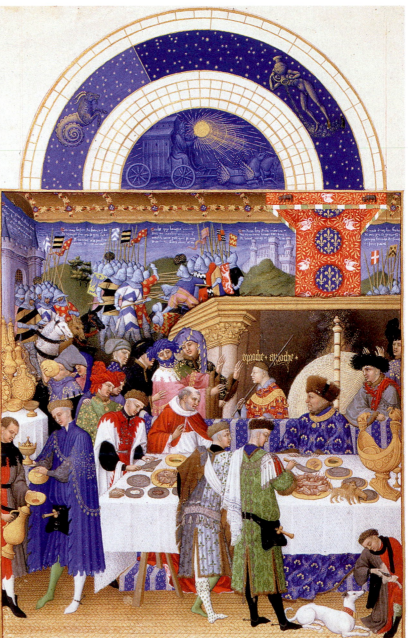

20-15 LIMBOURG BROTHERS (POL, HERMAN, JEAN), *January,* from *Les Très Riches Heures du Duc de Berry,* 1413–1416. Colors and ink on vellum, $8\frac{7}{8}$" × $5\frac{3}{8}$". Musée Condé, Chantilly.

The sumptuous pictures in *Les Très Riches Heures* depict characteristic activities of each month. The prominence of genre subjects reflects the increasing integration of religious and secular art.

1 in.

acteristics as illusionistic scenes. Increased contact with Italy, where Renaissance artists had revived the pictorial principles of classical antiquity, may have influenced French painters' interest in illusionism.

LIMBOURG BROTHERS The most innovative early-15th-century manuscript illuminators were the three LIMBOURG BROTHERS— POL, HERMAN, and JEAN—from Nijmegen in the Netherlands. They were nephews of Jean Malouel, the court artist of Philip the Bold (see page 558). Following in the footsteps of earlier illustrators such as Jean Pucelle (FIGS. 13-35 and 13-35A), the Limbourg brothers expanded the illusionistic capabilities of illumination. Trained in the Netherlands, the brothers moved to Paris no later than 1402, and between 1405 and their death in 1416, probably from the plague, they worked in Paris and Bourges for Jean, duke of Berry (r. 1360–1416) and brother of Philip the Bold of Burgundy and King Charles V (r. 1364–1380) of France.

Jean ruled the western French regions of Berry, Poitou, and Auvergne (MAP 20-1). The duke was an avid art patron and focused on collecting manuscripts, jewels, and rare artifacts. Among the

more than 300 manuscripts he owned were Pucelle's *Belleville Breviary* (FIG. 13-35) and the *Hours of Jeanne d'Évreux* (FIG. 13-35A) as well as *Les Très Riches Heures du Duc de Berry* (*The Very Sumptuous Hours of the Duke of Berry*; FIGS. 20-15 and 20-16), which he commissioned the Limbourg brothers to produce. A *Book of Hours*, like a *breviary*, was a book used for reciting prayers (see "Medieval Books," page 316). As prayer books, they replaced the traditional *psalters* (books of psalms), which were the only liturgical books in private hands until the mid-13th century. The centerpiece of a Book of Hours was the "Office [prayer] of the Blessed Virgin," which contained liturgical passages to be read privately at set times during the day, from *matins* (dawn prayers) to *compline* (the last of the prayers recited daily). An illustrated calendar containing local religious feast days usually preceded the Office of the Blessed Virgin. Penitential psalms, devotional prayers, litanies to the saints, and other prayers, including those of the Holy Cross and for the dead, followed the centerpiece. Books of Hours became favorite possessions of the northern European aristocracy during the 14th and 15th centuries. These costly books eventually became available to affluent merchants and contributed to the decentralization of religious practice that was one factor in the Protestant Reformation in the early 16th century (see page 680).

The full-page calendar pictures of *Les Très Riches Heures* are the most famous in the history of manuscript illumination. They represent the 12 months in terms of the associated seasonal tasks, alternating scenes of nobility and peasantry, and featuring the duke's relationship with his courtiers and peasants. Above each picture is a *lunette* in which the Limbourgs depicted the zodiac signs and the chariot of the sun as it makes its yearly cycle through the heavens. Beyond its function as a religious book, *Les Très Riches Heures* also furnishes a picture of life in the territory the duke ruled—a picture designed to flatter the Limbourgs' patron. For example, the colorful calendar picture for January (FIG. **20-15**) portrays a New Year's reception at court. The duke appears as magnanimous host, his head circled by the fire screen, almost halolike, behind him. His chamberlain stands next to him, urging the guests forward with the words "*aproche, aproche.*" The lavish spread of food on the table and the large tapestry on the back wall augment the richness and extravagance of the setting and the occasion.

In contrast, the illustration for October (FIG. **20-16**) focuses on the peasantry. Here, the Limbourg brothers depicted a sower, a man plowing on horseback, and washerwomen, along with city dwellers, who promenade in front of the Louvre (the French king's residence at the time, now one of the world's great art museums). The peasants do not appear

1 in.

20-16 LIMBOURG BROTHERS (POL, HERMAN, JEAN), *October,* from *Les Très Riches Heures du Duc de Berry,* 1413–1416. Colors and ink on vellum, $8\frac{7}{8}" \times 5\frac{3}{8}"$. Musée Condé, Chantilly.

The Limbourg brothers expanded the illusionistic capabilities of manuscript painting with their care in rendering architectural details and their convincing depiction of cast shadows.

discontented as they go about their various tasks. Surely, this imagery flattered the duke's sense of himself as a compassionate master. The growing artistic interest in naturalism is evident here in the careful way the painter recorded the architectural details of the Louvre and in the convincing shadows of the people and objects (such as the archer scarecrow and the horse) in the scene.

As a whole, *Les Très Riches Heures* reinforced the image of the duke of Berry as a devout man, cultured *bibliophile* (lover of books), sophisticated art patron, and powerful and magnanimous leader. Further, the expanded range of subject matter, especially the prominence of *genre* subjects in a religious book, reflected the increasing integration of religious and secular concerns in both art and life at the time. Although all three Limbourg brothers worked on *Les Très Riches Heures*, art historians have never been able to ascertain definitively which brother painted which images. (One scholar has suggested that because the book was left unfinished at the time the brothers died, some of the details are the work of a fourth artist, who completed the illustrations around the middle of the century.) Given the common practice of collaboration on artistic projects at this time, however, the determination of specific authorship is not very important. Together, the *Très Riches Heures* illuminators reoriented the art of manuscript illumination to approximate more closely the art of panel painting, treating the pages of books as if they were windows onto the world of 15th-century northern Europe.

MARY OF BURGUNDY The Limbourgs' most accomplished successor at the end of the century was an anonymous illuminator known as the MASTER OF MARY OF BURGUNDY. Some scholars identify him as ALEXANDER BENING (ca. 1444–1519) of Ghent, a painter in the circle of Hugo van der Goes (FIG. 20-12). The two facing pages illustrated here (FIG. **20-17**) are the opening full-page illumination and one of the daily prayers in the private devotional Book of Hours that belonged to Mary, the last duchess of Burgundy (r. 1477–1482) and daughter of Charles the Bold. She is the elegantly dressed woman sitting in a private chapel with her pet dog on her lap, reading from a prayer book of the same size and format as the one in which her portrait appears. On a ledge to her left are her rosary beads and a tall vase with purple irises, flowers associated with the Virgin Mary. The masterful representation of rich fabrics, of Mary's transparent veil, and of the still life of flowers all attest to this painter's skill and powers of observation.

Even more remarkable is the illuminator's meticulously detailed depiction—at only half the size of Jan van Eyck's *Madonna in a Church* (FIG. 20-6A)—of the Gothic church seen through the window of Mary's chapel. The scene presented to the viewer through the chapel window within the page's "window onto the world"— a brilliant conception in itself—is the realization of Mary's prayers. The duchess has been granted a private audience with the Virgin without any interceding priest. She, accompanied by her ladies-in-

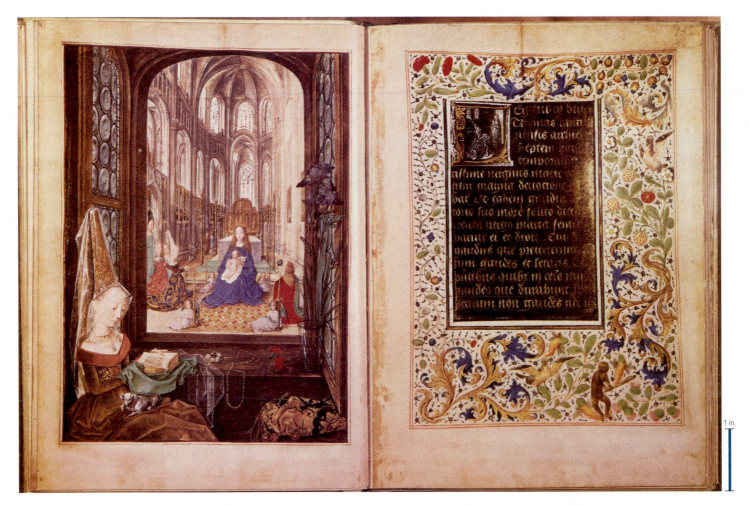

20-17 MASTER OF MARY OF BURGUNDY, *Mary of Burgundy at Prayer*, folios 14 verso and 15 recto of the *Hours of Mary of Burgundy*, ca. 1477. Colors and ink on parchment, illumination on left page 7 3/8" × 5 1/8". Österreichische Nationalbibliothek, Vienna.

In this Book of Hours, the page became literally a window onto the world. Mary of Burgundy prays in a private chapel. Seen through a window is the answer to her prayers—an audience with the Virgin.

waiting, kneels before the Virgin, who sits before the church altar, attended by angels and holding the Christ Child in her lap. Both holy figures turn their heads to look at the duchess. The illumination has few peers in the history of art as an image of pious devotion.

Panel Painting

In addition to illustrated books, independent paintings were popular in France, as in Flanders, for private devotional use. The preferred medium was oil paint on wood panels.

JEAN FOUQUET Among the French artists whose paintings were in high demand was JEAN FOUQUET (ca. 1425–1478). Fouquet's workshop was in Tours, and he received important commissions from King Charles VII (r. 1422–1461, the patron and client of Jacques Coeur; FIG. 13-30) and from the duke of Nemours and other elite members of the French aristocracy. Fouquet painted a diptych (FIG. 20-18) for Étienne Chevalier, who, despite his lowly birth as the son of one of Charles VII's secretaries, rose to become royal treasurer in 1452. In the left panel of the *Melun Diptych* (named for its original location in Melun Cathedral), Chevalier appears with his patron saint, Saint Stephen (Étienne in French). Appropriately, Fouquet's donor portrait of Chevalier depicts his prominent patron as devout—kneeling, with hands clasped in prayer. The representation of the pious donor with his standing saint recalls Flemish art, as do the three-quarter stances and the realism of Chevalier's portrait.

The artist portrayed Saint Stephen, whose head also has a portrait-like quality, holding the stone symbolizing his martyrdom (death by stoning) atop a volume of the holy scriptures, thereby ensuring that viewers can properly identify the saint. Fouquet rendered the entire image in meticulous detail and included a highly ornamented architectural setting.

In its original diptych form (the two panels are now in different museums), the viewer would follow the gaze of Chevalier and Saint Stephen over to the right panel, which depicts the *Virgin Mary and Christ Child* in a most unusual way—with marblelike flesh, surrounded by red and blue *cherubs* (chubby winged child angels). The juxtaposition of these two images enabled the patron to bear witness to the sacred. The integration of sacred and secular (especially the political or personal), prevalent in other Northern Renaissance artworks, also emerges here, which complicates the reading of this diptych. Agnès Sorel (1421–1450), the mistress of King Charles VII (see page 393), was Fouquet's model for the Virgin Mary, whose left breast is exposed, presumably to nurse the infant Jesus, but she does not look at her son or the viewer. (Mary as nursing mother is a rare although not unique way of representing the Virgin in northern Europe; compare FIG. 20-1.) Chevalier commissioned this painting after Sorel's death, probably by poisoning while pregnant with the king's child. Thus, in addition to the religious interpretation of this diptych, there is surely a personal and political narrative here as well, made all the more complex given that Sorel gave birth to three of the king's daughters, but never a son.

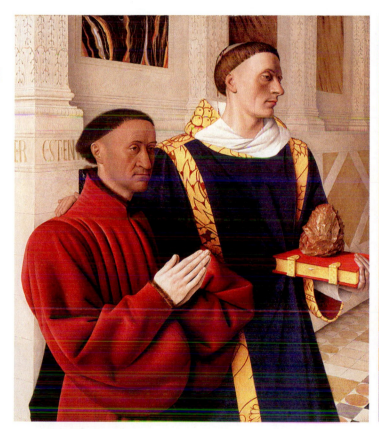 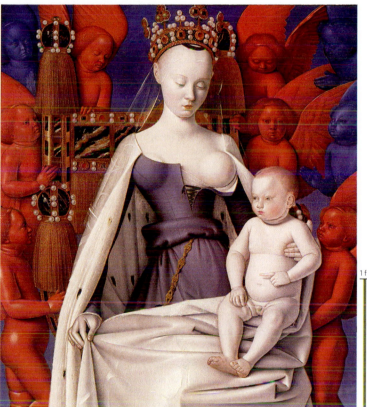

1 ft.

20-18 JEAN FOUQUET, *Melun Diptych*, ca. 1452. Left wing: *Étienne Chevalier and Saint Stephen*. Oil on wood, 3' $\frac{1}{2}$" × 2' 9$\frac{1}{2}$". Gemäldegalerie, Staatliche Museen zu Berlin, Berlin. Right wing: *Virgin and Child*. Oil on wood, 3' 1$\frac{1}{4}$" × 2' 9$\frac{1}{2}$". Koninklijk Museum voor Schone Kunsten, Antwerp.

Fouquet's meticulous representation of a pious kneeling donor with a standing patron saint recalls Flemish painting, as do the three-quarter stances and the realism of the donor's portrait head.

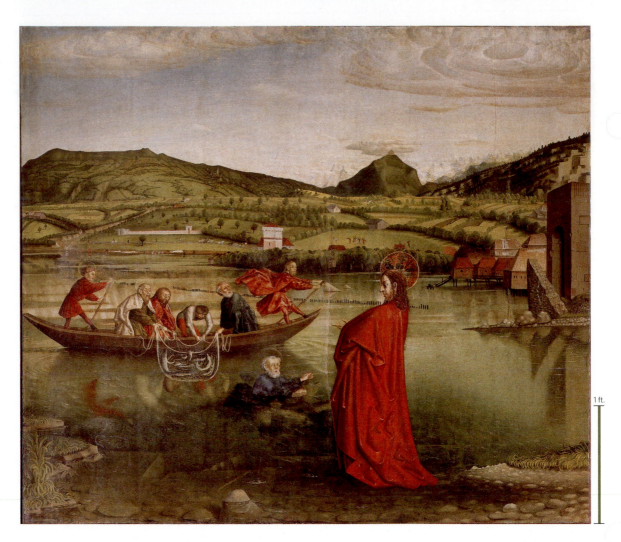

20-19 KONRAD WITZ, *Miraculous Draft of Fish*, exterior wing of *Altarpiece of Saint Peter*, from the Chapel of Notre-Dame des Maccabées, Cathedral of Saint Peter, Geneva, Switzerland, 1444. Oil on wood, 4' 3" × 5' 1". Musée d'Art et d'Histoire, Geneva.

Konrad Witz set this biblical story on Lake Geneva. The painting is one of the first 15th-century works depicting a specific locale and is noteworthy for the painter's skill in rendering water effects.

1 ft.

HOLY ROMAN EMPIRE

Because the Holy Roman Empire (whose core was Germany) did not participate in the drawn-out saga of the Hundred Years' War, its economy remained stable and prosperous. Without a dominant court to commission artworks, wealthy merchants and clergy became the primary German art patrons during the 15th century.

Panel Painting

The art of the early Northern Renaissance in the Holy Roman Empire displays a pronounced stylistic diversity. Some artists followed developments in Flemish painting, and large-scale altarpieces featuring naturalistically painted biblical themes were familiar sights in the Holy Roman Empire.

KONRAD WITZ Among the most notable 15th-century German altarpieces is the *Altarpiece of Saint Peter,* painted by KONRAD WITZ (ca. 1400–1446) for the chapel of Notre-Dame des Maccabées in the Cathedral of Saint Peter in Geneva, Switzerland. Signed by "Magister Conradus of Basel" and dated 1444, the altarpiece is a triptych featuring Witz's paintings on both the exterior and interior. *Miraculous Draft of Fish* (FIG. 20-19) appears on one of the exterior wings. The other (not illustrated) depicts the release of Saint Peter from prison. The central panel is lost. On the interior wings, Witz painted scenes of the adoration of the magi and of

Saint Peter's presentation of the donor (Bishop François de Mies) to the Virgin and Child. *Miraculous Draft of Fish* shows Peter, the first pope, unsuccessfully trying to emulate Christ walking on water. The choice of this episode from among others in Peter's life (see "Early Christian Saints," page 236) may be a commentary on the part of Witz's patron, the Swiss cardinal, on the limited power of the pope in Rome.

The painting is particularly significant because of the landscape's prominence. Witz showed precocious skill in the study of water effects—the shimmering sky on the slowly moving lake surface, the mirrored reflections of the figures in the boat, and the transparency of the shallow water in the foreground. He observed and represented the landscape so carefully that art historians have been able to determine the exact location shown. Witz presented a view of the shores of Lake Geneva, with the town of Geneva on the right and Le Môle Mountain in the distance behind Christ's head. This painting is one of the first 15th-century works depicting a specific, identifiable site. The work of other leading German painters of the mid-15th century—for example, STEFAN LOCHNER (ca. 1400–1451)—retained medieval features to a much greater degree, as is immediately evident in a comparison between Witz's landscape and Lochner's *Madonna in the Rose Garden* (FIG. 20-19A).

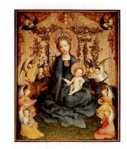

20-19A LOCHNER, *Madonna in the Rose Garden*, ca. 1435–1440.

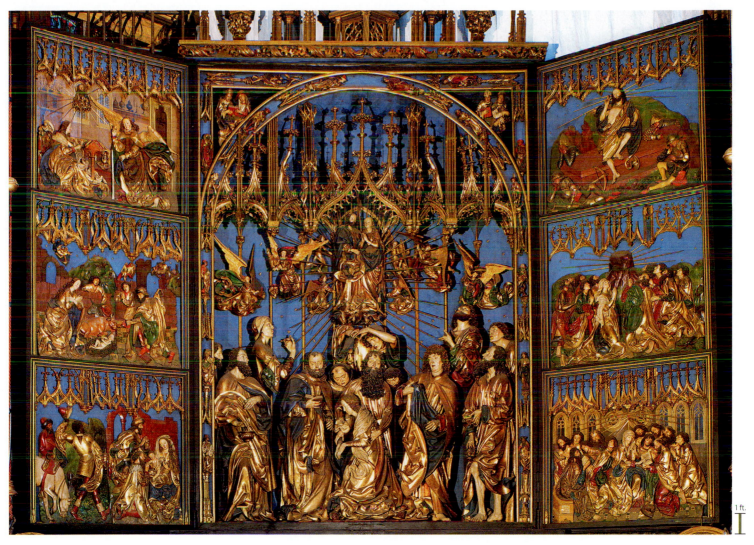

20-20 VEIT STOSS, *Death and Assumption of the Virgin*, center panel of the *Altarpiece of the Virgin Mary* (with wings open), Church of Saint Mary, Kraków, Poland, 1477–1489. Painted and gilded lime-wood, central panel 23' 9" high.

In this huge painted and gilded sculptured wood altarpiece, Stoss used every figural and ornamental element from the vocabulary of Gothic art to heighten the emotion and glorify the sacred event.

Sculpture

In contrast to Flanders, where painted altarpieces were the norm, in the Holy Roman Empire many of the leading 15th-century artists specialized in carving large wood retables. These grandiose sculpted altarpieces reveal the lingering power of the Late Gothic style.

VEIT STOSS The sculptor VEIT STOSS (ca. 1447–1533) trained in the Upper Rhine region, possibly in Strasbourg, but settled in Kraków (in present-day Poland) in 1477. In that year, he began work on a monumental altarpiece for the church of Saint Mary in Kraków, paid for by the city's citizens. In the central boxlike shrine is *Death and Assumption of the Virgin* (FIG. 20-20), peopled by huge carved, painted, and gilded figures, some 9 feet high. (An altarpiece of this kind may have inspired Rogier van der Weyden's *Deposition* [FIG. 20-9].) On both the outer and inner faces of the wings, Stoss portrayed scenes from the lives of Christ and Mary. The altar forcefully expresses the intense piety of Gothic culture in its late phase, when artists used every figural and ornamental motif in the repertoire of Gothic art to heighten the emotion and to glorify sacred

events. In the center panel of the Kraków altarpiece, Christ's disciples congregate around the Virgin, who collapses, dying. One of them supports her, while another wrings his hands in grief. Above, Mary rises to Heaven with the resurrected Christ. Stoss posed others in attitudes of woe and psychic shock, striving for realism in every minute detail. He engulfed the figures in restless, twisting, and curving swaths of drapery whose broken and writhing lines unite the whole tableau in a vision of agitated emotion. The artist's massing of sharp, broken, and pierced forms that dart flamelike through the composition—at once unifying and animating it—recalls the design principles of Late Gothic architecture (FIG. 13-27). Indeed, in the Kraków altarpiece, Stoss merged sculpture and architecture, enhancing their union with paint and gilding.

The Kraków altarpiece gives modern viewers the opportunity to appreciate the polychromy that was standard in ancient and medieval sculpture in both wood and stone. Examples such as this one are unfortunately rare. The vast majority of preserved statues and reliefs from antiquity and the Middle Ages give a false impression of their original appearance (compare FIGS. 3-13A and 5-63A) because the paint has disappeared.

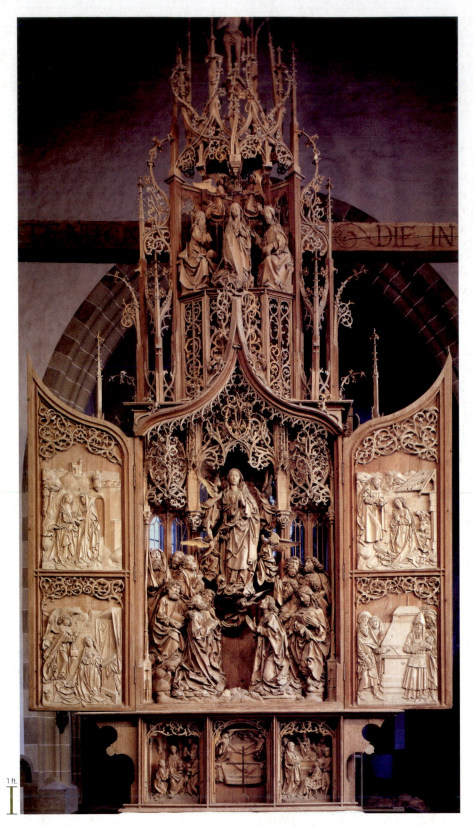

20-21 Tilman Riemenschneider, *Assumption of the Virgin* (*Creglingen Altarpiece*), Herrgottskirche, Creglingen, Germany, ca. 1495–1505. Lime-wood, 30' 2" high.

Riemenschneider specialized in carving large wood retables. His works feature intricate Gothic tracery and religious figures whose bodies are almost lost within their swirling garments.

TILMAN RIEMENSCHNEIDER *Assumption of the Virgin* is also the center panel of the *Creglingen Altarpiece* (FIG. **20-21**), carved by Tilman Riemenschneider (ca. 1460–1531) of Würzburg for a parish church in Creglingen, Germany. Riemenschneider incorporated

intricate Gothic forms, especially in the altarpiece's elaborate canopy, but unlike Stoss, he did not paint the figures or the background. By employing an endless and restless line running through the garments of the figures, the Würzburg master succeeded in setting the whole design into fluid motion, and no individual element functions without the rest. The draperies float and flow around bodies lost within them, serving not as descriptions but as design elements that tie the figures to one another and to the framework. A look of psychic strain, a facial expression common in Riemenschneider's work, heightens the spirituality of the figures, immaterial and weightless as they appear.

Graphic Arts

A new age blossomed in the 15th century with a sudden technological advance that had widespread effects—the invention by Johannes Gutenberg (ca. 1400–1468) of moveable type around 1450 and the development of the printing press. Printing had been known in China centuries before, but had never fostered, as it did in 15th-century Europe, a revolution in written communication and in the generation and management of information. Printing provided new and challenging media for artists, and the earliest form was the *woodcut*. Artists produced inexpensive woodcuts such as the *Buxheim Saint Christopher* (FIG. **20-21A**) before the development

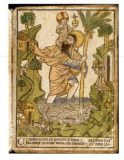

↗ **20-21A** *Buxheim Saint Christopher*, 1423(?).

of moveable-type printing. But when a rise in literacy and the improved economy necessitated the production of illustrated books on a grand scale, artists met the challenge of bringing the woodcut picture onto the same letterpress text pages (see "How to Illustrate Printed Books," page 577).

MARTIN SCHONGAUER The woodcut medium hardly had matured when printmakers introduced the technique of *engraving* (see "Engraving and Etching," page 578). Begun in the 1430s and well developed by 1450, engraving proved much more flexible than woodcut. Predictably, in the second half of the century, engraving began to replace the woodcut process for making both book illustrations and widely popular single prints. Not surprisingly, many of the earliest engravers were professional goldsmiths, who easily applied their training to the new art form.

Martin Schongauer (ca. 1430–1491) of Colmar, a painter and the son of a goldsmith, was the most skilled and subtle northern

PROBLEMS AND SOLUTIONS
How to Illustrate Printed Books

With the invention of moveable type in the 15th century and the new widespread availability of paper from commercial mills, the art of print-making developed rapidly in Europe. A *print* is an artwork on paper, usually produced in multiple impressions. The set of prints an artist creates from a single print surface is called an *edition*. Like the manufacturing of books on a press, the printmaking process involves the transfer of ink from a printing surface to paper. This can be accomplished in several ways. The oldest and simplest is the *relief* method—carving the design into a surface, usually a soft wood, such as pear. Relief printing requires artists to conceptualize their images in reverse—that is, they must draw mirror images of the intended design on the wood block. They then remove the surface areas around the drawn lines using a gouging instrument. Thus, when the printmaker inks the ridges that correspond to the original (reversed) drawing, the hollow areas remain dry, and a correctly oriented image results when the artist presses the printing block against paper. Because artists produce *woodcuts* through a subtractive process (removing parts of the material), it is difficult to create very thin, fluid, and closely spaced lines. Moreover, if the ridges are too thin, they will break during printing. As a result, woodcut prints (for example, FIGS. I-9, 20-21A, and 20-22) tend to exhibit stark contrasts between the dark lines and the blank background.

During the later 15th century, publishers realized that the wood-cut was the ideal medium for solving the problem of illustrating their new printed books. The new technology quickly led to the demise of the manuscript illuminator as well as the scribe, both of whom had been essential for the production of illustrated books through the late Middle Ages, whether they were monks working in monastic *scriptoria* or lay professionals employed in the for-profit workshops of Paris and other cities.

The most ambitious early effort to produce low-cost mass-produced printed books was the so-called *Nuremberg Chronicle*, a history of the world produced in Nuremberg by ANTON KOBERGER (ca. 1445–1513), with more than 650 illustrations furnished by the workshop of MICHAEL WOLGEMUT (1434–1519). The hand-colored page illustrated here (FIG. 20-22) represents *Madeburga* (modern Magdeburg, Germany). The blunt, simple lines of the woodcut technique give a detailed perspective of Magdeburg, its harbor and shipping, its walls and towers, its churches and municipal buildings, and a statue-topped columnar monument. Despite the numerous architectural structures, this illustration is not an accurate depiction of the city but the product of the artist's fanciful imagination. Wolgemut often used the same image to illustrate different cities, even those with very little in common—for example, Verona, Italy, and Damascus, Syria. This depiction of Magdeburg is a generic view of a late medieval German town, not a portrait of a specific place. Regardless, the *Nuremberg Chronicle* is a monument to a new craft, which expanded in concert with the art of the printed book.

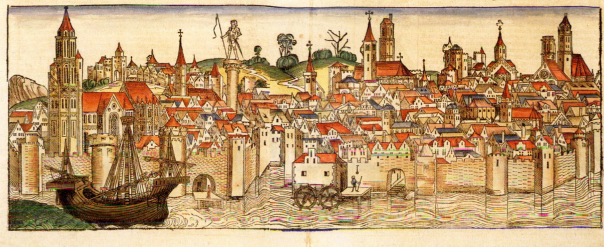

20-22 MICHAEL WOLGEMUT and workshop, *Madeburga*, page from the *Nuremberg Chronicle*, 1493. Woodcut, 1' 6$\frac{1}{8}$" × 2' 1$\frac{5}{8}$". Printed by ANTON KOBERGER.

The *Nuremberg Chronicle* is an early example of woodcut illustrations in printed books. The more than 650 pictures include detailed views of towns, but they are generic rather than specific portrayals.

MATERIALS AND TECHNIQUES
Engraving and Etching

In contrast to the production of relief prints, in the *intaglio* method of printmaking, the artist *incises* (cuts) the lines on a metal plate, often copper, rather than cuts away the area around the lines, as the relief printer does. The image can be created on the plate manually (*engraving* or *drypoint*; for example, FIG. 20-23) using a tool (a *burin* or *stylus*) or chemically (*etching*; for example, FIG. 25-16). In the etching process, an acid bath eats into the exposed parts of the plate where the artist has drawn through an acid-resistant coating. When the artist inks the surface of the intaglio plate and wipes it clean, the ink is forced into the incisions. Then the artist runs the plate and paper through a roller press, and the paper absorbs the remaining ink, creating the print. Because the artist "draws" the image onto the plate, intaglio prints differ in character from relief prints, such as woodcuts. Engravings, drypoints, and etchings generally present a wider variety of linear effects, as is immediately evident in a comparison of the roughly contemporaneous woodcut (FIG. 20-22) by Michael Wolgemut and an engraving (FIG. 20-23) by Martin Schongauer. Intaglio prints also often reveal to a greater extent evidence of the artist's touch, the result of the hand's changing pressure and shifting directions.

The paper and inks that artists use also affect the finished look of the printed image. During the 15th and 16th centuries, European printmakers used papers produced from cotton and linen rags that papermakers mashed with water into a pulp. The papermakers then applied a thin layer of this pulp to a wire screen and allowed it to dry to create the paper. As contact with Asia increased, printmakers made greater use of what was called Japan paper (of mulberry fibers) and China paper. Artists, then as now, could select from a wide variety of inks. The type and proportion of the ink ingredients affect the consistency, color, and oiliness of inks, which various papers absorb differently.

Paper is lightweight, and the portability of prints has been an important factor in their appeal to artists. The opportunity to produce numerous impressions from the same print surface also made printmaking attractive to 15th- and 16th-century artists. In addition, prints can be sold at much lower prices than paintings or sculptures. Consequently, prints reached a far wider audience than did one-of-a-kind artworks. The number and quality of existing 15th- and 16th-century European prints attest to the importance of the new print medium.

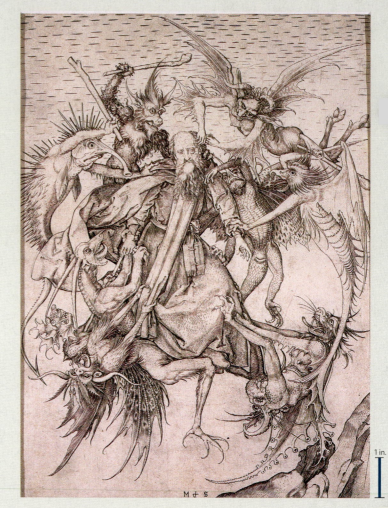

20-23 MARTIN SCHONGAUER, *Saint Anthony Tormented by Demons*, ca. 1480. Engraving, 1' $\frac{1}{4}$" × 9". Fondazione Magnani Rocca, Corte di Mamiano.

Schongauer was the most skilled of the early masters of metal engraving. By using a burin to incise lines in a copper plate, he was able to create a marvelous variety of tonal values and textures.

European master of metal engraving. His *Saint Anthony Tormented by Demons* (FIG. 20-23) shows both the versatility of the medium and the artist's mastery of it. The stoic saint is caught in a revolving thornbush of spiky demons, who claw and tear at him furiously. With unsurpassed skill and subtlety, Schongauer incised lines of varying thickness and density into a metal plate and created marvelous distinctions of tonal values and textures—from smooth skin to rough cloth, from the furry and feathery to the hairy and scaly. The use of *cross-hatching* (sets of engraved lines at right angles) to describe forms, which Schongauer probably developed, became standard among German graphic artists. The Italians preferred *parallel hatching* (FIG. 21-29) and rarely adopted cross-hatching, which, in keeping with the general Northern Renaissance approach to art, tends to describe the surfaces of things rather than their underlying structures.

Schongauer probably engraved *Saint Anthony* around the year 1480. By then, the political geography of Europe had changed dramatically. Charles the Bold, who had assumed the title of duke of Burgundy in 1467, died in 1477, bringing to an end the Burgundian dream of forming a strong middle kingdom between France and the Holy Roman Empire. After Charles's death at the battle of Nancy, the French monarchy reabsorbed the southern Burgundian lands, and the Netherlands passed to the Holy Roman Empire by virtue of the dynastic marriage of Charles's daughter, Mary of Burgundy (FIG. 20-17), to Maximilian of Habsburg, inaugurating a new political and artistic era in northern Europe (see page 676). The next two chapters, however, explore Italian developments in painting, sculpture, and architecture during the 15th and 16th centuries.

LATE MEDIEVAL AND EARLY RENAISSANCE NORTHERN EUROPE

Burgundy and Flanders

- The most powerful rulers north of the Alps during the first three quarters of the 15th century were the dukes of Burgundy. They controlled Flanders, which derived its wealth from wool and banking, and were great art patrons. Duke Philip the Bold (r. 1363–1404) endowed the Carthusian monastery at Champmol, near Dijon, which became a ducal mausoleum. The head of Philip's sculptural workshop was Claus Sluter, whose *Well of Moses* features innovative statues of prophets with portraitlike features and realistic costumes.

- Flemish artists popularized the use of oil paints on wood panels. By superimposing translucent glazes, painters could create richer colors than possible using tempera or fresco. One of the earliest examples of oil painting is Melchior Broederlam's *Retable de Champmol* (1339), painted for Philip the Bold.

- A major art form in churches and private homes alike was the altarpiece with folding wings. In Robert Campin's *Mérode Altarpiece*, the Annunciation takes place in a Flemish home. The work's donors, depicted on the left wing, are anachronistically present as witnesses to the sacred event. As is typical of "Northern Renaissance" art, the everyday objects in the triptych often have symbolic significance.

- Jan van Eyck, Rogier van der Weyden, and others established portraiture as an important art form in 15th-century Flanders. Their subjects were successful businessmen, both Flemish and foreign, and occasionally themselves. Jan portrayed himself wearing a red turban, and Rogier represented himself in the guise of Saint Luke drawing the Virgin.

- Among the other major Flemish painters were Petrus Christus and Hans Memling of Bruges, Dieric Bouts of Louvain, and Hugo van der Goes of Ghent, all of whom produced both altarpieces for churches and portraits for the homes of wealthy merchants.

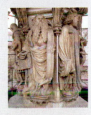

Sluter, *Well of Moses*, 1396–1406

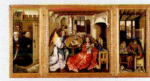

Campin, *Mérode Altarpiece*, ca. 1425–1428

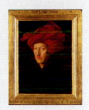

Van Eyck, *Man in a Red Turban*, 1433

France

- During the 15th century, the Hundred Years' War crippled the French economy, but dukes and members of the royal court still commissioned some notable artworks.

- The Limbourg brothers expanded the illusionistic capabilities of manuscript illumination in the Book of Hours they produced for Jean, duke of Berry (r. 1360–1416) and brother of King Charles V (r. 1364–1380). Their full-page calendar pictures alternately represent the nobility and the peasantry, always in seasonal, naturalistic settings with realistically painted figures.

- French court art—for example, Jean Fouquet's *Melun Diptych*—owes a large debt to Flemish painting in style and technique as well as in the integration of sacred and secular themes.

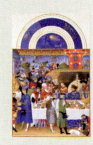

Limbourg brothers, *Les Très Riches Heures du Duc de Berry*, 1413–1416

Holy Roman Empire

- The Late Gothic style remained popular in 15th-century Germany for large carved wood retables featuring highly emotive figures amid Gothic tracery. The leading sculptors were Veit Stoss and Tilman Riemenschneider.

- The major German innovation of the 15th century was the development of the printing press, which publishers soon used to produce books with woodcut illustrations. Woodcuts are relief prints in which the artist carves out the areas around the lines to be printed.

- German artists, such as Martin Schongauer, were also the earliest masters of engraving. The intaglio technique allows for a wider variety of linear effects because the artist incises the image directly onto a metal plate.

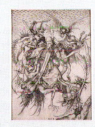

Schongauer, *Saint Anthony*, ca. 1480

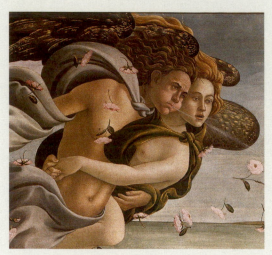

◀ **21-1a** Inspired by a poem by Angelo Poliziano, Botticelli painted *Birth of Venus* for the Medici between 1484 and 1486. At the left, Zephyrus, carrying Chloris, blows Venus on a cockleshell to Cyprus.

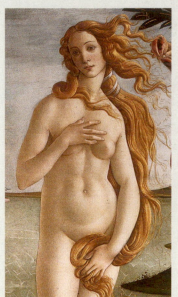

◀ **21-1b** Botticelli's revival of the theme of the female nude, largely absent from medieval art, was consistent with the Neo-Platonic view that beholding physical beauty prompts the contemplation of spiritual beauty.

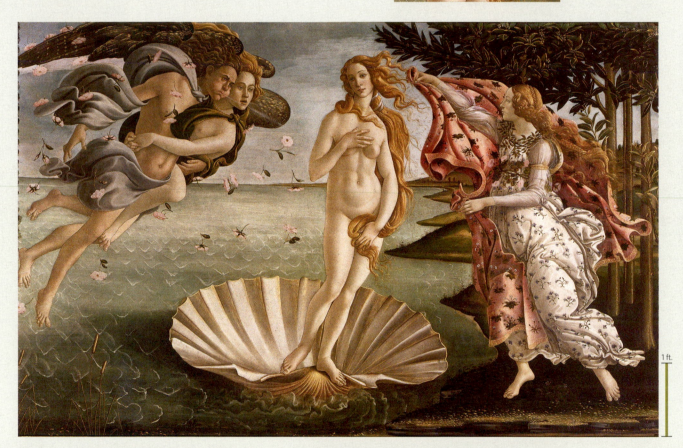

■ **21-1** **SANDRO BOTTICELLI**, *Birth of Venus*, ca. 1484–1486. Tempera on canvas, 5' 9" × 9' 2". Galleria degli Uffizi, Florence.

1 ft.

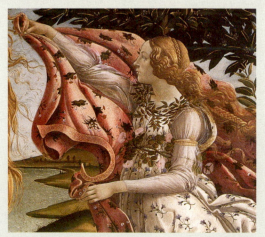

◀ **21-1c** Awaiting the newborn goddess of love on her sacred island is the nymph Pomona, who runs to meet Venus with a brocaded mantle. Her draperies undulate loosely in the gentle gusts of wind.

The Renaissance in Quattrocento Italy

THE MEDICI, BOTTICELLI, AND CLASSICAL ANTIQUITY

The name of one family—the Medici of Florence—has become synonymous with the extraordinary cultural phenomenon called the Italian Renaissance. By early in the 15th century (the 1400s, or *Quattrocento* in Italian), the banker Giovanni di Bicci de' Medici (ca. 1360–1429) had established the family fortune. His son Cosimo (1389–1464) became a great patron of art and of learning in the broadest sense. Cosimo's grandson Lorenzo (1449–1492), called *Il Magnifico* (the Magnificent), gathered about him a galaxy of artists and gifted men in all fields as a member of the Platonic Academy of Philosophy. Lorenzo spent lavishly on buildings, paintings, and sculptures. Indeed, scarcely a single great Quattrocento architect, painter, sculptor, philosopher, or humanist scholar failed to enjoy Medici patronage.

Of all the Florentine masters the Medici employed, perhaps the most famous today is SANDRO BOTTICELLI (1444–1510). His work is a testament to the intense interest that Quattrocento humanist scholars and the Medici had in the art, literature, and mythology of the Greco-Roman world—often interpreted in terms of Christianity according to the philosophical tenets of *Neo-Platonism*.

Botticelli painted *Birth of Venus* (FIG. 21-1) for the Medici based on a poem by Angelo Poliziano (1454–1494), a leading humanist of the day. In Botticelli's representation of Poliziano's version of the Greek myth, Venus (the Roman equivalent of the Greek goddess Aphrodite), born of the sea foam (*aphros*), stands on a floating cockleshell at the center of the painting. Zephyrus, the west wind, carrying the *nymph* Chloris, blows Venus to her sacred island, Cyprus. There, the nymph Pomona runs to meet her with a brocaded mantle. Zephyrus's breath moves all the figures without effort. Draperies undulate easily in the gentle gusts, perfumed by rose petals that fall on the whitecaps.

The most remarkable aspect of *Birth of Venus* is that Botticelli used as a model for his Venus an ancient statue similar to the *Aphrodite of Knidos* (FIG. 5-62) by the famed Greek sculptor Praxiteles. The nude, especially the female nude, was exceedingly rare during the Middle Ages. The artist's depiction of Venus unclothed (especially on such a large scale—roughly life-size) could have drawn harsh criticism. But in the more accommodating Renaissance culture and under the protection of the powerful Medici, Botticelli's nude Venus went unchallenged, in part because his painting was susceptible to a Neo-Platonic reading. Marsilio Ficino (1433–1499), for example, made the case in his treatise *On Love* (1469) that those who embrace the contemplative life of reason—including, of course, the humanists in the Medici circle—will immediately contemplate spiritual and divine beauty whenever they behold physical beauty. In this manner, Italian Renaissance patrons made classical learning and Christian faith compatible.

RENAISSANCE HUMANISM

The humanism that Petrarch and Boccaccio promoted during the 14th century (see page 418) fully blossomed in the 15th century. Increasingly, Italians in elite circles embraced the tenets underlying humanism—an emphasis on education and on expanding knowledge (especially of classical antiquity), the exploration of individual potential and a desire to excel, and a commitment to civic responsibility and moral duty. Quattrocento Italy also enjoyed an abundance of artistic talent. The fortunate coming together of artistic genius, the spread of humanism, and economic prosperity nourished the Renaissance, forever changing the direction and perception of art in the Western world.

For the Italian humanists, the quest for knowledge began with the legacy of the Greeks and Romans—the writings of Plato, Aristotle, Ovid, and others. The development of a vernacular literature based on the commonly spoken Tuscan dialect expanded the audience for humanist writings. Further, the invention of moveable metal type in Germany around 1445 (see page 576) facilitated the printing and wide distribution of books. Italians greeted this new printing process enthusiastically. By 1464, Subiaco (near Rome) boasted a press, and by 1469, Venice had established one as well. Among the first books printed in Italy using this new technology was Dante's *Divine Comedy,* his epic about Heaven, Purgatory, and Hell. The production of editions in Foligno (1472), Mantua (1472), Venice (1472), Naples (1477 and 1478–1479), and Milan (1478) testifies to the widespread popularity of Dante's work.

The humanists also avidly acquired information in a wide range of fields, including botany, geology, geography, optics, medicine, and engineering. Leonardo da Vinci's phenomenal expertise in many fields—from art and architecture to geology, aerodynamics, hydraulics, botany, and military science, among many others (see page 624)—still defines the modern notion of the "Renaissance man." Humanism also fostered a belief in individual potential and encouraged personal achievement, as well as civic responsibility. Whereas people in medieval society accorded great power to divine will in determining the events that affected lives, those in Renaissance Italy adopted a more secular stance. Humanists not only encouraged individual improvement but also rewarded excellence with fame and honor. Achieving and excelling through hard work became moral imperatives.

Quattrocento Italy witnessed constant fluctuations in its political and economic spheres, including shifting power relations among the numerous city-states and the rise of princely courts (see "Art in the Princely Courts of Renaissance Italy," page 613). *Condottieri* (military leaders) with large numbers of mercenary troops at their disposal played a major role in the ongoing struggle for power. At Urbino, Mantua, and elsewhere, courts headed by dukes and condottieri emerged as cultural and artistic centers alongside the great civic art centers of the 14th century, especially the Republic of Florence. The association of humanism with education and culture appealed to accomplished individuals of high status, and humanism had its greatest impact among the elite and powerful—the most influential art patrons—whether in the republics or the princely courts. As a result, humanist ideas came to permeate Italian Renaissance art. The intersection of art with humanist doctrines during the Renaissance is evident in the popularity of subjects selected from classical history or mythology (for example, FIG. 21-1), in the increased concern with developing perspective systems and depicting anatomy accurately, in the revival of portraiture and other self-promoting forms of patronage, and in citizens' extensive commissions of civic and religious art.

FLORENCE

Because high-level patronage required significant accumulated wealth, those individuals, whether princes or merchants, who had managed to prosper came to the fore in artistic circles. The best-known Italian Renaissance art patrons were the Medici, the leading bankers of the Republic of Florence (see "The Medici," page 581), yet the earliest important artistic commission in 15th-century Florence (MAP 21-1, page 603) was not a Medici project but rather a competition held by the Cathedral of Santa Maria del Fiore and sponsored by the city's guild of wool merchants.

Sculpture

In 1401, at a time when Florence was threatened from without, the cathedral's art directors held a competition to make bronze doors for the east portal of the Baptistery of San Giovanni (Saint John the Baptist; FIG. 12-30). In the late 1390s, Giangaleazzo Visconti, the first duke of Milan (r. 1378–1395), had begun a military campaign to take over the Italian peninsula. By 1401, when the cathedral's art directors initiated the baptistery doors competition, Visconti's troops had surrounded Florence, and its independence was in serious jeopardy. Despite dwindling water and food supplies, Florentine officials exhorted the public to defend the city's freedom. For example, the humanist chancellor Coluccio Salutati (1331–1406) urged his fellow citizens to adopt the republican ideal of civil and political liberty associated with ancient Rome and to identify themselves with its spirit. To be a citizen of the Florentine Republic was to be Roman. Freedom was the distinguishing virtue of both societies. The decision to beautify the city's baptistery in the face of Visconti's threat was an expression of Florentine freedom and defiance—and an opportunity for the wool merchants to assert their preeminence among Florentine guilds. In 1402, when Visconti died suddenly, Florence retained its independence, and the wool guild proceeded with the baptistery doors.

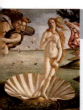

THE RENAISSANCE IN QUATTROCENTO ITALY

1400–1425
- Ghiberti wins the competition to design new doors for Florence's baptistery
- Nanni di Banco, Donatello, and others create statues for Or San Michele
- Masaccio carries Giotto's naturalism further in the Brancacci chapel
- Brunelleschi develops linear perspective and designs the Ospedale degli Innocenti, the first Renaissance building

1425–1450
- Ghiberti installs the *Gates of Paradise* facing Florence Cathedral
- Donatello revives freestanding nude male statuary
- Michelozzo builds the new Medici palace in Florence
- Alberti publishes his treatise on painting
- Marino Contarini builds his "House of Gold" in Venice

1450–1475
- Federico da Montefeltro brings Piero della Francesca to the Urbino court
- Alberti applies the principles of his *On the Art of Building* to architectural projects in Florence and Mantua
- Mantegna creates illusionistic paintings for the Camera Picta in Mantua
- Pietro Lombardo and his sons carve tombs for the doges of Venice

1475–1500
- Botticelli paints Neo-Platonic mythological allegories for the Medici
- Savonarola condemns humanism, and the Medici flee Florence
- Pope Sixtus IV employs leading painters to decorate the Sistine Chapel
- Bellini founds the Venetian High Renaissance school of painting

SACRIFICE OF ISAAC The Florentines considered the baptistery doors commission singularly prestigious because the east entrance to the baptistery faced the cathedral (FIG. 14-19). The competition is historically important not only for the quality of the work submitted by those seeking the commission but also because it showcased several key elements associated with mature Renaissance art: personal or, in this case, guild patronage as both a civic duty and a form of self-promotion; the esteem accorded to individual artists; and the development of a new pictorial illusionism.

Between 1330 and 1335, Andrea Pisano had designed the south doors (FIG. 14-20) of the baptistery with reliefs framed by Gothic quatrefoils. The jurors of the 1401 competition for the second set of doors required each entrant to submit a similarly framed relief panel depicting the sacrifice of Isaac. This episode from the book of Genesis (22:2–13) centers on God's order to Abraham to sacrifice his son Isaac as a demonstration of Abraham's devotion (see "Jewish Subjects in Christian Art," page 238). As Abraham was about to comply, an angel intervened and stopped him from plunging the knife into his son's throat. Because of the parallel between Abraham's willingness to sacrifice Isaac and God's sacrifice of his son, Jesus, to redeem humankind, Christians viewed the sacrifice of Isaac as a *prefiguration* (prophetic forerunner) of Jesus's crucifixion.

BRUNELLESCHI AND GHIBERTI The jury selected seven semifinalists from among the many artists who entered the widely advertised competition. Only the panels of the two finalists, FILIPPO BRUNELLESCHI (1377–1446) and LORENZO GHIBERTI (1378–1455),

have survived. At 24 and 23 years old respectively, they were also the two youngest entrants in the competition. As instructed, both artists used the same French-style frames and depicted the same moment of the narrative—the angel's interruption of the action. Brunelleschi's entry (FIG. 21-2) is a vigorous interpretation of the theme and recalls the emotional agitation of Giovanni Pisano's relief sculptures (FIG. 14-4). Abraham seems suddenly to have summoned the dreadful courage needed to murder his son at God's command. He lunges forward, robes flying, and exposes the terrified Isaac's throat to the knife. Matching Abraham's energy, the saving angel flies in from the left, grabbing Abraham's arm to stop the killing. Brunelleschi's figures demonstrate his ability to represent faithfully and dramatically all the elements in the biblical narrative.

Whereas Brunelleschi imbued his image with violent movement and high emotion, Ghiberti emphasized grace and smoothness. In Ghiberti's panel (FIG. 21-3), Abraham appears in a typically Gothic pose with outthrust hip (compare FIG. 13-26) and seems to contemplate the act he is about to perform, even as he draws back his arm to strike. The figure of Isaac, beautifully posed and rendered, recalls Greco-Roman statuary, and many art historians cite it as the first classical nude since antiquity. (Compare, for example, the torsion of Isaac's body and the dramatic turn of his head with the posture of the ancient statue of a Gaul plunging a sword into his own chest, FIG. 5-81.) Unlike his medieval predecessors, Ghiberti revealed a genuine appreciation of the nude male form and a deep interest in how the muscular system and skeletal structure move the human body. Even the altar on which Isaac kneels displays Ghiberti's

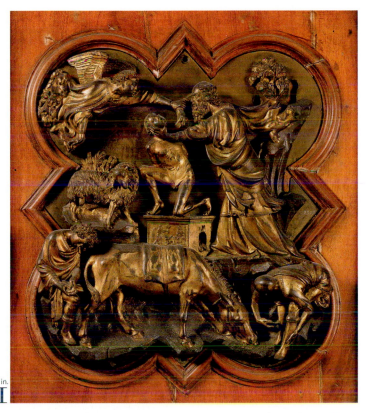

1 in.

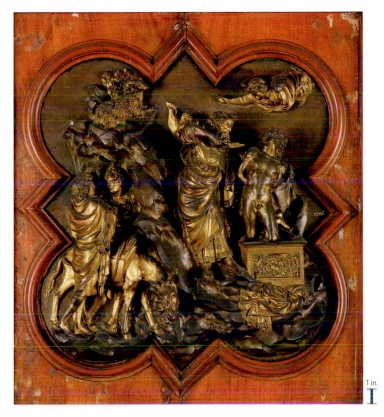

1 in.

21-2 FILIPPO BRUNELLESCHI, *Sacrifice of Isaac*, competition panel for the east doors of the Baptistery of San Giovanni, Florence, Italy, 1401–1402. Gilded bronze, 1' 9" × 1' 5½". Museo Nazionale del Bargello, Florence.

Brunelleschi's entry in the competition to create new bronze doors for the Florentine baptistery shows a frantic angel about to halt an emotional, lunging Abraham clothed in swirling Gothic robes.

21-3 LORENZO GHIBERTI, *Sacrifice of Isaac*, competition panel for the east doors of the Baptistery of San Giovanni, Florence, Italy, 1401–1402. Gilded bronze, 1' 9" × 1' 5⅐". Museo Nazionale del Bargello, Florence.

In contrast to Brunelleschi's panel (FIG. 21-2), Ghiberti's entry in the baptistery competition features gracefully posed figures that recall classical statuary. Isaac's altar has a Roman acanthus frieze.

ARTISTS ON ART

The *Commentarii* of Lorenzo Ghiberti

In addition to his many achievements as an artist, Lorenzo Ghiberti was also the first Renaissance art historian. His *Commentarii* in three books opens with an admiring account of the naturalistic art of classical antiquity that is heavily dependent on Pliny the Elder (see page 129) and Vitruvius (see "Vitruvius's *Ten Books on Architecture*," page 199). Book 2 deals with the art of his own time and the previous century and notably includes the earliest preserved autobiography of an artist. The third book enumerates the disciplines that a successful sculptor must master, including anatomy and optics.

Ghiberti's account of Early Renaissance art in his second *Commentary,* like Vasari's later biographies (see page 636), centers on individual artists. It opens with the author's lament that Constantine's embrace of Christianity brought an end to the glorious art of classical antiquity chronicled in the first *Commentary*. In Ghiberti's view, art "began to rise again" only when Cimabue, who painted "in the Greek [that is, Byzantine] manner" discovered Giotto drawing in a field and took him into his workshop. Ghiberti describes Giotto as having "brought about the new art; he left behind the coarseness of the Greeks" and was "the inventor and discoverer of so much knowledge which had been buried for around six hundred years" (2.3). Among the other 13th- and 14th-century masters whom Ghiberti singled out for praise were Pietro Cavallini, Andrea Orcagna, Ambrogio Lorenzetti, Simone Martini, and Duccio, although Ghiberti tempers his praise of Duccio by noting that he, like Cimabue, "adhered to the Greek manner" (2.15). The sculptors whom Ghiberti admired included Giovanni and Andrea Pisano (FIGS. 14-4 and 14-20).

In the spirit of Quattrocento humanism, Ghiberti frequently quotes from classical literature and dates the artists he discusses according to Olympiads, reviving the ancient Greek practice of dating events to four-year periods corresponding to the Olympic Games, which had not been held since 390 (see page 250). Ghiberti inserts himself into the history of art beginning in the year 1400 and describes how he

> tried to investigate how nature manifests itself and, in order to approximate nature, how appearances reach the eye and how the visual faculties work and how visual things function and in what way the theory of statuary art and of painting should be put into practice (2.18).

Then follows Ghiberti's account of the Florentine baptistery doors competition, culminating in his boast about the outcome, which also reveals the fame and glory increasingly accorded to individual achievement in 15th-century Italy:

> The palm of the victory was granted to me by all the skilled men and by all those who had competed with me. The glory was universally conceded to me without any exception. To all it appeared that I had surpassed the others at that time without any exception, after very great deliberation and examination by learned men. . . . There were thirty-four judges from the city and the other surrounding regions; by all the confirmation of victory was given in my favor (2.19).*

*All translations by Christie Knapp Fengler, *Lorenzo Ghiberti's* Second Commentary: *The Translation and Interpretation of a Fundamental Renaissance Treatise on Art* (Diss. University of Wisconsin, 1974), 16-19, 45, 54, 57-58.

---

emulation of antique models. Decorating it are acanthus scrolls of a type that commonly adorned Roman temple friezes in Italy and throughout the former Roman Empire (for example, FIG. 7-32). These classical references reflect the influence of humanism in Quattrocento Italy. Ghiberti's entry in the baptistery competition is also noteworthy for the artist's interest in spatial illusion. The rocky landscape seems to emerge from the blank panel toward the viewer, as does the strongly foreshortened angel. Brunelleschi's image, in contrast, emphasizes the planar orientation of the surface.

Ghiberti's training included both painting and metalwork. His careful treatment of the gilded bronze surfaces, with their sharply and accurately incised detail, proves his skill as a goldsmith. That Ghiberti cast his panel in only two pieces (thereby reducing the amount of bronze needed) no doubt also impressed the selection committee. Brunelleschi's panel consists of several cast pieces. Thus, not only would Ghiberti's doors, as proposed, be lighter. They also represented a significant cost savings. The younger artist's submission clearly had much to recommend it, both stylistically and technically, and the judges awarded the commission to him—an achievement that he noted with exceptional pride in his *Commentaries* (see "The *Commentarii* of Lorenzo Ghiberti," above).

OR SAN MICHELE A second major Florentine sculptural project of the early 1400s was the placement of statues on the exterior of Or San Michele (FIG. 14-20A), an early-14th-century building prominently located on the main street connecting the Palazzo della Signoria (FIG. 14-19B; seat of Florence's governing council) and the Duomo (cathedral; FIG. 14-19; see MAP 21-1, page 603). At various

times, Or San Michele housed a church, a granary, and the headquarters of Florence's guilds. City officials had assigned the niches on the building's four sides to specific guilds, instructing each guild to place a statue of its patron saint in its niche.

Nearly a century after completion of Or San Michele, however, the guilds had filled only 5 of the 14 niches. In 1406, the Signoria ordered the guilds to comply with the original plan to embellish their assigned niches. A few years later, Florence was once again under siege, this time by King Ladislaus (r. 1399–1414) of Naples. Ladislaus had marched north, occupied Rome and the Papal States (MAP 14-1) by 1409, and threatened to overrun Florence. As they had done when Visconti was at the city's doorstep, Florentine officials urged citizens to stand firm and defend the republic from tyranny. Once again, Florence escaped unscathed. Ladislaus, on the verge of military success in 1414, fortuitously died. The guilds may well have viewed this new threat as an opportunity to perform their civic duty by rallying their fellow Florentines while also promoting their own importance and position in Florentine society. By 1423, statues by Ghiberti and other leading Florentine artists were on display in the nine remaining niches of Or San Michele.

NANNI DI BANCO Among the niches filled during the Neapolitan king's siege was the one assigned to the Florentine guild of stone- and woodworkers. They chose a guild member, the sculptor NANNI DI BANCO (ca. 1384–1421), to create four life-size marble statues of the guild's martyred patron saints. (Below the statues is a relief depicting guild members at work.) These four Early Christian sculptors had defied an order from Diocletian (r. 284–305; see page 223)

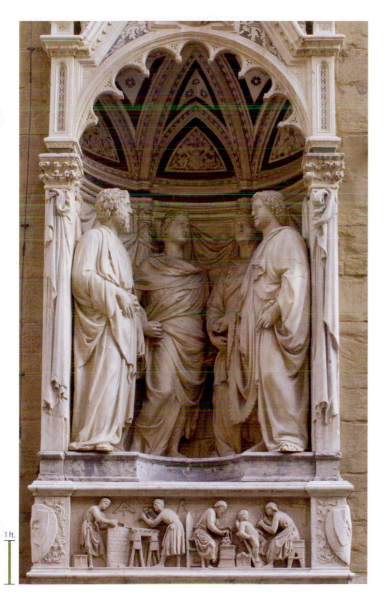

21-4 Nanni di Banco, *Four Crowned Saints,* niche on the north side of Or San Michele, Florence, Italy, ca. 1410–1414. Marble, figures 6' high. Modern copy; original sculpture in museum on second floor of Or San Michele, Florence.

Nanni's group representing the four martyred patron saints of Florence's sculptors' guild is an early example of Renaissance artists' attempt to liberate statuary from its architectural setting.

to carve a statue of a Roman deity. In response, the emperor ordered them put to death. Because they placed their faith above all else, these saints, in addition to representing the sponsoring guild, were perfect role models for the 15th-century Florentines whom city leaders exhorted to stand fast in the face of Ladislaus's armies.

Nanni's sculptural group, *Four Crowned Saints* (FIG. **21-4**), is an early Renaissance attempt to solve the problem of integrating figures and architecture on a monumental scale. The artist's positioning of the figures, which stand in a niche that is *in* but confers some separation *from* the wall, furthered the gradual emergence of sculpture from its architectural setting. This process began with works such as the 13th-century statues (FIG. 13-24) on the jambs of the west facade portals of Reims Cathedral. At Or San Michele, the niche's spatial recess presented Nanni di Banco with a dramatic new possibility for the interrelationship of the figures. By placing them in a semicircle within their deep niche and relating them to one another by their

postures and gestures, the Quattrocento sculptor arrived at a unified spatial composition. A remarkable psychological unity also connects these unyielding figures, whose bearing expresses the discipline and integrity necessary to face adversity. As the figure on the right speaks, pointing to his right, the two men opposite listen, and the one next to him (carved from the same block of marble) looks out into space, pondering the meaning of the words and reinforcing the formal cohesion of the figural group with psychological cross-references.

Four Crowned Saints, consistent with the renewed interest in ancient statues, also reveals Nanni's close study of Roman portraits. The emotional intensity of the faces of the two inner saints owes much to the extraordinarily moving portrayals in stone of third-century Roman emperors (FIGS. 7-66 and 7-66A), and the bearded heads of the outer saints make evident Nanni's familiarity with second-century imperial portraiture (FIGS. 7-57 and 7-57A). Renaissance artists seeking to portray individual personalities often turned to ancient Roman models for inspiration, but they did not simply copy them. Rather, they strove to interpret or offer commentary on their classical models in the manner of humanist scholars dealing with classical texts.

DONATELLO Another sculptor who carved statues for Or San Michele's niches was Donato di Niccolo Bardi, called DONATELLO (ca. 1386–1466), a former apprentice in Ghiberti's workshop, who incorporated Greco-Roman sculptural principles in his *Saint Mark* (FIG. **21-5**), executed for the guild of linen makers and

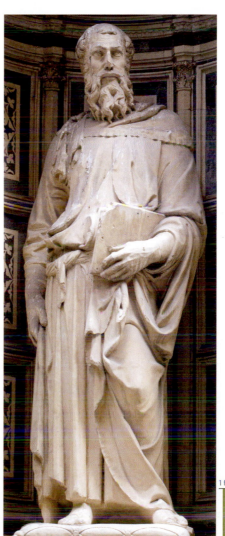

21-5 Donatello, *Saint Mark,* niche on the south side of Or San Michele, Florence, Italy, ca. 1411–1413. Marble, figure 7' 9" high. Modern copy; original sculpture in museum on second floor of Or San Michele, Florence.

In this statue carved for the guild of linen makers and tailors, Donatello introduced classical contrapposto into Quattrocento sculpture. The drapery falls naturally and moves with the body.

21-6 DONATELLO, *Saint George,* niche on the north side of Or San Michele, Florence, Italy, ca. 1415–1418. Marble, figure 6' 10" high. Modern copy; original in Museo Nazionale del Bargello, Florence.

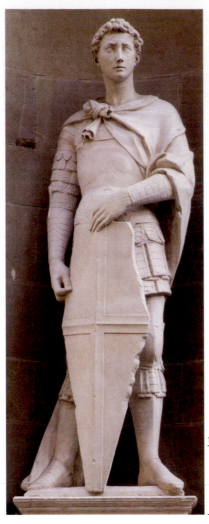

Donatello's statue for the armorers' guild once had a bronze sword and helmet. The warrior saint stands defiantly, ready to spring from his niche to defend Florence, his sword pointed at the spectator.

tailors. (The saint stands on one of the guild's pillows. Below him [not visible in FIG. 21-5] is his symbol, the lion; see "The Four Evangelists," page 318.) In this sculpture, Donatello took a fundamental step toward depicting motion in the human figure by recognizing the principle of weight shift, or *contrapposto.* Greek sculptors of the fifth century BCE were the first to grasp that the act of standing requires balancing the position and weight of the different parts of the human body, as they demonstrated in works such as *Kritios Boy* (FIG. 5-35) and *Doryphoros* (FIG. 5-41). In contrast to earlier sculptors, Greek artists recognized that the human body is not a rigid mass but a flexible structure that moves by continuously shifting its weight from one supporting leg to the other. Donatello reintroduced this concept into Renaissance statuary. As the saint's body "moves," his garment "moves" with it, hanging and folding naturally from and around different body parts so that the viewer senses the figure as a nude human wearing clothing, not as a stone statue with arbitrarily composed drapery folds. Donatello's *Saint Mark* is

the first Renaissance statue whose voluminous robe (the pride of the Florentine guild that paid for the statue) does not conceal but accentuates the movement of the arms, legs, shoulders, and hips. This development further contributed to the sculpted figure's independence from its architectural setting. Saint Mark's stirring limbs, shifting weight, and mobile drapery suggest impending movement out of the niche.

SAINT GEORGE For the Or San Michele niche assigned to the guild of armorers and sword makers, Donatello created *Saint George* (FIG. 21-6). The saintly knight stands proudly with his shield in front of him. He once held a bronze sword in his right hand and wore a bronze helmet on his head, both fashioned by the sponsoring guild. The statue continues the Gothic tradition of depicting warrior saints on church facades, as seen in the statue of Saint Theodore (FIG. 13-19) on the westernmost jamb of the south *transept* portal of Chartres Cathedral, but here it has a civic role to play. Saint George stands in a defiant manner—ready to spring from his niche to defend Florence against attack from another Visconti or Ladislaus, his sword jutting out threateningly at all passersby. The saint's body is taut, and Donatello gave him a face filled with nervous energy.

Directly below the statue's base is Donatello's marble relief (FIG. 21-7) representing Saint George slaying a dragon to rescue a princess (see "Early Christian Saints," page 237). The relief marks a turning point in Renaissance sculpture. Even the landscapes in the baptistery competition reliefs (FIGS. 21-2 and 21-3) are modeled forms seen against a blank background. In *Saint George and the Dragon,* Donatello created an atmospheric effect by using incised lines. It is impossible to talk about a background plane in this work. The landscape recedes into distant space, and the depth of that space cannot be measured. The sculptor conceived the relief as a window onto an infinite vista. To create that effect, Donatello used a pictorial device already known to the ancients—*atmospheric perspective* (see page 191). Artists (painters more frequently than sculptors) using atmospheric perspective (sometimes called *aerial perspective*) exploit the principle that the farther back an object is in space, the blurrier and less detailed it appears. In Donatello's *Saint George and the Dragon,* the foreground figures are much sharper than the landscape elements in the background.

FEAST OF HEROD Donatello's mastery of perspective in relief sculpture is also evident in *Feast of Herod* (FIG. 21-8), a bronze relief on the baptismal font in Siena Cathedral's baptistery. Appropriately, the subject of the relief is an episode in the life of John the Baptist. Salome, a figure based on a popular classical motif, dances before

21-7 DONATELLO, *Saint George and the Dragon,* relief below the statue of Saint George (FIG. 21-6), Or San Michele, Florence, Italy, ca. 1417–1420. Marble, 1' 3¼" × 3' 11¼". Modern copy; original relief in Museo Nazionale del Bargello, Florence.

Donatello's relief marks a turning point in Renaissance sculpture. He took a painterly approach, creating an atmospheric effect by using incised lines. The depth of the background cannot be measured.

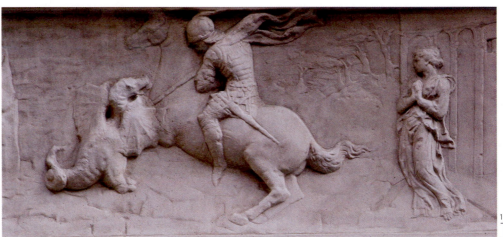

PROBLEMS AND SOLUTIONS
Linear Perspective

In the 14th century, Italian artists, such as Giotto, Duccio, and the Lorenzetti brothers (see Chapter 14), had used several devices to indicate distance, but with the development of *linear perspective,* Quattrocento artists acquired a way to make the illusion of distance certain and consistent. To solve the problem of representing depth in a two-dimensional painting or relief, Renaissance artists conceived the picture plane as a transparent window through which the observer looks to see the constructed pictorial world. (The literal meaning of *perspective* is "to see through.") This discovery was enormously important, for it made possible what has been called the "rationalization of sight." It brought all random and infinitely various visual sensations under a simple rule that could be expressed mathematically. Indeed, Renaissance artists' interest in linear perspective reflects the emergence at this time of modern science itself. Of course, 15th-century artists were not primarily scientists. They simply found perspective an effective way to order and clarify their compositions. Nonetheless, there can be little doubt that linear perspective, with its new mathematical certitude, conferred a kind of aesthetic legitimacy on painting and relief sculpture by making the picture measurable and exact. The projection of measurable objects on flat surfaces not only influenced the character of Renaissance paintings and reliefs but also made possible scale drawings, maps, charts, graphs, and diagrams—means of exact representation that laid the foundation for modern science and technology.

Renaissance artists were not the first to focus on depicting illusionistic space. Both the Greeks and the Romans were well versed in perspective rendering. Many of the frescoes that adorn the walls of Roman houses represent buildings and colonnades (for example, FIG. 7-19, *right*) using a Renaissance-like system of converging lines. However, the Renaissance rediscovery of and interest in perspective contrasted sharply with the portrayal of space during the Middle Ages, when spiritual concerns superseded the desire to depict objects illusionistically.

Developed by Filippo Brunelleschi, linear perspective enables artists to determine mathematically the relative size of rendered objects to correlate them with the visual recession into space. The artist first must identify a horizontal line that marks, in the image, the horizon in the distance (hence the term *horizon line*). The artist then selects a *vanishing point* on that horizon line (often located at the exact center of the line). By drawing *orthogonals* (diagonal lines) from the edges of the picture to the vanishing point, the artist creates a structural grid that organizes the image and determines the size of objects within the image's illusionistic space. Among the Quattrocento works that provide clear examples of linear perspective are Donatello's *Feast of Herod* (FIG. 21-8), Ghiberti's *Isaac and His Sons* (FIG. 21-9), Masaccio's *Holy Trinity* (FIG. 21-20), and Perugino's *Christ Delivering the Keys of the Kingdom to Saint Peter* (FIG. 21-41).

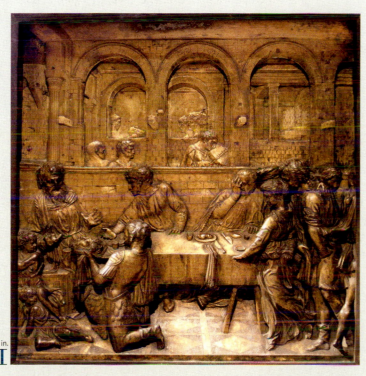

1 in.

21-8 DONATELLO, *Feast of Herod,* panel on the baptismal font of the baptistery, Siena Cathedral, Siena, Italy, 1423–1427. Gilded bronze, 1' 11½" × 1' 11½".

Donatello's *Feast of Herod* marked the introduction of rationalized perspective space in Renaissance relief sculpture. Two arched courtyards of diminishing size open the space of the action into the distance.

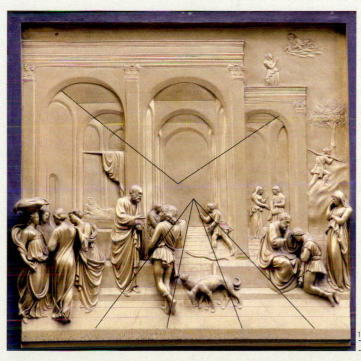

1 in.

21-9 LORENZO GHIBERTI, *Isaac and His Sons* (detail of FIG. 21-10, with overlay of perspective orthogonals), east doors (*Gates of Paradise*) of the Baptistery of San Giovanni, Florence, Italy, 1425–1452. Gilded bronze, 2' 7½" × 2' 7½". Museo dell'Opera del Duomo, Florence.

All the orthogonals of the floor tiles in this early example of linear perspective converge on a vanishing point on the central axis of the composition, but the orthogonals of the architecture do not.

King Herod. At the left, Salome's wish granted, the kneeling executioner delivers John's severed head to the king. The other figures recoil in horror in two groups. At the right, one man covers his face with his hand. At the left, Herod and two terrified children shrink back in dismay. The psychic explosion drives the human elements apart, leaving a gap across which the emotional electricity crackles.

Forming the backdrop for this dramatic staging of the biblical story are two successive arched courtyards in Herod's palace. Donatello's rendition of the architectural setting in the *Feast of Herod* marks the introduction of rationalized perspective in Renaissance art. As in *Saint George and the Dragon* (FIG. 21-7), Donatello opened the space of the action well into the distance. But, instead of atmospheric perspective, he employed the new mathematically based science of *linear perspective,* in which the size of the piers and arches and even the bricks in the walls as well as the figures in the courtyards decrease in size systematically with increasing distance from the viewer (see "Linear Perspective," page 587).

The inventor (or rediscoverer) of linear perspective was Filippo Brunelleschi. In his biography of the Florentine artist, written around 1480, Antonio Manetti (1423–1497) described Brunelleschi's perspective system as a new "science":

> [Filippo Brunelleschi] propounded and realized what painters today call perspective, since it forms part of that science which, in effect, consists of setting down properly and rationally the reductions and enlargements of near and distant objects as perceived by the eye of man: buildings, plains, mountains, places of every sort and location, with figures and objects in correct proportion to the distance in which they are shown. He originated the rule that is essential to whatever has been accomplished since his time in that area. We do not know whether centuries ago the ancient painters . . . knew about perspective or employed it rationally. If indeed they employed it by rule (I did not previously call it a science without reason) as he did later, . . . [no] records about it have been discovered. . . . Through industry and intelligence [Brunelleschi] either rediscovered or invented it.[1]

GATES OF PARADISE Lorenzo Ghiberti, Brunelleschi's chief rival in the baptistery competition, was, with Donatello, among the first artists to embrace Brunelleschi's scientific system for representing space. Ghiberti's enthusiasm for perspective illusion is on display in the new east doors (FIG. 21-10) for Florence's baptistery (FIG. 12-30), which the cathedral officials commissioned him to make in 1425. Ghiberti's patrons moved his first pair of doors to the north entrance to make room for the new

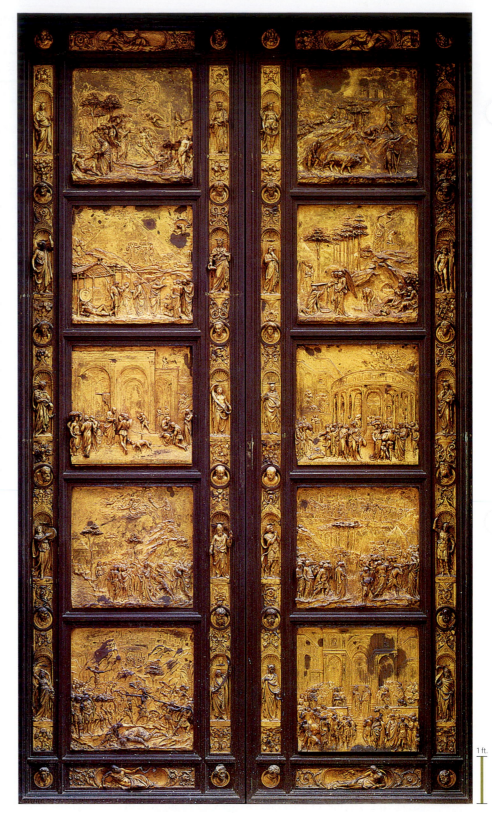

21-10 LORENZO GHIBERTI, east doors (*Gates of Paradise*) of the Baptistery of San Giovanni, Florence, Italy, 1425–1452. Gilded bronze, 17' high. Modern replica, 1990. Original panels in Museo dell'Opera del Duomo, Florence.

In Ghiberti's later doors for the Florentine baptistery, the sculptor abandoned Gothic quatrefoil frames for the biblical scenes (compare FIG. 21-3) and employed painterly illusionistic devices.

ones that they commissioned him to make for the prestigious east side. Michelangelo later declared Ghiberti's second doors as "so beautiful that they would do well for the gates of Paradise."[2] In the *Gates of Paradise,* as the doors have been called since then, Ghiberti abandoned the quatrefoil frames of Andrea Pisano's south doors (FIG. 14-20) and his own earlier doors and reduced the number of panels from 28 to 10. Each panel contains a relief set in plain molding and depicts an episode from the Old Testament. The complete gilding of the reliefs creates an effect of great splendor and elegance.

The individual panels, such as *Isaac and His Sons* (FIG. 21-9), clearly recall painting techniques in their depiction of space as well as in their treatment of the narrative. Some exemplify more fully than painting many of the principles that the architect and theorist Leon Battista Alberti formulated in his 1435 treatise, *On Painting*. In his relief, Ghiberti created the illusion of space partly through the use of linear perspective and partly by sculptural means. He represented the pavement on which the figures stand according to a painter's vanishing-point perspective construction (note the overlay of orthogonal lines in FIG. 21-9), but the figures themselves appear almost fully in the round. In fact, some of their heads stand completely free. As the eye progresses upward, the relief increasingly flattens, concluding with the architecture in the background, which Ghiberti depicted using barely raised lines. As Donatello did in *Feast of Herod* (FIG. 21-8), Ghiberti here employed atmospheric perspective, making the forms appear less distinct the deeper they are in space. Regardless of the height of the reliefs, however, the size of each figure decreases in exact correspondence to its distance from the foreground, just as do the dimensions of the floor tiles, as specified in Alberti's treatise.

Ghiberti described his employment of perspective in the baptistery's east doors as follows:

> I strove to imitate nature as closely as I could, and with all the perspective I could produce [to have] excellent compositions rich with many figures. In some scenes I placed about a hundred figures, in some less, and in some more. . . . There were ten stories, all in frames because the eye from a distance measures and interprets the scenes in such a way that they appear round. The scenes are in the lowest relief and the figures are seen in the planes; those that are near appear large, those in the distance small, as they do in reality. I executed this entire work with these principles.[3]

In the reliefs of the *Gates of Paradise*, Ghiberti achieved a greater sense of depth than had previously seemed possible in sculpture. His principal figures do not occupy the architectural space he created for them. Rather, the artist arranged them along a parallel plane in front of the grandiose architecture. (According to Alberti, the grandeur of the architecture reflects the dignity of the events shown in the foreground.)

Ghiberti's figure style mixes a Gothic patterning of rhythmic line, classical poses and motifs, and a new realism in characterization, movement, and surface detail. But the Florentine sculptor retained the medieval narrative method of presenting several episodes within a single frame. In *Isaac and His Sons*, the women in the left foreground attend the birth of Esau and Jacob in the left background. In the central foreground, Isaac sends Esau and his dogs to hunt game. In the right foreground, Isaac blesses the kneeling Jacob as Rebecca looks on. Yet viewers experience little confusion because of Ghiberti's careful and subtle placement of each scene. The figures, in varying degrees of projection, gracefully twist and turn, appearing to occupy and move through a convincing stage space, which Ghiberti deepened by showing some figures from behind.

Ghiberti's classicism derived from his close study of ancient art. The artist admired and collected classical sculpture, bronzes, and coins. Their influence appears throughout the *Isaac and His Sons*

panel, particularly in the figure of Rebecca, which Ghiberti based on a popular Greco-Roman statuary type. The emerging practice of collecting classical art in the 15th century had much to do with the incorporation of classical motifs and the emulation of classical style in Renaissance art (compare Botticelli's Venus [FIG. 21-1], based on an ancient statue).

DONATELLO, *DAVID* The use of perspective systems in relief sculpture and painting represents only one aspect of the Renaissance revival of classical principles and values in the arts. Another was the revival of the freestanding nude statue. The first Renaissance sculptor to portray the nude male figure in statuary was Donatello. He probably cast his bronze *David* (FIG. 21-11) sometime between 1440 and 1460 for display in the courtyard (FIG. 21-36) of the Medici palace in Florence. In the Middle Ages, the clergy regarded nude statues as both indecent and idolatrous, and, as noted in the opening discussion of *Birth of Venus* (page 581), nudity in general appeared only rarely in medieval art—and then only in biblical or moralizing contexts, such as the story of Adam and Eve or depictions of sinners in Hell. With *David*, Donatello reinvented the classical nude. His subject, however, was not a Greco-Roman god, hero, or athlete but the youthful biblical slayer of Goliath who had become the symbol of the Florentine Republic—and therefore an ideal choice of subject for the residence of the most powerful family in Florence. The Medici were aware of Donatello's earlier *David* in Florence's town

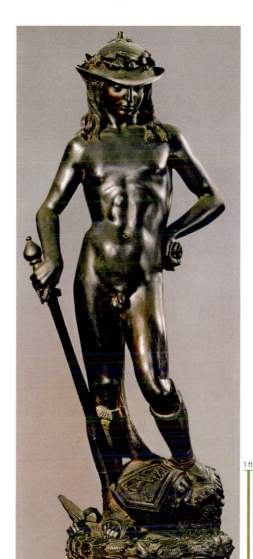

21-11 DONATELLO, *David*, from the Palazzo Medici, Florence, Italy, ca. 1440–1460. Bronze, 5' 2$\frac{1}{4}$" high. Museo Nazionale del Bargello, Florence.

Donatello's *David* possesses both the relaxed contrapposto and the sensuous beauty of nude Greek gods (FIG. 5-63). The revival of classical statuary style appealed to the sculptor's patrons, the Medici.

hall (FIG. 14-19B), which the artist had produced during the threat of invasion by King Ladislaus. Their selection of the same subject suggests that the Medici identified themselves with Florence or, at the very least, shared Florence's ideals and the Florentine desire for freedom and independence. To underscore that association, the Medici added an inscription to the base of the *David* statue:

The victor is whoever defends the fatherland. God crushes the wrath of an enormous foe. Behold! A boy overcame a great tyrant. Conquer, O citizens![4]

The invoking of classical poses and formats also appealed to the Medici as humanists. Donatello's *David* possesses both the relaxed classical contrapposto stance and the proportions and sensuous beauty of the gods that Praxiteles portrayed in his statues (FIG. 5-63). These qualities were, not surprisingly, absent from medieval figures—and they are also lacking, for different reasons, in Donatello's depiction of the aged Mary Magdalene. The contrast between the sculptor's *David* and his *Penitent Mary Magdalene* (FIG. 21-11A) demonstrates the extraordinary versatility of this Florentine master.

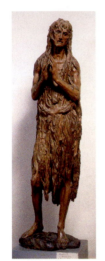

⊿ 21-11A
DONATELLO, *Penitent Mary Magdalene*, ca. 1455.

VERROCCHIO Another *David* (FIG. 21-12), by ANDREA DEL VERROCCHIO (1435–1488), one of the most important sculptors during the second half of the 15th century, reaffirms the Medici family's identification with the heroic biblical king and with Florence. A painter as well as a sculptor, Verrocchio directed a flourishing *bottega* (workshop) in Florence that attracted many students, among them Leonardo da Vinci. Verrocchio's *David* contrasts strongly in its narrative realism with the quiet classicism of Donatello's *David*. Verrocchio's hero is a sturdy, wiry youth clad in a leather doublet who stands with a jaunty pride. As in Donatello's version, Goliath's head lies at David's feet. He poses like a hunter with his kill. The easy balance of the weight and the lithe, still thinly adolescent musculature, with prominent veins, show how closely Verrocchio read the biblical text and how clearly he knew the psychology of brash young men. The Medici eventually sold Verrocchio's bronze *David* to the Florentine Republic for placement in the Palazzo della Signoria. After the expulsion of the Medici from Florence, civic officials appropriated Donatello's *David* for civic use and moved it to the city hall as well.

POLLAIUOLO The Renaissance interest in classical culture naturally also led to the revival of Greco-Roman mythological themes in art. The Medici were Florence's leading patrons in this sphere as well, and Botticelli (FIGS. 21-1 and 21-28) was only one of the artists they hired to produce artworks with classical myths for subjects. Around 1470, ANTONIO DEL POLLAIUOLO (ca. 1431–1498), who was also an important painter and engraver (FIG. 21-29), received a Medici commission to produce a small-scale sculpture, *Hercules and Antaeus* (FIG. 21-13). The mythological subject matter and the emphasis on human anatomy reflect the Medici preference for humanist imagery. Even more specifically, the Florentine seal had featured Hercules since the end of the 13th century. As commissions such as the two *David* sculptures demonstrate, the Medici clearly embraced every opportunity to associate themselves with the glory of the Florentine Republic and claimed much of the credit for its preeminence.

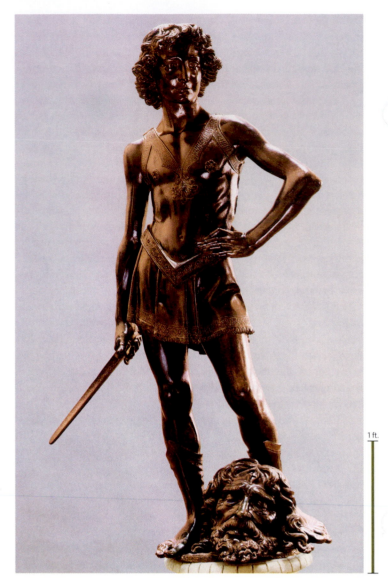

1 ft.

21-12 ANDREA DEL VERROCCHIO, *David,* from the Palazzo della Signoria, Florence, Italy, ca. 1465–1470. Bronze, 4' 1½" high. Museo Nazionale del Bargello, Florence.

Verrocchio's *David,* also made for the Medici, displays a brash confidence. The statue's narrative realism contrasts strongly with the quiet classicism of Donatello's *David* (FIG. 21-11).

In contrast to the quiet stance of Donatello's *David* (FIG. 21-11), Pollaiuolo's bronze statuette exhibits the stress and strain of the human figure in violent action. The 18-inch-tall *Hercules and Antaeus* departs dramatically from the convention of frontality that had dominated statuary during the Middle Ages and the Early Renaissance. Indeed, by placing the two wrestling figures on an unusual triangular pedestal, Pollaiuolo established three possible "fronts" for the statuette, encouraging the viewer to look at it from different angles. The group illustrates the wrestling match between Antaeus (Antaios), a giant and son of the goddess Earth, and Hercules (Herakles), a theme the Greek painter Euphronios had represented on an ancient Greek vase (FIG. 5-23) 2,000 years before. The subject embodies the ferocity and vitality of elemental physical conflict. According to the Greek myth, each time Hercules threw him down, Antaeus sprang up again, his strength renewed by contact with the earth. Finally, Hercules held him aloft—so that Antaeus could not touch the ground—and strangled him around the waist.

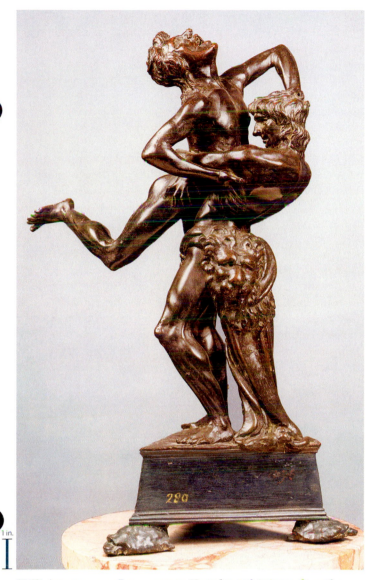

21-13 ANTONIO DEL POLLAIUOLO, *Hercules and Antaeus*, from the Palazzo Medici, Florence, Italy, ca. 1470–1475. Bronze, 1' 6" high with base. Museo Nazionale del Bargello, Florence.

The Renaissance interest in classical culture led to the revival of Greco-Roman mythological themes in art. *Hercules and Antaeus* exhibits the stress and strain of the human figure in violent action.

Pollaiuolo strove to convey the final excruciating moments of the struggle—the strained sinews of the combatants, the clenched teeth of Hercules, and the kicking and screaming of Antaeus. The figures intertwine and interlock as they fight, and the flickering reflections of light on the dark gouged bronze surface contribute to a fluid play of planes and the effect of agitated movement.

TOMB OF LEONARDO BRUNI Given the increased emphasis on individual achievement and recognition that humanism fostered, it is not surprising that portraiture enjoyed a revival in the 15th century. In addition to likenesses of elite individuals made during their lifetime, commemorative portraits of the deceased were common in Quattrocento Italy, as in ancient Rome. Leonardo Bruni (1369–1444) of Arezzo was one of the leading Early Renaissance humanist scholars. Around 1403, he wrote a *laudatio* (essay of praise) in honor of Florence, celebrating the city as the heir of the ancient Roman Republic. His most ambitious work, published

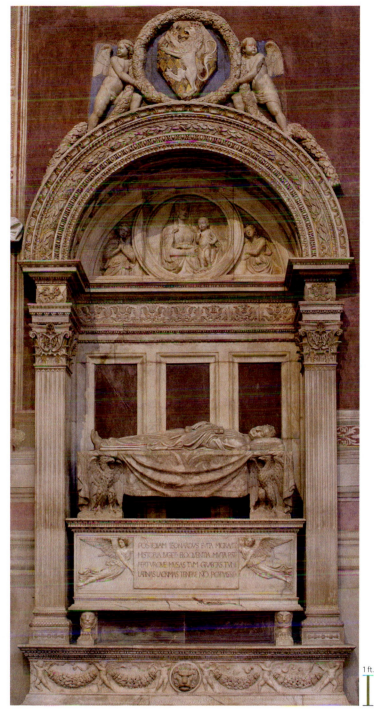

21-14 BERNARDO ROSSELLINO, tomb of Leonardo Bruni, Santa Croce, Florence, Italy, ca. 1444–1450. Marble, 23' 3½" high.

Rossellino's tomb in honor of the humanist scholar and chancellor Leonardo Bruni combines ancient Roman and Christian motifs. It established the pattern for Renaissance wall tombs (FIG. 21-39).

in 1429 when he served as Florence's chancellor (1427–1444), was a history of the Florentine Republic. When Bruni died on March 9, 1444, the Signoria ordered a state funeral "according to ancient custom," during which the eminent humanist Giannozzo Manetti (1396–1459) delivered the eulogy and placed a laurel wreath on the head of Bruni's toga-clad corpse. The Florentine government also commissioned BERNARDO ROSSELLINO (1409–1464) to carve a monumental tomb (FIG. 21-14) for the right wall of the nave of Santa Croce (FIG. I-4) honoring the late chancellor. Rossellino was the most prominent member of a family of stonecutters from Settignano, a town near Florence noted for its quarries.

Rossellino's monument in honor of Leonardo Bruni established the wall tomb as a major genre of Italian Renaissance sculpture. Later examples include Pietro Lombardo's tomb of Pietro Mocenigo (FIG. 21-39) in Venice and Michelangelo's tombs of the Medici (FIG. 22-16) in Florence and of Pope Julius II (FIGS. 22-14 and 22-15) in Rome. Bruni's tomb is rich in color—white, black, and red marbles with selective gilding. Rossellino based his effigy of Bruni on ancient Roman sarcophagi (FIG. 7-59). The chancellor lies on a funerary bier supported by Roman eagles atop a sarcophagus resting on the foreparts of lions. Bruni, dressed in a toga and crowned with a laurel wreath, as during his state funeral, holds one of his books, probably his history of Florence. The realism of Bruni's head has led many scholars to postulate that Rossellino based his portrait on a wax death mask following ancient Roman practice (see "Roman Ancestor Portraits," page 183). Two winged Victories hold aloft a plaque with a Latin inscription stating that History mourns the death of Leonardus, Eloquence is now silenced, and the Greek and Latin muses cannot hold back their tears. Framing the effigy is a round-arched niche with Corinthian *pilasters*. The base of the tomb is a frieze of *putti* (cupids) carrying garlands, a standard motif on Roman sarcophagi, which also commonly have lions as supports (FIG. 7-68). The classically inspired tomb stands in sharp contrast to the Gothic tomb (FIG. 13-42A) of King Edward II in Gloucester Cathedral. But the Renaissance tomb is a creative variation of classical models, not a copy, and the motifs are a mix of classical and Christian themes. In the lunette beneath the arch is a *tondo* of the Madonna and Child between praying angels. Above the arch, two putti hold up a wreath circling the lion of the Florentine Republic. A lion's head is also the central motif in the putto-and-garland frieze below the deceased's coffin.

GATTAMELATA The grandest and most costly Quattrocento portraits in the Roman tradition were over-life-size bronze equestrian statues. The supremely versatile Donatello also excelled in this genre. In 1443, he left Florence for northern Italy to accept a lucrative commission from the Republic of Venice to create a commemorative monument (FIG. 21-15) in honor of the recently deceased Venetian condottiere Erasmo da Narni (1270–1443), nicknamed Gattamelata ("honeyed cat," a wordplay on his mother's name, Melania Gattelli). Condottieri played a major role in the power politics of Quattrocento Italy. Because Florence, Venice, and other republics barred their citizens from bearing arms, those states hired mercenary armies to fight on their behalf. They often owed the condottieri who commanded those armies a debt of gratitude as well as payment for their services. Although Gattamelata's family bore the cost of the

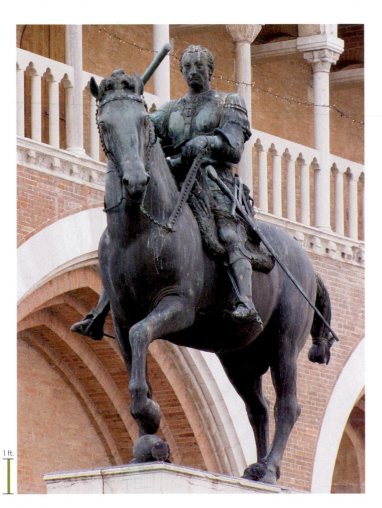

21-15 DONATELLO, *Gattamelata* (equestrian statue of Erasmo da Narni), Piazza del Santo, Padua, Italy, ca. 1445–1453. Bronze, 12′ 2″ high.

Donatello based his gigantic portrait of a Venetian general on equestrian statues of ancient Roman emperors (FIG. 7-57). Together, man and horse convey an overwhelming image of irresistible strength.

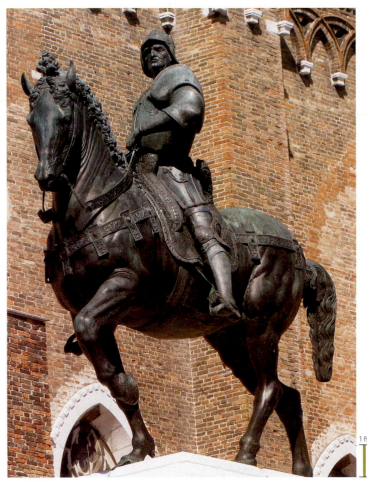

21-16 ANDREA DEL VERROCCHIO, *Bartolommeo Colleoni* (equestrian statue), Campo dei Santi Giovanni e Paolo, Venice, Italy, ca. 1481–1495. Bronze, 13′ high.

Eager to compete with Donatello's *Gattamelata* (FIG. 21-15), Bartolommeo Colleoni provided the funds in his will for his own equestrian statue, which stands on a pedestal even taller than *Gattamelata*'s.

general's equestrian portrait, the Venetian senate had to authorize its placement in the square in front of the church of Sant'Antonio in Padua, the condottiere's birthplace. Equestrian statues occasionally had been set up in Italy in the late Middle Ages, but Donatello's *Gattamelata* was the first since antiquity to rival the grandeur of Roman imperial mounted portraits, such as that of Marcus Aurelius (FIG. 7-57), which the artist must have seen in Rome. Donatello's contemporaries, one of whom described Gattamelata as sitting on his horse "with great magnificence like a triumphant Caesar,"[5] recognized this reference to antiquity. The statue stands on a lofty elliptical base, set apart from its surroundings, celebrating the Renaissance liberation of sculpture from architecture. Massive and majestic, the great horse bears the armored general easily, for, unlike the sculptor of the Marcus Aurelius statue, Donatello did not represent the Venetian commander as superhuman and disproportionately larger than his horse. Gattamelata dominates his mighty steed by force of character rather than sheer size. The Italian rider, his face set in a mask of dauntless resolution and unshakable will, is the very portrait of the Renaissance individualist. Such a man—intelligent, courageous, ambitious, and frequently of humble origin—could, by his own resourcefulness and on his own merits, rise to a commanding position in the world, even become a head of state (see page 612). Together, man and horse convey an overwhelming image of irresistible strength and unlimited power—an impression Donatello reinforced visually by placing the left forefoot of the horse on an orb, reviving a venerable ancient symbol for domination of the world (compare FIG. 11-13). The imperial imagery is all the more remarkable because Erasmo da Narni was not an emperor, king, or duke.

BARTOLOMMEO COLLEONI Verrocchio also received a commission to fashion an equestrian statue of a Venetian condottiere, Bartolommeo Colleoni (1400–1475). His portrait (FIG. **21-16**) provides a counterpoint to Donatello's statue. Eager to garner the same fame that the *Gattamelata* portrait achieved, Colleoni provided funds in his will for his own statue. Because both Donatello and Verrocchio executed their statues after the deaths of their subjects, neither artist knew personally the individual he portrayed. The result is a fascinating difference of interpretation (like that between their two *Davids*) as to the demeanor of a professional captain of armies. Verrocchio placed the statue of the bold equestrian general on a pedestal even taller than the one Donatello used for *Gattamelata*, elevating it so that viewers could see the dominating, aggressive figure from all approaches to the piazza (the Campo dei Santi Giovanni e Paolo). In contrast with the near repose of *Gattamelata*, the *Colleoni* horse moves in a prancing stride, arching and curving its powerful neck, while the commander seems suddenly to shift his whole weight to the stirrups and rise from the saddle with a violent twist of his body. The artist depicted both horse and rider with an exaggerated tautness—the animal's bulging muscles and the man's fiercely erect and rigid body together convey brute strength. In *Gattamelata*, Donatello created a portrait of a grim commander. Verrocchio's *Bartolommeo Colleoni* is a portrait of merciless might.

Painting

In Quattrocento Italy, humanism and the celebration of classical artistic values also largely determined the character of panel and mural painting. The new Renaissance style did not, however, immediately displace all vestiges of the Late Gothic style. In particular, the *International Gothic* style, the dominant mode in painting around 1400 (see page 424), persisted well into the 15th century.

GENTILE DA FABRIANO The leading Quattrocento master of the International Gothic style was GENTILE DA FABRIANO (ca. 1370–1427), who in 1420 moved his workshop from Brescia in northern Italy to Florence, where he hoped to share in the opportunities to work for the city's many wealthy patrons. Three years later, Gentile painted *Adoration of the Magi* (FIG. **21-17**) as the altarpiece for the family

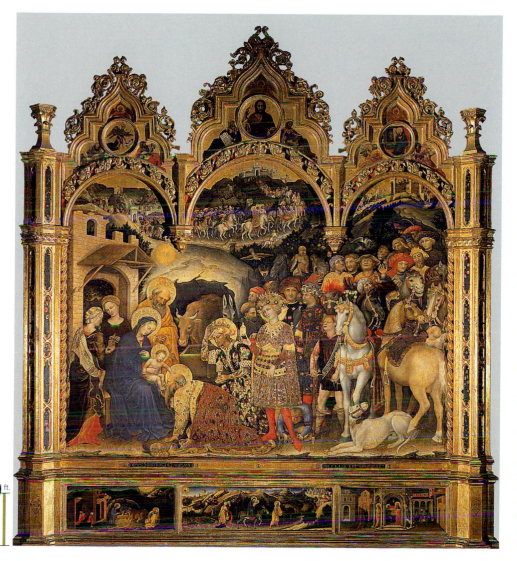

21-17 GENTILE DA FABRIANO, *Adoration of the Magi*, altarpiece from the Strozzi chapel, Santa Trinità, Florence, Italy, 1423. Tempera on wood, 9′ 11″ × 9′ 3″. Galleria degli Uffizi, Florence.

Gentile was the leading Florentine painter working in the International Gothic style. He successfully blended naturalistic details with late medieval splendor in color, costume, and framing ornamentation.

ART AND SOCIETY

Imitation and Emulation in Renaissance Art

Although many of the values championed by Renaissance humanists endure to the present day, the premium that modern Western society places on artistic originality is a fairly recent phenomenon. In contrast, imitation and emulation were among the concepts that Renaissance artists most valued. Many 15th- and 16th-century artists, of course, developed unique, recognizable styles, but convention, in terms of both subject matter and representational practices, predominated. In Italian Renaissance art, certain themes, motifs, and compositions appear with great regularity, fostered by training practices that emphasized the importance of tradition for aspiring Renaissance artists.

- **Imitation** The starting point in a young artist's training (see "Artistic Training in Renaissance Italy," page 426) was imitation. Italian Renaissance artists believed that the best way to learn was to copy the works of masters. Accordingly, much of an apprentice's training consisted of copying exemplary artworks.

For example, even a supreme master such as Leonardo da Vinci filled his sketchbooks with drawings of well-known sculptures and frescoes, and the boldly original Michelangelo spent days sketching artworks in churches around Florence and Rome.

- **Emulation** The next step was emulation, which involved modeling one's art after that of another artist. Although imitation provided the foundation for this practice, an artist used features of another's art only as a springboard for improvements or innovations. Thus, developing artists went beyond previous artists and attempted to prove their own competence and skill by improving on the work of established and recognized masters. Comparison and a degree of competition were integral to emulation. To evaluate the "improved" artwork, viewers had to be familiar with the original "model."

Renaissance artists believed that young artists would ultimately develop their own distinctive, if related, style through this process of imitation and emulation. But the boldest of them would quickly break away from their masters' influence, and some, like Massaccio (FIGS. 21-18 to 21-20), would redirect the history of art through brilliant innovation.

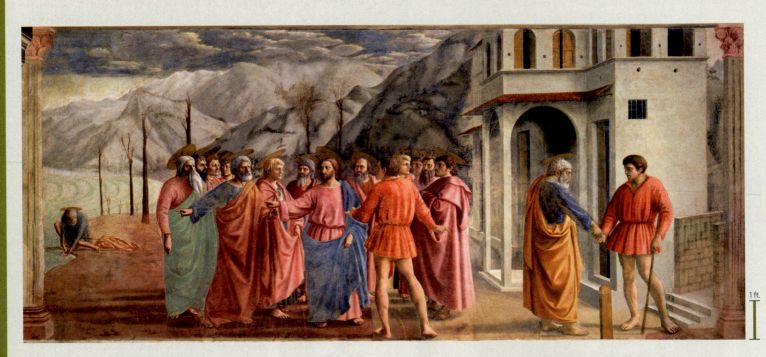

21-18 MASACCIO, *Tribute Money*, Brancacci chapel, Santa Maria del Carmine, Florence, Italy, ca. 1424–1427. Fresco, 8' 4$\frac{1}{8}$" × 19' 7$\frac{1}{8}$".

Masaccio's figures recall Giotto's in their simple grandeur, but they convey a greater psychological and physical credibility. He modeled his figures with light coming from a source outside the picture.

chapel of Palla Strozzi (1372–1462) in the church of Santa Trinità in Florence. At the beginning of the 15th century, the Strozzi family was the richest in the city. The altarpiece, with its elaborate gilded Gothic frame, is testimony to the patron's lavish tastes. So too is the painting itself, with its gorgeous surface and sumptuously costumed kings, courtiers, captains, and retainers (among whom, according to some sources, are portraits of Palla Strozzi and his father). Accompanying the kings and their entourage is a menagerie of exotic animals. Gentile portrayed all these elements in a rainbow of color with extensive use of gold. The painting presents all the pomp and ceremony of chivalric etiquette in a religious scene centered on the Madonna and Child.

Although the style is fundamentally International Gothic, Gentile inserted striking naturalistic details. For example, the artist depicted animals from a variety of angles and foreshortened the forms convincingly, most notably the horse at the far right seen in a three-quarter rear view. Gentile did the same with human figures, such as the kneeling man removing the spurs from the standing *magus* in the center foreground. In the left panel of the predella, Gentile painted what may have been the first nighttime nativity scene with the central light source—the radiant Christ Child—introduced into the picture itself. Although predominantly conservative, Gentile demonstrated that he was not oblivious to Quattrocento experimental trends and could blend naturalistic and inventive elements skillfully and subtly into a traditional composition without sacrificing Late Gothic splendor in color, costume, and framing ornamentation.

MASACCIO The artist who personifies the innovative spirit of early-15th-century Florentine painting was Tommaso di ser Giovanni di Mone Cassai, known as MASACCIO (1401–1428). Although his presumed teacher, Masolino da Panicale (see "Italian Artists' Names," page 413), had worked in the International Gothic style, Masaccio broke sharply from the normal practice of imitating his master's style (see "Imitation and Emulation in Renaissance Art," page 594). He moved suddenly, within the short span of six years, into unexplored territory. Most art historians recognize no other painter in history to have contributed so much to the development of a new style as quickly as Masaccio, whose untimely death at age 27 cut short his brilliant career. Masaccio was the artistic descendant of Giotto (see page 418), whose calm, monumental style he carried further by introducing a whole new repertoire of representational devices that generations of Renaissance painters later studied and developed.

BRANCACCI CHAPEL The frescoes Masaccio painted in the family chapel that Felice Brancacci (1382–1447) sponsored in Santa Maria del Carmine in Florence provide excellent examples of his innovations. In *Tribute Money* (FIG. **21-18**), painted shortly before his death, Masaccio depicted an episode from the Gospel of Matthew (17:24–27). As the tax collector confronts Jesus at the entrance to the Roman town of Capernaum, Jesus directs Saint Peter to the shore of Lake Galilee. There, as Jesus foresaw, Peter finds the tribute coin in the mouth of a fish and returns to pay the tax. Masaccio divided the story into three parts within the fresco. In the center, Jesus, surrounded by his disciples, tells Peter to retrieve the coin from the fish, while the tax collector stands in the foreground, his back to spectators and hand extended, awaiting payment. At the left, in the middle distance, Peter extracts the coin from the fish's mouth, and, at the right, he thrusts the coin into the tax collector's hand.

Masaccio's figures recall Giotto's in their simple grandeur, but they convey a greater psychological and physical credibility. Masaccio created the figures' bulk through modeling not with a flat, neutral light lacking an identifiable source but with a light coming from a specific source outside the picture. The light comes from the right (as if through a real window in the chapel wall) and strikes the figures at an angle, illuminating the parts of the solids obstructing its path and leaving the rest in shadow, producing the illusion of deep sculptural relief. Between the extremes of light and dark, the light appears as a constantly active but fluctuating force highlighting the scene in varying degrees. In his frescoes, Giotto used light only to model the masses. In Masaccio's works, light has its own nature, and the masses are visible only because of its direction and intensity. The viewer can imagine the light as playing over forms—revealing some and concealing others, as the artist directs it. The individual figures in *Tribute Money* are solemn and weighty, but they also move freely and reveal body structure, as do Donatello's statues. Masaccio's representations adeptly suggest bones, muscles, and the pressures and tensions of joints. Each figure conveys a maximum of contained energy. *Tribute Money* provides support for Giorgio Vasari's assessment of Masaccio's place in the history of art: "[T]he works made before his [Masaccio's] day can be said to be painted, while his are living, real, and natural."[6]

Masaccio's arrangement of the figures is equally inventive. They do not stand in a line in the foreground. Instead, the artist,

probably inspired by Nanni di Banco's *Four Crowned Saints* (FIG. 21-4), grouped them in circular depth around Jesus, and he placed the whole group in a spacious landscape, rather than in the confined stage space of earlier frescoes. The group itself generates the foreground space, and the architecture on the right amplifies it. Masaccio depicted the building in perspective, locating the vanishing point, where all the orthogonals converge, at Jesus's head. He also diminished the brightness of the colors as the distance increases, an aspect of atmospheric perspective understood and applied only by the most skilled painters. Although ancient Roman painters used aerial perspective (FIG. 7-20), medieval artists had abandoned it. Thus it virtually disappeared from art until Masaccio and his contemporaries rediscovered it. They came to realize that the light and air interposed between viewers and what they see are two parts of the visual experience called "distance."

In an awkwardly narrow space at the entrance to the Brancacci chapel, to the left of *Tribute Money*, Masaccio painted *Expulsion of Adam and Eve from Eden* (FIG. 21-19), a fresco that also displays the representational innovations seen in *Tribute Money*. For example, the sharply slanted light from an outside source creates deep relief, with lights placed alongside darks, and acts as a strong unifying agent. Masaccio also presented the figures with convincing structural accuracy, thereby suggesting substantial body weight. Further,

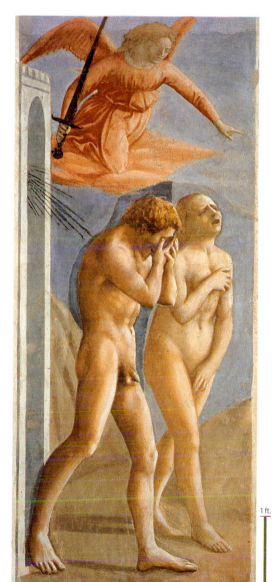

21-19

MASACCIO, *Expulsion of Adam and Eve from Eden*, Brancacci chapel, Santa Maria del Carmine, Florence, Italy, ca. 1424–1427. Fresco, 7' × 2' 11".

Adam and Eve, expelled from Eden, stumble on blindly, driven by the angel's will and their own despair. The hazy background specifies no locale but suggests a space around and beyond the figures.

1 ft.

the hazy background specifies no locale but suggests a space around and beyond the figures. Adam's feet, clearly in contact with the ground, mark the human presence on earth, and the cry issuing from Eve's mouth voices her anguish. The angel does not force them physically from Eden. Rather, they stumble on blindly, the angel's will and their own despair driving them. The composition is starkly simple, its message incomparably eloquent.

HOLY TRINITY Masaccio's *Holy Trinity* (FIG. **21-20**) in Santa Maria Novella, another of the young artist's masterworks, is the premier early-15th-century example of the application of mathematics to the depiction of space. In this fresco, Masaccio painted the composition on two levels of unequal height. Above, in a barrel-vaulted chapel reminiscent of a Roman *triumphal arch* (FIGS. 7-40 and 7-44A; compare FIG. 21-49A), the Virgin Mary and Saint John appear on either side of the crucified Christ. (Mary, unlike in almost all other representations of the crucifixion, appears as an older woman, her true age at the time of her adult son's death.) God the Father emerges from behind Christ, supporting the arms of the cross and presenting his son to the worshiper as a devotional object. Christ's blood runs down the cross onto the painted ledge below—a reference to the symbolic blood of the wine of the Eucharist on the church's altar. The dove of the Holy Spirit hovers between God's head and Christ's head. Masaccio also included portraits of the donors of the painting, Lorenzo Lenzi and his wife, who kneel just in front of the pilasters framing the chapel's entrance. Below, the artist painted a tomb containing a skeleton. An inscription in Italian above the skeleton reminds the spectator, "I was once what you are, and what I am you will become."

The illusionism of *Holy Trinity* is breathtaking, a brilliant demonstration of the principles and potential of Brunelleschi's new science of perspective. Indeed, some art historians have suggested that Brunelleschi may have collaborated with Masaccio on this commission. The vanishing point of the composition is at the foot of the cross. With this point at eye level, spectators look up at the Trinity and down at the tomb. About 5 feet above the floor level, the vanishing point pulls the two views together, creating the illusion of a real structure transecting the wall's vertical plane. Whereas the tomb seems to project forward into the church, the chapel recedes visually behind the wall and appears as an extension of the spectator's space. This adjustment of the picture's space to the viewer's position was an important innovation in illusionistic painting that other artists of the Renaissance and the later Baroque period would develop further. Masaccio was so exact in his metrical proportions that it is possible to calculate the dimensions of the chapel (for example, the span of the painted vault is 7 feet, and the depth of the chapel is 9 feet). Thus he achieved not only a successful illusion but also a rational measured coherence that is responsible for the unity and harmony of the fresco.

Holy Trinity is, however, much more than a highly successful application of Brunelleschi's perspective system or a showpiece for the painter's ability to represent fully modeled figures bathed in light. In this painting, Masaccio also powerfully conveyed one of the central tenets of Christian faith. The ascending pyramid of figures leads viewers from the despair of death to the hope of resurrection and eternal life through Christ's crucifixion. Masaccio's *Holy Trinity* clearly reveals that humanism and religion were not mutually exclusive.

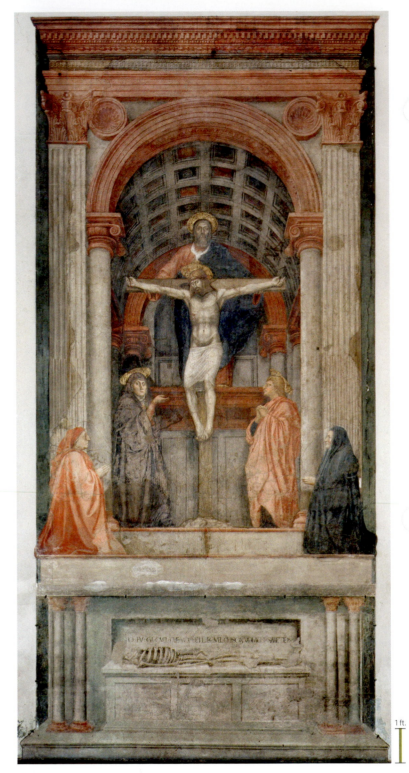

1 ft.

21-20 MASACCIO, *Holy Trinity*, Santa Maria Novella, Florence, Italy, ca. 1424–1427. Fresco, 21' 10$\frac{5}{8}$" × 10' 4$\frac{3}{4}$".

Masaccio's pioneering *Holy Trinity* is the premier early-15th-century example of the application of mathematics to the depiction of space according to Filippo Brunelleschi's system of perspective.

FRA ANGELICO For many other Quattrocento Italian artists, humanist concerns were not a primary consideration, however. The art of FRA ANGELICO (ca. 1400–1455) focused on serving the Roman Catholic Church. In the late 1430s, the abbot of the Dominican monastery of San Marco (Saint Mark) in Florence asked Fra Angelico to produce a series of frescoes for the order's Florentine compound. The Dominicans (see "Mendicant Orders," page 415) of

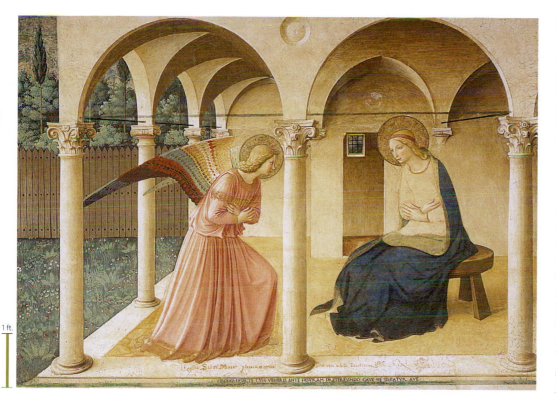

Painted for the Dominican monks of San Marco, Fra Angelico's fresco is simple and direct. Its figures and architecture have a pristine clarity befitting the fresco's function as a devotional image.

San Marco had dedicated themselves to lives of prayer and work, and their monastery was mostly spare and austere to encourage the monks to immerse themselves in their devotional lives. Fra Angelico's *Annunciation* (FIG. 21-21) appears at the top of the stairs leading to the friars' sleeping cells. Appropriately, Fra Angelico presented the scene of the Virgin Mary and the Archangel Gabriel with simplicity and serenity. The two figures appear in a plain *loggia* resembling the *portico* of San Marco's *cloister,* and the artist painted all the fresco elements with a pristine clarity. The figures do not cast shadows, however. Although Fra Angelico constructed the loggia according to the rules of Renaissance perspective (but with too few

columns to support the vaults), the unnatural lighting removes the sacred event from the everyday world. Underscoring the devotional function of the image, Fra Angelico included a small inscription at the base of the fresco admonishing the friars: "As you venerate, while passing before it, this figure of the intact Virgin, beware lest you omit to say a Hail Mary." Like most of Fra Angelico's paintings, *Annunciation,* with its simplicity and directness, still has an almost universal appeal and fully reflects the artist's simple, humble character.

ANDREA DEL CASTAGNO Fra Angelico's younger contemporary ANDREA DEL CASTAGNO (ca. 1421–1457) also accepted a commission to produce a series of frescoes for a religious establishment. Castagno's *Last Supper* (FIG. 21-22) in the *refectory* (dining hall) of Sant'Apollonia in Florence, a convent for Benedictine nuns, faithfully follows the biblical narrative, although the lavishly appointed, marble-revetted room that Jesus and his 12 disciples occupy has no basis in the Gospels. The setting Castagno chose reflected his

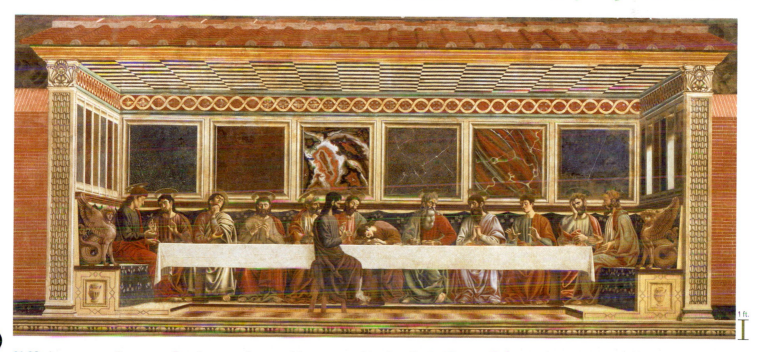

21-22 ANDREA DEL CASTAGNO, *Last Supper*, refectory of the convent of Sant'Apollonia, Florence, Italy, 1447. Fresco, 15' 5" × 32'.

In this *Last Supper* on the wall of a nuns' dining room, Judas sits isolated. Castagno's depiction of the setting for the apostles' meal reflects his preoccupation with the new science of perspective.

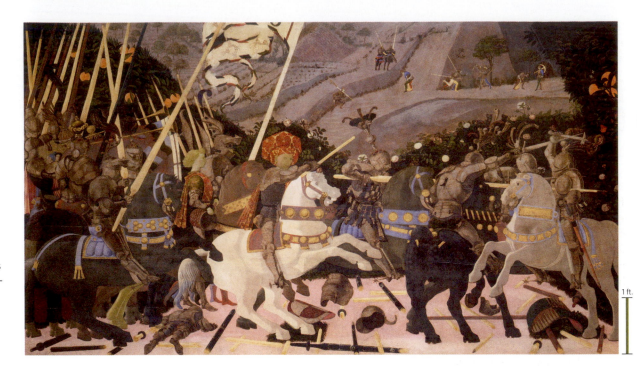

In this panel once in Lorenzo de' Medici's bedchamber, Niccolò da Tolentino leads the charge against the Sienese. The foreshortened spears and figures reveal Uccello's fascination with perspective.

1 ft.

interest in employing linear perspective to create the illusion of three-dimensional space, but close scrutiny reveals inconsistencies in his application of Brunelleschian principles. For example, in the Florentine perspective system, it is impossible to see both the ceiling from inside and the roof from outside, as Castagno depicted. The two side walls also do not appear parallel.

In placing the figures inside the biblical dining room, Castagno chose a conventional compositional format, with Jesus and the apostles seated at a horizontally placed table. The painter derived the apparent self-absorption of most of the disciples and the menacing features of Judas (who sits alone on the outside of the table) from the Gospel of Saint John, rather than the more familiar version of the Last Supper recounted in the Gospel of Saint Luke. Castagno's dramatic and spatially convincing depiction of the event no doubt was a powerful presence for the nuns during their daily meals.

PAOLO UCCELLO A much rarer genre of Quattrocento Florentine art was history painting. A masterpiece of this secular side of Renaissance art is *Battle of San Romano* (FIG. 21-23) by PAOLO UCCELLO (1397–1475), who trained in the International Gothic style. The large panel painting is one of three that Lorenzo de' Medici acquired for his bedchamber in the palatial Medici residence (FIGS. 21-35 and 21-36) in Florence. There is some controversy about the date of the painting because documents have been discovered suggesting that Lorenzo may have purchased at least two of the paintings from a previous owner instead of commissioning the full series himself. The scenes commemorate the Florentine victory over the Sienese in 1432 and must have been painted no earlier than the mid-1430s. The traditional date assigned to the commission is 1455, but a date around 1435 is more likely. In the panel illustrated here, Niccolò da Tolentino (ca. 1350–1435), a friend and supporter of Cosimo de' Medici, leads the charge against the Sienese. Mounted on a white horse and wearing an elegant red hat in place of a more practical helmet, Niccolò cuts a dashing figure.

In *Battle of San Romano*, Uccello created a composition that recalls the processional splendor of Gentile da Fabriano's International Gothic–style *Adoration of the Magi* (FIG. 21-17) yet also

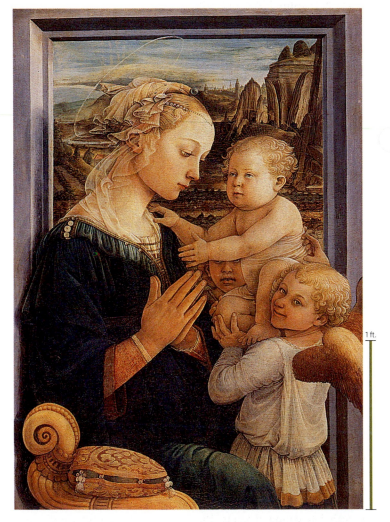

1 ft.

21-24 FRA FILIPPO LIPPI, *Madonna and Child with Angels*, ca. 1460–1465. Tempera on wood, 2' 11½" × 2' 1". Galleria degli Uffizi, Florence.

Fra Filippo, a monk guilty of many misdemeanors, represented the Madonna and Christ Child in a distinctly worldly manner, carrying the humanization of the holy family further than any artist before him.

21-25 Piero della Francesca, *Resurrection*, Palazzo Comunale, Borgo San Sepolcro, Italy, ca. 1463–1465. Fresco, 7' 4⅝" × 6' 6¼".

Christ miraculously rises from his tomb while the Roman guards sleep. The viewer sees the framing portico and the soldiers from below, but has a head-on view of the seminude muscular figure of Christ.

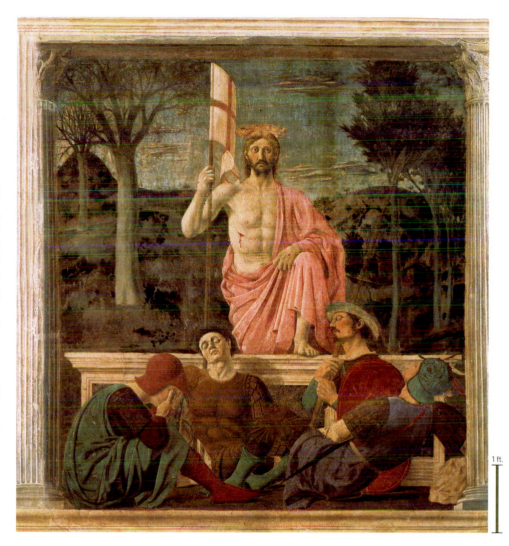

reflects Uccello's obsession with perspective. In contrast with Gentile, who emphasized surface decoration, Uccello painted life-size, classically inspired figures arranged in the foreground and, in the background, a receding landscape resembling the low cultivated hillsides between Florence and Lucca. He foreshortened broken spears, lances, and a fallen soldier and carefully placed them along the converging orthogonals of the perspective system (compare FIG. 21-9) to create a base plane akin to a checkerboard, on which he then placed the larger volumes in measured intervals. The rendering of three-dimensional form, used by other painters for representational or expressive purposes, became for Uccello a preoccupation. For him, it had a magic of its own, which he exploited to satisfy his inventive and original imagination.

FRA FILIPPO LIPPI Another younger contemporary of Fra Angelico, FRA FILIPPO LIPPI (ca. 1406–1469), was also a friar—but there all resemblance ends. Fra Filippo was unsuited for monastic life. He indulged in misdemeanors ranging from forgery and embezzlement to the abduction of a pretty nun, Lucretia, who became his mistress and the mother of his son, the painter Filippino Lippi (1457–1504). Only the intervention of the Medici on his behalf at the papal court preserved Fra Filippo from severe punishment and total disgrace. An orphan, Fra Filippo spent his youth in a monastery adjacent to the church of Santa Maria del Carmine, and when he was still in his teens, he must have met Masaccio there and witnessed the decoration of the Brancacci chapel. Fra Filippo's early work survives only in fragments, but these show that he tried to work with Masaccio's massive forms. Later, probably under the influence of Ghiberti's and Donatello's relief sculptures, he developed a linear style that emphasized the contours of his figures and enabled him to suggest movement through flying and swirling draperies.

In a painting from Fra Filippo's later years, *Madonna and Child with Angels* (FIG. **21-24**), the Virgin sits in prayer at a slight angle to the viewer. Her body casts a shadow on the window frame behind her. But the painter's primary interest was not in space but in line, which unifies the composition and contributes to the precise and smooth delineation of forms. The Carmelite brother interpreted his subject in a surprisingly worldly manner. The Madonna is a beautiful young mother, albeit with a transparent halo, in an elegantly furnished Florentine home, and neither she nor the Christ Child, whom two angels hold up, has a solemn expression. One of the angels, in fact, sports the mischievous, puckish grin of a boy refus-

ing to behave for the pious occasion. Significantly, all of the figures reflect the use of live models (perhaps Lucretia for the Madonna). Fra Filippo plainly relished the charm of youth and beauty as he found it in this world. He preferred the real in landscape also. The background, seen through the window, incorporates recognizable features of the Arno valley. Compared with the earlier Madonnas by Giotto (FIG. 14-8) and Duccio (FIG. 14-10), this work shows how far artists had carried the humanization of this traditional religious theme. Whatever the ideals of spiritual perfection may have meant to artists in past centuries, Renaissance artists realized those ideals in terms of the sensuous beauty of this world.

PIERO DELLA FRANCESCA One of the most renowned painters in 15th-century Italy was PIERO DELLA FRANCESCA (ca. 1420–1492), a native of Borgo San Sepolcro in southeastern Tuscany, who worked for diverse patrons, including the Medici in Florence and Federico de Montefeltro in Urbino (see page 614). In Tuscany, his commissions included the frescoes *Resurrection* (FIG. 21-25) for the town hall of his birthplace and *Legend of the True Cross* (FIG. **21-25A**) for the church of San Francesco at Arezzo. He painted

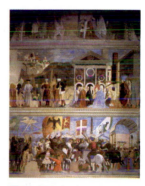

21-25A PIERO DELLA FRAN-CESCA, *Legend of the True Cross*, ca. 1450-1455.

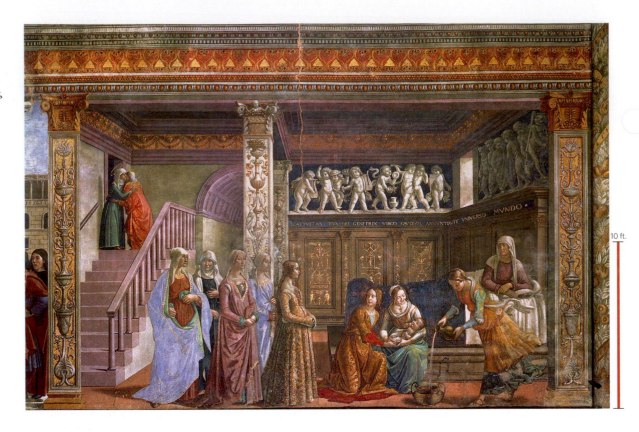

21-26 Domenico Ghirlandaio, *Birth of the Virgin*, Cappella Maggiore, Santa Maria Novella, Florence, Italy, ca. 1485–1490. Fresco, 24' 4" × 14' 9".

Ludovica Tornabuoni holds as prominent a place in Ghirlandaio's fresco as she must have held in Florentine society—evidence of the secularization of sacred themes in 15th-century Italian painting.

10 ft.

Resurrection on the wall facing the entrance to Borgo San Sepol-cro's newly remodeled Palazzo Comunale at the request of the civic council. Normally, the subjects chosen for city halls were scenes of battles, townscapes, or allegories of enlightened governance, as in Siena's Palazzo Pubblico (FIGS. 14-16A, 14-17, and 14-18). But the San Sepolcro council chose a religious subject instead. The town's name—Holy Sepulcher—derived from the legend that two 10th-century saints, Arcanus and Egidius, brought a fragment of Christ's tomb to the town from the Holy Land. (Christ's resurrection was also the subject of the central panel of the altarpiece painted between 1346 and 1348 by the Sienese painter Niccolò di Segna for the cathedral of San Sepolcro.)

In Piero's *Resurrection,* the viewer witnesses the miracle of the risen Christ through the *Corinthian columns* of a classical portico (preserved only in part because the painting was trimmed during its installation in a new location). Piero chose a viewpoint corresponding to the viewer's position and depicted the architectural frame at a sharp angle from below. The Roman soldiers who have fallen asleep when they should be guarding the tomb are also seen from below in a variety of foreshortened poses. (The bareheaded guard second from the left with his head resting on Christ's sarcophagus may be a self-portrait of the artist.) The soldiers form the base of a compositional triangle culminating at Christ's head. For Christ, Piero violated the perspective of the rest of the fresco and used a head-on view of the resurrected savior, imbuing the figure with an iconic quality. Christ's muscular body has the proportions of Greco-Roman nude statues. His pastel cloak stands out prominently from the darker colors of the soldiers' costumes. Christ holds the banner of his victory over death and displays his wounds. His face has portraitlike features. The tired eyes and somber expression are the only indications of his suffering on the cross.

DOMENICO GHIRLANDAIO Although projects undertaken with church, civic, and Medici patronage were significant sources of income for Florentine artists, other wealthy families also offered attractive commissions. Toward the end of the 15th century, DOMENICO

GHIRLANDAIO (1449–1494) received the contract for an important project for Giovanni Tornabuoni, one of the wealthiest Florentines of his day. Tornabuoni asked Ghirlandaio to paint a cycle of frescoes depicting scenes from the lives of the Virgin and Saint John the Baptist for the choir of Santa Maria Novella (FIG. 14-5B), the Dominican church where Masaccio had earlier painted his revolutionary *Holy Trinity* (FIG. 21-20). In *Birth of the Virgin* (FIG. **21-26**), Mary's mother, Saint Anne (see "Early Christian Saints," page 236), reclines in a palatial Renaissance room embellished with fine wood inlay and sculpture, while midwives prepare the infant's bath. From the left comes a solemn procession of women led by a young Tornabuoni family member, probably Ludovica, Giovanni's only daughter. Ghirlandaio's composition effectively summarizes the goals of Quattrocento Florentine painting: clear spatial representation, statuesque figures, and rational order and logical relations among all figures and objects. If any remnant of earlier traits remains here, it is the arrangement of the figures, which still cling somewhat rigidly to layers parallel to the picture plane. New, however, and in striking contrast to the dignity and austerity of Fra Angelico's frescoes (FIG. 21-21) for the Dominican monastery of San Marco, is the dominating presence of the donor's family in the religious tableau. Ludovica holds as prominent a place in the composition (close to the central axis) as she must have held in Florentine society. Her appearance in the painting (a different female member of the house appears in each fresco) is conspicuous evidence of the secularization of sacred themes—and of the importance of women in Florence's elite families. Artists depicted living women and men of high rank not only as present at biblical dramas (as Masaccio did in *Holy Trinity*) but also even stealing the show from the saints—as here, where the Tornabuoni women upstage the Virgin and Child. The display of patrician elegance tempers the biblical narrative and subordinates the fresco's devotional nature.

Ghirlandaio also painted individual portraits of wealthy Florentines. His 1488 panel painting (FIG. **21-27**) of an aristocratic young woman is probably a portrait of Giovanna Tornabuoni, a member of the powerful Albizzi family and wife of Lorenzo Tornabuoni, one

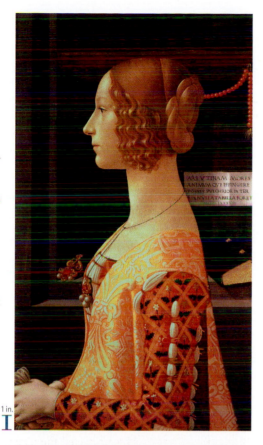

Renaissance artists
revived the ancient
art of portraiture. This
portrait reveals the
wealth, courtly man-
ners, and humanistic
interest in classical
literature that lie
behind much 15th-
century Florentine art.

1 in.

of Lorenzo de' Medici's cousins. Although artists at this time were beginning to employ three-quarter and full-face views for portraits (FIG. 21-28A) in place of the more traditional profile pose, Ghirlandaio used the older format. This did not prevent him from conveying a character reading of the sitter. His portrait reveals the proud bearing of a sensitive and beautiful young woman. It also tells viewers much about the advanced state of culture in Florence, the value and careful cultivation of beauty in life and art, the breeding of courtly manners, and the great wealth behind it all. In addition, the painting shows the powerful attraction that classical literature held for Italian humanists. In the background, an epitaph (Giovanna Tornabuoni died in child-birth in 1488 at age 20) quotes the ancient Roman poet Martial:

> If art could depict character and soul,
> No painting on earth would be more beautiful.[7]

BOTTICELLI, *PRIMAVERA* The appeal of Greek and Latin litera-ture to the elite families of Quattrocento Florence is most evident, however, in the paintings produced by Sandro Botticelli for mem-bers of the Medici family in the 1480s (see "The Medici, Botticelli, and Classical Antiquity," page 581). Botticelli painted *Primavera* (FIG. 21-28) for Lorenzo di Pierfrancesco de' Medici (1463–1503), one of Lorenzo the Magnificent's cousins, probably a couple of years before *Birth of Venus* (FIG. 21-1). The artist made reference to his patron by setting the scene in a grove of orange fruit—*mela medica* (Italian, "medicinal apples"). Because the name Medici means "doc-tors," this fruit was a fitting symbol of the family.

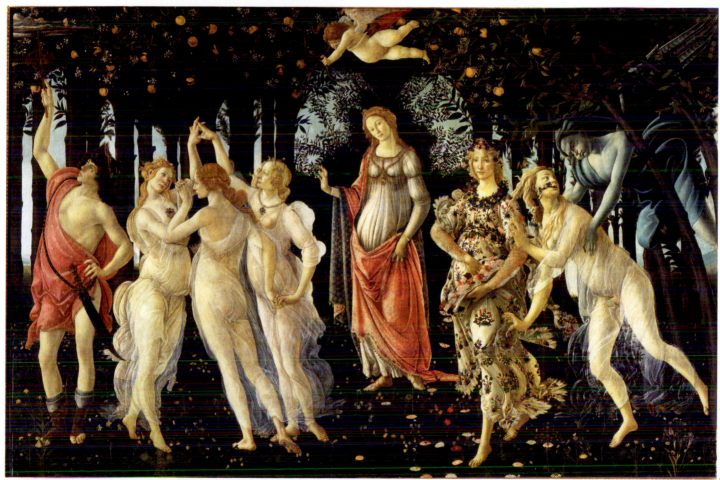

1 ft.

21-28 SANDRO BOTTICELLI, *Primavera*, ca. 1482. Tempera on wood, 6' 8" × 10' 4". Galleria degli Uffizi, Florence.

In Botticelli's lyrical painting celebrating love in springtime, the blue, ice-cold Zephyrus, the west wind, carries off and marries the nymph Chloris, whom he transforms into Flora, goddess of spring.

Venus stands just to the right of center with her son Cupid hovering above her head. Botticelli drew attention to the goddess of love by opening the landscape behind her to reveal a portion of sky that forms a kind of halo around Venus's head. To her right (the viewer's left) are the dancing Three Graces, who seem to be the target of Cupid's arrow. Botticelli's Graces are based closely on ancient prototypes, but they are clothed, albeit in thin, transparent garments. At the right are two of the key figures in *Birth of Venus*. The blue ice-cold Zephyrus is about to carry off and marry Chloris, whom he transforms into Flora, goddess of spring, appropriately shown wearing a rich floral gown. At the far left, Mercury turns away from all the others and reaches up with his distinctive staff, the *caduceus*, perhaps to dispel storm clouds. The sensuality of the representation, the appearance of Venus in springtime, and the abduction and marriage of Chloris all suggest that the occasion for the painting was young Lorenzo's wedding to Semiramide d'Appiani in May 1482. But the painting also sums up the Neo-Platonists' view that earthly love is compatible with Christian theology. In their reinterpretation of classical mythology, Venus as the source of love provokes desire through Cupid. Desire can lead either to lust and violence (Zephyrus) or, through reason and faith (Mercury), to the love of God. *Primavera*, read from right to left, served to urge the newlyweds to seek God through love.

Botticelli's paintings stand apart from those of the many other Quattrocento artists who sought to comprehend humanity and the natural world through a rational, empirical order. Indeed, Botticelli's elegant and beautiful linear style (he was a pupil of Fra Filippo Lippi, FIG. 21-24) seems removed from all the scientific knowledge 15th-century artists had gained in the areas of perspective and anatomy. For example, the seascape in *Birth of Venus* (FIG. 21-1) is a flat backdrop devoid of atmospheric perspective. Botticelli's style paralleled the Florentine allegorical pageants that were chivalric tournaments structured around allusions to classical mythology. The same trend is evident in the poetry of the 1470s and 1480s. Artists and poets at this time did not directly imitate classical antiquity but used the myths, with delicate perception of their charm, in a way still tinged with medieval romance. Ultimately, Botticelli created a style of visual poetry parallel to the love poetry of Lorenzo de' Medici. His paintings possess a lyricism and courtliness that appealed to cultured Florentine patrons, whether the Medici themselves or associates of the family (FIG. 21-28A).

21-28A BOTTICELLI, *Young Man Holding a Medal*, ca. 1474–1475.

ENGRAVING Although the most prestigious commissions in 15th-century Florence were for large-scale panel paintings and frescoes and for monumental statues and reliefs, some artists also produced important small-scale works, such as Pollaiuolo's *Hercules and Antaeus* (FIG. 21-13). Pollaiuolo also experimented with the new medium of engraving, which northern European artists had pioneered around the middle of the century. But whereas German graphic artists, such as Martin Schongauer (FIG. 20-23), described their forms with hatching that followed the forms, Italian engravers, such as Pollaiuolo, preferred parallel hatching. The former method was in keeping with the general Northern Renaissance approach to art, which tended to describe surfaces of forms rather than their underlying structures, whereas the latter better suited the anatomical studies that preoccupied Pollaiuolo and his Italian contemporaries.

Battle of Ten Nudes (FIG. 21-29), like Pollaiuolo's *Hercules and Antaeus* (FIG. 21-13), reveals the artist's interest in the realistic presentation of human figures in action. Earlier artists, such as Donatello (FIG. 21-11) and Masaccio (FIG. 21-19), had dealt effectively with the problem of rendering human anatomy, but they usually depicted their figures at rest or in restrained motion. As is evident in his engraving as well as in his sculpture, Pollaiuolo took delight in showing violent action. He conceived the body as a powerful machine and liked to display its mechanisms, such as knotted muscles and taut sinews that activate the skeleton as ropes pull levers. To show this to best effect, Pollaiuolo developed a figure so lean and muscular that it appears as if it has no skin. Pollaiuolo's figures also have strongly accentuated delineations at the wrists, elbows, shoulders, and knees. *Battle of Ten Nudes*—which has no identifiable subject or protagonists—shows this figure type in a variety of poses and from numerous viewpoints, enabling Pollaiuolo to demonstrate his prowess in rendering the nude male figure. In this, he was a kindred spirit of late-sixth-century Greek vase painters, such as Euthymides (FIG. 5-24), whose experiments with foreshortening also took precedence over narrative content. Even though the figures in *Ten Nudes* hack and slash at each other without mercy, they nevertheless seem somewhat stiff and frozen because Pollaiuolo depicted *all* the muscle groups at maximum tension. Not until several decades later did an even greater anatomist, Leonardo da Vinci (see page 629), observe that only some of the body's muscle groups participate in any one action, while the others remain relaxed.

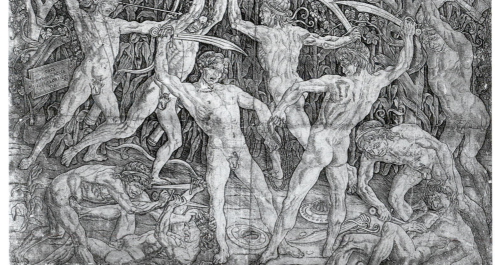

21-29 ANTONIO DEL POLLAIUOLO, *Battle of Ten Nudes*, ca. 1465. Engraving, 1' 3$\frac{1}{8}$" × 1' 11$\frac{1}{4}$". Metropolitan Museum of Art, New York (bequest of Joseph Pulitzer, 1917).

Pollaiuolo was fascinated by how muscles and sinews activate the human skeleton. He delighted in showing nude figures in violent action and from numerous foreshortened viewpoints.

1 in.

Architecture

Filippo Brunelleschi's ability to codify a system of linear perspective derived in part from his skill as an architect. Although according to his biographer, Antonio Manetti, Brunelleschi turned to architecture out of disappointment over the loss to Lorenzo Ghiberti of the commission for the baptistery doors (FIGS. 21-2 and 21-3), he continued to work as a sculptor for several years and received commissions for sculpture as late as 1416. It is true, however, that as the 15th century progressed, Brunelleschi's interest turned increasingly toward architecture—a field that he would reorient. Several trips to Rome (the first in 1402, probably with his friend Donatello), where the ruins of ancient Rome captivated him, heightened his fascination with buildings. His close study of Roman monuments and his effort to make an accurate record of what he saw may have been the catalyst that led Brunelleschi to develop his revolutionary system of linear perspective.

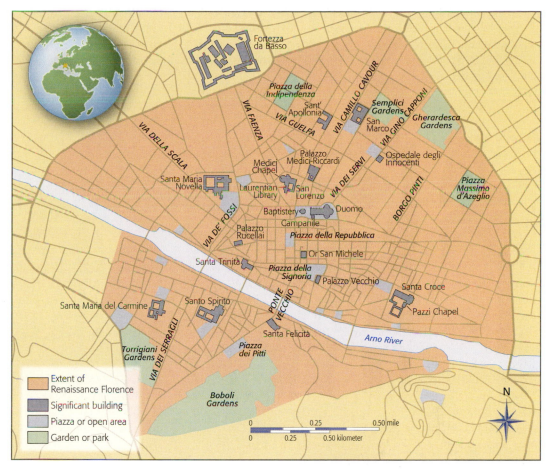

MAP 21-1
Renaissance Florence.

OSPEDALE DEGLI INNOCENTI At the end of the second decade of the 15th century, Brunelleschi received two important architectural commissions in Florence (MAP 21-1)—to construct a dome (FIGS. **21-29A** and **21-29B**) for the city's late medieval cathedral (FIG. 14-19) and to design the Ospedale degli Innocenti (Hospital of the Innocents, FIG. **21-30**), a home for Florentine orphans and foundlings. The orphanage commission came from Florence's guild of silk manufacturers and goldsmiths, of which Brunelleschi, a goldsmith, was a member. The site chosen, adjacent to the church of the Santissima Annunziata (Most Holy Annunciation), was appropriate. The church housed a miracle-working *Annunciation* that attracted large numbers of pilgrims. With the construction of the new foundling hospital, the Madonna would now watch over

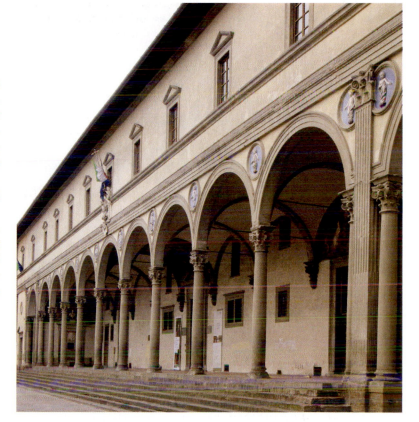

21-30 FILIPPO BRUNELLESCHI, loggia of the Ospedale degli Innocenti (Foundling Hospital; looking northeast), Florence, Italy, begun 1419.

Often called the first Renaissance building, the loggia of the orphanage sponsored by Florence's silk and goldsmith guild features a classically austere design based on a module of 10 braccia.

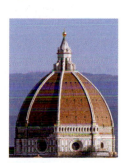

🔗 **21-29A** BRUNELLESCHI, Florence Cathedral dome, 1420–1436.

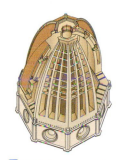

🔗 **21-29B** BRUNELLESCHI, Florence Cathedral dome, cutaway.

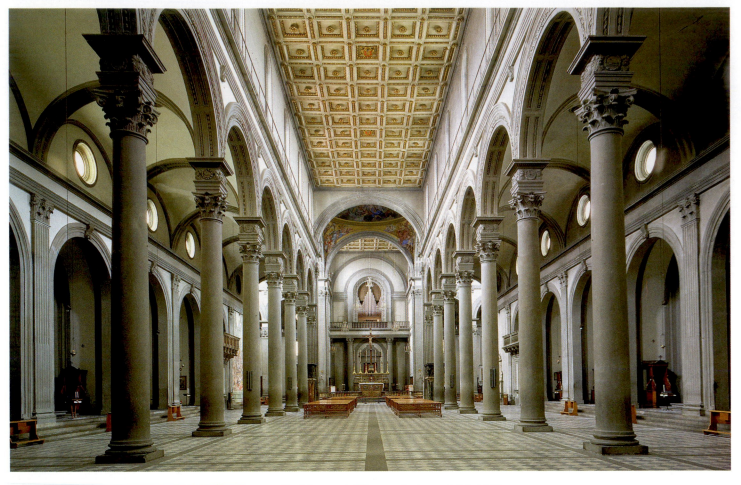

21-31 FILIPPO BRUNELLESCHI, interior of San Lorenzo (looking east), Florence, Italy, ca. 1421–1469.

The mathematical clarity and austerity of the decor of San Lorenzo are key elements of Brunelleschi's classically inspired architectural style, which contrasts sharply with the soaring drama of Gothic churches.

infants as well, assisted by the guild, which supported the orphanage with additional charitable donations.

Most scholars regard Brunelleschi's Ospedale degli Innocenti as the first building to embody the new Renaissance architectural style. As in earlier similar buildings, the facade of the Florentine orphanage is a loggia opening onto the street, a sheltered portico where, in this case, parents could anonymously deliver unwanted children to the care of the foundling hospital. Brunelleschi's arcade consists of a series of round arches on slender Corinthian columns. Each bay is a domed compartment with a *pediment*-capped window above. Both plan and elevation conform to a *module* that embodies the rationality of classical architecture. Each column is 10 *braccia* (approximately 20 feet; 1 braccia, or arm, equals 23 inches) tall. The distance between the columns of the facade and the distance between the columns and the wall are also 10 braccia. Thus each of the bays is a cubical unit 10 braccia wide, deep, and high. The height of the columns also equals the diameter of the arches (except in the two outermost bays, which are slightly wider and serve as framing elements in the overall design). The color scheme, which would become a Brunelleschi hallmark, is austere: white stucco walls with gray pietra serena ("serene stone") columns and moldings.

SAN LORENZO In 1418, the year before Brunelleschi began work on the Ospedale degli Innocenti, Giovanni de' Medici became the official banker of the Vatican, a position that enabled him and his heirs to amass both wealth and power (see "The Medici," page 581).

Giovanni became the leader of a group of Florentine citizens that financed the rebuilding of the church of San Lorenzo (Saint Lawrence; FIG. **21-31**). The church, one of the largest in the city, had a venerable history. The original church was dedicated in 393, but an 11th-century Romanesque church that replaced the Early Christian *basilica* still stood on the site in the early 15th century. In 1421, the commission for the new church went to Brunelleschi, who did not live to see his design executed in full. In fact, at the time of his death in 1446, not a single column of the nave was yet in place.

San Lorenzo is one of two basilican churches in Florence designed by Brunelleschi, and its plan and elevation closely resemble those of Santo Spirito (FIGS. **21-31A** and **21-31B**), begun about a decade later on the opposite side of the Arno River (MAP 21-1). Both churches embody the new Renaissance spirit of the Florentine orphanage loggia in their austerity and rationality. As in the

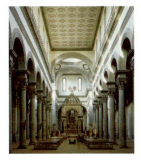

🔼 **21-31A** BRUNELLESCHI, Santo Spirito interior, begun 1446.

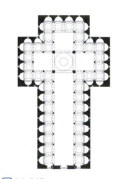

🔼 **21-31B** BRUNELLESCHI, Santo Spirito plan, begun 1446.

Italian Renaissance Family Chapel Endowments

During the 14th through 16th centuries in Italy, wealthy families regularly endowed chapels in or adjacent to major churches. These family chapels were usually situated on either side of the choir near the altar at the church's east end. Very wealthy families sponsored chapels in the form of separate buildings constructed adjacent to churches. For example, the Medici Chapel (Old Sacristy) abuts San Lorenzo in Florence. The Pazzi family commissioned a chapel (FIGS. 21-32 to 21-34) adjacent to Santa Croce. Other powerful banking families—the Baroncelli, Bardi, and Peruzzi—each sponsored chapels inside the church. The Brancacci family paid for the decorative program (FIGS. 21-18 and 21-19) of their chapel in Santa Maria del Carmine, and the Strozzi for their family chapel in Santa Trinità (FIG. 21-17).

These families and many others, not only in Florence but throughout Italy, endowed chapels to ensure the well-being of the souls of individual family members and ancestors. The chapels served as burial sites and as spaces for liturgical celebrations and commemorative services. Chapel owners sponsored Masses for the dead, praying to the Virgin Mary and the saints for intercession on behalf of their deceased loved ones.

Changes in Christian doctrine prompted these concerted efforts to enhance donors' chances for eternal salvation. Until the 13th century, most Christians believed that after death, souls went either to Heaven or to Hell. In the late 1100s and early 1200s, the concept of Purgatory—a way station between Heaven and Hell where souls could atone for sins before judgment day—increasingly won favor. Pope Innocent III (1198–1216) officially recognized the existence of such a place in 1215. Because Purgatory represented a chance for the faithful to improve the likelihood of eventually gaining admission to Heaven, Christians eagerly embraced this opportunity.

When the Church extended to the living the concept of earning salvation in Purgatory, charitable work, good deeds, and devotional practices proliferated. Family chapels provided the space necessary for the performance of devotional rituals. Most chapels included altars, as well as chalices, vestments, candlesticks, and other objects used in the

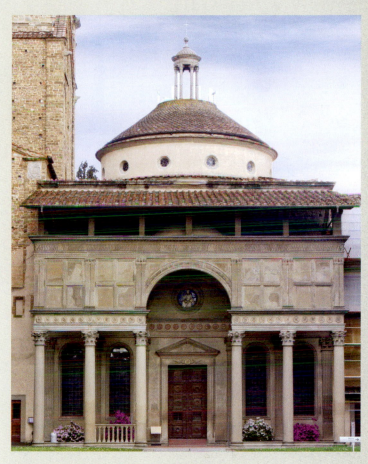

21-32 FILIPPO BRUNELLESCHI, west facade of the Pazzi Chapel, Santa Croce, Florence, Italy, begun 1433.

The Pazzi family erected this chapel as a gift to the Franciscan church of Santa Croce. It served as the monks' chapter house and is one of the first independent Renaissance central-plan buildings.

Mass. In consultation with the relevant church officials, most patrons also commissioned decorations, such as painted altarpieces, frescoes on the walls, and sculptural objects. The chapels were therefore not only expressions of piety and devotion but also opportunities for donors to enhance their stature in the larger community.

---

earlier building, Brunelleschi adopted an all-encompassing modular design for the church that extended even to the diameter of the shafts of the nave columns and the dimensions of their Corinthian capitals. The nave has a simple two-story elevation (nave arcade and clerestory) with a flat, coffered timber roof. The columns support *impost blocks* from which round arches spring. Ample light enters through the arcuated clerestory windows and through *oculi* in the aisle walls, one over each chapel opening onto the domed aisle bays. The restrained color scheme of white stucco wall surfaces and moldings in gray *pietra serena* became standard in Florentine churches for 500 years.

The calculated logic of the design echoes that of ancient Roman buildings, but contrasts sharply with the soaring drama and spirituality of the nave arcades and vaults of Gothic churches (for example, FIGS. 13-20 and 13-21). San Lorenzo's rational interior even deviates from Florence Cathedral's nave (FIG. 14-19A), whose verticality is restrained in comparison to its northern European counterparts. San Lorenzo fully expresses the new Renaissance spirit that placed its faith in reason rather than in the emotions.

PAZZI CHAPEL Shortly after Brunelleschi began work on San Lorenzo, the Pazzi family commissioned him to design the chapel (FIGS. 21-32 to 21-34) they intended to donate to the Franciscan church of Santa Croce in Florence (see "Italian Renaissance Family Chapel Endowments," above). The project was not completed, however, until the 1460s, long after Brunelleschi's death, and the exterior (FIG. 21-32) probably does not reflect his original design. The loggia, admirable as it is, likely was added as an afterthought, perhaps by the sculptor-architect Giuliano da Maiano (1432–1490). The Pazzi Chapel served as the *chapter house* (meeting hall) of the local chapter of Franciscan monks. Historians have suggested that the monks needed the expansion to accommodate more of their brethren.

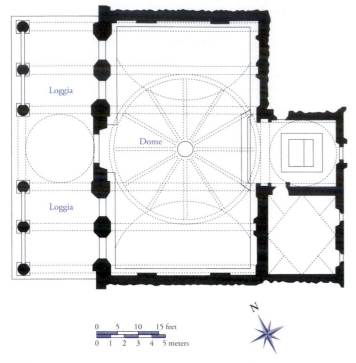

21-33 FILIPPO BRUNELLESCHI, plan of the Pazzi Chapel, Santa Croce, Florence, Italy, begun 1433.

Although the Pazzi Chapel is rectangular, rather than square or round, Brunelleschi created a central plan by placing all emphasis on the dome-covered space at the heart of the building.

Behind the loggia stands one of the first independent Renaissance buildings conceived basically as a *central-plan* structure (compare FIGS. 8-11 and 8-12), so called because the various aspects of the interior resemble one another, no matter where an observer stands, in contrast to the *longitudinal plan* of basilican churches. Although the Pazzi Chapel's plan (FIG. **21-33**) is rectangular, rather than square or round, Brunelleschi placed all emphasis on the central dome-covered space. The short *barrel-vaulted* sections bracing the dome on two sides appear to be incidental appendages. The interior trim (FIG. **21-34**) is Brunelleschi's favorite gray pietra serena, which stands out against the white stuccoed walls and crisply defines the modular relationships of plan and elevation. As he did in his design for the Ospedale degli Innocenti (FIG. 21-30) and later for Santo Lorenzo (FIG. 21-31), Brunelleschi used a basic unit that enabled him to construct a balanced, harmonious, and regularly proportioned space.

Circular medallions (tondi) in the dome's *pendentives* (see "Placing a Dome over a Square," page 264) consist of *terracotta* reliefs representing the four evangelists. The technique for manufacturing these baked clay reliefs was of recent invention. Around 1430, LUCA DELLA ROBBIA (1400–1482) perfected the application of vitrified (heat-fused) colored potters' *glazes* to sculpture (FIG. **21-34A**). Inexpensive, durable, and decorative, these ceramic

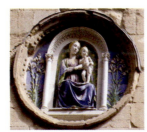

📷 **21-34A** LUCA DELLA ROBBIA, *Madonna and Child*, ca. 1455–1460.

sculptures became extremely popular and provided the basis for a lucrative family business. Luca's nephew Andrea della Robbia (1435–1525) produced *roundels* of babies in swaddling clothes for

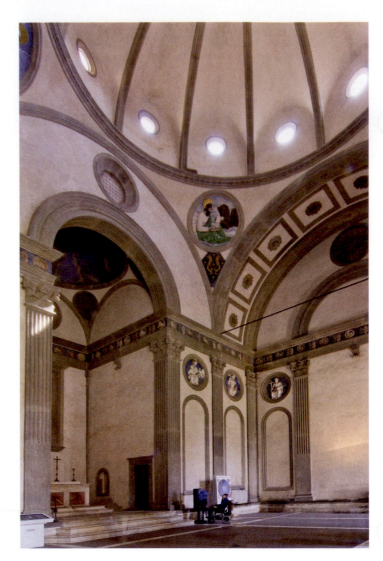

21-34 FILIPPO BRUNELLESCHI, interior of the Pazzi Chapel (looking southeast), Santa Croce, Florence, Italy, begun 1433.

The interior trim of the Pazzi Chapel is gray pietra serena, which stands out against the white stuccoed walls and crisply defines the modular relationships of Brunelleschi's plan and elevation.

Brunelleschi's loggia of the Ospedale degli Innocenti (FIG. 21-30) in 1487 (the only indication on the building's facade of its charitable function), and Andrea's sons, Giovanni della Robbia (1469–1529) and Girolamo della Robbia (1488–1566), carried on this tradition well into the 16th century. Most of the tondi in the Pazzi Chapel are the work of Luca della Robbia himself. Together with the images of the 12 apostles on the pilaster-framed wall panels, they add striking color accents to the tranquil interior.

PALAZZO MEDICI It seems curious that Brunelleschi, the most renowned architect of his time, did not participate in the upsurge of palace building that Florence experienced in the 1430s and 1440s. This proliferation of *palazzi* testified to the stability of the Florentine economy and to the affluence and confidence of the city's leading citizens. Brunelleschi, however, confined his efforts in this field to work on the Palazzo di Parte Guelfa (headquarters of Florence's then-ruling "party") and to a rejected model for a new palace that Cosimo de' Medici intended to build. When the Medici returned to Florence in 1434 after a brief exile imposed upon them by other elite families who resented the Medicis' consolidation of power, Cosimo,

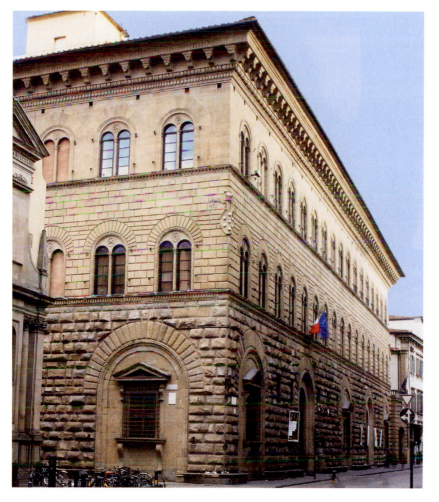

aware of the importance of public perception, attempted to maintain a lower profile and to wield his power from behind the scenes. In all probability, this attitude accounted for his rejection of Brunelleschi's design for the new Medici residence, which he evidently found too imposing and ostentatious to be politically wise. Cosimo eventually awarded the commission to MICHELOZZO DI BARTOLOMMEO (1396–1472), a young architect who had been Donatello's collaborator in several sculptural enterprises. Although Cosimo passed over Brunelleschi, the architect's style nevertheless deeply influenced Michelozzo. To a limited extent, the Palazzo Medici (FIG. 21-35) reflects Brunelleschian principles.

Later bought by the Riccardi family (hence the name Palazzo Medici-Riccardi), who almost doubled the façade's length in the 18th century, the palace, in both its original and its extended form, is a simple, massive structure. Heavy *rustication* (rough, unfinished masonry) on the ground floor accentuates its strength. Michelozzo divided the building block into stories of decreasing height by using long, unbroken *stringcourses* (horizontal bands), which give it coherence. *Dressed masonry* (smooth, finished) *ashlar* blocks on the second level and an even smoother surface on the top story modify the severity of the ground floor and make the building appear progressively lighter as the eye moves upward. The extremely heavy *cornice*, which Michelozzo related not to the top story but to the building as a whole, dramatically reverses this effect. Like the ancient Roman cornices that served as Michelozzo's models (compare FIGS. 7-32, 7-40, and 7-44A), the Palazzo Medici-Riccardi cornice is a very effective lid for the structure, clearly and emphatically defining its proportions. Michelozzo perhaps also was inspired by the many extant examples of Roman rusticated masonry, and Roman precedents even exist for the juxtaposition of rusticated and dressed

21-35 MICHELOZZO DI BARTOLOMMEO, Palazzo Medici-Riccardi (looking northwest), Florence, Italy, begun 1445.

The Medici palace, with its combination of dressed and rusticated masonry and classical moldings, draws heavily on ancient Roman architecture, but Michelozzo creatively reinterpreted his models.

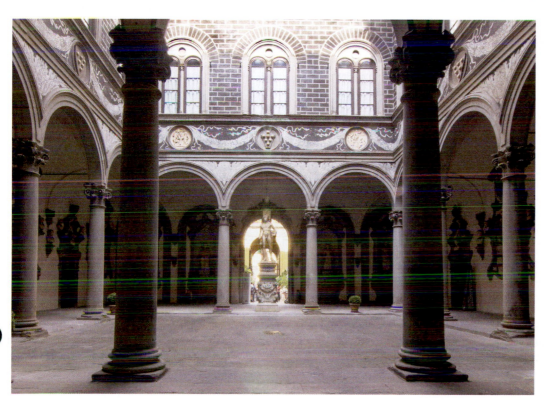

21-36 MICHELOZZO DI BARTOLOMMEO, interior court of the Palazzo Medici-Riccardi (looking west), Florence, Italy, begun 1445.

The Medici palace's interior court surrounded by a round-arched colonnade was the first of its kind, but the austere design clearly reveals Michelozzo's debt to Brunelleschi (FIG. 21-30).

Leon Battista Alberti's *On the Art of Building*

Although he wrote treatises on painting and sculpture, Leon Battista Alberti's most ambitious work, modeled on Vitruvius's *Ten Books on Architecture* (see page 199) was *De re aedificatori libri X (On the Art of Building in Ten Books)*, written about 1450 and published in 1486. Alberti was the first to study Vitruvius's treatise in detail, and his knowledge of it, combined with his own archaeological investigations, made him the first Renaissance architect to understand classical architecture in depth. His own buildings (FIGS. **21-36A**, **21-37,** and 21-45 to 21-47), however, are not ancient replicas but highly original designs.

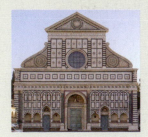

▣ **21-36A** ALBERTI, Santa Maria Novella, Florence, 1456–1470.

Alberti's treatise, in addition to serving as a practical manual for architects, also celebrated and sought to ennoble the profession of architect. In his prologue, Alberti argued that

> The security, dignity, and honor of the republic depend greatly on the architect: it is he who is responsible for our delight, entertainment, and health while at leisure, and our profit and advantage while at work, and in short, that we live in a dignified manner, free from any danger. In view then of the delight and wonderful grace of his works, and of how indispensable they have proved, and in view of the benefit and convenience of his inventions, and their service to posterity, he should no doubt be accorded praise and respect, and be counted among those most deserving of mankind's honor and recognition.*

Alberti believed that architectural design should reflect the laws of nature and conform to mathematical formulas for beautiful proportions.

> The great experts of antiquity . . . have instructed us that a building is very like an animal, and that Nature must be imitated when we delineate it. . . . Beauty is a form of sympathy and consonance of the parts within a body, according to definite number, outline, and position, . . . the absolute and fundamental rule of Nature. This is the main object of the art of building, and the source of her dignity, charm, authority, and worth (IX.5).

Alberti shared this conviction with Brunelleschi, and this fundamental dependence on classically derived mathematics distinguished their architectural work from that of most of their medieval predecessors. They believed in the eternal and universal validity of numerical ratios as the source of beauty. In this respect, Alberti and Brunelleschi revived the true spirit of the High Classical age of ancient Greece, following the lead of the architect Iktinos and the sculptor Polykleitos, who produced canons of proportions for the perfect temple and the perfect statue (see "The Perfect Temple," page 103, and "Polykleitos's Prescription for the Perfect Statue," page 129).

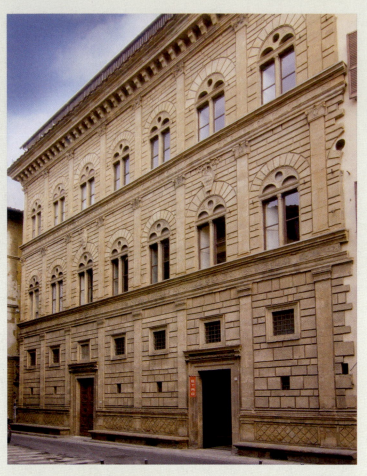

21-37 LEON BATTISTA ALBERTI and BERNARDO ROSSELLINO, Palazzo Rucellai (looking northwest), Florence, Italy, ca. 1452–1470.

Alberti was an ardent student of classical architecture. By adapting the Roman use of different orders for each story, he created the illusion that the Palazzo Rucellai becomes lighter toward its top.

Two of Alberti's prescriptions for good architectural design are of particular interest. In contrast to the long tradition of building basilican churches with nave arcades, Alberti believed that the central plan was the ideal form for churches and that arches should not rest on columns.

> It is obvious from all that is fashioned, produced, or created under her influence that Nature delights primarily in the circle. Need I mention the earth, the stars, the animals, their nests, and so on, all of which she has made circular. . . . The round plan is defined by the circle (VII.4).

> For arched colonnades quadrangular columns are required. The work would be defective with round columns (VII.131).

Many later architects took both suggestions to heart.

*All passages translated by Joseph Rykwert, Neil Leach, and Robert Tavernor, *Leon Battista Alberti: On the Art of Building in Ten Books* (Cambridge, Mass.: MIT Press, 1988), 5, 196, 236, 301, 303.

---

stone masonry on the same facade (FIG. 7-34). However, nothing in the ancient world precisely compares with Michelozzo's design. The Palazzo Medici exemplifies the simultaneous respect for and independence from the antique that characterizes the Early Renaissance in Italy.

The heart of the Palazzo Medici is an open colonnaded court (FIG. **21-36**) that clearly shows Michelozzo's debt to Brunelleschi. The round-arched colonnade, although more massive in its proportions, closely resembles Brunelleschi's foundling-hospital loggia (FIG. 21-30) and the nave colonnades of San Lorenzo (FIG. 21-31) and Santo Spirito (FIG. 21-31A). As in Brunelleschi's loggia and the Pazzi Chapel (FIG. 21-34), roundels (here framing Medici coats-of-arms) are prominent motifs in the arcades, although in the Palazzo Medici they appear in the frieze above the arcade, alternating with garlands, a popular motif in ancient Roman architecture (for example, FIG. 7-4). The Palazzo Medici's internal court surrounded by an arcade was the first of its kind in Renaissance architecture and influenced a long line of descendants in Italian domestic architecture (for example, FIG. 22-27).

LEON BATTISTA ALBERTI Although he entered the profession of architecture rather late in life, LEON BATTISTA ALBERTI (1404–1472) made a major contribution to architectural design (see "Leon Battista Alberti's *On the Art of Building*," page 608). Alberti's architectural style represents a scholarly application of classical elements to contemporaneous buildings. Most architectural historians believe that he designed the Palazzo Rucellai (FIG. 21-37) in Florence, although his pupil and collaborator, Bernardo Rossellino (FIG. 21-14), constructed the building using Alberti's plans and sketches. The facade of the palace is much more severe than that of the Palazzo Medici-Riccardi (FIG. 21-35). Pilasters define each story, and a classical cornice crowns the whole. Between the smooth pilasters are subdued and uniform wall surfaces. Alberti created the sense that the structure becomes lighter in weight toward its top by adapting the ancient Roman manner of using different capitals for the pilasters of each story. He chose the severe capitals of ancient *Tuscan columns* (the Etruscan variant of the Greek *Doric order* [FIG. 5-13, *left*], used also by the Romans) for the ground floor, capitals of his own invention with acanthus leaves and *palmettes* (palm leaves) for the second story, and Corinthian capitals for the third floor. Alberti modeled his facade on the most imposing Roman ruin of all, the Colosseum (FIG. 7-37), but he was no slavish copyist. On the Colosseum's facade, the capitals employed are, from the bottom up, Tuscan, Ionic, and Corinthian. Moreover, Alberti adapted the Colosseum's varied surface to a flat facade, which does not allow the deep penetration of the building's mass that is so effective in the Roman structure. By converting his ancient model's *engaged columns* (half-round columns attached to a wall) into shallow pilasters that barely project from the wall, Alberti created a large-meshed linear net. Stretched tightly across the front of his building, it not only unifies the three levels but also emphasizes the wall's flat, two-dimensional qualities.

GIROLAMO SAVONAROLA In the 1490s, Florence underwent a political, cultural, and religious upheaval. Florentine artists and their fellow citizens responded then not only to humanist ideas but also to the incursion of French armies and especially to the preaching of the Dominican monk Girolamo Savonarola (1452–1498), the reformist priest-dictator who denounced the humanistic secularism of the Medici and their artists, philosophers, and poets. Savonarola exhorted the people of Florence to repent their sins, and when Lorenzo de' Medici died in 1492, the priest prophesied the downfall of the city and of Italy and assumed absolute control of the state. As did a large number of citizens, Savonarola believed that the Medici family's political, social, and religious power had corrupted Florence and invited the scourge of foreign invasion. In his sermons, Savonarola condemned the worldly and irreverent representation of holy figures—for example, Fra Filippo Lippi's *Madonna and Child with Angels* (FIG. 21-24)—and those families who spent their fortunes on chapels dedicated to perpetuating their memory instead of aiding the poor (see "Family Chapel Endowments," page 605).

He encouraged citizens to burn their classical texts, scientific treatises, and philosophical publications. The Medici fled in 1494.

Scholars still debate the significance of Savonarola's brief span of power. Apologists for the undoubtedly sincere monk deny that his actions played a role in the decline of Florentine culture at the end of the 15th century. But the puritanical spirit that moved Savonarola must have dampened considerably the enthusiasm for classical antiquity of the Florentine Early Renaissance. Certainly, Savanarola's condemnation of humanism as heretical nonsense, and his banishing of the Medici, Tornabuoni, and other wealthy families from Florence, deprived local artists of some of their major patrons, at least in the short term. There were, however, commissions aplenty for artists elsewhere in Italy—beginning long before Savonarola launched his attacks on Florentine humanism.

VENICE

At the dawn of the Renaissance, Venice was one of the richest states in Italy and the major commercial and cultural link to the Byzantine Empire. In the realm of architecture, it boasted one of the greatest churches in Europe, the five-domed mosaic-filled Saint Mark's (FIG. 9-27) dedicated to the city's patron saint, and one of the gems of late medieval secular architecture, the palace (FIG. 14-23) of the city's ruling *doges* (dukes). The design of the seat of Venetian power contrasts vividly with Florence's fortresslike Palazzo della Signoria (FIG. 14-19B) and reflects the fact that Venice, unlike Florence, was free of civil conflict.

CA D'ORO That happy state of affairs also dictated the design of private palaces. The most spectacular 15th-century Venetian palace (FIG. 21-38) looks nothing like the Palazzo Medici (FIG. 21-35). It belonged to Marino Contarini, the scion of one of the city's wealthiest merchant families. Built between 1421 and 1437, the Palazzo Contarini has an asymmetrical three-story facade facing Venice's

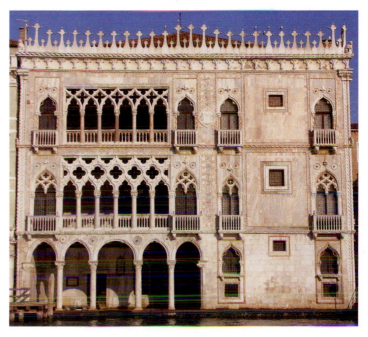

21-38 Palazzo Contarini (Ca d'Oro; looking northeast), Venice, Italy, 1421–1437.

In vivid contrast to the fortresslike Florentine Palazzo Medici (FIG. 21-35), Marino Contarini's "House of Gold" displays the Venetian's taste for flowery painted and gilded Gothic ornamentation.

WRITTEN SOURCES
The Tomb of Doge Pietro Mocenigo

Upon entering the basilican church in Venice dedicated to Saints John and Paul, visitors today are greeted by so many tombs of the city's former rulers that the church has been dubbed the "pantheon of the doges." The tombs impressed earlier tourists as well, including Felix Faber (ca. 1441–1502), a Dominican theologian who stopped in Venice in 1480 during a pilgrimage to Jerusalem and recorded what he saw in his diary. The doges' tombs in Santi Giovanni e Paolo made a profound impression on Faber, especially that of Pietro Mocenigo (FIG. 21-39), carved by Pietro Lombardo and his workshop. The focus of Mocenigo's tomb is his portrait in armor, framed by a triumphal arch. The statue rests on the doge's sarcophagus, held aloft by three warriors of different ages and decorated with reliefs commemorating major achievements of his short reign as duke. More statues of soldiers stand in superposed niches to the left and right. Below are reliefs depicting the Labors of Hercules. At the summit is the resurrected Christ above a relief representing the Three Marys at the Savior's empty tomb.

Faber took special interest in the combination of Christian iconography and classical mythology on Mocenigo's tomb—a distinctive feature of much Italian Renaissance art—and the ease with which those not schooled in Greco-Roman art and literature could confuse antique heroes with Old and New Testament figures.

> The Dominican church in Venice has the tombs of many doges. Never have I beheld tombs so full of beauty and pomp. Not even the tombs of the popes in Rome stand up by comparison. The tombs are embedded in the wall above the floor and are completely covered in various marbles and sculptures and decorated in gold and silver more than is proper. There are images of Christ, the Blessed Virgin, the Apostles, martyrs and other saints all according to the wish of the patrons. . . . To the right of the church entrance I saw the precious tomb of [Doge Pietro Mocenigo], upon which is carved the image of Hercules fighting. He is portrayed as usual but is wearing the skin of a lion he has killed rather than a cloak. Then there is another image of Hercules wrestling the hydra, a fearful monster which immediately grows seven new heads as soon as one of the old ones is chopped off. . . . Many of these pagan images alternate with those of our redemption, and thus it is that simple souls, believing they are saints, worship Hercules, mistaking him for Samson, and Venus, taking her for Mary Magdalene, and so on.*

*Quoted by Wolfgang Wolters in Giandomencio Romanelli, ed., *Venice: Art & Architecture* (Cologne: Könemann, 2005), 202–203.

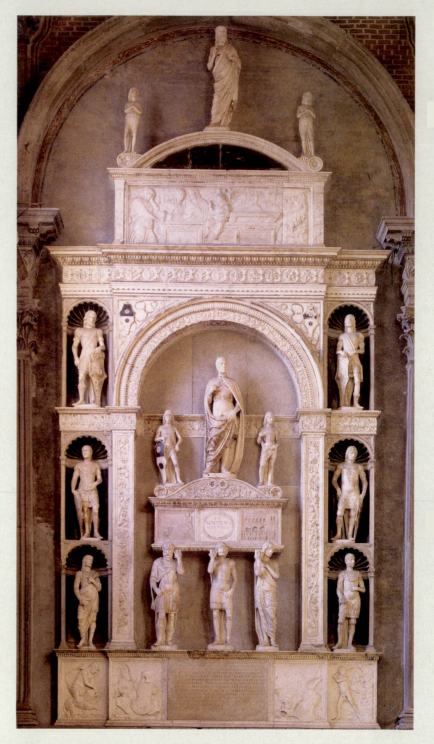

21-39 PIETRO LOMBARDO, tomb of Doge Pietro Mocenigo, Santi Giovanni e Paolo, Venice, 1476–1480.

This immense wall tomb by the leading Quattrocento Venetian sculptor and his sons presents Doge Pietro Mocenigo as a conquering warrior and incorporates both Christian and classical mythological themes.

primary waterway, the Grand Canal. The lowest floor—it cannot accurately be called the "ground" floor—has a simple loggia with wide bays for the unloading of goods from boats. Behind it is a corridor running the length of the house flanked by storerooms and a small courtyard and garden. (The palace was Contarini's warehouse as well as residence.) On the main (second) floor—the *piano nobile* ("noble floor")—were the public reception rooms behind a loggia

of ornate Late Gothic multilobed arches. The family's private chambers were on the third floor.

Detailed building accounts show that Contarini spared no expense in making his home a showcase of his wealth. He instructed painters to decorate the facade in white and blue enamel and stonemasons to oil the red Veronese marble blocks to make them shine brightly. Most of the intricately carved architectural ornamentation was gilded—hence the palace's longstanding nickname: Ca d'Oro (House of Gold). To achieve the look and quality he sought, Contarini hired artists from far and wide, including Matteo Raverti, one of the sculptors who worked at Milan Cathedral, and the French painter known in Italy as Zuan di Franza. The Ca d'Oro is a testimonial not only to Contarini's financial success but also to the survival of flowery Gothic taste in Venice at the same time that Filippo Brunelleschi was designing classically austere buildings (FIGS. 21-30 to 21-34) in Florence.

PIETRO LOMBARDO The leading sculptural workshop of Renaissance Venice was established around 1467 by PIETRO LOMBARDO (ca. 1435–1515), whose sons, Tullio and Antonio, continued to win major commissions in the 16th century. The specialty of the family workshop was funerary sculpture, particularly the grandiose wall tomb (compare FIG. 21-14). The basilica of Santi Giovanni e Paolo in Venice (next to which Colleoni's equestrian statue [FIG. 21-16] stands on a towering pedestal) became a showcase for their work. The church housed the wall tombs of several doges, of which probably the most impressive is that of Pietro Mocenigo (r. 1474–1476; FIG. **21-39**), carved by Pietro, assisted by his sons and others, between 1476 and 1481 (see "The Tomb of Doge Pietro Mocenigo," page 610).

GIOVANNI BELLINI In the 16th century, Venice emerged as one of three great centers of Renaissance painting in Italy, along with Florence and Rome. The man credited with establishing the Venetian High Renaissance school of painting was GIOVANNI BELLINI (ca. 1430–1516). Trained in the International Gothic style by his father, Jacopo, a student of Gentile da Fabriano (FIG. 21-17), Giovanni worked in the family shop and did not develop his own style until after his father's death in 1470 (see "Imitation and Emulation in Renaissance Art," page 594). His early independent works show the dominant influence of his brother-in-law Andrea Mantegna (FIGS. 21-48 to 21-50). But in the late 1470s, he came into contact with the work of the Sicilian-born painter Antonello da Messina (ca. 1430–1479). Antonello received his early training in Naples, where he must have encountered Flemish painting and mastered using mixed oil (see "Tempera and Oil Painting," page 559). This more flexible medium is wider in coloristic range than either tempera or fresco. Antonello arrived in Venice in 1475 and during his two-year stay introduced his Venetian colleagues to the possibilities that the new oil technique offered.

In *Saint Francis in the Desert* (FIG. **21-40**), Bellini's most famous work of this period, the Venetian master depicted the founder of the Franciscan order as a hermit in the wilderness—although not

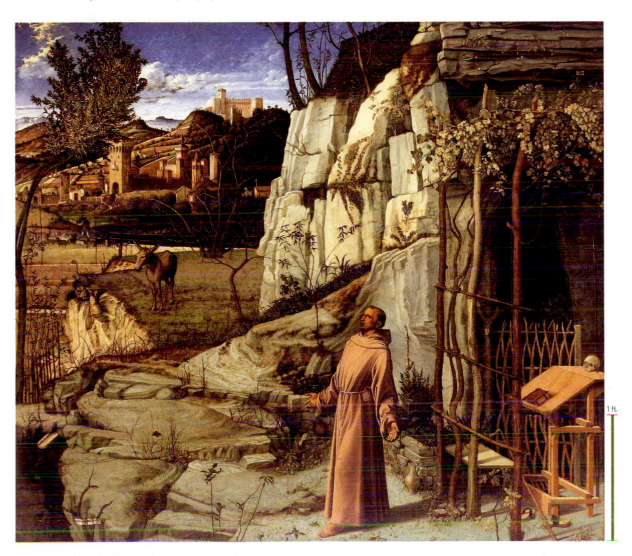

21-40 GIOVANNI BELLINI, *Saint Francis in the Desert*, ca. 1477–1479. Oil and tempera on wood, 4' 1" × 4' 7$\frac{7}{8}$".
Frick Collection, New York (Henry Clay Frick Bequest).

Mixing tempera and oil, Bellini depicted Saint Francis communing with God in a landscape filled with references to the crucifixion and to Moses, whom the Franciscans identified with their founder.

too far removed from the medieval Italian town that Bellini placed in the background. Saint Francis has stepped out of his cave home, where he has set up beneath a grape bower a simple wooden desk with a skull on it (symbolic of the crucifixion and the blood of Christ). He spreads his arms, displaying his *stigmata,* the marks of his identification with Christ (see page 416), and gazes skyward at a burst of golden light (at the upper left corner of the panel) that signals God's presence.

Emulating Netherlandish masters, Bellini filled his painting of Saint Francis's ecstatic communion with God with symbols and allusions. The Franciscans viewed their founding saint as a new Moses, who had communed with God in the desert before the burning bush, perhaps alluded to by the windblown tree before the burst of light. Certainly, the water trickling from a spout in the rocks at the lower left beneath the quivering tree is a reference to the water that miraculously appeared when Moses struck the rock at Mount Horeb with his staff. Francis also stands barefoot (his sandals are beside his desk), just as Moses did in the desert when God commanded him to remove his shoes because he stood on sacred ground. The donkey, a traditional symbol of patience appropriate for a hermit saint, may also refer to Francis's description of his own body as Brother Ass.

Bellini painted *Saint Francis in the Desert* using a mixture of tempera and oil, following the lead of Antonello da Messina. He soon became a master of the new medium and developed a sensuous coloristic manner destined to characterize Venetian painting of the 16th century (see page 650).

THE PRINCELY COURTS

The governments, churches, guilds, and merchants of the republics of Florence and Venice were not the only sponsors of the "rebirth" of art in Quattrocento Italy. The "princely courts" in Rome, Urbino, Mantua, and elsewhere were also instrumental in nurturing Renaissance art, whether the "prince" was a duke, marquis, count, condottiere, or pope. In the 15th century, princely courts proliferated throughout the Italian peninsula (MAP 14-1), notably in Rome and the papal states (FIGS. 21-40A, 21-41, and 21-42), Milan, Naples, Ferrara, Savoy, Urbino (FIGS. 21-43, 21-44, and 21-44A), and Mantua (FIGS. 21-45 to 21-50).

The efficient functioning of a princely court required a sophisticated administrative structure. Each prince employed an extensive household staff, ranging from counts, nobles, cooks, waiters, stewards, footmen, stable hands, and ladies-in-waiting to dog handlers, leopard keepers, pages, and runners. The duke of Milan had more than 40 chamberlains to attend to his personal needs alone. Each prince also needed an elaborate bureaucracy to oversee political, economic, and military operations and to ensure his continued control. These officials included secretaries, lawyers, captains, ambassadors, and condottieri. Burgeoning international diplomacy and trade made each prince the center of an active and privileged sphere. Their domains extended to the realm of culture, for they saw themselves as more than political, military, and economic leaders (see "Art in the Princely Courts of Renaissance Italy," page 613).

Rome and the Papal States

Although not a secular ruler, the pope in Rome was the head of a court with enormous wealth at his disposal. With the election of a French pope in 1305 (see "The Great Schism," page 415), however, papal commissions in Rome had ceased, and for more than a century, the once-glorious city became an artistic backwater. Even with the succession of Martin V (r. 1417–1431) and the return of papal power to Rome from Avignon, significant papal patronage did not resume immediately. Upon his election in 1471, however, Pope Sixtus IV (r. 1471–1484) initiated a major building campaign in Rome that included the restoration of churches, bridges, streets, and aqueducts; the construction in 1475 of a new papal library in the Vatican; and a new chapel bearing his name (the Sistine Chapel; FIG. 22-1).

PERUGINO Between 1481 and 1483, Sixtus IV summoned a group of artists to Rome to decorate the walls of his new chapel. Among the artists the pope employed were Botticelli, Ghirlandaio, and Pietro Vannucci, known as PERUGINO (ca. 1450–1523) after his birthplace—Perugia, in Umbria. The project followed immediately the completion of the new Vatican library, which the pope also ordered decorated with frescoes by MELOZZO DA FORLÌ (1438–1494; FIG. 21-40A) and others. Perugino's contribution to the Sistine Chapel fresco cycle was *Christ Delivering the Keys of the Kingdom to Saint Peter* (FIG. 21-41). The papacy had, from the beginning,

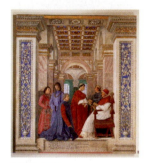

🔼 **21-40A** MELOZZO DA FORLÌ, *Sixtus IV Confirming Platina,* ca. 1477–1481.

based its claim to infallible and total authority over the Roman Catholic Church on this biblical event, and therefore the subject was one of obvious appeal to Sixtus IV.

In Perugino's fresco, Christ hands the keys to Saint Peter, who stands amid an imaginary gathering of the 12 apostles and Renaissance contemporaries. These figures occupy the apron of a great stage space that extends into the distance to a point of convergence in the doorway of a central-plan temple. (Perugino used parallel and converging lines in the pavement to mark off the intervening space; compare FIG. 21-9.) The smaller figures in the middle distance enhance the sense of depth and also act out important New Testament stories—for example (at the left), the episode of Jesus, Peter, and the tribute money (compare FIG. 21-18).

At the corners of the great piazza, duplicate triumphal arches serve as the base angles of a distant compositional triangle whose apex is in the central building. Perugino modeled the arches closely on the Arch of Constantine (FIG. 7-73) in Rome. Although anachronisms in a painting depicting a scene from Jesus's life, the arches served to underscore the close ties between Saint Peter and Constantine, the first Christian emperor of Rome and builder of the great basilica (FIG. 8-9) over Saint Peter's tomb. In fact, the inscriptions on the arches compare Sixtus IV to Constantine. Christ and Peter flank the triangle's central axis, which runs through the temple's doorway, the vanishing point of Perugino's perspective scheme. Brunelleschi's new spatial science enabled the Umbrian artist to organize the action systematically. The composition interlocks both two-dimensional and three-dimensional space, and the placement of central actors emphasizes the axial center.

LUCA SIGNORELLI Another Umbrian painter whom Sixtus IV employed for the decoration of the Sistine Chapel was LUCA SIGNORELLI (ca. 1445–1523), in whose work the fiery passion of Savonarola's sermons found its pictorial equal. Signorelli further

Art in the Princely Courts of Renaissance Italy

As the wealthiest individuals in their regions, Renaissance princes possessed the means to commission numerous artworks and buildings. In addition to being a source of visual pleasure, art functioned in several capacities in the princely courts—as evidence of princely sophistication and culture, as a form of prestige or commemoration, as a demonstration of wealth, and even as propaganda. For example, in the mural (FIG. 21-41) that Pope Sixtus IV commissioned Perugino to paint for the Sistine Chapel in the Vatican, the subject chosen glorified the papacy itself.

Princes and their advisers carefully researched the reputations and styles of the artists and architects they employed because the quality of the work reflected not solely on the artist but on the patron as well. Sometimes, princes bestowed on selected individuals the title of "court artist." Serving as a court artist had its benefits, among them a guaranteed salary (not always paid), living quarters in the palace, liberation from guild restrictions, and, on occasion, status as a member of the prince's inner circle, perhaps even a knighthood. For artists struggling to elevate their profession from the ranks of craftspeople, working for a prince presented an unparalleled opportunity. Until the 16th century, artists had limited status, and most people considered them in the same class as small shopkeepers and petty merchants. Indeed, at court dinners, artists usually sat with the other members of the salaried household: tailors, cobblers, barbers, and upholsterers. Thus the possibility of social advancement was a powerful and constant incentive in addition to the income received from princely commissions.

In return for the salaries and lofty titles they offered, princes demanded a great deal from court artists. Artists not only created the frescoes, portraits, and sculptures that have become their legacies but also designed tapestries, seat covers, costumes, masks, and decorations for various court festivities. Because princes constantly received ambassadors and dignitaries and needed to maintain a high profile to reinforce their authority, lavish social functions were the norm. Artists often created gifts for visiting nobles and potentates. Recipients judged these gifts on the quality of both the work and the materials. By using expensive materials—gold leaf, silver leaf, lapis lazuli (a rich azure-blue stone imported from Afghanistan), silk, and velvet brocade—and employing the best artists—princes could impress others with their wealth and good taste.

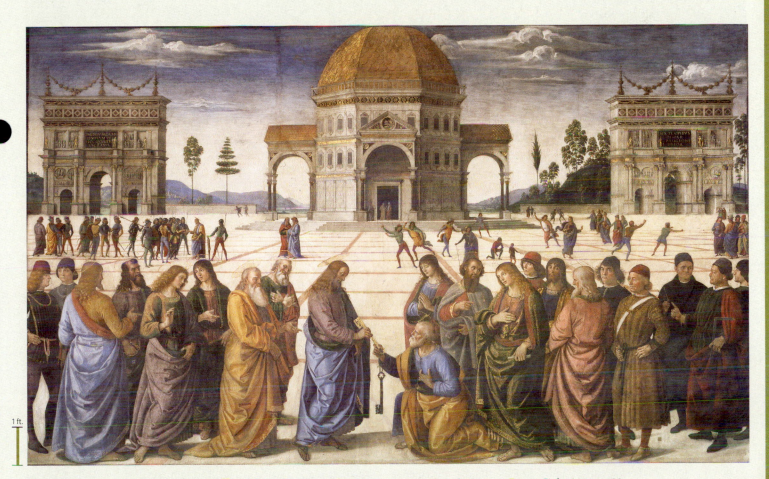

1 ft.

21-41 PERUGINO, *Christ Delivering the Keys of the Kingdom to Saint Peter*, Sistine Chapel, Vatican, Rome, Italy, 1481–1483. Fresco, 11' $5\frac{1}{2}$" × 18' $8\frac{1}{2}$".

Painted for the Vatican, this fresco depicts the event on which the papacy bases its authority. The converging lines of the pavement connect the action in the foreground with the background.

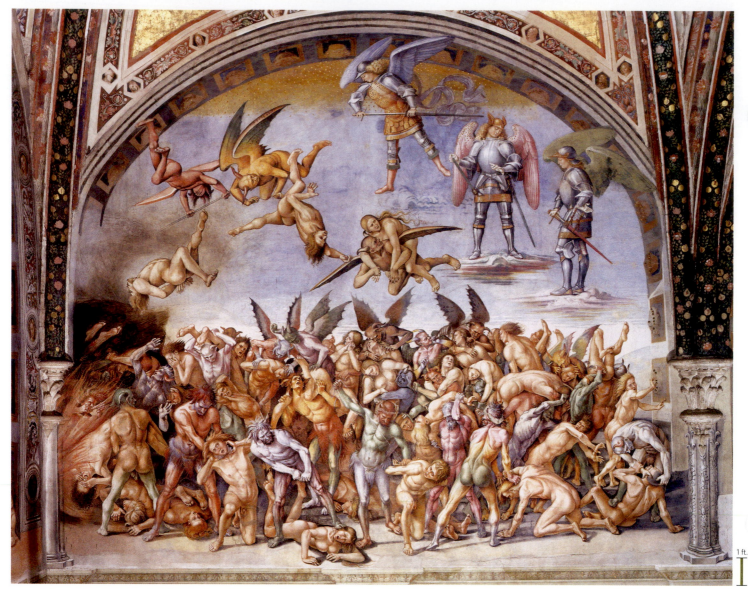

21-42 Luca Signorelli, *The Damned Cast into Hell,* San Brizio chapel, Orvieto Cathedral, Orvieto, Italy, 1499–1502. Fresco, 23' wide.

Few figure compositions of the 15th century match the psychic impact of Signorelli's fresco in Orvieto Cathedral showing writhing, foreshortened muscular bodies tortured by demons in Hell.

developed Pollaiuolo's interest in the depiction of muscular bodies in violent action in a wide variety of poses and foreshortenings. In the San Brizio chapel in the cathedral (FIG. 14-13) of the papal city of Orvieto (MAP 14-1), Signorelli painted for Pope Alexander VI (r. 1492–1503) scenes depicting the end of the world, including *The Damned Cast into Hell* (FIG. **21-42**). Few Quattrocento figure compositions equal Signorelli's in psychic impact. Saint Michael and the hosts of Heaven hurl the damned into Hell, where, in a dense, writhing mass, they are vigorously tortured by demons, some winged. The horrible consequences of a sinful life had not been so graphically depicted since Gislebertus carved his vision of the Last Judgment (FIG. 12-15) in the west *tympanum* of Saint-Lazare at Autun around 1130. The figures—nude, lean, and muscular—assume every conceivable posture of anguish. Signorelli was a master both of foreshortening the human figure and depicting bodies in violent movement. Although each figure is clearly a study from a model, Signorelli incorporated the

individual studies into a convincing and coherent narrative composition. Terror and rage pass like storms through the wrenched and twisted bodies. The fiends, their hair flaming and their bodies the color of putrefying flesh, lunge at their victims in ferocious frenzy.

Urbino

Under the patronage of the condottiere Duke Federico da Montefeltro (1422–1482), Urbino, southeast of Florence across the Apennines (MAP 14-1), became an important center of Renaissance art and culture. In fact, the humanist writer Paolo Cortese (1465–1540) described Federico as one of the two greatest artistic patrons of the 15th century (the other was Cosimo de' Medici). Federico was so renowned for his military expertise that he was in demand by popes and kings, and soldiers came from across Europe to study under his direction.

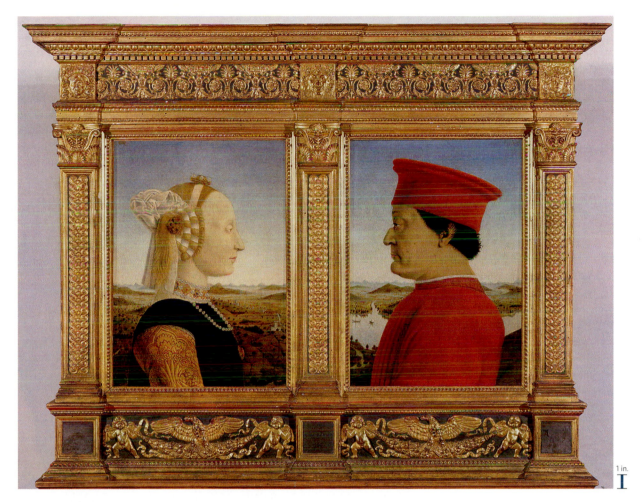

21-43 PIERO DELLA FRANCESCA, *Battista Sforza and Federico da Montefeltro*, ca. 1472–1474. Oil and tempera on wood in modern frame, each panel 1' 6½" × 1' 1". Galleria degli Uffizi, Florence.

Piero's portraits of Federico da Montefeltro and his recently deceased wife, Battista Sforza, combine the profile views on Roman coins with the landscape backgrounds of Flemish portraiture (FIG. 20-14).

PIERO DELLA FRANCESCA One of the artists who received several commissions from Federico was Piero della Francesca, who had already established a major reputation in his native Tuscany (FIGS. 21-25 and 21-25A). Among the works Piero produced for Federico is a double portrait (FIG. **21-43**) of the count and his second wife, Battista Sforza (1446–1472), whom he married in 1460 when she was 14 years old. The daughter of Alessandro Sforza (1409–1473), lord of Pesaro and brother of the duke of Milan (see page 620), Battista was a well-educated humanist who proved to be an excellent administrator of Federico's territories during his frequent military campaigns. She gave birth to eight daughters in 11 years and finally, on January 25, 1472, to the male heir for which the couple had prayed. When the countess died of pneumonia five months later at age 26, Federico went into mourning for virtually the rest of his life. He never remarried.

Federico commissioned Piero della Francesca to paint their double portrait shortly after Battista's death to pay tribute to her and to have a memento of their marriage. The present frame is a 19th-century addition. Originally, the two portraits formed a hinged diptych. The format—two bust-length portraits with a landscape background—followed Flemish models, such as the portraits by Hans Memling (FIGS. 20-14 and 20-14A), as did Piero's use of oil-based pigment (see "Tempera and Oil Painting," page 559). Piero would have been familiar with the latest artistic developments in northern Europe because Federico employed Flemish painters at his court. But Piero depicted the Urbino count and countess in profile, in part to emulate the profile portraits on Roman coins (FIGS. 7-10 and 7-79, *left*) that Renaissance humanists avidly collected, and in part to conceal the disfigured right side of Federico's face. (He lost his right eye and part of the bridge of his nose in a tournament in 1450.) That injury also explains why Federico is on the right in left profile (compare FIG. 21-44). Roman coins normally show the emperor in right profile, and Renaissance marriage portraits almost always place the husband at the viewer's left.

Piero probably based Battista's portrait on her death mask, and the pallor of her skin may be a reference to her death. Latin inscriptions on the reverse of the two portraits refer to Federico in the present tense and to Battista in the past tense, confirming the posthumous date of her portrait. The backs of the panels (not illustrated) also bear paintings. They represent Federico and Battista in triumphal chariots accompanied by personifications of their respective virtues, including Justice, Prudence, and Fortitude (Federico) and Faith, Charity, and Chastity (Battista). The placement of scenes of triumph on the reverse of profile portraits also emulates ancient Roman coinage.

21-44 Piero della Francesca, *Enthroned Madonna and Saints Adored by Federico da Montefeltro* (*Brera Altarpiece*), ca. 1472–1474. Oil on wood, 8' 2" × 5' 7". Pinacoteca di Brera, Milan.

The illusionism of Piero's *Brera Altarpiece* is so convincing that the viewer is compelled to believe in Federico da Montefeltro's presence before the Virgin Mary, Christ Child, and saints.

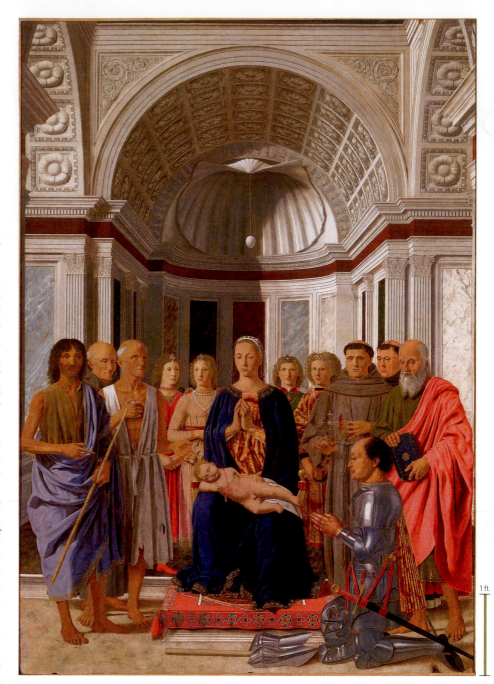

1 ft.

BRERA ALTARPIECE Federico also appears in left profile in Piero's altarpiece (FIG. 21-44) now in the collection of the Brera Pinacoteca (picture gallery) in Milan. The condottiere, clad in armor, kneels piously at the feet of the enthroned Madonna. Directly behind him stands Saint John the Evangelist, his patron saint. Where the viewer would expect to see Federico's wife (on the lower left, kneeling and facing her husband), no figure is present. Battista had died shortly before Federico commissioned Piero to paint the *Brera Altarpiece*. Thus her absence clearly announced his loss. Piero further called attention to it by depicting Saint John the Baptist, Battista's patron saint, at the far left. The ostrich egg suspended from a shell over Mary's head was common over altars dedicated to the Virgin. The figures appear in the space below the intersection of illusionistically painted coffered barrel vaults, perhaps corresponding to part of the interior of the church of San Bernadino degli Zoccolanti near Urbino, the painting's intended location. If so, the viewer would be compelled to believe in Federico's presence in the church before the Virgin, Christ Child, and saints.

The *Brera Altarpiece* reveals Piero's deep interest in the properties of light and color. In his effort to make the clearest possible distinction among forms, he flooded his pictures with light, imparting a silver-blue tonality. To avoid heavy shadows, he illuminated the dark sides of his forms with reflected light. By moving the darkest tones of his modeling toward the centers of his volumes, he separated shapes from their backgrounds. Because of this technique, Piero's paintings lack some of Masaccio's relieflike qualities but gain in spatial clarity, as each shape forms an independent unit surrounded by an atmospheric envelope and moveable to any desired position, akin to a figure on a chessboard. The precise placement of figures in space also characterizes Piero's most difficult-to-interpret painting, *Flagellation* (FIG. 21-44A), which he may also have painted for Federico da Montefeltro.

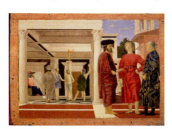

▶ **21-44A** Piero della Francesca, *Flagellation*, ca. 1455–1465.

Mantua

Marquis Ludovico Gonzaga (1412–1478) ruled the court of Mantua in northeastern Italy (MAP 14-1) during the mid-15th century. A famed condottiere like Federico da Montefeltro, Gonzaga established his reputation as a fierce military leader while general of the Milanese armies. The visit of Pope Pius II (r. 1458–1464) to Mantua in 1459 stimulated the marquis's determination to transform his city into one that all Italy would envy.

SANT'ANDREA One of the major projects Gonzaga instituted was the redesign of the church of Sant'Andrea (FIGS. 21-45 to 21-47) to replace an 11th-century church. Gonzaga turned to the renowned architect Leon Battista Alberti (FIGS. 21-36A and 21-37) for this important commission. The facade (FIG. 21-45) that Alberti designed incorporated two major ancient Roman architectural motifs—the

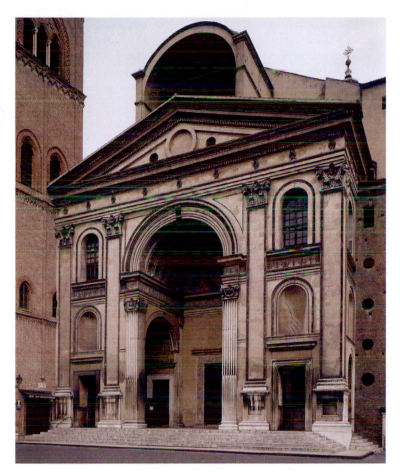

Alberti's design for Sant'Andrea reflects his study of ancient Roman architecture. Employing a colossal order, the architect combined a triumphal arch and a Roman temple front with pediment.

temple front and the triumphal arch. The combination was already a familiar feature of Roman buildings still standing in Italy. For example, many triumphal arches, including a late-first-century BCE arch at Rimini on Italy's northeast coast, feature a pediment over the arcuated passageway and engaged columns, but there is no close parallel in antiquity for Alberti's eclectic and ingenious design. The Renaissance architect's concern for proportion (see "Alberti's *On the Art of Building,*" page 608) led him to equalize the vertical and horizontal dimensions of the facade, which left it considerably shorter than the church behind it. Because of the primary importance of visual appeal, many Renaissance architects made this concession not only to the demands of a purely visual proportionality in the facade but also to the facade's relation to the small square in front of it, even at the expense of continuity with the body of the building. Yet structural correspondences to the building do exist in Sant'Andrea's facade. The pilasters are the same height as those on the nave's interior walls; and the large barrel vault over the central portal, with smaller barrel vaults branching off at right angles, introduces on a smaller scale the arrangement of the church's nave and chapels (FIGS. **21-46** and **21-47**). The facade pilasters, as part of the wall, run uninterrupted

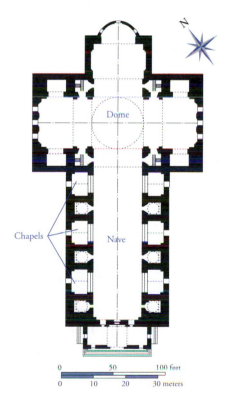

21-46 LEON BATTISTA ALBERTI, plan of Sant'Andrea, Mantua, Italy, designed 1470, begun 1472.

In *On the Art of Building,* Alberti criticized the traditional basilican plan as impractical. He designed Sant'Andrea as a single huge hall with independent chapels branching off at right angles.

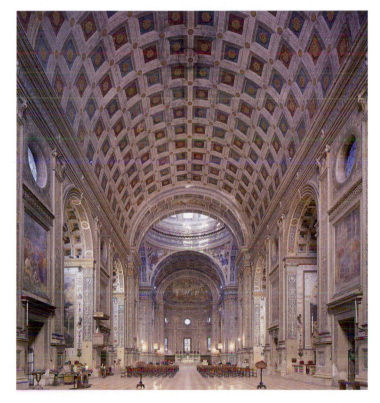

21-47 LEON BATTISTA ALBERTI, interior of Sant'Andrea (looking east), Mantua, Italy, designed 1470, begun 1472.

For the nave of Sant'Andrea, Alberti abandoned the traditional columnar arcade. The tremendous vaults suggest that Constantine's Basilica Nova (FIG. 7-76) in Rome may have served as a prototype.

through three stories in an early application of the *colossal* or *giant order* (pilasters that extend through more than one level) that became a favorite motif of Michelangelo (FIG. 22-25).

The tremendous vaults in the interior of Sant'Andrea suggest that Alberti's model may have been Constantine's Basilica Nova (FIG. 7-76) in Rome—erroneously thought in the Middle Ages and Renaissance to be a Roman temple. Consistent with his belief that arches should not be used with freestanding columns (see page 608), Alberti abandoned the medieval columnar arcade that Brunelleschi still used in San Lorenzo (FIG. 21-31) and Santo Spirito (FIG. 21-31A). Thick walls alternating with vaulted chapels, interrupted by a massive dome over the crossing, support the huge coffered barrel vault. Because FILIPPO JUVARA (1678–1736) added the present dome in the 18th century, the effect may be somewhat different from what Alberti planned. Regardless, the vault calls to mind the vast interior spaces and dense enclosing masses of Roman architecture. In *On the Art of Building,* Alberti criticized the traditional basilican plan (with continuous aisles flanking the central nave) as impractical because the colonnades conceal

the ceremonies from the faithful in the aisles. For this reason, he designed a single huge hall (FIG. 21-47) with independent chapels branching off at right angles (FIG. 21-46). This break with a Christian building tradition that had endured for a thousand years was extremely influential in later Renaissance and Baroque church planning.

ANDREA MANTEGNA Like other princes, Ludovico Gonzaga believed that it was important to surround himself with humanist scholars and talented artists, and he made Mantua one of Europe's leading cultural centers. The marquis also knew that an impressive palace was an important visual expression of his authority. One of the most spectacular rooms in the Palazzo Ducale (Ducal Palace) is Ludovico's bedchamber and audience hall, the so-called Camera degli Sposi (Room of the Newlyweds), originally the Camera Picta (Painted Chamber; FIG. 21-48). ANDREA MANTEGNA (ca. 1431–1506) of Padua took almost nine years to complete the extensive fresco program in which he sought to glorify Ludovico Gonzaga and his family. The particulars of each scene are still a matter

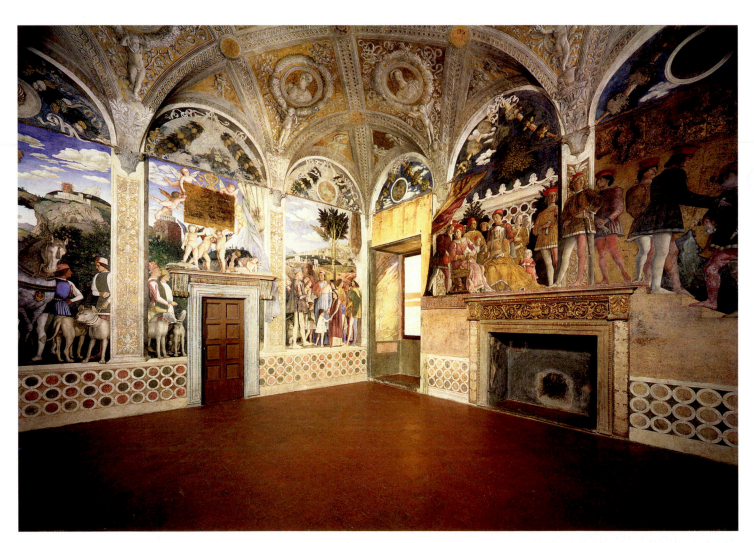

21-48 ANDREA MANTEGNA, interior of the Camera Picta (Painted Chamber), Palazzo Ducale, Mantua, Italy, 1465–1474. Fresco.

Working for Ludovico Gonzaga, who established Mantua as a great art city, Mantegna produced for the duke's palace the first completely consistent illusionistic decoration of an entire room.

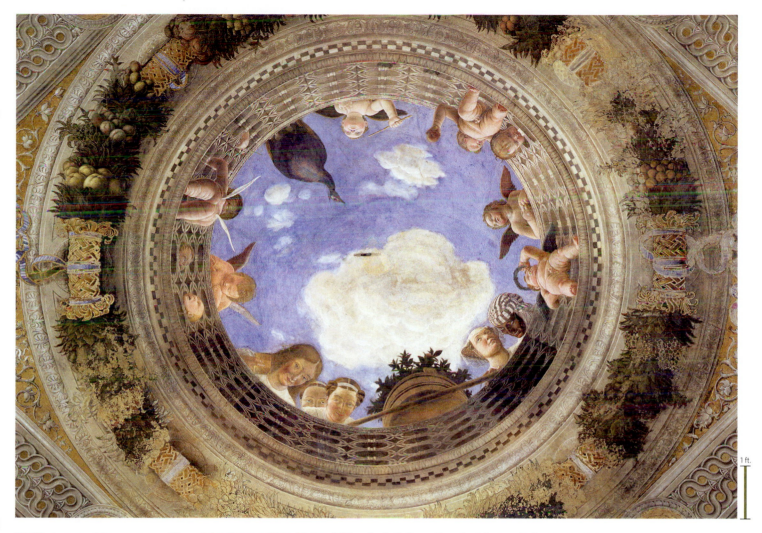

21-49 ANDREA MANTEGNA, ceiling of the Camera Picta (Painted Chamber), Palazzo Ducale, Mantua, Italy, 1465–1474. Fresco, 8' 9" in diameter.

Inside the Camera Picta, the viewer becomes the viewed as figures gaze into the room from a painted oculus opening onto a blue sky. This is the first perspective view of a ceiling from below.

of scholarly debate, but any viewer standing in the Camera Picta surrounded by the spectacle and majesty of courtly life cannot help but be thoroughly impressed by both the commanding presence and elevated status of the patron and the dazzling artistic skills of Mantegna.

In the Camera Picta, Mantegna performed a triumphant feat by producing the first completely consistent illusionistic decoration of an entire room. By integrating real and painted architectural elements, Mantegna illusionistically dissolved the room's walls in a manner foretelling 17th-century Baroque decoration (see page 720). The Camera Picta recalls the efforts more than 15 centuries earlier by Italian painters on the Bay of Naples to merge mural painting and architecture in frescoes of the so-called Second Style of Roman painting (FIGS. 7-18 and 7-19). Mantegna's *trompe l'oeil* (French, "deceives the eye") design, however, went far beyond anything preserved from ancient Italy. The Renaissance painter's daring experimentalism led him to complete the room's decoration with the first perspective of a ceiling (FIG. 21-49) seen from below (called, in Italian, *di sotto in sù*, "from below upward"). Baroque ceiling decorators (FIGS. 24-22 to 24-24) later broadly developed this technique. Inside the Camera Picta, the viewer becomes the viewed as figures

look down into the room from the painted *oculus* ("eye"). Seen against the convincing illusion of a cloud-filled blue sky, several putti, strongly foreshortened, set the amorous mood of the Room of the Newlyweds, as the painted spectators (who are not identified and include an exotic black man wearing a turban) smile down on the scene. The prominent peacock, perched precariously as if ready to swoop down into the room, is an attribute of Juno, Jupiter's bride, who oversees lawful marriages. This brilliant feat of illusionism is the climax of decades of experimentation with perspective representation by numerous Quattrocento artists as well as by Mantegna himself—for example, in his frescoes (FIG. 21-49A) in the Church of the Eremitani (Church of the Hermits) in Padua.

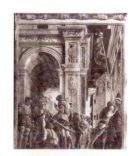

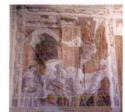

⬈ **21-49A** MANTEGNA, *Saint James Led to Martyrdom*, 1454–1457.

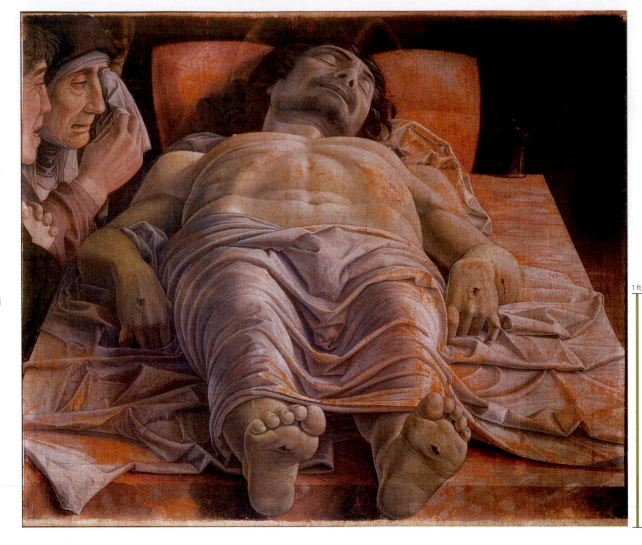

21-50 ANDREA MANTEGNA, *Foreshortened Christ* (*Lamentation over the Dead Christ*), ca. 1500. Tempera on canvas, 2' 2¾" × 2' 7⅞". Pinacoteca di Brera, Milan.

In this work of overwhelming emotional power, Mantegna presented both a harrowing study of a strongly foreshortened cadaver and an intensely poignant depiction of a biblical tragedy.

1 ft.

FORESHORTENED CHRIST One of Mantegna's later paintings (FIG. 21-50) is another example of the artist's mastery of perspective. In fact, Mantegna seems to have set up for himself difficult problems in perspective simply for the joy he took in solving them. The painting often called *Lamentation over the Dead Christ* but recorded under the name *Foreshortened Christ* at the time of Mantegna's death is a work of overwhelming power. At first glance, as its 16th-century title implies, this painting seems to be a strikingly realistic study in foreshortening. Careful examination, however, reveals that Mantegna reduced the size of Christ's feet, which, as he surely knew, would cover much of the body if properly represented according to the rules of perspective, in which the closest objects, people, or body parts are the largest. Thus, tempering naturalism with artistic license, Mantegna presented both a harrowing study of a strongly foreshortened cadaver and an intensely poignant depiction of a biblical tragedy. Remarkably, in the supremely gifted

hands of Mantegna, all of Quattrocento science here served the purpose of devotion.

Milan

The leading city of northwestern Italy at this time was Milan (MAP 14-1), ruled by the powerful Sforza family, which also sought to lure the best artists to its court. In 1481, Ludovico Sforza (1451–1508) accepted a proposal from Leonardo da Vinci that the famed artist leave Florence for Milan to work for the Milanese court as military engineer, architect, sculptor, and painter. Several of Leonardo's early masterworks, including his world-famous *Last Supper* (FIG. 22-4), date to the closing years of the 15th century when he was in Milan. A discussion of those works opens the examination of the High Renaissance in Italy in Chapter 22.

THE RENAISSANCE IN QUATTROCENTO ITALY

Florence

- The fortunate coming together of artistic genius, the spread of humanism, and economic prosperity nourished the flowering of the new artistic culture that historians call the Renaissance—the rebirth of classical values in art and life. The greatest center of Renaissance art in the 15th century was Florence, home of the powerful Medici, who were among the most ambitious art patrons in history.

- Some of the earliest examples of the new Renaissance style in sculpture are the statues that Nanni di Banco and Donatello made for Or San Michele. Donatello's later *David*, which emulates classical contrapposto, was the first nude male statue since antiquity. Donatello was also a pioneer in relief sculpture, the first to incorporate the principles of linear and atmospheric perspective, devices also employed brilliantly by Lorenzo Ghiberti in his *Gates of Paradise*.

- The Renaissance interest in classical culture naturally also led to the revival of Greco-Roman mythological themes in art—for example, Antonio del Pollaiuolo's *Hercules and Antaeus*—and to the revival of equestrian portraits, such as Donatello's *Gattamelata* and Andrea del Verrocchio's *Bartolommeo Colleoni*.

- Although some painters continued to work in the late medieval International Gothic style, others broke fresh ground by exploring new modes of representation. Masaccio's figures recall Giotto's, but have a greater psychological and physical credibility, and the light shining on Masaccio's figures comes from a source outside the picture. His *Holy Trinity* owes its convincing illusionism to Filippo Brunelleschi's new science of linear perspective.

- The secular side of Quattrocento Italian painting is on display in historical works, such as Paolo Uccello's *Battle of San Romano,* and in portraiture—for example, Domenico Ghirlandaio's *Giovanna Tornabuoni*. The humanist love of classical themes comes to the fore in the works of Sandro Botticelli, whose lyrical *Primavera* and *Birth of Venus* were inspired by poetry and Neo-Platonic philosophy.

- Italian architects also revived the classical style. Brunelleschi's San Lorenzo conforms to a strict modular scheme and showcases the Roman-inspired rationality of 15th-century Florentine architecture. The treatise of the ancient Roman architect Vitruvius was the model for Leon Battista Alberti's *On the Art of Building*.

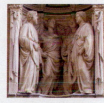

Nanni di Banco, *Four Crowned Saints*, ca. 1410–1414

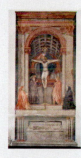

Masaccio, *Holy Trinity*, ca. 1424–1427

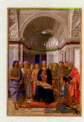

Brunelleschi, San Lorenzo, ca. 1421–1469

Venice and the Princely Courts

- Quattrocento architecture in Venice was still essentially Late Gothic, but at the end of the century, Giovanni Bellini founded the Venetian High Renaissance school of painting, which rivaled the schools of Florence and Rome.

- Among the important papal commissions of the Quattrocento was the decoration of the walls of the Sistine Chapel with frescoes, including Perugino's *Christ Delivering the Keys of the Kingdom to Saint Peter*, a prime example of the application of Renaissance linear perspective.

- Under the patronage of Federico da Montefeltro, Urbino became a major center of Renaissance art and culture. The leading painter in Federico's employ was Piero della Francesca, a master of color and light and the author of the first theoretical treatise on perspective.

- Mantua became an important art center under Marquis Ludovico Gonzaga, who commissioned Alberti to rebuild the church of Sant'Andrea. Alberti applied the principles that he had developed in his architectural treatise to the project and freely adapted forms from Roman religious and civic architecture. Gonzaga also hired Andrea Mantegna, who painted the Camera Picta of the ducal palace, producing the first completely consistent illusionistic decoration of an entire room.

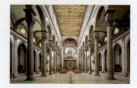

Piero della Francesca, *Brera Altarpiece*, ca. 1472–1474

Alberti, Sant'Andrea, Mantua, 1470

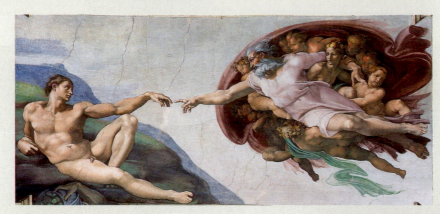

22-1a Michelangelo, the Renaissance genius who was primarily a sculptor, reluctantly spent almost four years painting the ceiling of the Sistine Chapel under commission from Pope Julius II.

22-1b The fresco cycle illustrates the creation and fall of humankind as related in Genesis. Michelangelo always painted with a sculptor's eye. His heroic figures resemble painted statues.

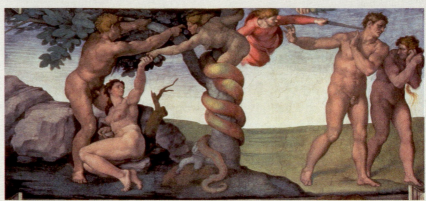

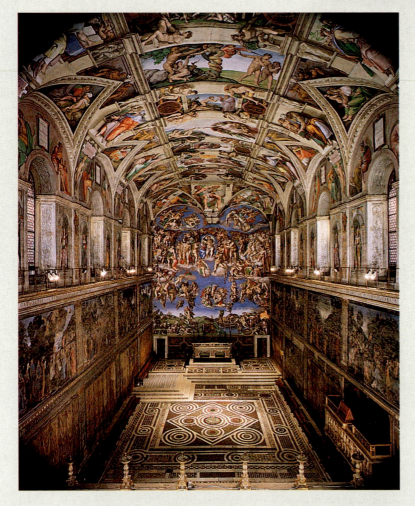

22-1 Interior of the Sistine Chapel (looking west), Vatican City, Rome, Italy, built 1473; ceiling and altar wall frescoes by MICHELANGELO BUONARROTI, 1508–1512 and 1536–1541, respectively.

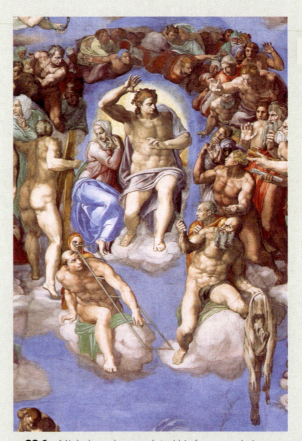

▲ 22-1c Michelangelo completed his fresco cycle in the Sistine Chapel for another pope—Paul III—with this terrifying vision of the fate awaiting sinners. The Last Judgment includes his self-portrait.

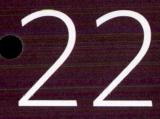

22

FRAMING THE ERA

Renaissance and Mannerism in Cinquecento Italy

MICHELANGELO IN THE SERVICE OF JULIUS II

The first artist in history whose exceptional talent and brooding personality matched today's image of the temperamental artistic genius was MICHELANGELO BUONARROTI (1475–1564). The Florentine artist's self-imposed isolation, creative furies, proud independence, and daring innovations led Italians of his era to speak of the charismatic personality of the man and the expressive character of his works in one word—*terribilità,* the sublime shadowed by the fearful. Yet, unlike most modern artists, who create works in their studios and offer them for sale later, Michelangelo and his contemporaries produced most of their paintings and sculptures under contract for wealthy patrons who dictated the content—and sometimes the form—of their artworks.

In Italy in the 1500s—the *Cinquecento*—the greatest art patron was the Catholic Church headed by the pope in Rome. Michelangelo's most famous work today—the ceiling of the Sistine Chapel (FIG. **22-1**) in the Vatican—was, in fact, a commission he did not want. His patron was Julius II (r. 1503–1513), an immensely ambitious man who sought to extend his spiritual authority into the temporal realm, as other medieval and Renaissance popes had done. Julius selected his name to associate himself with Julius Caesar and found inspiration in ancient Rome. His enthusiasm for engaging in battle earned Julius the designation "warrior-pope," but his ten-year papacy was most notable for his patronage of the arts. Julius fully appreciated the propagandistic value of visual imagery and, upon his election, immediately commissioned artworks that would present an authoritative image of his rule and reinforce the primacy of the Catholic Church.

When Julius asked Michelangelo to take on the challenge of providing frescoes for the ceiling of the Sistine Chapel, the artist insisted that painting was not his profession—a protest that rings hollow after the fact, but Michelangelo's major works until then had been in sculpture. The artist had no choice, however, but to accept the pope's assignment.

In the Sistine Chapel frescoes, as in his sculptures, Michelangelo relentlessly concentrated his expressive purpose on the human figure. To him, the body was beautiful not only in its natural form but also in its spiritual and philosophical significance. The body was the manifestation of the character of the soul. In the *Creation of Adam, Fall of Man,* and *Last Judgment* frescoes, Michelangelo represented the body in its most elemental aspect—in the nude or simply draped, with almost no background and no ornamental embellishment. He always painted with a sculptor's eye for how light and shadow reveal volume and surface. It is no coincidence that many of the figures in the Sistine Chapel seem to be painted statues.

HIGH AND LATE RENAISSANCE

The art and architecture of 16th-century Italy built on the foundation of the Early Renaissance of the 15th century, but no single artistic style characterized Italian 16th-century art, and regional differences abounded, especially between central Italy (Florence and Rome) and Venice. The period opened with the brief era that art historians call the High Renaissance—the quarter century between 1495 and the deaths of Leonardo da Vinci in 1519 and Raphael in 1520. The Renaissance style and the interest in classical culture, perspective, proportion, and human anatomy dominated the remainder of the 16th century (the Late Renaissance), but a new style, called *Mannerism,* challenged Renaissance naturalism almost as soon as Raphael had been laid to rest (inside the ancient Roman Pantheon, FIG. 7-51). The one constant in Cinquecento Italy is the astounding quality, both technical and aesthetic, of the art and architecture produced.

Indeed, the modern notion of the "fine arts" and the exaltation of the artist-genius originated in Renaissance Italy. Humanist scholars and art patrons alike eagerly adopted the ancient Greek philosopher Plato's view of the nature of poetry and of artistic creation in general: "All good poets . . . compose their beautiful poems not by art, but because they are inspired and possessed. . . . For not by art does the poet sing, but by power divine."[1] In Cinquecento Italy, the pictorial arts achieved the high status formerly held only by poetry, and painters and sculptors became international celebrities for the first time. None achieved greater fame than Leonardo da Vinci, Raphael, and Michelangelo, the three greatest masters of the High Renaissance, although even they could not create totally freely but had to satisfy the wishes of their patrons (see "Michelangelo in the Service of Julius II," page 623).

Leonardo da Vinci

Born in the small town of Vinci, near Florence, LEONARDO DA VINCI (1452–1519) trained in the studio of Andrea del Verrocchio (FIGS. 21-12 and 21-16). The quintessential "Renaissance man," Leonardo possessed unequaled talent and an unbridled imagination. Art was but one of his innumerable interests, the scope and depth of which were without precedent. His unquenchable curiosity is evident in the voluminous notes he interspersed with sketches in his notebooks dealing with botany, geology, geography, cartography, zoology, military engineering, animal lore, anatomy, and aspects of physical science, including hydraulics and mechanics. Leonardo stated repeatedly that his scientific investigations made him a better painter. That is undoubtedly the case. For example, Leonardo's in-depth exploration of optics provided him with a thorough understanding of perspective, light, and color. Leonardo was a true artist-scientist. Indeed, his scientific drawings (FIG. 22-6) are themselves artworks.

Leonardo's great ambition in his painting, as well as in his scientific endeavors, was to discover the laws underlying the processes and flux of nature. With this end in mind, he also studied the human body and contributed immeasurably to the fields of physiology and psychology. Leonardo believed that reality in an absolute sense is inaccessible and that humans can know it only through its changing images. He considered the eyes the most vital organs and sight the most essential function. Better to be deaf than blind, he argued, because through the eyes, individuals can grasp reality most directly and profoundly.

LEONARDO IN MILAN In 1482, Leonardo left Florence for Milan after offering his services to Ludovico Sforza (1451–1508). The political situation in Florence was uncertain, and Leonardo must have felt that his particular skills would be in greater demand in one of Italy's princely courts (see "Art in the Princely Courts of Renaissance Italy," page 613). He clearly believed that the Sforza court in Milan could provide him with increased financial security. The letter that Leonardo wrote to Ludovico seeking employment in Milan is preserved and is, at first sight, surprising. The Florentine artist devoted most of the letter to advertising his qualifications as a military engineer, mentioning only at the end his abilities as a painter and sculptor. The letter illustrates the breadth of Leonardo's competence and also underscores the decisive role that individual patrons played in the history of Renaissance art.

> And in short, according to the variety of cases, I can contrive various and endless means of offense and defense. . . . In time of peace I believe I can give perfect satisfaction and to the equal of any other in architecture and the composition of buildings, public and private; and in guiding water from one place to another. . . . I can carry out sculpture in marble, bronze, or clay, and also I can do in painting whatever may be done, as well as any other, be he whom he may.[2]

That Leonardo selected expertise in military engineering as his primary attraction for the Sforzas is an index of the period's instability. In any event, Ludovico accepted Leonardo's offer, although he did not give the Florentine artist a salaried position until several years later. Leonardo remained in Milan for the next 17 years, during which he created the masterpieces that are the basis for his lofty reputation then and now.

MADONNA OF THE ROCKS Shortly after settling in Milan, Leonardo painted *Madonna of the Rocks* (FIG. **22-2**) as the central panel of an altarpiece for the chapel of the Confraternity of the Immaculate Conception in San Francesco Grande. Leonardo presented the Madonna, Christ Child, infant John the Baptist, and angel in a pyramidal grouping. The four figures pray, point, and bless, and these

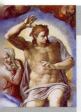

RENAISSANCE AND MANNERISM IN CINQUECENTO ITALY

1495–1520
- Leonardo da Vinci paints *Last Supper* in Milan and *Mona Lisa* in Florence
- High Renaissance art emerges in Rome under Pope Julius II
- Raphael paints *School of Athens* for the papal apartments
- Michelangelo carves *David* for the Palazzo della Signoria in Florence and paints the ceiling of the Sistine Chapel in Rome

1520–1550
- Paul III launches the Counter-Reformation
- Michelangelo paints *Last Judgment* in the Sistine Chapel
- In Venice, Titian uses rich colors and establishes oil on canvas as the preferred medium of Western painting
- Mannerism emerges as an alternative to High Renaissance style in the work of Pontormo, Parmigianino, Bronzino, and Giulio Romano

1550–1575
- The Council of Trent defends religious art
- Andrea Palladio becomes chief architect of the Venetian Republic
- Giorgio Vasari publishes his *Lives* of the leading Italian painters, sculptors, and architects, from Cimabue to Titian

1575–1600
- Tintoretto is the leading Venetian Mannerist painter
- Veronese creates a huge illusionistic ceiling painting for the Doge's Palace
- Giovanni da Bologna uses spiral compositions for Mannerist statuary groups
- The Jesuits construct Il Gesù in Rome

ARTISTS ON ART

Leonardo and Michelangelo on Painting versus Sculpture

Both Leonardo da Vinci and Michelangelo produced work in a variety of artistic media, earning enviable reputations not just as painters and sculptors but also as architects. The two disagreed, however, on the relative merits of the different media. In particular, Leonardo, with his intellectual and analytical mind, preferred painting (FIGS. 22-2, 22-4, and 22-5) to sculpture, which he regarded as lowly manual labor. In contrast, Michelangelo, who worked in a more intuitive manner, saw himself primarily as a sculptor. Two excerpts from their writings reveal their positions on the relationship between the two media.

Leonardo da Vinci wrote the following in his so-called *Treatise on Painting*:

> Painting is a matter of greater mental analysis, of greater skill, and more marvelous than sculpture, since necessity compels the mind of the painter to transform itself into the very mind of nature, to become an interpreter between nature and art. Painting justifies by reference to nature the reasons of the pictures which follow its laws: in what ways the images of objects before the eye come together in the pupil of the eye; which, among objects equal in size, looks larger to the eye; which, among equal colors will look more or less dark or more or less bright; which, among things at the same depth, looks more or less low; which, among those objects placed at equal height, will look more or less high, and why, among objects placed at various distances, one will appear less clear than the other.

> This art comprises and includes within itself all visible things such as colors and their diminution, which the poverty of sculpture cannot include. Painting represents transparent objects but the sculptor will show you the shapes of natural objects without artifice. The painter will show you things at different distances with variation of color due to the air lying between the objects and the eye; he shows you mists through which visual images penetrate with difficulty; he shows you rain which discloses within it clouds with mountains and valleys; he shows the dust which discloses within it and beyond it the combatants who stirred it up; he shows streams of greater or lesser density; he shows fish playing between the surface of the water and its bottom; he shows the polished pebbles of various colors lying on the washed sand at the bottom of rivers, surrounded by green plants; he shows the stars at various heights above us, and thus he achieves innumerable effects which sculpture cannot attain.*

As if in response, although decades later, Michelangelo wrote these excerpts in a letter to Benedetto Varchi (1502–1565), a Florentine poet best known for his 16-volume history of Florence:

> I believe that painting is considered excellent in proportion as it approaches the effect of relief, while relief is considered bad in proportion as it approaches the effect of painting.

> I used to consider that sculpture was the lantern of painting and that between the two things there was the same difference as that between the sun and the moon. But . . . I now consider that painting and sculpture are one and the same thing.

> Suffice that, since one and the other (that is to say, both painting and sculpture) proceed from the same faculty, it would be an easy matter to establish harmony between them and to let such disputes alone, for they occupy more time than the execution of the figures themselves. As to that man [Leonardo] who wrote saying that painting was more noble than sculpture, if he had known as much about the other subjects on which he has written, why, my serving-maid would have written better![†]

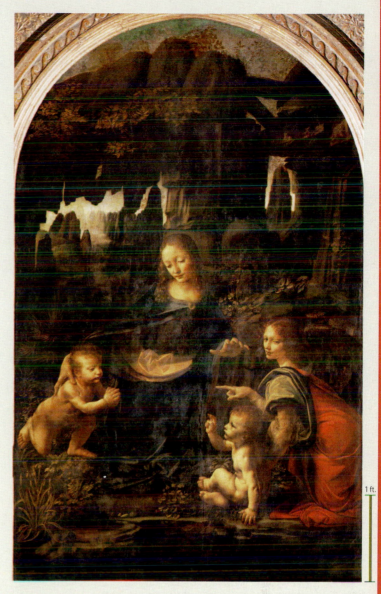

22-2 LEONARDO DA VINCI, *Madonna of the Rocks*, from San Francesco Grande, Milan, Italy, 1483–1490. Oil on wood (transferred to canvas), 6' 6$\frac{1}{2}$" × 4'. Musée du Louvre, Paris.

In this groundbreaking work, Leonardo demonstrated the oil painter's ability to represent all the figures sharing the same light-infused environment, something impossible to achieve in sculpture.

---

*Leonardo da Vinci, *Treatise on Painting*, 51, Robert Klein and Henri Zerner, *Italian Art 1500–1600. Sources and Documents* (Evanston, Ill.: Northwestern University Press, 1966), 7–8.
[†]Michelangelo to Benedetto Varchi, Rome, 1549. Klein and Zerner, 13–14.

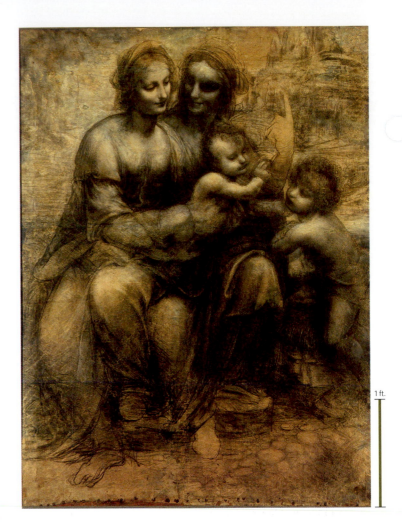

22-3 LEONARDO DA VINCI, cartoon for *Madonna and Child with Saint Anne and the Infant Saint John*, ca. 1505–1507. Charcoal heightened with white on brown paper, 4' 6" × 3' 3". National Gallery, London.

In this cartoon for a painting of the Madonna and Child and two saints, Leonardo drew a scene of tranquil grandeur filled with monumental figures reminiscent of classical statues of goddesses.

acts and gestures, although their meanings are uncertain, visually unite the individuals portrayed. The angel points to the infant John and, through his outward glance, involves the viewer in the tableau. John prays to the Christ Child, who blesses him in return. The Virgin herself completes the series of interlocking gestures, her left hand reaching toward the Christ Child and her right hand resting protectively on John's shoulder. The melting mood of tenderness, which the caressing light enhances, suffuses the entire composition. Indeed, Leonardo's most notable achievement in *Madonna of the Rocks* was to paint the figures as sharing the same environment. Leonardo built on Masaccio's understanding and usage of *chiaroscuro,* the subtle play of light and dark. The biblical figures emerge through nuances of light and shade from the half-light of the mysterious cavernous landscape. Light simultaneously veils and reveals the forms, immersing them in a layer of atmosphere. Leonardo's groundbreaking achievement—the unified representation of objects in an atmospheric setting—was a manifestation of his scientific curiosity about the invisible substance surrounding things. It was also in large part due to his mastery of the relatively new medium of oil painting, which had previously been used mostly by northern European painters (see "Tempera and Oil Painting," page 559). Oil-based pigments enabled Leonardo to realize the full potential of the painter's craft, which he considered superior to sculpture (see "Leonardo and Michelangelo on Painting versus Sculpture," page 625). By creating an emotionally compelling, visually unified,

and spatially convincing image, Leonardo achieved what he believed to be the two chief goals of a good painter: "to paint man and the intention of his soul. The former is easy, the latter hard, for it must be expressed by gestures and the movement of the limbs."[3]

***MADONNA AND CHILD* CARTOON** Leonardo's style fully emerges in *Madonna and Child with Saint Anne and the Infant Saint John* (FIG. 22-3), a preliminary drawing (*cartoon*) for a painting (see

22-4 LEONARDO DA VINCI, *Last Supper*, ca. 1495–1498. Oil and tempera on plaster, 13' 9" × 29' 10". Refectory, Santa Maria delle Grazie, Milan.

Jesus has just announced that one of his disciples will betray him, and each one reacts. He is both the psychological focus of Leonardo's fresco and the focal point of all the converging perspective lines.

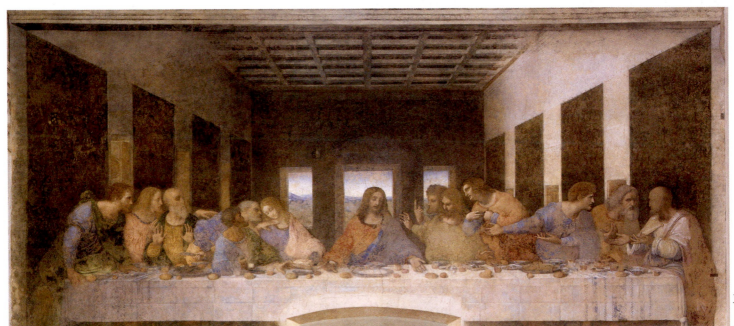

"Renaissance Drawings," page 628) he made in 1505 or shortly thereafter. Here, the glowing light falls gently on the majestic forms in a scene of tranquil grandeur and balance. Leonardo ordered every part of his cartoon with an intellectual pictorial logic that results in an appealing visual unity. The figures are robust and monumental, the stately grace of their movements reminiscent of the Greek statues of goddesses (FIG. 5-49) in the pediments of the Parthenon. However, Leonardo's infusion of the principles of classical art into his designs cannot be attributed to specific knowledge of Greek monuments. He and his contemporaries never visited Greece. Their acquaintance with classical art extended only to Etruscan and Roman monuments, Roman copies of Greek statues in Italy, and ancient texts describing Greek and Roman works of art and architecture.

LAST SUPPER For Ludovico Sforza, Leonardo painted *Last Supper* (FIG. 22-4) in the refectory of the church of Santa Maria delle Grazie in Milan. Both formally and emotionally, *Last Supper* is Leonardo's most impressive work. It is also his largest. On the wall opposite a *Crucifixion* with portraits of Ludovico and his family, Leonardo painted Jesus and his 12 disciples sitting at a long table placed parallel to the picture plane in a simple, spacious room. The austere setting amplifies the painting's highly dramatic action. Jesus, with outstretched hands, has just said, "One of you is about to betray me" (Matt. 26:21). A wave of intense excitement passes through the group as each disciple asks himself and, in some cases, his neighbor, "Is it I?" (Matt. 26:22). Leonardo visualized a sophisticated coupling of the dramatic "One of you is about to betray me" with the initiation of the ancient liturgical ceremony of the Eucharist, when Jesus, blessing bread and wine, said, "This is my body, which is given for you. Do this for a commemoration of me. . . . This is the chalice, the new testament in my blood, which shall be shed for you" (Luke 22:19–20).

In the center, Jesus appears isolated from the disciples and in perfect repose, the calm eye of the swirling emotion around him. The central window at the back, whose curved pediment arches above his head, frames his figure. The pediment is the only curve in the architectural framework, and it serves here, along with the diffused light, as a halo. Jesus's head is the focal point of all converging perspective lines in the composition. Thus the still, psychological focus and cause of the action is also the perspective focus, as well as the center of the two-dimensional surface. In Leonardo's *Last Supper*, the two-dimensional, the three-dimensional, and the psychodimensional focuses are the same.

Leonardo presented the agitated disciples in four groups of three, united among and within themselves by the figures' gestures and postures. The artist sacrificed traditional iconography to pictorial and dramatic consistency by placing Judas on the same side of the table as Jesus and the other disciples (compare FIG. 21-22). Judas's face is in shadow (the light source in the painting corresponds to the windows in the Milanese refectory). He clutches a money bag in his right hand as he reaches his left forward to fulfill Jesus's declaration: "But yet behold, the hand of him that betrayeth me is with me on the table" (Luke 22:21). The two disciples at the table ends are quieter than the others, as if to bracket the energy of the composition, which is more intense closer to Jesus, whose serenity both halts and intensifies it. The disciples register a broad range of emotional responses, including fear, doubt, protestation, rage, and love. Leonardo's numerous preparatory studies—using live models—suggest that he thought of each figure as carrying a particular charge and type of emotion. Like a stage director, he read the Gospel story carefully, and scrupulously cast his actors as the Bible described their roles. In this work, as in his other religious paintings, Leonardo revealed his extraordinary ability to apply his voluminous knowledge about the observable world to the pictorial representation of a religious scene, resulting in a psychologically complex and compelling painting.

Leonardo's *Last Supper* is unfortunately in poor condition today, even after the completion in 1999 of a cleaning and restoration project lasting more than two decades. In a bold experiment in mural painting, instead of using fresco, which has a matte surface, Leonardo mixed oil and tempera, and applied much of it *a secco* (to dried, rather than wet, plaster) in order to create a surface appearance that more closely approximated oil painting on canvas or wood. But because the wall did not absorb the pigment as in the *buon fresco* technique, the paint quickly began to flake (see "Fresco Painting," page 419). The humidity of Milan further accelerated the deterioration. The restoration involved extensive scholarly, chemical, and computer analysis. Like similar projects elsewhere, however, most notably in the Sistine Chapel (FIGS. 22-1 and 22-18B), this one was not without controversy. One scholar has claimed that 80 percent of what is visible today is the work of the modern restorers, not Leonardo.

MONA LISA Leonardo's *Mona Lisa* (FIG. 22-5) is probably the world's most famous portrait. In his biography of Leonardo, Vasari

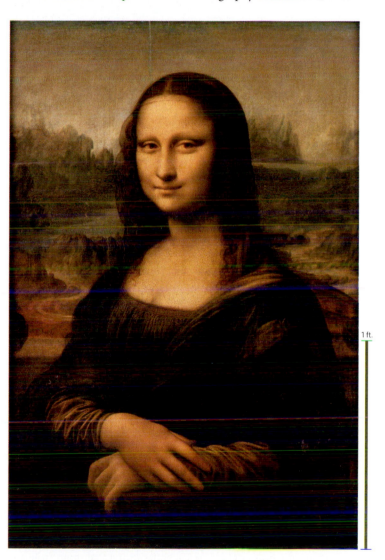

1 ft.

22-5 LEONARDO DA VINCI, *Mona Lisa*, ca. 1503–1505. Oil on wood, 2' 6¼" × 1' 9". Musée du Louvre, Paris.

Leonardo's skill with chiaroscuro and atmospheric perspective is on display in this new kind of portrait depicting the sitter as an individual personality who engages the viewer psychologically.

MATERIALS AND TECHNIQUES
Renaissance Drawings

In Cinquecento Italy, drawing assumed a position of greater artistic prominence than ever before. Until the late 15th century, the expense of drawing surfaces and their lack of availability limited the production of preparatory sketches. Most artists drew on *parchment* (prepared from the skins of calves, sheep, and goats) or on *vellum* (made from the skins of young animals; FIG. 13-36). Because of the high cost of these materials, drawings in the 14th and 15th centuries tended to be extremely detailed and meticulously executed. Artists often drew using a silverpoint stylus (FIG. 20-1) because of the fine line it produced and the sharp point it maintained. The introduction in the late 15th century of less expensive paper made of fibrous pulp produced for the developing printing industry (see "Printed Books," page 577) enabled artists to experiment more and to draw with greater freedom. As a result, sketches proliferated. Artists executed these drawings in pen and ink (FIGS. **22-5A** and **22-6**), chalk, charcoal (FIG. 22-3), brush, and graphite or lead.

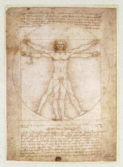

⬈22-5A LEONARDO, *Vitruvian Man*, ca. 1485–1490.

During the Renaissance, the importance of drawing transcended the mechanical or technical possibilities that it afforded artists. The Italian term for drawing—*disegno*—refers also to design, an integral component of good art. Design was the foundation of art, and drawing was the fundamental element of design. In his 1607 treatise *L'idea de' pittori, scultori ed architteti*, Federico Zuccari (1542–1609), director of the Accademia di San Luca (Academy of Saint Luke), the Roman painting academy, summed up this philosophy when he stated that drawing is the external physical manifestation (*disegno esterno*) of an internal intellectual idea or design (*disegno interno*).

The design dimension of art production became increasingly important as artists cultivated their own styles. The early stages of artistic training largely focused on imitation and emulation (see "Imitation and Emulation," page 594), but to achieve widespread recognition, artists had to develop their own styles. Although the artistic community and public at large acknowledged technical skill, the conceptualization of the artwork—its theoretical and formal development—was paramount. Disegno, or design in this case, represented

an artist's conceptualization and intention. In the Italian literature of the period, the terms often invoked to praise esteemed artists included *invenzione* (invention), *ingegno* (innate talent), *fantasia* (imagination), and *capriccio* (originality).

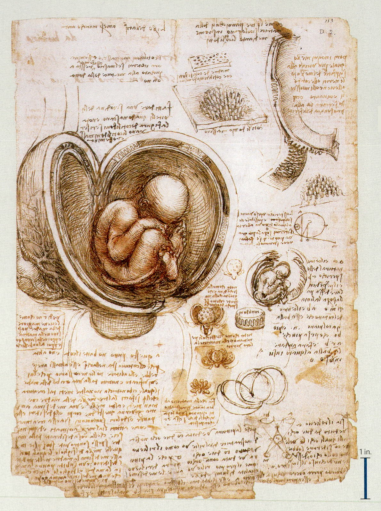

22-6 LEONARDO DA VINCI, *The Fetus and Lining of the Uterus*, ca. 1511–1513. Pen and ink with wash over red chalk and traces of black chalk on paper, $1' \times 8\frac{5}{8}"$. Royal Library, Windsor Castle.

The introduction of less expensive paper in the late 15th century enabled artists to draw more frequently. Leonardo's analytical anatomical studies exemplify the scientific spirit of the Renaissance.

(see "Giorgio Vasari's *Lives*," page 636) identified the woman portrayed as Lisa di Antonio Maria Gherardini, the wife of Francesco del Giocondo, a wealthy Florentine—hence, "Mona (an Italian contraction of *ma donna*, "my lady") Lisa." Unlike earlier portraits, Leonardo's representation of Gherardini, who was about 25 years old when she posed for Leonardo, does not serve solely as an icon of status. Indeed, Gherardini wears no jewelry and holds no attribute associated with wealth. Leonardo's concern was rather to paint a convincing representation of a specific individual, both in terms of appearance and personality. Mona Lisa sits quietly, her hands folded, her mouth forming a gentle smile, and her gaze directed at the viewer. Renaissance etiquette dictated that a woman should not look directly into a man's eyes. Leonardo's portrayal of this self-assured young woman without the trappings of power but engaging

the audience psychologically is unprecedented and accounts in large part for the painting's unparalleled reputation today.

The enduring appeal of *Mona Lisa* also derives from Leonardo's decision to set his subject against the backdrop of a mysterious uninhabited landscape. This setting, with roads and bridges seemingly leading nowhere, recalls that of his *Madonna of the Rocks* (FIG. 22-2). The composition also resembles Fra Filippo Lippi's *Madonna and Child with Angels* (FIG. 21-24) with figures seated in front of a window through which the viewer glimpses a distant landscape. Originally, the artist represented Gherardini in a loggia. A later owner trimmed the painting, eliminating the columns, but partial column bases remain to the left and right of Mona Lisa's shoulders.

The painting is darker today than 500 years ago, and the colors are less vivid, but *Mona Lisa* still reveals Leonardo's fascination and skill with chiaroscuro and atmospheric perspective. The portrait is a prime example of the artist's famous smoky *sfumato* (misty haziness)—his subtle adjustment of light and blurring of precise planes.

ANATOMICAL STUDIES *Mona Lisa* is also exceptional because Leonardo completed very few paintings. His perfectionism, relentless experimentation, and far-ranging curiosity diffused his efforts. However, the drawings (see "Renaissance Drawings," page 628) in his notebooks preserve an extensive record of his ideas. His interests focused increasingly on science in his later years, and he embraced knowledge of all facets of the natural world. His investigations in anatomy, based in part on dissection, yielded drawings of great precision and beauty of execution. *The Fetus and Lining of the Uterus* (FIG. 22-6), although it does not meet 21st-century standards for accuracy (for example, Leonardo regularized the uterus's shape to a sphere, and his characterization of the lining is incorrect), was an astounding achievement in its day. Leonardo's analytical anatomical studies exemplify the scientific spirit of the Renaissance, establishing that era as a prelude to the modern world and setting it in sharp contrast to the preceding Middle Ages. Although Leonardo may not have been the first scientist of the modern world (at least not in today's sense of the term), he did originate the modern method of scientific illustration incorporating *cutaway* views. Scholars have long recognized the importance of his drawings for the development of anatomy as a science, especially in an age predating photographic methods such as X-rays.

ARCHITECTURE AND SCULPTURE Leonardo also won renown in his time as both architect and sculptor, although no extant buildings or sculptures can be definitively attributed to him. Like many of his contemporaries, he studied the ancient Roman architectural treatise by Vitruvius (see "Vitruvius's *Ten Books on Architecture*," page 199, and FIG. 22-5A). From his many drawings of central-plan structures (FIG. **22-6A**), it is evident that he shared the interest of other Renaissance architects in this building type. As for Leonardo's sculptures, numerous drawings of monumental equestrian statues survive, and he made a full-scale model for a monument to Francesco Sforza (1401–1466), Ludovico's father. The French used the statue as a target and shot it to pieces when they occupied Milan in 1499. The defacement of ruler portraits, documented at least as far back as the third millennium BCE (FIG. 2-12), is eloquent testimony to the power of images in public life.

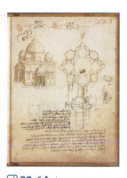

22-6A LEONARDO, central-plan church, ca. 1487–1490.

Leonardo left Milan when the French captured the city. He served for a while as a military engineer for Cesare Borgia (1476–1507), who, with the support of his father, Pope Alexander VI (r. 1492–1503), tried to conquer the cities of the Romagna region in north-central Italy and create a Borgia duchy. Leonardo eventually returned to Milan in the service of the French. At the invitation of King Francis I (see "Francis I, Royal Art Patron and Collector," page 693), he then went to France, where he died at the château of Cloux in 1519.

Raphael

Alexander VI's successor was Julius II. Among the many projects that the ambitious new pope sponsored were a design for a modern Saint Peter's (FIGS. 22-22 and 22-23) to replace the timber-roofed fourth-century basilica (FIG. 8-9), the decoration of the papal apartments (FIG. 22-9), and the construction of his tomb (FIGS. 22-14 and 22-15), in addition to commissioning Michelangelo to paint the Sistine Chapel ceiling (see "Michelangelo in the Service of Julius II," page 623, and FIG. 22-1).

In 1508, Julius II called Raffaello Santi (or Sanzio), known as RAPHAEL (1483–1520) in English, to the papal court in Rome, which would soon displace Florence, Urbino, and Mantua as the leading Italian patron of art and architecture (see "Art in the Princely Courts of Renaissance Italy," page 613). Born in a small town in Umbria near Urbino, Raphael probably learned the rudiments of his art from his father, Giovanni Santi (d. 1494), a painter connected with the ducal court of Federico da Montefeltro (see page 614), before entering the studio of Perugino (FIG. 21-41) in Perugia. Although strongly influenced by Perugino, Leonardo, and others, Raphael developed an individual style that embodied the ideals of High Renaissance art. Although he died at an early age, Raphael completed a large body of work, and several of his assistants became leaders of the next generation of Italian artists, extending his influence well into the century.

MARRIAGE OF THE VIRGIN Among Raphael's early works is *Marriage of the Virgin* (FIG. **22-7**), which he painted for the chapel of Saint Joseph in the church of San Francesco in Città di Castello,

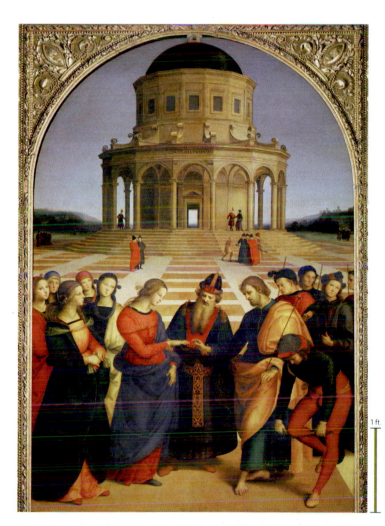

22-7 RAPHAEL, *Marriage of the Virgin,* from the Albizzini chapel, San Francesco, Città di Castello, Italy, 1504. Oil on wood, 5' 7" × 3' 10½". Pinacoteca di Brera, Milan.

In this early work depicting the marriage of the Virgin to Saint Joseph, Raphael demonstrated his mastery of foreshortening and of the perspective system he learned from Perugino (FIG. 21-41).

southeast of Florence. The subject was a fitting one for Saint Joseph (see "Early Christian Saints," page 236). According to the *Golden Legend* (a 13th-century collection of stories about the lives of the saints), Joseph competed with other suitors for Mary's hand. The high priest was to give the Virgin to whichever suitor presented to him a rod that had miraculously bloomed. Raphael depicted Joseph with his flowering rod in his left hand. In his right hand, Joseph holds the wedding ring he is about to place on Mary's finger. Other virgins congregate at the left, and the unsuccessful suitors stand on the right. One of them breaks his rod in half over his knee in frustration, giving Raphael an opportunity to demonstrate his mastery of foreshortening. The perspective system he used is the one he learned from Perugino (compare FIG. 21-41). The temple in the background is Raphael's version of a centrally planned building, featuring Brunelleschian arcades (FIG. 21-30).

MADONNA IN THE MEADOW Raphael spent the four years from 1504 to 1508 in Florence. There, still in his early 20s, he discovered that the painting style he had learned so painstakingly from Perugino was already outmoded (as was Brunelleschi's Early Renaissance architectural style). Florentine crowds flocked to the church of Santissima Annunziata to see Leonardo's recently unveiled cartoon of the Virgin, Christ Child, Saint Anne, and Saint John (probably an earlier version of FIG. 22-3). Under Leonardo's influence, Raphael began to modify the Madonna compositions he had employed in Umbria. In *Madonna in the Meadow* (FIG. 22-8) of 1505–1506, Raphael adopted Leonardo's pyramidal composition and modeling of faces and figures in subtle chiaroscuro. Yet the Umbrian artist placed the large, substantial figures in a Peruginesque landscape, with his former master's typical feathery trees in the middle ground. Although Raphael experimented with Leonardo's dusky modeling, he tended to return to Perugino's lighter tonalities and blue skies. Raphael preferred clarity to obscurity, not fascinated, as Leonardo was, with mystery. Raphael quickly achieved fame for his Madonnas, which depict Mary as a beautiful young mother tenderly interacting with her young son. In *Madonna of the Meadow*, Mary almost wistfully watches Jesus play with John the Baptist's cross-shaped staff, as if she has a premonition of how her son will die. Raphael's work, as well as Leonardo's, deeply influenced the slightly younger ANDREA DEL SARTO (1486–1530), whose most famous painting is *Madonna of the Harpies* (FIG. 22-8A).

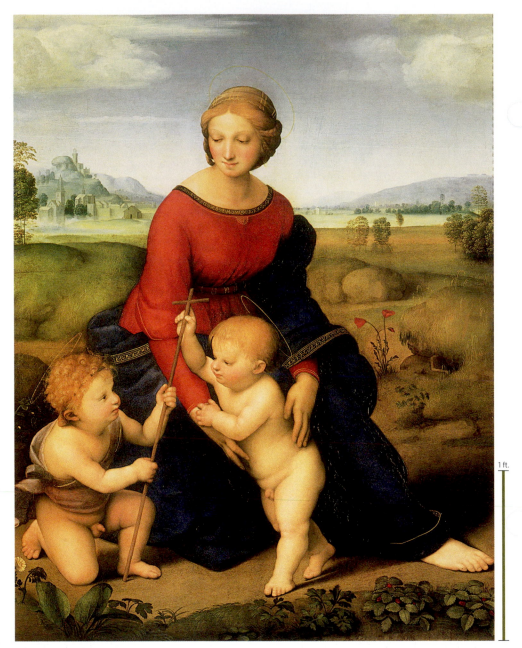

22-8 RAPHAEL, *Madonna in the Meadow*, 1505–1506. Oil on wood, 3' 8$\frac{1}{2}$" × 2' 10$\frac{1}{4}$". Kunsthistorisches Museum, Vienna.

Emulating Leonardo's pyramidal composition (FIG. 22-2) but rejecting his dusky modeling and mystery, Raphael set his Madonna in a well-lit landscape and imbued her with grace, dignity, and beauty.

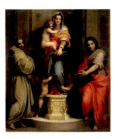

🔲 **22-8A** ANDREA DEL SARTO, *Madonna of the Harpies*, 1517.

SCHOOL OF ATHENS Three years after completing *Madonna in the Meadow*, Raphael received one of the most important painting commissions that Julius II awarded—the decoration of the papal apartments in the Apostolic Palace of the Vatican (MAPS 22-1 and 24-1). Of the suite's several rooms (*stanze*), Raphael painted the room that came to be called the Stanza della Segnatura (Room of the Signature—Julius's papal library, where later popes signed official documents) and the Stanza d'Eliodoro (Room of Heliodorus—the pope's private audience room, named for one of the paintings there). His pupils completed the others following his sketches. On the four walls of the Stanza della Segnatura, Raphael presented images symbolizing the four branches of human knowledge and wisdom under the headings *Theology*, *Law* (*Justice*), *Poetry*, and *Philosophy*—the learning required of a Renaissance pope. Given Julius II's desire for recognition as both a spiritual and temporal leader, the *Theology*

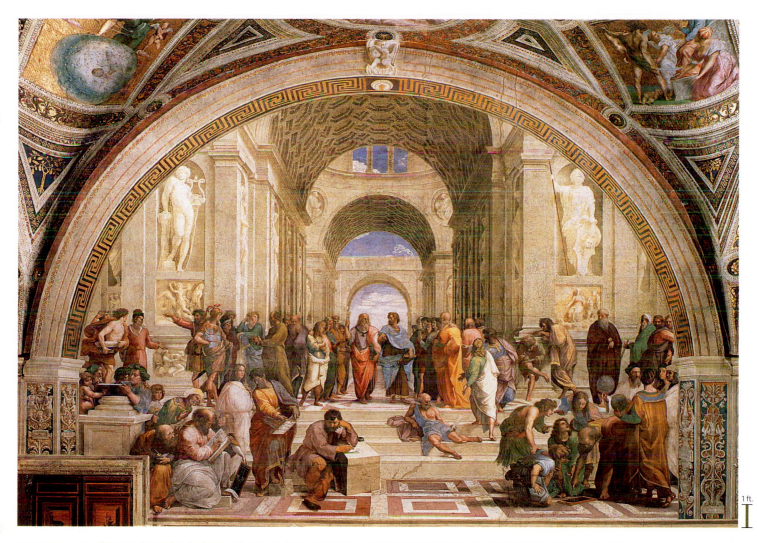

22-9 RAPHAEL, *Philosophy* (*School of Athens*), Stanza della Segnatura, Apostolic Palace, Vatican City, Rome, Italy, 1509–1511. Fresco, 19' × 27'.

Raphael included himself in this gathering of great philosophers and scientists whose self-assurance conveys calm reason. The setting recalls the massive vaults of the ancient Basilica Nova (FIG. 7-76).

and *Philosophy* frescoes face each other. The two images present a balanced picture of the pope—as a cultured, knowledgeable individual and as a wise, divinely ordained religious authority.

In Raphael's *Philosophy* mural (commonly called *School of Athens*, FIG. **22-9**), the setting is not a "school" but a congregation of the great philosophers and scientists of the ancient world. Raphael depicted these luminaries, revered by Renaissance humanists, conversing and explaining their various theories and ideas. The setting is a vast hall covered by massive vaults that recall ancient Roman architecture, especially the much-admired coffered barrel vaults of the Basilica Nova (FIG. 7-76). Colossal statues of Apollo and Athena, patron deities of the arts and of wisdom, oversee the interactions. Plato and Aristotle are the central figures around whom Raphael carefully arranged the others. Plato holds his book *Timaeus* and points to Heaven, the source of his inspiration, while Aristotle carries his book *Nichomachean Ethics* and gestures toward the earth, from which his observations of reality sprang. Appropriately, ancient philosophers, men concerned with the ultimate mysteries that transcend this world, stand on Plato's side. On Aristotle's side are the philosophers and scientists concerned with practical matters, such as mathematics. At the lower left, Pythagoras writes as a servant holds up the harmonic scale. In the foreground, Heraclitus (probably a portrait of Michelangelo) broods alone. Diogenes sprawls on the steps. At the right, students surround Euclid, who demonstrates a theorem. Euclid may be a portrait of the architect Bramante, whom Julius II had recently commissioned to design the new church (FIGS. 22-22 and 22-23) to replace Constantine's 1,200-year-old Saint Peter's (FIG. 8-9). (*School of Athens* probably reflects Bramante's 1505 design for the interior of Saint Peter's; compare FIG. 24-5. According to Vasari, Bramante advised Raphael about the architectural setting.) At the extreme right, just to the right of the astronomers Zoroaster and Ptolemy, both holding globes, is a young man wearing a black hat—Raphael's self-portrait.

The groups appear to move easily and clearly, with eloquent poses and gestures that symbolize their doctrines and present an engaging variety of figural positions. The self-assurance and natural dignity of the figures convey calm reason, balance, and measure—those qualities that Renaissance thinkers admired as the heart of philosophy. Significantly, Raphael placed himself among the mathematicians and scientists in *School of Athens*. Certainly, the evolution of pictorial science approached perfection in this fresco in which Raphael convincingly depicted a vast space on a two-dimensional surface.

High and Late Renaissance   **631**

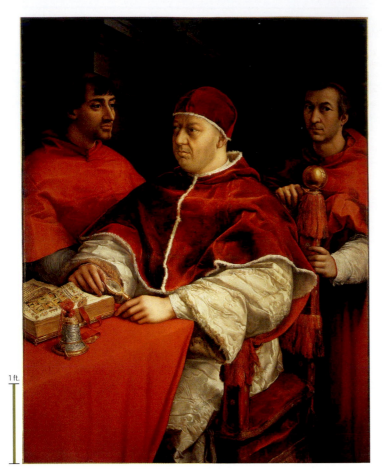

22-10 RAPHAEL, *Pope Leo X with Cardinals Giulio de' Medici and Luigi de' Rossi*, ca. 1517. Oil on wood, 5' $\frac{5}{8}$" × 3' 10 $\frac{7}{8}$". Galleria degli Uffizi, Florence.

In this dynastic portrait of the Medici pope and two Medici cardinals, Raphael depicted Leo X as an art collector and man of learning. The meticulous details reveal a debt to Netherlandish painting.

1 ft.

Medici to Florence following nearly two decades of exile (see page 606), and Leo used his position to advance the family's interests. The portrait (FIG. 22-10) that he commissioned Raphael to paint in 1517—a few years after the artist portrayed the famed courtier Baldassare Castiglione (FIG. 22-10A)—is, in essence, a dynastic portrait. Appropriately, the pope dominates the composition, seated in his study before a table with an illuminated 14th-century manuscript, the magnifying glass he required because of his impaired eyesight, and a bell engraved with classical decorative motifs. Raphael portrayed Leo as he doubtless wished to be represented—as a man of learning and a collector of beautiful objects rather than as a head of state. To the

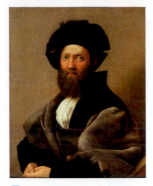

22-10A RAPHAEL, *Baldassare Castiglione*, ca. 1514.

pope's right is his cousin Cardinal Giulio de' Medici, who became Pope Clement VII (r. 1523–1534). Behind Leo's chair is Luigi de' Rossi (1474–1519), his cousin on his mother's side, whom the pope appointed cardinal. The three men look neither at one another nor at the painter or spectator, but are absorbed in their own thoughts.

Raphael's mastery of the oil technique is evident in every detail. His depiction of the rich satin, wool, velvet, and fur garments skillfully conveys their varied textures. His reproduction of the book on the pope's desk is so meticulous that scholars have been able to identify it as the *Hamilton Bible* in the Berlin Staatsbibliothek, open to folio 400 verso, the beginning of the Gospel of Saint John with illustrations of Christ's passion. The light illuminating the scene comes from the right—from a window reflected in the spherical brass finial of the pope's chair, in which the viewer can also see the indistinct form of the painter. In details such as these, Raphael revealed his knowledge and admiration of Netherlandish painting, especially the works of Jan van Eyck (compare the mirror in FIG. 20-7).

School of Athens also reveals Raphael's matured psychological insight. As in Leonardo's *Last Supper* (FIG. 22-4), all the characters communicate moods that reflect their beliefs, and the artist's placement of each figure tied these moods together. From the center, where Plato and Aristotle stand, Raphael arranged the groups of figures in an ellipse with a wide opening in the foreground. Moving along the floor's perspective pattern, the viewer's eye penetrates the assembly of philosophers and continues, by way of the reclining Diogenes, up to the here-reconciled leaders of the two great opposing camps of Renaissance philosophy. The vanishing point falls on Plato's left hand, drawing attention to *Timaeus*. In the Stanza della Segnatura, Raphael reconciled and harmonized not only the Platonists and Aristotelians but also classical humanism and Christianity, surely a major factor in the fresco's appeal to Julius II.

LEO X Succeeding Julius II as Raphael's patron was Pope Leo X (r. 1513–1521). By this time, Raphael had achieved renown throughout Italy and moved in the highest circles of the papal court. The new pope entrusted the Umbrian artist with so many projects in Rome, including overseeing construction of Saint Peter's, that Raphael became a wealthy man at a young age. Leo himself (Giovanni de' Medici) was a scion of Italy's most famous family. The second son of Lorenzo the Magnificent, he received a princely humanistic education. His election as pope came only a year after the return of the

GALATEA As a star at the papal court, Raphael also enjoyed the patronage of other prominent figures in Rome. Agostino Chigi (1465–1520), an immensely wealthy banker who managed the Vatican's financial affairs, commissioned Raphael to decorate his palace on the Tiber River with scenes from classical mythology. Outstanding among the frescoes Raphael painted in the small but splendid Villa Farnesina is *Galatea* (FIG. 22-11), which he based on *Stanzas for the Joust of Giuliano de' Medici* by Angelo Poliziano, whose poetry had earlier inspired Botticelli to paint *Birth of Venus* (FIG. 21-1). In Raphael's fresco, Galatea flees on a shell drawn by leaping dolphins to escape her uncouth lover, the cyclops Polyphemus (painted on another wall by a different artist). Sea creatures and playful cupids surround her. The painting is an exultant song in praise of human beauty and zestful love. Compositionally, Raphael enhanced the liveliness of the image by placing the sturdy figures around Galatea in bounding and dashing movements that always return to her as the energetic center. The cupids, skillfully foreshortened, repeat the circling motion. Raphael conceived his figures sculpturally, and Galatea's body—supple, strong, and vigorously in motion—contrasts with Botticelli's delicate, hovering, almost dematerialized Venus while suggesting the spiraling compositions of Hellenistic statuary (FIG. 5-81). In *Galatea*, classical myth presented in monumental form, in vivacious movement, and in a spirit of passionate delight resurrects the naturalistic art and poetry of the Greco-Roman world.

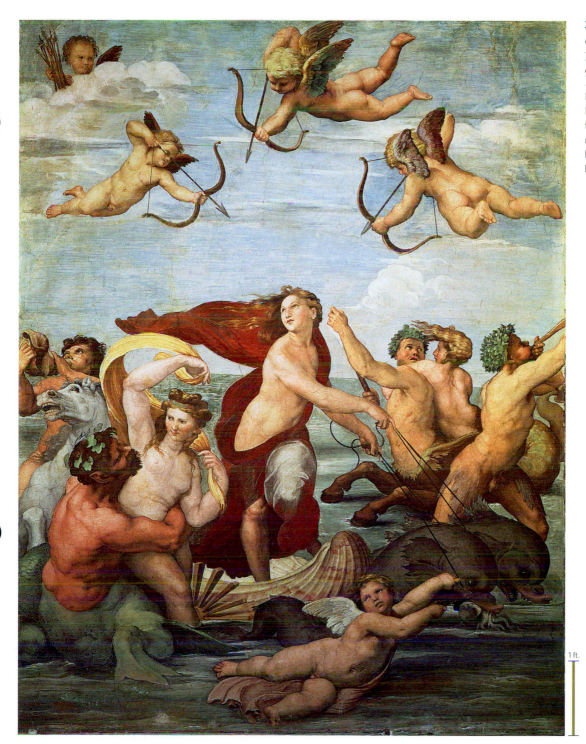

22-11 RAPHAEL, *Galatea*, Sala di Galatea, Villa Farnesina, Rome, Italy, ca. 1513. Fresco, 9' 8" × 7' 5".

Based on a poem by Poliziano, Raphael's fresco depicts Galatea fleeing Polyphemus. The painting, made for the palace of Vatican banker Agostino Chigi, celebrates human beauty and zestful love.

1 ft.

Michelangelo

Although Michelangelo is most famous today as the painter of the Sistine Chapel frescoes (FIG. 22-1), he was also an architect, poet, engineer, and, first and foremost, sculptor. Michelangelo considered sculpture superior to painting because the sculptor shares in the divine power to "make man" (see "Leonardo and Michelangelo on Painting versus Sculpture," page 625). Drawing a conceptual parallel to Plato's ideas, Michelangelo believed that the image which the artist's hand produces must come from the idea in the artist's mind. The idea, then, is the reality that the artist's genius has to bring forth. But artists are not the creators of the ideas they conceive. Rather, they find their ideas in the natural world, reflecting the absolute idea, which, for the artist, is beauty. One of Michelangelo's best-

known observations about sculpture is that the artist must proceed by finding the idea—the image—locked in the stone. By removing the excess stone, the sculptor extricates the idea from the block (FIG. I-16), bringing forth the living form. The artist, Michelangelo felt, works for many years to discover this unceasing process of revelation and "arrives late at novel and lofty things."[4]

Michelangelo did indeed arrive "at novel and lofty things," for he broke sharply from the lessons of his predecessors and contemporaries in one important respect: he mistrusted the application of mathematical methods as guarantees of beauty in proportion. Measure and proportion, he believed, should be "kept in the eyes." Vasari quoted Michelangelo as declaring that "it was necessary to have the compasses in the eyes and not in the hand, because the hands work and the eye judges."[5] Thus Michelangelo set aside Vitruvius,

Alberti, Leonardo, and others who tirelessly sought the perfect measure, and insisted that the artist's inspired judgment could identify other pleasing proportions. In addition, Michelangelo argued that the artist must not be bound, except by the demands made by realizing the idea. This assertion of the artist's authority was typical of Michelangelo and anticipated the modern concept of the right to a self-expression of talent limited only by the artist's own judgment. The artistic license to aspire far beyond the "rules" was, in part, a manifestation of the pursuit of fame and success that humanism fostered. In this context, Michelangelo created works in architecture, sculpture, and painting that departed from High Renaissance regularity. He put in its stead a style of vast, expressive strength conveyed through complex, eccentric, and often titanic forms that loom before the viewer in tragic grandeur.

As a youth, Michelangelo was an apprentice in the studio of the painter Domenico Ghirlandaio (FIGS. 21-26 and 21-27), but he left before completing his training. Although Michelangelo later claimed that he owed nothing artistically to anyone, he made detailed drawings based on the work of the great Florentines Giotto and Masaccio. Early on, he came to the attention of Lorenzo the Magnificent and studied sculpture under one of Lorenzo's favorite artists, Bertoldo di Giovanni (ca. 1420–1491), a former collaborator of Donatello's. When Lorenzo died in 1492 and the Medici fell two years later, Michelangelo left Florence for Venice and then Bologna, where the sculptures of the Sienese artist Jacopo della Quercia (1367–1438) impressed him.

PIETÀ Michelangelo made his first trip to Rome in the summer of 1496, and two years later, still in his early 20s, he produced his first masterpiece there: a *Pietà* (FIG. **22-12**) for Jean de Bilhères Lagraulas (1439–1499), Cardinal of Saint-Denis and the French king's envoy to the Vatican. The cardinal commissioned the statue to be placed in the rotunda attached to the south transept of Old Saint Peter's (not shown in FIG. 8-9) in which he was to be buried beside other French churchmen. (The work is now on view in the new church [FIG. 24-4] that replaced the fourth-century basilica.) The theme—Mary cradling the dead body of Christ in her lap—was a staple in the repertoire of French and German artists, and Michelangelo's French patron doubtless chose the subject. The Italian sculptor, however, rendered the northern European theme in an unforgettable manner. Michelangelo transformed marble into flesh, hair, and fabric with a sensitivity for texture almost without parallel. The best photographs can capture something of the luminosity of the marble surface, but the exquisite nature of Michelangelo's carving and polishing can be fully appreciated only in the presence of the original. Also breathtaking is the tender sadness of the beautiful and youthful Mary as she mourns the death of her son. In fact, her age—seemingly less than that of Christ—was a subject of controversy from the moment the statue was unveiled. Michelangelo explained Mary's ageless beauty as an integral part of her purity and virginity. Beautiful, too, is the son whom she holds. (In fact, Michelangelo's figure of the adult Christ is too small in relation to the size of Mary. This may be an intentional allusion to the imagery of the Madonna and Child subject of innumerable artworks.) Christ seems less to have died a martyr's crucifixion than to have drifted off into peaceful sleep in Mary's maternal arms. His wounds are barely visible. It is hard to imagine a starker contrast in conception and style than that between the *Röttgen Pietà* (FIG. 13-50) and Michelangelo's.

DAVID Michelangelo returned to Florence in 1501. In 1495, during the Medici exile, the Florentine Republic had ordered the transfer of Donatello's *David* (FIG. 21-11) from the Medici residence to the Palazzo della Signoria to join Verrocchio's *David* (FIG. 21-12) there. The importance of David as a civic symbol led the Florence Cathedral building committee to invite Michelangelo to work a great block of marble left over from an earlier aborted commission into still another *David* for the Signoria. The colossal statue (FIG. **22-13**)—Florentines referred to it as "the Giant"—that Michelangelo created from that block forever assured his reputation as an extraordinary talent. Vasari, a great admirer of Michelangelo's (see "Giorgio Vasari's *Lives*," page 636), extolled the work, claiming:

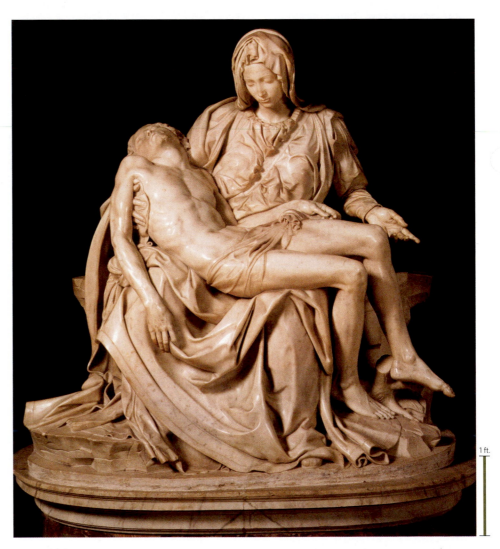

1 ft.

22-12 MICHELANGELO, *Pietà*, ca. 1498–1500. Marble, 5' 8½" high. Saint Peter's, Vatican City, Rome.

Michelangelo's representation of Mary cradling Christ's corpse captures the sadness and beauty of the young Virgin but was controversial because the Madonna seems younger than her son.

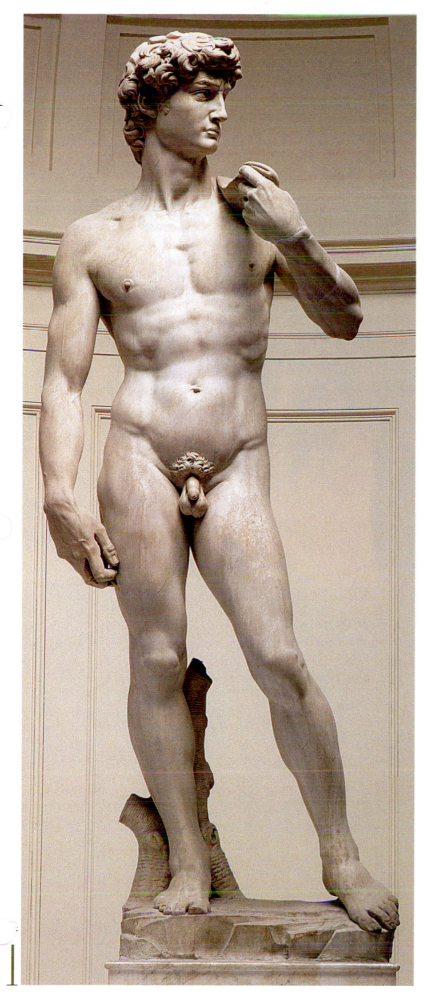

without any doubt [Michelangelo's *David*] has put in the shade every other statue, ancient or modern, Greek or Roman . . . [The statue] was intended as a symbol of liberty [in front of Florence's city hall], signifying that just as David had protected his people and governed them justly, so whoever ruled Florence should vigorously defend the city and govern it with justice.[6]

Despite the traditional association of David with heroic triumph over a fearsome adversary, Michelangelo chose to represent the young biblical warrior not after his victory, with Goliath's head at his feet (as Donatello and Verrocchio had done), but before the encounter, with David sternly watching his approaching foe. *David* exhibits the characteristic representation of energy in reserve that imbues Michelangelo's later figures with the tension of a coiled spring. The anatomy of David's body plays an important part in this prelude to action. His rugged torso, sturdy limbs, and large hands and feet alert viewers to the triumph to come. Each swelling vein and tightening sinew amplifies the psychological energy of David's pose.

Michelangelo doubtless had the classical nude in mind when he conceived his *David*. Like many of his colleagues, he greatly admired Greco-Roman statues, in particular the skillful and precise rendering of heroic physique. Without strictly imitating the antique style, which he studied firsthand in Rome, the Renaissance sculptor captured in his portrayal of the biblical hero the tension that is a key ingredient of the athletes (FIG. 5-65) of the Late Classical sculptor Lysippos, and the psychological insight and emotionalism of Hellenistic statuary (FIGS. 5-81, 5-82, and 5-90). His *David* differs from Donatello's and Verrocchio's creations in much the same way that later Hellenistic statues departed from their Classical predecessors (see Chapter 5). Michelangelo abandoned the self-contained compositions of the 15th-century *David*s by abruptly turning the hero's head toward his gigantic adversary. This *David* is compositionally and emotionally connected to an unseen presence beyond the statue, a feature also of Hellenistic sculpture (FIG. 5-86). As early as 1501, then, Michelangelo invested his efforts in presenting towering, pent-up emotion rather than calm, ideal beauty. He transferred his own doubts, frustrations, and passions into the great figures he created or planned.

TOMB OF JULIUS II The formal references to classical antiquity in Michelangelo's *David* surely appealed to Julius II, who associated himself with the humanists and with Roman emperors. Thus this sculpture and the fame that accrued to Michelangelo on its completion called the artist to the pope's attention, leading shortly thereafter to major papal commissions (see "Michelangelo in the Service of Julius II," page 623). The first project that Julius II commissioned from Michelangelo was the pontiff's tomb, to be placed in

22-13 MICHELANGELO BUONARROTI, *David*, from Piazza della Signoria, Florence, Italy, 1501–1504. Marble, 17' high. Galleria dell'Accademia, Florence.

In this colossal statue for the Florentine Signoria, Michelangelo represented David in heroic classical nudity, capturing the tension of Lysippos's athletes and the emotionalism of Hellenistic statuary.

WRITTEN SOURCES
Giorgio Vasari's *Lives*

Giorgio Vasari (1511–1574) of Arezzo was an architect and painter who trained in Michelangelo's Florentine workshop. He enjoyed considerable success, especially as an architect, and received several major commissions, most notably to design the complex of offices next to the Palazzo della Signoria in Florence—the Uffizi—that now houses the world's greatest collection of Italian Renaissance art. Vasari's most significant achievement, however, was as a biographer and art historian. Sometimes called "the father of art history," Vasari published *Lives of the Most Excellent Painters, Sculptors, and Architects* in 1530. A second, definitive edition appeared in 1568. Vasari's *Lives* is far more than a compendium of facts and anecdotes about Italian artists. Vasari virtually created the discipline of art history, and the story of Renaissance art that art historians tell today remains rooted in Vasari's account.

Indeed, art historians, and the general public as well, owe the very concept of the "Renaissance" to Vasari. In his preface, Vasari placed all the biographies to follow in the context of his view that the history of art had three major periods: the glorious Greco-Roman age; the Middle Ages, when only inferior art was produced; and the Renaissance, when, beginning in the 14th century, classical art was reborn (see pages 374 and 416).

> What was the most infinitely harmful and damaging to those professions [painting, sculpture, and architecture] . . . was the fervent zeal of the new Christian religion . . . [which] cast to the ground all the marvelous statues, sculptures, paintings, mosaics, and ornaments of the false pagan gods, but it also . . .
>
> destroy[ed] the most honored temples of the pagan idols. . . . Once [today's artists] have seen how art reached the summit of perfection . . . and how it had fallen into complete ruin . . . [and how the arts], like human bodies, are born, grow up, become old, and die, they will now be able to recognize more easily the progress of art's rebirth and the state of perfection to which it has again ascended in our own times.*

Vasari also divided the Renaissance into three ages—the era of Cimabue and Giotto, when artists broke away from the *maniera greca* (see page 415); the Quattrocento, when artists began to employ linear perspective and produced works exhibiting greater naturalism (the ultimate goal of art, according to Vasari); and the Cinquecento, when Leonardo, Raphael, and especially Michelangelo achieved perfection.

Consistent with his view that the excellence of Renaissance art was due to the inspired genius and limitless talent of individual artists—a celebratory biographical approach to the history of art that persists even today—Vasari's *Lives* is often unrestrained in its flattery of the artists he admired most (Florentine artists above all others). Some brief excerpts:

Leonardo da Vinci: Truly wondrous and divine was Leonardo. . . . [W]ith his birth, Florence truly received the greatest of all gifts, and at his death, the loss was incalculable. To the art of painting, he added a kind of shadowing to the method of coloring with oils which has enabled the moderns to endow their figures with great energy and relief.[†]

Raphael: [A]lthough other paintings may be called paintings, those of Raphael are living things: for the flesh in his figures seems palpable, they breathe, their pulses beat. . . . [B]ecause of Raphael, the arts of painting, coloring, and invention were harmoniously brought to a stage of completion and perfection that could hardly be hoped for.[‡]

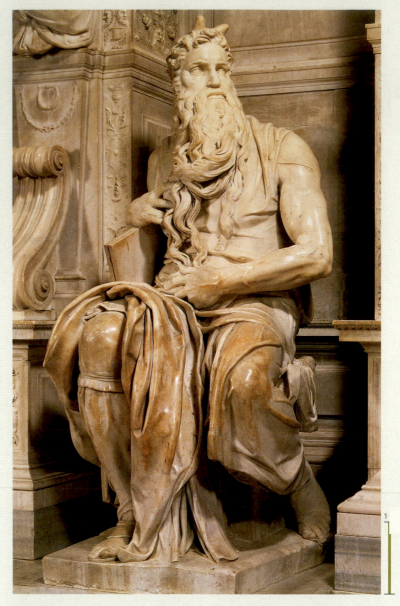

22-14 MICHELANGELO BUONARROTI, *Moses*, from the tomb of Pope Julius II, Rome, Italy, ca. 1513–1515. Marble, 7' 8½" high. San Pietro in Vincoli, Rome.

Not since Hellenistic times had a sculptor captured as much emotional and physical energy in a seated statue as Michelangelo did in *Moses*. Vasari believed that God bequeathed Michelangelo to Florence.

Michelangelo: [T]he most benevolent Ruler of Heaven . . . decided . . . to send to earth a spirit who, working alone, was able to demonstrate in every art and every profession the meaning of perfection in the art of design . . . and because He saw that in the practice of . . . painting, sculpture, and architecture, Tuscan minds were always among the greatest, . . . He wanted to bequeath [Michelangelo] to . . . Florence, the most worthy among all the other cities, so that the perfection Florence justly achieved with all her talents might finally reach its culmination in one of her own citizens.[§]

*Translated by Julia Conaway Bondanella and Peter Bondanella, *Giorgio Vasari: The Lives of the Artists* (New York: Oxford University Press, 1991), 5–6.
[†]Ibid., 284, 298.
[‡]Ibid., 325, 332.
[§]Ibid., 415–416.

Old Saint Peter's. The sculptor's original 1505 design called for a freestanding, two-story structure with more than 40 statues. The proposed monument, of unprecedented size and complexity, would have given Michelangelo the latitude to sculpt numerous human figures while providing Julius II with a grandiose memorial that would associate the Cinquecento pope with the first pope, Peter himself. Shortly after Michelangelo began work on this project, however, the pope interrupted the commission, possibly because funds had to be diverted to the rebuilding of Saint Peter's. After Julius II's death in 1513, Michelangelo reluctantly reduced the scale of the project step-by-step until, in 1542, a final contract specified a simple wall tomb (compare FIGS. 21-14 and 21-39) with fewer than one-third of the originally planned figures. Michelangelo completed the tomb in 1545 and saw it placed in San Pietro in Vincoli (MAP 22-1), where Julius II had served as cardinal before his accession to the papacy. Given Julius's ambitions, it is safe to say that had he seen the final design of his tomb or known where it would eventually be located, he would have been bitterly disappointed.

The spirit of the tomb may be summed up in *Moses* (FIG. **22-14**), which Michelangelo carved between 1513 and 1515 during one of his sporadic resumptions of work on the project. Meant to be seen from below and to be balanced with seven other massive forms related to it in spirit, *Moses* in its final comparatively paltry setting does not convey the impact originally intended. Michelangelo depicted the Old Testament prophet seated, the Tablets of the Law under one arm and his hands gathering his voluminous beard. The horns on Moses's head were a convention in Christian art (based on a mistranslation of the Hebrew word for "rays") and helped Renaissance viewers identify the prophet (compare FIGS. 12-38 and 20-2). Here, as in his *David,* Michelangelo used the device of the turned head, in this case to concentrate the expression of awful wrath stirring in the prophet's mighty frame and eyes. Moses's muscles bulge, his veins swell, and his great legs seem to begin slowly to move. Not since Hellenistic times (FIGS. 5-85 and 5-86) had a sculptor imbued a seated figure with so much torsion and emotionalism.

Michelangelo also intended to incorporate in the pope's tomb some 20 statues of captives, popularly known as slaves, in various attitudes of revolt and exhaustion. Art historians have traditionally believed that *Bound Slave,* or *Rebellious Prisoner* (FIG. **22-15**), and the unfinished statue shown in FIG. I-16 to be two of those destined for Julius's tomb. Some scholars now doubt this attribution, and some even reject the identification of the statues as "slaves" or "captives." Whatever their identity, these statues, like Michelangelo's *David* and *Moses,* testify to the sculptor's ability to create figures embodying powerful emotional states. In *Bound Slave,* the defiant figure's violent contrapposto is the image of frantic but impotent struggle. Michelangelo based his whole art on his conviction that whatever can be said greatly through sculpture and painting must be said through the human figure.

TOMB OF GIULIANO DE' MEDICI Following the death of Julius II, Michelangelo, like Raphael, went into the service of Leo X and his successor, Clement VII. These Medici popes chose not to spend their resources on their predecessor's unfinished tomb. Instead, immediately following the death in May 1519 of Lorenzo de' Medici (1492–1519), duke of Urbino, they (Pope Leo X and the then-cardinal Giulio de' Medici; FIG. 22-10) commissioned Michelangelo to design a funerary chapel, the New Sacristy, attached to Brunelleschi's San Lorenzo (FIG. 21-31) in Florence, to house twin tombs of Lorenzo and Giuliano de' Medici (1478–1516), duke of Nemours (south of Paris), who had died three years before.

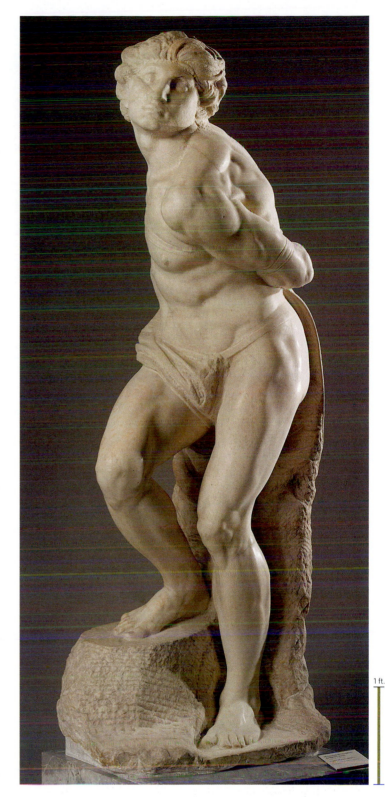

1 ft.

22-15 MICHELANGELO BUONARROTI, *Bound Slave* (*Rebellious Prisoner*), from the tomb of Pope Julius II, Rome, Italy, ca. 1513–1516. Marble, 7' $\frac{5}{8}$" high. Musée du Louvre, Paris.

For Pope Julius II's grandiose tomb, Michelangelo planned a series of statues of captives or slaves in various attitudes of revolt and exhaustion. This defiant figure exhibits violent contrapposto.

The chapel was also to contain the tombs of the dukes' namesakes, Lorenzo the Magnificent and his murdered brother, Giuliano, and was intended as a dynastic mausoleum for Florence's leading family. Michelangelo finished neither tomb. Today, the tombs of Lorenzo

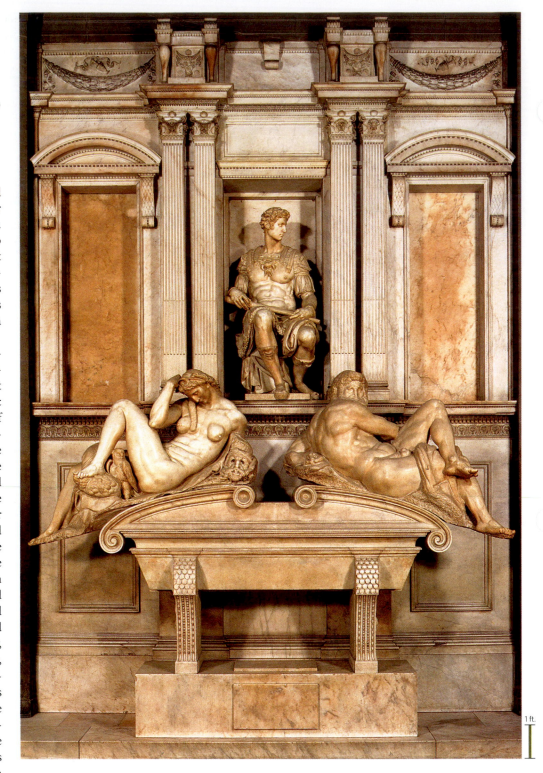

22-16 MICHELANGELO BUONARROTI, tomb of Giuliano de' Medici, New Sacristy (Medici Chapel), San Lorenzo, Florence, Italy, 1519–1534. Marble, central figure 5' 11" high.

Michelangelo depicted the deceased Giuliano de' Medici in Roman armor, the model of the active and decisive man. Below him are the anguished, twisting figures of Night and Day.

1 ft.

and Giuliano (FIG. **22-16**), as completed by the master's pupils, face each other on opposite walls of the New Sacristy. Scholars believe that Michelangelo intended to place pairs of recumbent river gods at the bottom of the sarcophagi, balancing the pairs of figures resting on the sloping sides, but his grand design for the tombs remains a puzzle.

According to the traditional interpretation, the arrangement Michelangelo planned mirrors the soul's ascent through the levels of the Neo-Platonic universe. Neo-Platonism, the school of thought based on Plato's idealistic, spiritualistic philosophy, embraced in the 15th century by the humanists in the Medici circle, experienced a renewed popularity in the 16th century. The lowest level of the tomb, which the river gods represent, would have signified the Underworld of brute matter, the source of evil. The two statues on the sarcophagi would symbolize the realm of time—the specifically human world of the cycles of dawn, day, evening, and night. Humanity's state in this world of time was one of pain and anxiety, of frustration and exhaustion. At left, the muscular female Night—Michelangelo used male models even for his female figures—and, at right, the male Day appear to be chained into never-relaxing tensions. Both exhibit the anguished twisting of the body's masses in contrary directions seen also in Michelangelo's *Bound Slave* (FIG. 22-15; compare FIG. I-16) and in his Sistine Chapel paintings (FIGS. 22-18 and 22-18A). This contortion is a staple of Michelangelo's figural art. Day, with a body the thickness of a great tree and the anatomy of Hercules (or of a reclining Greco-Roman river god that may have inspired Michelangelo's statue), strains his huge limbs against each other, his unfinished visage rising menacingly above his shoulder. Night, the symbol of rest, twists as if in troubled sleep, her posture wrenched and feverish. The artist surrounded her with an owl, poppies, and a hideous mask symbolic of nightmares. Some scholars argue, however, that the Night and Day personifications allude not to humanity's pain but to the life cycle and the passage of time leading ultimately to death.

On their respective tombs, seated statues of Lorenzo and Giuliano appear in niches at the apex of the structures. Transcending worldly existence, they represent the two ideal human types—the contemplative man (Lorenzo) and the active man (Giuliano; FIG. 22-16). The latter wears the armor of a Roman general and holds a commander's baton, his head turned alertly as if in council (he looks toward the statue of the Virgin at one end of the chapel). Across the room, Lorenzo appears deep in thought, his face in shadow. Together, they symbolize the two ways that human beings might achieve union with God—through meditation or through the active life fashioned after that of Christ. In this sense, they are not individual portraits. Indeed, Michelangelo declined to

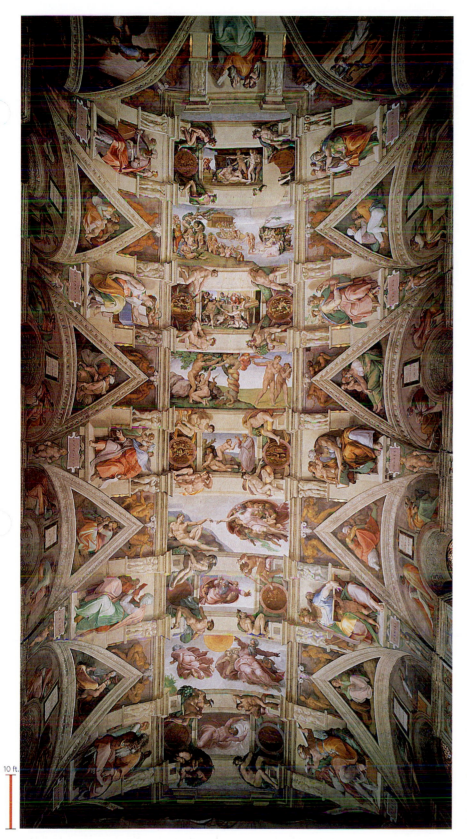

22-17 MICHELANGELO BUONARROTI, ceiling of the Sistine Chapel, Vatican City, Rome, Italy, 1508–1512. Fresco, 128' × 45'.

Michelangelo labored almost four years for Pope Julius II on the frescoes for the ceiling of the Sistine Chapel (FIG. 22-1). He painted more than 300 figures illustrating the creation and fall of humankind.

SISTINE CHAPEL CEILING When Julius II suspended work on his tomb, the pope offered the bitter Michelangelo the commission to paint the ceiling (FIG. **22-17**) of the Sistine Chapel (FIG. 22-1) in 1508. The chapel, built by Sixtus IV in 1479 to 1481 between the Vatican's apostolic palace and Saint Peter's (see page 644 and MAPS 22-1 and 24-1), served as the private chapel of the pope and the papal court. It was also the place where the College of Cardinals gathered after the death of a pope to select his successor. Some of the leading Quattrocento painters had provided frescoes (FIG. 21-41) for its walls, but the commission for the ceiling dwarfed the earlier mural projects in both size and complexity. Michelangelo faced enormous difficulties: the ceiling's dimensions (some 5,800 square feet), its height above the pavement (almost 70 feet), and the complicated perspective problems that the vault's height and curve presented—in addition to his inexperience in the fresco technique. (Michelangelo had to redo the first section he completed because of faulty preparation of the intonaco; see "Fresco Painting," page 419.) Yet, in less than four years, the Florentine sculptor produced an extraordinary series of frescoes incorporating his patron's agenda, Church doctrine, and his own interests. In depicting the most august and solemn themes of all, the creation, fall, and redemption of humankind—subjects most likely selected by Julius II with input from Michelangelo and Cardinal Marco Vigerio della Rovere (1446–1516)—Michelangelo spread a colossal compositional scheme across the vast surface. He succeeded in weaving together more than 300 figures in an ultimate grand drama of the human race.

Nine narrative panels describing the creation, as recorded in Genesis, run along the crown of the vault, from *God's Separation of Light and Darkness* (above the altar) to *Drunkenness of Noah* (nearest the entrance to the chapel). Thus as viewers enter the chapel, look up, and walk toward the altar, they review, in reverse order, the history of the fall of humankind. (When facing those assembled in the chapel, the presiding priest—the pope—sees the narrative scenes in the correct order, but upside down.) The Hebrew prophets and ancient *sibyls* (FIG. 22-18B) who foretold the coming of Christ appear seated in large thrones on both sides of the central row of scenes from Genesis, where the vault curves down. In the four corner pendentives, Michelangelo placed four Old Testament scenes with David, Judith, Haman, and Moses and the Brazen Serpent. Scores of lesser figures also appear. The ancestors of Christ fill the triangular compartments above the windows, nude youths punctuate the corners of the central panels, and small pairs of putti

sculpt likenesses of Lorenzo and Giuliano. Who, he asked, would care what they looked like in a thousand years? The rather generic visages of the two Medici captains of the Church are consistent with Michelangelo's lifelong approach to figural art, in painting as well as sculpture. Throughout his career, he demonstrated less concern for facial features and expressions than for the overall human form. Michelangelo's "portraits" are thus fundamentally different from those of Leonardo (FIG. 22-5) and Raphael (FIGS. 22-10 and 22-10A).

10 ft.

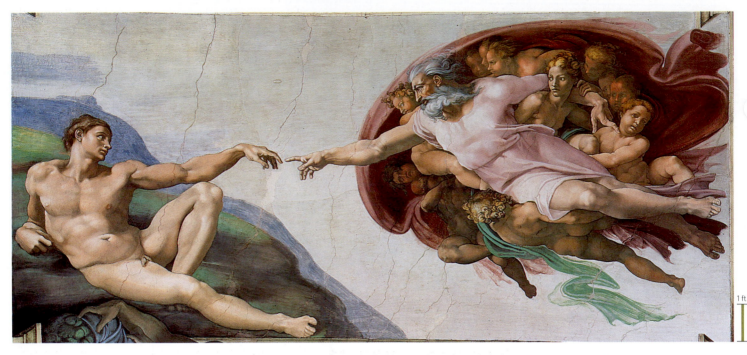

22-18 MICHELANGELO BUONARROTI, *Creation of Adam*, detail of the ceiling of the Sistine Chapel (FIG. 22-17), Vatican City, Rome, Italy, 1511–1512. Fresco, 9' 2" × 18' 8".

Life leaps to Adam like a spark from the extended hand of God in this fresco, which recalls the communication between gods and heroes in the classical myths that Renaissance humanists greatly admired.

in *grisaille* (to imitate sculpture) support the painted cornice surrounding the entire central corridor. The overall conceptualization of the ceiling's design and narrative structure not only presents a sweeping chronology of Christianity but also is in keeping with Renaissance ideas about Christian history. These ideas included interest in the conflict between good and evil and between the energy of youth and the wisdom of age. The conception of the entire ceiling was astounding in itself, and the articulation of it in its thousands of details was a superhuman achievement.

Unlike Andrea Mantegna's decoration of the ceiling of the Camera Picta (FIGS. 21-48 and 21-49) in Mantua, the strongly marked unifying architectural framework in the Sistine Chapel does not construct "picture windows" framing illusions within them. Rather, the viewer focuses on figure after figure, each sharply outlined against the neutral tone of the architectural setting or the plain background of the panels.

CREATION OF ADAM The two central panels of Michelangelo's ceiling are *Creation of Adam* (FIG. **22-18**) and *Fall of Man* (FIG. **22-18A**). In both cases, Michelangelo rejected traditional iconographical convention in favor of bold new interpretations of these momentous events. In *Creation of Adam*, God and Adam confront each other in a primordial unformed landscape of which Adam is still a

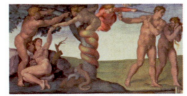

↗ 22-18A MICHELANGELO, *Fall of Man*, ca. 1510.

material part, heavy as earth. The Lord transcends the earth, wrapped in a billowing cloud of drapery and borne up by his powers. Life leaps to Adam like a spark from the extended and mighty hand of God. The communication between gods and heroes, so familiar in classical myth, is here concrete. This blunt depiction of the Lord as ruler of Heaven in the classical, Olympian sense indicates how easily High

Renaissance thought joined classical and Christian traditions. Yet the classical trappings do not obscure the essential Christian message.

Beneath the Lord's sheltering left arm is a woman, apprehensively curious but as yet uncreated. Scholars traditionally believed that she is Eve, but many now think she is the Virgin Mary (with the Christ Child at her knee). If the second identification is correct, it suggests that Michelangelo incorporated into his fresco one of the essential tenets of Christian faith—the belief that Adam's original sin eventually led to the sacrifice of Christ, which in turn made possible the redemption of all humankind (see "Jewish Subjects in Christian Art," page 238).

As God reaches out to Adam, the viewer's eye follows the motion from right to left, but Adam's extended left arm leads the eye back to the right, along the Lord's right arm, shoulders, and left arm to his left forefinger, which points to the Christ Child's face. The focal point of this right-to-left-to-right movement—the fingertips of Adam and the Lord—is dramatically off-center. Michelangelo replaced the straight architectural axes found in Leonardo's compositions with curves and diagonals. For example, the bodies of the two great figures are complementary—the concave body of Adam fitting the convex body and billowing "cloak" of God. Thus motion directs not only the figures but also the whole composition. The reclining positions of the figures, the heavy musculature, and the twisting poses are all intrinsic parts of Michelangelo's style.

The photographs of the Sistine Chapel reproduced here record the appearance of Michelangelo's frescoes after the completion of a 12-year cleaning project (1977–1989). The painstaking restoration (FIG. **22-18B**) elicited considerable controversy because it revealed vivid colors that initially shocked art historians, producing accusations that

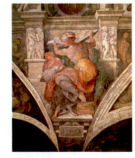

↗ 22-18B Sistine Chapel restoration, 1977–1989.

the restorers were destroying Michelangelo's masterpieces. That reaction, however, was largely attributable to the fact that for centuries everyone had seen Michelangelo's frescoes only in their soot-and-grime-covered state. Today, all can see that Michelangelo's true palette—so different from Leonardo's (FIGS. 22-2 to 22-5)—resembles, not surprisingly, the colors favored by Quattrocento Florentine fresco painters such as Masaccio (FIG. 21-19) and Piero della Francesca (FIG. 21-25).

THE COUNTER-REFORMATION Paul III (r. 1534–1549) succeeded Clement VII as pope in 1534 at a time of widespread dissatisfaction with the leadership and policies of the Roman Catholic Church. Led by clerics such as Martin Luther and John Calvin in the Holy Roman Empire (see page 680), early-16th-century reformers directly challenged papal authority, especially regarding secular issues. Disgruntled Catholics voiced concerns about the sale of *indulgences* (pardons for sins, reducing the time a soul spent in purgatory), nepotism (the appointment of relatives to important positions; compare FIG. 22-10), and high Church officials pursuing personal wealth. This Reformation movement resulted in the establishment of Protestantism, with sects such as Lutheranism and Calvinism. Central to Protestantism was a belief in personal faith rather than

adherence to decreed Church practices and doctrines. Because the Protestants believed that the only true religious relationship was the personal relationship between an individual and God, they were, in essence, eliminating the need for Church intercession, which is central to Catholicism.

The Catholic Church, in response, mounted a full-fledged campaign to counteract the defection of its members to Protestantism. Led by Paul III, this response, the Counter-Reformation, consisted of numerous initiatives. The Council of Trent, which met intermittently from 1545 through 1563, was a major component of this effort (see "The Council of Trent," page 642). Composed of cardinals, archbishops, bishops, abbots, and theologians, the Council of Trent dealt with issues of Church doctrine, including many that the Protestants contested. Many papal art commissions during this period should be viewed as an integral part of the Counter-Reformation effort. Popes long had been aware of the power of visual imagery to construct and reinforce ideological claims, and 16th-century popes exploited this capability.

LAST JUDGMENT Among Paul III's first papal commissions was an enormous (48-foot-tall) fresco for the Sistine Chapel. Michelangelo agreed to paint *Last Judgment* (FIG. 22-19) on the chapel's altar (west) wall. Here, the artist depicted Christ as the stern judge of the world, but—in vivid contrast to both the Byzantine (FIG. 9-24) and European medieval (FIG. 12-15) traditions—as a twisting, almost nude, giant who raises his mighty right arm in a gesture of damnation so broad and universal as to suggest that he will destroy all creation. The choirs of Heaven surround the youthful judge and pulse with anxiety and awe. Crowded into the space below are trumpeting angels, the ascending figures of the saved, and the downward-hurtling figures of the damned. The Virgin is already in Heaven, on Christ's right side, the side of the blessed. On the opposite side, demons, whose gargoyle masks and burning eyes revive the demons of Romanesque tympana, torment the damned.

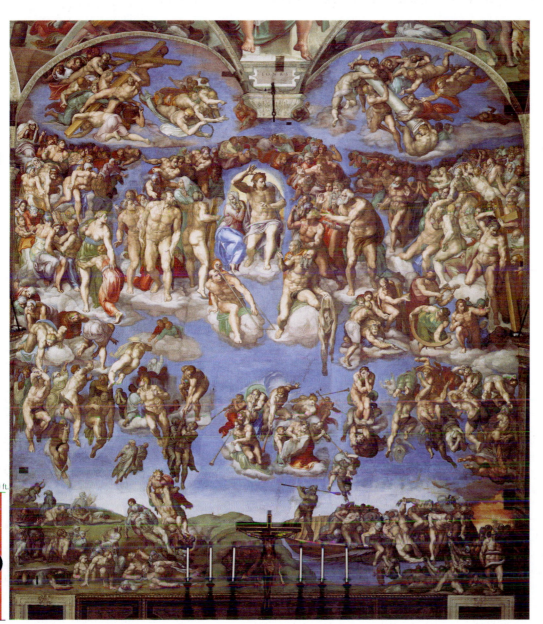

10 ft.

22-19 MICHELANGELO BUONARROTI, *Last Judgment,* altar wall of the Sistine Chapel, Vatican City, Rome, Italy, 1536–1541. Fresco, 48' × 44'.

Michelangelo completed his fresco cycle in the Sistine Chapel with this terrifying vision of the fate awaiting sinners. Near the center, he placed his own portrait on the flayed skin that Saint Bartholomew holds.

The Council of Trent

Both Catholics and Protestants took seriously the role of devotional imagery in religious life. However, their views differed dramatically. Catholics deemed art valuable for cultivating piety. Protestants believed that religious imagery encouraged idolatry and distracted the faithful from the goal of developing a personal relationship with God (see page 681). As part of the Counter-Reformation effort, Pope Paul III convened the Council of Trent in 1545 to review controversial Church doctrines. At its conclusion in 1563, the council issued the following edict regarding the Church's role as patron of paintings and sculptures:

> The holy council commands all bishops and others who hold the office of teaching and have charge of the *cura animarum* ["care of souls"—the responsibility of laboring for the salvation of souls], that in accordance with the usage of the Catholic and Apostolic Church, received from the primitive times of the Christian religion, and with the unanimous teaching of the holy Fathers and the decrees of sacred councils, they above all instruct the faithful diligently in matters relating to intercession and invocation of the saints, the veneration of relics, and the legitimate use of images. . . . Moreover, that the images of Christ, of the Virgin Mother of God, and of the other saints are to be placed and retained especially in the churches, and that due honor and veneration is to be given them; . . . because the honor which is shown them is referred to the prototypes which they represent, so that by means of the images which we kiss and before which we

uncover the head and prostrate ourselves, we adore Christ and venerate the saints whose likeness they bear. That is what was defined by the decrees of the councils, especially of the Second Council of Nicaea, against the opponents of images.

> Moreover, let the bishops diligently teach that by means of the stories of the mysteries of our redemption portrayed in paintings and other representations the people are instructed and confirmed in the articles of faith, which ought to be borne in mind and constantly reflected upon; also that great profit is derived from all holy images, not only because the people are thereby reminded of the benefits and gifts bestowed on them by Christ, but also because through the saints the miracles of God and salutary examples are set before the eyes of the faithful, so that they may give God thanks for those things, may fashion their own life and conduct in imitation of the saints and be moved to adore and love God and cultivate piety. . . . That these things may be the more faithfully observed, the holy council decrees that no one is permitted to erect or cause to be erected in any place or church, howsoever exempt, any unusual image unless it has been approved by the bishop.*

In taking this position, the Catholic Church reaffirmed its role as the greatest art patron of the Cinquecento and assured that it would retain that status throughout the succeeding Baroque era, both in Europe and in Spain's vast territories in the New World.

*Canons and Decrees of the Council of Trent, December 3–4, 1563. Robert Klein and Henri Zerner, *Italian Art 1500–1600: Sources and Documents* (Evanston, Ill.: Northwestern University Press, 1966), 120–121.

Michelangelo's terrifying vision of the fate awaiting sinners goes far beyond even Signorelli's gruesome images (FIG. 21-42). Martyrs who suffered especially agonizing deaths crouch below the judge. One of them, Saint Bartholomew, who was skinned alive, holds the flaying knife and the skin, its face a grotesque self-portrait of Michelangelo. The figures are huge and violently twisted, with small heads and contorted features. Yet while this frightening fresco impresses on viewers Christ's wrath on judgment day, it also holds out hope. A group of saved souls—the elect—crowd around Christ, and on the far right appears a figure with a cross, most likely the Good Thief (crucified with Christ) or a saint martyred by crucifixion, such as Saint Andrew.

UNFINISHED *PIETÀ* Six years after completing the *Last Judgment* fresco and nearly 50 years after carving the *Pietà* (FIG. 22-12) for the burial chapel of Cardinal Bilhères Lagraulas, Michelangelo, already in his 70s, began work on another *Pietà* (FIG. **22-20**), this one destined for his own tomb in Santa Maria Maggiore in Rome. For this *Pietà*, the aged master set for himself an unprecedented technical challenge—to surpass the sculptors of the ancient *Laocoön* (FIG. 5-89) and carve four life-size figures from a single marble block.

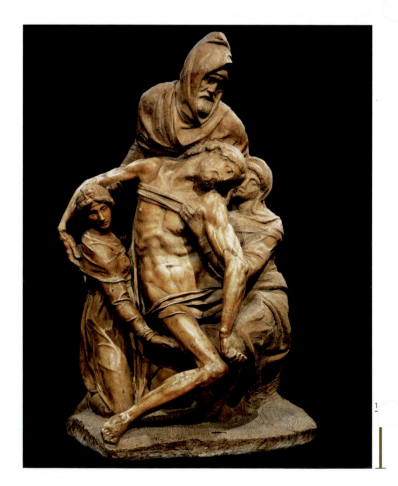

22-20 MICHELANGELO BUONARROTI, *Pietà*, ca. 1547–1555. Marble, 7' 8" high. Museo dell'Opera del Duomo, Florence.

Left unfinished, this *Pietà*, begun when Michelangelo was in his 70s and intended for his own tomb, includes a self-portrait of the sculptor as Nicodemus supporting the lifeless body of the Savior.

He did not succeed. Christ's now-missing left leg became detached, perhaps because of a flaw in the marble, and in 1555 Michelangelo abandoned the project and began to smash the statue. His assistants intervened, and he eventually permitted one of them, Tiberio Calcagni (1532–1565), to repair some of the damage and finish the work in part.

In composition and tone, the Santa Maria Maggiore *Pietà*—really a *Deposition* (see "The Life of Jesus in Art," page 241)—stands in stark contrast to the work of Michelangelo's youth. The composition is vertical, with three figures—the Virgin, Mary Magdalene, and Nicodemus—supporting the lifeless body of Christ. The Virgin is now a subsidiary figure, half hidden by her son, whose left leg originally rested on her left thigh. The undersized Mary Magdalene is in a kneeling position. Forming the apex of the composition is the hooded Nicodemus, a self-portrait of Michelangelo. This late work is therefore very personal in nature, not surprising when the artist was also the patron.

Architecture: Rome

Michelangelo was an accomplished architect as well as a sculptor and painter, and his Vatican commissions included work on a new church to replace the basilica that Constantine had erected over the site of Saint Peter's burial place (Old Saint Peter's, FIG. 8-9 and MAPS 22-1 and 24-1). By the 15th century, it was obvious that the ancient timber-roofed church was insufficient for the needs and aspirations of the Renaissance papacy. Rebuilding the fourth-century basilica would occupy several popes and some of the leading architects of Italy for more than a century.

BRAMANTE The first in the distinguished line of architects of the new Saint Peter's was DONATO D'ANGELO BRAMANTE (1444–1514). Born in Urbino and trained as a painter (perhaps by Piero della Francesca), Bramante went to Milan in 1481 and, as Leonardo did, stayed there until the French captured the city in 1499. In Milan, Bramante abandoned painting to become his generation's most renowned architect. Under the influence of Filippo Brunelleschi, Leon Battista Alberti, and perhaps Leonardo, all of whom strongly favored the art and architecture of classical antiquity, Bramante developed the High Renaissance form of the central-plan church.

The architectural style Bramante championed was, consistent with the humanistic values of the day, based on ancient Roman models. Bramante's first major work in the classical mode was the small architectural gem known as the Tempietto (FIG. 22-21) on the Janiculum hill overlooking the Vatican. The building received its name because, to contemporaries, it had the look of a small ancient temple. "Little Temple" is, in fact, a perfect nickname for the structure, because the round temples of Roman Italy, including two in Rome—one in the Roman Forum and another on the east bank of the Tiber—and a third at nearby Tivoli (FIG. 7-4), directly inspired Bramante's design. King Ferdinand (r. 1479–1516) and Queen Isabella of Spain commissioned the Tempietto to mark what they believed was the spot of Saint Peter's crucifixion. (The Vatican cemetery in which Peter was buried lies at the northern foot of the Janiculum.) Bramante undertook the project in 1502, but construction may not have begun until the end of the decade. Today, the Tempietto stands inside the rectangular cloister of the monastery of San Pietro in Montorio, but Bramante planned, although never executed, a circular colonnaded courtyard to frame the "temple." His intent was to coordinate the Tempietto and its surrounding portico by aligning the columns of the two structures.

The Tempietto's design is severely rational and features a stately circular *stylobate* (stepped temple platform) and austere *Tuscan col-*

umns. Bramante achieved a wonderful balance and harmony in the relationship of the parts (dome, drum, and base) to one another and to the whole. Conceived as a tall domed cylinder projecting from the lower, wider cylinder of its colonnade, the "temple" is in some respects more a monument than a building. Bramante's sculptural eye is most evident in the rhythmic play of light and shadow around the columns and balustrade and across the deep-set rectangular windows alternating with shallow shell-capped niches in the *cella* (central room of a temple), walls, and drum. Although the Tempietto, superficially at least, may resemble a Greco-Roman *tholos* (a circular shrine; FIG. 5-72), and although antique models (for example, FIG. 7-4) provided the inspiration for all its details, the combination of parts and details was new and original. (Classical tholoi, for instance, were never two-story structures and had neither a drum nor a balustrade.)

One of the main differences between the Early and High Renaissance styles of architecture is the former's emphasis on adorning flat wall surfaces versus the latter's sculptural handling of architectural masses. Bramante's Tempietto initiated the High Renaissance era in architecture. Andrea Palladio, a brilliant theorist as well as a major later 16th-century architect (FIGS. 22-28 to 22-31), included the Tempietto in his survey of ancient temples because Bramante was "the first to bring back to light the good and beautiful architecture that from antiquity to that time had been hidden."[7] (Note the kinship with Ghiberti's and Vasari's views of the history of painting; see pages 584 and 636.) Round in plan and elevated on a base that isolates it from its surroundings, the Tempietto conforms to Alberti's and Palladio's strictest demands for an ideal church, although it is far too small to house a congregation.

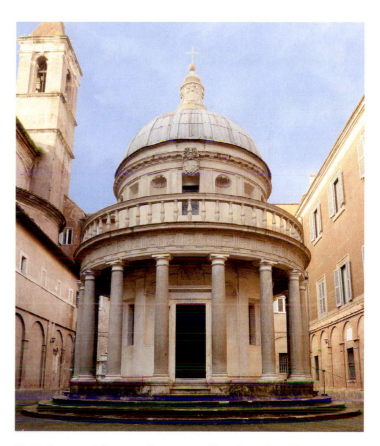

22-21 DONATO D'ANGELO BRAMANTE, Tempietto, San Pietro in Montorio, Rome, Italy, begun 1502.

Contemporaries celebrated Bramante as the first architect to revive the classical style. Roman temples (FIG. 7-4) inspired his "little temple," but Bramante combined the classical parts in new ways.

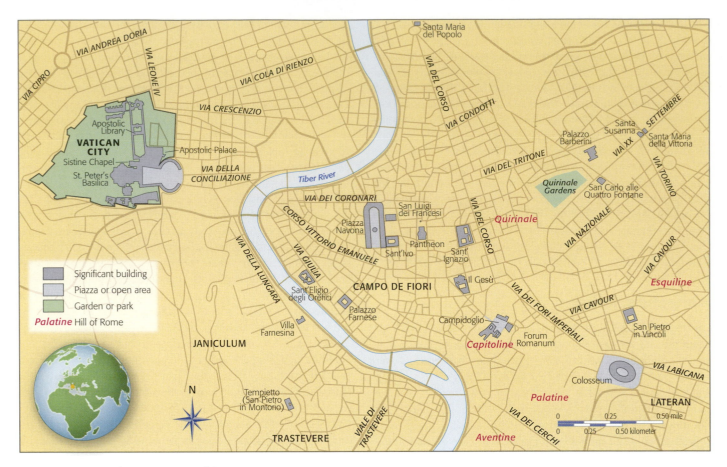

MAP 22-1 Rome with Renaissance and Baroque monuments.

SAINT PETER'S As noted, Bramante was the architect whom Julius II selected to design a replacement for the basilica of Old Saint Peter's (FIG. 8-9). The fourth-century building had fallen into considerable disrepair and, in any event, did not suit the ambitious pope's taste for the colossal. Many members of the papal *Curia* ("court") opposed tearing down the venerable shrine, but Julius could not be dissuaded. He dreamed of gaining control over all Italy and making the Rome of the popes the equal of (if not more

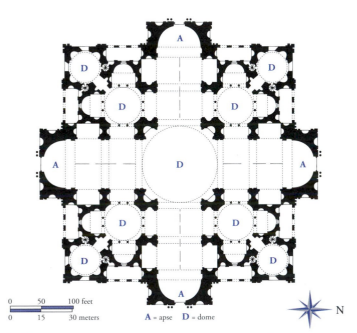

0 50 100 feet
0 15 30 meters   A = apse   D = dome   N

22-22 DONATO D'ANGELO BRAMANTE, plan for Saint Peter's, Vatican City, Rome, Italy, 1505.

Bramante proposed to replace the Constantinian basilica of Saint Peter's (FIG. 8-10) with a central-plan church featuring a cross with arms of equal length, each of which terminated in an apse.

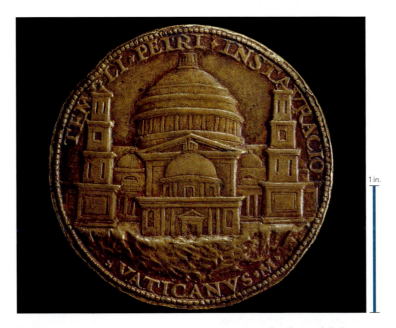

1 in.

22-23 CRISTOFORO FOPPA CARADOSSO, reverse side of a medal showing Bramante's design for Saint Peter's, 1506. Bronze, 2¼" diameter. British Museum, London.

Bramante's unexecuted 1506 design for Saint Peter's called for a large dome over the crossing, smaller domes over the subsidiary chapels, and a boldly sculptural treatment of the walls and piers.

splendid than) the Rome of the caesars (see "Julius II," page 623). A crumbling basilica did not serve his purposes. A magnificent new church did, especially one that revived the classical architectural vocabulary of imperial Rome. Like its predecessor, the new Saint Peter's was to serve as a *martyrium* to mark the apostle's grave, but Julius also intended to install his own tomb (FIGS. 22-14 and 22-15) in the church. Constantine's basilica was not large enough to house the mammoth tomb that the pope envisioned (see page 637).

Bramante's ambitious design (FIG. 22-22) for the new Saint Peter's consisted of a cross with arms of equal length, each terminating in an apse. A large dome would have covered the crossing, and smaller domes over subsidiary chapels would have capped the diagonal axes of the roughly square plan. Bramante's design also called for a boldly sculptural treatment of the walls and piers under the dome. The organization of the interior space was complex in the extreme: nine interlocking crosses, five of them supporting domes. The scale of Bramante's Saint Peter's was gigantic. The architect boasted that he would place the dome of the Pantheon (FIGS. 7-49 to 7-51) over the Basilica Nova (Basilica of Constantine; FIG. 7-76).

A commemorative medal (FIG. 22-23) by CRISTOFORO FOPPA CARADOSSO (ca. 1452–1526) shows how Bramante planned to accomplish that feat. As in the Pantheon, Saint Peter's dome would be hemispherical, but Bramante broke up the massive unity of the ancient temple by adding two towers and a medley of domes and porticos. In light of Julius II's interest in the Roman Empire, it is not surprising that the pope approved using the Pantheon as a model for the new church. That Bramante's design appeared on a commemorative medal is in itself noteworthy. Such medals proliferated in the 15th century (FIG. 21-28A), reviving the ancient Roman practice of placing images of important imperial building projects on the reverse side of coins. The fronts of those coins bore portraits of the emperors who commissioned the buildings. Predictably, a portrait of Julius II, not Bramante, appears on the front of the Caradosso medal.

MICHELANGELO, SAINT PETER'S During Bramante's lifetime, construction of Saint Peter's did not advance beyond the erection of the crossing piers and the lower choir walls. After his death, the work passed from one architect to another and, in 1546, to Michelangelo, whom Pope Paul III had already put in charge of the reorganization of the Capitoline Hill (FIG. 22-23A) in Rome. With the Church facing challenges to its supremacy, the pope surely felt a sense of urgency about the completion of this project. Michelangelo's work on Saint Peter's became a long-term show of dedication, thankless and without pay. Among Michelangelo's difficulties was his struggle to preserve and carry through Bramante's original plan (FIG. 22-22), which he praised and chose to retain as the basis for his own design (FIGS. 22-24 and 22-25). Michelangelo shared Bramante's conviction that a central plan was the ideal form for a church. Always a sculptor at heart, Michelangelo carried his obsession with human form over to architecture and reasoned that buildings should follow the form of the human body. This meant organizing their units symmetrically around a central axis, as the arms relate to the body or the eyes to the nose. "For it is an established fact," he wrote, "that the members of architecture resemble the members of man. Whoever neither has been nor is a master at figures, and especially at anatomy, cannot really understand architecture."[8]

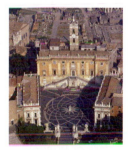

⬀ **22-23A** MICHELANGELO, Campidoglio, Rome, 1538–1564.

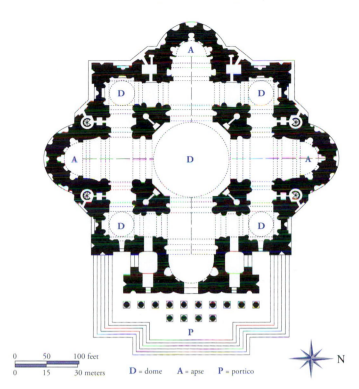

22-24 MICHELANGELO BUONARROTI, **plan for Saint Peter's, Vatican City, Rome, Italy, 1546.**

Michelangelo admired Bramante's plan (FIG. 22-22) for Saint Peter's, but modified it. He replaced the core of interlocking crosses in Bramante's design with a compact domed Greek cross inscribed in a square.

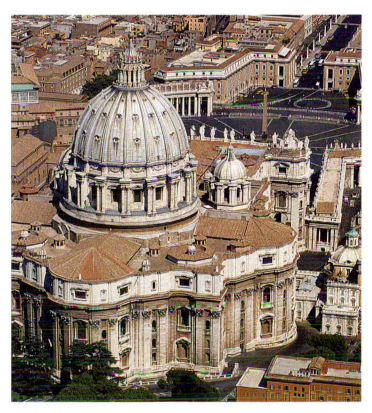

22-25 MICHELANGELO BUONARROTI, **aerial view of Saint Peter's (looking northeast), Vatican City, Rome, Italy, 1546–1564. Dome completed by** GIACOMO DELLA PORTA, **1590.**

The west end of Saint Peter's offers the best view of Michelangelo's intentions. The giant pilasters of his colossal order march around the undulating wall surfaces of the central-plan building.

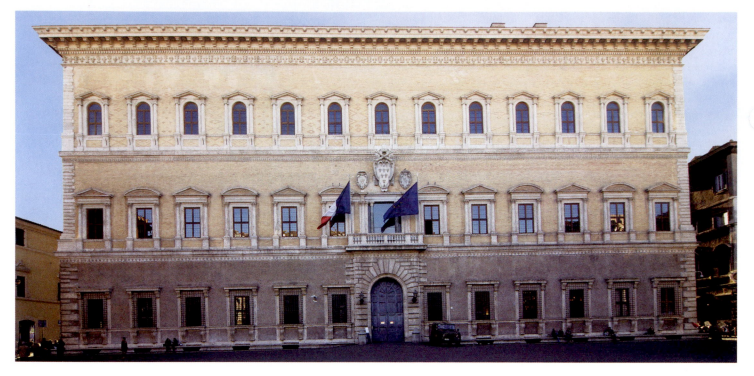

22-26 Antonio da Sangallo the Younger, Palazzo Farnese (looking southwest), Rome, Italy, 1517–1546; completed by Michelangelo Buonarroti, 1546–1550.

Pope Paul III commissioned this lavish palace when he was Cardinal Farnese. The facade features a rusticated central doorway and quoins and alternating triangular and segmental pediments.

In his modification of Bramante's plan, Michelangelo replaced the core of interlocking crosses in Bramante's design with a compact domed *Greek cross* inscribed in a square and fronted with a double-columned portico. Without destroying the centralizing features of Bramante's plan, Michelangelo, with a few strokes of the pen, converted its crystalline complexity into massive, cohesive unity. His treatment of the building's exterior further reveals his interest in creating a unified design. Because of later changes to the front of the church, the west (apse) end (FIG. 22-25) offers the best view of Michelangelo's style and intention. His design incorporated the colossal order, the two-story pilasters first seen in more reserved fashion in Alberti's Mantuan church of Sant'Andrea (FIG. 21-45). The giant pilasters seem to march around the undulating wall surfaces, confining the movement without interrupting it. The architectural sculpturing here extends up from the ground through the attic stories and into the drum and dome, unifying the whole building from base to summit.

The domed west end—as majestic as it is today and as influential as it has been on architecture throughout the centuries—is not quite as Michelangelo intended it. Originally, he had planned a dome with an ogival section, like the one Brunelleschi designed for Florence Cathedral (FIGS. 14-19, 21-29A, and 21-29B). But in his final version, he decided on a hemispherical dome to temper the verticality of the design of the lower stories and to establish a balance between dynamic and static elements. However, when Giacomo della Porta (FIG. 22-57) executed the dome (FIGS. 22-25 and 24-4) after Michelangelo's death, he restored the earlier high design, ignoring Michelangelo's later version. Giacomo's reasons were probably the same ones that had impelled Brunelleschi to use an ogival section for the Florentine dome—greater stability and ease of construction. The result is that the dome seems to rise from its base,

rather than rest firmly on it—an effect Michelangelo might not have approved.

PALAZZO FARNESE Another architectural project Michelangelo took over at the request of Paul III was to complete the construction of the lavish palace (FIG. 22-26) the pope had commissioned when he was Cardinal Alessandro Farnese. The future pope had selected Antonio da Sangallo the Younger (1483–1546) as the architect. Antonio, the youngest of a family of architects, arrived in Rome around 1503 and became Bramante's draftsman and assistant. He is the perfect example of the professional architect. Indeed, his family constituted an architectural firm, often planning and drafting for other architects.

The broad, majestic front of the Palazzo Farnese asserts to the public the exalted station of a great family. It is significant that Paul chose to enlarge the original rather modest palace to its present grandiose form after his election as head of the Catholic Church in 1534—a reflection of his ambitions both for his family and for the papacy. Facing a spacious paved square, the facade is the very essence of princely dignity in architecture. The *quoins* (rusticated building corners) and cornice firmly anchor the rectangle of the smooth front, and lines of windows (the central row with alternating triangular and curved [*segmental*] pediments, in Bramante's fashion) mark a majestic march across it. The window frames are not flush with the wall, as in the Palazzo Medici-Riccardi (FIG. 21-35), but project from its surface, so instead of being a flat, thin plane, the facade is a spatially active three-dimensional mass. The rusticated doorway and second-story balcony, surmounted by the Farnese coat of arms, emphasize the central axis and bring the design's horizontal and vertical forces into harmony. Those centralizing features are absent from the palaces of Michelozzo (FIG. 21-35) and Alberti

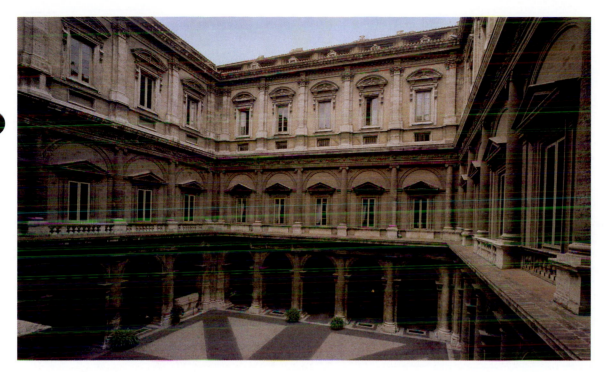

22-27 Antonio da Sangallo the Younger, courtyard of the Palazzo Farnese (looking south), Rome, Italy, ca. 1517–1546. Third story and attic by Michelangelo Buonarroti, 1546–1550.

The interior courtyard of the Palazzo Farnese set the standard for later Italian palaces. It fully expresses the order, regularity, simplicity, and dignity of the High Renaissance style in architecture.

(FIG. 21-37). In the Palazzo Farnese, the portal is the external end of a central corridor axis running through the entire building and continuing in the garden beyond. Around this axis, Sangallo arranged the rooms with strict regularity.

The interior courtyard (FIG. **22-27**) displays stately column-framed arches on the first two levels, as in the Colosseum (FIG. 7-37). On the third level, Michelangelo, after Sangallo's death in 1546, incorporated his sophisticated variation on that theme (based in part on the Colosseum's fourth-story Corinthian pilasters), with overlapping pilasters replacing the weighty columns of Sangallo's design. The Palazzo Farnese set the standard for Italian Renaissance palaces and fully expresses the classical order, regularity, simplicity, and dignity of the High Renaissance architectural style.

Architecture: Venice

For centuries a major Mediterranean port, Venice served as the gateway to the Orient. After reaching the height of its commercial and political power during the 15th century, the city saw its fortunes decline in the 16th century. Even so, Venice and the Papal States were the only Italian sovereignties to retain their independence during the century of strife. Either France or Spain dominated all others. Although the discoveries in the New World and the economic shift from Italy to areas such as the Netherlands were largely responsible for the decline of Venice, even more immediate and pressing events drained its wealth and power. After their conquest of Constantinople (see page 258), the Turks began to vie with the Venetians for control of the eastern Mediterranean. The Ottoman Empire evolved into a constant threat to Venice. Early in the century, the European powers of the League of Cambrai also attacked the Italian port city. Formed and led by Pope Julius II, who coveted Venetian holdings on Italy's mainland, the league included Spain, France, and the Holy Roman Empire, in addition to the Papal States. Despite these challenges, Venice developed a flourishing, independent, and influential school of artists and architects.

ANDREA PALLADIO The chief architect of the Venetian Republic from 1570 until his death a decade later was Andrea di Pietro of Padua, known as ANDREA PALLADIO (1508–1580). (The surname derives from Pallas Athena, Greek goddess of wisdom, an appropriate reference for an architect schooled in the classical tradition of Alberti and Bramante.) Palladio began his career as a stonemason and decorative sculptor in Vicenza. At age 30, however, he turned to architecture, engineering, military science, and the ancient literature on architecture. In order to study the ancient buildings firsthand, Palladio made several trips to Rome. In 1556, he illustrated Daniele Barbaro's edition of Vitruvius's *De architectura* (see page 199) and later wrote his own treatise on architecture, *I quattro libri dell'architettura* (*The Four Books of Architecture*), originally published in 1570. That work had wide-ranging influence on succeeding generations of architects throughout Europe. Palladio's influence outside Italy, most significantly in England and in colonial America (see pages 787 and 789), was stronger and more lasting than any other architect's.

Palladio accrued his significant reputation from his many designs for *villas*, built on the Venetian mainland. Nineteen still stand, and they especially influenced later architects. The same spirit that prompted the ancient Romans to build villas in the countryside motivated a similar villa-building boom in 16th-century Venice, which, with its very limited space, was highly congested. But a longing for the countryside was not the only motive. Declining fortunes prompted the Venetians to develop their mainland possessions with new land investment and reclamation projects. Citizens who could afford to do so set themselves up as aristocratic farmers and developed swamps into productive agricultural land. The villas were thus the elegant residential centerpieces of income-producing farms surrounded by service outbuildings (like the much later American plantations, which emulated many aspects of Palladio's architectural style). Palladio generally arranged the outbuildings in long, low wings branching out from the main building and enclosing a large rectangular court area.

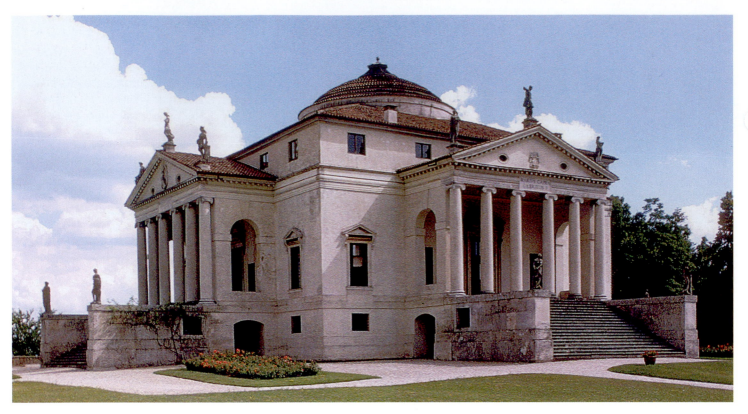

22-28 ANDREA PALLADIO, Villa Rotonda (looking southwest), near Vicenza, Italy, ca. 1550–1570.

The Villa Rotonda has four identical facades, each one resembling a Roman temple with a columnar porch. In the center is a great dome-covered rotunda modeled on the Pantheon (FIG. 7-49).

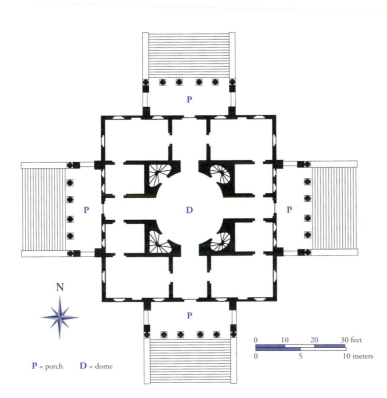

22-29 ANDREA PALLADIO, plan of the Villa Rotonda, near Vicenza, Italy, ca. 1550–1570.

Andrea Palladio published an influential treatise on architecture in 1570. Consistent with his design theories, all parts of the Villa Rotonda relate to one another in terms of mathematical ratios.

VILLA ROTONDA Palladio's most famous villa, Villa Rotonda (FIG. 22-28), near Vicenza, is exceptional because the architect did not build it for an aspiring gentleman farmer but for a retired monsignor in the papal court in Rome, Paolo Almerico, who wanted a villa for social events. Palladio planned and designed Villa Rotonda, located on a hilltop, as a kind of *belvedere* (literally "beautiful view"; in architecture, a structure with a view of the countryside or the sea), without the usual wings of secondary buildings. It has a central plan (FIG. 22-29) featuring four identical facades with projecting porches, each of which resembles a Roman Ionic temple. In placing a traditional temple porch in front of a dome-covered unit, Palladio doubtless had the Pantheon (FIG. 7-49) in mind. (The villa's name "La Rotonda," proposed by Almerico, is a reference to Santa Maria Rotonda in Rome—the name of the Pantheon after its remodeling as a church with twin bell towers added to its ancient facade.) But, as Bramante did in his Tempietto (FIG. 22-21), Palladio transformed his model into a new design without parallel in antiquity, rotating the plan 45 degrees from the cardinal points in order for natural sunlight to illuminate every room. Each of the villa's four porches doubles as a columnar facade and a platform for enjoying a different view of the surrounding landscape. In this design, the central dome-covered rotunda logically functions as a circular reception area from which visitors may turn in any direction for the preferred view. The result is a building with functional parts systematically related to one another in terms of calculated mathematical relationships. Villa Rotonda embodies all the qualities of self-sufficiency and formal completeness that most Renaissance architects sought.

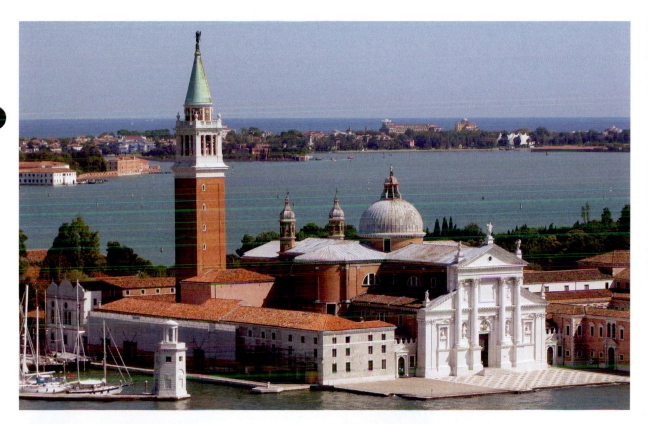

22-30 ANDREA PALLADIO, San Giorgio Maggiore (looking southeast), Venice, Italy, begun 1566.

Dissatisfied with earlier solutions to the problem of integrating a high central nave and lower aisles into a unified facade, Palladio superimposed a tall and narrow classical porch on a low broad one.

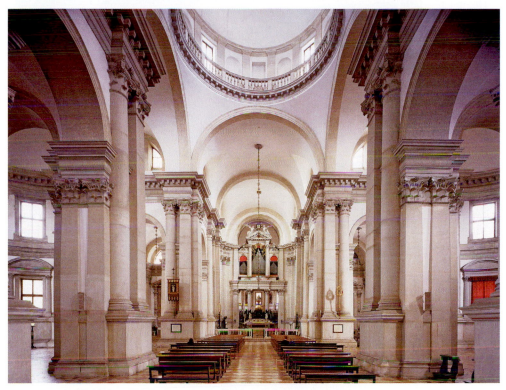

22-31 ANDREA PALLADIO, interior of San Giorgio Maggiore (looking east), Venice, Italy, begun 1566.

In contrast to the somewhat irrational intersection of two temple facades on the exterior of San Giorgio Maggiore, Palladio's interior is strictly logical, consistent with classical architectural theory.

SAN GIORGIO MAGGIORE One of the most dramatically placed buildings in Venice is San Giorgio Maggiore (FIGS. **22-30** and **22-31**), directly across the Grand Canal from Piazza San Marco. Palladio began work on the church a few years before he succeeded JACOPO SANSOVINO (1486–1570; FIG. **22-31A**) as Venice's official

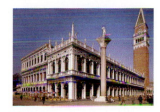

22-31A SANSOVINO, Mint and Library, Venice, begun 1536.

architect. Dissatisfied with earlier solutions to the problem of integrating a high central nave and lower aisles into a unified facade design, Palladio solved it by superimposing a tall and narrow classical porch on a low broad one. This solution reflects the building's interior arrangement (dome-covered nave and single-story aisles) and in that sense is strictly logical, but the intersection of two temple facades is irrational and ambiguous, consistent with contemporaneous developments in Mannerist architecture (see page 668). Palladio's design also created the illusion of three-dimensional depth, an effect intensified by the strong projection of the central columns and the shadows they cast. The play of shadow across the building's surfaces, its reflection in the water, and its gleaming white against sea and sky create a remarkably colorful effect. The interior of the church lacks the ambiguity of the facade and exhibits strong roots in High Renaissance architectural style. Light floods the interior and crisply defines the contours of the rich wall moldings with their archaeologically correct profiles, an exemplar of classical architectural theory.

Venetian Painting

The leading Venetian painter at the turn of the century was Giovanni Bellini (FIG. 21-40). Bellini developed a coloristic oil painting style that became the foundation of the distinctive High Renaissance style of the maritime republic, setting Cinquecento Venetian art apart from Florentine and Roman art.

SAN ZACCARIA ALTARPIECE Bellini earned great recognition for his many Madonnas, which he painted both in half-length (with or without accompanying saints) on small devotional panels and in full-length on monumental altarpieces representing a *sacra conversazione* (holy conversation). In the sacra conversazione, which became a popular theme for religious paintings from the middle of the 15th century on, saints from different epochs occupy the same space and seem to converse either with each other or with the audience. (Raphael employed much the same concept in his *School of Athens* [FIG. 22-9], where he gathered Greek philosophers of different eras.)

Bellini carried on the tradition in the *San Zaccaria Altarpiece* (FIG. **22-32**), which he painted in 1505, already in his 70s. (He died in his mid-80s in 1516. Bellini's long career explains in part his profound influence on the next generation of Venetian painters.) In an architectural setting that Bellini carefully coordinated with the church's real columns, pilasters, and arches, the Virgin Mary sits enthroned, holding the Christ Child, with saints flanking her. Attributes aid the identification of all the saints: Saint Lucy holds a tray with her plucked-out eyes displayed on it; Peter, his key and book; Catherine, the palm of martyrdom and a broken wheel; and Jerome, a book (representing his translation of the Bible into Latin). At the foot of the throne sits an angel playing a viol. The painting radiates a feeling of serenity and spiritual calm. Viewers derive this sense less from the figures (no interaction occurs among them) than from Bellini's harmonious and balanced presentation of color and light. Line is not the chief agent of form, as it generally is in paintings produced in Rome and Florence. Indeed, outlines dissolve in light and shadow. Glowing color produces a soft radiance that envelops the forms with an atmospheric haze and enhances their majestic serenity.

22-32 GIOVANNI BELLINI, *Madonna and Child with Saints* (*San Zaccaria Altarpiece*), 1505. Oil on wood transferred to canvas, 16' 5½" × 7' 9". San Zaccaria, Venice.

In this *sacra conversazione* uniting saints from different eras, Bellini created a feeling of serenity and spiritual calm through the harmonious and balanced presentation of color and light.

FEAST OF THE GODS Painted a decade later, *Feast of the Gods* (FIG. **22-33**) is one of Bellini's acknowledged masterpieces. By this time, the aged master was already looking to the work of some of his students for inspiration. *Feast of the Gods* draws upon the poetic "Arcadian" landscapes of Giorgione (FIG. 22-34). Derived from Arcadia, a region in southern Greece, the term *Arcadian* referred, by the time of the Renaissance, to an idyllic place of rustic peace and simplicity. After Giorgione's premature death, Bellini embraced his student's interests and, in *Feast of the Gods,* developed a new kind of mythological painting. The duke of Ferrara, Alfonso d'Este (r. 1505–1534), commissioned this work for the Camerino d'Alabastro (Alabaster Room), a private apartment in the Palazzo Ducale complex. Alfonso hired four painters—Bellini, Titian (Bellini's greatest student; FIGS. 22-35 to 22-41), Raphael, and Fra Bartolommeo (1472–1517) of Florence—to provide four paintings of related mythological subjects for the room, carefully selected for the duke by the humanist scholar Mario Equicola (1470–1515). Both Raphael and Fra Bartolommeo died before fulfilling the commission.

For his painting, Bellini drew some of the figures from the standard repertoire of Greco-Roman art—most notably, the nymph carrying a vase on her head and the sleeping nymph in the lower

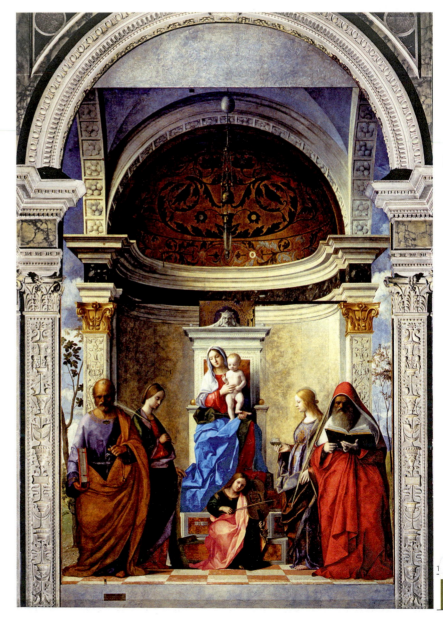

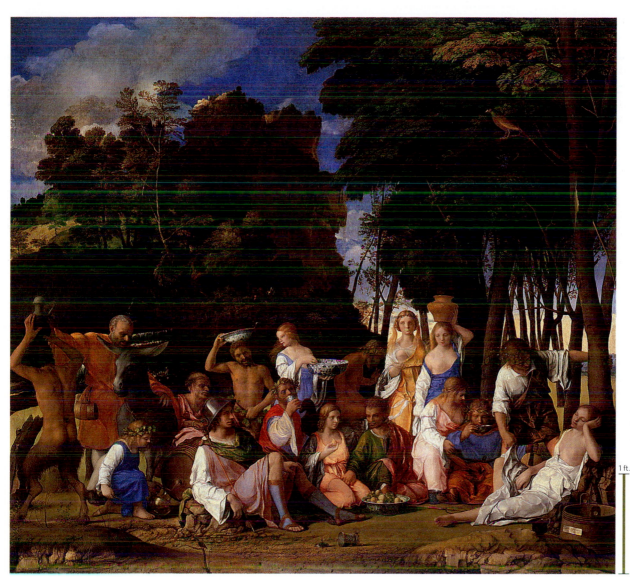

1 ft.

right corner. But Bellini's Olympian gods appear as peasants enjoying a picnic in a shady glade. The ancient literary source was the *Fasti* (1:391–440; 6:319–348) by the Roman poet Ovid, who described banquets of gods. In Bellini's painting, satyrs attend the gods, nymphs bring jugs of wine, and couples engage in love play. At the far right, Priapus lifts the dress of the sleeping nymph with exposed breast. (All four paintings in the Camerino centered on Venus or Bacchus, the Roman gods of love and wine.) The mellow light of a long afternoon glows softly around the gathering, caressing the surfaces of colorful fabrics, smooth flesh, and polished metal. Here, Bellini communicated the delight that the Venetian school took in the beauty of texture revealed by the full resources of gently and subtly harmonized color. Behind the warm, lush tones of the figures, a background of cool green tree-filled glades extends into the distance. At the right, a screen of trees—painted in 1529 by Titian—creates a verdant shelter. The atmosphere is idyllic, a lush countryside providing a setting for the never-ending pleasure of the immortal gods.

With Bellini, Venetian art became the great complement of the schools of Florence and Rome. The Venetians' instrument was color, that of the Florentines and Romans sculpturesque form. Scholars often distill the contrast between these two approaches down to *colorito* (colored or painted) versus *disegno* (drawing and design).

Whereas most central Italian artists emphasized careful design preparation based on preliminary drawing (see "Renaissance Drawings," page 628), Venetian artists focused on color and the process of paint application. Vasari, who held the artists of his native Florence in greater esteem than Venice's, disapprovingly drew attention to the different working methods of the Venetians and attributed them largely to Giorgione (FIG. 22-34):

> Giorgione of Castelfranco . . . made use of live and natural objects and copied them as best he knew how with colors, tinting them with the crude and soft colors that Nature displays, without making preliminary drawings since he was firmly convinced that painting alone with its colors, and without any other preliminary study of designs on paper, was the truest and best method of working.[9]

In addition, the general thematic focus of Venetian artists differed from those of Florence and Rome. The Venetians painted the poetry of the senses and delighted in nature's beauty and the pleasures of humanity. Florentine and Roman artists gravitated toward more intellectual themes—the epic of humanity, the masculine virtues, the grandeur of the ideal, and the lofty conceptions of religion involving the heroic and sublime. Much of the history of later Western art involves a dialogue between these two traditions.

The subject of this painting featuring a nude woman in a lush landscape beneath a stormy sky is uncertain, contributing, perhaps intentionally, to the painting's intriguing air of mystery.

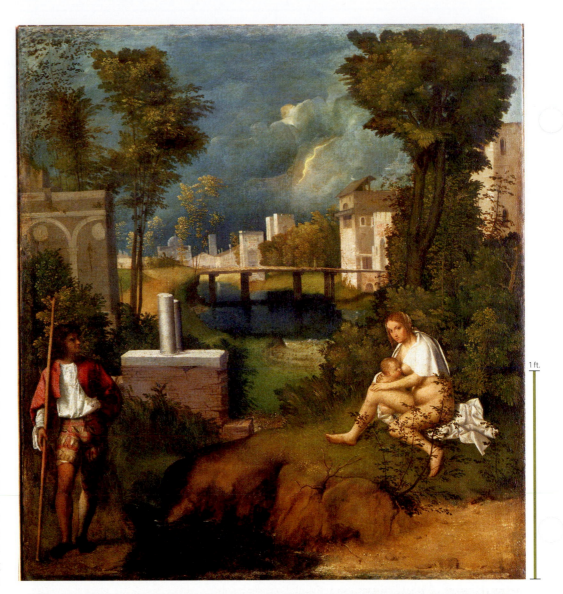

GIORGIONE Describing Venetian art as "poetic" is particularly appropriate, given the development of *poesia,* or painting meant to operate in a manner similar to poetry. Both classical and Renaissance poetry inspired Venetian artists, and their paintings focused on the lyrical and sensual. Thus, in many Venetian artworks, identifying specific subjects is impossible. That is certainly the case with *The Tempest* (FIG. **22-34**), a painting that continues to defy interpretation. It is the greatest work attributed to the short-lived Giorgione da Castelfranco (ca. 1477–1510), the Venetian artist who deserves much of the credit for developing the poetic manner of painting and whose lush landscapes served as an inspiration for his teacher, Bellini, in works such as *Feast of the Gods.* In Giorgione's *Tempest,* stormy skies and lightning in the middle background threaten the tranquility of the pastoral setting, however. And, in contrast to Bellini, Giorgione pushed off to both sides the few human figures depicted—a young woman nursing a baby in the right foreground and, on the left, a man with a staff.

Giorgione painted *The Tempest* for a wealthy private collector, Gabriele Vendramin, and much scholarly debate has centered on the painting's subject, fueled by X-rays of the canvas, which revealed that the Venetian master altered many of the details as

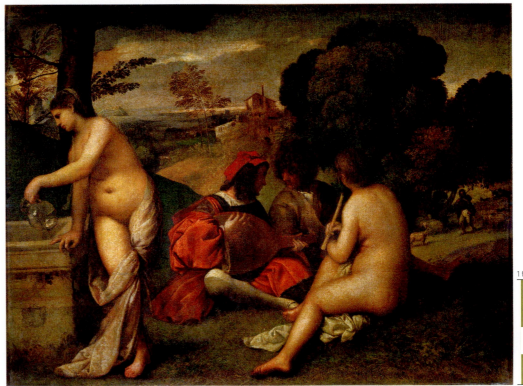

Venetian art conjures poetry. In this painting, Titian so eloquently evoked the pastoral mood that the inability to decipher the picture's meaning is not distressing. The mood and rich color are enough.

work progressed. Most notably, a seated nude woman originally occupied the position where Giorgione subsequently placed the standing man, whose elegant garb is out of place in this rustic setting. The changes the painter made have led many art historians to believe that Giorgione did not intend the painting to have a definitive narrative, which is appropriate for a Venetian poetic rendering. Other scholars have suggested various mythological and biblical narratives. The uncertainty about the subject contributes to the painting's intriguing air, however.

TITIAN Giorgione's masterful handling of light and color and his interest in landscape, poetry, and music—Vasari reported that he was an accomplished lutenist and singer—influenced not only his much older yet constantly inquisitive teacher, Bellini, but also his younger contemporary, Tiziano Vecelli, called TITIAN (ca. 1490–1576) in English. Indeed, a masterpiece long attributed to Giorgione—*Pastoral Symphony* (FIG. **22-35**)—is now widely believed to be an early work of Titian. Out of dense shadow emerge the soft forms of figures and landscape. Titian, a supreme colorist and master of the oil medium, cast a mood of tranquil reverie and dreaminess over the entire scene, evoking the landscape of a lost but never forgotten paradise. As in Giorgione's *Tempest*, the theme is as enigmatic as the lighting. Two nude women occupy the foreground. The seated one resembles the woman in *The Tempest*, but seen from behind. Accompanying them are two clothed young men, the lute player wearing elegant city clothes, the other dressed like a shepherd. The four figures occupy a bountiful landscape. In the middle ground is a shepherd and his sheep. In the distance, a villa crowns a hill.

Titian so eloquently evoked the pastoral mood that the viewer does not find the uncertainty about the picture's precise meaning distressing. The mood is enough. The musician symbolizes the poet. The pipes and lute symbolize his poetry. The two women may be thought of as the young men's invisible inspiration, their muses. One turns to lift water from the sacred well of poetic inspiration. Smoky shadow softly models the voluptuous bodies of the women. The fullness of their figures became the standard in Venetian art and contributes to their effect as poetic personifications of nature's abundance. Venetian painters, unlike their counterparts in Florence and Rome, generally painted directly on the canvas without preparatory drawings. Their nudes are neither precise anatomical studies nor idealized forms based on mathematics and geometry.

ASSUMPTION OF THE VIRGIN On Bellini's death in 1516, the Republic of Venice appointed Titian as its official painter. Shortly thereafter, the prior of the Franciscan basilica of Santa Maria Gloriosa dei Frari commissioned Titian to paint a gigantic altarpiece (nearly 23 feet high) for the high altar of the church. In *Assumption of the Virgin* (FIG. **22-36**), a fitting theme for the shrine of the "glorious Saint Mary," Titian's remarkable coloristic sense and his ability to convey light

through color are again on display. The subject is the ascent of the Virgin to Heaven on a great white cloud borne aloft by putti. Above, golden clouds, so luminous that they seem to glow and radiate light into the church, envelop the Virgin, whose head is on the vertical axis of the composition and is the center of a circle formed by the arched frame and the U-shaped band of clouds. God the Father appears above, slightly off-center, awaiting Mary with open arms. Below, closest to the viewer, over-life-size apostles gesticulate wildly as they witness the glorious event. Many have their backs to the worshipers, who join the apostles as observers looking up with them at the Virgin's miraculous ascent. Through his mastery of the oil medium—fresco was not a good choice for Venetian churches because of the dampness and salinity of this city with saltwater streets—Titian used vibrant color to infuse the image with intensity and amplify the drama.

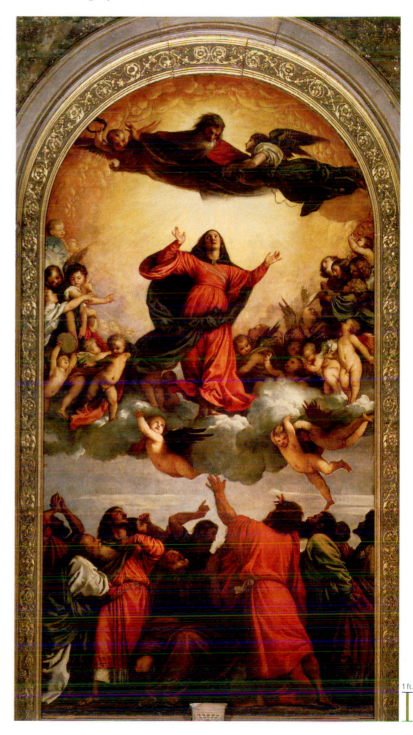

22-36 TITIAN, *Assumption of the Virgin*, 1515–1518. Oil on wood, 22′ 7½″ × 11′ 10″. Santa Maria Gloriosa dei Frari, Venice.

Titian won renown for his skill in conveying light through color. In this dramatic depiction of the Virgin Mary's ascent to Heaven, the golden clouds seem to glow and radiate light into the church.

1 ft.

PESARO MADONNA A year after installing *Assumption of the Virgin* in the main altar of the Venetian church of the Frari, Titian received a commission to paint *Madonna of the Pesaro Family* (FIG. **22-37**) for the same church. Jacopo Pesaro (d. 1547), bishop of Paphos in Cyprus and commander of the papal fleet, had led a successful expedition in 1502 against the Turks during the Venetian-Turkish war. He dedicated a family chapel in Santa Maria Gloriosa and donated Titian's altarpiece in gratitude. In a stately sunlit setting in what may be the Madonna's palace in Heaven, Mary receives the commander, who kneels dutifully at the foot of her throne. A soldier (Saint George?) behind the commander carries a banner with the *escutcheons* (shields with coats of arms) of the Borgia pope, Alexander VI, and of Pesaro. Behind him is a turbaned Turk, a prisoner of war of the Christian forces. Saint Peter appears on the steps of the throne, and Saint Francis introduces other Pesaro family members,

who kneel solemnly in the right foreground. (All of the kneeling figures are male. Italian depictions of donors in this era typically excluded women and children.) Thus Titian entwined the human and the heavenly, depicting the Madonna and saints honoring the achievements of a specific man. A quite worldly transaction takes place (albeit beneath a heavenly cloud bearing angels) between a queen and her court and loyal servants, consistent with Renaissance protocol and courtly splendor.

A prime characteristic of High Renaissance painting is the massing of monumental figures, singly and in groups, within a weighty and majestic architecture. But here Titian did not compose a horizontal and symmetrical arrangement, as did Leonardo in *Last Supper* (FIG. 22-4) and Raphael in *School of Athens* (FIG. 22-9). Rather, he placed the figures on a steep diagonal, positioning the Madonna, the focus of the composition, well off the central axis. Titian drew attention to her with the perspective lines, the inclination of the figures, and the directional lines of gaze and gesture. The banner that forms a diagonal accent at the left beautifully brings the design into equilibrium, balancing the rightward and upward tendencies of its main direction. This kind of composition is more dynamic than most High Renaissance examples and foreshadowed a new kind of pictorial design—one built on movement rather than rest. It also anticipated some of the most daring illusionistic mural and ceiling paintings of the Baroque era in taking the viewer's position into consideration (see page 720). The Pesaro *Madonna* is on the wall in the left aisle of the Frari church. Worshipers approach the painting from the left and look up at the Virgin in the same way Jacopo Pesaro does. Then, if they turn to the right and look at the apse, they see Titian's *Assumption of the Virgin* (FIG. 22-36).

BACCHUS AND ARIADNE After the deaths of Raphael and Fra Bartolommeo, Titian took over their commissions to paint *bacchanal* scenes for Alfonso d'Este's Camerino d'Alabastro, in addition to his own assignment. Titian also contributed the landscape background to Bellini's *Feast of the Gods* (FIG. 22-33). Completed in 1523, *Meeting of Bacchus and Ariadne* (FIG. **22-38**), based on an ancient Latin poem by Catullus, is a roughly 6-foot-square canvas in which Bacchus, accompanied by a boisterous group, arrives on the island of Naxos in a leopard-drawn chariot to save Ariadne, whom Theseus had abandoned there. Consistent with the mythological subject, Titian looked to classical art for models and derived one of the figures, the snake-entwined satyr, from the recently unearthed *Laocoön* (FIG. 5-89), a marble statue that also made an indelible impression on Michelangelo and many others. Titian's rich and luminous colors, especially his lavish use of ultramarine, the most expensive oil pigment, add greatly to the sensuous appeal of the painting, making it perfect for what Alfonso called his "pleasure chamber."

VENUS OF URBINO In 1538, at the height of his powers, Titian painted the so-called *Venus of Urbino* (FIG. **22-39**), probably for Guidobaldo II, who became the duke of Urbino the following year (r. 1539–1574). The title (given to the painting later) elevates to the status of classical mythology what is probably a representation of a sensual Italian woman in her bedchamber. Whether the nude woman is divine or mortal, Titian based his version on an earlier (and pioneering) painting of Venus (not illustrated) by Giorgione. Here, Titian established the compositional elements and the standard for paintings of the reclining female nude. This "Venus" reclines on the gentle slope of her luxurious pillowed couch. Her softly rounded body contrasts with the sharp vertical edge of the curtain behind her, which serves to direct the viewer's attention to her left hand

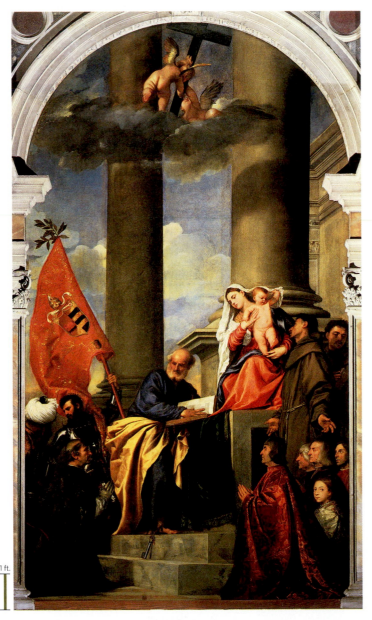

22-37 TITIAN, *Madonna of the Pesaro Family*, 1519–1526. Oil on canvas, 15' 11" × 8' 10". Pesaro Chapel, Santa Maria Gloriosa dei Frari, Venice.

In this dynamic composition foreshadowing a new kind of pictorial design, Titian placed the figures on a steep diagonal, positioning the Madonna, the focus of the composition, well off the central axis.

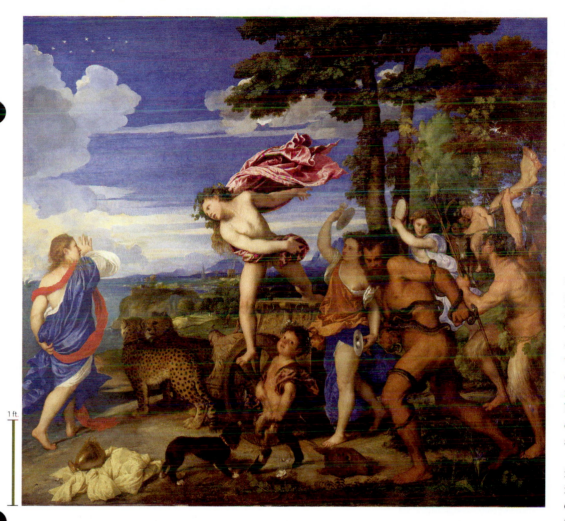

22-38 TITIAN, *Meeting of Bacchus and Ariadne,* from the Camerino d'Alabastro, Palazzo Ducale, Ferrara, Italy, 1522–1523. Oil on canvas, 5' 9" × 6' 3". National Gallery, London.

Titian's rich and luminous colors add greatly to the sensuous appeal of this mythological painting in which he based one of the figures on the recently unearthed *Laocoön* (FIG. 5-89).

a chest, apparently searching for garments (Renaissance households stored clothing in carved wood chests called *cassoni*) to clothe their reclining nude mistress. Beyond them, a smaller vista opens into a landscape. Titian masterfully constructed the view backward into the room and the division of the space into progressively smaller units.

As in other Venetian paintings, color plays a prominent role in *Venus of Urbino.* The red tones of the matron's skirt and the muted reds of the tapestries against the neutral whites of the matron's sleeves and the kneeling girl's gown echo the deep Venetian reds set off against the pale neutral whites of the linen and the warm ivory gold of the flesh. The viewer must study the picture carefully to realize the subtlety of color planning.

For instance, the two deep reds (in the foreground cushions and in the background skirt) play a critical role in the composition as a gauge of distance and as indicators of an implied diagonal opposed to the real one of the reclining figure. Here, Titian used color not simply to record surface appearance but also to organize his placement of forms.

and pelvis as well as to divide the foreground from the background. At the woman's feet is a slumbering lapdog—where Cupid would be if this were Venus (compare FIG. 7-59). In the right background, near the window opening onto a landscape, two servants bend over

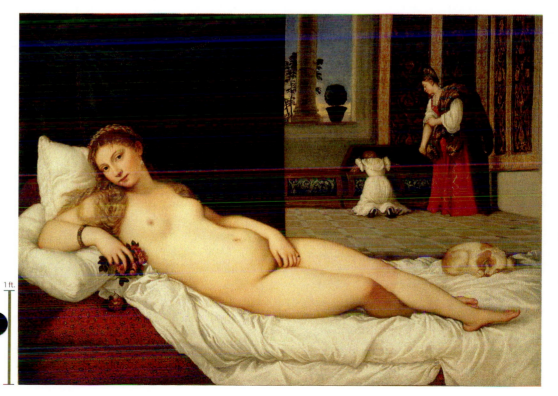

22-39 TITIAN, *Venus of Urbino,* 1536–1538. Oil on canvas, 3' 11" × 5' 5". Galleria degli Uffizi, Florence.

Titian established oil-based pigment on canvas as the preferred painting medium in Western art. Here, he also set the standard for representations of the reclining female nude, whether divine or mortal.

ART AND SOCIETY

Women in the Renaissance Art World

The Renaissance art world was decidedly male-dominated. Few women could become professional artists because of the many obstacles they faced. In particular, training practices requiring residence in a master's house (see "Artists' Guilds," page 422) prevented women from gaining the necessary experience to establish their own studios and attract patrons. In addition, social proscriptions, such as those barring women from drawing from nude models, hampered an aspiring woman artist's advancement through the accepted avenues of artistic training in Renaissance Europe.

Still, some determined Renaissance women surmounted these barriers and produced not only considerable bodies of work but earned enviable reputations as well. One was Sofonisba Anguissola (FIG. 22-47), the first Italian woman to have ascended to the level of international art celebrity. LAVINIA FONTANA (1552–1614; FIG. 22-40A) also achieved notable success, and her paintings constitute the largest surviving body of work by any woman artist before 1700.

Perhaps more challenging for women than the road to becoming a professional painter was the mastery of sculpture, made more difficult by the physical demands of the medium. Yet Properzia de' Rossi (ca. 1490–1530)

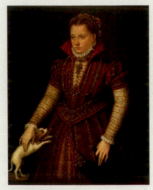

⊿ **22-40A** FONTANA, *Portrait of a Noblewoman*, ca. 1580.

established herself as a professional sculptor and was the only woman artist that Vasari included in his *Lives*. Active in the early 16th century, she died of the plague in 1530, bringing her promising career to an early end.

Beyond the realm of art production, Renaissance women exerted significant influence as art patrons—and probably to a much greater degree than the available evidence suggests, because women often wielded their influence and decision-making power behind the scenes. Many of them attained their positions through marriage. Their power was thus indirect and provisional, based on their husbands' wealth and status. Thus documentation of the networks within which women patrons operated and of the processes they used to exert power in a society dominated by men is meager compared to what is known about male patrons.

Nonetheless, there can be no doubt that one of the most important Renaissance art patrons, male or female, was Isabella d'Este (1474–1539), the marquess of Mantua, one of the leading art centers of Renaissance Italy (see page 616). The daughter of Ercole d'Este, duke of Ferrara (r. 1471–1505), and brought up in the cultured princely court there, Isabella married Marquis Francesco Gonzaga of Mantua in 1490. The marriage gave Isabella access to the position and wealth necessary to become a major force in the Renaissance art world. An avid collector, she enlisted the aid of agents who scoured Italy for appealing artworks. Isabella did not limit her collection to painting and sculpture but included ceramics, glassware, gems, cameos, medals, classical texts, musical manuscripts, and musical instruments. She also commissioned several portraits of herself from the most esteemed artists of her day—Leonardo da Vinci, Andrea Mantegna, and Titian (FIG. 22-40). The detail and complexity of many of Isabella's contracts with artists reveal her insistence on control over the diverse series of works she paid for.

Other Renaissance women also positioned themselves as serious art patrons. One was Caterina Sforza (1462–1509), daughter of Galeazzo Maria Sforza (heir to the duchy of Milan), who married Girolamo Riario (1443–1488) in 1484. The death of her husband, lord of Imola and count of Forlì, gave Sforza, who survived him by two decades, access to power denied most women. Another female art patron was Lucrezia Tornabuoni (1425–1482), who married Piero di Cosimo de' Medici (1416–1469), one of many Medici, both men and women, who earned reputations as lavish art patrons.

Further archival investigation of women's roles in Renaissance Italy undoubtedly will produce more evidence of how women established themselves as patrons and artists and the extent to which they contributed to the careers of various artists and the development of Renaissance art in general.

22-40 TITIAN, *Isabella d'Este*, 1534–1536. Oil on canvas, 3' 4$\frac{1}{8}$" × 2' 1$\frac{3}{16}$". Kunsthistorisches Museum, Vienna.

Isabella d'Este, marquess of Mantua, was one of the most powerful women of the Renaissance era. When, at age 60, she hired Titian to paint her portrait, she insisted that the artist depict her in her 20s.

Palma il Giovane on Titian

An important change occurring in the mid-16th century was the almost universal adoption of canvas, primed with a coat of white to furnish a smooth surface, in place of wood panels for paintings. The most famous painter of the time was Titian, and his works established oil-based pigment on canvas as the standard medium of the Western pictorial tradition thereafter. Palma il Giovane, one of Titian's students, who completed the *Pietà* (FIG. 22-41) that Titian intended for his tomb in Santa Maria Gloriosa dei Frari in Venice, wrote a valuable account of his teacher's working methods and of how Titian used the new medium to great advantage:

> Titian [employed] a great mass of colors, which served . . . as a base for the compositions. . . . I too have seen some of these, formed with bold strokes made with brushes laden with colors, sometimes of a pure red earth, which he used, so to speak, for a middle tone, and at other times of white lead; and with the same brush tinted with red, black and yellow he formed a highlight; and observing these principles he made the promise of an exceptional figure appear in four brushstrokes. . . . Having constructed these precious foundations he used to turn his pictures to the wall and leave them there without looking at them, sometimes for several months. When he wanted to apply his brush again he would examine them with the utmost rigor . . . to see if he could find any faults. . . . In this way, working on the figures and revising them, he brought them to the most perfect symmetry that the beauty of art and nature can reveal. . . . [T]hus he gradually covered those quintessential forms with living flesh, bringing them by many stages to a state in which they lacked only the breath of life. He never painted a figure all at once and . . . in the last stages he painted more with his fingers than his brushes.*

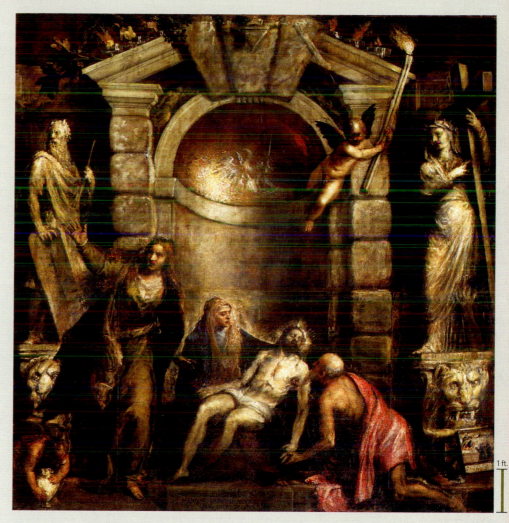

22-41 TITIAN and PALMA IL GIOVANE, *Pietà,* ca. 1570–1576. Oil on canvas, 11' 6" × 12' 9". Galleria dell'Accademia, Venice.

In this late work characterized by broad brushstrokes and a thick impasto, Titian portrayed himself as Saint Jerome kneeling before the dead Christ. Titian intended the work for his own tomb.

*Francesco Valcanover, *Titian: Prince of Painters* (Venice: Marsilio, 1990), 23–24.

ISABELLA D'ESTE Titian was also a highly esteemed portraitist. More than 50 portraits by his hand survive, reflecting the great demand for his services by wealthy patrons desirous of immortalizing themselves. One of Titian's best portraits is of Isabella d'Este (FIG. 22-40), one of the most prominent women of the Renaissance (see "Women in the Renaissance Art World," page 656). Isabella was the sister of Alfonso d'Este, for whom Titian painted three mythological scenes for the Ferrara ducal palace. At 16, she married Francesco Gonzaga, marquis of Mantua (1466–1519; see page 616), and through her patronage of art and music was instrumental in developing the Mantuan court into an important cultural center. Portraits by Titian generally emphasize his psychological reading of the subject's head and hands. Thus here Titian sharply highlighted Isabella's face, whereas her black dress fades into the undefined darkness of the background. The unseen light source also illuminates the sitter's hands, and Titian painted the sleeves of Isabella's elegant gown with incredible detail to further draw viewers' attention to her hands. This portrait reveals not only Titian's skill but the patron's wish too. Painted when Isabella was 60 years old, the portrait depicts her in her 20s—at her specific request. Titian used an earlier likeness of her as his guide, but his portrait is no copy. Rather, *Isabella d'Este* is a distinctive portrayal of the artist's poised and self-assured patron that owes little to its model.

PIETÀ As Michelangelo had done late in his life, Titian began to contemplate death and salvation, and around 1570 he decided to create a memorial for his tomb. Titian, too, chose *Pietà* (FIG. 22-41) as the theme, albeit for a painting, not a statuary group, as in Michelangelo's case (FIG. 22-20). Intended for the altar of his burial chapel in the right aisle of Santa Maria Gloriosa dei Frari in Venice, which housed two of his earlier altarpieces (FIGS. 22-36 and 22-37), Titian's *Pietà* remained unfinished when he died of the plague in 1576. His assistant, Jacopo Negretti, known as PALMA IL GIOVANE (1548–1628)—Palma the Younger—completed the painting.

Titian set the scene of grief over Christ's death in a rusticated niche reminiscent of the bays of Sansovino's Venetian Mint (FIG. 22-31A, *left*). The Virgin cradles her son's body, while Mary Magdalene runs forward with her right arm raised in a gesture of extreme distress. (Echoing her form, but in reverse, is the torch-carrying angel added by Palma.) The other penitent mourner is Saint Jerome, seen from behind kneeling at the Savior's side. His head has the features of the aged, balding Titian—another parallel with Michelangelo's *Pietà*. Both artists apparently wanted to portray themselves touching Christ's body, hoping for salvation.

For this huge (roughly 12-foot-square) canvas, Titian employed one of his favorite compositional devices (compare FIG. 22-37), creating a bold diagonal movement beginning at Jerome's feet and leading through Christ, the Virgin, and Mary Magdalene to the statue of Moses with the Ten Commandments at the left. (The other statue represents Faith. The votive painting leaning against its pedestal depicts Titian and his son Orazio, who also died of the plague in 1576, praying before another *Pietà*.) But unlike Titian's early and mature works, in which he used smooth and transparent oil glazes, this *Pietà* features broken brushstrokes and rough, uneven patches of pigment built up like paste (*impasto*) so that they catch the light, like his other late paintings. Many Baroque painters, especially Peter Paul Rubens (FIGS. 25-2 to 25-4) and Rembrandt van Rijn (FIGS. 25-12 to 25-15A), subsequently adopted Titian's innovative and highly expressive manner of applying thick paint to canvas (see "Palma il Giovane on Titian," page 657).

MANNERISM

The High Renaissance styles of Rome, Florence, and Venice dominated Italian painting, sculpture, and architecture for most of the 16th century, but as early as the 1520s, leading artists of the post-Leonardo, post-Raphael generation began to explore new modes of artistic expression. Art historians long ago dubbed the work of these artists *Mannerist*, a term derived from the Italian word *maniera*, meaning "style" or "manner," which in turn derives from *mano* ("hand"). In the field of art history, the term *style* usually refers to a characteristic or representative mode, especially of an artist or period (for example, Titian's style or Gothic style; see page 3). Style can also refer to an absolute quality of fashion (for example, someone "has style" or "is stylish"). The first art historians to adopt the term argued that Mannerism's style (or representative mode) was characterized by style (being stylish, cultured, elegant).

The term is unfortunate in many respects. First, when originally applied to the artworks examined in the next section, "Mannerism" had negative connotations, just as "Gothic" did when first used by Giorgio Vasari (see page 374). Mannerist works are not, however, of inferior quality compared to High Renaissance works, although they are unquestionably different. Second, Mannerism is not a unified style. It encompasses diverse contemporaneous personal styles, even if they all represent a break from High Renaissance norms. Nonetheless, "Mannerism," like "Gothic," is too firmly entrenched in art history to be discarded.

Painting

What specifically constitutes Mannerism in art? Among the features most closely associated with Mannerism is artifice. Of course, all art involves artifice, in the sense that art is not "natural." It is something fashioned by human hands. But many artists, including High Renaissance painters such as Leonardo and Raphael, chose to conceal that artifice by using devices such as perspective and shading to make their representations of the world look natural. In contrast, Mannerist painters consciously revealed the constructed nature of their art. In other words, Renaissance artists generally strove to create art that appeared natural, whereas Mannerist artists were less inclined to disguise the contrived nature of art production. This is why artifice is a central feature of discussions about Mannerism, and why Mannerist works can seem, appropriately, "mannered." The conscious display of artifice in Mannerism often reveals itself

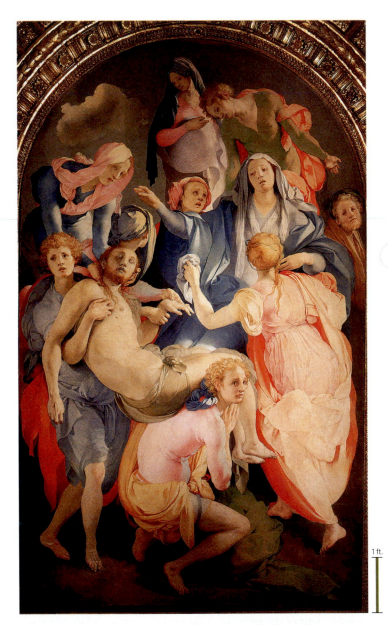

1 ft.

22-42 JACOPO DA PONTORMO, *Entombment of Christ*, Capponi chapel, Santa Felicità, Florence, Italy, 1525–1528. Oil on wood, 10' 3" × 6' 4".

Mannerist paintings such as this one represent a departure from the compositions of the earlier Renaissance. Instead of concentrating masses in the center of the painting, Pontormo left a void.

in imbalanced compositions and unusual complexities, both visual and conceptual. Ambiguous space, departures from expected conventions, and unusual presentations of traditional themes also surface frequently in Mannerist art.

PONTORMO *Entombment of Christ* (FIG. 22-42) by the Florentine painter Jacopo Carucci, known as JACOPO DA PONTORMO (1494–1557) after his birthplace, exhibits almost all the stylistic features characteristic of Mannerism's early phase in painting—as does *Fall of the Rebel Angels* (FIG. 22-42A) by Pontormo's older contemporary DOMENICO BECCAFUMI (1481–1551). Christ's descent from the cross and subsequent entombment had frequently been depicted in art, and Pontormo exploited the familiarity 16th-century viewers would have had by playing off their expectations. For example, he omitted from the painting both the cross and the tomb, and consequently scholars debate whether the artist meant to represent Christ's descent from the cross or his entombment. Also, instead of presenting the action

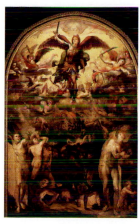

⟐ **22-42A** BECCAFUMI, *Fall of the Rebel Angels*, ca. 1524.

as taking place across the perpendicular picture plane, as Rogier van der Weyden did (FIG. 20-9; compare FIG. 14-9), Pontormo rotated the conventional figural groups along a vertical axis. Several of the figures seem to float in the air. Those that touch the ground do so on tiptoes, enhancing the sense of weightlessness. Unlike High Renaissance artists, who concentrated their masses in the center of the painting, Pontormo left a void. This emptiness accentuates the grouping of hands filling that hole, calling attention to the void—symbolic of loss and grief. The artist enhanced the painting's ambiguity with the curiously anxious glances that the figures cast in all directions. (The bearded young man at the upper right who looks out at the viewer is probably a self-portrait of Pontormo.) Many of the figures have elastically elongated limbs and undersized heads, and move unnaturally. For example, the torso of the foreground figure bends in an anatomically impossible way. The contrasting colors, primarily light blues and pinks, add to the dynamism and complexity of the work. The painting represents a pronounced departure from the balanced, harmoniously structured compositions of the High Renaissance.

PARMIGIANINO Nine years younger than Pontormo, Girolamo Francesco Maria Mazzola of Parma, known as PARMIGIANINO (1503–1540), achieved a reputation as a gifted painter while still in his teens, and at age 21, he made a deep impression on Pope Clement VII with an unconventional self-portrait (FIG. 22-43; see "How to Impress a Pope," below). Parmigianino's best-known work,

PROBLEMS AND SOLUTIONS
How to Impress a Pope

Because Renaissance artists depended on commissions from churches, town councils, princes, and wealthy merchants, attracting the attention of a prominent patron early in one's career was essential if the artist was going to enjoy success. When he was 21, Parmigianino, who soon became a leading figure among the "Mannerists" who were exploring stylistic alternatives to the classical art of Raphael, devised an unusual way to impress Pope Clement VII with his skill. During a visit to a barber's shop, Parmigianino saw his reflection in a convex mirror, which inspired him to paint a self-portrait (FIG. 22-43) of unconventional format with the intention of presenting it to Pope Clement VII as a demonstration of his virtuosity.

To imitate the appearance of a convex mirror, Parmigianino had a carpenter prepare a section of a wood sphere of the same size and shape as a barber's mirror (about 10 inches in diameter) and used oil glazes to produce a surface luster that heightened the illusion of the viewer looking into a mirror and not at a painting. The viewer in this case is also the painter, whose handsome countenance Giorgio Vasari described as an angel's, not a man's. The pope remarked that Parmigianino's portrait of himself in his studio was "a marvel" and "astonishing" in its success in creating the appearance of someone gazing at his reflection. As in a real convex mirror, the artist's face—at the center of the reflective surface and some distance from it—is free of distortion, but his hand and sleeve are of exaggerated size. The emphasis on the hand no doubt is also a statement on Parmigianino's part about the supreme importance of the painter's hand in fashioning an artwork. That emphasis on artifice as the essence of painting is the core principle of Mannerism.

Parmigianino, whom Vasari described as possessing charm as well as good looks and precocious artistic talent, quickly became the favorite painter of the elite in Rome, the successor to Raphael, who had died just four years before Parmigianino's arrival at the papal court.

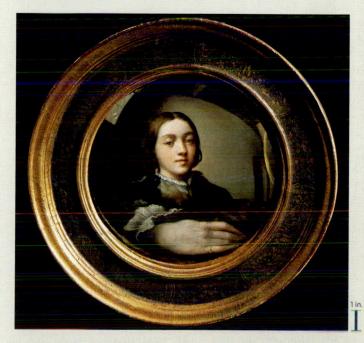

1 in.
I

22-43 PARMIGIANINO, *Self-Portrait in a Convex Mirror*, 1524. Oil on wood, 9⅝" diameter. Kunsthistorisches Museum, Vienna.

Painted to impress Pope Clement VII with his virtuosity, Parmigianino's self-portrait brilliantly reproduces the young Mannerist's distorted appearance as seen in a barber's convex mirror.

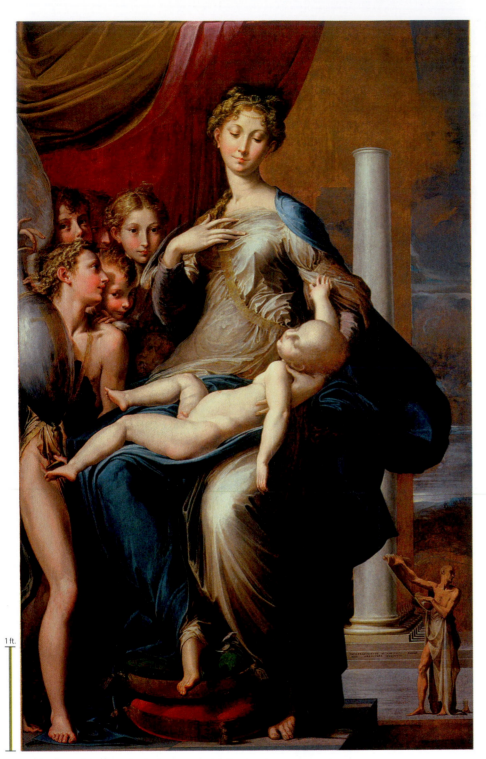

1 ft.

Parmigianino's Madonna displays the stylish elegance that was a principal aim of Mannerism. Mary has a small oval head, a long and slender neck, attenuated hands, and a sinuous body.

and a mysterious figure with a scroll, perhaps Saint James, whose distance from the foreground is immeasurable and ambiguous—the antithesis of rational Renaissance perspective diminution of size with distance.

Although the elegance and sophisticated beauty of the painting are due in large part to the Madonna's attenuated neck and arms, that exaggeration is not solely decorative in purpose. *Madonna with the Long Neck* takes its subject from a simile in medieval hymns comparing the Virgin's neck with a great ivory tower or column, such as the one Parmigianino depicted to the right of the Madonna.

BRONZINO *Venus, Cupid, Folly, and Time* (FIG. **22-45**), by Agnolo di Cosimo, called BRONZINO (1503–1572), also displays all the chief features of Mannerist painting. A pupil of Pontormo, Bronzino was a Florentine and painter to the first grand duke of Tuscany, Cosimo I de' Medici (r. 1537–1574). In this painting, which Cosimo commissioned as a gift for King Francis I of France (see "Francis I, Royal Art Patron and Collector," page 693), Bronzino demonstrated the Mannerists' fondness for learned allegories that often had lascivious undertones, a shift from the simple and monumental statements and forms of the High Renaissance. Bronzino depicted Cupid—here not an infant but an adolescent who has reached puberty—fondling his mother, Venus, while provocatively thrusting his buttocks at the viewer. Folly prepares to shower the "couple" with rose petals. Time, who appears in the upper right corner, draws back the curtain to reveal the playful incest in progress. Other figures in the painting represent other human qualities and emotions, including Envy. The masks, a favorite device of the Mannerists, symbolize deceit.

Bronzion's *Venus, Cupid, Folly, and Time* seems to suggest that love—accompanied by envy and plagued by inconstancy—is foolish and that lovers will discover its folly in time. But as in many Mannerist paintings, the meaning here is ambiguous, and interpretations of the painting vary. Compositionally, Bronzino placed the figures around the front plane, and they almost entirely block

however, is *Madonna with the Long Neck* (FIG. **22-44**), which exemplifies the elegant stylishness that was a principal aim of Mannerism. In Parmigianino's hands, this traditional, usually sedate, religious subject became a picture of exquisite grace and precious sweetness. The Madonna's small oval head, her long and slender neck, the otherworldly attenuation and delicacy of her hand, and the sinuous, swaying elongation of her frame—all are marks of the aristocratic, sumptuously courtly taste of Mannerist artists and patrons alike. Parmigianino amplified this elegance by expanding the Madonna's form as viewed from head to toe. On the left stands a bevy of angelic creatures, melting with emotions as soft and smooth as their limbs. On the right, the artist included a line of columns without capitals

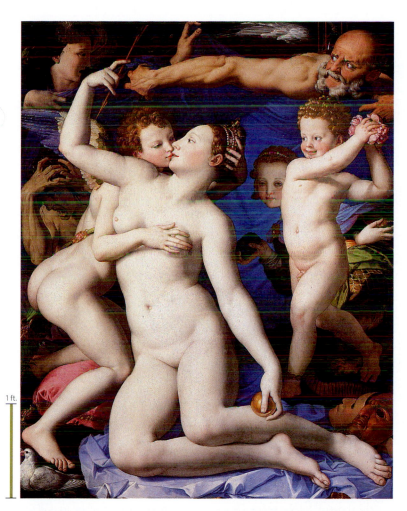

1 ft.

22-45 BRONZINO, *Venus, Cupid, Folly, and Time*, ca. 1546. Oil on wood, 5' 1" × 4' 8¼". National Gallery, London.

In this painting of Cupid fondling his mother, Venus, Bronzino demonstrated a fondness for learned allegories with lascivious undertones. As in many Mannerist works, the meaning is ambiguous.

the space. The contours are strong and sculptural, the surfaces of enamel smoothness. Of special interest are the heads, hands, and feet, for the Mannerists considered the extremities to be the carriers of grace, and the clever depiction of them evidence of artistic skill.

ELEANORA OF TOLEDO In 1540, Cosimo I de' Medici married Eleanora of Toledo (1519–1562), daughter of Charles V's viceroy in Naples, and thereby cemented an important alliance with the Spanish court. Several years later, Cosimo asked Bronzino to paint Eleanora and their second son, Giovanni (FIG. **22-46**), who then was about three years old. Bronzino painted dozens of portraits of members of the Medici family, but never portrayed Eleanora with any of her daughters (she and Cosimo had three daughters as well as eight sons). This painting therefore should be seen as a formal dynastic portrait intended to present the duke's wife as the mother of one of his heirs.

As in other Bronzino portraits (FIG. **22-46A**), the subjects appear aloof and emotionless. Bronzino idealized both Eleanora and Giovanni, giving both of them perfect features and blemishless skin that glows like alabaster. Eleanora's figure takes up most of the panel's surface, and Bronzino further underscored her primacy by lightening the blue background around her head, creating a halolike frame for her face and perhaps associating the mother and son with the Madonna and Christ Child.

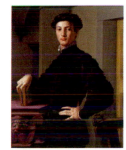

⬧ **22-46A** BRONZINO, *Portrait of a Young Man*, ca. 1530–1545.

Seated with one arm around Giovanni and the other resting on her lap, Eleanora looks out at the viewer with cool detachment. She is richly attired in a brocaded gown and wears a costly pearl necklace and a tiara. The painter reproduced the various textures of fabric, jewels, hair, and flesh with supreme skill. The boy stands stiffly, staring forward, suppressing all playful thoughts in order to behave as expected on this formal occasion. Bronzino's portrayal of Eleanora and Giovanni is in some ways less a portrait of a mother and child than of a royal audience.

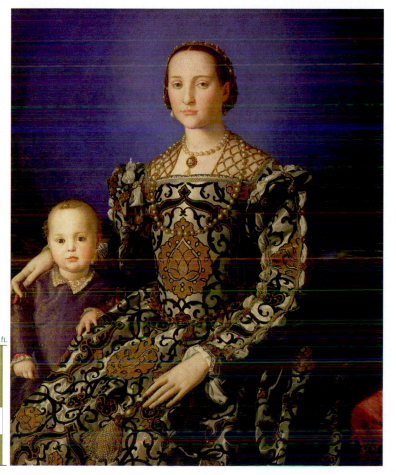

1 ft.

22-46 BRONZINO, *Eleanora of Toledo and Giovanni de' Medici*, ca. 1546. Oil on wood, 3' 9¼" × 3' 1¾". Galleria degli Uffizi, Florence.

Bronzino was the official portraitist of Grand Duke Cosimo de' Medici. His portrayal of Cosimo's Spanish wife and their second son features rich costumes and coolly detached personalities.

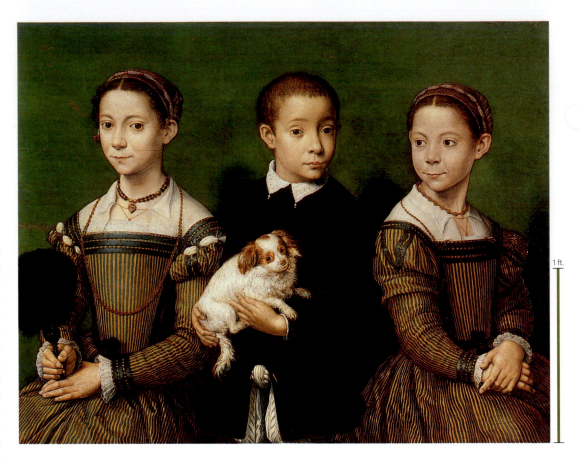

22-47 Sofonisba Anguissola, *Portrait of the Artist's Sisters and Brother,* ca. 1555. Oil on wood, 2' 5¼" × 3' 1½". Methuen Collection, Corsham Court, Wiltshire.

Anguissola was the leading woman artist of her time. Her contemporaries admired her use of relaxed poses and expressions in intimate and informal group portraits such as this one of her family.

SOFONISBA ANGUISSOLA The aloof formality of Bronzino's dynastic portrait is much relaxed in the portraiture of SOFONISBA ANGUISSOLA (ca. 1532–1625) of Cremona in northern Italy. Anguissola introduced a new kind of group portrait of irresistible charm, characterized by an informal intimacy and by subjects that are often moving, conversing, or engaged in activities. Like many of the other works she produced before settling in Spain in 1559, the portrait illustrated here (FIG. 22-47) represents members of her family. Against a neutral ground, Anguissola placed her two sisters and brother in an affectionate pose meant not for official display but for private showing. The sisters, wearing matching striped gowns, flank their brother, who caresses a lapdog. The older sister (at the left) summons the dignity required for the occasion, while the boy looks quizzically at the portraitist with an expression of naive curiosity, and the other girl diverts her attention toward something or someone to the painter's left.

Anguissola's use of relaxed poses and expressions, her sympathetic personal presentation, and her graceful treatment of the forms brought her international acclaim (see "Women in the Renaissance Art World," page 656). She received praise from the aged Michelangelo, was court painter to Phillip II (r. 1556–1598) of Spain, and, at the end of her life, gave advice on art to a young admirer of her work, Anthony Van Dyck (FIG. 25-5), the great Flemish master.

TINTORETTO Venetian painting of the later 16th century built on established High Renaissance Venetian ideas, but incorporated many elements of the Mannerist style. Jacopo Robusti, known as TINTORETTO (1518–1594), claimed to be a student of Titian and aspired to combine Titian's color with Michelangelo's drawing, but art historians consider Tintoretto the outstanding Venetian representative of Mannerism. He adopted many Mannerist pictorial devices, which he employed to produce works imbued with dramatic power, depth of spiritual vision, and glowing Venetian color schemes.

Toward the end of Tintoretto's life, his art became spiritual, even visionary, as solid forms melted away into swirling clouds of dark shot through with fitful light. In Tintoretto's *Last Supper* (FIG. 22-48), painted for the right wall next to the high altar in Andrea Palladio's church of San Giorgio Maggiore (FIG. 22-31), the figures appear in a dark interior illuminated by a single light in the upper left of the image. The shimmering halos establish the biblical nature of the scene. The ability of this dramatic scene to engage viewers was fully in keeping with Counter-Reformation ideals (see "The Council of Trent," page 642) and the Catholic Church's belief in the didactic nature of religious art.

Tintoretto's *Last Supper* incorporates many Mannerist devices, including an imbalanced composition and visual complexity. In terms of design, the contrast with Leonardo's *Last Supper* (FIG. 22-4) is both extreme and instructive. Leonardo's composition, balanced and symmetrical, parallels the picture plane in a geometrically organized and closed space. The figure of Jesus is the tranquil center of the drama and the perspective focus. In Tintoretto's painting, Jesus is above and beyond the converging perspective lines racing diagonally away from the picture surface, creating disturbing effects of limitless depth and motion. The viewer locates Tintoretto's Jesus via the light flaring, beaconlike, out of darkness. The contrast of the two pictures reflects the direction Renaissance painting took in the 16th century, as it moved away from architectonic clarity of space and neutral lighting toward the dynamic perspectives and dramatic chiaroscuro of the coming Baroque.

VERONESE Among the great Venetian masters was Paolo Caliari of Verona, called PAOLO VERONESE (1528–1588). Whereas Tintoretto gloried in monumental drama and deep perspectives, Veronese specialized in splendid pageantry painted in superb color and set within majestic classical architecture. Like Tintoretto, Veronese painted on a huge scale, with canvases often as large as 20 by 30 feet or more. His usual subjects, painted for the refectories of wealthy monasteries, afforded him an opportunity to display magnificent companies at table.

Veronese painted *Christ in the House of Levi* (FIG. 22-49), originally called *Last Supper,* for the dining hall of Santi Giovanni e Paolo

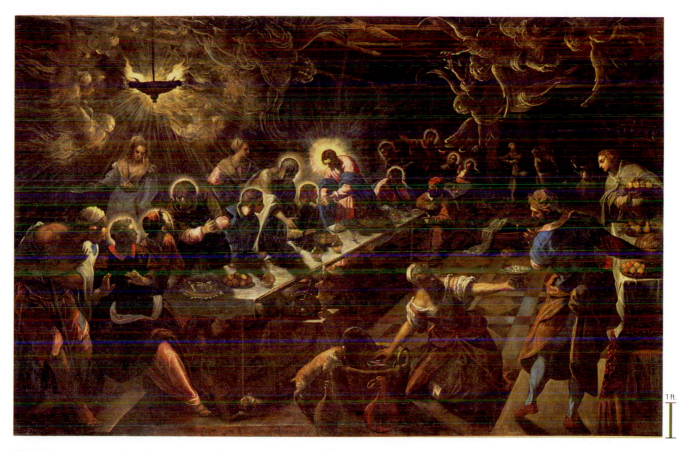

22-48 TINTORETTO, *Last Supper*, 1594. Oil on canvas, 12' × 18' 8". San Giorgio Maggiore, Venice.

Tintoretto adopted many Mannerist pictorial devices to produce oil paintings imbued with emotional power, depth of spiritual vision, glowing Venetian color schemes, and dramatic lighting.

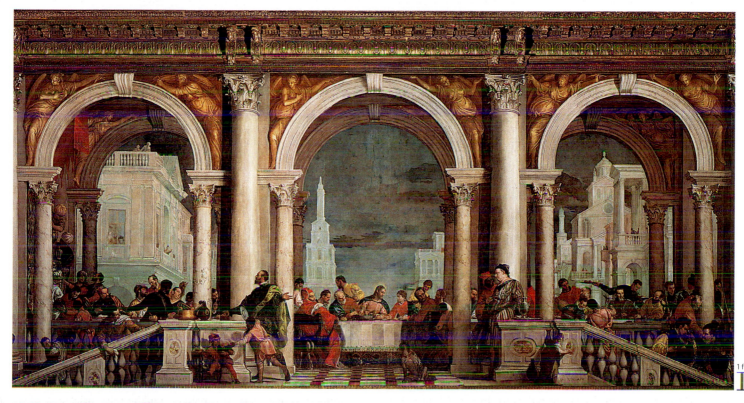

22-49 PAOLO VERONESE, *Christ in the House of Levi*, from the refectory of Santi Giovanni e Paolo, Venice, Italy, 1573. Oil on canvas, 18' 3" × 42'. Galleria dell'Accademia, Venice.

Veronese's paintings feature superb color and majestic classical settings. The Catholic Church accused him of impiety for including dogs and dwarfs near Christ in this work originally titled *Last Supper*.

22-50 PAOLO VERONESE, *Triumph of Venice*, ca. 1585. Oil on canvas, 29' 8" × 19'. Hall of the Grand Council, Doge's Palace, Venice.

Veronese's immense oval ceiling painting presents a tableau of Venice crowned by Fame amid columns, clouds, and personifications. Baroque painters adopted this 45-degree view from the ground.

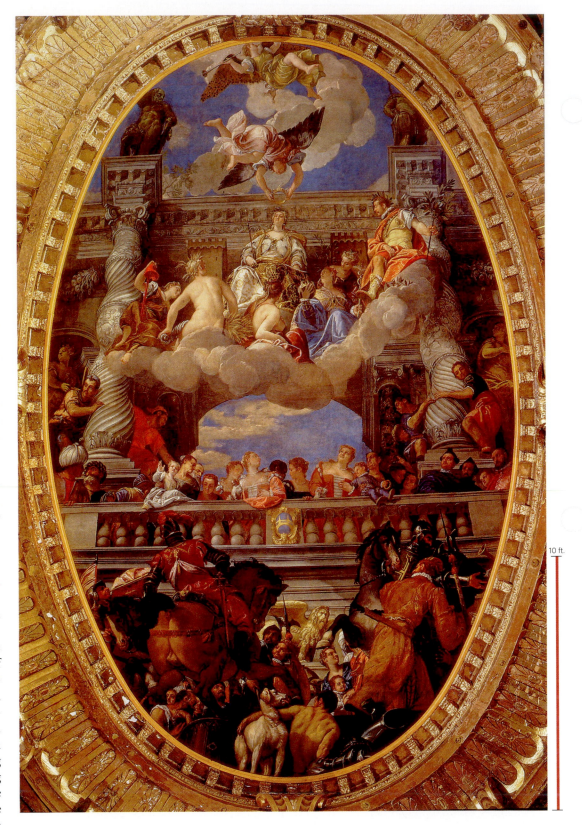

10 ft.

in Venice. As Palladio looked to the example of classically inspired High Renaissance architecture, so Veronese returned to High Renaissance composition, its symmetrical balance, and its ordered architectonics. His shimmering colors span the whole spectrum, although he avoided solid colors in favor of half shades (light blues, sea greens, lemon yellows, roses, and violets), creating veritable flowerbeds of tone. In a great open loggia framed by three monumental arches, Christ sits at the center of the splendidly garbed elite of Venice. In the foreground, with a courtly gesture, the very image of gracious grandeur, the chief steward welcomes guests. Robed lords, their colorful retainers, dogs, and dwarfs crowd into the spacious loggia. Also present are exotic figures wearing turbans, and others of African descent. Painted in 1573 during the Counter-Reformation, this depiction prompted criticism from the Catholic Church. The Holy Office of the Inquisition put the painter on trial, accusing Veronese of impiety for painting "lowly creatures" so close to the Lord and ordering him to make changes at his own expense within three months. Reluctant to do so, he simply changed the painting's title, converting the subject to a less solemn one. His patrons were quite amenable to this solution, for they found nothing objectionable in the painting. Magnificent feasts and carnivals were a source of pride for Venetians.

TRIUMPH OF VENICE Veronese, like Tintoretto, also received prestigious commissions from the Venetian Republic itself. Both artists were hired to decorate the grand chambers and council rooms of the Doge's Palace (FIG. 14-23). In *Triumph of Venice* (FIG. 22-50) in the grandiose Hall of the Grand Council, Veronese revealed himself a master of illusionistic ceiling compositions. Within an oval frame, he presented personified Venice, crowned by Fame, enthroned between two great twisted columns in a balustrade-capped loggia, garlanded with clouds, and attended by figures symbolic of the maritime republic's glories. Unlike Mantegna's *di sotto in sù* (FIG. 21-49) perspective, Veronese's is not a projection directly up from below,

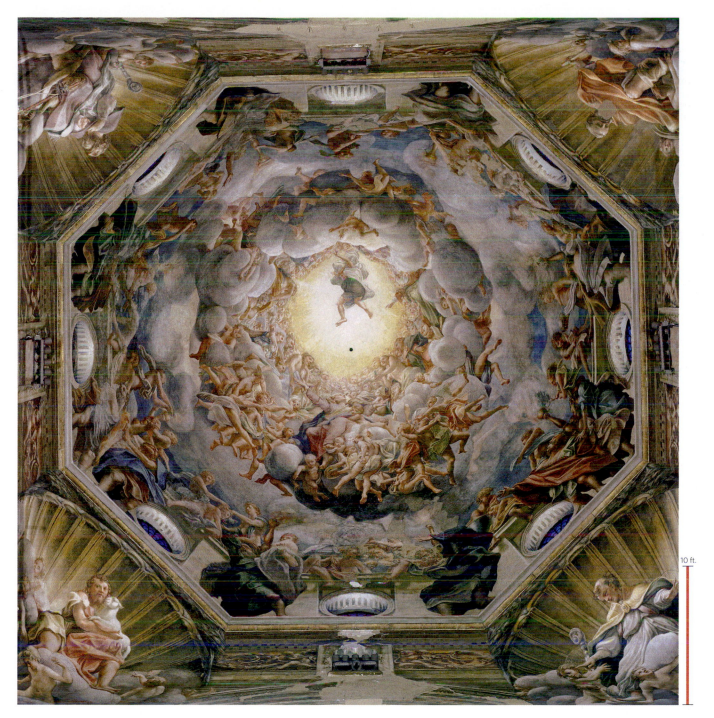

10 ft.

22-51 CORREGGIO, *Assumption of the Virgin*, 1526–1530. Fresco, 35' 10" × 37' 11". Parma Cathedral, Parma.

Working long before Veronese, Correggio, the teacher of Parmigianino, won little fame in his day, but his illusionistic ceiling designs, such as this one in Parma Cathedral, inspired many Baroque painters.

but at a 45-degree angle to spectators, a technique used by many later Baroque decorators (for example, FIGS. 24-22 to 24-24).

CORREGGIO One painter who developed a personal style almost impossible to classify was Antonio Allegri, known as CORREGGIO (ca. 1489–1534) from his birthplace near Parma. The teacher of Parmigianino, Correggio pulled together many stylistic trends, including those of Leonardo, Raphael, and the Venetians. His most enduring contribution was the further development of illusionistic ceiling perspective painting. In Parma Cathedral, he painted away the entire dome with his *Assumption of the Virgin* (FIG. 22-51; see

"How to Make a Ceiling Disappear," page 720). Opening up the *cupola*, the artist showed worshipers a view of the sky, with concentric rings of clouds where hundreds of soaring figures perform a wildly pirouetting dance in celebration of the Assumption. Versions of these angelic creatures became permanent tenants of numerous Baroque churches in later centuries. Correggio was also an influential painter of religious panels, anticipating in them many other Baroque compositional devices. Correggio's *Assumption of the Virgin* predates Veronese's *Triumph of Venice* by more than a half century, but contemporaries expressed little appreciation for his achievement. Later, during the 17th century, Baroque painters recognized him as a kindred spirit.

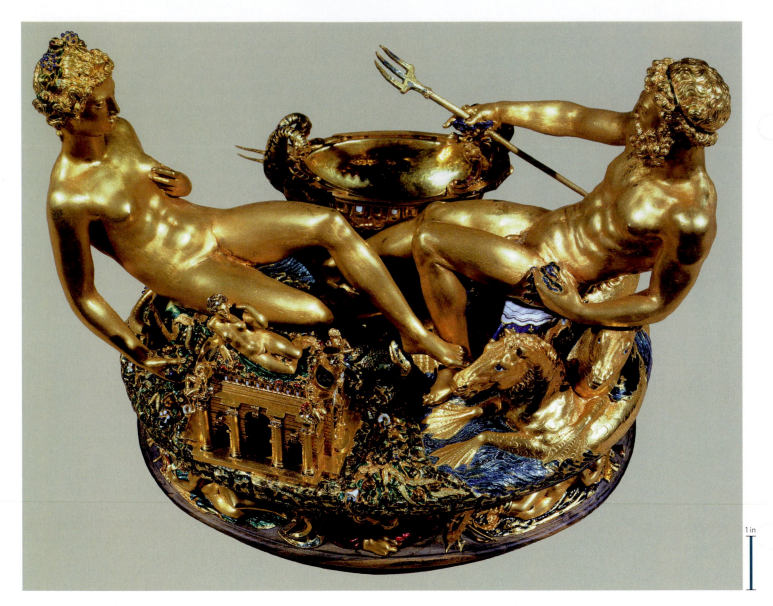

22-52 BENVENUTO CELLINI, *Saltcellar of Francis I,* 1540–1543. Gold, enamel, and ebony, $10\frac{1}{4}$" × 1' $1\frac{1}{8}$". Kunsthistorisches Museum, Vienna.

Famed as a master goldsmith, Cellini fashioned this costly saltcellar for the table of Francis I of France. The elongated proportions of the figures clearly reveal Cellini's Mannerist approach to form.

Sculpture

Mannerism extended beyond painting. Artists translated its principles into sculpture and architecture as well.

BENVENUTO CELLINI Among those who made their mark as Mannerist sculptors was BENVENUTO CELLINI (1500–1571), the author of a fascinating autobiography. It is difficult to imagine a medieval artist composing an autobiography. Only in the Renaissance, with the birth of the notion of individual artistic genius, could a work such as Cellini's (or Vasari's *Lives*) have been conceived and written. Cellini's literary self-portrait presents him not only as a highly accomplished artist but also as a statesman, soldier, and lover, among many other roles.

Cellini was, first of all, a goldsmith, but only one of his major works in that medium survives, the saltcellar (FIG. **22-52**) he made for the royal table of Francis I (see "Francis I, Royal Art Patron and

Collector," page 693). The king had hired Cellini with a retainer of an annual salary, supplemented by fees for the works he produced—for example, his *Genius of Fontainebleau* (FIG. **22-52A**) for the royal hunting lodge outside Paris. The price Francis paid Cellini for the luxurious

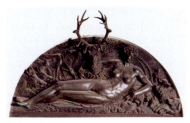

↗ **22-52A** CELLINI, *Genius of Fontainebleau,* 1542–1543.

gold-and-*enamel* saltcellar illustrated here was almost 50 percent greater than the artist's salary for the year.

The two sculpted figures of Cellini's saltcellar are Neptune and Tellus (or, as the artist named them, Sea—the source of salt—and Land). They recline atop an ebony base decorated with relief figures of Dawn, Day, Twilight, Night, and the four winds—some based on Michelangelo's statues in the New Sacristy (FIG. **22-16**) attached to

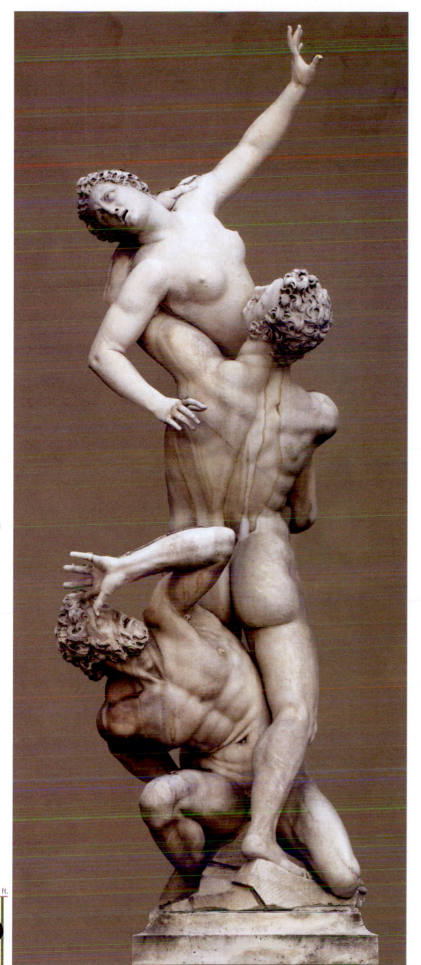

San Lorenzo. The boat next to Neptune's right leg is the salt container, and the triumphal arch (compare FIG. 7-73) next to the right leg of the earth goddess held the pepper. The elongated proportions of the figures, especially the slim, small-breasted figure of Tellus, whom ancient artists always represented as a matronly woman (FIG. 7-30), reveal Cellini's Mannerist approach to form.

GIOVANNI DA BOLOGNA The lure of Italy drew a brilliant young Flemish sculptor, Jean de Boulogne, to Italy, where he practiced his art under the equivalent Italian name of Giovanni da Bologna or, in its more common contracted form, GIAMBOLOGNA (1529–1608). His *Abduction of the Sabine Women* (FIG. **22-53**) exemplifies Mannerist principles of figure composition. Drawn from the legendary history of early Rome, the group of figures received its current title—relating how the Romans abducted wives for themselves from the neighboring Sabines—only after its exhibition. Earlier, it was *Paris Abducting Helen,* among other mythological titles. In fact, Giambologna did not intend to depict any particular subject. He created the group as a demonstration piece. His goal was to achieve a dynamic spiral figural composition involving an old man, a young man, and a woman, all nude in the tradition of ancient statues portraying deities and mythological figures.

Although Giambologna would have known Antonio Pollaiuolo's *Hercules and Antaeus* (FIG. 21-13), whose Greek hero lifts his opponent off the ground, he turned directly to ancient sculpture for inspiration, especially to the much-admired *Laocoön* (FIG. 5-89), discovered in Rome earlier in the century. *Abduction of the Sabine Women* includes references to that ancient statue in the crouching old man and in the woman's up-flung arm. The three bodies interlock on a vertical axis, creating an ascending spiral movement.

To appreciate *Abduction of the Sabine Women* fully, the viewer must walk around the statuary group, because the work changes radically according to the viewing point. One factor contributing to the shifting imagery is the prominence of open spaces passing through the masses (for example, the space between an arm and a body), which have as great an effect as the solids. This sculpture was the first large-scale group since classical antiquity designed to be seen from multiple viewpoints, although Giambologna's figures do not break out of the spiral vortex but remain as if contained within a cylinder.

22-53 GIAMBOLOGNA, *Abduction of the Sabine Women,* Loggia dei Lanzi, Piazza della Signoria, Florence, Italy, 1579–1583. Marble, 13' 5½" high.

This sculpture was the first large-scale group since classical antiquity designed to be seen from multiple viewpoints. The three bodies interlock to create a vertical spiral movement.

1 ft.

Federigo Gonzaga, Giulio Romano, and the Palazzo del Tè

As during the Middle Ages, when the clergy were the primary source of artistic commissions, Renaissance patrons, whether popes, dukes, or bankers, had a powerful—often a controlling—voice in the content and even the form of the artworks they paid for (see "Art in the Princely Courts of Renaissance Italy," page 613, and "Michelangelo in the Service of Julius II," page 623). But there were also many instances of a give-and-take between artists and patrons. One well-documented example is the relationship between Federigo Gonzaga, duke of Mantua, and Giulio Romano, the painter and architect he lured to northern Italy in 1524. Giorgio Vasari describes in detail how Gonzaga showered Giulio with gifts and then accepted the artist's proposal to construct a grandiose palace when the duke had planned only to invest in a modest retreat:

> Giulio was celebrated as the best artist in Italy after the death of Raphael, and Count Baldassare Castiglione [FIG. 22-10A], in Rome at that time as the ambassador of Federigo Gonzaga, . . . was ordered to procure an architect . . . and the count worked at

this so diligently with entreaties and promises that Giulio declared he would go at any time provided it was by the leave of Pope Clement. Once this permission had been obtained, . . . Castiglione presented Giulio to [Federigo] who, after many acts of kindness, gave Giulio an honorably furnished home and provided a salary and food for him. . . . [and] sent Giulio several lengths of velvet and satin, as well as other kinds of cloth and fabric for his clothing. And afterwards, learning that Giulio had no horse, he had one of his own favorite horses, called Luggieri, brought out and gave it to Giulio, and when Giulio had mounted the horse, they went off . . . to where His Excellency had a place and some stables call the Tè in the middle of a meadow. . . . [Federigo declared] he would like to prepare a small place where he could go and take refuge on occasion to have lunch or amuse himself at dinner. . . . Giulio surveyed everything, took the ground-plan for the site, and set to work. . . . [Federigo] later decided, after such a humble beginning, to make the entire edifice into a grand palace [FIGS. 22-54 and 22-55], for Giulio executed a very beautiful model, its courtyard rusticated inside and out, which pleased that ruler so much that he ordered an ample provision of money.*

*Giorgio Vasari, "The Life of Giulio Romano, Painter," translated by Julia Conaway Bondanella and Peter Bondanella, *Giorgio Vasari: The Lives of the Artists* (New York: Oxford University Press, 1991), 366–367.

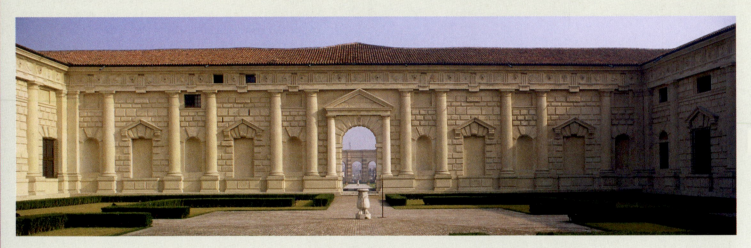

22-54 GIULIO ROMANO, courtyard of the Palazzo del Tè (looking southeast), Mantua, Italy, 1525–1535.

Federico Gonzaga was greatly pleased by Giulio's Mannerist divergences from architectural convention in the Palazzo del Tè. The design constitutes a parody of Bramante's classical style.

Architecture

Mannerist architects used classical architectural elements in a highly personal and unorthodox manner, rejecting the balance, order, and stability that were the hallmarks of the High Renaissance style, and aiming instead to reveal the contrived nature of architectural design.

GIULIO ROMANO Applying that unorthodox approach was the goal of GIULIO ROMANO (ca. 1499–1546) when he designed the Palazzo del Tè (FIG. 22-54) in Mantua and, with it, formulated almost the entire architectural vocabulary of Mannerism. Early in his career, Giulio was Raphael's chief assistant in decorating the Vatican stanze. After Raphael's premature death in 1520, Giulio became

his master's artistic executor, completing Raphael's unfinished frescoes and panel paintings. In 1524, Giulio went to Mantua (opening an opportunity at the papal court for Parmigianino), having been courted by Duke Federigo Gonzaga (r. 1530–1540), for whom he built and decorated the Palazzo del Tè between 1525 and 1535 (see "Federigo Gonzaga, Giulio Romano, and the Palazzo del Tè," above). Gonzaga intended the palace to serve as both suburban summer residence and stud farm for his famous stables. Originally planned as a relatively modest country villa, Giulio's building so pleased his patron that Gonzaga soon commissioned the architect to enlarge the structure. In a second building campaign, Giulio expanded the villa to a palatial scale by adding three wings, which he placed around a square central court. This once-paved court, which functions both as a passage and as the focal point of the design, has a nearly urban character. Its surrounding buildings form a self-enclosed unit with a large garden, flanked by a stable, attached to it on the east side.

Giulio's Mannerist style is on display in the facades facing the palace's courtyard (FIG. 22-54), where the divergences from architectural convention are pronounced. Indeed, the Palazzo del Tè constitutes an enormous parody of Bramante's classical style, a veritable Mannerist manifesto announcing the artifice of architectural design. In a building laden with structural surprises and contradictions, the courtyard is the most unconventional of all. The *keystones* (central *voussoirs*), for example, either have not fully settled or seem to be slipping from the arches—and, even more eccentrically, Giulio placed voussoirs in the pediments over the rectangular niches, where no arches exist. The massive Tuscan columns flanking these niches carry incongruously narrow *architraves*. That these architraves break midway between the columns stresses their apparent structural insufficiency, and they seem unable to support the weight of

the *triglyphs* of the *Doric frieze* above (see "Doric and Ionic Orders," page 114 and FIG. 5-13), which threaten to crash down on the head of anyone foolish enough to stand beneath them. To be sure, only a highly sophisticated observer can appreciate Giulio's witticism. Recognizing some quite subtle departures from the norm presupposes a thorough familiarity with the established rules of classical architecture. That the duke delighted in Giulio's mannered architectural inventiveness speaks to his cultivated taste.

SALA DEI GIGANTI Federigo also entrusted Giulio with the interior decoration of his suburban pleasure palace. In the Sala dei Giganti (Room of the Giants; FIG. **22-55**), painted to serve as the reception hall for the second visit to Mantua of Charles V, frescoes cover every square inch of the walls and ceiling. At the top (almost entirely out of view in the photograph reproduced here) is an illusionistic oculus that pays tribute to, but is a Mannerist commentary on, Mantegna's earlier *tromple-l'oeil* ceiling in the Camera Picta (FIG. 21-49) of

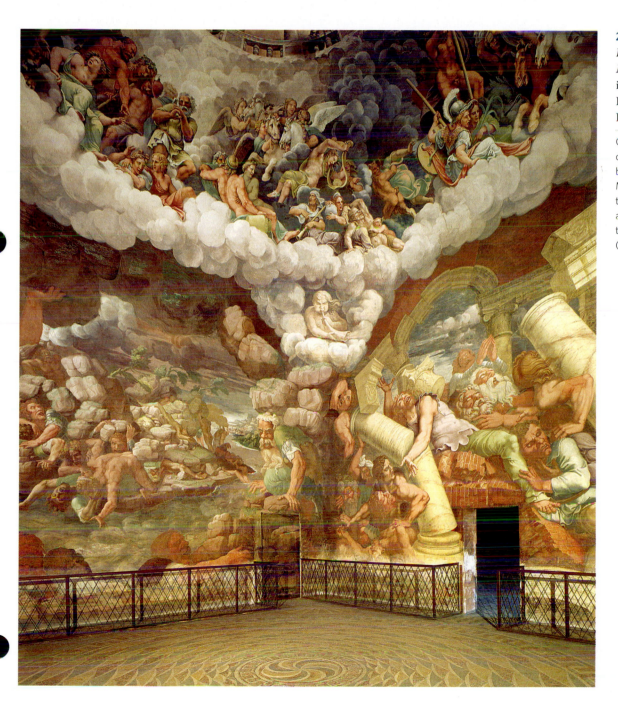

22-55 GIULIO ROMANO, *Fall of the Giants from Mount Olympus,* fresco in the Sala dei Giganti, Palazzo del Tè, Mantua, Italy, 1530–1532.

Giulio Romano's dramatic ceiling fresco of giants battling the Greek gods of Mount Olympus continues the theme of collapsing architecture that he used on the Palazzo del Tè's exterior (FIG. 22-54).

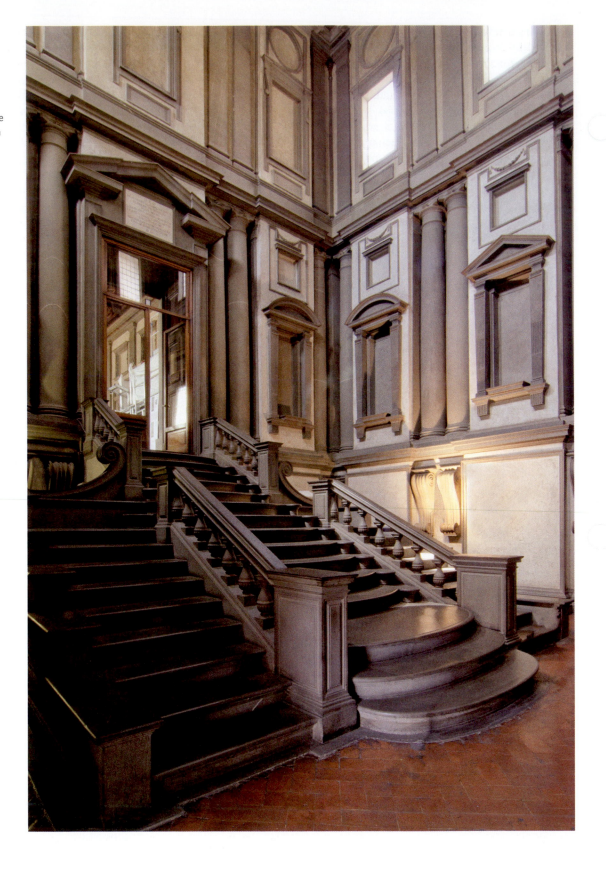

22-56 MICHELANGELO
BUONARROTI, vestibule of the
Laurentian Library, Florence,
Italy, 1524–1534; staircase,
1558–1559.

With his customary independence
of spirit, Michelangelo, working in
a Mannerist mode in the Laurentian Library vestibule, disposed
willfully of almost all the rules of
classical architecture.

the ducal palace in Mantua. The *Fall of the Giants from Mount
Olympus* revives the venerable classical theme of the *gigantomachy*
(battle of gods and giants), which was popular in ancient Greece
(FIGS. 5-18 and 5-80) because the defeat of the giants at the hands
of the Olympian gods served as an allegory of the triumph of
Greek civilization over barbarism. In Renaissance Mantua, Duke
Federigo may have seen himself as a modern-day Zeus/Jupiter,
who in Giulio's fresco hurls thunderbolts at the giants who have

stormed Mount Olympus, causing them to fall back to earth amid
collapsing classical temples.

The gigantic fresco merits comparison with Michelangelo's dramatic vision in his *Last Judgment* (FIG. 22-19), painted later in the
decade for the east wall of the Sistine Chapel in Rome. But despite
the tumultuous details of Michelangelo's fresco of heroically nude
cloud-borne figures, the composition retains classical balance and
symmetry, whereas Giulio's fresco embodies the instability and

asymmetry that Mannerist artists and patrons alike preferred. In the Palazzo del Tè, where the architect and the painter were the same man and had the full support of his ducal patron, Giulio carried his critical and whimsical commentary on classical architecture indoors. Visitors to the pleasure palace surely would have been reminded of the triglyphs about to crash down from the Doric frieze of the building's exterior (FIG. 22-54) when they encountered the collapsing entablatures and crumbling columns of the frescoes in the Sala dei Giganti.

LAURENTIAN LIBRARY Although for most people, Michelangelo personifies the High Renaissance artist, he, like Giulio Romano, also experimented with architectural designs that flouted most of the classical rules of order and stability. The restless nature of Michelangelo's genius is evident in the vestibule (FIG. 22-56) he designed for the Medici library adjoining the Florentine church of San Lorenzo. The Laurentian Library had two contrasting spaces that Michelangelo had to unite: the long horizontal of the library proper and the vertical of the vestibule. The need to place the vestibule windows up high (at the level of the reading room) determined the narrow verticality of the vestibule's elevation and proportions. Much taller than it is wide, the vestibule gives the impression of a vertically compressed, shaft-like space. Anyone schooled exclusively in the classical architecture of Bramante and the High Renaissance would have been appalled by Michelangelo's indifference here to classical norms in proportion and

in the application of the rules of the classical orders. For example, he used columns in pairs and sank them into the walls, where they perform no supporting function. Michelangelo also split columns in halves around corners. Elsewhere, he placed scroll *corbels* on the walls beneath columns. They seem to hang from the moldings, holding up nothing. He arbitrarily broke through pediments as well as through cornices and stringcourses. He sculpted pilasters that taper downward instead of upward. In short, the High Renaissance master, working in a Mannerist mode, disposed willfully and abruptly of classical architecture. Moreover, in the vast, flowing stairway (the latest element of the vestibule) that protrudes tonguelike into the room from the "mouth" of the doorway to the library, Michelangelo foreshadowed the dramatic movement of Baroque architecture (see page 702). With his customary trailblazing independence of spirit, Michelangelo created an interior space that conveyed all the strains and tensions found in his statuary and in his painted figures.

Michelangelo's art began in the style of the Quattrocento, became emblematic of High Renaissance art, and, at the end, moved toward Mannerism. He was 89 when he died in 1564, still hard at work on Saint Peter's and other projects. Few artists, then or since, could escape his influence.

IL GESÙ Probably the most influential building of the later Cinquecento was the mother church of the Jesuit order, Il Gesù, or Church of Jesus (FIGS. 22-57 and 22-58) in Rome. The activity of the Society of Jesus, known as the Jesuits, was an important component of the Counter-Reformation (see page 641). Ignatius of Loyola (1491–1556), a Spanish nobleman who dedicated his life to the service of God, founded the Jesuits in 1534 with preaching and missionary work as the key components of their spiritual assignment. In 1540, Pope Paul III formally recognized his group as a religious order. The Jesuits were the papacy's invaluable allies in its quest to reassert the supremacy of the Catholic Church. Particularly

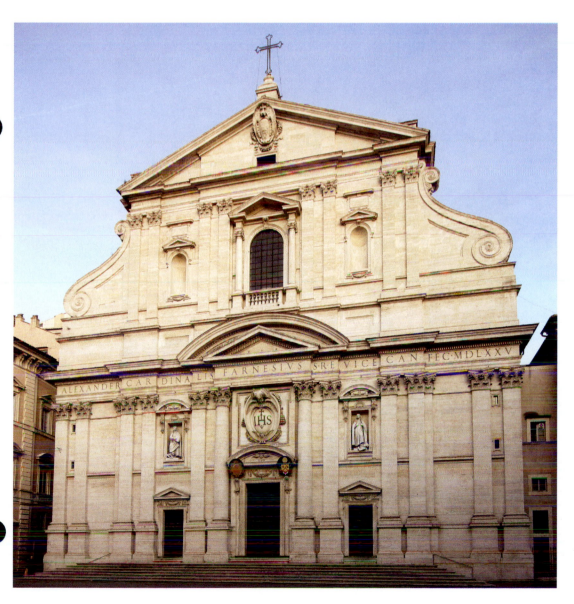

22-57 GIACOMO DELLA PORTA, west facade of Il Gesù, Rome, Italy, begun 1568.

In Giacomo della Porta's innovative design, the march of pilasters and columns builds to a climax at the central bay. Many Roman Baroque church facades are architectural variations of Il Gesù.

PROBLEMS AND SOLUTIONS
Rethinking the Basilican Church

As a major participant in the Counter-Reformation, the Jesuit order needed a church appropriate to its new prominence. In 1568, with the financial backing of Cardinal Alessandro Farnese (1520–1589), the order turned to GIACOMO DA VIGNOLA (1507–1573), who designed Il Gesù's plan (FIG. 22-58), and GIACOMO DELLA PORTA (ca. 1533–1602), who was responsible for the facade (FIG. 22-57)—and who later designed the dome of Saint Peter's (FIG. 22-25).

The plan of the Church of Jesus in Rome is a monumental expansion of Alberti's scheme for Sant'Andrea (FIGS. 21-46 and 21-47) in Mantua. In Il Gesù, the nave (FIG. 22-57) takes over the main volume of space, making the structure a great hall with side chapels. The transept is no wider than the nave and chapels, and Vignola also eliminated the normal deep choir in front of the altar. Consequently, all worshipers have a clear view of the celebration of the Eucharist. The wide acceptance of Vignola's plan in the Catholic world, even in modern times, speaks to its suitability for the performance of Catholic rituals.

The opening of the church building into a single great hall provides an almost theatrical setting for large promenades and processions (which combined social with priestly functions). Above all, the ample space could accommodate the great crowds that gathered to hear the eloquent preaching of the Jesuits.

The facade of Il Gesù (FIG. 22-57) was also not entirely original, but it too had an enormous influence on later church design. The union of the lower and upper stories, achieved by scroll buttresses, harks back to Alberti's Santa Maria Novella (FIG. 21-36A). Its classical pediment is familiar in Alberti's work (FIG. 21-45), as well as in Palladio's (FIGS. 22-28 and 22-30). The paired pilasters appear in Michelangelo's design for Saint Peter's (FIG. 22-25). Della Porta skillfully synthesized these existing motifs and unified the two stories. The horizontal march of the pilasters and columns builds to a dramatic climax at the central bay, and the bays of the facade snugly fit the nave-chapel system behind them. Many Roman church facades of the 17th century are architectural variations on della Porta's design. Chronologically and stylistically, Il Gesù belongs to the Late Renaissance, but its enormous influence on later basilican churches marks it as one of the most significant monuments for the development of Italian Baroque ecclesiastical architecture.

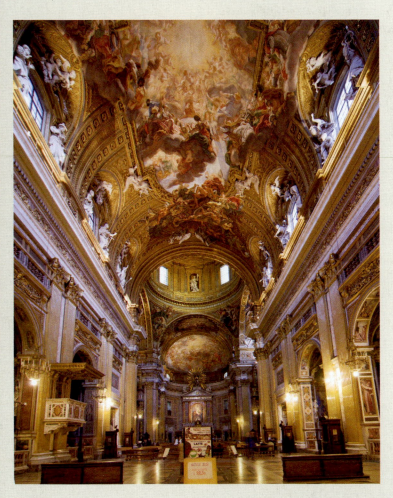

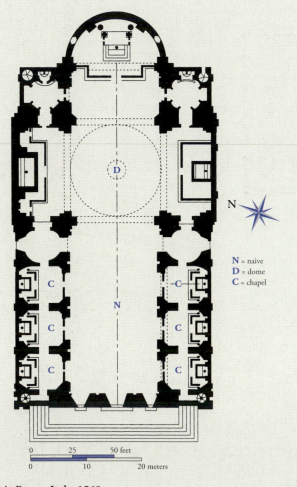

N = naive
D = dome
C = chapel

22-58 GIACOMO DA VIGNOLA, interior looking east (*left*) and plan (*right*) of Il Gesù, Rome, Italy, 1568.

Giacomo da Vignola's plan for Il Gesù, with its exceptionally wide nave with side chapels instead of aisles—ideal for grand processions—won wide acceptance in the Catholic world.

successful in the field of education, the order established numerous schools. In addition, its members were effective missionaries and carried the message of Catholicism to the Americas, Asia, and Africa.

The Jesuits also made their mark in the history of architecture with the construction of Il Gesù (see "Rethinking the Basilican Church," above), which had an enormous influence on church design in the Baroque era, discussed in detail in the next chapter.

RENAISSANCE AND MANNERISM IN CINQUECENTO ITALY

High and Late Renaissance 1495–1600

- During the High (1500–1520) and Late (1520–1600) Renaissance periods in Italy, artists, often in the employ of the papacy, further developed the interest in classical cultures, perspective, proportion, and human anatomy that had characterized Quattrocento Italian art.

- Leonardo da Vinci, the quintessential "Renaissance man," won renown as a painter for his sfumato (misty haziness) and for his psychological insight in depicting biblical narrative (*Last Supper*) and contemporary personalities (*Mona Lisa*).

- Raphael favored lighter tonalities than Leonardo and clarity over obscurity. His sculpturesque figures appear in landscapes under blue skies (*Madonna of the Meadows*) or in grandiose architectural settings rendered in perfect perspective (*School of Athens*).

- Michelangelo was a pioneer in several media, including architecture, but his first love was sculpture. He carved (*David, Moses*) and painted (Sistine Chapel ceiling) emotionally charged figures with heroic physiques, preferring pent-up energy to Raphael's calm, ideal beauty.

- Whereas most Florentine and Roman artists emphasized careful design preparation based on preliminary drawing (disegno), Venetian artists, such as Giovanni Bellini and Giorgione, focused on color and the process of paint application (colorito), landscape, and a poetic approach to painting (poesia).

- The greatest master of the Venetian painting school was Titian, famed for his rich surface textures and dazzling display of color in all its nuances. In paintings such as *Venus of Urbino,* he established oil color on canvas as the standard medium of the Western pictorial tradition.

- The leading architect of the early 16th century was Bramante, who championed the classical style of the ancients. He based his design for the Tempietto—the first High Renaissance building—on antique models, but the combination of parts was new and original.

- Andrea Palladio, an important theorist as well as architect, carried on Bramante's classical style during the Late Renaissance. Famed for his villa designs, he had a lasting influence on later European and American architecture.

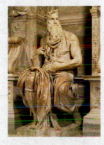

Michelangelo, *Moses*, ca. 1513–1515

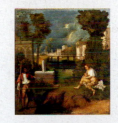

Giorgione, *The Tempest*, ca. 1509–1510

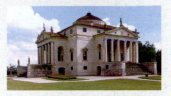

Palladio, Villa Rotonda, ca. 1550–1570

Mannerism 1520–1600

- Mannerism emerged in the 1520s as an alternative to the High Renaissance style. A prime feature of Mannerist art is artifice. Renaissance artists generally strove to create art that appeared natural, whereas Mannerist artists were less inclined to disguise the contrived nature of art production. Ambiguous space, departures from expected conventions, and unusual presentations of traditional themes are hallmarks of Mannerist painting.

- Parmigianino's *Madonna with the Long Neck* exemplifies the elegant stylishness of Mannerist painting. The elongated proportions of the figures, the enigmatic line of columns without capitals, and the ambiguous position of the figure with a scroll are the antithesis of High Renaissance classical proportions, clarity of meaning, and rational perspective.

- Mannerism was also a sculptural style. Benvenuto Cellini created a costly saltcellar for the table of the French king Francis I. The figures, based on antique statuary, have the slim waists and long limbs that appealed to Mannerist taste.

- The leading Mannerist architect was Giulio Romano, who rejected the balance, order, and stability of the High Renaissance style. In the Palazzo del Tè in Mantua, the divergences from architectural convention parody Bramante's classical style and include triglyphs that slip out of the Doric frieze.

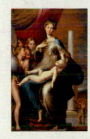

Parmigianino, *Madonna with the Long Neck*, 1534–1540

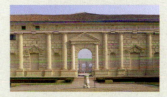

Giulio Romano, Palazzo del Tè, 1525–1535

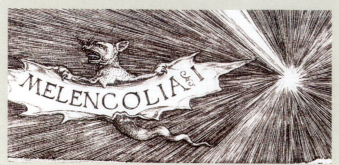

23-1a The Roman numeral on the bat's banner refers to the first level of melancholy: artistic melancholy. However, the burst of light suggests that artists can overcome depression and produce great art.

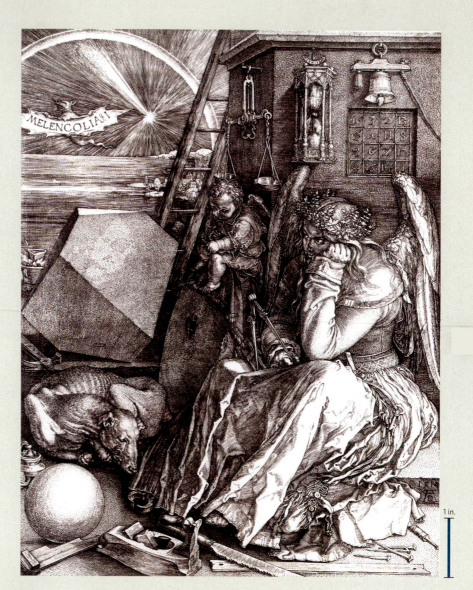

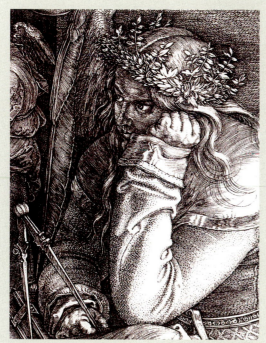

▲ 23-1b In this "self-portrait" of his artistic personality, Dürer represented Melancholy as a brooding winged woman. Melancholy's face is obscured by shadow, underscoring her state of mind.

1 in.

23-1 ALBRECHT DÜRER, *Melencolia I*, 1514. Engraving, $9\frac{3}{8}'' \times 7\frac{1}{2}''$. Victoria & Albert Museum, London.

▶ 23-1c All around Dürer's seated personification of Melancholy are the tools of the artist and builder—compass, hammer, saw, and nails among them— but the melancholic artist is incapable of using them.

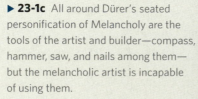

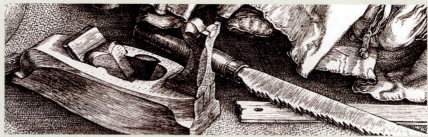

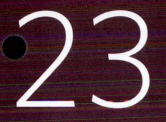

23

High Renaissance and Mannerism in Northern Europe and Spain

FRAMING THE ERA

ALBRECHT DÜRER, MELANCHOLIC GENIUS

In northern Europe, as in Italy, one by-product of the Renaissance was the celebration of artistic genius, accompanied in many cases by probing introspection (literally "looking inside") on the part of individual artists. One German artist who looked within was ALBRECHT DÜRER (1471–1528) of Nuremberg, the first artist outside Italy to become an international celebrity. Dürer was a highly skilled painter, but his reputation today as in his own time rests primarily on his graphic art, which he promoted with an astute businessman's skill. With the aid of his wife, his mother, and an agent, Dürer aggressively marketed his engravings and woodcuts and became a wealthy man. Moreover, in 1506, to protect his financial interests, Dürer filed the first lawsuit in history over artistic copyright, accusing an Italian artist of copying his prints.

One of Dürer's most famous works, *Melencolia I* (FIG. **23-1**), reveals not only his unsurpassed skill with the engraver's burin but also a great deal about his psyche as a Renaissance artist. In *Melencolia I,* Dürer took up the theme of melancholy, one of the temperaments associated with the "four humors"— the fluids that were the basis of the theories about body functions developed by the ancient Greek physician Hippocrates and practiced in medieval physiology. The Italian humanist Marsilio Ficino (1433–1499) had written an influential treatise (*De vita triplici,* 1482–1489) in which he asserted that artists were distinct from the population at large because they were born under the sign of the planet Saturn, named for the ancient Roman god. They shared that deity's melancholic temperament because they had an excess of black bile (one of the four humors) in their systems. Artists therefore were "saturnine"—eccentric and capable both of inspired artistic frenzy and melancholic depression. Raphael had depicted Michelangelo in the guise of the brooding Heraclitus in his *School of Athens* (FIG. 22-9), and Dürer used a similarly posed female figure for his winged personification of Melancholy.

In 1510, in *De occulta philosophia,* Heinrich Cornelius Agrippa (1486–1535) of Nettesheim identified three levels of melancholy. The first was artistic melancholy, which explains the Roman numeral on the banner carried by the bat—a creature of the dark—in Dürer's engraving. Above the brooding figure of Melancholy is an hourglass with the sands of time running out. All around her are the tools of the artist and builder (compare FIG. 13-32)—compass, hammer, nails, and saw among them. However, those tools are useless to the frustrated artist while suffering from melancholy. Melancholy's face is obscured by shadow, underscoring her state of mind. But Dürer also included a burst of light on the far horizon behind the bat, an optimistic note suggesting that artists can overcome their depression and produce works of genius—such as this engraving.

675

NORTHERN EUROPE IN THE 16TH CENTURY

The dissolution of the Burgundian Netherlands in 1477 led in the early 16th century to a realignment in the European geopolitical landscape (MAP 23-1, page 678). France and the Holy Roman Empire absorbed the former Burgundian territories and increased their power. But by the end of the century, through calculated marriages, military exploits, and ambitious territorial expansion, Spain was the dominant European state. Throughout the Continent, monarchs increasingly used art and architecture to glorify their reigns and to promote a stronger sense of cultural and political unity among their subjects, thereby laying the foundation for today's European nations. Wealthy merchants also cultivated art as a status symbol, and the commissioning and collecting of artworks became less and less the exclusive province of the aristocracy.

These important societal changes occurred against the backdrop of a momentous religious crisis. Concerted attempts to reform Church practices led to the Reformation and the establishment of Protestantism (as distinct from Catholicism), which in turn prompted the Church of Rome's response, the Counter-Reformation (see page 641). Ultimately, the Reformation split Christendom in half and produced a hundred years of civil war between Protestants and Catholics.

NORTHERN HUMANISM The tumultuous religious conflict engulfing 16th-century Europe did not, however, prevent—and may even have accelerated—the exchange of intellectual and artistic ideas, because artists frequently moved from one area to another in search of religious freedom and lucrative commissions. Catholic Italy and the (mostly) Protestant Holy Roman Empire shared in a lively commerce—economic and cultural—and 16th-century art throughout Europe was a major beneficiary of that exchange. Humanism filtered up from Italy and spread throughout northern Europe. Humanists north of the Alps, like their southern counterparts, cultivated knowledge of classical cultures and literature, but they focused more on reconciling humanism with Christianity.

Among the most influential of these "Christian humanists" were the Dutchman Desiderius Erasmus (1466–1536) of Rotterdam and the Englishman Sir Thomas More (1478–1535). Erasmus demonstrated his interest in both Italian humanism and religion with his "philosophy of Christ," emphasizing education and scriptural knowledge. Both an ordained priest and an avid scholar, Erasmus wrote (in Latin) his most famous essay, *In Praise of Folly*, in 1509, which he published two years later. In this widely read work, Erasmus satirized not just the Church of Rome but various social classes as well. His ideas were to play an important role in the development of the Reformation, but he consistently declined to join any of the Reformation sects. Equally well educated was Thomas More, who served King Henry VIII (r. 1509–1547; FIG. 23-11A). Henry eventually ordered More's execution because of More's opposition to England's break with the Catholic Church. In France, François Rabelais (ca. 1494–1553), a former monk who advocated rejecting stagnant religious dogmatism, disseminated the humanist spirit.

The turmoil emerging during the 16th century lasted well into the 17th century and permanently affected the face of Europe. The concerted challenges to established authority and the persistent philosophical inquiry eventually led to the rise of new political systems (for example, the nation-state) and new economic systems (such as capitalism).

GERMANY

Although at the opening of the 16th century many Christians in the Holy Roman Empire expressed dissatisfaction with the Church of Rome, Martin Luther had not yet posted his *Ninety-five Theses*, which launched the Protestant Reformation. The Catholic clergy in Germany still offered artists important commissions.

MATTHIAS GRÜNEWALD Matthias Neithardt, known conventionally as MATTHIAS GRÜNEWALD (ca. 1480–1528), worked for the archbishops of Mainz in several capacities, from court painter and decorator to architect, hydraulic engineer, and superintendent of works. Grünewald eventually moved to northern Germany, where he settled at Halle in Saxony. Around 1512, he began work on the *Isenheim Altarpiece* (FIG. 23-2), a complex and fascinating polyptych reflecting Catholic beliefs and incorporating several references to Catholic doctrines, such as the lamb (symbol of the son of God), whose wound spurts blood into a chalice in the *Crucifixion* (FIG. 23-2, *top*) on the exterior of the altarpiece.

Created for the monastic hospital order of Saint Anthony of Isenheim, the *Isenheim Altarpiece* takes the form of a carved wood shrine by NIKOLAUS HAGENAUER (active 1493–1538) featuring large painted and gilded statues of Saints Anthony Abbot, Augustine, and Jerome in the main zone, and smaller statues of Christ and the 12 apostles in the predella (FIG. 23-2, *bottom*). To Hagenauer's centerpiece, carved around 1505, Grünewald added between 1512 and 1515 two pairs of painted moveable wings that open at the center. Hinged at the sides, one pair stands directly behind the other. The exterior panels of the first pair (visible when the altarpiece is closed, FIG. 23-2, *top*) are *Crucifixion* in the center, *Saint Sebastian* on the left, *Saint Anthony Abbot* on the right, and *Lamentation* in the predella. When these exterior wings are open, four additional scenes (not illustrated)—*Annunciation, Angelic Concert, Madonna and Child,* and *Resurrection*—appear. Opening this second pair of wings exposes Hagenauer's interior shrine, flanked by Grünewald's *Meeting of Saints Anthony and Paul* and *Temptation of Saint Anthony* panels (FIG. 23-2, *bottom*).

HIGH RENAISSANCE AND MANNERISM IN NORTHERN EUROPE AND SPAIN

1500–1530

- In Catholic countries, commissions for religious works, such as the *Isenheim Altarpiece,* continue, but, consistent with Reformation values, Protestant patrons prefer secular themes, such as portraiture, classical mythology, and the macabre, including death and witchcraft
- Albrecht Dürer achieves international fame (and wealth) as a master printmaker

1530–1560

- Netherlandish painters inject moralizing religious messages into seemingly secular genre paintings
- Hans Holbein, Caterina van Hemessen, and Levina Teerlinc achieve renown as portrait painters
- In France under Henry II (r. 1547–1559), architectural designs are a mix of Italian and Northern Renaissance elements

1560–1600

- Pieter Bruegel the Elder, the greatest Netherlandish artist of the mid-16th century, produces masterful landscapes that nonetheless focus on human activities
- Greek-born El Greco settles in Toledo and creates paintings that are a uniquely personal mix of Byzantine and Italian Mannerist elements. His hybrid style captured the fervor of Spanish Catholicism

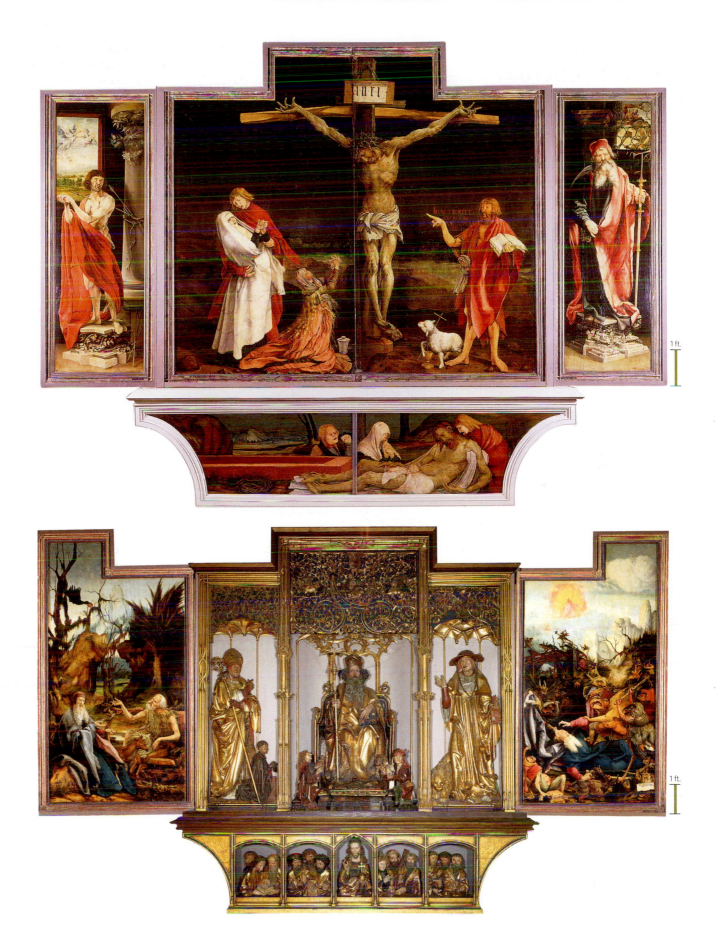

23-2 MATTHIAS GRÜNEWALD, *Isenheim Altarpiece* (*top:* closed; *bottom:* open), from the chapel of the Hospital of Saint Anthony, Isenheim, France, ca. 1512–1515. Oil on wood, center panel 9' 9$\frac{1}{2}$" × 10' 9", each wing 8' 2$\frac{1}{2}$" × 3' $\frac{1}{2}$", predella 2' 5$\frac{1}{2}$" × 11' 2". Shrine carved by NIKOLAUS HAGENAUER, ca. 1505. Painted and gilt limewood, 9' 9$\frac{1}{2}$" × 10' 9". Musée d'Unterlinden, Colmar.

Befitting its setting in a monastic hospital, Matthias Grünewald's *Isenheim Altarpiece* includes painted panels depicting suffering and disease but also miraculous healing, hope, and salvation.

MAP 23-1 Europe in the early 16th century.

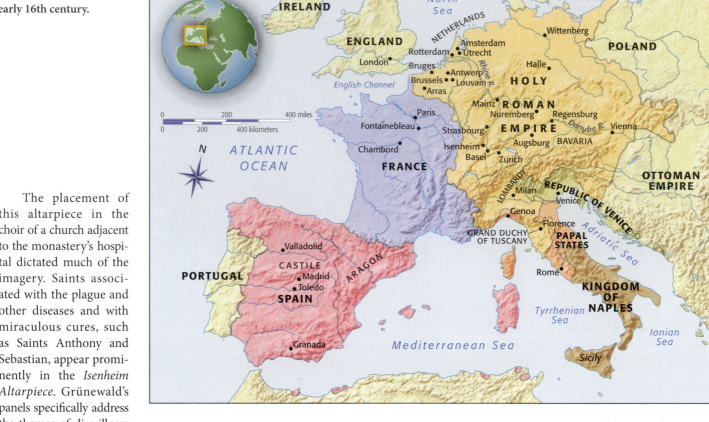

The placement of this altarpiece in the choir of a church adjacent to the monastery's hospital dictated much of the imagery. Saints associated with the plague and other diseases and with miraculous cures, such as Saints Anthony and Sebastian, appear prominently in the *Isenheim Altarpiece*. Grünewald's panels specifically address the themes of dire illness and miraculous healing and accordingly emphasize the suffering of the order's patron saint, Anthony Abbot (see "Early Christian Saints," page 237). The painted images served as warnings, encouraging increased devotion from monks and hospital patients. They also functioned therapeutically by offering some hope to the afflicted. Indeed, Saint Anthony's legend emphasized his dual role as vengeful dispenser of justice (by inflicting disease) and benevolent healer.

One of the most memorable scenes is *Temptation of Saint Anthony* (FIG. 23-2, *bottom right*). It is a terrifying image of the five temptations (lack of faith, despair, impatience, spiritual pride, and avarice), depicted as an assortment of ghoulish and bestial creatures in a dark landscape, attacking the saint. In the foreground, Grünewald painted a grotesque image of a man, whose oozing boils, withered arm, and distended stomach all suggest a horrible disease. Medical experts have connected these symptoms with ergotism (a disease caused by ergot, a fungus that grows especially on rye). Doctors did not discover the cause of this disease until about 1600. People lived in fear of its recognizable symptoms (convulsions and gangrene) and called the illness "Saint Anthony's Fire." Ergotism was one of the major diseases treated at the Isenheim hospital. Indeed, Grünewald depicted Christ's skin covered with sores. Furthermore, ergotism often compelled amputation, and viewers of the *Isenheim Altarpiece* have noted that the two moveable halves of the altarpiece's predella (FIG. 23-2, *top*), if slid apart, make it appear as if Christ's legs have been amputated. The same observation applies to the two main exterior panels. Due to the off-center placement of the cross, opening the left panel "severs" one arm from the crucified figure.

Thus Grünewald carefully selected and presented his altarpiece's iconography to be particularly meaningful for patients at this hospital. In the interior shrine, the artist balanced the horrors of the disease and the punishments awaiting those who did not repent with scenes such as *Meeting of Saints Anthony and Paul*, depicting the two saints, healthy and aged, conversing peacefully. Even the exterior panels (the closed altarpiece; FIG. 23-2, *top*) convey these same concerns. *Crucifixion* emphasizes Christ's pain and suffering, but the knowledge that this act redeemed humanity tempers the misery. In addition, Saint Anthony appears in the right wing as a devout follower of Christ who, like Christ, endured intense suffering for his faith. Saint Anthony's appearance on the exterior thus reinforces the themes that Grünewald intertwined throughout this entire work—themes of pain, illness, and death, as well as those of hope, comfort, and salvation. Grünewald also brilliantly used color to enhance the effect of the painted scenes of the altarpiece. He intensified the contrast of horror and hope by playing subtle tones and soft harmonies against shocking dissonances of color.

ALBRECHT DÜRER A slightly older contemporary of Grünewald was Albrecht Dürer (FIG. 23-1), who put the younger artist in charge of his studio during one of his trips to Italy. Dürer was the most famous northern European artist of his generation and one of the greatest printmakers of any era. Unlike Grünewald, Dürer traveled extensively, visiting and studying in Colmar, Basel, Strasbourg, Venice, Antwerp, and Brussels, among other locales. As a result, Dürer met many of the leading humanists and artists of his time, including Erasmus of Rotterdam and the Venetian master Giovanni Bellini (FIGS. 21-40, 22-32, and 22-33). Fascinated with the classical ideas of the Italian Renaissance, Dürer was among the first Northern Renaissance artists to travel to Italy expressly to study Italian art and its underlying theories at their source. After his first journey in 1494–1495 (the second was in 1505–1506), he incorporated many Italian developments into his prints and paintings. Art historians have acclaimed Dürer as the first artist north of the Alps to understand fully the basic aims of the Renaissance in Italy. Like Leonardo da Vinci, Dürer wrote theoretical treatises on a variety of subjects, including perspective, fortification, and the ideal in human proportions. Unlike Leonardo, he both finished and published his writings. Dürer also was the first northern European artist to leave a record of his life and career through his correspondence, a detailed diary, and a series of self-portraits.

SELF-PORTRAITS Dürer's earliest preserved self-portrait—a silverpoint drawing now in the Albertina in Vienna—dates to 1484, when he was only 13, two years before he began his formal education as an apprentice in the workshop of Michael Wolgemut (FIG. 20-22). In 1498, a few years after his first visit to Italy, he painted a likeness of himself in the Italian mode—a seated half-length portrait in three-quarter view in front of a window through which the viewer sees a landscape. The *Self-Portrait* reproduced here (FIG. 23-3), painted just two years later, is markedly different in character. Inscribed with his monogram and the date (*left*) and four lines (*right*) stating that the painting depicts him at age 28, the panel portrays the artist in a fur-trimmed coat in a rigid frontal posture against a dark background. Dürer has a short beard and shoulder-length hair, and the portrait intentionally evokes medieval devotional images of Christ. The position of Dürer's right hand resembles but does not duplicate (which would have been blasphemous) Christ's standard gesture of blessing in Byzantine icons (FIG. 9-34). The focus on the hand is also a reference to the artist's hand as a creative instrument. Doubtless deeply affected by the new humanistic view that had

emerged in Renaissance Italy of the artist as a divinely inspired genius (see "Albrecht Dürer, Melancholic Genius," page 675), Dürer responded by painting himself as a Christlike figure. He also embraced Italian artists' interest in science, as is evident in his botanically accurate 1503 watercolor study *Great Piece of Turf* (FIG. 23-3A).

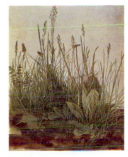

⦿ **23-3A** DÜRER, *Great Piece of Turf*, 1503.

FALL OF MAN Trained as a goldsmith by his father before he took up painting and printmaking, Dürer developed an extraordinary proficiency in handling the burin. This technical ability, combined with his extraordinary skill in drawing, enabled Dürer to produce a body of graphic work that few artists have rivaled for quality and number. Many of his prints were book illustrations, and Dürer also sold prints in single sheets, which people of ordinary means could buy, expanding his audience considerably and, as noted, making him a wealthy man. Erasmus praised Dürer as "the Apelles [the most renowned ancient Greek painter] of black lines,"[1] and the German artist's mastery of all aspects of printmaking is evident also in his woodcuts (FIG. I-9).

One of Dürer's early masterpieces, *Fall of Man* (*Adam and Eve*; FIG. 23-4), represents the first distillation of his studies of the Vitruvian theory of human proportions (compare FIG. 22-5A),

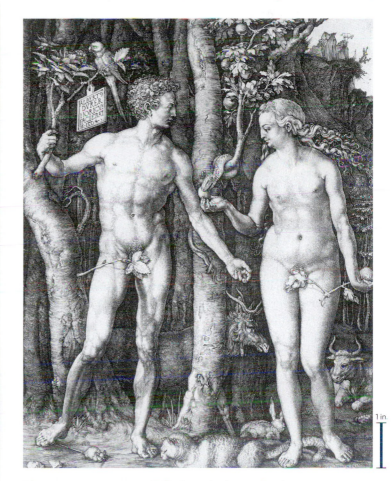

23-3 ALBRECHT DÜRER, *Self-Portrait*, 1500. Oil on wood, 2′ 2¼″ × 1′ 7¼″. Alte Pinakothek, Munich.

Dürer here presents himself as a frontal Christlike figure reminiscent of medieval icons. It is an image of the artist as a divinely inspired genius, a concept inconceivable before the Renaissance.

23-4 ALBRECHT DÜRER, *Fall of Man* (*Adam and Eve*), 1504. Engraving, 9⅞″ × 7⅝″. Museum of Fine Arts, Boston (centennial gift of Landon T. Clay).

Dürer was the first Northern Renaissance artist to achieve international celebrity. *Fall of Man*, with two figures based on ancient statues, reflects his studies of the Vitruvian theory of human proportions.

a theory based on arithmetic ratios. Clearly outlined against the dark background of a northern European forest, the two idealized figures of Adam and Eve stand in poses reminiscent of specific classical statues of Apollo and Venus. Preceded by numerous geometric drawings in which the artist attempted to systematize sets of ideal human proportions in balanced contrapposto poses, the final print presents Dürer's concept of the "perfect" male and female figures. Yet he tempered this idealization with naturalism, demonstrating his well-honed observational skills in his rendering of the background foliage and animals (compare FIGS. 23-3A and **23-4A**). The gnarled bark of the trees and the feathery leaves authenticate the scene, as do the various creatures skulking underfoot. The animals populating the print are symbolic. The choleric cat, the melancholic elk, the sanguine rabbit, and the phlegmatic ox represent humanity's temperaments based on the four humors (see page 675), which, prior to the fall of man, are in balance. Nonetheless, the tension between the cat and the mouse in the foreground symbolizes the relation between Adam and Eve at the crucial moment before they commit the original sin.

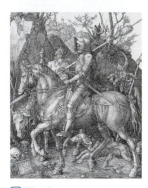

▣ **23-4A** DÜRER, *Knight, Death, and the Devil*, 1513.

FOUR APOSTLES Dürer's major work in the oil medium is *Four Apostles* (FIG. **23-5**), a two-panel painting he produced without commission and presented to the city fathers of Nuremberg in 1526 to be hung in the city hall. Saints John and Peter appear on the left panel, Mark and Paul on the right (see "Early Christian Saints," pages 236–237). In addition to showcasing Dürer's mastery of the oil technique, his brilliant use of color and light and shade, and his ability to imbue the four saints with individual personalities and portraitlike features, *Four Apostles* documents Dürer's support for the German theologian Martin Luther (1483–1546), who sparked the Protestant Reformation. Dürer conveyed his Lutheran sympathies by his positioning of the figures. He relegated Saint Peter (as representative of the pope in Rome) to a secondary role by placing him behind John the Evangelist (compare Konrad Witz's earlier treatment of Peter in *Miraculous Draft of Fish* [FIG. 20-19], widely interpreted as a commentary on the limited powers of the pope). John assumed particular prominence for Luther because of the evangelist's focus on Jesus as a person in his Gospel. In addition, Peter and John both read from the Bible, the single authoritative source of religious truth, according to Luther. Dürer emphasized the Bible's centrality by depicting it open to the passage "In the beginning was the Word, and the Word was with God, and the Word was God" (John 1:1). At the bottom of the panels, Dürer included quotations from the four apostles' books, using Luther's German translation of the New Testament. The excerpts warn against the coming of perilous times and the preaching of false prophets who will distort God's word.

LUTHER AND THE REFORMATION The Protestant Reformation, which came to fruition in the early 16th century, had its roots in long-term, growing dissatisfaction with the Catholic Church's leadership. The deteriorating relationship between the faithful and the Church of Rome's hierarchy stood as an obstacle for the millions who sought a meaningful religious experience. Particularly damaging was the perception that the Roman popes concerned themselves more with temporal power and material wealth than

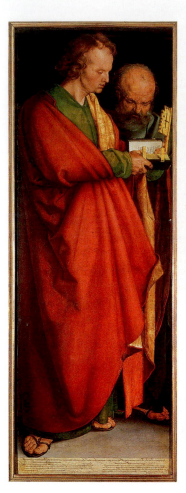
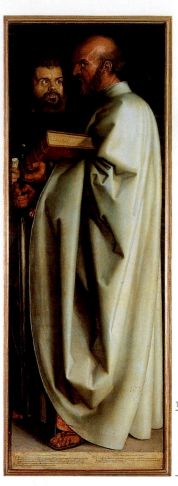

1 ft.

23-5 ALBRECHT DÜRER, *Four Apostles,* from the city hall, Nuremberg, Germany, 1526. Oil on wood, each panel 7' 1" × 2' 6". Alte Pinakothek, Munich.

Dürer's support for Lutheranism surfaces in his portraitlike depictions of four saints on two painted panels. Peter, representative of the pope in Rome, plays a secondary role behind John the Evangelist.

with the salvation of their Christian flock. The fact that many 15th-century popes and cardinals came from wealthy families, such as the Medici, intensified this perception. It was not only those at the highest levels who seemed to ignore their spiritual duties. Archbishops, bishops, and abbots began to accumulate numerous offices, thereby increasing their revenues but making it more difficult for them to fulfill all of their responsibilities. By 1517, dissatisfaction with the Roman Church had grown so widespread that Luther felt free to openly challenge papal authority by posting on October 31 in Wittenberg his *Ninety-five Theses,* in which he enumerated his objections to Catholic practices, especially the sale of indulgences. *Indulgences* were Church-sanctioned remittances (or reductions) of time Catholics had to spend in Purgatory for confessed sins. The increasing frequency of their sale suggested that those who could afford to purchase indulgences were buying their way into Heaven.

Luther's goal was significant reform and clarification of major spiritual issues, but his ideas ultimately led to splitting Western Christendom apart. According to Luther, the Catholic Church's extensive ecclesiastical structure needed casting out, for it had no basis in scripture. The Bible and nothing else could serve as the foundation for Christianity. Luther called the pope the Antichrist (for which Pope Leo X excommunicated him in 1520) and the Church of Rome the "whore of Babylon." He denounced ordained

RELIGION AND MYTHOLOGY

Catholic versus Protestant Views of Salvation

A central concern of the Protestant reformers was the question of how Christians achieve salvation. Rather than perceive salvation as something for which weak and sinful humans must constantly strive through good deeds performed under the watchful eye of a punitive God, Martin Luther argued that faithful individuals attained redemption solely by God's bestowal of his grace. Therefore, people cannot earn salvation. Further, no ecclesiastical machinery with all its miraculous rites and Church-sanctioned indulgences could save sinners face-to-face with God. Only absolute faith in Christ could redeem sinners and ensure salvation. Redemption by faith alone, with the guidance of holy scripture, was the fundamental doctrine of Protestantism.

In *Law and Gospel* (FIG. 23-6), a woodcut dated about a dozen years after Luther set the Reformation in motion with his *Ninety-five Theses*, Lucas Cranach the Elder gave visual expression to the doctrinal differences between Protestantism and Catholicism. Cranach contrasted Catholicism (based on Old Testament law, according to Luther) and Protestantism (based on the Gospel belief in God's grace) in two images separated by a centrally placed tree that has leafy branches only on the Protestant side. On the left half, judgment day has arrived, as represented by Christ's appearance at the top of the scene, hovering amid a cloud halo and accompanied by angels and saints. Christ raises his left hand in the traditional gesture of damnation, and, below, a skeleton drives off a terrified person to burn for eternity in Hell. This person tried to live a good and honorable life, but despite his efforts, he fell short. Moses stands to the side, holding the tablets of the law—the Ten Commandments, which Catholics follow in their attempt to attain salvation.

In contrast to this Catholic reliance on good works and clean living, Protestant doctrine emphasized God's grace as the source of redemption. Accordingly, God showers the sinner in the right half of the print with grace, as streams of blood flow from the crucified Christ. At the far left are Adam and Eve, whose original sin necessitated Christ's sacrifice. In the lower right corner of the woodcut, Christ emerges from the tomb and promises salvation to all who believe in him.

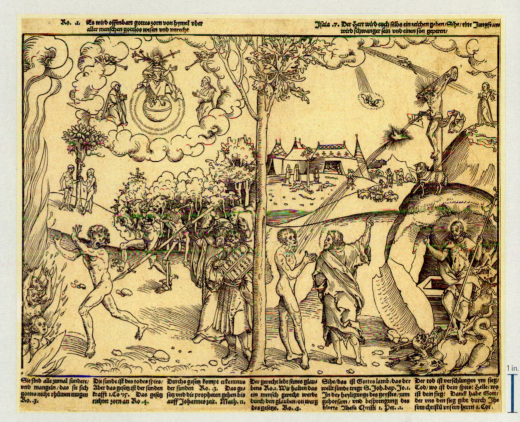

23-6 LUCAS CRANACH THE ELDER, *Law and Gospel*, ca. 1530. Woodcut, $10\frac{5}{8}$" × 1' $\frac{3}{4}$". British Museum, London.

Lucas Cranach was a close friend of Martin Luther, whose *Ninety-five Theses* launched the Protestant Reformation in 1517. This woodcut contrasts Catholic and Protestant views of how to achieve salvation.

priests and also rejected most of Catholicism's sacraments other than baptism and communion, decrying them as obstacles to salvation (see "Catholic versus Protestant Views of Salvation," above, and FIG. 23-6). Luther maintained that for Christianity to be restored to its original purity, the Catholic Church needed cleansing of all the doctrinal impurities that had collected through the ages. Luther advocated the Bible as the source of all religious truth. The Bible—the sole scriptural authority—was the word of God, which did not exist in the Church's councils, law, and rituals. Luther facilitated the lay public's access to biblical truths by publishing the first translation of the Bible in a vernacular language.

ART AND THE REFORMATION In addition to doctrinal differences, Catholics and Protestants took divergent stances on the role of visual imagery in religion. Catholics embraced church decoration as an aid to communicating with God (see "The Council of Trent," page 642). In contrast, Protestants believed that images of Christ, the Virgin, and saints could lead to idolatry and distracted viewers from focusing on the real reason for their presence in church—to communicate directly with God. Because of this belief, Protestant churches were relatively bare, and the extensive church pictorial programs found especially in Italy but also in northern Europe (FIGS. 20-18, 20-19, and 23-2) were not as prominent in Protestant churches.

The Protestant concern over the role of religious imagery escalated at times to outright *iconoclasm*—the objection to and destruction of religious imagery, a revival of an attitude that, centuries before, led to an outright ban on religious art in the Byzantine Empire (see "Icons and Iconoclasm," page 271). In encouraging a more personal relationship with God, Protestant leaders spoke out against much of the religious art being produced. In his 1525 tract *Against the Heavenly Prophets in the Matter of Images and*

Sacraments, Martin Luther explained his attitude toward religious imagery:

> I approached the task of destroying images by first tearing them out of the heart through God's Word and making them worthless and despised. . . . For when they are no longer in the heart, they can do no harm when seen with the eyes. . . . I have allowed and not forbidden the outward removal of images. . . . And I say at the outset that according to the law of Moses no other images are forbidden than an image of God which one worships. A crucifix, on the other hand, or any other holy image is not forbidden.[2]

In fact, Luther approved the inclusion of illustrations in his translations of the Bible as well as painted altarpieces in churches, which he believed served a didactic purpose. However, two influential Protestant theologians based in Switzerland—Huldrych (Ulrich) Zwingli (1484–1531) and French-born John Calvin (Jean Cauvin, 1509–1564)—were more vociferous in cautioning their followers about the potentially dangerous nature of all religious imagery. Zwingli and Calvin's condemnation of religious imagery often led to eruptions of iconoclasm. Particularly violent waves of iconoclastic fervor swept Basel, Zurich, Strasbourg, and Wittenberg in the 1520s. In an episode known as the Great Iconoclasm, bands of Calvinists visited Catholic churches in the Netherlands in 1566, shattering stained-glass windows, smashing statues, and destroying paintings and other artworks that they perceived as idolatrous. These strong reactions to art, which reflected the religious fervor of the time, also serve as dramatic demonstrations of the power of art—and of how much art matters in society.

LUCAS CRANACH THE ELDER The artist most closely associated with the Protestant Reformation and with Martin Luther in particular was LUCAS CRANACH THE ELDER (1472–1553), who provided the illustrations for Luther's vernacular Bible. Cranach and Luther were godfathers to each other's children, and many scholars have dubbed Cranach "the painter of the Reformation." Cranach was also an accomplished graphic artist who used the new, inexpensive medium of prints on paper to promote Lutheran ideology (FIG. 23-6). Cranach's work encompasses a wide range of themes, however. For example, for aristocratic Saxon patrons he produced a large number of paintings of classical myths featuring female nudes in suggestive poses.

One classical theme that Cranach depicted several times was *Judgment of Paris,* of which the small panel (FIG. **23-7**) now in Karlsruhe is the best example. Homer recorded the story in the eighth century BCE, but Cranach's source was probably the elaboration of the Greek tale in Roman times by Lucian (ca. 120–ca. 180). Mercury chose a handsome young shepherd named Paris to be the judge of a beauty contest among three goddesses—Juno, wife of Jupiter; Minerva, Jupiter's virgin daughter and goddess of wisdom and war; and Venus, the goddess of love (see "The Gods and Goddesses of Mount Olympus," page 105). According to Lucian, each goddess attempted to bribe Paris with rich rewards if he chose her. Venus won by offering Paris the most beautiful woman in the world, Helen of Troy, and thus set in motion the epic war between the Greeks and Trojans recounted in Homer's *Iliad* (see page 84).

No one, however, could confuse Cranach's painting with an ancient depiction of the myth. The setting is a German landscape with a Saxon castle in the background, and the seated shepherd is a knight in full armor wearing a fashionable hat. Mercury, an aged man (as he never is in ancient art), also wearing armor, bends over to draw Paris's attention to the three goddesses. They are nude save

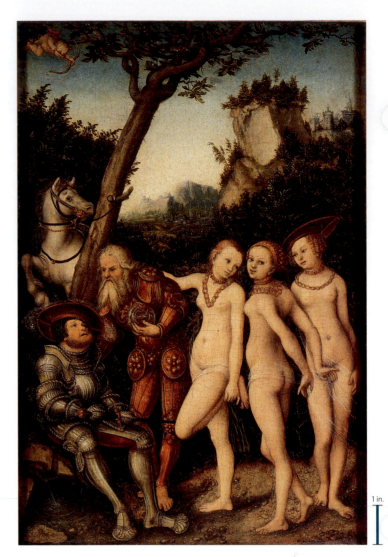

23-7 LUCAS CRANACH THE ELDER, *Judgment of Paris,* 1530. Oil on wood, 1' 1½" × 9½". Staatliche Kunsthalle, Karlsruhe.

For aristocratic German patrons, Cranach painted many classical myths featuring seductive female nudes. In his *Judgment of Paris,* the Greek shepherd is a knight in armor in a Saxon landscape.

for their transparent veils, their fine jewelry, and, in the case of Juno, an elegant hat. Cranach's goddesses are loosely based on classical representations of the Three Graces (compare FIG. 21-28), although ancient artists never depicted Juno or Minerva undressed. The German painter's figures also do not have the proportions (or modesty) of Praxiteles's *Aphrodite of Knidos* (FIG. 5-62) or Botticelli's *Venus* (FIG. 21-1). Slender, with small heads and breasts and long legs, they pose seductively before the judge. Venus performs a dance for Paris, but he seems indifferent to all three goddesses. Only the rearing horse appears to be excited by the spectacle—a touch of humor characteristic of Cranach.

HANS BALDUNG GRIEN When Albrecht Dürer undertook his second trip to Italy in 1505, he placed his most gifted assistant, HANS BALDUNG GRIEN (ca. 1484–1545), in charge of his studio. The son of a prosperous attorney and the brother of a university professor, Baldung chose to pursue printmaking (FIG. **23-8**) and painting (FIG. **23-9**) as a profession rather than the law or letters. He eventually settled in Strasbourg, a center of humanistic learning, where he enjoyed a long and successful career. Baldung produced some religious works, although none on the scale of Grünewald's

ART AND SOCIETY

Witchcraft, Disease, Plague, and Death

In an age when the normal life span was only about 40 years and disease, plague, and superstitious fear were commonplace, it is natural that these themes would figure prominently in some artworks, such as Matthias Grünewald's *Isenheim Altarpiece* (FIG. 23-2), painted for the Hospital of Saint Anthony in Isenheim. Death figures prominently too in the work of Grünewald's contemporary, Hans Baldung Grien, who also explored exotic and erotic subjects, including witchcraft.

Witchcraft was a counter-religion in the 15th and 16th centuries involving magical rituals, secret potions, and Devil worship. Witches prepared brews that they inhaled or rubbed into their skin, sending them into hallucinogenic trances in which they allegedly flew through the night sky on broomsticks or goats. The popes condemned all witches, and Church inquisitors vigorously pursued these demonic heretics and subjected them to torture to wrest confessions from them. People also feared witches because they thought that they could create storms and hailstorms that ruined crops and caused famines. Witchcraft fascinated Baldung, and he turned to the subject repeatedly. For him and his contemporaries, witches were evil forces in the world, threats to man—as was Eve herself, whom Baldung also frequently depicted as a temptress responsible for original sin.

In *Witches' Sabbath* (FIG. 23-8), Baldung depicted a night scene in a forest featuring a coven of nude witches, although 16th-century witches performed their rites clothed. Female nudity and macabre scenes were popular with men, who avidly purchased the relatively inexpensive prints that Baldung created in large numbers. The coven in the *Witches' Sabbath* woodcut includes both young seductresses and old hags. They gather around a covered jar from which a fuming concoction escapes into the air. One young witch rides through the night sky on a goat. She sits backward—Baldung's way of suggesting that witchcraft is the inversion of the true religion, Christianity.

Witches' Sabbath does not address death and illness directly, but the inevitability of old age and death, which, with a strong dose of eroticism, are the central elements in Baldung's *Three Ages of Woman and Death* (FIG. 23-9), a subject he returned to repeatedly during his career. Albrecht Dürer—in whose workshop Baldung trained—had portrayed Death and Famine (FIG. I-9) in his woodcuts, and the emaciated figure of Death in Baldung's painting owes a debt to his master's work, as does the beautiful nude young woman Death approaches from behind. She is a variation on Dürer's Eve in *Fall of Man* (FIG. 23-4), an engraving Dürer produced while Baldung was his apprentice. Baldung's oil painting is a commentary on *vanitas* (Latin, "vanity," especially with regard to the transience of life), another popular subject.

The voluptuous, fair-skinned young woman gazes at her reflection in a mirror as she combs her long hair, oblivious that Death pursues her. The maiden appears two more times in the same painting at two different ages—as an infant who plays with one end of the young woman's transparent mantle and as a wrinkled, dark-skinned old woman who rushes in from the left to try to push Death away. Baldung tells the viewer that the old woman will not succeed in warding off Death. Indeed, the sand in the hourglass that Death holds mockingly over the maiden's head will run out too soon. (An hourglass also looms over Dürer's personified Melancholy in *Melencolia I*, FIG. 23-1.)

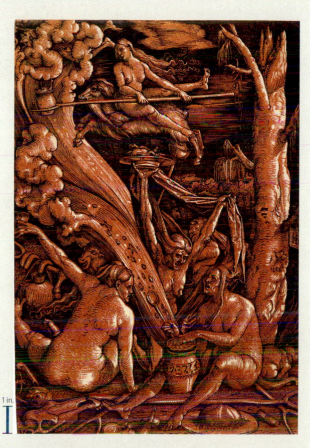

23-8 HANS BALDUNG GRIEN, *Witches' Sabbath*, 1510. Chiaroscuro woodcut, 1' 2⅞" × 10¼". British Museum, London.

Baldung's woodcut depicts witches gathered around a cauldron containing a secret potion. One witch flies mounted backward on a goat, suggesting that witchcraft is the inversion of Christianity.

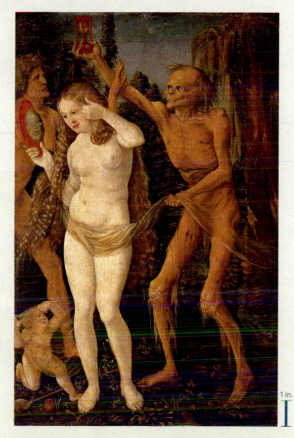

23-9 HANS BALDUNG GRIEN, *Three Ages of Woman and Death*, 1510. Oil on wood, 1' 3¾" × 1' ¾". Kunsthistorisches Museum, Vienna.

Baldung often explored macabre themes featuring female nudity. Here, Death approaches a maiden as she admires her reflection. Beside her are an old woman and an infant—the maiden at different ages.

Isenheim Altarpiece (FIG. 23-2). His reputation rested primarily on his exploration of nontraditional subjects, such as witchcraft (see "Witchcraft, Disease, Plague, and Death," page 683).

Witches' Sabbath (FIG. 23-8) is a *chiaroscuro woodcut,* a recent innovation usually attributed to the Flemish woodcutter Jost de Negker (ca. 1485–ca. 1544). The technique requires the use of two blocks of wood instead of one. The printmaker carves and inks one block (the *key block*) in the usual way in order to produce a traditional black-and-white print (see "Printed Books," page 577). Then the artist cuts a second block (the *tone block*) consisting of broad highlights to be inked in grays or colors and printed over the first

block's impression. Chiaroscuro woodcuts therefore incorporate some of the qualities of painting and feature tonal subtleties absent in traditional woodcuts.

ALBRECHT ALTDORFER Although Dürer, Cranach, and Baldung sold their artworks primarily to private patrons, other artists in 16th-century Germany, as elsewhere in Europe, earned their income in the employ of rulers, and their work promoted the political agendas of their patrons. In 1529, for example, the duke of Bavaria, Wilhelm IV (r. 1508–1550), commissioned ALBRECHT ALTDORFER (ca. 1480–1538) of Regensburg to paint *Battle of Issus* (FIG. 23-10)

23-10 ALBRECHT ALTDORFER, *Battle of Issus*, 1529. Oil on wood, 5' 2$\frac{1}{4}$" × 3' 11$\frac{1}{4}$". Alte Pinakothek, Munich.

Interweaving landscape, history, and 16th-century politics, Altdorfer painted Alexander the Great's defeat of the Persians for a patron who had just embarked on a military campaign against the Ottoman Turks.

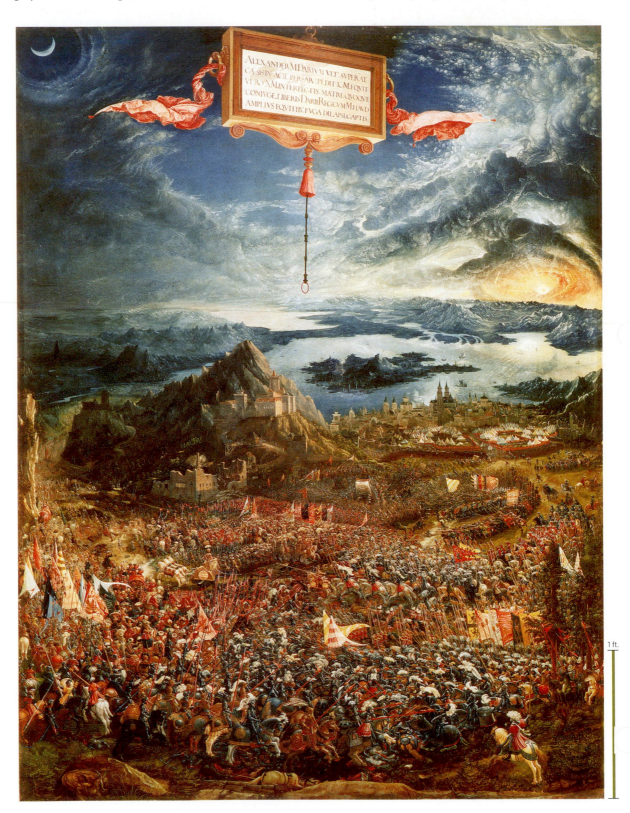

1 ft.

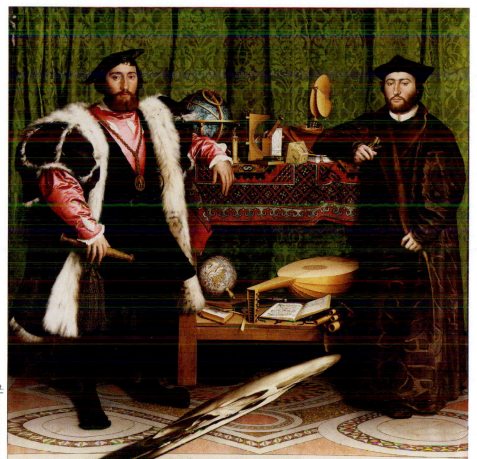

23-11 HANS HOLBEIN THE YOUNGER, *The French Ambassadors,* 1533. Oil and tempera on wood, 6' 8" × 6' 9½". National Gallery, London.

In this double portrait, Holbein depicted two humanists with a collection of objects reflective of their worldliness and learning, but he also included an anamorphic skull, a reminder of death.

HANS HOLBEIN Also in the employ of the rich and powerful for much of his career was HANS HOLBEIN THE YOUNGER (ca. 1497–1543), who excelled as a portraitist. Born in Augsburg, Germany, and trained by his father, Holbein produced many of his best portraits in England. The surfaces of Holbein's paintings are as lustrous as enamel, and the details are exact and exquisitely drawn, consistent with the tradition of 15th-century Flemish art. Yet he also incorporated Italian ideas about monumental composition and sculpturesque form. Holbein is a leading example of the increasingly international outlook of 16th-century European artists.

Holbein began his artistic career in Basel, where he became a master in the painter's guild in 1519 and met Erasmus of Rotterdam, whose portrait he painted several times. Because of the immediate threat of a religious civil war in Basel, Erasmus suggested that Holbein leave for England and gave him a recommendation to Thomas More, chancellor of England under Henry VIII. Holbein arrived in England in 1526 and quickly obtained important commissions—for example, to paint More's portrait. Holbein returned to Basel in 1528 but went back to England in 1532 and remained there until his death in 1543. In 1533, he painted one of his most ambitious works, a double portrait (FIG. 23-11) of the French ambassadors to England, Jean de Dinteville (1504–1557) and Georges de Selve (1509–1542). A few years later (1536), Holbein became the King's Painter and produced numerous portraits of Henry VIII (FIG. 23-11A).

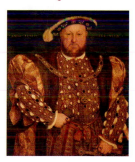

23-11A HOLBEIN THE YOUNGER, *Henry VIII,* 1540.

The French Ambassadors (FIG. 23-11) exhibits Holbein's considerable talents—his strong sense of composition, his subtle linear patterning, his gift for recording likenesses, his marvelous sensitivity to color, and his faultless technique. The two men, both ardent humanists, stand at opposite ends of a side table covered with an oriental rug and a collection of objects reflective of their worldliness and their interest in learning and the arts. These include mathematical and astronomical models and implements (compare FIG. 26-24), a lute with a broken string, compasses, a sundial, flutes, globes, and an open hymnbook with Luther's translation of *Veni, Creator Spiritus* and of the Ten Commandments.

Of particular interest is the long gray shape that slashes diagonally across the picture plane and interrupts the stable, balanced, and serene composition. This form is an *anamorphic image,* a distorted image recognizable only when viewed with a special device, such as a cylindrical mirror, or by looking at the painting at an

at the commencement of his military campaign against the invading Ottoman Turks (see page 300). The panel depicts Alexander the Great's defeat of King Darius III of Persia in 333 BCE near a town called Issus on the Pinarus River. Altdorfer announced the subject—which the Greek painter Philoxenos of Eretria (FIG. 5-70) had represented two millennia before—in the Latin inscription suspended in the sky. The parallels between the historical and contemporary conflicts were no doubt significant to the duke. Both involved Western societies engaged in battles against Eastern foes with different values—the Persians in antiquity and the Ottomans in 1528. Altdorfer reinforced this connection by attiring the figures in 16th-century armor (many of the "Persian" soldiers wear Turkish turbans) and depicting them battling in 16th-century military formations.

Altdorfer was one of the first to draw and paint landscapes as subjects in their own right, and *Battle of Issus* reveals his interest in recording natural locales. The battle takes place in an almost cosmological setting. From a bird's-eye view, the clashing armies swarm in the foreground. In the distance, craggy mountain peaks rise next to still bodies of water. Amid swirling clouds, a blazing sun descends. Although the spectacular topography may appear invented, Altdorfer derived his depiction of the landscape from a map of the Mediterranean world published in 1493 in the *Nuremberg Chronicle* (see page 577). Specifically, the viewer sees the terrain and sea from the mountains of Greece to the Nile Valley in Egypt. In addition, Altdorfer may have acquired his information about this battle from the German scholar Johannes Aventinus (1477–1534), whose account of Alexander's victory describes the bloody daylong battle. Appropriately, given Alexander's designation as the "sun god," the sun sets over the victorious Greeks on the right, while a small crescent moon (a symbol of ancient Persia) hovers in the upper left corner over the retreating enemy forces.

acute angle. In this case, if the viewer stands off to the right, the distorted image becomes a skull. Although scholars disagree on the skull's precise meaning, it certainly refers to death. Artists commonly incorporated skulls into paintings as reminders of mortality. Indeed, Holbein depicted a skull on the metal medallion on Jean de Dinteville's hat. Holbein may have intended the skulls, in conjunction with the crucifix that appears half hidden behind the curtain in the upper left corner, to encourage viewers to ponder death and resurrection. (A faint image of a skull appears on the polygonal block at the left in Dürer's *Melencolia I* [FIG. 23-1].)

Holbein's portrait of the two ambassadors may also allude to the growing tension between secular and religious authorities. Jean de Dinteville was a titled landowner, Georges de Selve a bishop. The inclusion of Luther's translations next to the lute with the broken string (a symbol of discord) may subtly refer to this religious strife. In any case, *The French Ambassadors* is a painting of supreme artistic achievement. Holbein rendered the still-life objects with the same meticulous care as he did the men themselves, the woven design of the deep emerald curtain behind them, and the Italian marble-inlay floor, drawn in perfect perspective.

THE NETHERLANDS

With the demise of the duchy of Burgundy in 1477 and the division of that territory between France and the Holy Roman Empire (MAP 23-1), the Netherlands at the beginning of the 16th century consisted of 17 provinces (corresponding to modern Holland, Belgium, and Luxembourg). The Netherlands was among the most commercially advanced and prosperous countries in Europe. Its extensive network of rivers and easy access to the Atlantic Ocean provided a

setting that encouraged overseas trade, and shipbuilding was one of the Netherlands' most profitable enterprises. The region's commercial center shifted toward the end of the 15th century, partly because of the buildup of silt in the Bruges estuary. Traffic relocated to Antwerp, which became the hub of economic activity in the Netherlands after 1510. As many as 500 ships a day passed through Antwerp's harbor, and large trading companies from Germany, Italy, Spain, Portugal, and England established themselves in the city.

During the second half of the 16th century, Philip II of Spain (r. 1556–1598) controlled the Netherlands. Philip had inherited the region from his father, Charles V (r. 1516–1556), and he sought to force the entire population to become Catholic. His heavy-handed tactics and repressive measures led in 1579 to revolt and the formation of two federations: the Union of Arras, a Catholic union of southern Netherlandish provinces, which remained under Spanish dominion, and the Union of Utrecht, a Protestant union of northern provinces, which became the Dutch Republic (MAP 25-1).

As in Germany (FIG. 23-2) at the opening of the 16th century, Netherlandish artists continued to receive commissions from Catholic churches for large-scale altarpieces and other religious works. But with the rise of Protestantism, most artists in the Netherlands focused on secular subjects. Netherlandish art of this period provides a wonderful glimpse into the lives of various levels of society, from nobility to peasantry, capturing their activities, environment, and values.

HIERONYMUS BOSCH The leading Netherlandish painter of the early 16th century was HIERONYMUS BOSCH (ca. 1450–1516), one of the most fascinating artistic personalities in history. Bosch's most famous painting, the *Garden of Earthly Delights* (FIG. 23-12), is also

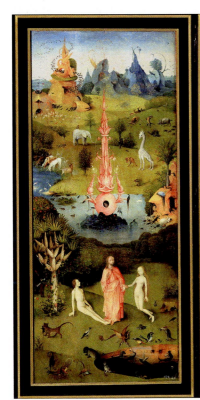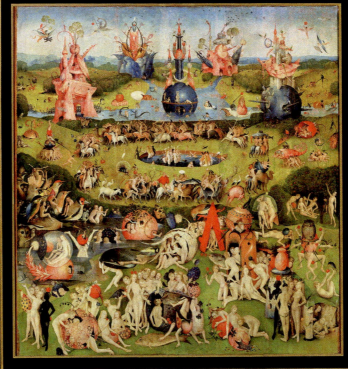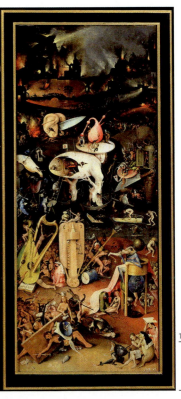

1 ft.

23-12 HIERONYMUS BOSCH, *Garden of Earthly Delights,* 1505–1510. Oil on wood, center panel 7' 2⅝" × 6' 4¾", each wing 7' 2⅝" × 3' 2¼". Museo del Prado, Madrid.

In the fantastic sunlit landscape that is Bosch's Paradise, scores of nude people in the prime of life blithely cavort. The horrors of Hell include sinners enduring tortures tailored to their conduct while alive.

his most puzzling, and no interpretation has ever won universal acceptance. Although the work is a large triptych, which would suggest a religious function as an altarpiece, *Garden of Earthly Delights* was on display in the palace of Count Henry III of Nassau-Breda (r. 1516–1538) no later than seven years after its completion. This suggests that the triptych was a secular commission, and some scholars have proposed that given the work's central themes of sex and procreation, the painting may commemorate a wedding. Marriage was a familiar theme in Netherlandish painting. Fifteenth-century examples include *Giovanni Arnolfini and His Wife* (FIG. 20-7) and *A Goldsmith in His Shop* (FIG. 20-10). Any similarity to those earlier paintings ends there, however. Whereas Jan van Eyck and Petrus Christus grounded their depictions of betrothed couples in contemporary Netherlandish life and custom, Bosch's image portrays a visionary world of fantasy and intrigue—a painted world without close parallel until the advent of Surrealism more than 400 years later (see page 921).

In the left panel, God (in the form of Christ) presents Eve to Adam in a landscape, presumably the Garden of Eden. Bosch's wildly imaginative setting includes an odd pink fountainlike structure in a body of water and an array of fanciful and unusual animals, including a giraffe, an elephant, and winged fish.

The central panel is a continuation of Paradise, a sunlit landscape filled with nude people, including exotic figures of African descent, who frequently appear in Renaissance paintings (for example, FIG. 21-49), both north and south of the Alps. All those in Paradise are in the prime of youth. They blithely cavort amid bizarre creatures and unidentifiable objects. Some of the youths exuberantly stand on their hands or turn somersaults. The numerous fruits and birds in the scene are fertility symbols and suggest procreation. Indeed, many of the figures pair off as couples.

In contrast to the orgiastic overtones of the central panel is the terrifying image of Hell in the right wing, where viewers must search through the inky darkness to find all of the fascinating though repulsive details that Bosch recorded. Beastly creatures devour people, while other condemned souls endure tortures tailored to their conduct while alive. A glutton must vomit eternally. A miser squeezes gold coins from his bowels. A spidery monster fondles a promiscuous woman while toads bite her.

Scholars have traditionally interpreted Bosch's triptych as a warning to viewers of the fate awaiting the sinful, decadent, and immoral, but as a secular work, *Garden of Earthly Delights* may have been intended for a learned audience fascinated by *alchemy*—the medieval study of seemingly magical chemical changes. (Witchcraft also involved alchemy; see page 683.) Details throughout the triptych are based on chemical apparatus of the day, which Bosch knew well because his in-laws were pharmacists.

QUINTEN MASSYS Antwerp's growth and prosperity, along with its wealthy merchants' propensity for collecting and purchasing art, attracted artists to the city. Among them was QUINTEN MASSYS (ca. 1466–1530), who became Antwerp's leading master after 1510. The son of a Louvain blacksmith, Massys demonstrated a willingness to explore the styles and modes of a variety of models, from Jan van Eyck and Rogier van der Weyden to Albrecht Dürer, Hieronymous Bosch, and Leonardo da Vinci. Yet his eclecticism was subtle and discriminating, enriched by an inventiveness that gave a personal stamp to his paintings.

In *Money-Changer and His Wife* (FIG. **23-13**), Massys presented a professional man transacting business. He holds scales, checking the weight of coins on the table. The artist's detailed rendering of the figures, setting, and objects suggests a fidelity to observable fact, and provides insight into developing commercial practices. But *Money-Changer and His Wife* is also a commentary on Netherlandish values and mores. The painting highlights the financial transactions that were an increasingly prominent part of 16th-century secular life in the Netherlands and that distracted Christians from their religious duties. The banker's wife, for example, shows more interest in watching her husband weigh money than in reading her prayer book. Massys incorporated into his painting numerous references to the importance of a moral, righteous, and spiritual life, including a carafe with water and a candlestick, traditional religious symbols. The couple

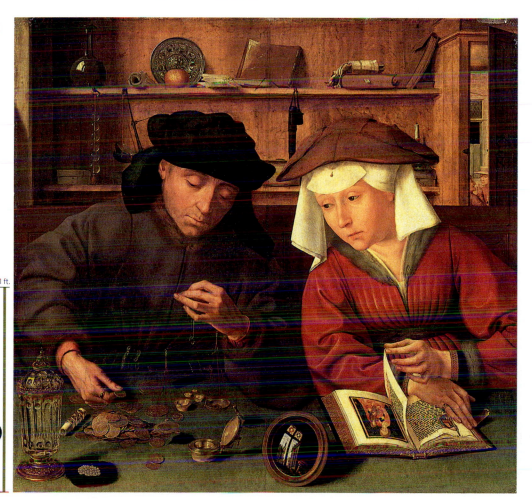

1 ft.

23-13 QUINTEN MASSYS, *Money-Changer and His Wife,* 1514. Oil on wood, 2' 3$\frac{3}{4}$" × 2' 2$\frac{3}{8}$". Musée du Louvre, Paris.

Massys's depiction of a secular financial transaction is also a commentary on Netherlandish values. The banker's wife shows more interest in the money-weighing than in her prayer book.

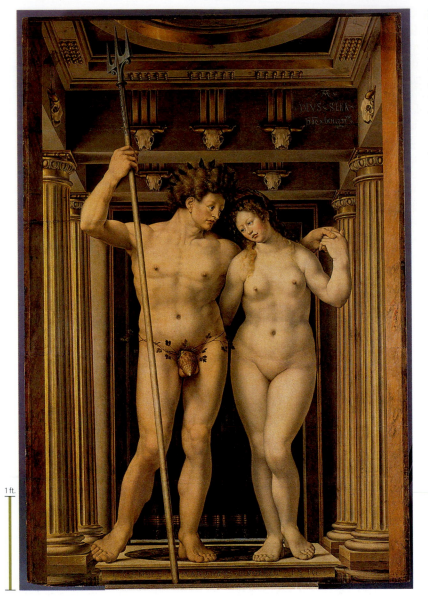

23-14 Jan Gossaert, *Neptune and Amphitrite*, 1516. Oil on wood, 6' 2" × 4' $\frac{3}{4}$". Gemäldegalerie, Staatliche Museen zu Berlin, Berlin.

Dürer's *Fall of Man* (FIG. 23-4) inspired the poses of Gossaert's classical deities, but the architectural setting is probably based on the sketches that Gossaert made of ancient buildings during his trip to Rome.

1 ft.

writing about 15 years after Gossaert's death, claimed that "Giovanni di Mabuse [Jan Gossaert] was almost the first to bring from Italy into Flanders the true method of making scenes full of nude figures."[3]

In fact, Gossaert derived much of his classicism from Albrecht Dürer, whose *Fall of Man* (FIG. 23-4) inspired the composition and poses in Gossaert's *Neptune and Amphitrite* (FIG. 23-14). However, in contrast to Dürer's exquisitely small engraving, Gossaert's painting is more than 6 feet tall and 4 feet wide. The artist executed the painting with characteristic Netherlandish polish, skillfully drawing and carefully modeling the life-size figures. Gossaert depicted the sea god with his traditional attribute, the *trident* (see "The Gods and Goddesses of Mount Olympus," page 105), and wearing a laurel wreath and an ornate conch shell in place of Dürer's fig leaf. Amphitrite is fleshy and, like Neptune, stands in a contrapposto stance. The architectural frame, which resembles the *cella* of a classical temple (FIG. 5-46), is an unusual mix of Doric and Ionic elements and *bucrania* (ox skull decorations), a common motif in ancient architectural ornamentation. Gossaert likely based the classical setting on sketches he had made of ancient buildings while in Rome. (Several of his drawings of ancient statues and of the Colosseum are preserved.)

Gossaert had traveled to Italy as part of an official delegation to Pope Julius II led by Philip, Admiral of Burgundy (1498–1517) and Bishop of Utrecht (1517–1524), who commissioned Gossaert to paint *Neptune and Amphitrite*. The subject must have held special appeal for the admiral, but Philip did not display the work publicly. He kept the representation of the nude god and goddess in the innermost room of his castle.

ignores them, focusing solely on money. On the right, through a window, an old man talks with another man, a reference to idleness and gossip. The reflected image in the convex mirror on the counter offsets this image of sloth and foolish chatter. There, a man reads what is most likely a Bible or prayer book. Behind him is a church steeple. An inscription on the original frame (now lost) read, "Let the balance be just and the weights equal" (Lev. 19:36), an admonition that applies both to the money-changer's professional conduct and eventually to judgment day. Nonetheless, the couple in this painting has tipped the balance in favor of the pursuit of wealth.

JAN GOSSAERT Bosch and Massys spent their entire careers in the Netherlands, but many of their contemporaries succumbed to the lure of Italy. JAN GOSSAERT (ca. 1478–1535), known to his contemporaries as "the Apelles of our age," was one of those who traveled to Italy (in 1508–1509) and became fascinated with classical antiquity and mythology (FIG. 23-14), although he also painted traditional Christian themes (FIG. 23-14A). Giorgio Vasari (see "Vasari's *Lives*," page 636),

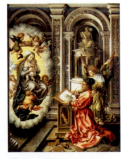

23-14A GOSSAERT, *Saint Luke Drawing the Virgin*, ca. 1520–1525.

PIETER AERTSEN Gossaert's *Neptune and Amphitrite* is exceptional in treating a Greco-Roman subject. More typical, and another example of the Netherlandish tendency to inject reminders about spiritual well-being into paintings of everyday life, is *Butcher's Stall* (FIG. 23-15) by PIETER AERTSEN (ca. 1507–1575) of Amsterdam, who became a master in Antwerp's Guild of Saint Luke in 1535 and a citizen of his adopted city in 1542. He returned to Amsterdam in 1557 and worked there until his death two decades later.

Butcher's Stall is one of the *genre* scenes (paintings of daily life) for which Aertsen achieved fame. On display is an array of meat products—a side of a hog, chickens, sausages, a stuffed intestine, pig's feet, meat pies, a cow's head, a hog's head, and hanging entrails. Also visible are fish, pretzels, cheese, and butter. But, like Massys, Aertsen embedded strategically placed religious images in his painting. In the background (FIG. 23-15, *center left*), Joseph leads a donkey carrying Mary and the Christ Child. The holy family stops to offer alms to a beggar and his son, while the people behind the holy family wend their way toward a church. Furthermore, the crossed fishes on the platter and the pretzels and wine in the rafters on the upper left all refer to "spiritual food" (pretzels were often served as

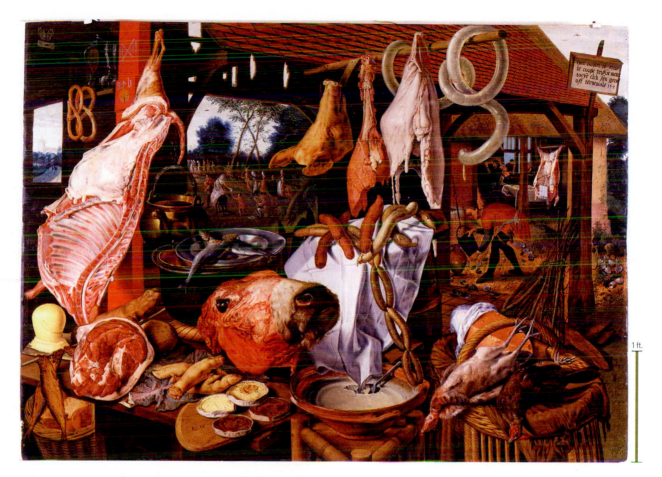

23-15 PIETER AERTSEN, *Butcher's Stall,* 1551. Oil on wood, 4' $\frac{3}{8}$" × 6' 5 $\frac{3}{4}$". Uppsala University Art Collection, Uppsala.

Butcher's Stall appears to be a genre painting, but in the background, Joseph leads a donkey carrying Mary and the Christ Child. Aertsen balanced images of gluttony with allusions to salvation.

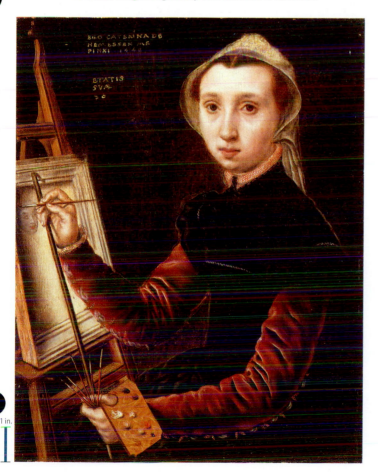

bread during Lent). Aertsen accentuated these allusions to salvation through Christ by contrasting them to their opposite—a life of gluttony, lust, and sloth. He represented this degeneracy with the oyster and mussel shells (which Netherlanders believed possessed aphrodisiacal properties) scattered on the ground on the painting's right side, along with the people seen eating and carousing nearby under the roof. Underscoring the general theme is the placard at the right advertising land for sale—Aertsen's moralistic reference to a recent scandal involving the transfer of land from an Antwerp charitable institution to a land speculator.

CATERINA VAN HEMESSEN With the accumulation of wealth in the Netherlands, private portraits increased in popularity. The example illustrated here (FIG. **23-16**), by CATERINA VAN HEMESSEN (1528–1587), is the first known northern European self-portrait by a woman. The artist signed the work "Caterina van Hemessen painted me / 1548 / her age 20" and confidently presented herself as a painter who interrupts her work at her easel to look toward the viewer. She holds brushes, a palette, and a *maulstick* (a stick used to steady the hand while painting) in her left hand, and delicately applies pigment to the panel with her right hand. Professional women artists remained unusual in the 16th century in

23-16 CATERINA VAN HEMESSEN, *Self-Portrait,* 1548. Oil on wood, 1' $\frac{3}{4}$" × 9 $\frac{7}{8}$". Kunstmuseum Basel, Basel.

In this first known northern European self-portrait by a woman, Caterina van Hemessen represented herself as a confident artist momentarily interrupting her work to look out at the viewer.

The Netherlands **689**

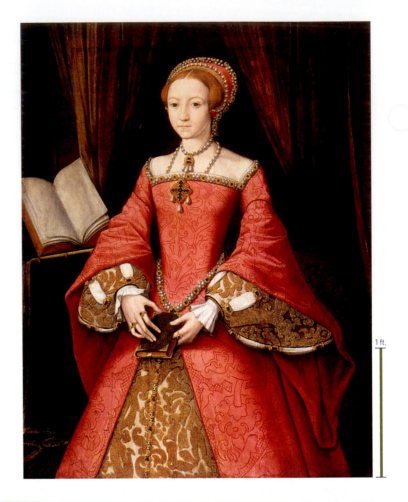

23-17 Attributed to Levina Teerlinc, *Elizabeth I as a Princess*, ca. 1559. Oil on wood, 3' 6¾" × 2' 8¼". Royal Collection, Windsor Castle, Windsor.

Teerlinc received greater compensation for her work for the British court than did her male contemporaries. Her considerable skill is evident in this life-size portrait of Elizabeth I as a young princess.

large part because of the difficulty in obtaining formal training (see "The Artist's Profession in Flanders," page 566). Caterina was typical in having been taught by her father, Jan Sanders van Hemessen (ca. 1500–1556), a well-known painter in Antwerp who had traveled in Italy in the 1520s. She acquired an enviable reputation for her portraits of women and enjoyed the patronage of Mary, queen consort of Hungary (1505–1558).

LEVINA TEERLINC Another Netherlandish woman painter was Levina Teerlinc (ca. 1515–1576) of Bruges. She established such a high reputation that Henry VIII (FIG. 23-11A) invited her to England and appointed her royal *paintrix* in 1546, three years after the death of Hans Holbein the Younger. Teerlinc became a formidable rival of her male contemporaries at the court and received greater compensation for her work than they did for theirs. Teerlinc's considerable skill is evident in a life-size portrait (FIG. 23-17) attributed to her, which depicts Elizabeth I as a composed, youthful princess. Daughter of Henry VIII and Anne Boleyn, Elizabeth was probably in her late 20s when she posed for this portrait. Appropriate to her station in life, Elizabeth wears an elegant brocaded gown, extravagant jewelry, and a headdress based on a style popularized by her mother.

1 ft.

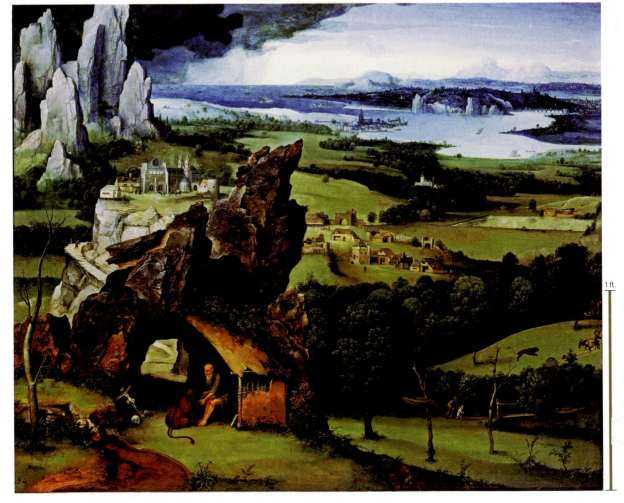

23-18 Joachim Patinir, *Landscape with Saint Jerome*, ca. 1520–1524. Oil on wood, 2' 5⅛" × 2' 11⅞". Museo del Prado, Madrid.

Joachim Patinir, a renowned Netherlandish landscape painter, subordinated the story of Saint Jerome to the depiction of craggy rock formations, verdant rolling fields, and expansive bodies of water.

1 ft.

That Teerlinc enjoyed such success is a testament to her determination and skill, given the difficulties that women faced in a profession dominated by men. Women also played an important role as patrons in 16th-century northern Europe. Politically powerful women such as Mary of Hungary, van Hemessen's patron, and Margaret of Austria (1480–1530), regent of the Netherlands during the early 16th century, were active collectors and patrons, and contributed significantly to the thriving state of the arts. As did other art patrons, these women collected and commissioned art not only for the aesthetic pleasure it provided but also for the status it bestowed on them and the cultural sophistication it represented.

JOACHIM PATINIR In addition to portrait and genre painting, landscape painting flourished in the 16th-century Netherlands. Particularly well known for his landscapes was JOACHIM PATINIR (ca. 1480–1524), who became a master in Antwerp's painters' guild in 1515. In fact, the word *Landschaft* (landscape) first emerged in German literature as a characterization of an artistic category when Dürer described Patinir as a "good landscape painter." In *Landscape with Saint Jerome* (FIG. 23-18), Patinir subordinated the saint, who removes a thorn from a lion's paw in the foreground, to the exotic and detailed landscape populated by other figures and animals. As is typical of his work, in this painting Patinir depicted the countryside from a high vantage point in order to achieve a broad and distant panorama. Craggy rock formations, verdant rolling fields, villages with church steeples, expansive bodies of water, and a dramatic sky fill most of the panel. Although nature figures more prominently in his religious paintings than do the biblical protagonists, Patinir had little interest in exploring Italian linear perspective. In fact, his bird's-eye views are inconsistent: the terrain is represented from above, but individual features, such as trees and rocky outcroppings, are seen head-on. He did, however, use different blues, making them paler with increasing distance to suggest recession.

PIETER BRUEGEL THE ELDER The greatest Netherlandish painter of the mid-16th century was PIETER BRUEGEL THE ELDER (ca. 1528–1569). Trained in Antwerp and influenced by Patinir, although he was an apprentice in a different studio, Bruegel was also a landscape painter. In Brueghel's paintings, however, no matter how huge a slice of the world the artist depicted, human activities remain the dominant theme. Like many of his contemporaries, Bruegel traveled to Italy, where between 1551 and 1554 he went as far south as Sicily, and was in Rome in 1553. Unlike other artists, however, Bruegel chose not to incorporate classical elements into his paintings. He settled in Brussels in 1563.

Bruegel's *Netherlandish Proverbs* (FIG. 23-19), painted several years after the artist returned to Antwerp from Italy, depicts a Netherlandish village populated by a wide range of people, encompassing nobility, peasants, and clerics. Seen from the kind of bird's-eye view that Patinir favored is a mesmerizing array of activities reminiscent of the topsy-turvy scenes of Bosch (FIG. 23-12). In fact, contemporaries referred to Bruegel as "a second Bosch." Nonetheless, *Netherlandish Proverbs* is unlike anything Bosch ever painted, and the purpose and meaning of Bruegel's anecdotal details are clear, whereas Bosch's are difficult to interpret, at least for modern viewers. By illustrating more than a hundred proverbs in this one painting, the artist indulged his Netherlandish audience's obsession with proverbs, passion for detailed and clever imagery, and interest in human folly—the subject of Erasmus's most famous work, *In Praise of Folly*.

As the viewer scrutinizes the myriad vignettes within the painting, Bruegel's close observation and deep understanding of human nature become apparent. The proverbs depicted include, on the far left, a man in blue gnawing on a pillar. "He who bites a church pillar" is a religious zealot engaged in folly. To his right, a man "beats his head against a wall" (a frustrated idiot who has attempted something impossible). On the roof a man "shoots one arrow after the

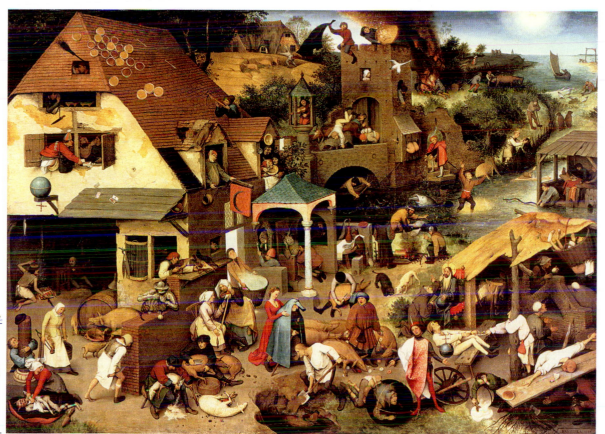

23-19 PIETER BRUEGEL THE ELDER, *Netherlandish Proverbs*, 1559. Oil on wood, 3' 10" × 5' 4$\frac{1}{8}$". Gemäldegalerie, Staatliche Museen zu Berlin, Berlin.

In this painting of a Netherlandish village, Bruegel indulged his audience's obsession with proverbs and passion for clever imagery, and demonstrated his deep understanding of human nature.

1 ft.

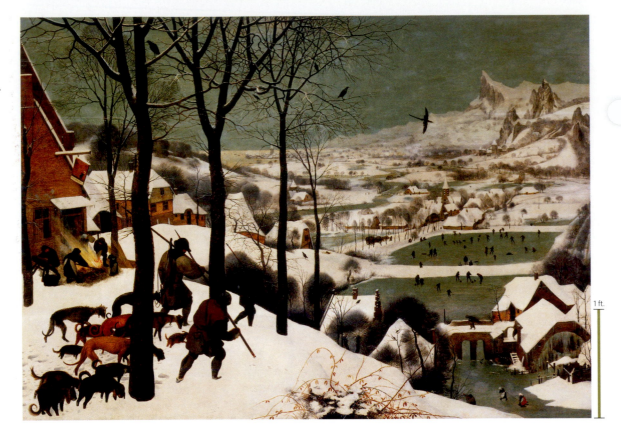

1 ft.

other, but hits nothing" (a fool who throws good money after bad). In the far distance, near the burst of sunlight, the "blind lead the blind"—a subject to which Bruegel returned several years later in one of his most famous paintings.

In contrast to Patinir's Saint Jerome, lost in the landscape, the vast cast of often comical characters in Bruegel's *Netherlandish Proverbs* fills the panel, so much so that the artist almost shut out the sky. *Hunters in the Snow* (FIG. 23-20) and *Fall of Icarus* (FIG. 23-20A) are very different in character and illustrate the dynamic variety of Bruegel's work. *Hunters* is one of a series of six paintings he produced in Brussels illustrating sea-

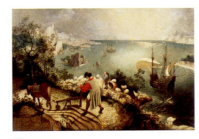

23-20A BRUEGEL THE ELDER, *Fall of Icarus*, ca. 1555–1556.

sonal changes, with each painting representing not a season but a pair of months. The paintings were a private commission and hung in the home of Nicolaes Jongelinck, a wealthy Antwerp merchant. The series, which Bruegel completed in a single year, grew out of the tradition of depicting months and peasants in Books of Hours (FIGS. 20-15 and 20-16). The painting, which must represent December/January, shows human figures and landscape locked in winter cold, reflecting the particularly severe winter of 1565. The weary hunters return with their hounds, women build fires, skaters skim the frozen pond, and the town and its church huddle in their mantle of snow. Bruegel rendered the landscape in an optically accurate manner. It develops smoothly from foreground to background and draws the viewer diagonally into its depths, starting with the row of bare trees in the left foreground. The painter's supreme skill in using line and shape and his subtlety in tonal harmony make this one of the great landscape paintings in Western art.

FRANCE

As Holbein's *French Ambassadors* (FIG. 23-11) illustrates, France in the early 16th century continued its efforts to secure widespread recognition as a political power and cultural force. Under Francis I (r. 1515–1547), the French established a firm foothold in Milan and its environs, and waged a campaign (known as the Habsburg-Valois Wars) against Charles V, King of Spain and Holy Roman Emperor. These wars, which occupied Francis for most of his reign, involved disputed territories—southern France, the Netherlands, the Rhineland, northern Spain, and Italy—and reflect France's central role in the shifting geopolitical landscape (MAP 23-1).

The French king also took a strong position in the religious controversies of his day. By the mid-16th century, the split between Catholics and Protestants had become so pronounced that subjects often felt compelled either to accept the religion of their sovereign or emigrate to a territory where the sovereign's religion corresponded with their own. France was predominantly Catholic, and in 1534, Francis declared Protestantism illegal. The state persecuted its Protestants—the Huguenots, a Calvinist sect—and drove them underground. Calvin himself fled from France to Switzerland two years later. The Huguenots' commitment to Protestant Calvinism eventually led to one of the bloodiest religious massacres in European history when the Huguenots and Catholics clashed in Paris in August 1572. The violence quickly spread throughout France with the support of many nobles, which presented a serious threat to the king's authority.

JEAN CLOUET As the rulers of antiquity and other Renaissance monarchs had done, Francis commissioned portraits of himself to assert his authority. The finest is the portrait that JEAN CLOUET (ca. 1485–1541) painted about a decade after Francis became king. Clouet probably came from the Netherlands to France during the

THE PATRON'S VOICE
Francis I, Royal Art Patron and Collector

With the coming of age of Francis I, the Catholic Church, the primary patron of art and architecture in medieval France, yielded that position to the French monarchy. The patronage of Francis I, extensively chronicled in a rich trove of contemporary documents, is an illuminating case study of what can result from the confluence of vast wealth, absolute power, and sophisticated taste.

Francis expended especially large sums on building projects, including a royal hunting lodge at Chambord (FIG. 23-22). After his decision in 1528 to relocate to Paris from the Loire valley, he undertook the remodeling of the Louvre, then a medieval fortress (FIG. 20-16), and constructed new palaces in the Bois du Boulogne forest outside Paris, at Saint-Germain-en-Laye, and most significantly at Fontainebleau.

Francis favored art that was at once elegant, erotic, and unorthodox. Appropriately, Mannerism held great appeal for him, and he hired three prominent Italian Mannerists to create artworks for his pleasure and to decorate the new palace at Fontainebleau: Benvenuto Cellini (FIGS. 22-52 and 22-52A), Rosso Fiorentino (1494–1540), and Francesco Primaticcio (1504–1570). Francis had earlier enticed Leonardo da Vinci to come to France after the king won control of Milan in 1516 (see page 629). Leonardo was given a generous pension and an elegant home at Cloux, where he died three years later (without having produced any important works for the king).

Anecdotes abound attesting to Francis's deep personal interest in the artists in his employ. The king was capable of both extravagant praise and harsh criticism. On one occasion he rebuked Cellini for not living up to his promises and warned the artist about the consequences if he did not change his ways:

> I gave you express orders to make me twelve silver statues. . . . You have chosen to execute a saltcellar [FIG. 22-52], and vases and busts and doors, and a heap of other things. . . . You have neglected my wishes and worked for the fulfillment of your own. . . . I tell you, therefore, plainly: do your utmost to obey my commands; for if you stick to your own fancies you will run your head against a wall.*

Francis probably made his greatest mark, however, as a collector. Through diplomatic gifts that he received and the artworks that his agents commissioned or acquired on his behalf in Italy, Francis formed a magnificent collection. With some horror, Giorgio Vasari, the great chronicler of Renaissance artists' lives (see "Giorgio Vasari's *Lives*," page 636), took note in his biography of Andrea del Sarto (FIG. 22-8A) of the king's ravenous appetite for Italian art and of how the artistic patrimony of Vasari's beloved Florence was being exported to France:

> In Florence . . . Giovanbattista della Palla . . . was not only having executed all the sculptures and pictures he could, to send to France for King Francis I, but was also buying antiques of all sorts and pictures of every kind, provided only that they were by the hands of good masters; and every day he was packing them up and sending them off.†

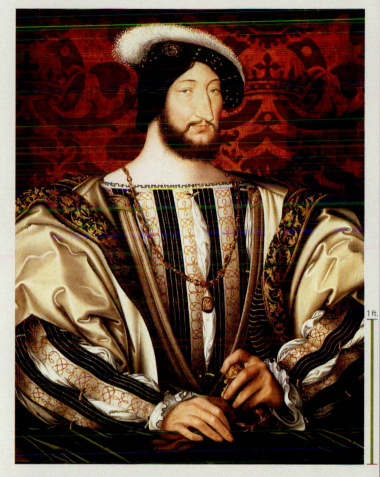

23-21 JEAN CLOUET, *Francis I*, ca. 1525–1530. Tempera and oil on wood, 3' 2" × 2' 5". Musée du Louvre, Paris.

Clouet's portrait of the elegantly dressed Francis I reveals the artist's skill, but the flattening of the king's features and disproportion between his head and body give the painting a formalized quality.

Francis's art treasures became the core of one of the world's greatest museums, the Musée du Louvre. A brief list just of the works in *Art through the Ages* that Francis once owned will suffice to indicate the quality of his collection: Leonardo da Vinci's *Madonna of the Rocks* (FIG. 22-2) and *Mona Lisa* (FIG. 22-5); Bronzino's *Venus, Cupid, Folly, and Time* (FIG. 22-45); Michelangelo's *Bound Slave* (FIG. 22-15); and Cellini's saltcellar (FIG. 22-52) and *Genius of Fontainebleau* (FIG. 22-52A). In addition, Francis's collection boasted works by Perugino, Raphael, Andrea del Sarto, Titian, Giulio Romano, and Rosso Fiorentino, as well as tapestries and ancient statues.

*Quoted by Robert J. Knecht, *Renaissance Warrior and Patron: The Reign of Francis I.* (New York: Cambridge University Press, 1994), 456.
†Translated by Janet Cox-Rearick, *The Collection of Francis I: Royal Treasures* (New York: Abrams, 1996), 87.

reign of Louis XII (r. 1498–1515). He soon established a studio specializing in portraiture and received royal commissions. In *Francis I* (FIG. 23-21), Clouet presented the French monarch as a worldly ruler magnificently bedecked in silks and brocades, wearing a gold chain with a medallion of the Order of Saint Michael, a French order founded by Louis XI in 1469. Francis appears suave and confident, with his hand resting on the pommel of a dagger. Despite the careful detail, the portrait also exhibits an elegantly formalized quality, the result of Clouet's suppression of modeling, which flattens features, seen particularly in Francis's neck. The disproportion between the

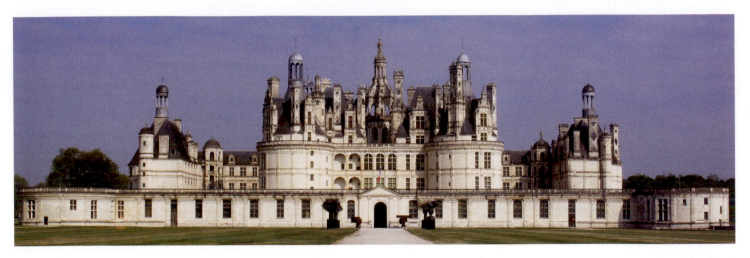

23-22 Château de Chambord (looking northwest), Chambord, France, begun 1519.

French Renaissance châteaux, which developed from medieval castles, served as country houses for royalty. King Francis I's Château de Chambord reflects Italian palazzo design, but it has a Gothic roof.

king's small head and his broad body, swathed in heavy layers of fabric, adds to the formalized nature.

Portraiture was, however, a relatively minor interest of Francis's. He was a great patron of sculpture and the decorative arts; a passionate collector of paintings, especially those of Italian masters; and a builder on a grand scale (see "Francis I, Royal Art Patron and Collector," page 693).

CHÂTEAU DE CHAMBORD Among Francis's architectural commissions is the grandiose Château de Chambord (FIG. 23-22). As a building type, the *château* developed from medieval castles, but, reflecting more peaceful times, Renaissance châteaux served as country houses for royalty, who usually built them near forests for use as hunting lodges. Many, including Chambord, still featured protective surrounding moats, however. Construction of the Château de Chambord began in 1519, but Francis I never saw its completion. Chambord's plan, originally drawn by a pupil of Giuliano da Sangallo (FIGS. 22-26 and 22-27), includes a central square block with four corridors in the shape of a cross, and a broad central stair-

case that gives access to groups of rooms—ancestors of the modern suite of rooms or apartments. At each of the four corners, a round tower punctuates the square plan. From the exterior, Chambord presents a carefully contrived horizontal accent on three levels, with continuous moldings separating its floors. Windows align precisely, one exactly over another. The Italian Renaissance palazzo served as the model for this matching of horizontal and vertical features, but above the third level, the structure's lines break chaotically into a jumble of high *dormers* (projecting gable-capped windows), chimneys, and turrets that are the heritage of French Gothic residential architecture—for example, the Louvre palace (FIG. 20-16) in Paris.

LOUVRE, PARIS Chambord, despite its Italian elements, is essentially a French building. During the reign of Francis's successor, Henry II (r. 1547–1559), however, translations of Italian architectural treatises appeared, and Italian architects themselves came to work in France. Moreover, the French turned to Italy for study and travel. These exchanges caused a more extensive revolution in style than had transpired earlier, although certain French elements derived from

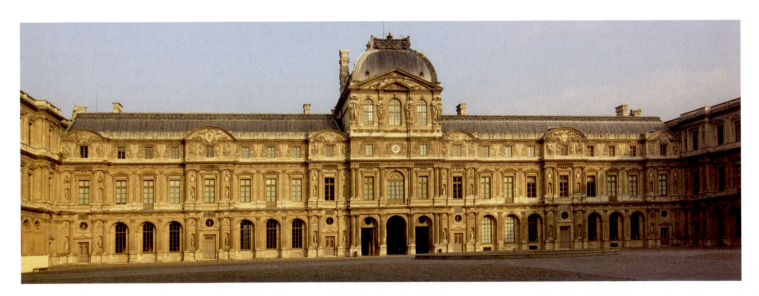

23-23 PIERRE LESCOT, west wing of the Cour Carrée (Square Court; looking west) of the Louvre, Paris, France, begun 1546.

Pierre Lescot's design for the Louvre palace reflects Italian Renaissance architectural models, but the decreasing height of the stories, large windows, and steep roof are northern European features.

the Gothic tradition persisted. This incorporation of Italian architectural ideas characterizes the redesigned Louvre in Paris, originally a medieval palace and fortress (FIG. 20-16). Since Charles V's renovation of the Louvre in the mid-14th century, the castle had fallen into a state of disrepair. Francis I initiated the project to renovate the royal palace (see "Francis I," page 693) when he decided in 1528 to move his court to Paris from the Loire valley. It was not until 1546, however, that Francis commissioned PIERRE LESCOT (1510–1578) to build a new palace. Francis died the following year, but work continued under Henry II, who greatly enlarged the project, enabling Lescot to design a palace that has become synonymous with the classical style of 16th-century French architecture.

Lescot and his associates were familiar with the architectural style of Bramante and his school. In the west wing of the Cour Carrée (Square Court; FIG. 23-23) of the Louvre, each of the stories forms a complete order, and the cornices project enough to furnish a strong horizontal accent. The arcading on the ground story reflects the ancient Roman use of arches and produces more shadow than in the upper stories due to its recessed placement, thereby strengthening the design's visual base. On the second story, the pilasters rising from bases and the alternating curved and angular pediments have direct antecedents in several High Renaissance palaces—for example, the Palazzo Farnese (FIG. 22-26) in Rome. Yet the decreasing height of the stories, the scale of the windows (proportionately much larger than in Italian Renaissance buildings), and the steep roof are northern European elements. Especially French are the pavilions jutting from the wall. A motif that the French long favored—double columns framing a niche—punctuates the pavilions. The richly articulated wall surfaces feature relief sculptures by JEAN GOUJON (ca. 1510–1565), who had previously collaborated with Lescot on the Fountain of the Innocents (FIG. 23-23A) in Paris.

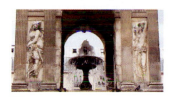

23-23A GOUJON, Fountain of the Innocents, 1547-1549.

Other northern European countries imitated this French classical manner—its double-columned pavilions, tall and wide windows, profuse statuary, and steep roofs—although with local variations. The modified classicism that the French embraced became the model for building projects north of the Alps through most of the 16th century.

SPAIN

Spain's ascent to power in Europe began in the mid-15th century with the marriage of Isabella of Castile (1451–1504) and Ferdinand of Aragon (1452–1516) in 1469. By the end of the 16th century, Spain had emerged as the dominant European power. Under the Habsburg rulers Charles V and Philip II, the Spanish Empire controlled a territory greater in extent than any ever known—a large part of Europe, the western Mediterranean, a strip of North Africa, and vast expanses in the New World. Spain acquired many of its New World colonies through aggressive overseas exploration. Among the most notable conquistadors sailing under the Spanish flag were Christopher Columbus (1451–1506), Vasco Núñez de Balboa (ca. 1475–1517), Ferdinand Magellan (1480–1521), Hernán Cortés (1485–1547), and Francisco Pizarro (ca. 1470–1541). The Habsburg Empire, enriched by New World plunder, supported the most powerful military force in Europe. Spain defended and then promoted the interests of the Catholic Church in its battle against the inroads of the Protestant Reformation. Indeed, Philip II earned

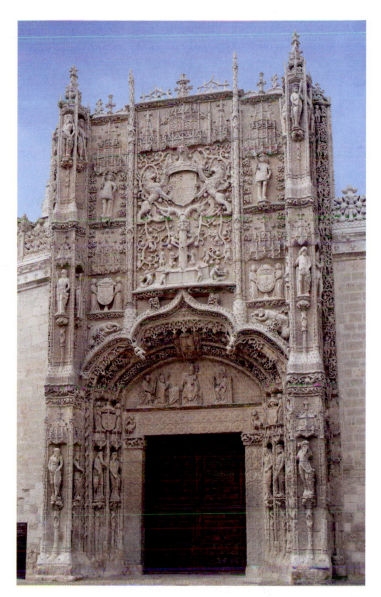

23-24 Portal, Colegio de San Gregorio, Valladolid, Spain, ca. 1498.

The Plateresque architectural style takes its name from *platero* (Spanish, "silversmith"). At the center of this portal's Late Gothic tracery is the coat of arms of King Ferdinand and Queen Isabella.

the title "Most Catholic King." Spain's crusading spirit, nourished by centuries of war with Islam (see page 298), prepared the country to assume the role of the most Catholic civilization of Europe and the Americas. In the 16th century, for good or for ill, Spain left the mark of its power, religion, language, and culture on two hemispheres.

COLEGIO DE SAN GREGORIO During the 15th century and well into the 16th, a Late Gothic style of architecture, the Plateresque, prevailed in Spain. *Plateresque* derives from the Spanish word *platero* ("silversmith"), and delicately executed ornamentation resembling metalwork is the defining characteristic of the Plateresque style. The Colegio de San Gregorio (Seminary of Saint Gregory; FIG. 23-24) in the Castilian city of Valladolid handsomely exemplifies the Plateresque manner, which Spanish expansion into the Western Hemisphere also brought to New Spain (FIG. 23-24A). Great

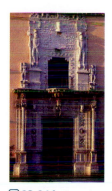

23-24A Casa de Montejo, Mérida, 1549.

carved retables, like the German altarpieces that influenced them (FIGS. 20-20, 20-21, and 23-2, *bottom*), appealed to church patrons and architects in Spain, and the portals of Plateresque facades often resemble elegantly carved retables set into an otherwise blank wall.

The Plateresque entrance of San Gregorio is a lofty sculptured stone screen bearing no functional relation to the architecture behind it. On the entrance level, lacelike tracery reminiscent of Moorish design hems the flamboyant ogival arches. (Spanish hatred of the Moors did not discourage Spanish architects from adapting Moorish motifs—a habit that dates to the Visigothic age; see page 320.) A great screen, paneled into sculptured compartments, rises above the tracery. In the center, the branches of a huge pomegranate tree (symbolizing Granada, the Moorish capital of Spain, which the Habsburgs captured in 1492) wreathe the coat of arms of King Ferdinand and Queen Isabella. Cupids play among the tree branches, and, flanking the central panel, niches frame armed pages of the court, heraldic wild men symbolizing aggression, and armored soldiers, attesting to Spain's proud new militancy. In typical Plateresque and Late Gothic fashion, the activity of a thousand intertwined motifs unifies the whole design, which, in sum, creates an exquisitely carved panel greatly expanded in scale from the retables that inspired it.

EL ESCORIAL Under Philip II, the Plateresque style gave way to an Italian-derived classicism that also characterized 16th-century French architecture (FIG. 23-23). The Italian style is on display in the expansive complex called El Escorial (FIG. **23-25**), which JUAN BAUTISTA DE TOLEDO (d. 1567) and JUAN DE HERRERA (ca. 1530–1597), principally the latter, constructed for Philip II. In his will, Charles V stipulated that a "dynastic pantheon" be built to house the remains of past and future monarchs of Spain. Philip II, obedient to

his father's wishes, chose a site some 30 miles northwest of Madrid in rugged terrain with barren mountains. Here, he built El Escorial, not only a royal mausoleum but also a church, a monastery, and a palace. Legend has it that the gridlike plan for the enormous complex, 625 feet wide and 520 feet deep, symbolized the gridiron on which Saint Lawrence, El Escorial's patron saint, suffered his martyrdom (see "Early Christian Saints," page 237).

The vast structure is in keeping with Philip's austere character, his passionate Catholicism, his proud reverence for his dynasty, and his stern determination to impose his will worldwide. He insisted that in designing El Escorial, the architects should focus on simplicity of form, severity in the whole, nobility without arrogance, and majesty without ostentation. The result is a classicism of Doric severity, ultimately derived from Italian architecture and with the grandeur of Saint Peter's (FIGS. 24-3 and 24-4) implicit in the scheme, but without close parallel in European architecture.

Only the three entrances, with the dominant central portal framed by *superimposed orders* and topped by a pediment in the Italian fashion, break the long sweep of the structure's severely plain walls. Massive square towers punctuate the four corners. The stress is on the central axis, echoed in the two flanking portals. The construction material for the entire complex (including the church)—granite, a difficult stone to work—conveys a feeling of starkness and gravity. The church's imposing facade and the austere geometry of the interior complex, with its blocky walls and ponderous arches, produce an effect of overwhelming strength and weight. The entire complex is a monument to the collaboration of a great king and remarkably understanding architects. El Escorial stands as the overpowering architectural expression of Spain's spirit in its heroic epoch and of the character of Philip II, the extraordinary ruler who directed it.

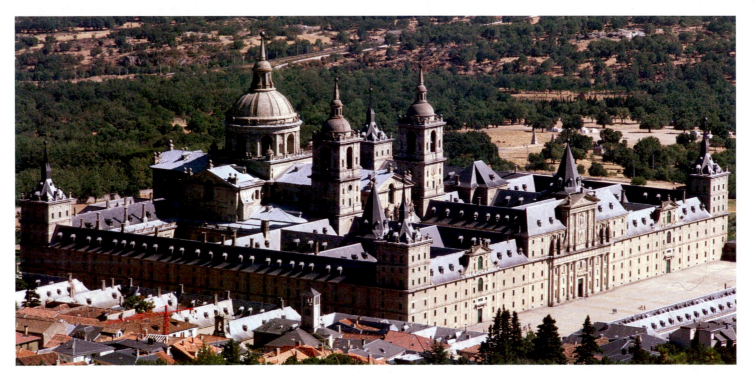

23-25 JUAN DE HERRERA and JUAN BAUTISTA DE TOLEDO, aerial view (looking southeast) of El Escorial, near Madrid, Spain, 1563–1584.

Conceived by Charles V and built by Philip II, El Escorial is a royal mausoleum, church, monastery, and palace in one. The complex is classical in style, with severely plain walls and massive towers.

EL GRECO Reflecting the increasingly international character of European art as well as the mobility of artists, the greatest Spanish painter of the era was not a Spaniard. Born on Crete, Domenikos Theotokopoulos, called EL GRECO (ca. 1547–1614), emigrated to Italy as a young man. In his youth, he absorbed the traditions of Late Byzantine frescoes and mosaics. While still young, El Greco went to Venice, where he worked in Titian's studio, although Tintoretto's paintings (FIG. 22-48) seem to have made a stronger impression on him. A brief trip to Rome explains the influences of Roman and Florentine Mannerism on his work. By 1577, he had left for Spain to spend the rest of his life in Toledo.

El Greco's art is a strong personal blending of Byzantine and Mannerist elements. The intense emotionalism of his paintings, which naturally appealed to Spanish piety, and a great reliance on and mastery of color bound him to 16th-century Venetian art and to Mannerism. El Greco's art was not strictly Spanish, for it had no Spanish antecedents and little effect on later Spanish painters. Nevertheless, El Greco's hybrid style captured the fervor of Spanish Catholicism.

VIEW OF TOLEDO El Greco's singular vision is evident in *View of Toledo* (FIG. 23-26), the only pure landscape he ever painted. As does

so much of El Greco's work, this painting breaks sharply with tradition. The Greek-born artist depicted the Spanish city from a nearby hilltop and drew attention to the great spire of Toledo's cathedral by leading the viewer's eye along the diagonal line of the bridge crossing the Tajo River and continuing with the city's walls. El Greco knew Toledo intimately, and every building is recognizable, although he rearranged some of their positions. For example, he moved the Alcazar palace to the right of the cathedral. Yet El Greco rendered no structure in meticulous detail, as most Renaissance painters would have done, and the color palette is not true to nature but limited to greens and grays. The atmosphere is eerie. Dramatic bursts of light in the stormy sky cast a ghostly pall over the city. The artist applied oil pigment to canvas in broad brushstrokes typical of his late, increasingly abstract painting style, with the result that the buildings and trees do not have sharp contours and almost seem to shake.

Art historians have compared *View of Toledo* to Giorgione da Castelfranco's *Tempest* (FIG. 22-34) and the dramatic lighting to works by Tintoretto (FIG. 22-48), and indeed, El Greco's Venetian training is evident. Still, the closest parallels lie not in the past but in the future—in paintings such as Vincent van Gogh's *Starry Night* (FIG. 28-19) and in 20th-century Expressionism and Surrealism (see pages 885 and 921).

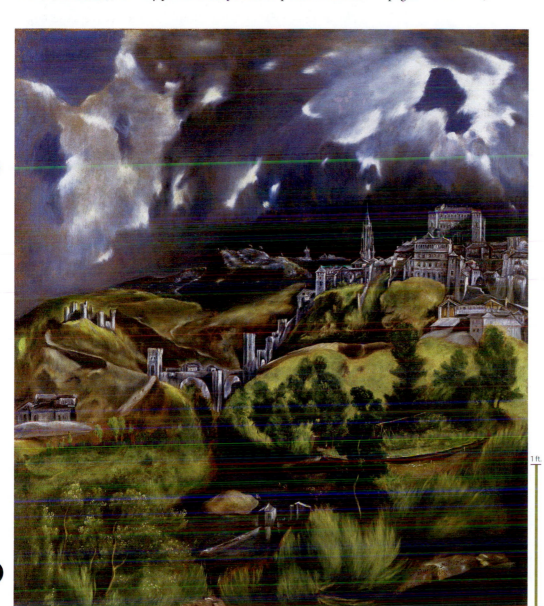

23-26 EL GRECO, *View of Toledo*, ca. 1610. Oil on canvas, 3' 11 $\frac{3}{4}$" × 3' 6 $\frac{3}{4}$". Metropolitan Museum of Art, New York (H. O. Havemeyer Collection. Bequest of Mrs. H. O. Havemeyer, 1929).

View of Toledo is the only pure landscape El Greco ever painted. The dark, stormy sky casts a ghostly pall over the Spanish city. The painted exemplifies the artist's late, increasingly abstract, style.

1 ft.

23-27 El Greco, *Burial of Count Orgaz*, 1586. Oil on canvas, 16' × 12'. Santo Tomé, Toledo.

El Greco's art is a blend of Byzantine and Italian Mannerist elements. His intense emotional content captured the fervor of Spanish Catholicism, and his dramatic use of light foreshadowed the Baroque style.

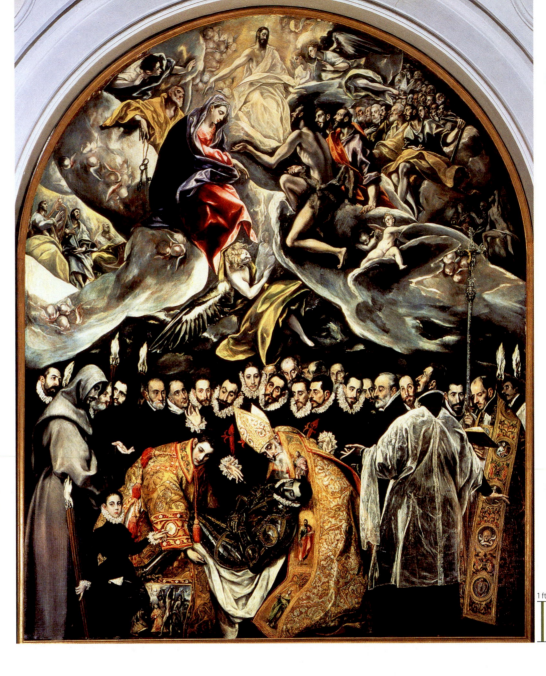

1 ft.

BURIAL OF COUNT ORGAZ More typical of El Greco's work is *Burial of Count Orgaz* (FIG. 23-27), painted in 1586 for the church of Santo Tomé in Toledo. El Greco based the painting on the legend of the count of Orgaz, who had died some three centuries before and who had been a great benefactor of Santo Tomé. According to the legend, Saints Stephen and Augustine miraculously descended from Heaven to lower the count's body into its sepulcher in the church. In the painting, El Greco carefully distinguished the terrestrial and celestial spheres. The brilliant Heaven above irradiates the earthly burial scene below. The painter represented the terrestrial realm with a firm realism, whereas he depicted the celestial, in his quite personal manner, with elongated undulating figures, fluttering draperies, and a visionary swirling cloud. Below, the two saints lovingly lower the count's armor-clad body, the armor and heavy draperies painted with all the rich sensuousness of the Venetian school. A solemn chorus of personages dressed in black fills the background. Among the witnesses to the miracle are El Greco himself; his young son, Jorge Manuel; the priest who commissioned the painting; and the Spanish king Philip II. In the carefully individualized features of these figures, El Greco demonstrated that he was also a great portraitist.

The upward glances of some of the figures below and the flight of an angel above link the painting's lower and upper spheres. The action of the angel, who carries the count's soul in his arms as Saint John and the Virgin intercede for it before the throne of Christ, reinforces this connection. El Greco's deliberate change in style to distinguish between the two levels of reality gives the viewer an opportunity to see the artist's early and late manners in the same work, one below the other. His relatively sumptuous and realistic presentation of the earthly sphere is still strongly rooted in Venetian art, but the abstractions and distortions that El Greco used to show the immaterial nature of the heavenly realm characterize his later style. His elongated figures existing in undefined spaces, bathed in a cool light of uncertain origin, explain El Greco's usual classification as a Mannerist, but his art is impossible to classify using conventional labels. Although El Greco used Mannerist formal devices, his primary concerns were conveying emotion and religious fervor and arousing those feelings in viewers. The forcefulness of his paintings is the result of his unique, highly developed expressive style, which foreshadowed developments of the Baroque era in Spain and Italy, examined in the next chapter.

HIGH RENAISSANCE AND MANNERISM IN NORTHERN EUROPE AND SPAIN

Germany

- Widespread dissatisfaction with the Church in Rome led to the Protestant Reformation, splitting Christendom in half. Protestants, led by Martin Luther, objected to the sale of indulgences and rejected most of the sacraments of the Catholic Church. They also condemned ostentatious church decoration as a form of idolatry that distracted the faithful from communication with God.

- As a result, Protestant churches were relatively bare, but art, especially prints, still played a role in Protestantism. Lucas Cranach the Elder, for example, effectively used visual imagery to contrast Catholic and Protestant views of salvation in his woodcut *Law and Gospel*.

- The greatest German printmaker of the 16th century was Albrecht Dürer, who was also a painter. His works range from biblical to botanical subjects and reflect his studies of classical statuary and of the Vitruvian theory of human proportions. Dürer's engravings rival painting in tonal quality.

- Other German artists, such as Matthias Grünewald and Hans Baldung Grien, explored disease, death, witchcraft, and eroticism in their art. Hans Holbein was a renowned portraitist who became court painter in England.

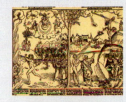

Cranach, *Law and Gospel*, ca. 1530

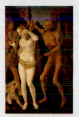

Baldung Grien, *Three Ages of Woman and Death*, 1510

The Netherlands

- The Netherlands was one of the most commercially advanced and prosperous countries in 16th-century Europe. Much of Netherlandish art of this period provides a picture of contemporary life and values. Quentin Massys's *Money-Changer and His Wife*, for example, is a commentary on a couple's obsession with wealth. Pieter Aertsen's *Butcher's Stall* seems to be a straightforward genre scene, but includes the holy family offering alms to a beggar in the background, providing a stark contrast between gluttony and religious piety.

- Landscapes were the specialty of Joachim Patinir. Pieter Bruegel's repertoire also included landscape painting. His *Hunters in the Snow* is one of a series of paintings depicting seasonal changes and the activities associated with them, as in traditional Books of Hours.

- Women artists of the period include Caterina van Hemessen, who painted the earliest northern European self-portrait of a woman, and Levina Teerlinc, who produced portraits for the English court.

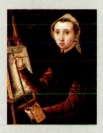

Van Hemessen, *Self-Portrait*, 1548

France

- King Francis I fought against Holy Roman Emperor Charles V and declared Protestantism illegal in France. An admirer of Italian art, he invited several prominent Mannerists to work at his court and decorate his palace at Fontainebleau. His art collection formed the core of the Musée du Louvre.

- French architecture of the 16th century mixes Italian and Northern Renaissance elements, as in Pierre Lescot's design of the renovated Louvre palace and Francis's château at Chambord, which combines classical motifs derived from Italian palazzi with a Gothic roof silhouette.

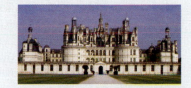

Château de Chambord, begun 1519

Spain

- At the end of the 16th century, Spain was the dominant power in Europe, with an empire greater in extent than any ever known, including vast territories in the New World. The Spanish Plateresque style of architecture, which spread to New Spain, takes its name from *platero* ("silversmith") and features delicate ornamentation resembling metalwork.

- Under Philip II, the Plateresque style gave way to an Italian-derived classicism, seen at its best in El Escorial, a royal mausoleum, monastery, and palace complex near Madrid.

- The leading painter of 16th-century Spain was the Greek-born El Greco, who combined Byzantine style, Italian Mannerism, and the religious fervor of Catholic Spain in such works as *Burial of Count Orgaz*.

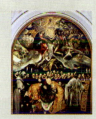

El Greco, *Burial of Count Orgaz*, 1586

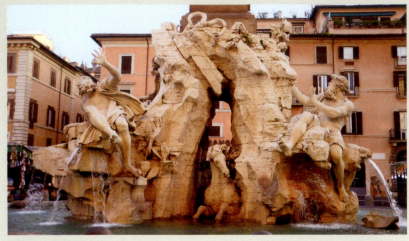

▲ **24-1a** As water flows from a travertine grotto supporting an ancient Egyptian obelisk, Bernini's marble personifications of major rivers of four continents twist and gesticulate emphatically.

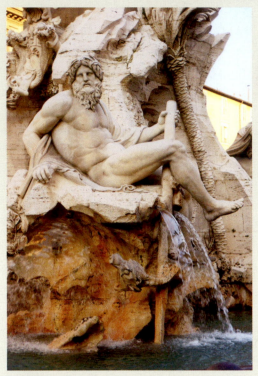

▲ **24-1b** Each of the four rivers has an identifying attribute. The Ganges (Asia) most closely resembles a Greco-Roman river god. Bernini's personification of the easily navigable Ganges holds an oar.

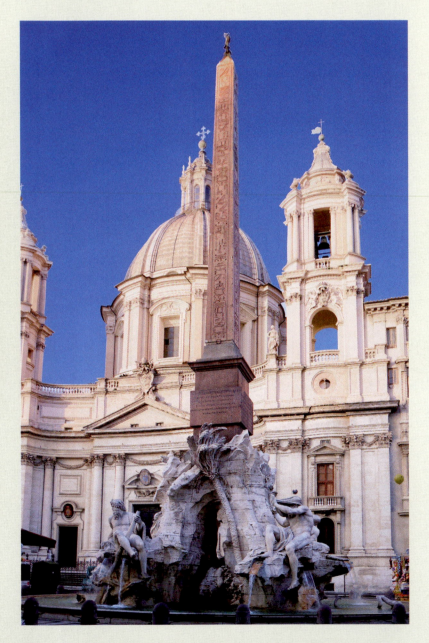

| 24-1 | **GIANLORENZO BERNINI, Fountain of the Four Rivers (looking southwest with Sant'Agnese in Agone in the background), Piazza Navona, Rome, Italy, 1648–1651.** |

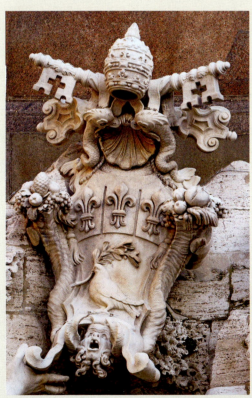

▲ **24-1c** Crowning the grotto is Pope Innocent X's coat of arms, with the Pamphili family's dove symbolizing the Holy Spirit and the triumph of the Church in all parts of the then-known world.

The Baroque in Italy and Spain

BAROQUE ART AND SPECTACLE

One of the most popular tourist attractions in Rome is the Fountain of the Four Rivers (FIG. **24-1**) in Piazza Navona, by GIANLORENZO BERNINI (1598–1680). Architect, painter, sculptor, playwright, and stage designer, Bernini was one of the most important and imaginative artists of the Baroque era in Italy and its most characteristic and sustaining spirit. Nonetheless, the fountain's patron, Pope Innocent X (r. 1644–1655), did not want Bernini to win this commission. Bernini had been the favorite sculptor of the Pamphili pope's predecessor, Urban VIII (r. 1623–1644), who spent so extravagantly on art and himself and his family that he nearly bankrupted the Vatican treasury. Innocent emphatically opposed the excesses of the Barberini pope and shunned Bernini, awarding new papal commissions to other sculptors and architects. Bernini was also in disgrace at the time because of his failed attempt to erect bell towers for the new facade (FIG. 24-3) of Saint Peter's. When Innocent announced a competition for a fountain in Piazza Navona (MAP 22-1), site of the Pamphili family's palace and parish church, Sant'Agnese in Agone (FIG. 24-1, *rear*), he pointedly did not invite Bernini to submit a design. However, the renowned sculptor succeeded in having a model of his proposed fountain placed where the pope would see it. When Innocent examined it, he was so captivated that he declared that the only way anyone could avoid employing Bernini was not to look at his work.

Bernini's bold design, executed in large part by his assistants, called for a sculptured travertine grotto supporting an ancient *obelisk* that Innocent had transferred to Piazza Navona from the *circus* (chariot racecourse) of the Roman emperor Maxentius (r. 305–312) on the Via Appia. The piazza was once the site of the *stadium* of Domitian (r. 81–96), a long and narrow theater-like structure for footraces and other athletic contests, which explains the piazza's unusual shape and the church's name (*agone* means "foot race" in Italian). Water rushes from the artificial grotto into a basin filled with marble statues personifying major rivers of four continents—the Danube (Europe), Nile (Africa), Ganges (Asia), and Plata (Americas). The reclining figures twist and gesticulate, consistent with the Italian Baroque taste for artworks incorporating movement and drama. The Nile covers his face—Bernini's way of acknowledging that the Nile's source was unknown at the time. The Rio de la Plata has a hoard of coins, signifying the wealth of the New World. The Ganges, easily navigable, holds an oar. The Danube, awestruck, reaches up to the papal coat of arms. A second reference to Innocent X is at the apex of the obelisk, where the Pamphili dove also symbolizes the Holy Spirit and the triumph of Christianity in all parts of the then-known world. The scenic effect of the cascading water would have been heightened whenever Piazza Navona was flooded for festival pageants. Bernini's fountain epitomizes the Baroque era's love for uniting art and spectacle.

"BAROQUE" ART AND ARCHITECTURE

Art historians traditionally describe 17th-century European art as *Baroque*, but the term is problematic because the period encompasses a broad range of styles and genres. Although its origin is unclear, "Baroque" may have come from the Portuguese word *barroco*, meaning an irregularly shaped pearl. Use of the term can be traced to the late 18th century, when critics disparaged the Baroque period's artistic production, in large part because of perceived deficiencies in comparison to the art of the Italian Renaissance. Over time, this negative connotation faded, but the term stuck. "Baroque" remains useful to describe the distinctive new style that emerged during the early 1600s—a style of complexity and drama seen especially in Italian art of this period. Whereas Renaissance artists reveled in the precise, orderly rationality of classical models, Baroque artists embraced dynamism, theatricality, and elaborate ornamentation, all used to spectacular effect, often on a grandiose scale, as in Bernini's Four Rivers Fountain (FIG. 24-1).

ITALY

Although in the 16th century the Roman Catholic Church launched the Counter-Reformation in response to—and as a challenge to—the Protestant Reformation, the considerable appeal of Protestantism continued to preoccupy the popes throughout the 17th century. The Treaty of Westphalia (see page 732) in 1648 formally recognized the principle of religious freedom, serving to validate Protestantism, predominantly in the German states. With the Catholic Church as the leading art patron in 17th-century Italy, the aim of much of Italian Baroque art was to restore Roman Catholicism's predominance and centrality. The Council of Trent, one 16th-century Counter-Reformation initiative, firmly resisted Protestant objections to using images in religious worship, insisting on their necessity for teaching the laity (see "The Council of Trent," page 642). Baroque art and architecture in Italy, especially in Rome, embodied the renewed energy of the Counter-Reformation and the papacy's zeal to communicate the Catholic message to the populace.

Architecture and Sculpture

At the end of the 16th century, Pope Sixtus V (r. 1585–1590) had played a key role in the Catholic Church's lengthy campaign to reestablish its preeminence. He augmented the papal treasury and intended to rebuild Rome as an even more magnificent showcase of Church power. Between 1606 and 1667, several strong and ambitious popes—Paul V, Urban VIII, Innocent X, and Alexander VII—made many of Sixtus V's dreams a reality. Rome still bears the marks of their patronage everywhere.

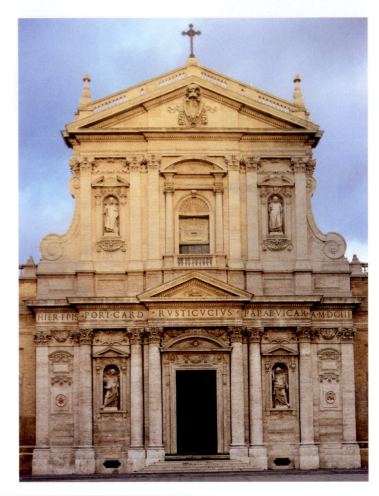

24-2 CARLO MADERNO, facade of Santa Susanna (looking north), Rome, Italy, 1597–1603.

Santa Susanna's facade is one of the earliest manifestations of the Baroque spirit. The rhythm of the columns and pilasters mounts dramatically toward the emphatically stressed vertical axis.

SANTA SUSANNA The facade (FIG. 24-2) that CARLO MADERNO (1556–1629) designed at the turn of the century for the Roman church of Santa Susanna stands as one of the earliest manifestations of the Baroque artistic spirit. In its general appearance, Maderno's facade resembles Giacomo della Porta's immensely influential design for Il Gesù (FIG. 22-57), the church of the Jesuits in Rome. But the later facade has a greater verticality that concentrates and dramatizes the major features of its model. The tall central section projects forward from the horizontal lower story, and the scroll buttresses connecting the two levels are narrower and set at a sharper angle. The elimination of an arch framing the pediment over the doorway further enhances the design's vertical thrust. The rhythm

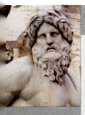

THE BAROQUE IN ITALY AND SPAIN

1600-1625	1625-1650	1650-1675	1675-1700
■ Paul V commissions Maderno to complete Saint Peter's ■ Carracci introduces quadro riportato fresco painting in the Palazzo Farnese ■ Caravaggio pioneers tenebrism in Baroque painting ■ Bernini creates *David* and *Apollo and Daphne* for Cardinal Scipione Borghese	■ Borromini designs San Carlo alle Quattro Fontane and the Chapel of Sant'Ivo in Rome ■ Gentileschi, the leading woman artist of the 17th century, achieves international renown ■ Ribera and Zurburán paint scenes of martyrdom in Catholic Spain ■ Philip IV of Spain appoints Velázquez court painter	■ Bernini designs the colonnaded oval piazza in front of Saint Peter's ■ Murillo creates the canonical image of the Immaculate Virgin ■ Velázquez paints *Las Meninas* ■ Catholic churches in New Spain emulate but do not copy European models	■ Gaulli and Pozzo paint illusionistic ceiling frescoes in Il Gesù and Sant'Ignazio in Rome ■ Guarini brings the Baroque architectural style of Rome to Turin

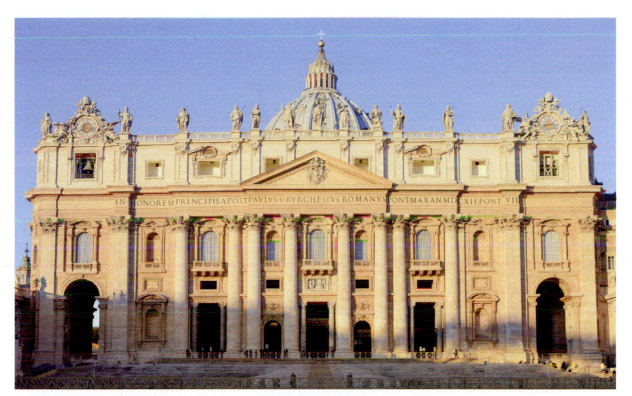

For the facade of Saint Peter's, Maderno elaborated on his design for Santa Susanna (FIG. 24-2). The two outer bays with bell towers were not part of his plan and detract from the verticality he sought.

of Santa Susanna's vigorously projecting columns and pilasters mounts dramatically toward the emphatically stressed central axis. The recessed niches, which contain statues and create pockets of shadow, heighten the sculptural effect.

MADERNO AND SAINT PETER'S The drama inherent in Santa Susanna's facade appealed to Pope Paul V (r. 1605–1621), who commissioned Maderno in 1606 to complete Saint Peter's in Rome. As the symbolic seat of the papacy, the church that Constantine originally built over the first pope's tomb (see page 243) was the very emblem of Western Christendom. In light of Counter-Reformation concerns, the Baroque popes wanted to conclude the already century-long rebuilding project and reap the prestige embodied in the mammoth new church. In many ways, Maderno's facade (FIG. 24-3) is a gigantic expansion of the elements of Santa Susanna's first level. But the compactness and verticality of the smaller church's facade are not as prominent because Saint Peter's enormous breadth counterbalances them. Special circumstances must be taken into consideration when assessing Maderno's design, however. Because he had to match the preexisting core of an incomplete building, Maderno did not have the luxury of formulating a totally new concept for Saint Peter's. Moreover, the facade's two outer bays with bell towers were not part of the architect's original design. Hence, had the facade been constructed according to Maderno's initial concept, it would have exhibited greater verticality and visual coherence.

Maderno's plan (MAP 24-1) also departed from the Renaissance central plans for Saint Peter's designed by Bramante (FIG. 22-22) and, later, by Michelangelo (FIG. 22-24). Paul V asked Maderno to add three nave bays to the earlier nucleus because Church officials had decided that the central plan was too closely associated with ancient temples, such as the Pantheon (FIG. 7-49). Further, the spatial organization of the longitudinal basilican plan of the original fourth-century church (FIG. 8-9) reinforced the symbolic distinction between clergy and laity and also was much better suited for religious processions. Lengthening the nave, however, pushed the dome farther back from the

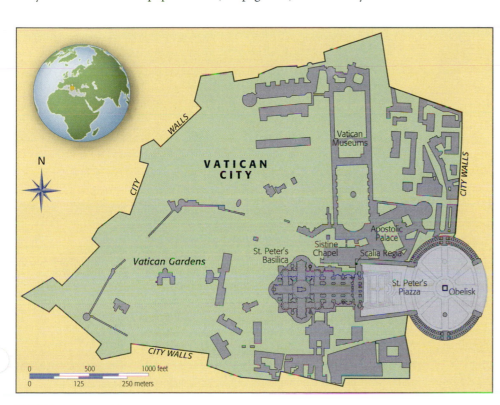

MAP 24-1 Vatican City.

PROBLEMS AND SOLUTIONS
Completing Saint Peter's

Old Saint Peter's had a large forecourt, or *atrium* (FIG. 8-10, no. 6), in front of the church proper, and in the mid-17th century, Gianlorenzo Bernini, who had long before established his reputation as a supremely gifted architect and sculptor (see page 701), received the prestigious commission to construct a monumental colonnade-framed piazza (FIG. 24-4) in front of Maderno's facade. Bernini's design had to incorporate two preexisting structures on the site—an obelisk that the ancient Romans had brought from Egypt (which Pope Sixtus V had moved to its present location in 1585 as part of his vision of Christian triumph in Rome) and a fountain that Maderno constructed in front of the church. Bernini's solution was to co-opt these features to define the long axis of a vast oval embraced by two colonnades joined to Maderno's facade.

Four rows of huge *Tuscan columns* make up the two colonnades, which terminate in classical temple fronts. The colonnades extend a dramatic gesture of embrace to all who enter the piazza, symbolizing the welcome that the Roman Catholic Church gave its members during the Counter-Reformation. Bernini himself referred to his colonnades as the welcoming arms of Saint Peter's.

Beyond their symbolic resonance, the colonnades served visually to counteract the natural perspective and bring the facade closer to the viewer. Emphasizing the facade's height in this manner, Bernini subtly and effectively compensated for its extensive width. Thus a Baroque transformation expanded the compact central designs of Bramante and Michelangelo into a dynamic complex of axially ordered elements that reach out and enclose spaces of vast dimension. By its sheer scale and theatricality, the completed Saint Peter's fulfilled the desire of the Counter-Reformation Church to present an awe-inspiring and authoritative vision of itself.

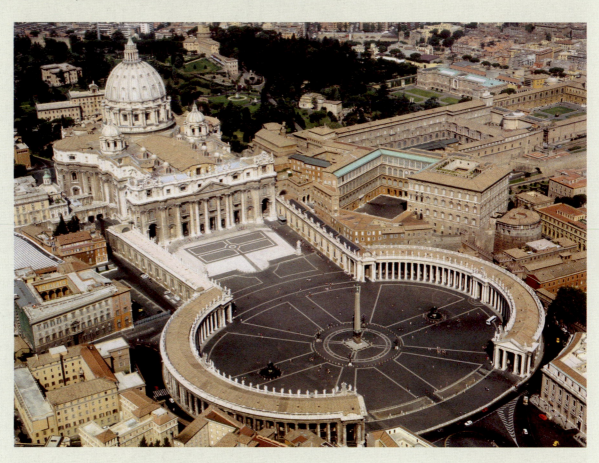

24-4 Aerial view of Saint Peter's (looking northwest), Vatican City, Rome, Italy. Piazza designed by GIANLORENZO BERNINI, 1656–1667.

The dramatic gesture of embrace that Bernini's colonnade makes as worshipers enter Saint Peter's piazza symbolizes the welcome the Catholic Church wished to extend during the Counter-Reformation.

facade, and all but destroyed the effect Michelangelo had planned—a structure pulled together and dominated by its dome. When viewed at close range (FIG. 24-3), the dome barely emerges above the facade's soaring frontal plane. Seen from farther back, standing in the great piazza (FIG. 24-4) erected later by Bernini (see "Completing Saint Peter's," above), Maderno's dome appears to have no drum. Visitors must move back quite a distance from the front (or fly over the church, FIG. 24-4) to see the dome and drum together. Today, visitors to the Vatican can appreciate the effect Michelangelo intended only by viewing Saint Peter's from the back (FIG. 22-25).

BALDACCHINO Bernini's colonnaded piazza in front of Saint Peter's was neither his first nor his last project for the Vatican. For Pope Alexander VII (r. 1665–1667) he tackled the difficult prob-

lem of designing a stairway in the papal palace, the Scala Regia (FIG. 24-4A). Within the great basilica itself, he erected a gigantic bronze *baldacchino* (FIG. 24-5) directly beneath Giacomo della Porta's dome (FIG. 22-25). Completed between 1624 and 1633, the canopy-like structure (*baldacco* is Italian for "silk from Baghdad," such as for a cloth canopy) stands almost 100 feet high (the height of an average eight-story building) and serves both functional and symbolic purposes. It marks the high altar in the nave and the tomb of Saint Peter beneath the basilica,

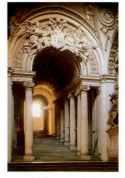

↗ 24-4A BERNINI, Scala Regia, Vatican, 1663-1666.

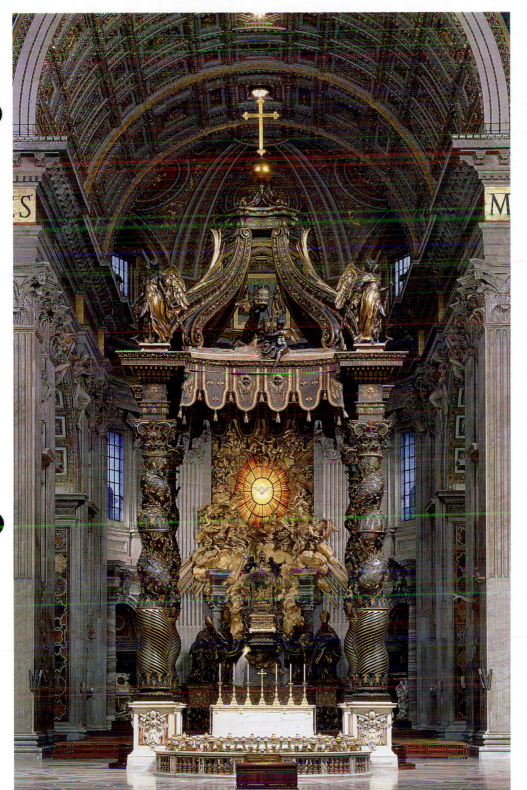

24-5 Gianlorenzo Bernini, baldacchino (looking west), Saint Peter's, Vatican City, Rome, Italy, 1624–1633.

Bernini's baldacchino serves both functional and symbolic purposes. It marks Saint Peter's tomb and the high altar, and it visually bridges the marble floor and the lofty vaults and dome above.

thereby invoking the past to reinforce the primacy of the Church of Rome in the 17th century. At the top of the vine-entwined columns, four colossal angels stand guard at the upper corners of the canopy. Forming the canopy's apex are four serpentine brackets that elevate the orb and the cross. Since the time of Constantine (FIG. 7-79, *right;* compare FIG. 9-2), the orb and the cross had served as symbols of the Church's triumph. The baldacchino also features numerous bees, symbols of Urban VIII's family, the Barberini. Bernini's design thus effectively gives visual form to the triumph of Christianity and to the papal claim to supremacy in formulating Church doctrine.

The construction of the baldacchino was itself a remarkable feat. Each of the bronze columns consists of five sections cast from wood models using the *lost-wax process* (see "Hollow-Casting," page 127). Although Bernini did some of the work himself, including cleaning and repairing the wax molds and doing the final cleaning and *chasing* (engraving and embossing) of the bronze casts, he contracted out much of the project to experienced bronze-casters and sculptors. The superstructure is predominantly cast bronze, although some of the sculptural elements are brass or wood. The enormous scale of the baldacchino required a considerable amount of bronze. On Urban VIII's orders, workmen dismantled the portico of the ancient Roman temple of all gods, the Pantheon (FIG. 7-49), to acquire the bronze for the baldacchino—an ideologically appropriate act, given the Church's rejection of polytheism.

The concepts of triumph and grandeur permeate every aspect of the 17th-century design of Saint Peter's. Suggesting a great and solemn procession, the main axis of the complex traverses the piazza (marked by the central obelisk; FIG. 24-4) and enters Maderno's nave. It comes to a temporary halt at the altar beneath Bernini's baldacchino (FIG. 24-5), but it continues on toward its climactic destination at another great altar in the apse.

and provides a dramatic, compelling presence at the crossing, visually bridging the marble floor and the lofty vaults and dome above. Its columns also serve as a frame for the elaborate sculpture representing the throne of Saint Peter (the Cathedra Petri) at the far end of the nave (FIG. 24-5, *rear*).

On a symbolic level, the baldacchino's decorative elements speak to the power of the Catholic Church and of Pope Urban VIII. Partially fluted and wreathed with vines, the structure's four spiral columns are Baroque versions of the comparable columns of the ancient baldacchino over the same spot in Old Saint Peter's,

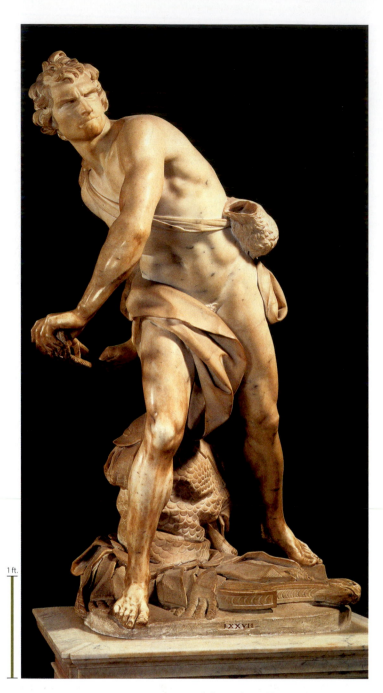

1 ft.

24-6 GIANLORENZO BERNINI, *David,* from the Villa Borghese, Rome, Italy, 1623. Marble, 5′ 7″ high. Galleria Borghese, Rome.

Bernini's sculptures are expansive and theatrical, and the element of time plays an important role in them. His emotion-packed *David* seems to be moving through both time and space.

DAVID Bernini's baldacchino is, like his Four Rivers Fountain (FIG. 24-1), a masterpiece of the sculptor's craft even more than the architect's. In fact, although Bernini achieved an international reputation as an architect, his fame rests primarily on his sculpture. The biographer Filippo Baldinucci (1625–1696) observed: "[T]here was perhaps never anyone who manipulated marble with more facility and boldness. He gave his works a marvelous softness . . . making the marble, so to say, flexible."[1] Bernini's sculpture is expansive and theatrical, and the element of time usually plays an important role in it, as in the pronounced movement of the personified rivers—and the cascading water—in his Piazza Navona fountain.

A sculpture that predates both the Four Rivers Fountain and the baldacchino in Saint Peter's is Bernini's *David* (FIG. 24-6). The Baroque master surely knew the Renaissance statues of the biblical hero fashioned by Donatello (FIG. 21-11), Verrocchio (FIG. 21-12), and Michelangelo (FIG. 22-13). Bernini's *David* differs fundamentally from those earlier masterpieces, however. Michelangelo portrayed David before his encounter with his larger-than-life adversary, and Donatello and Verrocchio depicted David after his triumph over Goliath. Bernini chose to represent the combat itself and aimed to capture the split-second of maximum action. Bernini's *David* has his muscular legs firmly planted, straddling his lyre (David is here psalmist as well as hero). The body armor at David's feet is the protection King Saul offered him but that David rejected because he placed his faith in the Lord.

In Bernini's statue, David begins the violent, pivoting motion that will launch the stone from his sling. (A bag full of stones is at David's left hip, suggesting that he thought the fight would be tough and long.) Unlike Myron, the fifth-century BCE Greek sculptor who froze his *Discus Thrower* (FIG. 5-40) at a fleeting moment of inaction, Bernini selected the most dramatic of an implied sequence of poses, requiring the viewer to think simultaneously of the continuum and of this tiny fraction of it. The suggested continuum imparts a dynamic quality to the statue. The energy that is confined in Michelangelo's figures (FIGS. 22-14 and 22-15) bursts forth in Bernini's *David*. The Baroque statue seems to be moving through time and through space. This kind of sculpture cannot be inscribed in a cylinder or confined in a niche. Its unrestrained action demands space around it. Nor is it self-sufficient in the Renaissance sense, as its pose and attitude direct attention beyond it to the unseen Goliath. Bernini's *David* moves out into the space surrounding it, as do Apollo and Daphne in the marble group (FIG. 24-6A) that he carved for the same patron, Cardinal Scipione Borghese (1576–1633). Further, the expression of intense concentration on David's face contrasts vividly with the classically placid visages of Donatello's and Verrocchio's versions and is more emotionally charged even than Michelangelo's. The tension in David's face augments the dramatic impact of Bernini's sculpture.

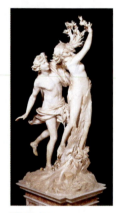

24-6A BERNINI, *Apollo and Daphne,* 1623-1624.

ECSTASY OF SAINT TERESA Another work displaying the motion and emotion that are hallmarks of Italian Baroque art is Bernini's *Ecstasy of Saint Teresa* in the Cornaro chapel (FIG. 24-7) of the Roman church of Santa Maria della Vittoria (Saint Mary of Victory, so named because of the Virgin's aid in a 1620 Catholic victory near Prague during the Thirty Years' War). The work exemplifies the Baroque master's refusal to limit his statues to firmly defined spatial settings. For this commission, Bernini marshaled the full capabilities of architecture, sculpture, and painting to charge the entire chapel with palpable tension. In the Cornaro chapel, Bernini drew on the considerable knowledge of the theater that he derived from writing plays and producing stage designs.

The marble sculpture (FIG. 24-8) that serves as the chapel's focus depicts Saint Teresa of Avila (1515–1582), a nun of the Carmelite order and one of the great mystical saints of the Spanish Counter-Reformation, who only recently had been canonized by the Catholic Church. Teresa's conversion occurred after the death

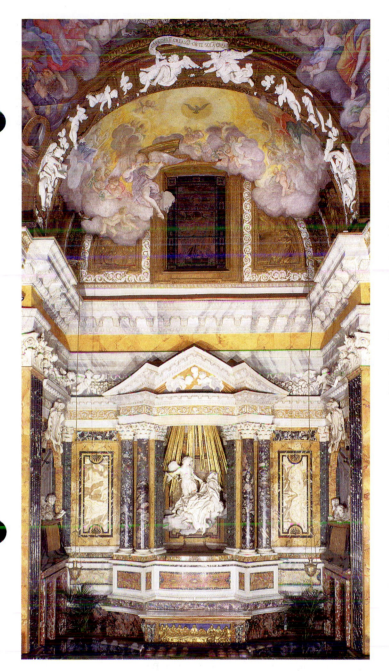

24-7 GIANLORENZO BERNINI, Cornaro chapel, Santa Maria della Vittoria, Rome, Italy, 1645–1652.

In the Cornaro chapel, Bernini, the quintessential Baroque artist, marshaled the full capabilities of architecture, sculpture, and painting to create an intensely emotional experience for worshipers.

of her father, when she fell into a series of trances, saw visions, and heard voices. Feeling a persistent pain, she attributed it to the fire-tipped arrow of divine love that an angel had thrust repeatedly into her heart. In her writings, Saint Teresa described this experience as making her swoon in delightful anguish.

In Bernini's hands, the entire Cornaro chapel became a theater for the production of this mystical drama. The niche in which it takes place appears as a shallow *proscenium* (the part of the stage in front of the curtain) crowned with a broken Baroque pediment and ornamented with polychrome marble. On either side of the chapel, sculpted portraits of members of the family of Cardinal Federico Cornaro (1579–1673) watch the heavenly drama unfold

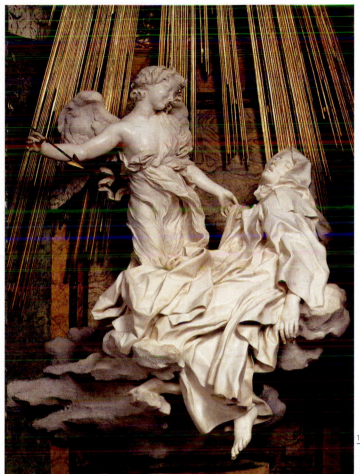

24-8 GIANLORENZO BERNINI, *Ecstasy of Saint Teresa*, Cornaro chapel, Santa Maria della Vittoria, Rome, Italy, 1645–1652. Marble, height of group 11' 6".

The passionate drama of Bernini's depiction of Saint Teresa correlated with the ideas of Ignatius Loyola, who argued that the re-creation of spiritual experience would encourage devotion and piety.

from choice balcony seats. Bernini depicted the saint in ecstasy, unmistakably a mingling of spiritual and physical passion, swooning back on a cloud, while the smiling angel aims his arrow. The sculptor's supreme technical virtuosity is evident in the visual differentiation in texture among clouds, rough cloth and gauzy material, smooth flesh, and feathery wings—all carved from the same white marble. Light from a hidden window of yellow glass pours down in golden rays suggesting the radiance of Heaven, whose painted representation covers the vault.

The passionate drama of Bernini's *Ecstasy of Saint Teresa* correlated with the ideas disseminated earlier by Ignatius Loyola (1491–1556), who founded the Jesuit order in 1534 (see page 671) and whom the Catholic Church canonized as Saint Ignatius in 1622. In his book *Spiritual Exercises*, Ignatius argued that the re-creation of spiritual experiences in artworks would do much to increase devotion and piety. Thus theatricality and sensory impact were useful vehicles for achieving Counter-Reformation goals (see "The Council of Trent," page 642). Bernini was a devout Catholic, which undoubtedly contributed to his understanding of those goals. His inventiveness, technical skill, sensitivity to his patrons' needs, and energy made him the quintessential Italian Baroque artist.

PROBLEMS AND SOLUTIONS
Rethinking the Church Facade

Although Carlo Maderno incorporated sculptural elements in his designs for the facades of Santa Susanna (FIG. 24-2) and Saint Peter's (FIG. 24-3), those church fronts still develop along relatively lateral planes, the traditional approach to facade design. In contrast, Francesco Borromini rethought the very nature of a church facade. In his design for San Carlo alle Quattro Fontane (FIG. 24-9) in Rome, he set the building's front in undulating motion, creating a dynamic counterpoint of concave and convex elements on two levels (for example, the sway of the cornices). He enhanced the three-dimensional effect with deeply recessed niches. Borromini's facade therefore stands in sharp opposition to the idea, which has its roots in antiquity, that a facade should be a flat frontispiece that defines a building's outer limits. In Borromini's hands, the church facade became a pulsating, engaging screen inserted between interior and exterior space, designed not to separate but to provide a fluid transition between the two.

In fact, San Carlo has not one but two facades, underscoring the functional interrelation of the building and its environment. The second facade (FIG. 24-9, *left*), a narrow bay crowned with its own small tower, turns away from the main facade (FIG. 24-9, *right*) and, following the curve of the street, faces an intersection.

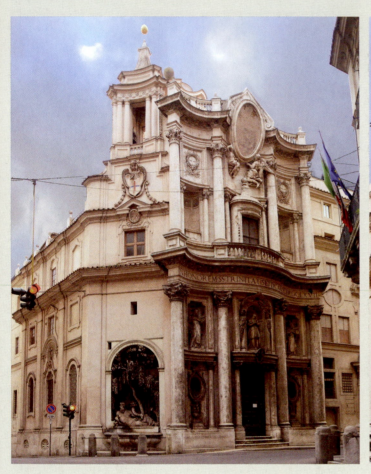 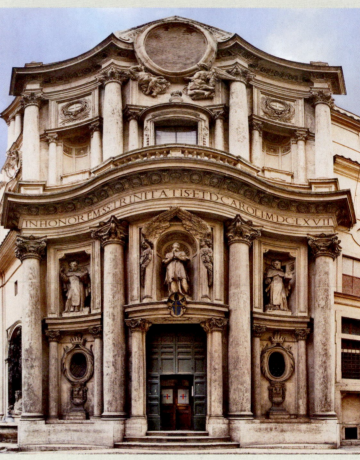

24-9 FRANCESCO BORROMINI, two views of the facade of San Carlo alle Quattro Fontane (*left:* looking south; *right:* looking southeast), Rome, Italy, 1638–1641.

Borromini rejected the notion that a church should have a flat frontispiece. He set San Carlo's facade in undulating motion, creating a dynamic counterpoint of concave and convex elements.

SAN CARLO ALLE QUATTRO FONTANE As gifted as Bernini was as an architect, FRANCESCO BORROMINI (1599–1667) took Italian Baroque architecture to even greater dramatic heights. In the little church of San Carlo alle Quattro Fontane (Saint Charles at the Four Fountains; FIG. 24-9), Borromini went much further than any of his predecessors or contemporaries in emphasizing a building's sculptural qualities, both inside and out (see "Rethinking the Church Facade," above). His innovative style had an enormous influence on later Baroque architects throughout Italy and beyond. The Palazzo Carignano (FIG. 24-9A) in Turin, for example, designed by GUARINO GUARINI (1624–1683), depends heavily on Borromini's work in Rome.

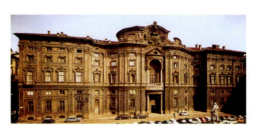

⬈ **24-9A** GUARINI, Palazzo Carignano, Turin, 1679–1692.

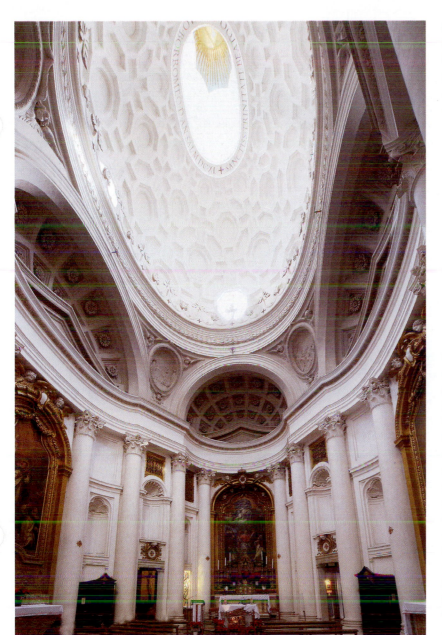

24-10 FRANCESCO BORROMINI, interior of San Carlo alle Quattro Fontane (looking northwest and up into the dome), Rome, Italy, 1638–1641.

The plan of San Carlo is a hybrid of a Greek cross and an oval. The walls pulsate in a way that reverses the facade's movement. The molded, dramatically lit space flows from entrance to altar.

The interior (FIG. **24-10**) of San Carlo alle Quattro Fontane is as remarkable as its exterior. The radical design is in part Borromini's ingenious response to an awkward site, but it is also a provocative variation on the theme of the centrally planned church. In plan (FIG. **24-11,** *left*), San Carlo is a hybrid of a *Greek cross* (a cross with four arms of equal length) and an oval, with a long axis between entrance and apse. The side walls move in an undulating flow that reverses the facade's motion. Vigorously projecting columns define the space into which they protrude just as much as they accent the walls to which they are attached. Capping this molded interior space is a deeply coffered oval dome (FIG. 24-11, *right*) that seems to float on the light entering through windows hidden in its base. Rich variations on the basic theme of the oval—dynamic curves relative to the static circle—create an interior that flows from entrance to altar, unimpeded by the segmentation so characteristic of Renaissance buildings.

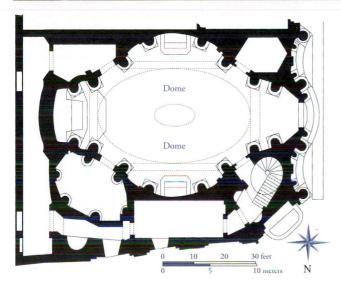

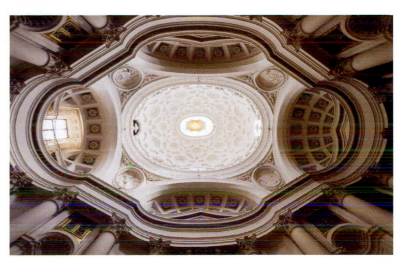

24-11 FRANCESCO BORROMINI, plan (*left*) and view of dome from below (*right*), San Carlo alle Quattro Fontane, Rome, Italy, 1638–1641.

Instead of using a traditional round dome, Borromini capped the interior of San Carlo with a deeply coffered oval dome that seems to float on the light entering through windows hidden in its base.

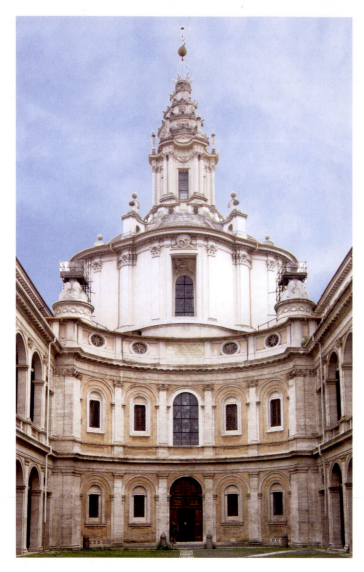

24-12 FRANCESCO BORROMINI, facade of Sant'Ivo alla Sapienza (looking east), Rome, Italy, begun 1642.

In characteristic fashion, Borromini played concave against convex forms on the upper level of the Chapel of Saint Ives. Pilasters restrain the forces that seem to push the bulging forms outward.

CHAPEL OF SAINT IVO Borromini carried the unification of interior space even further in Sant'Ivo alla Sapienza (FIG. **24-12**), the chapel dedicated to Saint Ives, the patron saint of jurists, at the east end of the courtyard of the "Sapienza," the 17th-century seat of the University of Rome (*sapienza* means "wisdom" or "learning"). In his characteristic manner, Borromini played concave against convex forms on the upper level of the chapel's exterior. The arcaded courtyard, which frames the lower levels of the chapel's facade, had already been constructed when Borromini began work, and he adjusted his design to achieve a harmonious merging of the new and older parts of the college. Above the inward-curving lower two stories of the Saint Ives chapel rises a convex drumlike structure that supports

24-14 FRANCESCO BORROMINI, view of dome from below, Sant'Ivo alla Sapienza, Rome, Italy, begun 1642.

Unlike Renaissance domes, Borromini's Baroque dome is an organic form that evolves out of and shares the qualities of the supporting walls, and it cannot be separated from them.

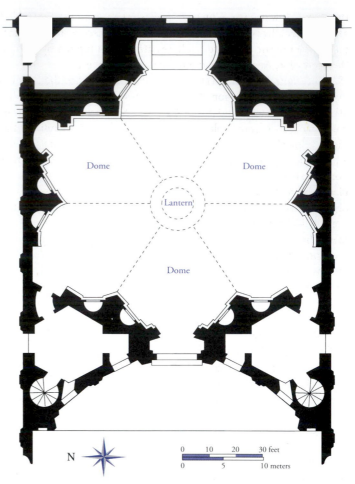

24-13 FRANCESCO BORROMINI, plan of Sant'Ivo alla Sapienza, Rome, Italy, begun 1642.

The interior elevation of Borromini's Saint Ives chapel fully reflects all the elements of its highly complex plan, which is star-shaped with rounded points and apses on all sides.

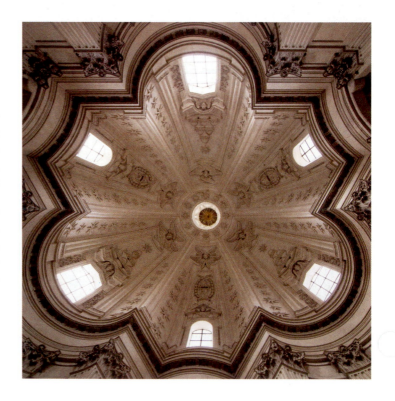

the dome's lower parts. Clusters of pilasters restrain the forces that seem to push the bulging forms outward. Buttresses above the pilasters curve upward to brace a tall, ornate *lantern* topped by a spiral that, screwlike, seems to fasten the structure to the sky.

The centralized plan (FIG. 24-13) of the interior of the Sant'Ivo chapel is that of a hexagonal star with rounded points and apses on all sides. Indentations and projections along the angled, curving walls create a highly complex plan, with all the elements fully reflected in the interior elevation. From floor to lantern, the wall panels rise in a continuously tapering sweep halted only momentarily by a single horizontal cornice (FIG. 24-14). Thus the dome is not a separate unit placed on a supporting block, as in Renaissance buildings. It is an organic part that evolves out of and shares the qualities of the supporting walls, and it cannot be separated from them. This carefully designed progression up through the lantern creates a dynamic and cohesive shell that encloses and energetically molds a scalloped fragment of space. Few architects have matched Borromini's ability to translate extremely complicated designs into masterfully unified structures, but some later architects, including Guarini, an accomplished mathematician as well as architect, designed even more complex domes (FIG. 24-14A).

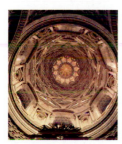

🔼 **24-14A** GUARINI, Chapel of the Holy Shroud, Turin, 1667–1694.

Painting

Although architecture and sculpture provided the most obvious vehicles for manipulating space and creating theatrical effects, painting continued to be an important art form in 17th-century Italy.

Among the most noted Italian Baroque painters were Annibale Carracci and Caravaggio, whose styles, although quite different, were both thoroughly in accord with the period.

ANNIBALE CARRACCI A native of Bologna, ANNIBALE CARRACCI (1560–1609) received much of his training at an art academy founded there by several members of his family, among them his cousin Ludovico Carracci (1555–1619) and brother Agostino Carracci (1557–1602). The Bolognese academy was the first significant institution of its kind in the history of Western art. The Carracci established it on the premises that art can be taught—the basis of any academic philosophy of art—and that art instruction must include the classical and Renaissance traditions in addition to the study of anatomy and life drawing.

In *Flight into Egypt* (FIG. 24-15), based on the biblical narrative from Matt. 2:13–14, Annibale Carracci created the "ideal" or "classical" landscape, in which nature appears ordered by divine law and human reason. Tranquil hills and fields, quietly gliding streams, serene skies, unruffled foliage, shepherds with their flocks—all the props of the pastoral scene and mood familiar in Venetian Renaissance paintings (FIG. 22-35)—expand to fill the picture space in *Flight into Egypt* and similar paintings. Carracci regularly included screens of trees in the foreground, dark against the sky's even light. In contrast to many Renaissance artists, he did not create the sense of deep space through linear perspective but rather by varying light and shadow to suggest expansive atmosphere. In *Flight into Egypt*, streams or terraces, carefully placed one above the other and narrowed, zigzag through the terrain, leading the viewer's eyes back to the middle ground. As in many Venetian Renaissance paintings, the background of Carracci's *Flight into Egypt* is filled with walled towns or citadels, towers, temples, monumental tombs, and villas.

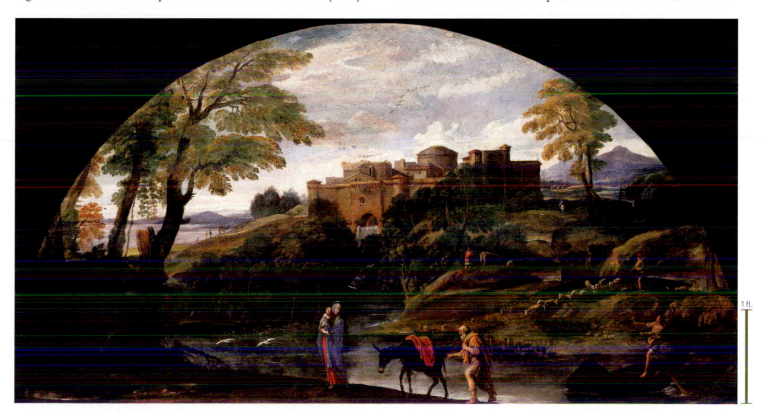

1 ft.

24-15 ANNIBALE CARRACCI, *Flight into Egypt*, 1603–1604. Oil on canvas, 4' × 7' 6". Galleria Doria Pamphili, Rome.

Carracci's landscapes idealize antiquity and the idyllic life. Here, the pastoral setting takes precedence over the narrative of Mary, the Christ Child, and Saint Joseph wending their way slowly to Egypt.

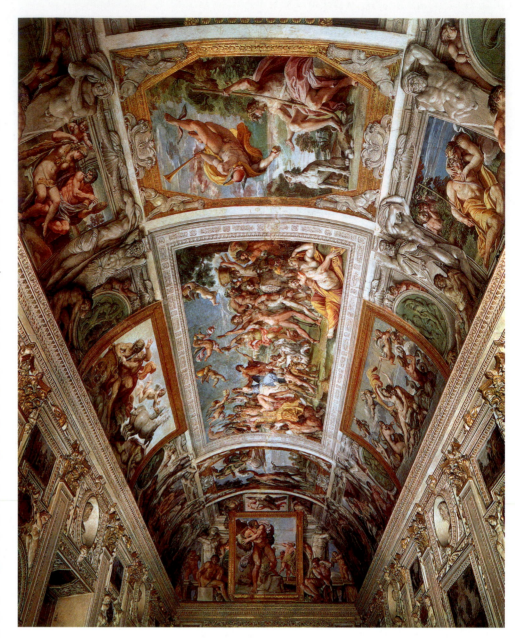

24-16 ANNIBALE CARRACCI, *Loves of the Gods,* ceiling frescoes in the gallery, Palazzo Farnese (FIG. 22-26), Rome, Italy, 1597–1601.

On the shallow curved vault of this gallery in the Palazzo Farnese, Annibale Carracci arranged the mythological scenes in a quadro riportato format resembling easel paintings on a wall.

These constructed environments captured idealized antiquity and the idyllic life. Although the artists often took the subjects for these classically rendered scenes from religious or heroic stories, they favored pastoral landscapes over narratives. Here, Annibale greatly diminished the size of Mary, the Christ Child, and Saint Joseph, who simply become part of the landscape as they wend their way slowly to Egypt after having been ferried across a stream.

LOVES OF THE GODS Carracci's most notable works are his frescoes (FIG. **24-16**) in the Palazzo Farnese in Rome. Cardinal Odoardo Farnese (1573–1626)—a wealthy descendant of Pope Paul III, who built the palace (FIGS. 22-26 and 22-27) in the 16th century—commissioned Annibale to decorate the ceiling of the palace's gallery to celebrate the wedding of the cardinal's brother. Appropriately, the title of the fresco's iconographic program is *Loves of the Gods*—interpretations of the varieties of earthly and divine love, based on Ovid's *Metamorphoses.*

Carracci arranged the scenes in a format resembling framed easel paintings on a wall, but in the Farnese gallery, the paintings cover a shallow curved vault. The term for this type of simulation of easel painting for ceiling design is *quadro riportato* ("transferred framed panel"). By adapting the northern European and Venetian tradition of easel painting to the Florentine and Roman fresco tradition, Carracci reoriented the direction of painting in central Italy. He made the quadro riportato format fashionable for more than a century.

Flanking the framed pictures are polychrome seated nude youths, who turn their heads to gaze at the scenes around them, and standing Atlas figures painted to resemble marble statues. Carracci derived these motifs from the Sistine Chapel ceiling (FIG. 22-17), but he did not copy Michelangelo's figures. Notably, the chiaroscuro of the Farnese gallery frescoes differs for the pictures and the figures surrounding them. Carracci modeled the figures inside the panels in an even light. In contrast, light from beneath illuminates the outside figures, as if they were tangible three-dimensional beings or statues lit by torches in the gallery below. This interest in illusion, already manifest in the Renaissance, continued in the grand ceiling compositions (FIGS. 24-21 to 24-24) of the mature Baroque. In the crown of the vault, the long panel, *Triumph of Bacchus,* is an ingenious mixture of Raphael's drawing style and lighting and Titian's more sensuous and animated figures. Carracci succeeded in adjusting their authoritative styles to create something of his own—no easy achievement.

CARAVAGGIO Michelangelo Merisi, known as CARAVAGGIO (1573–1610) after his northern Italian birthplace, developed a distinctive personal style that had tremendous influence throughout Europe. His outspoken disdain for the classical masters (probably more rhetorical than real) drew bitter criticism from many painters, one of whom denounced him as the "anti-Christ of painting." Giovanni Pietro Bellori, the most influential critic of the age and an admirer of Annibale Carracci, believed that Caravaggio's refusal to emulate the models of his distinguished predecessors threatened the whole classical tradition of Italian painting that had reached its zenith in Raphael's work (see "Giovanni Pietro Bellori on Annibale Carracci and Caravaggio," page 713). Yet despite this criticism and the problems in Caravaggio's troubled life (police records are an important source of information about the artist), Caravaggio received many commissions, both public and private, and numerous painters paid him the supreme compliment of borrowing from his innovations. His influence on later artists, as much outside Italy as within, was immense.

WRITTEN SOURCES
Giovanni Pietro Bellori on Annibale Carracci and Caravaggio

The written sources to which art historians turn as aids in understanding the art of the past are invaluable, but they reflect the personal preferences and prejudices of the writers. Pliny the Elder, for example, claimed in the first century CE that "art ceased" after the death of Alexander the Great—a remark usually interpreted as expressing his disapproval of Hellenistic art in contrast to Classical art.* Giorgio Vasari, the biographer and champion of Italian Renaissance artists (see "Giorgio Vasari's *Lives*," page 636), condemned Gothic art as "monstrous and barbarous," and considered medieval art in general a distortion of the noble art of the Greeks and Romans (see page 374).[†] Giovanni Pietro Bellori (1613–1696), the leading biographer of Baroque artists, similarly recorded his admiration for Renaissance classicism as well as his distaste for Mannerism and realism in his opposing evaluations of Annibale Carracci and Caravaggio.

In the opening lines of his *Vita* (*Life*) of Carracci, Bellori praised "the divine Raphael . . . [whose art] raised its beauty to the summit, restoring it to the ancient majesty of . . . the Greeks and the Romans" and lamented that soon after, "artists, abandoning the study of nature, corrupted art with the *maniera*, that is to say, with the fantastic idea based on practice and not on imitation." But fortunately, Bellori observed, just "when painting was drawing to its end," Annibale Carracci rescued "the declining and extinguished art."[‡]

Bellori especially lauded Carracci's Palazzo Farnese frescoes (FIG. 24-16):

No one could imagine seeing anywhere else a more noble and magnificent style of ornamentation, obtaining supreme excellence in the compartmentalization and in the figures and executed with the grandest manner in the design with the just proportion and the great strength of chiaroscuro. . . . Among modern works they have no comparison.[§]

In contrast, Bellori characterized Caravaggio as talented and widely imitated but misguided in his rejection of classicism in favor of realism.

[Caravaggio] began to paint according to his own inclinations; not only ignoring but even despising the superb statuary of antiquity and the famous paintings of Raphael, he considered nature to be the only subject fit for his brush. As a result, when he was shown the most famous statues of [the ancient sculptors] Phidias [FIG. 5-46] and Glykon [FIG. 5-66] in order that he might use them as models, his only answer was to point toward a crowd of people, saying that nature had given him an abundance of masters. . . . [W]hen he came upon someone in town who pleased him he made no attempt to improve on the creations of nature.**

[Caravaggio] claimed that he imitated his models so closely that he never made a single brushstroke that he called his own, but said rather that it was nature's. Repudiating all other rules, he considered the highest achievement not to be bound to art. For this innovation he was greatly acclaimed, and many talented and educated artists seemed compelled to follow him . . . Nevertheless he lacked *invenzione*, decorum, *disegno*, or any knowledge of the science of painting. The moment the model was taken from him, his hand and his mind became empty. . . . Thus, as Caravaggio suppressed the dignity of art, everybody did as he pleased, and what followed was contempt for beautiful things, the authority of antiquity and Raphael destroyed. . . . Now began the imitation of common and vulgar things, seeking out filth and deformity.[††]

*Pliny, *Natural History*, 25.52.
[†]Giorgio Vasari, *Introduzione alle tre arti del disegno* (1550), ch. 3.
[‡]Giovanni Pietro Bellori, *Le vite de' pittori, scultori e architetti moderni* (Rome, 1672). Translated by Catherine Enggass, *The Lives of Annibale and Agostino Carracci by Giovanni Pietro Bellori* (University Park: Pennsylvania University Press, 1968), 5–6.
[§]Ibid., 33.
**Translated by Howard Hibbard, *Caravaggio* (New York: Harper & Row, 1983), 362.
[††]Ibid., 371–372.

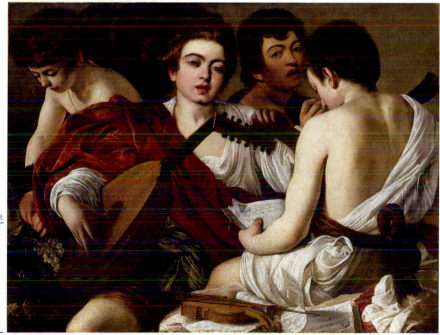

1 ft.

MUSICIANS One of Caravaggio's earliest major works is *Musicians* (FIG. **24-17**), which portrays four figures, including three musicians. The promising artist painted the canvas around 1595 when he was living in the household of Francesco Maria Bourbon Del Monte (1549–1627), whom Sixtus V appointed cardinal in 1588. Del Monte was a lover of art and music who headed a papal committee to study the reform of liturgical music and who oversaw the Sistine Choir, at that time an all-male ensemble of castrated singers. Caravaggio moved into Del

24-17 CARAVAGGIO, *Musicians,* from the Palazzo Madama, Rome, Italy, ca. 1595. Oil on canvas, 3' $\frac{1}{4}$" × 3' 10 $\frac{5}{8}$". Metropolitan Museum of Art, New York (Rogers Fund, 1952).

While Caravaggio lived in the home of Cardinal Del Monte, a lover of the good life and a patron of art and music, he painted this canvas depicting three androgynous musicians and Cupid plucking grapes.

24-18 CARAVAGGIO, *Calling of Saint Matthew*, ca. 1597–1601. Oil on canvas, 11' 1" × 11' 5". Contarelli chapel, San Luigi dei Francesi, Rome.

The stark contrast of light and dark is a key feature of Caravaggio's style. Here, Christ, cloaked in mysterious shadow, summons Levi the tax collector (Saint Matthew) to a higher calling.

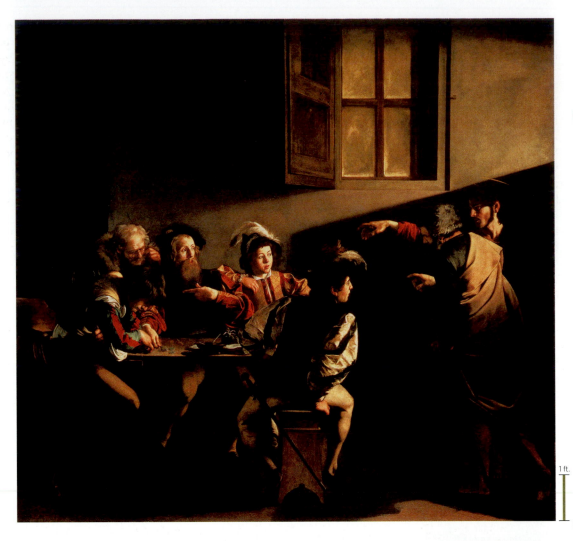

1 ft.

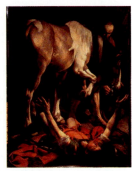

24-18A CARAVAGGIO, *Conversion of Saint Paul*, ca. 1601.

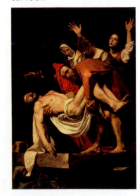

24-18B CARAVAGGIO, *Entombment*, ca. 1603.

Monte's home in the Palazzo Madama and drew a salary from the cardinal in return for producing an unspecified number of paintings while in his employ. This arrangement assured the gifted young painter a steady income for the first time and permitted him to hire a servant, who also lived in the cardinal's palace. Contemporaneous accounts describe Caravaggio at that time as a frequenter of taverns who always carried a sword, an illegal act for which he was arrested at least twice. (The police dropped the charges each time upon learning of his relationship to Del Monte.)

In *Musicians,* Caravaggio presented a tableau of four tightly cropped life-size half-length figures. The central figure is a young lute player who looks seductively directly at the viewer—that is, at Cardinal Del Monte, because this was a private commission for his personal collection. The horn player in the background is a self-portrait of Caravaggio. With his mostly bare back to the viewer, a third musician (his violin is in the foreground next to his left leg) studies a musical score. The fourth figure, in the upper left corner of the canvas, has wings and a quiver of arrows. He is Cupid, the adolescent god of love, who picks grapes, a reference to Bacchus, wine, and feasting— all themes that Caravaggio addressed repeatedly in his paintings of the 1590s. Caravaggio even painted a portrait of himself in the guise of Bacchus. Art historians have frequently cited the markedly homoerotic nature of this portrayal of sensual, partially undraped, androgynous young men with full lips as evidence of the cardinal's alleged homosexuality and of the artist's bisexuality, but secure evidence is lacking. Nonetheless, the painting's subject and Caravaggio's rendition of it undoubtedly appealed to the cardinal's well-documented

interest in "the good life" alongside his ecclesiastical duties.

CALLING OF SAINT MATTHEW Del Monte's home in Rome was next to the church of San Luigi dei Francesi (Saint Louis of the French), and the cardinal was instrumental in obtaining for Caravaggio the commission to provide paintings honoring Saint Matthew for the Contarelli chapel in the left aisle near the apse of the church. *Calling of Saint Matthew* (FIG. 24-18) is one of them. The painting is characteristic of Caravaggio's mature style and displays all the qualities for which he became famous—and for which he received scathing criticism (see "Giovanni Pietro Bellori," page 713).

In *Calling of Saint Matthew* and his other religious paintings—for example *Conversion of Saint Paul* (FIG. 24-18A) and *Entombment* (FIG. 24-18B)—Caravaggio injected naturalism into the representation of sacred subjects, reducing them to human dramas played out in the harsh and dingy settings of his time and place. The unidealized figures that he selected from the fields and the streets of Italy, however, were effective precisely because of their familiarity. The commonplace setting of *Calling of Saint Matthew*—a tavern with unadorned walls—is typical of Caravaggio's mature canvases. Into this mundane environment, cloaked in mysterious shadow and almost unseen, Christ, identifiable initially only by his indistinct halo, enters from the right. With a commanding gesture, he summons Levi, the Roman tax collector, to a higher calling (see "Early Christian Saints," page 237). The astonished Levi—his face highlighted for the viewer by the beam of light emanating from an unspecified source above Christ's head and outside the picture—points to himself in disbelief. Although Christ's extended arm is reminiscent of the Lord's in Michelangelo's *Creation of Adam* (FIG. 22-18), the position of his hand and wrist is similar to Adam's. This reference was highly appropriate, because the Church considered Christ to be the second Adam. Whereas Adam was responsible for the fall of humankind, Christ is the vehicle of its redemption. The conversion of Levi (who became Matthew) brought his salvation.

In Caravaggio's many paintings of religious scenes, the figures are still heroic, with powerful bodies and clearly delineated contours in the Renaissance tradition (see especially FIGS. 24-18A and 24-18B), but the stark and dramatic contrast of light and dark, which at first shocked and then fascinated his contemporaries, obscures the more traditional aspects of his style. Art historians call Caravaggio's use of dark settings that envelop their occupants— which profoundly influenced European art, especially in Spain and the Netherlands—*tenebrism*, from the Italian word *tenebroso*, or "shadowy" manner. In Caravaggio's work, tenebrism also contributed greatly to the essential meaning of his pictures. In *Calling of Saint Matthew*, the beam of light directing the viewer's attention to the seated tax collector is the divine light beckoning him to join the Son of God in his earthly mission.

ARTEMISIA GENTILESCHI Caravaggio's combination of naturalism and drama appealed both to patrons and to artists, and he had many followers. Among them was the most celebrated woman artist of the era, ARTEMISIA GENTILESCHI (ca. 1593–1653), whose father, Orazio (1563–1639), her teacher, was himself strongly influenced by Caravaggio. The daughter's successful career, pursued in Florence, Venice, Naples, and Rome, helped disseminate Caravaggio's style throughout the peninsula.

In *Judith Slaying Holofernes* (FIG. 24-19), Gentileschi adopted the tenebrism and what might be called the "dark" subject matter Caravaggio favored. Significantly, she chose a narrative involving a

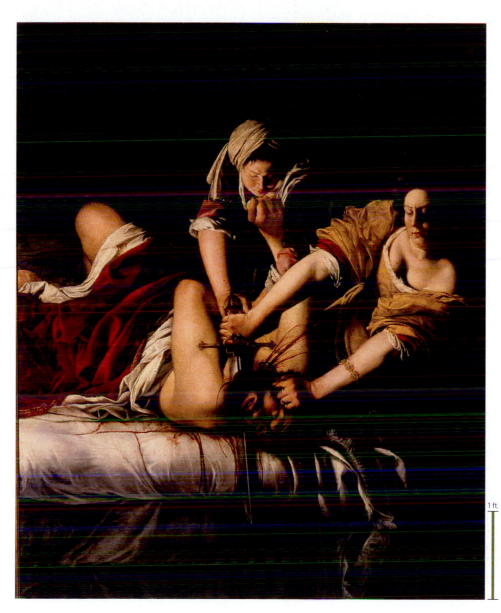

24-19 ARTEMISIA GENTILESCHI, *Judith Slaying Holofernes*, ca. 1614–1620. Oil on canvas, 6' 6$\frac{1}{3}$" × 5' 4". Galleria degli Uffizi, Florence.

Narratives involving heroic women were a favorite theme of Gentileschi. In *Judith Slaying Holofernes*, the dramatic lighting of the action in the foreground emulates Caravaggio's tenebrism.

1 ft.

ARTISTS ON ART

The Letters of Artemisia Gentileschi

Artemisia Gentileschi (FIG. 24-20) was the most renowned—although by no means the only—woman painter in 17th-century Europe (see "Women in the Renaissance Art World," page 656). Among the others who had highly successful careers was perhaps most notably Gentileschi's younger contemporary Elisabetta Sirani (1638–1665) of Bologna. Famed for the speed with which she completed paintings, Sirani produced some 200 canvases and prints during her short-lived career and took over the direction of her father's workshop when he became ill.

Gentileschi was the first woman ever admitted to membership in Florence's Accademia del Disegno (Academy of Design). Like Sirani and other women who could not become apprentices in all-male studios (see "The Artist's Profession," page 566), she learned her craft from her father. Never forgotten in subsequent centuries, Artemisia owes her modern fame to the seminal 1976 exhibition catalogue *Women Artists: 1550–1950,*[*] which brought to the fore many other notable artists and opened a new chapter in feminist art history.

In addition to scores of paintings created for wealthy patrons, among them the king of England and the grand duke of Tuscany, Gentileschi left behind 28 letters, some of which reveal that she believed that patrons treated her differently because of her gender. Three 1649 letters written in Naples to Don Antonio Ruffo (1610–1678) in Messina make her feelings explicit.

> I fear that before you saw the painting you must have thought me arrogant and presumptuous. . . . [I]f it were not for Your Most Illustrious Lordship . . . I would not have been induced to give it for one hundred and sixty, because everywhere else I have been I was paid one hundred *scudi* per figure. . . . You think me pitiful, because a woman's name raises doubts until her work is seen.[†]

> I was mortified to hear that you want to deduct one third from the already very low price that I had asked. . . . It must be that in your heart Your Most Illustrious Lordship finds little merit in me.[‡]

> As for my doing a drawing and sending it, [tell the gentleman who wishes to know the price for a painting that] I have made a solemn vow never to send my drawings because people have cheated me. In particular, just today I found myself [in the situation] that, having done a drawing of souls in Purgatory for the Bishop of St. Gata, he, in order to spend less, commissioned another painter to do the painting using my work. If I were a man, I can't imagine it would have turned out this way, because when the concept has been realized and defined with lights and darks, and established by means of planes, the rest is a trifle.[§]

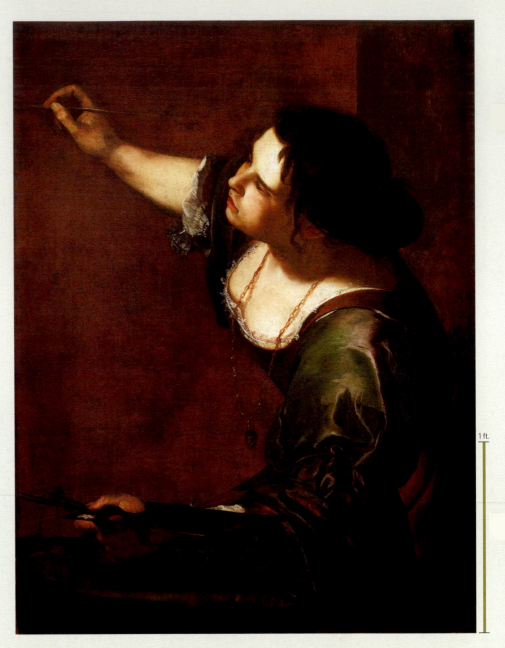

24-20 ARTEMISIA GENTILESCHI, *Self-Portrait as the Allegory of Painting*, ca. 1638–1639. Oil on canvas, 3' 2$\frac{7}{8}$" × 2' 5$\frac{5}{8}$". Royal Collection, Kensington Palace, London.

Gentileschi here portrayed herself in the guise of La Pittura (Painting) with brush and palette. To paint a self-portrait from the side, Gentileschi had to set up a pair of mirrors to record her features.

1 ft.

[*]Ann Sutherland Harris and Linda Nochlin, *Women Artists: 1550–1950* (Los Angeles: Los Angeles County Museum of Art, 1976), 118–124.
[†]Letter dated January 30, 1649. Translated by Mary D. Garrard, *Artemisia Gentileschi: The Image of the Female Hero in Italian Baroque Art* (Princeton, N.J.: Princeton University Press, 1989), 390.
[‡]Letter dated October 23, 1649. Ibid., 395–396.
[§]Letter dated November 13, 1649. Ibid., 397–398.

heroic woman, a favorite theme of hers. The story, from the book of Judith, relates the delivery of Israel from the Assyrians. Having succumbed to Judith's charms, the Assyrian general Holofernes invited her to his tent for the night. When he fell asleep, Judith cut off his head. In this version of the scene (Gentileschi produced more than one painting of the subject), Judith and her maidservant behead Holofernes. Blood spurts everywhere as the two women summon all their strength to wield the heavy sword. The tension and strain are palpable. The controlled highlights on the action in the foreground recall Caravaggio's work and heighten the drama here as well.

LA PITTURA During the brief period that Orazio Gentileschi was the official painter of the English king Charles I (r. 1625–1649), Artemisia painted perhaps her most unusual work, an allegory of Painting (*La Pittura;* FIG. **24-20**). Most art historians believe that the painting, which was in the collection of the king at the time of his execution in 1649, is a self-portrait.

Gentileschi's personified image of Painting as a woman closely follows the prescription for representing La Pittura set forth by Cesare Ripa (d. 1622) in his widely circulated handbook called *Iconologia,* published in 1593. Until the 16th century, only Poetry and Music had a fixed iconography. The inclusion of Painting in *Iconologia* reflects the newly elevated status that painters held during the Renaissance. Ripa described La Pittura as a beautiful woman with disheveled hair painting with her brush in one hand and holding her palette in the other. She wears a gold chain with a pendant in the form of a mask, because masks imitate faces and painting is the art of imitation. The chain symbolizes the continuous linkage of master to pupil from generation to generation. Gentileschi incorporated all of these traits into her painting, but instead of representing La Pittura as a frontal, emblematic figure, she portrayed her as actively engaged in her craft, seen from her left side. The viewer's eye follows the line of her left arm through the curve of her shoulders and

right arm to her right hand, the instrument of artistic genius. It is noteworthy that the canvas in this painting is blank. This is not a self-portrait of the artist at work on a specific painting (compare FIGS. 23-16, 25-11, 26-16, and 26-17) but a portrait of Gentileschi as Painting herself.

In almost all Renaissance and Baroque self-portraits, the artist gazes at the viewer. The frontal view not only provides the fullest view of the artist's features, but it is also the easiest to paint because the artist needs only to look in a mirror in order to record his or her features (FIG. 22-43). To create this self-portrait, however, Gentileschi had to set up two mirrors to paint her likeness from an angle, a highly original break from tradition and an assertion of her supreme skill in a field dominated by men (see "The Letters of Artemisia Gentileschi," page 716).

GUIDO RENI Caravaggio was not the only early-17th-century painter to win a devoted following. GUIDO RENI (1575–1642), known to his many admirers as "the divine Guido," trained in the Bolognese art academy founded by the Carracci family. The influence of Annibale Carracci and Raphael is evident in *Aurora* (FIG. **24-21**), a ceiling fresco in the Casino Rospigliosi in Rome. Aurora (Dawn) leads Apollo's chariot, while the Hours dance about it. Guido conceived *Aurora* as a quadro riportato, following the format of the paintings in Annibale's *Loves of the Gods* (FIG. 24-16), and provided the quadro with a complex and convincing illusionistic frame. The fresco exhibits a fluid motion, soft modeling, and sure composition, although without Raphael's sculpturesque strength. It is an intelligent interpretation of the Renaissance master's style. Consistent with the precepts of the Bolognese academy, the painter also looked to antiquity for models. The ultimate sources for the *Aurora* composition were Roman reliefs (FIG. 7-42) and coins depicting emperors in triumphal chariots accompanied by flying Victories and other personifications.

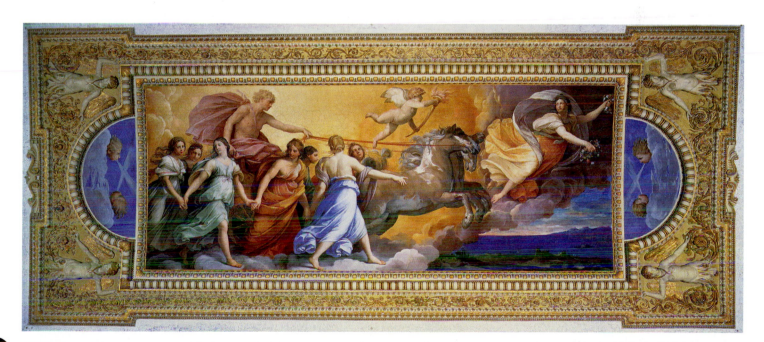

24-21 GUIDO RENI, *Aurora,* ceiling fresco in the Casino Rospigliosi, Rome, Italy, 1613–1614.

The "divine Guido" conceived *Aurora* as a quadro riportato, reflecting his training in the Bolognese art academy. The scene of Dawn leading Apollo's chariot derives from ancient Roman reliefs.

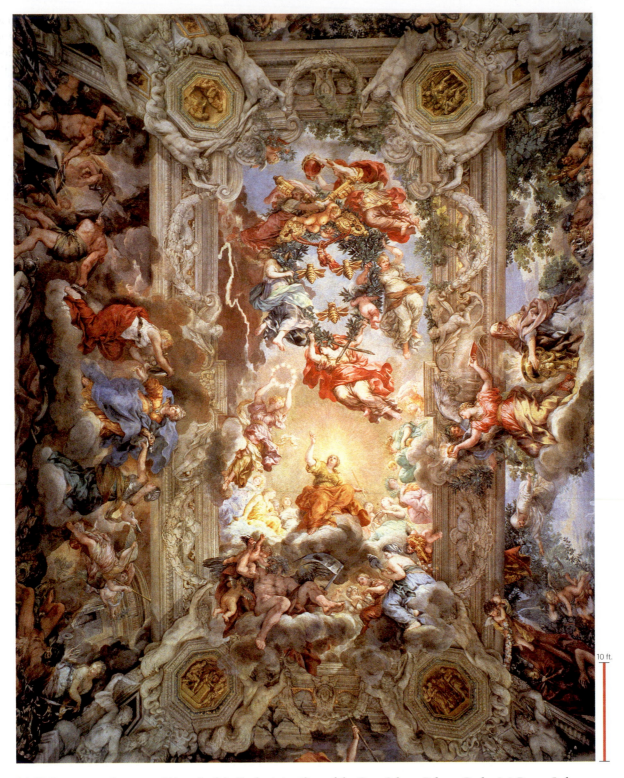

24-22 PIETRO DA CORTONA, *Triumph of the Barberini,* ceiling of the Gran Salone, Palazzo Barberini, Rome, Italy, 1633–1639. Fresco, 78' × 46'.

In this dramatic ceiling fresco, Divine Providence appears in a halo of radiant light directing Immortality, holding a crown of stars, to bestow eternal life on the family of Pope Urban VIII.

PIETRO DA CORTONA Looking up at a painting is different from viewing a painting hanging on a wall, even in the case of quadro riportato ceiling designs. The considerable height and expansive scale of most ceiling frescoes induce a feeling of awe. Patrons who wanted to burnish their public image or control their legacy found grandiose ceiling frescoes to be perfect vehicles. In 1633, Pope Urban VIII commissioned a ceiling fresco for the Gran Salone (the main reception hall) of the Palazzo Barberini in Rome. The most important decorative commission of the 1630s, the lucrative assignment went to PIETRO DA CORTONA (1596–1669), a Tuscan architect and painter who had moved to Rome two decades before. The immense (78-by-46-foot) *Triumph of the Barberini* (FIG. **24-22**) overwhelms spectators with the glory of the Barberini family (and Urban VIII in particular). The iconographic program for this fresco, designed

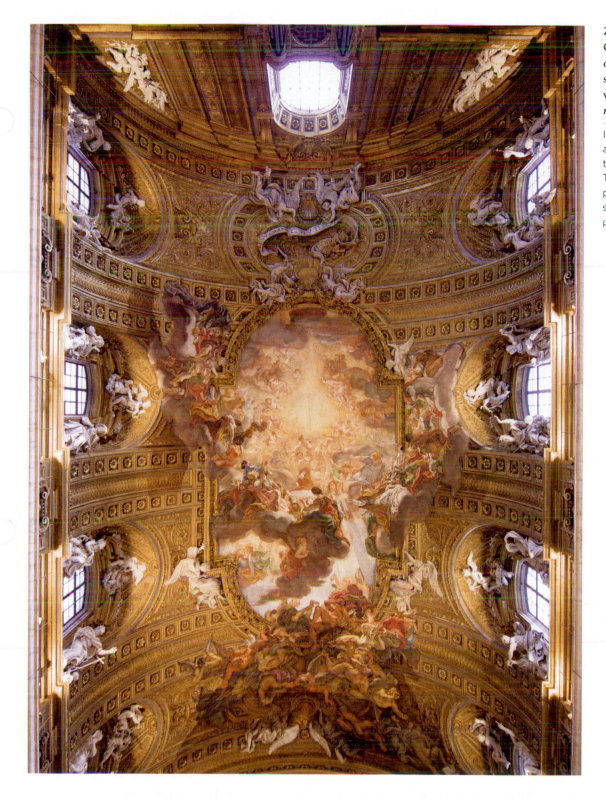

24-23 Giovanni Battista Gaulli, *Triumph of the Name of Jesus,* ceiling fresco with stucco figures on the nave vault of Il Gesù (FIG. 22-58, *right*), Rome, Italy, 1676–1679.

In the nave of Il Gesù, gilded architecture opens up to offer the faithful a glimpse of Heaven. To heighten the illusion, Gaulli painted figures on stucco extensions that project outside the painting's frame.

by the poet Francesco Bracciolini (1566–1645), centered on the accomplishments of the Barberini. Divine Providence appears in a halo of radiant light directing Immortality, holding a crown of stars, to bestow eternal life on the family. The virtues Faith, Hope, and Charity hold aloft a gigantic laurel wreath (also a symbol of immortality), which frames three bees (the Barberini family's symbols, which also appeared in Bernini's baldacchino, FIG. 24-5). Also present are the papal tiara and keys announcing the personal triumphs of Urban VIII.

GIOVANNI BATTISTA GAULLI *Triumph of the Name of Jesus* (FIG. **24-23**) in the nave of Il Gesù (FIG. 22-58) vividly demonstrates

the dramatic impact that Baroque ceiling frescoes could have in ecclesiastical contexts. As the mother church of the Jesuit order, Il Gesù played a prominent role in Counter-Reformation efforts. In this monumental fresco by GIOVANNI BATTISTA GAULLI (1639–1709), gilded architecture opens up in the center of the ceiling to offer the faithful a stunning glimpse of Heaven. Gaulli represented Jesus as a barely visible monogram (IHS) floating heavenward in a blinding radiant light. In contrast, sinners experience a violent descent back to Earth. The painter glazed the gilded architecture to suggest shadows, thereby enhancing the scene's illusionistic quality. To further heighten the illusion, Gaulli painted many of the sinners on three-dimensional stucco extensions projecting outside the painting's frame.

PROBLEMS AND SOLUTIONS
How to Make a Ceiling Disappear

The effectiveness of Italian Baroque religious art depended on the drama and theatricality of individual images, as well as on the interaction and fusion of architecture, sculpture, and painting. Sound enhanced this experience. Architects designed churches with acoustical effects in mind, and in an Italian Baroque church filled with music, the power of both image and sound must have been very moving. Through simultaneous stimulation of the senses of both sight and hearing, the faithful might well have been transported into a trancelike state that would, indeed, as the great English poet John Milton (1608–1674) eloquently stated in *Il Penseroso* (1631), "bring all Heaven before [their] eyes."*

Seventeenth-century ecclesiastical officials keenly realized that spectacular paintings high above the ground offered perfect opportunities to impress on worshipers the glory and power of the Catholic Church. In conjunction with the theatricality of Italian Baroque architecture and sculpture, grandiose frescoes on church ceilings contributed to creating transcendent spiritual environments well suited to the needs of the Catholic Church in Counter-Reformation Rome.

As Giovanni Battista Gaulli did in his *Triumph of the Name of Jesus* (FIG. 24-23) for Il Gesù, in his fresco (FIG. 24-24) for the ceiling of the nave of the Roman church honoring Saint Ignatius, Fra Andrea Pozzo created the illusion of Heaven opening up above the congregation. To accomplish this, the artist painted an extension of the church's architecture into the vault so that the roof seems to be lifted off. As Heaven and earth commingle, Christ receives Saint Ignatius in the presence of figures personifying the four corners of the world. A disk in the nave floor marks the spot where the viewer should stand to gain the whole perspective illusion. For worshipers looking up from this point, the vision is complete. They find themselves in the presence of the heavenly and spiritual, the ultimate goal of Italian Baroque ecclesiastical art and architecture.

*John Milton, *Il Penseroso* (1631, published 1645), 166.

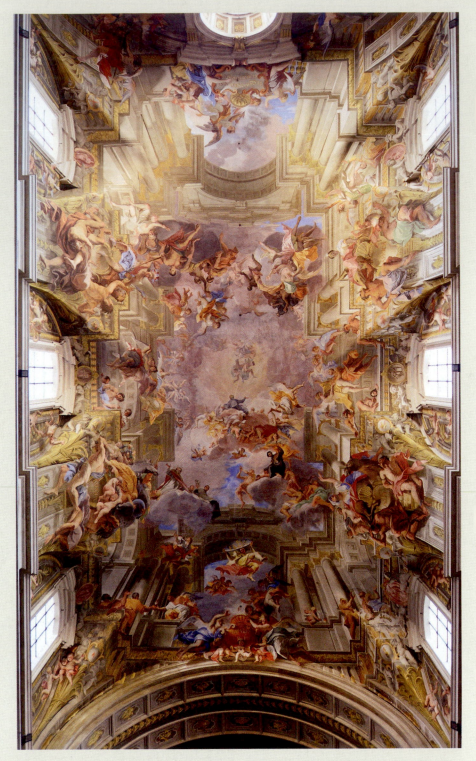

24-24 FRA ANDREA POZZO, *Glorification of Saint Ignatius,* ceiling fresco in the nave of Sant'Ignazio, Rome, Italy, 1691–1694.

By merging real and painted architecture, Pozzo created the illusion that the vaulted ceiling of Sant'Ignazio has been lifted off and that the nave opens to Heaven above the worshipers' heads.

FRA ANDREA POZZO Another master of ceiling decoration was FRA ANDREA POZZO (1642–1709), a lay brother of the Jesuit order and a master of perspective, on which he wrote an influential treatise. Pozzo designed and executed the vast ceiling fresco *Glorification of Saint Ignatius* (FIG. 24-24) for the church of Sant'Ignazio in Rome (see "How to Make a Ceiling Disappear," above). Like Il Gesù, Sant'Ignazio was a prominent Counter-Reformation church because of its dedication to the founder of the Jesuit order. The Jesuits played a major role in Catholic education and sent legions of missionaries to the New World and Asia.

SPAIN AND NEW SPAIN

During the 16th century, Spain had established itself as an international power. The Habsburg kings had built a dynastic state encompassing Portugal, part of Italy, the Netherlands, and extensive areas of the New World (see pages 695 and 1084). By the beginning of the 17th century, however, the Habsburg Empire was in decline, and although Spain mounted an aggressive effort during the Thirty Years' War (see page 732), by 1660 the imperial age of the Spanish Habsburgs was over. In part, the demise of the Habsburg Empire was due to economic woes. The military campaigns that Philip III (r. 1598–1621) and his son Philip IV (r. 1621–1665) waged during the Thirty Years' War were costly and led to the imposition of higher taxes. The increasing tax burden placed on Spanish subjects in turn incited revolts and civil war in Catalonia and Portugal in the 1640s, further straining an already fragile economy.

Painting and Sculpture

Although the dawn of the Baroque period found the Spanish kings struggling to maintain control of their dwindling empire, both Philip III and Philip IV understood the prestige that great artworks brought and the value of visual imagery in communicating effectively with a wide audience. Thus both kings continued to spend lavishly on art.

JUAN SÁNCHEZ COTÁN One painter who made a major contribution to the development of Spanish art, although he did not receive any royal commissions, was JUAN SÁNCHEZ COTÁN (1560–1627). Born in Orgaz, outside Toledo, Sánchez Cotán moved to Granada and became a Carthusian monk in 1603. Although he painted religious subjects, his greatest works are the *still lifes* (paintings of artfully arranged inanimate objects) that he produced before entering monastic life (and never thereafter). Few in number, they nonetheless established still-life painting as an important genre in 17th-century Spain.

Still Life with Game Fowl (FIG. **24-25**) is one of Sánchez Cotán's most ambitious compositions, but it conforms to the pattern he adopted for all his still lifes. A niche or a window—the artist clearly wished the setting to be indeterminate—fills the entire surface of the canvas. At the bottom, fruits and vegetables, including a melon—cut open with a slice removed—rest on a ledge. Above, suspended on strings from a nail or hook outside the frame, are a quince and four game fowl. All are meticulously rendered and brightly illuminated, enhancing the viewer's sense of each texture, color, and shape, yet the background is impenetrable shadow. The sharp and unnatural contrast between light and dark imbues the still life with a sense of mystery that is absent, for example, in Dutch still-life paintings (FIGS. 23-15, 25-21, 25-22, and 25-23). There may, in fact, be a religious reference. Sánchez Cotán once described his 11 paintings of fruits, vegetables, and birds as "offerings to the Virgin"—probably a reference to the Virgin as the *fenestra coeli* ("window to Heaven") and the source of spiritual food for the faithful.

JOSÉ DE RIBERA In the 17th century, Spain maintained its passionate commitment to Catholic orthodoxy, and, as in Counter-Reformation Italy, Spanish Baroque artists sought ways to move viewers and encourage greater devotion and piety. Scenes of death and martyrdom had great appeal in Spain. They provided artists with opportunities both to depict extreme emotion and to elicit passionate feelings. Spain prided itself on its saints—Saint Teresa of Avila (FIG. 24-8) and Saint Ignatius Loyola (FIG. 24-24) were both Spanish-born—and martyrdom scenes appear frequently in Spanish Baroque art.

As a young man, JOSÉ (JUSEPE) DE RIBERA (ca. 1588–1652) emigrated to Naples and fell under the spell of Caravaggio, whose

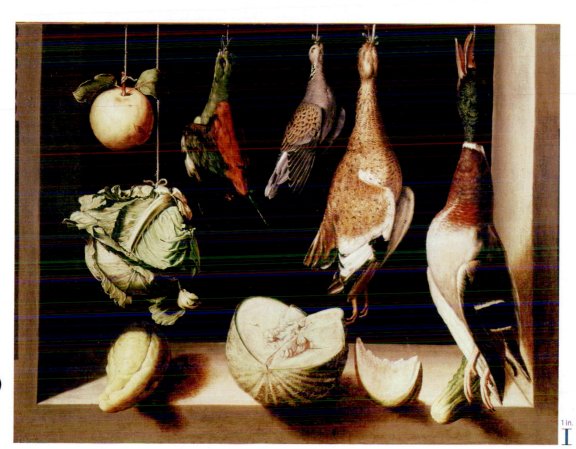

24-25 JUAN SÁNCHEZ COTÁN, *Still Life with Game Fowl*, ca. 1600–1603. Oil on canvas, 2' 2¾" × 2' 10⅞". Art Institute of Chicago, Chicago (gift of Mr. and Mrs. Leigh B. Block).

Sánchez Cotán established still life as an important genre in Spain. His compositions feature brightly illuminated fruits, vegetables, and birds, hanging or on a ledge, against a dark background.

Martyrdom scenes were popular in Counter-Reformation Spain. Scorning idealization of any kind, Ribera represented Philip's executioners hoisting him into position to die on a cross.

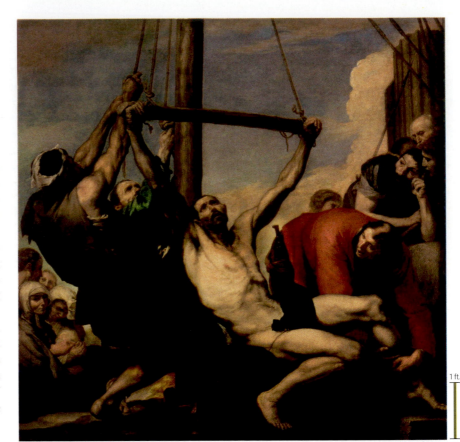

innovative style he introduced to Spain. Emulating Caravaggio, Ribera made naturalism and compelling drama primary ingredients of his paintings, which often embraced brutal themes, reflecting the harsh times of the Counter-Reformation and the Spanish taste for stories showcasing courage and devotion. Ribera's *Martyrdom of Saint Philip* (FIG. **24-26**) is grim and dark in both subject and form. Scorning idealization of any kind, Ribera represented Philip's executioners hoisting him into position after tying him to a cross, the instrument of Christ's own martyrdom. The saint's rough, heavy body and swarthy, plebeian features express a kinship between him and his tormentors, who are similar to the types of figures found in Caravaggio's paintings. The patron of this painting is unknown, but it is possible that Philip IV commissioned the work, because Saint Philip was the king's patron saint.

FRANCISCO DE ZURBARÁN Another prominent Spanish painter of dramatic works was FRANCISCO DE ZURBARÁN (1598–1664), whose primary patrons throughout his career were rich Spanish monastic orders. Many of his paintings are quiet and contemplative, appropriate for prayer and devotional purposes. Zurbarán painted *Saint Serapion* (FIG. **24-27**) as a devotional image for the funerary chapel of the monastic Order of Mercy in Seville, which was founded to aid Christians who had been taken prisoner by the Moors. The saint, who participated in the Third Crusade of 1196, suffered martyrdom while preaching the Gospel to Muslims. According to one account, the monk's captors tied him to a tree and then tortured and decapitated him. The Order of Mercy dedicated itself to self-sacrifice, and Serapion's membership in this order amplified the resonance of Zurbarán's painting. In *Saint Serapion,* the monk emerges from a dark background and fills the foreground. The bright light shining on him calls attention to the saint's tragic death and increases the dramatic impact of the image. In the background are two barely visible tree branches. A small note next to the saint identifies him for viewers. The coarse features of the Spanish monk label him as common (Serapion had not yet been declared a saint at the time Zurbarán portrayed him), no doubt evoking empathy from a wide audience.

JUAN MARTÍNEZ MONTAÑÉS The drama and fervor of Spanish Baroque religious painting have parallels in 17th-century Spanish sculpture. Especially noteworthy is the work of JUAN MARTÍNEZ MONTAÑÉS (1568–1649), the leading sculptor of Seville. Variously called by his contemporaries "the Sevillian Phidias" and "the Andalusian Lysippos," references to two of the most famous ancient Greek sculptors, Montañés was primarily known as "the god of wood" because of his mastery of the art of *polychrome* (painted) and gilded wood sculptures.

One of the major commissions that Montañés received during his long career (he died at age 81 in the 1649 plague in Seville) was to

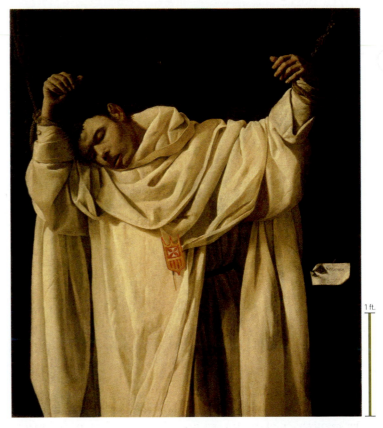

24-27 Francisco de Zurbarán, *Saint Serapion,* 1628. Oil on canvas, 3' 11½" × 3' 4¾". Wadsworth Atheneum Museum of Art, Hartford (The Ella Gallup Sumner and Mary Catlin Sumner Collection Fund).

The light shining on Serapion calls attention to his tragic death and increases the painting's dramatic impact. The monk's coarse features label him as common, evoking empathy from a wide audience.

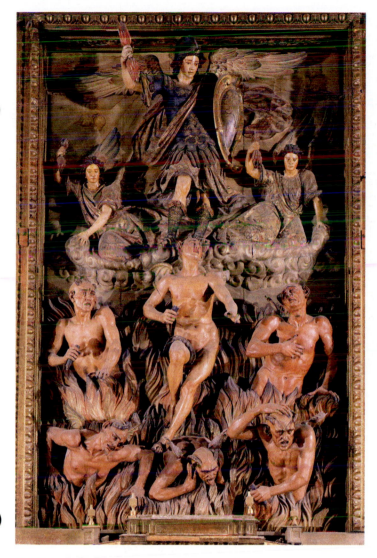

24-28 JUAN MARTÍNEZ MONTAÑÉS, *Battle of Demons and Angels,* main panel of the retablo in the apse of San Miguel, Jerez de la Frontera, Spain, ca. 1609–1613. Painted and gilded wood.

Montañés was the leading Spanish Baroque sculptor. This polychrome and gilded wood retablo panel of the archangel Michael defeating the rebel angels may be an allegory of Catholicism's triumph over Protestantism.

provide relief sculptures for the enormous multistory *retablo* (Spanish, "altarpiece") that fills the apse of the church of San Miguel (Saint Michael) at Jerez de la Frontera in southern Spain (MAP 25-1). The retablo is the work of several sculptors and took decades to complete. The main panel (FIG. **24-28**), by Montañés, celebrates the victory of the archangel Michael, the church's namesake, over the rebel angels. Contemporaries viewed the biblical story as an allegory of the triumph of Catholicism over Protestantism. In the Spanish sculptor's conception of the theme (compare Domenico Beccafiumi's *Fall of the Rebel Angels,* FIG. 22-42A), Michael and his angels are handsome and beautifully proportioned, classically inspired figures who attack from above (that is, from Heaven) the ugly, writhing agents of the Devil. The arrangement of the demons from Hell owes a debt to the famous Hellenistic-style *Laocoön* (FIG. 5-89) statuary group discovered in Rome in 1506. Although stylistically related to Baroque sculpture in Italy, Spanish Baroque sculpture is a distinct regional variation. Compared to the pure white marble statues of Bernini and his Italian contemporaries, the lifelike polychrome wood statues and reliefs of 17th-century Spain elicit a very different reaction from the viewer.

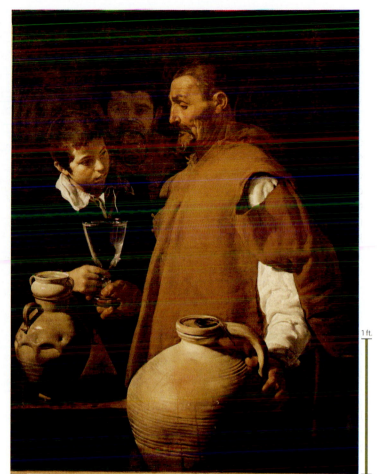

24-29 DIEGO VELÁZQUEZ, *Water Carrier of Seville,* ca. 1619. Oil on canvas, 3' 5½" × 2' 7¾". Victoria & Albert Museum, London.

In this early work—a genre scene that seems to convey a deeper significance—the contrast of darks and lights, and the plebeian nature of the figures, reveal Velázquez's debt to Caravaggio.

DIEGO VELÁZQUEZ The foremost Spanish painter of the Baroque age—and the greatest beneficiary of royal patronage—was DIEGO VELÁZQUEZ (1599–1660). An early work, *Water Carrier of Seville* (FIG. **24-29**), reveals Velázquez's impressive command of the painter's craft when he was only about 20 years old. In this genre scene that seems to convey a deeper significance, Velázquez rendered the figures with clarity and dignity, and his careful and convincing depiction of the water jugs in the foreground, complete with droplets of water, adds to the scene's credibility. The plebeian nature of the figures and the contrast of darks and lights again reveal the influence of Caravaggio, whose work Velázquez had studied.

Like many other Spanish artists, Velázquez produced religious pictures—for example, *Christ on the Cross* (FIG. **24-29A**)—as well as genre scenes, but his renown in his day rested primarily on the works he painted for King Philip IV (see "Velázquez and Philip IV," page 724). After the king appointed Velázquez court painter, the artist largely abandoned both religious and genre subjects in favor of royal portraits (FIG. 24-30A) and canvases recording historical events.

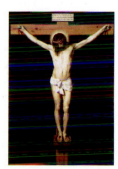

▶ **24-29A** VELÁZQUEZ, *Christ on the Cross,* ca. 1631–1632.

Trained in Seville, Diego Velázquez was quite young when he came to the attention of Philip IV. The painter's immense talent impressed the king, and Philip named him chief court artist and palace chamberlain, a position that also involved overseeing the rapidly growing royal art collection and advising the king on acquisitions and display. Among the works in Philip IV's possession were paintings by Titian, Annibale Carracci, Guido Reni, Albrecht Dürer, and Velázquez's famous Flemish contemporary, Peter Paul Rubens (see page 732).

With the exception of two extended trips to Italy and a few excursions, Velázquez remained in Madrid for the rest of his life. His close relationship with Philip IV and his high office as chamberlain gave him prestige and a rare guaranteed income. But, like most artists before the modern era, Velázquez above all had to please his patron and consequently had little opportunity to choose his own subjects. One sign of Velázquez's fertile imagination as well as mastery of the brush is that he, like Michelangelo (see "Michelangelo in the Service of Julius II," page 623), was able to create timeless artworks from the assignments he received.

A case in point is the painting Velázquez produced on the king's orders to commemorate the Spanish victory over the Dutch in 1625. Painted in 1635, *Surrender of Breda* (FIG. **24-30**) was part of an extensive program of decoration for the Hall of Realms in Philip IV's new secondary pleasure palace in Madrid, the Palacio del Buen Retiro. The huge canvas (more than 12 feet long and almost as tall) was one of 10 paintings celebrating recent Spanish military successes, not only in Europe but in the New World as well. Among the most troublesome situations for Spain was the conflict in the Netherlands. Determined to escape Spanish control, the northern Netherlands broke from the Habsburg Empire in the late 16th century. Skirmishes continued to flare up along the border between the northern (Dutch) and southern (Spanish) Netherlands, and in 1625, Philip IV sent General Ambrogio di Spínola to Breda to reclaim the town for Spain.

Velázquez depicted the victorious Spanish troops, organized and well armed, on the right side of the painting. In sharp contrast, the defeated Dutch on the left appear bedraggled and disorganized. In the

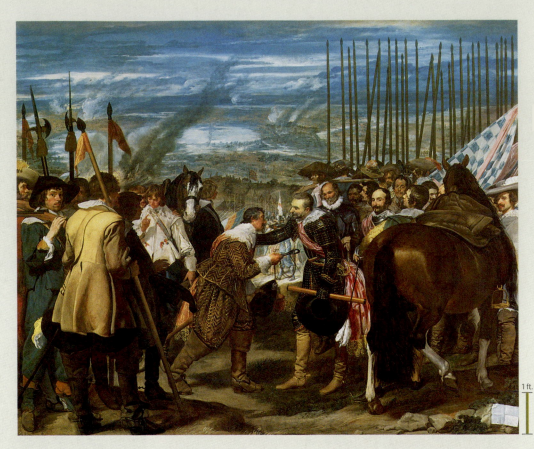

24-30 DIEGO VELÁZQUEZ, *Surrender of Breda*, 1634–1635. Oil on canvas, 10' 1" × 12' $\frac{1}{2}$". Museo del Prado, Madrid.

As Philip IV's court artist, Velázquez produced many history paintings, including fictional representations such as this one depicting the Dutch mayor of Breda surrendering to a Spanish general.

center foreground, the mayor of Breda, Justinus of Nassau, hands the city's keys to the Spanish general—although no encounter of this kind ever occurred. Velázquez's fictional record of the event glorifies not only the strength of the Spanish military but also the benevolence of Spínola. Velázquez did not portray the Spanish general astride his horse, lording over the vanquished Dutch mayor, but rather painted him standing and magnanimously stopping Justinus from kneeling. Indeed, the terms of surrender were notably lenient, and Spínola allowed the Dutch to retain their arms—which they used to recapture the city in 1637.

Velázquez also painted dozens of portraits of Philip IV (FIG. **24-30A**) and his family and retinue, including *Las Meninas* (FIG. 24-31), one of the greatest paintings in the history of Western art, a work that Philip admired so much that he displayed it in his personal office.

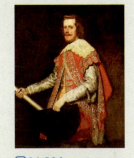

24-30A VELÁZQUEZ, *Philip IV*, 1644.

LAS MENINAS After an extended visit to Rome from 1648 to 1651, Velázquez returned to Spain. In 1656, he painted his greatest work, *Las Meninas* (*The Maids of Honor*; FIG. **24-31**). The setting is the artist's studio in the palace of the Alcázar, the official royal residence in Madrid. After the death of Prince Baltasar Carlos in 1646, Philip

IV ordered part of the prince's chambers converted into a studio for Velázquez. The painter represented himself standing before a large canvas. The young Infanta (Princess) Margarita appears in the foreground with her two maids-in-waiting, her favorite dwarfs, and a large dog. In the middle ground are a woman in widow's attire and

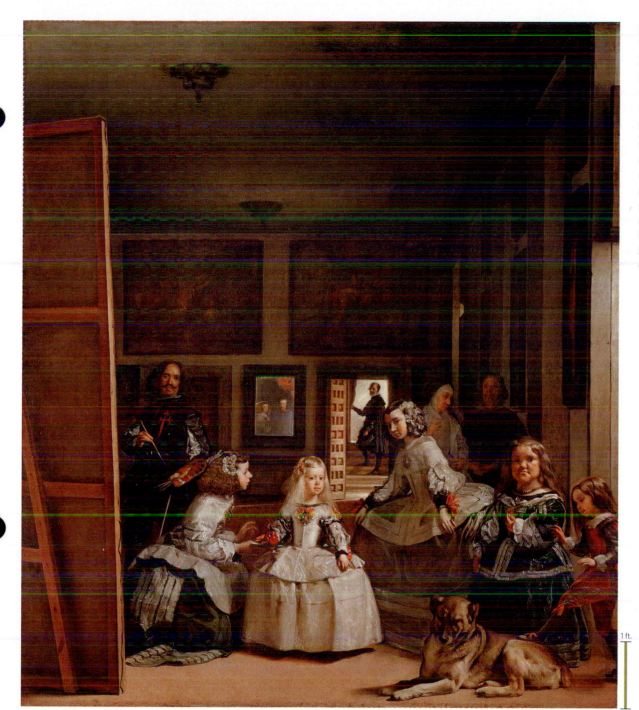

24-31 Diego Velázquez, *Las Meninas* (*The Maids of Honor*), 1656. Oil on canvas, 10' 5" × 9'. Museo del Prado, Madrid.

Velázquez intended this huge and complex work, with its cunning contrasts of real, mirrored, and picture spaces, to elevate both himself and the profession of painting in the eyes of Philip IV.

1 ft.

a male escort. In the background, a chamberlain stands in a brightly lit open doorway. Scholars have been able to identify everyone in the room, including the two meninas and the dwarfs.

Las Meninas is noteworthy for its visual and narrative complexity. Indeed, art historians have yet to agree on any particular reading or interpretation. A central issue preoccupying scholars has been what, exactly, is taking place in *Las Meninas*. What is Velázquez depicting on the huge canvas in front of him? He may be painting this very picture—an informal image of the infanta and her entourage. Alternately, Velázquez may be painting a portrait of King Philip IV and Queen Mariana, whose reflections appear in the mirror on the far wall. If so, that would suggest the presence of the king and queen in the viewer's space, outside the confines of the picture. Other scholars have proposed that the mirror image is not a reflection of the royal couple standing in Velázquez's studio but a

reflection of the portrait the artist is in the process of painting on the canvas before him. This question will probably never be definitively resolved.

More generally, *Las Meninas* is Velázquez's attempt to elevate both himself and his profession. As first painter to the king and as chamberlain of the palace, Velázquez was conscious not only of the importance of his court office but also of the honor and dignity belonging to his profession as a painter. Throughout his career, Velázquez hoped to be ennobled by royal appointment to membership in the ancient and illustrious Order of Santiago (Saint James). Because he lacked a sufficiently noble lineage, he gained entrance only with difficulty at the very end of his life, and then only through the pope's dispensation. In the painting, Velázquez wears the order's red cross on his doublet, painted there, legend says, by Philip IV. In all likelihood, Velázquez painted it. In the artist's mind, *Las Meninas* might have embodied the idea of the great king visiting his studio, as Alexander the Great visited the studio of the painter Apelles in ancient times. The figures in the painting all appear to acknowledge the royal presence. Placed among them in equal dignity is Velázquez, face-to-face with his sovereign.

The location of the completed painting reinforced this act of looking—of seeing and being seen. *Las Meninas* hung in Philip IV's personal office in another part of the palace. Thus, although occasional visitors admitted to the king's private quarters may have seen this painting, Philip was the primary audience. Each time he stood before the canvas, he again participated in the work as the probable subject of Velázquez's painting within the painting and as the object of the figures' gazes. In *Las Meninas*, Velázquez elevated the art of painting, in the person of the painter, to the highest status. The king's presence enhanced this status—either in person as the viewer of *Las Meninas* or as a reflected image in the painting itself. The paintings that appear in *Las Meninas* further reinforced this celebration of the painter's craft. On the wall above the doorway and the mirror, two faintly recognizable pictures are copies made by Velázquez's son-in-law, Juan del Mazo (ca. 1612–1667), of paintings by Peter Paul Rubens. The paintings depict the immortal gods as the source of art. Ultimately, Velázquez sought ennoblement not for himself alone but for his art as well.

Las Meninas is extraordinarily complex visually. Velázquez's optical report of the event, authentic in every detail, pictorially summarizes the various kinds of images in their different levels and degrees of reality. He portrayed the realities of image on canvas, of mirror image, of optical image, and of the two painted images. This work—with its cunning contrasts of real spaces, mirrored spaces, picture spaces, and pictures within pictures—itself appears to have been taken from a large mirror reflecting the entire scene. This would mean that the artist did not paint the princess and her suite as the main subjects of *Las Meninas* but himself in the process of painting them. *Las Meninas* is a pictorial summary and a commentary on the essential mystery of the visual world, as well as on the ambiguity that results when different states or levels interact or are juxtaposed.

Velázquez employed several devices in order to achieve this visual complexity. For example, the extension of the composition's pictorial depth in both directions is noteworthy. The open doorway and its ascending staircase lead the eye beyond the artist's studio, and the mirror and the outward glances of several of the figures incorporate the viewer's space into the picture as well. (Compare how the mirror in Jan van Eyck's *Giovanni Arnolfini and His Wife* [FIG. 20-7] similarly incorporates the area in front of the canvas into the picture, although less obviously and without a comparable extension of space beyond the rear wall of the room.) Velázquez also masterfully observed and represented form and shadow. Instead of putting lights abruptly beside darks, following Caravaggio, Velázquez allowed a great number of intermediate values of gray to come between the two extremes. His matching of

tonal gradations approached effects later discovered in the age of photography.

BARTOLOMÉ ESTEBAN MURILLO No Spanish painter of the second half of the 17th century could challenge Velázquez in stature or quality, but one painter, BARTOLOMÉ ESTEBAN MURILLO (1617–1682), had an influence on later painters that was in some ways more pervasive than Velázquez's. Murillo was born in Seville, where in 1645 he received his first important commission—a series of paintings of the life of Saint Francis for the cloister of San Francisco el Grande. His most famous works, however, depict the Immaculate Virgin (for example, *Immaculate Conception of the Escorial*, FIG. 24-32), an immensely popular theme in fervently Catholic Spain. For centuries, the Spanish Church had lobbied the popes in Rome to certify that the Virgin, like Christ, had been conceived

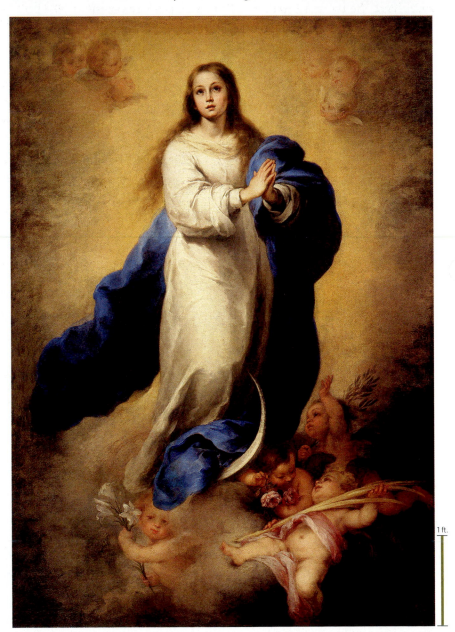

1 ft.

24-32 BARTOLOMÉ ESTEBAN MURILLO, *Immaculate Conception of the Escorial*, ca. 1661–1670. Oil on canvas, 6' 9 $\frac{1}{8}$" × 4' 8 $\frac{5}{8}$". Museo del Prado, Madrid.

Murillo established the canonical image of the Immaculate Virgin—a beautiful young praying woman ascending to Heaven on clouds, accompanied by angels bearing symbols of her purity.

without sin, a position supported by the Franciscan order. The Dominicans, in contrast, insisted that the Virgin had not been miraculously conceived but was purified while in her mother's womb. Many Spanish painters received commissions to paint Mary's immaculate conception in accord with the standard Counter-Reformation iconography. In Murillo's painting, the Virgin, wearing a white gown and a blue cloak, rises heavenward on clouds, riding on a crescent moon (as described in the Apocalypse) and accompanied by angels carrying attributes referring to her purity (roses, lilies, a mirror) and her suffering (palm fronds).

Murillo's many *Virgin of the Immaculate Conception* paintings set the standard for representations of this subject. The *Immaculate Conception of the Escorial* (FIG. 24-32) is probably his best. In 1661, Pope Alexander VII officially decreed that Mary was free of original sin, causing great celebration in Spain and putting an end to the controversy. The Escorial *Immaculate Conception* has fewer angels and attributes than Murillo's earlier versions. The Spanish master represented Mary as a beautiful, humble young woman, her hands clasped in prayer, slowly ascending to Heaven. By using light colors and making the angels in the upper half of the canvas almost disappear in the clouds, Murillo imbued the scene with a sense of weightlessness. His formulation of the theme became canonical, not only in Spain but in the Spanish colonies in the New World.

Architecture

The Baroque architecture of Spain and its colonies in the Western Hemisphere has closer affinities to the lavish surface decoration of the Plateresque style of the late 15th and 16th centuries (FIGS. 23-24 and 23-24A) than to the more severe style of El Escorial (FIG. 23-25). The important Romanesque church of Saint James at Santiago de Compostela (FIG. 12-7A), for example, received a new Baroque-style facade in the 17th century, and Baroque taste also determined the look of the churches that the Spanish conquerors erected in the New World. As in Rome at the same time, the richest and most influential architectural patron in Latin America was the Catholic Church.

MEXICO CITY The largest building constructed anywhere in New Spain during the colonial period was Metropolitan Cathedral of the Assumption of Mary (FIG. 24-33) in Mexico City. The project began shortly after the victory of Hernàn Cortès over the Aztec Empire (see page 1084) on the site of the Templo Mayor (FIG. 35-3), the ceremonial and religious center of the Aztec capital city of Tenochtitlán (see MAP 35-1). The cathedral building campaign lasted nearly three centuries, completed only in 1817. Most of the present enormous (360-foot-long and 179-foot-wide) structure dates to the 17th century

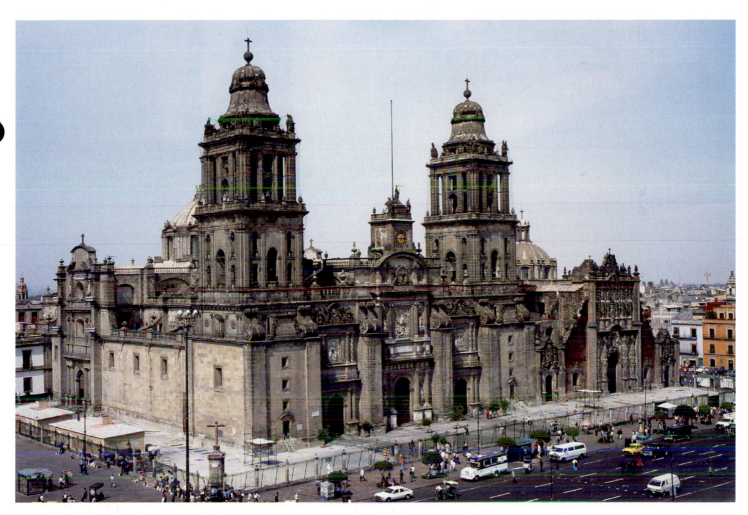

24-33 CLAUDIO DE ARCINIEGA and others, Metropolitan Cathedral of the Assumption of Mary (looking northeast), Mexico City, Mexico, 1573–1817.

The largest building in colonial Latin America is Mexico City's Metropolitan Cathedral, built on the site of the religious center of the conquered Aztec capital. The design reflects Roman Baroque church exteriors.

24-34 JEAN-BAPTISTE GILLES or MARTINEZ DE OVIEDO, west facade of the Iglesia La Compañía de Jesús (Church of the Society of Jesus), Cuzco, Peru, 1650–1668.

The Baroque facade of the Jesuits' church in the former capital of the Inka Empire is a distinctive colonial variation without close parallels in Europe. The design resembles a grandiose Spanish retablo.

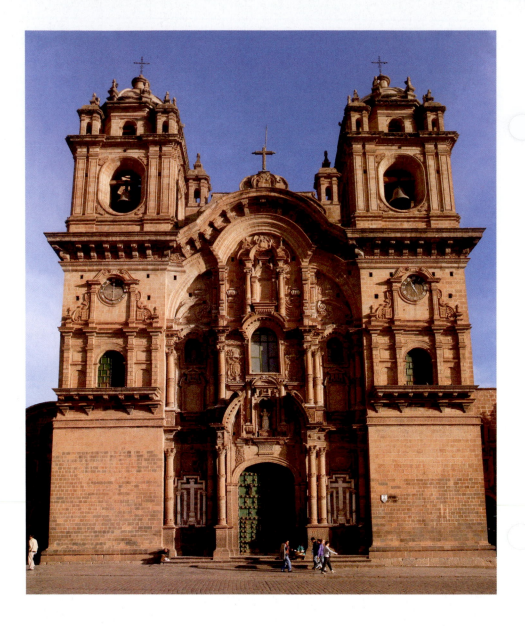

and follows the plan drawn by CLAUDIO DE ARCINIEGA (ca. 1520–1593) in 1569. Construction commenced in 1573, using stones from the Aztec pyramid-temple of Huitzilopochtl. Dominating the wide facade are twin cupola-capped towers that date to the 18th century. The articulation of the lower facade, erected during the second half of the 17th century, reflects the style of the churches of Baroque Rome.

CUZCO A purer example of Baroque style in New Spain is the Church of the Society of Jesus (FIG. **24-34**) in Cuzco, Peru (see MAP 35-2), erected during a concentrated period of 18 years after an earthquake in 1650 destroyed an earlier church at the heart of the former Inka capital (see page 1091). Designed either by the Flemish Jesuit architect-priest JEAN-BAPTISTE GILLES (1596–1675) or the Spanish retablo master MARTINEZ DE OVIEDO (d. 1670), the church's facade, which resembles a grandiose retablo framed by comparatively plain twin bell towers, is a distinctive colonial variation of Baroque architecture without close parallels in Europe. The design captures the dynamic projecting and receding elements of the facades of contemporaneous Roman churches without copying any of them. The predominantly curvilinear motifs rise in waves to a crescendo in the richly carved upper cornice, which also unites the towers with the center of the facade.

The churches of New Spain are eloquent symbols of the triumph of Christianity, and specifically of the Catholic Church, in the Western Hemisphere, and, more generally, of the subjugation of the native populations and their cultural values by the kings of Spain and their armies, priests, and artists.

THE BAROQUE IN ITALY AND SPAIN

Italy

- Art historians call the art of 17th-century Italy and Spain "Baroque," a term that probably derives from the Portuguese word for an irregularly shaped pearl. Baroque art is dynamic and theatrical, in vivid contrast to the precision and orderly rationality of Renaissance classicism.

- Baroque architects emphatically rejected the classical style. Gianlorenzo Bernini's colonnade framing the piazza in front of Saint Peter's is not a traditional rectangular atrium but two curving arms welcoming worshipers.

- Francesco Borromini emphasized the sculptural qualities of buildings. The facades of his churches—for example, San Carlo alle Quattro Fontane—are not flat frontispieces but undulating surfaces that provide a fluid transition from exterior to interior space. The interiors of his buildings pulsate with energy and feature complex domes that grow organically from curving walls.

- Bernini achieved even greater renown as a sculptor. His *David* represents the biblical hero in action, hurling stones at Goliath. In *Ecstasy of Saint Teresa*, Bernini marshaled the full capabilities of architecture, sculpture, and painting to create an intensely emotional experience for worshipers, consistent with the Counter-Reformation principle of using artworks to inspire devotion and piety.

- In painting, Caravaggio broke new ground by employing stark and dramatic contrasts of light and dark (tenebrism) and by setting religious scenes in everyday locales filled with rough-looking common people. Caravaggio's combination of drama and realism attracted both admiring followers—including Artemisia Gentileschi, the leading woman painter of the 17th century—and harsh critics. The biographer Giovanni Pietro Bellori, for example, deplored Caravaggio's abandonment of the noble style of Raphael and the ancients and his "suppression of the dignity of art." Bellori preferred the more classical style of Annibale Carracci and the Bolognese art academy.

- Illusionistic ceiling paintings were very popular in Baroque Italy. The major ceiling painters were Pietro da Cortona, Giovanni Battista Gaulli, and Fra Andrea Pozzo. In Sant'Ignazio in Rome, by merging the church's architecture with the painted nave vault, Pozzo created the illusion that Heaven is opening up above worshipers' heads.

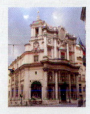

Borromini, San Carlo alle Quattro Fontane, Rome, 1638–1641

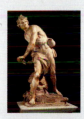

Bernini, *David*, 1623

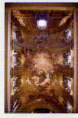

Gaulli, *Triumph of the Name of Jesus*, 1676–1679

Spain and New Spain

- Although the power of the Habsburg kings declined during the 17th century, the royal family, which was devoutly Catholic, continued to spend lavishly on art.

- Spanish artists eagerly embraced the drama and emotionalism of Italian Baroque art. Scenes of death and martyrdom were popular in Counter-Reformation Spain. Painters such as José de Ribera and Francisco de Zurbarán adopted Caravaggio's lighting and realism to produce moving images of martyred saints.

- The greatest Spanish Baroque artist was Diego Velázquez, court painter to Philip IV. Velázquez depicted themes ranging from genre and religious subjects to royal portraits and historical events, such as *Surrender of Breda*. His masterwork, *Las Meninas*, is extraordinarily complex and mixes real spaces, mirrored spaces, picture spaces, and pictures within pictures. It is a celebration of the art of painting itself.

- The paintings, sculptures, and buildings of 17th-century Spain profoundly influenced the art and architecture of the Spanish colonies in the Western Hemisphere, but the buildings of New Spain—for example, the Church of the Jesuits in Cuzco—have no close parallels in Europe.

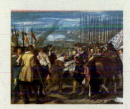

Velázquez, *Surrender of Breda*, 1634–1635

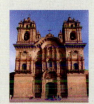

Church of the Jesuits, Cuzco, 1650–1668

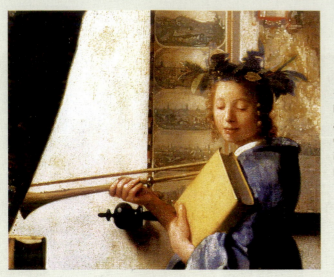

25-1a Vermeer's model wears a laurel wreath and holds a trumpet and book, traditional attributes of Clio, the muse of history. The light illuminating her may allude to the light of artistic inspiration.

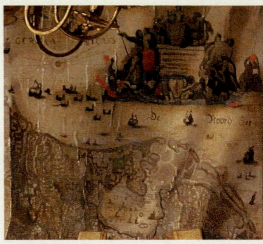

▲ 25-1b Proud Dutch patrons adorned their homes with worldly goods, including maps of the newly independent United Provinces of the Netherlands, and domestic scenes became a popular painting genre.

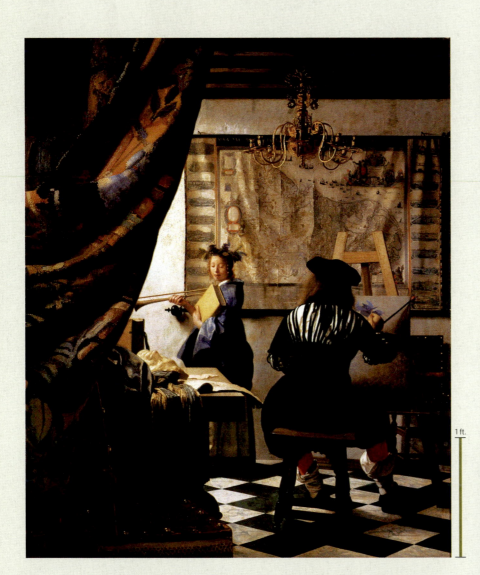

25-1 Jan Vermeer, *Allegory of the Art of Painting*, 1670–1675. Oil on canvas, 4' 4" × 3' 8". Kunsthistorisches Museum, Vienna.

1 ft.

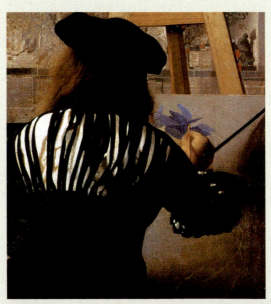

▲ 25-1c Usually interpreted as an allegory of the art of painting inspired by history, this canvas shows Vermeer at work with his back to the viewer, dressed in clothing reminiscent of historical Burgundian attire.

The Baroque in Northern Europe

THE ART OF PAINTING IN A DUTCH HOME

In 1648, after decades of continuous border skirmishes with the Spaniards, the northern Netherlands achieved official recognition as the United Provinces of the Netherlands (the Dutch Republic; MAP 25-1, page 737). The new independent republic owed its ascendance largely to its success in international trade. Dutch ships laden with goods roamed the world, sailing as far as North and South America, western Africa, China, Japan, and the Pacific islands, spreading prosperity to a greatly expanded middle class.

Although steeped in the morality and propriety central to the Calvinist ethic, members of the Dutch middle class sought ways to announce their success and newly acquired status. House furnishings, paintings, tapestries, and porcelain were among the items they collected and displayed in their homes. Those homes also became a popular subject for artworks. Many Dutch patrons collected small paintings depicting intimate domestic scenes of family members engaged in the activities of daily life. Dutch taste thus presents a sharp contrast with the Italian Baroque penchant for dazzling, large-scale ceiling frescoes and opulent room decoration (see Chapter 24). Indeed, the stylistic, as opposed to the chronological, designation "Baroque" is ill suited to these 17th-century northern European artworks.

The leading Dutch painter of interior scenes was JAN VERMEER (1632–1675), whose most complex and intriguing painting is *Allegory of the Art of Painting* (FIG. 25-1). The artist himself appears in the painting, with his back to the viewer and dressed in clothing reminiscent of historical Burgundian attire. He is hard at work on a painting of the model standing before him. She wears a laurel wreath and holds a trumpet and book, traditional attributes of Clio, the muse of history. The map of the provinces (an increasingly common wall adornment in Dutch homes) on the back wall serves as yet another reference to history.

As in many of Vermeer's domestic scenes, the viewer is outside the space of the action, looking in through the drawn curtain, which also separates the artist in his studio from the rest of the house. Some art historians have suggested that the light radiating from an unseen window on the left, illuminating both the model and the canvas being painted, alludes to the light of artistic inspiration. Accordingly, many scholars have interpreted this painting as an allegory—a reference to painting inspired by history. Vermeer's mother-in-law confirmed this allegorical reading in 1677 when, after Vermeer's death, 26 of his works were scheduled for sale to pay his widow's debts. In her written claim to retain the painting for herself, she described the painting as "the piece . . . wherein the Art of Painting is portrayed."[1]

WAR AND TRADE IN NORTHERN EUROPE

During the 17th and early 18th centuries, numerous geopolitical shifts occurred in Europe as the fortunes of individual countries rose and fell. Pronounced political and religious friction resulted in widespread unrest and warfare. Indeed, between 1562 and 1721, all of Europe was at peace for a mere four years. The major conflict of this period was the Thirty Years' War (1618–1648), which ensnared Spain, France, Sweden, Denmark, the Netherlands, Germany, Austria, Poland, the Ottoman Empire, and the Holy Roman Empire. Although the outbreak of the war had its roots in the conflict between militant Catholics and militant Protestants, the driving force quickly shifted to secular, dynastic, and nationalistic concerns. Among the major political entities vying for expanded power and authority in Europe were the Bourbon dynasty of France and the Habsburg dynasties of Spain and the Holy Roman Empire. The war, which concluded with the Treaty of Westphalia in 1648, was largely responsible for the political restructuring of Europe (MAP 25-1, page 737). As a result, the United Provinces of the Netherlands (the Dutch Republic), Sweden, and France expanded their authority. Spanish and Danish power diminished. In addition to reconfiguring territorial boundaries, the Treaty of Westphalia in essence granted freedom of religious choice throughout Europe. This treaty thus marked the abandonment of the idea of a united Christian Europe, and accepted the practical realities of secular political systems. The building of today's nation-states was emphatically under way.

The 17th century also brought heightened economic competition to Europe. Much of the foundation for worldwide mercantilism—extensive voyaging and geographic exploration, improved mapmaking, and advances in shipbuilding—had been laid in the previous century. In the 17th century, however, changes in financial systems, lifestyles, and trading patterns, along with expanding colonialism, fueled the creation of a worldwide marketplace. The Dutch founded the Bank of Amsterdam in 1609, which eventually became the center of European transfer banking. By establishing a system in which merchant firms held money on account, the bank relieved traders of having to transport precious metals as payment. Trading practices became more complex. Rather than simple reciprocal trading, triangular trade (trade among three parties) facilitated access to a larger pool of desirable goods. Exposure to an ever-growing array of goods affected European diets and lifestyles. Tea (from China) and, later, coffee (from island colonies) became popular beverages over the course of the 17th century. Equally explosive was the growth of sugar use. Sugar, tobacco, and rice were slave crops, and the slave trade expanded to meet the demand for these goods. Traders captured and enslaved Africans and shipped them to European colonies and the Americas to provide the requisite labor force for producing these commodities.

The resulting worldwide mercantile system permanently changed the face of Europe. The prosperity that international trade generated affected social and political relationships, necessitating new rules of etiquette and careful diplomacy. With increased disposable income, more of the newly wealthy spent money on art, significantly expanding the market for artworks, especially small-scale paintings for private homes, the specialty of Jan Vermeer (FIG. 25-1), among other leading artists of the era.

FLANDERS

In the 16th century, the Netherlands had come under the crown of Habsburg Spain when Emperor Charles V retired, leaving the Spanish kingdoms, their Italian and American possessions, and the Netherlandish provinces to his only legitimate son, Philip II (r. 1556–1598). (Charles bestowed his imperial title and German lands on his brother.) Philip's repressive measures against the Protestants led the northern provinces to break from Spain and establish the Dutch Republic. The southern provinces remained under Spanish control and retained Catholicism as their official religion. The political distinction between modern Holland and Belgium more or less reflects this original separation, which in the 17th century signaled not only religious but also artistic differences.

Painting

The major artistic medium of 17th-century Flanders (the Spanish Netherlands) was oil painting, as during the Renaissance (see "Oil Painting," page 559). Flemish Baroque painters retained close connections to the Baroque art of Catholic Europe. In contrast, the Dutch schools of painting developed their own subjects and styles, consistent with their reformed religion and the new political, social, and economic structure of the Dutch Republic.

PETER PAUL RUBENS The greatest 17th-century Flemish painter was PETER PAUL RUBENS (1577–1640), a towering figure in the history of Western art. Rubens built on the innovations of the Italian Renaissance and Baroque masters to formulate the first truly pan-European painting style. Rubens's art is an original and powerful synthesis of the manners of many masters, especially Michelangelo, Titian, Carracci, and Caravaggio. His style had wide appeal, and his influence was international. Among the most learned individuals of his time, Rubens possessed an aristocratic education and a courtier's manner, diplomacy, and tact, which, with his facility for language, made him the associate of princes and scholars. He became court painter to the dukes of Mantua (descended from Mantegna's patrons), friend of King Philip IV (r. 1621–1665) of Spain and his adviser on collecting art, painter to Charles I (r. 1625–1649) of England and Marie de' Medici (1573–1642) of France, and permanent court

THE BAROQUE IN NORTHERN EUROPE

1600–1625
- Peter Paul Rubens is the leading painter in Catholic Flanders
- The founding of the Bank of Amsterdam in 1609 initiates an era of Dutch preeminence in international trade
- In the northern Netherlands, Calvinist patrons favor genre scenes, portraits, and still lifes

1625–1650
- Frans Hals achieves renown for his group portraits of Dutch burghers
- Rembrandt, the foremost Dutch Baroque painter, is also a master of etching
- The Treaty of Westphalia concludes the Thirty Years' War in 1648

1650–1675
- Jacob van Ruisdael and other Dutch artists specialize in landscape painting
- Jan Vermeer uses a camera obscura as an aid in painting domestic interiors
- Nicolas Poussin champions classical "grand manner" painting in Rome

1675–1700
- Louis XIV, the Sun King, builds a grandiose palace and garden complex at Versailles
- Sir Christopher Wren designs Saint Paul's Cathedral in London

painter to the Spanish governors of Flanders. Rubens also won the confidence of his royal patrons in matters of state, and they often entrusted him with diplomatic missions of the highest importance.

To produce a steady stream of paintings for a rich and powerful international clientele, Rubens employed scores of assistants. He also became a highly successful art dealer, buying and selling contemporary artworks and classical antiquities for royal and aristocratic clients throughout Europe, who competed with one another in amassing vast collections of paintings and sculptures. One of those collections became the subject of a painting (FIG. **25-1A**) by Rubens and JAN BRUEGEL THE ELDER (1568–1625). Rubens's many enterprises made him a rich man, able to afford a magnificent townhouse in Antwerp and a castle in the countryside.

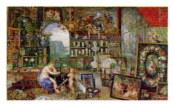
⤴ **25-1A** BRUEGHEL and RUBENS, *Allegory of Sight*, ca. 1617–1618.

Rubens, like Raphael, was a successful and renowned artist, a consort of kings, a shrewd man of the world, and a learned philosopher.

ELEVATION OF THE CROSS When he was 23 years old, Rubens departed Flanders for Italy and remained there from 1600 until 1608. During these years, he studied the works of Italian Renaissance and Baroque masters and laid the foundations of his mature style. Shortly after returning home, he painted *Elevation of the Cross* (FIG. **25-2**) for the church of Saint Walburga in Antwerp. Later moved to the city's cathedral, the altarpiece in the form of a triptych is one of numerous commissions for religious works that Rubens received at this time. By investing in sacred art, Flemish churches sought to affirm their allegiance to Catholicism and Spanish Habsburg rule after a period of Protestant iconoclastic fervor in the region.

Rubens's interest in Italian art, especially the works of Michelangelo and Caravaggio, is evident in the Saint Walburga triptych. The choice of this episode from the passion cycle provided Rubens with the opportunity to depict heavily muscled men in unusual poses straining to lift the heavy cross with Christ's body nailed to it. Here, as in his *Lion Hunt* (FIG. I-13), Rubens, deeply impressed by Michelangelo's heroic twisting sculpted and painted nude male figures, showed his prowess in representing foreshortened anatomy and the contortions of violent action. Rubens placed the body of Christ on the cross as a diagonal that cuts dynamically across the picture while inclining back into it. The whole composition seethes with a power that comes from strenuous exertion, from elastic human sinew taut with effort. The tension is emotional as well as physical, as reflected not only in Christ's face but also in the features

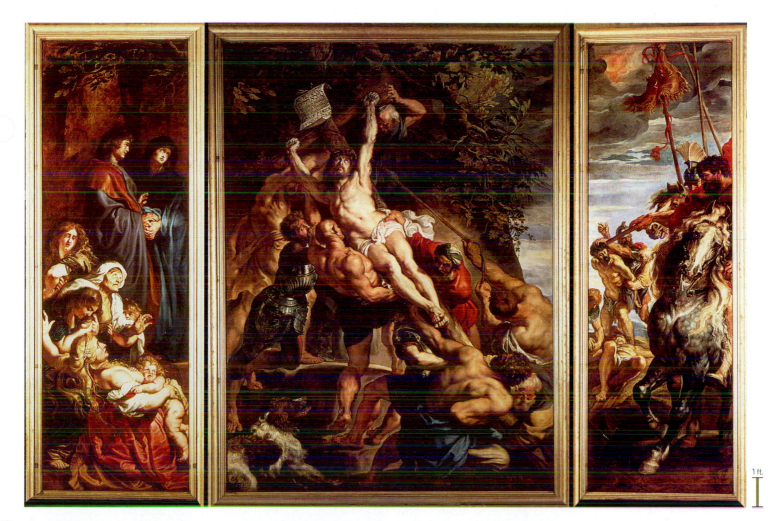

25-2 PETER PAUL RUBENS, *Elevation of the Cross*, from Saint Walburga, Antwerp, 1610. Oil on wood, 15' 1$\frac{7}{8}$" × 11' 1$\frac{1}{2}$" (center panel), 15' 1$\frac{7}{8}$" × 4' 11" (each wing). Antwerp Cathedral, Antwerp.

In this triptych, Rubens explored foreshortened anatomy and violent action. The whole composition seethes with a power that comes from heroic exertion. The tension is emotional as well as physical.

1 ft.

of his followers. Bright high-lights and areas of deep shadow inspired by Caravaggio's tenebrism (see page 715), hallmarks of Rubens's work at this stage of his career, enhance the drama.

Although Rubens later developed a much subtler coloristic style in paintings such as *Garden of Love* (FIG. **25-2A**),

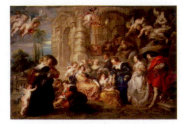

25-2A RUBENS, *Garden of Love,* 1630–1632.

the human body in action, draped or undraped, male or female, remained the focus of his art. This interest, combined with his voracious intellect, led Rubens to copy the works of classical antiquity and of the Italian masters. During his last two years in Rome, Rubens made many black-chalk drawings of great artworks, including figures in Michelangelo's Sistine Chapel frescoes (FIG. 22-17) and the ancient marble group (FIG. 5-89) of Laocoön and his two sons. In a Latin treatise he wrote titled *De imitatione statuarum* (*On the Imitation of Statues*), Rubens stated: "I am convinced that in order to achieve the highest perfection one needs a full understanding

ARTISTS ON ART
Rubens on *Consequences of War*

In the ancient and medieval worlds, artists rarely wrote commentaries on the works they produced. (The Greek sculptor Polykleitos is a notable exception; see "Polykleitos's Prescription for the Perfect Statue," page 129.) Beginning with the Renaissance, however, the increased celebrity that artists enjoyed and the ready availability of paper encouraged artists to record their intentions in letters to friends and patrons.

In March 1638, Peter Paul Rubens wrote a letter to Justus Sustermans (1597–1681), court painter of Grand Duke Ferdinando II de' Medici of Tuscany, explaining his *Consequences of War* (FIG. 25-3) and his attitude toward the European military conflicts of his day.

> The principal figure is Mars, who has left the open temple of Janus (which in time of peace, according to Roman custom, remained closed) and rushes forth with shield and blood-stained sword, threatening the people with great disaster. He pays little heed to Venus, his mistress, who, accompanied by Amors and Cupids, strives with caresses and embraces to hold him. From the other side, Mars is dragged forward by the Fury Alekto, with a torch in her hand. Near by are monsters personifying Pestilence and Famine, those inseparable partners of War. On the ground, turning her back, lies a woman with a broken lute, representing Harmony, which is incom-

patible with the discord of War. There is also a mother with her child in her arms, indicating that fecundity, procreation and charity are thwarted by War, which corrupts and destroys everything. In addition, one sees an architect thrown on his back, with his instruments in his hand, to show that which in time of peace is constructed for the use and ornamentation of the City, is hurled to the ground by the force of arms and falls to ruin. I believe, if I remember rightly, that you will find on the ground, under the feet of Mars a book and a drawing on paper, to imply that he treads underfoot all the arts and letters. There ought also to be a bundle of darts or arrows, with the band which held them together undone; these when bound form the symbol of Concord. Beside them is the caduceus and an olive branch, attribute of Peace; these are also cast aside. That grief-stricken woman clothed in black, with torn veil, robbed of all her jewels and other ornaments, is the unfortunate Europe who, for so many years now, has suffered plunder, outrage, and misery, which are so injurious to everyone that it is unnecessary to go into detail. Europe's attribute is the globe, borne by a small angel or genius, and surmounted by the cross, to symbolize the Christian world.*

Given the allegorical complexity of *Consequences of War*, the compositional unity and unbridled energy of the personified figures in the painting are all the more remarkable.

*Translated by Kristin Lohse Belkin, *Rubens* (London: Phaidon, 1998), 288–289.

25-3 PETER PAUL RUBENS, *Consequences of War*, 1638–1639. Oil on canvas, 6' 9" × 11' 3$\frac{7}{8}$". Galleria Palatina, Palazzo Pitti, Florence.

Since the Renaissance, artists have left behind many letters shedding light on their lives and work. In a 1638 letter, Rubens explained the meaning of each figure in this allegorical painting.

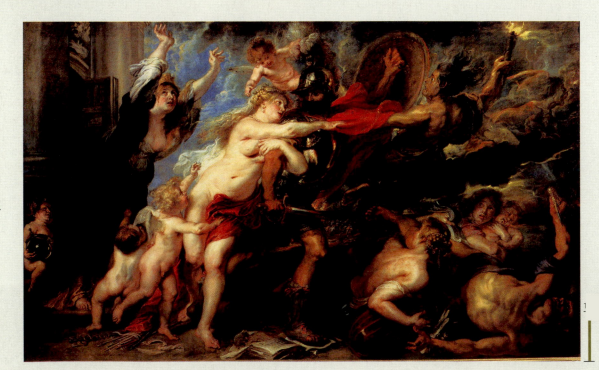

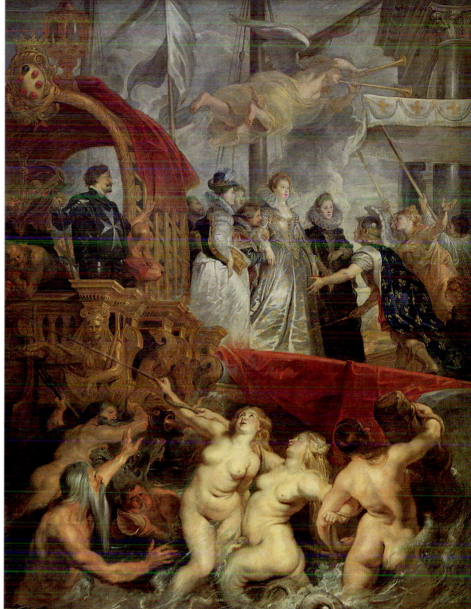

25-4 PETER PAUL RUBENS, *Arrival of Marie de' Medici at Marseilles*, from the Luxembourg Palace, Paris, France, 1622–1625. Oil on canvas, 12' 11½" × 9' 7". Musée du Louvre, Paris.

Rubens painted 24 large canvases glorifying Marie de' Medici's career. In this historical-allegorical picture of robust figures in an opulent setting, the sea and sky rejoice at the queen's arrival in France.

1 ft.

of the [ancient] statues, indeed a complete absorption in them; but one must make judicious use of them and before all avoid the effect of stone."[2]

CONSEQUENCES OF WAR Once Rubens established his reputation, commissions from kings, queens, dukes, and other elite patrons throughout Europe soon followed. One of these commissions was *Consequences of War* (FIG. 25-3), which Rubens painted in 1638 for Ferdinando II de' Medici, the grand duke of Tuscany (r. 1621–1670). Like *Elevation of the Cross* (FIG. 25-2), *Consequences of War* is a chaotic scene filled with twisting, straining, foreshortened male and female bodies, but Rubens used the commission from the Medici duke as an opportunity to express his desire for peace in an age when war was constant. *Consequences of War* is a commentary on the Thirty Years' War (see "Rubens on *Consequences of War*," page 734).

MARIE DE' MEDICI Rubens's interaction with royalty and aristocracy provided the Flemish master with an understanding of the ostentation and spectacle of Baroque (particularly Italian) art that appealed to the wealthy and privileged. Rubens, the born courtier, reveled in the pomp and majesty of royalty. Likewise, those in power embraced the lavish spectacle that served the Catholic Church so well in Italy. The magnificence and splendor of Baroque imagery reinforced the authority and right to rule of the highborn. Among Rubens's royal patrons was Marie de' Medici, a member of the famous Florentine banking family and widow of Henry IV (r. 1589–1610), the first Bourbon king of France. She commissioned Rubens to paint a series of huge canvases memorializing and glorifying her career. Between 1622 and 1626, Rubens, working with amazing creative energy, produced with the aid of his many assistants 21 historical-allegorical pictures and three portraits designed to hang in the queen's new palace, the Luxembourg, in Paris. (Today, they are on display in a huge exhibition hall in the Louvre, the former palace of the kings of France.) Remarkably, each of the paintings, although conceived as an instrument of royal propaganda to flatter the queen and impress her subjects and foreign envoys, is also a great work of art—a supreme testimony to Rubens's skill and the talents of his small army of assistants.

In *Arrival of Marie de' Medici at Marseilles* (FIG. **25-4**), a 13-foot-tall tableau that may be the best of the series, Marie disembarks at that southern French port after her sea voyage from Italy. An allegorical personification of France, draped in a cloak decorated with the *fleur-de-lis* (the floral symbol of French royalty; compare FIG. 25-24), welcomes her. The sea and sky rejoice at the queen's safe arrival. Neptune and the Nereids (daughters of the sea god Nereus) salute her, and the winged and trumpeting personified Fame swoops overhead. Conspicuous in the galley's opulently carved stern-castle, under the Medici coat of arms, stands the imperious commander of the vessel, the only immobile figure in the composition. In black and silver, this figure makes a sharp accent amid the swirling ivory, gold, and red brushstrokes. Rubens enriched the surfaces with a decorative splendor that pulls the whole composition together. The audacious vigor that customarily enlivens the painter's figures, beginning with the muscle-bound twisting sea creatures, vibrates through the entire design.

ANTHONY VAN DYCK Most of the leading painters of the next generation in Flanders were at one time trained or employed in Rubens's studio. The master's most famous pupil was ANTHONY VAN DYCK (1599–1641). Early on, the younger man, unwilling to be overshadowed by Rubens's undisputed stature, left his native

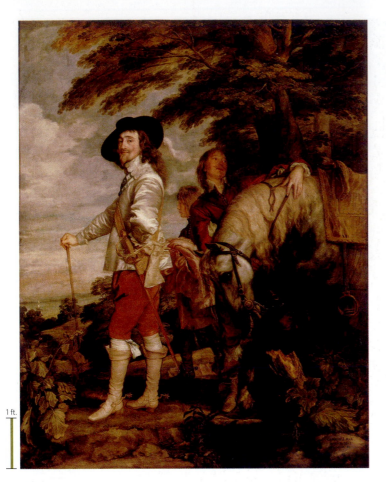

25-5 ANTHONY VAN DYCK, *Charles at the Hunt*, ca. 1635. Oil on canvas, 8' 11" × 6' 11½". Musée du Louvre, Paris.

Van Dyck specialized in court portraiture. In this painting, he depicted the absolutist monarch Charles I at a sharp angle so that the king, a short man, appears to be looking down at the viewer.

Antwerp for Genoa and then London, where he became court portraitist to Charles I and was awarded a knighthood. Although Van Dyck created dramatic compositions of high quality, his specialty became the portrait. He developed a courtly manner of great elegance that influenced many artists throughout Europe and resounded in English portrait painting well into the 19th century.

In one of his finest works, *Charles I at the Hunt* (FIG. **25-5**), the ill-fated English king stands on a hillock with the Thames River in the background. An equerry and a page attend him. The portrait is a stylish image of relaxed authority, as if the king is out for a casual ride in his park, but no one can mistake the regal poise and the air of

25-6 CLARA PEETERS, *Still Life with Flowers, Goblet, Dried Fruit, and Pretzels*, 1611. Oil on panel, 1' 7¾" × 2' 1¼". Museo del Prado, Madrid.

Peeters was a pioneer of still-life painting. In this breakfast piece, she reveals her virtuosity in depicting a variety of objects. She laid the groundwork for many Dutch still-life painters.

absolute authority that Charles's Parliament resented and was soon to rise against. Here, the king turns his back on his attendants as he surveys his domain. Van Dyck's placement of the monarch is exceedingly artful. He stands off center, but as the sole figure seen against the sky and with the branches of the trees pointing to him, he is the immediate focus of the viewer's attention, whose gaze the king returns. In this masterful composition, Van Dyck also managed to make Charles I, who was of short stature, seem taller than his attendants and even his horse. The painter also portrayed the king looking down on the observer, befitting his exalted position.

CLARA PEETERS Some 17th-century Flemish artists specialized in still-life painting, as did Sánchez Cotán (FIG. 24-25) in Spain. A pioneer of this genre was CLARA PEETERS (1594–ca. 1657), a native of Antwerp who spent time in Holland and laid the groundwork for Pieter Claesz (FIG. 25-21), Willem Kalf (FIG. 25-22), Rachel Ruysch (FIG. 25-23), and other Dutch masters of still-life painting. Peeters won renown for her depictions of food and flowers together, and for still lifes featuring bread and fruit, known as *breakfast pieces*. In *Still Life with Flowers, Goblet, Dried Fruit, and Pretzels* (FIG. **25-6**), Peeters's considerable skills are evident. One of a series of four paintings, each of which depicts a typical early-17th-century meal, this breakfast piece reveals Peeters's virtuosity in depicting a wide variety of objects convincingly, from the smooth, reflective surfaces of the glass and silver goblets to the soft petals of the blooms in the vase. Peeters often painted the objects in her still lifes against a dark background, thereby negating any sense of deep space (compare FIG. 24-25). In this breakfast piece, she enhanced the sense of depth in the foreground by placing the leaves of the flower on the stone ledge as though they were encroaching into the viewer's space.

DUTCH REPUBLIC

With the founding of the Bank of Amsterdam in 1609, Amsterdam emerged as the financial center of the Continent. In the 17th century, the city had the highest per capita income in Europe. The Dutch economy also benefited enormously from the country's expertise on the open seas, which facilitated establishing lucrative

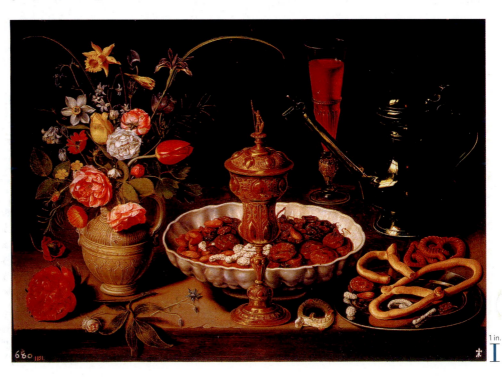

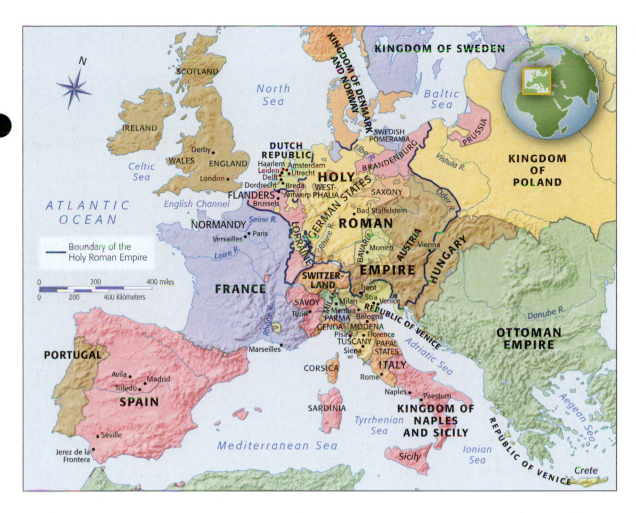

MAP 25-1 Europe in 1648 after the Treaty of Westphalia.

trade routes to ports as far away as Japan, Africa, and South America (see page 748). Due to this prosperity and in the absence of an absolute ruler, political power increasingly passed into the hands of a wealthy class of merchants and manufacturers, especially in cities such as Amsterdam, Haarlem, and Delft (MAP 25-1). All of these bustling cities were located in Holland (the largest of the seven United Provinces), which explains why many historians informally use the name "Holland" to refer to the entire country.

Ter Brugghen and van Honthorst

Religious differences were a major consideration during the northern Netherlands' insistent quest for independence in the 16th and early 17th centuries. Whereas Spain and the southern Netherlands were Catholic, the people of the northern Netherlands were predominantly Protestant. The prevailing Calvinism demanded a puritanical rejection of art in churches, and thus artists produced relatively little religious art in the Dutch Republic at this time (especially compared with the volume of commissions created in the wake of the Counter-Reformation in areas dominated by Catholicism; see "The Council of Trent," page 642, and "Middle-Class Patronage," page 738).

HENDRICK TER BRUGGHEN Some artists in the Dutch Republic did produce religious art, however. HENDRICK TER BRUGGHEN (1588–1629) of Utrecht, for example, painted *Calling of Saint Matthew* (FIG. 25-7) in 1621 after returning from a trip to Italy, selecting as his subject a theme Caravaggio had painted (FIG. 24-18) for the church of San

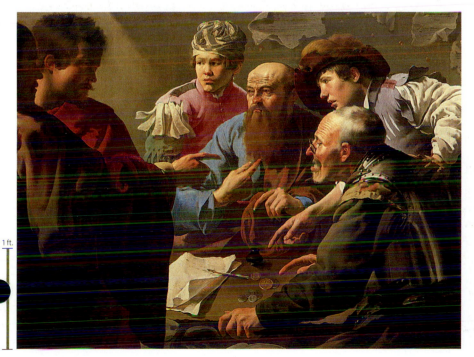

25-7 HENDRICK TER BRUGGHEN, *Calling of Saint Matthew*, 1621. Oil on canvas, 3' 4" × 4' 6". Centraal Museum, Utrecht.

Although middle-class patrons in the Protestant Dutch Republic preferred genre scenes, still lifes, and portraits, some artists, including Hendrick ter Brugghen, also painted religious scenes.

Middle-Class Patronage and the Art Market in the Dutch Republic

Throughout history, the wealthy have been the most avid art collectors. Indeed, the money necessary to commission major artworks from leading artists can be considerable. During the 17th century in the Dutch Republic, however, the prosperity that a large proportion of the population enjoyed expanded the range of art patrons significantly. As a result, one distinguishing hallmark of Dutch art production during this period was how it catered to the tastes of a middle-class audience, broadly defined. An aristocracy and an upper class of shipowners, rich businesspeople, high-ranking officers, and directors of large companies still existed, and these groups continued to be major patrons of the arts. But as the Dutch economy expanded, new patrons—traders, craftspeople, bureaucrats, and soldiers—also commissioned and collected art.

Although the financial success that the middle class increasingly enjoyed resulted in sharply higher investment in home furnishings and art (see "The Art of Painting in a Dutch Home," page 731), the Calvinist disdain for excessive ostentation led these new Dutch collectors to favor small, low-key works—portraits of bourgeois men and women (FIGS. 25-9, 25-10, 25-12, and 25-13), still lifes (FIGS. 25-21, 25-22, and 25-23), genre scenes (FIGS. 25-8, 25-19, and 25-20), and landscapes (FIGS. 25-17, 25-18, 25-18A, and 25-18B). This focus contrasted with the Italian Baroque penchant for gigantic ceiling frescoes and oil paintings with religious subjects (see Chapter 24). Stylistically, the art of northern Europe, although also called "Baroque" by art historians, differs markedly from Italian Baroque art.

It is risky to generalize about the spending and collecting habits of the Dutch middle class, but probate records, contracts, and archived inventories reveal some interesting facts. These records suggest that an individual earning between 1,500 and 3,000 guilders a year could live quite comfortably. A house could be purchased for 1,000 guilders.

Another 1,000 guilders could buy all the necessary furnishings for a middle-class home, including a significant amount of art, particularly paintings. Although there was, of course, considerable variation in prices, many artworks were very affordable. Prints, for example, were extremely cheap because of the high number of copies artists produced of each picture. Paintings of interior and genre scenes were relatively inexpensive in 17th-century Holland, perhaps costing one or two guilders each. Small landscapes fetched between three and four guilders. Commissioned portraits were the most costly. The size of the work and quality of the frame (see "Framed Paintings," page 564), as well as the reputation of the artist, were other factors in determining the price of a painting, regardless of the subject.

With the exception of portraits, Dutch artists produced most of their paintings for an anonymous market, hoping to appeal to a wide audience. To ensure success, artists in the United Provinces adapted to the changed conditions of art production and sales. They marketed their paintings in many ways, selling their works directly to buyers who visited their studios and through art dealers, exhibitions, fairs, auctions, and even lotteries. Because of the uncertainty of these sales mechanisms (as opposed to the certainty of an ironclad contract for a commission from a church, king, or duke), artists became more responsive to market demands. Specialization became common among Dutch artists. For example, painters might limit their practice to portraits, still lifes, or landscapes—the most popular genres among middle-class patrons.

Artists did not always sell their paintings. Frequently, they used their work to pay off loans or debts. Tavern debts, in particular, could be settled with paintings, which may explain why many art dealers, including Jan Vermeer (FIG. 25-1) and his father before him, were also innkeepers. This connection between art dealing and other businesses eventually solidified, and innkeepers, for example, often would have art exhibitions in their taverns hoping to make a sale. The institutions of today's open art market—dealers, galleries, auctions, and estate sales—owe their establishment to the emergence in the 17th century of a prosperous middle class in the Dutch Republic.

25-8 GERRIT VAN HONTHORST, *Supper Party*, 1620. Oil on canvas, 4' 8" × 7'. Galleria degli Uffizi, Florence.

Genre scenes were popular subjects among middle-class Dutch patrons. Gerrit van Honthorst's *Supper Party* may also have served as a Calvinist warning against the sins of gluttony and lust.

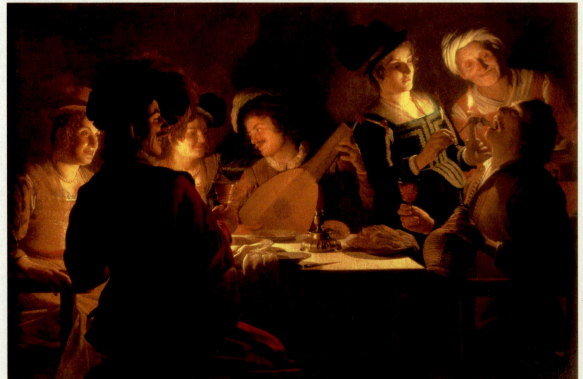

1 ft.

Luigi dei Francesi in Rome. The moment of the narrative chosen and the naturalistic depiction of the figures echo Caravaggio's work. But although ter Brugghen was an admirer of the Italian master, he dispensed with Caravaggio's stark contrasts of dark and light and instead presented the viewer with a more colorful palette of soft tints. Further, the Dutch painter compressed the figures into a small but well-lit space, creating an intimate effect compared with Caravaggio's more spacious setting.

MERCANTILIST PATRONAGE Given the absence of an authoritative ruler and the Calvinist concern for the potential misuse of religious art, commissions from royalty or the Catholic Church, prominent in the art of other European countries, were uncommon in the United Provinces. With the new prosperity, however, an expanding class of merchants with different tastes emerged as art patrons. In contrast to Italian, Spanish, and Flemish Baroque art, 17th-century Dutch art centered on genre scenes, landscapes, portraits of middle-class men and women, and still lifes, all of which appealed to the newly prosperous Dutch merchants (see "Middle-Class Patronage and the Art Market in the Dutch Republic," page 738).

GERRIT VAN HONTHORST Typical of 17th-century Dutch genre scenes is *Supper Party* (FIG. **25-8**) by GERRIT VAN HONTHORST (1590–1656). In this painting, van Honthorst presented an informal gathering of unidealized figures. While a musician serenades the group, his companions delight in watching a young woman feeding a piece of chicken to a man whose hands are both occupied—one holds a jug and the other a glass. Van Honthorst spent several years in Italy, and while there he carefully studied Caravag-

gio's work, as did fellow Utrecht painter Hendrick ter Brugghen. The Italian artist's influence surfaces in the mundane tavern setting and the nocturnal lighting of *Supper Party*. Fascinated by nighttime effects, van Honthorst frequently placed a hidden light source in his pictures and used it as a pretext to work with dramatic and starkly contrasting dark and light effects.

Seemingly lighthearted genre scenes were popular in Baroque Holland, but Dutch viewers could also interpret them moralistically. For example, *Supper Party* can be read as a warning against the sins of gluttony (represented by the man on the right) and lust (the woman feeding the glutton is, in all likelihood, a prostitute with her aged procuress at her side). Or perhaps the painting represents the loose companions of the Prodigal Son (Luke 15:13; see FIG. 25-14)—panderers and prostitutes drinking, singing, strumming, and laughing. Strict Dutch Calvinists no doubt approved of such interpretations. Others simply took delight in the immediacy of the scenes or the skill of artists such as van Honthorst.

Hals and Leyster

Many Dutch artists excelled in painting portraits, which were in high demand. Two of the most important portrait specialists were FRANS HALS (ca. 1581–1666), the leading painter in Haarlem, and Judith Leyster.

FRANS HALS In addition to individual patrons, groups of Dutch citizens often asked Hals to paint portraits of them. Representing the members of a group, such as the Haarlem regents of an old men's home (FIG. **25-9**) or the Saint Hadrian militia (FIG. 25-10),

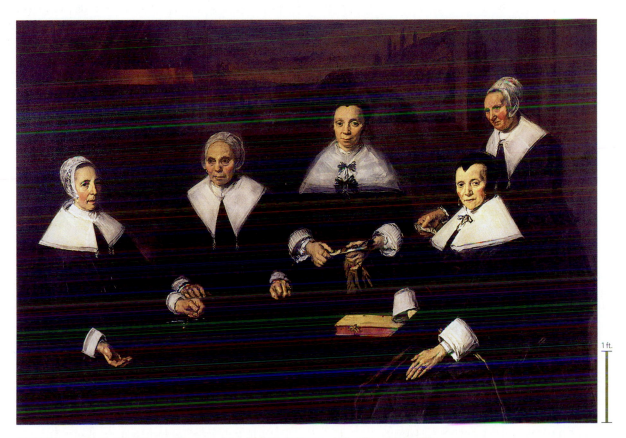

25-9 FRANS HALS, *The Women Regents of the Old Men's Home at Haarlem,* 1664. Oil on canvas, 5' 7" × 8' 2". Frans Halsmuseum, Haarlem.

Dutch women played a major role in public life as regents of charitable institutions. A stern puritanical sensibility suffuses Hals's group portrait of the regents of Haarlem's old men's home.

PROBLEMS AND SOLUTIONS
Frans Hals's Group Portraits

Portrait artists traditionally relied heavily on convention—for example, specific poses, settings, attire, and furnishings—to convey a sense of the sitter. Because the subject was usually someone of status or note, such as a pope, king, duchess, condottiere, or wealthy banker, the artist's goal was to produce an image appropriate to the subject's station in life. With the increasing number of Dutch middle-class patrons, portrait painting became more challenging. The Calvinists shunned ostentation, instead wearing subdued and dark clothing with little variation or decoration (FIG. 25-9), and the traditional conventions became inappropriate and thus unusable. Despite these difficulties, or perhaps because of them, Frans Hals produced lively portraits that seem far more relaxed than traditional formulaic portraiture. He injected an engaging spontaneity into his images and conveyed the individuality of his sitters as well. His manner of execution, using light and rapid brushstrokes, intensified the casualness, immediacy, and intimacy in his paintings. The poses of his figures, the highlights on their clothing, and their facial expression all seem instantaneously created.

Hals's most ambitious portraits reflect the widespread popularity in the Dutch Republic of very large canvases commemorating the participation of Dutch burghers in civic organizations. These commissions presented greater difficulties to the painter than requests to depict a single sitter. Hals rose to the challenge and achieved great success

with this new portrait genre. His *Archers of Saint Hadrian* (FIG. 25-10) is typical in that the subject is one of the many Dutch civic militia groups that claimed credit for liberating the Dutch Republic from Spain. As did other companies, each year the Archers met in dress uniform for a grand banquet on their saint's feast day. The celebrations sometimes lasted an entire week, prompting an ordinance limiting them to three or four days. These events often included sitting for a group portrait.

In *Archers of Saint Hadrian*, Hals attacked the problem of how to represent each militia member satisfactorily yet retain action and variety in the composition. Whereas earlier group portraits in the Netherlands were rather ordered and regimented images, Hals sought to enliven the depictions. In his portrait of the Saint Hadrian militiamen, each member is both part of the troop and an individual with unique features. The sitters' movements and moods vary markedly. Some engage the viewer directly. Others look away or at a companion. Some are stern, others animated. Each archer is equally visible and clearly recognizable. The uniformity of attire—black military dress, white ruffs, and sashes—did not deter Hals from injecting spontaneity into the work. Indeed, he used those elements to create a lively rhythm extending throughout the composition and energizing the portrait. The impromptu effect—the preservation of every detail and fleeting facial expression—is, of course, the result of careful planning. Yet Hals's vivacious brush appears to have moved instinctively, directed by a plan in his mind but not traceable in any preparatory scheme on the canvas. The result is a portrait that is less a record of "sitters posing for the painter" than it is a snapshot of a social gathering.

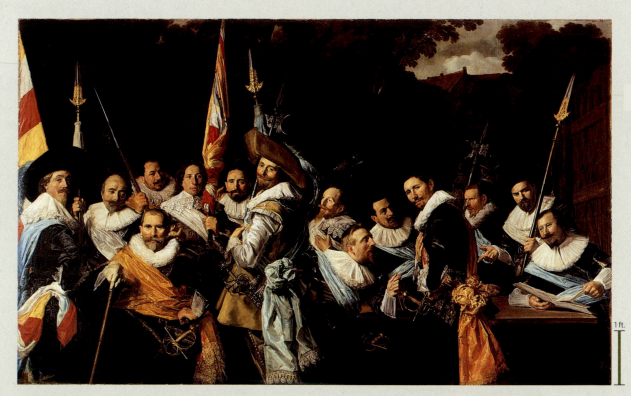

25-10 FRANS HALS, *Archers of Saint Hadrian,* ca. 1633. Oil on canvas, 6' 9" × 11'. Frans Halsmuseum, Haarlem.

In this brilliant composition, Hals succeeded in solving the problem of portraying each individual in a group portrait while retaining action and variety in the painting as a whole.

1 ft.

rather than separate individuals, presented a special problem for the painter, but Hals quickly became a master of the new genre of group portraiture (see "Frans Hals's Group Portraits," above).

Hals's *The Women Regents of the Old Men's Home at Haarlem* (FIG. 25-9) is the finest of his group portraits of Calvinist women engaged in charitable works. Although Dutch women had primary responsibility for the welfare of the family and the orderly opera-

tion of the home, they also populated the labor force in the cities. Among the more prominent roles that educated Dutch women played in public life were as regents of orphanages, hospitals, old age homes, and prisons. In Hals's portrait, the Haarlem regents sit quietly in a manner becoming devout Calvinists. Unlike the more relaxed, seemingly informal character of his other group portraits, a stern, puritanical, and composed sensibility suffuses Hals's

accents of the clothing, contributes to the painting's restraint. Both the coloration and the mood of Hals's portrait are appropriate for this commission. Recording the likenesses of the Haarlem regents called for a very different kind of portrait than those Hals made of men at festive militia banquets (FIG. 25-10).

JUDITH LEYSTER Some of Hals's followers developed thriving careers of their own as portraitists. One was JUDITH LEYSTER (1609–1660), who may not have been Hals's pupil, but was a close associate who fully absorbed the master's innovations in technique and composition. In fact, Leyster's *Self-Portrait* (FIG. 25-11) was once thought to have been painted by Hals himself. The canvas is detailed, precise, and accurate, but also imbued with the spontaneity found in Hals's works. In her self-portrait, Leyster succeeded at communicating a great deal about herself. She depicted herself as an artist, seated in front of a painting on an easel. The palette in her left hand and brush in her right announce the painting as her creation. She thus invites the viewer to evaluate her skill, which both the fiddler on the canvas and the image of herself demonstrate as considerable. Although she produced a wide range of paintings, including still lifes and floral pieces, her specialty was genre scenes such as the comic image seen on the easel. Leyster's quick smile and relaxed pose as she stops her work to meet the viewer's gaze reveal her self-assurance. Although presenting herself as an artist, Leyster did not paint herself wearing the traditional artist's smock, as her more famous contemporary Rembrandt did in his 1659–1660 self-portrait (FIG. 25-15). Her elegant attire distinguishes her socially as a member of a well-to-do family, another important aspect of Leyster's identity.

Rembrandt

REMBRANDT VAN RIJN (1606–1669), Hals's younger contemporary and the leading Dutch painter of his time, was an undisputed genius—an artist of great versatility, a master of light and shadow, and a unique interpreter of the Protestant conception of holy scripture. Born in Leiden, he moved to Amsterdam around 1631, where he could attract a more extensive clientele than possible in his native city.

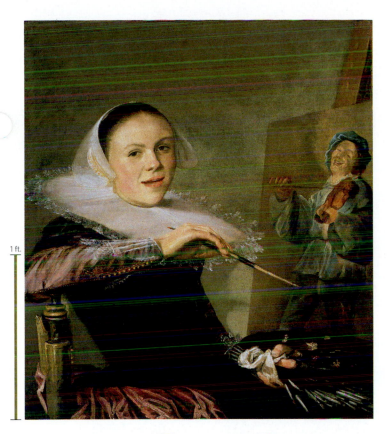

25-11 JUDITH LEYSTER, *Self-Portrait*, ca. 1630. Oil on canvas, 2′ 5 3/8″ × 2′ 1 5/8″. National Gallery of Art, Washington, D.C. (gift of Mr. and Mrs. Robert Woods Bliss).

Although presenting herself as an artist specializing in genre scenes, Leyster wears elegant attire instead of a painter's smock, placing her socially as a member of a well-to-do family.

portrayal of these regents. The women—all carefully distinguished as individuals—gaze out from the painting with expressions ranging from dour disinterest to kindly concern. The somber and virtually *monochromatic* (one-color) palette, punctuated only by the white

Rembrandt had trained as a history painter in Leiden, but in Amsterdam he immediately entered the lucrative market for portraiture and soon became renowned for that genre.

ANATOMY LESSON OF DR. TULP In a painting he completed shortly after he arrived in Amsterdam, *Anatomy Lesson of Dr. Nicolaes Tulp* (FIG. 25-12), Rembrandt deviated even further from the traditional staid group portrait than Hals. Despite Hals's determination to enliven his portraits, he still evenly spread his subjects across the canvas. In contrast, Rembrandt chose to portray the members of the surgeons' guild (who commissioned

25-12 REMBRANDT VAN RIJN, *Anatomy Lesson of Dr. Nicolaes Tulp*, 1632. Oil on canvas, 5′ 3 3/4″ × 7′ 1 1/4″. Mauritshuis, The Hague.

In this early work, Rembrandt used an unusual composition, arranging members of Amsterdam's surgeons' guild clustered on one side of the painting as they watch Dr. Tulp dissect a corpse.

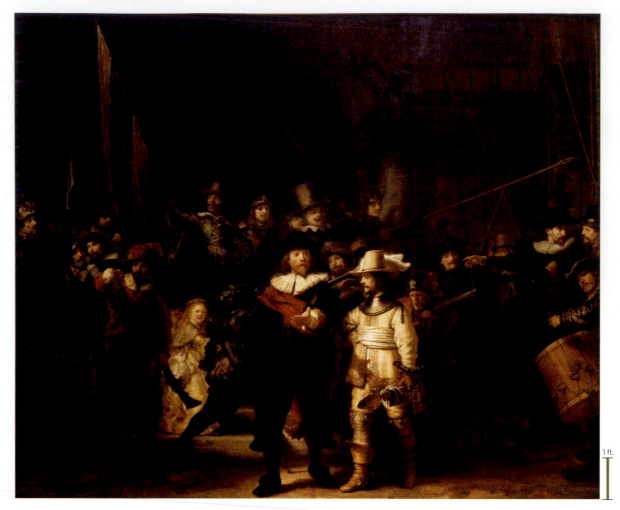

25-13 REMBRANDT VAN RIJN, *The Company of Captain Frans Banning Cocq* (*Night Watch*), from the Musketeers Hall, Amsterdam, Netherlands, 1642. Oil on canvas, 11′ 11″ × 14′ 4″ (trimmed from original size). Rijksmuseum, Amsterdam.

Rembrandt's dramatic use of light contributes to the animation of this militia group portrait in which the artist showed the company members rushing to organize themselves for a parade.

this group portrait) clustered on the painting's left side. In the foreground appears the corpse that Dr. Tulp, a noted physician, is in the act of dissecting. Rembrandt diagonally placed and foreshortened the corpse, activating the space by disrupting the strict horizontal, planar orientation typical of traditional portraiture. He depicted each of the "students" specifically, and although they wear virtually identical attire, their poses and facial expressions suggest the varying degrees of intensity with which they watch Dr. Tulp's demonstration—or ignore it. One, at the apex of Rembrandt's triangular composition of bodies, gazes at the viewer instead of at the operating table. Another directs his attention to the open book (an anatomy manual) at the cadaver's feet. Rembrandt produced this painting when he was 26 and just beginning his career. His innovative approach to group portraiture is therefore all the more noteworthy.

NIGHT WATCH Rembrandt amplified the complexity and energy of the group portrait in *The Company of Captain Frans Banning Cocq* (FIG. **25-13**), better known as *Night Watch*. This more commonly used title is a misnomer, however. The painting is not a nocturnal scene, nor are the figures portrayed posted on a watch in defense of their city. It features dramatic lighting, but the painting's darkness (which explains in part the commonly used title) is the result of the varnish the artist used, which darkened considerably over time.

It was not the painter's intention to portray his subjects moving about at night.

Night Watch was one of six paintings by different artists commissioned by various groups around 1640 for the assembly and banquet room of Amsterdam's new Musketeers Hall, the largest and most prestigious interior space in the city. From the limited information available about the commission, it appears that two officers, Captain Frans Banning Cocq and Lieutenant Willem van Ruytenburch, along with 16 members of their militia, contributed to Rembrandt's fee. The canvas also includes 16 additional figures, among them a girl just to the left of center, whom scholars have never been able to identify, despite her prominence in the composition.

Unfortunately, in 1715, when city officials moved Rembrandt's painting to Amsterdam's town hall, they trimmed it on all sides (by as much as 2 feet). Even in its truncated form, *The Company of Captain Frans Banning Cocq* is still a huge canvas (nearly 15 feet wide), but it is an incomplete record of the artist's resolution of the challenge of portraying 18 patrons at once. Rembrandt's apparent goal was to capture the excitement and frenetic activity of men preparing for a parade, and he succeeded brilliantly. Comparing this militia group portrait to Hals's *Archers of Saint Hadrian* (FIG. 25-10) reveals Rembrandt's inventiveness in enlivening what was, by then, becoming a conventional format for Dutch group portraits. Rather than present assembled men posed in orderly fashion, the younger artist chose to portray the company members rushing about in the act of organizing themselves, thereby animating the image considerably. At the same time, he managed to record the three most important stages of using a musket—loading, firing, and readying the weapon for reloading—details that must have pleased his patrons.

RETURN OF THE PRODIGAL SON The Calvinist injunction against religious art did not prevent Rembrandt from making a series of religious paintings and prints. In the Dutch Republic, paintings depicting biblical themes were not objects of devotion, but they still brought great prestige, and Rembrandt and other artists vied to demonstrate their ability to represent in dramatic new ways the stories narrated in holy scripture. One of Rembrandt's earliest biblical paintings, *Blinding of Samson* (FIG. 25-13A), reveals the young artist's debt to Rubens and Caravaggio. His mature works, however, differ markedly from the religious art of Baroque Italy and Flanders. Rembrandt had a

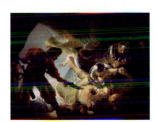

◉ **25-13A** REMBRANDT, *Blinding of Samson*, 1636.

special interest in probing the states of the human soul. The spiritual stillness of his later religious paintings is that of inward-turning contemplation, far from the choirs and trumpets and the heavenly tumult of Bernini (FIG. 24-7) or Pozzo (FIG. 24-24).

The Dutch artist's psychological insight and his profound sympathy for human affliction produced, at the end of his life, one of the most moving pictures in the history of biblical art, *Return of the Prodigal Son* (FIG. 25-14). In this Old Testament parable, the younger of two sons leaves his home and squanders his wealth on a life of sin. When he becomes poor and hungry and sees the error of his ways, he returns home. In Rembrandt's painting, the forgiving father tenderly embraces his lost son, who crouches before him in weeping contrition, while three figures, immersed to varying degrees in the soft shadows, note the lesson of mercy. The light, everywhere mingled with shadow, directs the viewer's attention by illuminating the father and son and largely veiling the witnesses (see "Rembrandt's Use of Light and Shade," below). Its focus is the beautiful, spiritual face of the old man. Secondarily, the light touches the contrasting stern face of the foremost witness. The painting demonstrates the degree to which Rembrandt developed a personal style completely in tune with the simple eloquence of the biblical passage.

MATERIALS AND TECHNIQUES
Rembrandt's Use of Light and Shade

Among the hallmarks of the style of Rembrandt van Rijn, the leading painter in the 17th-century Dutch Republic, is his masterful use of light and shade. Rembrandt's pictorial method involved refining light and shade into finer and finer nuances until they blended with one another. Earlier painters' use of abrupt lights and darks gave way, in the work of artists such as Rembrandt and Velázquez (FIGS. 24-29 to 24-31), to gradation. Although these later artists sacrificed some of the dramatic effects of sharp chiaroscuro, a greater fidelity to appearances more than offsets those sacrifices. In fact, the recording of light in small gradations is closer to reality because the eye perceives light and dark not as static but as always subtly changing.

In general, Renaissance artists represented forms and faces in a flat, neutral modeling light (even Leonardo's shading is of a standard kind). They represented the *idea* of light, rather than showed how humans perceive light. Artists such as Rembrandt discovered gradations of light and dark as well as degrees of differences in pose, in the movements of facial features, and in psychic states. They arrived at these differences optically, not conceptually or in terms of some ideal. Rembrandt found that by manipulating the direction, intensity, and distance of light and shadow, and by varying the surface texture with tactile brushstrokes, he could render subtle nuances of character and mood, both in individuals and whole scenes, as in his touching portrayal of the prodigal son's return (FIG. 25-14). He discovered for the modern world that variations of light and shade, subtly modulated, can be read as emotional differences. In the visible world, light, dark, and the wide spectrum of values between the two are charged with meanings and feelings that sometimes are independent of the shapes and figures they modify. The theater and the photographic arts have used these discoveries to great dramatic effect.

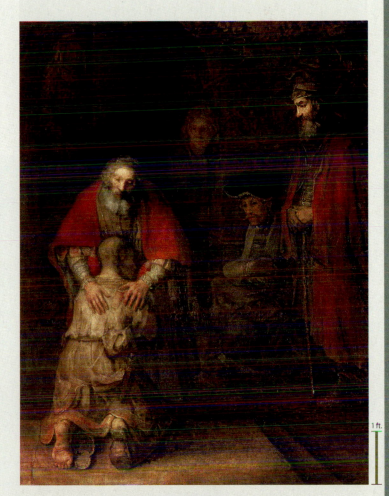

1 ft.

25-14 REMBRANDT VAN RIJN, *Return of the Prodigal Son*, ca. 1665. Oil on canvas, 8' 8" × 6' 9". State Hermitage Museum, Saint Petersburg.

In Rembrandt's moving representation of this biblical parable, light mingled with shadow directs the viewer's attention by illuminating the father and son while largely veiling the witnesses.

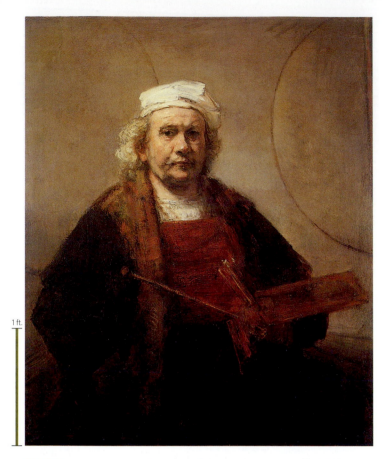

25-15 REMBRANDT VAN RIJN, *Self-Portrait,* ca. 1659–1660. Oil on canvas, 3' 8¾" × 3' 1". Kenwood House, London (Iveagh Bequest).

In this late self-portrait, Rembrandt's interest in revealing the soul is evident in the attention given to his expressive face. The controlled use of light and the nonspecific setting contribute to this focus.

SELF-PORTRAITS Rembrandt carried over the spiritual quality of his religious works into his later portraits (FIGS. **25-15** and **25-15A**) by the same means—what could be called the "psychology of light." Light and dark are not in conflict in his portraits. They are reconciled, merging softly and subtly to produce the visual equivalent of quietness. Their prevailing mood is one of tranquil meditation, of philosophical resignation, of musing recollection—indeed, a whole cluster of emotional tones heard only in silence.

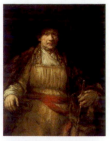

🔲 **25-15A** REMBRANDT, *Self-Portrait,* 1658.

In his self-portrait now in Kenwood House (FIG. 25-15), the light source outside the upper left of the painting bathes the painter's face in soft highlights, leaving the lower part of his body in shadow. The artist depicted himself as possessing dignity and strength, and the portrait serves as a summary of the many stylistic and professional concerns that occupied him throughout his career. Rembrandt's distinctive use of light is evident, as is the assertive brushwork suggesting his confidence and self-assurance. He presented himself as a working artist holding his brushes, palette, and maulstick (compare FIG. 23-16) and wearing his studio garb—a smock and painter's turban. The circles on the wall behind him (the subject of much scholarly debate) may allude to a legendary sign of artistic virtuosity—the ability to draw a perfect circle freehand. Rembrandt's abiding interest in revealing the human soul emerges here in his careful focus on his expressive visage. His controlled use of light and the nonspecific setting contribute to this focus.

X-rays of the painting have revealed that Rembrandt originally depicted himself in the act of painting. His final resolution, with the viewer's attention drawn to his face, produced a portrait not just of the artist but of the man as well. Indeed, Rembrandt's nearly 70 self-

25-16 REMBRANDT VAN RIJN, *Christ with the Sick around Him, Receiving the Children* (*Hundred-Guilder Print*), ca. 1649. Etching and engraving, 11" × 1' 3¼". Pierpont Morgan Library, New York.

Rembrandt's mastery of the newly perfected medium of etching is evident in his expert use of light and dark to draw attention to Christ as he preaches compassionately to the blind and lame.

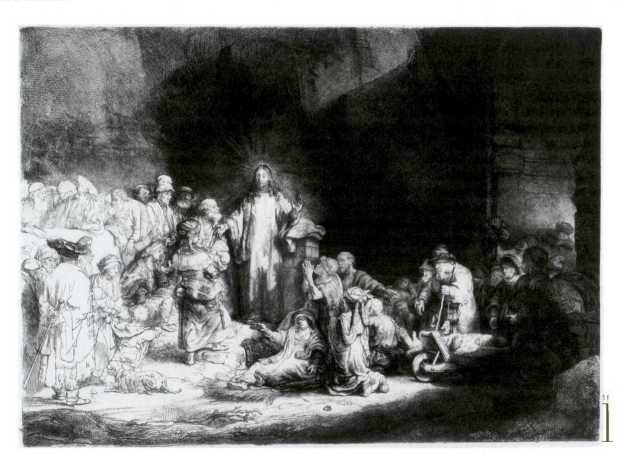

portraits in various media have no parallel in sheer quantity. They reflect the artist's deeply personal connection to his craft.

ETCHINGS Rembrandt's virtuosity also extended to the graphic media, especially etching (see "Engraving and Etching," page 578). Many printmakers adopted etching after its perfection early in the 17th century, because the technique afforded greater freedom in drawing the design than engraving did. The etcher covers a copper plate with a layer of wax or varnish, and then incises the design into this surface with a pointed tool, exposing the metal below but not cutting into its surface. Next, the artist immerses the plate in acid, which etches, or eats away, the exposed parts of the metal, acting in the same way the burin does in engraving. The wax's softness gives etchers greater carving freedom than woodcutters and engravers have working directly in more resistant wood and metal. If Rembrandt had never painted, he still would be acclaimed, as he principally was in his lifetime, for his prints. Prints were a major source of income for Rembrandt, as they were for Albrecht Dürer (see page 675), and he often reworked the plates so that they could be used to produce a new issue or edition. This constant reworking was unusual within the context of 17th-century printmaking practices.

HUNDRED-GUILDER PRINT One of Rembrandt's most celebrated graphic works is *Christ with the Sick around Him, Receiving the Children* (FIG. 25-16). Indeed, the title by which this print has been known since the early 18th century—the *Hundred-Guilder Print*— refers to the high sale price it brought during Rembrandt's lifetime. (As noted, a comfortable house could be purchased for 1,000 guilders.) *Christ with the Sick* demonstrates the artist's mastery of all aspects of the printmaker's craft, for Rembrandt used both engraving and etching to depict the figures and the setting. As in his other religious works, Rembrandt suffused this print with a deep and abiding piety, presenting the viewer not the celestial triumph of the Catholic Church but the humanity and humility of Jesus.

Christ appears in the center preaching compassionately to, and simultaneously blessing, the blind, the lame, and the young, who are spread throughout the composition in a dazzling array of standing, kneeling, and lying positions. Also present is a young man in elegant garments with his head in his hand, lamenting Christ's insistence that the wealthy need to give their possessions to the poor in order to gain entrance to Heaven. The tonal range of the print is remarkable. At the right, the figures near the city gate are in deep shadow. At the left, the figures, some rendered almost exclusively in outline, are in bright light—not the light of day but the illumination radiating from Christ himself. A second, unseen source of light comes from the right and casts the shadow of the praying man's arms and head onto Christ's tunic. Technically and in terms of its humanity, Rembrandt's *Hundred-Guilder Print* is his supreme achievement as a printmaker.

Cuyp and Ruisdael

After gaining independence from Spain, the Dutch undertook an extensive land reclamation project lasting almost a century. Dikes and drainage systems cropped up across the countryside, affecting Dutch social and economic life. The marshy and swampy nature of much of the terrain made it less desirable for large-scale exploitation, so the extensive feudal landowning system elsewhere in Europe never developed in the United Provinces. Most Dutch families owned and worked their own farms, cultivating a feeling of closeness to the land. Consequently, landscape scenes abound in 17th-century Dutch art.

AELBERT CUYP One Dutch artist who established his reputation as a specialist in landscape painting was AELBERT CUYP (ca. 1620– 1691). His works were the products of careful observation and a deep respect for and understanding of Dutch topography. *Distant View of Dordrecht, with a Milkmaid and Four Cows, and Other Figures* (FIG. 25-17) reveals Cuyp's skillful use of the oil medium to record nature, but as was the norm at the time, Cuyp painted his canvases in his studio, not outdoors. Unlike the idealized classical landscapes in many Italian Renaissance paintings, Cuyp's Dordrecht landscape is particularized. The church in the background, for example, is a faithful representation of the city's Grote Kerk (Great Church). The dairy cows, shepherds, and milkmaid in the foreground refer to a cornerstone of the Dutch economy—dairy products such as butter and cheese, the demand for which increased with the development of urban centers. The credibility of this and similar paintings rests on Cuyp's pristine rendering of each detail.

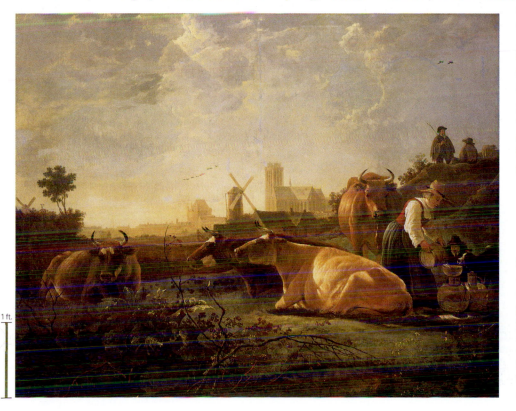

1 ft.

25-17 AELBERT CUYP, *Distant View of Dordrecht, with a Milkmaid and Four Cows, and Other Figures* (*The "Large Dort"*), late 1640s. Oil on canvas, 5' 1" × 6' 4$\frac{7}{8}$". National Gallery, London.

Unlike idealized Italian Renaissance landscapes, Cuyp's painting portrays a particular locale. The cows, shepherds, and milkmaid refer to the Dutch Republic's important dairy industry.

25-18 JACOB VAN RUISDAEL, *View of Haarlem from the Dunes at Overveen,* ca. 1670. Oil on canvas, 1' 10" × 2' 1". Mauritshuis, The Hague.

In this painting, Ruisdael succeeded in capturing a specific, realistic view of Haarlem, its windmills, and Saint Bavo church, but he also imbued the landscape with a quiet serenity approaching the spiritual.

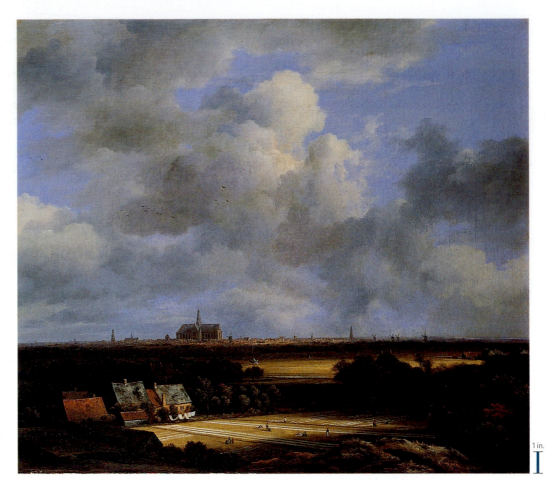

JACOB VAN RUISDAEL Depicting the Dutch landscape with precision and sensitivity was also a specialty of JACOB VAN RUISDAEL (ca. 1628–1682). In *View of Haarlem from the Dunes at Overveen* (FIG. 25-18), Ruisdael provided an overarching view of this major Dutch city. The specificity of the artist's image—the Saint Bavo church in the background, the numerous windmills that refer to the land reclamation efforts, and the figures in the foreground stretching linen to be bleached (a major industry in Haarlem)—reflects the pride Dutch painters took in recording their homeland and the activities of their fellow citizens. Nonetheless, in this painting the inhabitants and dwellings are so small that they blend into the land itself, unlike the figures in Cuyp's view of Dordrecht. Moreover, the horizon line is low, so the sky fills almost three-quarters of the canvas surface, and the sun illuminates the landscape only in patches, where it has broken through the clouds above. In *View of Haarlem,* Ruisdael not only captured the appearance of a specific locale but also succeeded in imbuing the work with a quiet serenity that is almost spiritual. Less typical of his work, but also one of the great landscape paintings of the 17th century, is Ruisdael's allegorical *Jewish Cemetery* (FIG. 25-18A).

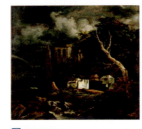

🔲 **25-18A** RUISDAEL, *Jewish Cemetery,* ca. 1655–1660.

Vermeer

Although he also painted landscapes, such as *View of Delft* (FIG. 25-18B), Jan Vermeer made his reputation as a painter of interior scenes, another popular subject among middle-class patrons (see "The Art of Painting in a Dutch Home," page 731). These paintings offer the viewer glimpses into the private lives of prosperous, responsible, and cultured citizens of the United

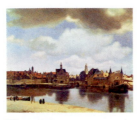

🔲 **25-18B** VERMEER, *View of Delft,* ca. 1661.

Provinces. Despite his fame as a painter today, Vermeer derived much of his income from his work as an innkeeper and art dealer in Delft (see "Middle-Class Patronage and the Art Market," page 738), and he completed no more than 35 paintings that can be definitively attributed to him. He began his career as a painter of biblical and historical themes, but soon abandoned those traditional subjects in favor of domestic scenes. Flemish artists of the 15th century also had painted domestic interiors, but sacred personages often occupied those scenes (for example, FIG. 20-4). In contrast, Vermeer and his contemporaries composed neat, quietly opulent interiors of Dutch middle-class dwellings featuring women especially but also men and occasionally children engaging in household tasks or at leisure.

WOMAN HOLDING A BALANCE In two of Vermeer's finest paintings—*The Letter* (FIG. 25-18C) and *Woman Holding a Balance* (FIG. 25-19)—women are the primary occupants of the Dutch homes. Both paintings are highly idealized depictions of the social values of the burghers of his day. In *Woman Holding a Balance,* a beautiful young woman wearing a veil and a fur-trimmed jacket stands in a room in her home. Light coming from a window illuminates the scene, as in many of the artist's paintings (compare FIG. 25-1). The woman stands before a table on which are spread her most precious possessions—

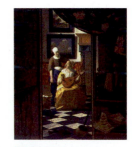

🔲 **25-18C** VERMEER, *The Letter,* 1666.

pearl necklaces, gold chains, and gold coins, which reflect the sunlight that also shines on the woman's face and the fingers of her right hand. In fact, the perspective orthogonals direct the viewer's

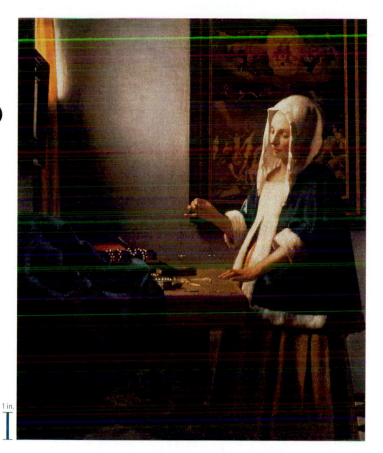

25-19 JAN VERMEER, *Woman Holding a Balance*, ca. 1664. Oil on canvas, 1' 3⅞" × 1' 2". National Gallery of Art, Washington, D.C. (Widener Collection).

Vermeer's woman holding empty scales in perfect balance, ignoring pearls and gold on the table, is probably an allegory of the temperate life. On the wall behind her is a depiction of the Last Judgment.

attention neither to the woman's head nor to her treasures but to the hand in which she holds a balance for weighing gold. The scales, however, are empty—in perfect balance, the way Ignatius of Loyola advised Catholics (Vermeer was a Catholic convert in the Protestant Dutch Republic) to lead a temperate, self-aware life and to balance one's sins with virtuous behavior. The mirror on the wall may refer to self-knowledge, but it may also symbolize, as do the pearls and gold, the sin of vanity. Bolstering that interpretation is the large framed *Last Judgment* painting on the back wall in which Christ, weigher of souls, appears in a golden aureole directly above the young woman's head. Therefore, this serene domestic scene is pregnant with hidden meaning. The woman holds the scales in balance and contemplates the kind of life (one free from the temptations of worldly riches) that she must lead in order to be judged favorably on judgment day.

Vermeer, like Rembrandt (see page 743), was a master of pictorial light and used it with immense virtuosity. He could render space so convincingly through his depiction of light that in his works, the picture surface functions as an invisible glass pane through which the viewer looks into the constructed illusion. Art historians believe that Vermeer used as tools both mirrors and the *camera obscura*, an ancestor of the modern camera based on passing light through a tiny pinhole or lens to project an image on a screen or the wall of a room. (In later versions, artists projected the image on a ground-glass wall of a box whose opposite wall contained the pinhole or lens.) Vermeer did not simply copy the camera's image, however. Instead, the camera obscura and the mirrors helped him obtain

results that he reworked compositionally, enabling him to achieve, for example, a beautiful stability of rectilinear shapes by carefully positioning the figures and furniture in a room. Vermeer's compositions evoke a matchless classical serenity.

Enhancing this quality are colors so true to the optical facts and so subtly modulated that they suggest that Vermeer was far ahead of his time in color science. For example, Vermeer realized that shadows are not colorless and dark, that adjoining colors affect each other, and that light is composed of colors. Thus he painted reflections off of surfaces in colors modified by others nearby. Some scholars have suggested that Vermeer also perceived the phenomenon that modern photographers call "circles of confusion," which appear on out-of-focus negatives. Vermeer could have seen them in images projected by the camera obscura's primitive lenses. He approximated these effects with light dabs that, in close view, give the impression of an image slightly "out of focus." When the observer draws back a step, however, as if adjusting the lens, the color spots cohere, giving an astonishingly accurate illusion of the third dimension.

Steen

Whereas Vermeer's paintings reveal the charm and beauty of Dutch domesticity, the works of JAN STEEN (ca. 1625–1679) provide a counterpoint. In *Feast of Saint Nicholas* (FIG. **25-20**), instead of depicting a tidy, calm Dutch household, Steen opted for a scene of chaos and disruption. Saint Nicholas has just visited this residence, and the children are in an uproar as they search their shoes

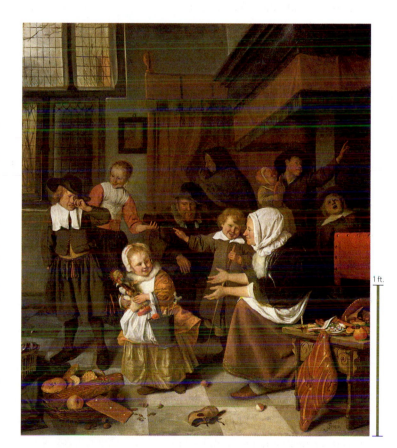

25-20 JAN STEEN, *Feast of Saint Nicholas*, ca. 1660–1665. Oil on canvas, 2' 8¼" × 2' 3¾". Rijksmuseum, Amsterdam.

Steen's lively scene of Dutch children discovering their Christmas gifts may also have an allegorical dimension. *Feast of Saint Nicholas* probably alludes to selfishness, pettiness, and jealousy.

Dutch *Vanitas* Still-Life Paintings

Peter Mundy, a widely traveled Englishman, commented in 1640 on the irony that the Dutch Republic produced almost nothing on its own land, yet because of its success in international trade, Dutch citizens enjoyed great wealth and could afford rare commodities from around the world:

> For although the land (and that with much labor) is brought only to pasture . . . yet by means of their shipping they are plentifully supplied with what the earth affords for the use of man . . . from any part of the world . . . Europe, Asia, Africa or America . . . with the most precious and rich commodities of those parts.*

The prosperous Dutch were justifiably proud of their accomplishments, and the popularity of still-life paintings—particularly images of accumulated goods, such as *Still Life with a Late Ming Ginger Jar* (FIG. 25-22)—reflected this pride. These paintings of worldly possessions marked the emergence of an important new class of art patrons—wealthy merchants—who had tastes distinctly different from those of the leading patrons elsewhere in Baroque Europe, namely royalty and the Catholic Church. Dutch still lifes, which were well suited to the Protestant ethic rejecting most religious art, are among the finest

ever painted. They are meticulously crafted images both scientific in their optical accuracy and poetic in their beauty and lyricism.

One of the best Dutch paintings of this genre is *Vanitas Still Life* (FIG. 25-21) by Pieter Claesz, in which the painter presented the material possessions of a prosperous household strewn across a tabletop or dresser. The ever-present morality and humility central to the Calvinist faith tempered Dutch pride in worldly goods, however. Thus, although Claesz fostered the appreciation and enjoyment of the beauty and value of the objects he depicted, he also reminded the viewer of life's transience by incorporating references to death. Art historians call works of this type *vanitas* ("vanity") paintings, and each features a *memento mori* ("reminder of death"). In *Vanitas Still Life*, references to mortality include the skull, timepiece, tipped glass, and cracked walnut. All suggest the passage of time or someone or something that was here but now is gone. Claesz emphasized this element of time (and demonstrated his technical virtuosity) by including a self-portrait reflected in the glass ball on the left side of the table. He appears to be painting this still life. But in an apparent challenge to the message of inevitable mortality that vanitas paintings convey, the portrait serves to immortalize the artist.

*Quoted in Julie Berger Hochstrasser, *Still Life and Trade in the Dutch Golden Age* (New Haven, Conn.: Yale University Press, 2007), 16.

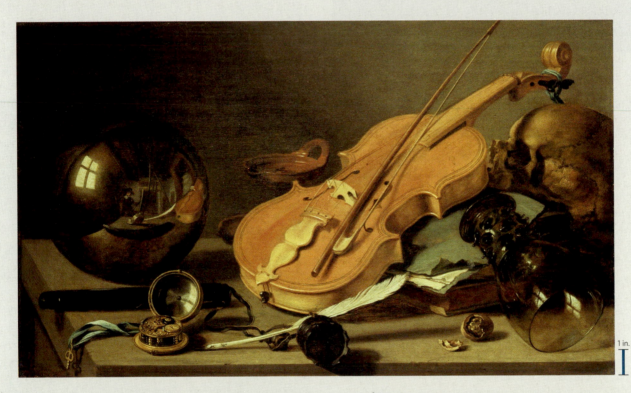

25-21 PIETER CLAESZ, *Vanitas Still Life*, 1630s. Oil on panel, 1' 2" × 1' 11 ½". Germanisches Nationalmuseum, Nuremberg.

In the 17th century, an important new class of patrons emerged in the Dutch Republic—successful merchants who took pride in their material possessions, the fruit of worldwide trade.

for the Christmas gifts he has left. Steen masterfully recorded the children's personalities. Some of them are delighted. The little girl in the center clutches her gifts, clearly unwilling to share with the other children despite her mother's pleas. Others are disappointed. The boy on the left is in tears because he received only a birch rod. An appropriately festive atmosphere reigns, which contrasts sharply

with the decorum prevailing in Vermeer's works. Like the paintings of other Dutch artists, Steen's lively scenes often take on an allegorical dimension and moralistic tone. Steen frequently used children's activities as satirical comments on foolish adult behavior. *Feast of Saint Nicholas* is not his only allusion to selfishness, pettiness, and jealousy.

Claesz, Kalf, and Ruysch

As already discussed (see "Middle-Class Patronage," page 738), the rise of a new class of art patrons in the Dutch Republic prompted artists to focus on a new range of subjects. Still-life painting was one of the most popular. The leading Dutch practitioners of this genre were PIETER CLAESZ (1597–1660; FIG. 25-21), Willem Kalf (FIG. 25-22), and Rachel Ruysch (FIG. 25-23). Often, these still-life paintings had a double appeal to Dutch patrons as celebrations of their prosperity and as reminders of the transience of life (see "Dutch *Vanitas* Still-Life Paintings," page 748).

WILLEM KALF As Dutch prosperity increased, precious objects and luxury items made their way into still-life paintings. *Still Life with a Late Ming Ginger Jar* (FIG. 25-22) by WILLEM KALF (1619–1693) reflects both the wealth that Dutch citizens had accrued and the painter's exquisite skills, both technical and aesthetic. Kalf highlighted the breadth of Dutch maritime trade through his depiction of the Persian floral carpet, the Chinese jar used to store ginger (a luxury item), and the Mediterranean orange and peeled lemon. He delighted in recording the lustrous sheen of fabric and the light glinting off reflective surfaces. As is evident in this image, Kalf's works present an array of ornamental objects, such as the Venetian and Dutch glassware and the silver plate. The inclusion of the watch suggests that this work, like Claesz's *Vanitas Still Life* (FIG. 25-21), may also be a vanitas painting, if less obviously so.

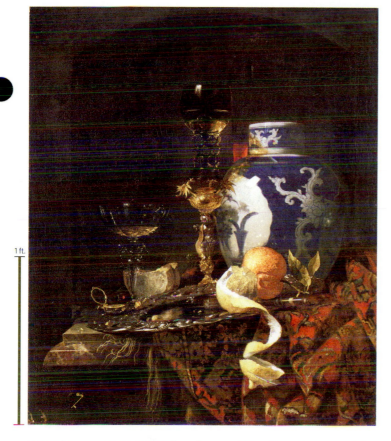

25-22 WILLEM KALF, *Still Life with a Late Ming Ginger Jar*, 1669. Oil on canvas, 2' 6" × 2' 1¾". Indianapolis Museum of Art, Indianapolis (gift in commemoration of the 60th anniversary of the Art Association of Indianapolis, in memory of Daniel W. and Elizabeth C. Marmon).

The opulent objects, especially the Persian carpet and Chinese jar, attest to the prosperous Dutch maritime trade. Kalf's inclusion of a watch suggests that this painting may be a vanitas still life.

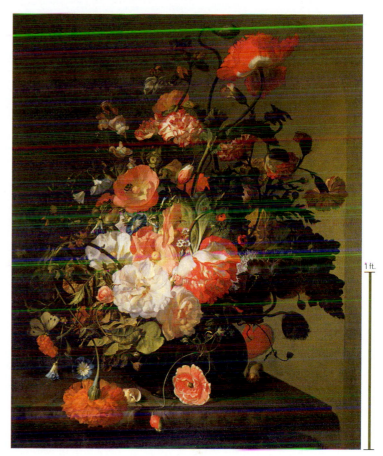

25-23 RACHEL RUYSCH, *Flower Still Life*, after 1700. Oil on canvas, 2' 5¾" × 1' 11⅞". Toledo Museum of Art, Toledo (purchased with funds from the Libbey Endowment, gift of Edward Drummond Libbey).

Flower paintings were very popular in the Dutch Republic. Ruysch achieved international renown for her lush paintings of floral arrangements, noted also for their careful compositions.

RACHEL RUYSCH As living objects that soon die, flowers, particularly cut blossoms, appeared frequently in vanitas paintings. However, floral painting as a distinct genre also enjoyed great popularity in the Dutch Republic because the Dutch were the leading growers and exporters of flowers in 17th-century Europe. One of the major practitioners of flower painting was RACHEL RUYSCH (1664–1750), who from 1708 to 1716 served as court painter to the elector Palatine (the ruler of the Palatinate, a former division of Bavaria) in Düsseldorf, Germany. Ruysch's father was a professor of botany and anatomy, which may account for her interest in and knowledge of plants and insects. She acquired an international reputation for her lush paintings and was able to charge very high prices for her work. *Flower Still Life* (FIG. 25-23) is one of her finest paintings. In this canvas, the lavish floral arrangement is so full, many of the blossoms seem to be spilling out of the vase. However, Ruysch's floral still lifes are not pictures of real floral arrangements, but idealized groupings of individually studied flowers, often combining perfect specimens of flowers that bloomed at different times of the year and could never be placed on a table at the same time. Her careful composition of the individual elements in the illustrated example is evident in her arrangement of the flowers to create a diagonal running from the lower left to the upper right corner of the canvas, offsetting the opposing diagonal of the table edge.

FRANCE

In France, monarchical authority had been increasing for centuries, culminating in the reign of Louis XIV (r. 1661–1715), who sought to determine the direction of French society and culture. Although its economy was not as expansive as the Dutch Republic's, France became Europe's largest and most powerful nation in the 17th century. Against this backdrop, the arts flourished.

Louis XIV

The preeminent French art patron of the 17th century was King Louis XIV himself. Determined to consolidate and expand his power, Louis was a master of political strategy and propaganda. He established a carefully crafted and nuanced relationship with the nobility, granting them sufficient benefits to keep them pacified but simultaneously maintaining rigorous control to avoid insurrection or rebellion. He also ensured subservience by anchoring his rule in *divine right* (belief in a king's absolute power as God's will), rendering Louis's authority incontestable. So convinced was Louis of his importance and centrality to the French kingdom that he eagerly adopted the title "le Roi Soleil" ("the Sun King"). Like the planets and the sun, all of France revolved around Louis XIV.

The Sun King's desire for control extended to all realms of French life, including art. Louis and his principal adviser, Jean-Baptiste Colbert (1619–1683), strove to organize art and architecture in the service of the state. They fully appreciated the power of art as propaganda and the value of visual imagery for cultivating a public persona, and they spared no expense to raise great monuments celebrating the king's absolute power. Louis and Colbert sought to regularize taste and establish the classical style as the preferred French manner. The founding of the Royal Academy of Painting and Sculpture in 1648 served to advance this goal.

PORTRAITURE Louis XIV maintained a workshop of artists, each with a specialization—for example, faces, fabric, architecture, landscapes, armor, or fur. Thus many of the king's portraits were a group effort. *Louis XIV* (FIG. **25-24**) by HYACINTHE RIGAUD (1659–1743) is probably largely the work of his assistants, but he designed the composition and painted the king's face himself—on paper, affixed to the canvas after the rest of the painting was complete. Rigaud's portrait successfully conveys the image of an absolute monarch. The king, age 63 when he commissioned this portrait, stands with his left hand on his hip and gazes directly at the viewer. His elegant ermine-lined fleur-de-lis coronation robes (compare FIG. 25-4) hang loosely from his left shoulder, suggesting an air of haughtiness. Louis also draws his garment back to expose his legs. (The king was a ballet dancer in his youth and was proud of his well-toned legs.) The portrait's majesty derives in large part from the composition. The Sun King is the unmistakable focal point of the image, and Rigaud placed him so that he seems to look down on the viewer. (Louis XIV was only 5 feet, 4 inches tall—a fact that drove him to design the red-heeled shoes he wears in this painting.) The carefully detailed environment in which the king stands also contributes to the portrait's stateliness and grandiosity, as does the painting's sheer size (more than 9 feet tall).

Rigaud's portrait was originally intended as a gift to Louis's grandson, Philip V of Spain, but the Sun King was so pleased with it that he kept it for his own collection. Only three years later did Louis commission Rigaud to produce a copy for Philip. The image soon became iconic, and Rigaud's studio produced more copies for various European aristocrats.

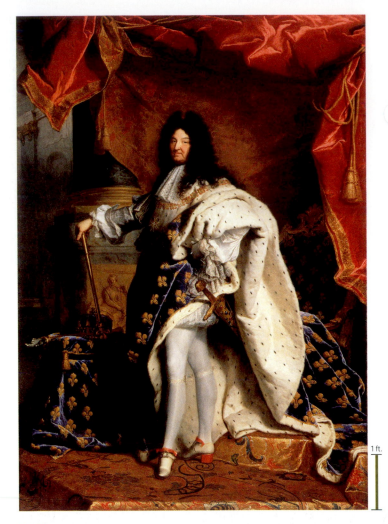

25-24 HYACINTHE RIGAUD, *Louis XIV,* 1701. Oil on canvas, 9' 2" × 6' 3". Musée du Louvre, Paris.

In this portrait set against a stately backdrop, Rigaud portrayed the 5' 4" Sun King wearing red high-heeled shoes and with his ermine-lined coronation robes thrown over his left shoulder.

THE LOUVRE The first great architectural project that Louis XIV and his adviser Colbert undertook was the closing of the east side of the Louvre's Cour Carré (FIG. 23-23), left incomplete by Pierre Lescot in the 16th century. The king summoned the renowned architect and sculptor Gianlorenzo Bernini (see page 701) from Rome to submit plans, but Bernini envisioned an Italian palace on a monumental scale, which would have involved the demolition of all previous work. His plan rejected, Bernini indignantly returned home. Louis then turned to three French architects—CLAUDE PERRAULT (1613–1688), LOUIS LE VAU (1612–1670), and CHARLES LE BRUN (1619–1690)—for the Louvre's east facade (FIG. **25-25**). The design is a brilliant synthesis of French and Italian classical elements, culminating in a new and definitive formula. The facade has a central and two corner projecting columnar pavilions resting on a stately podium. The central pavilion is in the form of a classical temple front. To either side is a giant colonnade of paired columns, resembling the columned flanks of a temple folded out like wings. The designers favored an even roofline, balustraded and broken only by the central pediment, over the traditional French pyramidal roof of the Louvre's west wing (FIG. 23-23). The emphatically horizontal sweep of the 17th-century facade brushed aside all memory of Gothic verticality. The stately proportions and monumentality

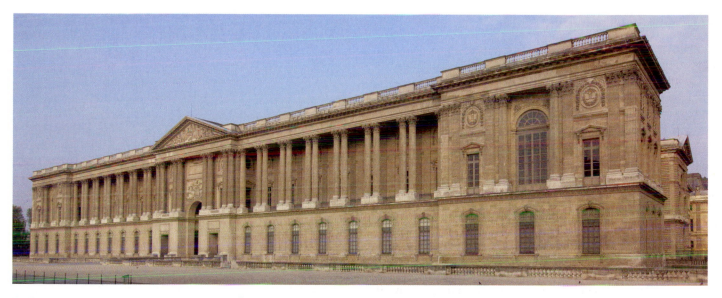

25-25 CLAUDE PERRAULT, LOUIS LE VAU, and CHARLES LE BRUN, east facade of the Louvre (looking southwest), Paris, France, 1667–1670.

The design of the Louvre's east facade is a brilliant synthesis of French and Italian classical elements, including a central pavilion resembling an ancient temple front with a pediment.

of the Baroque design were both an expression of the new official French taste and a symbol of centrally organized authority.

VERSAILLES Work on the Louvre had barely begun when Louis XIV decided to convert a royal hunting lodge at Versailles, south of Paris, into a great palace (see "The Sun King's Palace at Versailles," page 752, and FIG. **25-26**). The enormous palace might appear unbearably ostentatious were it not for its extraordinary setting in a vast park, which makes the palace seem almost an adjunct. The park of Versailles must rank among the world's greatest artworks in both

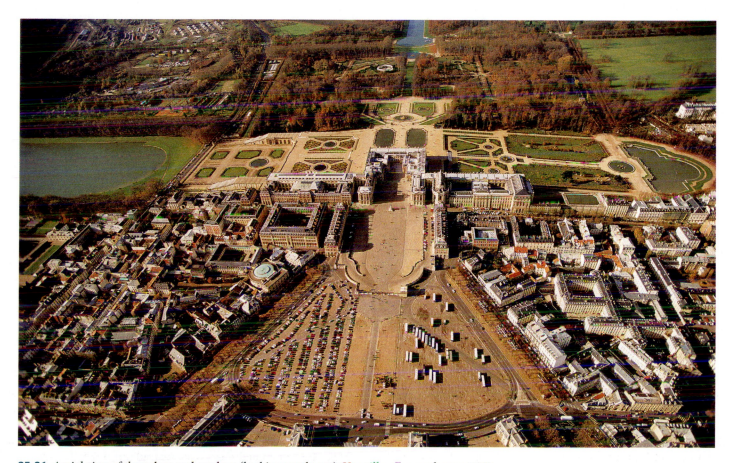

25-26 Aerial view of the palace and gardens (looking northwest), Versailles, France, begun 1669.

Louis XIV ordered his architects to convert a royal hunting lodge at Versailles into a gigantic palace and vast park with a satellite city with three radial avenues whose axes intersect in the king's bedroom.

ART AND SOCIETY

The Sun King's Palace at Versailles

To realize his vision of a grandiose palace worthy of a "Sun King," Louis XIV assembled a veritable army of architects, decorators, sculptors, painters, and landscape designers under the general management of Charles Le Brun to design and construct his new royal residence at Versailles (FIG. 25-26). At the king's direction, Le Brun and his team converted the remodeling of a simple hunting lodge into the greatest architectural project of the age—a defining statement of French Baroque style and a grandiose symbol of Louis XIV's power and ambition.

Planned on a gigantic scale, the project called not only for a large palace flanking a vast park but also for the construction of a satellite city to house court and government officials, military and guard detachments, courtiers, and servants (thereby keeping them all under the king's close supervision). Le Brun laid out this town to the east of the palace along three radial avenues that converge on the palace. Their axes, in a symbolic assertion of the ruler's absolute power over his domains, intersected in the king's spacious bedroom, which served as an official audience chamber. The palace itself, more than a quarter-mile long, is perpendicular to the dominant east-west axis running through the associated city and park.

Every detail of the extremely rich decoration of the palace's interior received careful attention. The architects and decorators designed everything from wall paintings to doorknobs in order to reinforce the splendor of Versailles and to exhibit the very finest sense of artisanship. Of the literally hundreds of rooms within the palace, the most famous is the Galerie des Glaces, or Hall of Mirrors (FIG. **25-27**), designed by JULES HARDOUIN-MANSART (1646-1708) and Le Brun. This hall overlooks Le Nôtre's

25-27 JULES HARDOUIN-MANSART and CHARLES LE BRUN, Galerie des Glaces (Hall of Mirrors), palace of Versailles, Versailles, France, ca. 1680.

In this grandiose hall overlooking the park of the Sun King's palace at Versailles, hundreds of mirrors illusionistically extend the room's width and once reflected its gilded and jeweled furnishings.

park (FIG. 25-26) from the second floor and extends along most of the width of the central block. Although deprived of its original sumptuous furniture, which included gold and silver chairs and bejeweled trees, the 240-foot-long Galerie des Glaces retains much of its splendor today. Hundreds of mirrors, set into the wall opposite the windows, alleviate the hall's tunnel-like quality and illusionistically extend the width of the room. The mirror, that ultimate source of illusion, was a favorite element of Baroque interior design. Here, it also enhanced the dazzling extravagance of the great festivals that Louis XIV was so fond of hosting. From the Galerie des Glaces, the king and his guests could enjoy a sweeping vista down the tree-lined central axis of the Versailles park and across terraces, lawns, pools, and lakes toward the horizon.

As a symbol of absolute power, Versailles has no equal. It also expresses, in the most monumental terms of its age, the rationalistic creed—based on scientific advances, such as the physics of Sir Isaac Newton (1642-1727) and the mathematical philosophy of René Descartes (1596-1650)—that all knowledge must be systematic and all science must be the consequence of the intellect imposed on matter. The majestic and rational design of Versailles proudly proclaims the mastery of human intelligence (and the mastery of Louis XIV) over the disorderliness of nature.

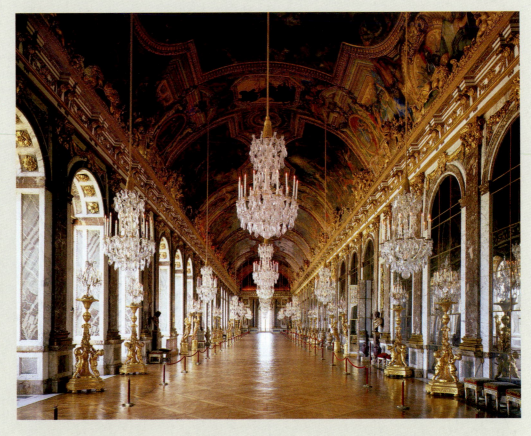

size and concept. Here, ANDRÉ LE NÔTRE (1613–1700) transformed an entire forest into a park. Although its geometric plan may appear stiff and formal, the park in fact offers an almost unlimited assortment of vistas, as the French architect used not only the multiplicity of natural forms but also the terrain's slightly rolling contours with stunning effectiveness.

The formal gardens near the palace provide a transition from the frozen architectural forms to the natural living ones. Here, the elegant shapes of trimmed shrubs and hedges define the tightly designed geometric units. Each unit is different from its neighbor and has a focal point in the form of a sculptured group, a pavilion, a reflecting pool, or a fountain. Farther away from the palace, the design loosens as trees, in shadowy masses, screen or frame views of open countryside. Le Nôtre carefully composed all vistas for maximum effect. Light and shadow, formal and informal, dense growth and open meadows—all play against one another in unending combinations and variations. No photograph or series of photographs can reveal the design's full richness. The park unfolds itself only to

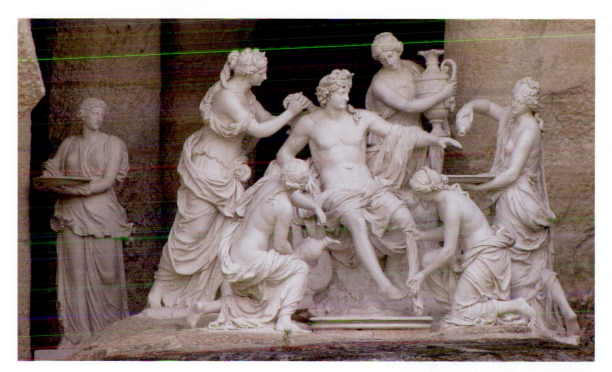

25-28 FRANÇOIS GIRARDON and THOMAS REGNAUDIN, *Apollo Attended by the Nymphs of Thetis*, Grotto of Thetis, park of Versailles, Versailles, France, 1664–1670. Marble, life-size.

Girardon's study of ancient sculpture and Poussin's figural compositions influenced the design of this mythological group. Apollo, often equated with the sun, alludes to Louis XIV, the Sun King.

those walking through it. In this respect, it is a temporal artwork. Its aspects change with the time of day, the seasons, and the relative position of the observer.

GROTTO OF THETIS Scattered through the vast Versailles park are allegorical references to the Sun King in the form of statues of the Greek god Apollo, who was often identified with the sun (see "The Gods and Goddesses of Mount Olympus," page 105). Perhaps the finest of these is *Apollo Attended by the Nymphs of Thetis* (FIG. 25-28) by FRANÇOIS GIRARDON (1628–1715) with additional statues by THOMAS REGNAUDIN (1622–1706), which in the 18th century were moved by HUBERT ROBERT (1773–1808) to an artificial grotto above a dramatic waterfall (FIG. 25-28A). Both stately and graceful, the nymphs have a compel-

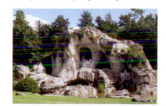

25-28A ROBERT, Baths of Apollo, Versailles, 1777–1781.

ling charm as they minister to Apollo at the end of the day. Girardon, who also won the commission to make a bronze equestrian statue of the Sun King, had spent time in Rome, and his close study of Greco-Roman sculpture heavily influenced his design of the central group. (Girardon based his Apollo on one of the most famous ancient statues then known, the *Apollo Belvedere* in the Vatican.) The figural compositions of the most renowned French painter of the era, Nicolas Poussin (FIG. 25-31), inspired Girardon's arrangement of the statues as a group. The sculptor's classical style and mythological symbolism well suited France's glorification of royal majesty.

ROYAL CHAPEL In 1698, Hardouin-Mansart received the commission to add a Royal Chapel to the Versailles palace complex. The chapel's interior (FIG. 25-29) is essentially rectangular, but because its apse is as high as the nave, the fluid central space takes on a curved, Baroque quality. However, the light entering through the large clerestory windows lacks the directed dramatic effect of the Italian Baroque, instead illuminating the interior's precisely chiseled details brightly and evenly. Pier-supported arcades carry a majestic

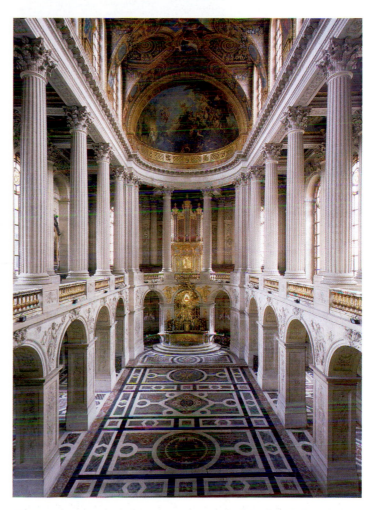

25-29 JULES HARDOUIN-MANSART, interior of the Royal Chapel, with ceiling decorations by ANTOINE COYPEL, palace of Versailles, Versailles, France, 1698–1710.

Because the apse is as high as the nave, the central space of the Royal Chapel at Versailles has a curved, Baroque quality. Louis XIV could reach the royal pew directly from his apartments.

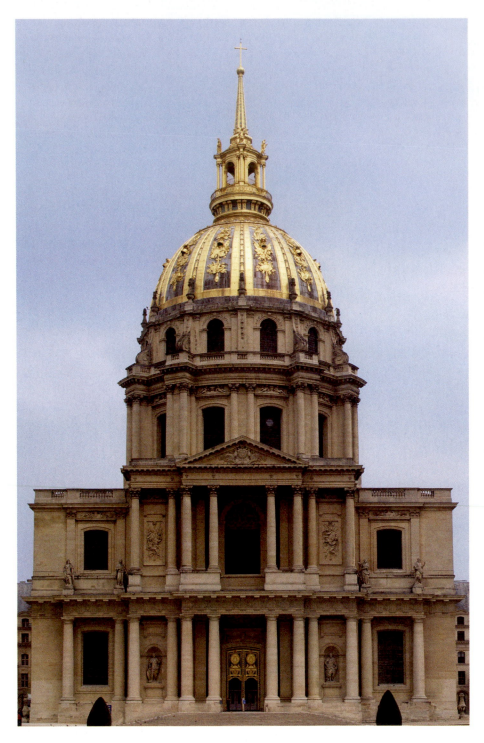

25-30 JULES HARDOUIN-MANSART, Église du Dôme (looking north), Church of the Invalides, Paris, France, 1676–1706.

Hardouin-Mansart's church marries the Italian and French architectural styles. The grouping of the orders is similar to the Italian Baroque manner but without the dramatic play of curved surfaces.

frame is not unlike that in Italian Baroque architecture but without the dramatic play of curved surfaces characteristic of many 17th-century Italian churches—for example, Borromini's San Carlo (FIG. 24-9) in Rome. The compact facade is low and narrow in relation to the vast drum and dome, seeming to serve simply as a base for them. The overpowering dome, conspicuous on the Parisian skyline, is itself expressive of the Baroque love for dramatic magnitude, as is the way its designer aimed for theatrical effects of light and space. The dome consists of three shells, the lowest cut off so that a visitor to the interior looks up through it to the one above, which is filled with light from hidden windows in the third, outermost dome. CHARLES DE LA FOSSE (1636–1716) painted the second dome in 1705 with an Italian-inspired representation of the heavens opening up to receive Saint Louis, patron of France (see page 390).

Poussin and Claude Lorrain

Louis XIV's embrace of classicism enticed many French artists to study Rome's ancient and Renaissance monuments. But even before the Sun King ascended to the throne in 1661, NICOLAS POUSSIN (1594–1665) of Normandy had spent most of his life in Rome, where he produced grandly severe paintings modeled on those of Titian and Raphael. He also carefully formulated a theoretical explanation of his method and was ultimately responsible for establishing classical painting as an important ingredient of 17th-century French art (see "Poussin's Notes for a Treatise on Painting," page 755). His classical style presents a striking contrast to the contemporaneous Baroque style of his Italian counterparts in Rome, underscoring the multifaceted character of the art of 17th-century Europe.

row of Corinthian columns defining the royal gallery. The royal pew is at the rear, accessible directly from the king's apartments. Amid the restrained decoration, only the illusionistic ceiling paintings, added in 1708 and 1709 by ANTOINE COYPEL (1661–1722), suggest the drama and complexity of Italian Baroque art.

ÉGLISE DU DÔME, PARIS Another of Hardouin-Mansart's masterworks, the Église du Dôme (FIG. 25-30), or Church of the Invalides, in Paris, also marries the Italian Baroque and French classical architectural styles. An intricately composed domed square of great scale, the church adjoins the veterans hospital that Louis XIV established for the disabled soldiers of his many wars. Two firmly separated levels, the upper one capped by a pediment, compose the frontispiece. The grouping of the orders and of the bays they

ET IN ARCADIA EGO Poussin's *Et in Arcadia Ego* (*Even in Arcadia, I* [am present]; FIG. 25-31) exemplifies the "grand manner" of painting that the artist advocated. It features a lofty subject rooted in the classical world and figures based on antique statuary. Rather than depicting dynamic movement and intense emotions, as his Italian contemporaries in Rome did, Poussin emulated the rational order and stability of Raphael's paintings. Dominating the foreground are three shepherds living in the idyllic land of Arcadia. They study an

Poussin's Notes for a Treatise on Painting

As the leading proponent of classical painting in 17th-century Rome, Nicolas Poussin outlined the principles of classicism in notes for an intended treatise on painting, left incomplete at his death. In those notes, Poussin described the essential ingredients necessary to produce a beautiful painting in "the grand manner":

> The grand manner consists of four things: subject-matter or theme, thought, structure, and style. The first thing that, as the foundation of all others, is required, is that the subject-matter shall be grand, as are battles, heroic actions, and divine things. But assuming that the subject on which the painter is laboring is grand, his next consideration is to keep away from minutiae . . . [and paint only] things magnificent and grand . . . Those who elect mean subjects take refuge in them because of the weakness of their talents.*

The idea of beauty does not descend into matter unless this is prepared as carefully as possible. This preparation consists of three things: arrangement, measure, and aspect or form. Arrangement means the relative position of the parts; measure refers to their size; and form consists of lines and colors. Arrangement and relative position of the parts and making every limb of the body hold its natural place are not sufficient unless measure is added, which gives to each limb its correct size, proportionate to that of the whole body [compare "Polykleitos's Prescription for the Perfect Statue," page 129], and unless form joins in, so that the lines will be drawn with grace and with a harmonious juxtaposition of light and shadow.†

Poussin applied these principles in paintings such as *Et in Arcadia Ego* (FIG. 25-31), a work peopled with perfectly proportioned statuesque figures attired in antique garb.

*Translated by Robert Goldwater and Marco Treves, eds., *Artists on Art*, 3d ed. (New York: Pantheon Books, 1958), 155.
†Ibid., 156.

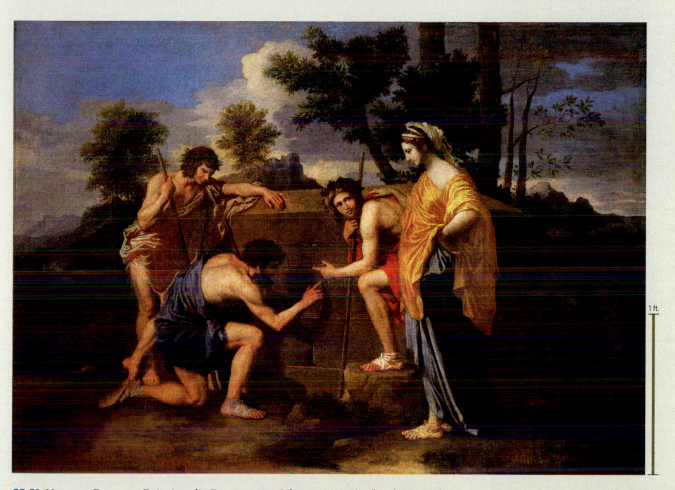

1 ft.

25-31 NICOLAS POUSSIN, *Et in Arcadia Ego*, ca. 1655. Oil on canvas, 2' 10" × 4'. Musée du Louvre, Paris.

Poussin was the leading proponent of classicism in 17th-century Rome. His "grand manner" paintings are models of "arrangement and measure" and incorporate figures inspired by ancient statuary.

inscription on a tomb as a statuesque female figure quietly places her hand on the shoulder of one of them. She may be the spirit of death, reminding these mortals, as does the inscription, that death is found even in Arcadia, supposedly a spot of paradisiacal bliss. The countless draped female statues surviving in Italy from Roman times supplied the models for this figure, and the posture of the youth with one foot resting on a boulder derives from Greco-Roman statues of Neptune, the sea god, leaning on his trident. The classically compact and balanced grouping of the figures, the even light, and the thoughtful and reserved mood complement Poussin's classical figure types.

25-32 Nicolas Poussin, *Landscape with Saint John on Patmos,* 1640. Oil on canvas, 3' 3½" × 4' 5⅝". Art Institute of Chicago, Chicago (A. A. Munger Collection).

Poussin placed Saint John in a classical landscape amid broken columns, an obelisk, and a ruined temple, suggesting the decay of great civilizations and the coming of the new Christian era.

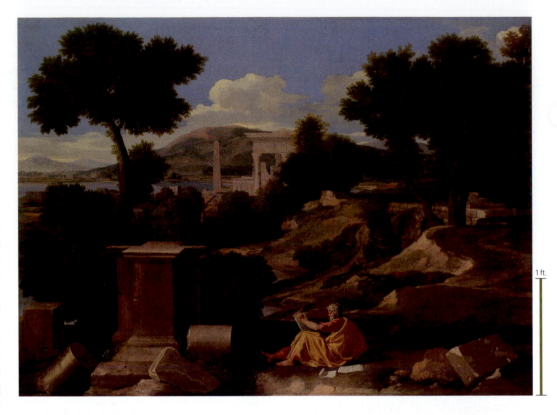

SAINT JOHN ON PATMOS In *Et in Arcadia Ego,* monumental figures dominate the landscape setting, but the natural world looms large in many of Poussin's paintings. *Landscape with Saint John on Patmos* (FIG. **25-32**) is one of a pair of canvases Poussin painted for Gian Maria Roscioli (d. 1644), secretary to Pope Urban VIII. The second landscape represents Saint Matthew, reclining in right profile, who faced Saint John when the two canvases, now in different museums on different continents, hung side by side in Rome. An eagle stands behind John, just as an angel, Matthew's attribute, stands beside him (see "The Four Evangelists," page 318). John, near the end of his life on the Greek island of Patmos, composed the book of Revelation, his account of the end of the world and the second coming of Christ, a prophetic vision of violent destruction and the Last Judgment (see "Early Christian Saints," page 237).

Poussin's setting, however, is a serene classical landscape beneath a sunny sky. (He created a similar setting in *Burial of Phocion* [FIG. **25-32A**], which he painted later in the decade.) Saint John reclines in the foreground, posed like a Greco-Roman river god, amid shattered columns and a pedestal for a statue that disappeared long ago. In the middle ground, two oak trees frame the ruins of a classical temple and an Egyptian obelisk, many of which the

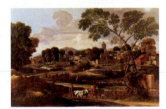

25-32A Poussin, *Burial of Phocion,* 1648.

25-33 Claude Lorrain, *Landscape with Cattle and Peasants,* 1629. Oil on canvas, 3' 6" × 4' 10½". Philadelphia Museum of Art, Philadelphia (George W. Elkins Collection).

Claude used atmospheric and linear perspective to transform the rustic Roman countryside filled with peasants and animals into an ideal classical landscape bathed in sunlight in infinite space.

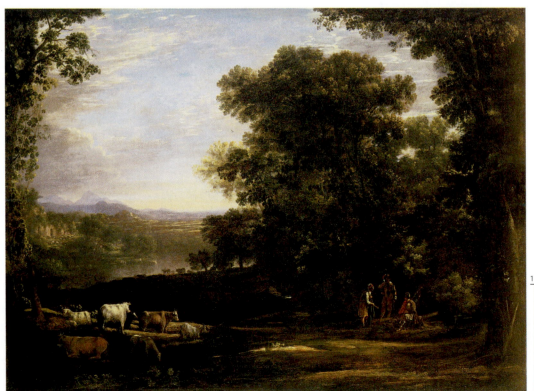

Romans brought to their capital from the Nile and the popes reused in their building projects—for example, in the piazza in front of Saint Peter's (FIG. 24-4) and in Bernini's Fountain of the Four Rivers (FIG. 24-1). The decaying buildings suggest the decline of great empires—to be replaced by Christianity in a new era. In the distance are hills, sky, and clouds, all of which Poussin represented with pristine clarity, ignoring the rules of atmospheric perspective. His landscapes are not portraits of specific places, as are the Dutch landscapes of Ruisdael (FIG. 25-18) and Vermeer (FIG. 25-18B). Rather, they are imaginary settings constructed according to classical rules of design. Poussin's clouds, for example, echo the contours of his hills.

CLAUDE LORRAIN Claude Gellée, called CLAUDE LORRAIN (1600–1682) after his birthplace in the duchy of Lorraine, which was technically independent from the French monarchy during this period, rivaled Poussin in fame. Claude modulated in a softer style Poussin's disciplined rational art, with its sophisticated revelation of the geometry of landscape. Unlike the figures in Poussin's pictures, those in Claude's landscapes tell no dramatic story, point out no moral, praise no hero, and celebrate no saint. Indeed, the figures in Claude's paintings often appear to be added as mere excuses for the radiant landscape itself. For the French artist, painting involved essentially one theme—the beauty of a broad sky suffused with the golden light of dawn or sunset glowing through a hazy atmosphere and reflecting brilliantly off rippling water.

In *Landscape with Cattle and Peasants* (FIG. **25-33**), the figures in the right foreground chat in animated fashion. In the left foreground, cattle relax contentedly. In the middle ground, cattle amble slowly away. The well-defined foreground, distinct middle ground, and dim background recede in serene orderliness, until all form dissolves in a luminous mist. Atmospheric and linear perspective reinforce each other to turn a vista into a typical Claudian vision, an ideal classical world bathed in sunlight in infinite space (compare FIG. I-1).

Claude's formalizing of nature with balanced groups of architectural masses, screens of trees, and sheets of water followed the great tradition of classical landscape. It began with the backgrounds of Venetian paintings (FIGS. 22-33 to 22-35) and continued in the art of Annibale Carracci (FIG. 24-15) and Poussin (FIGS. 25-32 and 25-32A). Yet Claude, like the Dutch painters, studied the light and the atmospheric nuances of nature, making an important contribution. He recorded carefully in hundreds of sketches the look of the Roman countryside, its gentle terrain accented by stone-pines, cypresses, and poplars and by the ever-present ruins of ancient aqueducts, tombs, and towers. He made these the fundamental elements of his compositions. Claude's landscapes owe their timeless appeal to the distinctive combination of the natural beauty of the outskirts of Rome and the mystique of the past.

Claude achieved his marvelous effects of light by painstakingly placing on his canvas tiny brushstrokes representing small value gradations, which imitated, though on a very small scale, the range of values of outdoor light and shade. Avoiding the problem of high-noon sunlight overhead, Claude preferred, and convincingly rendered, the sun's rays as they gradually illuminated the morning sky or, with their dying glow, set the pensive mood of evening. Thus he matched the moods of nature with those of human subjects. Claude's infusion of nature with human feeling and his recomposition of nature in a calm equilibrium greatly appealed to many landscape painters of the 18th and early 19th centuries.

Le Nain, Callot, La Tour

Although classicism was an important element of French art during the 17th and early 18th centuries, not all artists embraced the "grand manner." The works of LOUIS LE NAIN (ca. 1593–1648) have more in common with contemporaneous Dutch art than Renaissance or ancient art. Nevertheless, subjects that in Dutch painting were opportunities for boisterous good humor (FIG. 25-20), Le Nain treated with somber stillness. *Family of Country People* (FIG. **25-34**) reflects the thinking of 17th-century French social theorists who celebrated the natural virtue of peasants who worked

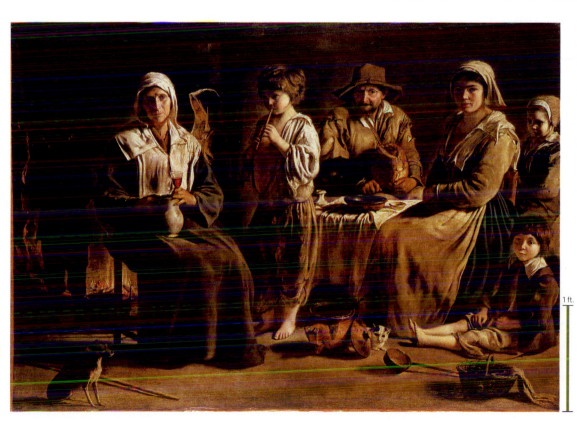

25-34 LOUIS LE NAIN, *Family of Country People*, ca. 1640. Oil on canvas, 3' 8" × 5' 2". Musée du Louvre, Paris.

Le Nain's painting expresses the grave dignity of a peasant family made stoic by hardship. It reflects 17th-century French social theory, which celebrated the natural virtue of those who worked the soil.

1 ft.

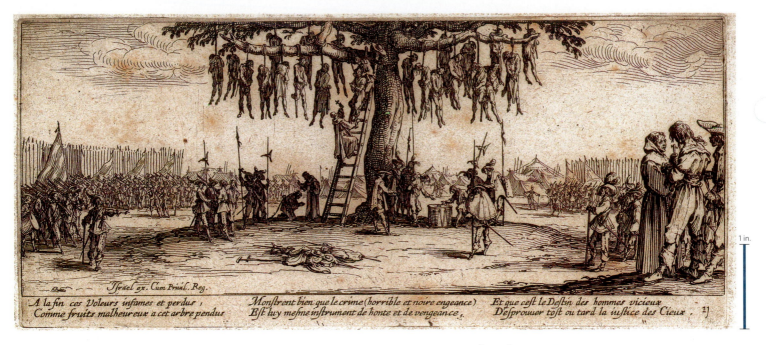

1 in.

25-35 JACQUES CALLOT, *Hanging Tree,* from the *Miseries of War* series, 1629–1633. Etching, $3\frac{3}{4}" \times 7\frac{1}{4}"$. Bibliothèque Nationale, Paris.

Callot's *Miseries of War* etchings were among the first realistic pictorial records of the human disaster of military conflict. *Hanging Tree* depicts a mass execution of thieves in the presence of an army.

the soil. Le Nain's painting expresses the grave dignity of one peasant family made stoic and resigned by hardship. These drab country folk surely had little reason for merriment. The peasant's lot, never easy, was miserable during the Thirty Years' War. The anguish and frustration of the peasantry, suffering from the cruel depredations of unruly armies living off the countryside, often erupted in violent revolts that the same armies savagely suppressed. This family, however, is pious, docile, and calm. Because Le Nain depicted peasants with dignity and quiet resignation, despite their harsh living conditions, some scholars have suggested that he intended his paintings to please wealthy urban patrons.

JACQUES CALLOT Two other prominent artists from Lorraine were Jacques Callot and Georges de La Tour. JACQUES CALLOT (ca. 1592–1635) conveyed a sense of military life during these troubled times in a series of prints called *Miseries of War.* Callot confined himself almost exclusively to the art of etching and was widely influential. Rembrandt was among those who knew and learned from his work. Callot developed a very hard surface for the copper plate to enable fine and precise delineation with the needle. His

quick, vivid touch and faultless drawing produced panoramas sparkling with sharp details of life—and death—despite their small size (roughly 4 by 7 inches). In the *Miseries of War* series, he observed these details coolly, presenting without comment images based on events he must have witnessed in the wars in Lorraine.

In *Hanging Tree* (FIG. **25-35**), Callot depicted a mass execution of thieves (identified in the text at the bottom of the etching). The event takes place in the presence of a disciplined army, drawn up on parade with banners, muskets, and lances, their tents in the

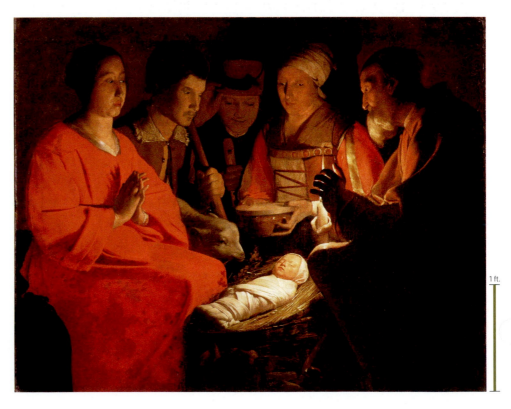

1 ft.

25-36 GEORGES DE LA TOUR, *Adoration of the Shepherds,* 1645–1650. Oil on canvas, 3' 6" × 4' 6". Musée du Louvre, Paris.

Without the aid of the title, this candlelit nighttime scene could be a genre painting instead of a biblical narrative. La Tour did not even paint halos around the heads of the holy personages.

background. Hanged men sway in clusters from the branches of a huge cross-shaped tree. A monk climbs a ladder, holding up a crucifix to a man while the executioner adjusts the noose around the man's neck. At the foot of the ladder, another victim kneels to receive absolution. Under the crucifix-tree, men roll dice on a drumhead, hoping to win the belongings of the executed. (This may be an allusion to the soldiers who cast lots for the garments of the crucified Christ.) In the right foreground, a hooded priest consoles a bound man. Callot's *Miseries of War* etchings are among the first realistic pictorial records of the human disaster of armed conflict.

GEORGES DE LA TOUR France, unlike the Dutch Republic, was a Catholic country, and religious themes, although not as common as in Italian and Spanish Baroque art, occupied some 17th-century French painters. Among the French artists who painted biblical subjects was GEORGES DE LA TOUR (1593–1652). His work, particularly his use of light, suggests a familiarity with Caravaggio's art (see page 715), which he may have learned about from painters in Utrecht, such as ter Brugghen and van Honthorst (FIGS. 25-7 and 25-8). Although La Tour used the devices of Caravaggio's Dutch followers, his effects are strikingly different from theirs. His *Adoration of the Shepherds* (FIG. 25-36) makes use of the night setting favored by the Utrecht school, much as van Honthorst portrayed it. But here, the light, its source shaded by an old man's hand, falls upon a very different company in a very different mood. A group of humble men and women, coarsely clad, gather in prayerful vigil around a luminous baby Jesus. Without the aid of the title, this work might be construed as a genre piece, a narrative of some event from peasant life. Nothing in the environment, placement, poses, dress, or attributes of the figures distinguishes them as the Virgin Mary, Joseph, Christ Child, or shepherds. The artist did not even give the religious personages halos. The light is not spiritual but material: it comes from a candle.

La Tour's scientific scrutiny of the effects of light, as it throws precise shadows on surfaces intercepting it, nevertheless had religious intention and consequence. The light illuminates a group of ordinary people held in a mystic trance induced by their witnessing the miracle of the incarnation. In this timeless tableau of simple people, La Tour eliminated the dogmatic significance and traditional iconography of the birth of the Savior. Still, these people reverently contemplate something they regard as holy. The devout of any religious persuasion can read this painting, regardless of their familiarity with the biblical account.

The supernatural calm pervading *Adoration of the Shepherds* is characteristic of the mood of Georges de La Tour's art. He achieved this by eliminating motion and emotive gesture (only the light is dramatic), by suppressing surface detail, and by simplifying body volumes. These stylistic traits are among those associated with classical and Renaissance art. Thus several apparently contradictory elements meet in the work of La Tour: classical composure, fervent spirituality, and genre realism.

ENGLAND

In England, in sharp distinction to France, the common law and the Parliament kept royal power in check. England also differed from France (and Europe in general) in other significant ways. Although an important part of English life, religion was not the contentious issue it was on the Continent. The religious affiliations of the English included Catholicism, Anglicanism, Protestantism, and Puritanism (the English version of Calvinism). In the economic realm, England was the one country (other than the Dutch Republic) to take advantage of the opportunities that overseas trade offered. As an island, Britain (which after 1603 consisted of England, Wales, and Scotland), like the Dutch Republic, possessed a large and powerful navy, as well as excellent maritime capabilities.

Jones and Wren

In the realm of art, the most significant English achievements were in the field of architecture, much of it, as in France, incorporating classical elements.

INIGO JONES The most important English architect of the first half of the 17th century was INIGO JONES (1573–1652), architect to Kings James I (r. 1603–1625) and Charles I (FIG. 25-5). Jones spent considerable time in Italy. He greatly admired the classical authority and restraint of Andrea Palladio's buildings and studied with great care his treatise on architecture (see page 647). Jones took many motifs from Palladio's villas and palaces, and he adopted Palladio's basic design principles for his own architecture, which transformed the medieval city of London. The nature of Jones's achievement is evident in the buildings he designed for his royal patrons, among them the Banqueting House (FIG. 25-37) at Whitehall, used, as its name reveals, for royal banquets and other festive occasions.

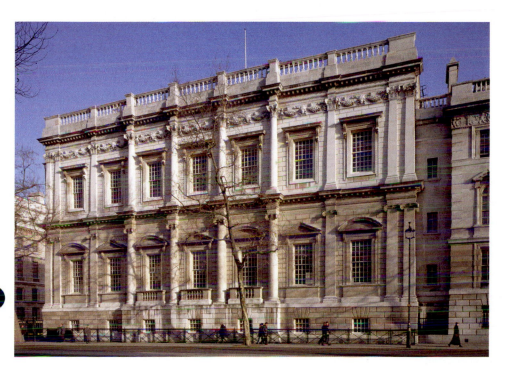

25-37 INIGO JONES, **Banqueting House (looking northeast), Whitehall, London, England, 1619–1622.**

Jones was a great admirer of the classical architecture of Palladio, and he adopted motifs from the Italian architect's villas and palaces for the buildings he designed for his royal patrons.

(Adorning the ceiling of the grand interior hall is a 1634–1636 painting by Rubens depicting the apotheosis of James I.) For this structure, a symmetrical block of great clarity and dignity, Jones superimposed two orders (Ionic below, Corinthian above), using columns in the center and pilasters near the ends. The balustraded roofline, uninterrupted in its horizontal sweep, predates the Louvre's east facade (FIG. 25-25) by more than 40 years. Palladio would have recognized and approved all of the design elements, but the building as a whole is not a copy of his work. Although relying on the revered Italian's architectural vocabulary and syntax, Jones retained his independence as a designer. For two centuries, his influence in English architecture was almost as authoritative as Palladio's.

CHRISTOPHER WREN London's majestic Saint Paul's Cathedral (FIG. **25-38**) is the work of England's most renowned architect, CHRISTOPHER WREN (1632–1723). A mathematical genius and skilled engineer whose work won Isaac Newton's praise, Wren became professor of astronomy at Gresham College in London at age 25. Mathematics led to architecture, and Charles II (r. 1649–1685) asked Wren to prepare a plan for restoring the old Gothic church dedicated to Saint Paul. Wren proposed to remodel the building based on Roman structures. Within a few months, the Great Fire of London, which destroyed the old structure and many other churches in the city in 1666, gave Wren his opportunity. Although Jones's work strongly influenced him, Wren also traveled in France, where the splendid palaces and state buildings being created in and around Paris at the time of the expansion of the Louvre palace (FIG. 25-25) must have impressed him. Wren also closely studied prints illustrating Baroque architecture in Italy. In Saint Paul's, he harmonized Palladian, French, and Italian Baroque features.

In view of its size, Saint Paul's Cathedral was built with remarkable speed—in little more than 30 years—and Wren lived to see it completed. The building's form underwent constant refinement during construction, and Wren did not determine the final appearance of the towers until after 1700. In the splendid skyline composition, two foreground towers act effectively as foils to the great dome. Wren must have known similar schemes that Italian architects had devised for Saint Peter's (FIG. 24-4) in Rome to solve the problem of the relationship between the facade and dome. Certainly, the influence of Borromini (FIGS. 24-1, rear, and 24-12) is evident in the upper levels and lanterns of the towers. The lower levels owe a debt to Palladio (FIG. 22-30), and the superposed paired columnar porticos recall the Louvre's east facade (FIG. 25-25). Wren's skillful eclecticism brought all these foreign features into a monumental unity.

Wren designed many other London churches after the Great Fire. Even today, Wren's towers and domes punctuate the skyline of London. Saint Paul's dome is the tallest of all. Wren's legacy was significant and long-lasting, both in England and in colonial America, as examined in the next chapter.

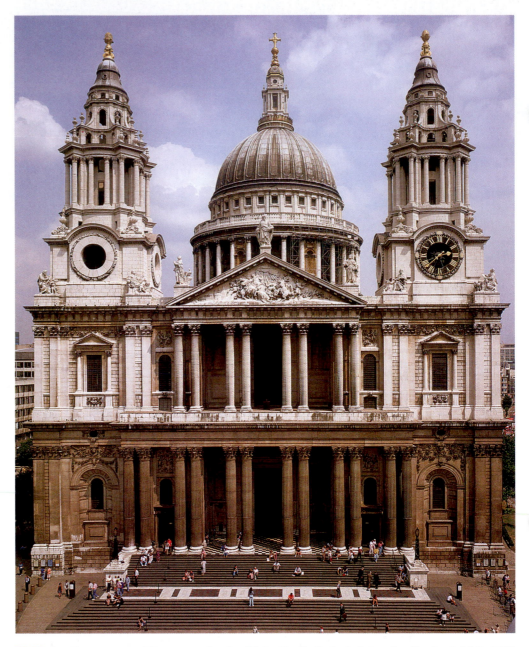

25-38 Sir Christopher Wren, west facade of Saint Paul's Cathedral, London, England, 1675–1710.

Wren's cathedral replaced an old Gothic church. The facade design owes much to Palladio (FIG. 22-30) and Borromini (FIG. 24-12). The great dome recalls Saint Peter's in Rome (FIGS. 22-25 and 24-4).

THE BAROQUE IN NORTHERN EUROPE

Flanders

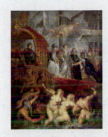

Rubens, *Marie de' Medici at Marseilles*, 1622–1625

- In the 17th century, Flanders remained Catholic and under Spanish control. Flemish Baroque art was more closely tied to the Baroque art of Italy than was the art of much of the rest of northern Europe.
- The leading Flemish painter of this era was Peter Paul Rubens, whose work and influence were international in scope. A diplomat as well as an artist, he counted kings and queens among his patrons and friends. His paintings, for example, the series of huge canvases he painted for Marie de'Medici to glorify her career, exhibit Baroque splendor in color and ornament, and feature robust and foreshortened figures in swirling motion.

Dutch Republic

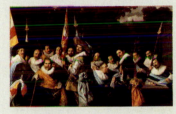

Hals, *Archers of Saint Hadrian*, ca. 1633

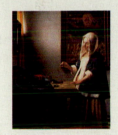

Vermeer, *Woman Holding a Balance*, ca. 1664

- The Dutch Republic received official recognition of its independence from Spain in the Treaty of Westphalia of 1648. Worldwide trade and banking brought prosperity to its predominantly Protestant citizenry, which largely rejected church art in favor of private commissions of portraits, genre scenes, landscapes, and still lifes.
- Frans Hals produced innovative portraits of middle-class patrons in which a lively informality replaced the formulaic patterns of traditional portraiture. Aelbert Cuyp and Jacob van Ruisdael specialized in landscapes depicting specific places, not idealized Renaissance settings. Pieter Claesz, Willem Kalf, and others specialized in still lifes featuring meticulous depictions of worldly goods, sometimes amid reminders of death.
- Rembrandt van Rijn, the greatest Dutch artist of the age, treated a broad range of subjects, including religious themes and portraits. His oil paintings are notable for their dramatic impact and subtle gradations of light and shade as well as the artist's ability to convey human emotions. Rembrandt was also a master printmaker.
- Jan Vermeer specialized in painting the occupants of serene, comfortable Dutch homes. His convincing representation of interior spaces depended in part on his employment of a camera obscura. Vermeer was also a master of light and color and understood that shadows are not colorless.

France and England

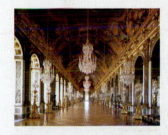

Galerie des Glaces, Versailles, ca. 1680

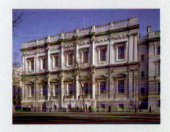

Jones, Banqueting House, London, 1619–1622

- The major art patron in 17th-century France was the Sun King, the absolutist monarch Louis XIV, who expanded the Louvre in Paris and built a vast palace and garden complex at nearby Versailles featuring sumptuous furnishings and sweeping vistas. Among the architects that Louis employed were Charles Le Brun and Jules Hardouin-Mansart, who succeeded in marrying Italian Baroque and French classical styles.
- The leading French proponent of classical painting was Nicolas Poussin, who spent most of his life in Rome and championed the "grand manner" of painting. This style called for heroic or divine subjects and classical compositions with figures often modeled on ancient statues.
- Claude Lorrain, whose fame rivaled Poussin's, specialized in classical landscapes rendered in linear and atmospheric perspective. His compositions often incorporated ancient ruins.
- In 17th-century England, architecture was the most important art form. Two architects who achieved international fame were Inigo Jones and Christopher Wren. They harmonized the architectural principles of Andrea Palladio with the Italian Baroque and French classical styles in buildings such as the Banqueting House (Jones) and Saint Paul's Cathedral (Wren) in London.

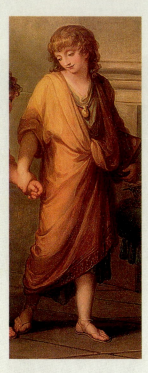

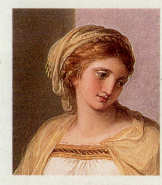

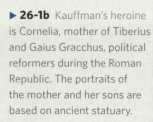

◀ **26-1a** The Enlightenment fascination with classical antiquity gave rise to the art movement called Neoclassicism. In this painting, Kauffman chose a classical subject and clothed her figures in Roman garb.

▶ **26-1b** Kauffman's heroine is Cornelia, mother of Tiberius and Gaius Gracchus, political reformers during the Roman Republic. The portraits of the mother and her sons are based on ancient statuary.

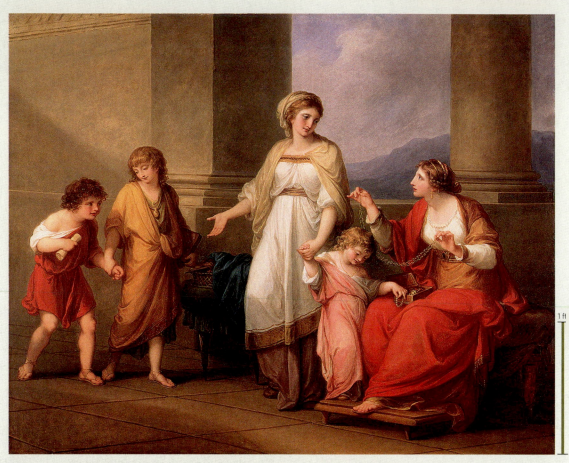

1 ft

26-1 ANGELICA KAUFFMAN, *Cornelia Presenting Her Children as Her Treasures,* or *Mother of the Gracchi,* ca. 1785. Oil on canvas, 3' 4" × 4' 2". Virginia Museum of Fine Arts, Richmond (Adolph D. and Wilkins C. Williams Fund).

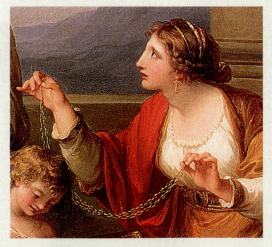

◀ **26-1c** The painting is an Enlightenment *exemplum virtutis* ("example of virtue"). When a visitor shows Cornelia her jewelry and asks to see Cornelia's, the mother of the Gracchi presents her children as her jewels.

Rococo to Neoclassicism: The 18th Century in Europe and America

THE ENLIGHTENMENT, ANGELICA KAUFFMAN, AND NEOCLASSICISM

The dawn of the *Enlightenment* in the 18th century brought a new way of thinking critically about the world and about men and women, independently of religion, myth, or tradition. Enlightenment thinkers rejected unfounded beliefs in favor of empirical evidence and promoted the questioning of all assertions. This new worldview was a major factor in the revolutionary political, social, and economic changes that swept Europe and America in the mid- to late 1700s. Among these were the wars for independence in America and France, the Industrial Revolution in England, and a renewed admiration in both Europe and America for the art and architecture of classical antiquity. The Enlightenment's emphasis on rationality in part explains this classical focus, because the geometric harmony of classical art and architecture embodied Enlightenment ideals. Moreover, Greece and Rome represented the pinnacle of civilized society—paragons of enlightened political organization. With their traditions of liberty, civic virtue, morality, and sacrifice, these cultures were ideal models during a period of political upheaval.

The Enlightenment interest in classical antiquity in turn gave rise to the artistic movement known as *Neoclassicism*, which incorporated the subjects and styles of Greek and Roman art. One of the pioneers of Neoclassical painting was ANGELICA KAUFFMAN (1741–1807). Born in Switzerland and trained in Italy, Kauffman spent many of her productive years in England. In an era when nearly all successful artists were men, Kauffman enjoyed an enviable reputation and was a founding member of the British Royal Academy of Arts.

Cornelia Presenting Her Children as Her Treasures, or *Mother of the Gracchi* (FIG. 26-1), is perhaps Kauffman's best-known work. The theme of the painting is the virtue of Cornelia, mother of the future political leaders Tiberius and Gaius Gracchus, who, in the second century BCE, attempted to reform the Roman Republic. Cornelia reveals her character in this scene, which takes place after a visitor has shown off her fine jewelry and then haughtily insists that Cornelia show hers. Instead of taking out her own precious adornments, Cornelia brings her sons forward, presenting them as her jewels. *Mother of the Gracchi* is a characteristic example of the Enlightenment embrace of the values of the classical world, an *exemplum virtutis* ("example of virtue") drawn from Greek and Roman history and literature.

To give her retelling of the story an authentic air, Kauffman studied ancient statuary and then clothed her actors in ancient Roman garb and posed them in statuesque attitudes within Roman interiors. The architectural setting is severe, and the composition and drawing have the simplicity and firmness of low-relief carving, qualities that became hallmarks of the Neoclassical style.

A CENTURY OF REVOLUTIONS

In 1700, Louis XIV still ruled France as the Sun King (see page 750), presiding over his realm and French culture from his palatial residence at Versailles (FIG. 25-26). The French king's palace inspired the construction of many other grandiose homes on the Continent and across the English Channel during the early 18th century, including Blenheim Palace (FIG. 26-1A), which SIR JOHN VANBRUGH (1664–1726) and NICHOLAS HAWKSMOOR (1661–

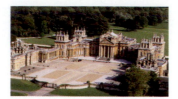

🡵 **26-1A** VANBRUGH and HAWKSMOOR, Blenheim Palace, 1705–1725.

1736) designed for the duke of Marlborough. By 1800, however, revolutions had overthrown the monarchy in France and achieved independence for the British colonies in America. The 18th century also gave birth to a revolution of a different kind—the Industrial Revolution, which began in England and soon transformed the economies of continental Europe and North America and eventually the world.

Against this backdrop of revolutionary change, social as well as political, economic, and technological, came major transformations in the arts. Compare, for example, Antoine Watteau's 1717 *Pilgrimage to Cythera* (FIG. 26-7), which unfolds in a lush landscape and celebrates the romantic dalliances of the moneyed elite, with Angelica Kauffmann's 1785 *Mother of the Gracchi* (FIG. 26-1), set in an austere home of classical columns and piers and glorifying the maternal virtue of an ancient Roman woman. The two works have little in common other than that both are horizontally oriented oil paintings. In the 18th century, shifts in style and subject matter were both rapid and significant.

ROCOCO

The death of Louis XIV in 1715 brought many changes in French high society. The elite quickly abandoned the court of Versailles for the pleasures of town life. Although French citizens still owed allegiance to a monarch, the early 18th century brought a resurgence of aristocratic social, political, and economic power. Members of the nobility not only exercised their traditional privileges (for example, exemption from certain taxes and from forced labor on public works) but also sought to expand their power. In the cultural realm, aristocrats reestablished their predominance as art patrons. The *hôtels* (elegant private townhouses) of Paris soon became the centers of a new, softer style called *Rococo*. Associated with the regency (1715–1723) following the death of Louis XIV and with the reign of Louis XV (r. 1723–1774), the Rococo style in art and architecture

was the perfect expression of the lighthearted elegance that the wealthy cultivated in their opulent homes (see "Femmes Savantes and Salon Culture," page 765).

Architecture

Rococo appeared in France around 1700, primarily as a style of interior design. The French Rococo exterior was most often simple, or even plain, but Rococo exuberance took over the interior. The term derived from the French word *rocaille* ("pebble"), but it referred especially to the small stones and shells used to decorate grotto interiors. Shells or forms resembling shells were the principal motifs in Rococo ornamentation.

SALON DE LA PRINCESSE A typical French Rococo room is the Salon de la Princesse (FIG. 26-2) in the Hôtel de Soubise in Paris, designed by GERMAIN BOFFRAND (1667–1754) in collaboration with the painter JOSEPH NATOIRE (1700–1777) and the sculptor JEAN-BAPTISTE LEMOYNE (1704–1778). Parisian salons such as this one were the center of Rococo social life. They usurped the role that Louis XIV's Versailles palace (FIG. 25-26) played in the 17th century, when the Sun King set the tone for French culture. In the early 18th century, the centralized and grandiose palace-based culture of Baroque France gave way to a much more intimate and decentralized culture based in private homes.

The new architectural style mirrored this social and cultural shift. A comparison between the Salon de la Princesse and the Galerie des Glaces (FIG. 25-27) at Versailles reveals how Boffrand softened the strong architectural lines and panels of the earlier style into flexible, sinuous curves. The walls melt into the vault. Irregular painted shapes, topped by sculpture and separated by rocaille shells, replace the hall's cornices. Painting, architecture, and sculpture combine to form a single ensemble. The profusion of curving tendrils and sprays of foliage blend with the shell forms to give an effect of freely growing nature, suggesting that the designer permanently bedecked the Rococo room for a festival.

French Rococo interiors were lively total works of art. Exquisitely wrought furniture, enchanting small sculptures (FIG. 26-10), ornamented mirror frames, crystal chandeliers, delightful ceramics and silver plates and goblets, small paintings, and decorative *tapestries* complemented the architecture, relief sculptures, and mural paintings. Unfortunately, the Salon de la Princesse has lost most of the moveable furnishings that once contributed so much to its total ambience. Visitors can nonetheless imagine how this and similar Rococo rooms—with their alternating gilded moldings, vivacious relief sculptures, and daintily colored ornamentation of flowers and garlands, all visually multiplied by their mirror reflections—must have harmonized with the chamber music played in them, with

WRITTEN SOURCES
Femmes Savantes and Salon Culture

The feminine look of the Rococo style reflects the taste and social initiative of women, and to a large extent, women dominated the cultural sphere during the Rococo age. In the 18th century, aristocratic women—including Madame de Pompadour (1721–1764), mistress of Louis XV of France; Maria Theresa (1717–1780), archduchess of Austria and queen of Hungary and Bohemia; and Empresses Elizabeth (r. 1741–1762) and Catherine the Great (r. 1762–1796) of Russia—held some of the most influential positions in Europe. Female taste also was a defining factor in numerous smaller courts as well as in the private sphere.

In the early 1700s, Paris was the social capital of Europe, and the Rococo salon (FIG. 26-2) was the center of Parisian society. Wealthy, ambitious, and clever society hostesses competed to attract the most famous and accomplished people to their salons. The medium of social intercourse was conversation spiced with wit and as quick and deft as a fencing match. Artifice reigned supreme, and participants considered enthusiasm or sincerity in bad taste.

The women who hosted these salons, whether in Paris or elsewhere in Europe (FIG. 26-3), referred to themselves as *femmes savants* ("learned women"). Chief among them was Julie de Lespinasse (1732–1776), one of the most articulate, urbane, and intelligent French women of the time. She held daily salons from five o'clock until nine in the evening. The memoirs of Jean François Marmontel (1723–1799), published in 1827, documented the liveliness of these gatherings and the remarkable nature of this hostess.

The circle was formed of persons who were not bound together. She [Julie de Lespinasse] had taken them here and there in society, but so well assorted were they that once [in her salon] they fell into harmony like the strings of an instrument touched by an able hand. Following out that comparison, I may say that she played the instrument with an art that came of genius; she seemed to know what tone each string would yield before she touched it; I mean to say that our minds and our natures were so well known to her that in order to bring them into play she had but to say a word. Nowhere was conversation more lively, more brilliant, or better regulated than at her house. It was a rare phenomenon indeed, the degree of tempered, equable heat which she knew so well how to maintain, sometimes by moderating it, sometimes by quickening it. The continual activity of her soul was communicated to our souls, but measurably; her imagination was the mainspring, her reason the regulator. Remark that the brains she stirred at will were neither feeble nor frivolous. . . . Her talent for casting out a thought and giving it for discussion to men of that class, her own talent in discussing it with precision, sometimes with eloquence, her talent for bringing forward new ideas and varying the topic—always with the facility and ease of a fairy . . . these talents, I say, were not those of an ordinary woman. It was not with the follies of fashion and vanity that daily, during four hours of conversation, without languor and without vacuum, she knew how to make herself interesting to a wide circle of strong minds.*

*Jean François Marmontel, *Memoirs of Marmontel* (1827), translated by Brigit Patmore (London: Routledge, 1930), 270.

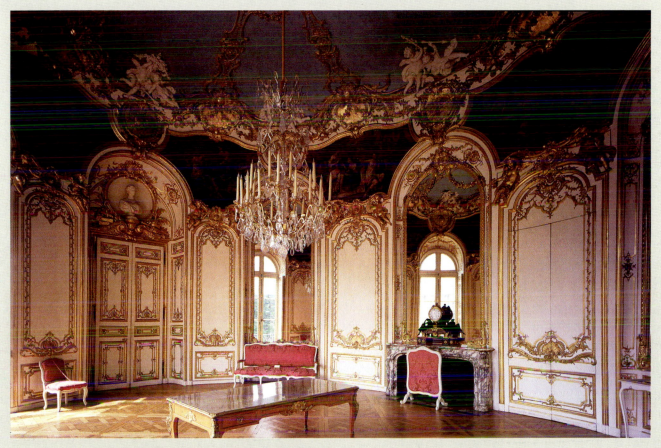

26-2 GERMAIN BOFFRAND, Salon de la Princesse, with paintings by CHARLES-JOSEPH NATOIRE and sculpture by JEAN-BAPTISTE LEMOYNE, Hôtel de Soubise, Paris, France, 1737–1740.

Rococo rooms such as this one, featuring sinuous curves, gilded moldings and mirrors, small sculptures and paintings, and floral ornamentation, were the center of Parisian social and intellectual life.

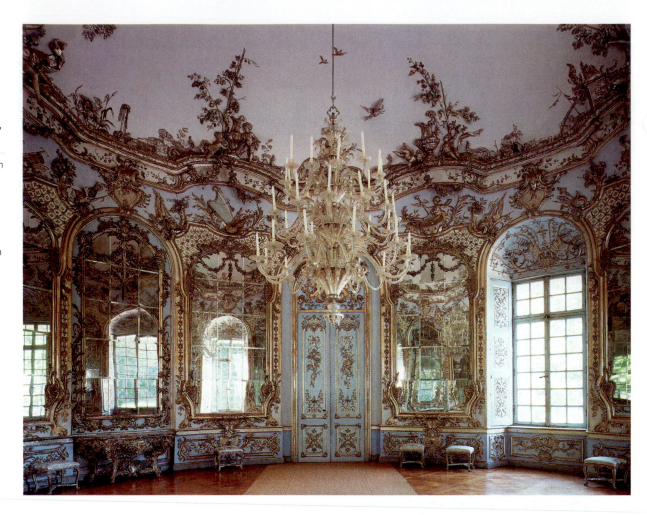

26-3 FRANÇOIS DE CUVILLIÉS, Hall of Mirrors, the Amalienburg, Nymphenburg Palace park, Munich, Germany, early 18th century.

Designed by a French architect, this circular hall in a German lodge displays the Rococo architectural style at its height, dazzling the eye with the organic interplay of mirrors, crystal, and stucco relief.

the elaborate costumes of satin and brocade, and with the equally elegant etiquette and sparkling wit of the people who graced them.

AMALIENBURG The French Rococo style quickly spread beyond Paris. The Amalienburg, a small lodge that the French architect FRANÇOIS DE CUVILLIÉS (1695–1768) built in the park of the Nymphenburg Palace in Munich, is a prime example of Germany's adoption of the Parisian style. The most spectacular room in the lodge is the circular Hall of Mirrors (FIG. **26-3**), a silver-and-blue ensemble of architecture, stucco relief, silvered bronze mirrors, and crystal. The hall dazzles the eye with myriad scintillating motifs, forms, and figurations, and showcases the full ornamental repertoire of the Rococo style at the height of its popularity. Silvery light, reflected and amplified by windows and mirrors, bathes the room and creates shapes and contours that weave rhythmically around the upper walls and the ceiling coves. Everything seems organic, growing, and in motion, an ultimate refinement of illusion with virtuoso flourishes created by the team of architects, artists, and artisans.

VIERZEHNHEILIGEN Rococo style was not exclusively a domestic phenomenon, however. Although some early-18th-century archi-

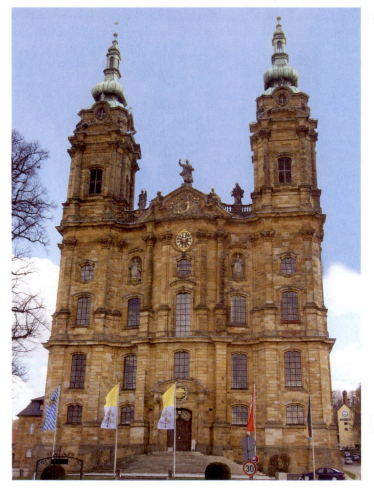

26-4 BALTHASAR NEUMANN, facade of the pilgrimage church of Vierzehnheiligen (looking east), near Bad Staffelstein, Germany, 1743–1772.

The facade of Neumann's pilgrimage church of Vierzehnheiligen (Fourteen Saints) features the undulating surfaces of Italian Baroque architecture, but its Rococo interior (FIG. 26-6) lacks Baroque drama.

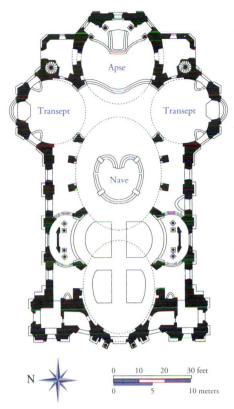

26-5 BALTHASAR NEUMANN, plan of the pilgrimage church of Vierzehnheiligen, near Bad Staffelstein, Germany, 1743–1772.

Vierzehnheiligen's plan features undulating lines and a dynamic composition of tangent ovals and circles. It is even more complex than Borromini's influential church plans (FIGS. 24-11 and 24-13).

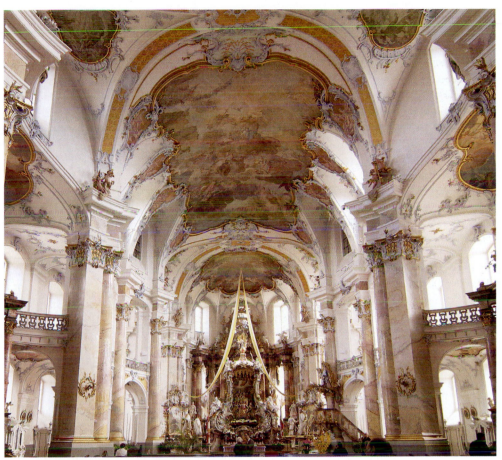

26-6 BALTHASAR NEUMANN, interior of the pilgrimage church of Vierzehnheiligen (looking east), near Bad Staffelstein, Germany, 1743–1772.

Neumann adapted the intimate Rococo style to ecclesiastical architecture. Vierzehnheiligen's interior is light and delicate, whereas Italian Baroque church designs are heavy and dynamic.

tects, such as JOHANN BERNHARD FISCHER VON ERLACH (1656–1723), continued to design churches incorporating Baroque and classical elements—for example, Karlskirche (FIG. 26-3A) in Vienna—others eagerly adopted the Rococo style for ecclesiastical architecture. One of the most splendid examples is the pilgrimage church of Vierzehnheiligen (Fourteen Saints; FIGS. 26-4, 26-5, and 26-6) near Bad Staffelstein (MAP 25-1), which the German architect BALTHASAR NEUMANN (1687–1753) began as construction was about to be concluded on the grandiose palace (FIG. 26-6A) he had designed in 1719 for the prince-bishops of Würzburg.

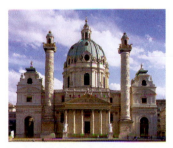

26-3A FISCHER VON ERLACH, Karlskirche, Vienna, 1716–1737.

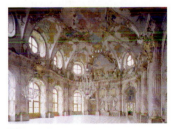

26-6A NEUMANN, Kaisersaal, Würzburg, 1719–1744.

Vierzehnheiligen's undulating facade (FIG. 26-4) and curve-filled plan (FIG. 26-5) and interior (FIG. 26-6) reveal the influence of the great Italian Baroque architect Francesco Borromini (FIGS. 24-10 to 24-14). Neumann's plan, however, is even more complex than

the plans of Borromini's churches in Rome. The German architect deliberately banished all straight lines. The composition, made up of tangent ovals and circles, achieves a quite different interior effect within the essential outlines of a traditional rectilinear basilican church with a nave, transept, and apse. Undulating space is in continuous motion, creating unlimited vistas that are bewildering in their variety and surprise effects, as is also true of the contemporaneous Wieskirche (Church of the Meadow; FIG. 26-6B) by DOMINIKUS ZIMMERMANN (1685–1766). Numerous large windows in Vierzehnheiligen's richly decorated walls flood the interior with an even, bright, and cheerful light. The feeling is one of lightness

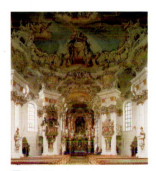

26-6B ZIMMERMANN, Wieskirche, Füssen, 1745–1754.

and delicacy. The church's walls and vaults pulse, flow, and commingle as if they were ceaselessly in the process of being molded. The design's fluidity of line, the floating and hovering surfaces, the interwoven spaces, and the dematerialized masses combine to suggest a "frozen" counterpart to the intricacy of voices in a Baroque fugue by Johann Sebastian Bach (1685–1750). The Bad Staffelstein pilgrimage church is a brilliant ensemble of architecture, painting, sculpture, and music that dissolves the boundaries among the arts.

Poussinistes and Rubénistes

Pilgrimage to Cythera (FIG. 26-7), the first great fête galante painting, was Antoine Watteau's entry for admission to the French Royal Academy of Painting and Sculpture (see "Academic Salons," page 844). In 1717, the fête galante was not an acceptable category for submission, but rather than reject Watteau's candidacy, the Academy created a new category to accommodate his entry.

At the turn of the 18th century, two competing doctrines sharply divided the membership of the French Royal Academy. Many members followed Nicolas Poussin (FIGS. 25-31, 25-32, and 25-32A) in teaching that form was the most important element in painting, whereas "colors in painting are as allurements for persuading the eyes."* Colors, argued Poussin's admirers, were additions for effect and not really essential. The other group took Rubens (FIGS. 25-2, 25-2A, 25-3, and 25-4) as its model and proclaimed the natural supremacy of color and the coloristic style as the artist's proper guide.

Depending on which doctrine they supported, members of the French Academy were classified as either *Poussinistes* or *Rubénistes*. Watteau was Flemish, and Rubens's coloristic style heavily influenced his work. With Watteau in their ranks, the Rubénistes carried the day, establishing Rococo painting as the preferred style in early-18th-century France.

*Translated by Robert Goldwater and Marco Treves, eds., *Artists on Art*, 3d ed. (New York: Pantheon Books, 1958), 157.

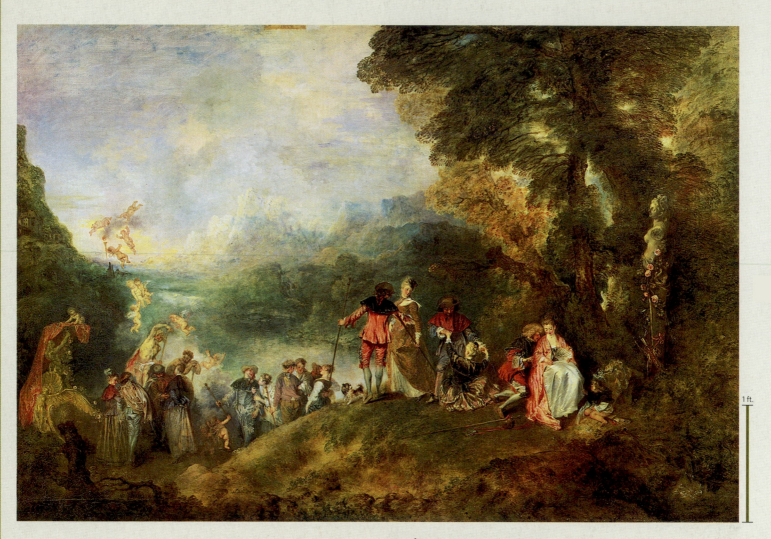

26-7 ANTOINE WATTEAU, *Pilgrimage to Cythera*, 1717. Oil on canvas, 4' 3" × 6' 4 1/2". Musée du Louvre, Paris.

Watteau's fête galante paintings depict the outdoor amusements of French upper-class society. The haze of color suited the new Rococo taste and was the hallmark of the Royal Academy's Rubénistes.

Painting and Sculpture

The unification of diverse artistic media that characterizes the Rococo style did not preclude the rise to prominence of painters of independent works. Chief among them were Antoine Watteau, François Boucher, and Jean-Honoré Fragonard in France.

ANTOINE WATTEAU The painter whom scholars most closely associate with French Rococo is ANTOINE WATTEAU (1684–1721). Watteau was largely responsible for creating a specific type of Rococo painting genre called a *fête galante* ("amorous festival") (see "Poussinistes and Rubénistes," above). Fête galante paintings depicted the outdoor entertainment or amusements of French high society. The premier example is Watteau's masterpiece (painted in two versions), *Pilgrimage to Cythera* (FIG. **26-7**). The canvas presents luxuriously costumed lovers who have made a "pilgrimage" to Cythera, the island of eternal youth and love, sacred to Aphrodite. (Some art historians think the lovers are returning from Cythera rather than having just arrived. Watteau provided few clues to settle the question definitively.)

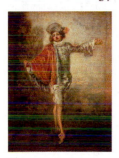

🔗 **26-7A** WATTEAU, *L'Indifférent*, ca. 1716.

The elegant figures move gracefully from the protective shade of a woodland park filled with playful cupids and voluptuous statuary. The poses of the figures, which blend elegance and sweetness, are hallmarks of Watteau's style, both in ambitious multifigure compositions such as *Pilgrimage to Cythera* and in single-figure studies such as *L'Indifférent* (FIG. **26-7A**).

Watteau prepared his paintings using albums of drawings in which he sought to capture slow movement from difficult and unusual angles, searching for the smoothest, most poised, and most refined attitudes. As he experimented with nuances of posture and movement, Watteau also strove for the most exquisite shades of color difference, defining in a single stroke the shimmer of silk at a bent knee or the shine appearing on a glossy surface as it emerges from shadow. The haze of color, the subtly modeled shapes, the gliding motion, and the air of suave gentility tinged with nostalgia

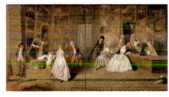

🔗 **26-7B** WATTEAU, *Signboard of Gersaint*, 1721.

appealed greatly to Watteau's wealthy patrons, whom, as he was dying from tuberculosis, he still depicted as carefree and at leisure in his most unusual painting, *Signboard of Gersaint* (FIG. **26-7B**).

FRANÇOIS BOUCHER After Watteau's death at age 36 brought his brilliant career to a premature end, FRANÇOIS BOUCHER (1703–1770) rose to the dominant position in French painting, in large part because he was Madame de Pompadour's favorite artist. Although Boucher was an excellent portraitist, his success rested primarily on his graceful canvases depicting shepherds, nymphs, and goddesses cavorting in shady glens engulfed in pink and sky-blue light. *Cupid a Captive* (FIG. **26-8**) presents a rosy pyramid of infant and female flesh set off against a cool, leafy background, with fluttering draperies both hiding and revealing the nudity of the figures. Boucher used the full range of Italian and French Baroque devices—the dynamic play of crisscrossing diagonals, curvilinear forms, and slanting recessions—to create his masterful composition. But he dissected powerful Baroque curves into a multiplicity of decorative flourishes, dissipating Baroque drama into sensual playfulness. Lively and lighthearted, Boucher's artful Rococo fantasies became mirrors for his well-to-do French patrons to behold the ornamental reflections of their cherished pastimes.

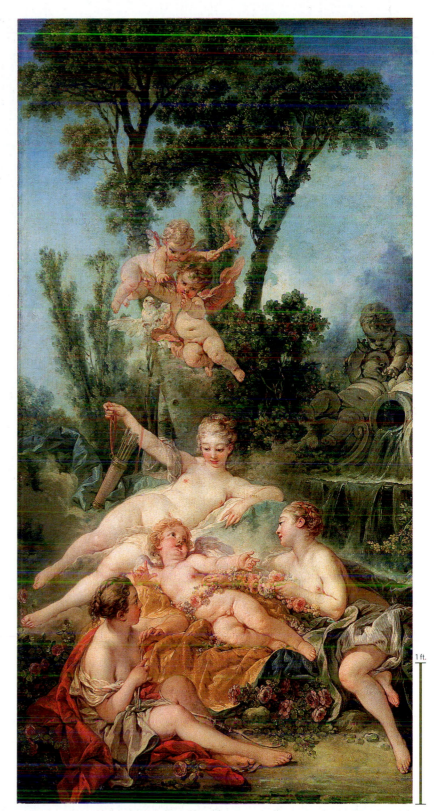

1 ft.

26-8 FRANÇOIS BOUCHER, *Cupid a Captive*, 1754. Oil on canvas, 5′ 6″ × 2′ 10″. Wallace Collection, London.

Boucher was Madame de Pompadour's favorite artist. In this Rococo tableau, he painted a pyramid of rosy infant and female flesh and fluttering draperies set off against a cool, leafy background.

JEAN-HONORÉ FRAGONARD Boucher's greatest student, JEAN-HONORÉ FRAGONARD (1732–1806), was a first-rate colorist whose decorative skill almost surpassed his master's. An example of his

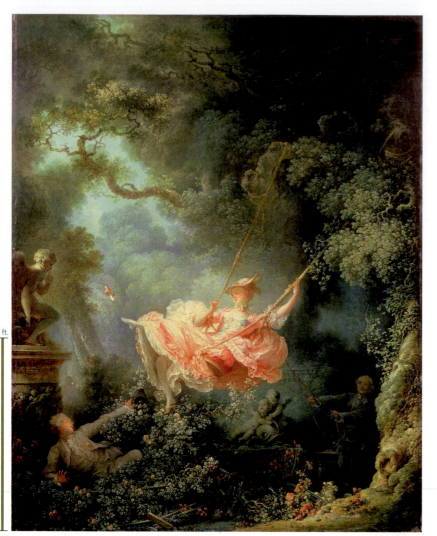

Fragonard's *Swing* exemplifies Rococo style. Pastel colors and soft light complement a scene in which a young lady flirtatiously kicks off her shoe at a statue of Cupid while her lover gazes at her.

Italian Mannerist sculpture. His small group *Nymph and Satyr Carousing* (FIG. **26-10**) depicts two followers of Bacchus, the Roman god of wine. The sensuous nymph who rushes to pour wine from a cup into the open mouth of a semihuman goat-legged satyr is reminiscent of the nude female figures of Benvenuto Cellini (FIGS. 22-52 and 22-52A), who worked at Fontainebleau for Francis I (see page 693), and of Giambologna (FIG. 22-53), a French Mannerist sculptor who moved to Italy. The erotic playfulness of Boucher and Fragonard is also evident in Clodion's 2-foot-tall terracotta group destined for display on a marble tabletop in an elegant Rococo salon.

GIAMBATTISTA TIEPOLO Also small are *The Swing*—less than 3 feet in height—and Watteau's *L'Indifférent* (FIG. 26-7A), which is barely 10 inches tall. Even the figure-packed landscape *Pilgrimage to Cythera* (FIG. 26-7) is only a little more than 4 feet high. But the intimate Rococo style could also be adapted for paintings of huge size, as the work of GIAMBATTISTA TIEPOLO (1696–1770) demonstrates. A Venetian, Tiepolo worked for patrons in Austria, Germany (FIG. 26-4A), and Spain, as well as in Italy. He was a master of illusionistic ceiling decoration in the Baroque tradition, but favored the bright,

manner can stand as characteristic not only of his work but also of the later Rococo in general. In *The Swing* (FIG. **26-9**), a young gentleman has convinced an unsuspecting old bishop to swing the young man's pretty sweetheart higher and higher, while her lover (and the work's patron), in the lower left corner, stretches out to admire her from a strategic position on the ground. The young lady flirtatiously kicks off her shoe toward the little statue of Cupid. The infant love god holds his finger to his lips. The landscape emulates Watteau's—a luxuriant perfumed bower in a park that very much resembles a stage scene for comic opera. The glowing pastel colors and soft light convey, almost by themselves, the theme's sensuality.

CLODION Rococo was a style best suited for small-scale works projecting a mood of sensual intimacy. Claude Michel, called CLODION (1738–1814), specialized in small, lively sculptures representing sensuous Rococo fantasies. Clodion lived and worked in Rome for several years after winning a cherished Prix de Rome (Rome Prize) from the French Royal Academy to study art and paint or sculpt in the Eternal City. Clodion's work incorporates echoes of

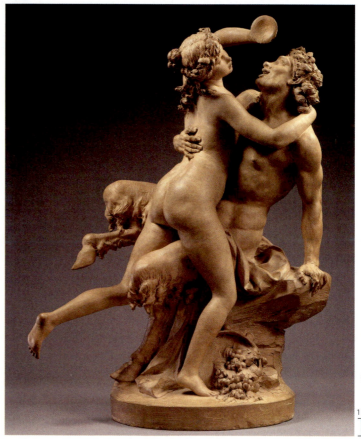

26-10 CLODION, *Nymph and Satyr Carousing*, ca. 1780–1790. Terracotta, 1' 11¼" high. Metropolitan Museum of Art, New York (bequest of Benjamin Altman, 1913).

The erotic playfulness of Boucher and Fragonard is evident in Clodion's tabletop terracotta sculptures representing sensuous fantasies often involving satyrs and nymphs, the followers of Bacchus.

THE ENLIGHTENMENT

The aristocratic culture celebrated in Rococo art did not go unchallenged during the 18th century. Indeed, the feudal system that served as the foundation of social and economic life in Europe dissolved, and the rigid social hierarchies that provided the basis for Rococo art and patronage relaxed. By the end of the 18th century, revolutions had erupted in France and America. A major factor in these political, social, and economic changes was the Enlightenment.

Philosophy and Science

Enlightenment thinkers rejected faith in favor of reason and championed an approach to the acquisition of knowledge based on empirical observation and scientific experimentation. Enlightenment-era science had roots in the work of René Descartes (1596–1650), Blaise Pascal (1623–1662), Isaac Newton (1642–1727), and Gottfried Wilhelm von Leibniz (1646–1716) in the 17th century. England and France were the principal centers of the Enlightenment, though its maxims influenced the thinking of intellectuals throughout Europe and in the American colonies. Benjamin Franklin (1706–1790), Thomas Jefferson (1743–1826), and other American notables embraced its principles.

NEWTON AND LOCKE Of particular importance for Enlightenment thought was the work of Isaac Newton and John Locke (1632–1704) in England. In his scientific studies, Newton insisted on empirical proof of his theories and encouraged others to avoid metaphysics and the supernatural—realms that extended beyond the natural physical world. This emphasis on both tangible data and concrete experience became a cornerstone of Enlightenment thought. In addition, Newton's experiments revealed rationality in the physical world, and Enlightenment thinkers transferred that concept to the sociopolitical world by promoting a rationally organized society. Locke, whose works acquired the status of Enlightenment gospel, developed these ideas further. According to Locke's "doctrine of empiricism," knowledge comes through sensory perception of the material world. From these perceptions alone, people form ideas.

Locke asserted that human beings are born good, not cursed by original sin. The laws of nature grant them the natural rights of life, liberty, and property as well as the right to freedom of conscience. Government is by contract, and the purpose of the government is to protect these rights. If and when government abuses these rights, the citizenry has the further natural right of revolution. Locke's ideas empowered people to take control of their own destinies.

PHILOSOPHES The work of Newton and Locke also inspired many French intellectuals, or *philosophes*. These thinkers conceived of individuals and societies as parts of physical nature. They shared the conviction that the ills of humanity could be remedied by

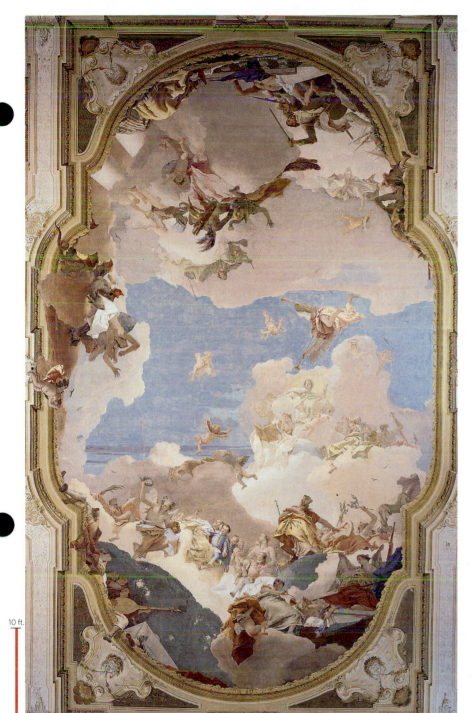

26-11 GIAMBATTISTA TIEPOLO, *Apotheosis of the Pisani Family*, ceiling painting in the Villa Pisani, Stra, Italy, 1761–1762. Fresco, 77' 1" × 44' 3".

A master of illusionistic ceiling painting in the Baroque tradition, Tiepolo adopted the bright and cheerful colors and weightless figures of Rococo easel paintings for huge frescoes.

cheerful colors and relaxed compositions of Rococo easel paintings. In *Apotheosis of the Pisani Family* (FIG. **26-11**), a ceiling fresco in the Villa Pisani at Stra in northern Italy (MAP 25-1), Tiepolo depicted seemingly weightless figures fluttering through vast sunlit skies and fleecy clouds, their forms casting dark accents against the brilliant light of high noon. The painter elevated Pisani family members to the rank of gods in a heavenly scene recalling the ceiling paintings of Pozzo (FIG. 24-24). But while retaining 17th-century illusionism in his works, Tiepolo softened the rhetoric and created pictorial schemes of great elegance and grace, unsurpassed for their sheer effectiveness as decor.

ART AND SOCIETY

Joseph Wright of Derby and the Industrial Revolution

The scientific advances of the Enlightenment era affected the lives of everyone, and most people enthusiastically responded to the wonders of the Industrial Revolution such as the steam engine, which gave birth to the modern manufacturing economy and the prospect of a seemingly limitless supply of goods and services.

The fascination that science held for ordinary people as well as for the learned was a favorite subject of the English painter Joseph Wright of Derby (FIGS. **26-11A** and **26-12**). Wright studied painting near Birmingham (MAP 27-2), the center of the Industrial Revolution, and specialized in dramatically lit scenes showcasing modern scientific instruments and experiments.

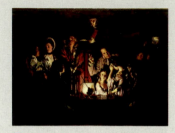

26-11A WRIGHT OF DERBY, *Experiment on a Bird,* 1768.

A characteristic example of Wright's work is *A Philosopher Giving a Lecture at the Orrery.* In this painting, a scholar demonstrates a mechanical model of the solar system called an *orrery,* in which each planet (represented by a metal orb) revolves around the sun (a lamp) at the correct relative velocity. Light from the lamp pours forth from in front of the boy silhouetted in the foreground to create shadows that heighten the drama of the scene. Curious children crowd close to the tiny orbs representing the planets within the curving bands symbolizing their orbits. An earnest listener makes notes, while the lone woman seated at the left and the two gentlemen at the right pay rapt attention. Scientific knowledge mesmerizes everyone in Wright's painting. The artist visually reinforced the fascination with the orrery by composing his image in a circular fashion, echoing the device's orbital design. The postures and gazes of all the participants and observers focus attention on the cosmic model. Wright scrupulously and accurately rendered every detail of the figures, the mechanisms of the orrery, and even the books and curtain in the shadowy background.

Wright's choice of subjects and realism in depicting them appealed to the great industrialists of his day, including Josiah Wedgwood (1730–1795), who pioneered many techniques of mass-produced pottery, and Sir Richard Arkwright (1732–1792), whose spinning frame revolutionized the textile industry. Both men often purchased paintings by Wright featuring scientific advances. To them, the Derby artist's elevation of the theories and inventions of the Industrial Revolution to the plane of history painting was exciting and appropriately in tune with the new era of Enlightenment.

26-12 JOSEPH WRIGHT OF DERBY, *A Philosopher Giving a Lecture at the Orrery,* ca. 1763–1765. Oil on canvas, 4' 10" × 6' 8". Derby Museums and Art Gallery, Derby.

Wright specialized in dramatically lit paintings celebrating the modern scientific instruments of the Industrial Revolution. Here, a scholar demonstrates an orrery, a revolving model of the solar system.

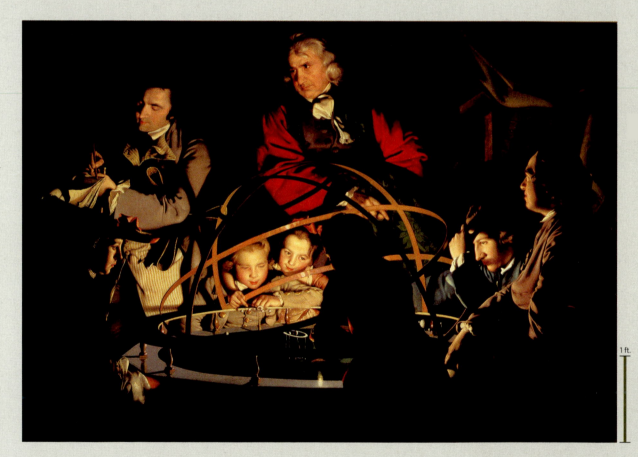

1 ft.

applying reason and common sense to human problems. They criticized the powers of Church and State as irrational limits placed on political and intellectual freedom. They were convinced that by accumulating and propagating knowledge, humanity could advance by degrees to a happier state than it had ever known. This conviction matured into the "doctrine of progress" and its corollary doctrine, the "perfectibility of humankind." Previous societies, for the most part, perceived the future as inevitable—the cycle of life and death. They believed that religious beliefs determined fate. The notion of progress—the systematic and planned improvement of society—first developed during the 18th century and still influences 21st-century thought.

DIDEROT Animated by their belief in human progress and perfectibility, the philosophes took on the task of gathering knowledge and making it accessible to all who could read. Their program was, in effect, the democratization of knowledge. Denis Diderot (1713–1784) greatly advanced the Enlightenment's rationalistic and materialistic thinking. He became editor of the pioneering *Encyclopédie*, a compilation of articles written by more than a hundred contributors, including all the leading philosophes. The *Encyclopédie* was truly comprehensive (its formal title was *Systematic Dictionary of the Sciences, Arts, and Crafts*) and included all available knowledge—historical, scientific, and technical as well as religious and moral—and political theory. (The *Encyclopédie*'s 21st-century descendant is Wikipedia, which has a similar goal of collecting all that is known and making that knowledge universally available.) The first installment of Diderot's 35-volume illustrated encyclopedia appeared in 1751 and the last in 1780. Other Enlightenment authors produced different compilations of knowledge. Diderot's contemporary Georges-Louis Leclerc (1707–1788) undertook a kind of encyclopedia of the natural sciences. His *Natural History*, a monumental work of 44 volumes, was especially valuable for its zoological content. At the same time, Swedish botanist Carolus Linnaeus (1707–1778) established a system of plant classification.

The political, economic, and social consequences of this increase in knowledge and of the doctrine of progress were explosive. It is no coincidence that the French Revolution, the American Revolution, and the Industrial Revolution in England all occurred during this period. These upheavals precipitated yet other major changes, including the growth of cities and of an urban working class, and the expansion of colonialism as the demand for cheap labor and raw materials increased. This enthusiasm for growth gave birth to the doctrine of Manifest Destiny (see page 814)—the ideological justification for continued territorial expansion. Thus the Enlightenment ushered in a new way of thinking and affected historical developments worldwide.

VOLTAIRE François Marie Arouet, better known as Voltaire (1694–1778), was the most representative figure—almost the personification—of the Enlightenment spirit. Voltaire was instrumental in introducing Newton and Locke to the French intelligentsia. He hated, and attacked through his writings, the arbitrary despotic rule of kings, the selfish privileges of the nobility and the Church, religious intolerance, and, above all, the injustice of the French *ancien régime* (the "old order"). In his numerous books and pamphlets, which the authorities regularly condemned and burned, he protested against government persecution of the freedoms of thought and religion. Voltaire believed that people could never be happy until an enlightened society removed the traditional obstructions to the progress of the human mind. His personal and public involvement in the struggle against established political and religious authority gave authenticity to his ideas. Voltaire persuaded a whole generation that fundamental changes were necessary, paving the way for a revolution in France that he never intended, and probably would not have approved. For example, Voltaire did not believe that "all men are created equal," the credo of Jean-Jacques Rousseau, Thomas Jefferson, and the American Declaration of Independence.

INDUSTRIAL REVOLUTION The Enlightenment emphasis on scientific investigation and technological invention opened up new possibilities for human understanding of the world and for control of its material forces. Research into the phenomena of electricity and combustion, along with the discovery of oxygen and the power of steam, had enormous consequences. Steam power as an adjunct to, or replacement for, human labor initiated a new era in world history. These and other technological advances—admiringly recorded in the paintings of JOSEPH WRIGHT OF DERBY (1734–1797; see "Joseph Wright of Derby and the Industrial Revolution," page 772, and FIGS. 26-11A and 26-12)—exemplified the Enlightenment notion of progress and gave birth to the Industrial Revolution. Most scholars mark the dawn of that technological revolution in the 1740s with the invention in England of steam engines for industrial production. By 1850, England could boast the world's first manufacturing economy. Within a century, the harnessed power of steam, coal, oil, iron, steel, and electricity, working in concert, transformed Europe. These scientific and technological advances also affected the arts, particularly through the invention of photography (see page 832) and the use of new materials for constructing buildings.

COALBROOKDALE BRIDGE The first use of iron in bridge design was in the cast-iron bridge (FIG. 26-13) built over the Severn River, near Coalbrookdale in England (MAP 30-1), where ABRAHAM DARBY III (1750–1789), one of the bridge's two designers, ran his family's cast-iron business. The Darby family had spearheaded

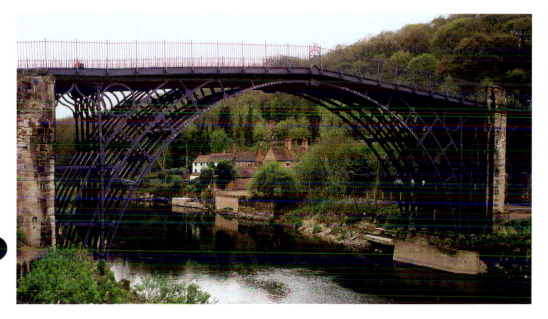

26-13 ABRAHAM DARBY III and THOMAS F. PRITCHARD, iron bridge (looking northwest), Coalbrookdale, England, 1776–1779.

The first use of iron in bridge design was in this bridge over the Severn River. The Industrial Revolution brought engineering advances and new materials that permanently changed architectural construction.

Diderot on Chardin and Boucher

Denis Diderot was a pioneer in the field of art criticism as well as in the encyclopedic compilation of human knowledge. Between 1759 and 1781, he contributed reviews of the biennial Salon of the French Royal Academy of Painting and Sculpture (see "Academic Salons," page 844) to the Parisian journal *Correspondence littéraire*. In his review of the 1763 Salon, Diderot had the following praise for Chardin's still lifes and for naturalism in painting.

> There are many small pictures by Chardin at the Salon, almost all of them depicting fruit with the accoutrements for a meal. This is nature itself. The objects stand out from the canvas and they are so real that my eyes are fooled by them. . . . In order to look at other people's paintings, I feel as though I need different eyes; but to look at Chardin's, I need only keep the ones nature gave me and use them properly. If I had painting in mind as a career for my child, I'd buy this one [and have him copy it]. . . . Yet nature itself may be no more difficult to copy. . . . O Chardin, it's not white, red or black pigment that you grind on your palette but rather the very substance of objects; it's real air and light that you take onto the tip of your brush and transfer onto the canvas. . . . It's magic, one can't understand how it's done: thick layers of color, applied one on top of the other, each one filtering through from underneath to create the effect. . . . Close up, everything blurs, goes flat and disappears. From a distance, everything comes back to life and reappears.*

While Diderot lavished praise on some of the leading artists of his day, he wrote scathing reviews of others. He admired Chardin (FIG. 26-14) because his work was the antithesis of the Rococo manner in painting, which Diderot deplored. Here, for example, is what Diderot had to say about François Boucher (FIG. 26-8), who also exhibited in the Salon of 1763, and his younger protégés emulating his Rococo style:

> What a misuse of talent! How much time gone to waste! You could have had twice the effect for half the effort. . . . When one writes, does one have to write everything? And when one paints, does one have to paint everything? . . . This man is the ruination of all young apprentice painters. Barely able to handle a brush and hold a palette, they torture themselves stringing together infantile garlands, painting chubby crimson bottoms, and hurl themselves headlong

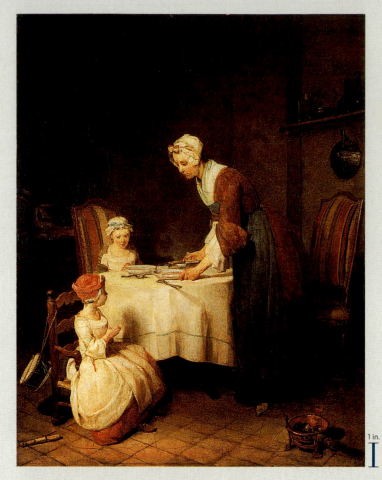

26-14 JEAN-BAPTISTE-SIMÉON CHARDIN, *Grace*, 1740. Oil on canvas, 1' 7" × 1' 3". Musée du Louvre, Paris.

Chardin embraced naturalism and celebrated the simple goodness of ordinary people, especially mothers and children, who lived in a world far from the frivolous Rococo salons of Paris.

> into all kinds of follies which cannot be redeemed by originality, fire, tenderness nor by any magic in their models. For they lack all of these.[†]

*Translated by Kate Tunstall, in Charles Harrison, Paul Wood, and Jason Gaiger, eds., *Art in Theory 1648-1815: An Anthology of Changing Ideas* (Oxford: Blackwell, 2000), 604.
[†]Ibid., 603–604.

the evolution of the iron industry in England, and they vigorously supported the investigation of new uses for the material. The fabrication of cast-iron rails and bridge elements inspired Darby to work with architect THOMAS F. PRITCHARD (1723–1777) in designing the Coalbrookdale Bridge. The cast-iron armature supporting the roadbed springs from stone pier to stone pier until it leaps the final 100 feet across the Severn River gorge. The style of the graceful center arc echoes the grand arches of Roman *aqueducts* (FIG. 7-33). At the same time, the exposed structure of the bridge's cast-iron parts prefigured the skeletal use of iron and steel in the 19th century, when exposed structural armatures became expressive factors in the design of buildings such as the Crystal Palace (FIG. 27-47) in England and the Eiffel Tower (FIG. 28-40) in France.

"NATURAL" ART

The second key figure of the French Enlightenment, who was also instrumental in preparing the way ideologically for the French Revolution, was Jean-Jacques Rousseau (1712–1778). Voltaire believed that the salvation of humanity lay in the advancement of science and the rational improvement of society. In contrast, Rousseau argued that the arts and sciences, society, and civilization in general had corrupted "natural man"—people in their primitive state. He was convinced that humanity's only salvation lay in a return to something like "the ignorance, innocence and happiness" of its original condition. According to Rousseau, human capacity for feeling, sensibility, and emotions came before reason: "To exist is to feel; our feeling is undoubtedly earlier than our intelligence, and we had feelings before we had ideas." Nature alone must be the guide: "All our natural inclinations are right." Fundamental to Rousseau's thinking was the notion that "Man by nature is good . . . he is depraved and perverted by society." He rejected the idea of progress, insisting that "our minds have been corrupted in proportion as the arts and sciences have improved."[1] Rousseau's elevation of feeling above reason as the most primitive—and hence the most "natural"—human expression led him to exalt as the ideal the peasant's simple life, with its honest and unsullied emotions.

Rousseau's views, popular and widely read, were largely responsible for the turning away from the Rococo sensibility in the arts and the formation of a taste for the "natural," as opposed to the artificial and frivolous.

CHARDIN Reflecting Rousseau's values, Jean-Baptiste-Siméon Chardin (1699–1779) painted quiet scenes of domestic life in the tradition of 17th-century Dutch genre scenes (see pages 746–747). These subjects offered Chardin the opportunity to praise the simple goodness of ordinary people, especially mothers and young children, who in spirit, occupation, and environment lived far from corrupt society. In *Grace* (FIG. 26-14), Chardin ushers the viewer into a modest room where a mother and her small daughters are about to dine. The mood of quiet attention is at one with the hushed lighting and mellow color and with the closely studied still-life accessories whose worn surfaces tell their own humble domestic history. The viewer witnesses a moment of social instruction, when mother and older sister supervise the younger sister in the simple, pious ritual of giving thanks to God before a meal. The simplicity of the composition reinforces the subdued charm of this scene, with the three figures highlighted against the dark background. Chardin was the poet of the commonplace and the master of its nuances. A gentle sentiment

prevails in all his pictures, an emotion not contrived and artificial but born of the painter's honesty, insight, and sympathy. Chardin's paintings had wide appeal, even in unexpected places. Louis XV, the royal personification of the Rococo in his life and tastes, once owned *Grace*. The painter was also a favorite of Diderot, the leading art critic of the day as well as the editor of the *Encyclopédie* (see "Diderot on Chardin and Boucher," page 774).

JEAN-BAPTISTE GREUZE The sentimental narrative in art became the specialty of French artist Jean-Baptiste Greuze (1725–1805), whose most popular work, *Village Bride* (FIG. 26-15), sums up the characteristics of the genre. The setting is an unadorned room in a rustic dwelling. In a notary's presence, the elderly father has passed his daughter's dowry to her youthful husband-to-be and blesses the pair, who gently take each other's arms. The old mother tearfully gives her daughter's arm a farewell caress, while the youngest sister melts in tears on the shoulder of the demure bride. An envious older sister broods behind her father's chair. Rosy-faced, healthy children play around the scene. The picture's story is simple—the happy climax of a rural romance. The picture's moral is just as clear—happiness is the reward of "natural" virtue.

Greuze produced this work at a time when the audience for art was expanding. The strict social hierarchy that provided the foundation for Rococo art and patronage gave way to a bourgeois economic and social system. The newly important middle class embraced art, and paintings such as *Village Bride* particularly appealed to ordinary hard-working people. They carefully analyzed each gesture and each nuance of sentiment and reacted with tumultuous enthusiasm. At the 1761 Salon of the Royal Academy, Greuze's picture received enormous attention. Diderot, who reviewed the exhibition for *Correspondence littéraire*, reported that it was difficult to get near the canvas because of the throngs of admirers.

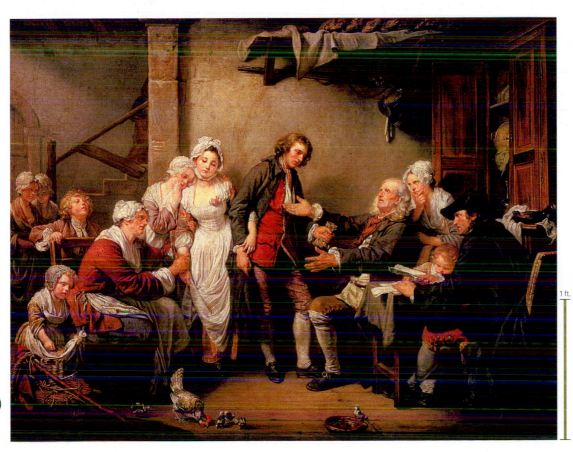

26-15 Jean-Baptiste Greuze, *Village Bride*, 1761. Oil on canvas, 3' × 3' 10½". Musée du Louvre, Paris.

Greuze was a master of sentimental narrative, which appealed to a new audience that admired "natural" virtue. Here, in an unadorned room, a father blesses his daughter and her husband-to-be.

ART AND SOCIETY

Vigée-Lebrun, Labille-Guiard, and the French Royal Academy

The two most successful woman artists in 18th-century France were Élisabeth-Louise Vigée-Lebrun (FIGS. **26-15A** and 26-16) and Adélaïde Labille-Guiard (FIG. 26-17). Although they shared the honor of admission to the French Royal Academy of Painting and Sculpture and enjoyed royal patronage, their careers differed in some significant ways.

Vigée-Lebrun began painting as a young girl under the tutelage of her father, Louis Vigée (1715–1767), a successful portrait painter. By the time she was 15,

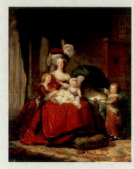

26-15A VIGÉE-LEBRUN, *Marie Antoinette*, 1787.

she had already received portrait commissions of her own. After her marriage to Jean-Baptiste Lebrun, a prominent Parisian art dealer, she began to attract wealthy and important clients, whom the couple entertained in salons at their fashionable home. Vigée-Lebrun soon became the favorite painter of Queen Marie Antoinette, whose influence gained the 28-year-old artist admission to the Royal Academy in 1783. She eventually painted some 30 portraits of the queen. Vigée-Lebrun

was famous for the force and grace of her portraits of highborn ladies and royalty throughout Europe. Her induction into the Royal Academy was short-lived, however. After the French Revolution, the Academy rescinded her membership because women were no longer welcome. Nonetheless, Vigée-Lebrun enjoyed continued success owing to her talent, wit, and ability to forge connections with those in power in the postrevolutionary period.

Six years older than Vigée-Lebrun, Labille-Guiard never achieved the renown enjoyed by her younger contemporary. She trained with François-Élie Vincent (1708–1790) and later with his son François-André Vincent (1746–1816), whom she married after her divorce from her first husband, Louis-Nicolas Guiard, a clerk. Like Vigée-Lebrun, Labille-Guiard boasted royal patronage, but not of the same order. She became the official painter of the "mesdames"—the aunts of King Louis XVI—in 1787, four years after she was admitted to the French painting academy on the same day as Vigée-Lebrun. The two painters captured the remaining two of four memberships reserved for women, a quota that Labille-Guiard worked hard to lift after gaining admission. The two artists took opposite sides during the French Revolution, and Labille-Guiard painted portraits of some of the uprising's leaders, including one of the few known portraits of Maximilien Robespierre (1758–1794), the most prominent figure calling for the death of King Louis XVI.

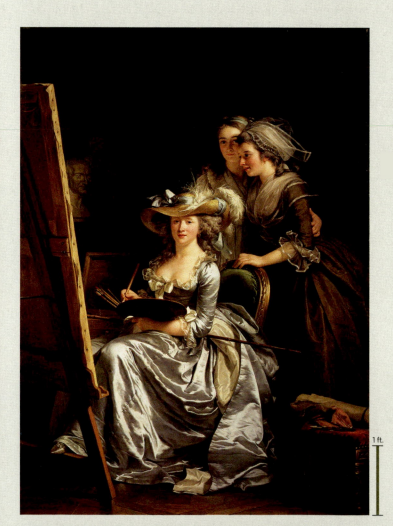

26-16 ÉLISABETH-LOUISE VIGÉE-LEBRUN, *Self-Portrait*, 1790. Oil on canvas, 8' 4" × 6' 9". Galleria degli Uffizi, Florence.

Vigée-Lebrun was one of the few women admitted to the Royal Academy of Painting and Sculpture. In this self-portrait, she depicted herself confidently painting the likeness of Queen Marie Antoinette.

26-17 ADÉLAÏDE LABILLE-GUIARD, *Self-Portrait with Two Pupils*, 1785. Oil on canvas, 6' 11" × 4' 11½". Metropolitan Museum of Art, New York (gift of Julia A. Berwind, 1953).

In contrast to Vigée-Lebrun (FIG. 26-16), Labille-Guiard, her older contemporary, depicted herself as a teacher. Her father's bust portrait serves as her muse in a reversal of traditional gender roles.

ÉLISABETH-LOUISE VIGÉE-LEBRUN Another manifestation of the "naturalistic" impulse in 18th-century French art was the emergence of a new more personal and less pretentious mode of portraiture. *Self-Portrait* (FIG. 26-16) by ÉLISABETH-LOUISE VIGÉE-LEBRUN (1755–1842) is a characteristic example of the genre. The painter looks directly at viewers and pauses in her work to return their gaze. Although her mood is lighthearted and her costume's details echo the serpentine curve that Rococo artists and wealthy patrons loved, nothing about Vigée-Lebrun's pose appears contrived. Hers is the self-confident, natural stance of a woman whose art has won her an independent role in society (see "Vigée-Lebrun, Labille-Guiard, and the French Royal Academy," page 776). She portrayed herself in a close-up, intimate view at work on one of the many portraits (for example, FIG. 26-15A) that she painted of her most important patron, Queen Marie Antoinette (1755–1793).

ADÉLAÏDE LABILLE-GUIARD After Vigée-Lebrun, the second most important woman painter in Paris at the end of the 18th century was ADÉLAÏDE LABILLE-GUIARD (1749–1803). A comparison between Labille-Guiard's *Self-Portrait with Two Pupils* (FIG. 26-17) and Vigée-Lebrun's *Self-Portrait* (FIG. 26-16) is instructive. It underscores the two women's different self-images. The younger painter presented herself at work on a portrait of her most important patron, Marie Antoinette. The subject of the canvas that Labille-Guiard is painting is unknown. Her self-portrait focuses instead on her role as a teacher. She had as many as nine women in her studio

at one time. Here, two apprentices—dressed more simply than their elegantly clad instructor—cluster behind her, one intently studying the painting in progress, the other, like Labille-Guiard, gazing at the viewer. The three figures form a classical pyramidal composition, echoed by the easel. In the V formed by the two triangles is a portrait bust of the artist's father. Appropriately for this early feminist, her muse is a man, a reversal of the traditional gender roles.

WILLIAM HOGARTH Across the Channel, a truly English style of painting emerged with WILLIAM HOGARTH (1697–1764), who satirized the lifestyle of the newly prosperous middle class with comic zest. Traditionally, the British imported painters from the Continent—Holbein, Rubens, and Van Dyck among them. Hogarth waged a lively campaign throughout his career against the English feeling of dependence on, and inferiority to, these artists. Although Hogarth would have been the last to admit it, his own painting owed much to the work of his contemporaries in France, the Rococo artists. Yet his subject matter, frequently moral in tone, was distinctively English. This was the great age of English satirical writing, and Hogarth—who admired that literary genre and included Henry Fielding (1701–1754), the author of *Tom Jones* (1749), among his closest friends—clearly saw himself as translating satire into the visual arts.

Hogarth's favorite device was to make a series of narrative paintings and prints, in a sequence similar to chapters in a book or scenes in a play, following a character or group of characters in their encounters with some social evil. *Breakfast Scene* (FIG. 26-18),

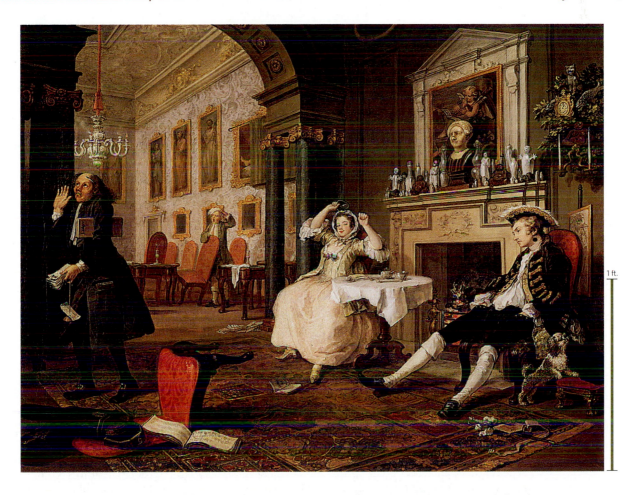

26-18 WILLIAM HOGARTH, *Breakfast Scene,* from *Marriage à la Mode,* ca. 1745. Oil on canvas, 2′ 4″ × 3′. National Gallery, London.

Hogarth won fame for his paintings and prints satirizing English life with comic zest. This is one of a series of six paintings in which he chronicled the marital immoralities of the moneyed class.

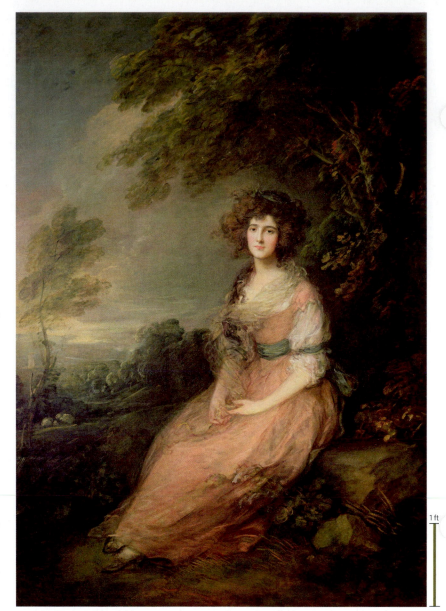

26-19 THOMAS GAINSBOROUGH, *Mrs. Richard Brinsley Sheridan,* 1787. Oil on canvas, 7' 2⅝" × 5' ⅝". National Gallery of Art, Washington, D.C. (Andrew W. Mellon Collection).

In this life-size portrait, Gainsborough sought to match Mrs. Sheridan's natural beauty with that of the landscape. The rustic setting, soft-hued light, and feathery brushwork recall Rococo painting.

1 ft

from *Marriage à la Mode,* is one in a sequence of six paintings satirizing the marital immoralities of the moneyed classes in England. In it, the marriage of a young viscount is just beginning to founder. The husband and wife are tired after a long night spent in separate pursuits. While the wife stayed at home for an evening of cards and music-making, her young husband had been away from the house enjoying the company of another woman. He thrusts his hands deep into the empty money-pockets of his breeches, while his wife's small dog sniffs inquiringly at the other woman's lacy cap protruding from his coat pocket. A steward, his hands full of unpaid bills, raises his eyes in despair at the actions of his noble master and mistress.

The couple's home is palatial, but Hogarth filled it with witty clues to the dubious taste of its occupants. For example, the row of pious religious paintings on the upper wall of the distant room concludes with a curtained canvas undoubtedly depicting an erotic subject. According to the custom of the day, ladies could not view this discretely hidden painting, but at the pull of a cord, the master and his male guests could enjoy a tableau of cavorting figures. In *Breakfast Scene,* as in all his work, Hogarth proceeded as a novelist might, elaborating on his subject with carefully chosen detail, the discovery of which heightens the comedy.

Hogarth designed the marriage series to be published as a set of engravings. The prints of this and his other moral narratives were so popular that unscrupulous entrepreneurs produced unauthorized versions almost as fast as the artist created his originals. The popularity of these prints speaks not only to the appeal of their subjects but also to the democratization of knowledge and culture that the Enlightenment fostered and to the exploitation of new printing technologies that opened the way for a more affordable and widely disseminated visual culture.

THOMAS GAINSBOROUGH A contrasting blend of "naturalistic" representation and Rococo setting is found in *Mrs. Richard Brinsley Sheridan* (FIG. 26-19), a characteristic portrait by British painter THOMAS GAINSBOROUGH (1727–1788). Gainsborough presented Mrs. Sheridan as a lovely, informally dressed woman seated in a rustic landscape faintly reminiscent of Watteau (FIG. 26-7) in its soft-hued light and feathery brushwork. Gainsborough's goal was to match the natural, unspoiled beauty of the landscape with that of his sitter. Mrs. Sheridan's dark brown hair blows freely in the slight wind, and her clear "English complexion" and air of ingenuous sweetness contrast sharply with the pert sophistication of the subjects of Continental Rococo portraits. Gainsborough planned to give the picture a more pastoral air by adding several sheep, but he did not live long enough to complete the canvas. Even without the sheep, the painting clearly expresses Gainsborough's deep interest in the landscape setting. Although he won greater fame in his time for his portraits, as did his slightly older contemporary, SIR JOSHUA REYNOLDS (1723–1792; see "Grand Manner Portraiture," page 779, and FIG. 26-20), Gainsborough had begun as a landscape painter and always preferred painting scenes of nature to depicting individual likenesses.

BENJAMIN WEST Some American artists also became well known in England. BENJAMIN WEST (1738–1820), born in Pennsylvania on what was then the colonial frontier, traveled to Europe early in life to study art and then went to England, where he met with almost immediate success. One of the 36 founding members of the Royal Academy of Arts, West succeeded Sir Joshua Reynolds as its president. He became official painter to George III (r. 1760–1801) and retained that position even during the strained period of the American Revolution.

In *Death of General Wolfe* (FIG. 26-21), West depicted the mortally wounded young English commander just after his defeat of the French in the decisive battle of Quebec in 1759, which gave Canada to Great Britain. Because his subject was a recent event, West

PROBLEMS AND SOLUTIONS
Grand Manner Portraiture

The Enlightenment concept of "nobility," especially in the view of Rousseau (page 774), referred to character, not to aristocratic birth. In an era of revolutions, the virtues of courage and resolution, patriotism, and self-sacrifice assumed greater importance. Having risen from humble origins, the modern military hero joined the well-born aristocrat as a major patron of portrait painting.

Sir Joshua Reynolds was one of those who often received commissions to paint likenesses of key participants in the great events of the latter part of the 18th century. Indeed, he soon specialized in what became known as *Grand Manner portraiture*, echoing the term that Nicolas Poussin used in the previous century to describe his paintings of "grand subjects" (see page 755). Although clearly depicting specific individuals, Grand Manner portraits elevated the sitters by conveying refinement and elegance. Reynolds and other painters communicated a person's grace and class through certain standardized conventions, such as the large scale of the figure relative to the canvas, the controlled pose, the landscape setting, and the low horizon line.

Reynolds painted *Lord Heathfield* (FIG. 26-20) in 1787. The sitter was a perfect subject for a Grand Manner portrait—a burly, ruddy English officer, the commandant of the fortress at Gibraltar. Heathfield had doggedly defended the British stronghold against the Spanish and French, and later received the honorary title Baron Heathfield of Gibraltar. Here, he holds the huge key to the fortress, the symbol of his victory. He stands in front of a curtain of dark smoke rising from the battleground, flanked by one cannon pointing ineffectively downward and another whose tilted barrel indicates that it lies uselessly on its back. Reynolds portrayed the features of the general's heavy, honest face and his uniform with unidealized realism. But Lord Heathfield's posture and the setting dramatically suggest the heroic themes of battle, courage, and patriotism.

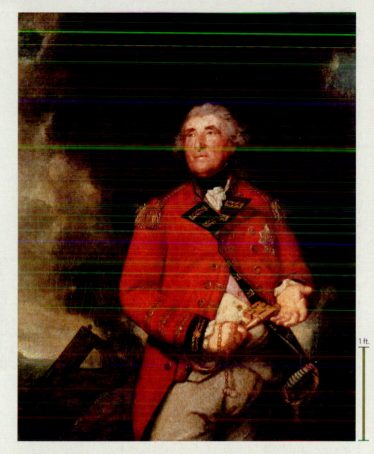

1 ft.

26-20 SIR JOSHUA REYNOLDS, *Lord Heathfield*, 1787. Oil on canvas, 4' 8" × 3' 9". National Gallery, London.

In this Grand Manner portrait, Reynolds depicted the English commander who defended Gibraltar. As is typical for this genre, Heathfield stands in a dramatic pose, and his figure takes up most of the canvas.

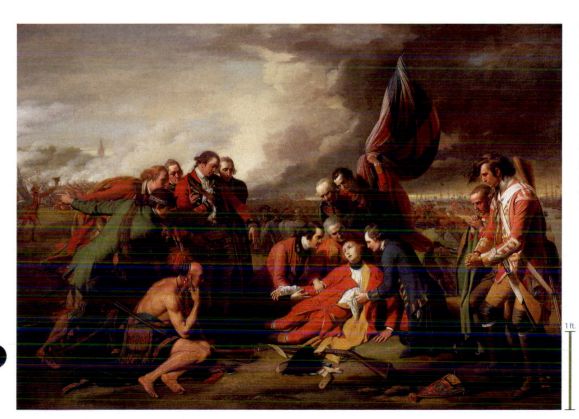

1 ft.

26-21 BENJAMIN WEST, *Death of General Wolfe*, 1771. Oil on canvas, 4' 11 $\frac{1}{2}$" × 7'. National Gallery of Canada, Ottawa (gift of the Duke of Westminster, 1918).

West's major innovation was to blend contemporary subject matter and costumes with the grand tradition of history painting. Here, the painter likened General Wolfe's death to that of a martyred saint.

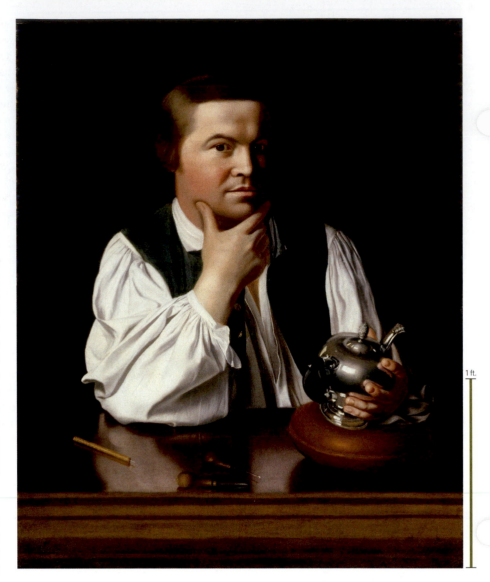

26-22 John Singleton Copley, *Paul Revere*, ca. 1768–1770. Oil on canvas, 2' 11⅛" × 2' 4". Museum of Fine Arts, Boston (gift of Joseph W., William B., and Edward H. R. Revere).

In contrast to Grand Manner portraits, Copley's *Paul Revere* emphasizes the subject's down-to-earth character, differentiating this American work from its European counterparts.

1 ft.

clothed his characters in contemporary costumes (although the military uniforms are not accurate in all details) and included a rare glimpse for his English audience of a Native American warrior, depicted as an exemplary "noble savage." However, West blended this realism of detail with the grand tradition of history painting by arranging his figures in a complex and theatrically ordered composition. His modern hero dies among grieving officers on the field of victorious battle in a way that suggests the death of a saint. (The composition, in fact, derives from paintings of the lamentation over the dead Christ; compare fig. 20-9.) West wanted to present this hero's death in the service of the state as a martyrdom charged with religious emotions. His innovative and highly effective combination of the conventions of traditional heroic painting with a look of modern realism influenced history painting well into the 19th century.

JOHN SINGLETON COPLEY American artist John Singleton Copley (1738–1815) matured as a painter in the Massachusetts Bay Colony. Like West, Copley later emigrated to England, where he absorbed the fashionable English portrait style. But unlike Grand Manner portraits, Copley's *Paul Revere* (fig. **26-22**), painted before the artist left Boston, conveys a sense of directness and faithfulness to visual fact that marked the taste for honesty and plainness noted by many late-18th- and 19th-century visitors to America. When Copley painted his likeness, Revere was not yet the familiar hero of the American Revolution. In this picture, he is a working professional silversmith. The setting is plain, the lighting clear and revealing. Revere sits in his shirtsleeves, bent over a teapot in progress. He pauses and turns his head to look the observer straight in the eyes. The painter treated the reflections in the polished wood of the tabletop with as much care as he did Revere's figure, his tools, and the teapot resting on its leather graver's pillow. Copley gave special prominence to Revere's eyes by reflecting intense reddish light onto the darkened side of his face and hands. The informality and the sense of the moment link this painting to contemporaneous English and Continental portraits. But the spare style and the emphasis on the sitter's down-to-earth character differentiate this American work from its European counterparts.

THE GRAND TOUR The 18th-century public also sought "naturalness" in artists' depictions of landscapes. Documentation of specific places became popular, in part due to growing travel opportunities and expanding colonialism. These depictions of geographic settings also served the needs of the many scientific expeditions mounted during the century and satisfied the desires of genteel tourists for

mementos of their journeys. By this time, a "Grand Tour" of the major sites of Europe was an essential part of every well-bred person's education (see "The Grand Tour and Veduta Painting," page 781). Those who embarked on a tour of the Continent wished to return with souvenirs to help them remember their experiences and impress those at home with the wonders they had seen. The English were especially eager collectors of travel pictures. Venetian artists in particular found it profitable to produce paintings of the most characteristic *vedute* ("scenic views") of their city to sell to British visitors. Chief among those artists was Antonio Canaletto (1697–1768), whose works—for example, *Riva degli Schiavoni, Venice (Bank of the Slaves, Venice;* fig. **26-23**)—English tourists avidly acquired as evidence of their visit to Italy's magical city of water.

POMPEO BATONI Some of those who embarked on the Grand Tour sought to obtain a more personalized memento of their cultural journey than a portrait of Venice: a portrait of themselves painted by the leading Italian portrait painter of the day, Pompeo Batoni (1708–1787). Born in Lucca and trained in Rome, where he eventually became curator of the papal art collection, Batoni received commissions for "Grand Tour portraits" from prosperous visitors of various nationalities, but especially from Englishmen. More than 150 of Batoni's portraits of English gentlemen with Italian backdrops are in museums and private collections today.

ART AND SOCIETY

The Grand Tour and Veduta Painting

Although travel throughout Europe was commonplace in the 18th century, Italy became an especially popular destination. This "pilgrimage" of aristocrats, the wealthy, politicians, and diplomats from France, England, Germany, Flanders, Sweden, Russia, Poland, Hungary, and even the British colonies in America came to be known as the Grand Tour. Italy's allure fueled the revival of classicism, and the popularity of Neoclassical art drove the fascination with Italy. One British observer noted, "All our religion, all our arts, almost all that sets us above savages, has come from the shores of the Mediterranean."*

The Grand Tour was not simply leisure travel. The education available in Italy to the inquisitive mind made such a tour an indispensable experience for anyone who wished to make a mark in society. The Enlightenment had made knowledge of ancient Greece and Rome imperative, and a steady stream of Europeans and Americans traveled to Italy in the late 18th and early 19th centuries. These tourists aimed to increase their knowledge of literature, the visual arts, architecture, theater, music, history, customs, and folklore. Given this extensive agenda, it is not surprising that a Grand Tour could take a number of years to complete. Most travelers moved from location to location, following an established itinerary, not unlike the pilgrimages to saints' shrines in the late Middle Ages (see "Pilgrimage Roads in France and Spain," page 342).

The British were the most avid travelers, and they conceived the initial "tour code," including required itineraries to important destinations. Although they designated Rome early on as the primary destination in Italy, visitors traveled as far north as Venice and as far south as Naples. Eventually, Paestum, Sicily, Florence, Siena, Pisa, Genoa, Milan, Bologna, and Parma (MAP 25-1) all appeared in guidebooks and in paintings. Joseph Wright of Derby (FIGS. 26-11A and 26-12) and Joseph Mallord William Turner (FIG. 27-22) were among the many British artists to undertake a Grand Tour.

Many visitors to Italy returned home from their Grand Tour with a painting by Antonio Canaletto, the leading painter of scenic views (*vedute*) of Venice. It must have been very cheering on a gray winter afternoon in England to look up and see a sunny, panoramic view such as that in Canaletto's *Riva degli Schiavoni, Venice* (FIG. 26-23), with its cloud-studded sky, picturesque water traffic, and well-known Venetian landmarks painted in scrupulous perspective and minute detail. (The Doge's Palace [FIG. 14-23] is at the left in *Riva degli Schiavoni*.)

Canaletto usually made drawings "on location" to take back to his studio and use as sources for paintings. To help make the on-site drawings true to life, he often used a *camera obscura,* as Vermeer (FIG. 25-18B) did before him. These instruments were darkened chambers (some of them virtually portable closets) with optical lenses fitted into a hole in one wall through which light entered to project an inverted image of the subject onto the chamber's opposite wall. The artist could trace the main details from this image for later reworking and refinement. The camera obscura enabled artists to create convincing representations incorporating the variable focus of objects at different distances. Canaletto's paintings give the impression of capturing every detail, with no "editing." In fact, he presented each site according to Renaissance perspective conventions and exercised great selectivity about which details to include and which to omit to make a coherent and engagingly attractive veduta.

*Cesare de Seta in Andrew Wilton and Ilaria Bignamini, eds., *Grand Tour: The Lure of Italy in the Eighteenth Century* (London: Tate Gallery, 1996), 13.

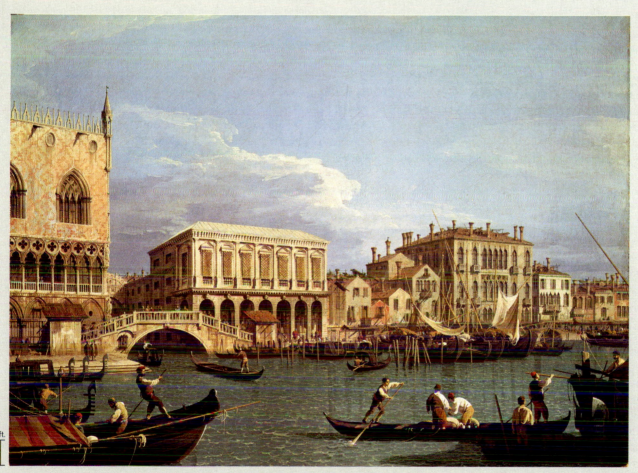

26-23 **ANTONIO CANALETTO**, *Riva degli Schiavoni, Venice*, ca. 1735–1740. Oil on canvas, $1' 6\frac{1}{2}'' \times 2' 7\frac{7}{8}''$. Toledo Museum of Art, Toledo.

Canaletto was the leading painter of Venetian vedute, which were treasured souvenirs for 18th-century travelers visiting Italy on a Grand Tour. He used a camera obscura for his on-site drawings.

1 ft.

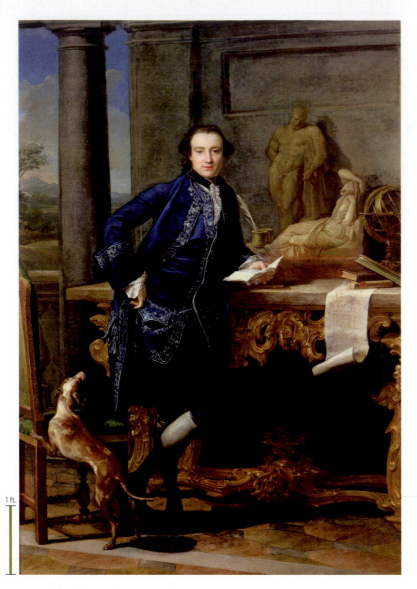

26-24 POMPEO BATONI, *Charles John Crowle*, ca. 1761–1762. Oil on canvas, 8' 1⅝" × 5' 7¾". Musée du Louvre, Paris.

Prosperous visitors to Rome on the Grand Tour frequently commissioned Batoni to paint their portraits. Here, an English gentleman poses with items attesting to his learning and passion for antiquity.

1 ft.

the excavations of Herculaneum and Pompeii, which the volcanic eruption of Mount Vesuvius had buried (see "The Excavations of Herculaneum and Pompeii," page 783). Soon, murals based on the paintings unearthed in the excavations began to appear in European townhouses, such as the Etruscan Room (FIG. **26-25**) by ROBERT ADAM (1728–1792) in Osterley Park House in Middlesex, begun in 1761.

GIBBON AND WINCKELMANN The enthusiasm for classical antiquity also permeated much of the scholarship of the time. In the late 18th century, the ancient world increasingly became the focus of academic research. For example, a visit to Rome inspired Edward Gibbon (1737–1794) to begin his monumental *Decline and Fall of the Roman Empire*, which appeared between 1776 and 1788. The classical world, and specifically classical art, became the lifelong focus of Johann Joachim Winckelmann (1717–1768), whom scholars widely recognize as the first modern art historian (see "Winckelmann and the History of Classical Art," page 784).

Painting

The Enlightenment idea of a participatory and knowledgeable citizenry lay behind the revolt against the French monarchy in 1789, but the immediate causes of the French Revolution were France's economic crisis and the clash between the Third Estate (bourgeoisie, peasantry, and urban and rural workers) and the First and Second Estates (the clergy and nobility, respectively). They fought over the issue of representation in the legislative body, the Estates-General, which had been convened to discuss taxation as a possible solution to the economic problem. However, the ensuing revolution revealed the instability of the monarchy and of French society's traditional structure and resulted in a succession of republics and empires as France struggled to find a way to adjust to these fundamental changes.

JACQUES-LOUIS DAVID The artist who became the painter-ideologist of the French Revolution was JACQUES-LOUIS DAVID (1748–1825). Mengs (FIG. 26-25A) and Kauffman (FIG. 26-1) were pioneers of Neoclassical painting, but David is generally considered the greatest Neoclassical master. A distant relative of François Boucher (FIG. 26-8), David followed the Rococo painter's style until a period of study in Rome won the younger man over to the classical art tradition. David favored academic teachings about using the art of the ancients and of the great Renaissance masters as models. He, like Winckelmann, rebelled against Rococo style as an "artificial taste" and exalted the "perfect form" of Greek art (see "David on Greek Style and Public Art," page 784).

OATH OF THE HORATII David concurred with the Enlightenment belief that the subject of an artwork should have a moral. Paintings representing noble deeds in the past could inspire virtue in the

Batoni's portrait (FIG. **26-24**) of Charles John Crowle (1738–1811) is a characteristic example of the type of portrait that his patrons found so appealing. Crowle, a second-generation member of the British Parliament from Yorkshire, stands in a palatial columnar study with a view of the Roman countryside behind him. Attended by his faithful dog, Crowle is surrounded by abundant evidence of his learning and passion for antiquity. Most prominent are copies of reduced size of the *Farnese Hercules* (FIG. 5-66) in Naples and of a statue of the sleeping Ariadne in the Vatican. On the elegant table on which Crowle leans is an astronomical model (compare FIG. 26-12) and an unrolled plan of Saint Peter's (FIG. 24-4). In 1764, after returning from Rome, Crowle was elected a member of the Society of Dilettanti, a prestigious group of British connoisseur-admirers of Greco-Roman art.

NEOCLASSICISM

As Batoni's *Charles John Crowle* (FIG. 26-24) vividly illustrates, the popularity of the Grand Tour among the cultural elite of Europe both reflected and contributed to the heightened interest in classical antiquity during the Enlightenment. Exposure to the art treasures of Italy was also a major factor in the rise of Neoclassicism as the leading art movement of the late 18th century (see "The Enlightenment, Angelica Kauffman, and Neoclassicism," page 763). Further whetting the public appetite for classicism were

ART AND SOCIETY

The Excavations of Herculaneum and Pompeii

Among the developments stimulating the European fascination with classical antiquity was the initiation of systematic excavations at two ancient Roman towns on the Bay of Naples—Herculaneum and Pompeii—in 1738 and 1748, respectively. The violent eruption of Mount Vesuvius in August 79 had buried both sites under volcanic ash and lava (see "An Eyewitness Account of the Eruption of Mount Vesuvius," page 186), protecting the towns for hundreds of years from looters and the ravages of nature. Consequently, the 18th-century excavations yielded an unprecedented number of well-preserved paintings, sculptures, vases, and other household objects, and provided rich evidence for reconstructing Roman art and life. As a result, European ideas about and interest in ancient Rome expanded tremendously, and collectors eagerly acquired as many of the newly discovered antiquities as they could. One of the most avid collectors was Sir William Hamilton (1731–1803), British consul in Naples from 1764 to 1800, who purchased numerous painted vases and other ancient objects soon after taking up his post. Because Hamilton sold his collection to the British Museum in 1772, the finds at Pompeii and Herculaneum quickly became available to a wide public.

"Pompeian" style soon became all the rage in England, as evident, for example, in Robert Adam's Etruscan Room (FIG. 26-25) at Osterley Park House, which was inspired by the frescoes of the Third and early Fourth Styles of Roman mural painting (FIGS. 7-21 and 7-34A). Adam took decorative motifs (medallions, urns, vine scrolls, sphinxes, and tripods) from Roman art and arranged them sparsely within broad, neutral spaces and slender margins, as in his elegant, linear ancient models. This new Neoclassical style almost entirely displaced the curvilinear Rococo (FIGS. 26-2 and 26-3) in the homes of the wealthy after midcentury. Adam was also an archaeologist, and he had explored and written accounts of the ruins of Diocletian's palace (FIG. 7-72) at Split. Kedleston House in Derbyshire, Adelphi Terrace in London, and a great many other structures that he designed show how the Split palace influenced his work.

The archaeological finds from Herculaneum and Pompeii also affected garden and landscape design, fashion, and tableware. Clothing based on classical garb became popular, and Emma, Lady Hamilton (1761–1815), Sir William's wife, often gave lavish parties dressed in delicate Greek-style drapery (compare the costumes in Angelica Kauffman's Mother of the Gracchi; FIG. 26-1).

Neoclassical taste also determined the pottery designs of John Flaxman (1755–1826) and Josiah Wedgwood. Wedgwood established his reputation in the 1760s with his creamware inspired by ancient art. He eventually produced vases based on what were then thought to be Etruscan designs (they were, in fact, imported Greek vases deposited in Etruscan tombs; see page 108) and expanded his business by producing small busts of classical figures as well as cameos and medallions adorned with copies of antique reliefs and statues.

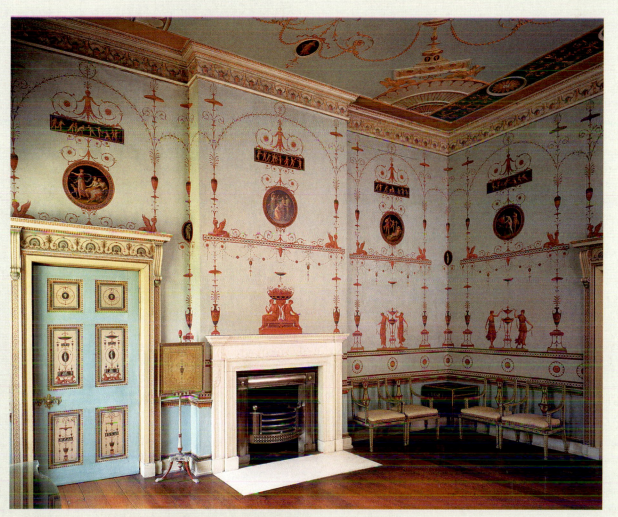

26-25 ROBERT ADAM, Etruscan Room, Osterley Park House, Middlesex, England, begun 1761. Reconstructed in the Victoria & Albert Museum, London.

Inspired by archaeological discoveries at Herculaneum and Pompeii in the mid-18th century, Adam incorporated decorative motifs from Roman mural painting into his Etruscan Room at Osterley Park.

Winckelmann and the History of Classical Art

In 1755, Johann Joachim Winckelmann published his groundbreaking *Reflections on the Imitation of Greek Works in Painting and Sculpture*. In this treatise, the German scholar unequivocally designated Greek art as the most perfect to come from human hands. For Winckelmann, classical art was far superior to the "natural" art of his day.

> Good taste, which is becoming more prevalent throughout the world, had its origins under the skies of Greece. . . . The only way for us to become great . . . is to imitate the ancients. . . . In the masterpieces of Greek art, connoisseurs and imitators find not only nature at its most beautiful but also something beyond nature, namely certain ideal forms of its beauty. . . . A person enlightened enough to penetrate the innermost secrets of art will find beauties hitherto seldom revealed when he compares the total structure of Greek figures with most modern ones, especially those modeled more on nature than on Greek taste.*

In his later *History of Ancient Art* (1764), Winckelmann carefully described major works of classical art and positioned each one within a huge inventory organized by subject, style, and period. Before Winckelmann, art historians had focused on biography, as did Giorgio Vasari and Giovanni Pietro Bellori in the 16th and 17th centuries (see "Giorgio Vasari's *Lives*," page 636, and "Giovanni Pietro Bellori on Annibale

Carracci and Caravaggio," page 713). Winckelmann thus initiated one modern art historical method thoroughly in accord with Enlightenment ideas of ordering knowledge—a system of description and classification that provided a pioneering model for the understanding of stylistic evolution.

As was the norm at that time, Winckelmann's familiarity with classical art derived predominantly from Roman works and Roman copies of Greek art in Italy. Yet Winckelmann was instrumental in bringing to scholarly attention the differences between Greek and Roman art. Thus he paved the way for more thorough study of the distinct characteristics of the art and architecture of these two cultures.

Winckelmann's influence extended beyond the world of scholarship. He also was instrumental in promoting Neoclassicism as a major stylistic movement in late-18th-century painting. He was, for example, the scholar who advised his countryman ANTON RAPHAEL MENGS (1728–1779) on classical iconography when Mengs painted *Parnassus* (FIG. 26-25A), the fresco that many art historians regard as the first Neoclassical painting. It predates Angelica Kauffman's *Mother of the Gracchi* (FIG. 26-1) by almost a quarter century.

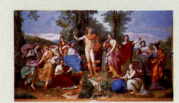

26-25A MENGS, *Parnassus*, 1761.

*Translated by Elfriede Heyer and Roger C. Norton in Charles Harrison, Paul Wood, and Jason Gaiger, eds., *Art in Theory 1648–1815: An Anthology of Changing Ideas* (Oxford: Blackwell, 2000), 451–453.

present. A milestone painting in the Neoclassical master's career, *Oath of the Horatii* (FIG. 26-26), depicts a story from pre-Republican Rome, the heroic phase of Roman history. The topic was not too obscure for David's audience. Pierre Corneille (1606–1684) had retold this story of conflict between love and patriotism, recounted by the ancient Roman historian Livy, in a play performed in Paris several years earlier. According to the story, the leaders of the warring cities of Rome and Alba decided to resolve their conflicts in a series of encounters waged by three representatives from each side.

The Romans chose as their champions the three Horatius brothers, who had to face the three sons of the Curatius family from Alba. A sister of the Horatii, Camilla, was the bride-to-be of one of the Curatius sons, and the wife of the youngest Horatius was the sister of the Curatii. David's painting shows the Horatii as they swear on their swords, held high by their father, to win or die for Rome, oblivious to the anguish and sorrow of the Horatius women.

Oath of the Horatii is a paragon of the Neoclassical style. Not only does the subject matter deal with a narrative of patriotism

David on Greek Style and Public Art

Jacques-Louis David was the leading Neoclassical painter in France at the end of the 18th century. He championed a return to Greek style and the painting of inspiring heroic and patriotic subjects. In 1796, he made the following statement to his pupils:

> I want to work in a pure Greek style. I feed my eyes on antique statues, I even have the intention of imitating some of them. The Greeks had no scruples about copying a composition, a gesture, a type that had already been accepted and used. They put all their attention and all their art on perfecting an idea that had been already conceived. They thought, and they were right, that in the arts the way in which an idea is rendered, and the manner in which it is expressed, is much more important than the idea itself. To give a body and a perfect form to one's thought, this—and only this—is to be an artist.*

David also strongly believed that paintings depicting noble events in ancient history, such as his *Oath of the Horatii* (FIG. 26-26), would serve to instill patriotism and civic virtue in the public at large in post-revolutionary France. In November 1793, he wrote:

> [The arts] should help to spread the progress of the human spirit, and to propagate and transmit to posterity the striking examples of the efforts of a tremendous people who, guided by reason and philosophy, are bringing back to earth the reign of liberty, equality, and law. The arts must therefore contribute forcefully to the education of the public. . . . The arts are the imitation of nature in her most beautiful and perfect form. . . . [T]hose marks of heroism and civic virtue offered the eyes of the people [will] electrify the soul, and plant the seeds of glory and devotion to the fatherland.†

*Translated by Robert Goldwater and Marco Treves , eds., *Artists on Art*, 3d ed. (New York: Pantheon Books, 1958), 206.
†Ibid., 205.

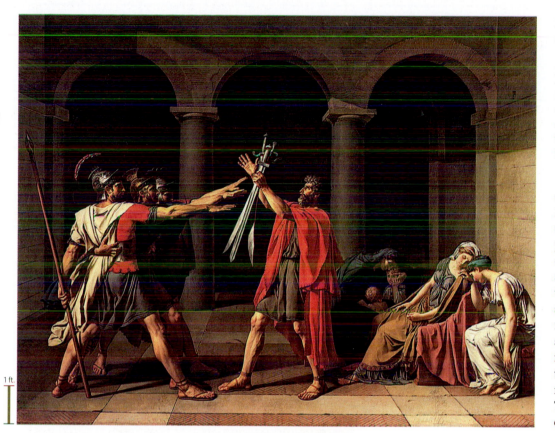

26-26 JACQUES-LOUIS DAVID, *Oath of the Horatii*, 1784. Oil on canvas, 10' 10" × 13' 11". Musée du Louvre, Paris.

David was the Neoclassical painter-ideologist of the French Revolution. This huge canvas celebrating ancient Roman patriotism and sacrifice features statuesque figures and classical architecture.

and sacrifice excerpted from Roman history, but the painter also employed formal devices to present the image with force and clarity. The action unfolds in a shallow space much like a stage setting, defined by a severely simple architectural framework (compare FIG. 26-1). David deployed his statuesque and carefully modeled figures across the space, close to the foreground, in a manner reminiscent of ancient relief sculpture. The rigid, angular, and virile forms of the men on the left effectively contrast with the soft curvilinear shapes of the distraught women on the right. This juxtaposition visually pits the virtues that Enlightenment leaders ascribed to men, such as courage, patriotism, and unwavering loyalty to a cause, against the emotions of love, sorrow, and despair expressed by the women in the painting. The French viewing audience perceived such emotionalism as characteristic of the female nature. The message was clear and of a type readily identifiable to the pre-revolutionary French public.

The picture created a sensation at its first exhibition in Paris in 1785. Although David had painted it under royal patronage and did not intend the painting as a revolutionary statement, *Oath of the Horatii* aroused his audience to patriotic zeal. The Neoclassical style soon became the semiofficial voice of the French Revolution.

DEATH OF MARAT When the revolution broke out in 1789, David threw in his lot with the Jacobins, the radical and militant revolutionary faction. He accepted the role of de facto minister of propaganda, organizing political pageants and ceremonies requiring floats, costumes, and sculptural props. David believed that art could play an important role in educating the public and that dramatic paintings emphasizing patriotism and civic virtue would prove effective as rallying calls. However, rather than continuing to create artworks focused on scenes from antiquity, David began to portray scenes from the French Revolution itself.

In 1793, David painted *Death of Marat* (FIG. 26-27), which he wanted not only to serve as a record of an important event in the struggle to overthrow the monarchy but also to provide inspiration and encouragement to the revolutionary forces. The painting commemorates the assassination that year of Jean-Paul Marat (1743–1793), an influential writer who was David's friend. The artist depicted the martyred revolutionary still holding a quill pen in his right hand after Charlotte Corday (1768–1793), a member of a rival political faction, stabbed him to death while Marat was immersed in a bathtub as he worked. (Marat suffered from a

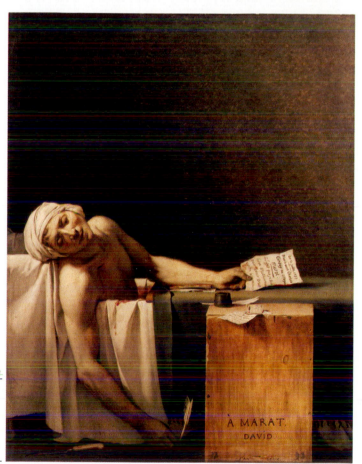

26-27 JACQUES-LOUIS DAVID, *Death of Marat*, 1793. Oil on canvas, 5' 5" × 4' 2½". Musées Royaux des Beaux-Arts de Belgique, Brussels.

David depicted the revolutionary Marat as a tragic martyr, stabbed to death in his bath. Although the painting displays severe Neoclassical spareness, its convincing realism conveys pain and outrage.

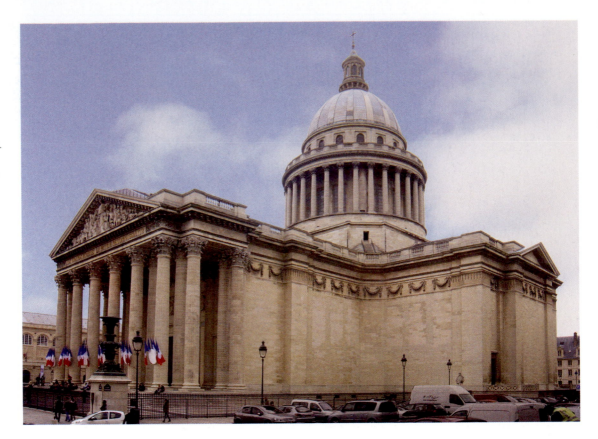

26-28 Jacques-Germain Soufflot, Panthéon (Sainte-Geneviève; looking northeast), Paris, France, 1755–1792.

Soufflot's Panthéon is a testament to the Enlightenment admiration for Greece and Rome. It combines a portico based on an ancient Roman temple with a colonnaded dome and a Greek-cross plan.

painful skin disease and required frequent medicinal baths.) His "desk" was a board placed across the tub with a wood stand next to it for his writing materials. David presented the scene with directness and clarity. The cold neutral space above Marat's figure slumped in the tub produces a chilling oppressiveness. The painter vividly placed all narrative details in the foreground—the knife, the wound, the blood, the letter with which Corday gained entrance—to sharpen the sense of pain and outrage. David masterfully composed the painting to present Marat as a tragic martyr who died in the service of the revolution. Indeed, the writing stand, which bears the words "To Marat, David," resembles a tombstone, and David based Marat's figure on the dead Christ in Michelangelo's *Pietà* (FIG. 22-12) in Saint Peter's in Rome. The reference to Christ's martyrdom made the painting a kind of "altarpiece" for the new civic "religion," inspiring the French people with the saintly dedication of their slain leader.

Architecture and Sculpture

Architects in the Enlightenment era also formed a deep admiration for the Greco-Roman past. Fairly early in the 18th century, they began to turn away from the theatricality and ostentation of Baroque design, still evident in grandiose structures such as Blenheim Palace (FIG. 26-1A) in England and Karlskirche (FIG. 26-3A) in Austria, as well as from the delicate flourishes of Rococo salons (FIGS. 26-2 and 26-3), palaces (FIG. 26-6A), and churches (FIGS. 26-4 and 26-6B). The style they instead embraced offered a more streamlined antique look.

PANTHÉON The Parisian church of Sainte-Geneviève (FIG. 26-28), now the Panthéon, designed by JACQUES-GERMAIN SOUFFLOT (1713–1780) stands as testament to the revived interest in classical

architecture. The Roman ruins at Baalbek in Syria, especially the gigantic colonnade of the temple of Jupiter, provided much of the inspiration for Soufflot's Neoclassical church. The columns, reproduced with studied archaeological precision, stand out from walls that are severely blank, except for a repeated garland motif near the top. The colonnaded dome, a Neoclassical version of the domes of Saint Peter's (FIG. 22-25) in Rome, the Église du Dôme (FIG. 25-30) in Paris, and Saint Paul's (FIG. 25-38) in London, rises above a Greek-cross plan. Both the dome and the vaults rest on an interior grid of splendid freestanding Corinthian columns, as if the portico's colonnade continued within. Although the whole effect, inside and out, is Roman, the structural principles employed were essentially Gothic. Soufflot was one of the first 18th-century builders to apply the logical engineering of Gothic cathedrals (see "The

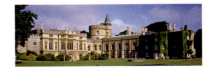

26-28A Walpole, Strawberry Hill, Twickenham, 1749–1777.

Gothic Cathedral," page 381) to modern buildings. With few exceptions, however, such as Strawberry Hill (FIG. 26-28A), owned and largely designed by HORACE WALPOLE (1717–1797), the revival of interest in the Gothic architectural style did not take hold until the following century (see page 828 and FIGS. 27-43 and 27-43A).

CHISWICK HOUSE The appeal of classical architecture extended well beyond French borders. The popularity of Greek and Roman cultures was due not only to their association with morality, rationality, and integrity but also to their connection to political systems ranging from Athenian democracy to Roman imperial rule. Thus parliamentary England joined revolutionary France in embracing Neoclassicism. In England, Neoclassicism's appeal also was due to its clarity and simplicity. These characteristics provided a stark

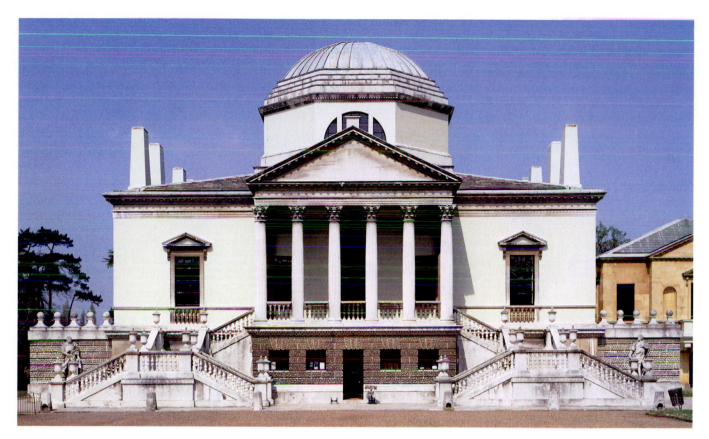

26-29 RICHARD BOYLE and WILLIAM KENT, Chiswick House (looking northwest), near London, England, begun 1725.

For this English villa, Boyle and Kent emulated the simple symmetry and unadorned planes of the Palladian architectural style. Chiswick House is a free variation on the Villa Rotonda (FIG. 22-28).

contrast to the complexity and opulence of Baroque art, then associated with the flamboyant rule of absolute monarchy. In English architecture, the preference for a simple and rational style derived indirectly from the authority of the ancient Roman architect Vitruvius (see "Vitruvius's *Ten Books on Architecture*," page 199) through Andrea Palladio (FIGS. 22-28 to 22-31) in the 16th century and Inigo Jones (FIG. 25-37) in the 17th.

RICHARD BOYLE (1695–1753), earl of Burlington, strongly restated Jones's Palladian doctrine in the new Neoclassical idiom in Chiswick House (FIG. **26-29**), which he built on London's outskirts with the help of WILLIAM KENT (ca. 1686–1748). Paving the way for this shift in style was, among other things, the publication of Colin Campbell's *Vitruvius Britannicus* (1715), three volumes of engravings of ancient buildings, prefaced by a denunciation of the Italian Baroque style and high praise for Palladio and Jones. Chiswick House is a free variation on the theme of Palladio's Villa Rotonda (FIG. 22-28). The exterior design provided a clear alternative to the colorful splendor of Versailles (FIG. 25-26). In its simple symmetry, unadorned planes, right angles, and precise proportions, Chiswick House looks very classical and rational. But the Palladian-style villa's setting within informal gardens, where a charming irregularity of layout and freely growing uncropped foliage dominate the scene, balances the classical severity and rationality of the architecture. Just as the owners of English villas cultivated irregularity in the landscaping surrounding their homes, they sometimes preferred interiors ornamented in a style more closely related to Rococo decoration. At Chiswick House, the interior design creates a luxurious Baroque foil to the stern symmetry of the exterior and the plan.

Palladian classicism prevailed in English architecture until about 1760, when it began to evolve into Neoclassicism. Playing a pivotal role in the shift from a dependence on Renaissance examples to ancient models was the publication in 1762 of the first volume of *Antiquities of Athens* by two British painters and architects, JAMES STUART

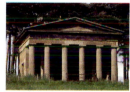

26-29A STUART, Doric Portico, Hagley Park, 1758.

(1713–1788) and Nicholas Revett (1720–1804). Indeed, the purest expression of Greek-inspired architecture in 18th-century England was Stuart's design for the Doric portico (FIG. **26-29A**) at Hagley Park.

STOURHEAD PARK English architects also made a significant contribution to the history of architecture by developing the *picturesque garden* in the 18th century, a garden designed in accord with the Enlightenment taste for the "natural." This approach to landscape architecture was in strong opposition to the formality and symmetry of Continental gardens such as those of the palace at Versailles (FIG. 25-26), which expressed the French monarch's power to impose rational order on untamed nature. Despite their "unordered" appearance, 18th-century English gardens, like Chinese gardens (see "Planning an Unplanned Garden," page 1055), were carefully planned. But unlike Chinese gardens, English gardens of the Enlightenment era often made allusions to classical antiquity, satisfying the demands of their patrons to surround themselves with mementos of the Grand Tour (see "The Grand Tour," page 781) they undertook in their youth.

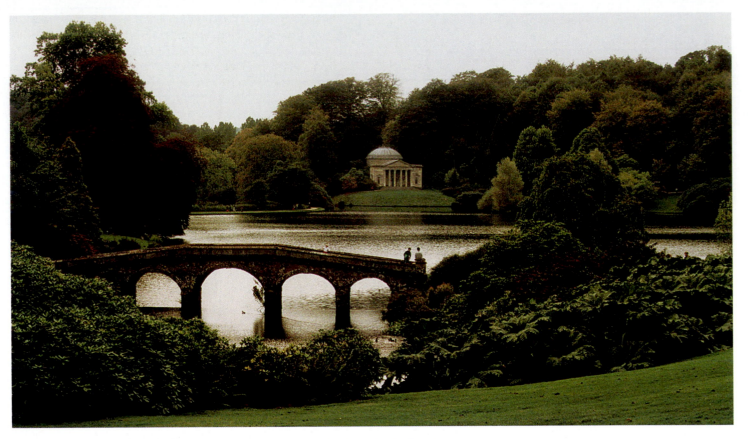

26-30 Henry Flitcroft and Henry Hoare, the park at Stourhead, England, 1743–1765.

Flitcroft's design for Hoare's Wiltshire estate included a replica of the Pantheon overlooking an artificial lake, and a grotto alluding to Aeneas's journey to the Underworld from Lake Avernus.

An early masterpiece of this genre is the park at Stourhead (FIG. 26-30), designed by Henry Flitcroft (1697–1769) in collaboration with the property's owner, Henry Hoare (1705–1785), the son of a wealthy banker. Hoare's country estate in Wiltshire overlooked a lush valley in which Flitcroft created an irregularly shaped artificial lake by damming up the Stour River. Around it, he placed a winding path leading to and from a grotto adorned with statues of a river god and a nymph. The twisting road and the grotto conjured for Hoare the voyage of Aeneas and the entrance to the Underworld in Virgil's *Aeneid,* required reading (in the original Latin) for any properly educated British gentleman. Flitcroft also placed around

Hoare's version of Lake Avernus a bridge with five arches modeled on Andrea Palladio's bridge at Vicenza and pavilions that are free variations on famous classical buildings, including the Temple of Venus (FIG. 7-70) at Baalbek and the Pantheon (FIG. 7-49) in Rome. Flitcroft sited all the structures strategically to create vistas resembling those in the paintings of Claude Lorrain (FIG. 25-33), beloved by those who had completed a Grand Tour. In fact, the view reproduced here of Flitcroft's Pantheon beyond the Palladian bridge on the far side of the lake at Stourhead specifically emulates Claude's 1672 *Landscape with Aeneas at Delos* in the National Gallery in London, in turn inspired by the *Aeneid.* Still, consistent with the eclectic

26-31 Thomas Jefferson, Monticello, Charlottesville, Virginia, 1770–1806.

Jefferson led the movement to adopt Neoclassicism as the architectural style of the United States. Although built of local materials, his Palladian Virginia home recalls Chiswick House (FIG. 26-29).

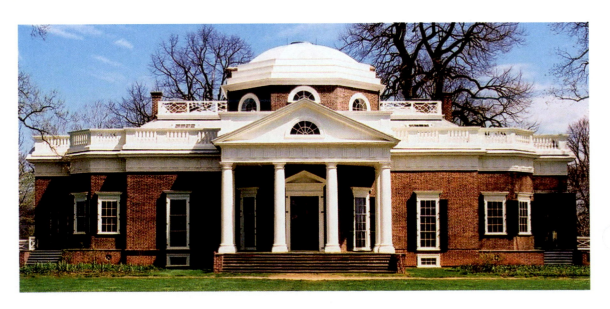

THE PATRON'S VOICE
Thomas Jefferson, Patron and Practitioner

Thomas Jefferson's advocacy of Neoclassicism as the architectural style of the newly independent United States of America was an extension of the Enlightenment belief in the perfectibility of human beings and in the power of art to help achieve that perfection. An accomplished architect in his own right (FIGS. 26-31 and 26-32), as president, Jefferson personally selected Benjamin Latrobe (1764–1820) to complete the commission for the U.S. Capitol in Washington, D.C., specifying that Latrobe use a Roman style. Jefferson's choice reflected in part his admiration for the beauty of the Roman buildings he had seen in Europe and in part his association of those buildings with an idealized Roman republican government and, through that, with the democracy of ancient Greece. As early as 1791, as the first secretary of state under President George Washington, Jefferson expressed his preference for the future design of the Capitol in a letter to Pierre Charles L'Enfant (1754–1825), whom Washington had asked to prepare a plan for the new national capital on the Potomac River.

> Whenever it is proposed to prepare plans for the Capitol, I should prefer the adoption of some one of the models of antiquity, which have had the approbation of thousands of years.*

In his own designs for public buildings, Jefferson also looked to Rome for models. He modeled the State Capitol in Richmond, Virginia, on the Maison Carrée (FIG. 7-32), which he described in 1786 as "the most perfect and precious remain of antiquity in existence."† For the University of Virginia, which he founded, Jefferson turned to the Pantheon (FIG. 7-49). The Rotunda (FIG. **26-32**) is the centerpiece of Jefferson's "academical village" in Charlottesville. It sits on an elevated platform at one end of a grassy quadrangle ("the Lawn"), framed by Neoclassical pavilions and colonnades—just as temples in Roman fora (FIGS. 7-12 and 7-44) stood at one short end of a colonnaded square. Each of the ten pavilions (five on each side) resembles a small classical temple. No two are exactly alike. Jefferson experimented with variations of all the different classical orders in his pavilions. He had thoroughly absorbed the principles of classical architecture and clearly delighted in borrowing motifs from major buildings. Jefferson was no mere copyist, however. His designs were highly original—and, in turn, frequently emulated. And, as president and patron, he put his stamp on the character of Washington, D.C., forever.

*Letter of Thomas Jefferson to the commission overseeing the plans for Washington, D.C., January 26, 1786, quoted in Leland M. Roth, ed., *America Builds: Source Documents in American Architecture and Planning* (New York: Harper & Row, 1983), 29.

†Letter of Thomas Jefferson to Madame de Tessé, March 20, 1787, quoted in Harry Francis Mallgrave, ed., *Architectural Theory, Volume I: An Anthology from Vitruvius to 1870* (Malden, Mass.: Blackwell, 2006), 427.

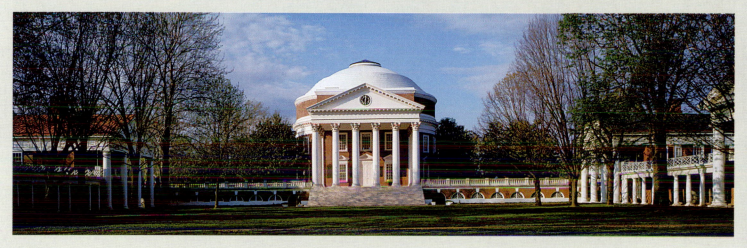

26-32 THOMAS JEFFERSON, Rotunda and Lawn (looking north), University of Virginia, Charlottesville, Virginia, 1819–1826.

Modeled on the Pantheon (FIG. 7-49), Jefferson's Neoclassical Rotunda sits like a temple in a Roman forum on an elevated platform overlooking the colonnaded Lawn of the University of Virginia.

tastes of 18th-century patrons, Hoare's park also contains Chinese bridges, a Turkish tent, and a Gothic tower.

THOMAS JEFFERSON Because the appeal of Neoclassicism was due in part to the values with which it was associated—morality, idealism, patriotism, and civic virtue—it is not surprising that in the new American republic, THOMAS JEFFERSON (1743–1826) spearheaded a movement to adopt Neoclassicism as the national architectural style. Jefferson—economist, educational theorist, gifted amateur architect, as well as statesman (see "Thomas Jefferson, Patron and Practitioner," above)—admired Palladio immensely and read carefully the Italian architect's *Four Books of Architecture*. Later, while minister to France, he studied 18th-century French classical architecture and city planning and visited the Maison Carrée (FIG. 7-32), an ancient Roman temple at Nîmes. After his European sojourn, Jefferson decided to completely remodel Monticello (FIG. **26-31**), his home near Charlottesville, Virginia, which he originally had designed in a different style. The final version of Monticello is somewhat reminiscent of Palladio's Villa Rotonda (FIG. 22-28) and of Chiswick House (FIG. 26-29), but its materials are the local wood and brick used in Virginia. The single-story home with an octagonal dome set above the central drawing room behind a pediment-capped columnar porch sits on a wooded plot of land with mountain vistas all around. (Monticello means "hillock" or "little mountain" in Italian.) The setting fulfilled another of Jefferson's goals—to build for himself a country villa inspired by the ones described by the first-century Roman author Pliny (see page 186).

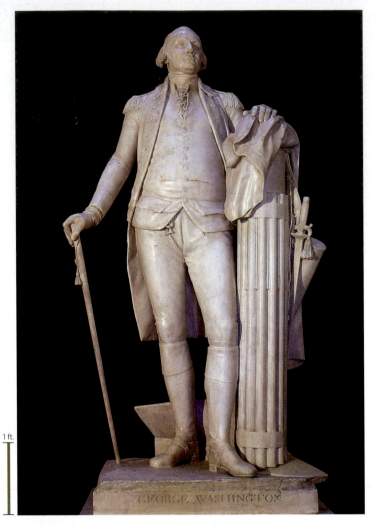

26-33 JEAN-ANTOINE HOUDON, *George Washington*, 1788–1792. Marble, 6' 2" high. State Capitol, Richmond.

Houdon portrayed Washington in contemporary garb, but he incorporated the Roman fasces and Cincinnatus's plow in the statue, because Washington similarly had returned to his farm after his war service.

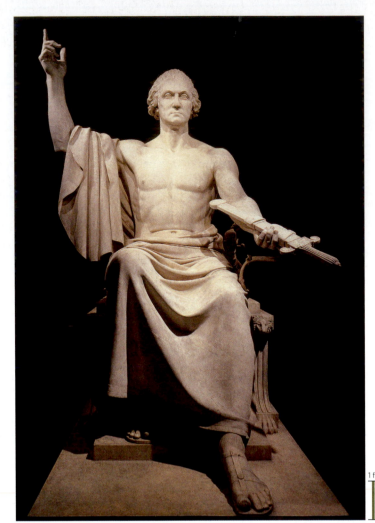

26-34 HORATIO GREENOUGH, *George Washington*, 1840. Marble, 11' 4" high. Smithsonian American Art Museum, Washington, D.C.

In this posthumous portrait, Greenough likened Washington to a god by depicting him seminude and enthroned in the manner of Phidias's Olympian statue of Zeus, king of the Greek gods.

JEAN-ANTOINE HOUDON Neoclassicism also became the preferred style for public sculpture in the new American republic. When members of the Virginia legislature wanted to erect a life-size marble statue of Virginia-born George Washington (1732–1799), they awarded the commission to the leading French Neoclassical sculptor of the late 18th century, JEAN-ANTOINE HOUDON (1741–1828). Houdon had already carved a bust portrait of Benjamin Franklin (1706–1790) when Franklin was America's ambassador to France. Houdon's portrait of Washington (FIG. 26-33) is the sculptural equivalent of a painted Grand Manner portrait (FIG. 26-20). But although Washington wears 18th-century garb, the statue makes overt reference to the Roman Republic. The "column" on which Washington leans is a bundle of rods with an ax attached—the ancient Roman *fasces,* an emblem of authority—used much later as the emblem of Mussolini's Fascist government in 20th-century Italy. ("Fascist" derives from "fasces.") The 13 rods symbolize the 13 original states. The plow behind Washington alludes to Cincinnatus, a *patrician* of the early Roman Republic who was elected *dictator* during a time of war and resigned his position as soon as victory had been achieved in order to return to his farm. Washington wears the badge of the Society of the Cincinnati (visible beneath the

bottom of his waistcoat), an association founded in 1783 for officers in the revolutionary army who had resumed their peacetime roles. Tellingly, Washington no longer holds his sword in Houdon's statue.

HORATIO GREENOUGH After his death, Washington gradually took on almost godlike stature as the "father of his country." In 1840, the U.S. Congress commissioned American sculptor HORATIO GREENOUGH (1805–1852) to create a statue (FIG. 26-34) of the country's first president for the Capitol. Greenough used Houdon's portrait as his model for the head, but he portrayed Washington as seminude and enthroned, as Phidias depicted Zeus in the famous lost statue he made for the god's temple at Olympia in ancient Greece. The colossal statue—Washington is more than 11 feet tall, seated—is a supreme example of the Neoclassical style, but it did not win favor with either the Congress that commissioned it or the public. Although no one ever threw Greenough's statue into the Potomac River, as one congressman suggested, the legislators never placed it in its intended position beneath the Capitol dome. In fact, by 1840, the Neoclassical style itself was no longer in vogue. The leading artists of Europe and America had already embraced a new style, *Romanticism,* examined in the next chapter.

ROCOCO TO NEOCLASSICISM:
THE 18TH CENTURY IN EUROPE AND AMERICA

Rococo

- In the early 18th century, the centralized and grandiose palace-based culture of Baroque France gave way to the much more intimate Rococo culture based in the townhouses of Paris. There, aristocrats and intellectuals gathered for witty conversation in salons featuring delicate colors, sinuous lines, gilded mirrors, elegant furniture, and small paintings and sculptures.

- The leading Rococo painter was Antoine Watteau, whose usually small canvases feature light colors and elegant figures in ornate costumes moving gracefully through lush landscapes. His fête galante paintings depict the outdoor amusements of French high society.

- Watteau's successors included François Boucher and Jean-Honoré Fragonard, who carried on the Rococo style late into the 18th century. In Italy, Giambattista Tiepolo adapted the Rococo manner to huge ceiling frescoes in the Baroque tradition.

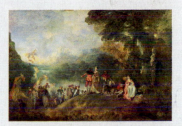

Watteau, *Pilgrimage to Cythera*, 1717

The Enlightenment

- By the end of the 18th century, revolutions had overthrown the monarchy in France and achieved independence for the British colonies in America. A major factor was the Enlightenment, a new way of thinking critically about the world independently of religion and tradition.

- The Enlightenment promoted scientific questioning of all assertions and embraced the doctrine of progress, exemplified by the Industrial Revolution, which began in England in the 1740s. The paintings of Joseph Wright of Derby celebrated the scientific inventions of the Enlightenment era.

- The Enlightenment also made knowledge of ancient Rome imperative for the cultured elite, and Europeans and Americans in large numbers undertook a Grand Tour of Italy. Among the most popular souvenirs of the Grand Tour were Antonio Canaletto's cityscapes of Venice rendered in precise Renaissance perspective with the aid of a camera obscura.

- Rejecting the idea of progress, Rousseau, one of the leading French philosophes, argued for a return to natural values and exalted the simple, honest life of peasants. His ideas had a profound impact on such artists as Jean-Baptiste-Siméon Chardin and Jean-Baptiste Greuze, who painted sentimental narratives about rural families.

- The taste for naturalism also led to the popularity of portrait paintings with landscape backgrounds, a specialty of Thomas Gainsborough, and to a reawakening of interest in realism. Benjamin West represented the protagonists in his history paintings wearing contemporary costumes.

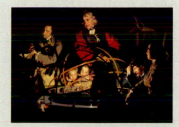

Wright, *A Lecture at the Orrery*, ca. 1763–1765

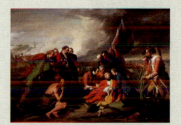

West, *Death of General Wolfe*, 1771

Neoclassicism

- The Enlightenment revival of interest in Greece and Rome, which spurred systematic excavations at Herculaneum and Pompeii, also gave rise in the late 18th century to the artistic movement known as Neoclassicism, which incorporated the subjects and styles of ancient art.

- One pioneer of the new style was Angelica Kauffman, who often chose subjects drawn from Roman history for her paintings. Jacques-Louis David, who exalted classical art as "the imitation of nature in her most beautiful and perfect form," also favored ancient Roman themes. Painted on the eve of the French Revolution, *Oath of the Horatii*, set in a severe classical hall, served as an example of patriotism and sacrifice.

- Architects also eagerly embraced the Neoclassical style. Ancient Roman and Italian Renaissance structures inspired Jacques-Germain Soufflot's Panthéon in Paris and Richard Boyle's Chiswick House near London. A Greek temple in Athens was the model for James Stuart's Doric portico in Worcestershire.

- In the United States, Thomas Jefferson adopted the Neoclassical style in his designs for Monticello and the University of Virginia. He championed Neoclassicism as the official architectural style of the new American republic because it represented for him idealism, patriotism, and civic virtue.

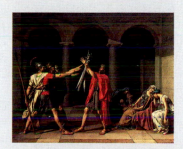

David, *Oath of the Horatii*, 1784

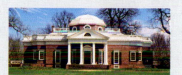

Jefferson, Monticello, 1770–1806

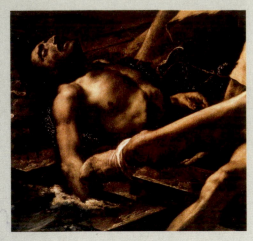

◀ **27-1a** In this gigantic painting, Géricault rejected Neoclassical compositional principles and, in the Romantic spirit, presented a jumble of writhing bodies in every attitude of suffering, despair, and death.

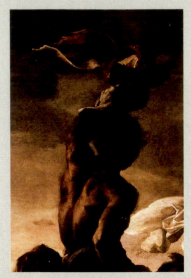

◀ **27-1b** At the apex of a diagonal axis stretching from the lower left, a heroic seminude black man, one of the few survivors, waves a tattered garment in the hope of attracting the attention of the rescue ship.

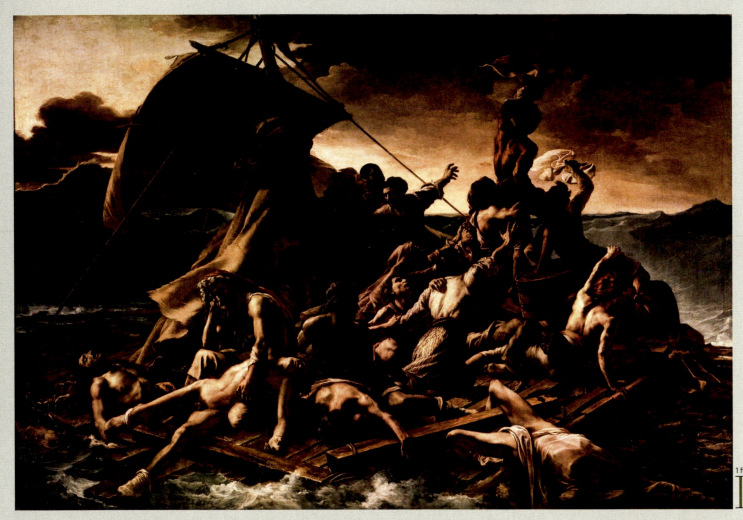

1 ft.

27-1 THÉODORE GÉRICAULT, *Raft of the Medusa*, 1818–1819. Oil on canvas, 16' 1" × 23' 6". Musée du Louvre, Paris.

▶ **27-1c** Barely visible in the distance is the ship *Argus,* which would eventually rescue the *Medusa's* 15 survivors, who told Géricault the story of the captain's incompetence and described the horrors of the raft.

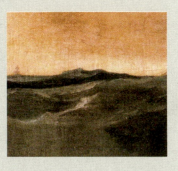

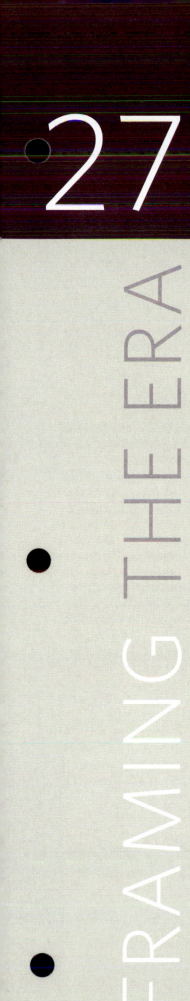

27

FRAMING THE ERA

Romanticism, Realism, Photography: Europe and America, 1800 to 1870

THE HORROR—AND ROMANCE—OF DEATH AT SEA

At the close of the 18th century, Neoclassicism was the dominant artistic style in Europe, but it soon gave way to a movement that historians of art, music, and literature call *Romanticism*. In France, one of the pioneering Romantic painters was THÉODORE GÉRICAULT (1791–1824). Although Géricault retained an interest in the heroic and the epic, and studied drawing in the studio of Neoclassical painter Pierre-Narcisse Guérin (1774–1833), he chafed at the rigidity of the Neoclassical style, instead producing works that captivate viewers with their drama, visual complexity, and emotional force.

Géricault's most ambitious project was *Raft of the Medusa* (FIG. **27-1**), an immense (23-foot-wide) canvas with figures larger than life. The painting immortalized the July 2, 1816, shipwreck off the Mauritanian coast of the French frigate *Medusa*, which ran aground on a reef due to the incompetence of its inexperienced captain, a political appointee. The captain and his officers safely abandoned the ship. In an attempt to survive, 147 passengers built a makeshift raft from pieces of the disintegrating frigate. The raft drifted for 13 days, and the starving survivors dwindled to 15, in part because of cannibalism. Finally, the ship *Argus* spotted the raft and rescued those still alive. This horrendous event was political dynamite once it became public knowledge.

In *Raft of the Medusa*, Géricault chose to represent the moment when some of those still alive summon what little strength they have left to flag down the *Argus* far on the horizon, not knowing if the ship's crew could see their raft. Géricault sought to capture accurately the horror, chaos, and emotion of the tragedy yet invoke the grandeur and impact of Neoclassical history painting. He visited hospitals and morgues to study the bodies of the dying and dead, interviewed survivors, and had a model of the raft constructed in his studio. The legacy of Neoclassicism is still evident in the incongruously muscular bodies of the starving. But Géricault rejected Neoclassical composition principles and instead presented a jumble of writhing bodies. He arranged the survivors and several corpses in a powerful X-shaped composition, and piled one body on another in every attitude of suffering, despair, and death. One light-filled diagonal axis stretches from the bodies at the lower left up to the black man raised on his comrades' shoulders and waving a tattered garment toward the horizon. Yet the man, seen from the back and faceless, is an anonymous antihero, in striking contrast to the protagonists of the historical and mythological works then in vogue. The cross axis descends from the dark, billowing sail at the upper left to the shadowed upper torso of the body trailing in the open sea. Géricault's bold decision to place the raft at a diagonal so that a corner juts outward makes it seem as though some of the corpses are sliding off the raft into the viewer's space. *Raft of the Medusa*, like the event itself, caused a sensation. It established Géricault's reputation and reoriented the history of painting.

MAP 27-1

The Napoleonic
Empire in 1812.

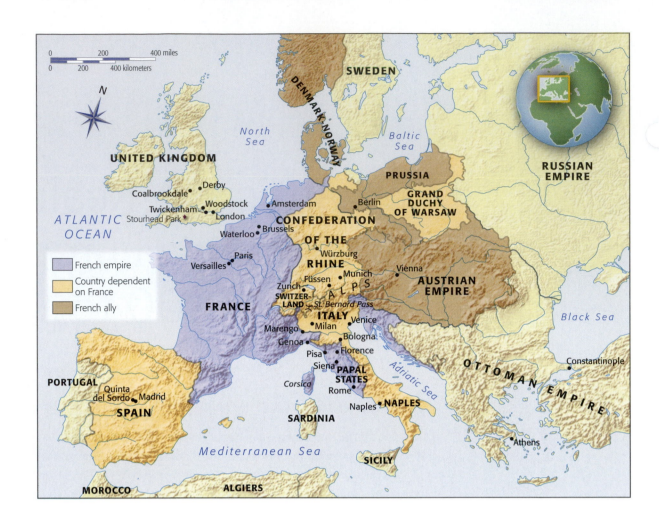

MAP 27-1 The Napoleonic Empire in 1812.

POLITICAL, INDUSTRIAL, AND ARTISTIC REVOLUTIONS

The revolution of 1789 initiated a new era in France, but the overthrow of the monarchy also opened the door for Napoleon Bonaparte (1769–1821) to exploit the resulting disarray and establish a different kind of monarchy with himself at its head. In 1800, after serving in various French army commands and leading major campaigns in Italy and Egypt, Napoleon assumed a newly created position—First Consul of the French Republic, a title with clear and intentional links to the ancient Roman Republic (see page 179).

During the next 15 years, the ambitious general gained control of almost all of continental Europe in name or through alliances (MAP 27-1). In May 1804, for example, he became king of Italy. Later that year, the pope journeyed to Paris for Napoleon's coronation as Emperor of the French (FIG. 27-3). In 1812, however, Napoleon launched a disastrous invasion of Russia that ended in retreat, and

in 1815 he suffered a devastating defeat at the hands of the British at Waterloo in present-day Belgium. Forced to abdicate the imperial throne, Napoleon went into exile on the island of Saint Helena in the South Atlantic, where he died six years later.

After Napoleon's death, the political geography of Europe changed dramatically (MAP 27-2), but in many ways the more significant changes during the first half of the 19th century were technological and economic. The Industrial Revolution caused a population boom in European cities, and railroads spread to many parts of the Continent, facilitating the transportation of both goods and people.

Transformation also occurred in the art world. The century opened with Neoclassicism still supreme, but by 1870, Romanticism and Realism in turn had captured the imagination of artists and public alike. New construction techniques had a major impact on architectural design, and the invention of photography revolutionized picture making of all kinds.

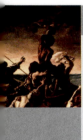

ROMANTICISM, REALISM, PHOTOGRAPHY: EUROPE AND AMERICA, 1800 TO 1870

1800-1815
- Napoleon appoints David as First Painter of the Empire and brings Italian sculptor Canova to Paris
- Vignon models La Madeleine, Napoleon's Neoclassical "temple of glory," on ancient Roman temples
- David's students Gros, Girodet, and Ingres form a bridge between Neoclassicism and Romanticism

1815-1840
- Romanticism is the leading art movement in Europe. Delacroix and other painters favor exotic and fantastic subjects featuring unleashed emotion, vibrant color, and bold brushstrokes
- Friedrich, Turner, Cole, and other Romantic artists specialize in painting transcendental landscapes
- The Gothic style enjoys a revival in architecture
- Daguerre in France and Talbot in England invent photography

1840-1870
- Courbet exhibits his work in the Pavilion of Realism. He and other Realist painters in Europe and America insist that people and events of their own time are the only valid subjects for art
- Manet's paintings get a hostile reception because of their shocking subjects and nonillusionistic style
- Paxton pioneers prefabricated glass-and-iron construction in the Crystal Palace
- Technological advances enable artists to make on-the-spot photographs of the Civil War

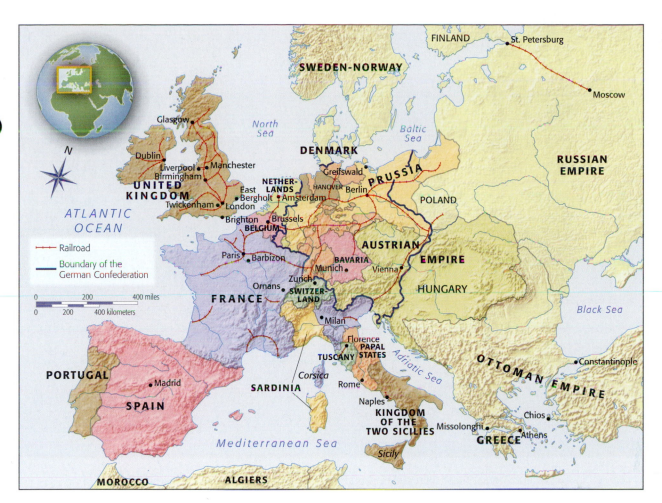

MAP 27-2
Europe around 1850.

ART UNDER NAPOLEON

As soon as Napoleon had consolidated his power, he enlisted France's leading artists and architects to construct a public image of his reign. Not surprisingly, Napoleon, who aspired to rule an empire that might one day rival ancient Rome's, embraced Neoclassicism as the ideal stylistic vehicle for linking his rule with the classical past and for expressing his imperial authority. Napoleon's architectural commissions in Paris included a grandiose triumphal arch (FIG. 27-18A), a commemorative column in the Place Vendôme modeled on the Column of Trajan (FIG. 7-45) in Rome, and a Neoclassical temple.

LA MADELEINE In 1807, Napoleon resumed construction of the church of La Madeleine (Mary Magdalene; FIG. 27-2) in Paris, which had been interrupted in 1790. However, the new emperor converted the building into a "temple of glory" for France's imperial armies. (The structure reverted again to a church after Napoleon's defeat and long before its completion in 1842.) Designed by PIERRE-ALEXANDRE BARTHÉLÉMY VIGNON (1763–1828), the

grandiose Napoleonic temple includes a high podium and a broad flight of stairs leading to a deep porch in the front. These architectural features, coupled with the Corinthian columns, recall Roman temples in France, such as the Maison Carrée (FIG. 7-32) at Nîmes, making La Madeleine a symbolic link between the Napoleonic and Roman empires. Curiously, the building's classical shell surrounds an interior covered by a sequence of three domes, a feature found in Byzantine and Romanesque churches. Vignon in essence clothed a traditional church in the costume of imperial Rome.

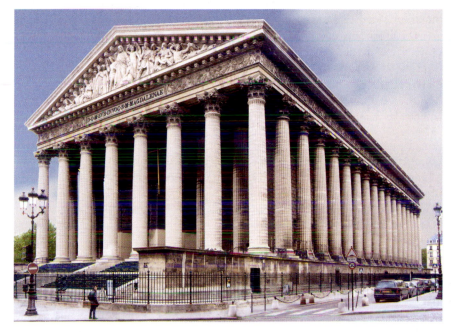

27-2 PIERRE-ALEXANDRE BARTHÉLÉMY VIGNON, La Madeleine, Paris, France, 1807–1842.

Napoleon constructed La Madeleine as a "temple of glory" for his armies. Based on ancient temples (FIG. 7-32) in France, Vignon's Neoclassical design linked the Napoleonic and Roman empires.

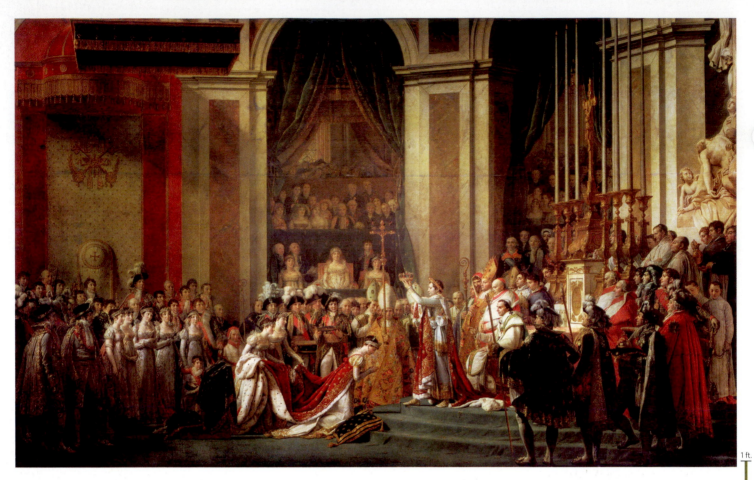

27-3 JACQUES-LOUIS DAVID, *Coronation of Napoleon,* 1805–1808. Oil on canvas, 20' 4½" × 32' 1¾". Musée du Louvre, Paris.

At his patron's insistence, David recorded Napoleon at his 1804 coronation crowning his wife with the pope as witness, thus underscoring the emperor's authority and independence from the Church.

NAPOLEON AND DAVID At the fall of the French revolutionary Maximilien Robespierre and his party in 1794, Jacques-Louis David, who had aligned himself personally and through his work (FIGS. 26-26 and 26-27) with the revolutionary forces, barely escaped with his life. He stood trial and went to prison. After his release in 1795, he worked hard to resurrect his career—for example, by painting a series of portraits of Napoleon on horseback crossing the Alps (FIG. **27-2A**). When the new emperor approached David immediately after his 1804 coronation and offered him the position of First Painter of the Empire, David seized the opportunity. The most grandiose work David produced for his new imperial patron was an immense (20-by-32-foot) canvas (FIG. **27-3**) documenting the pomp and pageantry of that coronation (see "The Coronation of Napoleon," page 797). The work took the artist three years to complete.

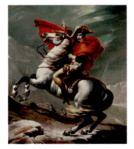

27-2A DAVID, *Napoleon Crossing Saint-Bernard,* 1800-1801.

ANTONIO CANOVA Neoclassical sculpture also was in vogue under Napoleon. His favorite sculptor was ANTONIO CANOVA (1757–1822), who somewhat reluctantly left his native Italy to settle in Paris and serve the emperor. Canova had gained renown for his sculptures of classical gods and heroes (for example, *Cupid and Psyche,* FIG. **27-3A**). In Paris, he made numerous portraits of the emperor and his family in the Neoclassical style, including a nude statue of the emperor in the guise of the Roman war god Mars. The most famous portrait that Canova carved is, however, the marble statue (FIG. **27-4**) of Napoleon's sister Pauline Borghese (1780–1825) in the guise of Venus Victorious. Initially, Canova had suggested depicting Pauline clothed as Diana, goddess of the hunt. She demanded, however, that she be portrayed nude as Venus, the goddess of love. Thus Pauline appears, reclining on a divan and gracefully holding the golden apple, the symbol of the goddess's triumph in the judgment of Paris. Canova clearly based his work on Greek statuary—the sensuous pose and seminude body recall Hellenistic works such as *Venus de Milo* (FIG. 5-84)—and the reclining figure has parallels on Roman sarcophagus lids (FIG. 7-59; compare FIG. 6-6).

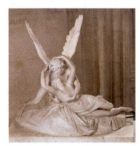

27-3A CANOVA, *Cupid and Psyche,* 1787-1793.

The French public never had the opportunity to admire Canova's portrait, however. Napoleon had arranged the marriage of his sister to an heir of the noble Roman Borghese family. Once Pauline was in Rome, she took several lovers, and the public gossiped extensively about her affairs. Pauline's insistence on being represented

Every thumbnail illustration has a corresponding full-size Bonus Image and accompanying Bonus Essay online.

THE PATRON'S VOICE
The Coronation of Napoleon

Napoleon's coronation on December 2, 1804, was a carefully staged pageant filled with symbolism. By securing the participation of Pope Pius VII (r. 1800–1823), Napoleon legitimized his assumption of absolute power by linking his crowning to Charlemagne's coronation as Roman emperor by Pope Leo III (r. 795–816) almost exactly 1,000 years before. Moreover, to dissociate himself from the monarchy, Napoleon held his ceremony in Notre-Dame Cathedral (FIG. 13-10) in Paris instead of in Reims Cathedral (FIGS. 13-1 and 13-23A), the traditional setting for the coronation of French kings (see page 373). Napoleon's crown, made for the occasion, also broke with royal tradition. He chose a gold laurel wreath of the kind worn by Roman emperors.

To a large extent, in *Coronation of Napoleon* (FIG. 27-3) First Painter David adhered to historical fact in depicting the event, duly recording, for example, the appearance of the interior of Paris's Notre-Dame Cathedral as the emperor's architects Charles Percier (1764–1838) and Pierre-François-Léonard Fontaine (1762–1853) had decorated it for the occasion. David also faithfully portrayed those in attendance: scores of people, all at approximately life size, including Napoleon; his wife Josephine (1763–1814), who kneels to receive her crown; the pope, seated behind Napoleon; Joseph (1768–1814) and Louis (1778–1846) Bonaparte; Napoleon's ministers; the retinues of the emperor and empress; a representative group of the clergy; and David himself, seated among the rows of spectators in the balconies.

Preliminary studies and drawings reveal, however, that, at Napoleon's direction, David made changes to his initially accurate record of the event. For example, the emperor insisted that the painter depict the pope with his hand raised in blessing, instead of as the inactive witness he was. Further, Napoleon's mother, who had refused to attend the coronation, appears prominently in the center background. The *Gazette nationale* of January 16, 1808, diplomatically described Napoleon's "suggestions" as follows:

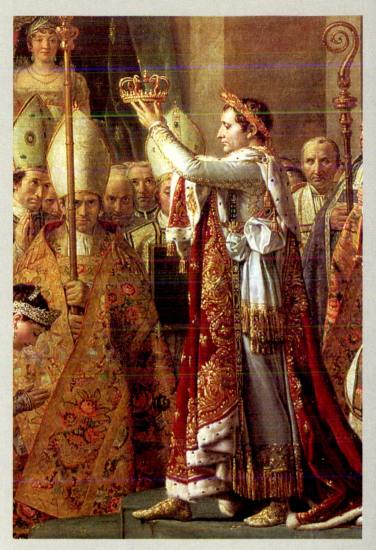

Detail of *Coronation of Napoleon* (FIG. 27-3).

> His Majesty, employing expressions full of kindness and taking the most delicate care, communicated to Monsieur David several observations. The painter, recognizing the fine tact, the exquisite taste, and the profound thinking that His Majesty the Emperor manifests in all his engagements with the sciences and the arts, took it upon himself to conform it to these opinions that enlightened him and thus to perfect his painting.*

Given the number of figures and details David had to incorporate in his painting, it is remarkable that he was able to impose upon the lavish pageant the structured composition that was central to the Neoclassical style. As in his *Oath of the Horatii* (FIG. 26-26), David presented the action as if on a theater stage—which in this instance was literally the case, even if the stage Percier and Fontaine constructed was inside a church. In addition, as he did in his arrangement of the men and women in *Oath of the Horatii,* David conceptually divided the painting to highlight polarities. The pope, prelates, and priests representing the Catholic Church appear on the right. The members of Napoleon's imperial court are on the left. The relationship between Church and State was one of this period's most contentious issues. Napoleon's decision to crown himself, rather than to allow the pope to perform the coronation, as was traditional, reflected Napoleon's concern about the Church-State power relationship. For the painting commemorating the occasion, David had initially planned to show Napoleon crowning himself. But the emperor insisted that the artist instead depict the

moment after, when Napoleon placed a crown on his wife's head, further underscoring his authority and independence from the Church. Moreover, Napoleon instructed David to portray Josephine as looking younger than her real age. David also reduced the scale of Notre-Dame so that the protagonists would not seem dwarfed by the towering interior of the cathedral.

Thus, although this painting appears at first to be a detailed, objective record of a historical event, it is, in fact, a carefully crafted tableau designed to present Napoleon in the way he wished to be seen. In

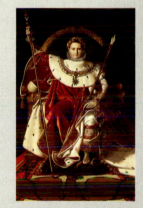

27-3B INGRES, *Napoleon on His Imperial Throne*, 1806.

that respect, as well as stylistically, David was emulating the artists in the employ of the ancient Roman emperors (see Chapter 7), as was his pupil, Ingres, in a contemporaneous portrait (FIG. 27-3B) of Napoleon enthroned.

*Todd Porterfield and Susan L. Siegfried, *Staging Empire: Napoleon, Ingres, and David* (University Park: Pennsylvania State University Press, 2006), 196.

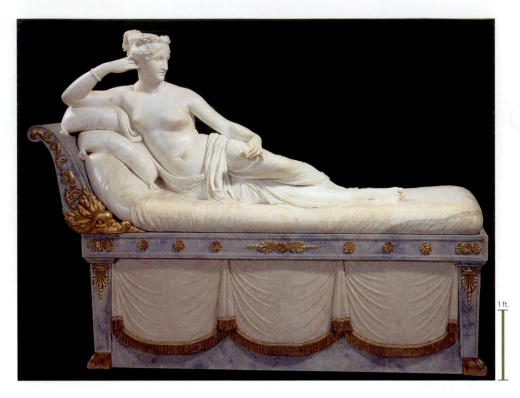

27-4 ANTONIO CANOVA, *Pauline Borghese as Venus Victorious,* from the Villa Borghese, Rome, Italy. 1808. Marble, 6′ 7″ long. Galleria Borghese, Rome.

Canova was Napoleon's favorite sculptor. Here, the artist depicted the emperor's sister—at her insistence—as the nude Roman goddess of love in a marble statue inspired by classical models.

1 ft.

as the goddess of love erotically posed on a 19th-century couch, meticulously reproduced by Canova, reflected her self-perception. Because of his wife's notoriety, Prince Camillo Borghese (1775–1832), the work's official patron, kept the sculpture in his palatial villa in Rome, now the Galleria Borghese, a public museum. The prince allowed relatively few people to see the portrait, and only at night by torchlight.

DAVID'S STUDENTS Given David's stature as an artist in Napoleonic France, along with the popularity of Neoclassicism, it is not surprising that the First Painter attracted numerous students and developed an active and flourishing teaching studio (see "David on Greek Style," page 784). He gave practical instruction to and deeply influenced many important artists of the period. So strong was David's commitment to classicism that he encouraged all his students to learn Latin, the better to immerse themselves in and understand classical culture. David even initially demanded that his pupils select their subjects from Plutarch, the ancient author of *Lives of the Noble Greeks and Romans* and a principal source of Neoclassical subject matter. Due to this thorough classical foundation, David's students all produced work that at its core retains Neoclassical elements. Yet the work of his three most famous students—Ingres (FIGS. 27-3B, 27-7, and 27-8), Gros (FIG. 27-5), and Girodet-Trioson (FIGS. 27-6 and 27-6A)—represents a departure from the structured confines of Neoclassicism. David's pupils laid the foundation for the Romantic movement (see page 801) by exploring the realm of the exotic and the erotic, and often by turning to fictional narratives for the subjects of their paintings, as the Romantic artists would also do.

ANTOINE-JEAN GROS As did his teacher, ANTOINE-JEAN GROS (1771–1835) produced several paintings that contributed to Napoleon's growing mythic status. In *Napoleon Visiting the Plague-Stricken in Jaffa* (FIG. 27-5), the artist, on commission from Napoleon, recorded an incident during an outbreak of the bubonic plague in the course of the general's Syrian campaign of 1799. This fearsome disease struck Muslim and French forces alike, and to quell the growing panic and hysteria, on March 11, 1799, Napoleon himself visited the mosque at Jaffa that had been converted into a hospital for those who had contracted the dreaded disease. Gros depicted Napoleon's staff officers covering their noses against the stench of the place, whereas Napoleon, amid the dead and dying, is fearless and in control. He comforts those still alive, who are clearly awed by his presence and authority. Indeed, by depicting the French leader as having removed his glove to touch the sores of a French plague victim, Gros implied that Napoleon possessed the miraculous power

to heal. The composition recalls scenes of the doubting Thomas touching Christ's wound. Here, however, Napoleon is not Saint Thomas but a Christlike figure tending to the sick, as in Rembrandt's *Hundred-Guilder Print* (FIG. 25-16), which Gros certainly knew. The French painter also based the despairing seated Arab figure at the lower left on the comparable figure (one of the damned) in Michelangelo's *Last Judgment* (FIG. 22-19). The kneeling nude Frenchman with extended arm at the right recalls the dead Christ in Michelangelo's late *Pietà* (FIG. 22-20).

The action in *Napoleon in Jaffa* unfolds against the exotic backdrop of the horseshoe arches and Moorish arcades of the mosque-hospital's courtyard (compare FIG. 10-11). On the left are Muslim doctors distributing bread and ministering to plague-stricken Arabs in the shadows. On the right, in radiant light, are Napoleon and his soldiers in their splendid tailored uniforms. David had used this polarized compositional scheme and an arcaded backdrop to great effect in his *Oath of the Horatii* (FIG. 26-26), and Gros emulated those features in this painting, but employed brighter colors and looser brushstrokes. The younger artist's fascination with the exoticism of the Muslim world, as is evident in his attention to the details of architecture and costume, also represented a departure from his teacher's Neoclassicism and reflects a growing interest among the French in the Near East and North Africa, spurred in large measure by Napoleon's eastern campaigns. Historians and art historians alike refer to this European curiosity about the decidedly non-Western culture of the East as *Orientalism*. The setting of *Napoleon in Jaffa,* along with Gros's emphasis on death, suffering, and an emotional rendering of the scene, also foreshadowed core elements of the artistic movement that would soon displace Neoclassicism—Romanticism.

GIRODET-TRIOSON *Burial of Atala* (FIG. 27-6) by ANNE-LOUIS GIRODET-TRIOSON (1767–1824) is an important bridge between Neoclassicism and Romanticism. Girodet based the painting on *The Genius of Christianity,* a novel by François René de Chateaubriand (1768–1848). The section of the novel dealing with Atala appeared as an excerpt a year before the publication of the entire book in 1802.

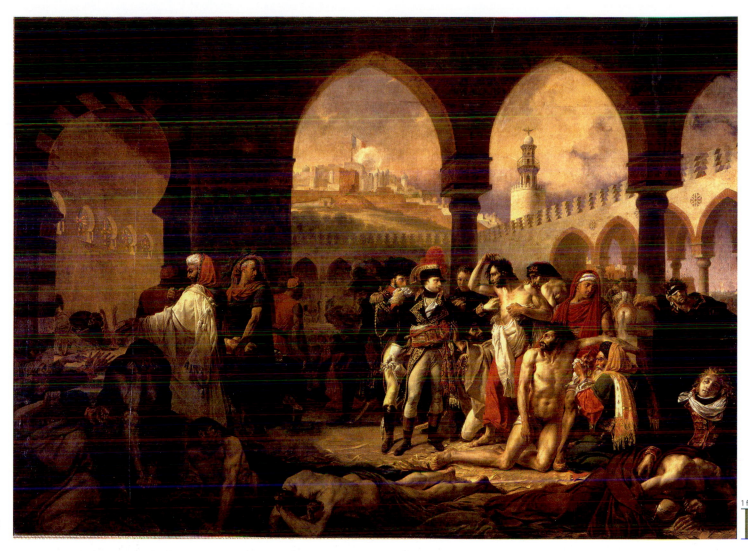

27-5 ANTOINE-JEAN GROS, *Napoleon Visiting the Plague-Stricken in Jaffa*, 1804. Oil on canvas, 17' 5" × 23' 7". Musée du Louvre, Paris.

In his depiction of Napoleon as a Christlike healer, Gros foreshadowed Romanticism by recording the exotic people, costumes, and architecture of Jaffa, including the striped horseshoe arches of the mosque-hospital.

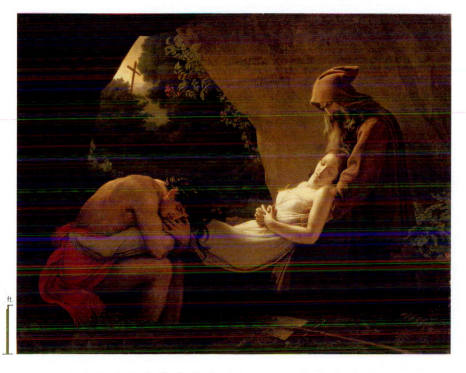

27-6 ANNE-LOUIS GIRODET-TRIOSON, *Burial of Atala*, 1808. Oil on canvas, 6' 11" × 8' 9". Musée du Louvre, Paris.

Girodet's depiction of Native American lovers in the Louisiana wilderness appealed to the French public's fascination with what it perceived as the passion and primitivism of the New World.

Both the excerpt and the novel were enormously successful, and as a result, Atala became almost a cult figure. The exoticism and eroticism integral to the narrative accounted in large part for the public's interest in *The Genius of Christianity*. Set in Louisiana, Chateaubriand's story focuses on the young Native American Chactas and Atala, a Christian girl of mixed European and Native American descent, who had promised her mother on her deathbed that, like the Virgin Mary, she would remain chaste her entire life. However, she falls in love with Chactas, and they run away together through the wilderness. Erotic passion permeates the story, and Atala finally commits suicide rather than break her oath. Girodet's painting depicts this tragedy. Atala's grief-stricken lover, Chactas, buries the heroine in the shadow of a cross. Assisting in the burial is a cloaked priest, whose presence is appropriate given Chateaubriand's emphasis on the revival of Christianity (and the Christianization of the New World) in his novel. Like Gros's depiction of the exotic Muslim world of Jaffa (FIG. 27-5), Girodet's representation of Native American lovers in the Louisiana wilderness appealed to the public's fascination (whetted by the Louisiana Purchase in 1803) with what it perceived as the passion and primitivism of native life in the New World. *Burial of Atala* speaks here to emotions, rather than inviting philosophical meditation or revealing some grand order of nature and form. Unlike David's appeal in *Oath of the Horatii* (FIG. 26-26) to feelings that inspire public action, the appeal here is to the viewer's private world of fantasy and emotion. But Girodet-Trioson also occasionally addressed contemporary themes in his work, as he did in his portrait (FIG. 27-6A) of Jean-Baptiste Belley, a French legislator and former slave.

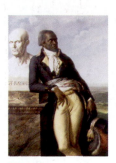

🔲 **27-6A** GIRODET-TRIOSON, *Jean-Baptiste Belley,* 1797.

J.-A.-D. INGRES David's greatest pupil, JEAN-AUGUSTE-DOMINIQUE INGRES (1780–1867), arrived at David's studio in the late 1790s after Girodet-Trioson had left to establish an independent career. Ingres's study there was to be short-lived, however, as he soon broke with David on matters of style. Ingres adopted what he believed to be a truer and purer Greek style than David's Neoclassical manner. The younger artist employed linear forms approximating those found in Greek vase painting (for example, FIGS. 5-23, 5-23A, 5-24, and 5-24A), and often placed the main figures in the foreground of his composition, emulating classical low-relief sculpture.

APOTHEOSIS OF HOMER Ingres exhibited *Apotheosis of Homer* (FIG. 27-7) at the Salon of 1827 (see "Academic Salons," page 844). The huge painting, intended for a ceiling in the Louvre, incorporates none of the perspective devices of Baroque ceiling painting. Rather, the canvas presents in a single statement the Neoclassical doctrines of ideal form and composition. It is the artist's attempt to wed the styles of Raphael and classical antiquity. Winged Victory (or Fame) crowns the epic poet Homer, who sits like a god on a throne before an Ionic temple. At Homer's feet are two statuesque women, personifications of the *Iliad* (holding a sword) and the *Odyssey* (holding an oar), the offspring of his imagination. Symmetrically grouped about him is a company of the "sovereign geniuses"—as Ingres called them—who expressed humanity's highest ideals in philosophy, poetry, music, and art. To Homer's left are the Greek poet Pindar with his lyre, Phidias with his sculptor's hammer, the philosophers Plato and Socrates, and other ancient worthies of different eras. They gather together in the painter's world of suspended time as Raphael united them in *School of Athens* (FIG. 22-9), which was the inspiration for *Apotheosis of Homer*. To the far right in Ingres's assembly of literary and artistic giants are the Roman poets Horace and Vergil, and two Italians: Dante, and, conspicuously, Raphael. Among the forward group on the painting's left side are Poussin (pointing) and Shakespeare (half concealed). At the right are French writers Jean Baptiste Racine, Molière, Voltaire, and François de Salignac de la Mothe Fénelon. Ingres had planned a much larger and more inclusive group, but limited the cast of characters for the Salon exhibition.

GRANDE ODALISQUE Despite his commitment to ideal form and careful compositional structure, Ingres also produced works that, like those of Gros and Girodet, his contemporaries saw as departures from Neoclassicism. The most famous is *Grande Odalisque* (FIG. 27-8), painted for Napoleon's sister Caroline Murat

27-7 JEAN-AUGUSTE-DOMINIQUE INGRES, *Apotheosis of Homer,* 1827. Oil on canvas, 12' 8" × 16' 10¾". Musée du Louvre, Paris.

Inspired by *School of Athens* (FIG. 22-9) by Raphael, Ingres's favorite painter, this huge canvas is a Neoclassical celebration of Homer and other ancient worthies, Dante, and select French authors.

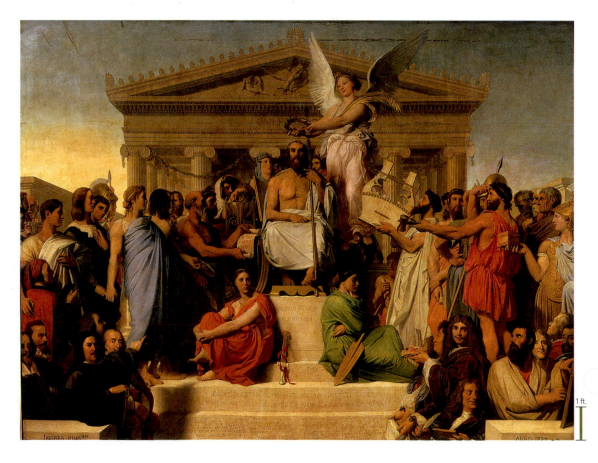

1 ft.

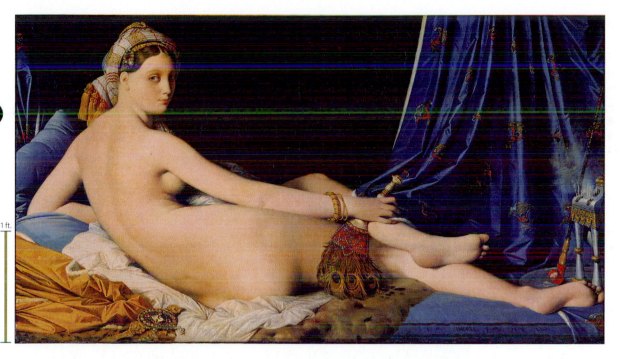

27-8 Jean-Auguste-Dominique Ingres, *Grande Odalisque*, 1814. Oil on canvas, $2' 11\frac{7}{8}"$ × 5' 4". Musée du Louvre, Paris.

The reclining female nude was a Greco-Roman subject, but Ingres converted his Neoclassical figure into an odalisque in a Turkish harem, consistent with the new Romantic taste for the exotic.

(1782–1839), queen of Naples. The subject—the reclining nude female figure—followed the grand tradition of antiquity and the Renaissance (FIGS. 22-16 and 22-39) in sculpture as well as painting, as did Canova's *Pauline Borghese as Venus* (FIG. 27-4). *Grande Odalisque* again shows Ingres's admiration for Raphael in his borrowing of that master's type of female head (FIGS. 22-7 and 22-8). The figure's languid pose, small head, and elongated limbs and torso, and the generally cool color scheme reveal the painter's debt to Parmigianino (FIG. 22-44) and the Italian Mannerists, sculptors (FIGS. 22-52 and 22-52A) as well as painters. However, by converting the figure to an *odalisque* (woman in a Turkish harem), Ingres, unlike Canova, made a strong concession to the burgeoning Romantic taste for Orientalist subjects.

This rather strange mixture of artistic allegiances—the combination of precise classical draftsmanship, Mannerist proportions, and Romantic themes—prompted confusion, and when Ingres first exhibited *Grande Odalisque* in 1814, the painting drew acid criticism. Critics initially saw Ingres as a rebel in terms of both the form and content of his works. They did not cease their attacks until the mid-1820s, when a greater enemy of David's Neoclassical style, Eugène Delacroix, appeared on the scene (see page 805). Critics suddenly perceived that Ingres's art, despite its innovations and deviations, still contained crucial elements adhering to the Neoclassical taste for the ideal. In fact, on the basis of works such as *Apotheosis of Homer* (FIG. 27-7), Ingres soon became the leader of the academic forces in their battle against the "barbarism" of Delacroix, Théodore Géricault, and the Romantic movement.

ROMANTICISM

Whereas Neoclassicism's rationality reinforced Enlightenment thought (see page 763), particularly Voltaire's views, Romanticism owed much to the ideas of Jean-Jacques Rousseau (see page 774). Rousseau's exclamation "Man is born free, but is everywhere in chains!"—the opening line of his *Social Contract* (1762)—summarizes a fundamental Romantic premise. Romanticism emerged from a desire for freedom—not only political freedom but also freedom of thought, feeling, action, worship, speech, and taste. Romantics

asserted that freedom was the right and property of all. They believed that the path to freedom was through imagination and feeling rather than reason.

The allure of the Romantic spirit grew dramatically during the late 18th century, when the term originated among German literary critics. Their aim was to distinguish peculiarly "modern" traits from the Neoclassical traits that already had displaced Baroque and Rococo design elements. Consequently, some scholars refer to Romanticism as a phenomenon that began around 1750 and ended about 1850, but most use the term more narrowly to denote an art movement that flourished from about 1800 to 1840, between Neoclassicism and Realism.

Roots of Romanticism

The transition from Neoclassicism to Romanticism represented a shift in emphasis from reason to feeling, from calculation to intuition, and from objective nature to subjective emotion. Among the leading manifestations of Romanticism was heightened interest in the medieval period and in the sublime. For people living in the 18th century, the Middle Ages were the "dark ages," a time of barbarism, superstition, mystery, and miracle. The Romantic imagination stretched its perception of the Middle Ages into all the worlds of fantasy open to it, including the ghoulish, infernal, terrible, nightmarish, grotesque, and sadistic—the imagery that comes from the chamber of horrors when reason sleeps. Related to the imaginative sensibility was the period's notion of the sublime. Among the individuals most involved in studying the sublime was the British politician and philosopher Edmund Burke (1729–1797). In *A Philosophical Enquiry into the Origins of Our Ideas of the Sublime and Beautiful* (1757), Burke articulated his definition of the sublime—feelings of awe mixed with terror. Burke observed that pain or fear evoked the most intense human emotions and that these emotions could also be thrilling. Thus raging rivers and great storms at sea could be sublime to their viewers. Accompanying this taste for the sublime was the taste for the fantastic, the occult, and the macabre—for the adventures of the soul voyaging into the dangerous reaches of the imagination.

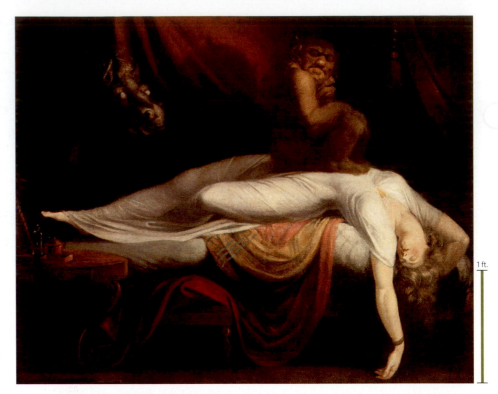

27-9 John Henry Fuseli, *The Nightmare*, 1781. Oil on canvas, 3' 3¾" × 4' 1½". Detroit Institute of the Arts (Founders Society purchase with funds from Mr. and Mrs. Bert L. Smokler and Mr. and Mrs. Lawrence A. Fleishman).

The transition from Neoclassicism to Romanticism marked a shift in emphasis from reason to feeling. Fuseli was among the first painters to depict the dark terrain of the human subconscious.

JOHN HENRY FUSELI The concept of the nightmare is the subject of a 1781 painting (FIG. **27-9**) by the Swiss painter Johann Heinrich Fuseli, better known by his English name JOHN HENRY FUSELI (1741–1825). Fuseli lived in Rome from 1770 to 1778 and settled in England in 1799 and eventually became a member of the Royal Academy and one of its instructors. Largely self-taught, he contrived a distinctive manner to express the fantasies of his vivid imagination. Fuseli specialized in night moods of horror and in dark fantasies—in the demonic, the macabre, and often the sadistic. In *The Nightmare*, a beautiful young woman lies asleep, draped across the bed with her limp arm dangling over the side. An *incubus*, a demon believed in medieval times to prey, often sexually, on sleeping women, squats ominously on her body. In the background, a ghostly horse with flaming eyes bursts into the scene from beyond the curtain. Despite the temptation to see the painting's title as a pun because of this horse, the word *nightmare* in fact derives from "night" and "Mara." Mara was a spirit in Scandinavian mythology who tormented and suffocated sleepers. Fuseli was among the first to attempt to depict the dark terrain of the human subconscious that became fertile ground for later artists.

WILLIAM BLAKE In their images of the sublime and the terrible, Romantic artists often combined something of Baroque dynamism with naturalistic details in their quest for grippingly moving visions. These elements became the mainstay of Romantic art and contrasted with the more intellectual, rational Neoclassical themes and compositions. The two were not mutually exclusive, however. Gros, Girodet-Trioson, and Ingres effectively integrated elements of Neoclassicism with Romanticism. So, too, did the visionary English poet, painter, and engraver WILLIAM BLAKE (1757–1827). Blake greatly admired ancient Greek art because it exemplified for him the mathematical and thus the eternal, and his work often incorporated

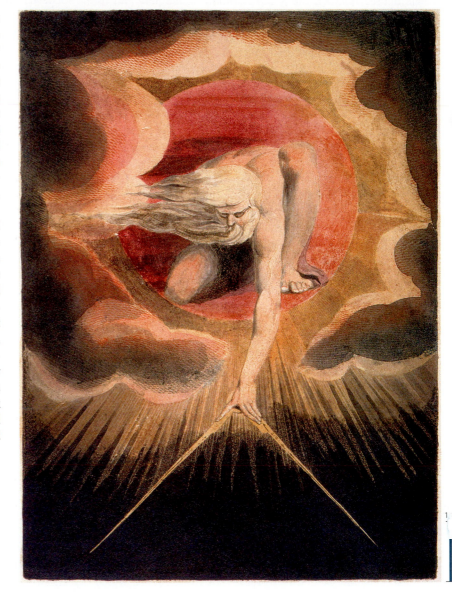

27-10 William Blake, *Ancient of Days*, frontispiece of *Europe: A Prophecy*, 1794. Metal relief etching, hand colored, 9½" × 6¾". Pierpont Morgan Library, New York.

Although art historians classify Blake as a Romantic artist, he incorporated classical references in his works. Here, ideal classical anatomy merges with the inner dark dreams of Romanticism.

classical references. Yet Blake did not align himself with prominent Enlightenment figures. As did many other Romantic artists, he also found the art of the Middle Ages appealing. Blake derived the inspiration for many of his paintings and poems from his dreams. The importance he attached to these nocturnal experiences led him to believe that the rationalist search for material explanations of the world stifled the spiritual side of human nature. He also believed that the stringent rules of behavior that orthodox religions imposed had killed the individual creative impulse.

Blake's vision of the Almighty in *Ancient of Days* (FIG. **27-10**) combines his ideas and interests in a highly individual way. For Blake, this figure united the concept of the Creator with that of wisdom as a part of God. He chose *Ancient of Days* as the frontispiece for his book *Europe: A Prophecy,* and juxtaposed it with a quotation ("When he set a compass upon the face of the deep") from Proverbs 8:27. The speaker is Wisdom, who tells the reader how she was with the Lord through all the time of the creation (Prov. 8:22–23, 27–30). Energy fills Blake's composition. The Almighty leans forward from a fiery orb, peering toward earth and unleashing power through his outstretched left arm into twin rays of light. These emerge between his spread fingers like an architect's measuring instrument—a conception of creation with precedents in Gothic manuscript painting (FIG. 13-32). Here, however, a mighty wind surges through the

Creator's thick hair and beard. Only the strength of his Michelangelesque physique keeps him firmly planted on his heavenly perch. In this image Blake merged ideal classical anatomy with the inner dark dreams of Romanticism.

Spain and France

From its roots in the work of Fuseli, Blake, and other late-18th-century artists, Romanticism gradually displaced Neoclassicism as the dominant painting style of the first half of the 19th century. Romantic artists, including Francisco Goya in Spain and Théodore Géricault (FIG. 27-1) and Eugène Delacroix in France, reveled in exploring the exotic, erotic, and fantastic.

FRANCISCO GOYA Although FRANCISCO JOSÉ DE GOYA Y LUCIENTES (1746–1828) was David's contemporary, their work has little in common. Goya spent more than a year in Italy in 1770–1771 and worked with the influential Neoclassical painter Anton Raphael Mengs (FIG. 26-25A) in Madrid. He did not arrive at his general dismissal of Neoclassicism without considerable thought about the Enlightenment and the Neoclassical penchant for rationality and order. In *The Sleep of Reason Produces Monsters* (FIG. **27-11**), an etching from a series titled *Los Caprichos* (*The Caprices*), Goya depicted an artist, probably himself, asleep, slumped onto a desk, while threatening creatures converge on him, at least in his dream. The subject is a variation on the theme of Fuseli's *Nightmare* (FIG. 27-9), but without that painting's sexuality. Seemingly poised to attack the artist are owls (symbols of folly) and bats (symbols of ignorance). The viewer might read this as a portrayal of what emerges when reason is suppressed and, therefore, as advocating Enlightenment ideals. However, the print is ambiguous, probably intentionally so. *The Sleep of Reason* can also be interpreted as Goya's commentary on the creative process and a testament to his embrace of the Romantic spirit—the unleashing of imagination, emotions, and even nightmares. Goya's explanatory caption for the print reads: "Imagination abandoned by reason produces impossible monsters; united with her, she is the mother of the arts and the source of their wonders."

THIRD OF MAY, 1808 Much of Goya's multifaceted work deals not with Romantic fantasies but with contemporary events. In 1786, he became an official artist in the court of Charles IV (r. 1788–1808) and produced portraits of the king and his family (FIG. **27-11A**). Dissatisfaction with the king's rule increased dramatically during Goya's tenure at the court, and the Spanish people eventually threw their support behind the king's son, Ferdinand VII, in the hope that he would initiate reform. To overthrow

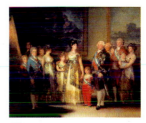

🔎 **27-11A** GOYA, *Family of Charles IV*, 1800.

27-11 FRANCISCO GOYA, *The Sleep of Reason Produces Monsters,* no. 43 from *Los Caprichos*, ca. 1798. Etching and aquatint, $8\frac{1}{2}" \times 5\frac{7}{8}"$. Metropolitan Museum of Art, New York (gift of M. Knoedler & Co., 1918).

In this print, Goya depicted himself asleep while threatening creatures converge on him, revealing his embrace of the Romantic spirit—the unleashing of imagination, emotions, and nightmares.

1 in.

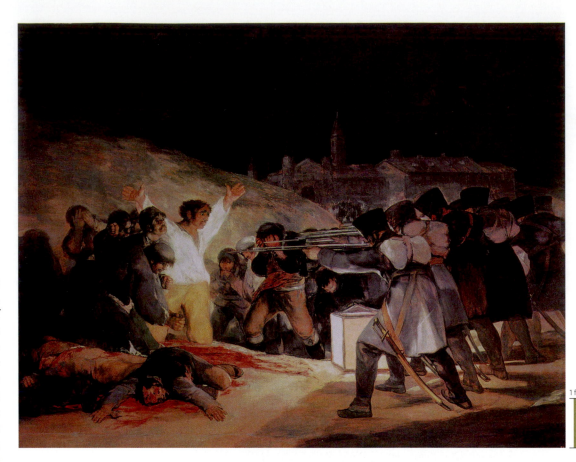

1 ft.

his father and mother, Queen Maria Luisa (1751–1819), Ferdinand enlisted the aid of Napoleon Bonaparte. Because he had designs on the Spanish throne, Napoleon readily agreed to send French troops to Spain. Not surprisingly, as soon as he ousted Charles IV, Napoleon installed his brother Joseph Bonaparte (r. 1808–1813) on the Spanish throne as his surrogate.

The Spanish people, finally recognizing the French as invaders, sought a way to expel the foreign troops. On May 2, 1808, Spaniards attacked Napoleon's soldiers in a chaotic and violent clash. In retaliation and as a show of force, the French responded the next day by rounding up and executing Spanish citizens. This tragic event is the subject of Goya's most famous painting, *Third of May, 1808* (FIG. 27-12), commissioned in 1814 by Ferdinand VII (r. 1813–1833), who had reclaimed the throne after the ouster of the French. In emotional fashion, following the lead of Callot (FIG. 25-35) in the 18th century, Goya depicted the anonymous murderous wall of Napoleonic soldiers ruthlessly executing the unarmed and terrified Spanish peasants. The artist encouraged empathy for the Spaniards by portraying horrified expressions and anguish on their faces, endowing them with a humanity lacking in the faceless French firing squad in the shadows. Moreover, the peasant about to be shot throws his arms out in a cruciform gesture reminiscent of Christ's position on the cross. (The anonymous martyr's right hand also bears Christ's stigmata.) Goya enhanced the emotional drama of the massacre by sharply contrasting the darkness of the night with the focused illumination of the French squad's lantern and by extending the time frame depicted. Although Goya captured the specific moment when one man is about to be executed, he also recorded the bloody bodies of others lying dead on the ground. Still others have been herded together to be shot in a few moments. The horrible massacre will continue indefinitely.

SATURN Goya painted *Third of May* when he was already totally deaf as a result of a mysterious illness he suffered in 1792 that also rendered him temporarily blind and paralyzed as well. Although he recovered all but his hearing, over time Goya became increasingly disillusioned and pessimistic. This state of mind emerges forcefully especially in his late works known as the "Black Paintings," frescoes

he painted on the walls of his farmhouse called Quinta del Sordo (House of the Deaf Man), outside Madrid. Because Goya created the Black Paintings solely on his terms and for his private viewing, they provide great insight into the artist's outlook, which is terrifying and disturbing.

Saturn Devouring One of His Children (FIG. 27-13) depicts the raw carnage and violence of Saturn (the Greek god Kronos; see "The Gods and Goddesses of Mount Olympus," page 105), wild-eyed and monstrous, as he consumes one of his sons in reaction to a prophecy that one of his children would dethrone him. Because of the similarity of Kronos and *khronos* (the Greek word for "time"), Saturn has come to be associated with time. This has led some to interpret Goya's painting as an expression of the artist's despair over the passage of time. Despite the simplicity of the image, it conveys a wildness, boldness, and brutality that evoke an elemental response from all viewers. Goya's work, rooted both in personal and national history, presents darkly emotional images well in keeping with Romanticism.

THÉODORE GÉRICAULT In a tragically brief career lasting only a dozen years, Théodore Géricault (see page 793) had a major influence on the course of French painting in the 19th century. Independently wealthy, he spent only a short time as an apprentice in painting studios, preferring to learn his craft by studying in the Louvre. The former royal palace then housed the recently installed Musée Napoléon and its treasure trove of works by Jan van Eyck, Titian, Caravaggio, Rembrandt, and Peter Paul Rubens, which the emperor had triumphantly brought to Paris as the spoils of his successful military campaigns. Géricault was drawn especially to Rubens, in whose canvases the young painter saw an alternative to the classical compositions, smooth finish, and invisible brushstrokes of David. Géricault also studied Renaissance and Baroque art in Florence, Rome, and

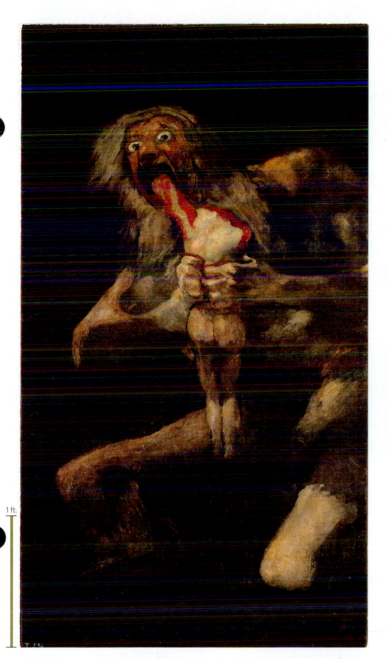

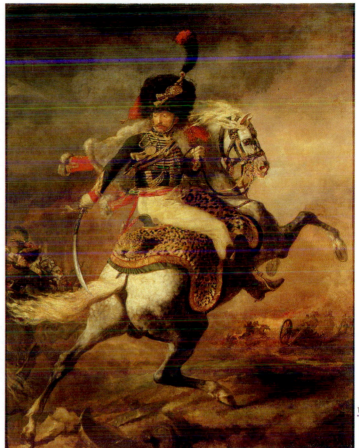

27-14 THÉODORE GÉRICAULT, *Charging Chasseur*, 1812. Oil on canvas, 11' 5" × 8' 8$\frac{3}{4}$". Musée du Louvre, Paris.

Painted when he was 21, Géricault's huge canvas, with its foreshortened rider and loose brushwork influenced by Rubens, differs sharply from David's equestrian portrait of Napoleon (FIG. 27-2A).

27-13 FRANCISCO GOYA, *Saturn Devouring One of His Children*, from Goya's Quinto del Sordo farmhouse, near Madrid, Spain, 1819–1823. Fresco, later detached and mounted on canvas, 4' 9$\frac{1}{8}$" × 2' 8$\frac{5}{8}$". Museo Nacional del Prado, Madrid.

This disturbing fresco from Goya's farmhouse uses a mythological tale to express the aging artist's despair over the passage of time. Saturn's Greek name, Kronos, is similar to the Greek word for "time."

Naples in 1816 on a self-funded trip to Italy after failing to win a Rome Prize, but he also explored themes with few if any precedents—for example, portraits of the insane (FIG. 27-13A).

At the time of his death at age 32, Géricault had exhibited only three works in the Parisian Salons. The last, in 1819, was his greatest work, *Raft of the Medusa* (FIG. 27-1). The first, submitted to the Salon of 1812, was *Charging Chasseur* (FIG. 27-14). Painted

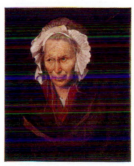

27-13A GÉRICAULT, *Insane Woman*, 1822-1823.

when he was 21, the gigantic (more than 11-foot-tall) canvas depicts a French cavalry officer (*chasseur*). Because Géricault had to enter the work in the portrait category, he identified the chasseur as Lieutenant Alexandre Dieudonné, but the painting could represent any heroic French soldier during Napoleon's Russian campaign. The chasseur and his rearing horse seen in a three-quarter view from behind fill almost the entire canvas. Inspired by Rubens's boldly foreshortened figures (FIG. I-13) as well as the Flemish master's palette and brushwork, Géricault's painting recalls but differs markedly from David's portrait of Napoleon on horseback (FIG. 27-2A), in which the emperor and his steed occupy a narrow space parallel to the picture plane, as in classical relief sculpture (FIG. 5-50, *top*). Amid the tumult and horror of the raging battle, the officer twists on his mount to fend off an attack from behind. The high drama and violent action disguise how carefully Géricault posed the chasseur and his horse, creating, for example, a continuous arc from the officer's sword to the horse's head and forming three parallel lines from the chasseur's right leg and the horse's two right legs. *Charging Chasseur* impressed the judges at the 1812 Salon and earned the then-unknown Géricault a gold medal.

EUGÈNE DELACROIX Art historians often present the history of painting during the first half of the 19th century as a contest between two major artists—Ingres, the Neoclassical draftsman, and EUGÈNE DELACROIX (1798–1863), the Romantic colorist. Their

The Romantic Spirit in Art, Music, and Literature

The appeal of Romanticism, with its emphasis on freedom and feeling, extended well beyond the realm of the visual arts. The imagination and vision that characterized Romantic paintings and sculptures were equally moving and riveting in musical or written form. In European music, literature, and poetry, the Romantic spirit was a dominant presence during the late 18th and early 19th centuries. Composers and authors alike rejected classicism's structured order in favor of the emotive and expressive. In music, the compositions of Franz Schubert (1797–1828), Franz Liszt (1811–1886), Frédéric Chopin (1810–1849), and Johannes Brahms (1833–1897) emphasized the melodic or lyrical. For these composers, music had the power to express what cannot be expressed with words and to communicate the subtlest and most powerful human emotions.

In literature, Romantic poets such as John Keats (1795–1821), William Wordsworth (1770–1850), and Samuel Taylor Coleridge (1772–1834) published volumes of poetry manifesting the Romantic interest in lyrical drama. *Ozymandias*, by Percy Bysshe Shelley (1792–1822), transported readers to faraway, exotic locales. The setting of Lord Byron's *Sardanapalus* is the ancient Assyrian Empire (see page 48). Byron's poem conjures images of eroticism and fury unleashed—images Eugène Delacroix made concrete in his painting *Death of Sardanapalus* (FIG. 27-15). One of the best examples of the Romantic spirit is the engrossing novel *Frankenstein,* written in 1818 by Shelley's wife, Mary Wollstonecraft Shelley (1797–1851). This fantastic tale of a monstrous creature run amok remains popular to the present day. As was true of many Romantic artworks, the novel not only embraced emotionalism but also rejected the rationalism underlying Enlightenment thought. Dr. Frankenstein's monster was a product of science, and the novel is an indictment of the deep faith in science that Voltaire and other Enlightenment thinkers promoted. *Frankenstein* served as a cautionary tale of the havoc that could result from unrestrained scientific experimentation and from the arrogance of scientists.

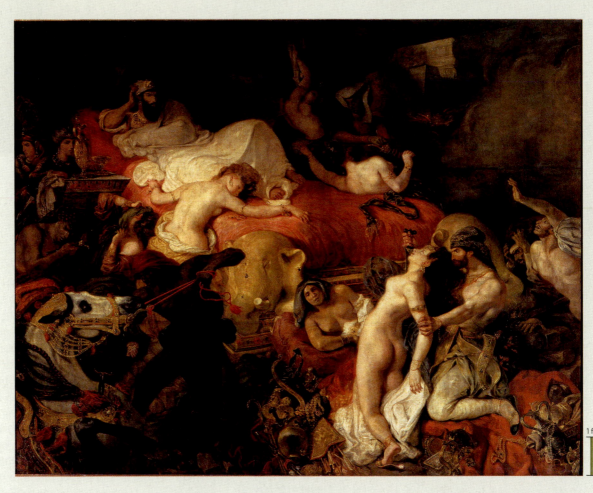

27-15 Eugène Delacroix, *Death of Sardanapalus,* 1827. Oil on canvas, 12' 1$\frac{1}{2}$" × 16' 2$\frac{7}{8}$". Musée du Louvre, Paris.

Inspired by Lord Byron's 1821 poem, Delacroix painted the Romantic spectacle of an Assyrian king on his funeral pyre. The richly colored and emotionally charged canvas is filled with exotic figures.

1 ft.

dialogue recalls the quarrel between the Poussinistes and the Rubénistes at the end of the 17th century and the beginning of the 18th (see "Poussinistes and Rubénistes," page 768). The Poussinistes were conservative defenders of academism who insisted that drawing was superior to color, whereas the Rubénistes proclaimed the importance of color over line (line quality being more intellectual and thus more restrictive than color). Delacroix's works were products of his view that the artist's powers of imagination would in turn capture and inflame the viewer's imagination. Literature of imagi-

native power served Delacroix (and many of his contemporaries) as a useful source of subject matter (see "The Romantic Spirit in Art, Music, and Literature," above). Théophile Gautier (1811–1872), the prominent Romantic critic and novelist, recalled:

> In those days painting and poetry fraternized. The artists read the poets, and the poets visited the artists. We found Shakespeare, Dante, Goethe, Lord Byron and Walter Scott in the studio as well as in the study. There were as many splashes of color as there were blots of ink

in the margins of those beautiful books which we endlessly perused. Imagination, already excited, was further fired by reading those foreign works, so rich in color, so free and powerful in fantasy.[1]

DEATH OF SARDANAPALUS Delacroix's 1827 *Death of Sardanapalus* (FIG. **27-15**) is perhaps the grandest Romantic pictorial drama ever painted. Although inspired by the 1821 narrative poem *Sardanapalus* by Lord Byron (George Gordon Byron, 1788–1824), the painting does not illustrate that text faithfully. Delacroix depicted the last hour of the Assyrian king Ashurbanipal (r. 668–627 BCE; FIG. 2-23), whom the Greeks called Sardanapalus. The king has just received news of his army's defeat and the enemy's entry into his city. The setting that Delacroix painted is much more tempestuous and crowded than Byron described, and orgiastic destruction has replaced the sacrificial suicide of the poem. Sardanapalus reclines on his funeral pyre, soon to be set alight, and gloomily watches the carrying out of his order to destroy all of his most precious possessions—his women, slaves, horses, and treasure. The king's favorite concubine throws herself on the bed, determined to go up in flames with her master. The Assyrian ruler presides like a genius of evil over the tragic scene. Most conspicuous are the tortured and dying bodies of the harem women. In the foreground, a muscular slave plunges his knife into the neck of one woman. Delacroix filled this awful spectacle of suffering and death with the most daringly difficult and tortuous poses, and chose the richest intensities of hue. With its exotic and erotic overtones and violent Orientalist subject, *Death of Sardanapalus* tapped into the Romantic fantasies of 19th-century viewers.

Although *Death of Sardanapalus* is a seventh-century BCE drama, Delacroix, like Géricault, also turned to current events, particularly tragic or sensational ones, for his subject matter. For example, he produced several images based on the Greek War for Independence (1821–1829), including a huge canvas that he painted while the war was still in progress recording the Turkish massacre of the Greeks of Chios (FIG. **27-15A**). The French perception of the Greeks as locked in a brutal **struggle** for freedom from the cruel and exotic Ottoman Turks generated great interest in Romantic circles.

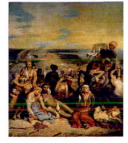

27-15A DELACROIX, *Massacre at Chios*, 1822–1824.

LIBERTY LEADING THE PEOPLE Closer to home, Delacroix captured the passion and energy of the 1830 revolution in *Liberty Leading the People* (FIG. **27-16**). Based on the July 27–29, 1830, Parisian uprising against Charles X (r. 1824–1830), it is at once a record of a contemporaneous event and a Romantic allegory. Dominating the composition is the bare-breasted personification of Liberty defiantly thrusting forth the republic's tricolor banner as she urges the masses to fight on. She wears a scarlet Phrygian cap (the symbol of a freed slave in antiquity), reinforcing the urgency of this struggle. Arrayed around Liberty are bold Parisian types—the street boy brandishing his pistols, the menacing worker with a cutlass, and the intellectual dandy in top hat brandishing a musket. As in Géricault's *Raft of the Medusa* (FIG. 27-1), dead bodies are all around. In the background, the towers of Notre-Dame (FIG. 13-10) rise through the smoke and haze. The painter's inclusion of this recognizable Parisian landmark announces the specificity of locale and event, balancing historical fact with poetic allegory.

WOMEN OF ALGIERS An enormously influential event in Delacroix's life that affected his art in both subject and form was his visit to North Africa in 1832. Delacroix was the official artist in the entourage of the count of Mornay, who led a diplomatic mission to Morocco to seek the support of Sultan Abd al-Rahman (r. 1822–1859) for the French annexation of Algeria. What Delacroix saw in North Africa excited his imagination with fresh impressions that lasted throughout his life and resulted in paintings such as *Tiger Hunt* (FIG. **27-16A**), which he completed more than two decades after his trip.

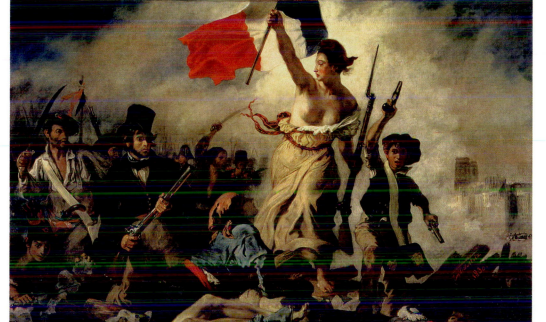

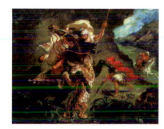

27-16A DELACROIX, *Tiger Hunt*, 1854.

27-16 EUGÈNE DELACROIX, *Liberty Leading the People*, 1830. Oil on canvas, 8′ 6″ × 10′ 8″. Musée du Louvre, Paris.

In a balanced mix of history and poetic allegory, Delacroix captured the passion and energy of the 1830 revolution in this painting of Liberty leading the Parisian uprising against Charles X.

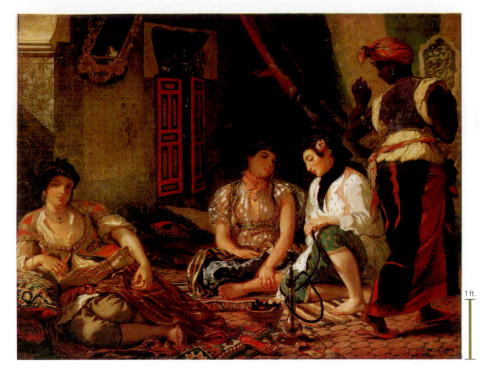

Among the canvases Delacroix painted immediately upon his return to France is *Women of Algiers* (FIG. **27-17**), which captivated the public when exhibited in the 1834 Salon. For viewers of the exhibition, the painting was their first "eyewitness account" of a harem—an exotic locale that had special appeal because Western men were normally not permitted to enter harems. (Delacroix was able to gain entry because of the official nature of his visit to Morocco. The seated woman at the left seems to acknowledge the artist's presence.) The painting depicts three odalisques—modestly dressed, unlike the harem girl in Ingres's earlier imaginary and coolly classical rendition of the same theme (FIG. 27-8)—and a black servant in an incense-filled room with tiled walls and sumptuous carpets. The woman at the left reclines languorously. Her two seated companions share the intoxicating smoke of a *hookah* (water pipe). Delacroix's "documentation" of the opulent interior of a harem reinforced all the stereotypes that his countrymen held dear, especially their fantasies about Oriental harems as places where men could freely indulge their sexual appetites in the company of exotic women.

Delacroix's style perfectly suits this sensuous subject. Relying on large patches of rich color to define his figures, in striking contrast to Ingres's emphasis on line and contour, his technique is as lush as the harem. What Delacroix knew about color he passed on to later painters of the 19th century, particularly the Impressionists (see page 843). He observed that pure colors are as rare in nature as lines and that color appears only in an infinitely varied scale of different tones, shadings, and reflections, which he tried to re-create in his paintings. He recorded his observations in his journal, which became for later painters and scholars a veritable handbook of pre-Impressionist color theory. Although Delacroix anticipated the later development of Impressionist color science, that art-science had to await the discoveries by Michel Eugène Chevreul (1786–1889) and Hermann von Helmholtz (1821–1894) of the laws of light decomposition and the properties of complementary colors. Only then could the problems of color perception and juxtaposition in painting be properly formulated (see "19th-Century Color Theory," page 855). Nevertheless, Delacroix's observations were significant, and he advised other artists not to fuse their brushstrokes, as those strokes would appear to fuse naturally from a distance.

No other painter of the time explored the domain of Romantic subject and mood as thoroughly and definitively as Delacroix. His technique was impetuous, improvisational, and instinctive, rather than deliberate, studious, and cold. It exemplified Romantic colorist painting, catching the impression quickly and developing it in the execution process. His contemporaries commented on how furiously Delacroix worked once he had an idea, keeping the whole painting progressing at once. One critic described Delacroix's brushwork as painting "with a drunken broom." The fury of the artist's attack matched the fury of his imagination and his subjects.

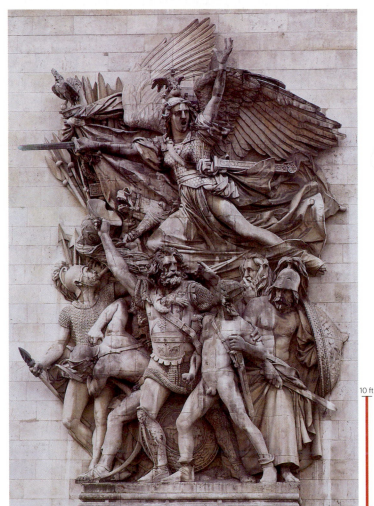

27-18 FRANÇOIS RUDE, *Departure of the Volunteers of 1792* (*La Marseillaise*), northeast pier relief of the Arc de Triomphe, Paris, France, 1833–1836. Limestone, 41' 8" high.

This historical-allegorical sculpture features the Roman war goddess Bellona, but the violent motion, jagged contours, and densely packed masses typify Romantic painting compositions.

FRANÇOIS RUDE The Romantic spirit pervaded all media during the early 19th century. As did the painters of the period, many sculptors produced work incorporating both Neoclassical and Romantic elements. The colossal limestone group *Departure of the Volunteers of 1792* (FIG. 27-18), also called *La Marseillaise*, is one example. The relief, the work of FRANÇOIS RUDE (1784–1855), decorates one of the gigantic piers of the Arc de Triomphe (FIG. 27-18A) in Paris, designed for Napoleon by JEAN-FRANÇOIS-THÉRÈSE CHALGRIN (1739–1811). The sculpture depicts the volunteers of 1792 departing from Marseilles to defend France's borders against the foreign enemies of the revolution. A composite personification of Bellona, the Roman goddess of war;

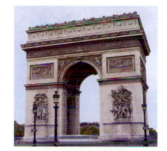

27-18A CHALGRIN, Arc de Triomphe, Paris, 1806–1836.

Liberty; and the Marseillaise, the revolutionary hymn that since 1879 has been France's national anthem, soars above patriots of all ages, exhorting them forward with a thundering battle cry emerging from her wide-open mouth. The figures recall David's classically armored (FIG. 26-26) or nude heroes, as do the rhetorical gestures of the wide-flung arms and the striding poses. Yet the violence of motion, the jagged contours, and the densely packed, overlapping masses relate more closely to the compositional method of dramatic Romanticism, as found in the canvases of Géricault (FIG. 27-1) and Delacroix (FIG. 27-16). Indeed, the allegorical figure in *La Marseillaise* is the spiritual sister of Delacroix's Liberty. Rude's stone figure shares the same Phrygian cap, the badge of liberty, with Delacroix's earlier painted figure, but Rude's soldiers wear classical costumes or are heroically nude, whereas those in Delacroix's painting appear in modern Parisian dress. Both works are allegorical, but one looks to the past and the other to the present.

Landscape Painting

Landscape painting came into its own in the 19th century as a fully independent and respected genre. Briefly eclipsed at the century's beginning by the taste for ideal form, which favored figural composition and history, landscape painting flourished as leading painters adopted the genre as their specialty. Increasing tourism, which came courtesy of improved and expanded railway systems both in Europe (MAP 27-2) and America, contributed to the popularity of landscape painting. So too did the growth of cities. As urban populations expanded, city dwellers increasingly took pleasure in "picturesque" views of the unspoiled countryside. To be sure, earlier artists, especially in the 18th century, regarded the comforting, aesthetic mood that nature inspired as making the landscape itself picturesque—that is, worthy of being painted. But Romantic painters often used nature as allegory and embraced landscape as a vehicle to comment on spiritual, moral, historical, or philosophical issues.

In the early 19th century, most northern European landscape painting to some degree expressed the Romantic view (first extolled by Rousseau) of nature as a "being" that included the totality of existence in organic unity and harmony. German painters, who were primarily Lutherans, were especially attracted to nature, where they could communicate directly with God without the need of a Catholic priest as intermediary. In nature—"the living garment of God," as German poet and dramatist Johann Wolfgang von Goethe (1749–1832) called it—artists found an ideal subject to express the Romantic theme of the soul unified with the natural world. As all nature was mysteriously permeated by "being," landscape artists had the task of interpreting the signs, symbols, and emblems of universal spirit disguised within visible material things. Artists no longer merely beheld a landscape but participated in its spirit, becoming translators of nature's transcendent meanings.

CASPAR DAVID FRIEDRICH Among the first northern European artists to depict the Romantic transcendental landscape was CASPAR DAVID FRIEDRICH (1774–1840), who was born in Greifswald, Germany, near the Baltic Sea; studied art in Copenhagen; and settled in Dresden. For Friedrich, the personal experience of nature led to a deeper understanding of God, nature's creator. The reverential mood of his works demands from the viewer the silence appropriate to sacred places filled with a divine presence.

Abbey in the Oak Forest (FIG. 27-19) is a characteristic example. It is the pictorial equivalent of a solemn requiem. Under a winter sky, through the leafless oaks of a snow-covered cemetery, a procession

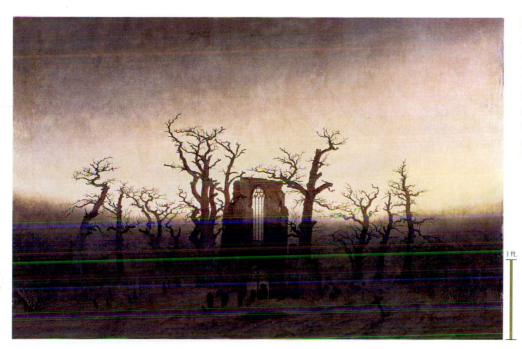

27-19 CASPAR DAVID FRIEDRICH, *Abbey in the Oak Forest*, 1810. Oil on canvas, 4' × 5' 8½". Alte Nationalgalerie, Staatliche Museen zu Berlin, Berlin.

Friedrich was a master of the Romantic transcendental landscape. The reverential mood of this winter scene with a ruined Gothic church and cemetery demands the silence appropriate to sacred places.

1 ft.

WRITTEN SOURCES
Friedrich's *Wanderer above a Sea of Mist*

In *Abbey in the Oak Forest* (FIG. 27-19) and most of Caspar David Friedrich's landscapes, the human figure plays an insignificant role. Indeed, in many instances the human actors are difficult even to discern. But in other paintings, one or more figures seen from behind gazing at the natural vista dominate the canvas. In *Wanderer above a Sea of Mist* (FIG. 27-20), probably Friedrich's most famous painting, a solitary man dressed in German attire suggestive of a bygone era stands on a rocky promontory and leans on his cane. He surveys a vast panorama of clouds, mountains, and thick mist. Because Friedrich chose a point of view on the level of the man's head, the viewer has the sensation of hovering in space behind him—an impossible position that enhances the aura of mystery that the scene conveys. Art historians dispute whether Friedrich intended the viewer to identify with the man seen from behind or if he wanted the viewer to contemplate the man gazing at the misty landscape. Some think that the man is not an anonymous hiker but a specific Prussian war hero contemplating the scenery of his native land. In any interpretation, the painter communicated an almost religious awe at the beauty and vastness of the natural world.

Carl Gustav Carus (1789–1869), a German physician and sometime painter who was a friend of Friedrich's, published in Dresden in 1831 *Nine Letters on Landscape Painting, Written in the Years 1815 to 1824*. In one of the letters, he described the essence of Friedrich's approach to landscape painting in a passage that could serve as a description of *Wanderer above a Sea of Mist*:

> [T]he solid earth, with all of its varied shapes and features like rocks and mountains, valleys and plains, its placid and its rushing waters, the clouds and airy breezes, these are more or less the forms through which the life of the earth reveals itself to us; a life of such immeasurable dimensions in comparison with our own small-ness . . . Go up then to the summit of the mountain, look out across all the distant hilly peaks, contemplate the steady progress of the rivers and every splendor that reveals itself to your gaze, and what feeling is it that then seizes hold of you? There is a quiet sense of devotion within you, you lose yourself in boundless space, your whole being experiences a gentle elevation and purification, your very self vanishes away, you are nothing and God is everything.*

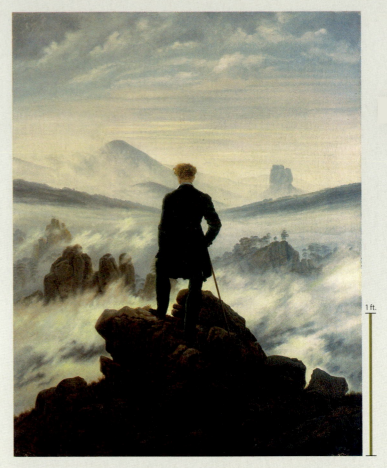

27-20 CASPAR DAVID FRIEDRICH, *Wanderer above a Sea of Mist*, 1817–1818. Oil on canvas, 3' 1¾" × 2' 5⅜". Hamburger Kunsthalle, Hamburg.

Friedrich's painting of a solitary man on a rocky promontory gazing at a vast panorama of clouds, mountains, and thick mist perfectly expresses the Romantic notion of the sublime in nature.

Wanderer above a Sea of Mist perfectly expresses the Romantic notion of the sublime in nature.

*Translated by Nicholas Walker, in Charles Harrison, Paul Wood, and Jason Gaiger, *Art in Theory 1815–1900: An Anthology of Changing Ideas* (Oxford: Blackwell, 1998), 104.

---

of monks bears a coffin into the ruins of a Gothic church that Friedrich based on the remains of Eldana Abbey near Greifswald. The emblems of death are everywhere—the season's desolation, the leaning crosses and tombstones, the black of mourning that the grieving wear, the skeletal trees, and the destruction that time has wrought on the church. The painting is a kind of meditation on human mortality. As Friedrich himself remarked: "Why, it has often occurred to me to ask myself, do I so frequently choose death, transience, and the grave as subjects for my paintings? One must submit oneself many times to death in order some day to attain life everlasting."[2] The artist's sharp-focused rendering of details demonstrates his keen perception of everything in the physical environment relevant to his message. Friedrich's work balances inner and outer experience. "The artist," he wrote, "should paint not only what he sees before him, but also what he sees within him. If, however, he sees nothing within him, then he should also refrain from painting that which he sees before him."[3] Although *Abbey in the Oak Forest* and Friedrich's other works—for

example, *Wanderer above a Sea of Mist* (FIG. 27-20)—may not have the theatrical energy of the paintings of Géricault or Delacroix, a resonant and deep emotion pervades them (see "Friedrich's *Wanderer above a Sea of Mist*," above).

JOHN CONSTABLE In England, one of the most momentous developments in Western history—the Industrial Revolution—had a profound impact on the evolution of Romantic landscape painting. Although discussion of the Industrial Revolution invariably focuses on technological advances, factory development, and growth of urban centers (see page 773), industrialization had no less pronounced an effect on the countryside and the land itself. The detrimental economic effect that the Industrial Revolution had on prices for agrarian products created significant unrest in the English countryside. In particular, increasing numbers of farmers could no longer afford to farm their small plots and had to abandon their land.

ARTISTS ON ART
John Constable on Landscape Painting

In the early 1820s, John Constable corresponded with his friend John Fisher, the archdeacon of Salisbury Cathedral (FIGS. 13-39 to 13-41), on various topics, including his views on landscape painting. The following excerpts from a letter he wrote to Fisher on October 23, 1821, provide invaluable insight into the artist's goals and values.

> I am most anxious to get into my London painting-room. . . . I have done a good deal of skying, for I am determined to conquer all difficulties. . . . The landscape painter who does not make his skies a very material part of his composition, neglects to avail himself of one of his greatest aids. . . . Certainly, if the sky is obtrusive, as mine are, it is bad; but if it is evaded, as mine are not, it is worse; it must and always shall with me make an effectual part of the composition. . . . The sky is the force of light in nature, and governs every thing; even our common observations on the weather of every day are altogether suggested by it. . . . Shakespeare could make every thing poetical; he tells us of poor Tom's haunts among "sheep cotes and mills." As long as I do paint, I shall never cease to paint such places. . . . Still I should paint my own places best; painting is with me but another word for feeling, and I associate "my careless boyhood" with all that lies on the banks of the Stour; those scenes made me a painter, and I am grateful.*

*Charles Harrison, Paul Wood, and Jason Gaiger, *Art in Theory 1815–1900: An Anthology of Changing Ideas* (Oxford: Blackwell, 1998), 118–119.

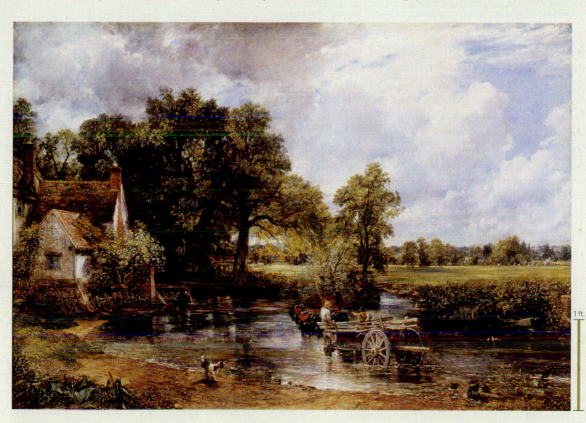

27-21 JOHN CONSTABLE, *The Hay Wain*, 1821. Oil on canvas, 4' $3\frac{1}{4}$" × 6' 1". National Gallery, London.

The Hay Wain is a nostalgic view of the disappearing English countryside during the Industrial Revolution. Constable had a special gift for capturing the texture that climate and weather give to landscapes.

1 ft.

JOHN CONSTABLE (1776–1837) devoted his career to painting the English countryside during this agrarian crisis. He made countless studies from nature for each of his canvases, which helped him produce in his paintings a convincing sense of reality. In his quest for the authentic landscape, Constable studied nature as a meteorologist (he was an accomplished amateur "weatherman"). Although he produced his paintings in his London studio, the norm at the time, he was one of the first to make his sketches outdoors using oil paints instead of watercolors or pencil drawings. His special gift was for capturing the texture that climate and weather, which delicately veil what is seen, give to landscapes. Constable's oil studies of clouds under different weather conditions are especially remarkable. His use of tiny dabs of local color, stippled with white, created a sparkling shimmer of light and hue across the canvas surface—the vibration itself suggestive of movement and process.

The Hay Wain (FIG. 27-21) is representative of Constable's art and reveals much about his outlook. His subjects are Romantic but not sublime. Here, a small cottage sits on the left of a serenely pastoral scene of the countryside. In the center foreground, a man slowly leads a horse and hay-filled wagon (a *hay wain*) across a shallow stretch of the Stour River. Billowy clouds float lazily across the sky. The muted greens and golds and the delicacy of Constable's brushstrokes complement the scene's tranquility. The artist portrayed the oneness with nature that the Romantic poets sought. The relaxed figures are not observers but participants in the landscape's "being."

In terms of content, *The Hay Wain* is significant for precisely what it does not show—the civil unrest of the agrarian working class and the resulting outbreaks of violence and arson. The people populating Constable's landscapes blend into the scenes and become one with nature. Rarely does the viewer see workers engaged in tedious labor (compare, in France, Jean-François Millet's portrayal of the menial and backbreaking work of women gathering scraps after a harvest; FIG. 27-28). Indeed, this painting has a nostalgic, wistful air to it, and reflects Constable's memories of a disappearing rural pastoralism.

Unleashing the Emotive Power of Color

The passion and energy of Turner's landscapes and seascapes reveal the sensibility that was the foundation for much of the art of the Romantic era, but Turner discovered a new means of capturing in painting Edmund Burke's concept of the sublime—awe mixed with terror.

Turner's *The Slave Ship* (FIG. 27-22), although strikingly different in form from Géricault's *Raft of the Medusa* (FIG. 27-1), also has as its subject a politically explosive disaster at sea. *The Slave Ship* depicts a 1781 incident reported in the widely read *History of the Abolition of the Slave Trade,* by Thomas Clarkson (1760–1846). Clarkson's account, reprinted in 1839, undoubtedly was the reason Turner chose this subject for this 1840 painting. The incident involved the slave ship *Zong,* en route from Africa to Liverpool. The ship's captain, on realizing that his insurance would reimburse him only for slaves lost at sea but not for those who died en route, ordered more than 50 sick and dying slaves to be thrown overboard. Appropriately, the painting's subtitle is *Slavers Throwing Overboard the Dead and Dying, Typhoon Coming On.* Slavery had been a powerful political issue in England for some time. For example, in the 1780s, fashionable women wore brooches depicting a kneeling, shackled African slave and carrying the words "Am I Not a Man and a Brother?"—the seal of the Society for the Abolition of Slavery in England. (Brooches and medallions bearing the motif were produced in great numbers in the ceramic factory of Josiah Wedgwood, much better known for his Neoclassical designs featuring Greco-Roman gods and heroes; see page 783.)

Turner's frenzied emotional depiction of the dumping of the sick slaves into the sea matches its barbaric nature. The artist transformed the sun into an incandescent comet amid flying scarlet clouds. The slave ship moves into the distance, leaving in its wake a turbulent sea choked with the bodies of slaves sinking to their deaths. The relative scale of the minuscule human forms compared with the vast sea and overarching sky reinforces the sense of the sublime, especially the immense power of nature over humans. *The Slave Ship* is the polar opposite of *Raft of the Medusa,* in which heroic, over-life-size bodies fill the canvas and block out most of the ocean. Almost lost in the boiling colors of Turner's painting are the event's particulars, but on close inspection, the viewer can discern the iron shackles and manacles around the wrists and ankles of the drowning slaves, cruelly denying them any chance of saving themselves from the predatory fish circling about them.

A key ingredient of Turner's highly personal style is the emotive power of pure color. The haziness of the painter's forms and the indistinctness of his compositions intensify the colors and energetic brushstrokes. Turner's innovation in works such as *The Slave Ship* was to release color from any defining outlines so as to express both the forces of nature and the painter's emotional response to them. In his paintings, the reality of color is at one with the reality of feeling.

Turner's methods had an incalculable effect on the later development of painting. His discovery of the aesthetic and emotive power of pure color and his pushing of the medium's fluidity to a point where the paint itself is almost the subject were important steps toward 20th-century Abstract Expressionist art, which dispensed with identifiable forms altogether (see page 953).

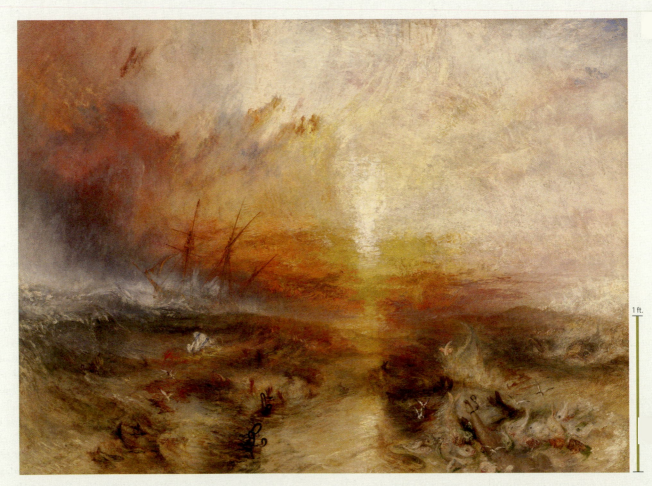

27-22 JOSEPH MALLORD WILLIAM TURNER, *The Slave Ship* (*Slavers Throwing Overboard the Dead and Dying, Typhoon Coming On*), 1840. Oil on canvas, 2' 11$\frac{1}{4}$" × 4'. Museum of Fine Arts, Boston (Henry Lillie Pierce Fund).

The essence of Turner's innovative style is the emotive power of color. He released color from any defining outlines to express both the forces of nature and the painter's emotional response to them.

1 ft.

Thomas Cole on the American Landscape

Although—or perhaps because—he was born in England, Thomas Cole (FIG. 27-23), the most prominent member of the Hudson River School of landscape painting, best defined those qualities that distinguished American landscapes from European ones. In his "Essay on American Scenery" published in the January 1836 issue of *American Monthly Magazine,* Cole described the unique nature of the American countryside.

> There are those who through ignorance or prejudice strive to maintain that American scenery possesses little that is interesting or truly beautiful, . . . that being destitute of those vestiges of antiquity, whose associations so strongly affect the mind, it may not be compared with European scenery. . . . I am by no means desirous of less-ening in your estimation the glorious scenes of the old world . . . over which time and genius have suspended an imperishable halo. No! But I would have it remembered that nature has shed over *this* land beauty and magnificence, and although the character of its scenery may differ from the old world's, yet inferiority must not therefore be inferred; for though American scenery is destitute of many of those circumstances that give value to the European, still it has features, and glorious ones, unknown to Europe. . . . The most distinctive, and perhaps the most impressive, characteristic of American scenery is its wildness. It is the most distinctive, because in civilized Europe the primitive features of scenery have long since been destroyed or modified . . . [In America] nature is still predominant . . . [T]hose scenes of solitude from which the hand of nature has never been lifted affect the mind with a more deep toned emotion than aught which the hand of man has touched. Amid them the consequent associations are of God the creator— they are his undefiled works, and the mind is cast into the contemplation of eternal things.*

*Charles Harrison, Paul Wood, and Jason Gaiger, *Art in Theory 1815–1900: An Anthology of Changing Ideas* (Oxford: Blackwell, 1998), 136–137.

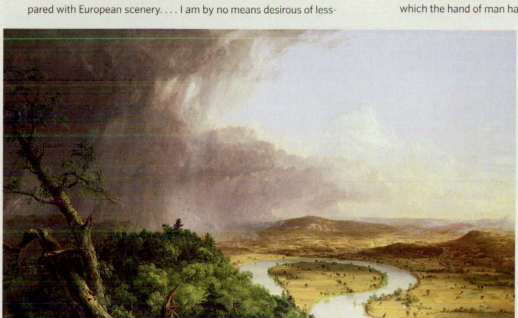

1 ft.

27-23 THOMAS COLE, *The Oxbow* (*View from Mount Holyoke, Northampton, Massachusetts, after a Thunderstorm*), 1836. Oil on canvas, 4' 3½" × 6' 4". Metropolitan Museum of Art, New York (gift of Mrs. Russell Sage, 1908).

Cole championed the idea of America having a landscape distinct from Europe's. Here, he contrasted dark wilderness on the left and sunlit civilization on the right, with a minuscule painter at the bottom center.

The artist's father was a successful miller and flour merchant and a rural landowner of considerable wealth. Many of the scenes that Constable painted (*The Hay Wain* included) depict his family's property near East Bergholt in Suffolk, East Anglia. This nostalgia, presented in such naturalistic terms, renders Constable's works Romantic in tone. That the painter felt a kindred spirit with the Romantic artists is revealed by his comment, "painting is with me but another word for feeling" (see "John Constable on Landscape Painting," page 811).

J.M.W. TURNER Constable's great contemporary in the English school of landscape painting was JOSEPH MALLORD WILLIAM TURNER (1775–1851). Both artists tirelessly sought to raise the prestige of landscape painting in the Royal Academy. However, whereas Constable's canvases are serene and precisely painted, and have as their exclusive subject the rural countryside of his birthplace, Turner's paintings have a much wider range of themes and, as in *The Slave Ship* (FIG. 27-22), feature turbulent swirls of frothy pigment (see "Unleashing the Emotive Power of Color," page 812).

THOMAS COLE In America, landscape painting was the specialty of a group of artists known as the Hudson River School, so named because its members drew their subjects primarily from the uncultivated regions of New York's Hudson River Valley, although many of these painters depicted scenes from across the country. As did the early-19th-century landscape painters in Germany and England, the artists of the Hudson River School not only presented Romantic panoramic landscape views but also participated in the ongoing exploration of the individual's and the country's relationship to the land. American landscape painters frequently focused on identifying qualities that made America unique. THOMAS COLE (1801–1848), often referred to as the leader of the Hudson River School, best articulated this idea (see "Thomas Cole on the American Landscape," above).

Another issue that surfaced frequently in Hudson River School paintings was the moral question of America's direction as a civilization. Cole addressed this question in *The Oxbow* (*View from Mount Holyoke, Northampton, Massachusetts, after a Thunderstorm;* FIG. 27-23). A splendid scene opens before the viewer, dominated

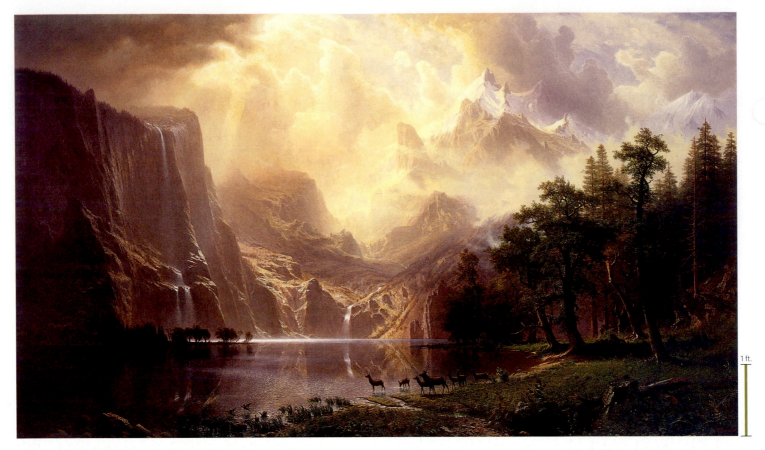

27-24 ALBERT BIERSTADT, *Among the Sierra Nevada Mountains, California,* 1868. Oil on canvas, 6' × 10'. National Museum of American Art, Smithsonian Institution, Washington, D.C.

Bierstadt's panoramic landscape presents the breathtaking natural beauty of the American West, reinforcing the 19th-century doctrine of Manifest Destiny, which justified America's western expansion.

by the lazy oxbow-shaped turning of the Connecticut River. Cole divided the composition in two, with the dark, stormy wilderness on the left and the more developed civilization on the right. The minuscule artist wearing a top hat in the bottom center of the painting, dwarfed by the landscape's scale, turns to the viewer as if to ask for input in deciding the country's future course. Cole's depictions of expansive wilderness incorporated reflections and moods romantically appealing to the public.

ALBERT BIERSTADT Other Hudson River artists used the landscape genre as an allegorical vehicle to address moral and spiritual concerns. ALBERT BIERSTADT (1830–1902) traveled west in 1858 and produced many paintings depicting the Rocky Mountains, Yosemite Valley, and other dramatic locales. These works, such as *Among the Sierra Nevada Mountains, California* (FIG. **27-24**), present breathtaking scenery and natural beauty. This panoramic view (the painting is 10 feet wide) is awe inspiring. Deer and waterfowl appear at the edge of a placid lake, and steep and rugged mountains soar skyward on the left and in the distance. A stand of trees, uncultivated and wild, frames the lake on the right. To underscore the transcendental nature of this scene, Bierstadt depicted the sun's rays breaking through the clouds overhead, suggesting a heavenly consecration of the land. That Bierstadt's focus was the American West is not insignificant. By calling national attention to the splendor and uniqueness of the regions beyond the Rocky Mountains,

Bierstadt's paintings reinforced the idea of Manifest Destiny. This popular 19th-century doctrine held that westward expansion across the continent was the logical destiny of the United States. As John L. O'Sullivan (1813–1895) expounded in the earliest known use of the term in 1845, "Our manifest destiny [is] to spread over and to possess the whole of the continent which Providence has given us for the development of the great experiment of liberty and federal development of self-government entrusted to us."[4] Paintings of the scenic splendor of the West helped to mute growing concerns over the realities of conquest, the displacement of Native Americans, and the exploitation of the environment. It should come as no surprise that among those most eager to purchase Bierstadt's work were mail-service magnates and railroad builders—entrepreneurs and financiers involved in westward expansion.

FREDERIC CHURCH Another painter usually associated with the Hudson River School was FREDERIC EDWIN CHURCH (1826–1900), but his interest in landscape scenes extended beyond America. He traveled widely—to South America, Mexico, Europe, the Middle East, Newfoundland, and Labrador. Church's paintings are firmly in the idiom of the Romantic sublime, yet they also reveal contradictions and conflicts in the constructed mythology of American providence and character. *Twilight in the Wilderness* (FIG. **27-25**) presents a panoramic view of the sun setting over the majestic landscape. Beyond Church's precise depiction of the magnificent

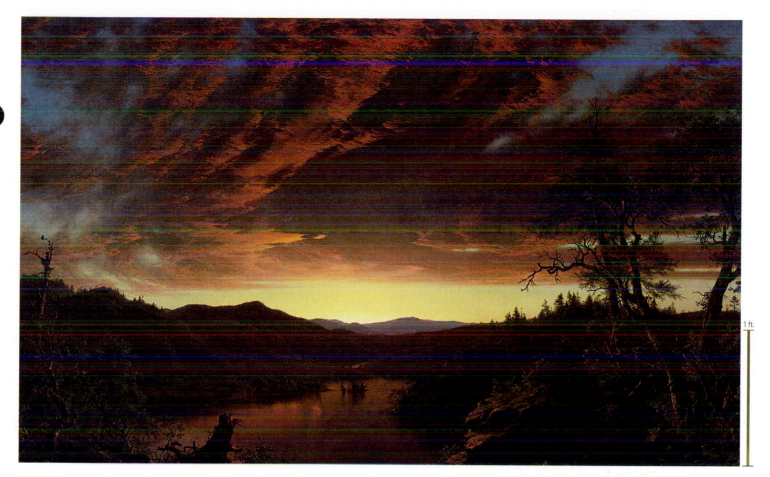

1 ft.

27-25 FREDERIC EDWIN CHURCH, *Twilight in the Wilderness,* 1860s. Oil on canvas, 3′ 4″ × 5′ 4″. Cleveland Museum of Art, Cleveland (Mr. and Mrs. William H. Marlatt Fund).

Church's paintings eloquently express the Romantic notion of the sublime. This wilderness landscape presents a glorious sunset in America, but the dead trees may be a reference to the Civil War.

spectacle of nature, the painting, like Constable's *Hay Wain* (FIG. 27-21), is remarkable for what it does not depict. Like Constable, Church and the other Hudson River School painters worked in a time of great upheaval. *Twilight in the Wilderness* dates to the 1860s, when the Civil War was tearing apart the no-longer-united states. Church's painting does not overtly display evidence of turbulence or discord. Indeed, it does not include even a single figure. But the view of nature that Church provides is not entirely comforting. Beside the rich vegetation and glorious sunset, there are also dead trees, perhaps symbolizing the casualties of the Civil War.

REALISM

Advances in industrial technology during the early 19th century reinforced Enlightenment faith in the connection between science and progress. Both intellectuals and the general public increasingly embraced *empiricism* and *positivism*. To empiricists, the basis of knowledge is observation and direct experience. Positivists ascribed to the philosophical model developed by Auguste Comte (1798–1857), who believed that scientific laws governed the environment and human activity and could be revealed through careful recording and analysis of observable data. Comte's followers promoted science as the mind's highest achievement and advocated a purely empirical approach to nature and society.

France

Realism was a movement that developed in France around mid-century against this backdrop of an increasing emphasis on science. Consistent with the philosophical tenets of the empiricists and positivists, Realist artists argued that only the contemporary world—what people can see—was "real." Accordingly, Realists focused their attention on the people and events of their own time and disapproved of historical and fictional subjects on the grounds that they were neither visible nor present and therefore were not real.

GUSTAVE COURBET The leading figure of the Realist movement in 19th-century art was GUSTAVE COURBET (1819–1877). In fact, even though he shunned labels, Courbet used the term *Realism* when exhibiting his own works (see "Gustave Courbet on Realism," page 816). The Realists' sincerity about scrutinizing their environment led them to paint mundane and trivial subjects that artists had traditionally deemed unworthy of depiction—for example, working-class laborers and peasants, and similar "low" themes. Moreover, by depicting these subjects on a scale and with a seriousness previously reserved for historical, mythological, and religious painting, Realist artists sought to establish parity between contemporary subject matter and the traditional themes of "high art."

ARTISTS ON ART
Gustave Courbet on Realism

The academic jury selecting work for the 1855 Salon (part of the Exposition Universelle in Paris that year) rejected 3 of the 14 paintings that Gustave Courbet submitted, declaring that his subjects and figures were too coarse (so much so as to be plainly "socialistic") and too large. Typical of Courbet's work are *The Stone Breakers* (FIG. 27-26), which depicts menial laborers, and *Burial at Ornans* (FIG. 27-27), which represents the funeral of an ordinary man and is nearly 22 feet long. In response to the jury's decision, Courbet withdrew all of his works, including those that had been accepted, and set up his own exhibition outside the grounds, calling it the Pavilion of Realism, featuring not 14 but 40 of his own works. This was in itself a bold action. Courbet was the first artist ever known to have staged a private exhibition of his own work. His pavilion and the statement he issued to explain the paintings shown there amounted to the Realist movement's manifesto. Although Courbet maintained that he founded no school and was of no school, he did, as the name of his pavilion suggests, accept the term *Realism* as descriptive of his art.

The statement that Courbet distributed at his pavilion reads in part:

> The title of "realist" has been imposed upon me. . . . Titles have never given a just idea of things; were it otherwise, the work would be superfluous. . . . I have studied the art of the ancients and the moderns, avoiding any preconceived system and without prejudice. I have no more wanted to imitate the former than to copy the latter; nor have I thought of achieving the idle aim of "art for art's sake." No! I have simply wanted to draw from a thorough

knowledge of tradition the reasoned and free sense of my own individuality. . . . To be able to translate the customs, ideas, and appearances of my time as I see them—in a word, to create a living art—this has been my aim.*

Six years later, on Christmas Day, 1861, Courbet wrote an open letter, published a few days later in the *Courier du dimanche*, addressed to prospective students. In the letter, the painter reflected on the nature of his art:

> [An artist must apply] his personal faculties to the ideas and the events of the times in which he lives. . . . [A]rt in painting should consist only of the representation of things that are visible and tangible to the artist. Every age should be represented only by its own artists, that is to say, by the artists who have lived in it. I also maintain that painting is an essentially concrete art form and can consist only of the representation of both real and existing things. . . . An abstract object, not visible, nonexistent, is not within the domain of painting.†

Courbet's most famous statement, however, is his blunt dismissal of academic painting, in which he concisely summed up the core principle of Realist painting:

> I have never seen an angel. Show me an angel, and I'll paint one.‡

---

*Translated by Robert Goldwater and Marco Treves, eds., *Artists on Art from the XIV to the XX Century* (New York: Pantheon, 1958), 295.
†Translated by Petra ten-Doesschate Chu, *Letters of Gustave Courbet* (Chicago: University of Chicago Press, 1992), 203–204.
‡Quoted by Vincent van Gogh in a July 1885 letter to his brother, Theo, in Ronald de Leeuw, *The Letters of Vincent van Gogh* (New York: Penguin, 1996), 302.

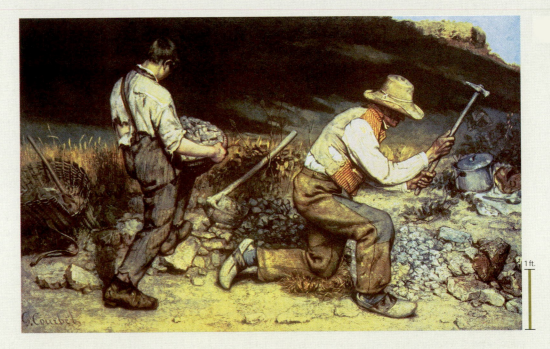

27-26 GUSTAVE COURBET, *The Stone Breakers*, 1849. Oil on canvas, 5' 3" × 8' 6". Formerly Gemäldegalerie, Dresden (destroyed in 1945).

Courbet was the leading figure in the Realist movement. Using a palette of dirty browns and grays, he conveyed the dreary and dismal nature of menial labor in mid-19th-century France.

1 ft.

STONE BREAKERS An early work that exemplifies Courbet's championing of everyday life as the only valid subject for the modern artist is *The Stone Breakers* (FIG. 27-26), in which the Realist painter presented a glimpse into the life of rural menial laborers. Courbet represented in a straightforward manner, and nearly at life size, two men—one about 70, the other quite young—in the decidedly nonheroic act of breaking stones to provide paving for provincial roads. Traditionally, this backbreaking, poorly paid work fell to the lowest members of French society, as the stone breakers' tattered garments and utensils for a modest meal of soup confirm. By juxtaposing youth and age, Courbet suggested that those born to poverty will remain poor their entire lives. The artist neither romanticized

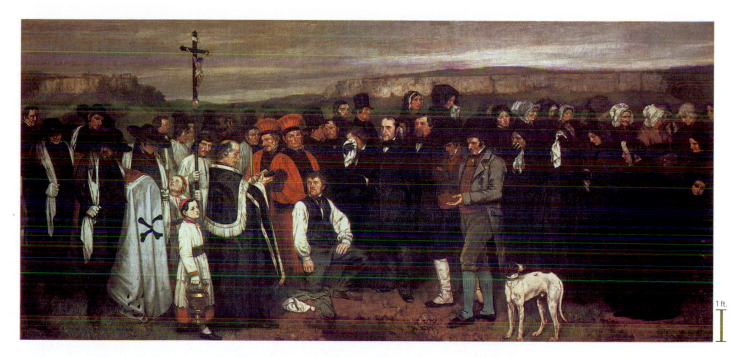

27-27 Gustave Courbet, *Burial at Ornans*, 1849. Oil on canvas, 10' 3½" × 21' 9½". Musée d'Orsay, Paris.

Although as imposing in scale as a traditional history painting, *Burial at Ornans* horrified critics because of the ordinary nature of the subject and Courbet's starkly antiheroic composition.

nor idealized the men's work but depicted their thankless toil with directness and accuracy. Courbet's palette of dirty browns and grays further conveys the dreary and dismal nature of the task, and the angular positioning of the older stone breaker's limbs suggests a mechanical monotony.

Courbet's interest in the working poor as subject matter had a special resonance for his mid-19th-century French audience. In 1848, laborers rebelled against the bourgeois leaders of the newly formed Second Republic and against the rest of the nation, demanding better working conditions and a redistribution of property. The army quelled the uprising in three days, but not without long-lasting trauma and significant loss of life. The 1848 revolution raised the issue of labor as a national concern. Courbet's depiction of stone breakers in 1849 was thus timely, populist, and, in the view of the conservative Salon jurors, "socialistic."

BURIAL AT ORNANS Many art historians regard Courbet's *Burial at Ornans* (FIG. 27-27) as his masterpiece. The huge (10-by-22-foot) canvas depicts a funeral set in a bleak provincial landscape outside the artist's hometown near Besançon in eastern France. Attending the funeral are the types of ordinary people that Honoré de Balzac (1799–1850) and Gustave Flaubert (1821–1880) presented in their novels. While a robed clergyman recites the Office of the Dead, those attending cluster around the excavated gravesite. Although the painting has the imposing scale of a traditional history painting, the subject's ordinariness and the starkly antiheroic composition horrified critics. *Burial at Ornans* is not a record of the burial of a Christian martyr or a heroic soldier. It commemorates a recurring event involving common folk, and it does not ennoble or romanticize death. No one had ever painted a genre subject on this scale. Furthermore, Courbet had the audacity to submit *Burial at Ornans* to the 1851 Salon in the category of history painting, but declined to identify the deceased.

Arranged in a wavering line extending across the enormous breadth of the canvas are three groups—the somberly clad women

at the back right; a semicircle of similarly clad men, including town officials and a hunting dog, by the open grave; and assorted churchmen at the left. The seemingly equal stature of all at the funeral also offended the hierarchical social sensibility of the Salon audience. This wall of figures blocks any view into deep space. The faces are portraits. Some of the models were Courbet's father, sisters, and friends. Behind and above the figures are bands of overcast sky and barren cliffs. The dark pit of the grave opens into the viewer's space in the center foreground.

Despite the unposed look of the figures, Courbet controlled the composition in a masterful way by his sparing use of bright color. In place of the heroic, the sublime, and the dramatic (the mourners are all emotionally detached), Courbet aggressively presented Salon viewers with the mundane realities of daily life and death. In 1857, Jules-François-Félix Husson Champfleury (1821–1889), one of the first critics to recognize and appreciate Courbet's work, wrote of *Burial at Ornans*, "[I]t represents a small-town funeral and yet reproduces the funerals of *all* small towns."[5] Unlike the theatricality of Romanticism, Realism captured the ordinary rhythms of daily life.

Of great importance for the later history of art, Realism also involved a reconsideration of the painter's primary goals and departed from the established emphasis on illusionism. Accordingly, Realists called attention to painting as a pictorial construction by the ways they applied pigment or manipulated composition. Courbet's intentionally simple and direct methods of expression in composition and technique seemed unbearably crude to many of his more traditional contemporaries, who called him a primitive. Although his bold, somber palette was essentially traditional, Courbet often used the *palette knife* to quickly place and unify large daubs of paint, producing a roughly wrought surface. His example inspired the young artists who worked for him (and later Impressionists such as Claude Monet and Auguste Renoir; see Chapter 28), but the public accused him of carelessness, and critics wrote of his "brutalities."

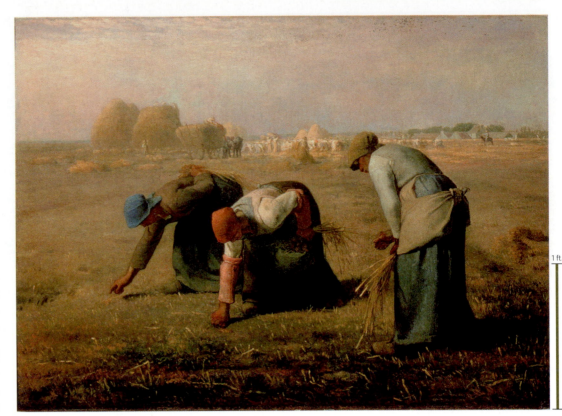

27-28 Jean-François Millet, *The Gleaners*, 1857. Oil on canvas, 2' 9" × 3' 8". Musée d'Orsay, Paris.

Millet and the Barbizon School painters specialized in depictions of French country life. Here, Millet portrayed three impoverished women gathering the scraps left in the field after a harvest.

JEAN-FRANÇOIS MILLET Like Courbet, Jean-François Millet (1814–1878) found his subjects in the people and occupations of the everyday world. Millet was one of a group of French painters of country life who, to be close to their rural subjects, settled near the village of Barbizon in the forest of Fontainebleau. This Barbizon School specialized in detailed pictures of forest and countryside. Millet, their most prominent member, was born into a prosperous farming family in Normandy, but was keenly aware of the hard lot of the country poor. In *The Gleaners* (FIG. 27-28), he depicted three impoverished women—members of the lowest level of peasant society—performing the backbreaking task of *gleaning*. Landowning nobles traditionally permitted peasants to glean, or collect, the wheat scraps left in the field after the harvest. Millet characteristically placed his large figures in the foreground, against a broad sky. Although the field stretches back to a rim of haystacks, cottages, trees, and distant workers and a flat horizon, the gleaners quietly doing their tedious and time-consuming work dominate the canvas. It is hard to imagine a sharper contrast with the almost invisible agricultural workers in Constable's *Hay Wain* (FIG. 27-21).

Although Millet's paintings evoke a sentimentality absent from Courbet's, the French public still reacted to his work with disdain and suspicion. In the aftermath of the 1848 revolution, Millet's investiture of the poor with solemn grandeur did not meet with approval from the prosperous classes. In particular, middle-class landowners resisted granting gleaning rights, and thus Millet's relatively dignified depiction of gleaning antagonized them. The middle class also linked the poor with the dangerous, newly defined working class, which was finding outspoken champions in men such as Karl Marx (1818–1883), Friedrich Engels (1820–1895), and the novelists Émile Zola (1840–1902) and Charles Dickens (1812–1870). Socialism was a growing movement, and both its views on property and its call for social justice, even economic equality, threatened and frightened the bourgeoisie. Millet's sympathetic portrayal of the poor seemed to much of the public to be a political manifesto.

HONORÉ DAUMIER Because people widely recognized the power of art to serve political ends, the political and social agitation accompanying the violent revolutions in France and the rest of Europe in the later 18th and early 19th centuries prompted the French people to suspect artists of subversive intentions. A person could be jailed for too bold a statement in the press, in literature, in art—even in music and drama. Realist artist Honoré Daumier (1808–1879) was a defender of the urban working class, and in his art he boldly confronted authority with social criticism and political protest. In response, the authorities imprisoned him. A painter, sculptor, and, like Dürer, Rembrandt, and Goya, one of history's great printmakers, Daumier produced *lithographs* (see "Lithography," page 819) that enabled him to create an unprecedented number of prints, thereby reaching an exceptionally large and broad audience. In addition to producing individual prints for sale, Daumier also contributed satirical lithographs to the widely read, liberal French Republican journal *Caricature*, further increasing the number of people exposed to his work. In *Caricature*, Daumier mercilessly lampooned the foibles and misbehavior of politicians, lawyers, doctors, and the rich bourgeoisie in general.

RUE TRANSNONAIN Daumier's lithograph *Rue Transnonain, April 15, 1834* (FIG. 27-29), published in the August 1834 issue of *L'association mensuelle*, a monthly French newspaper, had the same shocking impact as Goya's *Third of May, 1808* (FIG. 27-12). The title refers to the day when, on that street in Paris, an unknown sniper killed a civil guard, part of a government force trying to repress a worker demonstration. Because the fatal shot had come from a workers' housing block, the remaining guards immediately stormed the building and massacred all of its inhabitants. With Goya's power, Daumier created a view of the atrocious slaughter from a sharp angle of vision. But unlike Goya, he depicted not the dramatic moment of execution but the terrible, quiet aftermath. The limp bodies of the workers—and of a child crushed beneath his father's corpse—lie amid violent disorder. The print's power derives from its factualness. Daumier's pictorial manner is rough and spontaneous, and that approach to representation, which is a central characteristic of Realist art, accounts in large measure for the print's remarkable force.

MATERIALS AND TECHNIQUES
Lithography

In 1798, the German printmaker Alois Senefelder (1771–1834) created the first prints using stone instead of metal plates or wood blocks. In contrast to earlier printing techniques (see pages 577 and 578), in which the artist applied ink either to a raised or incised surface, in *lithography* (Greek, "stone writing or drawing") the printing and non-printing areas of the plate are on the same plane.

The chemical phenomenon fundamental to lithography is the repellence of oil and water. The lithographer uses a greasy, oil-based crayon to draw directly on a stone plate and then wipes water onto the stone, which clings only to the areas the drawing does not cover. Next, the artist rolls oil-based ink onto the stone, which adheres to the drawing but is repelled by the water. When the artist presses the stone against paper, only the inked area—the drawing—transfers to the paper. Color lithography requires multiple plates, one for each color, and the printmaker must take special care to make sure each impression lines up perfectly with the previous one so that each color prints in its proper place.

One of the earliest masters of this new printmaking process was Honoré Daumier, whose lithographs (FIGS. 27-29 and 27-49A), often published in leading French journals such as *Caricature* and *L'association mensuelle*, reached an audience of unprecedented size.

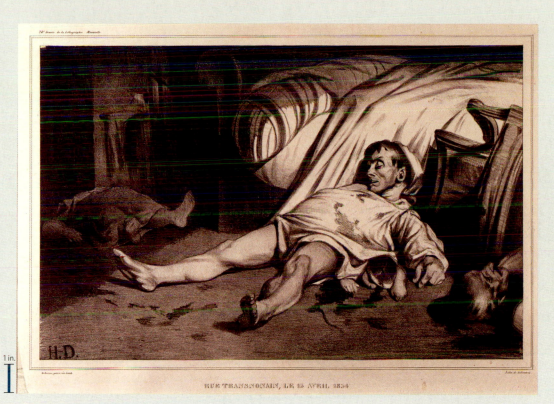

1 in.

27-29 HONORÉ DAUMIER, *Rue Transnonain, April 15, 1834*, 1834. Lithograph, 1' 1$\frac{3}{8}$" × 1' 6$\frac{1}{4}$". Yale University Art Gallery, New Haven (Everett V. Meeks, B.A. 1901, Fund).

Daumier used the recent invention of lithography to reach a wide audience for his social criticism and political protest. This print records the horrific 1834 massacre in a workers' housing block.

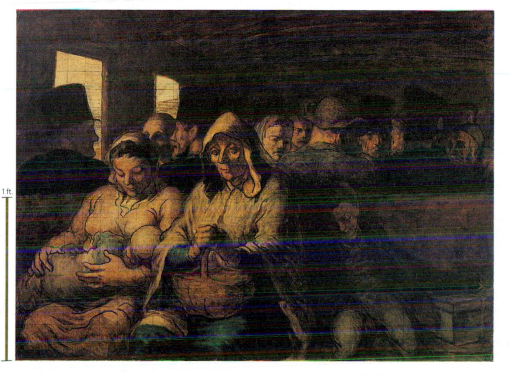

1 ft.

THIRD-CLASS CARRIAGE For his paintings, Daumier chose the same kind of subjects and representational manner as in his graphic work, especially after the 1848 revolution. His unfinished *Third-Class Carriage* (FIG. 27-30) provides a glimpse into the cramped and grimy railway cars of the 1860s. The riders are poor and can afford only third-class tickets. First- and second-class carriages had closed compartments, but third-class passengers had to cram

27-30 HONORÉ DAUMIER, *Third-Class Carriage*, ca. 1862. Oil on canvas, 2' 1$\frac{3}{4}$" × 2' 11$\frac{1}{2}$". Metropolitan Museum of Art, New York (H. O. Havemeyer Collection, bequest of Mrs. H. O. Havemeyer, 1929).

Daumier frequently depicted the plight of the disinherited masses, the victims of 19th-century industrialization. Here, he portrayed the anonymous poor cramped together in a grimy third-class railway carriage.

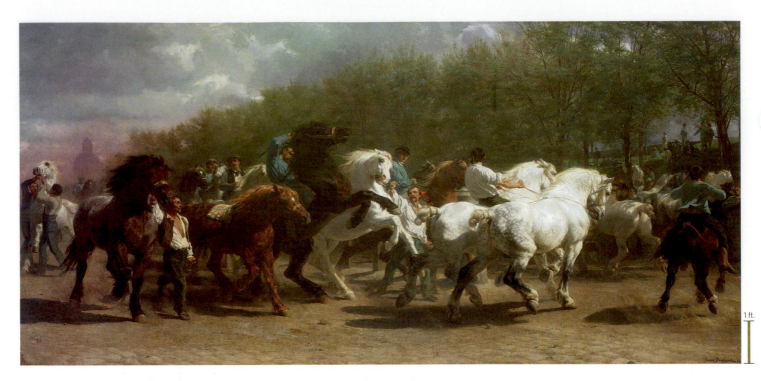

27-31 ROSA BONHEUR, *The Horse Fair,* 1853–1855. Oil on canvas, 8' $\frac{1}{4}$" × 16' 7 $\frac{1}{2}$". Metropolitan Museum of Art, New York (gift of Cornelius Vanderbilt, 1887).

Bonheur was the most celebrated woman artist of the 19th century. A Realist, she went to great lengths to record accurately the anatomy of living horses, even studying carcasses in slaughterhouses.

together on hard benches stretching from one end of their carriage to the other. The disinherited masses, the victims of 19th-century industrialization, were Daumier's indignant concern. He depicted them in the unposed attitudes and unplanned arrangements of the millions thronging the modern cities—anonymous, insignificant, dumbly patient with a lot they cannot change. Daumier saw people as they ordinarily appeared, their faces vague, impersonal, and blank—unprepared for any observers. He tried to achieve the real by isolating a random collection of the unrehearsed details of human existence from the continuum of ordinary life. Daumier's vision anticipated the spontaneity and candor of scenes captured with the camera at the end of the century.

ROSA BONHEUR The most celebrated woman artist of the 19th century was MARIE-ROSALIE (ROSA) BONHEUR (1822–1899). Born in Bordeaux, she won the gold medal at the Salon of 1848 and became the director of France's state-sponsored drawing school for women the same year, a post she held until 1859. (Admission to the École des Beaux-Arts was nearly impossible for women, as it was in Britain's Royal Academy.) In 1865, Bonheur became the first woman to be awarded the Grand Cross of the French Legion of Honor. As was typical for women since the Renaissance (see "The Artist's Profession," page 566), Bonheur received her artistic training from her father, Oscar-Raymond Bonheur (1796–1849), who was a proponent of *Saint-Simonianism,* an early-19th-century utopian socialist movement that championed the education and enfranchisement of women. As a result of her father's influence, Bonheur launched her career believing that as a woman, an artist, and a lesbian who frequently wore male attire, she had a special role to play in creating a new and perfect society. A Realist passion for accuracy in painting drove Bonheur, but she resisted depicting the problematic social and political themes seen in the work of Courbet, Millet, Daumier,

and other Realists. Rather, she turned to the animal world—not, however, to the exotic wild animals that so fascinated Delacroix (FIG. 27-16A), but to animals common in the French countryside, especially horses, but also rabbits, cows, and sheep. She went to great lengths to observe the anatomy of living horses at the twice-weekly Parisian horse market and spent long hours studying the anatomy of carcasses in the Paris slaughterhouses. (Women were not permitted in the French stockyards and slaughterhouses, but Bonheur's male garb gained her access.)

For *The Horse Fair* (FIG. **27-31**), Bonheur's best-known work, the artist chose a panoramic composition similar to that in Courbet's *Burial at Ornans* (FIG. 27-27). She filled her broad canvas with the sturdy farm Percherons of Normandy and their grooms on parade. Some horses, not quite broken, rear up. Others plod or trot, guided on foot or ridden by their keepers. Bonheur recorded the Percherons' uneven line of march, their thunderous pounding, and their seemingly overwhelming power based on her close observation of living animals, even though she acknowledged some inspiration from the Parthenon frieze (FIG. 5-50, *top*). The dramatic lighting, loose brushwork, and rolling sky also reveal her admiration of Géricault's style (FIG. 27-1 and 27-14). Bonheur's masterful depiction of horses at life size and seen from multiple angles captivated viewers, who eagerly bought engraved reproductions of *The Horse Fair,* making it one of the most popular artworks of the century.

ÉDOUARD MANET As pivotal a figure in 19th-century European art as Gustave Courbet was the painter ÉDOUARD MANET (1832–1883). Like Courbet, Manet was influential in articulating Realist principles, but the younger artist also played an important role in the development of Impressionism in the 1870s (see page 841). Manet's *Le Déjeuner sur l'Herbe* (*Luncheon on the Grass;* FIG. **27-32**), widely recognized only later as a seminal work in the history of art,

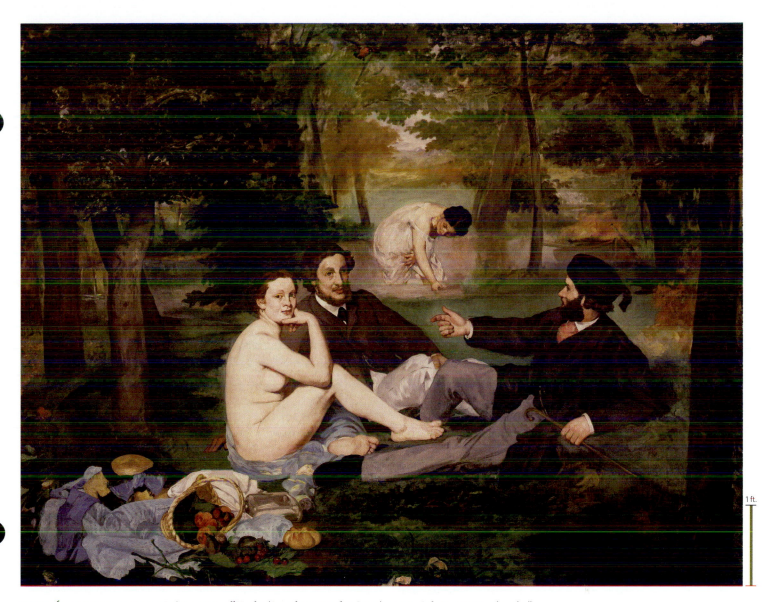

27-32 Édouard Manet, *Le Déjeuner sur l'Herbe* (*Luncheon on the Grass*), 1863. Oil on canvas, 7' × 8' 8".
Musée d'Orsay, Paris.

Manet shocked his contemporaries with both his subject matter and manner of painting. Moving away from illusionism, he used colors to flatten form and to draw attention to the painting surface.

was rejected by the jury for the 1863 Salon. It depicts two clothed men and one nude and one clothed woman at a picnic. Consistent with Realist principles, Manet depicted a contemporary genre scene and based all four figures on real people, including Victorine Meurent (1844–1927), Manet's favorite model at the time, and his brother. The two men wear fashionable Parisian attire of the 1860s. The nude woman—she has undressed in the park and tossed her clothes on the grass—is a distressingly unidealized figure who also seems completely unfazed by her nakedness. She gazes directly at the viewer without shame or flirtatiousness. Her companion looks in the same direction. Neither pays any attention to what the second man is saying to them. Nor is it clear what relationship, if any, the second woman has to the trio "at lunch." She appears to be looking for something in a pool of water, while attempting unsuccessfully to keep her garment dry. No one has any interest in the picnic food. This is no luncheon on the grass, although it may be the aftermath of a meal. Nor is this truly Realism, because the subject is incomprehensible—as Manet wished it to be. In this work, he sought to reassess the nature of painting. The composition contains

sophisticated references and allusions to many artistic genres—history painting, portraiture, pastoral scenes, nudes, and even religious scenes. *Le Déjeuner sur l'Herbe* is Manet's impressive synthesis and critique of the entire history of painting.

This audacious painting outraged the French public. Rather than a traditional pastoral scene—for example, Titian's *Pastoral Symphony* (FIG. 22-35), with which Manet no doubt wished his canvas to be compared—*Le Déjeuner* is not populated by anonymous idealized figures in an idyllic setting. Instead, it features ordinary men and promiscuous women in a Parisian park. One hostile critic, no doubt voicing public opinion, said: "A commonplace woman of the demimonde, as naked as can be, shamelessly lolls between two dandies dressed to the teeth. These latter look like schoolboys on a holiday, perpetrating an outrage to play the man. . . . This is a young man's practical joke—a shameful, open sore."[6]

The negative response to Manet's painting on the part of public and critics alike extended beyond subject matter. The painter's manner of presenting his figures also elicited severe criticism. He rendered the men and women in soft focus and broadly painted the

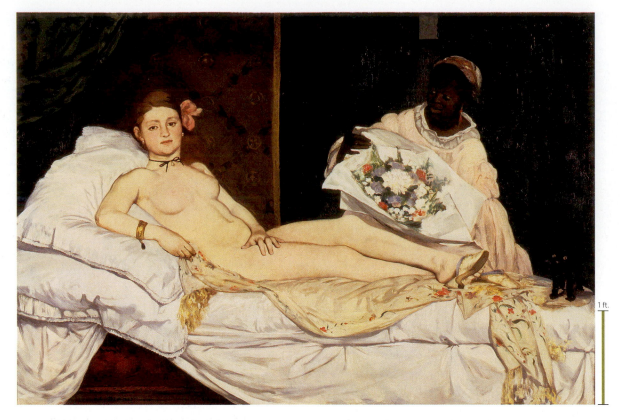

27-33 ÉDOUARD MANET, *Olympia,* 1863. Oil on canvas, 4' 3" × 6' 2$\frac{1}{4}$". Musée d'Orsay, Paris.

Manet's painting of a nude prostitute and her black maid carrying a bouquet from a client scandalized the public. Critics also faulted his rough brushstrokes and abruptly shifting tonalities.

landscape. The loose manner of painting contrasts with the clear forms of the harshly lit foreground trio and of the pile of discarded female clothes and picnic foods at the lower left. The lighting creates strong contrasts between dark and highlighted areas. In the main figures, many values are summed up in one or two lights or darks. The effect is both to flatten the forms and set them off sharply from the setting. Manet aimed to move away from illusionism toward an open acknowledgment of painting's properties, such as the flatness of the painting surface, which would become a core principle of many later 19th-century painters as well as their successors to the present day. The mid-19th-century French public, however, saw only a crude sketch lacking the customary finish of paintings exhibited in the Paris Salon. The style of the painting, coupled with the unorthodox subject matter, made *Le Déjeuner sur l'Herbe* one of the most controversial artworks ever created.

OLYMPIA Even more scandalous to the French viewing public, however, was Manet's *Olympia* (FIG. **27-33**), painted the same year and also loosely based on a painting by Titian—*Venus of Urbino* (FIG. 22-39). Manet's subject was a young white prostitute. (Olympia was a common "professional" name for prostitutes in 19th-century France.) She reclines on a bed that extends across the full width of the painting (and beyond) and is nude except for a thin black ribbon tied around her neck, a bracelet on her arm, an orchid in her hair, and fashionable slippers on her feet. Like the seated nude in *Le Déjeuner* (Victorine Meurent served again as Manet's model), Olympia meets the viewer's eye with a look of cool indifference. The only other figure in the painting is a black maid, who presents Olympia a bouquet of flowers from a client.

Olympia horrified the public and critics alike. One reviewer of the Salon of 1865 (remarkably, the jury accepted Manet's painting

for inclusion) described the painter as "the apostle of the ugly and repulsive."[7] Although images of prostitutes were not unheard of during this period, the shamelessness of Olympia and her look verging on defiance shocked viewers. The depiction of a black woman was also not new to painting, but the French public perceived Manet's inclusion of both a black maid and a nude prostitute as evoking moral depravity, inferiority, and animalistic sexuality. The contrast of the black servant with the fair-skinned courtesan also conjured racial divisions.

An anonymous critic in *Le Monde Illustré* described Olympia as "a courtesan, with dirty hands and wrinkled feet . . . her body has the livid tint of a cadaver displayed in the morgue; her outlines are drawn in charcoal and her greenish, bloodshot eyes appear to be provoking the public, protected all the while by a hideous Negress."[8] From this and similar reviews, it is clear that critics and the public were responding not solely to the subject matter but to Manet's artistic style as well. The painter's brushstrokes are much rougher and the shifts in tonality are far more abrupt than those found in traditional academic painting.

This departure from accepted practice exacerbated the audacity of the subject matter. *Olympia*—indeed, all of Manet's work—represented a radical departure from the academic style then in favor, as exemplified by the work of ADOLPHE-WILLIAM BOUGUEREAU (1825–1905; FIG. **27-33A**), an artist largely forgotten today, although he was a towering figure in the French art world during the second half of the 19th century.

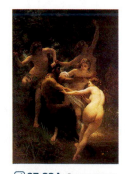

27-33A BOUGUEREAU, *Nymphs and a Satyr,* 1873.

Germany and the United States

Although French artists took the lead in promoting the depiction of the realities of modern life as the only valid goal for artists, the Realist movement was neither exclusively French nor confined to Europe.

WILHELM LEIBL In Germany, WILHELM LEIBL (1844–1900) shared the French Realists' commitment to representing the contemporary world and real people in his paintings. *Three Women in a Village Church* (FIG. 27-34) is Leibl's most famous work and characteristically depicts the life of rural peasants in Bavaria. The painting, which took three years to complete, records a sacred moment—the moment of prayer—in the life of three women of different generations. Dressed in rustic costume, their Sunday-church best, they quietly pursue their devotions in the village church, their prayer books held in large hands roughened by work. Their manners and their dress reflect their unaffected nature, untouched by the refinements of urban life. Leibl highlighted their natural virtues: simplicity, honesty, steadfastness, and patience. The picture is a moving expression of the artist's compassionate view of his subjects, a reading of character without sentimentality.

WINSLOW HOMER Realism received an especially warm welcome in the United States. One of the leading American Realist painters was WINSLOW HOMER (1836–1910) of Boston. Homer experienced at first hand the most momentous event of his era—the Civil War. In October 1862, he joined the Union campaign as an artist-reporter for *Harper's Weekly*. At the end of the war, he painted *Veteran in a New Field* (FIG. 27-35). Although it is simple and direct, Homer's painting is a significant commentary on the effects and aftermath of America's catastrophic national conflict. At the center of the canvas is a man with his back to the viewer, harvesting wheat. Homer identified him as a veteran by including his uniform and canteen carelessly thrown on the ground in the lower right corner. The man's current occupation, however, is as a farmer, and he has cast aside his former role as a soldier, as did the veterans of America's Revolutionary War in the previous century. The Civil War veteran's involvement in meaningful and productive work implies a smooth

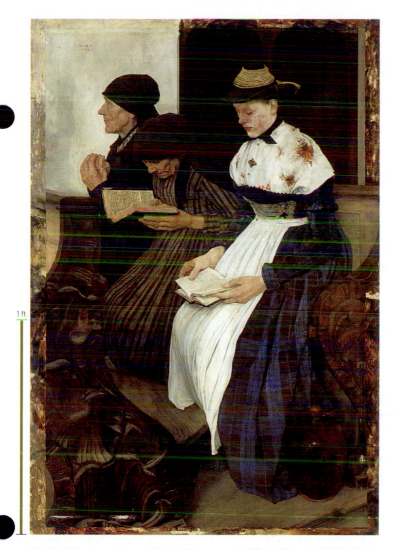

27-34 WILHELM LEIBL, *Three Women in a Village Church*, 1878–1882. Oil on canvas, 2′ 5″ × 2′ 1″. Kunsthalle, Hamburg.

French Realism spread quickly to Germany, where Leibl painted this moving depiction of simple peasant women of different generations holding their prayer books in hands roughened by work.

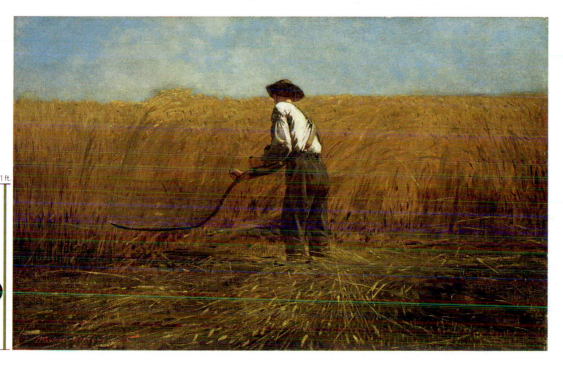

27-35 WINSLOW HOMER, *Veteran in a New Field*, 1865. Oil on canvas, 2′ $\frac{1}{8}$″ × 3′ 2 $\frac{1}{8}$″. Metropolitan Museum of Art, New York (bequest of Miss Adelaide Milton de Groot, 1967).

This veteran's productive work implies a smooth transition to peace after the Civil War, but Homer placed a single-bladed scythe—the Grim Reaper's tool—in his hands, symbolizing the deaths of soldiers.

transition from war to peace. This postwar transition to work and the fate of disbanded soldiers were national concerns. Echoing the sentiments behind Houdon's portrayal of George Washington as the new Cincinnatus (FIG. 26-33), the *New York Weekly Tribune* commented: "Rome took her great man from the plow, and made him a dictator—we must now take our soldiers from the camp and make them farmers."[9] America's ability to effect a smooth transition was seen as evidence of its national strength. "The peaceful and harmonious disbanding of the armies in the summer of 1865," wrote poet Walt Whitman (1819–1892), was one of the "immortal proofs of democracy, unequall'd in all the history of the past."[10] Homer's painting thus reinforced the perception of the country's greatness.

Veteran in a New Field also comments symbolically about death. By the 1860s, farmers used cradled scythes to harvest wheat. For this detail, however, Homer rejected realism in favor of symbolism. The former soldier's tool is a single-bladed scythe. The artist thus transformed the man who lived through the Civil War into a symbol of Death—the Grim Reaper himself. In addition to being a tribute to the successful transition to peace, *Veteran in a New Field* is an elegy to the thousands of soldiers who did not return from the war (compare FIG. 27-52). It may also be a lamentation on the recent assassination of President Abraham Lincoln.

THOMAS EAKINS Even more determined a Realist than Homer was Philadelphia-born THOMAS EAKINS (1844–1916), whose paintings reflect his keen appetite for recording the realities of the human experience. Eakins studied both painting and medical anatomy in Philadelphia before undertaking further study under French artist Jean-Léon Gérôme (1824–1904). Eakins aimed to paint things as he saw them rather than as the public might wish them portrayed. This attitude was very much in tune with 19th-century American taste, combining an admiration for accurate depiction with a hunger for truth.

The too-brutal Realism of Eakins's early masterpiece, *The Gross Clinic* (FIG. **27-36**), perhaps inspired by Rembrandt's *Anatomy Lesson of Dr. Nicolaes Tulp* (FIG. 25-12), prompted the art jury to reject it for the Philadelphia exhibition celebrating the American independence centennial in 1876. The painting portrays the renowned surgeon Dr. Samuel Gross in the operating amphitheater of the Jefferson Medical College in Philadelphia, where the painting

hung for 130 years until its sale in 2006 to raise funds for the college. Eakins's decision to depict an operation in progress reflects the public's increasing faith that scientific and medical advances could enhance—and preserve—lives. Dr. Gross, with bloody fingers and scalpel, lectures about his surgery on a young man's leg. The patient suffered from osteomyelitis, a bone infection. Watching the surgeon, acclaimed for his skill in this specific operation, are several colleagues—all of whom historians have identified—and the patient's mother, who covers her face. Eakins, who considered becoming a physician and studied at the college, included his self-portrait (in the doorway at the right) to underscore the accuracy of what he recorded as an eyewitness. Also present is an anesthetist, who holds a cloth over the patient's face. Anesthetics had been introduced in 1846, and their development eliminated a major obstacle to extensive surgery. The painting, made more dramatic by the lighting, is an unsparing description of an unfolding event, with a good deal more reality than many viewers could endure. "It is a picture," one critic said, "that even strong men find difficult to look at long, if they can look at it at all."[11]

Consistent with the dominance of empiricism in the latter half of the 19th century, Eakins believed that careful observation and, where relevant, scientific knowledge were prerequisites for his art,

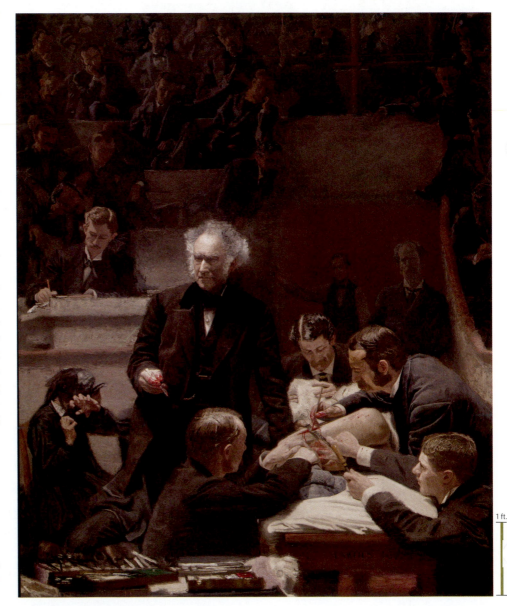

27-36 THOMAS EAKINS, *The Gross Clinic,* from Jefferson Medical College, Philadelphia, Pennsylvania, 1875. Oil on canvas, 8' × 6' 6". Philadelphia Museum of Art, Philadelphia.

The too-brutal realism of Eakins's depiction of a medical college operating amphitheater caused this painting's rejection from the Philadelphia exhibition celebrating America's centennial.

1 ft.

and he created his paintings in a deliberate, methodical way based on firsthand study of his subject. For example, Eakins's focus on anatomical correctness led him to investigate the human form and humans in motion, both with regular photographic apparatuses and with a special camera devised by the French kinesiologist (a person who studies the physiology of body movement) Étienne-Jules Marey (1830–1904). Eakins later collaborated with Eadweard Muybridge (FIG. 27-53) in the photographic study of animal and human action of all types, anticipating the 20th-century invention of the motion picture.

JOHN SINGER SARGENT The expatriate American artist JOHN SINGER SARGENT (1856–1925), born in Florence, Italy, was a younger contemporary of Eakins. Sargent developed a looser, more dashing Realist painting style, in contrast to Eakins's carefully rendered details. Sargent studied art in Paris before settling in London, where he won renown both as a cultivated and cosmopolitan gentle-man and as an accomplished portrait painter. He learned his adept application of paint in thin layers and his effortless achievement of quick and lively illusion from his study of Velázquez, whose masterpiece, *Las Meninas* (FIG. 24-31), may have influenced Sargent's family portrait *The Daughters of Edward Darley Boit* (FIG. **27-37**). The four girls (the children of one of Sargent's close friends) appear in a hall and small drawing room in their Paris home. The informal, eccentric arrangement of their slight figures suggests how much at ease they are within this familiar space and with objects such as the enormous Japanese vases, the red screen, and the fringed rug, whose scale subtly emphasizes the children's diminutive stature. Sargent must have known the Boit daughters well. Relaxed and trustful, they gave the artist an opportunity to record a gradation of young innocence. He sensitively captured the naive, wondering openness of the little girl in the foreground, the grave artlessness of the 10-year-old child, and the slightly self-conscious poise of the adolescents.

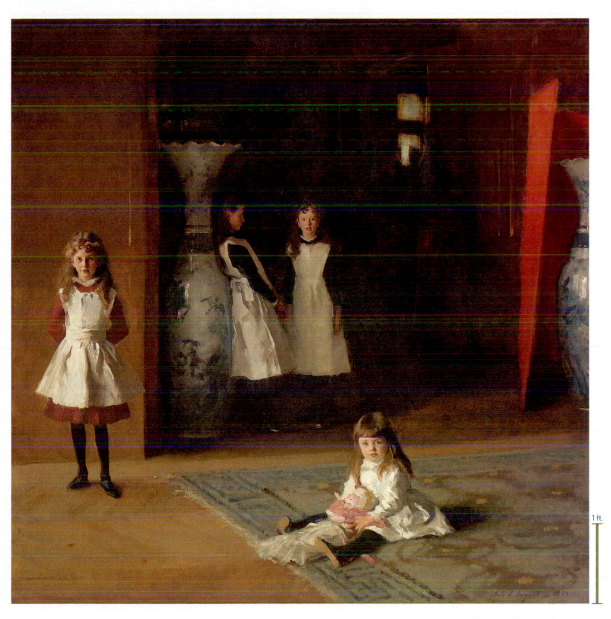

27-37 JOHN SINGER SARGENT, *The Daughters of Edward Darley Boit*, 1882. Oil on canvas, 7' 3 $\frac{3}{8}$" × 7' 3 $\frac{5}{8}$". Museum of Fine Arts, Boston (gift of Mary Louisa Boit, Florence D. Boit, Jane Hubbard Boit, and Julia Overing Boit, in memory of their father, Edward Darley Boit).

Sargent's casual positioning of the Boit sisters creates a sense of the momentary and spontaneous, consistent with Realist painters' interest in recording modern people in modern contexts.

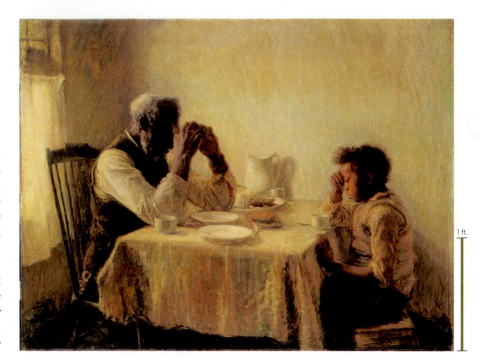

27-38 Henry Ossawa Tanner, *The Thankful Poor*, 1894. Oil on canvas, 2' 11½" × 3' 8¼". Collection of William H. and Camille Cosby.

Tanner combined the Realists' belief in careful study from nature with a desire to portray with dignity the life of African American families. The lighting reinforces the painting's reverent spirit.

Sargent's casual positioning of the figures and seemingly random choice of the setting communicate a sense of spontaneity. The children seem to be attending momentarily to an adult who has asked them to interrupt their activity. The painting embodies the Realist belief that the artist's business is to record modern people in modern contexts.

HENRY OSSAWA TANNER Typical of the Realist painter's desire to depict the lives of ordinary people engaged in everyday activities is *The Thankful Poor* (FIG. 27-38), an early work by African American artist Henry Ossawa Tanner (1859–1937). Tanner

ART AND SOCIETY
Edmonia Lewis, an African American Sculptor in Rome

About 15 years older than Henry Ossawa Tanner (FIG. 27-38), the sculptor Edmonia Lewis was the daughter of a Chippewa mother and African American father. Born in upstate New York and given the name Wildfire, Lewis became an orphan when she was four years old, and was raised by the Chippewa.

Lewis produced sculptures stylistically indebted to Neoclassicism but depicting contemporary Realist themes. *Forever Free* (FIG. 27-39) is a marble statue that she carved while living in Rome, surrounded by examples of both classical and Renaissance art. It represents two freed African American slaves immediately after President Lincoln's issuance of the Emancipation Proclamation. The man stands triumphantly in a contrapposto stance reminiscent of classical statues. His right hand rests on the shoulder of the kneeling woman with her hands clasped in thankful prayer. The man holds aloft in his left hand a broken manacle and chain as literal and symbolic references to his former servitude. Produced four years after Lincoln's proclamation, *Forever Free* (originally titled *The Morning of Liberty*) was widely perceived as an abolitionist statement. ("Forever free" is a phrase that Lincoln used in both his preliminary September 1862 and final January 1863 emancipation proclamations.) Although emancipated, the former slaves still have shackles attached, in contrast to those born free. However, other factors caution against an overly simplistic reading. For example, scholars have debated the degree to which the sculptor attempted to inject a statement about gender relationships into this statue and whether the kneeling position of the woman is a reference to female subordination in the African American community.

Lewis's accomplishments as a sculptor speak to the increasing access to training available to women in the 19th century. She adopted the name Edmonia Lewis in 1859 when she was admitted to Oberlin College (the first American college to grant degrees to women and among the first to admit African Americans). After Oberlin, Lewis became an apprentice in a sculpture studio in Boston. She financed her 1865 trip to Rome, which became her permanent home, with the sale of portrait medallions and marble busts, mostly representing abolitionist leaders. Lewis's success in a field dominated by white European and American men is a testament to both her artistic skill and her determination.

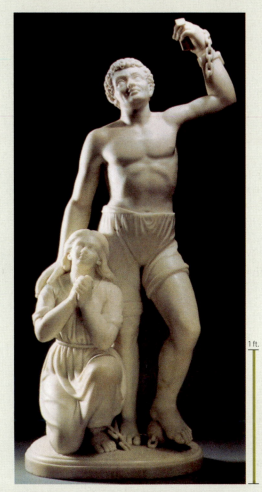

27-39 Edmonia Lewis, *Forever Free*, 1867. Marble, 3' 5¼" high. James A. Porter Gallery of Afro-American Art, Howard University, Washington, D.C.

African American–Chippewa Lewis's sculptures owe a stylistic debt to Neoclassicism but depict contemporary Realist themes. She carved *Forever Free* four years after Lincoln's Emancipation Proclamation.

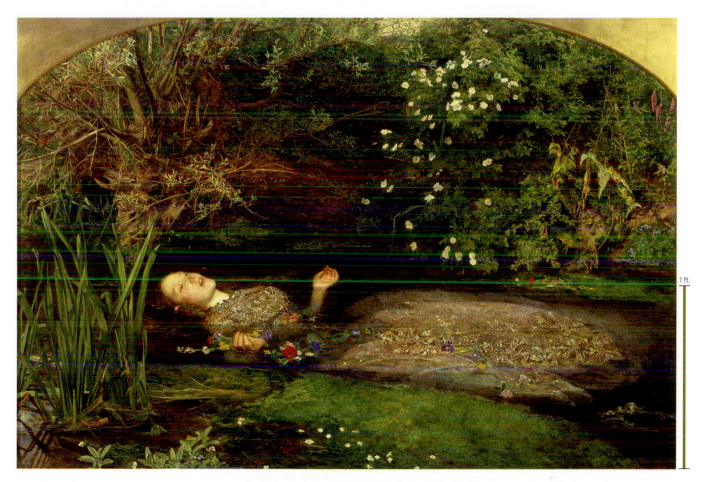

1 ft.

27-40 JOHN EVERETT MILLAIS, *Ophelia*, 1852. Oil on canvas, 2' 6" × 3' 8". Tate Gallery, London.

Millet was a founder of the Pre-Raphaelite Brotherhood, whose members refused to be limited to the contemporary scenes that strict Realists portrayed. The drowning of Ophelia is a Shakespearean subject.

studied art with Eakins at the Pennsylvania Academy of Fine Arts before moving to Paris in 1891. There he combined Eakins's belief in careful study from nature with a desire to portray with dignity the life of the working people he had been raised among as a minister's son in Pennsylvania. The mood in *The Thankful Poor* is one of quiet devotion not far removed from the Realism of Millet (FIG. 27-28) and Leibl (FIG. 27-34), but quite different from the mood of the sculptures of EDMONIA LEWIS (ca. 1844–ca. 1911), Tanner's older contemporary (see "Edmonia Lewis, an African American Sculptor in Rome," page 826, and FIG. 27-39). Tanner painted the grandfather, grandchild, and main objects in the room in great detail, whereas everything else dissolves into loose strokes of color and light. The lighting reinforces the painting's reverent spirit, with deep shadows intensifying the man's devout concentration. The golden rays pouring in the window illuminate the quiet expression of thanksgiving on the younger face. The deep sense of sanctity evoked here in terms of everyday experience became increasingly important for Tanner. Within a few years of completing *The Thankful Poor*, he began painting biblical subjects grounded in direct studies from nature and in the love of Rembrandt that had inspired him from his days as a Philadelphia art student.

Pre-Raphaelite Brotherhood

Realism did not appeal to all artists, of course. In England, a group of painters who called themselves the *Pre-Raphaelite Brotherhood* refused to be limited to the contemporary scenes that strict Realists portrayed. These artists chose instead to represent fictional, historical,

and fanciful subjects, but with a significant degree of convincing illusion. Organized in 1848, the Pre-Raphaelite artists wished to create fresh and sincere art, free from what its members considered the tired and artificial manner propagated in the academies by the successors of Raphael. Influenced by the critic, artist, and writer John Ruskin (1819–1900), the Pre-Raphaelites shared his distaste for the materialism and ugliness of the contemporary industrializing world. They also expressed appreciation for the spirituality and idealism (as well as the art and artisanship) of past times, especially the Early Renaissance.

JOHN EVERETT MILLAIS One of the founders of the Pre-Raphaelite Brotherhood was JOHN EVERETT MILLAIS (1829–1896). Millais's *Ophelia* (FIG. 27-40) garnered enthusiastic praise when the painter exhibited it in the Exposition Universelle in Paris in 1855—the exhibition at which Courbet set up his Pavilion of Realism. The subject, from Shakespeare's *Hamlet* (4.7.174–183), is the drowning of Ophelia, who, in her madness, is unaware of her plight:

> *When down her weedy trophies and herself*
> *Fell in the weeping brook. Her clothes spread wide;*
> *And, mermaid-like, awhile they bore her up . . .*
> *Till that her garments, heavy with their drink,*
> *Pull'd the poor wretch from her melodious lay*
> *To muddy death.*

To make the pathos of the scene visible, Millais became a faithful and feeling witness of its every detail, reconstructing it

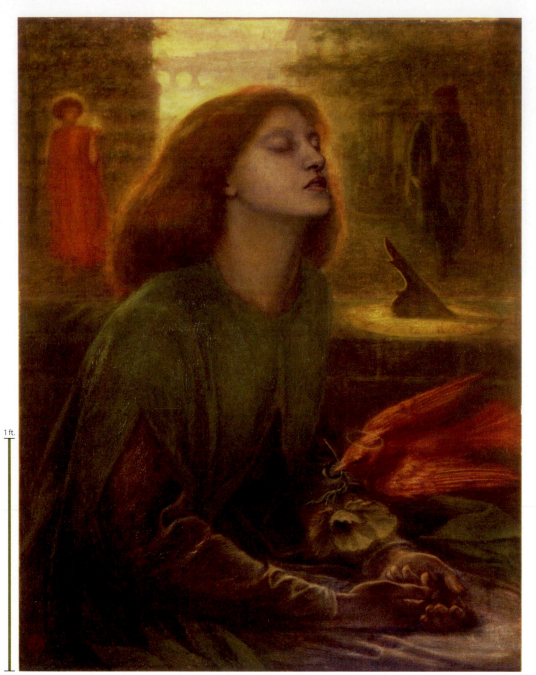

1 ft.

This painting of a beautiful and sensuous woman is ostensibly a literary portrait of Dante's Beatrice, but the work also served as a memorial to Rossetti's wife, who died of an opium overdose.

literary figure—Beatrice, from Dante's *Vita Nuova*. In Rossetti's painting, Dante's heroine overlooks Florence in a trance after being mystically transported to Heaven. Yet the portrait also had personal resonance for Rossetti. It served as a memorial to his wife, Elizabeth Siddal (1829–1862), the model for Millais's *Ophelia*. Siddal had died shortly before Rossetti began this painting in 1862. In the image, a red dove (a messenger of both love and death) deposits a poppy (symbolic of sleep and death) in the hands of the seated woman (Siddal-Beatrice), who has a faraway look on her face. Because Siddal died of an opium overdose, the presence of the poppy assumes greater significance.

ARCHITECTURE

At the opening of the 19th century, Napoleon had co-opted the classical style as the official architectural expression of his empire. Neoclassicism was in vogue elsewhere in Europe, especially in the Prussian capital of Berlin (see "The First Public Art Museum," page 829, and FIGS. 27-41A and 27-42) and in the new American republic too, but other historical styles, Gothic chief among them, also enjoyed revivals at the same time that architects were exploring the expressive possibilities that new construction technologies had made possible. The buildings constructed during the 19th century are consequently among the most stylistically diverse in history.

GOTHIC REVIVAL As 19th-century scholars gathered the documentary materials of European history in encyclopedic enterprises, each nation came to value its past as evidence of the validity of its ambitions and claims to greatness. Intellectuals appreciated the art of the remote past as a product of cultural and national genius. Italy, of course, had its Roman ruins, which had long inspired later architects. A reawakening of interest in Gothic architecture also surfaced at this time, even in France under Napoleon. In 1802, Chateaubriand published his influential *Genius of Christianity*—the source for

with a lyricism worthy of the original poetry. (Charles Baudelaire [1821–1867] called him "the poet of meticulous detail.") Although the scene is fictitious and therefore one that Realist painters would have rejected, Millais worked diligently to present it with unswerving fidelity to visual fact. He painted the background on site at a spot along the Hogsmill River in Surrey. For the figure of Ophelia, Millais had a friend lie in a heated bathtub full of water for hours at a time.

DANTE GABRIEL ROSSETTI Another founder of the Pre-Raphaelite Brotherhood was DANTE GABRIEL ROSSETTI (1828–1882), who established an enviable reputation as both a painter and poet. Like other members of the group, Rossetti focused on literary and biblical themes in his art. He also produced numerous portraits of women that projected an image of ethereal beauty and melded apparent opposites—for example, a Victorian prettiness with sensual allure. His *Beata Beatrix* (FIG. 27-41) is ostensibly a portrait of a

PROBLEMS AND SOLUTIONS
The First Public Art Museum

After the fall of Napoleon, who had occupied the Prussian capital of Berlin from 1806 to 1808, a fervent nationalistic spirit emerged in Germany. One manifestation of Prussian nationalism was the decision to build Europe's first public art museum to house the extensive and growing royal collection. The commission went to KARL FRIEDRICH SCHINKEL (1781–1841), who worked in many revival styles during his career. But which one would be the best choice for an art museum? Although he had designed buildings in the Romanesque, Gothic, and Italian Renaissance styles, Schinkel chose the Neoclassical style for what he and Crown Prince Friedrich Wilhelm III (1755–1861) conceived as a "temple of culture." (The prince's father, King Friedrich Wilhelm II [r. 1786–1797], had earlier commissioned one of the world's most famous Neoclassical monuments, Berlin's Brandenburg Gate [FIG. 27-41A], designed by CARL GOTTHARD LANGHANS [1732–1808].)

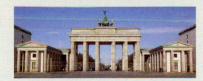

⬀ **27-41A** LANGHANS, Brandenburg Gate, Berlin, 1788–1791.

The Altes (Old) Museum (FIG. 27-42), constructed on an island in the Spree River across from the royal palace in Berlin, is not truly temple-like, however. Rather, with its broad facade of 18 Ionic columns on a high podium, it more closely resembles a Greek stoa (FIG. 5-78) than a pediment-capped classical temple. Noteworthy for its perfect proportions, Schinkel's austere design expresses nobility, tradition, and elite culture, now made accessible to the public in a building whose style Europeans associated with the democratic values of ancient Greece and Rome.

The Neoclassical facade masks a very practical plan that has no model in classical temples or stoas, however. A broad central staircase leads into a foyer and then a cubical central block, which projects above the facade's colonnade. The central block houses a sculpture-filled domed rotunda loosely based on the Pantheon (FIG. 7-51) in Rome (a mixing of historical sources characteristic of 19th-century European architecture in general). To either side is a courtyard whose windows provide light to the painting galleries all around. Large windows on the side and rear walls of the Altes Museum also illuminate the galleries.

The Altes Museum is also significant in terms of exhibition theory and practice. This first public art museum was also the first museum of any kind in which the artworks it contained were organized and displayed in chronological order, emphasizing the history of art, as opposed to simply exhibiting aesthetic treasures (compare FIG. 25-1A).

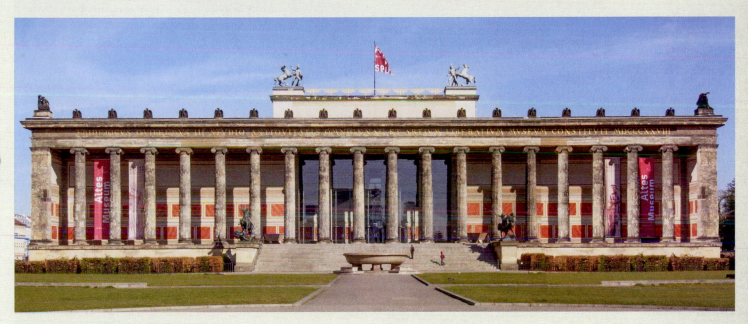

27-42 KARL FRIEDRICH SCHINKEL, Altes Museum (looking northwest), Berlin, Germany, 1822–1830.

Schinkel conceived the first public art museum in Europe as a Neoclassical "temple of culture." The Altes Museum's facade of 18 Ionic columns resembles an ancient Greek stoa (FIG. 5-78).

Girodet's *Burial of Atala* (FIG. 27-6)—which defended religion on the grounds of its beauty and mystery rather than on the grounds of truth. Gothic cathedrals, according to Chateaubriand, were translations of the sacred groves of the ancient Gauls into stone and should be cherished as manifestations of France's holy history. One result of this new nationalistic respect for the Gothic style was that Eugène Emmanuel Viollet-le-Duc (1814–1879) received a commission in 1845 to restore the interior of Paris's Notre-Dame

to its Gothic splendor after later alterations, including those made for Napoleon's coronation (see "The Coronation of Napoleon," page 797).

HOUSES OF PARLIAMENT England also celebrated its medieval heritage with *Neo-Gothic* buildings. In London, when the old Houses of Parliament burned in 1834, the Parliamentary Commission decreed that proposed designs for the

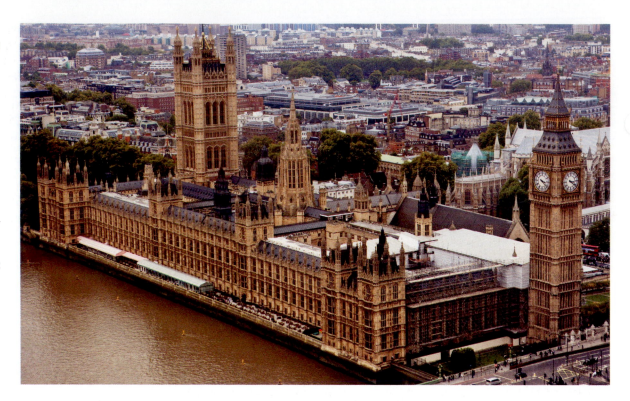

27-43 CHARLES BARRY and AUGUSTUS WELBY NORTHMORE PUGIN, Houses of Parliament (looking southwest), London, England, designed 1835.

During the 19th century, architects revived many historical styles, often reflecting nationalistic pride. The Houses of Parliament have an exterior veneer and towers that recall English Late Gothic style.

new building had to be either Gothic or Elizabethan. CHARLES BARRY (1795–1860), with the assistance of AUGUSTUS WELBY NORTHMORE PUGIN (1812–1852), won the commission for the new Houses of Parliament (FIG. 27-43) in 1835. By this time, architectural style had become a matter of selection from the historical past. Barry had traveled widely in Europe, Greece, Turkey, Egypt, and Palestine, studying the architecture of each place. He preferred the classical Renaissance styles, but he had designed some earlier Neo-Gothic buildings, and Pugin successfully influenced him in the direction of English Late Gothic. Pugin was one of a group of English artists and critics who saw moral purity and spiritual authenticity in the religious architecture of the Middle Ages and revered the careful medieval artisans who built the great cathedrals. The Industrial Revolution was flooding the market with cheaply made and ill-designed commodities. Machine work was replacing handicraft. Many, Pugin included, believed in the necessity of restoring the old artisanship, which they felt embodied honesty as well as quality. Pugin was also the author of the influential *True Principles of Pointed or Christian Architecture* (1841), which RICHARD UPJOHN (1802–1878) consulted for his Neo-Gothic Trinity Church (FIG. 27-43A) in New York City. The design of the Houses of Parliament, however, is not genuinely Gothic, despite its picturesque tower groupings (the Clock Tower, housing Big Ben, at one end, and the Victoria Tower at the other). The building has a formal axial plan and a kind of Palladian regularity beneath its Neo-Gothic detail. Pugin himself said of it, "All Grecian, Sir. Tudor [late English Gothic] details on a classical body."[12]

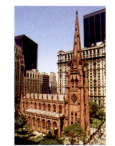

27-43A UPJOHN, Trinity Church, New York, 1841–1852.

ROYAL PAVILION Although the Neoclassical and Neo-Gothic styles dominated early-19th-century architecture, exotic new approaches of all manner soon began to appear, due in part to European imperialism and in part to the Romantic spirit permeating all the arts.

Great Britain's forays throughout the world, particularly in India, had exposed English culture to a broad range of non-Western artistic styles. The Royal Pavilion (FIG. 27-44), designed by JOHN NASH (1752–1835), exhibits a wide variety of these styles. Nash was an established architect, known for Neoclassical buildings in London, when the prince regent (later King George IV) asked him to design a royal pleasure palace in the seaside resort of Brighton. The architecture of Greece, Egypt, and China influenced the interior decor of the Royal Pavilion, but the fantastic exterior is a conglomeration of Islamic domes, minarets, and screens that some architectural historians describe as "Indian Gothic." Underlying the exotic facade is a cast-iron skeleton, an early (if hidden) use of this material in noncommercial construction. Nash also put this metal to fanciful use, creating life-size palm-tree columns in cast iron to support the Royal Pavilion's kitchen ceiling. The building, an appropriate enough backdrop for gala throngs pursuing pleasure by the seaside, has served as a prototype for countless playful architectural exaggerations still found in European and American resorts.

PARIS OPÉRA Another style that found favor in 19th-century architecture was the Baroque, because it was well suited to conveying a grandeur worthy of the riches that the European elite acquired during this age of expansion. The Paris Opéra (FIG. 27-45), designed by CHARLES GARNIER (1825–1898), is the leading example of *Neo-Baroque* architecture. Garnier, who had traveled extensively in Italy as a Rome Prize recipient, had submitted the winning design (out of 171 entrants) in a competition sponsored by Napoleon III. Garnier's opera house has a festive and spectacularly theatrical Neo-Baroque front and two wings resembling Baroque domed central-plan churches (not visible in FIG. 27-45). Inside, intricate arrangements of corridors, vestibules, stairways, balconies, alcoves, entrances, and exits facilitate easy passage throughout the building and provide space for entertainment and socializing at intermissions.

The Baroque grandeur of the layout and of the building's ornamental appointments is characteristic of an architectural style called

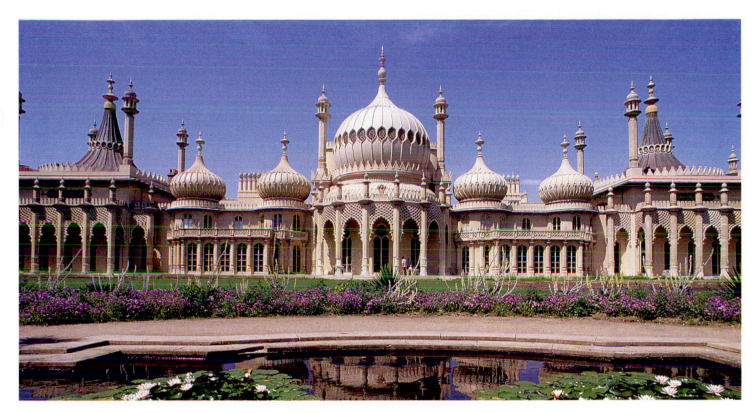

27-44 JOHN NASH, Royal Pavilion (looking northwest), Brighton, England, 1815–1818.

British territorial expansion brought a familiarity with many exotic styles. This palatial "Indian Gothic" seaside pavilion is a conglomeration of Islamic domes, minarets, and screens.

Beaux-Arts, which was most popular in the late 19th and early 20th centuries in France. Based on ideas taught at the dominant École des Beaux-Arts (School of Fine Arts) in Paris, the Beaux-Arts style incorporated classical principles (such as symmetry in design, including interior spaces extending radially from a central core or axis) and featured extensive exterior ornamentation. As an example of a Beaux-Arts building, Garnier's Opéra proclaims, through its majesty and lavishness, its function as a gathering place for fashionable audiences in an era of conspicuous wealth. The style was so attractive to the moneyed classes who supported the arts that theaters and opera houses continued to reflect the Paris Opéra's design until World War I transformed society.

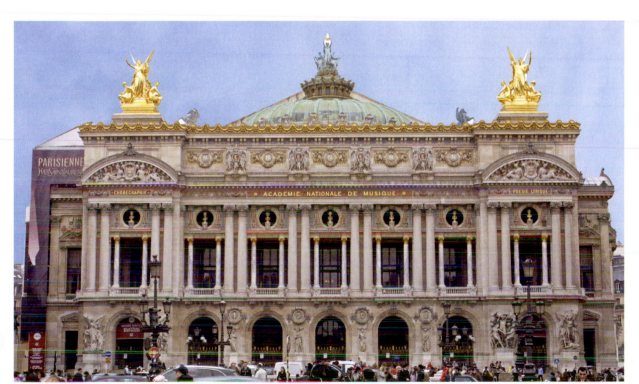

27-45 CHARLES GARNIER, Opéra (looking north), Paris, France, 1861–1874.

For Paris's opera house, Garnier chose a festive and spectacularly theatrical Neo-Baroque facade well suited to a gathering place for fashionable audiences in an age of conspicuous wealth.

27-46 HENRI LABROUSTE, reading room of the Bibliothèque Sainte-Geneviève, Paris, France, 1843–1850.

The exterior of this Parisian library looks like a Renaissance palazzo, but the interior has an exposed cast-iron skeleton, which still incorporates classical Corinthian capitals and Renaissance scrolls.

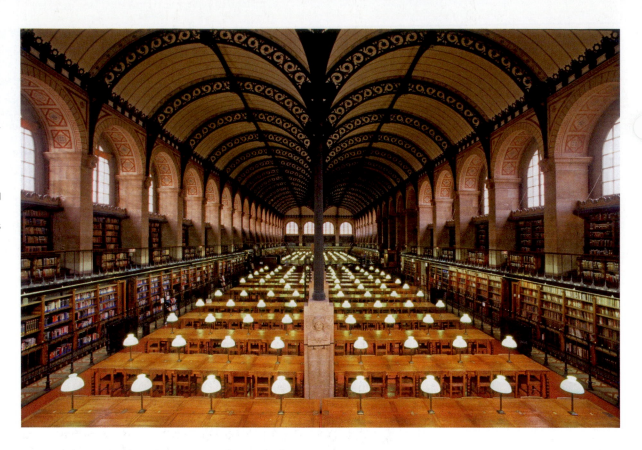

SAINTE-GENEVIÈVE LIBRARY Work on Garnier's opera house began in 1861, but by the middle of the 19th century, many architects had already abandoned sentimental and Romantic designs from the past. Since the 18th century, bridges had been constructed of cast iron (FIG. 26-13) because of its tensile strength and resistance to fire. Another new building material—steel—became available after 1860. Steel enabled architects to create new designs involving vast enclosed spaces, as in the great train sheds of railroad stations (FIG. 28-4) and in exposition halls. Most other utilitarian architecture— factories, warehouses, dockyard structures, mills, and the like—long had been built simply and without historical ornamentation.

The Bibliothèque Sainte-Geneviève, designed by HENRI LABROUSTE (1801–1875), is an interesting mix of Renaissance revival style and modern cast-iron construction. The library's two-story facade with arched windows recalls Renaissance *palazzo* designs, but Labrouste exposed the structure's metal skeleton on the interior. The lower story of the building housed the book stacks. The upper floor featured a spacious reading room (FIG. 27-46) consisting essentially of two barrel-vaulted halls, roofed in terracotta and separated by a row of slender cast-iron Corinthian columns on concrete pedestals. The columns support the iron roof arches pierced with intricate vine-scroll ornamentation derived from the Renaissance architectural repertoire. Labrouste's design highlights how the peculiar properties of the new structural material aesthetically transformed the shapes of traditional masonry architecture. But it is also clear how reluctant some 19th-century architects were to surrender traditional forms, even when fully aware of new possibilities for design and construction. Architects scoffed at "engineers'

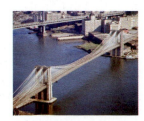

27-46A ROEBLING, Brooklyn Bridge, 1867–1883.

architecture" for many years and continued to clothe their steel-and-concrete structures in the Romantic "drapery" of a historical style. For example, the Brooklyn Bridge (FIG. 27-46A), designed and constructed by JOHN AUGUSTUS ROEBLING (1806–1869) and WASHINGTON ROEBLING (1837–1926), combined the latest steel technology with motifs from Gothic and Egyptian architecture. JOSEPH PAXTON (1801–1865) was an exception as a proponent of "undraped" architecture (see "Prefabricated Architecture," page 833, and FIG. 27-47).

PHOTOGRAPHY

A technological device of immense consequence for the modern experience was invented shortly before the mid-19th century: the camera, with its attendant art of photography. From the time Frenchman LOUIS-JACQUES-MANDÉ DAGUERRE (1789–1851) and Englishman William Henry Fox Talbot (1800–1877) announced the first practical photographic processes in 1839, people have celebrated photography's ability to make convincing pictures of people, places, and things. The relative ease of the process, even in its earliest and most primitive form, seemed a dream come true for 19th-century scientists and artists, who for centuries had grappled with less satisfying methods of capturing accurate images of their subjects. Photography also perfectly suited an age that saw the emergence of Realism as an art movement and a pronounced shift of artistic patronage away from the elite few toward a broader base of support. The growing and increasingly powerful middle class embraced both the comprehensible images of the new medium and their lower cost.

For the traditional artist, photography suggested new answers to the great debate about what is real and how to represent the real in art. Because photography easily and accurately enabled the reproduction of three-dimensional objects on a two-dimensional

PROBLEMS AND SOLUTIONS
Prefabricated Architecture

Completely "undraped" construction—that is, the erection of buildings that did not conceal their cast-iron structural skeletons—first became popular in the conservatories (greenhouses) of English country estates. Joseph Paxton built several of these structures for his patron, the duke of Devonshire. In the largest—300 feet long—he used an experimental system of glass-and-metal roof construction. Encouraged by the success of this system, Paxton submitted a winning glass-and-iron building design in the competition for the hall to house the 1851 Great Exhibition of the Works of Industry of All Nations in London.

As innovative as Paxton's use of modern materials in place of stone was his adoption of a new cost-effective way to erect his exhibition building, the Crystal Palace (FIG. 27-47). Paxton was the champion of *prefabricated architecture*—the use of structural elements manufactured in advance and transported to the construction site ready for assembly. In traditional stone architecture, masons carved the column capitals, moldings, and the like on site to ensure that these delicate features would not be damaged during transport. This slowed down construction considerably. Paxton's use of prefabricated parts—primarily glass panes in wood frames and cast-iron pillars and beams—for the Crystal Palace enabled workers to build the vast (18-acre) structure in the then unheard-of time of six months and to dismantle it quickly at the exhibition's closing to avoid permanent obstruction of the park. The building was the perfect expression of the new industrial age that the Great Exhibition celebrated.

Paxton's design, nonetheless, borrowed much from traditional architecture, especially Roman and Christian basilicas. The Crystal Palace had a central flat-roofed "nave" and a barrel-vaulted crossing "transept," providing ample interior space to contain displays of huge machines as well as to accommodate decorative touches in the form of large working fountains and giant trees. The public admired the Crystal Palace so much that the workers who dismantled it put up an enlarged version of the glass-and-iron exhibition hall at a new location on the outskirts of London at Sydenham, where it remained until fire destroyed it in 1936. Fortunately, a few old black-and-white photographs and several color lithographs (FIG. 27-47) preserve a record of the Crystal Palace's appearance.

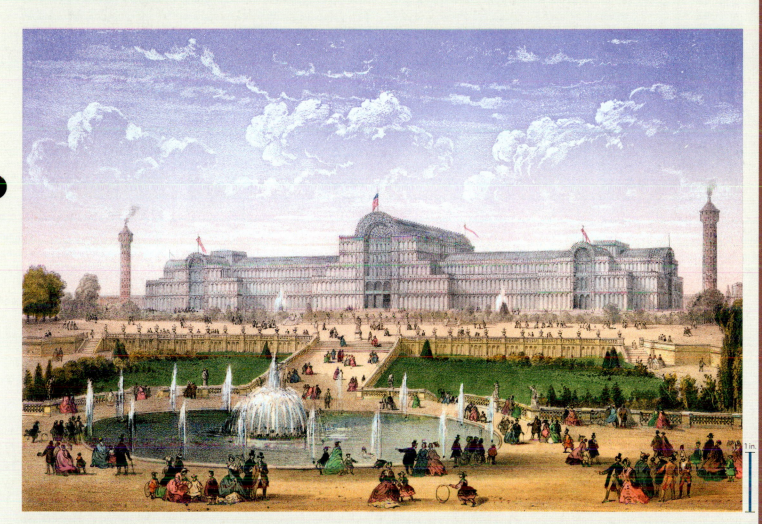

27-47 JOSEPH PAXTON, Crystal Palace, London, England, 1850–1851; enlarged and relocated at Sydenham, England, 1852–1854. Color lithograph, 8" × 11¾", by ACHILLE-LOUIS MARTINET, ca. 1862. Private collection.

The tensile strength of iron enabled Paxton to experiment with a new system of glass-and-metal roof construction. Constructed of prefabricated parts, the vast Crystal Palace required only six months to build.

MATERIALS AND TECHNIQUES
Daguerreotypes, Calotypes, and Wet-Plate Photography

The earliest photographic processes were the *daguerreotype* (FIGS. 27-48 and 27-49), named after L.J.M. Daguerre, and the *calotype* (FIG. 27-53).

Daguerre was an architect and theatrical set painter and designer. This background led Daguerre and a partner to open a popular entertainment called the Diorama. Audiences witnessed performances of "living paintings" created by changing the lighting effects on a "sandwich" composed of a painted backdrop and several layers of painted translucent front curtains. Daguerre used a camera obscura for the Diorama, but he wanted to find a more efficient and effective procedure. Through a mutual acquaintance, he met Joseph Nicéphore Niépce (1765–1833), who in 1826 had successfully made a permanent picture of the cityscape outside his upper-story window by exposing, in a camera obscura, a metal plate covered with a light-sensitive coating. Niépce's process, however, had the significant drawback that it required an eight-hour exposure time. After Niépce died in 1833, Daguerre continued his work, making two important discoveries. Latent development—that is, bringing out the image through treatment in chemical solutions—considerably shortened the length of time needed for exposure. Daguerre also discovered a better way to "fix" the image by chemically stopping the action of light on the photographic plate, which otherwise would continue to darken until the image turned solid black.

The daguerreotype reigned supreme in photography until the 1850s, but the second major photographic invention, the ancestor of the modern negative-print system, eventually replaced it. On January 31, 1839, less than three weeks after Daguerre unveiled his method in Paris, William Henry Fox Talbot presented a paper on his "photogenic drawings" to the Royal Institution in London. As early as 1835, Talbot made "negative" images by placing objects on sensitized paper and exposing the arrangement to light. This created a design of light-colored silhouettes recording the places where opaque or

translucent objects had blocked light from darkening the paper's emulsion. In his experiments, Talbot next exposed sensitized papers inside simple cameras and, with a second sheet, created "positive" images. He further improved the process with more light-sensitive chemicals and a chemical development of the negative image. This technique enabled multiple prints. However, in Talbot's process, which he named the *calotype* (from the Greek word *kalos*, "beautiful"), the photographic images incorporated the texture of the paper. This produced a slightly blurred, grainy effect very different from the crisp detail and wide tonal range available with the daguerreotype. Also discouraging widespread adoption of the calotype were the stiff licensing and equipment fees charged for many years after Talbot patented his new process in 1841.

One of the earliest masters of an improved kind of calotype photography was the multitalented Frenchman known as Nadar (FIGS. 27-49A and 27-50). He used glass negatives and albumen (egg-white-based) printing paper (FIGS. 27-51 and 27-52), which could record finer detail and a wider range of light and shadow than Talbot's calotype process. The new *wet-plate* technology (so named because the photographic plate was exposed, developed, and fixed while wet) almost at once became the universal way of making negatives until 1880. However, wet-plate photography had drawbacks. The plates had to be prepared and processed on the spot. Working outdoors meant taking along a portable darkroom—a wagon, tent, or box with light-tight sleeves for the photographer's arms.

Refinements of these early processes served photographers well for a century and a half, but have been almost completely supplanted today by digital photography (see page 1016).

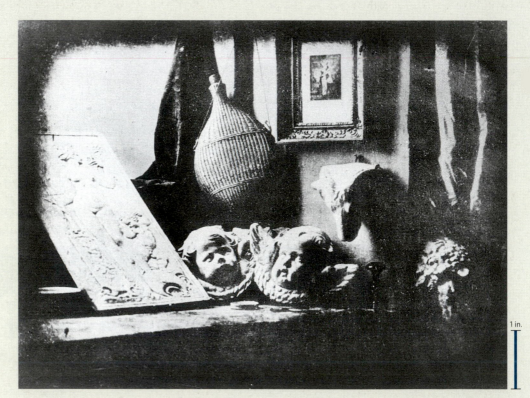

27-48 LOUIS-JACQUES-MANDÉ DAGUERRE, *Still Life in Studio*, 1837. Daguerreotype, $6\frac{1}{4}'' \times 8\frac{1}{4}''$. Société Française de Photographie, Paris.

One of the first plates Daguerre produced after perfecting his new photographic process was this still life, in which he was able to capture amazing detail and finely graduated tones of light and shadow.

1 in.

surface, the new medium also challenged the place of traditional modes of pictorial representation originating in the Renaissance. Artists as diverse as Delacroix, Ingres, Courbet, and the Impressionist Edgar Degas (see page 849) welcomed photography as a helpful auxiliary to painting. Other artists, however, feared that the camera was a mechanism that would displace the painstaking

work of skilled painters. From the moment of its invention, photography threatened to expropriate the realistic image, until then the exclusive property of painting. But just as some painters looked to the new medium of photography for answers on how best to render an image in paint, so some photographers looked to painting for suggestions about ways to imbue the photographic image with qualities beyond simple reproduction. Indeed, the first subjects that photographers chose to record were traditional painting themes—for example, still lifes and portraits—in part to establish photography as a legitimate artistic medium on a par with painting. A debate immediately began over whether the photograph was an art form or whether the camera was merely a scientific instrument. An 1862 court case provided the answer: photography was an art, and photographs were entitled to copyright protection (see FIG. 27-49A).

Artists themselves were instrumental in the development of the new photographic technology. The camera obscura was familiar to 18th-century artists. In 1807, the invention of the *camera lucida* (lighted room) replaced the enclosed chamber of the camera obscura. Now the photographer aimed a small prism lens, hung on a stand, downward at an object. The lens projected the image of the object onto a sheet of paper. Artists using either of these devices found the process long and arduous, no matter how accurate the resulting work. All yearned for a more direct way to capture a subject's image. Two very different scientific inventions that accomplished this—the *daguerreotype* and the *calotype* (see "Daguerreotypes, Calotypes, and Wet-Plate Photography," page 834)—appeared almost simultaneously in France and England in 1839.

DAGUERREOTYPES The French government presented the new daguerreotype process at the Academy of Science in Paris on January 7, 1839, with the understanding that its details would be made available to all interested parties without charge (although the inventor received a large annuity in appreciation). Soon, people worldwide began making pictures with the daguerreotype "camera" (a name shortened from camera obscura) in a process almost immediately christened "photography," from the Greek *photos* ("light") and *graphos* ("writing or drawing"). From the start, the possibilities of the process as a new art medium intrigued painters. Paul Delaroche (1797–1856), a leading academic painter of the day, wrote in an official report to the French government that anticipated the 1862 legal ruling:

Daguerre's process completely satisfies all the demands of art, carrying certain essential principles of art to such perfection that it must become a subject of observation and study even to the most accomplished painters. The pictures obtained by this method are as remarkable for the perfection of the details as for the richness and harmony of the general effect. Nature is reproduced in them not only with truth, but also with art.[13]

Unlike photographs that people make today, whether printed from traditional film negatives or from digital images, each daguerreotype is a unique work. *Still Life in Studio* (FIG. 27-48) is one of the first successful plates Daguerre produced after perfecting his method. The process captured every detail—the subtle forms, the varied textures, the finely graduated tones of light and shadow—in Daguerre's carefully constructed tableau. The three-dimensional forms of the sculptures, the basket, and the bits of cloth spring into high relief. The inspiration for the composition came from 17th-century Dutch *vanitas* still lifes, such as those of Pieter Claesz (FIG. 25-21). Like Claesz, Daguerre arranged his objects to reveal their textures and shapes clearly. Unlike a painter, Daguerre could not alter anything within his arrangement to create a stronger image. However, he could suggest a symbolic meaning through his choice of objects. Like the skull and timepiece in Claesz's painting, Daguerre's sculptural and architectural fragments and the framed print of a couple embracing suggest that even art is vanitas and will not endure forever.

HAWES AND SOUTHWORTH In the United States, photographers began to make daguerreotypes within two months of Daguerre's presentation in Paris. Two particularly avid and resourceful advocates of the new medium were JOSIAH JOHNSON HAWES (1808–1901), a painter, and ALBERT SANDS SOUTHWORTH (1811–1894), a pharmacist and teacher. Together, they ran a daguerreotype studio in Boston specializing in portraiture, then popular due to the shortened exposure time required for the process (although it was still long enough to require head braces to help subjects remain motionless while photographers recorded their images).

The partners also took their equipment outside the studio to record places and events of particular interest to them. One resultant image is *Early Operation under Ether, Massachusetts General Hospital* (FIG. 27-49).

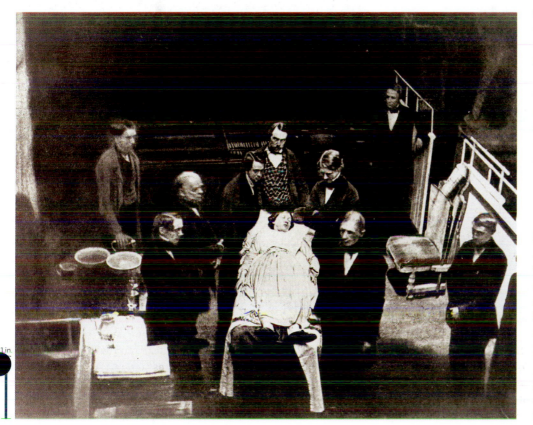

27-49 JOSIAH JOHNSON HAWES and ALBERT SANDS SOUTHWORTH, *Early Operation under Ether, Massachusetts General Hospital*, ca. 1847. Daguerreotype, $6\frac{1}{2}$" × $8\frac{1}{2}$". **Massachusetts General Hospital Archives and Special Collections, Boston.**

In this early daguerreotype, which predates Eakins's *Gross Clinic* (FIG. 27-36) by almost 30 years, Hawes and Southworth demonstrated the documentary power of the new medium of photography.

This daguerreotype, taken from the vantage point of the gallery of a hospital operating room, puts the viewer in the position of medical students looking down on the type of lecture-demonstration that was typical throughout the 19th century. An image of historical record, this early daguerreotype predates Eakins's *Gross Clinic* (FIG. 27-36) by almost three decades, but the theme had been explored in painting much earlier by Rembrandt (FIG. 25-12). The focus of attention in *Early Operation* is the white-draped patient surrounded by a circle of darkly clad doctors. The details of the figures and the room's furnishings are in sharp focus, but the slight blurring of several of the figures betrays motion during the exposure. The elevated viewpoint flattens the spatial perspective and emphasizes the relationships of the figures in ways that the Impressionists, especially Degas (FIG. 28-8), found intriguing.

NADAR Portraiture was one of the first photography genres to use the new wet-plate technology that improved on the calotype. Making portraits was an important economic opportunity for most photographers, as Southworth and Hawes proved, but the greatest early portrait photographer was undoubtedly Gaspar-Félix Tournachon. Known simply as NADAR (1820–1910), Tournachon was a French novelist, journalist, enthusiastic balloonist (FIG. 27-49A), and caricaturist, who became an early champion of photography. Photographic studies for his caricatures led Nadar to open a portrait

studio. So talented was he at capturing the essence of his subjects that the most important people in France, including Delacroix, Daumier, Courbet, and Manet, flocked to his studio to have their portraits made. Nadar said that he sought in his work "that instant of understanding that puts you in touch with the model—helps you sum him up, guides you to his habits, his ideas, and character and enables you to produce . . . a really convincing and sympathetic likeness, an intimate portrait."[14]

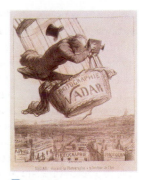

📷 **27-49A** DAUMIER, *Nadar Raising Photography*, 1862.

Nadar's *Eugène Delacroix* (FIG. 27-50) shows the painter at the height of his career. In this photograph, the artist appears with remarkable presence. Even in half-length, his gesture and expression create a mood that seems to reveal much about him. Perhaps Delacroix responded to Nadar's famous gift for putting his clients at ease by assuming the pose that best expressed his personality. The new photographic materials made possible the rich range of tones in Nadar's images.

JULIA MARGARET CAMERON Among the most famous portrait photographers in 19th-century England was JULIA MARGARET CAMERON (1815–1879), who did not take up photography seriously

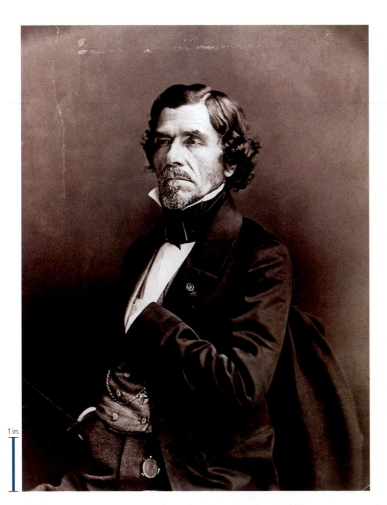

27-50 NADAR, *Eugène Delacroix*, ca. 1855. Modern print, $8\frac{1}{2}$" × $6\frac{2}{3}$", from the original negative. Bibliothèque Nationale, Paris.

Nadar was one of the earliest portrait photographers. His prints of the leading artists of the day, such as this one of Delacroix, reveal the sitters' personalities as well as record their features.

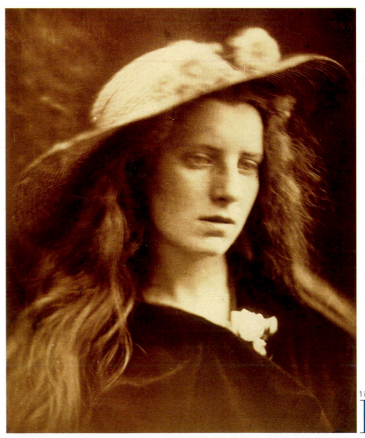

27-51 JULIA MARGARET CAMERON, *Ophelia, Study No. 2,* 1867. Albumen print, 1' 1" × $10\frac{2}{3}$". George Eastman House, Rochester (gift of Eastman Kodak Company; formerly Gabriel Cromer Collection).

Cameron was a prominent 19th-century photographer who often depicted her female subjects as characters in literary or biblical narratives. The slightly blurred focus is a distinctive feature of her work.

until the age of 48. Although she produced images of many well-known men of the period, including Charles Darwin, Alfred Tennyson, and Thomas Carlyle, she photographed more women than men, as was true of many women photographers. *Ophelia, Study No. 2* (FIG. 27-51) typifies her portrait style. Cameron often depicted her female subjects as characters in literary or biblical narratives. The slightly blurred focus also became a distinctive feature of her work—the by-product of photographing with a lens with a short focal length, which allowed only a small area of sharp focus. The blurriness adds an ethereal, dreamlike tone to the photographs, appropriate for Cameron's fictional "characters." Her photograph of Ophelia has a mysterious, fragile quality reminiscent of Pre-Raphaelite paintings (FIG. 27-41) of literary heroines.

TIMOTHY O'SULLIVAN Photographers were quick to realize the documentary power of their new medium. Thus began the story of photography's influence on modern life and of the immense changes it brought to communication and information management. With photography, historical events could for the first time be recorded in permanent form on the spot. The photographs taken of the Crimean War (1856) by Roger Fenton (1819–1869) and of the American Civil War by Mathew B. Brady (1823–1896), ALEXANDER GARDNER (1821–1882), and TIMOTHY O'SULLIVAN (1840–1882) remain unsurpassed as incisive accounts of military life, unsparing in their truthful detail and poignant as expressions of human experience.

Of the Civil War photographs, the most moving are the inhumanly objective records of combat deaths. Perhaps the most reproduced of these Civil War photographs is Gardner's print of O'Sullivan's *A Harvest of Death, Gettysburg, Pennsylvania* (FIG. 27-52). Although viewers could regard this image as simple reportage, it also functions to impress on people the high price of war. Corpses litter the battlefield as far and wide as the eye can see. As O'Sullivan's photograph modulates from the precise clarity of the bodies of Union soldiers in the foreground, boots stolen and pockets picked, to the indistinct corpses in the distance, the suggestion of innumerable other dead soldiers is unavoidable. This "harvest" is far more sobering and depressing than that in Winslow Homer's Civil War painting, *Veteran in a New Field* (FIG. 27-35). Though it was

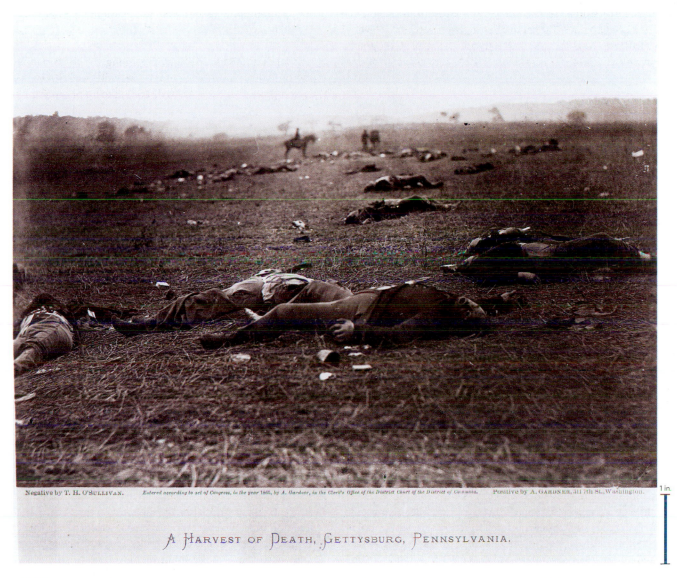

Negative by T. H. O'Sullivan.   Entered according to act of Congress, in the year 1865, by A. Gardner, in the Clerk's Office of the District Court of the District of Columbia.   Positive by A. GARDNER, 511 7th St., Washington.

A HARVEST OF DEATH, GETTYSBURG, PENNSYLVANIA.

27-52 TIMOTHY O'SULLIVAN, *A Harvest of Death, Gettysburg, Pennsylvania*, 1863. Negative by Timothy O'Sullivan. Albumen print by ALEXANDER GARDNER, $6\frac{3}{4}'' \times 8\frac{3}{4}''$. New York Public Library (Astor, Lenox and Tilden Foundations, Rare Books and Manuscript Division), New York.

Wet-plate technology enabled photographers to record historical events on the spot—and to comment on the high price of war, as in this photograph of dead Union soldiers at Gettysburg in 1863.

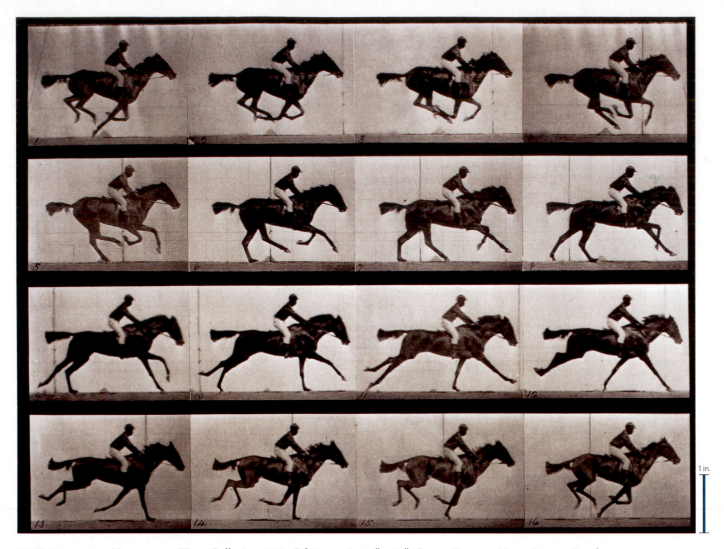

1 in.

27-53 EADWEARD MUYBRIDGE, *Horse Galloping,* 1878. Calotype print, 9" × 12". George Eastman House International Museum of Photography and Film, Rochester.

Muybridge specialized in photographic studies of the successive stages in human and animal motion—details too quick for the human eye to capture. Modern cinema owes a great deal to his work.

years before photolithography could reproduce photographs such as this one in newspapers, photographers exhibited them publicly. They made an impression that newsprint engravings never could.

EADWEARD MUYBRIDGE The Realist photographer and scientist EADWEARD MUYBRIDGE (1830–1904) came to the United States from England in the 1850s and settled in San Francisco, where he established a prominent international reputation for his photographs of the western United States. In 1872, the governor of California, Leland Stanford (1824–1893), sought Muybridge's assistance in settling a bet about whether, at any point in a stride, all four feet of a horse galloping at top speed are off the ground. Through his sequential photography, as seen in *Horse Galloping* (FIG. **27-53**), Muybridge proved that racing horses did in fact at times have all four feet in midair. This experience was the beginning of Muybridge's photographic studies of the successive stages in human and animal motion—details too quick for the human eye to capture. These investigations culminated in 1885 at the University of Pennsylvania with a series of multiple-camera motion studies that produced separate photographs of progressive moments in a single action. Muybridge's discoveries received extensive publicity

through the book *Animal Locomotion* (1887), and his motion photographs earned him a place in the history of science, as well as art. These sequential motion studies, along with those of Eakins and Marey (see page 825), influenced many other artists, including their contemporary, the painter and sculptor Edgar Degas (FIG. 28-8), and 20th-century artists such as Marcel Duchamp (FIG. 29-35).

Muybridge presented his work to scientists and general audiences with a device called the *zoopraxiscope,* which he invented to project his sequences of images (mounted on special glass plates) onto a screen. The result was so lifelike that one viewer said it "threw upon the screen apparently the living, moving animals. Nothing was wanting but the clatter of hoofs upon the turf."[15] The illusion of motion in Muybridge's photographic exhibits was the result of a physical fact of human eyesight called "persistence of vision." Stated simply, it means that the brain retains whatever the eye sees for a fraction of a second after the eye stops seeing it. Thus viewers saw a rapid succession of different images merging one into the next, producing the illusion of continuous change. This illusion lies at the heart of the motion-picture industry that debuted in the 20th century. Thus, with Muybridge's innovations in photography, yet another new art form was born—cinema.

ROMANTICISM, REALISM, PHOTOGRAPHY: EUROPE AND AMERICA, 1800 TO 1870

Art under Napoleon

- As Emperor of the French from 1804 to 1815, Napoleon embraced the Neoclassical style in order to associate his regime with the empire of ancient Rome. Roman temples were the models for La Madeleine in Paris, which Pierre Vignon built as a temple of glory for France's imperial armies.

- Napoleon chose Jacques-Louis David as First Painter of the Empire. His favorite sculptor was Antonio Canova, who carved marble Neoclassical portraits of the imperial family, including a reclining image of Napoleon's sister Pauline Borghese in the guise of Venus.

- The beginning of a break from Neoclassicism can already be seen in the work of several of David's students, including Gros, Girodet-Trioson, and Ingres, all of whom painted some exotic subjects reflecting Romantic taste.

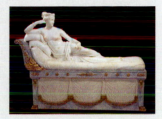

Canova, *Pauline Borghese as Venus*, 1808

Romanticism

- The roots of Romanticism are in the 18th century, but usually the term more narrowly denotes the artistic movement that flourished from 1800 to 1840, between Neoclassicism and Realism. Romantic artists gave precedence to feeling and imagination over Enlightenment reason. Romantic painters explored the exotic, erotic, and fantastic in their art.

- In Spain, Francisco Goya's *Caprichos* series celebrated the unleashing of imagination, emotions, and even nightmares. In France, Eugène Delacroix led the way in depicting Romantic narratives set in faraway places and distant times. Ancient Assyria, for example, is the subject of his *Death of Sardanapalus.*

- Romantic painters often chose landscapes as an ideal subject to express the theme of the soul unified with the natural world. Masters of the transcendental landscape include Friedrich in Germany, Constable and Turner in England, and Cole, Bierstadt, and Church in the United States.

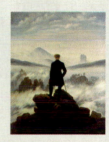

Friedrich, *Wanderer above a Sea of Mist*, 1817–1818

Realism

- Realism developed as an artistic movement in mid-19th-century France. Its leading proponent was Gustave Courbet, whose paintings of menial laborers and ordinary people exemplify his belief that painters should depict only their own time and place. Honoré Daumier boldly confronted authority with his satirical lithographs commenting on the plight of the urban working class. Édouard Manet shocked the public with his paintings' subjects—for example, promiscuous women—and with his technique, especially his rough brushstrokes, which emphasized the flatness of the painting surface, paving the way for modern abstract art.

- Among the leading American Realists were Winslow Homer, Thomas Eakins, and John Singer Sargent. Eakins's painting of surgery in progress was too brutally realistic for the Philadelphia art jury that rejected it.

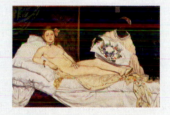

Manet, *Olympia*, 1863

Architecture

- Territorial expansion, the Romantic interest in exotic locales and earlier eras, and nationalistic pride led to the revival in the 19th century of older architectural styles, especially the Gothic, exemplified by London's Houses of Parliament.

- By the middle of the century, many architects had already abandoned sentimental and Romantic designs from the past in favor of exploring the possibilities of cast-iron construction, as in Henri Labrouste's Sainte-Geneviève Library in Paris and Joseph Paxton's prefabricated Crystal Palace in London.

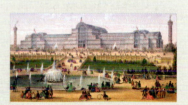

Paxton, Crystal Palace, London, 1850–1851

Photography

- In 1839, Daguerre in Paris and Talbot in London invented the first practical photographic processes. In 1862, a French court formally recognized photography as an art form subject to copyright protection. Many of the earliest photographers, including Nadar and Cameron, specialized in portrait photography, but others, including Hawes, Southworth, and O'Sullivan in the United States, quickly realized the documentary power of the new medium. Muybridge's sequential photos of human and animal motion were the forerunners of modern cinema.

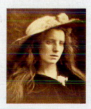

Cameron, *Ophelia*, 1867

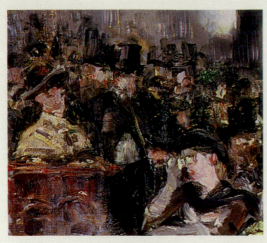

◀ 28-1a The Folies-Bergère was a popular café and music hall where Parisians enjoyed their leisure—a characteristic Impressionist subject that broke sharply with tradition, as did Manet's sketchy application of paint.

▶ 28-1b The central figure in *A Bar at the Folies-Bergère* is a young barmaid who looks out from the canvas but seems detached both from the viewer and the gentleman in a top hat who may be propositioning her.

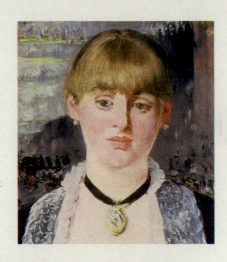

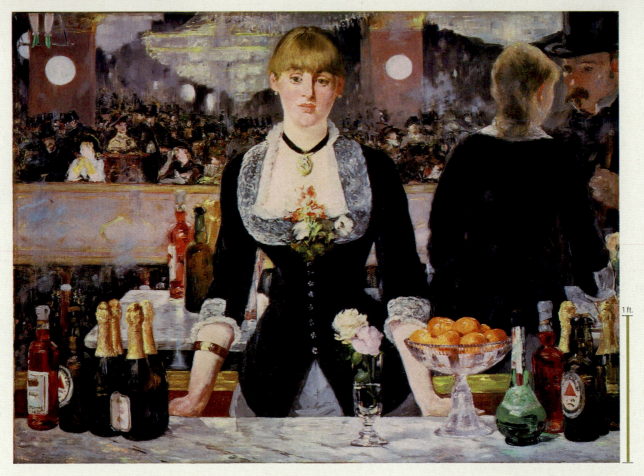

1 ft.

28-1 ÉDOUARD MANET, *A Bar at the Folies-Bergère*, 1882. Oil on canvas, 3' 1" × 4' 3". Courtauld Gallery, London.

▶ 28-1c In accord with modernist principles, Manet called attention to the canvas surface by creating spatial inconsistencies, such as the relationship between the barmaid and her apparent reflection in the mirror.

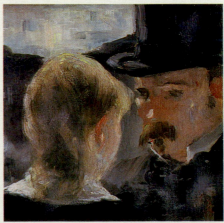

Impressionism, Post-Impressionism, Symbolism: Europe and America, 1870 to 1900

MODERNISM AT THE FOLIES-BERGÈRE

Between 1800 and 1900, the population of Europe's major cities exploded. In Paris, for example, the number of residents expanded from 500,000 to 2,700,000. It was there that the art movement called *Impressionism* was born, an aesthetic by-product of the sometimes brutal and chaotic transformation of French life, which made the world seem unstable and insubstantial. As the poet and critic Charles Baudelaire (1821–1867) observed in his 1860 essay *The Painter of Modern Life*: "[Modernity is] the ephemeral, the fugitive, the contingent, the half of art whose other half is the eternal and the immutable."[1] Accordingly, Impressionist painters built on the innovations of the Realists in turning away from traditional mythological and religious themes in favor of the daily life of the newly industrialized French capital and its suburbs along the Seine. But, in contrast to the Realists, the Impressionists sought to convey the elusiveness and impermanence of the subjects they portrayed.

One of the most popular Impressionist subjects was Paris's vibrant nightlife. The immensely versatile Édouard Manet (FIGS. 27-32 and 27-33), whose career bridged Realism and Impressionism, painted his last great work—*A Bar at the Folies-Bergère* (FIG. 28-1)—under the influence of the younger Impressionists. The Folies-Bergère was a popular café with music-hall performances, one of Paris's most fashionable gathering places. At the center of Manet's *Folies-Bergère* is a barmaid, who looks out from the canvas but seems disinterested or lost in thought, divorced from her patrons as well as from the viewer. In front of her, Manet painted a marvelous still life of bottles, flowers, and fruit—all for sale to the bar's customers. In the mirror is the reflection of a gentleman wearing a dapper top hat and carrying an elegant walking stick. He has approached the barmaid, perhaps to order a drink, but more likely to ask the price of her company after the bar closes. Also visible in the mirror, at the upper left corner of the canvas, are the lower legs of a trapeze artist and a woman in the nightclub's balcony watching some other performance through opera glasses.

What seems at first to be a straightforward representation of the bar, barmaid, and customers quickly fades as visual discrepancies immediately emerge. For example, is the reflection of the woman on the right the barmaid's? If both figures are the same person, it is impossible to reconcile the spatial relationship among the gentleman, the bar, the barmaid, and her seemingly displaced reflection. These visual contradictions complement Manet's blurred brushstrokes and rough application of paint. Together, they draw attention to the tactile surface of the canvas, consistent with late-19th-century artists' emerging insistence on underscoring the artifice of the act of painting, one of the central principles of *modernist* art.

MARXISM, DARWINISM, MODERNISM

The momentous developments of the early 19th century in Europe—urbanization, industrialization, and increased economic and political interaction worldwide—matured during the latter half of the century. The Industrial Revolution that began in England spread so rapidly to the Continent and the United States that historians often refer to the third quarter of the 19th century as the second Industrial Revolution. Whereas the first Industrial Revolution centered on textiles, steam, and iron, the second focused on steel, electricity, chemicals, and oil. The discoveries in these fields provided the foundation for developments in plastics, machinery, building construction, and automobile manufacturing and paved the way for the invention of the radio, telephone, electric lightbulb, and electric streetcar.

Expanding industrialization was closely tied to rapid urbanization. The number and size of European cities grew dramatically during the latter part of the 19th century, largely due to migration from the countryside. Farmers in large numbers relocated to urban centers because expanded agricultural enterprises squeezed smaller property owners from their land. The widely available work opportunities in the cities, especially in the factories, were also a major factor in this population shift. Improving health and living conditions in the cities further contributed to their explosive growth.

MARXISM AND DARWINISM The rise of the urban working class was fundamental to the ideas of Karl Marx (1818–1883), one of the era's dominant figures. Born in Trier, Germany, Marx received a doctorate in philosophy from the University of Berlin. After moving to Paris, he met fellow German Friedrich Engels (1820–1895), who became his lifelong collaborator. Together they wrote *The Communist Manifesto* (1848), which called for the working class to overthrow the capitalist system. Marx believed that in all societies, those who controlled the means of production conflicted with those whose labor they exploited for their own enrichment—a dynamic he called "dialectical materialism." Marx advocated the creation of a socialist state in which the working class seized power and destroyed capitalism. This new political, social, and economic system—Marxism—held great appeal for the working poor as well as for many intellectuals.

Equally influential was the English naturalist Charles Darwin (1809–1882), who postulated the theory of natural selection. Darwin and his compatriot Alfred Russel Wallace (1823–1913), working independently, proposed a rational model for the process of evolution, rather than attributing evolution to random chance or God's plan. They argued that evolution was the natural result of a competitive system in which only the fittest survived. Darwin's controversial ideas, as presented in *On the Origin of Species by Means of Natural Selection* (1859), contradicted the biblical narrative of creation and were greeted with hostility by many people.

MODERNISM Marx's emphasis on social conflict and Darwin's ideas about evolution were consistent with the growing sense of the world's impermanence and of a constantly shifting reality, which Baudelaire insisted was the essential characteristic of the modern world and the proper subject of a modernist painter (see page 841). *Modernism* in art, however, transcends the simple depiction of the contemporary world—the goal of Realism. Modernists also critically examine the premises of art itself, as Manet did in his groundbreaking 1863 painting *Le Déjeuner sur l'Herbe* (FIG. 27-32) and carried further in his 1882 *A Bar at the Folies-Bergère* (FIG. 28-1). Modernism thus implies certain concerns about art and aesthetics internal to art production, regardless of whether the artist is portraying modern life.

In an important 1965 article, Clement Greenberg (1909–1994), an influential American art critic who wrote about the revolutionary art movements of the decades following World War II (see "Greenbergian Formalism," page 954), explained modernism as follows:

> The essence of Modernism lies . . . in the use of the characteristic methods of a discipline to criticize the discipline itself—not in order to subvert it, but to entrench it more firmly in its area of competence. . . . [T]he unique and proper area of competence of each art coincide[s] with all that [is] unique to the nature of its medium. . . . Realistic, illusionist art had dissembled the medium, using art to conceal art. Modernism used art to call attention to art. The limitations that constitute the medium of painting—the flat surface, the shape of the support, the properties of pigment—were treated by the Old Masters as negative factors that could be acknowledged only implicitly or indirectly. Modernist painting has come to regard these same limitations as positive factors that are to be acknowledged openly. Manet's paintings became the first Modernist ones by virtue of the frankness with which they declared the surfaces on which they were painted. The Impressionists, in Manet's wake, abjured underpainting and glazing, to leave the eye under no doubt as to the fact that the colors used were made of real paint that came from pots or tubes.[2]

IMPRESSIONISM

A hostile critic applied the term *Impressionism* in response to *Impression: Sunrise* (FIG. 28-2), one of the paintings exhibited in the first Impressionist show in 1874 (see "Academic Salons and Independent Art Exhibitions," page 844). Although the critic intended

IMPRESSIONISM, POST-IMPRESSIONISM, SYMBOLISM: EUROPE AND AMERICA, 1870 TO 1900

1870–1880

- Claude Monet and the Impressionists mount their first independent exhibition in Paris
- The Impressionists paint subjects that capture the transitory nature of modern life in urbanized Paris and its suburbs
- European artists begin to collect Japanese prints and emulate Japanese compositions
- Gustave Moreau explores eroticism and fantasy in Symbolist paintings

1880–1890

- Édouard Manet completes his career with paintings in the Impressionist mode
- Georges Seurat investigates color theory and develops pointillism
- Vincent van Gogh moves to France and explores the expressive power of color
- Auguste Rodin receives the commission for *Gates of Hell*
- Alexandre-Gustave Eiffel builds the Eiffel Tower in Paris

1890–1900

- Henri de Toulouse-Lautrec pioneers the art of the poster
- Paul Cézanne seeks "to do Poussin over entirely from nature"
- The Art Nouveau movement emerges in architecture and the decorative arts
- Gustav Klimt's paintings epitomize fin-de-siècle culture in Austria
- Louis Sullivan builds steel, glass, and stone skyscrapers in America

PROBLEMS AND SOLUTIONS
Painting Impressions of Light and Color

In striking contrast to traditional studio artists, Monet began and completed *Impression: Sunrise* (FIG. **28-2**)—a view of the harbor of his boyhood home in Le Havre—outdoors. Closer to Paris, he often set up his easel on the banks of the Seine (FIG. **28-2A**) or in a boat on the river (FIG. **28-2B**). Painting *en plein air* was how Monet was able to meet his goal of capturing an instantaneous representation of atmosphere and climate, which he concluded was impossible to do in a studio. Of course, landscape painters had always drawn and made preliminary color studies outdoors and then used those sketches to produce formal paintings in their studios. Finishing as well as beginning his landscapes outdoors sharpened Monet's focus on the roles that light and color play in the way nature appears to the eye. The systematic investigation of light and color and the elimination of the traditional distinction between a sketch and a formal painting enabled Monet to paint images that truly conveyed a sense of the momentary and transitory. Lilla Cabot Perry (1848–1933), a student of Monet's late in his career, gave this description of Monet's approach:

> I remember his once saying to me: "When you go out to paint, try to forget what objects you have before you—a tree, a house, a field, or whatever. Merely think, here is a little square of blue, here an oblong of pink, here a streak of yellow, and paint it just as it looks

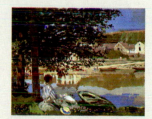

▣ **28-2A** MONET, *Bank of the Seine, Bennecourt*, 1868.

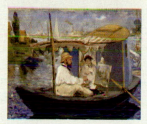

▣ **28-2B** MANET, *Monet in His Studio Boat*, 1874.

to you, the exact color and shape, until it gives your own naïve impression of the scene before you."*

Another factor encouraging Monet and some of his contemporaries to paint outdoors was the introduction of premixed pigments conveniently sold in easily portable tubes. The newly available oil paints gave artists new colors for their work and heightened their sensitivity to the multiplicity of colors in nature. After scrutinizing the effects of light and color on forms, Monet and other late-19th-century painters concluded that *local color*—an object's color in white light—becomes modified by the quality of the light shining on it, by reflections from other objects, and by the effects that juxtaposed colors produce. Shadows do not appear gray or black, as many earlier painters thought, but seem to be composed of colors modified by reflections or other conditions. If artists use complementary colors (see "19th-Century Color Theory," page 855) side by side over large enough areas, the colors intensify each other, unlike the effect of small quantities of adjoining mixed pigments, which blend into neutral tones. Furthermore, the "mixing" of colors by juxtaposing them directly on a white canvas without any preliminary sketch—also a sharp break from traditional painting practice—produces a more intense hue than the same colors mixed on the palette. Although it is not true, as some have maintained, that Monet exclusively used primary hues, placing them side by side to create secondary colors (blue and yellow, for example, to create green), he did achieve remarkably brilliant effects with his characteristically short, choppy brushstrokes, which so accurately catch the vibrating quality of light. The reason for much of the early adverse criticism leveled at Monet's paintings was that they lacked the polished surfaces and sharp contours of academic painting. In Monet's canvases, in sharp contrast to traditional oil paintings, the forms take on clarity only when the eye fuses the brushstrokes at a certain distance.

*Quoted in Linda Nochlin, *Impressionism and Post-Impressionism 1874–1904: Sources and Documents* (Englewood Cliffs, N.J.: Prentice Hall, 1966), 35.

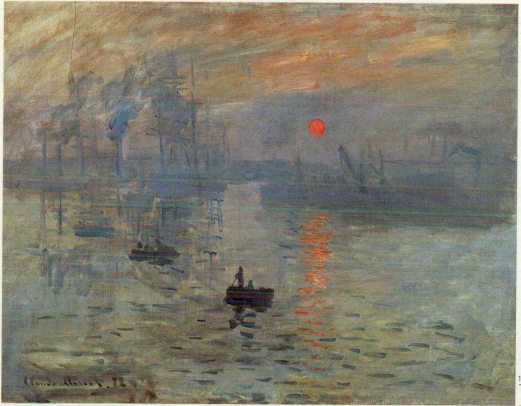

28-2 CLAUDE MONET, *Impression: Sunrise*, 1872. Oil on canvas, $1' 7\frac{1}{2}'' \times 2' 1\frac{1}{2}''$. Musée Marmottan, Paris.

Fascinated by reflected sunlight on water, Monet broke with traditional studio practice and painted his "impression" en plein air, using short brushstrokes of pure color on canvas without any preliminary sketch.

1 in.

Academic Salons and Independent Art Exhibitions

For both artists and art historians, modernist art stands in marked contrast to, indeed in forceful opposition to, academic art—that is, to the art promoted by the established art schools such as the Royal Academy of Painting and Sculpture in France (founded in 1648) and the Royal Academy of Arts in Britain (founded in 1768). These academies provided instruction for art students and sponsored exhibitions, exerting tight control over the art scene. The annual exhibitions, called "Salons" in France, were highly competitive, as was membership in these academies. Subsidized by the government, the French Royal Academy supported a limited range of artistic expression, focusing on traditional subjects and highly polished technique. Because of the challenges that modernist art presented to established artistic conventions, the juries for the Salons and other exhibitions routinely rejected the works that more adventurous artists wished to display, thereby preventing the public from viewing any art other than the officially sanctioned forms of expression. When, however, the 1855 jury rejected some of Gustave Courbet's paintings, the artist reacted by setting up his own Pavilion of Realism (see "Courbet on Realism," page 816). Years later, he wrote:

> [I]t is high time that someone have the courage to be an honest man and that he say that the Academy is a harmful, all-consuming institution, incapable of fulfilling the goal of its so-called mission.*

Growing dissatisfaction with the decisions of the French Academy's jurors prompted Napoleon III (r. 1852–1870) in 1863 to establish the Salon des Refusés (Salon of the Rejected) to show all of the works not accepted for exhibition in the regular Salon. Édouard Manet's *Le Déjeuner sur l'Herbe* (FIG. 27-32) was among them. The public greeted it and the entire exhibition with contempt. One reviewer of the rejected works summed up the prevailing attitude:

> This exhibition, at once sad and grotesque, . . . offers abundant proof . . . that the jury always displays an unbelievable leniency. Save for one or two questionable exceptions there is not a painting which deserves the honor of the official galleries . . . There is even something cruel about this exhibition; people laugh as they do at a farce.†

In 1867, after further rejections, Manet, following Courbet, mounted a private exhibition of 50 of his paintings outside the Paris World's Fair. Six years later, Claude Monet (FIGS. 28-2 to 28-4) and the other Impressionists formed their own society—essentially a painters' union modeled on other workers' unions of the era—and began mounting shows of their works in Paris. This action provided the Impressionists with great freedom because they did not have to contend with the Royal Academy's authoritative and confining viewpoint, which condemned not only the Impressionists' techniques but their modernist subject matter as well. Salon jurors regarded landscapes and cityscapes and the leisure pursuits of the middle class as unworthy themes for important artworks. The Impressionist exhibitions took place at one- or two-year intervals from 1874 until 1886. The Impressionists also displayed their work in private venues, such as the Parisian gallery owned by Paul Durand-Ruel (1831–1922), who was one of the first to recognize the important innovations of the Impressionists and who regularly exhibited their paintings.

Another group of artists unhappy with the official Salon's conservative nature adopted the same renegade idea. In 1884, these artists formed the Société des Artistes Indépendants (Society of Independent Artists) and held annual Salons des Indépendants. Georges Seurat's

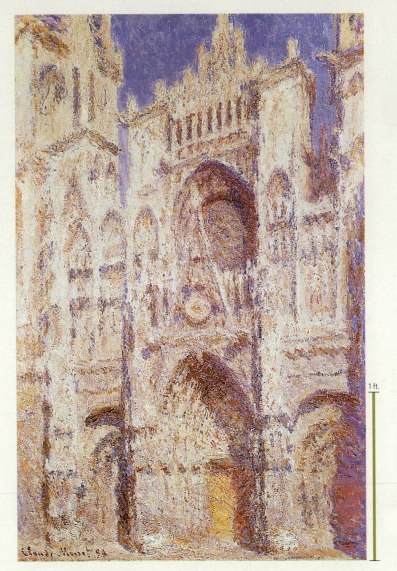

1 ft.

28-3 CLAUDE MONET, *Rouen Cathedral: The Portal (in Sun)*, 1894. Oil on canvas, 3' 3$\frac{1}{4}$" × 2' 1$\frac{7}{8}$". Metropolitan Museum of Art, New York (Theodore M. Davis Collection, bequest of Theodore M. Davis, 1915).

Monet exhibited 20 paintings of Rouen Cathedral in Paul Durand-Ruel's commercial art gallery in Paris. The canvases show the facade at different times of day and under various climatic conditions.

A Sunday on La Grande Jatte (FIG. 28-17) was one of the paintings in the Independents' 1886 Salon.

As the art market expanded, venues for the exhibition of art increased. Art circles and societies sponsored private shows in which both amateurs and professionals participated. Dealers became more aggressive in promoting the artists they represented by mounting exhibitions in a variety of spaces, some fairly intimate and small, others large and grandiose. Even nightclub owners displayed paintings for sale to their customers, following the example of Dutch innkeepers of the Baroque era (see "Middle-Class Patronage and the Art Market in the Dutch Republic," page 738). All of these proliferating opportunities for exhibition gave French artists alternatives to the traditional constraints of the Salon and provided fertile breeding ground for the development of radically new art forms and styles.

*Letter to Jules-Antoine Castagnary, October 17, 1868. Translated by Petra ten-Doesschate Chu, *Letters of Gustave Courbet* (Chicago: University of Chicago Press, 1992), 346.

†Maxime du Camp, in *Revue des deux mondes*, 1863, quoted in George Heard Hamilton, *Manet and His Critics* (New Haven: Yale University Press, New Haven, Conn., 1986), 42–43.

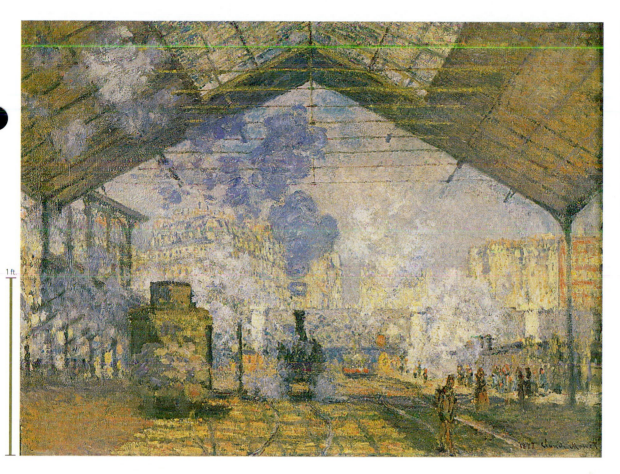

28-4 CLAUDE MONET, *Saint-Lazare Train Station*, 1877. Oil on canvas, 2' 5¾" × 3' 5". Musée d'Orsay, Paris.

The Impressionists often painted scenes of the new urbanized Paris, the heart of modern life in France. Monet's agitated application of paint contributes to the sense of energy in this railway terminal.

1 ft.

the label to be derogatory, by the third Impressionist show in 1878, the artists had embraced it and were calling themselves Impressionists. Both artists and critics had used the term before, but only in relation to sketches. Impressionist paintings do incorporate the qualities of sketches—abbreviation, speed, and spontaneity—but the artists considered their sketchlike works to be finished paintings, a radically modernist idea at the time.

CLAUDE MONET The painter of *Impression: Sunrise* was CLAUDE MONET (1840–1926), who grew up on the Normandy coast of France at Le Havre, the great seaport at the mouth of the Seine (MAP 28-1, page 846), where his father sold groceries in bulk to shipping companies. Monet began to paint at an early age, and moved to Paris in late 1862 to pursue a career as an artist, returning to Le Havre on several occasions. *Impression: Sunrise*, which is a view of that harbor, represented a sharp break from traditional landscape painting. In recording the boats, water, and sky, Monet made no attempt to disguise the brushstrokes or blend the pigment to create smooth tonal gradations and an optically accurate scene. This concern with acknowledging the paint and the canvas surface continued the modernist exploration that the Realists had begun.

The "impressionistic" application of paint is, however, only one aspect of Impressionism. Beyond its affinity with sketches, Impressionism operated at the intersection of what the artists saw and what they felt. In other words, the "impressions" these artists recorded in their paintings were neither purely objective descriptions of the exterior world nor solely subjective responses, but the interaction between the two. They were sensations, the Impressionists' subjective and personal responses to nature, formed and recorded *en plein air*—that is, outdoors (see "Painting Impressions of Light and Color," page 843).

ROUEN CATHEDRAL Monet's intensive study of the phenomena of light and color is especially evident in several series of paintings he made of the same subject. In one series, he painted more than 30 views of Rouen Cathedral, northwest of Paris, 20 of which he exhibited for sale in 1895 in a private commercial art gallery (see "Academic Salons and Independent Art Exhibitions," page 844). The subject evoked powerful associations in the popular imagination: the grandeur of France's Gothic past and of its great martyr saint, Joan of Arc, who was executed at Rouen in 1431. For each canvas in the series, Monet observed the cathedral from nearly the same viewpoint, but at different times of the day and under various climatic conditions. Often, he would work on as many as eight canvases at once, switching from one to another as the atmospheric conditions changed during the course of the day. In the painting illustrated here (FIG. 28-3), Monet depicted the church bathed in bright light. In the series as a whole, he carefully recorded the passing of time as seen in the movement of light over identical forms. To a certain degree, the real subject of Monet's painting—as the title *Rouen Cathedral: The Portal (in Sun)* implies—is not the cathedral, which he showed only in part, but the sunlight on the building's main portal. Consequently, many critics accused Monet of destroying form for fleeting atmospheric effects—an assertion that the painter probably would not have disputed, although he would have vigorously defended his approach to representation as well as his rejection of academic standards of judgment.

SAINT-LAZARE Most of the Impressionists painted scenes in and around Paris, the heart of modern life in France. Monet's *Saint-Lazare Train Station* (FIG. 28-4) depicts a characteristic aspect of the contemporary urban scene. The expanding railway network had made travel more convenient, bringing large numbers of people into Paris and enabling city dwellers to reach suburban areas, such as Bennecourt (FIG. 28-2A) and Argenteuil (FIG. 28-2B), quickly (MAP 28-1). In his "impression" of the Saint-Lazare railway terminal, Monet captured the energy and vitality of Paris's modern transportation hub. The train, emerging from the steam and smoke it emits, rumbles into the station. In the background haze are the tall buildings that were becoming a major component of the Parisian landscape. Monet's agitated paint application contributes to the sense of energy and conveys the atmosphere of urban life.

Georges Rivière (1855–1943), an art critic and friend of some of the Impressionists, saw this painting in the third Impressionist exhibition and recorded the essence of what Monet had tried to achieve:

> Like a fiery steed, stimulated rather than exhausted by the long trek that it has only just finished, [the locomotive] tosses its mane of smoke, which lashes the glass roof of the main hall. . . . We see the vast and manic movements at the station where the ground shakes with every turn of the wheel. The platforms are sticky with soot, and the air is full of that bitter scent exuded by burning coal. As we look at this magnificent picture, we are overcome by the same feelings as if we were really there, and these feelings are perhaps even more powerful, because in the picture the artist has conveyed his own feelings as well.[3]

GUSTAVE CAILLEBOTTE Monet was not the only Impressionist who considered the buildings and streets of contemporary Paris worthy subjects for their paintings. Manet, in fact, even proposed to the municipal authorities that he decorate Paris's remodeled city hall with murals depicting the metropolis's railroad stations and other emblems of modernity. (His proposal was rejected, however.) Indeed, a common interest in subjects drawn from contemporary city life bound the Impressionists together as a group more than did shared style and technique. The work of GUSTAVE CAILLEBOTTE (1849–1893), the heir to a fortune and an early collector of Impressionist paintings, is a case in point. The brushwork in his 1877 *Paris: A Rainy Day* (FIG. 28-5) bears little resemblance to Monet's or Manet's, but the subject is unmistakably Impressionist.

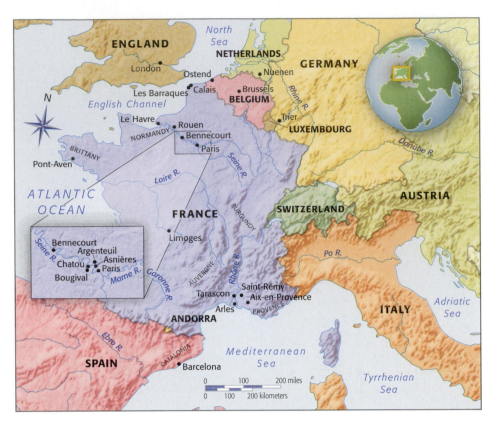

MAP 28-1 France around 1870 with towns along the Seine.

The setting of Caillebotte's painting is a junction of new boulevards resulting from the redesigning of Paris begun in 1852. The city's population had reached close to 1.5 million by midcentury and nearly doubled by 1900. To accommodate this congregation of humanity and relieve the overcrowding that many believed was a major cause of the cholera epidemic of 1849—and to facilitate the movement of troops in the event of another revolution—Napoleon III ordered Paris rebuilt. The emperor named Baron Georges Haussmann (1809–1891), superintendent of the Seine district, to oversee

28-5 GUSTAVE CAILLEBOTTE, *Paris: A Rainy Day,* 1877. Oil on canvas, 6' 9" × 9' 9". Art Institute of Chicago, Chicago (Worcester Fund).

Although Caillebotte did not use Impressionistic broken brushstrokes, in his view of the new "Haussmannized" Paris, the composition featuring cutoff buildings and figures suggests the transitory nature of modern life.

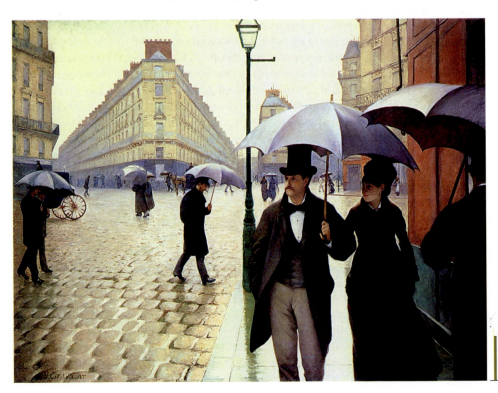

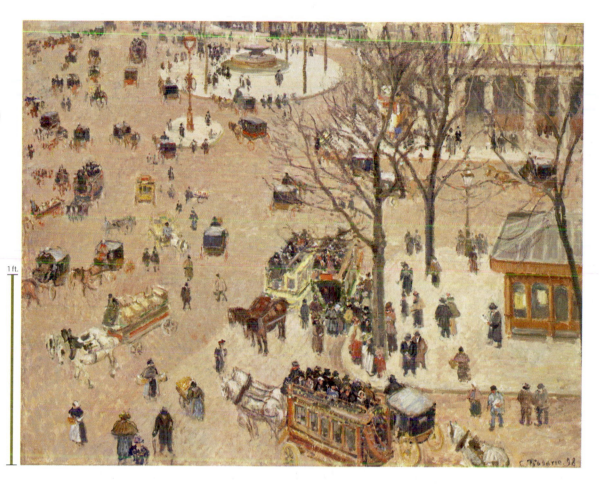

1 ft.

28-6 CAMILLE PISSARRO, *La Place du Théâtre Français*, 1898. Oil on canvas, 2' 4½" × 3' ½". Los Angeles County Museum of Art, Los Angeles (Mr. and Mrs. George Gard De Sylva Collection).

This Impressionist view of a busy Paris square seen from several stories above street level has much in common with photographs, especially the flattening spatial effect of the high viewpoint.

the entire project, which the emperor hoped would establish Paris as a world capital surpassing London. In addition to new water and sewer systems, new parks and paved plazas, street lighting, and new residential and commercial buildings, a major component of the new Paris was the creation of the wide, open boulevards seen in Caillebotte's painting. These great avenues, whose construction caused the demolition of thousands of old buildings and streets, transformed medieval Paris into the present-day city, with its superb vistas and wide, uninterrupted arteries for the flow of vehicular and pedestrian traffic. Caillebotte chose to focus on these markers of the new Paris and to commemorate them in a canvas of a size that rivaled traditional history painting.

Although Caillebotte did not dissolve his image into the broken color and brushwork characteristic of Monet's version of Impressionism, his composition is, save for the central lamppost, strongly asymmetrical and in violation of academic norms of design. The major building in the painting is at the upper left, a large empty space is at the lower left, and the largest figures are at the lower right. The frame also cuts off parts of Caillebotte's figures, underscoring that the men and women in this painting are moving and that this is a transitory moment in the life of the city and its residents. Significantly, those residents are all well-dressed Parisians of the leisure class—the only ones who could afford to live in the elegant new neighborhoods that Haussmann created. Thus, despite the sharp focus of *Paris: A Rainy Day*, the picture is the artist's "impression" of modern urban life. In fact, many city dwellers of the time complained that the new Paris was too impersonal and anonymous. Caillebotte incorporated that less celebratory view of the city by showing the pedestrians moving through Haussmann's Paris on a dreary, rainy day and by depicting all of them in similar dress and carrying identical umbrellas.

CAMILLE PISSARRO Other Impressionists also found the spacious boulevards and avenues that were the result of the "Haussmannization" of Paris attractive subjects for paintings. *La Place du Théâtre Français* (FIG. 28-6) is one of many panoramic scenes of the city painted by CAMILLE PISSARRO (1830–1903), the only Jewish member of the Impressionist movement and the only painter to submit his work to all eight Impressionist exhibitions. Born in the Danish West Indies, he settled in Paris in 1855 and was largely self-taught. Pissarro's approach to recording the new look of Paris was quite different from Caillebotte's. Using larger, rougher brushstrokes and a brighter palette, Pisarro captured his visual sensations of a crowded Parisian square viewed from several stories above street level. Unlike Monet, Pissarro did not seek to record fugitive light effects as much as the fleeting motion of street life, which he achieved through a seemingly casual arrangement of figures and horse-drawn carriages. Ironically, to accomplish this sense of spontaneity, Pissarro sometimes used photography to record the places he wished to paint, as did many of his fellow Impressionists. Indeed, the visual parallels between Impressionist paintings and photographs are striking, including, in *La Place du Théâtre Français*, the flattening spatial effect produced by the high viewpoint.

PIERRE-AUGUSTE RENOIR Ample time for leisure activities was another facet of the new, industrialized Paris, and, as noted in the opening discussion of Manet's *A Bar at the Folies-Bergère* (see page 841 and FIG. 28-1), scenes of dining and dancing, café-concerts, opera, ballet, and other forms of urban recreation became mainstays of Impressionism. Although seemingly unrelated, industrialization facilitated these pursuits. With the widespread adoption of set working hours, people's schedules became more regimented, enabling them to plan their favorite pastimes. One Impressionist

ARTISTS ON ART
Renoir on the Art of Painting

Many 19th-century artists were concerned with the theoretical basis of picture making. One of the most cogent statements on this subject is Pierre-Auguste Renoir's concise summary of how he, as an Impressionist, painted pictures and what he hoped to achieve as an artist.

> I arrange my subject as I want it, then I go ahead and paint it, like a child. I want a red to be sonorous, to sound like a bell; if it doesn't turn out that way, I add more reds and other colors until I get it. I am no cleverer than that. I have no rules and no methods; . . . I have no secrets. I look at a nude; there are myriads of tiny tints. I must find the ones that will make the flesh on my canvas live and quiver. [I]f they could explain a picture, it wouldn't be art. Shall I tell you what I think are the two qualities of art? It must be indescribable and it must be inimitable. . . . The work of art must seize upon you, wrap you up in itself, carry you away. It is the means by which the artist conveys his passions. . . . I want people to feel that neither the setting nor the figures are dull and lifeless.*

*Quoted in Eric Protter, ed., *Painters on Painting* (New York: Grosset & Dunlap, 1971), 145.

There is certainly nothing dull or lifeless about *Dance at Le Moulin de la Galette* (FIG. **28-7**), in which Renoir depicted throngs of ordinary working-class people gathered in the popular Parisian dance hall of that name. Some crowd the tables and chatter, while others dance energetically. So lively is the atmosphere that the viewer can virtually hear the sounds of music, laughter, and tinkling glasses. Unlike Manet's Folies-Bergère, a nightclub where people went to seek a new mate or the company of a prostitute, the Moulin de la Galette (Cake Mill) was a gathering place for friends, here seen on a sunny Sunday afternoon, their only day off from work. Renoir dappled the whole scene with sunlight and shade, artfully blurred into the figures to produce precisely the effect of floating and fleeting light that the Impressionists cultivated. The casual poses and asymmetrical placement of the figures and the suggested continuity of space, spreading in all directions and only accidentally limited by the frame, position the viewer as a participant rather than as an outsider. Whereas the artists favored by the French Academy frequently sought to express universal and timeless qualities (Baudelaire's "other half of art;" see page 841), the Impressionists attempted to depict just the opposite— the incidental, momentary, and passing aspects of reality. For Renoir's friends, that "reality" rang true. Several of them posed for individual figures in the painting.

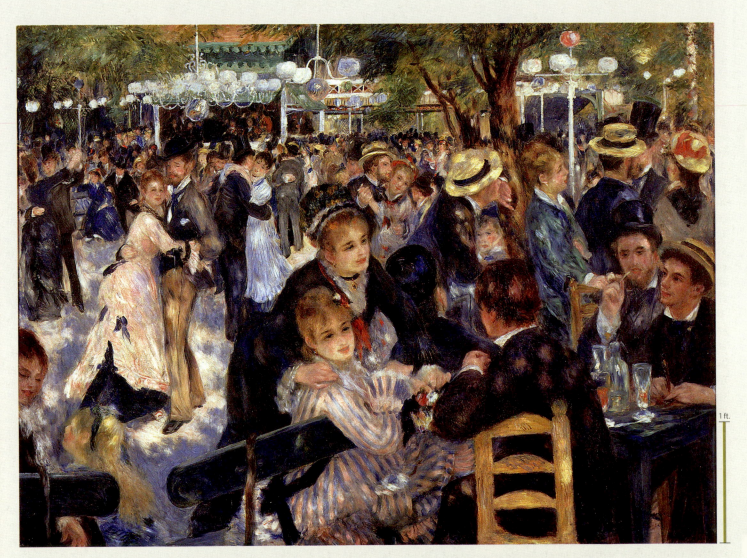

28-7 PIERRE-AUGUSTE RENOIR, *Dance at Le Moulin de la Galette*, 1876. Oil on canvas, 4' 3" × 5' 8". Musée d'Orsay, Paris.

Renoir's painting of this popular Parisian dance hall is dappled by sunlight and shade, artfully blurred into the figures to produce the effect of floating and fleeting light that many Impressionists cultivated.

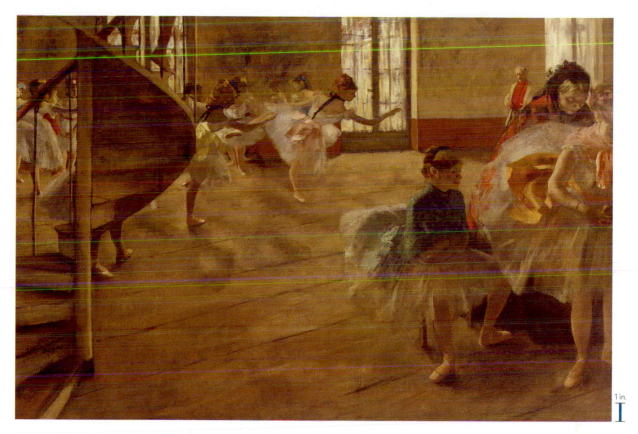

28-8 EDGAR DEGAS, *The Rehearsal*, 1874. Oil on canvas, 1' 11" × 2' 9". Glasgow Art Galleries and Museum, Glasgow (Burrell Collection).

Degas favored subjects, such as the Paris ballet, that gave him the opportunity to study the human body in motion. The high viewpoint and off-center placement of figures are characteristic aspects of his work.

who turned repeatedly to Parisian cafés and clubs for the subjects of his canvases was PIERRE-AUGUSTE RENOIR (1841–1919), whose father and mother, a tailor and dressmaker in Limoges, moved their large family to Paris in 1844 in search of a better future—the kind of individual decision that, multiplied hundreds of thousands of times, caused the population boom in Paris. Renoir trained as a porcelain painter and then entered the École des Beaux-Arts in 1862. In Paris, he met several of the Impressionists and, in 1874, painted en plein air alongside Monet and Manet at Argenteuil (FIG. 28-2B). In addition to achieving a reputation as one of the leading Impressionist painters, Renoir also became one of the most eloquent writers on the aims of Impressionism (see "Renoir on the Art of Painting," page 848). His *Dance at Le Moulin de la Galette* (FIG. 28-7) of 1876, shown in the third Impressionist exhibition, is a prime example of an Impressionist canvas portraying ordinary Parisians at leisure on Sunday afternoon at an open-air dance club. It was one of the paintings that Caillebotte purchased for himself and bequeathed to France in his will.

EDGAR DEGAS Dancing of a very different kind—ballet—was one of the favorite subjects of EDGAR DEGAS (1834–1917), the eldest son of a wealthy banker, who studied painting with a pupil of Ingres, attended the École des Beaux-Arts, and traveled extensively in Italy, but eventually rejected classicism in favor of Impressionism—or, at least, in favor of Impressionist subject matter. Unlike Monet, who personifies Impressionism for most museum-goers, Degas was not concerned with light and atmosphere. Indeed, he specialized in indoor subjects and made many preliminary studies for his finished paintings. Degas's interests were primarily recording body movement and exploring unusual angles of viewing. He was fascinated by

the formalized patterns of motion of the classical ballet performed at the Paris Opéra (FIG. 27-45) and with the training of ballerinas at its ballet school.

The Rehearsal (FIG. 28-8) is perhaps Degas's finest painting of this genre. In it and similar works, he recorded with care the unstable postures of the ballerinas, who stretch, bend, and swivel. But most of the dancers are hidden from the viewer by other figures or by the spiral stairway at the left. *The Rehearsal* is the antithesis of a classically balanced composition. The center is empty, and the floor takes up most of the canvas surface. At the margins, Degas arranged the ballerinas and their teachers in a seemingly random manner. As in other Impressionist paintings, the cutting off of figures at the left and right enhances the sense that the viewer is witnessing a fleeting moment. The implied position of that viewer is in a balcony looking down at the figures, as opposed to the head-on views of statuesque figures that were the norm in traditional paintings.

Because of his interest in patterns of movement, Degas became fascinated by photography and regularly used a camera to make preliminary studies for his works. Japanese *woodblock* prints, such as those by Suzuki Harunobu (FIG. 34-1), were another inspirational source for paintings such as *The Rehearsal*. Japanese artists used diverging lines not only to organize the flat shapes of figures but also to direct the viewer's attention into the picture space. The Impressionists, and later the Post-Impressionists, who became acquainted with these prints as early as the 1860s, greatly admired the spatial organization, familiar and intimate themes, and flat unmodeled color areas of the Japanese prints, and Degas and others avidly incorporated these features into their own paintings (see "Japonisme," page 850).

ART AND SOCIETY

Japonisme

Despite Europe's and America's extensive colonization in Asia, as elsewhere, during the 19th century, Japan's interactions with the West were very limited until 1853–1854, when Commodore Matthew Perry (1794–1858) and American naval forces exacted trading and diplomatic privileges from the Japanese court. Only then did Europeans become familiar with Japanese culture and Japanese art. The French in particular became so intrigued with everything Japanese that they coined a specific term—*Japonisme*—to describe the Japanese aesthetic, which, because of both its beauty and its exoticism, greatly appealed to the fashionable segment of Parisian society. In 1867 at the Exposition Universelle in Paris, the Japanese pavilion garnered enormous interest. Soon, Japanese kimonos, fans, lacquer cabinets, tea caddies, folding screens, tea services, and jewelry flooded Paris. Japanese-themed novels and travel books were immensely popular as well. As demand for Japanese merchandise grew in the West, the Japanese began to develop import-export businesses, and the foreign currency flowing into Japan helped finance much of its industrialization.

Artists in particular were great admirers of Japanese art. Among those influenced by the Japanese aesthetic were the Impressionists and Post-Impressionists, especially Manet, Degas, Mary Cassatt, James Abbott McNeill Whistler, Henri de Toulouse-Lautrec, Paul Gauguin, and Vincent van Gogh. Indeed, van Gogh collected and copied Japanese prints (FIG. 28-17B; compare FIG. 34-14), which were more readily available in the West than any other Asian art form. The Japanese presentation of space in woodblock prints (see "Japanese Woodblock Prints," page 1007) intrigued these artists. Because of the simplicity of the woodblock printing process, the Japanese prints feature broad areas of flat color with a limited amount of modulation or gradation. This flatness captured the imagination of modernist painters, who were seeking ways to call attention to the picture surface. The right side of Degas's *The Tub* (FIG. 28-9), for example, has this two-dimensional quality. Degas, in fact, owned a print by Japanese artist Torii Kiyonaga depicting eight women at a bath in various poses and states of undress. That print inspired Degas's painting. A comparison between Degas's bather and a detail (FIG. 28-10) of a bather from another of Kiyonaga's prints is striking, although Degas did not closely copy any of the Japanese artist's figures. But he did emulate Japanese compositional style and the distinctive angles that Japanese printmakers employed in representing human figures.

The decorative quality of Japanese images also appealed to the artists associated with the Arts and Crafts movement in England. Artists such as William Morris (FIG. 28-36) and Charles Rennie Mackintosh (FIG. 28-37) found Japanese prints attractive because those artworks intersected nicely with two fundamental Arts and Crafts principles: art should be available to the masses, and functional objects should be artistically designed.

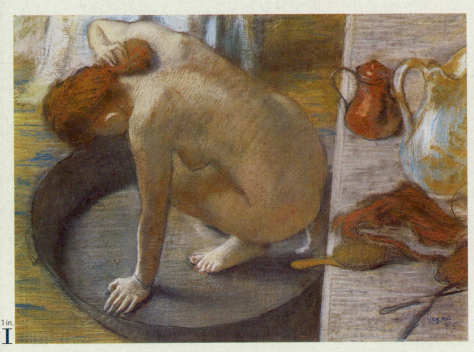

1 in.

28-9 EDGAR DEGAS, *The Tub*, 1886. Pastel, 1' 11½" × 2' 8⅜". Musée d'Orsay, Paris.

The Tub reveals the influence of Japanese prints, especially the sharp angles that artists such as Kiyonaga used in representing figures. Degas translated his Japanese model into the Impressionist mode.

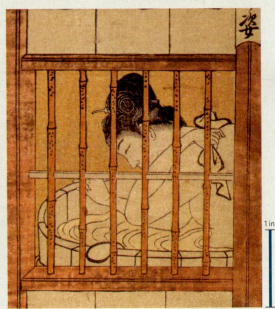

1 in.

28-10 TORII KIYONAGA, detail of *Two Women at the Bath*, ca. 1780. Color woodblock print; full print 10½" × 7½", detail 3¾" × 3½". Musée Guimet, Paris.

THE TUB The impact of Japanese prints on Degas is evident in *The Tub* (FIG. 28-9), inspired by a Japanese woodblock print similar to the one illustrated here (FIG. 28-10) by TORII KIYONAGA (1752–1815). In Degas's picture, a young woman crouches in a tub as she washes her neck with a sponge, unaware of the viewer's presence (also the case with the dancers in *The Rehearsal*). The angle of vision is so sharp that the floor and the tabletop or shelf at the right almost seem to be vertical surfaces parallel to the picture plane. Degas's combination of

ARTISTS ON ART

Whistler on "Artistic Arrangements"

Underscoring the emerging modernist idea, both in Europe and America, that paintings are independent two-dimensional artworks and not windows opening onto the three-dimensional world, American-born James Abbott McNeil Whistler, who produced his most famous works in London, named many of his paintings not according to the subjects they depicted but in abstract terms—for example, "arrangements" or "nocturnes." *Nocturne in Black and Gold* (FIG. 28-11) is a daring painting with gold flecks and splatters representing an exploded firework punctuating the darkness of the night sky. More interested in conveying the atmospheric effects than in providing details of the scene, Whistler emphasized creating a harmonious arrangement of shapes and colors on the rectangle of his canvas, an approach that many 20th-century artists adopted. Whistler's works angered conservative 19th-century critics, however. In England, John Ruskin (1819–1900) responded to *Nocturne in Black and Gold* by writing a scathing review accusing Whistler of "flinging a pot of paint in the public's face." In reply, Whistler sued Ruskin for libel. During the trial, Ruskin's attorney asked Whistler about the subject of *Nocturne*:

"What is your definition of a Nocturne?"

"It is an arrangement of line, form, and color first; . . . Among my works are some night pieces; and I have chosen the word Nocturne because it generalizes and amplifies the whole set of them. . . . The nocturne in black and gold is a night piece and represents the fireworks at Cremorne [Gardens in London]."

"Not a view of Cremorne?"

"If it were a view of Cremorne, it would certainly bring about nothing but disappointment on the part of the beholders. It is an artistic arrangement."*

The court transcript notes that the spectators in the courtroom laughed at that response, but Whistler won the case. However, his victory had sadly ironic consequences for him. The judge in the case, showing where his—and the public's—sympathies lay, awarded the artist only one farthing (less than a penny) in damages and required him to pay all of the court costs, which ruined him financially.

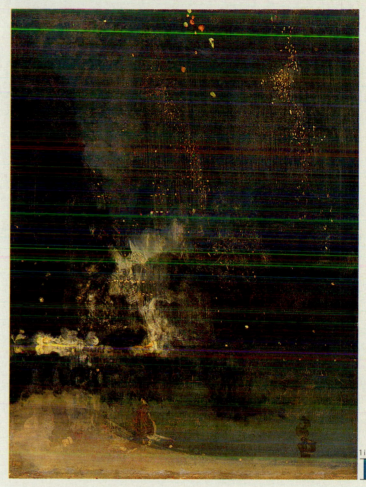

1 in.

28-11 JAMES ABBOTT MCNEILL WHISTLER, *Nocturne in Black and Gold (The Falling Rocket)*, ca. 1875. Oil on panel, 1' 11⅝" × 1' 6½". Detroit Institute of Arts, Detroit (gift of Dexter M. Ferry Jr.).

In this painting, Whistler displayed an Impressionist's interest in conveying the atmospheric effects of fireworks at night, but he also emphasized the abstract arrangement of shapes and colors.

*Quoted in Charles Harrison, Paul Wood, and Jason Gaiger, *Art in Theory, 1815–1900* (Oxford: Blackwell, 1998), 835–836.

---

the fully modeled figure of the bather and the flatness of the tub and shelf creates a visual perplexity fully consistent with the modernist exploration of the tension between illusionism and the acknowledgment that painting is a two-dimensional art form.

JAMES WHISTLER One of the important American expatriate artists in Europe during the closing decades of the 19th century was JAMES ABBOTT MCNEILL WHISTLER (1834–1903), who spent time in Paris before settling finally in London. He met several of the French Impressionists, and his art—for example, *Nocturne in Black and Gold,* or *The Falling Rocket* (FIG. 28-11)—incorporates some of their concerns and his own. Whistler shared the Impressionists' fondness for recording contemporary life and the sensations that color produces on the eye. To these interests he added his own

desire to create harmonies paralleling those achieved in music (see "Whistler on 'Artistic Arrangements,'" above). He believed that

> Nature contains the elements, in color and form, of all pictures, as the keyboard contains the notes of all music. But the artist is born to pick, and choose, and group with science, these elements, that the result may be beautiful—as the musician gathers his notes, and forms his chords, until he brings forth from chaos glorious harmony.[4]

CASSATT AND MORISOT The Impressionists were a diverse group of artists, women as well as men, from disparate economic, social, national, and religious backgrounds, united by a shared interest in the modern world that they experienced daily and a distaste for the stylistic constraints and restricted themes of academic art. The

Women Impressionists

Two of the best-known Impressionists were women. Although they came from very different backgrounds and their paintings could never be confused, both Mary Cassatt and Berthe Morisot brought a distinctively feminine viewpoint to their work, especially with regard to the subjects they chose and the way they portrayed women.

Cassatt, the daughter of a wealthy Philadelphia banker, was fortunate to live at a time when formerly all-male American colleges and art academies were opening their doors to women. She trained at the Pennsylvania Academy of the Fine Arts and then moved to Europe to study masterworks in France and Italy. Cassatt came to the attention of Degas when he saw a painting of hers in the Salon of 1874. Thereafter, she exhibited regularly with the Impressionists, but as a woman, she could not easily frequent the cafés with her male artist friends, and she had the responsibility of caring for her aging parents, who had moved to Paris to join her. Because of these restrictions, Cassatt's subjects were principally women and children, whom she presented with a combination of objectivity and genuine sentiment.

Cassatt's *The Child's Bath* (FIG. **28-12**) invites comparison with Degas's *The Tub* (FIG. 28-9). The two paintings have much in common stylistically. As in Degas's painting, the unseen artist looks down at the bathing scene from above and, similar to the contrast between the bather and the shelf in *The Tub*, the visual solidity of Cassatt's mother and child contrasts with the flattened patterning of the wallpaper and rug. Indeed, *The Child's Bath* owes much to the compositional devices of

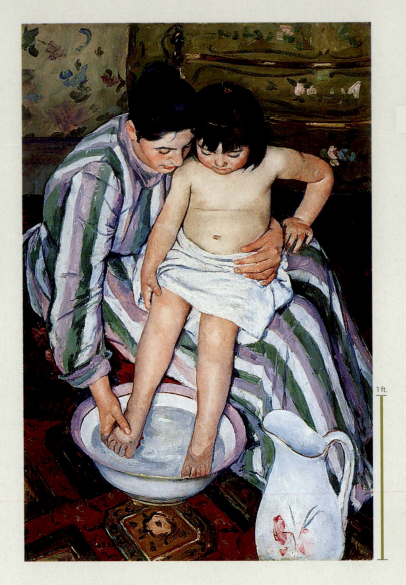

1 ft.

28-12 MARY CASSATT, *The Child's Bath*, 1893. Oil on canvas, 3' 3½" × 2' 2". Art Institute of Chicago, Chicago (Robert A. Walker Fund).

Cassatt's compositions owe much to Degas and Japanese prints, but her subjects differ from those of most Impressionists, in part because, as a woman, she could not frequent cafés with her male friends.

---

two most accomplished Impressionist women were MARY CASSATT (1844–1926), an American, who painted *The Child's Bath* (FIG. 28-12), and Frenchwoman BERTHE MORISOT (1841–1895), two of whose best paintings are *Summer's Day* (FIG. 28-13) and *In a Villa at the Seaside* (FIG. 28-13A). Their works, while having much in common with those of their male colleagues, differed from the paintings of Monet, Renoir, Degas, and the other Impressionists in important ways (see "Women Impressionists," pages 852–853).

POST-IMPRESSIONISM

By the mid-1880s, just as the Impressionists' sketchlike paintings of contemporary life in and around Paris were gaining wider acceptance, a group of younger painters—and even some of the Impressionists themselves—came to feel that in attempting to capture momentary sensations of light and color on canvas, too many important elements of traditional painting were being sacrificed. For example, in a conversation with the influential art dealer Ambroise Vollard (1866–1939) in about 1883, Renoir commented: "I had wrung Impressionism dry, and I finally came to the conclusion that I knew neither how to paint nor how to draw. In a word, Impressionism was a blind alley, as far as I was concerned."[5] Renoir's work took a different turn at that point, and other artists began to

examine more systematically the properties and expressive qualities of line, pattern, form, and color. Among them were Dutch-born Vincent van Gogh and the French painter Paul Gauguin, who focused their artistic efforts on exploring the expressive capabilities of formal elements, and Georges Seurat and Paul Cézanne, also from France, who were more analytical in orientation. Because their art had its roots in Impressionist precepts and methods, but was not stylistically homogeneous, these artists and others, including Henri de Toulouse-Lautrec, became known as the *Post-Impressionists*.

HENRI DE TOULOUSE-LAUTREC One Post-Impressionist who shared the keen interest of some of the Impressionists in Parisian nightlife was HENRI DE TOULOUSE-LAUTREC (1864–1901). His work, however, has an added satirical edge to it and often borders on caricature. Descended from the medieval counts of Toulouse, Toulouse-Lautrec began to paint as a child (his father and uncles were all amateur artists). He moved to Paris in 1882 and studied with two little-known painters, and in 1884, he set up his own studio in the Montmartre district. Genetic defects had stunted his growth and partially crippled him, leading to his self-exile from the high society that his ancient aristocratic name and wealth entitled him to enter. In Paris, he instead embraced the bohemian lifestyle and frequented Montmartre's cafés, dance halls, theaters, and brothels.

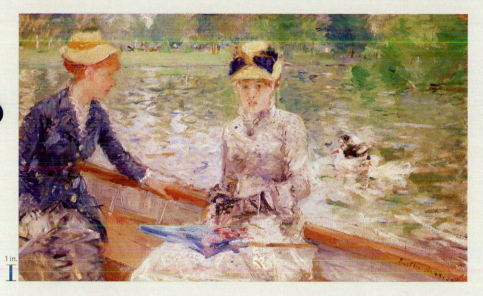

28-13 Berthe Morisot, *Summer's Day*, 1879. Oil on canvas, 1' 5$\frac{3}{4}$" × 2' 5$\frac{3}{8}$". National Gallery, London (Lane Bequest, 1917).

Morisot's subject (Parisians at leisure), bright palette, and sketchy brushstrokes typify Impressionism, but the people who inhabit her paintings are almost exclusively well-dressed, thoughtful women.

Degas as well as to Degas's sources—Japanese prints. But rather than providing a view of a nude woman unaware of the male artist-voyeur who has intruded into her private sphere, Cassatt's canvas celebrates the tender relationship between a mother and her child, both of whom gaze at their joint reflection in the tub of water.

In contrast to the expatriate American Cassatt, Morisot was raised in an upper-middle-class home in Paris, and she could not study painting at the École des Beaux-Arts because the European academies were still closed to women. Instead, she and her sister Edma took lessons from a private tutor. Berthe enjoyed some early success exhibiting in the official salons, but after meeting Édouard Manet in late 1867 or 1868 (she married his brother Eugène in 1874), she came in contact with the Impressionists and submitted nine paintings to their first exhibition in 1874 and many more to all but one of the next seven Impressionist shows.

Morisot's subject matter—the leisure activities of Parisians at resorts along the Seine or in Paris's great park called the Bois de

Boulogne—typifies the interests of many of the Impressionists. But the people who inhabit her canvases are almost exclusively women and their children, always well dressed and thoughtful, never frivolous or objects of male desire. *Summer's Day* (FIG. 28-13), originally titled *The Lake of the Bois de Boulogne* and shown in the fifth Impressionist exhibition of 1880, depicts two women in a boat on that lake. It is similar in spirit to Claude Monet's *On the Bank of the Seine, Bennecourt* (FIG. 28-2A), but Morisot's focus is the women, not the setting. Morisot herself is in the same boat, unseen, and she represented the women at a sharp angle, with parts of their bodies and most of the boat cut off by the frame, using the compositional format pioneered by Edgar Degas (FIG. 28-8) and adopted also by Cassatt. As in her other works (FIG. 28-13A), Morisot rejected contour lines in favor of patches of color that define the shapes of her figures. The sketchy brushstrokes used to paint the women merge with those of the water, unifying figure and ground in a striking two-dimensional composition that also captures all the freshness of a brightly lit summer day en plein air.

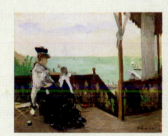

🔗 **28-13A** Morisot, *Villa at the Seaside*, 1874.

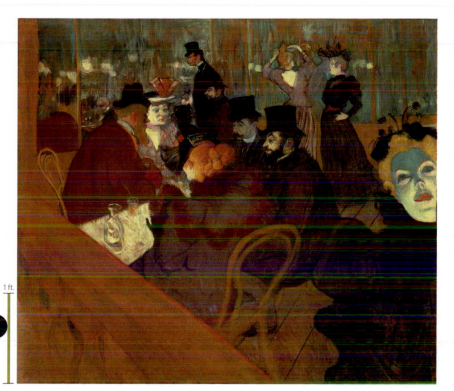

He became a denizen of the night world, consorting with the underclass of entertainers, prostitutes, and other social outcasts, bringing his sketchbook everywhere, and drinking heavily. Before dying of alcoholism at age 37, Toulouse-Lautrec devoted his brief career to depicting the city's after-hours entertainment centers, such as the Moulin Rouge (Red Mill), the subject of one of his best paintings.

At the Moulin Rouge (FIG. 28-14) reveals the influences of Degas, of Japanese prints, and of photography in the oblique and asymmetrical composition, the spatial diagonals, and the strong line patterns with added dissonant colors. But although Toulouse-Lautrec based everything he painted on firsthand

28-14 Henri de Toulouse-Lautrec, *At the Moulin Rouge*, 1892–1895. Oil on canvas, 4' × 4' 7". Art Institute of Chicago, Chicago (Helen Birch Bartlett Memorial Collection).

Toulouse-Lautrec devoted his brief career to depicting the bohemian lifestyle of Paris at night. The oblique composition, glaring lighting, masklike faces, and dissonant colors of *Moulin Rouge* typify his work.

observation, and the scenes he captured were already familiar to viewers in the work of the Impressionists, he so emphasized or exaggerated each element that the tone is new. Compare, for instance, the mood of *At the Moulin Rouge* with the relaxed and casual atmosphere of Renoir's *Dance at Le Moulin de la Galette* (FIG. 28-7). Toulouse-Lautrec's scene is decadent nightlife, with its glaring artificial light, brassy music, and assortment of corrupt, cruel, and masklike faces. (He included himself in the background—the diminutive man wearing a derby hat accompanying the very tall man, his cousin.) Such distortions by simplification of the figures and faces anticipated Expressionism (see page 885), when artists' use of formal elements—for example, brighter colors and bolder lines than ever before—increased the effect of the images on observers.

POSTER ART Toulouse-Lautrec produced many of his major works using oil-based paints on canvas, the preferred medium of Western art since the Renaissance (see "Tempera and Oil Painting," page 559), but he experimented with other media. Most notably, he explored the new art form of the poster, made possible by the perfection of multicolor lithography (see "Lithography," page 819) in the late 1870s and the development of printing presses capable of handling extra-large sheets of paper. Toulouse-Lautrec became the first great master of poster art, receiving numerous commissions from the concert-hall proprietors he befriended.

Jane Avril (FIG. 28-15), a five-color lithographic poster that appeared on hundreds of walls and windows in Paris in 1893, advertises the celebrated dancer who performed at the Jardin de Paris (Garden of Paris) cabaret. The composition reveals Toulouse-Lautrec's debt to Degas (FIGS. 28-8 and 28-9) in its oblique view from above, exaggerated foreshortening, and figures cut off by the frame. Most severely truncated is the bass viol player at the lower right, whom the artist reduced to a forearm and head and the upper part of his instrument. In fact, the musician and viol became in Toulouse-Lautrec's hands almost abstract shapes, and the lines extending from the instrument became the frame for the figure of Avril, whose left leg, kicking in the air, redirects the viewer's attention to the viol player. The composition, and especially the flat colors within prominent outlines, also owes a great deal to Japanese woodblock prints (FIGS. 34-1 and 34-12A), which late-19th-century French artists collected and admired (see "Japonisme," page 850) and even copied (FIG. 28-17B).

GEORGES SEURAT Of much more modest ancestry was the regrettably short-lived GEORGES SEURAT (1859–1891), the son of a customs official. He studied at the École des Beaux-Arts under one of Ingres's pupils, but was more intrigued by Delacroix's use of color. The subjects of Seurat's paintings of the 1880s were essentially Impressionist themes, but unlike the Impressionists and Toulouse-Lautrec, Seurat depicted modern life in a resolutely intellectual way. He devised a disciplined and painstaking system of painting focused on color analysis. Seurat was less concerned with the recording of immediate color sensations than he was with their careful and systematic organization into a new kind of pictorial order. He disciplined the free and fluent play of color characterizing Impressionism into a calculated arrangement based on scientific color theory. Seurat's system, which he called *divisionism,* but which is better known as *pointillism,* involves carefully observing color and separating it into its component parts (see "Pointillism and 19th-Century Color Theory," page 855). The artist then applies these pure component colors to the canvas in tiny dots (points) or daubs. Thus the shapes, figures, and spaces in the image become comprehensible only from a distance, when the viewer's eyes blend the many pigment dots.

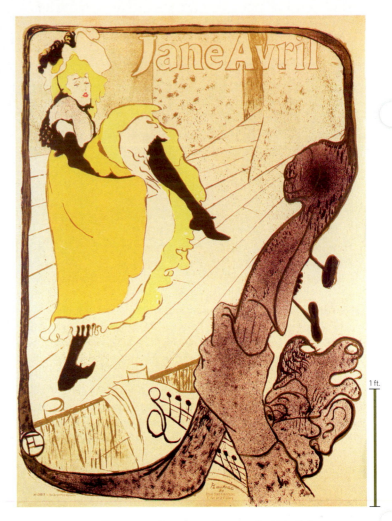

28-15 HENRI DE TOULOUSE-LAUTREC, *Jane Avril,* 1893. Color lithograph, 4' 2½" × 3' 1". San Diego Museum of Art, San Diego (gift of the Baldwin M. Baldwin Foundation).

Multicolor lithography made possible posters such as those Toulouse-Lautrec created to advertise Parisian nightclubs. The composition of *Jane Avril* owes a debt to Degas and Japanese prints.

Seurat introduced pointillism to the French public at the eighth and last Impressionist exhibition in 1886, where he displayed *A Sunday on La Grande Jatte* (FIGS. 28-16 and 28-17). According to one report, the painting attracted huge crowds, and it was impossible to get close enough to study it. La Grande Jatte (The Big Bowl) is an island in the Seine River near Asnières, one of late-19th-century Paris's rapidly growing industrial suburbs. It is the setting for a typically Impressionist recreational theme, populated by "modern people" from various classes and wearing different kinds of clothes. A sleeveless worker lounges in the left foreground next to a middle-class couple. In the center is a little girl in a spotless white dress accompanied by her fashionably attired nanny. Also present is a woman with a monkey on a leash who is almost certainly a prostitute. In short, the Sunday visitors to La Grande Jatte are a cross-section of Parisian society in the 1880s.

Seurat also shared the Impressionists' interest in analyzing light and color. But his rendition of Parisians at leisure is rigid and impersonal, unlike the spontaneous representations of Impressionism. Seurat's pointillism (FIG. 28-16) produced a carefully composed and painted image, in sharp contrast to Impressionist "sketches," incorporating repeated motifs—for example, similarly dressed women, identical parasols—to establish a rhythmic movement across the

MATERIALS AND TECHNIQUES
Pointillism and 19th-Century Color Theory

In the 19th century, advances in the sciences contributed to changing theories about color and how people perceive it. Many physicists and chemists immersed themselves in studying optical reception and the behavior of the human eye in response to light of differing wavelengths. They also investigated the psychological dimension of color. These new ideas about color and its perception provided a framework within which artists such as Georges Seurat (FIGS. 28-16 and 28-17) worked. Although historians do not know which publications on color Seurat himself read, he no doubt relied on aspects of these evolving theories to develop *pointillism*.

Discussions of color often focus on *hue* (for example, red, yellow, and blue), but it is important to consider the other facets of color—*saturation* (the hue's brightness or dullness) and *value* (the hue's lightness or darkness). Most artists during the 19th century understood the concepts of *primary colors* (red, yellow, and blue), *secondary colors* (orange, purple, and green), and *complementary colors* (red and green, yellow and purple, blue and orange; see page 7).

Chemist Michel-Eugène Chevreul (1786–1889) extended artists' understanding of color dynamics by formulating the law of *simultaneous contrasts* of colors. Chevreul asserted that juxtaposed colors affect the eye's reception of each, making the two colors as dissimilar as possible, both in hue and value. For example, placing light green next to dark green has the effect of making the light green look even lighter and the dark green darker. Chevreul further provided an explanation of *successive contrasts*—the phenomenon of colored afterimages. When a person looks intently at a color (green, for example) and then shifts to a white area, the fatigued eye momentarily perceives the complementary color (red).

Charles Blanc (1813–1882), who coined the term *optical mixture* to describe the visual effect of juxtaposed complementary colors, asserted that the smaller the areas of adjoining complementary colors, the greater the tendency for the eye to "mix" the colors, so that

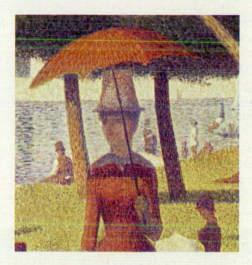

28-16 Detail of *A Sunday on La Grande Jatte* (FIG. 28-17).

Seurat's color system—pointillism—involved dividing colors into their component parts and applying those colors to the canvas in tiny dots. The forms become comprehensible only from a distance.

the viewer perceives a grayish or neutral tint. Seurat used this principle frequently in his paintings.

Also influential for Seurat was the work of physicist Ogden Rood (1831–1902), who published his ideas in *Modern Chromatics, with Applications to Art and Industry* in 1879. Expanding on the ideas of Chevreul and Blanc, Rood constructed an accurate and understandable diagram of contrasting colors. Further (and particularly significant to Seurat), Rood explored representing color gradation. He suggested that artists could achieve gradation by placing small dots or lines of color side by side, which he observed blended in the eye of the beholder when viewed from a distance.

The color experiments of Seurat and other late-19th-century artists were also part of a larger discourse about human vision and how people see and understand the world. The theories of physicist Ernst Mach (1838–1916) focused on the psychological experience of sensation. He believed that humans perceive their environments in isolated units of sensation that the brain then recomposes into a comprehensible world. Another scientist, Charles Henry (1859–1926), also pursued research into the psychological dimension of color—how colors affect people, and under what conditions. He went even further to explore the physiological effects of perception. Seurat's work, though characterized by a systematic and scientifically minded approach, also incorporated his concerns about the emotional tone of the images.

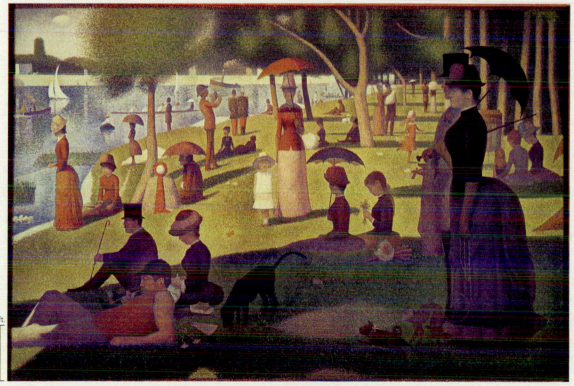

1 ft.

28-17 GEORGES SEURAT, *A Sunday on La Grande Jatte*, 1884–1886. Oil on canvas, 6' 9" × 10'. Art Institute of Chicago, Chicago (Helen Birch Bartlett Memorial Collection, 1926).

huge (almost 7-by-10-foot) canvas. Indeed, the scale of *A Sunday on La Grande Jatte* is firmly in the tradition of the Salon, unlike the intimate easel paintings of the Impressionists. Sunshine fills the picture, but Seurat did not break the light into transient patches of color. Light, air, people, and landscape are formal elements in an abstract design in which line, color, value, and shape cohere in a precise and tightly controlled organization.

VINCENT VAN GOGH In marked contrast to Seurat, VINCENT VAN GOGH (1853–1890) explored the capabilities of colors and distorted forms to express his emotions as he confronted nature. The son of a Dutch Protestant pastor, van Gogh believed he had a reli-

gious calling and did missionary work in the coal-mining area of Belgium. Repeated professional and personal failures brought him close to despair. Only after he turned to painting did he find a way to communicate his experiences. He completed his first major work, *The Potato Eaters* (FIG. **28-17A**), when he was 32 years old. Five years later, considering himself a failure as an artist and an outcast not only from artistic circles but also from society

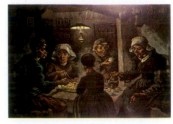

28-17A VAN GOGH, *The Potato Eaters,* 1885.

ARTISTS ON ART
The Letters of Vincent van Gogh

Throughout his life, Vincent van Gogh wrote letters to his brother Theo van Gogh (1857–1891), a Parisian art dealer, on matters both mundane and philosophical. The letters are precious documents of the vicissitudes of the painter's life and reveal his emotional anguish. In many of the letters, van Gogh also forcefully stated his views about art, including his admiration for Japanese prints (FIG. 28-17B). In one letter, he told Theo: "In both my life and in my painting, I can very well do without God but I cannot, ill as I am, do without something which is greater than I, . . . the power to create."*

For van Gogh, the power to create involved the expressive use of color. "Instead of trying to reproduce exactly what I have before my eyes, I use color more arbitrarily so as to express myself forcibly."† Color in painting, he argued, is "not locally true from the point of view of the delusive realist, but color suggesting some emotion of an ardent temperament."‡ "[It is better for a painter to] start from the colors on his palette than from the colors in nature. . . . I study nature, so as not to do foolish things . . . however, I don't care so much whether my color is exactly the same, as long as it looks beautiful on my canvas . . . I repeat, starting from one's palette, from one's knowledge of the harmony of colors is quite different from following nature mechanically and servilely."§

Some of van Gogh's letters contain vivid descriptions of his paintings, which are invaluable to art historians

in gauging his intentions and judging his success. For example, about *Night Café* (FIG. **28-18**), he wrote:

> I have tried to express the terrible passions of humanity by means of red and green. The room is blood-red and dark yellow with a green billiard table in the middle; there are four citron-yellow lamps with a glow of orange and green. Everywhere there is a clash and contrast of the most disparate reds and greens in the figures of little sleeping hooligans, in the empty, dreary room, in violet and blue. The blood-red and the yellow-green of the billiard table, for instance, contrast with the soft, tender Louis XV green of the counter, on which there is a pink nosegay. The white coat of the landlord, awake in a corner of that furnace, turns citron-yellow, or pale luminous green.**

*Vincent van Gogh to Theo van Gogh, September 3, 1888, in W. H. Auden, ed., *Van Gogh: A Self-Portrait. Letters Revealing His Life as a Painter* (New York: Dutton, 1963), 319.
†August 11, 1888. Ibid., 313.
‡September 8, 1888. Ibid., 321.
§October 2, 1885. Ibid., 253–254.
**September 8, 1888. Ibid., 320.

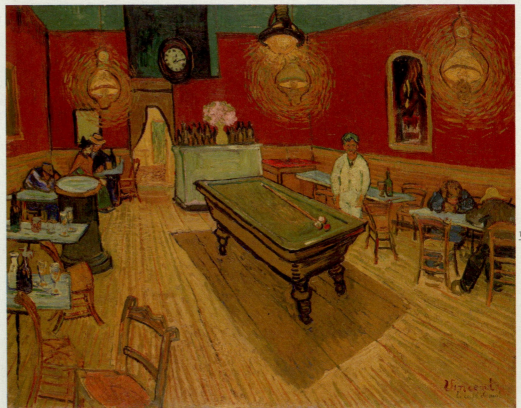

28-18 VINCENT VAN GOGH, *Night Café,* 1888. Oil on canvas, 2' 4½" × 3'. Yale University Art Gallery, New Haven (bequest of Stephen Carlton Clark).

In *Night Café,* van Gogh explored ways that colors and distorted forms can express emotions. The thickness, shape, and direction of the brushstrokes create a tactile counterpart to the intense colors.

1 ft.

at large, van Gogh fatally shot himself. He sold only one painting during his lifetime. Since his death, however, van Gogh's reputation and the appreciation of his art have grown dramatically. Subsequent painters, especially the Fauves and German Expressionists (see pages 883 and 885), built on van Gogh's expressive use of color. This kind of influence is an important factor in determining artistic significance, and it is no exaggeration to state that today van Gogh is one of the most revered artists in history.

NIGHT CAFÉ Van Gogh moved to Paris in 1886, where he began to collect—and copy (FIG. **28-17B**)—Japanese prints. In 1881, he relocated to Arles in southern France, where he painted *Night Café* (FIG. **28-18**), one of his most important and innovative canvases. Although the subject is apparently benign, van Gogh invested

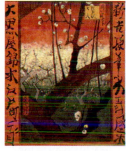

it with a charged energy. As he stated in a letter to his brother Theo (see "The Letters of Vincent van Gogh," page 856), he wanted the painting to convey an oppressive atmosphere—"a place where one can ruin one's self, go mad, or commit a crime. . . . [I want] to express the power of darkness in a low drinking spot . . . in an atmosphere like a devil's furnace."[6] The room is seen from above, and the floor takes up a large portion of the canvas, as in the paintings of Degas (FIG. 28-9). The ghostlike proprietor stands at the edge of the café's billiard table, disengaged from his customers, as they are from each other. Van Gogh depicted the billiard table in such a steeply tilted perspective that it threatens to slide out of the painting into the viewer's space. He communicated the "madness" of the place by selecting vivid hues whose juxtaposition augmented their intensity.

Van Gogh's insistence on the expressive values of color led him to develop a corresponding expressiveness in his paint application. The thickness, shape, and direction of his brushstrokes created a tactile counterpart to his intense color schemes. He moved the brush vehemently back and forth or at right angles, giving a textilelike effect, or squeezed dots or streaks onto the canvas directly from his paint tube. This bold, almost slapdash attack enhanced the intensity of his colors.

STARRY NIGHT Similarly illustrative of van Gogh's "expressionist" method is *Starry Night* (FIG. **28-19**), which the artist painted in 1889, the year before his death. At this time, van Gogh was living at the asylum of Saint-Paul-de-Mausole in Saint-Rémy, near Arles, where he had committed himself. In *Starry Night*, the artist did not represent the sky's appearance. Rather, he communicated his feelings about the electrifying vastness of the universe, filled with whirling and exploding stars, with the earth and humanity huddling beneath it. The church nestled in the center of the village is, perhaps, van Gogh's attempt to express or reconcile his conflicted views about religion. Although the style of *Starry Night* suggests a very personal vision, this work does correspond in many ways to the view available to the painter from the window of his room in Saint-Paul-de-Mausole. The existence of cypress trees and the placement of the constellations have been confirmed as matching the view visible to van Gogh during his stay in the asylum. Still, the artist translated everything he saw into his singular vision. Given van Gogh's determination to "use color . . . to express [him]self forcibly," the dark, deep blue suffusing the entire painting cannot be overlooked.

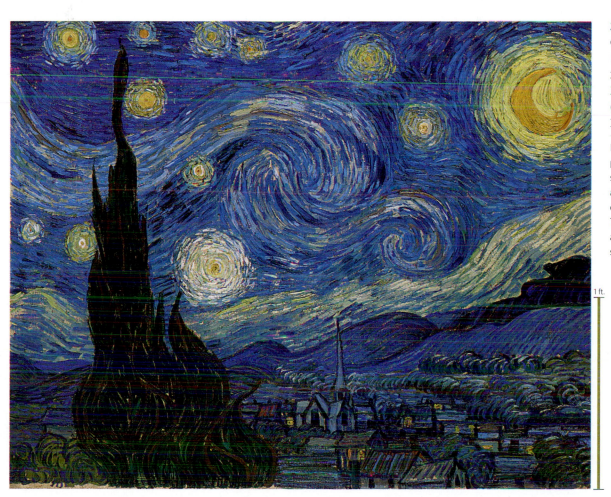

28-19 VINCENT VAN GOGH, *Starry Night*, 1889. Oil on canvas, 2' 5" × 3' $\frac{1}{4}$". Museum of Modern Art, New York (acquired through the Lillie P. Bliss Bequest).

In this late work, van Gogh painted the vast night sky filled with whirling and exploding stars, the earth huddled beneath it. The painting is an almost abstract pattern of expressive line, shape, and color.

1 ft.

Together with the turbulent brushstrokes, the color suggests a quiet but pervasive depression. A letter van Gogh wrote to his brother on July 16, 1888, reveals his contemplative state of mind:

> Perhaps death is not the hardest thing in a painter's life. . . . [L]ooking at the stars always makes me dream, as simply as I dream over the black dots representing towns and villages on a map. Why, I ask myself, shouldn't the shining dots of the sky be as accessible as the black dots on the map of France? Just as we take the train to get to Tarascon or Rouen, we take death to reach a star.[7]

PAUL GAUGUIN Until he lost his job in the stock market crash of 1882, PAUL GAUGUIN (1848–1903) was a stockbroker in Paris. In 1883, penniless, he decided to try to make his living as an artist, having painted as an amateur for many years. Three years later, attracted by Brittany's unspoiled culture, its ancient Celtic folkways, the still-medieval Catholic piety of its people, and its much lower cost of living, Gauguin moved to Pont-Aven, which had become a popular artists' colony. Although in the 1870s and 1880s, Brittany had been transformed into a profitable market economy focused on tourism, Gauguin still viewed the Bretons as "natural" men and women, perfectly at ease in what he regarded as their unspoiled peasant environment.

At Pont-Aven, Gauguin painted *Vision after the Sermon* (FIG. **28-20**), also known as *Jacob Wrestling with the Angel,* his most important early work. The painting shows Breton women, wearing their starched white Sunday caps and black dresses, visualizing the sermon they have just heard in church on Jacob's encounter with the Holy Spirit (Gen. 32:24–30). Joining the women, at the far right, is a tonsured monk who has Gauguin's features. The women and the monk pray devoutly before the apparition, as they would have before the roadside crucifix shrines that were characteristic features of the Breton countryside. Gauguin departed from optical realism and composed the picture elements to focus the viewer's attention on the idea and intensify its message. The images are not what the Impressionist eye would have seen and replicated but what Gauguin's memory recalled and his imagination modified. Thus the artist twisted the perspective and allotted most of the space to emphasize the innocent faith of the unquestioning women, and he shrank Jacob and the angel, wrestling in a ring enclosed by a Breton stone fence. Wrestling matches were regular features at the entertainment held after high mass, so Gauguin's women are spectators at a contest that was, for them, a familiar part of their culture.

28-20 PAUL GAUGUIN, *Vision after the Sermon (Jacob Wrestling with the Angel)*, 1888. Oil on canvas, 2′ 4 $\frac{3}{4}$″ × 3′ $\frac{1}{2}$″. National Gallery of Scotland, Edinburgh.

Gauguin admired Japanese prints, stained glass, and cloisonné enamels. Their influences are evident in this painting of Breton women, in which firm outlines enclose large areas of unmodulated color.

Gauguin did not unify the picture with a horizon perspective, light and shade, or naturalistic use of color. Instead, he abstracted the scene into a pattern, with the diagonal tree limb symbolically dividing the spiritual from the earthly realm. Pure unmodulated color fills flat planes and shapes bounded by firm line: white caps, black dresses, and the red field of combat. Gauguin admired Japanese prints and medieval *cloisonné* metalwork (see "Cloisonné," page 313) and *stained glass* (see "Stained-Glass Windows," page 384). These art forms contributed significantly to his daring experiment to transform traditional painting and Impressionism into abstract, expressive patterns of line, shape, and pure color. Like van Gogh, with whom he painted for a brief period in Arles in 1888, Gauguin rejected objective representation in favor of subjective expression. For Gauguin, the artist's power to determine the colors in a painting was a central element of creativity. However, whereas van Gogh's heavy, thick brushstrokes were an important component of his expressive style, Gauguin's color areas appear flatter, often visually dissolving into abstract patches or patterns.

WHERE DO WE COME FROM? In 1888, Gauguin, continuing his restless search for an inexpensive and unspoiled place to live, settled in Tahiti (MAP 36-1). The Polynesian island attracted Gauguin because he believed that it offered him a life far removed from materialistic Europe as well as an opportunity to reconnect with nature. On his arrival, he discovered that Tahiti, under French control since 1842, had been extensively colonized and that its capital, Papeete, was filthy and dangerous. Deeply disappointed, Gauguin tried to maintain his vision of an untamed paradise by moving to the Tahitian countryside, where he expressed his fascination with primitive life in a series of canvases in which he often based the design, though indirectly, on native motifs. The tropical flora of the island inspired the colors he chose for these paintings—unusual harmonies of lilac, pink, and lemon.

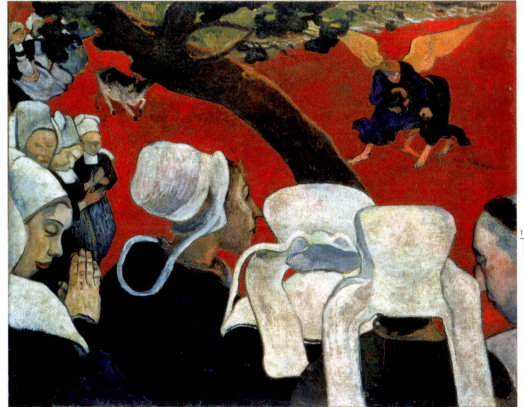

1 ft.

ARTISTS ON ART
Gauguin on *Where Do We Come From?*

Paul Gauguin's *Where Do We Come From? What Are We? Where Are We Going?* (FIG. 28-21), painted in Tahiti in 1897, was, in the artist's judgment, his most important work. The scene is a tropical landscape, populated with native women and children. Despite the setting, most of the canvas surface, other than the figures, consists of broad areas of flat color, which convey a lushness and intensity.

Two of Gauguin's letters to friends contain lengthy discussions of this work and shed important light on the artist's intentions and on the painting's meaning.

> Where are we going? Near to death an old woman.... What are we? Day to day existence.... Where do we come from? Source. Child. Life begins.... Behind a tree two sinister figures, cloaked in garments of somber color, introduce, near the tree of knowledge, their note of anguish caused by that very knowledge in contrast to some simple beings in a virgin nature, which might be paradise as conceived by humanity, who give themselves up to the happiness of living.*

> I wanted to kill myself. I went to hide in the mountains, where my corpse would have been eaten up by ants. I didn't have a revolver but I did have arsenic ... Was the dose too large, or was it the fact of vomiting, which overcame the effects of the poison by getting rid of it? I know not..... Before I died I wanted to paint a large canvas that I had worked out in my head, and all month long I worked day and night at fever pitch. I can assure you it's nothing like a canvas by Puvis de Chavannes [FIG. 28-24], with studies from nature, then a preparatory cartoon, etc. No, it's all done without a model, feeling my way with the tip of the brush on a piece of sackcloth that is full of knots and rough patches; so it looks terribly unpolished. People will say it is slipshod, unfinished ... [but] I do believe that not only is this painting worth more than all the previous ones but also that I will never do a better one or another like it. I put all my energy into it before dying, such painful passion amid terrible circumstances ... and life burst from it.†

Some details of the painting have resisted interpretation because Gauguin's symbolism is so personal, but the general meaning of *Where Do We Come From?* is clear. It is a sobering, pessimistic image of the inevitability of the life cycle, beginning, at the right, with infancy. At the center is a Polynesian Eve in the prime of youth picking fruit from a tree. At the left, with a Tahitian idol in the background, is a crouching old woman contemplating death.

It is noteworthy that, contrary to Gauguin's assertion in the quoted letter, he did make a detailed preliminary drawing, now in the Louvre, for *Where Do We Come From?* He is here altering the facts in order to establish a persona for himself as an inspired genius who created great works without recourse to traditional studio methods. Some scholars have even suggested that he intended his suicide attempt to fail.

*Letter to Charles Morice, March 1898. Translated by Belinda Thompson, *Gauguin by Himself* (Boston: Little, Brown, 1993), 270–271.

†Letter to Daniel de Monfreid, February 1898. Translated by Thompson, ibid., 257–258.

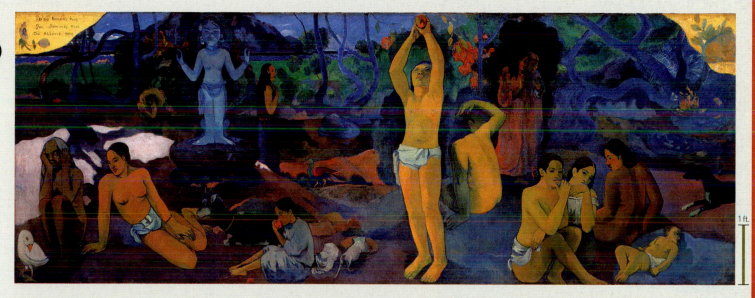

28-21 PAUL GAUGUIN, *Where Do We Come From? What Are We? Where Are We Going?* 1897. Oil on canvas, 4' 6¾" × 12' 3". Museum of Fine Arts, Boston (Tompkins Collection).

In search of a place far removed from European materialism, Gauguin moved to Tahiti, where he used native women and tropical colors to present a pessimistic view of the inevitability of the life cycle.

Despite the allure of the South Pacific, Gauguin continued to struggle with life. His health suffered, and his art had a hostile reception. In 1897, worn down by these obstacles, Gauguin decided to poison himself, but not before painting a mural-sized canvas titled *Where Do We Come From? What Are We? Where Are We Going?* (FIG. 28-21), which he wrote about in letters to his friends (see "Gauguin on *Where Do We Come From?*" above). His attempt to commit suicide in Tahiti was unsuccessful, but Gauguin died a few years later, in 1903, in the Marquesas Islands, his artistic genius still unrecognized.

PROBLEMS AND SOLUTIONS
Making Impressionism Solid and Enduring

Paul Cézanne's desire to "make of Impressionism something solid and enduring" led him to formulate a new approach to the art of painting, whether his subject was landscape (FIG. 28-22), still life (FIG. 28-23), or the human figure (FIG. 28-23A). Cézanne's distinctive way of studying nature is evident in *Mont Sainte-Victoire* (FIG. 28-22), one of many views that he painted of this mountain near his home in Aix-en-Provence. His aim was not truth in appearance, especially not photographic truth, nor was it the "truth" of Impressionism. Rather, he sought a lasting structure behind the formless and fleeting visual information that the eyes absorb. Instead of employing the Impressionists' random approach when he was face-to-face with nature, Cézanne, like Seurat, developed a more analytical style. His goal was to order the lines, planes, and colors of nature. He constantly and painstakingly checked his painting against the part of the scene—he called it the "motif"—that he was studying at the moment.

In a March 1904 letter, Cézanne stated his goal as a painter: "[to do] Poussin over entirely from nature . . . in the open air, with color and light, instead of one of those works imagined in a studio, where everything has the brown coloring of feeble daylight without reflections from the sky and sun."* He sought to achieve Poussin's effects of distance, depth, structure, and solidity, not by using traditional perspective and chiaroscuro, but rather by recording the color patterns that he deduced from an optical analysis of nature.

Cézanne set out to explore the properties of line, plane, and color, and their interrelationships. He studied the capacity of lines and planes to create the sensation of depth, the intrinsic qualities of color, and the power of colors to modify the direction and depth of lines and planes. To create the illusion of three-dimensional form and space, Cézanne focused on carefully selecting colors. He understood that the visual properties—hue, saturation, and value—of different colors vary (see "Color Theory," page 855). Cool colors tend to recede, whereas warm ones advance. By applying to the canvas small patches of juxtaposed colors, some advancing and some receding, Cézanne created volume and depth in his works. On occasion, the artist depicted objects chiefly in one hue and achieved convincing solidity by modulating the intensity (or saturation). At other times, he juxtaposed contrasting colors—for example, green, yellow, and red—of similar saturation to compose specific objects, such as fruit or bowls.

For example, in *Mont Sainte-Victoire*, Cézanne replaced the transitory visual effects of changing atmospheric conditions, effects that preoccupied Monet, with a more concentrated, lengthier analysis of the colors in large lighted spaces. The main space stretches out behind and beyond the canvas plane and includes numerous small elements, such as roads, fields, houses, and the viaduct at the far right, each seen from a slightly different viewpoint. Above this shifting, receding perspective—so different from traditional Renaissance perspective with the viewer standing in a fixed position and with a single vanishing point (see "Linear Perspective," page 587)—the largest mass of all, the mountain, seems simultaneously to be both near and far away, an effect achieved by equally stressing background and foreground contours. Cézanne's rendition of nature approximates the experience that a person has when viewing the forms of nature piecemeal. The relative proportions of objects vary, rather than being fixed by strict linear perspective. Cézanne immobilized the shifting colors of Impressionism into an array of clearly defined planes composing the objects and spaces in his scene. Describing his method in a letter to a fellow painter, he wrote:

> [T]reat nature by the cylinder, the sphere, the cone, everything in proper perspective so that each side of an object or a plane is directed towards a central point. Lines parallel to the horizon give breadth . . . Lines perpendicular to this horizon give depth. But nature for us men is more depth than surface, whence the need of introducing into our light vibrations, represented by reds and yellows, a sufficient amount of blue to give the impression of air.†

*Cézanne to Émile Bernard, March 1904. Quoted in Robert Goldwater and Marco Treves, eds., *Artists on Art, from the XIV to the XX Century* (New York: Pantheon, 1945), 363.
†Cézanne to Émile Bernard, April 15, 1904. Ibid., 363.

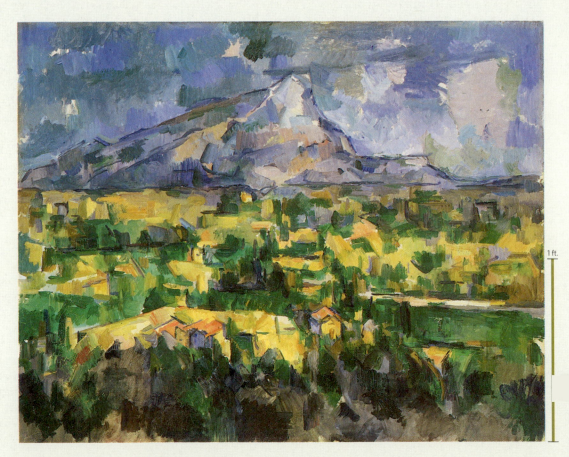

28-22 PAUL CÉZANNE, *Mont Sainte-Victoire*, 1902–1904. Oil on canvas, 2' 3½" × 2' 11¼". Philadelphia Museum of Art, Philadelphia (George W. Elkins Collection).

In his landscapes, Cézanne replaced the transitory visual effects of changing atmospheric conditions—the Impressionists' focus—with careful analysis of the lines, planes, and colors of nature.

1 ft.

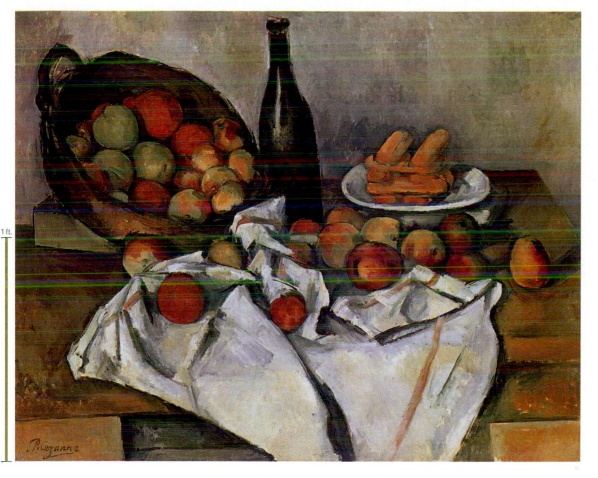

28-23 Paul Cézanne, *Basket of Apples*, ca. 1895. Oil on canvas, 2' 3/8" × 2' 7". Art Institute of Chicago, Chicago (Helen Birch Bartlett Memorial Collection, 1926).

Cézanne's still lifes reveal his analytical approach to painting. He captured the solidity of bottles and fruit by juxtaposing color patches, but the resulting abstract shapes are not optically realistic.

PAUL CÉZANNE Trained as a painter in his native Aix-en-Provence in southern France, Paul Cézanne (1839–1906) allied himself early in his career with the Impressionists, especially Pissarro (FIG. 28-6), and participated in the first (1874) and third (1877) Impressionist exhibitions in Paris. Initially, Cézanne accepted the Impressionists' color theories and their faith in subjects chosen from everyday life, but his own studies of traditional works of Western art in the Louvre persuaded him that Impressionism lacked form and structure. Cézanne declared that he wanted to "make of Impressionism something solid and enduring like the art in the museums."[8] In works such as *Mont Sainte-Victoire* (FIG. 28-22), he achieved that goal (see "Making Impressionism Solid and Enduring," page 860).

BASKET OF APPLES Still life, even more than landscape, proved to be a very effective vehicle for Cézanne's experiments in remaking Impressionism to emphasize the permanent instead of the transitory. In still-life painting, Cézanne could arrange a limited number of selected objects to provide a well-ordered point of departure. So analytical was Cézanne in preparing, observing, and painting still lifes (in contrast to the Impressionist emphasis on spontaneity) that he had to abandon using real fruit and flowers because they tended to rot. In *Basket of Apples* (FIG. 28-23), the objects have lost something of their individual character as bottles and fruit and have almost become cylinders and spheres. Cézanne captured the solidity of each object by juxtaposing color patches. His interest in the study of volume and solidity is evident from the disjunctures in the painting—the table edges are discontinuous, and various objects seem to be depicted from different vantage points. In his zeal to understand three-dimensionality and to convey the placement of forms relative to the space around them, Cézanne explored his still-life

arrangements from different viewpoints. This resulted in paintings that, though conceptually coherent, do not appear optically realistic.

Cézanne's approach to painting was consistent with the concern of 19th-century modernist painters with the integrity of the painting surface. Viewers of Cézanne's paintings are always aware that the three-dimensional forms they see are in reality two-dimensional patterns of line and color on a flat picture plane. Cézanne's legacy was significant. Especially his late works, such as the unfinished *The Large Bathers* (FIG. 28-23A), profoundly influenced the development of Cubism in the early 20th century (see page 892).

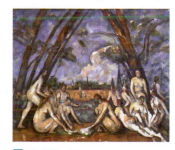

⊡ **28-23A** Cézanne, *Large Bathers*, 1906.

SYMBOLISM

The Impressionists and Post-Impressionists believed that their emotions and sensations were important elements for interpreting the world around them, but the depiction of what they could see—people, buildings and boulevards, landscapes, still lifes—remained their primary focus, as it had for the Realists before them. By the end of the 19th century, however, many artists turned their attention away from the real world to the imaginary. These artists, seeking to express their individual spirit, rejected the optical world of daily life in favor of a fantasy world, of forms they conjured in their free imagination. Color, line, and shape, divorced from conformity to the optical image, became symbols of personal emotions in response to

WRITTEN SOURCES
Albert Aurier on Symbolism

An early champion of Paul Gauguin, Albert Aurier published an influential essay in March 1891 in the journal *Mercure de France* in which he described the singular contribution of Gauguin to modern painting and used Gauguin's work to define Symbolism in painting. Aurier argued that

> The goal of painting . . . cannot be the direct representation of objects. Its end purpose is to express ideas as it translates them into a special language. Indeed, in the eyes of the artist . . . objects . . . have a significance only insofar as they are objects. The artist sees them only as *signs*, letters of an immense alphabet that only the genius knows how to read. To write one's thought, one's poem, with those signs, all the while remembering that the sign, however indispensable, is nothing in itself and the idea alone is everything—such appears to be the task of the artist whose eye can determine the evocative potential of tangible objects. . . . As a result, certain laws must govern pictorial imitation. The artist, in every form of art, must carefully avoid . . . concrete truth, illusionism, trompe-l'oeil. Indeed, he must not convey in his picture a false impression of nature that would act on the spectator like nature itself. . . . In consequence, the strict duty of the ideist painter is to make a reasoned selection from the multiple elements of objective reality, to use in his work only the lines, forms, general and distinctive colors that enable him to describe precisely the ideic significance of the object . . . To sum up and conclude, the work

of art as I have evoked it logically, is *Ideist* . . . *Symbolist* . . . *Synthetic* . . . and *Decorative*.*

Although he never formally identified himself with the Symbolists, the French painter PIERRE PUVIS DE CHAVANNES (1824–1898) became a major inspiration for those artists. In striking contrast to the Impressionists and Post-Impressionists, whose work was routinely rejected by the official Salons, Puvis served as a Salon juror until he resigned in 1872 to protest the narrowness of the other jurors. Puvis, nevertheless, was no admirer of Realism or Impressionism, producing instead an ornamental and reflective art incorporating classical imagery—a categorical rejection of the Realist and Impressionist focus on the everyday world.

In *Sacred Grove* (FIG. **28-24**), which may have influenced Seurat's *Grande Jatte* (FIG. 28-17), Puvis deployed statuesque figures in a tranquil landscape with a Greco-Roman shrine. Suspended in timeless poses, the figures have simple and sharp contours, and their modeling is as shallow as *bas-relief* sculpture. The calm and still atmosphere suggests some consecrated place where all movements and gestures have a permanent ritual significance. The stillness and simplicity of the forms, the linear patterns that their rhythmic contours create, and the suggestion of their symbolic weight constitute a type of anti-Realism. Puvis garnered support from a wide range of artists, from, at one extreme, the conservative members of the French Academy and the government, who applauded his classicism, to the Symbolists, who revered Puvis for his vindication of imagination and his independence from the capitalist world of materialism and the machine.

*Translated by Henri Dorra, ed., *Symbolist Art Theories: A Critical Anthology* (Berkeley and Los Angeles: University of California Press, 1995), 199–200.

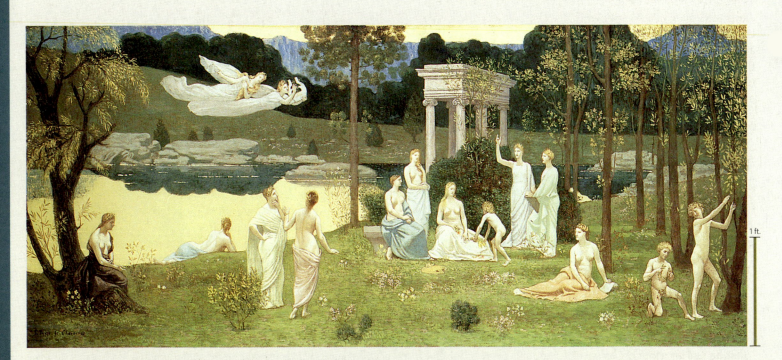

1 ft.

28-24 PIERRE PUVIS DE CHAVANNES, *Sacred Grove*, 1884. Oil on canvas, 2' 11½" × 6' 10". Art Institute of Chicago, Chicago (Potter Palmer Collection).

The Symbolists revered Puvis de Chavannes for his rejection of Realism. His statuesque figures in timeless poses inhabit a tranquil landscape, their gestures suggesting a symbolic ritual significance.

the world. Deliberately choosing to stand outside of convention and tradition, these artists spoke in signs and symbols.

Many of the artists following this path adopted an approach to subject and form that associated them with a general European movement called *Symbolism*. Symbolists, whether painters or writers, disdained Realism as trivial. The task of Symbolist artists, both visual and verbal, was not to see things but to see through them to a significance and reality far deeper than what superficial appearance revealed. In so doing, as the poet Arthur Rimbaud (1854–1891) insisted, artists became beings of extraordinary insight. (One group of Symbolist painters called itself the *Nabis*, the Hebrew word for "prophet.") Rimbaud, whose poems had great influence on the artistic community, went so far as to say, in his *Letter from a Seer* (1871), that to achieve the seer's insight, artists must become deranged. In effect, they must systematically unhinge and confuse the everyday faculties of sense and reason, which serve only to blur artistic vision. The artists' mystical vision must convert the objects of the commonsense world into symbols of a reality beyond that world and, ultimately, a reality from within the individual. Elements of Symbolism were already present in the works of van Gogh and especially Gauguin—for example, *Vision after the Sermon* (FIG. 28-20) and *Where Do We Come From?* (FIG. 28-21). In fact, one of the most coherent and influential definitions of Symbolist art appeared in an 1891 essay, "Symbolism in Painting: Paul Gauguin," by Albert Aurier (1865–1892), a leading Symbolist poet and art critic (see "Albert Aurier on Symbolism," page 862).

The extreme subjectivism of the Symbolists led them to cultivate all the resources of fantasy and imagination, no matter how deeply buried or obscure. Moreover, they urged artists to stand against the vulgar materialism and conventional values of industrial and middle-class society. Above all, the Symbolists wished to purge literature and art of anything utilitarian, to cultivate an exquisite aesthetic sensitivity. The subjects of the Symbolists, conditioned by this reverent attitude toward art and exaggerated aesthetic sensation, became increasingly esoteric and exotic, mysterious, visionary, dreamlike, and fantastic—the opposite of "concrete truth, illusionism, trompe-l'oeil." Perhaps not coincidentally, contemporary with the Symbolists, Sigmund Freud (1856–1939), the founder of psychoanalysis, began the age of psychiatry with his *Interpretation of Dreams* (1900), an introduction to the concept and the world of unconscious experience.

GUSTAVE MOREAU One of the foremost Symbolist painters was GUSTAVE MOREAU (1826–1898), who entered the École des Beaux-Arts at age 20. Toward the end of his career, in 1892, Moreau became a professor there, but he lived most of his life as a recluse in his townhouse at 14 rue de la Rochefoucauld in Paris, today the Musée Gustave Moreau. An admirer of Eugène Delacroix, Moreau loved exotic settings and rich colors, but his subjects, often drawn from classical mythology and the Bible, transcend those of Romanticism to embrace the world of imagination and spirituality celebrated by Symbolist writers.

The Apparition (FIG. 28-25), one of two versions of the same subject that Moreau submitted to the Salon of 1876, treats a theme that fascinated him and many of his contemporaries—the *femme fatale* ("fatal woman"), the destructive temptress of men. The seductive heroine here is the biblical Salome (Mark 6:21–28), who pleased her stepfather, King Herod, by dancing enticingly before him and demanded in return the head of Saint John the Baptist (compare FIG. 21-8). In Moreau's representation of the story, Herod sits in

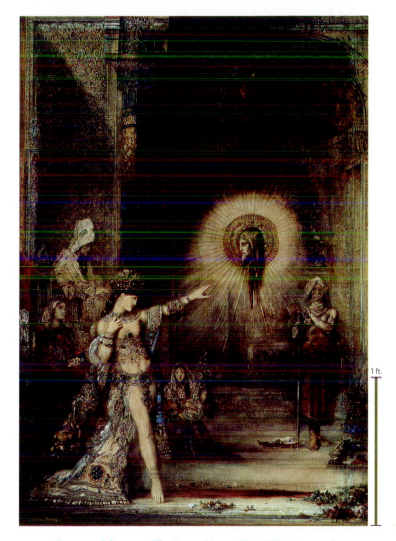

1 ft.

28-25 GUSTAVE MOREAU, *The Apparition*, 1874–1876. Watercolor on paper, 3' 5¾" × 2' 4⅜". Musée du Louvre, Paris.

Moreau's painting of Salome, a biblical femme fatale, combines hallucinatory imagery, eroticism, precise drawing, rich color, and an opulent setting—hallmarks of Moreau's Symbolist style.

the background, enthroned not in a Middle Eastern palace but in a classical columnar hall resembling a Roman triumphal arch. Salome is in the foreground, scantily clad in a gold- and gem-encrusted costume. She points to an apparition hovering in the air at the level of Herod's head. In a radiant circle of light is what Salome desired—the halo-framed head of John the Baptist, dripping with blood but with eyes wide open. The combination of hallucinatory imagery, eroticism, precise drawing, rich color, and opulent setting is the hallmark of Moreau's highly original style. *The Apparition* and Moreau's other major paintings—for example, *Jupiter and Semele* (FIG. **28-25A**)—foreshadow the work of the Surrealists in the next century (see page 921).

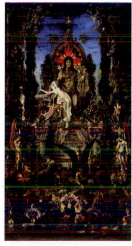

28-25A MOREAU, *Jupiter and Semele*, ca. 1875.

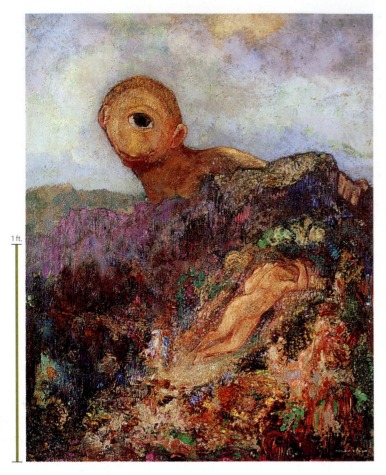

28-26 ODILON REDON, *The Cyclops,* 1898. Oil on canvas, 2' 1" × 1' 8". Kröller-Müller Foundation, Otterlo.

In *The Cyclops,* the Symbolist painter Odilon Redon represented the mythical one-eyed giant Polyphemus shyly observing the beautiful sleeping Galatea. The rich profusion of hues is the legacy of Impressionism.

ODILON REDON Like Moreau, fellow French Symbolist ODILON REDON (1840–1916) was a visionary. He had been aware of an intense inner world since childhood, and later wrote of "imaginary things" haunting him. Redon adapted the Impressionist palette and stippling brushstroke for a very different purpose—the representation of dreamlike narratives. In *The Cyclops* (FIG. **28-26**), Redon represented the mythological one-eyed giant Polyphemus emerging from behind a rocky outcropping in a landscape with a rich profusion of fresh saturated hues that harmonized with the mood that Redon felt fitted the subject. In Homer's *Odyssey,* Polyphemus is a monstrous giant whom the Greek hero Odysseus must vanquish on his journey home from Troy. Redon chose, however, the less familiar tale of Polyphemus's love for the nymph Galatea. Redon's Cyclops is a shy, simpering creature with its single huge loving eye set into a misshapen head. He rises baloonlike above the beautiful sleeping Galatea. The contrast with Raphael's representation of the same subject (FIG. 22-11) could hardly be more striking. As Redon himself observed: "All my originality consists . . . in making unreal creatures live humanly by putting, as much as possible, the logic of the visible at the service of the invisible."[9]

HENRI ROUSSEAU The imagination of HENRI ROUSSEAU (1844–1910) engaged a different but equally powerful world of personal fantasy. Gauguin had journeyed to the South Seas in search of primitive innocence. Rousseau was a "primitive" without leaving Paris—a self-taught amateur who turned to painting full-time only after his retirement from service in the French government. Nicknamed "Le Douanier" (The Customs Inspector), he first exhibited in the Salon of 1885 when he was 41. Derided by the critics, Rousseau turned to the Salon des Indépendants in 1886 and thereafter exhibited his works there almost every year until his death. Even in that more liberal showcase, Rousseau still received almost universally unfavorable reviews because of his lack of formal training, imperfect perspective, doll-like figures, and settings resembling constructed

28-27 HENRI ROUSSEAU, *Sleeping Gypsy,* 1897. Oil on canvas, 4' 3" × 6' 7". Museum of Modern Art, New York (gift of Mrs. Simon Guggenheim).

In *Sleeping Gypsy,* Rousseau depicted a doll-like but menacing lion sniffing at a recumbent dreaming figure in a mysterious landscape. The painting suggests the vulnerable subconscious during sleep.

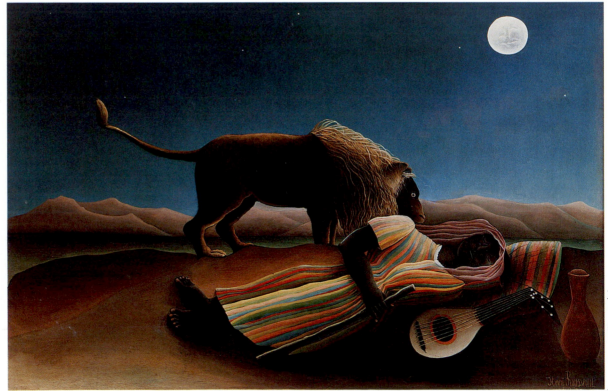

theater sets more than natural landscapes. Rousseau compensated for his apparent visual, conceptual, and technical naïveté with a natural talent for design and an imagination teeming with exotic, mysterious images.

Tropical landscapes are the setting for two of Rousseau's most famous works, *Sleeping Gypsy* (FIG. **28-27**) of 1897 and *The Dream* (FIG. **28-27A**), painted 13 years later. In the earlier painting, the recumbent figure occupies a desert world, silent and secret, and dreams beneath a pale, perfectly round moon. In the foreground, a lion resembling a stuffed, but somehow menacing, animal doll sniffs at the gypsy. A critical encounter impends—an encounter of the type that recalls the uneasiness of a person's vulnerable subconscious self during sleep—a subject of central importance to Rousseau's contemporary, Sigmund Freud. Rousseau's art of drama and fantasy has its own sophistication and, after the artist's death, influenced the development of Surrealism (see page 921).

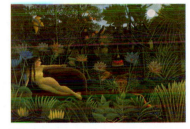

🔼 **28-27A** ROUSSEAU, *The Dream*, 1910.

JAMES ENSOR Although the Symbolist movement in art and literature began in France, it quickly expanded throughout Europe. The leading Belgian Symbolist was JAMES ENSOR (1860–1949), the son of an expatriate Englishman and a Flemish mother, who spent most of his life in the seaside resort village of Ostend, far from the artistic centers of Europe. In 1883 he cofounded Les Vingts (The Twenty), a group of Belgian artists who staged unjuried exhibitions in Brussels modeled on the independent salons of Paris. A fervent nationalist, he left the group when it began to exhibit the work of foreign artists. In fact, Ensor's most monumental work, *Christ's Entry into Brussels in 1889* (FIG. **28-28**), is very likely a critical response to Georges Seurat's *Grande Jatte* (FIG. **28-17**), exhibited by Les Vingt in 1887.

Whereas Seurat's canvas celebrates the leisure activities of contented bourgeois Parisians, a typical Impressionist theme, Ensor's even larger (14-foot-long) painting portrays an event that occurred only in the painter's imagination. In fact, it was a future event that Ensor imagined. *Christ's Entry into Brussels in 1889*, painted in 1888, is a socialist commentary on the decadence and alienation of urban life at the end of the 19th century. The mural-sized canvas is the artist's pessimistic vision of how Christ would be greeted if he entered the modern Belgian capital. Christ is a small and insignificant figure on a donkey in the background of the painting, ignored by the dense crowd of soldiers and citizens wearing grotesque masks inspired by the papier-mâché carnival masks that Ensor's family sold in their curio shop in Ostend. Some of the people carry banners and signs. One reads "Long Live Jesus, King of Brussels," another "Long Live the Socialist State." Complementing the ugly, grimacing masked faces of the anonymous crowd, which eloquently express Ensor's condemnation of the corrupt values of modern society, are the discordant combination of reds, blues, and greens and the coarse texture of the thickly applied oil pigment. As an indictment of the immorality of modern life, Ensor's *Christ's Entry* has few equals.

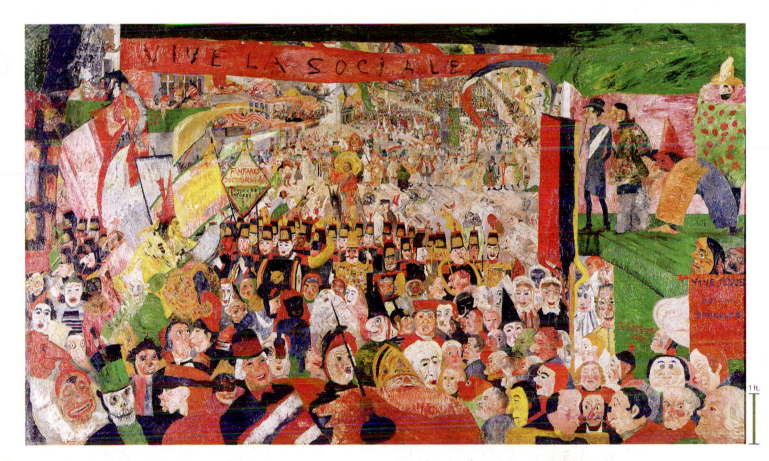

28-28 JAMES ENSOR, *Christ's Entry into Brussels in 1889*, 1888. Oil on canvas, 8' 3½" × 14' 1½". J. Paul Getty Museum, Los Angeles.

Ensor's mural-sized canvas is an indictment of corrupt modern values. Christ enters Brussels on a donkey in 1889, ignored by the dense crowd of soldiers and citizens wearing grotesque, grimacing masks.

EDVARD MUNCH Also linked in spirit to the Symbolists were the English artist AUBREY BEARDSLEY (1872–1898; FIG. 28-28A) and the Norwegian painter EDVARD MUNCH (1863–1944). Munch felt deeply the pain of human life and believed that people were powerless before the great natural forces of death and love. The emotions associated with those forces—jealousy, loneliness, fear, desire, despair—became the theme of most of his art (see "Painting Psychic Life," below).

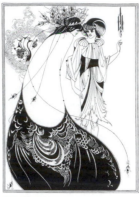

⬈ **28-28A** BEARDSLEY, *The Peacock Skirt*, 1894.

FIN-DE-SIÈCLE Historians have adopted the term *fin-de-siècle*, which literally means "end of the century," to describe European culture of the late 1800s. This designation is not merely chronological but also refers to a certain sensibility. At that time, the increasingly large and prosperous middle classes were aspiring to gain the advantages that the aristocracy traditionally enjoyed. The masses, striving to live "the good life," embraced a culture of decadence and indulgence. Characteristic of the fin-de-siècle period was an intense preoccupation with sexual drives, powers, and perversions. People at the end of the century also immersed themselves in the exploration of the unconscious. This culture was unrestrained and freewheeling, but the determination to enjoy life masked an anxiety prompted by significant political upheaval and an uncertain future. The country most closely associated with fin-de-siècle culture was Austria.

PROBLEMS AND SOLUTIONS
Painting Psychic Life

Few painters in history have been as successful as Edvard Munch in portraying primal emotions in works of art. In 1877, as a teenager, Munch endured the painful, slow death of his sister from tuberculosis, a wrenching experience that inspired his *Sick Child* of 1886. Munch's mother had died of the same disease a decade earlier, and those tragic events profoundly shaped the painter's outlook on life and his artistic vision.

Munch's goal as an artist was, in his own words, to describe the conditions of "modern psychic life." To achieve that goal, Realist and Impressionist techniques were inappropriate, focusing as they did on the tangible world. Instead, in the spirit of Symbolism, Munch used color, line, and figural distortion for expressive ends. Influenced by Gauguin, whose paintings he saw in an 1884 exhibition in Oslo, Munch produced both paintings and prints whose high emotional charge was a major source of inspiration for the German Expressionists in the early 20th century (see page 885).

Munch's *The Scream* (FIG. 28-29), painted in 1893 when he was 30 years old, exemplifies his style and remains to this day one of the most potent symbols of the unbearable pressures of modern life on individual people. The image—a man standing on a bridge—belongs to the real world. In fact, the inspiration for the painting came after Munch had experienced a fit of anxiety after walking, intoxicated, across an Oslo bridge on a summer evening. However, his depiction of the scene departs significantly from visual reality. *The Scream* evokes a powerful emotional response from the viewer because of the painter's dramatic presentation. The man in the foreground, simplified to almost skeletal form, emits a primal scream. The landscape's sweeping curvilinear lines reiterate the shapes of the man's mouth and head, almost like an echo, as the cry seems to reverberate through the setting. The fiery red and yellow stripes that give the sky an eerie glow also contribute to this work's resonance.

Munch wrote a revealing epigraph to accompany the painting:

> I was walking along the road with two friends. The sun was setting. I felt a breath of melancholy—Suddenly the sky turned blood-red. I stopped, and leaned against the railing, deathly tired—looking out across the flaming clouds that hung like blood and a sword over the blue-black fjord and town. My friends walked on—I stood there, trembling with fear. And I sensed a great, infinite scream pass through nature.*

Appropriately, the original title of this work was *Despair*.

*Quoted in Petra ten-Doesschate Chu, *Nineteenth-Century European Art*, 3d ed. (Upper Saddle River, N.J.: Pearson, 2011), 515.

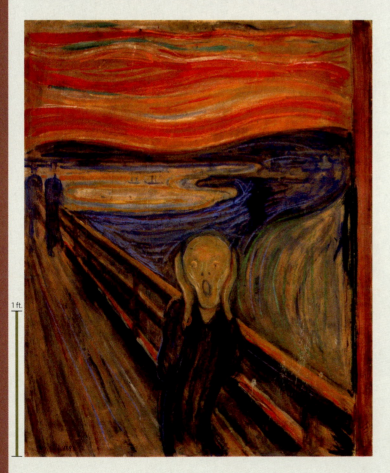

1 ft.

28-29 EDVARD MUNCH, *The Scream*, 1893. Tempera and pastels on cardboard, 2' 11¾" × 2' 5". National Gallery, Oslo.

Although grounded in the real world, *The Scream* departs significantly from visual reality. Munch used color, line, and figural distortion to evoke a strong emotional response from the viewer.

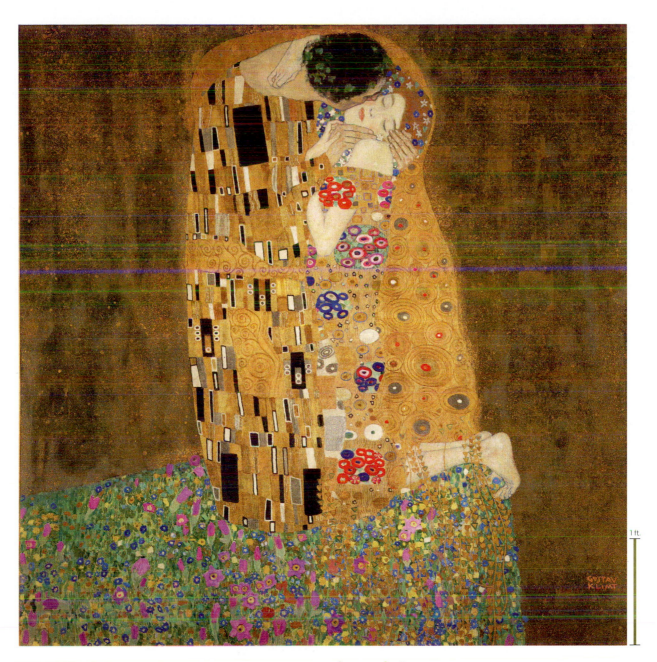

28-30 Gustav Klimt, *The Kiss,* 1907–1908. Oil on canvas, 5' 10¾" × 5' 10¾". Österreichische Galerie Belvedere, Vienna.

Klimt's paintings exemplify the Viennese fin-de-siècle spirit. In *The Kiss,* he revealed only a small segment of each lover's body. The rest of the painting dissolves into shimmering, extravagant flat patterning.

GUSTAV KLIMT The Viennese artist GUSTAV KLIMT (1863–1918) captured this period's flamboyance in his work, but tempered it with unsettling undertones. In *The Kiss* (FIG. **28-30**), his best-known work, Klimt depicted a kneeling couple locked in an embrace. The setting is ambiguous, an indeterminate place apart from time and space, perhaps a garden of flowers. Moreover, all the viewer sees of the embracing couple is a small segment of each body—and virtually nothing of the man's face. The rest of the canvas dissolves into shimmering, extravagant flat patterning. This patterning has clear ties to Art Nouveau and to the Arts and Crafts movement (discussed later) and also evokes the conflict between two- and three-dimensionality intrinsic to the work of Degas and other modernists. In *The Kiss,* however, those patterns also signify gender contrasts—rectangles for the man's garment, circles for the woman's. Yet the patterning

also unites the two lovers into a single formal entity, underscoring their erotic union.

GERTRUDE KÄSEBIER Photography, which during the 19th century most people regarded as the ultimate form of Realism, could also be manipulated by artists to produce effects more akin to painting than to factual records of contemporary life. After the first great breakthroughs (see page 834), which bluntly showed what was before the eye, some photographers began to pursue new ways of using the medium as a vehicle of artistic expression. A leading practitioner of what might be called the pictorial style in photography was the American GERTRUDE KÄSEBIER (1852–1934), who took up the camera in 1897 after raising a family and working as a portrait painter. She soon became famous for photographs with Symbolist themes, such

SCULPTURE

The names of the sculptors of the late 19th century are not as familiar as those of the painters of the same era, in part because their work was less revolutionary in nature, in part because their biographies are not as colorful as the tormented and nomadic lives of van Gogh and Gauguin. But the quality of the statues and reliefs created by the leading sculptors of this period is uncontested.

JEAN-BAPTISTE CARPEAUX In France, Jean-Baptiste Carpeaux (1827–1875) received his training as a sculptor at the École des Beaux-Arts under the direction of François Rude, best known for *La Marseillaise* (FIG. 27-18), his colossal relief on the Arc de Triomphe (FIG. 27-18A) in Paris. Although it took him a decade to achieve, Carpeaux won the Rome Prize in 1854 and spent the next eight years in Italy honing his technical skills. In his mature work, Carpeaux combined his love for the ancient, Renaissance, and Baroque sculpture he saw in Italy with a strong interest in Realism.

All of those sources are evident in his group *Ugolino and His Children* (FIG. 28-32), which he based on a passage in Dante's *Inferno* (33.58–75) in which Count Ugolino and his four sons starve to death while shut up in a tower. In Hell, Ugolino relates to Dante

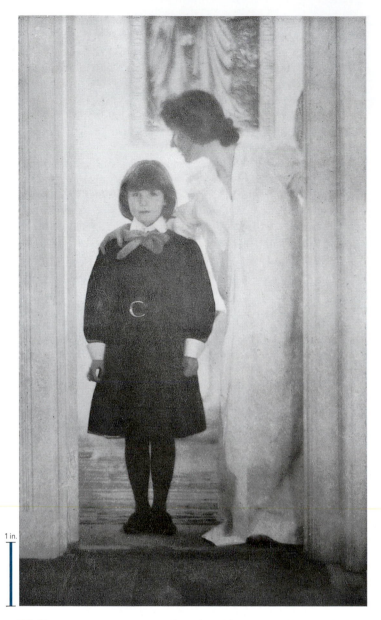

28-31 Gertrude Käsebier, *Blessed Art Thou among Women*, 1899. Platinum print on Japanese tissue, $9\frac{3}{8}" \times 5\frac{1}{2}"$. Museum of Modern Art, New York (gift of Mrs. Hermine M. Turner).

Symbolist Käsebier injected a sense of the spiritual and the divine into scenes from everyday life. The deliberately soft focus of this photograph invests the scene with an aura of otherworldly peace.

as *Blessed Art Thou among Women* (FIG. 28-31). The title repeats the phrase that the angel Gabriel used to announce to the Virgin Mary that she would be the mother of the Messiah. In the context of Käsebier's photography, the words suggest a parallel between the biblical Mother of God and the modern mother in the image, who both protects and sends forth her daughter from her secure home into the unfamiliar world at large. The white setting and the mother's pale gown shimmer in soft focus behind the girl, who wears darker tones and whom the photographer captured with sharper focus. Käsebier deliberately combined an out-of-focus background with a sharp or almost-sharp foreground, thereby blurring the entire image slightly. In *Blessed Art Thou*, the soft focus invests the scene with an aura of otherworldly peace. The photograph showcases Käsebier's ability to inject a sense of the spiritual and the divine into scenes from everyday life.

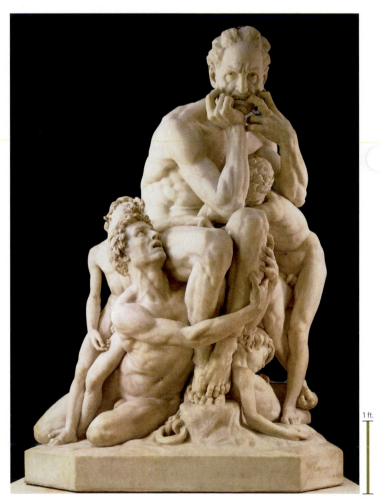

28-32 Jean-Baptiste Carpeaux, *Ugolino and His Children*, 1865–1867. Marble, 6' 5" high. Metropolitan Museum of Art, New York (Josephine Bay Paul and C. Michael Paul Foundation, Inc., and the Charles Ulrich and Josephine Bay Foundation, Inc., gifts, 1967).

As in Dante's *Inferno,* Carpeaux's Ugolino bites his hands in despair as he and his four sons await death by starvation. The twisted forms suggest the self-devouring torment of frustration.

how, in a moment of extreme despair, he bit both his hands in grief. His children, thinking he did it because of his hunger, offered him their own flesh as food. In Carpeaux's statuary group, the powerful forms—twisted, intertwined, and densely concentrated—suggest the self-devouring torment of frustration and despair wracking the unfortunate Ugolino. A careful student of Michelangelo's male figures, Carpeaux also said he had the ancient *Laocoön* (FIG. 5-89) in mind when he conceived *Ugolino and His Children*, which he hoped would be "a masterpiece of the human spirit." Certainly, the storm and stress captured in his *Ugolino* recall similar characteristics of the group of Laocoön and his two sons. Nevertheless, the sense of vivid reality in the anatomy of Carpeaux's figures shows that the artist had studied the human figure from life, not solely from other statues. However, the French public did not share Carpeaux's interest in Realism. They preferred the idealized bodies of classical sculptures—one of the reasons that Carpeaux was forced to remove another of his best works, *The Dance* (FIG. 28-32A), from the facade of the Paris opera house (FIG. 27-45).

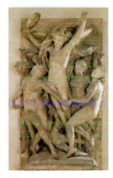

🔹 **28-32A** CARPEAUX, *The Dance*, 1867-1869.

AUGUSTE RODIN As talented as he was, Carpeaux was not the leading French sculptor of the later 19th century. That honor belongs to AUGUSTE RODIN (1840–1917), who conceived and executed his sculptures with a Realist sensibility. The human body in motion fascinated Rodin, as it did Eakins and Muybridge (FIG. 27-53) before him (see "Rodin on Movement in Art and Photography," below). Rodin was also well aware of the Impressionists' innovations. Although color was not a significant factor in Rodin's work, the influence of Impressionism is evident in the artist's interest in the effect of light on sculpted surfaces. When focusing on the human form, he joined his profound knowledge of anatomy and movement with special attention to the body's exterior, saying, "The sculptor must learn to reproduce the surface, which means all that vibrates on the surface, soul, love, passion, life. . . . Sculpture is thus the art of hollows and mounds, not of smoothness, or even polished planes."[10] Primarily a modeler of pliable material rather than a carver of hard wood or stone, Rodin worked his surfaces with fingers sensitive to the subtlest variations of texture, catching the fugitive play of constantly shifting light on metal. In his studio, he often would have a model move around in front of him while he created preliminary versions of his sculptures with coils of clay.

In *Walking Man* (FIG. 28-33), a preliminary study for the sculptor's *Saint John the Baptist Preaching*, Rodin succeeded in representing a fleeting moment in cast bronze. He portrayed a headless and armless figure in midstride at the moment when weight is transferred across the pelvis from the back leg to the front. In addition to capturing the sense of the transitory, Rodin demonstrated his mastery of realistic detail in his meticulous rendition of muscle, bone, and tendon.

ARTISTS ON ART
Rodin on Movement in Art and Photography

Photography had a profound effect on 19th-century art, and many artists used photographs as an aid in capturing "reality" on canvas or in stone. Eadweard Muybridge's photographs of a galloping horse (FIG. 27-53), for example, definitively established that at certain times, all four hooves of the animal are in the air. But not all artists believed that photography was "true to life." The sculptor Auguste Rodin (FIGS. 28-33, 28-33A, and 28-34) was one of the doubters.

> I have always sought to give some indication of movement [in my statues]. I have very rarely represented complete repose. I have always endeavored to express the inner feelings by the mobility of the muscles. . . . The illusion of life is obtained in our art by good modeling and by movement. . . . [M]ovement is the transition from one attitude to another. . . . Have you ever attentively examined instantaneous photographs of walking figures? . . . [Photographs] present the odd appearance of a man suddenly stricken with paralysis and petrified in his pose. . . . If, in fact, in instantaneous photographs, the figures, though taken while moving, seem suddenly fixed in mid-air, it is because, all parts of the body being reproduced exactly at the same twentieth or fortieth of a second, there is no progressive development of movement as there is in art. . . . [I]t is the artist who is truthful and it is photography which lies, for in reality time does not stop.*

*Translated by Robin Fedden, in Elizabeth Gilmore Holt, ed., *From the Classicists to the Impressionists: Art and Architecture in the 19th Century* (New Haven, Conn.: Yale University Press, 1966; reprint 1986), 406–409.

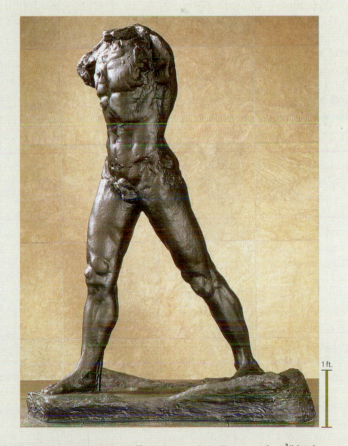

28-33 AUGUSTE RODIN, *Walking Man*, 1905. Bronze, 6' 11¾" high. Musée d'Orsay, Paris.

In this study for a statue of Saint John the Baptist, Rodin depicted a headless and armless figure in midstride. *Walking Man* demonstrates Rodin's mastery of anatomy and ability to capture transitory motion.

GATES OF HELL Rodin also made many nude and draped studies for each of the figures in two of his most ambitious works—the life-size group *Burghers of Calais* (FIG. **28-33A**) and the *Gates of Hell* (FIG. **28-34**), which occupied the sculptor for two decades. After he failed to gain admission to the École des Beaux-Arts, Rodin enrolled in the École Impériale Spéciale de Dessin et Mathématiques (Special Imperial School of Drawing and Mathematics), the French school of decorative arts, known as the "Petit École" (Little School) because it was a lesser version of the more prestigious Beaux-Arts academy. However, Rodin's talent could not be suppressed by rejection. He soon gained attention for the outstanding realism of some of his early sculptures, and on August 16, 1880, received a major governmental commission to design a pair of doors for a planned Museum of Decorative Arts in Paris. Rodin worked on the project for 20 years, but the museum was never built (the Musée d'Orsay now occupies the intended site). It was not until after the sculptor's death that others cast his still-unfinished doors in bronze.

The commission granted Rodin permission to choose his own subject. He selected *The Gates of Hell*, based on Dante's *Inferno* and Baudelaire's *Flowers of Evil*. Originally inspired by Lorenzo Ghiberti's *Gates of Paradise* (FIG. 21-10), which he had seen in Florence, Rodin quickly abandoned the idea of a series of framed narrative panels and decided instead to cover each of the doors with a continuous writhing mass of tormented men and women, sinners condemned to Dante's second circle of Hell for their lust. Because of the varying height of the relief, the complex poses, and the effect of light on the highly textured surfaces, the figures seem to be in flux, moving in and out of an undefined space in a reflection of their psychic turmoil. The dreamlike (or rather, the nightmarish) vision connects Rodin with the Symbolists, and

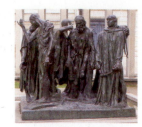

🔎 **28-33A** RODIN, *Burghers of Calais,* 1884–1889.

the pessimistic mood and sensuality embody the fin-de-siècle spirit. The swirling composition and emotionalism recall Delacroix's *Death of Sardanapalus* (FIG. 27-15) and Michelangelo's *Last Judgment* (FIG. 22-19). Rodin's work defies easy stylistic classification.

The nearly 200 figures of *The Gates of Hell* spill over onto the jambs and the lintel. Rodin also included freestanding figures, which, cast separately in multiple versions, are among his most famous works. Above the doors, *The Three Shades* is a trio of twisted nude male figures, essentially the same figure with elongated arms

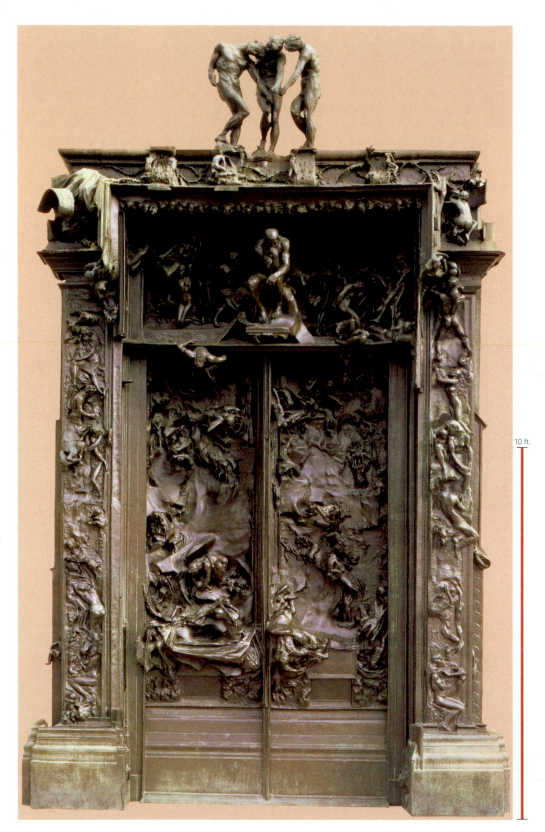

10 ft.

28-34 AUGUSTE RODIN, *The Gates of Hell,* 1880–1900 (cast in 1917). Bronze, 20′ 10″ × 13′ 1″. Musée Rodin, Paris.

Rodin's most ambitious work, inspired by Dante's *Inferno* and Ghiberti's *Gates of Paradise* (FIG. 21-10), presents nearly 200 tormented sinners in relief below *The Three Shades* and *The Thinker.*

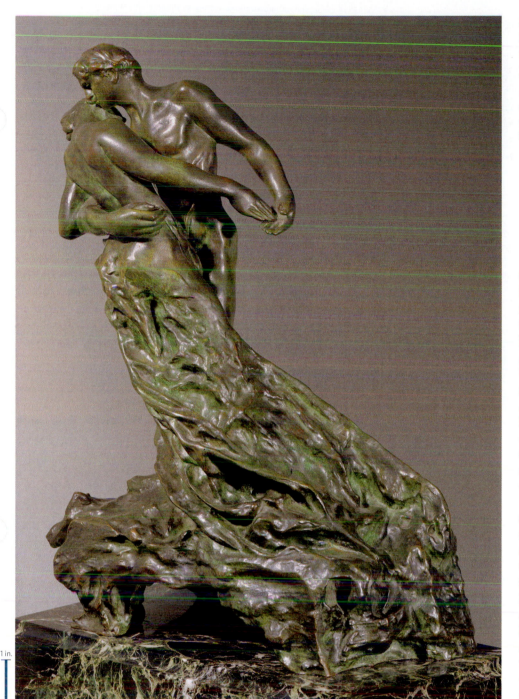

1 in.

28-35 CAMILLE CLAUDEL, *The Waltz*,
1895. Bronze, 1' 4⅞" high. Private collection, Paris.

The Waltz was a bold work for a woman artist
because it portrays male nudity. The textures
and movement are hallmarks of Rodin, but the
conception of spiritual and physical union is
Claudel's own.

CAMILLE CLAUDEL Because of the physical strength required for carving stone,
throughout history women who pursued careers as artists almost universally
became painters rather than sculptors.
An important exception is CAMILLE
CLAUDEL (1864–1943), who met Rodin
in 1883 when she was an apprentice in
another sculptor's studio. She became
his assistant, model, and lover in 1885.
Although Claudel produced life-size
sculptures for public commissions, she
specialized in small-scale bronzes for
display in private homes.

The Waltz (FIG. 28-35), produced over
several years in a number of variations, is
a characteristic, extremely bold work for
a woman artist of this era because it portrays male nudity. It deserves comparison
with Klimt's *Kiss* (FIG. 28-30) in its unbridled fin-de-siècle passion and eroticism. But unlike the Austrian painter's
kneeling lovers, Claudel's embracing
couple is swept up in the motion of
their dance, their spiraling movement
underscored and enhanced by the flowing drapery of the seminude woman.
The influence of Rodin is evident in the
variegated texture of the bronze statuette
and in Claudel's interest in the movement of the human body, but
The Waltz is her own conception of spiri-
tual as well as physical union between a
man and a woman.

in three different positions. The group evokes Carpeaux's *Ugolino
and His Children* (FIG. 28-32), as does *The Thinker*, Rodin's famous
seated nude man with a powerful body who rests his chin on his
clenched right hand, pondering the fate of the tormented souls on
the doors below. *The Thinker* is the alter-ego of both Dante and
Rodin.

The *Gates of Hell*, more than 20 feet tall, was Rodin's most ambitious project. It greatly influenced the painters and sculptors of the
Expressionist movements of the early 20th century (see page 885).
Rodin's ability to capture the quality of the transitory through his
highly textured surfaces while revealing larger themes and deeper,
lasting sensibilities is another reason he had a strong influence on
20th-century artists. Because many of his works, such as *Walking
Man*, were deliberate fragments, he was also instrumental in creating a taste for the incomplete, an aesthetic many later sculptors
embraced enthusiastically.

AUGUSTUS SAINT-GAUDENS Outside
France, the most renowned sculptor of
the late 19th century was an American,
AUGUSTUS SAINT-GAUDENS (1848–1907),
whose subjects and style differed markedly
from those of his French counterparts.
Saint-Gaudens produced monumental
statues expressing the majestic calm of
ancient Greek and Roman sculpture, such
as his *Adams Memorial* (FIG. 28-35A) in
Washington, D.C.

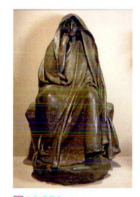

📥 28-35A SAINT-
GAUDENS, *Adams Memorial*,
1886–1891.

The Arts and Crafts Movement

One of the clearest cases in history of social, economic, and technological changes giving birth to new art forms is the Arts and Crafts movement in 19th-century England. This movement was shaped by the ideas of John Ruskin, the critic who skewered Whistler's "arrangements" (see "Whistler," page 851), and the artist William Morris. Both men shared a distrust of machines and industrial capitalism, which they believed alienated workers from their own nature. Accordingly, they advocated an art "made by the people for the people as a joy for the maker and the user."* This condemnation of capitalism and support for manual laborers were also consistent with the tenets of socialism, and many artists in the Arts and Crafts movement, especially in England, considered themselves socialists and participated in the labor movement.

This democratic, or at least populist, attitude carried over to the art they produced as well. Members of the Arts and Crafts movement dedicated themselves to making functional objects with high aesthetic value for a wide public. They advocated a style based on natural, rather than artificial, forms, which often consisted of repeated designs of floral or geometric patterns. For Ruskin, Morris, and others in the Arts and Crafts movement, who despised the inferior machine-made products that were flooding the market in England, high-quality artisanship and honest labor were crucial ingredients of superior works of decorative art.

To promote these ideals, Morris formed a decorating firm dedicated to Arts and Crafts principles: Morris, Marshall, Faulkner, and Company, Fine Arts Workmen in Painting, Carving, Furniture, and Metals. His company did a flourishing business producing wallpaper, textiles, tiles, furniture, books, rugs, stained glass, and pottery. In 1867,

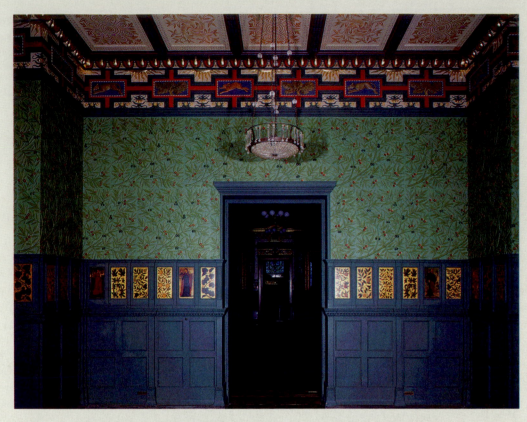

28-36 WILLIAM MORRIS, Green Dining Room, South Kensington Museum (now Victoria & Albert Museum), London, England, 1867.

William Morris was a founder of the Arts and Crafts movement. His Green Dining Room exemplifies the group's dedication to creating intricately patterned yet unified and functional environments.

Morris received the commission to decorate the Green Dining Room (FIG. 28-36) at London's South Kensington Museum (now the Victoria & Albert Museum), the center of public art education and home of decorative art collections. The range of room features that Morris created for this unified, beautiful, and functional environment was all-encompassing: wallpaper, ceiling panels, doors, *wainscoting* (paneling on the lower part of interior walls), and lighting. Nothing escaped his eye. Morris's design for this room also reveals the penchant of Arts and Crafts designers for intricate patterning of vegetal and floral motifs.

*Quoted in Eileen Boris, *Art and Labor: Ruskin, Morris, and the Craftsman Ideal in America* (Philadelphia: Temple University Press, 1986), 7.

ARCHITECTURE AND DECORATIVE ARTS

The decisive effects of industrialization were impossible to ignore, and although many artists embraced this manifestation of "modern life" or at least explored its effects, other artists decried the impact of rampant industrialism. Most notable were those associated with the Arts and Crafts movement in England, spearheaded by John Ruskin and WILLIAM MORRIS (1834–1896; see "The Arts and Crafts Movement," above, and FIG. 28-36).

CHARLES RENNIE MACKINTOSH Numerous Arts and Crafts societies in America, England, and Germany carried on the ideal of artisanship championed by Ruskin and Morris. In Scotland,

CHARLES RENNIE MACKINTOSH (1868–1929) designed a number of tea rooms, including the Ladies' Luncheon Room (FIG. 28-37) located in the Ingram Street Tea Room in Glasgow. The room decor is consistent with Morris's vision of functional, exquisitely designed art. The chairs, stained-glass windows, and large panels of colored *gesso* with twine, glass beads, thread, mother-of-pearl, and tin leaf—made by MARGARET MACDONALD MACKINTOSH (1864–1933), an artist-designer and Mackintosh's wife, who collaborated with him on many projects—are all pristinely geometric and rhythmical in design.

ART NOUVEAU An important international architectural and design movement that developed out of the ideas that the Arts and

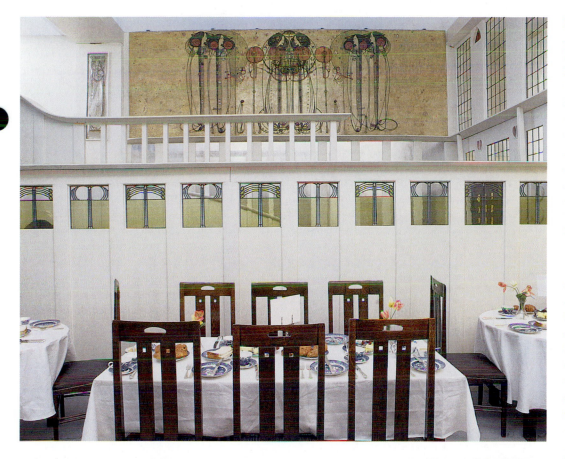

Crafts movement promoted was *Art Nouveau* (New Art), which took its name from a shop in Paris called L'Art Nouveau. Known by that name in France, Belgium, Holland, England, and the United States, the style had other names in other places: *Jugendstil* in Austria and Germany (after the magazine *Der Jugend,* "youth"), *Modernismo* in Spain, and *Stile Floreale* in Italy. Proponents of this movement tried to synthesize all the arts in a determined attempt to create art based on natural forms that could be mass-produced for a large audience. The Art Nouveau style adapted the twining-plant form to the needs of architecture, painting, sculpture, and all the decorative arts.

VICTOR HORTA The mature Art Nouveau style of the 1890s is on display in the houses designed by the Belgian architect VICTOR HORTA (1861–1947). A characteristic example is the staircase (FIG. **28-38**) in the Van Eetvelde House, which Horta built in Brussels in 1895, three years after designing the Tassel House

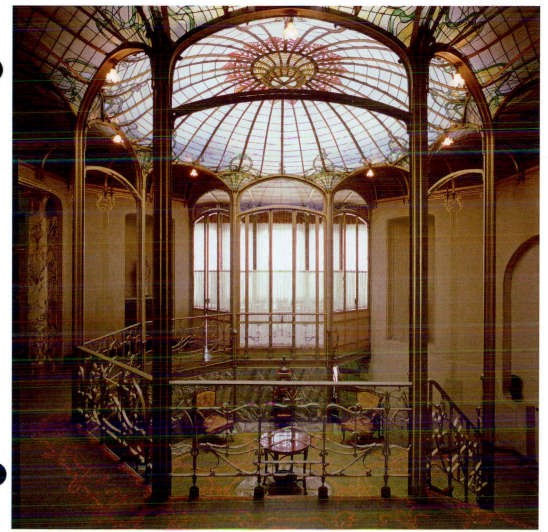

(FIG. 28-38A), his first major commission. Every detail of the Van Eetvelde interior functions as part of a living whole. Furniture, drapery folds, veining in the lavish stone paneling, and the patterning of the door moldings join with real plants to provide graceful counterpoints for the twining-plant theme. Metallic tendrils curl around the railings and posts, delicate metal tracery fills the glass dome, and floral and leaf motifs spread across the fabric panels of the screen. Flower and plant motifs also figure prominently in the immensely popular stained-glass lamps (FIG. 28-38B) of LOUIS COMFORT TIFFANY (1848–1933).

The Art Nouveau style reflects several influences. In addition to the rich, foliated two-dimensional ornamentation of Arts and Crafts design and that movement's respect for materials, the sinuous whiplash curve of Japanese print designs (FIG. 34-13) inspired Art Nouveau artists. Art Nouveau also borrowed from the expressively patterned styles

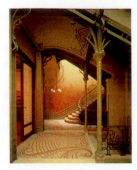

28-38A HORTA, Tassel House, Brussels, 1892–1893.

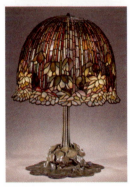

28-38B TIFFANY, water lily lamp, 1904–1915.

of van Gogh (FIGS. 28-18 and 28-19), Gauguin (FIGS. 28-20 and 28-21), and their Post-Impressionist and Symbolist contemporaries (compare, for example, Toulouse-Lautrec's posters [FIG. 28-15]). In addition, the style is a distant descendant of the Rococo aesthetic (see page 764), which was also derived from natural forms.

ANTONIO GAUDI Art Nouveau achieved its most personal expression in the work of the Spanish architect ANTONIO GAUDI (1852–1926). Before becoming an architect, Gaudi had trained as an ironworker. Like many young artists of his time, he longed to create a style both modern and appropriate to his country. Taking inspiration from Moorish architecture and from the simple architecture of his native Catalonia, Gaudi developed a distinctive personal aesthetic. He conceived a building as a whole and molded it almost as a sculptor might shape a figure from clay, approaching architectural design as if buildings were organic, living forms. Although work on his designs proceeded slowly under the guidance of his intuition and imagination, Gaudi was a master who invented many new structural techniques that facilitated construction of his visions.

Gaudi's Barcelona apartment house, Casa Milá (FIG. 28-39), is a wondrously free-form mass wrapped around a street corner. Lacy iron railings enliven the swelling curves of the cut-stone facade, which are echoed in the undulating walls of the interior courtyard. Dormer windows peep from the undulating tiled roof, from which fantastically writhing chimneys poke energetically into the air

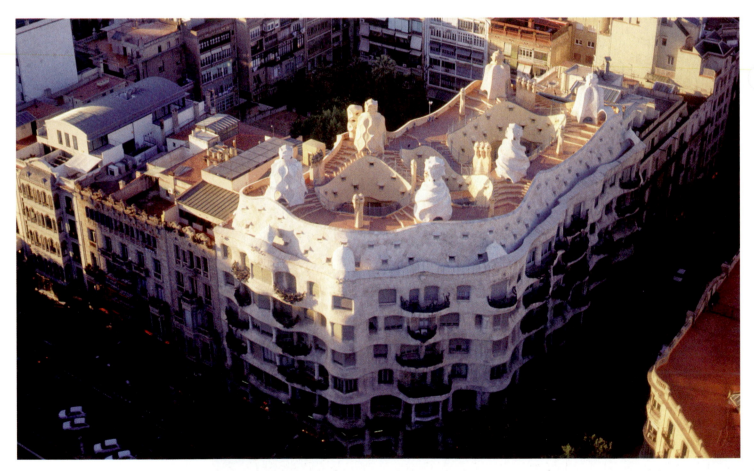

28-39 ANTONIO GAUDI, Casa Milá (looking north), Barcelona, Spain, 1907.

Spanish Art Nouveau architect Gaudi conceived this Barcelona apartment house as if it were a gigantic sculpture to be molded from clay. Twisting chimneys cap the undulating roof and walls.

above. The rough surfaces of the stone walls suggest naturally worn rock. The entrance portals look like eroded sea caves. Their design also may reflect the excitement that swept Spain following the 1879 discovery of Paleolithic cave paintings at Altamira (FIG. 1-8).

ALEXANDRE-GUSTAVE EIFFEL In the later 19th century, new technologies and the changing needs of urbanized, industrialized society affected architecture throughout the Western world. Since the 18th century, bridges had been built of cast iron (FIG. 26-13), which enabled engineering advancements in the construction of larger, stronger, and more fire-resistant structures. Steel, available after 1860, made it possible for architects to enclose ever larger spaces, such as those found in railroad stations (FIG. 28-4) and exposition halls. The Realist impulse also encouraged architectural designs that honestly expressed a building's purpose, rather than elaborately disguising its function.

The elegant metal-skeleton structures of the French engineer-architect ALEXANDRE-GUSTAVE EIFFEL (1832–1923) were responses to this idea, and they constituted an important contribution to the development of the 20th-century skyscraper. A native of Burgundy, Eiffel trained in Paris before beginning a distinguished career designing exhibition halls, bridges, and the interior armature for France's anniversary gift to the United States—the *Statue of Liberty* by Frédéric Auguste Bartholdi (1834–1904).

Eiffel designed his best-known work, the Eiffel Tower (FIG. 28-40), for an exhibition in Paris in 1889. Although the tower pays tribute to traditional architectural forms, such as the Roman

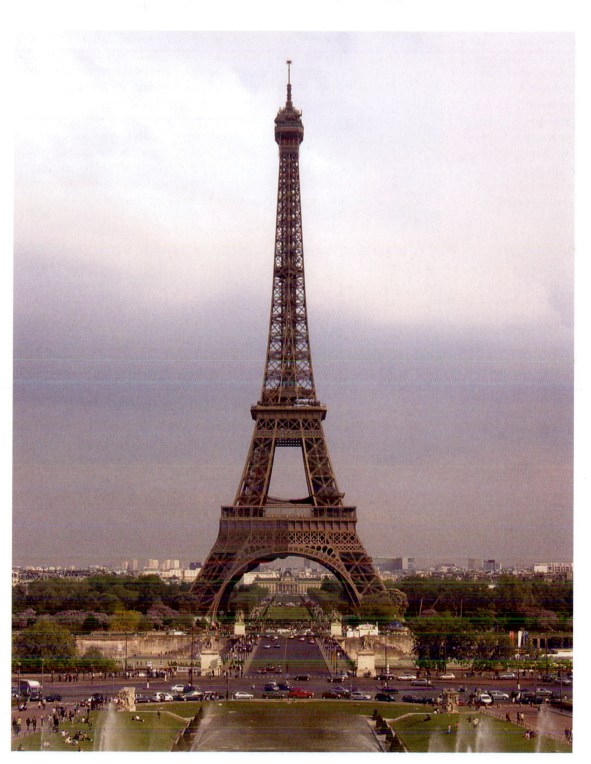

28-40 ALEXANDRE-GUSTAVE EIFFEL, Eiffel Tower (looking southeast), Paris, France, 1889.

New materials and technologies and the modernist aesthetic fueled radically new architectural designs in the late 19th century. Eiffel jolted the world with the exposed iron skeleton of his tower.

PROBLEMS AND SOLUTIONS
The First Skyscrapers

In cities, convenience required closely grouped buildings, and increased property values forced architects literally to raise the roof. Even an attic could command high rent if the builders installed one of the new elevators, used for the first time in the Equitable Building in New York, constructed between 1868 and 1871. Iron and steel, which could support these towering structures, gave birth to the American skyscraper.

One of the pioneers in designing these modern commercial towers was HENRY HOBSON RICHARDSON (1838–1886), but he also had a profound respect for earlier architectural styles. Because Richardson had a special fondness for the Romanesque architecture of the Auvergne area in France, he frequently used heavy round arches and massive masonry walls. Architectural historians sometimes consider his work to constitute a Romanesque revival related to the Neo-Gothic style (FIGS. 27-43 and 27-43A). This designation, however, does not do justice to the originality and quality of most of the buildings that Richardson designed during his brief 18-year practice. Trinity Church in Boston and his smaller public libraries, residences, railroad stations, and courthouses in New England and elsewhere best demonstrate his vivid imagination and the solidity (the sense of enclosure and permanence) so characteristic of his style.

Nevertheless, Richardson's most important and influential building was the Marshall Field wholesale store (FIG. 28-41) in Chicago, begun in 1885 and demolished in 1930. In this vast building, which occupied an entire city block, Richardson solved the problem of designing a structure to satisfy the needs of commerce while paying homage to historical styles without imitating them—an approach that would be revived a century later in *postmodern* architecture (see "After Modernism: Postmodernist Architecture," page 949). The tripartite elevation of a Renaissance palace (FIG. 21-35) or of the Roman aqueduct (FIG. 7-33) near Nîmes, France, may have influenced Richardson's design. But he used no classical ornamentation, made much of the massive courses of masonry, and, in the strong horizontality of the windowsills and the interrupted courses defining the levels,

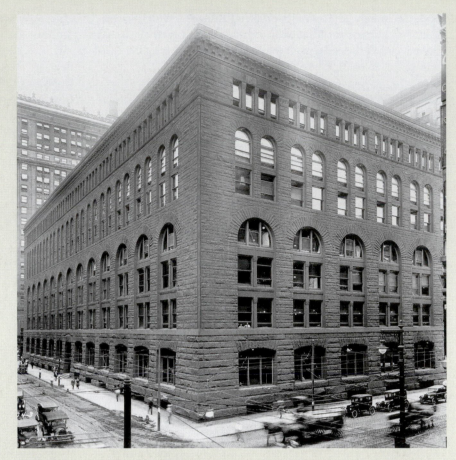

28-41 HENRY HOBSON RICHARDSON, Marshall Field wholesale store, Chicago, 1885–1887 (demolished 1930).

Richardson was a pioneer in designing commercial structures using a cast-iron skeleton encased in fire-resistant masonry. This construction technique enabled the insertion of large windows in the walls.

stressed the long sweep of the building's lines, as well as the edifice's ponderous weight. Although the structural frame still lay behind and in conjunction with the masonry screen, the great glazed arcades opened up the walls of the monumental store. They pointed the way to 20th-century skyscrapers characterized by the total penetration of walls and the transformation of them into mere screens or curtains that serve both to echo the underlying structural grid and to protect the interior spaces from the weather (compare FIG. 30-45).

arch and the Gothic spire, it immediately—and justly—became the iconic symbol of modern Paris. Eiffel's elegant iron tower thrusts its needle shaft 984 feet above the city, making it at the time of its construction until the erection of the Empire State Building in New York City in 1931 the world's tallest structure. The tower rests on four giant supports connected by gracefully arching open-frame skirts that provide a pleasing mask for the heavy horizontal girders needed to strengthen the legs as well as anchor the structure against powerful wind gusts. Visitors can take two successive elevators to the top, or they can use the internal staircase. Either way, the view of Paris and the Seine from the tower is incomparable, as is the design of the tower itself. The transparency of Eiffel's structure blurs the distinction between interior and exterior to an extent never before achieved or even attempted. This interpenetration of inner and outer space became a hallmark of 20th-century art and architecture. Eiffel's tower and the earlier iron skeletal frames designed by Labrouste (FIG. 27-46) and Paxton (FIG. 27-47) jolted the architectural profession into a realization that modern materials and processes could germinate a completely new style and a radically innovative approach to architectural design (see "Prefabricated Architecture," page 833).

AMERICAN SKYSCRAPERS The desire for greater speed and economy in building, as well as for a reduction in fire hazards, prompted

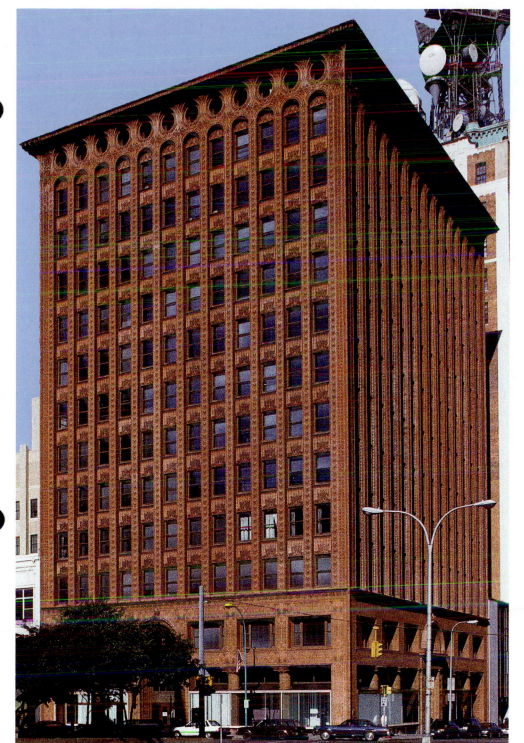

28-42 Louis Henry Sullivan, **Guaranty (Prudential) Building (looking southwest), Buffalo, New York, 1894–1896.**

Sullivan drew on the latest technologies to create this light-filled, well-ventilated Buffalo office building. He added ornate surface embellishments to impart a sense of refinement and taste.

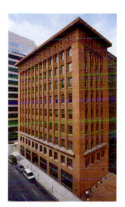

⬈ **28-42A** Sullivan, Wainwright Building, St. Louis, 1890–1891.

historians call the first truly modern architect, arrived at a synthesis of industrial structure and ornamentation that perfectly expressed the spirit of late-19th-century commerce. To achieve this, he used the latest technological developments to create light-filled, well-ventilated office buildings and adorned both exteriors and interiors with ornate embellishments. Such decoration served to connect commerce and culture, and imbued these white-collar workspaces with a sense of refinement and taste.

These characteristics are evident in Sullivan's Guaranty (Prudential) Building (FIG. **28-42**) in Buffalo, built between 1894 and 1896, and in his earlier Wainwright Building (FIG. **28-42A**) in St. Louis. The Buffalo skyscraper is steel, sheathed with terracotta. The imposing scale of the building and the regularity of the window placements served as an expression of the large-scale, refined, and orderly office work taking place within. Sullivan tempered the severity of the structure with lively ornamentation, both on the piers and cornice on the exterior of the building and on the stairway balustrades, elevator cages, and ceiling in the interior. The Guaranty Building illustrates Sullivan's famous dictum "form follows function," which became the slogan of many early-20th-century architects. Still, Sullivan did not advocate a rigid and doctrinaire correspondence between exterior and interior design. Rather, he espoused a free and flexible relationship—one that his pupil Frank Lloyd Wright (see page 917) later described as similar to that between the hand's bones and tissue.

the use of iron for many building programs, especially commercial ones. Designers in both England and the United States enthusiastically developed cast-iron architecture until a series of disastrous fires in the early 1870s in New York, Boston, and Chicago demonstrated that cast iron by itself was far from impervious to fire. This discovery led to encasing the metal in masonry, combining the first material's strength with the second's fire resistance (see "The First Skyscrapers," page 876, and FIG. **28-41**).

LOUIS HENRY SULLIVAN As skyscrapers proliferated, architects refined the visual vocabulary of the new inhabitable towers. Louis Henry Sullivan (1856–1924), whom many architectural

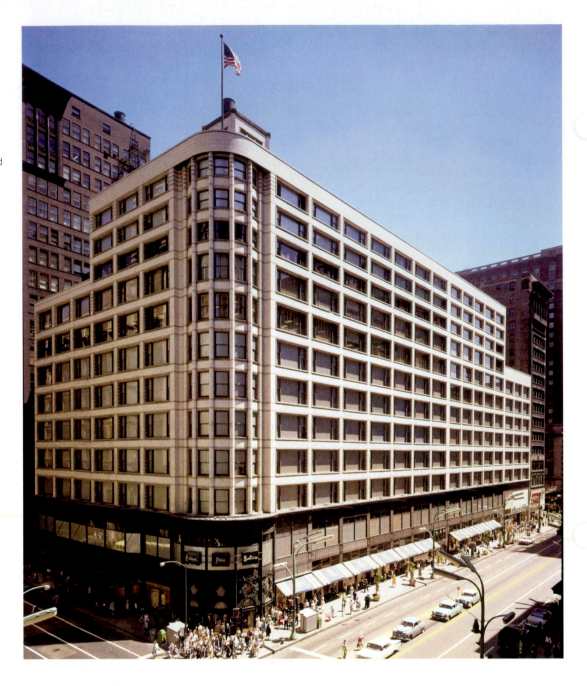

28-43 Louis Henry Sullivan, Carson, Pirie, Scott Building (looking southeast), Chicago, 1899–1904.

Sullivan's architectural motto was "form follows function." He tailored the design of this steel, glass, and stone Chicago department store to meet the needs of its employees and customers.

Sullivan also designed the Carson, Pirie, Scott Building (FIG. 28-43) in Chicago. Built between 1899 and 1904, this department store required broad, open, well-illuminated display spaces. Sullivan again used a minimal structural steel skeleton to achieve this goal. The architect gave over the lowest two levels of the building to an ornament in cast iron (of his invention) made of wildly fantastic motifs. He regarded the display windows as pictures, which merited elaborate frames. As in the Guaranty Building, Sullivan revealed his profound understanding of the maturing consumer economy and tailored the Carson, Pirie, Scott Building to meet the functional and symbolic needs of its users.

Thus, in architecture as well as in the pictorial arts, the late 19th century was a period during which artists challenged traditional modes of expression, often emphatically rejecting the past. Architects, painters, and sculptors as different as Sullivan, Monet, van Gogh, Cézanne, and Rodin, each in his own way, contributed significantly to the entrenchment of modernism as the new cultural orthodoxy of the early 20th century.

IMPRESSIONISM, POST-IMPRESSIONISM, SYMBOLISM: EUROPE AND AMERICA, 1870 TO 1900

Impressionism

- A hostile critic applied the term *Impressionism* to the paintings of Claude Monet because of their sketchy quality. The Impressionists—Monet, Pierre-Auguste Renoir, Edgar Degas, and others—were a diverse group. Some strove to capture fleeting moments and transient effects of light and climate on canvas. Others focused on recording the contemporary urban scene in Paris, frequently painting bars, dance halls, the ballet, wide boulevards, and railroad stations. What united them was not a uniform style or technique but an interest in depicting the transitory nature of modern life.

- Impressionist canvases vary in composition as well as technique, but many feature figures seen at sharply oblique angles and arbitrarily cut off by the frame. These compositions reflect the influence of Japanese prints and of photography.

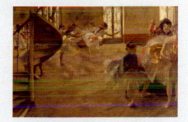

Degas, *The Rehearsal*, 1874

Post-Impressionism and Symbolism

- Post-Impressionism is not a unified style. The term refers to the group of late-19th-century artists, including Georges Seurat, Vincent van Gogh, Paul Gauguin, and Paul Cézanne, who followed the Impressionists and took painting in new directions. Seurat refined the Impressionist approach to color and light into pointillism—the disciplined application of pure color in tiny daubs. Van Gogh explored the capabilities of colors and distorted forms to express emotions. Gauguin moved away from Impressionism in favor of large areas of flat color bounded by firm lines, as in the Japanese prints that he and his contemporaries admired. Cézanne replaced the transitory visual effects of the Impressionists with a rigorous analysis of the lines, planes, and colors that make up landscapes and still lifes.

- Gustave Moreau, Odilon Redon, and Henri Rousseau were the leading French Symbolists. They disdained Realism as trivial and sought to depict a reality beyond that of the everyday world, rejecting materialism and celebrating fantasy and imagination. The subjects of their paintings were often mysterious, exotic, and sensuous.

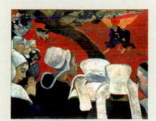

Gauguin, *Vision after the Sermon*, 1888

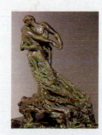

Rousseau, *Sleeping Gypsy*, 1897

Sculpture

- At the end of the 19th century, French artists also led the world in sculpture. Jean-Baptiste Carpeaux, an admirer of Michelangelo and Greco-Roman statuary, added a Realist dimension to his models in groups such as *Ugolino*. *The Waltz*, by Camille Claudel, exemplifies fin-de-siècle passion and eroticism.

- The leading sculptor of the era was Auguste Rodin, who explored Realist themes and the representation of movement. His vision of tormented, writhing figures in Hell connects his work with the Symbolists. Rodin also made statues that were deliberate fragments, creating a taste for the incomplete that appealed to many later sculptors.

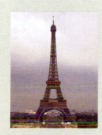

Claudel, *The Waltz*, 1895

Architecture and Decorative Arts

- Not all artists embraced the industrialization transforming daily life during the 19th century. The Arts and Crafts movement in England and the international Art Nouveau style formed in opposition to modern mass production. Both schools advocated natural forms and high-quality craftsmanship.

- New technologies and the changing needs of urbanized, industrialized society transformed architecture in the late 19th century. The exposed iron skeleton of the Eiffel Tower jolted architects into realizing that modern materials and processes could revolutionize architectural design. Henry Hobson Richardson and Louis Sullivan were pioneers in designing the first metal, stone, and glass skyscrapers.

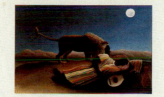

Eiffel, Eiffel Tower, Paris, 1889

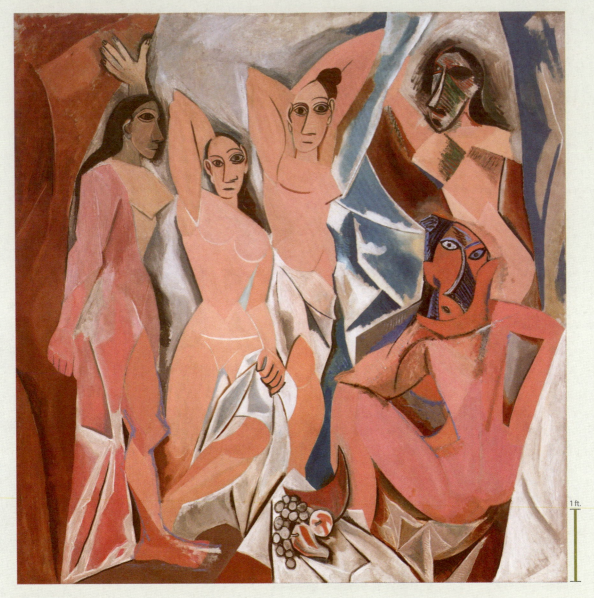

29-1 PABLO PICASSO, *Les Demoiselles d'Avignon*, 1907. Oil on canvas, 8' × 7' 8".
Museum of Modern Art, New York (acquired through the Lillie P. Bliss Bequest).

1 ft.

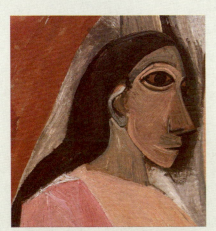

▲ **29-1a** "Primitive" art helped inspire Picasso's radical break with traditional Western norms of pictorial representation. Ancient Iberian sculptures were the sources of the features of the three young women at the left.

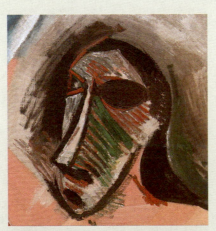

▲ **29-1b** The striated features of the distorted heads of the two young Avignon Street prostitutes at the right grew directly from Picasso's increasing fascination with African artworks, which he studied and collected.

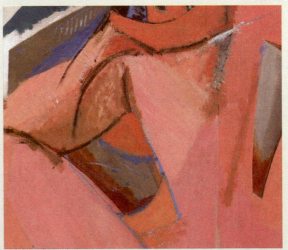

▲ **29-1c** By breaking the figures of the demoiselles into ambiguous planes, as if the viewer were seeing them from more than one place in space at once, Picasso disrupted the standards of Western art since the Renaissance.

Modernism in Europe and America, 1900 to 1945

PICASSO DISRUPTS THE WESTERN PICTORIAL TRADITION

An artist whose importance to the history of art is uncontested, PABLO PICASSO (1881–1973) was blessed with boundless talent and an inquisitive intellect that led him to make groundbreaking contributions to Western pictorial art. In 1907, with *Les Demoiselles d'Avignon* (*The Young Ladies of Avignon*; FIG. **29-1**), he opened the door to a radically new method of representing forms in space. Picasso began the work as a symbolic picture to be titled *Philosophical Bordello,* portraying two male clients (who, based on surviving drawings, had features resembling Picasso's) intermingling with women in the reception room of a brothel on Avignon Street in Barcelona. One was a sailor. The other carried a skull, an obvious reference to death. By the time the artist finished, he had eliminated both men and simplified the room's details to a suggestion of drapery and a schematic foreground still life. Picasso had become wholly absorbed in the problem of finding a new way to represent the five women in their interior space. Instead of depicting the figures as continuous volumes, he fractured their shapes and interwove them with the equally jagged planes representing drapery and empty space. Indeed, the space, so entwined with the bodies, is virtually illegible. The tension between Picasso's representation of three-dimensional space and his modernist conviction that a painting is a two-dimensional design on the surface of a stretched canvas is a tension between representation and abstraction.

The artist extended the radical nature of *Les Demoiselles d'Avignon* even further by depicting the figures inconsistently. Ancient Iberian sculptures inspired the calm, ideal features of the three prostitutes at the left. The energetic, violently striated features of the heads of the two women at the right emerged late in Picasso's production of the work and grew directly from his increasing fascination with African sculpture. Perhaps responding to the energy of these two new heads, Picasso also revised the women's bodies. He broke them into more ambiguous planes suggesting a combination of views, as if the observer sees the figures from more than one place in space at once. The woman seated at the lower right shows these multiple angles most clearly, seeming to present the observer simultaneously with a three-quarter back view from the left, another from the right, and a front view of the head that suggests seeing the figure frontally as well. Gone is the traditional Renaissance concept of an orderly, constructed, and unified pictorial space mirroring the world. In its place are the rudimentary beginnings of a new approach to representing the world—as a dynamic interplay of time and space. Picasso's *Les Demoiselles d'Avignon* was nothing less than a dramatic departure from and disruption of the Western pictorial tradition. It set the stage for many other artistic revolutions in the 20th century.

GLOBAL UPHEAVAL AND ARTISTIC REVOLUTION

The first half of the 20th century was a period of significant upheaval worldwide. Between 1900 and 1945, the major industrial powers fought two global wars (MAP 29-1); witnessed the rise of Communism, Fascism, and Nazism; and suffered the Great Depression.

These decades were also a time of radical change in the arts when painters and sculptors challenged some of the most basic assumptions about the purpose of art and what form an artwork should take. Throughout history, artistic revolution has often accompanied political, social, and economic upheaval, but never before had the new directions that artists explored been as pronounced or as long-lasting as those born during the first half of the last century (see "Picasso Disrupts the Western Pictorial Tradition," page 881).

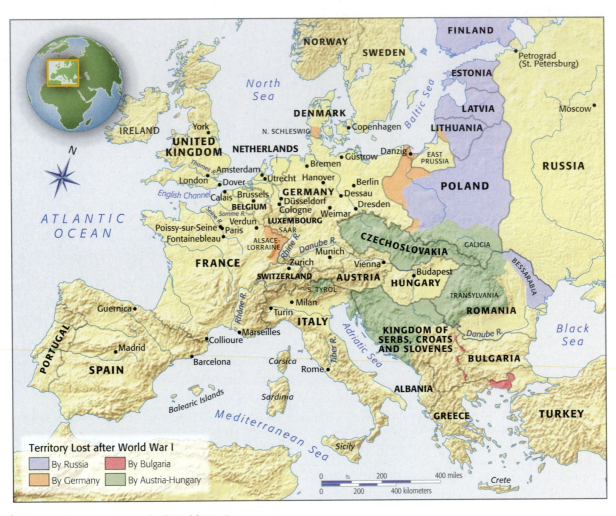

MAP 29-1 Europe at the end of World War I.

MODERNISM IN EUROPE AND AMERICA, 1900 TO 1945

1900-1910
- European artists build on the innovations of the Impressionists and Post-Impressionists and explore new avenues of artistic expression
- Henri Matisse and the Fauves free color from its descriptive function
- The expressive possibilities of color are also an important concern of the German Expressionists. Die Brücke artists produce paintings featuring distorted forms
- The "primitive" art of Africa and Oceania inspires Pablo Picasso and others to break away from traditional forms of representation in Western art
- In America, Frank Lloyd Wright promotes "organic architecture" in his expansive "prairie houses"

1910-1920
- Pablo Picasso and Georges Braque develop a radically new way of making pictures with their Cubist dissection of forms
- The Italian Futurists celebrate dynamic motion and modern technology in paintings and statues
- Vassily Kandinsky pursues abstraction in painting at the same time that scientists question Newtonian physics
- The Dadaists explore the role of chance in often irreverent artworks
- The Armory Show introduces American artists and the public to avant-garde developments in Europe

1920-1930
- In the wake of World War I, German Neue Sachlichkeit painters depict the horrors of global conflict
- The Surrealists seek ways to visualize the world of the unconscious and investigate automatism as a means of creating art
- De Stijl artists create "pure plastic art" using simple geometric forms and primary colors
- Constantine Brancusi and Barbara Hepworth promote abstraction in sculpture
- The Bauhaus advocates the integration of all the arts in its vision of "total architecture"
- Alfred Stieglitz and Edward Weston champion photography as an important art form

1930-1945
- Aaron Douglas and Jacob Lawrence explore African American history in the Harlem Renaissance
- Alexander Calder creates "mobiles"—colorful abstract sculptures with moving parts
- Grant Wood and the Regionalists reject European abstraction and realistically depict life in rural America
- José Orozco and Diego Rivera paint vast mural cycles recording Mexican history
- Dorothea Lange and Margaret Bourke-White achieve renown for their documentary photography

AVANT-GARDE As did other members of society, artists felt deeply the effects of the political and economic disruptions of the early 20th century. As the old social orders collapsed and new ones, from Communism to corporate capitalism, took their places, artists searched for new definitions of and uses for art in a changed world. This fundamental questioning of the nature and goals of artistic production had many precedents in the 19th century, when each successive modernist movement had challenged artistic conventions with ever-greater intensity. This relentless questioning of the status quo gave rise to the notion of an artistic *avant-garde.* The term, which means "front guard," derives from 19th-century French military usage. The avant-garde were the troops sent ahead of the army's main body to scout the enemy's position and strength. Politicians who deemed themselves visionary and forward-thinking subsequently adopted the term. It then migrated to the art world in the 1880s, when artists and critics used it to refer to the Realists, Impressionists, and Post-Impressionists—artists who were ahead of their time and who transgressed the limits of established art forms.

These trailblazing rebels rejected the classical and the academic, and questioned the premises and formal qualities of traditional Western painting, sculpture, and other media. Although the general public found avant-garde art incomprehensible, the principles underlying 19th-century modernism appealed to increasing numbers of artists as the 20th century dawned.

EUROPE, 1900 TO 1920

Avant-garde artists in all their diversity became a major force during the opening decades of the 20th century, beginning with the artistic movement known as *Fauvism.*

Fauvism

In 1905, at the third Salon d'Automne (Autumn Salon) in Paris, a group of young painters exhibited canvases so simplified in design and so shockingly bright in color that a startled critic, Louis Vauxcelles (1870–1943), described the artists as *fauves* (wild beasts). The Fauves were totally independent of the French Academy and the "official" Salon (see "Academic Salons and Independent Art Exhibitions," page 844). Driving the Fauve movement was a desire to develop an art having the directness of Impressionism but employing intense color juxtapositions for expressive ends.

Building on the legacy of artists such as Vincent van Gogh and Paul Gauguin (FIGS. 28-18 to 28-21), the Fauves went even further in liberating color from its descriptive function and exploring the effects that different colors have on emotions. The Fauves produced portraits, landscapes, still lifes, and nudes of spontaneity and verve, with rich surface textures, lively linear patterns, and, above all, bold colors. In an effort to release internal feelings, they employed startling contrasts of vermilion and emerald green and of cerulean blue and vivid orange held together by sweeping brushstrokes and bold patterns.

The Fauve painters never officially organized, and the looseness of both personal connections and stylistic affinities caused the Fauve movement to begin to disintegrate almost as soon as it emerged. Within five years, most of the artists had departed from a strict adherence to Fauve principles and developed their own more personal styles. During its brief existence, however, Fauvism made a remarkable contribution to the direction of art by demonstrating color's structural, expressive, and aesthetic capabilities.

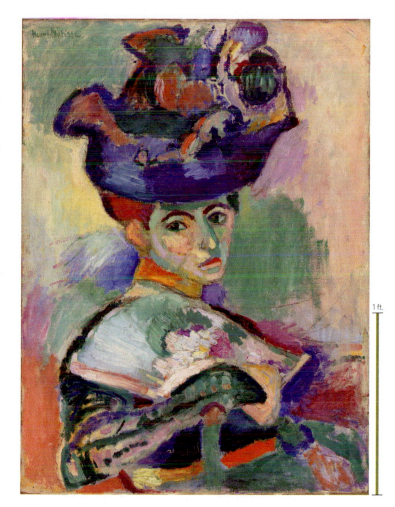

29-2 HENRI MATISSE, *Woman with the Hat,* 1905. Oil on canvas, 2' 7¾" × 1' 11½". San Francisco Museum of Modern Art, San Francisco (bequest of Elise S. Haas).

Matisse's portrayal of his wife, Amélie, features patches and splotches of seemingly arbitrary colors. He and the other Fauve painters used color not to imitate nature but to produce a reaction in the viewer.

HENRI MATISSE The dominant figure of the Fauve group was HENRI MATISSE (1869–1954), who believed that color could play a primary role in conveying meaning, and consequently focused his efforts on developing this notion. In an early painting, *Woman with the Hat* (FIG. **29-2**), Matisse depicted his wife, Amélie, in a rather conventional manner compositionally, but the seemingly arbitrary colors immediately startle the viewer, as does the sketchiness of the forms. The entire image—the woman's face, clothes, hat, and background—consists of patches and splotches of color juxtaposed in ways that sometimes produce jarring contrasts. Matisse explained his approach: "What characterized Fauvism was that we rejected imitative colors, and that with pure colors we obtained stronger reactions."[1] For Matisse and the Fauves, therefore, color became the formal element most responsible for pictorial coherence and the primary conveyor of meaning (see "Henri Matisse on Color," page 884, and FIG. **29-2A**).

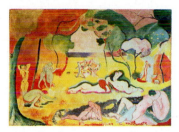

29-2A MATISSE, *Le Bonheur de Vivre,* 1905–1906.

Henri Matisse on Color

In an essay titled "Notes of a Painter," published in the Parisian journal *La Grande Revue* on Christmas Day 1908, Henri Matisse responded to his critics and set forth his principles and goals as a painter. The following excerpts help explain what Matisse was trying to achieve in paintings such as *Harmony in Red* (FIG. 29-3).

> What I am after, above all, is expression.... Expression, for me, does not reside in passions glowing in a human face or manifested by violent movement. The entire arrangement of my picture is expressive: the place occupied by the figures, the empty spaces around them, the proportions, everything has its share. Composition is the art of arranging in a decorative manner the diverse elements at the painter's command to express his feelings....

> Both harmonies and dissonances of color can produce agreeable effects.... Suppose I have to paint an interior: I have before me a cupboard; it gives me a sensation of vivid red, and I put down a red which satisfies me. A relation is established between this red and the white of the canvas. Let me put a green near the red, and make the floor yellow; and again there will be relationships between the green or yellow and the white of the canvas which will satisfy me.... A new combination of colors will succeed the first and render the totality of my representation. I am forced to transpose until finally my picture may seem completely changed when, after successive modifications, the red has succeeded the green as the dominant color. I cannot copy nature in a servile way; I am forced to interpret nature and submit it to the spirit of the picture. From the relationship I have found in all the tones there must result a living harmony of colors, a harmony analogous to that of a musical composition....

> The chief function of color should be to serve expression as well as possible.... My choice of colors does not rest on any scientific theory; it is based on observation, on sensitivity, on felt experiences.... I simply try to put down colors which render my sensation. There is an impelling proportion of tones that may lead me to change the shape of a figure or to transform my composition. Until I have achieved this proportion in all parts of the composition I strive towards it and keep on working. Then a moment comes when all the parts have found their definite relationships, and from then on it would be impossible for me to add a stroke to my picture without having to repaint it entirely.*

*Translated by Jack D. Flam, *Matisse on Art* (London: Phaidon, 1973), 32–40.

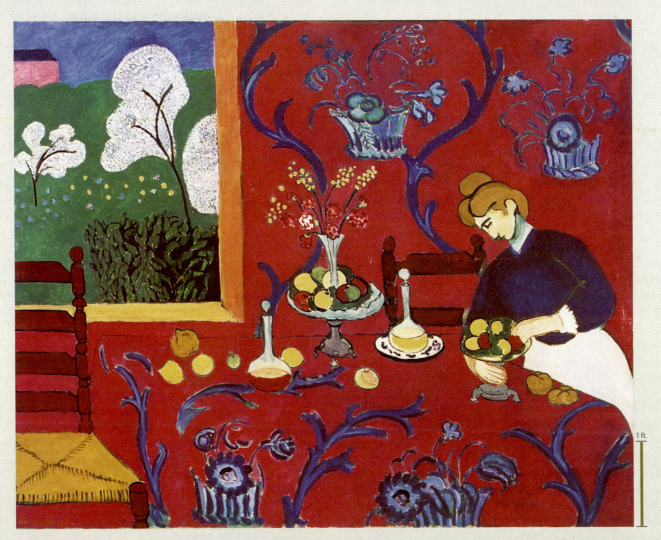

1 ft.

29-3 HENRI MATISSE, *Red Room* (*Harmony in Red*), 1908–1909. Oil on canvas, 5' 11" × 8' 1". State Hermitage Museum, Saint Petersburg.

Matisse believed that painters should choose compositions and colors that express their feelings. Here, the table and wall seem to merge because they are the same color and have identical patterning.

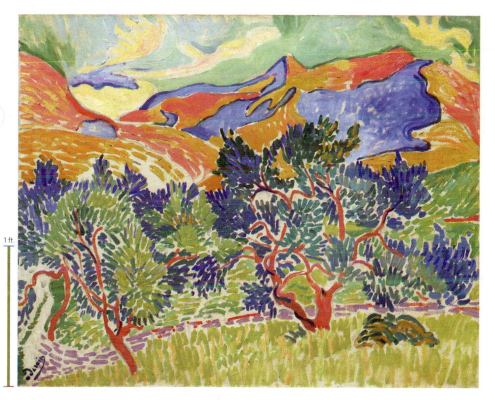

29-4 André Derain, *Mountains at Collioure*, 1905. Oil on canvas, 2' 8" × 3' 3½". National Gallery of Art, Washington, D.C. (John Hay Whitney Collection).

Mountains at Collioure owes much to the landscapes of the Impressionists, van Gogh, and Gauguin, but Derain went further in liberating color from its traditional role of imitating nature.

tance of color for striking the right chord in the viewer. Initially, this work was predominantly green. Then Matisse repainted it blue, but blue also did not seem appropriate to him. Not until he repainted the canvas red did Matisse feel that he had found the right color for the "harmony" he wished to compose.

ANDRÉ DERAIN The landscape setting of Matisse's *Le Bonheur de Vivre* (FIG. 29-2A) is Collioure, on the southeastern coast of France near the border with Spain. In 1905, Matisse painted there beside his friend and fellow Fauve, André Derain (1880–1954). Although Derain also produced many figure studies (for example, FIG. 29-5), at Collioure he frequently painted pure landscapes in the open air, as did the Impressionists before him. *Mountains at Collioure* (FIG. 29-4) is probably the best of that series. Much smaller than *Le Bonheur de Vivre,* Derain's representation of Collioure succeeds in capturing the vast panorama of the Mediterranean mountains, olive groves, and sky seen from a high vantage point. The painting owes much not only to Impressionism but also to Derain's close study of the Post-Impressionists. The short, energetic brushstrokes of pure color, for example, reveal Derain's familiarity with the landscapes of Vincent van Gogh (FIG. 28-19), whose influence is especially clear in the way Derain alternated staccato strokes of green with exposed white canvas in the foreground. The broad, flat areas of unmodulated color in the mountains and sky derive from Paul Gauguin (FIGS. 28-20 and 28-21).

Mountains at Collioure is no mere synthesis of earlier styles, however. Derain went further than either van Gogh or Gauguin in liberating color from its traditional role of imitating the appearance of nature. Like Matisse, Derain used color to create a mood—to express the energy he perceived in the landscape. In Derain's *The Dance* (FIG. 29-5), a lush landscape is merely the background for a study of several large figures, some nude, others clothed, which dominate the canvas.

HARMONY IN RED These color discoveries reached maturity in Matisse's *Red Room* (*Harmony in Red*; FIG. **29-3**). The subject is the interior of a comfortable, prosperous household with a maid placing fruit and wine on the table, but Matisse's canvas is radically different from traditional paintings of domestic interiors (for example, FIGS. 25-18C and 25-19). The Fauve painter depicted objects in simplified and schematized fashion and flattened out the forms. For example, Matisse eliminated the front edge of the table, rendering the table, with its identical patterning, as flat as the wall behind it. The window at the upper left could also be a painting on the wall, further flattening the space. Everywhere, the colors contrast richly and intensely. Matisse's process of overpainting reveals the impor-

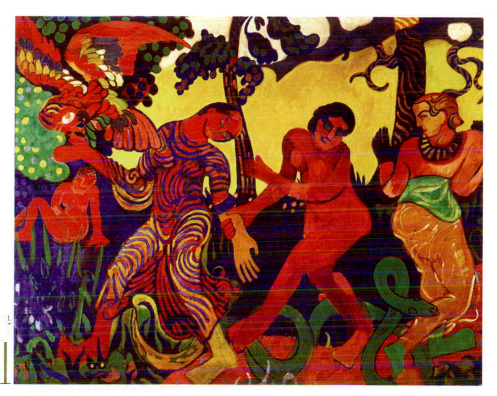

29-5 André Derain, *The Dance*, 1906. Oil on canvas, 6' ⅞" × 6' 10¼". Fridart Foundation, London.

Derain worked closely with Matisse, but the tropical setting and the bold colors of *The Dance* also reflect Derain's study of Gauguin's paintings (FIGS. 28-20 and 28-21), as does the flattened perspective.

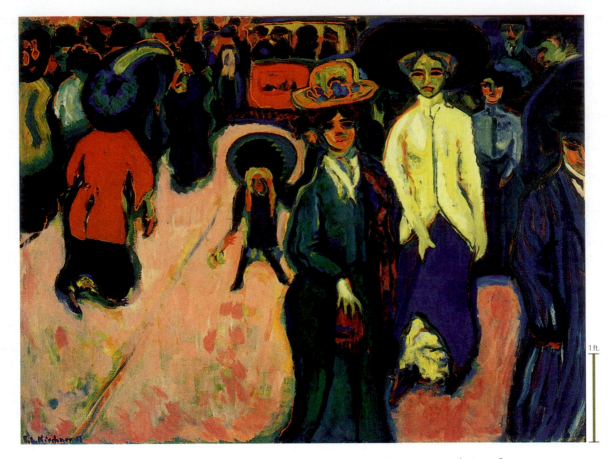

29-6 ERNST-LUDWIG KIRCHNER, *Street, Dresden,* 1908 (dated 1907). Oil on canvas, 4' 11$\frac{1}{4}$" × 6' 6$\frac{7}{8}$". Museum of Modern Art, New York.

Kirchner's perspective distortions, disquieting figures, and color choices reflect the influence of the Fauves and of Edvard Munch (FIG. 28-29), who made similar expressive use of formal elements.

The tropical setting and the bold colors again reflect Derain's study of Gauguin, as does the flattened perspective, but the the Fauve painter's colors are often jarring juxtapositions of complementary colors, which Derain referred to as "deliberate disharmonies." They are precisely what generated the hostility directed at the Fauves when they first presented their work to the public at the Salon d'Automne of 1905.

German Expressionism

The immediacy and boldness of the Fauve images appealed to many artists, including two groups of painters in Germany who called themselves *Die Brücke* ("the Bridge") and *Der Blaue Reiter* ("the Blue Rider"). Together, they produced dramatic and often emotional canvases that art historians classify under the general heading German *Expressionism*. However, although color plays a prominent role in German painting of the early 20th century, the "expressiveness" of many of the German images is due as much to the Expressionists' wrenching distortions of form, ragged outlines, and agitated brushstrokes.

ERNST LUDWIG KIRCHNER Die Brücke, the first group of German Expressionists, gathered in Dresden in 1905 under the leadership of ERNST LUDWIG KIRCHNER (1880–1938). The group members thought of themselves as paving the way for a more perfect age by bridging the old age and the new, hence their name. Kirchner's early studies in architecture, painting, and the graphic arts had instilled

in him a deep admiration for German medieval art. Like the British artists associated with the Arts and Crafts movement, such as William Morris (FIG. 28-36), Die Brücke artists modeled themselves on medieval craft guilds whose members lived together and practiced all the arts equally. Kirchner described their lofty goals in a ringing 1913 statement published in the form of a *woodcut* titled *Chronik der Brücke*:

> With faith in progress and in a new generation of creators and spectators we call together all youth. As youth, we carry the future and want to create for ourselves freedom of life and of movement against the long-established older forces. Everyone who reproduces that which drives him to creation with directness and authenticity belongs to us.[2]

Die Brücke artists protested the hypocrisy and materialistic decadence of those in power. Kirchner, in particular, focused much of his attention on the detrimental effects of industrialization, such as the alienation of individuals in cities, which he felt fostered a mechanized and impersonal society. The tensions leading to World War I further intensified the discomfort and anxiety of the German Expressionists.

Kirchner's *Street, Dresden* (FIG. 29-6) provides a glimpse into the frenzied urban activity of a bustling German city before World War I. Rather than offering the distant, panoramic urban view of the Impressionists (FIG. 28-5), Kirchner's street scene is jarring and dissonant in both composition and color, conveying the disquieting and alienating character of Dresden in the early 20th century. The women in the foreground loom large, approaching somewhat menacingly. The steep perspective of the street, which threatens to push the women directly into the viewer's space, increases their confrontational nature. Harshly rendered, the women's features make them appear ghoulish, and the garish, clashing colors—juxtapositions of bright orange, emerald green, chartreuse, and pink—add to the expressive impact of the image. Kirchner's perspective distortions, disquieting figures, and color choices reflect the influence of the work of Edvard Munch, who made similar expressive use of formal elements in *The Scream* (FIG. 28-29).

VASSILY KANDINSKY Der Blaue Reiter, the second major German Expressionist group, formed in Munich in 1911. The two founding members, Vassily Kandinsky and Franz Marc, whimsically selected this name because of their mutual interest in horses and the color blue. Like Die Brücke, this group produced paintings that captured their feelings in visual form while also eliciting intense emotional responses from viewers.

Born in Russia, VASSILY KANDINSKY (1866–1944) moved to Munich in 1896 and soon developed a spontaneous expressive style. Indeed, Kandinsky was one of the first artists to reject representation and explore abstraction as the "subject" of his paintings, as in *Improvisation 28* (FIG. **29-7**). Kandinsky's elimination of recognizable forms from his canvases grew in part from his interest in theosophy (a religious and philosophical belief system incorporating a wide range of tenets from, among other sources, Buddhism and mysticism) and the occult, but it also reflected his interest in the latest advances in science. A true intellectual, widely read in philosophy, religion, history, and the other arts, especially music, Kandinsky was also one of the few early modernist artists to read with some comprehension the new scientific theories of the era

ART AND SOCIETY
Science and Art in the Early 20th Century

In the early 20th century, radical new ways of thinking emerged in both science and art, forcing people to revise how they understood the world. In particular, the values and ideals that were the legacy of the Enlightenment (see page 771) began to yield to new perspectives. Intellectuals countered 18th- and 19th-century assumptions about progress and reason with ideas challenging traditional notions about the physical universe, the structure of society, and human nature. Modernist artists fully participated in this reassessment and formulated innovative theoretical bases for their work. Accordingly, much early-20th-century Western art is a rejection of traditional limitations and definitions both of art and of the universe.

Fundamental to the Enlightenment was faith in science (see "Joseph Wright of Derby and the Industrial Revolution," page 772). Because of its basis in empirical, or observable, fact, science provided a mechanistic conception of the universe, which reassured a populace that was finding traditional religions less certain. As promoted in the classic physics of Isaac Newton (1642-1727), the universe was a huge machine consisting of time, space, and matter. In the early 20th century, many scientists challenged this model of the universe in what amounted to a second scientific and technological revolution. Particularly noteworthy was the work of physicists Max Planck (1858-1947), Albert Einstein (1879-1955), Ernest Rutherford (1871-1937), and Niels Bohr (1885-1962). With their discoveries, each of these scientists shattered the

existing faith in the objective reality of matter and, in so doing, paved the way for a new model of the universe.

Planck's quantum theory (1900) raised questions about the emission of atomic energy. In his 1905 paper "The Electrodynamics of Moving Bodies," Einstein carried Planck's work further by introducing his theory of relativity. He argued that space and time are not absolute, as postulated in Newtonian physics. Rather, Einstein explained, time and space are relative to the observer and linked in what he called a four-dimensional space-time continuum. He also concluded that matter was not a solid, tangible reality, but another form of energy. Einstein's famous equation, $E = mc^2$, where E stands for energy, m for mass, and c for the speed of light, provided a formula for understanding atomic energy. Rutherford's and Bohr's exploration of atomic structure between 1906 and 1913 contributed to this new perception of matter and energy.

Together, all these scientific discoveries constituted a changed view of physical nature and contributed to the growing interest in abstraction, as opposed to naturalism—the representation of the world as it appears to the eye—among early-20th-century artists, especially Vassily Kandinsky (FIG. 29-7).

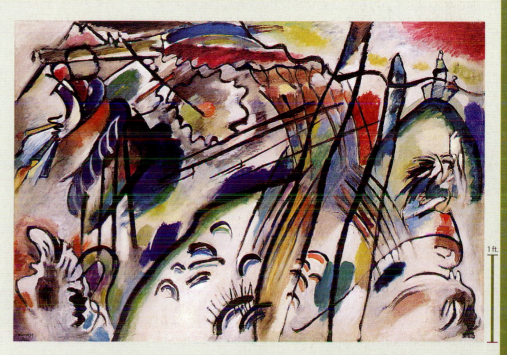

29-7 VASSILY KANDINSKY, *Improvisation 28* (second version), 1912. Oil on canvas, $3' 7\frac{7}{8}'' \times 5' 3\frac{7}{8}''$. Solomon R. Guggenheim Museum, New York (gift of Solomon R. Guggenheim, 1937).

1 ft.

The theories of Einstein and Rutherford convinced Kandinsky that material objects had no real substance. He was one of the first painters to reject representation in favor of abstraction in his canvases.

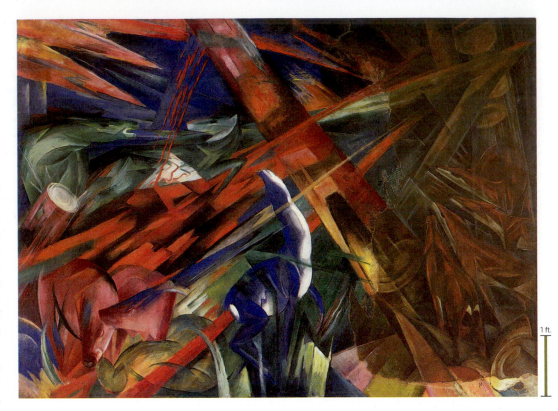

Marc developed a system of correspondences between specific colors and feelings or ideas. In this apocalyptic scene of animals trapped in a forest, the colors of severity and brutality dominate.

1 ft.

(see "Science and Art in the Early 20th Century," page 887). Scientists' exploration of atomic structure, for example, convinced Kandinsky that material objects had no real substance, thereby shattering his faith in a world of tangible things. He articulated his ideas in an influential treatise, *Concerning the Spiritual in Art,* published in 1912, the same year that he painted *Improvisation 28.* Artists, Kandinsky believed, must express their innermost feelings by orchestrating color, form, line, and space, much like composers create music out of notes, which do not mimic the sounds of nature. In his *Improvisation* series, Kandinsky sought to convey feelings solely by color juxtapositions, intersecting linear elements, and implied spatial relationships. Ultimately, Kandinsky saw these abstractions as evolving blueprints for a more enlightened and liberated society emphasizing spirituality.

FRANZ MARC Like many of the other German Expressionists, Franz Marc (1880–1916), the cofounder of Der Blaue Reiter, grew increasingly pessimistic about the state of humanity, especially as World War I loomed on the horizon. His perception of human beings as deeply flawed prompted him to turn to the animal world for his subjects. Animals, he believed, were more pure than humans and thus more appropriate vehicles for expressing an inner truth. In his quest to imbue his paintings with greater emotional intensity, Marc focused on color and developed a system of correspondences between specific colors and feelings or ideas. In a letter to a fellow "blue rider," Marc explained: "Blue is the *male* principle, severe and spiritual. Yellow is the *female* principle, gentle, happy and sensual. Red is *matter*, brutal and heavy."[3]

Fate of the Animals (FIG. **29-8**) represents the culmination of Marc's efforts to create, in a sense, an iconography of color. Painted in 1913, when the horrific tension of impending warfare had pervaded society, the animals appear trapped in a forest amid falling trees, some apocalyptic event destroying both the forest and the animals inhabiting it. The painter distorted the entire scene and shattered it into fragments. Significantly, the lighter and brighter colors—the passive, gentle, and cheerful ones—are absent, and the colors of severity and brutality dominate the work. On the back of the canvas, Marc wrote: "All being is flaming suffering." The artist discovered just how well his painting portended war's anguish and tragedy when he ended up at the front the following year. His experiences in battle prompted him to tell his wife in a letter: "[*Fate of the Animals*] is like a premonition of this war—horrible and shattering. I can hardly conceive that I painted it."[4] Marc's contempt for people's inhumanity and his attempt to express that through his art ended, with tragic irony, in his death in action in 1916.

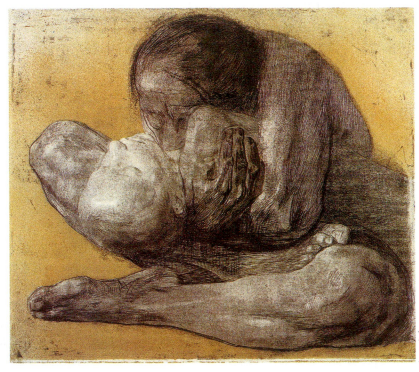

The theme of the mother mourning over her dead child comes from images of the *Pietà* in Christian art, but Kollwitz transformed it into a powerful universal statement of maternal loss and grief.

1 in.

KÄTHE KOLLWITZ The emotional range of German Expressionism extends from passionate protest and satirical bitterness to the poignantly expressed pity for the poor in the prints of KÄTHE KOLLWITZ (1867–1945)—for example, *Woman with Dead Child* (FIG. **29-9**). Kollwitz and her younger contemporary PAULA MODERSOHN-BECKER (1876–1907; FIG. **29-9A**) studied at the Union of Berlin Women Artists and had no formal association with any Expressionist group. Working in a variety of printmaking techniques, including woodcut, lithography, and etching, Kollwitz explored a range of issues from the overtly political to the deeply personal.

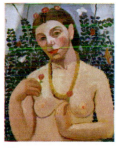

▣ **29-9A** MODERSOHN-BECKER, *Self-Portrait*, 1906.

One image that Kollwitz explored in depth, producing a number of print variations, was a mother with her dead child. Although she initially derived the theme from the Christian *Pietà*, Kollwitz transformed it into a universal statement of maternal loss and grief. In the etching and lithograph illustrated here (FIG. **29-9**), she replaced the reverence and grace pervading most depictions of Mary holding the dead Christ (FIG. 22-12) with an animalistic passion. The grieving mother ferociously grips the body of her dead child. The primal nature of the undeniably powerful image is in keeping with the aims of the Expressionists. Not since the Gothic age in Germany (FIG. 13-50) had any artist produced a mother-and-son group with a comparable emotional impact. Because Kollwitz used her younger son, Peter, as the model for the dead child, the image was no doubt all the more personal to her. The print stands as a poignant premonition. Peter died fighting in World War I at age 21.

EGON SCHIELE Another painter of highly expressive works featuring distorted forms but not associated with any German Expressionist group was the Austrian artist EGON SCHIELE (1890–1918), who during his tragically brief but prolific career produced more than 3,000 paintings and drawings. The bulk of them are nude figure studies of men and women in *gouache* and watercolor on paper, including approximately a hundred self-portraits exemplifying early-20th-century Expressionist painters' intense interest in emotional states. As a teenager, Schiele watched the slow, painful deterioration of his father, who contracted syphilis and died when Egon was 15. The experience had a profound impact on the artist, who ever after associated sex with physical and emotional pain and death.

Schiele began formal art training the year after his father died. He enrolled in Vienna's Academy of Fine Art in 1906, where he became a protégé of Gustav Klimt (FIG. 28-30), who invited Schiele to exhibit some of his works with his own and those of, among others, Vincent van Gogh and Edvard Munch. The emotional content of their work made a deep impression on Schiele, who nonetheless far surpassed van Gogh, Munch, and all of his contemporaries, including the sculptor WILHELM LEHMBRUCK (1881–1919; FIG. **29-9B**), in the portrayal of emaciated bodies and tormented

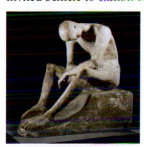

▣ **29-9B** LEHMBRUCK, *Seated Youth*, 1917.

psyches. Indeed, Schiele once spent 24 days in prison for producing what a judge ruled was pornographic art.

Schiele's 1910 nude portrait of himself grimacing (FIG. **29-10**) is a characteristic example of his mature work. He stands frontally, staring at himself in the large mirror he kept in his studio. There is no background. The edges of the paper sever his lower legs and right elbow. In some portraits, Schiele portrayed himself with amputated limbs, and his body is always that of a malnourished man whose muscles show through transparent flesh. The pose is awkward, twisted, and pained. The elongated fingers of the hands seem useless, incapable of holding anything. It is hard to imagine a nude body breaking more sharply with the classical tradition of heroic male nudity. Schiele's self-portrait is that of a martyr who has suffered both physically and psychologically. (He portrayed himself in several paintings as Saint Sebastian pierced by arrows.) Schiele's unhappy life ended when he contracted the Spanish flu in 1918. He was only 28 years old.

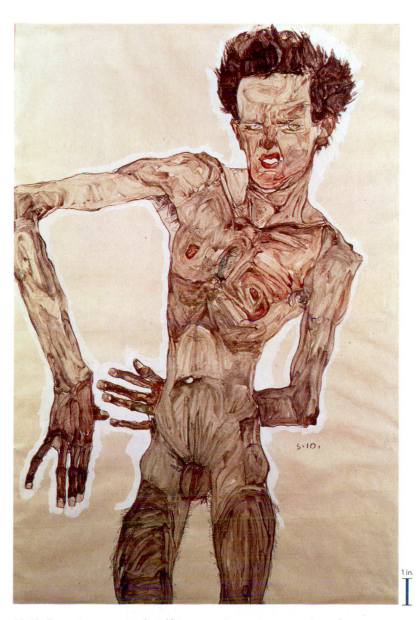

1 in.

29-10 EGON SCHIELE, *Nude Self-Portrait, Grimacing*, 1910. Gouache, watercolor, and pencil on paper, 1' 10" × 1' 2⅜". Albertina, Vienna.

Breaking sharply with the academic tradition of heroic male nudity, Schiele, a Viennese Expressionist, often portrayed himself with an emaciated body, twisted limbs, and a grimacing expression.

Primitivism and Cubism

The Expressionist departure from any strict adherence to illusionism in art was a path that other early-20th-century artists followed. Among those who most radically challenged prevailing artistic conventions and moved most deliberately into the realm of abstraction was Pablo Picasso (see "Picasso Disrupts the Western Pictorial Tradition," page 881).

PABLO PICASSO Born in Spain four years after Gustave Courbet's death, Picasso had mastered all aspects of late-19th-century Realist technique by the time he entered the Barcelona Academy of Fine Art in the late 1890s. His restless mind and limitless energy led him to experiment with a wide range of visual expression, first in Spain and then in Paris, where he settled in 1904. Perhaps the most prolific artist in history, Picasso explored virtually every artistic medium during his lengthy career, but remained a traditional artist in making careful preparatory studies for each major work. Nonetheless, Picasso exemplified modernism in his enduring quest for innovation, which resulted in sudden shifts from one style to another. By the time he settled permanently in Paris, Picasso's work had evolved from Spanish painting's sober Realism through an Impressionistic phase to the so-called Blue Period (1901–1904), when, in a melancholy state of mind, he used primarily blue colors to depict worn, pathetic, and alienated figures. In 1904, Picasso's palette changed to lighter and brighter colors during his Rose (or Pink) Period (1904–1906), but some of the canvases he painted during those years, such as *Family of Saltimbanques* (FIG. **29-10A**), retain the pessimistic overtones of the Blue Period.

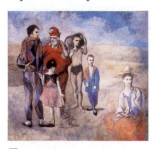

⬏ **29-10A** PICASSO, *Family of Saltimbanques*, 1905.

ART AND SOCIETY
Gertrude and Leo Stein and the Avant-Garde

One of the many unexpected developments in the history of art is that two Americans—Gertrude (1874-1946) and Leo (1872-1947) Stein—played pivotal roles in the history of the European avant-garde. The Steins provided a hospitable environment in their Paris home for artists, writers, musicians, collectors, and critics to socialize and discuss progressive art and ideas. Born in Pennsylvania, the Stein siblings moved to 27 rue de Fleurus in Paris in 1903. Gertrude's experimental writing stimulated her interest in the latest developments in the arts. Conversely, the avant-garde ideas discussed in her home influenced Gertrude's unique poetry, plays, and other works. She is perhaps best known for *The Autobiography of Alice B. Toklas* (1933), a unique memoir written in the persona of her lover and longtime companion.

The Steins' interest in the exciting and invigorating debates taking place in avant-garde circles led them to welcome visitors to their Saturday salons, which included lectures, thoughtful discussions, and spirited arguments. Often, these gatherings lasted until dawn and included not only their French friends but also visiting Americans, Britons, Swedes, Germans, Hungarians, Spaniards, Poles, and Russians. Among the hundreds who visited the Steins were artists Henri Matisse, Pablo Picasso, Georges Braque, Mary Cassatt, Marcel Duchamp, Alfred Stieglitz, and Arthur B. Davies; writers Ernest Hemingway, F. Scott Fitzgerald, John dos Passos, Jean Cocteau, and Guillaume Apollinaire; art dealers Daniel Kahnweiler and Ambroise Vollard; critics Roger Fry and Clive Bell; and collectors Sergei Shchukin and Ivan Morosov.

The Steins were themselves avid art collectors, and the works they hung in their home attracted many visitors. One of the first paintings Leo purchased was Matisse's notorious *Woman with the Hat* (FIG. 29-2), and he subsequently bought many more by Matisse—including *Le Bonheur de Vivre* (FIG. 29-2A)—along with works by Gauguin, Cézanne, Renoir, Picasso, and Braque. Sarah Stein and her husband, Michael, who was Leo and Gertrude's older brother, were also major, if more focused, collectors. They acquired many works by Matisse and lent some of them to the 1913 Armory Show in New York, which introduced avant-garde European art to America (see "The Armory Show," page 909).

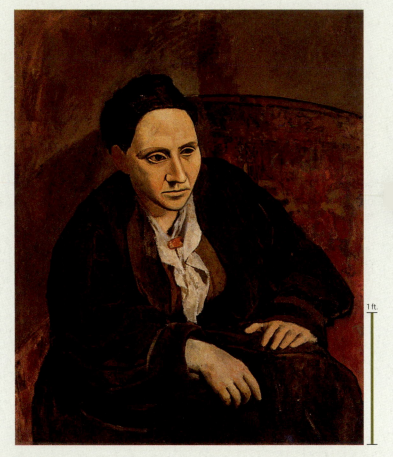

1 ft.

29-11 **PABLO PICASSO**, *Gertrude Stein*, 1906–1907. Oil on canvas, 3' 3 ⅜" × 2' 8". Metropolitan Museum of Art, New York (bequest of Gertrude Stein, 1947).

Picasso had left this portrait of his friend and patron unfinished until he decided to incorporate the planar simplicity of ancient Iberian stone sculptures into his depiction of her face.

Gertrude developed an especially close relationship with Picasso, who painted her portrait (FIG. 29-11) in 1907. Gertrude loved the painting so much that she kept it by her all her life and bequeathed it to the Metropolitan Museum of Art only upon her death in 1946.

GERTRUDE STEIN By 1906, Picasso was searching restlessly for new ways to depict form. He found clues in the ancient Iberian sculpture of his homeland and other "primitive" cultures. Inspired by these sources, Picasso returned to an unfinished portrait he had been preparing for Gertrude Stein (FIG. 29-11), his friend and patron (see "Gertrude and Leo Stein and the Avant-Garde," page 890). Stein had posed for more than 80 sittings earlier in the year, but Picasso was still not satisfied with the results. On resuming work, Picasso painted Stein's head as a simplified planar form, incorporating aspects derived from Iberian stone heads. Although the disparity between the style of the face and the rest of the figure is striking, together they provide an insightful portrait of a forceful, confident woman. More important, Picasso had discovered a new approach to the representation of the human form.

ART AND SOCIETY
Primitivism and Colonialism

The art of Africa, Oceania, and the native peoples of the Americas was a major source of inspiration for many early-20th-century modernist artists. Art historians refer to the incorporation of stylistic elements from these non-Western cultures as *primitivism*. Both "primitive" and "non-Western" are adjectives that imply the superiority of Western civilization and Western art, but many modernist artists admired the artworks of these cultures precisely because they embodied different stylistic preferences and standards. Some artists—for example Henri Matisse and Pablo Picasso (FIG. 29-12)—became enthusiastic collectors of "primitive art," but all of them could view non-Western objects in the many European and American anthropological and ethnographic museums that had begun to proliferate during the second half of the 19th century.

In 1882, the Musée d'Ethnographie du Trocadéro (now the Musée du quai Branly) in Paris opened its doors to the public. The Musée Permanent des Colonies (now the Musée National des Arts d'Afrique et d'Océanie) in Paris also provided the public with a wide array of objects—weapons, tools, basketwork, headdresses—from colonial territories, as did the Musée Africain in Marseilles. In Berlin, the Museum für Völkerkunde housed almost 10,000 African objects by 1886, when it opened for public viewing. Even the Expositions Universelles—regularly scheduled exhibitions in France designed to celebrate industrial progress—included products from Oceania and Africa after 1851. By the beginning of the 20th century, significant non-Western collections were on view in museums in Liverpool, Glasgow, Edinburgh, London, Hamburg, Stuttgart, Vienna, Berlin, Munich, Leiden, Copenhagen, and Chicago.

The formation of these collections was a by-product of the frenzied imperialist expansion central to the geopolitical dynamics of the 19th century and much of the 20th century. Most of the Western powers maintained colonies as sources of raw materials, as manufacturing markets, and as territorial acquisitions. For example, the United States, France, and Holland all kept a colonial presence in the Pacific. Britain, France, Germany, Belgium, Holland, Spain, and Portugal divided up the African continent. Social Darwinists, most notably Herbert Spencer (1820–1903), justified this colonization in terms of the survival of the most economically fit industrialized countries. Europeans and Americans often perceived the cultures they colonized as "primitive" and referred to many of the non-Western artifacts displayed in museums as "artificial curiosities" or "fetish objects." Indeed, the exhibition of these objects collected during expeditions to the colonies served to reinforce the "need" for a colonial presence in these countries. Colonialism often had a missionary dimension. These objects, which often depicted strange gods or creatures, reinforced the perception that these peoples were "barbarians" who needed to be "civilized" or "saved," and this perception justified colonialism and its missionary aspects worldwide.

Whether avant-garde artists were aware of the imperialistic implications of their appropriation of non-Western culture is unclear.

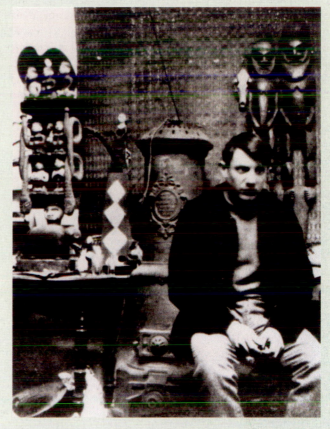

29-12 FRANK GELETT BURGESS, photograph of Pablo Picasso in his studio in the rue Ravignan, Paris, France, 1908. Musée Picasso, Paris.

Picasso was familiar with ancient Iberian art from his homeland and studied African and other "primitive" art in Paris's Trocadéro museum. He kept his own collection of primitive art in his studio.

Certainly, however, many artists reveled in the energy and freshness of non-Western images and forms. These different cultural products provided Western artists with new ways of looking at their own art. Matisse always maintained that he saw African sculptures as simply "good sculptures . . . like any other."[*] Picasso, in contrast, believed that "the masks weren't just like any other pieces of sculpture. Not at all. They were magic things. . . . mediators" between humans and the forces of evil, and he sought to capture their power as well as their forms in his paintings. "[In the Trocadéro] I understood why I was a painter. . . . All alone in that awful museum, with masks, dolls . . . *Les Demoiselles d'Avignon* [FIG. 29-1] must have come to me that day."[†] "Primitive art" seemed to embody a directness, closeness to nature, and honesty that appealed to modernist artists determined to reject conventional models. Non-Western art served as an important revitalizing and energizing force in Western art.

[*]Jean-Louis Paudrat, "From Africa," in William Rubin, ed., *"Primitivism" in 20th Century Art: Affinity of the Tribal and the Modern* (New York: Museum of Modern Art, 1984), 1:141.
[†]Ibid.

DEMOISELLES D'AVIGNON Later in 1907, Picasso carried his new approach to the representation of human form much further in his *Les Demoiselles d'Avignon* (FIG. 29-1). Although Picasso's painting incorporates references to the Western pictorial tradition—for example, a variation on an Archaic Greek *kouros* statue (FIG. 5-9) for the standing woman at the left and a doubtless intentional tribute to Manet's *Déjeuner sur l'Herbe* (FIG. 27-32) for the seated woman at the right—*Demoiselles* stands apart from that tradition not only in formal terms but in the representation of nude women as threatening rather than as passive figures on display for the pleasure of male viewers. However, Picasso's break with the formal vocabulary of Western art was far more radical than Manet's (see "Picasso Disrupts the Western Pictorial Tradition," page 881). Picasso's rethinking of the premises of Western art was largely inspired by his fascination with "primitive" art, which he had studied in Paris's Trocadéro ethnography museum and collected and kept in his Paris studio (see "Primitivism and Colonialism," page 891, and FIG. 29-12).

GEORGES BRAQUE AND CUBISM For many years, Picasso showed *Les Demoiselles* only to other painters. One of the first to see it was GEORGES BRAQUE (1882–1963), a Fauve painter who found it so challenging that he began to rethink his own painting style. Using the painting's revolutionary elements as a point of departure, together Braque and Picasso formulated *Cubism* around 1908 in the belief that the art of painting had to move far beyond the description of visual reality. Cubism represented a radical turning point in the history of art, nothing less than a dismissal of the pictorial illusionism that had dominated Western art since the Renaissance. The Cubists rejected naturalistic depictions, preferring compositions of shapes and forms abstracted from the conventionally perceived world. As Picasso once explained: "I paint forms as I think them, not as I see them."[5] Together, Picasso and Braque pursued the analysis of form central to Cézanne's artistic explorations (see page 860 and FIGS. 28-22 to 28-23A) by dissecting everything around them into its many constituent features, which they then recomposed, by a new logic of design, into a coherent, independent aesthetic picture. The Cubists' rejection of accepted artistic practice illustrates both the period's avant-garde critique of pictorial convention and the artists' dwindling faith in a safe, concrete Newtonian world in the face of the physics of Einstein and others (see "Science and Art," page 887).

The new style received its name after Matisse described some of Braque's work to the critic Louis Vauxcelles as having been painted "with little cubes." In his review, Vauxcelles described the new paintings as "cubic oddities."[6] The French writer and theorist Guillaume Apollinaire (1880–1918) summarized well the central concepts of Cubism in 1913:

> Authentic cubism [is] the art of depicting new wholes with formal elements borrowed not from the reality of vision, but from that of conception. This tendency leads to a poetic kind of painting which stands outside the world of observation; for, even in a simple cubism, the geometrical surfaces of an object must be opened out in order to give a complete representation of it.... Everyone must agree that a chair, from whichever side it is viewed, never ceases to have four legs, a seat and a back, and that, if it is robbed of one of these elements, it is robbed of an important part.[7]

ANALYTIC CUBISM Most art historians refer to the first phase of Cubism, developed jointly by Picasso and Braque, as *Analytic Cubism,* because in essence it is a painterly analysis of the structure of form. Because Cubists could not achieve the kind of total view Apollinaire described by the traditional method of drawing or painting models from one position, they began to dissect the forms of their subjects and to present their analysis of form across the canvas surface.

Georges Braque's painting *The Portuguese* (FIG. **29-13**) exemplifies Analytic Cubism. The subject is a Portuguese musician whom the artist recalled seeing years earlier in a bar in Marseilles. Braque dissected the man and his instrument and placed the resulting forms in dynamic interaction with the space around them. Unlike the Fauves and German Expressionists, who used vibrant colors, the Cubists chose subdued hues—here solely brown tones—in order to focus attention on form. In *The Portuguese,* Braque carried his analysis so far that viewers must work diligently to discover clues to the subject. The construction of large intersecting planes suggests the forms of a man and a guitar. Smaller shapes interpenetrate and hover in the large planes. The way Braque treated light and shadow reveals his departure from conventional artistic practice. Light and dark passages suggest both chiaroscuro modeling and transparent planes that enable viewers to see through one level to another. Solid forms emerge only to be canceled almost immediately by a different reading of the subject.

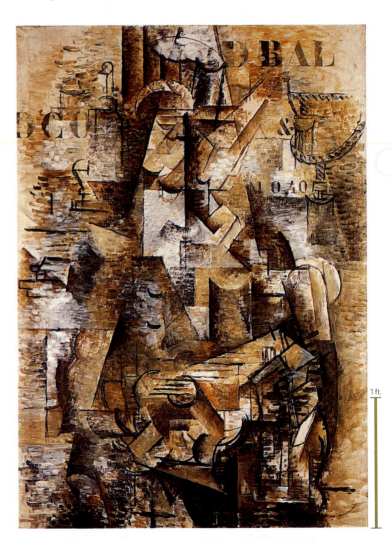

29-13 GEORGES BRAQUE, *The Portuguese,* 1911. Oil on canvas, 3' 10⅛" × 2' 8". Kunstmuseum Basel, Basel (gift of Raoul La Roche, 1952).

The Cubists rejected the pictorial illusionism that had dominated Western art for centuries. Here, Braque concentrated on dissecting form and placing it in dynamic interaction with space.

ARTISTS ON ART
Pablo Picasso on Cubism

In 1923, almost a decade after Picasso and Braque launched an artistic revolution with their Analytic (FIG. 29-13) and Synthetic (FIG. 29-14) Cubist paintings, Picasso granted an interview to the painter and critic Marius de Zayas (1880–1961). Born in Mexico, de Zayas had settled in New York City in 1907, and in 1911 had been instrumental in mounting the first exhibition in the United States of Picasso's works. In their conversation, the approved English translation of which appeared in the journal *The Arts* under the title "Picasso Speaks," the artist set forth his views about Cubism and the nature of art in general.

> We all know that Art is not truth. Art is a lie that makes us realize truth, at least the truth that is given us to understand. The artist must know the manner whereby to convince others of the truthfulness of his lies. . . . They speak of naturalism in opposition to modern painting. I would like to know if anyone has ever seen a natural work of art. Nature and art, being two different things, cannot be the same thing. Through art we express our conception of what nature is not. . . .
>
> Cubism is no different from any other school of painting. The same principles and the same elements are common to all. . . . Many think that Cubism is an art of transition, an experiment which is to bring ulterior results. Those who think that way have not understood it. Cubism is not either a seed or a foetus, but an art dealing primarily with forms, and when a form is realized it is there to live its own life. . . . Mathematics, trigonometry, chemistry, psychoanalysis, music, and whatnot, have been related to Cubism to give it an easier interpretation. All this has been pure literature, not to say nonsense, . . . Cubism has kept itself within the limits and limitations of painting, never pretending to go beyond it. Drawing, design, and color are understood and practiced

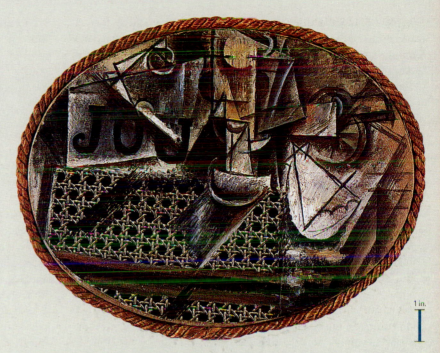

29-14 PABLO PICASSO, *Still Life with Chair-Caning*, 1912. Oil, oilcloth, and rope on canvas, $10\frac{5}{8}$" × 1' $1\frac{3}{4}$". Musée Picasso, Paris.

This painting includes a piece of oilcloth imprinted with the photolithographed pattern of a cane chair seat. Framed with a piece of rope, the still life challenges the viewer's understanding of reality.

> in Cubism in the spirit and manner that they are understood and practiced in all other schools. Our subjects might be different, as we have introduced into painting objects and forms that were formerly ignored. . . . [I]n our subjects, we keep the joy of discovery, the pleasure of the unexpected; our subject itself must be a source of interest.*

*Marius de Zayas, "Picasso Speaks," *The Arts* (May 1923), 315–326. Reprinted in Herschel B. Chipp, *Theories of Modern Art: A Source Book by Artists and Critics* (Berkeley and Los Angeles: University of California Press, 1968), 263–266.

The stenciled letters and numbers that Braque included add to the painting's complexity. Letters and numbers are flat shapes, but as elements of a Cubist painting such as *The Portuguese,* they enable the painter to play with the viewer's perception of two- and three-dimensional space. The letters and numbers lie flat on the painted canvas surface, yet the shading and shapes of other forms seem to flow behind and underneath them, pushing the letters and numbers forward into the viewing space. Occasionally, they seem attached to the surface of some object within the painting. Ultimately, the constantly shifting imagery makes it impossible to arrive at any definitive or final reading of the composition. Examining this kind of painting is a disconcerting excursion into ambiguity and doubt, especially because the letters and numbers seem to anchor the painting in the world of representation, thereby heightening the tension between representation and abstraction. Analytical Cubist paintings radically disrupt expectations about the representation of space and time.

SYNTHETIC CUBISM In 1912, Cubism entered a new phase that art historians have dubbed *Synthetic Cubism*. In this later Cubist style, instead of dissecting forms, artists constructed paintings and draw-ings from objects and shapes cut from paper or other materials. The work marking the point of departure for this new style was Picasso's *Still Life with Chair-Caning* (FIG. **29-14**), a mixed-media painting in which Picasso imprinted a photolithographed pattern of a cane chair seat on the canvas and then pasted a piece of oilcloth on it. Framed with rope, this work challenges the viewer's understanding of reality. The photographically replicated chair caning seems so "real" that the viewer expects the holes to break any brushstrokes laid on it. But the chair caning, although optically suggestive of the real, is only an illusion or representation of an object. In contrast, the painted abstract areas do not refer to tangible objects in the real world. Yet the fact that they do not imitate anything makes them more "real" than the chair caning. No pretense exists. Picasso extended the visual play by making the letter *U* escape from the space of the accompanying *J* and *O* and partially covering it with a cylindrical shape that pushes across its left side. The letters *JOU,* which appear in many Cubist paintings, formed part of the masthead of the daily French newspapers (*journaux*) often found among the objects represented. Picasso and Braque especially delighted in the punning references to *jouer* and *jouir*—the French verbs meaning "to play" and "to enjoy."

Although most discussions of Cubism focus on the formal innovations of Picasso and Braque, it is important to note that contemporary critics also viewed the revolutionary nature of Cubism in sociopolitical terms. Many considered Cubism's challenge to artistic convention and tradition a subversive attack on 20th-century society. In fact, many modernist artists and writers of the period did ally themselves with various anarchist groups whose social critiques and utopian visions appealed to progressive thinkers. It was, therefore, not difficult to see radical art, such as Cubism, as having political ramifications. The French press consistently equated Cubism's disdain for tradition with anarchism and revolution. Picasso himself, however, never viewed Cubism as a protest movement or even different in kind from traditional painting (see "Pablo Picasso on Cubism," page 893).

COLLAGE After *Still Life with Chair-Caning*, both Picasso and Braque continued to explore the medium of *collage* introduced into the realm of "high art" (as opposed to unself-conscious "folk art") in that work. From the French word *coller*, meaning "to stick," a collage is a composition of bits of objects, such as newspaper or cloth, glued to a surface. Braque's *Bottle, Newspaper, Pipe, and Glass* (FIG. **29-15**) is a type of collage called *papier collé* ("stuck paper") in which the artist glues assorted paper shapes to a drawing or painting. In Braque's papier collé, charcoal lines and shadows provide clues to the Cubist multiple views of various surfaces and objects. Roughly rectangular strips of printed and colored paper dominate the composition. The paper imprinted with wood grain and moldings provides an illusion whose concreteness contrasts with the lightly rendered objects on the right. Five pieces of paper overlap each other in the center of the composition to create a layering of flat planes that both echo the space that the lines suggest and establish the flatness of the work's surface. All shapes in the image seem to oscillate, pushing forward and dropping back in space. Shading seems to carve space into flat planes in some places and to turn planes into transparent surfaces in others. The pipe in the foreground illustrates this complex visual interplay especially well. Although it appears to lie on the newspaper, it is in fact a form cut through the printed paper to reveal the canvas surface, which Braque lightly modeled with charcoal. The artist thus kept his audience aware that *Bottle, Newspaper, Pipe, and Glass* is an artwork, a visual game to be deciphered, and not an attempt to reproduce nature.

Picasso explained the goals of Cubist collage in this way:

> Not only did we try to displace reality; reality was no longer in the object. . . . [In] the *papier collé* . . . [w]e didn't any longer want to fool the eye; we wanted to fool the mind. . . . If a piece of newspaper can be a bottle, that gives us something to think about in connection with both newspapers and bottles, too.[8]

Like all collage, the papier collé technique was modern in its medium—mass-produced materials never before found in high art—and modern in the way that the artist embedded the art's "message" in the imagery and in the nature of these everyday materials.

GUERNICA Picasso continued to experiment with different artistic styles and media right up until his death in 1973. Celebrated primarily for his brilliant formal innovations, in the late 1930s Picasso became openly involved in political issues as he watched his homeland descend into civil war. The result was *Guernica* (FIG. **29-16**), one of the greatest works of 20th-century art in any genre. At the time, Picasso declared: "[P]ainting is not made to decorate apartments. It is an instrument for offensive and defensive war against the enemy."[9] The artist got the opportunity to use his craft as a weapon in January 1937 when the Spanish Republican government-in-exile in Paris asked Picasso to produce a major work for the Spanish Pavilion at the Paris International Exposition that summer. He did not formally accept the invitation, however, until he received word that Guernica, the capital of the Basque region (an area in southern France and northern Spain populated by Basque speakers), had been almost totally destroyed in an air raid on April 26, 1937. Nazi pilots acting on behalf of the rebel general Francisco Franco (1892–1975) bombed the city at the busiest hour of a market day, killing or wounding many of Guernica's 7,000 citizens as well as leveling buildings. The event jolted Picasso into action. By the end of June, he had completed *Guernica*, a mural-sized canvas of immense power.

Despite the painting's title, Picasso made no specific reference to the event in *Guernica*. The imagery includes no bombs and no

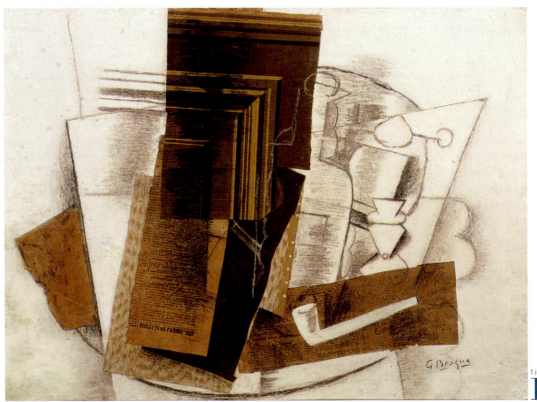

29-15 GEORGES BRAQUE, *Bottle, Newspaper, Pipe, and Glass*, 1913. Charcoal and various papers pasted on paper, 1' 6$\frac{7}{8}$" × 2' 1$\frac{1}{4}$". Private collection, New York.

This Cubist collage of glued paper is a visual game to be deciphered. The pipe in the foreground, for example, seems to lie on the newspaper, but it is a cutout revealing the canvas surface.

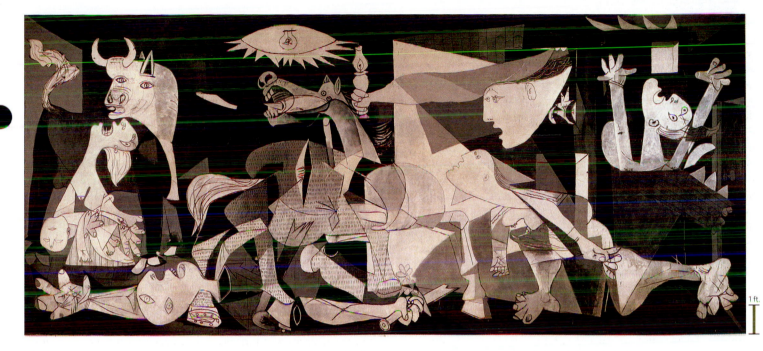

29-16 PABLO PICASSO, *Guernica*, 1937. Oil on canvas, 11' 5½" × 25' 5¾". Museo Nacional Centro de Arte Reina Sofía, Madrid.

Picasso used Cubist techniques, especially the fragmentation of objects and dislocation of anatomical features, to expressive effect in this condemnation of the Nazi bombing of the Basque capital.

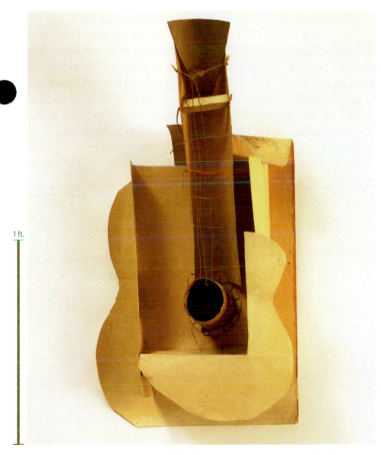

29-17 PABLO PICASSO, maquette for *Guitar*, 1912. Cardboard, string, and wire (restored), 2' 1¼" × 1' 1" × 7½". Museum of Modern Art, New York.

In this model for a sculpture of sheet metal, Picasso presented what is essentially a cutaway view of a guitar, enabling the viewer to examine both surface and interior space, both mass and void.

German planes. It is a universal outcry of human grief. In the center, along the lower edge of the painting, lies a slain warrior clutching a broken and useless sword. A gored horse tramples him and rears back in fright as it dies. On the left, a shrieking, anguished woman cradles her dead child. On the far right, a woman on fire runs screaming from a burning building, while another woman flees mindlessly. In the upper right corner, a woman, represented by only a head, emerges from the burning building, thrusting forth a light to illuminate the horror. Overlooking the destruction is a bull, which, according to the artist, represents "brutality and darkness."[10]

In *Guernica,* Picasso brilliantly used aspects of his earlier Cubist discoveries to expressive effect, particularly the fragmentation of objects and the dislocation of anatomical features. This Cubist fragmentation gave visual form to the horror of the aerial bombardment of the Basque people. What happened to these figures in the artist's act of painting—the dissections and contortions of the human form—paralleled what happened to them in real life. To emphasize the scene's severity and starkness, Picasso reduced his palette to black, white, and shades of gray, suppressing color once again, as he had in his Analytic Cubist works.

GUITAR Cubism not only opened new avenues for representing form on two-dimensional surfaces but also inspired new approaches to sculpture. Picasso created *Guitar* (FIG. 29-17) in 1912. Like his Cubist paintings, this sculpture operates at the intersection of two- and three-dimensionality. Picasso took the form of a guitar—an image that surfaces in many of his paintings as well, including *Three Musicians* (FIG. 29-17A)—and explored its volume using only flat pieces of cardboard. (The work reproduced in FIG. 29-17 is Picasso's *maquette*, or

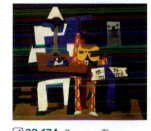

⬈ **29-17A** PICASSO, *Three Musicians*, 1921.

model. The finished sculpture was to be made of sheet metal.) By presenting what is essentially a *cutaway* view of a guitar, Picasso enabled the viewer to examine both surface and interior space, both mass and void. This, of course, was completely in keeping with the Cubist program. Some scholars have suggested that Picasso derived the cylindrical form that serves as the sound hole on the guitar from the eyes on masks from the Ivory Coast of Africa. African masks were a continuing and persistent source of inspiration for the artist (see "Primitivism," page 891). Here, however, Picasso seems to have transformed the anatomical features of African masks into a part of a musical instrument—dramatic evidence of his unique, innovative artistic vision. Ironically—and intentionally—the sound hole, the central void in a real guitar, is, in Picasso's *Guitar,* the only solid form.

ALEKSANDR ARCHIPENKO The Russian sculptor ALEKSANDR ARCHIPENKO (1887–1964) similarly explored the Cubist notion of spatial ambiguity and the relationship between solid forms and space. In *Woman Combing Her Hair* (FIG. **29-18**), Archipenko introduced, in place of the head, a void with a shape of its own that figures importantly in the whole design. Enclosed spaces have always existed in figurative sculpture—for example, the space between the arm and the body when the hand rests on the hip (FIG. 21-12). But in Archipenko's statuette, the space penetrates the figure's continuous mass and is a defined form equal in importance to the mass of the bronze. It is not simply the negative counterpart to the volume as it is in traditional statues. Archipenko's *Woman* shows the same fluid intersecting planes seen in Cubist painting, and the relation of the planes to each other is similarly complex. Thus, both in painting and sculpture, the Cubists broke through traditional limits and transformed these media.

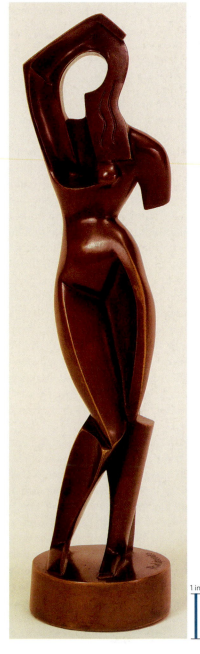

29-18 ALEKSANDR ARCHIPENKO, *Woman Combing Her Hair,* 1915. Bronze, 1' 1¾" high. Museum of Modern Art, New York (acquired through the Lillie P. Bliss Bequest).

....

In this statuette, Archipenko introduced, in place of the head, a void with a shape of its own that figures importantly in the whole design. The void is not simply the negative counterpart of the volume.

JULIO GONZÁLEZ Among the other notable sculptors of the early 20th century were JACQUES LIPCHITZ (1891–1973) and JULIO GONZÁLEZ (1876–1942). Lipchitz's works, such as *Bather* (FIG. **29-18A**), are three-dimensional equivalents of the Analytical Cubist canvases of Picasso and Braque (FIG. 29-13). González was a friend of Picasso who shared his interest in the artistic possibilities of new materials and new methods borrowed from both industrial technology and traditional metalworking. Born into a family of metalworkers in Barcelona, González helped Picasso construct a number of welded sculptures. This contact with Picasso in turn enabled González to refine his own sculptural vocabulary.

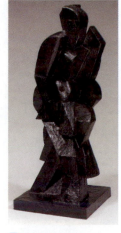

🔊 **29-18A** LIPCHITZ, *Bather,* 1917.

Using prefabricated bars, sheets, or rods of welded or wrought iron and bronze, González created dynamic sculptures with both linear elements and volumetric forms. A comparison between his *Woman Combing Her Hair* (FIG. **29-19**) and Archipenko's version of the same subject (FIG. 29-18) is instructive. Archipenko's figure still incorporates the basic shapes of a woman's body. González reduced his figure to an interplay of curves, lines, and planes—virtually a complete abstraction without any vestiges of traditional representational art. Although González's sculpture received only limited exposure during his lifetime, his work greatly influenced later abstract artists working in welded metal (FIG. 30-17).

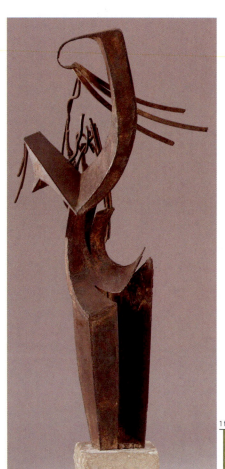

29-19 JULIO GONZÁLEZ, *Woman Combing Her Hair,* 1936. Iron, 4' 4" high. Museum of Modern Art, New York (Mrs. Simon Guggenheim Fund).

....

Using prefabricated metal pieces, González reduced his figure to an interplay of curves, lines, and planes—virtually a complete abstraction without any vestiges of traditional representational art.

PROBLEMS AND SOLUTIONS

Delaunay, Orphism, and the Representation of Modern Life

Robert Delaunay developed his ideas about color use in dialogue with his Russian-born wife, Sonia (1885–1974), also an important modernist artist. She created paintings, quilts and other textile arts, and book covers that exploited the expressive capabilities of color. As a result of their artistic explorations, both Delaunays became convinced that the best solution to the problem of representing the rhythms of modern life was to build on the Cubist breakthroughs of Picasso and Braque and enrich their approach to representation through the use of color harmonies and dissonances.

Delaunay called his method *Simultané-isme*, although it is better known under the name Guillaume Apollinaire proposed: *Orphism*. Simultaneity/Orphism for Delaunay meant the application of 19th-century theories about the perception and psychology of color (see "19th-Century Color Theory," page 855) to create spatial effects and kaleidoscopic movement solely through color contrasts. He insisted that color in painting was both form and subject, and as early as 1912 he began to paint purely abstract compositions with titles such as *Simultaneous Disks*, *Simultaneous Windows*, and *Simultaneous Contrasts*.

A salient feature of modern life for Delaunay was technological innovation, a belief he shared with the Futurists in Italy (see page 898). Consequently, the engineering marvels of the late 19th and early 20th centuries figure prominently in Delaunay's paintings. For example, in 1914, he immortalized the engineer, inventor, and aviator Louis Blériot (1872–1936) in one of his boldest Orphic canvases. *Homage to Blériot* (FIG. 29-20) is a mostly abstract composition that retains representational elements in celebration of Blériot's unprecedented achievement of flying across the English Channel. The 22-mile flight—in a monoplane of his own design—from Les Barraques, near Calais, France, to Dover, England, on July 25, 1909, lasted 37 minutes and made Blériot an instant international celebrity. It also brought him a prize of 1,000 British pounds, which a London newspaper had offered as a challenge to all aviators. At the time Delaunay commemorated the event, Blériot was manufacturing warplanes for use by French pilots and their allies during World War I. One of Blériot's planes appears at the upper right of Delaunay's painting, above another triumph of French engineering, the Eiffel Tower (FIG. 28-40), one of Delaunay's

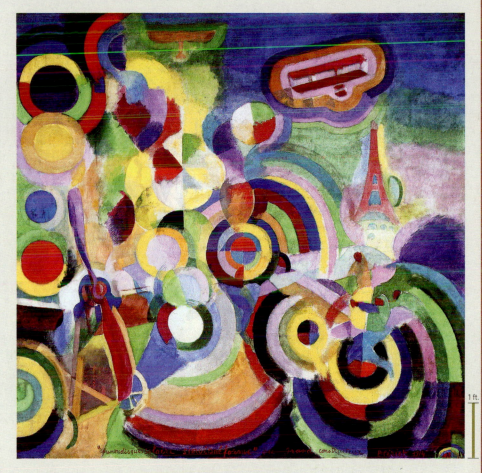

29-20 ROBERT DELAUNAY, *Homage to Blériot*, 1914. Oil on canvas, 8' 2½" × 8' 3". Kunstmuseum Basel, Basel (Emanuel Hoffman Foundation).

In this canvas celebrating modern technological innovation, Delaunay paid tribute to the first pilot to fly across the English Channel. The swirling shapes and bold colors convey explosive energy.

favorite subjects (FIG. 29-20A). Filling the rest of the canvas are a propeller (at the lower left) and mostly circular abstract shapes suggestive of whirling propellers and blazing suns. The swirling abstract and semiabstract shapes and the bold colors together convey explosive energy, and produce an exhilarating effect in the eye and mind of the viewer.

Delaunay's experiments with color dynamics strongly influenced the German Expressionists (he exhibited with Der Blaue Reiter as well as with Cubists)

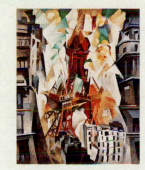

29-20A DELAUNAY, *Champs de Mars*, 1911.

and the Futurists. These artists found in his art means for intensifying expression by suggesting violent motion through shape and color.

ROBERT DELAUNAY AND ORPHISM Art historians generally regard the suppression of color as crucial to the success of Cubist painting, but ROBERT DELAUNAY (1885–1941), Picasso's and Braque's contemporary, worked toward a kind of color Cubism. Apollinaire gave the name *Orphism* to Delaunay's version of Cubism, after Orpheus, the mythical Greek musician. Apollinaire believed that art, like music, was distinct from the representation of the visible world. But Delaunay's own name for his art was *Simultanéisme* (see "Delaunay, Orphism, and the Representation of Modern Life," above, and FIGS. 29-20 and 29-20A).

PROBLEMS AND SOLUTIONS

Léger, the Machine Aesthetic, and the Representation of Modern Life

Robert Delaunay (FIGS. 29-20 and 29-20A) was by no means the only early-20th-century artist who sought to capture the dynamism of modern life on canvas. Another was the Purist Fernand Léger, a champion of the "machine aesthetic." But Léger's solution to the problem differed markedly from Delaunay's.

Léger devised an effective compromise of tastes, bringing together meticulous Cubist analysis of form with Purism's broad simplification and machinelike finish of the design components. He retained from his Cubist practice a preference for cylindrical and tube-shaped motifs, suggestive of machined parts such as pistons and cylinders. Léger's works have the sharp precision of the machine, whose beauty and quality he was one of the first artists to appreciate. For example, in his film *Ballet Mécanique* (*Mechanical Ballet*; 1924), Léger contrasted inanimate objects such as functioning machines with humans in dancelike variations.

Preeminently a painter of modern urban life, Léger incorporated into works such as *The City* (FIG. **29-21**) the massive effects of modern posters and billboard advertisements, the harsh flashing of electric lights, and the noise of traffic. The monumental scale of *The City*, an early work incorporating the aesthetic of Synthetic Cubism, suggests that Léger, had he been given the opportunity, would have been one of the great mural painters of his age. In a defini-

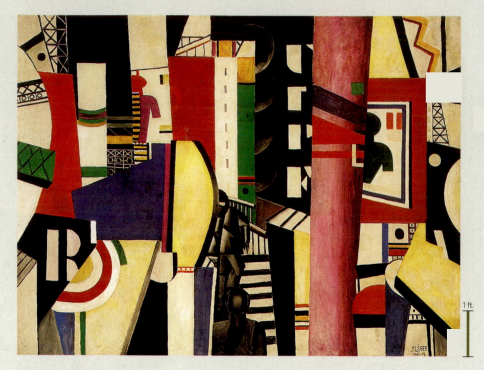

29-21 FERNAND LÉGER, *The City*, 1919. Oil on canvas, 7' 7" × 9' 9$\frac{1}{2}$". Philadelphia Museum of Art, Philadelphia (A. E. Gallatin Collection).

Léger championed the "machine aesthetic." In *The City*, he captured the mechanical commotion of urban life, incorporating the effects of billboard ads, flashing lights, and noisy traffic.

tive way, he depicted the mechanical commotion of urban life, including the robotic movements of mechanized people (FIG. **29-21A**).

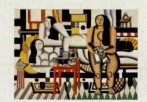

29-21A LÉGER, *Three Women*, 1921.

FERNAND LÉGER AND PURISM Best known today as one of the most important modernist architects, Le Corbusier (FIG. 29-69) was also a painter. In 1918, he founded a movement called *Purism*, which opposed Synthetic Cubism on the grounds that it was becoming merely an esoteric, decorative art out of touch with the machine age. Purists maintained that machinery's clean functional lines and the pure forms of its parts should direct artists' experiments in design, whether in painting, architecture, or industrially produced objects. This "machine aesthetic" inspired FERNAND LÉGER (1881–1955), a French artist who had painted with the Cubists (see "Léger, the Machine Aesthetic, and the Representation of Modern Life," above, and FIGS. 29-21 and 29-21A).

Futurism

Artists associated with another early-20th-century movement, *Futurism*, pursued many of the ideas that the Cubists explored. Equally important to the Futurists, however, was their well-defined sociopolitical agenda. Inaugurated and given its name by the charismatic Italian poet and playwright Filippo Tommaso Marinetti (1876–1944) in 1909, Futurism began as a literary movement but soon encompassed the visual arts, cinema, theater, music, and architecture. Indignant over the political and cultural decline of Italy, the Futurists published numerous manifestos in which they aggressively advocated revolution, both in society and in art (see "Futurist Manifestos," page 899). Like Die Brücke artists, the Futurists aimed at ushering in a new, more enlightened era.

In their quest to launch Italian society toward a glorious future, the Futurists championed war as a means of washing away the stagnant past. Indeed, they saw war as a cleansing agent. Marinetti declared: "We will glorify war—the only true hygiene of the world."[11] The Futurists agitated for the destruction of museums, libraries, and similar repositories of accumulated culture, which they described as mausoleums. They also called for radical innovation in the arts. Of particular interest to the Futurists were the speed and dynamism of modern technology, an interest shared by Delaunay (FIGS. 29-20 and 29-20A) and Léger (FIGS. 29-21 and 29-21A). Marinetti insisted that a racing "automobile adorned with great pipes like serpents with explosive breath . . . is more beautiful than the *Victory of Samothrace*"[12]—a reference to the Greek statue (FIG. 5-83) in the Louvre that for early-20th-century artists represented classicism and the glories of past civilizations. Appropriately, Futurist art often focused on motion in time and space, incorporating the Cubist discoveries derived from the analysis of form.

ARTISTS ON ART

Futurist Manifestos

On April 11, 1910, a group of young Italian artists published *Futurist Painting: Technical Manifesto* in Milan in an attempt to apply the writer Filippo Tommaso Marinetti's views on literature to the visual arts. Signed jointly by Giacomo Balla (FIG. **29-22**), Umberto Boccioni (FIG. **29-23**), Carlo Carrà, Luigi Russolo, and Gino Severini, the manifesto also appeared in an English translation supervised by Marinetti himself. It states in part:

> On account of the persistency of an image on the retina, moving objects constantly multiply themselves [and] their form changes . . . Thus a running horse has not four legs, but twenty. . . .

> What was true for the painters of yesterday is but a falsehood today. . . . To paint a human figure you must not paint it; you must render the whole of its surrounding atmosphere. . . . [T]he vivifying current of science [must] soon deliver painting from academic tradition. . . . The shadows which we shall paint shall be more luminous than the highlights of our predecessors, and our pictures, next to those of the museums, will shine like blinding daylight compared with deepest night. . . .

> We declare . . . that all forms of imitation must be despised, all forms of originality glorified . . . that all subjects previously used must be swept aside in order to express our whirling life of steel, of pride, of fever and of speed . . . that movement and light destroy the materiality of bodies.*

Two years later, Boccioni published a *Technical Manifesto of Futurist Sculpture*, in which he argued that traditional sculpture was "a monstrous anachronism" and modern sculpture should be

> a translation, in plaster, bronze, glass, wood or any other material, of those atmospheric planes which bind and intersect things. . . . Let's . . . proclaim the absolute and complete abolition of finite lines and the contained statue. Let's split open our figures and place the environment inside them. We declare that the environment must form part of the plastic whole.†

The sculptures of Boccioni (FIG. 29-23) and the paintings of Balla (FIG. 29-22) and Severini (FIG. 29-24) perfectly express these Futurist principles and goals.

Futurist Painting: Technical Manifesto (*Poesia*, April 11, 1910). Translated by Filippo Tommaso Marinetti, in Umbro Apollonio, ed. *Futurist Manifestos* (Boston: Museum of Fine Arts, 1970), 27–31.

†Translated by Robert Brain, in Apollonio, *Futurist Manifestos*, 51–65.

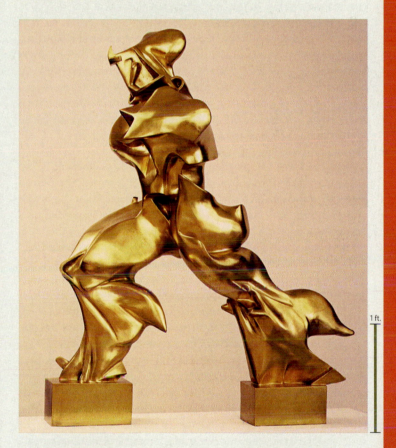

29-22 GIACOMO BALLA, *Dynamism of a Dog on a Leash*, 1912. Oil on canvas, 2' 11$\frac{3}{8}$" × 3' 7$\frac{1}{4}$". Albright-Knox Art Gallery, Buffalo (bequest of A. Conger Goodyear, gift of George F. Goodyear, 1964).

The Futurists' interest in motion and in the Cubist dissection of form is evident in Balla's painting of a passing dog and its owner. Simultaneity of views was central to the Futurist program.

29-23 UMBERTO BOCCIONI, *Unique Forms of Continuity in Space*, 1913 (cast 1931). Bronze, 3' 7$\frac{7}{8}$" high. Museum of Modern Art, New York (acquired through the Lillie P. Bliss Bequest).

Boccioni's Futurist manifesto for sculpture advocated abolishing the enclosed statue. This running figure's body is so expanded that it almost disappears behind the blur of its movement.

GIACOMO BALLA The Futurists' interest in motion and in the Cubist dissection of form is evident in *Dynamism of a Dog on a Leash* (FIG. 29-22), in which GIACOMO BALLA (1871–1958) represented a passing dog and its owner, whose skirts are just within visual range. Balla achieved the effect of motion by repeating shapes—for example, the dog's legs and tail and the swinging line of the leash. Simultaneity of views, as in Cubism, was central to the Futurist program.

UMBERTO BOCCIONI One of the cosigners of the Futurist manifesto (see "Futurist Manifestos," page 899) was UMBERTO BOCCIONI (1882–1916), who produced what is the definitive work of Futurist sculpture, *Unique Forms of Continuity in Space* (FIG. 29-23). This piece highlights the formal and spatial effects of motion rather than their source, the striding human figure. The figure is so expanded, interrupted, and broken in plane and contour that it almost disappears behind the blur of its movement—just as people, buildings, and stationary objects become blurred when seen from an automobile traveling at great speed on a highway or a train racing through the countryside along its steel rails. Boccioni's search for sculptural means of expressing dynamic movement reached definitive expression in *Unique Forms*. In its power and sense of vital activity, this sculpture surpasses similar efforts in Futurist painting to create images symbolic of the dynamic quality of modern life. Although Boccioni's figure bears a curious resemblance to the *Nike of Samothrace* (FIG. 5-83), the ancient sculptor suggested motion only through posture and agitated drapery, not through distortion and fragmentation of the human body—an approach to representation that is the antithesis of the core principles of classical art.

This Futurist representation of motion in sculpture has its limitations, however. The eventual development of the motion picture, based on the rapid sequential projection of fixed images (see page 838 and FIG. 27-53), produced more convincing illusions of movement. And several decades later, Alexander Calder (FIG. 29-79) pioneered the development of kinetic sculpture—sculptures with parts that really move. But in the early 20th century, Boccioni was unsurpassed for his ability to capture the sensation of motion in statuary.

GINO SEVERINI The painting *Armored Train* (FIG. 29-24) by GINO SEVERINI (1883–1966) also encapsulates the Futurist program—politically as well as artistically. Severini depicted a high-tech armored train with its rivets glistening and a huge booming cannon protruding from the top. Submerged in the bowels of the train, soldiers in a row point guns at an unseen target. In Cubist fashion, Severini depicted all of the elements of the painting, from the soldiers to the smoke emanating from the cannon, broken into facets and planes, suggesting action and movement. *Armored Train* reflects both the Futurists' passion for speed and the "whirling life of steel" and their faith in the cleansing action of war. Not only are the colors predominantly light and bright, but death and destruction—the tragic consequences of war—are absent from Severini's painting. This sanitized depiction of armed conflict contrasts sharply with Francisco Goya's *Third of May, 1808* (FIG. 27-12), which also depicts a uniform row of anonymous soldiers in the act of shooting. Goya, however, graphically presented the dead and those about to be shot, and the dark tones he used cast a dramatic and sobering pall.

Once World War I broke out, the Futurist group began to disintegrate, largely because so many of them felt compelled (given the Futurist support for the war) to join the Italian army. Some of them, including Umberto Boccioni, died in the war.

Dada

Although the Futurists celebrated World War I—the "Great War"—and the changes that they hoped it would effect, the mass destruction and chaos that the conflict unleashed horrified other artists. Humanity had never before witnessed such wholesale slaughter on so grand a scale over such an extended period. More than nine million soldiers died in four years. Millions more sustained grievous wounds in great battles. Britain alone lost 60,000 men on the opening day of the

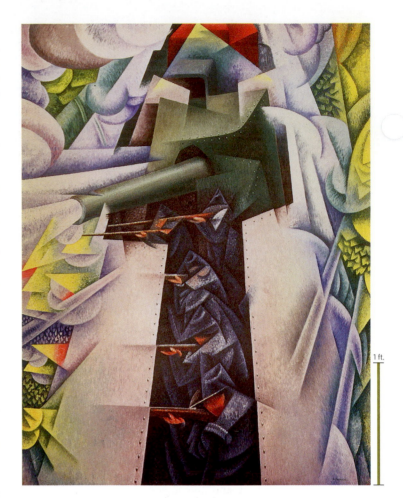

29-24 GINO SEVERINI, *Armored Train*, 1915. Oil on canvas, 3' 10" × 2' 10⅛". Collection of Richard S. Zeisler, New York.

Severini's glistening armored train with protruding cannon reflects the Futurist faith in the cleansing action of war. The painting captures the dynamism and motion central to the Futurist manifesto.

battle of the Somme in 1916. In the same year, the battle of Verdun, which lasted 10 months, produced half a million casualties. The new technology of armaments, bred of the age of steel, made the Great War a "war of the guns." In the face of massed artillery hurling millions of tons of high explosives and gas shells and in the sheets of fire from thousands of machine guns in armored vehicles of the kind celebrated in Severini's *Armored Train* (FIG. 29-24), attack was suicidal. Military campaigns no longer consisted of troop movements designed to capture territory. Warfare became a frustrating stalemate of soldiers holed up in trenches stretching from the English Channel almost to Switzerland. The mud, filth, and blood of the trenches, the pounding and shattering of incessant shell fire, and the terrible deaths and mutilations were a devastating psychological, as well as physical, experience for a generation brought up with the doctrine of progress and a belief in the fundamental values of civilization. The introduction of poison gas in 1915 added to the horror of humankind's inhumanity. The negotiated formal end of hostilities finally arrived in 1919, but peace could not erase the scars of a global conflict that had destroyed the lives of millions and altered the worldview of many millions more.

One major consequence of the Great War was the emergence of an artistic movement known as *Dada*. The Dadaists believed that Enlightenment reasoning had been responsible for the insane spectacle of collective homicide and global devastation that was World War I, and they concluded that the only route to salvation was through political anarchy, the irrational, and the intuitive. Although

Dada began independently in New York and Zurich, it also took root in Paris, Berlin, and Cologne, among other cities. Dada was more a mind-set or attitude than a single identifiable style. As André Breton (1896–1966), founder of the slightly later Surrealist movement (see page 922), explained: "Cubism was a school of painting, futurism a political movement: DADA is a state of mind."[13] Thus an element of absurdity is a cornerstone of Dada—reflected in the movement's very name. Many explanations exist for the choice of "Dada," but according to an oft-repeated anecdote, the Dadaists chose the word at random by sticking a knife into a French-German dictionary. Dada is French for a child's hobby horse. The word satisfied the Dadaists' desire for something nonsensical.

The Dadaists' pessimism and disgust surfaced in their disdain for convention and tradition. These artists made a concerted and sustained attempt to undermine cherished notions and assumptions about art. Because of this iconoclastic dimension, art historians often describe Dada as a destructive enterprise. Dada's negativity and derisive iconoclasm can be read at random from the Dadaists' numerous manifestos and declarations of intent. For example:

> Dada knows everything. Dada spits on everything. Dada says "knowthing," Dada has no fixed ideas. Dada does not catch flies. Dada is bitterness laughing at everything that has been accomplished, sanctified.... Dada is never right.... No more painters, no more writers, no more religions, no more royalists, no more anarchists, no more socialists, no more police, no more airplanes, no more urinary passages.... Like everything in life, Dada is useless, everything happens in a completely idiotic way.... We are incapable of treating seriously any subject whatsoever, let alone this subject: ourselves.[14]

Although cynicism and pessimism inspired the Dadaists, what they developed was phenomenally influential and powerful. By attacking convention and logic, the Dada artists unlocked new avenues for creative invention, thereby fostering a more serious examination of the basic premises of art than prior movements had. But the Dadaists could also be lighthearted in their subversiveness. Although horror and disgust about the war initially prompted Dada, an undercurrent of often irreverent humor and whimsy runs through much of the art. For example, Marcel Duchamp painted a moustache and goatee on a reproduction of Leonardo's *Mona Lisa* (FIG. 29-26A). The French painter Francis Picabia (1879–1953), Duchamp's collaborator in establishing Dada in New York, nailed a toy monkey to a board and labeled it *Portrait of Cézanne.*

In its emphasis on the spontaneous and intuitive, Dada paralleled the views of Sigmund Freud (1856–1939) and Carl Jung (1875–1961). Freud was a Viennese doctor who developed the fundamental principles for what became known as psychoanalysis. In his book *The Interpretation of Dreams* (1900), Freud argued that unconscious and inner drives (of which people are largely unaware) control human behavior. Jung, a Swiss psychiatrist who developed Freud's theories further, believed that the unconscious is composed of two facets, a personal unconscious and a collective unconscious. The collective unconscious comprises memories and associations that all humans share, such as archetypes and mental constructions. According to Jung, the collective unconscious accounts for the development of myths, religions, and philosophies.

Particularly interested in the exploration of the unconscious that Freud advocated, the Dada artists believed that art was a powerfully practical means of self-revelation and healing, and that the images arising out of the subconscious mind had a truth of their own, independent of conventional vision. A Dada filmmaker, Hans Richter (1888–1976), summarized the attitude of the Dadaists:

> Possessed, as we were, of the ability to entrust ourselves to "chance," to our conscious as well as our unconscious minds, we became a sort of public secret society.... We laughed at everything.... But laughter was only the expression of our new discoveries, not their essence and not their purpose. Pandemonium, destruction, anarchy, anti-everything of the World War? How could Dada have been anything but destructive, aggressive, insolent, on principle and with gusto?[15]

JEAN ARP One prominent Dada artist whose works illustrate Richter's element of chance was Zurich-based JEAN (HANS) ARP (1887–1966). Arp pioneered the use of chance in composing his images. Tiring of the look of the Cubist-related collages he was making, he took several sheets of paper, tore them into roughly shaped squares, haphazardly dropped them onto a sheet of paper on the floor, and glued them into the resulting arrangement. The rectilinearity of the shapes guaranteed a somewhat regular design (which Arp no doubt enhanced by adjusting the random arrangement into a quasi-grid), but chance had introduced an imbalance that seemed to Arp to restore to his work a special mysterious vitality that he wanted to preserve. *Collage Arranged According to the Laws of Chance* (FIG. 29-25) is one of the works that Arp created by this method. The operations of chance were for Dadaists a crucial part of this kind of

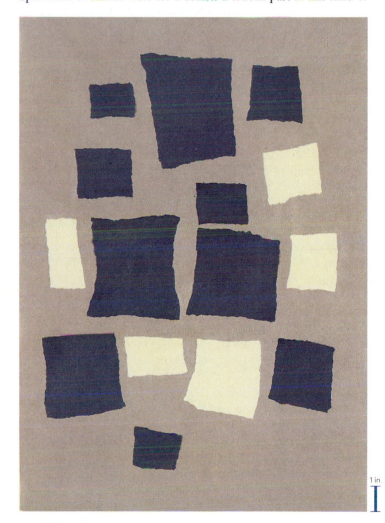

1 in

29-25 JEAN (HANS) ARP, *Collage Arranged According to the Laws of Chance*, 1916–1917. Torn and pasted paper, 1' 7$\frac{1}{8}$" × 1' 1$\frac{5}{8}$". Museum of Modern Art, New York.

In this collage, Arp dropped torn paper squares onto a sheet of paper and then glued them where they fell. His reliance on chance in composing images reinforced the anarchy inherent in Dada.

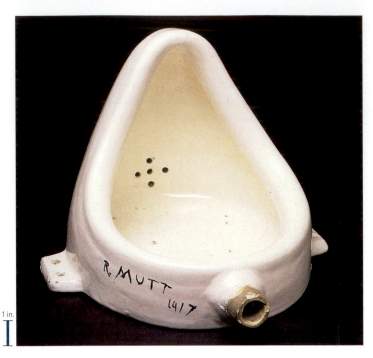

29-26 MARCEL DUCHAMP, *Fountain* (second version), 1950 (original version produced 1917). Glazed sanitary china with black paint, 1' high. Philadelphia Museum of Art, Philadelphia.

Duchamp's "readymade" sculptures were mass-produced objects that the Dada artist modified. In *Fountain,* he conferred the status of art on a urinal and forced people to see the object in a new light.

improvisation. As Richter stated: "For us chance was the 'unconscious mind' that Freud had discovered in 1900. . . . Adoption of chance had another purpose, a secret one. This was to restore to the work of art its primeval magic power and to find a way back to the immediacy it had lost through contact with . . . classicism."[16] Arp's renunciation of artistic control and reliance on chance when creating his compositions reinforced the anarchy and subversiveness inherent in Dada.

MARCEL DUCHAMP Perhaps the most influential Dadaist was MARCEL DUCHAMP (1887–1968), a Frenchman who became the central artist of New York Dada but was also active in Paris. In 1913, he exhibited his first "readymade" sculptures, which were mass-produced common objects—"found objects" that the artist selected and sometimes "rectified" by modifying their substance or combining them with another object. The creation of readymades, Duchamp insisted, was free from any consideration of either good or bad taste, qualities shaped by a society that he and other Dada artists found aesthetically bankrupt. Perhaps his most outrageous readymade was *Fountain* (FIG. **29-26**), a porcelain urinal presented on its back, signed "R. Mutt," and dated (1917). The "artist's signature" was, in fact, a witty pseudonym derived from the Mott plumbing company's name and that of the taller man of the then-popular Mutt and Jeff comic-strip duo. As with Duchamp's other readymades and "assisted readymades" such as *L.H.O.O.Q.* (FIG. **29-26A**), he did not select the urinal for exhibition because of its aesthetic qualities. The "art" of this "artwork" lay in the artist's choice of object, which had the effect of conferring the status of art on it and forcing viewers to

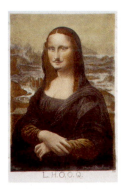

⬀ **29-26A** DUCHAMP, *L.H.O.O.Q.,* 1919.

see the object in a new light. As Duchamp wrote in a "defense" published in 1917, after an exhibition committee rejected *Fountain* for display: "Whether Mr. Mutt with his own hands made the fountain or not has no importance. He CHOSE it. He took an ordinary article of life, placed it so that its useful significance disappeared under the new title and point of view—created a new thought for that object."[17] It is hard to imagine a more direct challenge to artistic conventions than Dada works such as *Fountain.*

THE LARGE GLASS Among the most visually and conceptually challenging of Duchamp's works is *The Bride Stripped Bare by Her Bachelors, Even* (FIG. **29-27**), often called *The Large Glass.* Begun in 1915 and abandoned by Duchamp as unfinished in 1923, *The Large Glass* is a simultaneously playful and serious examination of humans as machines. Consisting of oil paint, wire, and lead foil sandwiched in between two large glass panels, the artwork presents an array of images, some apparently mechanical, others diagrammatic, and yet others seemingly abstract in nature. Duchamp provided some clues to the intriguing imagery in a series of notes accompanying the

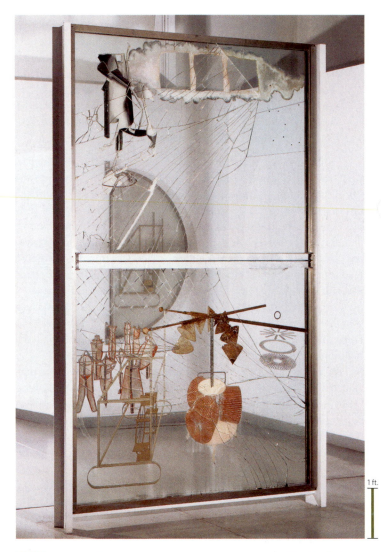

29-27 MARCEL DUCHAMP, *The Bride Stripped Bare by Her Bachelors, Even* (*The Large Glass*), 1915–1923. Oil, lead, wire, foil, dust, and varnish on glass, 9' $1\frac{1}{2}$" × 5' $9\frac{1}{8}$". Philadelphia Museum of Art, Philadelphia (Katherine S. Dreier Bequest).

The Large Glass is a simultaneously playful and serious examination of humans as machines. The bride is a motor fueled by "love gasoline," and the male figures in the lower half also move mechanically.

work. The top half of *The Large Glass* represents "the bride," whom Duchamp has depicted as "basically a motor" fueled by "love gasoline." In contrast, the bachelors appear as uniformed male figures in the lower half of the composition. They too move mechanically. The chocolate grinder in the center of the lower glass pane represents masturbation ("the bachelor grinds his own chocolate"). In *The Large Glass,* Duchamp provided his own whimsical but insightful reflections on desire and sexuality. In true Dadaist fashion, chance completed the work. During the transportation of *The Large Glass* from an exhibition in 1927, the glass panes shattered. Rather than replace the broken glass, Duchamp painstakingly pieced together the glass fragments. After encasing the reconstructed work, broken panes and all, between two heavier panes of glass, Duchamp declared the work completed "by chance."

Duchamp (and the generations of artists after him profoundly influenced by his art and especially his attitude) considered life and art matters of chance and choice freed from the conventions of society and tradition. In Duchamp's approach to art and life, each act was individual and unique. Every person's choice of found objects would be different, for example, and each person's throw of the dice would be at a different instant and would probably yield a different number. This philosophy of utter freedom for artists was fundamental to the history of art in the 20th century—in America as well as Europe. Duchamp spent much of World War I in New York, where he painted *Nude Descending a Staircase* (FIG. 29-35) and inspired a group of American artists and collectors with his radical rethinking of the role of artists and of the nature of art.

HANNAH HÖCH Dada spread throughout much of western Europe, arriving as early as 1917 in Berlin, where it soon took on an activist political edge, partially in response to the economic, social, and political chaos in that city in the years at the end of and immediately after World War I. The Berlin Dadaists developed to a new intensity a technique that had been used in private and popular arts long before the 20th century to create a composition by pasting together pieces of paper. A few years earlier, the Cubists had named the process "collage." The Berliners christened their version of the technique *photomontage.* Unlike Cubist collage, the parts of a Dada collage consisted almost entirely of "found" details, such as pieces of magazine photographs, usually combined into deliberately antilogical compositions. Collage lent itself well to the Dada desire to use chance when creating art—and anti-art—but not all Dada collage was as savagely aggressive as that of the Berlin photomontagists.

One of the Berlin Dadaists who perfected the photomontage technique was HANNAH HÖCH (1889–1978). Höch's photomontages advanced the absurd illogic of Dada by presenting the viewer with chaotic, contradictory, and satiric compositions. They also provided scathing and insightful commentary on two of the most dramatic developments during the Weimar Republic (1918–1933) in Germany— the redefinition of women's social roles and the explosive growth of mass print media. Höch, a passionate early feminist, revealed these combined themes in *Cut with the Kitchen Knife Dada through the Last Weimar Beer Belly Cultural Epoch of Germany* (FIG. **29-28**). In this work, whose title

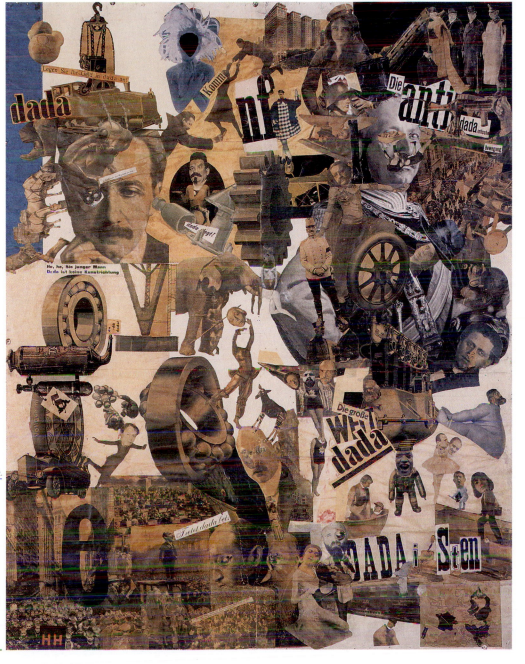

1 ft.

29-28 HANNAH HÖCH, *Cut with the Kitchen Knife Dada through the Last Weimar Beer Belly Cultural Epoch of Germany,* 1919–1920. Photomontage, 3′ 9″ × 2′ 11½″. Neue Nationalgalerie, Staatliche Museen zu Berlin, Berlin.

Photographs of some of Höch's fellow Dadaists appear among images of Marx and Lenin, and the artist juxtaposed herself with a map of Europe showing the progress of women's right to vote.

refers to the story that the name "Dada" resulted from thrusting a knife into a dictionary (see page 901), Höch arranged an eclectic mixture of cutout photos in seemingly haphazard fashion. Closer inspection, however, reveals the artist's careful selection and placement of the photographs. For example, the key figures in the Weimar Republic are together at the upper right (identified as the "anti-Dada movement"). Some of Höch's fellow Dadaists appear among images of Karl Marx and Vladimir Lenin, aligning Dada with other revolutionary forces in what she prominently labeled with cutout lettering *Die grosse Welt dada* ("the great Dada world"). Certainly, juxtaposing the heads of German military leaders with exotic dancers' bodies provided the wickedly humorous critique central to much of Dada. Höch also positioned herself in the topsy-turvy Dada world that she created. A photograph of her head appears in the lower right corner, juxtaposed with a map of Europe showing which countries had granted women the right to vote—a commentary on the power that both women and Dada had to destabilize society.

KURT SCHWITTERS In Hanover, KURT SCHWITTERS (1887–1948) followed a gentler muse. Inspired by Cubist collage but working nonobjectively, Schwitters found visual poetry in the cast-off junk of modern society and scavenged in trash bins for materials, which he pasted and nailed together into designs such as *Merz 19* (FIG. **29-29**). The term *Merz,* which Schwitters used as a generic title for a series of collages, derived nonsensically from the German word *Kommerzbank* ("commerce bank") and appeared as a word fragment in one of his compositions. Although nonobjective, his collages still resonate with the meaning of the fragmented found objects they contain. The recycled elements of Schwitters's collages, like Duchamp's readymades, acquire changed meanings through their new uses and locations. Elevating objects that are essentially trash to the status of high art certainly fits within the parameters of the Dada program and parallels the absurdist dimension of much of Dada art. Contradiction, paradox, irony, and even blasphemy were Dada's bequest to later artists.

Suprematism and Constructivism

Dada was a movement born of pessimism and cynicism. However, not all early-20th-century artists reacted to the profound turmoil of the times by retreating from society. Some artists promoted utopian ideals, believing staunchly in art's ability to contribute to improving society and all humankind. These efforts often surfaced in the face of significant political upheaval, as was the case with Suprematism and Constructivism in Russia.

KAZIMIR MALEVICH Despite Russia's distance from Paris, the center of the international art world in the early 20th century, Russians had a long history of cultural contact and interaction with western Europe. Wealthy Russians, such as Ivan Morozov (1871–1921) and Sergei Shchukin (1854–1936), amassed extensive collections of Impressionist, Post-Impressionist, and avant-garde paintings. Both Morozov and Shchukin had participated in the salons at the Steins' home in Paris (see "Gertrude and Leo Stein," page 890),

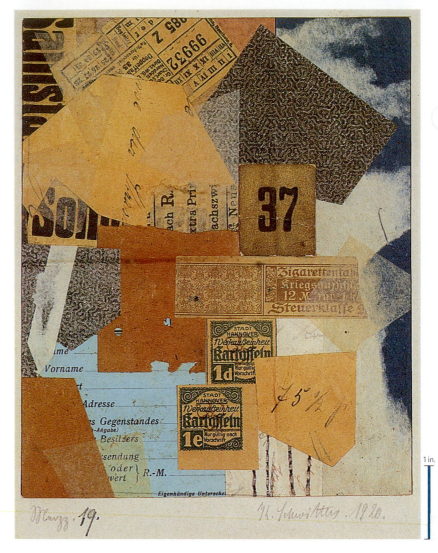

29-29 KURT SCHWITTERS, *Merz 19,* 1920. Paper collage, $7\frac{1}{4}'' \times 5\frac{7}{8}''$. Yale University Art Gallery, New Haven (gift of Collection Société Anonyme).

Inspired by Cubist collage but working nonobjectively, Schwitters found visual poetry in the cast-off junk of modern society, which he pasted and nailed together into striking Dada compositions.

and Shchukin became particularly enamored of the work of both Picasso and Matisse. By the mid-1910s, he had acquired 37 paintings by Matisse and 51 by Picasso. Because of their access to collections such as these, Russian artists were familiar with the latest artistic developments, especially Fauvism, Cubism, and Futurism.

One Russian artist who contributed significantly to the avant-garde nature of early-20th-century art was KAZIMIR MALEVICH (1878–1935). Malevich developed an abstract style to convey his belief that the supreme reality in the world is "pure feeling," which attaches to no object. Thus this belief called for new, nonobjective forms in art—shapes not related to objects in the visible world. Malevich had studied painting, sculpture, and architecture and had worked his way through most of the avant-garde styles of his youth before deciding that none could express pure feeling. He christened his new artistic approach *Suprematism,* explaining: "Under Suprematism I understand the supremacy of pure feeling in creative art. To the Suprematist, the visual phenomena of the objective world are, in themselves, meaningless; the significant thing is feeling, as such, quite apart from the environment in which it is called forth."[18]

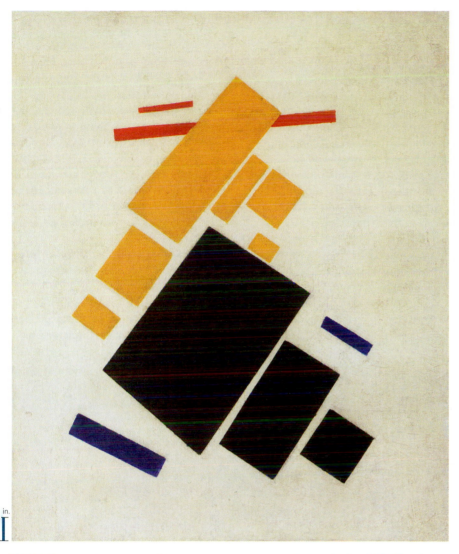

29-30 KAZIMIR MALEVICH, *Suprematist Composition: Airplane Flying*, 1915 (dated 1914). Oil on canvas, 1' 10 7/8" × 1' 7". Museum of Modern Art, New York.

Malevich developed an abstract style that he called Suprematism to convey that the supreme reality in the world is pure feeling. Here, the brightly colored rectilinear shapes float against white space.

The basic form of Malevich's new Suprematist nonobjective art was the square. Combined with its relatives, the straight line and the rectangle, the square soon filled his paintings, such as *Suprematist Composition: Airplane Flying* (FIG. **29-30**). In this work, the brightly colored shapes float against and within a white space, and the artist placed them in dynamic relationship to one another. Malevich believed that all peoples would easily understand his new art because of the universality of its symbols. It used the pure language of shape and color, to which everyone could respond intuitively.

RUSSIAN REVOLUTION In 1917, as a result of widespread dissatisfaction with the regime of Tsar Nicholas II (r. 1894–1917), Russian workers staged a general strike in protest, and the tsar abdicated in March. In late 1917, the Bolsheviks, a faction of Russian Social Democrats that promoted violent revolution, wrested control of the country from the ruling provisional government. Once in power, their leader, Vladimir Lenin (1870–1924), nationalized the land and turned it over to the local rural soviets (councils of workers' and soldiers' deputies). After extensive civil war, the Communists, as

they now called themselves, succeeded in retaining control of Russia and taking over an assortment of satellite countries in eastern Europe. This new state adopted the official name Union of Soviet Socialist Republics (USSR, or Soviet Union) in 1923.

Malevich, who held influential teaching posts in Vitebsk and Petrograd from 1919 to 1927, viewed the revolution as an opportunity to wipe out past traditions and begin a new culture. He believed that his art could play a major role in that effort because of its universal accessibility. But, after a short period during which the new regime tolerated avant-garde art, the political leaders of the Soviet Union decided that their new communist society needed a more "practical" art. Soviet authorities promoted a "realistic," illusionistic art that they thought a wide public could understand and that they hoped would teach citizens about their new government. This horrified Malevich. To him, true art could never have a practical connection with life:

> Every social idea, however great and important it
> may be, stems from the sensation of hunger; every
> art work, regardless of how small and insignificant it
> may seem, originates in pictorial or plastic feeling. It is
> high time for us to realize that the problems of art lie
> far apart from those of the stomach or the intellect.[19]

Disappointed and unappreciated by the public, Malevich continued to produce art but began to gravitate toward other disciplines, such as mathematical theory and geometry, logical fields given his interest in pure abstraction. His work and his theories, if ignored by the masses, nonetheless made a profound impression on other artists, especially in Russia. These included LYUBOV POPOVA (1889–1924), who joined Malevich's Suprematist movement in 1916. Popova's most notable works are the series of canvases she named *Architectonic Paintings* (FIG. **29-30A**).

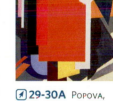

29-30A POPOVA, *Architectonic Painting*, 1916–1917.

NAUM GABO The Russian-born sculptor NAUM GABO (1890–1977) also wanted to create an innovative art to express a new reality, and like Malevich, he believed that art should spring from sources separate from the everyday world. For Gabo, the new reality was the space-time world described by early-20th-century scientists (see "Science and Art," page 887). As he wrote in *The Realistic Manifesto*, published with his brother Anton Pevsner (1886–1962) in 1920:

> Space and time are the only forms on which life is built and hence art
> must be constructed. . . . The realization of our perceptions of the world
> in the forms of space and time is the only aim of our pictorial and plas-
> tic art. . . . We renounce the thousand-year-old delusion in art that held
> the static rhythms as the only elements of the plastic and pictorial arts.
> We affirm in these arts a new element, the kinetic rhythms, as the basic
> forms of our perception of real time.[20]

Gabo was one of the Russian sculptors known as Constructivists. The name *Constructivism* may have come originally from the title *Construction*, which the Russian artist Vladimir Tatlin (FIG. 29-32) used for some relief sculptures he made in 1913 and 1914. Gabo explained that he called himself a Constructivist partly because he built up his sculptures piece by piece in space, instead of carving or modeling them in the traditional way. Although Gabo experimented briefly with real motion in his work, most of his sculptures relied on the relationship of mass and space to suggest the nature of space-time. To indicate the volumes of mass and space more clearly in his sculpture, Gabo used some of the new synthetic plastic materials, including celluloid, nylon, and Lucite, to create constructions whose space seems to flow through as well as around the transparent materials. In works such as *Column* (FIG. 29-31), Gabo opened up the column's circular mass so that the viewer can experience the volume of space it occupies. Two transparent planes extend through its diameter, crossing at right angles at the center of the implied cylindrical column shape. The opaque colored planes at the base and the inclined open ring set up counter-rhythms to the crossed upright planes. They establish the sense of dynamic kinetic movement that Gabo always sought to express as an essential part of reality.

Architecture

One of the goals of the Russian Constructivists was to design a better environment for human beings, a goal best achieved by architects.

VLADIMIR TATLIN The Russian Revolution was the signal to VLADIMIR TATLIN (1885–1953), as it had been to Malevich, that the hated old order was about to end. In utopian fashion, he aspired to play a significant role in creating a new world, one that would fully use the power of industrialization to benefit all people. Initially, like Malevich and Gabo, Tatlin believed that nonobjective art was ideal for the new society, free as such art was from any past symbolism. But after the 1917 revolution, Tatlin enthusiastically abandoned abstract art for "functional art" and designed products such as an efficient stove and workers' clothing.

Tatlin's most famous work is *Monument to the Third International* (FIG. 29-32), an architectural design that, in its reductive geometry, connects his work to the artistic programs of the Suprematists and Constructivists, although Tatlin was not a member of either group. Tatlin received the commission from the Department of Artistic Work of the People's Commissariat for Enlightenment

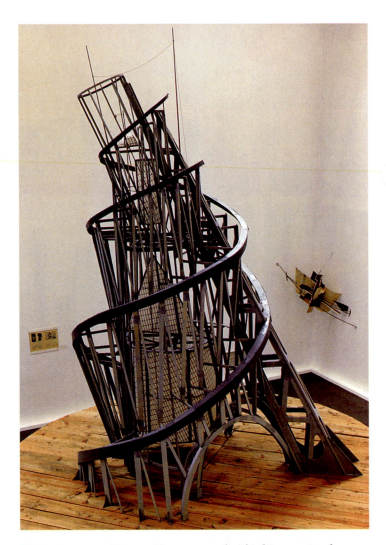

29-31 NAUM GABO, *Column*, ca. 1923 (reconstructed 1937). Perspex, wood, metal, and glass, 3' 5" × 2' 5" × 2' 5". Solomon R. Guggenheim Museum, New York.

Gabo's Constructivist sculptures rely on the relationship of mass and space to suggest the nature of space-time. Space seems to flow through as well as around the transparent materials he used.

29-32 VLADIMIR TATLIN, *Monument to the Third International*, 1919–1920. Reconstruction of the lost model, 1992–1993. Kunsthalle, Düsseldorf.

"Tatlin's Tower" was an ambitious avant-garde design for a Soviet governmental building with three geometrically shaped chambers rotating at different speeds within a dynamically tilted spiral cage.

in early 1919 to honor the Russian Revolution. He envisioned a huge glass-and-iron building that—at 1,300 feet—would have been one-third taller than the Eiffel Tower (FIG. 28-40). Widely influential, "Tatlin's Tower," as it became known, served as a model for those seeking to encourage socially committed and functional art. On its proposed site straddling the Moscow River at the center of the city, it would have functioned as a propaganda and news center for the Soviet people. Within a dynamically tilted spiral cage, three geometrically shaped chambers were to rotate around a central axis, each chamber housing facilities for a different type of governmental activity and rotating at a different speed. The one at the bottom, a huge cylindrical glass structure for lectures and meetings, was to revolve once a year. Higher up was a cone-shaped chamber that would rotate monthly and serve administrative functions. At the top, above a cubic information center designed to revolve daily, Tatlin placed an open-air news screen (illuminated at night) and a special instrument designed to project news bulletins and proclamations on the clouds on any overcast day. The proposed decreasing size of the chambers as visitors ascended the monument paralleled the decision-making hierarchy in the political system, with the most authoritative, smallest groups near the building's apex. Unfortunately, due to Russia's desperate economic situation in the 1920s, Tatlin's Tower was never built. But Tatlin worked out his ambitious design in now-lost metal and wood models exhibited on various official occasions. The only records of these models are a few drawings and photographs, but they have permitted faithful reconstructions of the design, such as the one reproduced in FIG. 29-32.

ADOLF LOOS In Germany, the most influential architectural theorist during the opening decades of the 20th century was ADOLF LOOS (1870–1933). Loos trained as an architect at the Dresden College of Technology and then traveled to the United States to attend the 1893 Columbia Exposition in Chicago. Although he apparently found no work as an architect in Chicago, he remained there three years. During that time, he became familiar with the buildings (FIGS. 28-42, 28-42A, and 28-43) and theories of Louis Sullivan, whose essay "Ornament in Architecture," published in *The Engineering Magazine* in August 1892, affected Loos profoundly. In that treatise, Sullivan suggested that architects consider banishing all ornamentation from their buildings for a period of years "in order that our thought might concentrate acutely upon the production of buildings well formed and comely in the nude."

Loos carried Sullivan's ideas even further in a series of essays in which he railed against the excesses of the Art Nouveau style (FIGS. 28-38 and 28-38A), which was the rage in Europe at the turn of the century. He published his major statement on the subject in 1908 under the title *Ornament and Crime.* Loos equated architec-

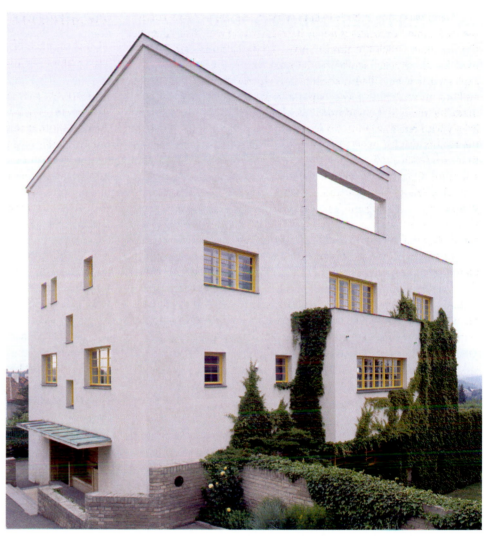

29-33 ADOLF LOOS, Villa Müller (looking north), Prague, Czech Republic, 1928–1930.

For Loos, decoration was a "criminal" waste of labor and materials. His Villa Müller is a white stucco cubical mass devoid of any ornamentation and without even moldings separating the floors.

tural ornamentation with the "amoral" tattoos of Papua New Guinea (see "Tattoo in Polynesia," page 1115, and FIGS. I-19 and 36-16) and asserted that modern men who tattooed themselves were either criminals or degenerates. Ornamentation in architecture was also a crime, both on aesthetic grounds and because it wasted labor and materials.

Loos put his ideas to work early on in his 1910 design for the Viennese home of the painter Lilly Steiner (1884–1962) and in many other buildings, of which the Villa Müller (FIG. 29-33) in Prague is perhaps the purest example of his architectural philosophy. The villa, restored to its former glory in 2000, was the grandiose private residence of the Czech engineer František Müller (1890–1951), the co-owner of a construction company that specialized in providing reinforced concrete for industrial projects and public buildings. Müller's new home was to be, in part, a showcase for the construction materials that brought him his personal fortune. Cubical in form, the Villa Müller has a reinforced-concrete skeleton and a severe white stucco shell without ornamentation of any kind, even moldings separating the floors. The only design elements breaking up the planar severity of the exterior walls are the windows and doors. Walter Gropius would later build on Loos's ideas about pure, functional architectural design at the Bauhaus (see "Walter Gropius and the Bauhaus," page 933, and FIG. 29-67), where he promoted "avoiding all romantic embellishment and whimsy."

UNITED STATES, 1900 TO 1930

Avant-garde experiments in the arts were not limited to Europe. Increasingly common transatlantic travel during the later 19th and early 20th centuries resulted in a lively exchange of artistic ideas among European and American artists. For example, John Singer Sargent (FIG. 27-37), James Abbott McNeil Whistler (FIG. 28-11), and Mary Cassatt (FIG. 28-12) spent much of their productive careers in Europe, whereas many European artists ended their careers in the United States, especially in anticipation of and, later, in the wake of World War I.

Painting and Sculpture

In the opening decade of the 20th century, when most American artists knew little about the revolutionary work of their European counterparts, the goal of many of the leading painters was to present a realistic, unvarnished look at American life. In this regard, their work parallels that of the French Realists in the mid-19th century (see page 815).

JOHN SLOAN AND THE EIGHT The most important group of American Realist artists was The Eight—eight painters who gravitated into the circle of the influential and evangelical artist and teacher Robert Henri (1865–1929). Henri urged his followers to make "pictures from life,"[21] and accordingly, these artists pursued with zeal the production of images depicting the rapidly changing urban landscape of New York City. Because these vignettes often captured the bleak and seedy aspects of city life, The Eight eventually became known as the Ash Can School. Some critics referred to them as "the apostles of ugliness."

A prominent member of The Eight was JOHN SLOAN (1871–1951). A self-described "incorrigible window watcher,"[22] Sloan constantly wandered the streets of New York, observing human drama. He focused much of his attention on the working class, which he perceived as embodying the realities of life. So sympathetic was Sloan to the plight of workers that he joined the Socialist Party in 1909 and eventually ran for public office on the Socialist ticket. In paintings such as *Sixth Avenue and 30th Street, New York City* (FIG. **29-34**), Sloan revealed his ability to capture both the visual and social realities of American urban life. When he painted this image in 1907, Sloan lived on West 23rd Street, on the outskirts of the Tenderloin District, an area cluttered with brothels, dance halls, saloons, gambling dens, and cheap hotels. *Sixth Avenue* depicts a bustling intersection. Bracketing the throngs of people filling the intersection are elevated train tracks on the left and a row of storefronts and apartment buildings on the right. These two defining elements of city life converge in the far center background of the painting.

Sloan's portrayals of New York also feature a cross-section of the population of the city at the opening of the 20th century. In the foreground of *Sixth Avenue,* Sloan prominently placed three women. One, in a shabby white dress, is a drunkard, stumbling along with her pail of beer. All around her are the residents of the Tenderloin, who barely take notice of her, save for two elegantly dressed women who are passing through the area on their way somewhere else. They stare at the disoriented woman with disdain. At a time when traditional art centered on genteel and proper society, the comfortable world of the two fashionable women, Sloan forthrightly depicted the street life of New York's underclass, for whom the painter clearly had deep sympathy.

ARMORY SHOW The relative isolation of American artists from developments across the Atlantic came to an abrupt end in early 1913 when the Armory Show opened in New York City (see "The Armory Show," page 909). Although later recognized as the foundational event in the development of American modernist art, the

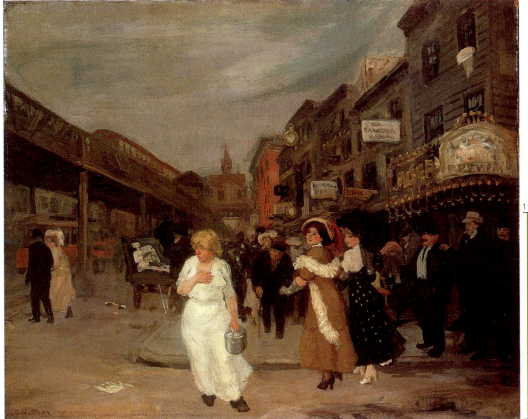

29-34 JOHN SLOAN, *Sixth Avenue and Thirtieth Street, New York City,* 1907. Oil on canvas, 2' $\frac{1}{4}$" × 2' 8". Philadelphia Museum of Art, Philadelphia (gift of Meyer P. Potamkin and Vivian O. Potamkin, 2000).

A prominent member of the American Realist group called The Eight, Sloan captured in his paintings the bleak and seedy aspects of the rapidly changing urban landscape of New York City.

1 ft.

ART AND SOCIETY

The Armory Show

From February 17 to March 15, 1913, the American public flocked in large numbers to view the International Exhibition of Modern Art at the 69th Regiment Armory in New York City. The "Armory Show," as it universally came to be called, was an ambitious endeavor organized primarily by two artists, Walt Kuhn (1877–1949) and Arthur B. Davies (1862–1928). The show included more than 1,600 artworks by American and European artists. Among the European artists represented were Matisse, Derain, Picasso, Braque, Duchamp (FIG. 29-35), Kandinsky, Kirchner, Lehmbruck, and Brancusi. In addition to exposing American artists and the public to the latest European artistic developments, the Armory Show also provided American artists with a prime showcase for their work. The foreword to the exhibition catalog spelled out the goals of the organizers:

> The American artists exhibiting here consider the exhibition of equal importance for themselves as for the public. The less they find their work showing signs of the developments indicated in the Europeans, the more reason they will have to consider whether or not painters or sculptors here have fallen behind . . . the forces that have manifested themselves on the other side of the Atlantic.*

On its opening, this provocative exhibition served as a lightning rod for commentary, immediately attracting heated controversy. The *New York Times* described the show as "pathological" and called the modernist artists "cousins to the anarchists," while the magazine *Art and Progress* compared them to "bomb throwers, lunatics, depravers."[†] Other critics demanded that the exhibition be closed as a menace to public morality. The *New York Herald,* for example, asserted: "The United States is invaded by aliens, thousands of whom constitute so many perils to the health of the body politic. Modernism is of precisely the same heterogeneous alien origin and is imperiling the republic of art in the same way."[‡]

Nonetheless, the exhibition was an important milestone in the history of art in the United States. The Armory Show traveled to Chicago and Boston after it closed in New York and was a significant catalyst for the reevaluation of the nature and purpose of American art.

*Quoted in Herschel B. Chipp, *Theories of Modern Art: A Source Book by Artists and Critics* (Berkeley and Los Angeles: University of California Press, 1968), 503.
[†]Quoted in Sam Hunter, John Jacobus, and Daniel Wheeler, *Modern Art,* rev. 3d. ed. (Upper Saddle River, N.J.: Prentice Hall, 2005), 250.
[‡]Quoted in Francis K. Pohl, *Framing America: A Social History of American Art,* 2d ed. (New York: Thames & Hudson, 2002), 341.

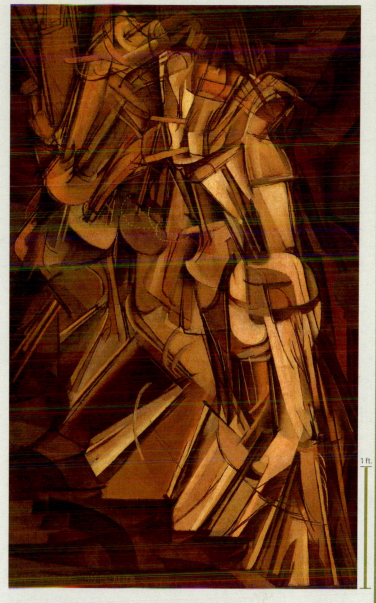

1 ft.

29-35 MARCEL DUCHAMP, *Nude Descending a Staircase, No. 2,* 1912. Oil on canvas, 4' 10" × 2' 11". Philadelphia Museum of Art, Philadelphia (Louise and Walter Arensberg Collection).

The Armory Show introduced European modernism to America. Duchamp's figure moving in a time continuum owes a debt to Cubism and Futurism. The press gave his painting a hostile reception.

---

exhibition received a hostile response from the press. The work that the journalists and critics most maligned was Marcel Duchamp's *Nude Descending a Staircase, No. 2* (FIG. 29-35). The painting represents a single figure moving in a time continuum and suggests the effect of a sequence of overlaid film stills. Unlike the Dada works by Duchamp (FIGS. 29-26, 29-26A, and 29-27), *Nude Descending a Staircase* shares many characteristics with the work of the Cubists and the Futurists. The monochromatic palette is reminiscent of Analytic Cubism, as is Duchamp's faceted presentation of the human form. The artist's interest in depicting the figure in motion reveals an affinity for the Futurists' ideas. One critic described this work as "an explosion in a shingle factory,"[23] and newspaper cartoonists delighted in lampooning the painting.

ARTHUR DOVE Among the American modernists who exhibited their work in the Armory Show was ARTHUR DOVE (1880–1946). After graduating from Cornell University, Dove worked briefly as a commercial artist in New York City and then in 1907 left for Paris, where he encountered the paintings of Henri Matisse (FIGS. 29-2, 29-2A, and 29-3) and André Derain (FIGS. 29-4 and 29-5). Dove returned to New York in 1910. He occupies a special place in the evolution of modernist art in the United States because he began painting completely nonobjective paintings at about the same time as Vassily Kandinsky but apparently without any knowledge of Kandinsky's *Improvisation* series (for example, FIG. 29-7).

Dove spent most of his life on farms in rural New York and Connecticut and loved the textures and colors of the American

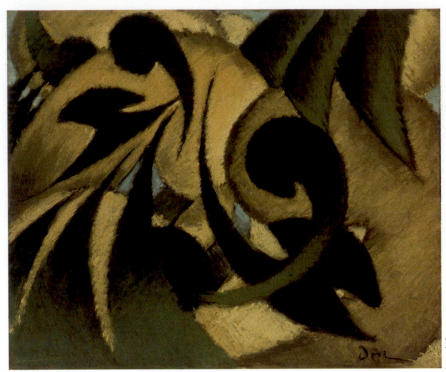

29-36 ARTHUR DOVE, *Nature Symbolized No. 2,* ca. 1911. Pastel on paper, 1' 6" × 1' 9$\frac{5}{8}$". Art Institute of Chicago, Chicago (Alfred Stieglitz Collection).

Dove was one of the first painters to produce completely nonobjective canvases. Using only abstract shapes and color, he sought to capture the essence of nature and of pulsating organic growth.

landscape. He sought to capture in his paintings the essence of nature, especially its pulsating energy, but without representing nature directly. A characteristic and aptly named example of his abstract renditions of fields, vegetation, and sky is *Nature Symbolized No. 2* (FIG. **29-36**), which he probably painted in 1911. Incorporating some of the principles and forms of Cubism but without representing any identifiable objects or landscape elements, Dove used swirling and jagged lines and a palette of mostly green, black, and sandy yellow to capture the essence of vegetation sprouting gloriously from fertile soil beneath patches of blue sky. He once described his goal as the creation of "rhythmic paintings" expressing nature's "spirit" through shape and color.

MAN RAY Another American artist who incorporated the latest European trends in his work was Emmanuel Radnitzky, who assumed the name MAN RAY (1890–1976). He was a close associate of Duchamp's in the 1920s and produced art having a decidedly Dada spirit, often incorporating found objects in his paintings, sculptures, movies, and photographs. Trained as an architectural draftsman, he earned his living as a graphic designer and portrait photographer, and developed an innovative photographic technique. In contrast to traditional photographs, Man Ray produced his images without using a camera by placing objects directly on photographic paper and then exposing the paper to light. He dubbed the resulting photographs, which in effect created themselves, *Rayographs*.

With many other artists of this period, Man Ray shared a keen interest in mass-produced objects and technology, as well as a dedication to exploring the psychological realm of human perception of the exterior world. Like Schwitters, he used the dislocation of ordinary things from their everyday settings to surprise the viewer into new awareness. His displacement of found objects was particularly effective in works such as *Cadeau* (*Gift*; FIG. **29-37**). For this sculpture, with characteristic Dada humor, he equipped a laundry iron with a row of wicked-looking tacks, subverting its proper function. Ray's "gift" would rip to shreds any garment that the recipient tried to press with it.

MARSDEN HARTLEY One American artist who developed a personal style influenced by European avant-garde art movements was MARSDEN HARTLEY (1877–1943). In 1912, Hartley traveled to Europe, visiting Paris, where he became acquainted with the work of the Cubists, and Munich, where he gravitated to the Blaue Reiter circle. Kandinsky's work particularly impressed Hartley, and he developed a style that he called "Cosmic Cubism." In 1913, he moved to Berlin. With the heightened militarism in Germany and the eventual outbreak of World War I, Hartley immersed himself in military imagery.

Portrait of a German Officer (FIG. **29-38**) is one of Hartley's best paintings of this period. It depicts an array of military-related images:

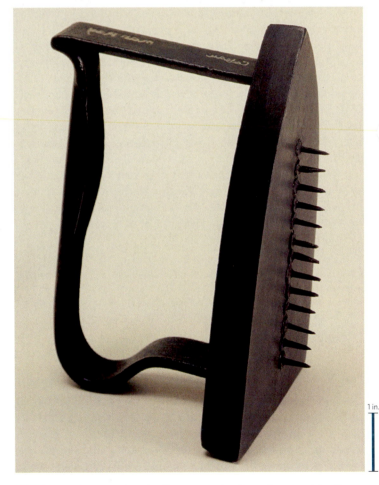

29-37 MAN RAY, *Cadeau* (*Gift*), ca. 1958 (replica of 1921 original). Painted flatiron with row of 13 tacks with heads glued to the bottom, 6$\frac{1}{8}$" × 3$\frac{5}{8}$" × 4$\frac{1}{2}$". Museum of Modern Art, New York (James Thrall Soby Fund).

With characteristic Dada humor, the American artist Man Ray equipped a laundry iron with a row of wicked-looking spikes, subverting its proper function of smoothing and pressing.

German imperial flags, regimental insignia, badges, and emblems such as the Iron Cross. Although this image resonates in the general context of wartime militarism, important elements in the painting had personal significance for Hartley. In particular, the painting includes references to his lover, Lieutenant Karl von Freyberg, who lost his life in battle a few months before Hartley painted this "portrait." Von Freyberg's initials appear in the lower left corner. His age when he died (24) appears in the lower right corner, and his regiment number (4) appears in the center of the painting. Also incorporated is the letter *E* for von Freyberg's regiment, the Bavarian Eisenbahn. The influence of Synthetic Cubism is evident in the flattened, planar presentation of the elements, which almost appear as abstract patterns. The somber black background against which the artist placed the colorful stripes, patches, and shapes casts an elegiac pall over the painting.

STUART DAVIS Philadelphia-born STUART DAVIS (1894–1964) created what he believed was a modern American art style by combining the flat shapes of Synthetic Cubism with his sense of jazz tempos and his perception of the energy of fast-paced American culture. *Lucky Strike* (FIG. 29-39) is one of several tobacco still lifes Davis began in 1921. Davis was a heavy smoker, and tobacco products and their packaging fascinated him. He insisted that the introduction of packaging in the late 19th century was evidence of high civilization and the progressiveness of American culture. Davis depicted the Lucky Strike package in fragmented form, reminiscent of Synthetic Cubist collages. However, the flat printed elements that the work incorporates are illusionistically painted, rather than glued onto the canvas. The discontinuities and the interlocking planes

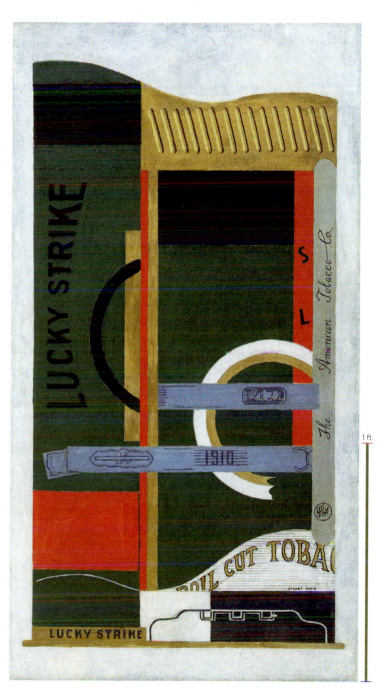

29-39 STUART DAVIS, *Lucky Strike*, 1921. Oil on canvas, 2' 9$\frac{1}{4}$" × 1' 6". Museum of Modern Art, New York (gift of the American Tobacco Company, Inc.). Art © Estate of Stuart Davis/Licensed by VAGA, New York.

Tobacco products fascinated Davis, a heavy smoker. In *Lucky Strike*, he depicted a cigarette package in fragmented form, recalling Cubism, and imbued his painting with an American jazz rhythm.

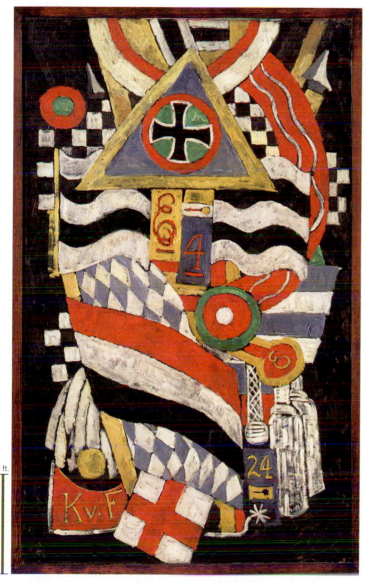

29-38 MARSDEN HARTLEY, *Portrait of a German Officer*, 1914. Oil on canvas, 5' 8$\frac{1}{4}$" × 3' 5$\frac{3}{8}$". Metropolitan Museum of Art, New York (Alfred Stieglitz Collection).

In this elegy to a lover killed in battle, Hartley arranged military-related images against a somber black background. The flattened, planar presentation reveals the influence of Synthetic Cubism.

ART AND SOCIETY

Aaron Douglas and the Harlem Renaissance

Spearheaded by writers and editors Alain Locke (1886–1953) and Charles Spurgeon Johnson (1883–1956), the Harlem Renaissance was a manifestation of the desire of African Americans to promote their cultural accomplishments. Locke and Johnson also aimed to cultivate pride among fellow African Americans and to foster racial tolerance across the United States. Expansive and diverse, the fruits of the Harlem Renaissance included the writings of authors such as Langston Hughes, Countee Cullen, and Zora Neale Hurston; the jazz and blues of Duke Ellington, Bessie Smith, Eubie Blake, Fats Waller, and Louis Armstrong; the photographs of James Van Der Zee and Prentice H. Polk; and the paintings and sculptures of Meta Warrick Fuller and Augusta Savage. The best-known artist associated with the Harlem Renaissance is, however, Aaron Douglas (FIGS. 29-40 and 29-40A).

Douglas arrived in New York City in 1924 and quickly became one of the most sought-after graphic artists in the African American community. Encouraged to create art that would express the cultural history of his race, Douglas incorporated motifs from African sculpture, broadly defined to include ancient Egyptian works, into compositions painted in a version of Synthetic Cubism stressing transparent angular planes. In 1927, Douglas observed:

> While it is absurd to take African sculpture and literally transplant it and inject it into Negro American life, we can go to African life and get . . . understanding, form and color and use this [in] an expression which interprets our life.*

Noah's Ark (FIG. **29-40**) is one of seven paintings Douglas produced based on a book of poems by James Weldon Johnson (1871–1938) called *God's Trombones: Seven Negro Sermons in Verse.* Egyptian influence is evident in Douglas's figures with rounded crania and frontal eyes in profile heads (compare FIG. 3-29). In *Noah's Ark,* he used flat planes to evoke a sense of mystical space and miraculous happenings. Lightning strikes and rays of light crisscross the pairs of animals entering the ark, while men load supplies in preparation for departure. Douglas suggested deep space by differentiating the size of the large human head and shoulders of the worker at the bottom and the small person at work on the far deck of the ship. Yet the composition's unmodulated color shapes create a pattern on the Masonite surface that cancels any illusion of three-dimensional depth. Here, Douglas used Cubism's formal language to express a powerful religious vision.

Seven years later, employed by the U.S. government to create murals for the Harlem branch of the New York Public Library, he addressed a contemporary rather than a biblical subject: the history of Africans in America (FIG. **29-40A**).

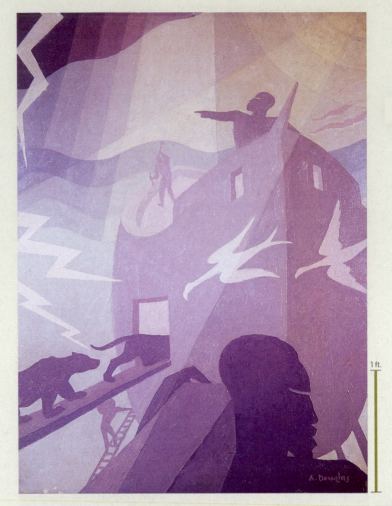

1 ft.

29-40 AARON DOUGLAS, *Noah's Ark,* ca. 1927. Oil on Masonite, 4' × 3'. Fisk University Galleries, University of Tennessee, Nashville.

In *Noah's Ark* and other paintings of the cultural history of African Americans, Douglas incorporated motifs from African sculpture and the transparent angular planes characteristic of Synthetic Cubism.

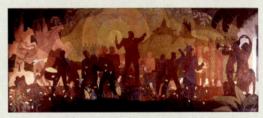

⬀ **29-40A** DOUGLAS, *Slavery through Reconstruction,* 1934.

*Quoted by Caroline Goeser, *Picturing the New Negro* (Lawrence: University of Kansas Press, 2007), 32.

---

imbue *Lucky Strike* with a dynamism and rhythm not unlike American jazz or the pace of life in a lively American metropolis. *Lucky Strike* is decidedly both American and modern.

AARON DOUGLAS Also deriving his personal style from Synthetic Cubism was African American artist AARON DOUGLAS (1898–1979), who used the style to represent symbolically the historical and cultural memories of African Americans. Born in Kansas, Douglas studied in Nebraska and Paris before settling in

New York City, where he became part of the flowering of art and literature in the 1920s known as the Harlem Renaissance (see "Aaron Douglas and the Harlem Renaissance," above).

PRECISIONISM One of the distinctly American art movements that developed in the post–Armory Show period was *Precisionism.* Although not an organized group, the Precisionists shared a fascination with the machine's "precision" and its importance in modern life. Although new technologies captured the imaginations of many

ART AND SOCIETY

Art "Matronage" in the United States

Until the 20th century, a leading reason for the dearth of women artists was that professional institutions restricted women's access to artistic training. For example, the proscription against women participating in life-drawing classes, a staple of academic artistic training, in effect denied women the opportunity to become professional artists. Another explanation for the absence of women from the traditional art historical canon is that art historians have not considered as "high art" many of the art objects that women have traditionally produced (for example, quilts or basketry).

By the early 20th century, however, many of the impediments to a woman's becoming a recognized artist had been removed. Today, women are a major presence in the art world, as the roster of artists discussed in Chapter 31 highlights. One of the developments in the early 20th century that laid the groundwork for this change was the prominent role that American women played as art patrons. These "art matrons" provided financial, moral, and political support to cultivate the advancement of the arts in America. Chief among them were Gertrude Vanderbilt Whitney, Lillie P. Bliss, Mary Quinn Sullivan, Abby Aldrich Rockefeller, Isabella Stewart Gardner, Peggy Guggenheim, and Jane Stanford.*

Gertrude Vanderbilt Whitney (1875–1942) was a practicing sculptor and enthusiastic collector. To assist young American artists such as Robert Henri and John Sloan (FIG. 29-34) in exhibiting their work, she opened the Whitney Studio in 1914. By 1929, dissatisfied with the recognition accorded young, progressive American artists, she offered her entire collection of 500 works to the Metropolitan Museum of Art in New York City. Her offer rejected, she founded her own museum in New York, the Whitney Museum of American Art, and provided funds to purchase additional works by American artists, such as Charles Demuth's *My Egypt* (FIG. **29-41**). She chose Juliana Force (1876–1948) as the first director, a visionary and energetic woman who inaugurated a pioneering series of monographs on living American artists, and organized lecture series by influential art historians and critics. Through the efforts of these two women, the Whitney Museum became a major factor in the enhanced prestige of American art.

A trip to Paris in 1920 whetted the interest of Peggy Guggenheim (1898–1979) in avant-garde art. Like Whitney, Guggenheim collected art and eventually opened a gallery in England to exhibit the work of innovative artists. She continued her support for modernist art after her return to the United States. Guggenheim's New York gallery, called Art of This Century, was instrumental in advancing the careers of many artists, including her husband, Max Ernst (FIG. 29-53). She eventually moved her art collection to a lavish Venetian palace, where the public can still view the important artworks that she acquired.

Other women who contributed significantly to the arts were Lillie P. Bliss (1864–1931), Mary Quinn Sullivan (1877–1939), and Abby Aldrich Rockefeller (1874–1948). Philanthropists, art collectors, and educators, these influential and farsighted women saw the need for a museum to collect and exhibit modernist art. Together they established the Museum of Modern Art in New York City in 1929, which became (and continues to be) the most influential museum of modern art in the world (see "The Museum of Modern Art," page 945).

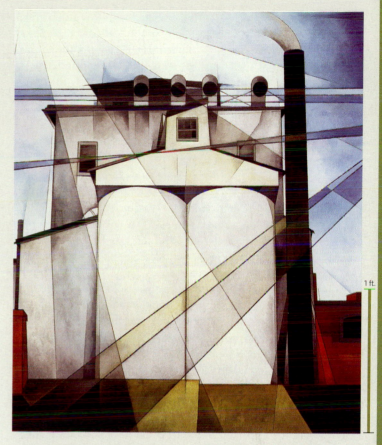

29-41 CHARLES DEMUTH, *My Egypt,* 1927. Oil on composition board, 2' 11$\frac{3}{4}$" × 2' 6". Whitney Museum of American Art, New York (purchased with funds from Gertrude Vanderbilt Whitney).

Demuth was one of the leading Precisionists—American artists who extolled the machine age. This painting depicts grain elevators reduced to geometric forms amid Cubist transparent diagonal planes.

Isabella Stewart Gardner (1840–1924) and Jane Stanford (1828–1905) also undertook the ambitious project of founding museums. The Isabella Stewart Gardner Museum in Boston, established in 1903, houses a well-chosen and comprehensive collection of art of many periods. The Stanford University Museum of Art (now the Iris B. and Gerald Cantor Center for Visual Arts), the first American museum west of the Mississippi, got its start in 1891 at the university that Leland Stanford Sr. and Jane Stanford founded after the tragic death of their son. The Cantor Center houses a wide range of objects, including archaeological and ethnographic artifacts. Both women committed much of their time, energy, and financial resources to ensure the success of their museums, and were intimately involved in their institutions' day-to-day operations.

The museums that these women established flourish today, attesting to the extraordinary vision of these "art matrons" and the remarkable contributions they made to the advancement of art in the United States.

*Art historian Wanda Corn coined the term "art matronage" in the catalog *Cultural Leadership in America: Art Matronage and Patronage* (Boston: Isabella Stewart Gardner Museum, 1997).

European artists, especially Delaunay, Léger, and the Futurists, Americans generally seemed more enamored of the prospects of a mechanized society than did Europeans. Even the Frenchman Francis Picabia, Duchamp's collaborator, noted: "Since machinery is the soul of the modern world, and since the genius of machinery attains its highest expression in America, why is it not reasonable to believe that in America the art of the future will flower most brilliantly?"[24] Precisionism, however, expanded beyond the exploration of machine imagery. Many artists associated with this group gravitated toward Synthetic Cubism's flat, sharply delineated planes as an appropriate visual idiom for their imagery, adding to the clarity and precision of their work. Eventually, Precisionism came to be characterized by a merging of a familiar native style in American architecture and artifacts with a modernist vocabulary derived largely from Synthetic Cubism.

CHARLES DEMUTH Two of the leading Precisionists hailed from Pennsylvania—Charles Sheeler (1883–1965) and CHARLES DEMUTH (1883–1935). Sheeler traveled to Italy and France in 1909, and Demuth spent the years 1912–1914 in Paris, but both artists rejected pure abstraction and favored American subjects, especially industrial landscapes. Demuth's *My Egypt* (FIG. 29-41) is one of many artworks acquired by Gertrude Vanderbilt Whitney, the leading patron of American modernist artists in the period between the two world wars (see "Art 'Matronage' in the United States," page 913). The painting incorporates the spatial discontinuities characteristic of Cubism into a typically Precisionist depiction of an industrial site near Lancaster, the painter's birthplace. Demuth reduced the John W. Eshelman and Sons grain elevators to simple geometric forms. The grain elevators remain recognizable and solid, but the "beams" of transparent planes and the diagonal force lines threaten to destabilize the image and recall Cubist fragmentation of space. The degree to which Demuth intended to extol the American industrial scene is unclear. The title, *My Egypt,* is sufficiently ambiguous in tone to accommodate differing readings. On the one hand, Demuth could have been suggesting a favorable comparison between the Egyptian pyramids and American grain elevators as cultural icons. On the other hand, the title could be read cynically, as a negative comment on the limitations of American culture. Or Demuth might have been making a biblical reference to Joseph's granaries, which fed Egypt during seven years of famine.

GEORGIA O'KEEFFE The work of Wisconsin-born GEORGIA O'KEEFFE (1887–1986) changed stylistically throughout her career. During the 1920s, O'Keeffe was a Precisionist. She had moved from the tiny town of Canyon, Texas, to New York City in 1918, and although she had visited the city before, what she found there excited her. "You have to live in today," she told a friend. "Today the city is something bigger, more complex than ever before in history. And nothing can be gained from running away. I couldn't even if I could."[25] While in New York, O'Keeffe met Alfred Stieglitz (FIGS. 29-43 and 29-43A), who played a major role in promoting the avant-garde in the United States. Stieglitz had established an art gallery at 291 Fifth Avenue in New York. In "291," as the gallery came to be called, he exhibited the latest in both European and American art. Thus 291, like the Armory Show, played an important role in the history of early-20th-century art in America. Stieglitz had seen and exhibited some of O'Keeffe's earlier work, and he drew her into his avant-garde circle of painters and photographers. He became one of O'Keeffe's staunchest supporters and, eventually, her husband. The interest of Stieglitz and his circle in capturing the sensibility of the machine age intersected with O'Keeffe's fascination with the fast pace of city life. During this period, she produced paintings such as *New York, Night* (FIG. **29-42**), featuring the soaring skyscrapers dominating the city, which, for many, were symbols of the modern world and of America's preeminence in architecture and engineering. Like other Precisionists, O'Keeffe reduced her images to simple planes, here punctuated by small rectangular windows that add rhythm and energy to the image, countering the monolithic darkness of the looming buildings.

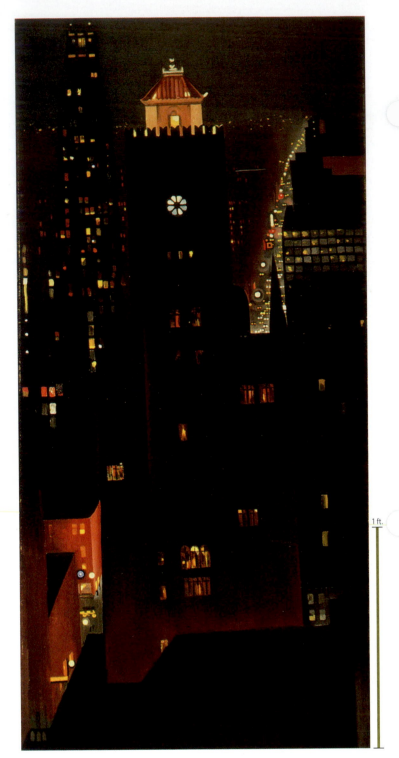

29-42 GEORGIA O'KEEFFE, *New York, Night,* 1929. Oil on canvas, 3' 4⅛" × 1' 7⅛". Sheldon Memorial Art Gallery, Lincoln (Nebraska Art Association, Thomas C. Woods Memorial Collection).

O'Keeffe's Precisionist representation of New York's soaring skyscrapers reduces the buildings to large, simple, dark planes punctuated by small windows that add rhythm and energy to the image.

Despite O'Keeffe's affiliation with the Precisionist movement and New York, she is best known for her paintings of cow skulls and of flowers. For example, in *Jack-in-the-Pulpit No. 4* (FIG. I-5), she reveals her interest in stripping subjects to their purest forms and colors to heighten their expressive power. In this work, O'Keeffe reduced the curved planes and contours of the flower to a symphony of basic

ARTISTS ON ART

Alfred Stieglitz on "Straight Photography"

Taking his camera everywhere he went, Alfred Stieglitz photographed whatever he saw around him, from the bustling streets of New York City to cloudscapes in upstate New York and the faces of friends and relatives. He believed in making only "straight, unmanipulated" photographs. Thus he exposed and printed them using basic photographic processes, without resorting to techniques such as double-exposure or double-printing that would add information absent in the subject when he released the shutter. Stieglitz said that he wanted the photographs he made with this direct technique "to hold a moment, to record something so completely that those who see it would relive an equivalent of what has been expressed."*

Stieglitz's photographic work is noteworthy for his insistence on seeing his subjects in terms of arrangements of forms and of the "colors" of his black-and-white materials. His aesthetic approach crystallized during the making of *The Steerage* (FIG. 29-43), a photograph he took during a sea voyage to Europe with his first wife and daughter in 1907. Traveling first class, Stieglitz rapidly grew bored with the company of the prosperous passengers in his section of the ship. He walked as far forward on the first-class level as he could, when the rail around the opening onto the lower deck brought him up short. This level was for the steerage passengers whom the government sent back to Europe after refusing them entrance into the United States. Later, Stieglitz described what happened next:

> The scene fascinated me: A round hat; the funnel leaning left, the stairway leaning right; the white drawbridge, its railing made of chain; white suspenders crossed on the back of a man below; circular iron machinery; a mast that cut into the sky, completing a triangle. I stood spellbound. I saw shapes related to one another—a picture of shapes, and underlying it, a new vision that held me: simple people; the feeling of ship, ocean, sky; a sense of release that I was away from the mob called rich. Rembrandt came into my mind and I wondered would he have felt as I did. . . . I had only one plate holder with one unexposed plate. Could I catch what I saw and felt? I released the shutter. If I had captured what I wanted, the photograph would go far beyond any of my previous prints. It would be a picture based on related shapes and deepest human feeling—a step in my own evolution, a spontaneous discovery.†

This description reveals Stieglitz's abiding interest in the formal elements of the photograph—an insistently modernist focus that

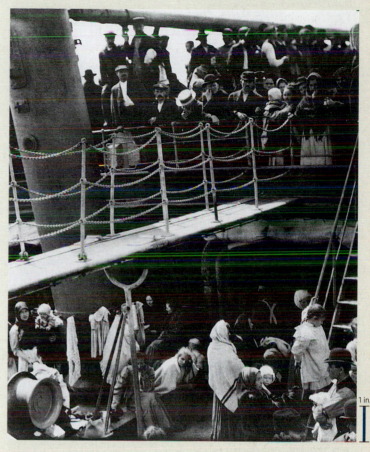

29-43 ALFRED STIEGLITZ, *The Steerage*, 1907 (print 1915). Photogravure (on tissue), 1' 3/8" × 10 1/8". Amon Carter Museum, Fort Worth.

Stieglitz waged a lifelong campaign for photography as a fine art. This 1907 "straight photographic" image taken on an ocean liner is a haunting mixture of human activity and found patterns of forms.

emerges in even more extreme form in his *Equivalent* series (FIG. 29-43A) of the 1920s. The finished print fulfilled Stieglitz's vision so well that it shaped his future photographic work, and its haunting mixture of found patterns and human activity has continued to stir viewers' emotions to this day.

*Dorothy Norman, *Alfred Stieglitz: An American Seer* (Millerton, N.Y.: Aperture, 1973), 9–10.
†Ibid., 161.

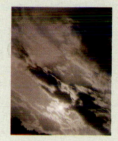

🔲 **29-43A** STIEGLITZ, *Equivalent*, 1923.

colors, shapes, textures, and vital rhythms, simplifying the forms almost to the point of complete abstraction. The fluid planes unfold like undulant petals from a subtly placed axis—the white jetlike streak—in a vision of the slow, controlled motion of growing life. O'Keeffe's painting, in its graceful, quiet poetry, reveals the organic reality of the object by strengthening its characteristic features.

Photography

Among the most significant artistic developments during the decades between the two world wars was the emergence of photography as a respected branch of the fine arts in the United States. The person most responsible for elevating the stature of photography was Alfred Stieglitz.

ALFRED STIEGLITZ While a student of photochemistry in Germany, ALFRED STIEGLITZ (1864–1946) began a lifelong campaign to win a place for photography among the fine arts. In New York, he founded the Photo-Secession group, which mounted traveling exhibitions in the United States and sent loan collections abroad, and he published an influential journal titled *Camera Work*. Stieglitz's many recorded comments on the art of photography clearly set forth his philosophy of picture making using film instead of paint (see "Alfred Stieglitz on 'Straight Photography,'" above).

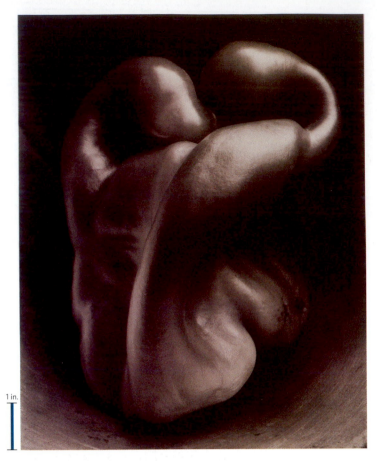

29-44 EDWARD WESTON, *Pepper No. 30,* 1930. Gelatin silver print, $9\frac{1}{2}'' \times 7\frac{1}{2}''$. Center for Creative Photography, University of Arizona, Tucson.

Weston "previsualized" his still lifes, choosing the exact angle, lighting, and framing he desired. His vegetables often resemble human bodies, in this case a seated nude seen from behind.

EDWARD WESTON Like Alfred Stieglitz, EDWARD WESTON (1886–1958) played a major role in establishing photography as an important artistic medium. But unlike Stieglitz, who worked outdoors and sought to capture transitory moments in his photographs, Weston meticulously composed his subjects in a controlled setting, whether he was doing still lifes of peppers, shells, and other natural forms of irregular shape, or figure studies. The 1930 photograph of a pepper illustrated here (FIG. **29-44**) is the 30th in a large series and an outstanding example of this genre. In contrast to Weston's photographs of sections of nude human bodies (FIG. **29-44A**), his still-life photographs show the entire object, albeit tightly framed. (Compare Georgia O'Keeffe's *Jack-in-the-Pulpit No. 4* [FIG. I-5] painted the same year.) The lighting accentuates the undulating surfaces and

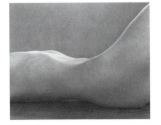

29-44A WESTON, *Nude,* 1925.

crevices of the vegetable. Weston left nothing to chance, choosing the exact angle and play of light over the object, "previsualizing" the final photographic print before snapping the camera's shutter.

In a kind of reversal of his approach to photographing nudes, which he often transformed into landscapes, Weston frequently chose peppers whose shapes reminded him of human bodies.

Pepper No. 30 looks like a seated nude figure seen from behind with raised arms emerging from broad shoulders. Viewers can read the vertical crease down the center of the vegetable as the spinal column leading to the buttocks. Although highly successful as a purely abstract composition of shapes and of light and dark, Weston's still life also conveys mystery and sensuality through its dramatic lighting and rich texture.

Architecture

Like other artists, many early-20th-century architects in the United States looked to Europe for inspiration, but distinctive American styles also emerged that in turn had a major influence on architectural design worldwide.

FRANK LLOYD WRIGHT One of the most striking personalities in the development of modern architecture on either side of the Atlantic was FRANK LLOYD WRIGHT (1867–1959). Born in Wisconsin, Wright moved to Chicago, where he eventually joined the firm headed by Louis Sullivan (FIGS. 28-42, 28-42A, and 28-43). Wright set out to create an American "architecture of democracy" (see "Frank Lloyd Wright on Organic Architecture," page 917).

Wright's vigorous originality emerged early, and by 1900 he had arrived at a style entirely his own. In his work during the first decade of the 20th century, his cross-axial plan and his fabric of continuous roof planes and screens defined a new American domestic architecture. He fully expressed these elements and concepts in the Robie House (FIG. **29-45**), built between 1907 and 1909. Like other buildings in the Chicago area that Wright designed at about the same time, he called this home a "prairie house." Wright conceived the long, sweeping, ground-hugging lines, unconfined by abrupt wall limits, as reaching out toward and capturing the expansiveness of the Midwest's great flatlands. Abandoning all symmetry, he eliminated a facade, extended the roofs far beyond the walls, and all but concealed the entrance. Wright filled the house's "wandering" plan (FIG. **29-46**) with intricately joined spaces (some large and open, others closed), grouped freely around a great central fireplace. (He believed strongly in the hearth's age-old domestic significance as well as in its ability to keep a house's inhabitants warm in Chicago's frigid winters.) Wright designed enclosed patios, overhanging roofs (essential to provide shade in the summer heat), and strip windows to provide unexpected light sources and glimpses of the outdoors as the inhabitants moved through the interior space. These elements, together with the open ground plan, created a sense of space in motion, inside and out. Wright matched his new and fundamental interior spatial arrangement in his exterior treatment. For example, the flow of interior space determined the sharp angular placement of exterior walls.

ART DECO Although Adolf Loos (FIG. 29-33) had strongly condemned ornamentation in the design of buildings, popular taste still favored decoration as an important element in architecture. *Art Deco* was a movement in the 1920s and 1930s whose adherents sought to upgrade industrial design in competition with "fine art." Proponents wanted to work new materials into decorative patterns that could be either machined or handcrafted and could, to a degree, reflect the simplifying trend in architecture. A remote descendant of Art Nouveau (see page 872), Art Deco acquired its name at the Exposition des Arts Décoratifs et Industriels Modernes (Exposition of Modern Decorative and Industrial Arts), held in Paris in 1925. Art Deco had universal application—to buildings, interiors,

ARTISTS ON ART
Frank Lloyd Wright on Organic Architecture

Always a believer in "natural" and "organic" buildings, Wright envisioned an "architecture of democracy"*—that is, buildings designed to serve free individuals who have the right to move within a "free" space. Wright equated free space with a nonsymmetrical design interacting spatially with its natural surroundings, as in his 1907–1909 Robie House (FIGS. 29-45 and 29-46) in Chicago. In his architectural designs, Wright sought to develop an organic unity of planning, structure, materials, and site, and identified the principle of "continuity" as fundamental to understanding his view of organic unity.

> Classic architecture was all fixation. . . . Now why not let walls, ceilings, floors become seen as component parts of each other? . . . You may see the appearance in the surface of your hand contrasted with the articulation of the bony structure itself. This ideal, profound in its architectural implications . . . I called . . . continuity.[†]

> In Organic Architecture . . . it is quite impossible to consider the building as one thing, its furnishings another and its setting and environment still another. The Spirit in which these buildings are conceived sees all these together at work as one thing. All are to be studiously foreseen and provided for in the nature of the structure. All these should become mere details of the character and completeness of the structure. . . . To thus make of a human dwelling-place a complete work of art, in itself expressive and beautiful, intimately related to modern life and fit to live in, lending itself more freely and suitably to the individual needs of the dwellers . . . this is the tall modern American opportunity in Architecture. True basis of a true Culture. . . . I believe this Ideal will become a new Tradition: a vast step in advance of the prescribed fashion in a day when a dwelling was a composite of cells arranged as separate rooms. . . . An organic-entity, this modern building as contrasted with that former insensate aggregation of parts. . . . One great thing instead of a quarrelling collection of so many little things.[‡]

*Quoted in Vincent Scully Jr., *Frank Lloyd Wright* (New York: Braziller, 1960), 18.

†Quoted in Edgar Kauffmann, ed., *Frank Lloyd Wright, An American Architecture* (New York: Horizon, 1955), 205, 208.

‡Quoted in Ulrich Conrads, ed., *Programs and Manifestoes on 20th-Century Architecture* (Cambridge, Mass.: MIT Press, 1970), 25.

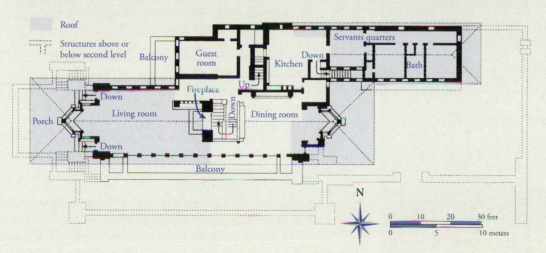

29-45 FRANK LLOYD WRIGHT, Robie House (looking northeast), Chicago, Illinois, 1907–1909.

The Robie House is an example of Wright's "architecture of democracy," in which free individuals move within a "free" space—a nonsymmetrical design interacting spatially with its natural surroundings.

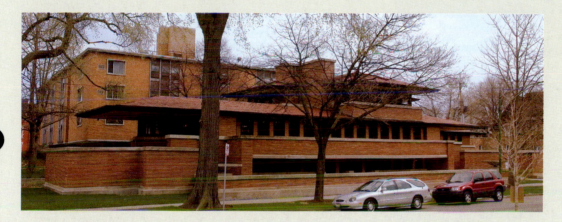

29-46 FRANK LLOYD WRIGHT, plan of the second (main) level of the Robie House, Chicago, Illinois, 1907–1909.

Typical of Wright's "prairie houses," the Robie House has a bold "wandering" asymmetrical plan with intricately joined open and closed spaces grouped freely around a great central fireplace.

furniture, utensils, jewelry, fashions, illustration, and commercial products of every sort. Art Deco products have a "streamlined," elongated symmetrical aspect. Simple, flat shapes alternate with shallow volumes in hard patterns. Derived from nature, these simple forms are inherently aerodynamic, making them technologically efficient (because of their reduced resistance as they move through air or water) as well as aesthetically pleasing. Designers adopted streamlined designs for trains and cars, and the popular appeal of these designs led to their use in an array of objects, from machines to consumer products.

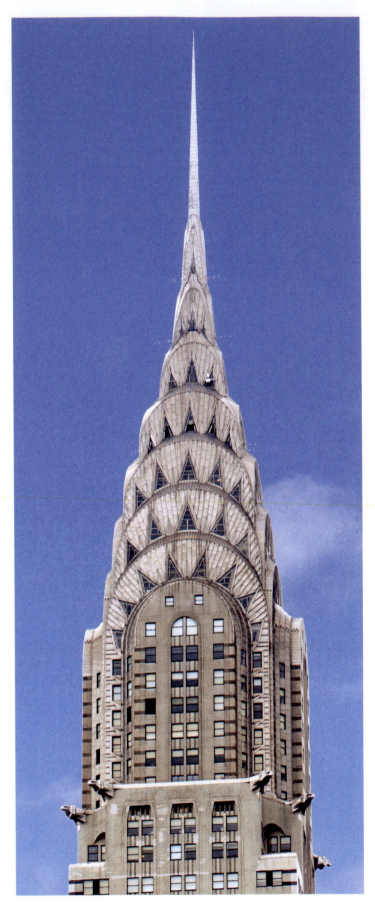

29-47 WILLIAM VAN ALEN, Chrysler Building (looking south), New York, New York, 1928–1930.

The Chrysler Building's stainless steel spire epitomizes Art Deco architecture. The skyscraper's glittering crown of diminishing fan shapes has a streamlined form popular in America during the 1920s.

Art Deco architecture's exemplary masterpiece is the stainless-steel spire of the Chrysler Building (FIG. **29-47**) in New York City, designed by WILLIAM VAN ALEN (1882–1954). The building and spire are monuments to the fabulous 1920s, when American millionaires and corporations competed with one another to raise the tallest skyscrapers in the biggest cities (compare FIG. 29-42). Built up of diminishing fan shapes, the spire glitters triumphantly in the sky, a resplendent crown honoring the business achievements of the great auto manufacturer. As a temple of commerce, the Chrysler Building celebrated the principles and success of American business before the onset of the Great Depression.

EUROPE, 1920 TO 1945

Because World War I was fought entirely on European soil, European artists experienced its devastating effects to a much greater degree than did American artists. The war had a profound effect on Europe's geopolitical terrain (MAP 29-1), on individual and national psyches, and on European art of the 1920s and 1930s.

Neue Sachlichkeit

In Germany, World War I gave rise to an artistic movement called *Neue Sachlichkeit* (New Objectivity). All of the artists associated with Neue Sachlichkeit served, at some point, in the German army. Their military experiences deeply influenced their worldviews and informed their art. "New Objectivity" captures the group's aim—to present a clear-eyed, direct, and honest image of the world, especially the "Great War" and its effects.

GEORGE GROSZ One of the leading Neue Sachlichkeit artists was GEORGE GROSZ (1893–1958), who was, for a time, associated with the Dada group in Berlin. Grosz observed the onset of World War I with horrified fascination that soon turned to anger and frustration:

> Of course, there was a kind of mass enthusiasm at the start. But this intoxication soon evaporated, leaving a huge vacuum. . . . And then after a few years when everything bogged down, when we were defeated, when everything went to pieces, all that remained, at least for me and most of my friends, were disgust and horror.[26]

Many of Grosz's paintings and drawings—for example, *Fit for Active Service* (FIG. **29-47A**)—depict the war itself. However, the largest canvas he ever painted— *The Eclipse of the Sun* (FIG. **29-48**)—does not, although it is a stinging indictment of the militarism and capitalism that Grosz believed were the root causes of the global conflict. *Eclipse of the Sun* takes its name from the large red German coin at the upper left blocking the sun and signifying

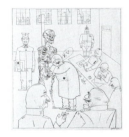

29-47A GROSZ, *Fit for Active Service*, 1916–1917.

that capitalism has brought darkness to the world. Also at the top are burning buildings. At the lower right are a skull and bones. Filling the rest of the canvas are the agents of this destruction seated at a table seen at a sharp angle from above. The main figure is the president of Germany, Paul von Hindenburg (r. 1925–1934), who wears his army uniform and war medals. His bloody sword is on the table before him, and on his head is the laurel wreath of victory. He presides over a meeting with four headless ministers—men who act on his orders without question. Grosz, however, also portrayed the president as a puppet leader. A wealthy industrialist wearing a top hat whispers

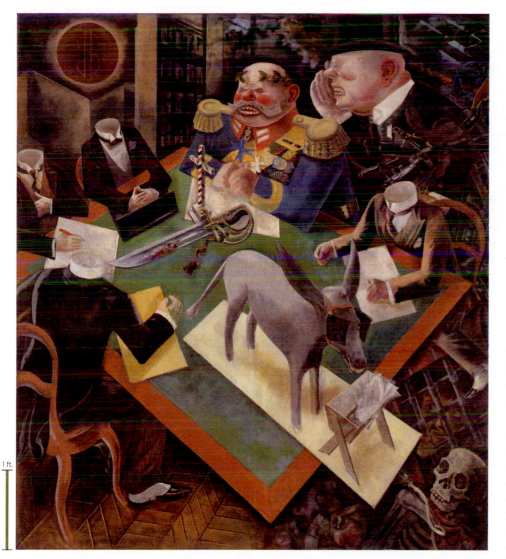

1 ft.

29-48 GEORGE GROSZ, *The Eclipse of the Sun*, 1926. Oil on canvas, 6' 9⅝" × 5' 11⅞". Heckscher Museum of Art, Huntington.

In Grosz's indictment of militarism and capitalism, an industrialist whispers instructions in the ear of the uniformed president of Germany, who meets with four of his headless ministers.

instructions in von Hindenburg's ear. The painting is also a commentary on the gullibility of the public, personified here as a donkey who eats newspapers—that is, as a mindless creature who swallows the propagandistic lies promoted by the government- and business-friendly press.

MAX BECKMANN Another major German artist who enlisted in the German army and initially rationalized the Great War was MAX BECKMANN (1884–1950). He believed that a better society would emerge from the chaos that the armed conflict unleashed, but over time the massive loss of life and widespread destruction increasingly disillusioned him. Soon Beckmann's work began to emphasize the horrors of war and of a society that he regarded as descending into madness. His disturbing view of wartime Germany is evident in *Night* (FIG. **29-49**), which depicts a cramped room that three intruders have forcefully invaded. A bound woman, apparently raped, is splayed across the foreground of the painting. Her husband appears on the left. One of the intruders hangs him, while another one twists his left arm out of its socket. An unidentified woman cowers in the background. On the far right, the third intruder prepares to flee with the child.

Although this image does not depict a war scene, the wrenching brutality and violence pervading the home are searing and horrifying comments on society's condition. Beckmann also injected a personal reference by using himself, his wife, and his son as the models for the three family members. The stilted angularity of the figures and the roughness of the paint surface contribute to the image's savageness. In addition, the artist's treatment of forms and space reflects the world's violence. Objects seem dislocated

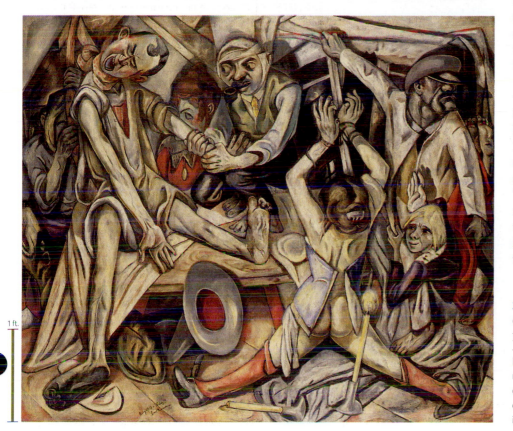

1 ft.

29-49 MAX BECKMANN, *Night*, 1918–1919. Oil on canvas, 4' 4⅜" × 5' ¼". Kunstsammlung Nordrhein-Westfalen, Düsseldorf.

Beckmann's treatment of forms and space in *Night* matched his view of the brutality of early-20th-century society. Objects seem dislocated and contorted, and the space appears buckled and illogical.

and contorted, and the space appears buckled and illogical. For example, the woman's hands are bound to the window opening from the room's back wall, but her body appears to hang vertically, rather than lying across the plane of the intervening table.

OTTO DIX The third artist most closely associated with Neue Sachlichkeit was OTTO DIX (1891–1969). Having served as both a machine gunner and an aerial observer, Dix was well acquainted with the Great War's effects. Like Grosz and Beckmann, Dix initially tried to find redeeming value in the apocalyptic event: "The war was a horrible thing, but there was something tremendous about it, too. . . . You have to have seen human beings in this unleashed state to know what human nature is. . . . I need to experience all the depths of life for myself, that's why I go out, and that's why I volunteered."[27] This idea of experiencing the "depths of life" stemmed from Dix's interest in the philosophy of Friedrich Nietzsche (1844–1900). In particular, Dix avidly read Nietzsche's *The Joyous Science*, deriving from it a belief in life's cyclical nature—procreation and death, building up and tearing down, and growth and decay.

As the war progressed, however, Dix's faith in the potential improvement of society faded, and he began to produce unflinchingly direct and provocative artworks. His triptych titled *Der Krieg* (*The War*; FIG. 29-50) vividly captures the panoramic devastation that war inflicts, both on the terrain and on humans. In the left panel,

armed and uniformed soldiers march off into the distance. Dix graphically displayed the horrific results in the center and right panels, where mangled bodies, many riddled with bullet holes, are scattered throughout the eerily lit apocalyptic landscape. As if to emphasize the intensely personal nature of this scene, the artist painted himself into the right panel as the ghostly but determined soldier who drags a comrade to safety. In the bottom panel, in a coffinlike bunker, lie sleeping—or perhaps dead—soldiers. Significantly, Dix chose to present this sequence of images in the format of an altarpiece, and the work recalls triptychs such as Matthias Grünewald's *Isenheim Altarpiece* (FIG. 23-2). However, Dix's "altarpiece" presents a bleaker outlook than Grünewald's. The hope of salvation extended to viewers of the *Isenheim Altarpiece* through Christ's eventual resurrection is absent from *Der Krieg*. As did his fellow Neue Sachlichkeit artists, Dix felt compelled to lay bare the realities of his time, which the war's violence dominated. Even years later, Dix still maintained:

> You have to see things the way they are. You have to be able to say yes to the human manifestations that exist and will always exist. That doesn't mean saying yes to war, but to a fate that approaches you under certain conditions and in which you have to prove yourself. Abnormal situations bring out all the depravity, the bestiality of human beings. . . . I portrayed states, states that the war brought about, and the results of war, as states.[28]

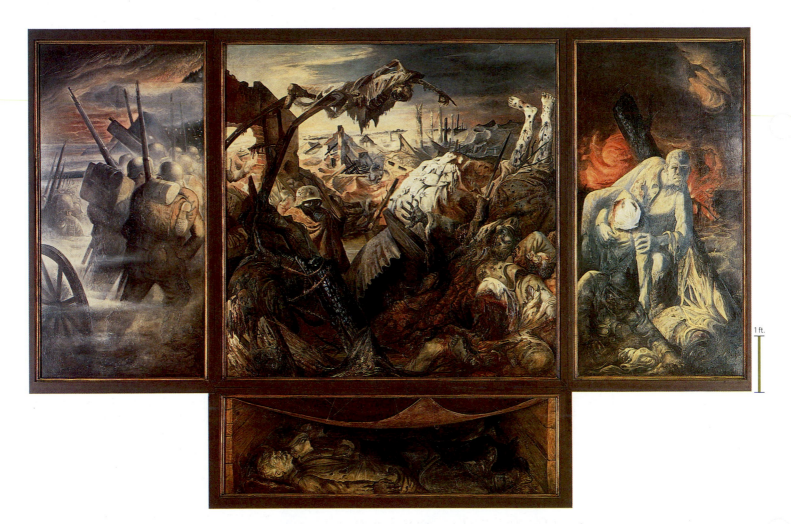

29-50 OTTO DIX, *Der Krieg* (*The War*), 1929–1932. Oil and tempera on wood, 8' 8" (including predella) × 13' 4¾". Staatliche Kunstsammlungen, Gemäldegalerie Neue Meister, Dresden.

In this triptych recalling earlier altarpieces, Dix captured the panoramic devastation that war inflicts on the terrain and on humans. He depicted himself as a soldier dragging a comrade to safety.

ERNST BARLACH A work more spiritual in its expression is the *War Monument* (FIG. 29-51) fashioned by the German sculptor ERNST BARLACH (1870–1938) for the cathedral in his hometown of Güstrow in 1927. Working often in wood, Barlach sculpted single figures usually dressed in flowing robes and portrayed in strong, simple poses embodying deep human emotions and experiences such as grief, vigilance, or self-comfort. Barlach's works combine sharp, smoothly planed forms with intense expression. The cast-bronze hovering figure of his *War Monument* is one of the most poignant memorials of World War I. Unlike traditional war memorials depicting heroic military figures, often engaged in battle, the hauntingly symbolic figure that Barlach created speaks to the experience of all caught in the conflict of war. The floating human form, suspended above a tomb inscribed with the dates 1914–1918 (and later also 1939–1945), suggests a dying soul at the moment when it is to awaken to everlasting life—the theme of death and transfiguration. The rigid economy of surfaces concentrates attention on the simple but expressive head. So powerful was this sculpture that the Nazis had it removed from the cathedral in 1937 and melted it down for ammunition. Luckily, a friend hid another version that Barlach had made. A Protestant parish in Cologne purchased it, and bronze workers made a new cast of the figure for the Güstrow cathedral.

Surrealism

The exuberantly aggressive momentum of the Dada movement that emerged during World War I lasted for only a short time. By 1924, with André Breton's publication in France of the *First Surrealist Manifesto,* most of the artists associated with Dada had joined the *Surrealism* movement, which had begun as a literary movement (see "André Breton's *First Surrealist Manifesto,*" page 922). The Surrealists were determined to explore ways to express in art the world of dreams and the unconscious. Not surprisingly, the Surrealists incorporated many of the Dadaists' improvisational techniques. They believed that these methods were important for engaging the elements of fantasy and activating the unconscious forces deep within every human being. Inspired in part by the ideas of the psychoanalysts Sigmund Freud and Carl Jung, the Surrealists focused on the inner world of the psyche and had a special interest in the nature of dreams, an interest already central to the Italian Metaphysical Painting movement of Giorgio de Chirico (FIG. 29-52). They viewed dreams as occurring at the level connecting all human consciousness and as constituting the arena in which people could move beyond their environment's constricting forces to reengage with the deeper selves that society had long suppressed.

Thus the Surrealists' dominant motivation was to bring the aspects of outer and inner "reality" together into a single position, in much the same way that life's seemingly unrelated fragments combine in the vivid world of dreams. The projection in visible form of this new conception required new techniques of pictorial construction. The Surrealists adapted some Dada devices and invented new methods such as automatic writing (spontaneous writing using free association), not so much to reveal a world without meaning as to provoke reactions closely related to subconscious experience.

Surrealism developed along two lines. In *Naturalistic Surrealism,* artists presented recognizable scenes that seem to have metamorphosed into a dream or nightmare image. The artists Salvador Dalí (FIG. 29-55) and René Magritte (FIGS. 29-56 and 29-56A) were the most famous practitioners of this variant of Surrealism. In contrast, some artists gravitated toward an interest in *Biomorphic Surrealism.* In Biomorphic ("life forms") Surrealism, *automatism*—the creation of art without conscious control—predominated. Biomorphic Surrealists such as Joan Miró (FIG. 29-58) produced largely abstract compositions, although the imagery sometimes suggests organisms or natural forms.

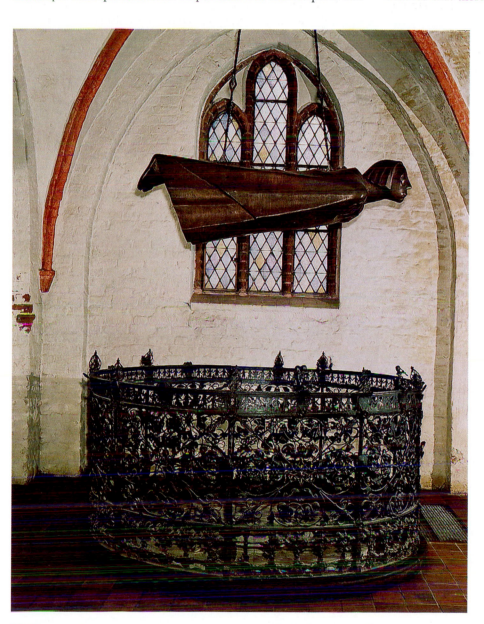

29-51 ERNST BARLACH, *War Monument,* Güstrow Cathedral, Güstrow, Germany, 1927. Bronze.

In this World War I memorial, which the Nazis melted down for ammunition, a human form floating above a tomb suggests a dying soul at the moment that it is about to awaken to everlasting life.

André Breton's *First Surrealist Manifesto*

A poet, novelist, and critic rather than a visual artist, André Breton nonetheless played a leading role in the formation of two of the 20th century's most important art movements: Dada (see page 900) and Surrealism. Although it was Guillaume Apollinaire who first proposed the term "Surrealism," the movement did not begin to take firm shape until 1924, when Breton published the *First Surrealist Manifesto* in the inaugural issue of *La revolution surréaliste*.

Some excerpts:

The mere word "freedom" is the only one that still excites me. . . . We are still living under the reign of logic . . . The absolute rationalism that is still in vogue allows us to consider only facts relating directly to our experience. . . . Under the pretense of civilization and progress, we have managed to banish from the mind everything that may rightly or wrongly be termed superstition, or fancy; forbidden is any kind of search for truth which is not in conformance with accepted practices. . . . [T]hanks to the discoveries of Sigmund Freud . . . [t]he imagination is perhaps on the point of reasserting itself, of reclaiming its rights. . . . Freud very rightly brought his critical faculties to bear upon the dream. . . . I have always been amazed at the way an ordinary observer lends so much more credence and attaches so much more importance to waking events than to those occurring in dreams. . . . I believe in the future resolution of these two states, dream and reality, which are seemingly so contradictory, into a kind of absolute reality, a "surreality," if one may so speak. It is in quest of this surreality that I am going . . .

Surrealism . . . is [p]sychic automatism in its pure state, by which one proposes to express—verbally . . . or in any other manner—the actual function of thought. . . . Surrealism is based on the belief in the superior reality of certain forms of previously neglected associations, in the omnipotence of dream, in the disinterested play of thought. It tends to ruin once and for all all other psychic mechanisms and to substitute itself for them in solving all the principal problems of life.*

*Translated by Richard Seaver and Helen R. Lane, *André Breton: Manifestoes of Surrealism* (Ann Arbor: University of Michigan Press, 1969), 3–47.

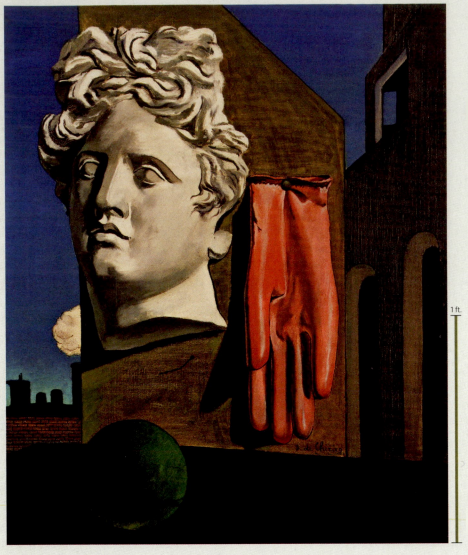

1 ft.

29-52 GIORGIO DE CHIRICO, *The Song of Love*, 1914. Oil on canvas, 2' 4$\frac{3}{4}$" × 1' 11$\frac{3}{8}$". Museum of Modern Art, New York (Nelson A. Rockefeller bequest).

De Chirico's Metaphysical Painting movement was a precursor of Surrealism. In this dreamlike scene set in a deserted square, a classical head of Apollo floats mysteriously next to a gigantic red glove.

GIORGIO DE CHIRICO The widely recognized precursor of Surrealism was the Italian painter GIORGIO DE CHIRICO (1888–1978). De Chirico's intentionally ambiguous paintings of cityscapes are the most famous examples of a movement called *Pittura Metafisica*, or Metaphysical Painting. Returning to Italy after studying in Munich, de Chirico found hidden reality revealed through strange juxtapositions, such as those seen on late autumn afternoons in the city of Turin, when the long shadows of the setting sun transformed vast open squares and silent public monuments into what the painter called "metaphysical towns."

De Chirico translated this vision into paint in works such as *The Song of Love* (FIG. 29-52), a dreamlike scene set in the deserted piazza of an Italian town. A huge marble head—a fragment of the famous *Apollo Belvedere* in the Vatican—is suspended in midair above a large green ball. To the right is a gigantic red glove nailed to a wall. The buildings and the three over-life-size objects cast shadows that direct the viewer's eye to the left and to a locomotive puffing smoke—a favorite Futurist motif, here shown in slow motion and incongruously placed near the central square. The choice of the term *metaphysical* to describe de Chirico's paintings

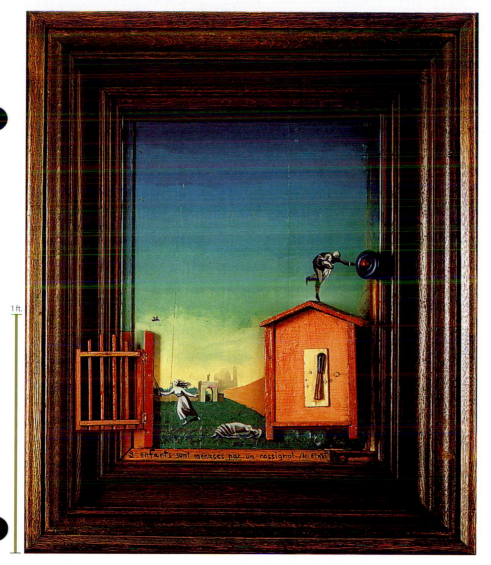

29-53 MAX ERNST, *Two Children Are Threatened by a Nightingale*, 1924. Oil on wood with wood construction, 2' 3½" × 1' 10½" × 4½". Museum of Modern Art, New York.

In this early Surrealist painting with an intentionally ambiguous title, Ernst used traditional perspective to represent the setting, but the three sketchily rendered figures belong to a dream world.

with marvels. In autobiographical notes, written mostly in the third person, he said of his birth:

> Max Ernst had his first contact with the world of sense on the 2nd April 1891 at 9:45 a.m., when he emerged from the egg which his mother had laid in an eagle's nest and which the bird had incubated for seven years.[30]

Ernst's service in the German army during World War I swept away his early success as an Expressionist. In his own words:

> Max Ernst died on 1st August 1914. He returned to life on 11th November 1918, a young man who wanted to become a magician and find the central myth of his age. From time to time he consulted the eagle which had guarded the egg of his prenatal existence. The bird's advice can be detected in his work.[31]

Before joining the Surrealists, Ernst explored every means of achieving the sense of the psychic in his art. Like other Dadaists, Ernst set out to incorporate found objects and chance into his works, often combining fragments of images that he had cut from old books, magazines, and prints to form one hallucinatory collage. He also began making paintings that shared the mysterious dreamlike effect of his collages.

In 1920, Ernst met Breton, who instantly recognized the German artist's affinity with the Surrealist group. In 1922, Ernst moved to Paris, where two years later he painted *Two Children Are Threatened by a Nightingale* (FIG. **29-53**). In it, Ernst displayed a private dream challenging the Renaissance idea that a painting should resemble a window looking into a "real" scene rendered illusionistically three-dimensional through mathematical perspective. He painted the landscape, the distant city, and the tiny flying bird in conventional fashion, following all the established rules of linear and atmospheric perspective. The three sketchily rendered figures, however, clearly belong to a dream world, and the literally three-dimensional miniature gate, the odd button knob, and the strange closed building "violate" the bulky frame's space. Additional dislocation occurs in the traditional museum identification label, which Ernst displaced into a cutaway part of the frame. Handwritten, it announces the work's title (taken from a poem that Ernst wrote before he painted this), adding another note of irrational mystery.

As is true of many Surrealist works, the title, *Two Children Are Threatened by a Nightingale,* is ambiguous and relates uneasily to what the spectator sees. The viewer must struggle to decipher connections between the image and the words. When Surrealists (and Dadaists and Metaphysical artists before them) used puzzling titles (for example, de Chirico's *Song of Love*), they intended the seeming contradiction between title and picture to knock the audience off balance with all their expectations challenged. Much of the impact of Surrealist works begins with the viewer's sudden awareness of the

suggests that these images transcend their physical appearances. *The Song of Love,* for all its clarity and simplicity, takes on a rather sinister air. The sense of strangeness that de Chirico could conjure with familiar objects and scenes recalls Nietzsche's "foreboding that underneath this reality in which we live and have our being, another and altogether different reality lies concealed."[29]

Reproductions of de Chirico's paintings appeared in periodicals almost as soon as he completed them, and his works quickly influenced artists outside Italy, including both the Dadaists and, later, the Surrealists. The incongruities in his work intrigued the Dadaists, whereas the eerie mood and visionary quality of paintings such as *The Song of Love* excited and inspired Surrealist artists who sought to portray the world of dreams.

MAX ERNST Originally a Dada activist in Germany, MAX ERNST (1891–1976) became one of the early adherents of the Surrealist circle anchored by André Breton. As a child living in a small community near Cologne, Ernst had found his existence fantastic and filled

ART AND SOCIETY

Degenerate Art

Although avant-garde artists often had to endure public ridicule both in Europe and America (see "The Armory Show," page 909), they suffered outright political persecution in Germany in the 1930s and 1940s. The most dramatic example of this persecution was the infamous *Entartete Kunst* (Degenerate Art) exhibition that Adolf Hitler (1889–1945) and the Nazis mounted in 1937.

Hitler aspired to become an artist himself and produced numerous drawings and paintings reflecting his firm belief that 19th-century realistic genre painting represented the zenith of Aryan art development. Accordingly, Hitler denigrated anything that did not conform to that standard—in particular, avant-garde art. Turning his criticism into action, Hitler ordered the confiscation of more than 16,000 artworks that he considered "degenerate." To publicize his condemnation of this art, he ordered his minister for public enlightenment and propaganda, Joseph Goebbels (1897–1945), to organize a massive exhibition of this "degenerate art." Hitler designated as degenerate those artworks that "insult German feeling, or destroy or confuse natural form, or simply reveal an absence of adequate manual and artistic skill."*

The term "degenerate" also had other specific connotations at the time. The Nazis used it to identify supposedly inferior racial, sexual, and moral types. Hitler's order to Goebbels to target 20th-century avant-garde art for inclusion in the *Entartete Kunst* exhibition aimed to impress on the public the general inferiority of the artists producing this work. To make that point all the more dramatic, Hitler ordered the organization of another exhibition, the *Grosse Deutsche Kunstausstellung* (Great German Art Exhibition), which ran concurrently and presented an extensive array of Nazi-approved conservative art.

Entartete Kunst opened in Munich on July 19, 1937, and included more than 650 paintings, sculptures, prints, and books. The exhibition was immensely popular. Roughly 20,000 people visited the show daily. By the end of its four-month run, it had attracted more than two million visitors, and nearly a million more viewed it as it traveled through Germany and Austria. Among the 112 artists whose works the Nazis presented for ridicule were Ernst Barlach, Max Beckmann, Otto Dix, Max Ernst, George Grosz, Vassily Kandinsky, Ernst Kirchner, Paul Klee, Wilhelm Lehmbruck, Franz Marc, and Kurt Schwitters. In a memorable photograph (FIG. 29-54) taken during Hitler's preview visit to the exhibition on July 16, 1937, the Nazi leader pauses in front of the Dada wall. Behind him are works by Schwitters, Klee, and Kandinsky, which the

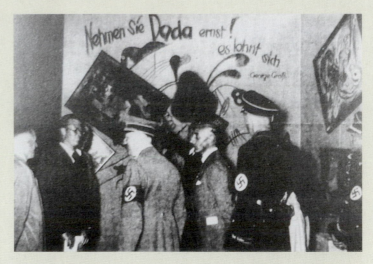

29-54 Adolf Hitler, accompanied by Nazi commission members, including photographer Heinrich Hoffmann, Wolfgang Willrich, Walter Hansen, and painter Adolf Ziegler, viewing the "Entartete Kunst" show on July 16, 1937.

For Hitler's visit, the curators deliberately hung askew the works of Kandinsky, Klee, and Schwitters. In Nazi Germany, no avant-garde artist was safe from persecution, and many fled the country.

organizers deliberately hung askew on the wall. (They subsequently straightened them for the duration of the exhibition.)

In Germany in the 1930s and 1940s, in the face of Nazi persecution, artists committed to pursuing avant-garde ideas required courage and a resoluteness that extended beyond issues of aesthetics and beyond the confines of the art world. No modernist artist was safe from Hitler's attack. (Only six of the artists in the exhibition were Jewish.) For example, despite his status as a charter member of the Nazi Party, the German Expressionist painter Emil Nolde (1867–1956) received particularly harsh treatment. The Nazis confiscated more than 1,000 of Nolde's works from German museums and included 27 of them in the exhibition, more than for almost any other artist. Max Beckmann and his wife fled to Amsterdam on the opening day of the *Entartete Kunst* exhibit, never to return to their homeland. Ernst Kirchner responded to the stress of Nazi pressure by destroying all his woodblocks and burning many of his works. A year later, in 1938, he committed suicide.

*Stephanie Barron, ed., "Degenerate Art": The Fate of the Avant-Garde in Nazi Germany (Los Angeles: Los Angeles County Museum of Art, 1991), 19.

---

incongruity and absurdity of what the artist pictured. These were precisely the qualities that subjected the Dadaists and Surrealists to public condemnation and, in Germany under Adolf Hitler (1889–1945), to governmental persecution (see "Degenerate Art," above, and FIG. **29-54**).

SALVADOR DALÍ The Surrealists' exploration of the human psyche and dreams reached new heights in the works of Spanish-born SALVADOR DALÍ (1904–1989). In his paintings, sculptures, jewelry, and designs for furniture and movies, Dalí probed a deeply erotic dimension, studying the writings of Richard von Krafft-Ebing (1840–1902) and Sigmund Freud, and inventing what he called the "paranoiac-critical method" to assist his creative process. As he described it, in his painting he aimed "to materialize the images of

concrete irrationality with the most imperialistic fury of precision . . . in order that the world of imagination and of concrete irrationality may be as objectively evident . . . as that of the exterior world of phenomenal reality."[32]

In *The Persistence of Memory* (FIG. **29-55**), Dalí created a haunting allegory of empty space where time has ended. An eerie, never-setting sun illuminates the barren landscape. An amorphous creature draped with a limp pocket watch sleeps in the foreground. Another watch hangs from the branch of a dead tree springing unexpectedly from a blocky architectural form. A third watch hangs half over the edge of the rectangular form, beside a small timepiece resting dial-down on the block's surface. Ants swarm mysteriously over the small watch, while a fly walks along the face of its large neighbor, almost as if this assembly of watches were decaying

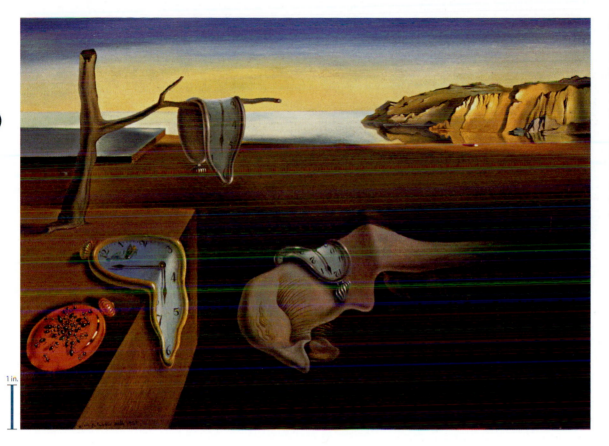

29-55 SALVADOR DALÍ, *The Persistence of Memory*, 1931. Oil on canvas, $9\frac{1}{2}$" × 1' 1". Museum of Modern Art, New York.

Dalí painted "images of concrete irrationality." In this realistically rendered landscape featuring three "decaying" watches, he created a haunting allegory of empty space where time has ended.

organisms—soft and sticky. Dalí rendered every detail of this dreamscape with precise control, striving to make the world of his paintings convincingly real—in his words, to make the irrational concrete.

RENÉ MAGRITTE The Belgian painter RENÉ MAGRITTE (1898–1967) encountered the work of Giorgio de Chirico (FIG. 29-52) in 1922. The Italian artist's disquieting combinations of motifs rendered in a realistic manner deeply impressed the younger artist, who produced his first Surrealist painting, *The Lost Jockey*, in 1926. The next year, Magritte moved to Paris, where he joined the intellectual circle of André Breton and remained in France until 1930. In 1929, Magritte

published an important essay in the Surrealist journal *La revolution surréaliste* in which he discussed the disjunction between objects, pictures of objects, and names of objects and pictures. The essay explains the intellectual basis for *The Treachery (or Perfidy) of Images* (FIG. 29-56), in which Magritte presented a meticulously rendered *trompe l'oeil* depiction of a briar pipe. The caption beneath the image, however, contradicts what seems obvious: "Ceci n'est pas une pipe" ("This is not a pipe"). The discrepancy between image and caption clearly challenges the assumptions underlying the reading of visual art. As is true of the other Surrealists' work, Magritte's paintings—for example, *The False Mirror* (FIG. 29-56A)—wreak havoc on the viewer's reliance on the conscious and the rational.

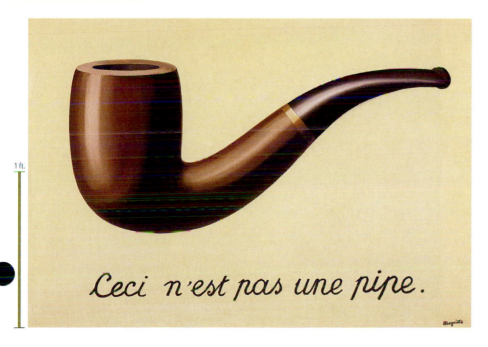

Ceci n'est pas une pipe.

29-56 RENÉ MAGRITTE, *The Treachery (or Perfidy) of Images*, 1928–1929. Oil on canvas, 1' $11\frac{5}{8}$" × 3' 1". Los Angeles County Museum of Art, Los Angeles (purchased with funds provided by the Mr. and Mrs. William Preston Harrison Collection).

The discrepancy between Magritte's meticulously painted briar pipe and his caption, "This is not a pipe," challenges the viewer's reliance on the conscious and rational in the reading of visual art.

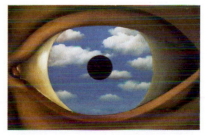

29-56A MAGRITTE, *The False Mirror*, 1928.

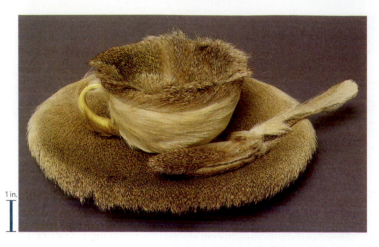

1 in.

29-57 Meret Oppenheim, *Object* (*Le Déjeuner en fourrure*), 1936. Fur-covered cup, $4\frac{3}{8}$" diameter; saucer, $9\frac{3}{8}$" diameter; spoon, 8" long. Museum of Modern Art, New York.

The Surrealists loved the concrete tangibility of sculpture, which made their art even more disquieting. Oppenheim's fur-covered object captures the Surrealist flair for magical transformation.

MERET OPPENHEIM Sculpture especially appealed to the Surrealists because its concrete tangibility made their art all the more disquieting. *Object* (FIG. 29-57), also called *Le Déjeuner en fourrure* (*Luncheon in Fur*), by Swiss artist MERET OPPENHEIM (1913–1985) captures the incongruity, humor, visual appeal, and, often, eroticism characterizing Surrealism. The artist presented a fur-lined teacup inspired by a conversation with Picasso. After admiring a bracelet that Oppenheim had made from a piece of brass covered with fur, Picasso noted that anything might be covered with fur. When her tea grew cold, Oppenheim responded to Picasso's comment by ordering "un peu plus de fourrure" (a little more fur), and the sculpture had its genesis. *Object* takes on an anthropomorphic quality, animated by the quirky combination of fur, exclusive to living organisms, with a stationary manufactured object. Further, the sculpture captures the Surrealist flair for alchemical, seemingly magical or mystical, transformation. It incorporates a sensuality and eroticism (seen here in the seductively soft, tactile fur lining the concave form) that are also components of much of Surrealist art.

JOAN MIRÓ Like the Dadaists, the Surrealists used many methods to free the creative process from reliance on the kind of conscious control that they believed society had shaped too much. Dalí used his paranoiac-critical approach to encourage the free play of association as he worked. Other Surrealists used automatism and various types of planned "accidents" to provoke reactions closely related to subconscious experience. Dalí's older countryman JOAN MIRÓ (1893–1983) was a master of this approach. Although Miró resisted formal association with any movement or group, including the Surrealists, André Breton identified him as "the most Surrealist of us all."[33]

29-58 Joan Miró, *Painting*, 1933. Oil on canvas, $5' 8\frac{1}{2}" \times 6' 5\frac{1}{4}"$. Museum of Modern Art, New York (Loula D. Lasker bequest by exchange).

Miró promoted automatism, the creation of art without conscious control. He began this painting with random doodles and completed the composition with forms suggesting floating amoebic organisms.

From the beginning, Miró's work contained an element of fantasy and hallucination. After Surrealist poets in Paris introduced him to the use of chance in the creation of art, the young Spaniard devised a new painting method that enabled him to create works such as *Painting* (FIG. 29-58). Miró began this painting by making random doodles. The abstract curvilinear forms became motifs that the artist freely reshaped on the canvas to create black silhouettes—solid or in outline, with dramatic accents of white and vermilion. They suggest, in the painting, a host of amoebic organisms or extraterrestrial constellations floating in an immaterial background space filled with soft reds, blues, and greens.

Miró described his creative process as a switching back and forth between unconscious and conscious image-making: "Rather than setting out to paint something, I begin painting and as I paint the picture begins to assert itself, or suggest itself under my brush. The form becomes a sign for a woman or a bird as I work. . . . The first stage is free, unconscious. . . . The second stage is carefully calculated."[34] Even the artist could not always explain the meanings of pictures such as *Painting*. They are, in the truest sense, spontaneous and intuitive expressions of the little-understood, submerged unconscious part of life.

PAUL KLEE Perhaps the most inventive artist using fantasy images to represent the nonvisible world was the Swiss-German painter PAUL KLEE (1879–1940). Like Miró, he shunned formal association with groups such as the Dadaists and Surrealists, but pursued their interest in the subconscious. Klee sought clues to humanity's deeper nature in primitive shapes and symbols. Like Jung, Klee seems to have accepted the existence of a collective unconscious that reveals itself in archaic signs and patterns and is everywhere evident in the art of "primitive" cultures (see "Primitivism," page 891). The son of a professional musician and himself an accomplished violinist, Klee thought of painting as similar to music in its ability to express feelings through color, form, and line. In 1920, Klee set down his "creative credo," which reads in part:

> Art does not reproduce the visible; rather it makes visible. . . . The
> formal elements of graphic art are dot, line, plane, and space—the last

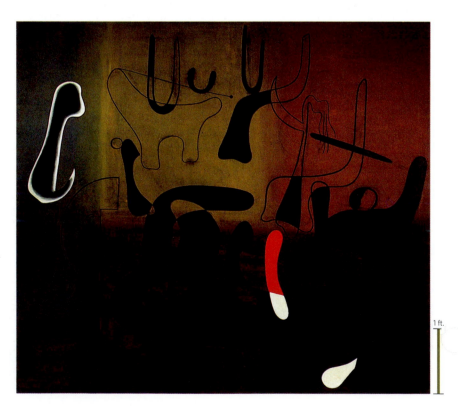

1 ft.

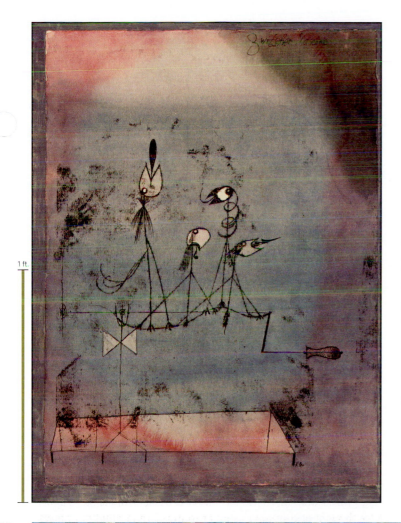

29-59 PAUL KLEE, *Twittering Machine*, 1922. Watercolor and pen and ink, on oil transfer drawing on paper, mounted on cardboard, 2' 1" × 1' 7". Museum of Modern Art, New York.

Although based on forms in the tangible world easily read as birds, Klee's *Twittering Machine* is a fanciful vision of a mysterious place presented in a simplified, almost childlike manner.

three charged with energy of various kinds. . . . Formerly we used to represent things visible on earth, things we either liked to look at or would have liked to see. Today we reveal the reality that is behind visible things.[35]

To penetrate "the reality behind visible things," Klee studied nature avidly, taking special interest in analyzing processes of growth and change. He coded these studies in diagrammatic form in notebooks. Thus the root of his work was nature, but nature filtered through his mind. Upon starting an image, Klee would allow the pencil or brush to lead him until an image emerged, to which he would then respond to complete the idea.

Twittering Machine (FIG. 29-59) reveals Klee's fanciful vision. The painting, although based on forms in the tangible world easily read as birds, is far from illusionistic. Klee presented the scene in a simplified, almost childlike manner, imbuing the work with a poetic lyricism. The inclusion of a crank-driven mechanism added a touch of whimsy. The small size of Klee's works enhances their impact. A viewer must draw near to decipher the delicately rendered forms and enter his mysterious dream world. Perhaps no other artist of the 20th century matched Klee's subtlety as he deftly created a world of ambiguity and understatement that draws each viewer into finding a unique interpretation of the work.

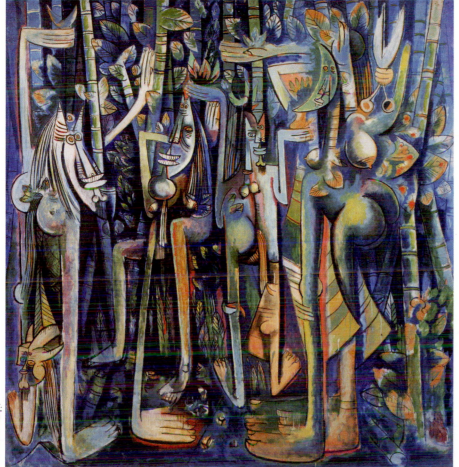

WIFREDO LAM Also loosely associated with the Surrealists was WIFREDO LAM (1902–1982), an artist whose work is as distinctive as his background. Cuban by birth, Lam was the son of a Chinese immigrant father and a mother of Cuban-African descent. He studied painting in Havana and later in Madrid, where he fought alongside the Republicans in the Spanish Civil War. That endeared Lam to Picasso, whom he met in Paris in 1938. Picasso introduced Lam to Braque and Breton and many other avant-garde artists and critics, and Lam's mature work, although the distinctive by-product of his Caribbean-African heritage, shows the influence of both Cubism and Surrealism.

After an 18-year sojourn in Europe, Lam returned to Havana in 1941, where two years later he produced *The Jungle* (FIG. 29-60), which

29-60 WIFREDO LAM, *The Jungle*, 1943. Gouache on paper mounted on canvas, 7' $10\frac{1}{4}$" × 7' $6\frac{1}{2}$". Museum of Modern Art, New York (Inter-American Fund).

In Lam's tropical jungle stand four composite creatures with long legs, prominent buttocks, and faces resembling African masks. The painting draws on Cubism, Surrealism, and Cuban religious ritual.

ARTISTS ON ART

Piet Mondrian on Neoplasticism

Initially attracted to the exciting efforts of the Cubists to rethink the Western pictorial tradition (see page 892), the Dutch De Stijl artist Piet Mondrian soon moved beyond Cubism because he felt that "Cubism did not accept the logical consequences of its own discoveries; it was not developing towards its own goal, the expression of pure plastics."* In 1914, he eloquently articulated his own view of what art should be.

> What first captivated us does not captivate us afterward (like toys). If one has loved the surface of things for a long time, later on one will look for something more. . . . The interior of things shows through the surface; thus as we look at the surface the inner image is formed in our soul. It is this inner image that should be represented. For the natural surface of things is beautiful, but the imitation of it is without life. . . . Art is higher than reality and has no direct relation to reality. . . . To approach the spiritual in art, one will make as little use as possible of reality, because reality is opposed to the spiritual. . . . [W]e find ourselves in the presence of an abstract art. Art should be above reality, otherwise it would have no value for man.[†]

Caught by the outbreak of hostilities while on a visit to Holland, Mondrian remained there during World War I, developing his theories for what he called *Neoplasticism*—the new "pure plastic art." He believed that all great art had polar but coexistent goals, the attempt to create "universal beauty" and the desire for "aesthetic expression of oneself."[‡] The first goal is objective in nature, whereas the second is subjective, existing within the individual's mind and heart. To create a universal expression, an artist must communicate "a real equation of the universal and the individual."[§]

To express this vision, Mondrian eventually limited his formal vocabulary to the three primary colors (red, yellow, and blue), the three primary values (black, white, and gray), and the two primary directions (horizontal and vertical). Basing his ideas on a combination of teachings, he concluded that primary colors and values are the purest colors and therefore are the perfect tools to help an artist construct a harmonious composition. Using this system, he created numerous paintings locking color planes into a grid of intersecting vertical and horizontal lines, as in *Composition with Red, Blue, and Yellow* (FIG. 29-61). In each of these paintings, Mondrian altered the grid patterns and the size and

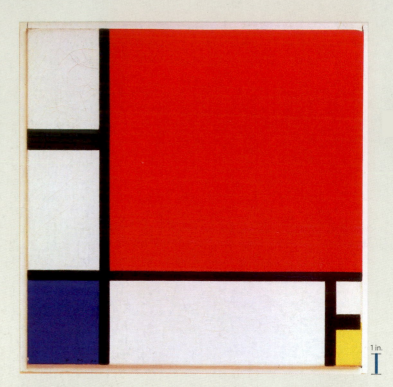

29-61 PIET MONDRIAN, *Composition with Red, Blue, and Yellow*, 1930. Oil on canvas, 1' 6⅛" × 1' 6⅛". Kunsthaus, Zürich. © 2014 Mondrian/ Holtzman Trust c/o HCR International USA.

Mondrian's "pure plastic" paintings consist of primary colors locked into a grid of intersecting vertical and horizontal lines. By altering the grid patterns, he created a "dynamic equilibrium."

placement of the color planes to create an internal cohesion and harmony. This did not mean inertia. Rather, Mondrian worked to maintain what he called a "dynamic equilibrium" in his paintings by precisely determining the size and position of lines, shapes, and colors.

*Piet Mondrian, *Plastic Art and Pure Plastic Art* (1937), quoted in George Heard Hamilton, *Painting and Sculpture in Europe, 1880–1940,* 6th ed. (New Haven, Conn.: Yale University Press, 1993), 319.

[†]Quoted in Michel Seuphor, *Piet Mondrian: Life and Work* (New York: Abrams, 1956), 117.

[‡]Mondrian, *Plastic Art*, quoted in Herschel B. Chipp, *Theories of Modern Art: A Source Book by Artists and Critics* (Berkeley and Los Angeles: University of California Press, 1968), 349.

[§]Ibid., 350.

many art historians consider his greatest work. The complex, crowded composition indeed suggests a dense jungle, populated by Surrealistic creatures whose fragmented forms recall Cubism. Inspired also by Santería, the Cuban religion that is a blend of African ritual and European Catholicism, *The Jungle* depicts four hybrid figures with long legs, prominent buttocks, and heads that resemble African masks. (Many scholars believe the painting is Lam's response, 35 years later, to Picasso's *Demoiselles d'Avignon* [FIG. 29-1].) Lam's composite creatures inhabit a tropical jungle of sugarcane and tobacco plants. Two of them have a horse's tail. The figure at the right holds a scissors—as if she, not the artist, is the one responsible for dismembering herself and her companions. In

many ways, *The Jungle* is a bridge between Cubism, Surrealism, and the nonrepresentational canvases of the New York School Abstract Expressionists of the 1940s and 1950s (see page 953).

De Stijl

The utopian spirit and ideals of the Suprematists and Constructivists (FIGS. 29-31 and 29-32) in Russia were shared in western Europe by a group of young Dutch artists. They formed a new movement in 1917 and began publishing a magazine, calling both the movement and magazine *De Stijl* (The Style). The group's cofounders were the painters Piet Mondrian (FIG. 29-61) and Theo van Doesburg

(1883–1931). In addition to promoting utopian ideals, De Stijl artists believed in the birth of a new age in the wake of World War I. They felt that it was a time of balance between individual and universal values, when the machine would assure ease of living. In their first manifesto of De Stijl, the artists declared: "There is an old and a new consciousness of time. The old is connected with the individual. The new is connected with the universal."[36] The goal, according to van Doesburg and architect Cor van Eesteren (1897–1988), was a total integration of art and life:

> We must realize that life and art are no longer separate domains. That is why the "idea" of "art" as an illusion separate from real life must disappear. The word "Art" no longer means anything to us. In its place we demand the construction of our environment in accordance with creative laws based upon a fixed principle. These laws, following those of economics, mathematics, technique, sanitation, etc., are leading to a new, plastic unity.[37]

PIET MONDRIAN Toward this goal of integration, PIET MONDRIAN (1872–1944) created a new style based on a single ideal principle. The choice of the term "De Stijl" reflected Mondrian's confidence that this style—*the* style—revealed the underlying eternal structure of existence. Accordingly, De Stijl artists reduced their artistic vocabulary to simple geometric elements. Time spent in Paris just before World War I introduced Mondrian to Cubism and other modes of abstraction. However, as his attraction to theological writings grew, Mondrian sought to purge his art of every overt reference to individual objects in the external world. He initially favored the teachings of theosophy, a tradition basing knowledge of nature and the human condition on knowledge of the divine nature or spiritual powers. (His fellow theosophist Vassily Kandinsky pursued a similar path.) Mondrian, however, quickly abandoned the strictures of theosophy and turned toward a conception of nonobjective design—"pure plastic art"—that he believed expressed universal reality (see "Piet Mondrian on Neoplasticism," page 928, and FIG. **29-61**).

Sculpture

It was impossible for early-20th-century artists to ignore the increasing expansion of mechanization and growth of technology in everyone's life. The Futurists had embraced these developments, but other artists did not. They attempted to overcome the predominance of mechanization in society by immersing themselves in a search for the organic and natural.

CONSTANTIN BRANCUSI One artist who was eager to produce works emphasizing the natural or organic was Romanian sculptor CONSTANTIN BRANCUSI (1876–1957). Brancusi sought to move beyond surface appearances to capture the essence or spirit of objects in rhythmic, elegant sculptures (see "Brancusi, Hepworth, and Moore on Abstract Sculpture," page 930). The softly curving surfaces and ovoid form of his sculptures refer, directly or indirectly, to the cycle of life. Brancusi's *The Newborn* (FIG. **29-61A**) is not a literal depiction of a head, nor does his *Bird in Space* (FIG. **29-62**) mimic a real bird's shape. The abstract form of both

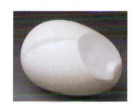

29-61A BRANCUSI, *The Newborn*, 1915.

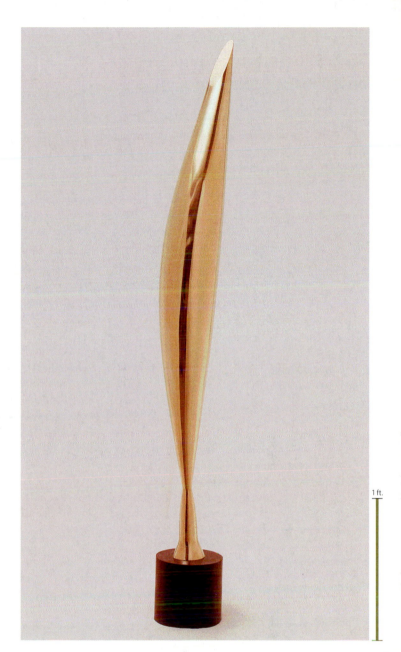

1 ft.

29-62 CONSTANTIN BRANCUSI, *Bird in Space*, 1924. Bronze, 4' 2 5/16" high. Philadelphia Museum of Art, Philadelphia (Louise and Walter Arensberg Collection, 1950).

Although not a literal depiction of a bird, Brancusi's softly curving light-reflecting abstract sculpture in polished bronze suggests a bird about to soar in free flight through the heavens.

works is the final result of a long process. For *Bird in Space*, Brancusi started with the image of a bird at rest with its wings folded at its sides, and ended with a gently curving columnar form sharply tapered at each end. Despite the abstraction, the sculpture retains the suggestion of a bird about to soar in free flight through the heavens. The highly reflective surface of the polished bronze does not allow the viewer's eye to linger on the sculpture itself (as do, for example, Rodin's agitated and textured surfaces; FIGS. 28-33, 28-33A, and 28-34). Instead, the eye follows the gleaming reflection along the delicate curves right off the tip of the work, thereby inducing a feeling of flight. Brancusi stated, "All my life I have sought the essence of flight. Don't look for mysteries. I give you pure joy. Look at the sculptures until you see them. Those nearest to God have seen them."[38]

ARTISTS ON ART
Brancusi, Hepworth, and Moore on Abstract Sculpture

Many early-20th-century sculptors rejected the notion that reproducing the physical world of nature was the purpose of sculpture. Instead, they championed abstraction as the sculptor's proper goal. Among those who not only produced enduring masterpieces of abstract sculpture but also wrote eloquently about the theoretical basis of their work were Constantin Brancusi (FIGS. 29-61A and 29-62), Barbara Hepworth (FIG. 29-63), and Henry Moore (FIG. 29-64). Some excerpts from their writings on sculpture illustrate their commitment to abstraction as their guiding principle.

- **Constantin Brancusi** Simplicity is not an objective in art, but one achieves simplicity despite oneself by entering into the real sense of things.* . . . What is real is not the external form but the essence of things. Starting from this truth it is impossible for anyone to express anything essentially real by imitating its exterior surface.[†]

- **Barbara Hepworth** The forms which have had special meaning for me since childhood have been the standing form (which is the translation of my feeling towards the human being standing in landscape); the two forms (which is the tender relationship of one living thing beside another); and the closed form, such as the oval, spherical, or pierced form (sometimes incorporating color) which translates for me the association and meaning of gesture in the landscape. . . . In all these shapes the translation of what one feels about man and nature must be conveyed by the sculptor in terms of mass, inner tension, and rhythm, scale in relation to our human size, and the quality of surface which speaks through our hands and eyes.[‡]

- **Henry Moore** Since the Gothic, European sculpture had become overgrown with moss, weeds—all sorts of surface excrescences which completely concealed shape. It has been Brancusi's special mission to get rid of this overgrowth, and to make us once more shape-conscious. To do this he has had to concentrate on very simple direct shapes . . . Abstract qualities of design are essen-

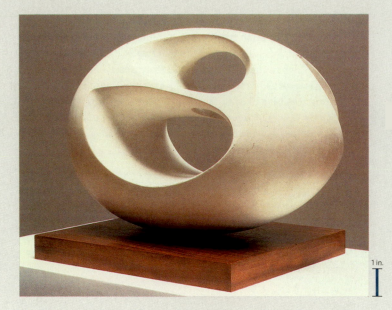

29-63 BARBARA HEPWORTH, *Oval Sculpture (No. 2)*, 1943. Plaster cast, $11\frac{1}{4}$" × 1' $4\frac{1}{4}$" × 10". Tate, London.

Hepworth's major contribution to the history of sculpture was the introduction of the hole, or negative space, as an abstract element that is as integral and important to the sculpture as its mass.

tial to the value of a work . . . Because a work does not aim at reproducing natural appearances, it is not, therefore, an escape from life—but may be a penetration into reality. . . . My sculpture is becoming less representational, less an outward visual copy . . . but only because I believe that in this way I can present the human psychological content of my work with greatest directness and intensity.[§]

*Quoted in Herschel B. Chipp, *Theories of Modern Art: A Source Book by Artists and Critics* (Berkeley and Los Angeles: University of California Press, 1968), 364–365.

[†]Quoted in George Heard Hamilton, *Painting and Sculpture in Europe, 1880–1940*, 6th ed. (New Haven, Conn.: Yale University Press, 1993), 426.

[‡]Barbara Hepworth, *A Pictorial Autobiography* (London: Tate, 1978), 9, 53.

[§]Quoted in Robert L. Herbert, *Modern Artists on Art*, 2d ed. (Mineola, N.Y.: Dover, 2000), 173–179.

BARBARA HEPWORTH In England, BARBARA HEPWORTH (1903–1975) developed her own kind of essential sculptural form, combining pristine shape with a sense of organic vitality. She sought a sculptural idiom that would express her sense both of nature and the landscape and of the person who is in and observes nature (see "Brancusi, Hepworth, and Moore," above). By 1929, Hepworth arrived at a breakthrough that evolved into an enduring and commanding element in her work from that point on. It represents her major contribution to the history of sculpture: the use of the hole, or void. Earlier sculptors, such as Archipenko (FIG. 29-18) had experimented with sculptural voids, but Hepworth introduced holes in her sculptures as abstract elements. The holes do not represent anything specific. They are simply negative space, but are as integral and important to the sculptures as their mass. *Oval Sculpture (No. 2)* is a plaster cast (FIG. 29-63) of an earlier wood sculpture that Hepworth carved in 1943. Pierced in four places, the work is as much defined by the smooth, curving edges of the holes as by the volume

of white plaster. Like the forms in all of Hepworth's mature works, those in *Oval Sculpture* are basic and universal, expressing a sense of timelessness.

HENRY MOORE Fellow Briton HENRY MOORE (1898–1986) shared Hepworth's interest in the hole, or void, as an important element in sculptural design, but his sculptures, such as *Reclining Figure* (FIG. 29-64), although abstracted, always remain recognizable. This statue is one of a long series of reclining female nudes inspired originally by a photograph that Moore acquired of a *chacmool* (FIG. 18-16) from pre-Columbian Mexico. Moore believed that the simple and massive shapes of his statues expressed a universal truth beyond the physical world (see "Brancusi, Hepworth, and Moore," above).

Reclining Figure is also characteristic of Moore's work in exploiting the natural beauty of different materials—here, elm. Moore maintained that every "material has its own individual qualities" and that these qualities could play a role in the creative process: "It is

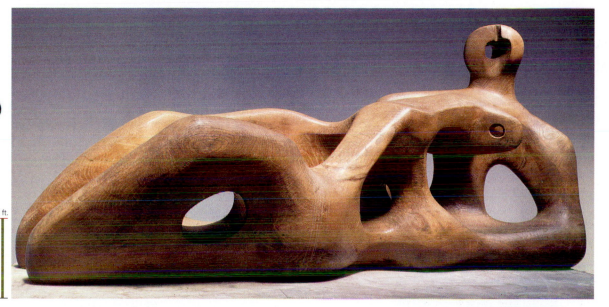

The reclining female figure was a major theme in Moore's sculptures. Inspired by a Mexican chacmool (FIG. 18-16), he simplified and abstracted the body form in a way that recalls Biomorphic Surrealism.

only when the sculptor works direct, when there is an active relationship with his material, that the material can take its part in the shaping of an idea."[39] Accordingly, the contours of *Reclining Figure* follow the grain of the wood. The abstracted shapes suggest Surrealist biomorphic forms (FIG. 29-58), but Moore's recumbent woman is also a powerful earth mother whose swelling forms and hollows suggest nurturing human energy. Similarly, the body shapes evoke the contours of the Yorkshire hills of Moore's childhood and the wind-polished surfaces of weathered wood and stone. Moore heightened the allusions to landscape (compare FIG. 29-44A) and to Surrealist organic forms in his work by interplaying mass and void, based on the intriguing qualities of cavities in nature. For Moore, the hole was not an abstract shape. It represented "the mysterious fascination of caves in hillsides and cliffs."[40] *Reclining Figure* uses the organic vocabulary central to Moore's philosophy—bone shapes, eroded rocks, and geologic formations—to describe the human form.

VERA MUKHINA Not all European sculptors of this period pursued abstraction. *Worker and Collective Farm Woman* (FIG. 29-65) by Russian artist VERA MUKHINA (1889–1963) presents a vivid contrast to the work of Brancusi, Hepworth, and Moore. Produced in 1937 for the International Exposition in Paris—the same venue in which Picasso displayed *Guernica* (FIG. 29-16)—Mukhina's over-life-size stainless-steel sculpture glorifies the communal labor of the Soviet people. Whereas Picasso employed Cubist abstraction to convey the horror of wartime bombing, Mukhina's representation of two exemplars of the Soviet citizenry was based on traditional figural sculpture. Specifically, Mukhina's primary source was an early-fifth-century BCE Greek group representing two Athenian citizens, Harmodios and Aristogeiton, who were celebrated for slaying a hated tyrant and restoring rule by the people—an appropriate model in the egalitarian Soviet state. Her statuary group, which stood on the top of the Soviet Pavilion at the exposition, depicts a male factory worker, holding aloft the tool of his trade, the hammer, and a farm woman, raising her sickle to the sky. The juxtaposed hammer and sickle at the apex of the sculpture replicate their appearance on the Soviet flag. Mukhina augmented the heroic tenor of the work by emphasizing the solidity of the figures, who stride forward with their clothes blowing dramatically behind them. Mukhina had studied in Paris and was familiar with abstraction,

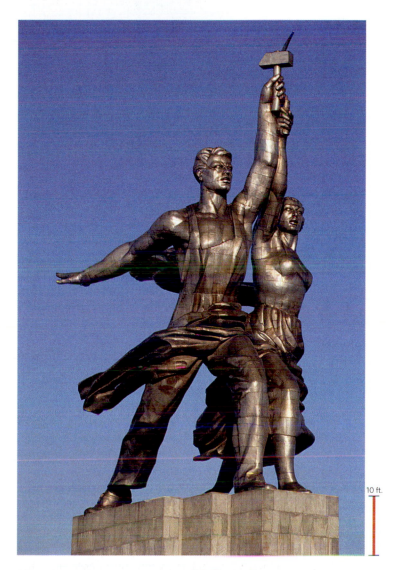

29-65 VERA MUKHINA, *Worker and Collective Farm Woman*, Soviet Pavilion, Paris Exposition, 1937. Stainless steel, 78' high. Art © Estate of Vera Mukhina/RAO, Moscow/VAGA, New York.

In contrast to contemporaneous abstract sculpture, Mukhina's realistic representation of a male factory worker and a female farm worker glorified the communal labor of the Soviet people.

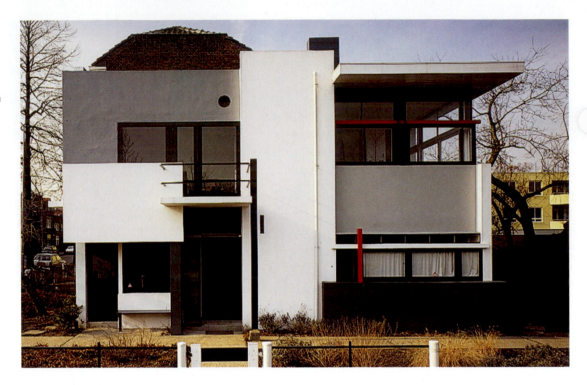

29-66 Gerrit Thomas Rietveld, Schröder House (looking northwest), Utrecht, the Netherlands, 1924.

The De Stijl Schröder House has an open plan and an exterior that is a kind of three-dimensional projection of the carefully proportioned flat color rectangles in Mondrian's paintings (FIG. 29-61).

especially Cubism, but felt that a commitment to realism tempered with idealism—note the muscled arms and chest of the man and the blemishless features of both faces—produced the most powerful sculpture. This approach to figural sculpture was, in fact, since 1934 the officially approved style of the Communist government. Mukhina's eager embrace of the official style, called Soviet Realism, earned high praise for her art and for this sculpture in particular. Indeed, Russian citizens cherished *Worker and Collective Farm Woman* as a national symbol for decades.

Architecture

As in the opening decades of the century, developments in European architecture after World War I closely paralleled the stylistic and theoretical concerns of painters and sculptors.

GERRIT RIETVELD The ideas that Piet Mondrian, Theo van Doesburg, and De Stijl artists advanced found their architectural equivalent in the designs of GERRIT THOMAS RIETVELD (1888–1964). His Schröder House (FIG. 29-66) in Utrecht, built in 1924, perfectly expresses van Doesburg's definition of De Stijl architecture:

> The new architecture is anti-cubic, i.e., it does not strive to contain the different functional space cells in a single closed cube, but it throws the functional space (as well as canopy planes, balcony volumes, etc.) out from the center of the cube, so that height, width, and depth plus time become a completely new plastic expression in open spaces. . . . The plastic architect . . . has to construct in the new field, time-space.[41]

The main public rooms of the Schröder House are on the second floor, with the private living quarters on the ground floor. Rietveld's house has an open plan and a relationship to nature more like the houses of American architect Frank Lloyd Wright (FIGS. 29-45 and 29-46). Rietveld designed the entire second floor with sliding partitions that can be closed to define separate rooms or pushed back to create one open space broken into units only by the furni-

ture arrangement. This shifting quality appears also on the outside, where railings, free-floating walls, and long rectangular windows give the effect of cubic units breaking up before the viewer's eyes. Rectangular planes seem to slide across each other on the Schröder House facade like movable panels, making this structure a kind of three-dimensional projection of the rigid but carefully proportioned flat color rectangles in Mondrian's paintings (FIG. 29-61).

WALTER GROPIUS De Stijl architects not only developed an appealing simplified geometric style but also promoted the notion that art should be thoroughly incorporated into living environments. As Mondrian had insisted, "[A]rt and life are *one*; art and life are both expressions of truth."[42] In Germany, WALTER GROPIUS (1883–1969) developed a particular vision of "total architecture." He made this concept the foundation of not only his own work but also the work of generations of pupils under his influence at a school called the *Bauhaus* (see "Walter Gropius and the Bauhaus," page 933, and FIG. **29-67**).

The building that Gropius designed for the Bauhaus in 1925 after the school relocated to Dessau was the Bauhaus's architectural manifesto. The Dessau Bauhaus consisted of workshop and class areas, a dining room, a theater, a gymnasium, a wing with studio apartments, and an enclosed two-story bridge housing administrative offices. Of the major wings, the most dramatic was the Shop Block (FIG. 29-67). Three stories tall, the Shop Block housed a printing shop and dye works facility, in addition to other work areas. The builders constructed the skeleton of reinforced concrete but set these supports well back, sheathing the entire structure in glass, creating a streamlined and light effect. This design's simplicity followed Gropius's dictum that architecture should avoid "all romantic embellishment and whimsy." Further, he realized the "economy in the use of space" articulated in his list of Bauhaus principles in his interior layout of the Shop Block, which consisted of large areas of free-flowing undivided space. Gropius believed that this kind of spatial organization encouraged interaction and the sharing of ideas.

ARTISTS ON ART

Walter Gropius and the Bauhaus

In 1919, Walter Gropius became the director of the Weimar School of Arts and Crafts in Germany, founded in 1906. Under Gropius, the school assumed a new name—Das Staatliche Bauhaus (State School of Building). Gropius's goal was to train artists, architects, and designers to accept and anticipate 20th-century needs. He developed an extensive curriculum based on certain principles set forth in the *Bauhaus Manifesto*, published in April 1919.

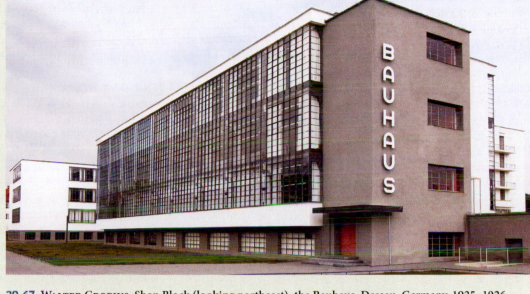

29-67 WALTER GROPIUS, Shop Block (looking northeast), the Bauhaus, Dessau, Germany, 1925–1926.

Gropius constructed this Bauhaus building by sheathing a reinforced concrete skeleton in glass. The design followed his dictum that architecture should avoid "all romantic embellishment and whimsy."

BAUHAUS MANIFESTO

The first principle that Gropius staunchly advocated in the 1919 manifesto was the importance of strong basic design (including principles of composition, two- and three-dimensionality, and color theory) and craftsmanship as fundamental to good art and architecture. He asserted that there was no essential difference between the artist and the craftsperson.

> The Bauhaus strives to coordinate all creative effort, to achieve, in a new architecture, the unification of all training in art and design. The ultimate, if distant, goal of the Bauhaus is the collective work of art—the Building—in which no barriers exist between the structural and the decorative arts.*

To encourage the elimination of those boundaries that traditionally separated art from architecture and art from craft, the Bauhaus offered courses in a wide range of artistic disciplines. These included carpentry, furniture design (by MARCEL BREUER [1902–1981]; FIG. **29-67A**), weaving (by GUNTA STÖLZL [1897–1983]; FIG. **29-67B**), pottery, bookbinding, metalwork, stained glass, mural painting, stage design, and advertising and typography, in addition to painting, sculpture, and architecture. Both a technical instructor and a "teacher of form"—an artist—taught in each department. Among the teachers whom Gropius hired were Vassily Kandinsky (FIG. 29-7) and Paul Klee (FIG. 29-59).

In addition, because Gropius wanted the Bauhaus to produce graduates who could design progressive environments that satisfied 20th-century needs, he emphasized thorough knowledge of machine-age technologies and materials. He felt that to produce truly successful designs, the artist-architect-craftsperson

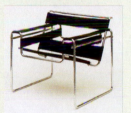

⚡ **29-67A** BREUER, Wassily chair, 1925.

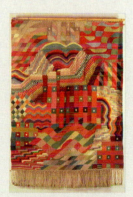

⚡ **29-67B** STÖLZL, Gobelin tapestry, 1927–1928.

had to understand industry and mass production. Ultimately, Gropius hoped for a marriage between art and industry—a synthesis of design and production. As did the De Stijl movement, the Bauhaus philosophy had its roots in utopian principles. Gropius's declaration reveals the idealism of the entire Bauhaus enterprise:

> Let us collectively desire, conceive, and create the new building of the future, which will be everything in one structure: architecture and sculpture and painting, which, from the million hands of craftsmen, will one day rise towards heaven as the crystalline symbol of a new and coming faith.†

In its reference to a unity of workers, this statement also reveals the undercurrent of socialism present in Germany at the time.

BAUHAUS IN DESSAU

After encountering increasing hostility from a new government elected in 1924, the Bauhaus moved north from Weimar to Dessau (FIG. 29-67) in early 1925. By this time, the Bauhaus program had matured. In a new statement, Gropius listed the school's goals more clearly:

- A decidedly positive attitude to the living environment of vehicles and machines
- The organic shaping of things in accordance with their own current laws, avoiding all romantic embellishment and whimsy
- Restriction of basic forms and colors to what is typical and universally intelligible
- Simplicity in complexity, economy in the use of space, materials, time, and money‡

*Quoted in Charles Harrison and Paul Wood, eds., *Art in Theory, 1900–2000: An Anthology of Changing Ideas*, 2d ed. (Oxford: Blackwell, 2003), 311.

†Translated by Charles W. Haxthausen, in Barry Bergdoll, ed., *Bauhaus 1919–1933* (New York: Museum of Modern Art, 2009), 64.

‡Quoted in John Willett, *Art and Politics in the Weimar Period: The New Sobriety, 1917–1933* (New York: Da Capo Press, 1978), 119.

LUDWIG MIES VAN DER ROHE In 1928, Gropius left the Bauhaus, and Ludwig Mies van der Rohe (1886–1969) eventually took over the directorship, moving the school to Berlin in 1932. Taking as his motto "less is more" and calling his architecture "skin and bones," the new Bauhaus director had already fully formed his aesthetic when he conceived the model (FIG. **29-68**) for a glass skyscraper building in 1921. In the glass model, which was on display at the first Bauhaus exhibition in 1923, three irregularly shaped towers flow outward from a central court designed to hold a lobby, a porter's room, and a community center. Two cylindrical entrance shafts rise at the ends of the court, each containing elevators, stairways, and toilets. Wholly transparent, the perimeter walls reveal the regular horizontal patterning of the cantilevered floor planes and their thin vertical supporting elements. The bold use of glass sheathing and inset supports was, at the time, technically and aesthetically adventurous. The weblike delicacy of the lines of the model, as well as the illusion of movement created by reflection and by light

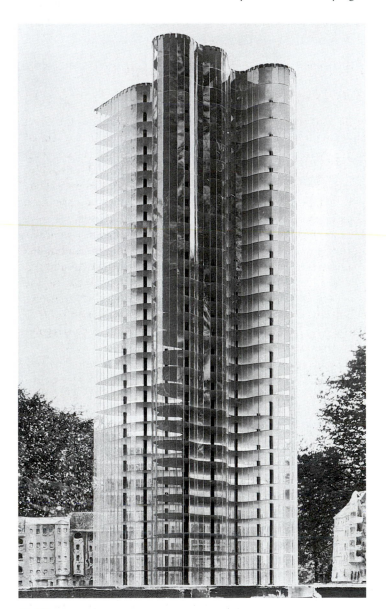

29-68 Ludwig Mies van der Rohe, model for a glass skyscraper, Berlin, Germany, 1922 (no longer extant).

In this technically and aesthetically adventurous design, the architect whose motto was "less is more" proposed a transparent building that revealed its cantilevered floor planes and thin supports.

changes seen through the glass, appealed to many other architects. A few years later, Gropius pursued it in his design for the Bauhaus building (FIG. 29-67) in Dessau. The legacy of Mies van der Rohe's design can be seen in the glass-and-steel skyscrapers found in major cities throughout the world today.

END OF THE BAUHAUS One of Hitler's first acts after coming to power was to close the Bauhaus in 1933. The student body had become radicalized, and the Nazis suspected that the school housed a press that printed Communist-inspired anti-Nazi brochures. During its 14-year existence, the beleaguered school graduated fewer than 500 students, yet it achieved legendary status. Its phenomenal influence extended beyond painting, sculpture, and architecture to interior design, graphic design, and advertising. Moreover, art schools everywhere began to structure their curricula in line with the program that the Bauhaus pioneered. The numerous Bauhaus instructors who fled Nazi Germany disseminated the school's philosophy and aesthetic. Many Bauhaus members came to the United States. Gropius and Breuer (FIG. 29-67A) ended up at Harvard University. Mies van der Rohe moved to Chicago and taught there.

LE CORBUSIER The simple geometric aesthetic developed by Gropius and Mies van der Rohe became known as the *International Style* because of its widespread popularity. The first and purest exponent of this style was the Swiss architect Charles-Edouard Jeanneret, who adopted his maternal grandfather's name—Le Corbusier (1887–1965). Trained in Paris and Berlin, he was also a painter, but Le Corbusier had the greatest influence as an architect and theorist on modern architecture. As such, he applied himself to designing a functional living space, which he described as a "machine for living."

Le Corbusier maintained that the basic physical and psychological needs of every human being were sun, space, and vegetation combined with controlled temperature, good ventilation, and insulation against harmful and undesired noise. He also advocated basing dwelling designs on human scale, because the house is humankind's assertion within nature. All these qualities characterize Le Corbusier's Villa Savoye (FIG. **29-69**), built at Poissy-sur-Seine near Paris on commission from Pierre Savoye, the director of a major insurance company. The country house, a place of retreat from the city for the wealthy businessman, sits at the center of a large plot of land cleared of trees and shrubs, but windows on all sides and the villa's roof-terrace provided Savoye and his wife, Emilie, with broad views of the surrounding landscape. Several colors appear on the exterior—originally, a dark-green base, cream walls, and a rose-and-blue windscreen on top. They were deliberately analogous to the colors in the machine-inspired Purist style of painting (FIG. 29-21) that Le Corbusier practiced.

A cube of lightly enclosed and deeply penetrated space, the Villa Savoye has only a partially confined ground floor (containing, originally, a three-car garage, bedrooms, a bathroom, and utility rooms, and today a ticket counter and small gift shop for visitors). Much of the house's interior is open space, with thin columns supporting the main living floor and the roof garden area. The major living rooms in the Villa Savoye are on the second floor, wrapping around an open central court. Strip windows running along the membranelike exterior walls provide illumination to the rooms as well as views out to nature. From the second-floor court, a ramp leads up to the roof-terrace and an interior garden protected by a curving windbreak along the north side.

The Villa Savoye has no traditional facade. The ostensible approach to the house does not define an entrance. Visitors must

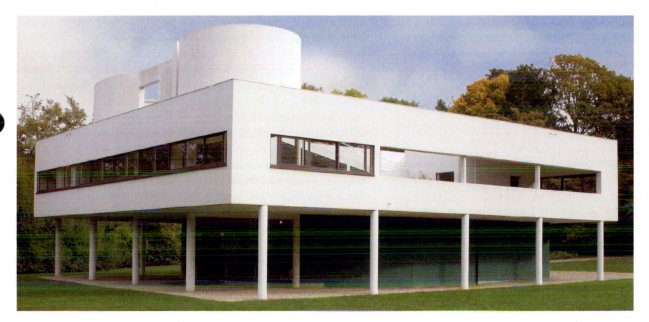

29-69 LE CORBUSIER, Villa Savoye (looking southeast), Poissy-sur-Seine, France, 1929.

Steel and ferroconcrete made it possible for Le Corbusier to invert the traditional practice of placing light architectural elements above heavy ones and to eliminate weight-bearing walls on the ground story.

walk around and through the house to comprehend its layout, which incorporates several changes of direction and spiral staircases. Spaces and masses interpenetrate so fluidly that inside and outside space intermingle. The machine-planed smoothness of the unadorned surfaces, the slender ribbons of continuous windows, and the buoyant lightness of the whole fabric—all combine to reverse the effect of traditional country houses (FIG. 22-28). By placing heavy elements above and light ones below, and by refusing to enclose the ground story of the Villa Savoye with masonry walls, Le Corbusier inverted traditional design practice. This openness, made possible by the use of steel and *ferroconcrete* (concrete strengthened by a skeleton of iron bars) as construction materials, makes the "load" of the Villa Savoye's upper stories appear to hover lightly on the slender columnar supports.

MARSEILLES AND CHANDIGARH As noted, Le Corbusier designed the Villa Savoye as a private home, but like De Stijl architects, he dreamed of extending his ideas of the house as a "machine for living" to designs for efficient and humane cities. He saw great cities as spiritual workshops, and he proposed to correct the deficiencies in existing cities caused by poor traffic circulation, inadequate living units, and the lack of space for recreation and exercise. He proposed replacing traditional cities with three types of new communities. Vertical cities would house workers and the business and service industries. Linear-industrial cities would run as belts along the routes between the vertical cities and would serve as centers for the people and processes involved in manufacturing. Finally, separate centers would be constructed for people involved in intensive agricultural activity. Le Corbusier's cities would provide for human cultural needs in addition to serving every person's need for physical, mental, and emotional comfort.

Later in his career, Le Corbusier designed a few vertical cities, most notably the Unité d'Habitation in Marseilles (1945–1952). He also created the master plan for the entire city of Chandigarh, the capital city of the Punjab, India (1950–1957). The ever-innovative architect ended his career with the Chapel of Notre Dame du Haut (FIGS. 30-41 and 30-42) at Ronchamp, France, one of the most adventurous building designs of the first half of the 20th century.

UNITED STATES AND MEXICO, 1930 TO 1945

In the 1930s, much of the Western world plunged into the Great Depression, which had a particularly acute effect in the United States. The decade following the catastrophic stock market crash of October 1929 dramatically changed the nation, and artists were among the millions of economic victims. The limited art market virtually disappeared, and museums curtailed both their purchases and exhibition schedules. Many artists sought financial support from the federal government, which established numerous programs to provide relief, assist recovery, and promote reform. Among the programs supporting artists were the Treasury Relief Art Project, founded in 1934 to commission art for federal buildings, and the Works Progress Administration (WPA), founded in 1935 to relieve widespread unemployment. Under the WPA, varied activities of the Federal Art Project paid artists, writers, and theater people a regular wage in exchange for work in their professions.

Despite the economic hardships facing artists during the Great Depression, the United States became a haven for European painters, sculptors, and architects seeking to escape from Hitler and the Nazis. Among those who abandoned their homelands for America during the years leading up to World War II were Léger, Lipchitz, Beckmann, Grosz, Ernst, and Dalí. This influx of European artists searching for freedom from political and religious persecution and a more hospitable environment for their art was as significant a factor in exposing American artists to modernist European art as the Armory Show of 1913 (see "The Armory Show," page 909).

A complementary factor was the desire on the part of American museums to demonstrate their familiarity and connection with the most progressive European art by mounting exhibitions centered on the latest European artistic developments. In 1938, for example, the City Art Museum of Saint Louis presented an exhibition of Beckmann's work, and the Art Institute of Chicago organized *George Grosz: A Survey of His Art from 1918–1938*. This interest in exhibiting the work of persecuted artists driven from their homelands also had political overtones. In the highly charged atmosphere of the late 1930s leading to the onset of World War II, Americans often perceived support for these artists and their work as support for freedom and democracy. For example, in 1942, Alfred H. Barr Jr. (1902–1981), the director of the Museum of Modern Art, stated:

> Among the freedoms which the Nazis have destroyed, none has been more cynically perverted, more brutally stamped upon, than the Freedom of Art. For not only must the artist of Nazi Germany bow to political tyranny, he must also conform to the personal taste of that great art connoisseur, Adolf Hitler. . . . But German artists of spirit and integrity have refused to conform. They have gone into exile or slipped into anxious obscurity. . . . Their paintings and sculptures, too, have been hidden or exiled. . . . But in free countries they can still be seen, can still bear witness to the survival of a free German culture.[43]

Despite this moral support for exiled artists, once the United States formally entered the war, Germany officially became the enemy. It became much more difficult for the American art world to promote German artists, however persecuted. Many émigré artists, including Léger, Grosz, Ernst, and Dalí, returned to Europe after the war ended. Their collective presence in the United States until then, however, was critical for the development of American art.

Painting

Although the political, social, and economic developments of the 1930s and 1940s brought many modernist European artists to the United States, the leading American painters of this period were primarily figural artists who had only a limited interest in abstract composition.

BEN SHAHN Born in Lithuania, BEN SHAHN (1898–1969) came to the United States in 1906 and trained as a lithographer before broadening the media in which he worked to include easel and mural painting and photography. He focused on the lives of ordinary people and the injustices often done to them by the structure of an impersonal, bureaucratic society. In the early 1930s, he completed a cycle of 23 paintings and prints inspired by the trial and execution of two Italian anarchists, Nicola Sacco and Bartolomeo Vanzetti. Accused of killing two men in a holdup in 1920 in South Braintree, Massachusetts, the Italians were convicted in a trial that

many people thought resulted in a grave miscarriage of justice. Shahn felt that he had found in this story a subject the equal of any in Western art history: "Suddenly I realized . . . I was living through another crucifixion."[44] Basing many of the works in this cycle on newspaper photographs of the events, Shahn devised a style that adapted his knowledge of Synthetic Cubism and his training in commercial art to an emotionally expressive use of flat, intense color in figural compositions filled with sharp, dry, angular forms. He called the major work in the series *The Passion of Sacco and Vanzetti* (FIG. I-6), drawing a parallel to Christ's passion. This tall, narrow painting condenses the narrative in terms of both time and space. The two executed men lie in coffins at the bottom of the composition. Presiding over them are the three members of the commission chaired by Harvard University president A. Laurence Lowell, who declared the original trial fair and cleared the way for the executions to take place. A framed portrait of Judge Webster Thayer, who handed down the initial sentence, hangs on the wall of a simplified government building. The gray pallor of the dead men, the stylized mask-faces of the mock-pious mourning commissioners, and the haughty judge all contribute to the mood of anguished commentary that Shahn sought. *The Passion of Sacco and Vanzetti* is one of the most powerful American artworks of the era.

EDWARD HOPPER Trained as a commercial artist, EDWARD HOPPER (1882–1967) studied painting and printmaking in New York and then in Paris. When he returned to the United States, he concentrated on scenes of contemporary American city and country life. His paintings depict buildings, streets, and landscapes that are curiously muted, still, and filled with empty spaces, evoking the national mindset during the Depression era. Hopper did not paint historically specific scenes. He took as his subject the more generalized theme of the overwhelming loneliness and echoing isolation of modern life in the United States. In his paintings, motion is stopped and time suspended.

From the darkened streets outside a restaurant in Hopper's *Nighthawks* (FIG. 29-70), the viewer glimpses the lighted interior through huge plate-glass windows, which lend the inner space the paradoxical sense of being both a safe refuge and a vulnerable place

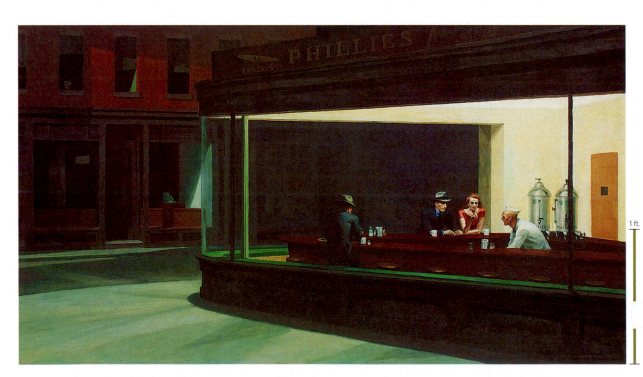

29-70 EDWARD HOPPER, *Nighthawks,* 1942. Oil on canvas, 2' 6" × 4' 8$\frac{11}{16}$". Art Institute of Chicago, Chicago (Friends of American Art Collection).

The seeming indifference of Hopper's characters to one another, and the echoing spaces surrounding them, evoke the overwhelming loneliness and isolation of Depression-era life in the United States.

1 ft.

ART AND SOCIETY

Jacob Lawrence's *Migration of the Negro*

Disillusioned with their lives in the South, hundreds of thousands of African Americans migrated north in the years following World War I, seeking improved economic opportunities and a more hospitable political and social environment. But the conditions that African Americans encountered both during their migration and in the North were often as difficult and discriminatory as those they had left behind in the South, as the artist Jacob Lawrence knew from his own experience. Lawrence was an African American whose family had migrated from the rural south to Atlantic City, New Jersey, where he was born. He moved to Harlem when he was 13 years old.

> I was part of the migration, as was my family, my mother, my sister, and my brother. . . . I grew up hearing tales about people "coming up," another family arriving. . . . I didn't realize what was happening until about the middle of the 1930s, and that's when the *Migration* series began to take form in my mind.*

Lawrence sought funding for his project from the Julius Rosenwald Fund. In his successful fellowship application, Lawrence argued that his proposal was of high educational value. He stated:

> It is important as a part of the evolution of America, since this Migration has affected the whole of America mentally, economically and socially. Since it has had this effect, I feel that my project would lay before the Negroes themselves a little of what part they have played in the History of the United States. In addition the whole of America might learn some of the history of this particular minority group, of which they know very little.†

His plan was to depict the history of the great African American migration northward in eight sections: Causes of the Migration; Stimulation of the Migration; The Spread of the Migration; The Efforts to Check the Migration; Public Opinion Regarding the Migration; The Effects of the Migration on the South; The Effects of the Migration on Various Parts of the North; and The Effects of the Migration on the Negro. The resulting series consists of 60 panels, all with explanatory captions—for example, "They did not always leave because they were promised work in the North. Many of them left because of Southern conditions, one of them being great floods that ruined the crops, and therefore they were unable to make a living where they were" (*No. 8*) and "They also found discrimination in the North although it was much different from that which they had known in the South" (*No. 49*; FIG. **29-71**).

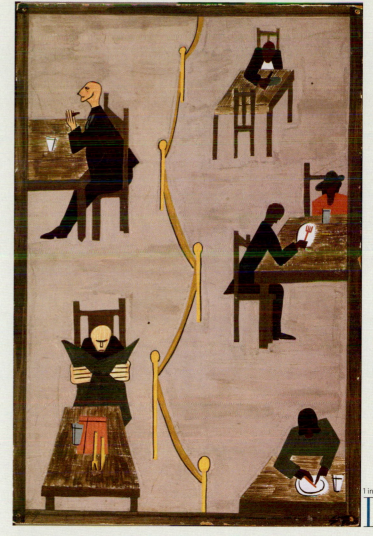

29-71 JACOB LAWRENCE, *No. 49* from *The Migration of the Negro*, 1940–1941. Tempera on Masonite, 1' 6" × 1'. Phillips Collection, Washington, D.C.

The 49th in a series of 60 paintings documenting African American life in the North, Lawrence's depiction of a segregated dining room underscored that the migrants had not left discrimination behind.

*Quoted in Henry Louis Gates Jr., "New Negroes, Migration, and Cultural Exchange," in Elizabeth Hutton Turner, ed., *Jacob Lawrence: The Migration Series* (Washington, D.C.: Phillips Collection, 1993), 20.

†Quoted in Patricia Hills, *Painting Harlem Modern: The Art of Jacob Lawrence* (Berkeley and Los Angeles: University of California Press, 2009), 98.

for the three customers and the man behind the counter. The seeming indifference of Hopper's characters to one another as well as the echoing spaces surrounding them evoke the pervasive loneliness of modern humans. In *Nighthawks* and other works, Hopper created a Realist vision recalling that of 19th-century artists such as Thomas Eakins (FIG. 27-36) and Henry Ossawa Tanner (FIG. 27-38), but in keeping with more recent trends in painting, he simplified the shapes, moving toward abstraction.

JACOB LAWRENCE African American artist JACOB LAWRENCE (1917–2000) moved to Harlem, New York, in 1927 while still a boy. There, he came under the spell of the African art and the African American history he found in lectures and exhibitions and in the special programs sponsored by the 135th Street branch of the New York Public Library, which had outstanding collections of African American art and archival data. Inspired by the politically oriented art of Goya (FIG. 27-12), Daumier (FIG. 27-29), and Orozco (FIG. 29-74), and influenced by the many artists and writers of the Harlem Renaissance whom he met, including Aaron Douglas (see "Aaron Douglas and the Harlem Renaissance," page 912, and FIGS. 29-40 and 29-40A), Lawrence found his subjects in the everyday life of Harlem and in African American history.

Grant Wood's *Revolt against the City*

Grant Wood and the Regionalists, sometimes referred to as the American Scene Painters, turned their attention away not only from Europe but also from America's cities. The Regionalists found their subjects instead in the rural life of America, which they considered its cultural backbone. Wood set forth his philosophy most clearly in *Revolt against the City*, a pamphlet he published in Iowa City in 1935, five years after completing his masterpiece, *American Gothic* (FIG. 29-72).

[American] painting has declared its independence from Europe, and is retreating from the cities to the more American village and country life. Paris is no longer the Mecca of the American artist. The American public, which used to be interested solely in foreign and imitative work, has readily acquired a strong interest in the distinctly indigenous art of its own land; and our buyers of paintings and patrons of art have naturally and honestly fallen in with the movement away from Paris and the American pseudo-Parisians.... This is no mere chauvinism. If it is patriotic, it is so because a feeling for one's own milieu and for the validity of one's own life and its surroundings is patriotic.... No longer is it necessary for [the American artist] to migrate even to New York, or to seek any great metropolis. No longer is it necessary for him to suffer the confusing cosmopolitanism, the noise, the too intimate gregariousness of the large city.

Let me try to state the basic idea of the regional movement. Each section has a personality of its own, in physiography, industry, psychology. Thinking painters and writers who have passed their formative years in these regions, will, by care-taking analysis, work out and interpret in their productions these varying personalities. When the different regions develop characteristics of their own, they will come into competition with each other; and out of this competition a rich American culture will grow.*

*Grant Wood, *Revolt against the City* (Iowa City: Frank Luther Mott, 1935). Reprinted in James M. Dennis, *Grant Wood: A Study in American Art and Culture* (New York: Viking, 1975).

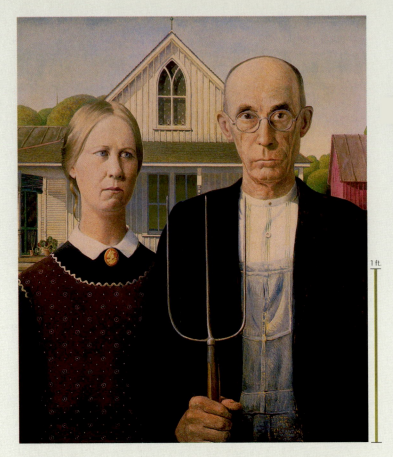

29-72 GRANT WOOD, *American Gothic*, 1930. Oil on beaverboard, 2' 5⅞" × 2' ⅞". Art Institute of Chicago, Chicago (Friends of American Art Collection).

In reaction to modernist abstract painting, the Midwestern Regionalism movement focused on American subjects. Wood's painting of an Iowa farmer and his daughter became an American icon.

In 1941, Lawrence began a 60-painting series titled *The Migration of the Negro* in which he defined his vision of the continuing African American struggle against discrimination (see "Jacob Lawrence's *Migration of the Negro*," page 937). Unlike his earlier historical paintings depicting important figures in American history, such as the abolitionists Frederick Douglass and Harriet Tubman, this series called attention to a contemporaneous event—the ongoing exodus of black labor from the southern United States.

Lawrence's *Migration* paintings provide numerous vignettes capturing the experiences of the African Americans who had moved to the North. Often, a sense of the bleakness and degradation of their new life dominates the images. In *No. 49* (FIG. 29-71), which tells of the unexpected and different kind of discrimination that African Americans encountered in the North, Lawrence depicted a blatantly segregated dining room with a barrier running down the room's center separating the whites on the left from the African Americans on the right. To ensure a continuity and visual integrity among all 60 paintings, Lawrence interpreted his themes systematically in rhythmic arrangements of bold, flat, and strongly colored shapes. His style drew equally from his interest in the push-pull effects of Cubist space and his memories of the patterns made by the colored scatter rugs brightening the floors of his childhood homes. He unified the narrative with a consistent palette of bluish green, orange, yellow, and grayish brown throughout the entire series.

GRANT WOOD Although many American artists, such as the Precisionists (FIGS. 29-41 and 29-42), preferred to depict the city or rapidly developing technological advances, others avoided subjects tied to modern life. At a 1931 arts conference, GRANT WOOD (1891–1942) announced a new movement developing in the Midwest, known as *Regionalism*, which he described as focused on American subjects and as standing in reaction to the modernist abstraction of Europe and New York. Four years later, Wood published a pamphlet titled *Revolt against the City*, which underscored their new focus (see "Grant Wood's *Revolt against the City*," above). Wood's paintings, for example, portray the people of rural Iowa, where he was born and raised.

The work that catapulted Wood to national prominence was *American Gothic* (FIG. **29-72**), which became an American icon. The artist depicted his dentist and his sister posing as a farmer and his spinster daughter standing in front of a neat house with a small *lancet* window, a motif originating in Gothic architecture and associated with churches and religious piety. The man and woman wear traditional attire. He appears in worn overalls and she in an apron trimmed with rickrack. The dour expression on both faces gives the painting a severe quality, which Wood enhanced with his meticulous brushwork. The public and professional critics agreed that *American Gothic* was "quaint, humorous, and AMERICAN" and embodied "strength, dignity, fortitude, resoluteness, integrity," qualities that represented the true spirit of America.[45]

Wood's Regionalist vision involved more than his subjects. It extended to a rejection of avant-garde styles in favor of a clearly readable, Realist style. Surely, this approach appealed to many people alienated by the increasing presence of abstraction in art. However, despite the accolades this painting received, it also attracted criticism. Not everyone saw the painting as a sympathetic portrayal of Midwestern life. Indeed, some Iowans considered the depiction of life in their state insulting. In addition, despite the seemingly reportorial nature of *American Gothic,* some viewed it as a political statement—one of staunch nationalism. In light of the problematic nationalism in Germany at the time, many observers found Wood's nationalistic attitude disturbing. Nonetheless, during the Great Depression, Regionalist paintings had a popular appeal because they often projected a reassuring image of America's heartland. The public saw Regionalism as a means of coping with the national crisis through a search for cultural roots. Thus people deemed acceptable any nostalgia implicit in Regionalist paintings or the mythologies these works perpetuated, because they served a larger purpose.

THOMAS HART BENTON Another major Regionalist artist was THOMAS HART BENTON (1889–1975). Whereas Wood focused his attention on Iowa, Benton turned to scenes from his native Missouri. He produced one of his major works, a series of murals titled *A Social History of the State of Missouri,* in 1936 for the Missouri State Capitol. The murals depict a collection of images from the state's historical and legendary past, such as primitive agriculture, horse trading, a vigilante lynching, an old-fashioned political meeting, and Mark Twain's Huckleberry Finn and Jim on their raft. Other scenes portray the mining industry, grain elevators, Native Americans, and family life. One segment, *Pioneer Days and Early Settlers* (FIG. **29-73**), shows a white man using whisky as a bartering tool with a Native American (*left*), along with scenes documenting the building of Missouri (*right*). Part documentary and part invention, Benton's images include both positive and negative aspects of Missouri's history, as these examples illustrate. Although the public perceived the Regionalists as dedicated to glorifying Midwestern life, that was not their aim. Indeed, Grant Wood observed, "Your true regionalist is not a mere eulogist; he may

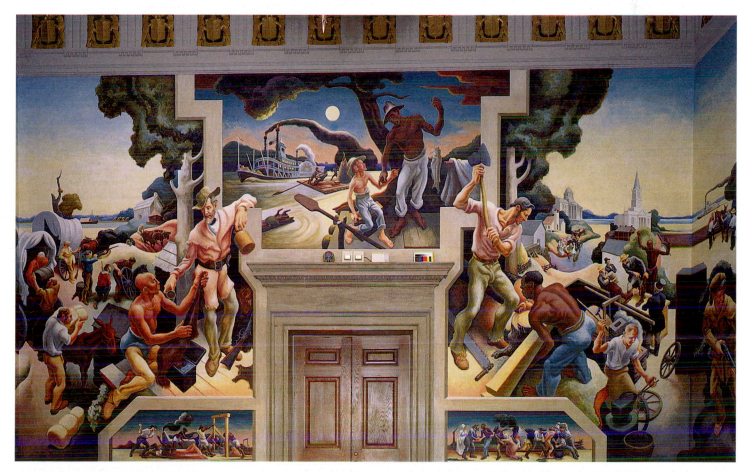

29-73 THOMAS HART BENTON, *Pioneer Days and Early Settlers,* fresco in the State Capitol, Jefferson City, Missouri, 1936.
Art © T. H. Benton and R. P. Benton Testamentary Trusts/UMB Bank Trustee/Licensed by VAGA, New York.

Benton's mural for Missouri's State Capitol is one of the major Regionalist artworks. Part documentary and part invention, the images include both positive and negative aspects of state history.

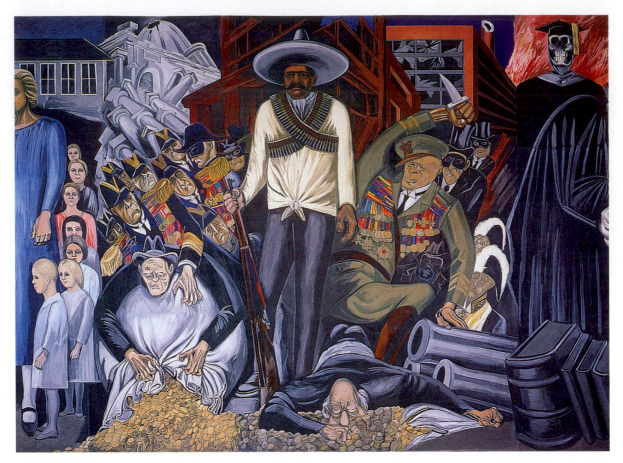

29-74 José Clemente Orozco, *Epic of American Civilization: Hispano-America* (panel 16), fresco in Baker Memorial Library, Dartmouth College, Hanover, New Hampshire, ca. 1932–1934. Art © Orozco Valladares Family/ SOMAAP, Mexico/Licensed by VAGA, New York.

One of 24 panels depicting the history of Mexico from ancient times, this scene focuses on a heroic peasant soldier of the Mexican Revolution surrounded by symbolic figures of his oppressors.

even be a severe critic."[46] Benton, like Wood, championed a visually accessible style, but he developed a highly personal aesthetic that included complex compositions, a fluidity of imagery, and simplified figures depicted with a rubbery distortion.

JOSÉ CLEMENTE OROZCO During the period between the two world wars, several Mexican painters achieved international renown for their work both in Mexico and the United States. The eldest was José Clemente Orozco (1883–1949), one of a group of Mexican artists determined to base their art on the indigenous history and culture existing in Mexico before the arrival of Europeans. The movement that these artists formed was part of the idealistic rethinking of society that occurred in conjunction with the Mexican Revolution (1910–1920) and the lingering political turmoil of the 1920s. Among the projects that these politically motivated artists undertook were vast mural cycles placed in public buildings to dramatize and validate the history of Mexico's native peoples. Orozco worked on one of the first major cycles, painted in 1922 on the walls of the National Training School in Mexico City. He carried the ideas of this mural revolution to the United States, completing many commissions for wall paintings between 1927 and 1934, notably a major mural cycle in the Baker Library at Dartmouth College in New Hampshire. The college let Orozco choose the subject, and he designed 14 large panels and 10 smaller ones that together formed a panoramic and symbolic history of ancient and modern Mexico.

The murals recount Mexican history from the early mythic days of the feathered-serpent god Quetzalcoatl (see pages 514 and 1088) to a contemporary and bitterly satiric vision of modern education.

The imagery in panel 16, *Epic of American Civilization: Hispano-America* (FIG. **29-74**), revolves around the monumental figure of a heroic Mexican peasant who has become a soldier in the Mexican Revolution. Looming on either side of him are mounds crammed with symbolic figures of his oppressors—bankers, government soldiers, officials, gangsters, and the rich. Money-grubbers empty huge bags of gold coins at the feet of the incorruptible armed peasant, cannons threaten him, and a general bedecked with medals raises a dagger to stab him in the back. Orozco's training as an architect gave him a sense of the framed wall surface, which he easily commanded, projecting his clearly defined figures onto the solid mural plane in monumental scale. In addition, Orozco's early experience as a maker of political prints and as a newspaper artist had taught him the rhetorical strength of graphic brevity, which he used here to assure that his allegory could be read easily. His skillful merging of the graphic and mural media effects gives his work an originality and force rarely seen in mural painting after the Renaissance and Baroque periods.

DIEGO RIVERA A second Mexican who received great acclaim for his murals, both in Mexico and in the United States, was Diego Rivera (1886–1957), who lived in Paris from 1911 to 1919 and

ARTISTS ON ART

Diego Rivera on Art for the People

Diego Rivera was an avid proponent of a social and political role for art in the lives of common people and wrote passionately about the proper goals for an artist—goals he fully met in his own murals depicting Mexican history (FIG. 29-75). Rivera's views stand in sharp contrast to the growing interest in abstraction on the part of many early-20th-century painters and sculptors.

> Art has always been employed by the different social classes who hold the balance of power as one instrument of domination—hence, as a political instrument. One can analyze epoch after epoch—from the stone age to our own day—and see that there is no form of art which does not also play an essential political role. . . . What is it then that we really need? . . . An art with revolution as its subject: because the principal interest in the worker's life has to be touched first. It is necessary that he find aesthetic satisfaction and the highest pleasure appareled in the essential interest of his life. . . . The subject is to the painter what the rails are to a locomotive. He cannot do without it. In fact, when he refuses to seek or accept a subject, his own plastic methods and his own aesthetic theories become his subject instead. . . . [H]e himself becomes the subject of his work. He becomes nothing but an illustrator of his own state of mind . . . That is the deception practiced under the name of "Pure Art."*

*Quoted in Robert Goldwater and Marco Treves, eds., Artists on Art from the XIV to the XX Century (New York: Pantheon, 1945), 475–477.

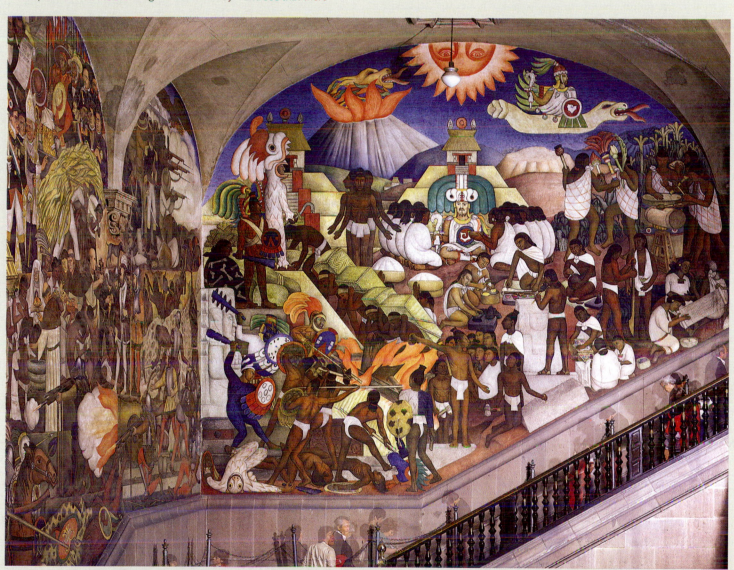

29-75 DIEGO RIVERA, *Ancient Mexico*, detail of *History of Mexico*, fresco in the Palacio Nacional, Mexico City, 1929–1935.

A staunch Marxist, Rivera painted vast mural cycles in public buildings to dramatize the history of his native land. This fresco depicts the conflicts between indigenous Mexicans and Spanish colonizers.

traveled to Italy to study Renaissance frescoes. A staunch Marxist, Rivera strove to develop an art that served his people's needs (see "Diego Rivera on Art for the People," above, and FIG. 29-75.). Toward that end, inspired in part by ancient murals in his homeland, he sought to create a national Mexican style focusing on Mexico's history and also incorporating a popular, generally accessible aesthetic in keeping with the socialist spirit of the Mexican Revolution. Rivera produced numerous large murals in public buildings, among them a series lining the staircase of the National Palace in Mexico City. In these images, painted between 1929 and 1935, he depicted scenes from Mexico's history, of which *Ancient Mexico* (FIG. 29-75) is one. This section of the mural represents the conflicts between the indigenous people and the Spanish colonizers. Rivera included portraits of important figures in Mexican history, especially those involved in the struggle for Mexican independence. Although the composition is complex, the simple monumental shapes and areas of bold color make the story easily legible.

FRIDA KAHLO Born to a Mexican mother and German father, the painter FRIDA KAHLO (1907–1954), who married Diego Rivera, used the details of her life as powerful symbols for the psychological pain of human existence. Art historians often consider Kahlo a Surrealist due to the psychic, autobiographical issues she dealt with in her art. Indeed, André Breton himself deemed her a Natural Surrealist. (The work of her older contemporary, RUFINO TAMAYO [1899–1991; FIG. 29-75A] has also been compared with Natural Surrealism.) Kahlo herself, however, rejected any association with the Surrealists. She began painting seriously as a young student, during convalescence from an accident that tragically left her in constant pain. Her life became a heroic and tumultuous battle for survival against illness and stormy personal relationships.

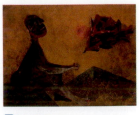

🔗 **29-75A** TAMAYO, *Friend of the Birds*, 1944.

Typical of her long series of unflinching self-portraits is *The Two Fridas* (FIG. 29-76), one of the few large-scale canvases Kahlo ever produced. The twin figures sit side by side on a low bench in a

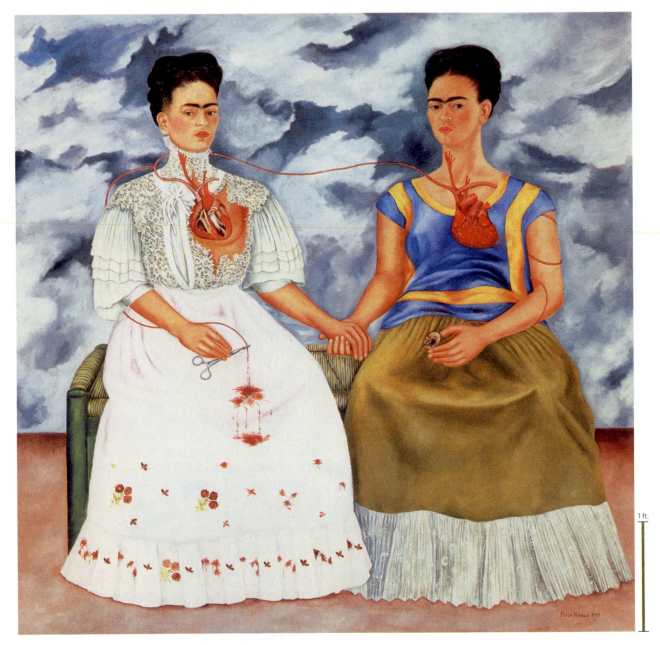

29-76 FRIDA KAHLO, *The Two Fridas*, 1939. Oil on canvas, 5′ 7″ × 5′ 7″. Museo de Arte Moderno, Mexico City.

Kahlo's deeply personal paintings touch sensual and psychological memories in her audience. Here, twin self-portraits linked by clasped hands and a common artery suggest two sides of her personality.

barren landscape under a stormy sky. The figures suggest different sides of the artist's personality, inextricably linked by the clasped hands and by the thin artery stretching between them, joining their exposed hearts. The artery ends on one side in surgical forceps and on the other in a miniature portrait of her husband as a child. Her deeply personal paintings touch sensual and psychological memories in her audience.

To read Kahlo's paintings solely as autobiographical overlooks the powerful political dimension of her art. Kahlo was deeply nationalistic and committed to her Mexican heritage. Politically active, she joined the Communist Party in 1927 and participated in public political protests. *The Two Fridas* incorporates Kahlo's commentary on the struggle facing Mexicans in the early 20th century in defining their national cultural identity. The Frida on the right (representing indigenous culture) appears in a Tehuana dress, the traditional costume of Zapotec women from the Isthmus of Tehuantepec, whereas the Frida on the left (representing imperialist forces) wears a European-style white lace dress. The heart, depicted here in such dramatic fashion, was an important symbol in the art of the Aztecs, whom Mexican nationalists idealized as the last inde-

pendent rulers of their land. Thus *The Two Fridas* represents both Kahlo's personal struggles and the struggles of her homeland.

Photography

Today, Frida Kahlo is the most famous female artist of her generation, but other women achieved prominence in the arts in the period between the two world wars. Especially noteworthy are the photographers Dorothea Lange and Margaret Bourke-White.

DOROTHEA LANGE One of the most important programs the U.S. government initiated during the 1930s was the Resettlement Administration (RA), better known by its later name, the Farm Security Administration. The RA oversaw emergency aid programs for farm families struggling to survive the Great Depression. The RA hired DOROTHEA LANGE (1895–1965) in 1935, and dispatched her to document the deplorable living conditions of the rural poor. At the end of an assignment photographing migratory pea pickers in California, Lange stopped at a camp in Nipomo and found the migrant workers there starving because the crops had frozen in the

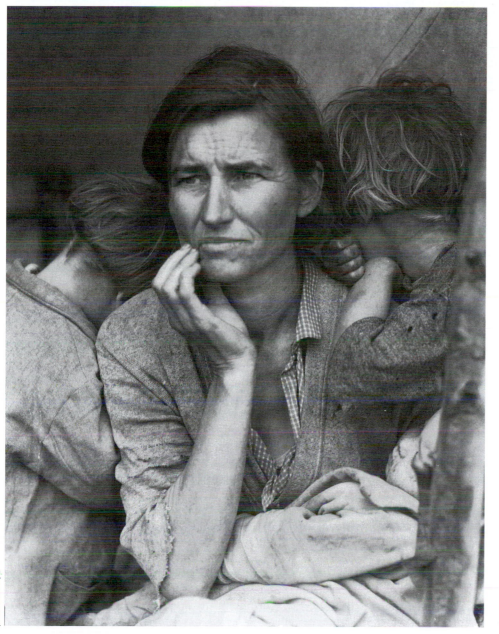

fields. Among the pictures Lange made on this occasion was *Migrant Mother, Nipomo Valley* (FIG. **29-77**), in which she captured the mixture of strength and worry in the raised hand and careworn face of a young mother, who holds a baby on her lap. Two older children cling to their mother trustfully while turning their faces away from the camera. Lange described how she got the picture:

> [I] saw and approached the hungry and desperate mother, as if drawn by a magnet. I do not remember how I explained my presence or my camera to her, but I remember she asked me no questions. I made five exposures, working closer and closer from the same direction. . . . There she sat in that lean-to tent with her children huddled around her, and she seemed to know that my pictures might help her, and so she helped me.[47]

Within days after Lange's photograph appeared in a San Francisco newspaper, people rushed food to Nipomo to feed the hungry workers.

29-77 DOROTHEA LANGE, *Migrant Mother, Nipomo Valley,* 1935. Gelatin silver print, 1' 1" × 9". Oakland Museum of California, Oakland (gift of Paul S. Taylor).

While documenting the lives of migratory farm workers during the Depression, Lange made this unforgettable photograph of a mother in which she captured the woman's strength and worry.

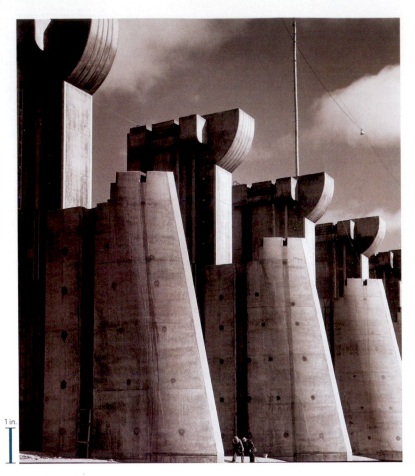

29-78 MARGARET BOURKE-WHITE, *Fort Peck Dam, Montana,* 1936. Gelatin silver print, 1' 1" × 10 ½". Metropolitan Museum of Art, New York (gift of Ford Motor Company and John C. Waddell, 1987).

Bourke-White's dramatic photograph of Fort Peck Dam graced the cover of the first issue of *Life* magazine and celebrated the achievements of American engineering during the depths of the Great Depression.

fortress.) She chose a sharp angle from below to communicate the dam's soaring height, underscoring the immense scale by including two dwarfed figures of men in the foreground. The tight framing, which shuts out all of the landscape and much of the sky, transforms the dam into an almost abstract composition, a kind of still life, like Edward Weston's peppers (FIG. 29-44). Bourke-White's photographs celebrate modern American engineering as heir to the architectural achievements of the ancient world's great civilizations, and bear comparison with the paintings of Charles Demuth (FIG. 29-41).

Sculpture

In striking contrast to the leading American painters and photographers of the 1930s, the most renowned sculptor of this period rose to international prominence because of his contributions to the development of abstract art.

MARGARET BOURKE-WHITE Almost 10 years younger than Dorothea Lange, MARGARET BOURKE-WHITE (1904–1971) also made her reputation as a photojournalist in Depression-era America. She was the first staff photographer that Henry Luce (1898–1967) hired to furnish illustrations for the magazines in his publishing empire. Beginning in 1929, Bourke-White worked for *Fortune,* then for *Life* when Luce launched the famous newsweekly in 1936. During her long career, she photographed Midwestern farmers in their drought-stricken fields, impoverished Southern sharecroppers, black gold miners in South Africa, the Nazi concentration camp at Buchenwald, and the Korean War.

Bourke-White's most famous photographs, however, were not of people or events but of the triumphs of 20th-century engineering, many of which appeared in Luce's magazines and served to instill pride in an American public severely lacking in confidence during the Depression. She photographed the Chrysler Building (FIG. 29-47) while it was under construction in New York, attracting media attention for her daring balancing act on steel girders high above the pavement. She also achieved renown as the first woman to fly a combat mission when she was an official U.S. Air Force photographer during World War II.

For the first issue of *Life* (November 23, 1936), Bourke-White not only provided the cover photograph—*Fort Peck Dam, Montana* (FIG. 29-78)—but also wrote and illustrated with 16 additional photographs the lead story on the town of New Deal, home to the workers who constructed the dam during the depths of the Depression. Fort Peck Dam was at the time the largest earth-filled dam in the world. Bourke-White photographed the still unfinished dam before the installation of the elevated highway at its summit. (The supports for that highway fortuitously conjure the image of a crenellated medieval

ALEXANDER CALDER The son and grandson of sculptors, ALEXANDER CALDER (1898–1976) initially studied mechanical engineering. Fascinated all his life by motion, he explored movement in relationship to three-dimensional form in much of his work. As a young artist in Paris in the late 1920s, Calder invented a circus full of wire-based miniature performers that mimicked the motion of their real-life counterparts. After a visit to Piet Mondrian's studio in the early 1930s, Calder set out to put the Dutch painter's brightly colored rectangular shapes (FIG. 29-61) into motion. (Marcel Duchamp, intrigued by Calder's early motorized and hand-cranked examples of moving abstract pieces, named them *mobiles.*) Calder soon used his engineering skills to fashion a series of balanced structures hanging from rods, wires, and colorful, organically shaped plates. This new kind of sculpture, which combined nonobjective organic forms and motion, succeeded in expressing the innate dynamism of the natural world.

An early Calder mobile is *Lobster Trap and Fish Tail* (FIG. **29-79**), which the artist created in 1939 under a commission from the Museum of Modern Art in New York City for the stairwell of the museum's new building on West 53rd Street (see "The Museum of Modern Art as Collector and Patron," page 945). Calder carefully planned each nonmechanized mobile so that any air current would set the parts moving to create a constantly shifting dance in space. Mondrian's work may have provided the initial inspiration for the mobiles, but their organic shapes resemble those in Joan Miró's Surrealist paintings (FIG. 29-58). Indeed, viewers can read Calder's forms as either geometric or organic. Geometrically, the lines suggest circuitry and rigging, and the shapes derive from circles and ovoid forms. Organically, the lines suggest nerve axons, and the shapes resemble cells, leaves, fins, wings, and other bioforms.

THE PATRON'S VOICE
The Museum of Modern Art as Collector and Patron

People understandably think of museums as repositories of artworks, often donated by wealthy private individuals. Indeed, the interests and tastes of donors can be the primary determinants of the character of a museum's collection. Although some world-famous museums—for example, the Metropolitan Museum of Art in New York and the Musée du Louvre in Paris—boast comprehensive art collections of all periods and places, most museums have much narrower acquisition policies. All museums, but especially the richest and largest, have the power to elevate the stature of individual artists or particular kinds of art by featuring them in exhibitions. And sometimes museums become influential patrons themselves by directly commissioning works of art.

The Museum of Modern Art (MoMA) in New York City is an excellent case study of the role of museums as art patrons. Established in 1929, MoMA owes its existence to a trio of women—Lillie P. Bliss, Mary Quinn Sullivan, and Abby Aldrich Rockefeller (see "Art 'Matronage' in the United States," page 913)—who saw the need for a museum to collect and exhibit modernist art. Within a short period of time, the institution that they founded became the most important museum of modern art in the world. Their success was extraordinary considering the skepticism and hostility greeting modernist art in the years before MoMA's inception. Indeed, few American museums then exhibited late-19th- and 20th-century art at all.

In its quest to expose the public to the energy and challenge of modernist, particularly avant-garde, art, MoMA developed ground-breaking, progressive exhibitions. Among those that the museum mounted during the early years of its existence were *Cubism and Abstract Art* and *Fantastic Art, Dada, Surrealism* (1936). Two other note-worthy shows were *American Sources of Modern Art (Aztec, Maya, Inca)* in 1933 and *African Negro Art* in 1935, both among the first exhibitions to deal with "primitive" artifacts in artistic rather than anthropological terms (see "Primitivism and Colonialism," page 891).

The organization of MoMA's administrative structure and the scope of the museum's early activities were also remarkable. The museum's first director, Alfred H. Barr Jr., insisted on establishing departments not only for painting and sculpture but also for photography, prints and drawing, architecture, and the decorative arts. He developed a library of books on modern art and a film library, both of which have become world-class collections, as well as an extensive publishing program.

It is the museum's art collection, however, that has drawn the most attention. By cultivating an influential group of benefactors, MoMA has developed an extensive and enviable collection of late-19th- and 20th-century art. The museum owns a long list of important works, such as van Gogh's *Starry Night* (FIG. 28-19), Picasso's *Les Demoiselles d'Avignon* (FIG. 29-1), and Dalí's *The Persistence of Memory* (FIG. 29-55), as well as many others illustrated in this book, including 23 in this chapter alone. MoMA has also played a role in the history of 20th-century art through its patronage of modernist artists. For example, in 1939, just a decade after the institution's founding, it commissioned Alexander Calder to produce the mobile *Lobster Trap and Fish Tail* (FIG. 29-79) for display in a prominent location in its midtown Manhattan building.

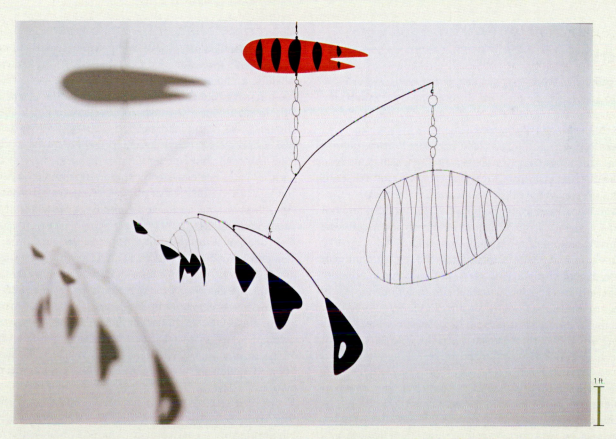

1 ft

29-79 ALEXANDER CALDER, *Lobster Trap and Fish Tail*, 1939. Painted sheet aluminum and steel wire, 8' 6" × 9' 6". Museum of Modern Art, New York.

Commissioned by the Museum of Modern Art, Calder used his thorough knowledge of engineering to create a new kind of sculpture—the mobile—that expressed nature's innate dynamism.

29-80 FRANK LLOYD WRIGHT, Kaufmann House (Fallingwater; looking northeast), Bear Run, Pennsylvania, 1936–1939.

Perched on a rocky hillside over a waterfall, Wright's Fallingwater has long, sweeping lines, unconfined by abrupt wall limits, reaching out and capturing the expansiveness of the natural environment.

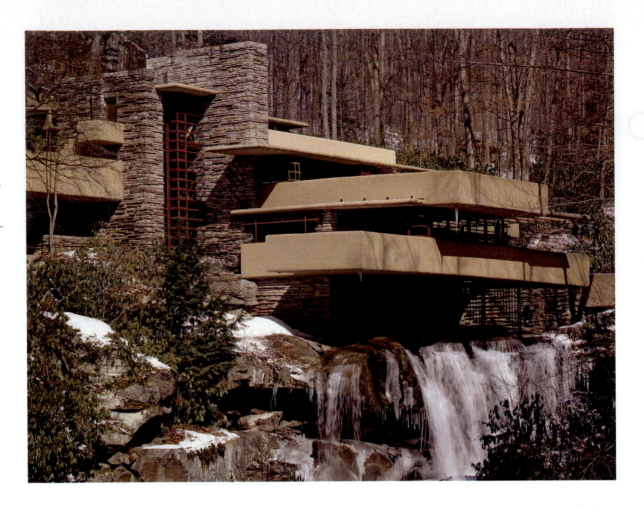

Architecture

The most influential American architect of the 1930s, as during the opening decades of the century, was the ever-inventive Frank Lloyd Wright.

FALLINGWATER Wright's universally acclaimed masterpiece of this period is the Kaufmann House (FIG. **29-80**), which he designed as a weekend retreat at Bear Run, Pennsylvania, for Pittsburgh department store magnate Edgar Kaufmann Sr. Perched on a rocky hillside over a small waterfall, the house, nicknamed Fallingwater, has become an icon of modernist architectural design. In keeping with his commitment to "organic architecture" (see page 917), Wright sought to find a way to incorporate the structure fully into its site in order to ensure a fluid, dynamic exchange between the interior of the house and the natural environment outside. Rather than build the house overlooking or next to the waterfall, Wright decided to build it over the waterfall, because he believed that the Kaufmanns would become desensitized to the waterfall's presence and power if they merely overlooked it. In Fallingwater, Wright took the blocky masses characterizing his earlier Robie House (FIGS. 29-45 and 29-46) and extended them in all four directions. To take advantage of the location, he designed a series of terraces that extend on three levels from a central core structure. The contrast in textures among concrete, painted metal, and natural stones in the house's terraces and walls enlivens its shapes, as does Wright's use of full-length strip windows to create a stunning interweaving of interior and exterior space.

The implied message of Wright's new architecture was space, not mass—a space designed to fit the patron's life and enclosed and divided as required. Wright took special pains to meet his clients' requirements, often designing all the accessories of a house (including, in at least one case, gowns for his client's wife). In the late 1930s, he acted on a cherished dream to provide good architectural design for less prosperous people by adapting the ideas of his prairie houses (see page 916) to plans for smaller, less expensive dwellings with neither attics nor basements. These residences, known as *Usonian* houses (for "United States of North America"), became templates for suburban housing developments in the post–World War II housing boom.

The publication of Wright's plans brought him a measure of fame in Europe, especially in Holland and Germany. The issuance in Berlin in 1910 of a portfolio of his work and an exhibition of his designs the following year stimulated younger architects to adopt some of his ideas about open plans that afforded clients freedom. Some 40 years before his career ended, his work was already of revolutionary significance. Mies van der Rohe wrote in 1940: "[The] dynamic impulse from [Wright's] work invigorated a whole generation. His influence was strongly felt even when it was not actually visible."[48]

Frank Lloyd Wright's influence in Europe was exceptional for any American artist before World War II. However, in the decades following that global conflict, American painters, sculptors, and architects often took the lead in establishing new styles that artists elsewhere quickly emulated. This new preeminence of the United States in the arts is the subject of Chapter 30.

MODERNISM IN EUROPE AND AMERICA, 1900 TO 1945

Europe 1900 to 1920

- In the early 1900s, avant-garde artists searched for new definitions of art in a changed world. Matisse and the Fauves used bold colors as the primary means of conveying feeling. German Expressionist paintings by Die Brücke featured clashing colors, disquieting figures, and perspective distortions.

- Pablo Picasso and Georges Braque radically challenged prevailing artistic conventions with Cubism. The Cubists dissected forms and placed them in interaction with the space around them.

- The Futurists focused on motion in time and space in their effort to create paintings and sculptures that captured the dynamic quality of modern life. The Dadaists celebrated the spontaneous and intuitive, exploring the role of chance in art and often incorporating found objects in their works.

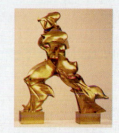

Boccioni, *Unique Forms of Continuity in Space,* 1913

United States 1900 to 1930

- The Armory Show of 1913 introduced avant-garde European art to American artists. Man Ray, for example, embraced Dada's fondness for the displacement of ordinary items, and Stuart Davis adopted the Cubist interest in fragmented form.

- The Harlem Renaissance brought African American artists to the forefront, including Aaron Douglas, whose paintings drew on Cubist principles. Charles Demuth, Georgia O'Keeffe, and the Precisionists used European modernist techniques to celebrate contemporary American subjects.

- Photography emerged as an important American art form in the work of Alfred Stieglitz and Edward Weston, who emphasized the careful arrangement of forms and patterns of light and dark.

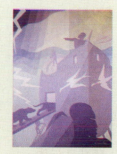

Douglas, *Noah's Ark,* ca. 1927

Europe 1920 to 1945

- World War I gave rise to the Neue Sachlichkeit movement in Germany. "New Objectivity" artists depicted the horrors of war and explored the themes of death and transfiguration.

- The Surrealists investigated ways to express in art the world of dreams and the unconscious. Natural Surrealists aimed for "concrete irrationality" in their naturalistic paintings of dreamlike scenes. Biomorphic Surrealists experimented with automatism and employed abstract imagery.

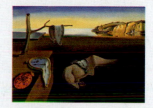

Dalí, *The Persistence of Memory,* 1931

- Many European modernists pursued utopian ideals. The Suprematists developed an abstract style to express pure feeling. The Constructivists used nonobjective forms to suggest the nature of space-time. De Stijl artists reduced their formal vocabulary to simple geometric forms in their search for "pure plastic art."

- Brancusi, Hepworth, Moore, and other sculptors increasingly turned to abstraction, often emphasizing voids as well as masses in their work.

- The Bauhaus in Germany promoted the vision of "total architecture," which called for the integration of all the arts in constructing modern living environments. Bauhaus buildings were unembellished glass and steel designs. In France, Le Corbusier used modern construction materials to build "machines for living"— houses with open plans and unadorned surfaces.

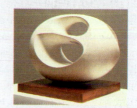

Hepworth, *Oval Sculpture (No. 2),* 1943

United States and Mexico 1930 to 1945

- Between the wars, Alexander Calder created mobiles (abstract sculptures with moving parts), but other American artists favored figural art. Lange and Shahn chronicled social injustice. Hopper explored the loneliness of life in the Depression era. Lawrence recorded the struggle of African Americans. Wood depicted life in rural Iowa.

- Mexican artists Orozco and Rivera painted epic mural cycles of the history of Mexico. Kahlo's powerful paintings explored the human psyche and were frequently autobiographical.

- The leading American architect of the first half of the 20th century was Frank Lloyd Wright, who promoted "organic architecture," in which free individuals move in a "free" space.

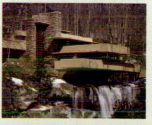

Wright, *Fallingwater,* 1936–1939

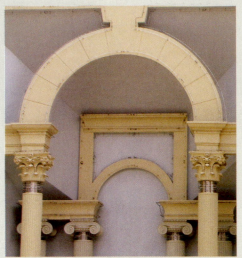

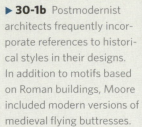

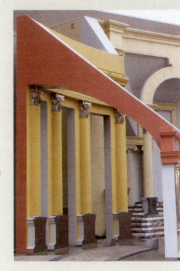

◄ **30-1a** Moore's circular postmodern Italian plaza incorporates elements drawn from classical architecture, including a portico inspired by ancient Roman fora and an exedra loosely based on a triumphal arch.

▶ **30-1b** Postmodernist architects frequently incorporate references to historical styles in their designs. In addition to motifs based on Roman buildings, Moore included modern versions of medieval flying buttresses.

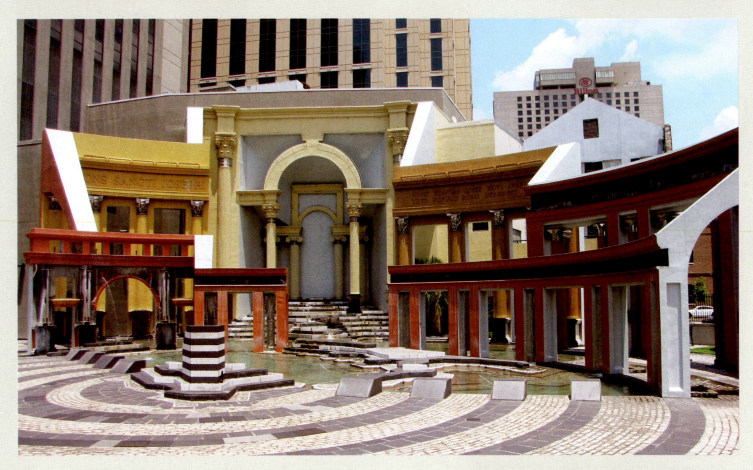

30-1 **CHARLES MOORE, Piazza d'Italia (looking northeast), New Orleans, 1976–1980.**

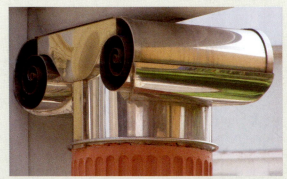

▲ **30-1c** Many of Moore's historical motifs are rendered in high-tech materials unavailable to earlier architects—for example, stainless-steel columns and capitals and neon lighting for multicolored nighttime illumination.

Modernism and Postmodernism in Europe and America, 1945 to 1980

AFTER MODERNISM: POSTMODERNIST ARCHITECTURE

One of the most significant developments in later-20th-century architecture (as well as in contemporaneous painting and sculpture) was *postmodernism*. Postmodernist architects rejected the severity and simplicity of the modernist idiom pioneered by Gropius (FIG. 29-67), Mies van der Rohe (FIG. 29-68), Le Corbusier (FIG. 29-69), and their postwar successors. Instead, they celebrated complexity and incorporated historical references in their designs, often rendered in high-tech materials unavailable to earlier architects.

An outstanding example of a postmodernist design that creates a dialogue between the past and the present is Piazza d'Italia (Plaza of Italy; FIG. **30-1**) in New Orleans by American architect CHARLES MOORE (1925–1993), dean of the Yale School of Architecture from 1965 to 1970. Designed in the late 1970s and restored after sustaining serious damage in the wake of Hurricane Katrina in 2005, Piazza d'Italia is dedicated to the city's Italian American community. Appropriately, Moore selected elements relating specifically to Italian history, all the way back to ancient Roman culture.

Piazza d'Italia is an open circular area partially formed by short segments of colonnades arranged in staggered concentric arcs, which direct the eye to the focal point of the composition—an *exedra*. This recessed area on a raised platform serves as a *rostrum* (speaker's platform) during the annual festivities of Saint Joseph's Day. Moore inlaid the piazza's pavement with a map of Italy centered on Sicily, from which the majority of the city's Italian families originated. From there, the map's Italian "boot" stretches to the steps, which correspond to the Alps, and ascends the rostrum.

The piazza's most immediate historical references are to the porticos of an ancient Roman forum (FIGS. 7-12 and 7-44) and to triumphal arches (FIGS. 7-40 and 7-44A), but the irregular placement of the concentrically arranged colonnade fragments inserts a note of instability into the design reminiscent of Mannerism (FIG. 22-56). Illusionistic devices, such as the continuation of the piazza's pavement design (apparently through a building and out into the street), are Baroque in character (FIG. 24-4). Moore incorporated all the classical orders—most with whimsical modifications, such as the stainless-steel columns and capitals, neon collars around the column necks, and neon lights framing various parts of the exedra and porticos for dramatic multicolored nighttime illumination. He even made references to medieval architecture by including modern versions of *flying buttresses,* and alternating white and gray-green stones in emulation of medieval buildings in Florence, Siena, and Orvieto (FIGS. 12-30, 12-30A, 14-13, and 14-13A). This kind of architectural eclecticism, especially rich in Piazza d'Italia, epitomizes postmodernism.

THE AFTERMATH OF WORLD WAR II

World War II, with the global devastation it unleashed on all dimensions of life—political, economic, and psychological—set the stage for the second half of the 20th century. The dropping of atomic bombs by the United States on the Japanese cities of Hiroshima and Nagasaki in 1945 signaled a turning point not only in the war itself but in the geopolitical balance and the nature of international conflict as well. For the postwar generation, nuclear attack became a very real threat. Indeed, the two nuclear superpowers, the United States and the Soviet Union, divided the world into spheres of influence, and each regularly intervened politically, economically, and militarily wherever and whenever it considered its interests to be at stake.

The cessation of global warfare did not bring global peace. On the contrary, regional conflicts erupted throughout the world during the decades after World War II. In 1947, the British left India, which precipitated a murderous Hindu-Muslim war that divided South Asia into two new hostile nations—India and Pakistan. After a bloody civil war, Communists came to power in China in 1949. North Korea invaded South Korea in 1950 and fought a grim war with the United States and its allies. The Soviets brutally suppressed uprisings in their subject nations—East Germany, Poland, Hungary, and Czechoslovakia. The United States intervened in disputes in Central and South America. Almost as soon as many of the colonial nations of Africa—Kenya, Uganda, Nigeria, Angola, Mozambique, the Sudan, Rwanda, and the Congo—won their independence, civil wars devastated them. In Indonesia, civil war left more than 100,000 dead. Algeria expelled France in 1962 after the French waged a prolonged war with Algeria's Muslim natives. After 15 years of bitter war in Southeast Asia, the United States suffered defeat in Vietnam.

The period from 1945 to 1980 also brought upheaval in the cultural sphere. In the United States, for example, the struggles for civil rights for African Americans, for free speech on university campuses, and for disengagement from the Vietnam War led to a rebellion of the young, who took to the streets in often raucous demonstrations, some with violent repercussions. The prolonged ferment produced a new system of values, a "youth culture," expressed in the radical rejection not only of national policies but often also of the society generating them. Young Americans mocked their elders' lifestyles and adopted unconventional dress, manners, habits, and morals deliberately subversive of mainstream social standards, a phenomenon that continues today in different forms—for example, "punk" fashion. The postwar youth era witnessed the sexual revolution, the widespread use and abuse of drugs, and the development of rock music, then an exclusively youthful art form. Young people "dropped out" of regulated society, embraced alternative belief systems, and rejected Western university curricula as irrelevant.

This counterculture had considerable societal impact. The civil rights movement of the 1960s and later the women's liberation movement of the 1970s reflected the spirit of rebellion, coupled with the rejection of racism and sexism. In keeping with the growing resistance to established authority, women systematically began to challenge the male-dominated culture, which they perceived as having limited their political power and economic opportunities for centuries. Feminists charged that the political, social, and economic institutions of Western society, as well as the traditional family unit headed by a patriarch, perpetuated male power and the subordination of women.

Increasingly, individuals and groups actively challenged the status quo and sought to change the balance of power. For example, by adapting strategies developed first in the civil rights movement and later in feminism, various ethnic groups and gays and lesbians mounted challenges to discriminatory policies and attitudes. These groups fought for recognition, respect, and legal protection and battled discrimination with political action, an effort that recently has begun to yield significant results—for example, in the increasing acceptance of same-sex marriage. In addition, the growing scrutiny in numerous academic fields—cultural studies, literary theory, and colonial and postcolonial studies—of the dynamics and exercise of power also contributed to the dialogue on these issues. As a result, identity (both individual and group) emerged as a potent arena for discussion and action—and as a persistent and compelling subject for artists.

PAINTING, SCULPTURE, AND PHOTOGRAPHY

The end of World War II in 1945 left devastated cities, ruptured economies, and governments in chaos throughout Europe. These factors, coupled with the massive loss of life and the indelible horrors of the bombing of Hiroshima and Nagasaki and of the Holocaust, in which six million Jews died at the hands of the Nazis, resulted in a pervasive sense of despair, disillusionment, and skepticism. Although many people (for example, the Futurists in Italy; see page 898) had tried to find redemptive value in World War I, it was nearly impossible to do the same with World War II, coming as it did so soon after the "war to end all wars." Further, the "Great War" was largely a European conflict that left roughly 10 million people dead, whereas World War II was a truly global catastrophe, claiming 35 million lives.

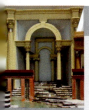

MODERNISM AND POSTMODERNISM, 1945 TO 1980

1945–1960

- European Expressionists capture in paintings and sculptures the revulsion and cynicism that emerged in the wake of World War II
- New York School painters develop Abstract Expressionism, emphasizing form and raw energy over subject matter
- Sleek, geometrically rigid modernist skyscrapers become familiar sights in cities throughout the world

1960–1970

- Post-Painterly Abstractionists reject the passion and texture of action painting and celebrate the flatness of pigment on canvas
- Op artists produce the illusion of motion and depth using only geometric forms
- Minimalists reduce sculpture to basic shapes and emphasize their works' "objecthood"
- Pop artists find inspiration in popular culture and represent commonplace commercial products
- Superrealists create paintings and sculptures characterized by scrupulous reproduction of the appearance of people and objects
- Performance artists replace traditional stationary artworks with temporal action-artworks

1970–1980

- Artists play a leading role in the feminist movement by promoting women's themes and employing materials traditionally associated with women, such as china and fabric
- Postmodern architects erect complex and eclectic buildings that often incorporate references to historical styles
- Environmental artists redefine what constitutes "art" by manipulating natural materials in monumental earthworks
- Artists increasingly embrace new media—video recorders, computers—as tools for creating artworks

Postwar Expressionism in Europe

The cynicism pervading Europe in the 1940s found a voice in *existentialism,* a philosophy asserting the absurdity of human existence and the impossibility of achieving certitude. Many who embraced existentialism also promoted atheism and questioned the possibility of situating God within a systematic philosophy. Scholars trace the roots of existentialism to the Danish theologian Søren Kierkegaard (1813–1855), but in the postwar period, the writings of French author Jean-Paul Sartre (1905–1980) most clearly captured the existentialist spirit. According to Sartre, if God does not exist, then individuals must constantly struggle in isolation with the anguish of making decisions in a world without absolutes or traditional values. This spirit of pessimism and despair emerged frequently in European art of the immediate postwar period. A brutality or roughness appropriately expressing both the artist's state of mind and the larger cultural sensibility characterized the work of many European sculptors and painters.

ALBERTO GIACOMETTI The sculptures of Swiss artist ALBERTO GIACOMETTI (1901–1966) perhaps best express the existentialist spirit. Although Giacometti never claimed that he pursued existentialist ideas in his art, his works brilliantly capture the spirit of that philosophy. Indeed, Sartre, Giacometti's friend, saw the artist's figurative sculptures as the personification of existentialist humanity—alienated, solitary, and lost in the world's immensity. Giacometti's sculptures of the 1940s, such as *Man Pointing No. 5* (FIG. 30-2), are thin, nearly featureless figures with rough, agitated surfaces. Rather than conveying the solidity and mass of conventional bronze sculpture, these thin and elongated figures seem

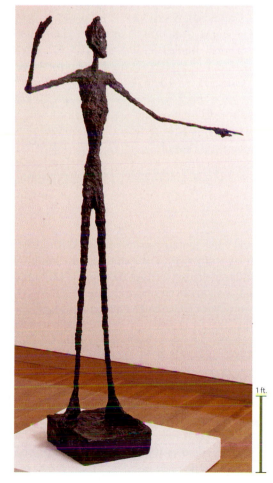

30-2 ALBERTO GIACOMETTI, *Man Pointing No. 5*, 1947. Bronze, 5' 10" high. Des Moines Art Center, Des Moines (Nathan Emory Coffin Collection).

The writer Jean-Paul Sartre saw Giacometti's thin and virtually featureless sculpted figures as the personification of existentialist humanity—alienated, solitary, and lost in the world's immensity.

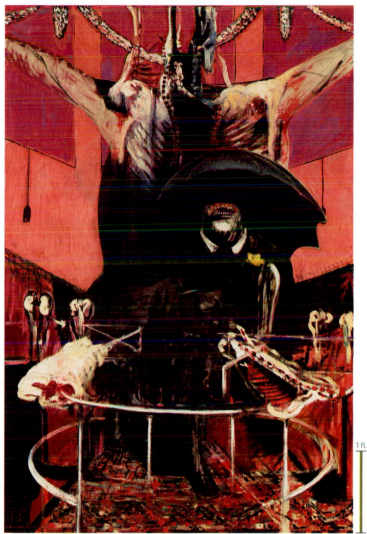

30-3 FRANCIS BACON, *Painting,* 1946. Oil and pastel on linen, 6' 5 $\frac{7}{8}$" × 4' 4". Museum of Modern Art, New York.

Painted in the aftermath of World War II, this intentionally revolting image of a powerful figure presiding over a slaughter is a reflection of war's butchery. It is Bacon's indictment of humanity.

swallowed up by the space surrounding them, imparting a sense of isolation and fragility. Giacometti's evocative sculptures spoke to the pervasive despair that emerged in the aftermath of world war.

FRANCIS BACON Although born in Dublin, Ireland, FRANCIS BACON (1910–1992) was the son of a well-to-do Englishman. He spent most of his life in London, where he experienced firsthand the destruction of lives and property that the Nazi bombing wrought on the city during World War II. *Painting* (FIG. 30-3) is characteristic of Bacon's work—a reflection of war's butchery and an indictment of humanity. The artist presented a compelling and revolting image of a powerful, stocky man with a gaping mouth and a vivid red stain on his upper lip, as if he were a carnivore devouring the raw meat sitting on the railing surrounding him (compare FIG. 30-3A). Bacon may have based his depiction of this central figure on news photos of similarly dressed European

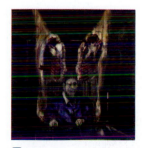

30-3A BACON, *Figure with Meat,* 1954.

Jean Dubuffet on Crude Art

In the introductory essay to the catalog of the Autumn 1949 group exhibition of the Compagnie de l'Art Brut at the Galerie René Drouin in Paris, Jean Dubuffet (FIG. 30-4) explained the rationale for Crude Art in what became the movement's manifesto:

> [T]he approved art of the museums, galleries and salons—let us call it "cultural art" . . . [is not] representative of art in general, rather merely the activity of a particular clique: a cohort of careerist intellectuals. . . . There are still people, particularly the intellectuals, who do not clearly see that the intelligent are hopeless cases, and one needs to rely on the so-called imbeciles for moments of lucidity . . . [I]n July 1945 we [the Compagnie de l'Art

Brut] undertook . . . methodical research into the relevant ways of producing that which we now call Crude Art. We understand by this works created by those untouched by artistic culture, in which copying has little part, unlike the art of intellectuals. Similarly, the artists take everything . . . from their own inner being, not from the canons of classical or fashionable art. We engage in an artistic enterprise that is completely pure, basic; totally guided in all its phases solely by the creator's own impulses.*

Not surprisingly, among the founding members of the Crude Art group was André Breton, the key intellectual champion of Dada and Surrealism (see "André Breton's First Surrealist Manifesto," page 922).

*Jean Dubuffet, *L'art brut préferé aux arts culturels* (Paris: Galerie René Drouin, 1949), n.p. Translated by Charles Harrison and Paul Wood, eds., *Art and Theory 1900–2000: An Anthology of Changing Ideas* (Malden, Mass.: Blackwell, 2002), 606–607.

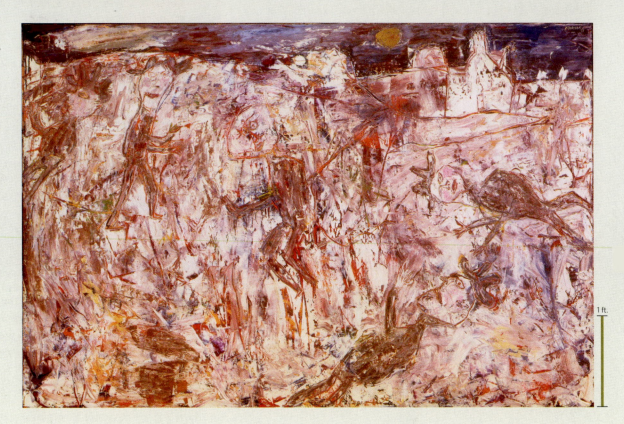

30-4 JEAN DUBUFFET, *Vie Inquiète* (*Uneasy Life*), 1953. Oil on canvas, 4' 3" × 6' 4". Tate Modern, London (gift of the artist, 1966).

Dubuffet expressed a tortured vision of the world through thickly encrusted painted surfaces and crude images of the kind that children and the insane produce. He called it Art Brut—untaught Crude Art.

1 ft.

and American officials. The umbrella in particular recalls images of Neville Chamberlain (1869–1940), the wartime British prime minister who frequently appeared in photographs with an umbrella. Bacon added to the gut-wrenching impact of the painting by depicting the flayed carcass hanging behind the central figure like a crucified human form. Although the specific sources for the imagery in *Painting* are uncertain, the work is unmistakably "an attempt to remake the violence of reality itself," as Bacon often described his art, based on what he referred to as "the brutality of fact."[1]

JEAN DUBUFFET Although less specific, the works of French artist JEAN DUBUFFET (1901–1985) also express a tortured vision of the world through manipulated materials. In works such as *Vie Inquiète* (*Uneasy Life*; FIG. 30-4), Dubuffet first built up an *impasto* (a layer of thickly applied pigment) of plaster, glue, sand, asphalt,

and other common materials, on which he painted or incised crude images of the kind that children, the insane, and scrawlers of graffiti produce. Scribblings interspersed with the images heighten the impression of smeared and gashed surfaces of crumbling walls and worn pavements marked by random individuals. Dubuffet believed that the art of children, the mentally unbalanced, prisoners, and outcasts was more direct and genuine because those who created it did so unrestrained by conventional standards of art. He promoted *Art Brut*—untaught *Crude Art* (see "Jean Dubuffet on Crude Art," above).

GERHARD RICHTER Artistic repercussions of the devastation of World War II were not confined to England and France. Powerful, frightening memories of the destruction wrought in Europe during the war lingered forever after in the minds of all who lived through it. Decades later in Germany, GERHARD RICHTER (b. 1932) would paint a series of grey "damaged landscapes"—for example, *Townscape Paris* (FIG. **30-4A**)—that conjured the aerial bombardments of the 1940s.

Abstract Expressionism

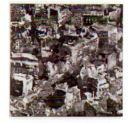
🔎 **30-4A** RICHTER, *Townscape Paris*, 1968.

The devastation that World War II had inflicted across Europe resulted in an influx of émigré artists escaping to the United States. In the 1950s, the center of the Western art world shifted from Paris to New York. It was there that the first major American avant-garde art movement—*Abstract Expressionism*—emerged. The most important forerunner of the Abstract Expressionists, however, was an Armenian immigrant who arrived in New York in 1924.

ARSHILE GORKY Born a Christian in Islamic Turkish Armenia, Vosdanik Manoog Adoian was four years old when his father escaped being drafted into the Turkish army by fleeing the country. His mother died of starvation in her 15-year-old son's arms in a refugee camp for victims of the Turkish campaign of genocide against the Christian minority. The penniless Vosdanik managed in 1920 to make his way to America, where a relative took him into his home near Boston. Four years later, then a young man, Vosdanik changed his name to ARSHILE GORKY (1904–1948)—"Bitter Achilles" in Russian—and moved to New York City, where he continued the art education that he had begun in Boston. In 1948, Gorky hanged himself after suffering a series of misfortunes: a fire destroyed much of his recent work, he discovered his wife's infidelity, and an automobile accident robbed him of the use of his right arm. The injury

might have been only temporary, but the depressed Gorky thought he would never be able to paint again. In a career lasting only two decades, the Armenian immigrant contributed significantly to the artistic revolution born in New York. His work is the bridge between the Biomorphic Surrealism of Joan Miró (FIG. 29-58) and the totally abstract canvases of Jackson Pollock (FIG. 30-6).

Garden in Sochi (FIG. **30-5**), painted in 1943, is the third in a series of canvases with identical titles named after a Black Sea resort but inspired by Gorky's childhood memories of the Garden of Wish Fulfillment in his birthplace. The women of the Armenian village of Khorkom believed that their wishes would be granted if they rubbed their bare breasts against a rock in that garden beneath a tree to which they tied torn strips of their clothing. The brightly colored and thinly outlined forms in *Garden in Sochi*, which initially appear to be purely abstract biomorphic shapes, are loose sketches representing, at the left, a bare-breasted woman, and, at the center, a tree trunk with fluttering fabric. At the bottom are two oversized shoes—the Armenian slippers that Gorky's father gave his son shortly before abandoning the family.

CLEMENT GREENBERG The few traces of representational art in Gorky's work disappeared in Abstract Expressionism. As the name suggests, the artists associated with the New York School of Abstract Expressionism produced paintings that are, for the most part, abstract but express the artist's state of mind, with the goal also of striking emotional chords in the viewer. The most important champion of this strict *formalism*—an emphasis on an artwork's visual elements rather than its subject—was the American art critic Clement Greenberg (1909–1994), who wielded considerable influence from the 1940s through the 1970s. Greenberg helped redefine the parameters of modernism by advocating the rejection of illusionism and the exploration of the properties of each artistic medium.

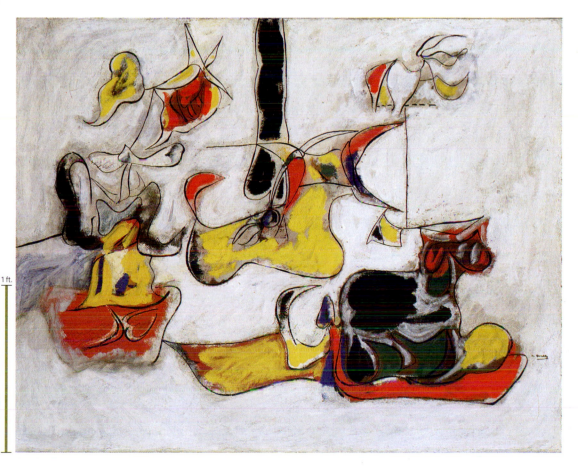

1 ft.

30-5 ARSHILE GORKY, *Garden in Sochi*, ca. 1943. Oil on canvas, 2' 7" × 3' 3". Museum of Modern Art, New York (acquired through the Lillie P. Bliss Bequest).

Gorky's paintings of the 1940s, which still incorporate recognizable forms, are the bridge between the Biomorphic Surrealist canvases of Miró and the Abstract Expressionist paintings of Pollock.

WRITTEN SOURCES
Greenbergian Formalism

Clement Greenberg, the most important critic of modern art in the postwar period, modified his complex ideas about art over the years, but consistently expounded certain basic concepts. He argued, for example, that Abstract Expressionism was no different than more traditional modes of painting in the sense that "abstract art like every other cultural phenomenon reflects the social and other circumstances of the age in which its creators live."* Greenberg championed abstract art because he believed that it represented purity in art: "Purity in art consists in the acceptance, willing acceptance, of the limitations of the medium of the specific art. . . . The purely plastic or abstract qualities of the work of art are the only ones that count."† In other words, Greenberg thought that artists should strive for a more explicit focus on the properties exclusive to each medium—for example, two-dimensionality or flatness in painting, and three-dimensionality in sculpture:

[T]he unique and proper area of competence of each art coincide[s] with all that [is] unique to the nature of its medium.‡

It follows that a modernist work of art must try, in principle, to avoid communication with any order of experience not inherent in the most literally and essentially construed nature of its medium. Among other things, this means renouncing illusion and explicit subject matter. The arts are to achieve concreteness, "purity," by

dealing solely with their respective selves—that is, by becoming "abstract" or nonfigurative.§

The Abstract Expressionists turned inward to create, and the resulting works convey a rough spontaneity and palpable energy. The New York School painters—Jackson Pollock (FIGS. 30-6 and 30-7), Mark Rothko (FIG. 30-11), and others—wanted the viewer to grasp the content of their art intuitively, in a mental state free from structured thinking. Rothko himself explained:

We assert man's absolute emotions. We don't need props or legends. We create images whose realities are self evident. Free ourselves from memory, association, nostalgia, legend, myth. Instead of making cathedrals out of Christ, man or life, we make it out of ourselves, out of our own feelings. The image we produce is understood by anyone who looks at it without nostalgic glasses of history.**

*Clement Greenberg, "Toward a Newer Laocoon," *Partisan Review* 7, no. 4 (July–August 1940): 296.

†Ibid., 305.

‡Clement Greenberg, "Sculpture in Our Time," *Arts Magazine* 32, no. 9 (June 1956): 22.

§Clement Greenberg, "Modernist Painting," *Art & Literature* 4 (Spring 1965): 195.

**Marcus Rothko and Adolph Gottlieb, quoted in Edward Alden Jewell, "The Realm of Art: A New Platform and Other Matters: 'Globalism' Pops into View," *New York Times*, June 13, 1943, 9.

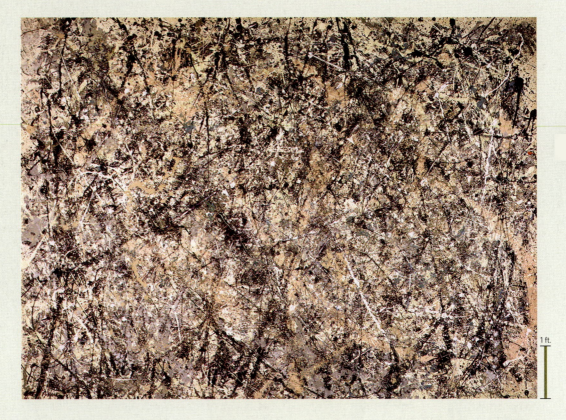

30-6 JACKSON POLLOCK, *Number 1, 1950* (*Lavender Mist*), 1950. Oil, enamel, and aluminum paint on canvas, 7' 3" × 9' 10". National Gallery of Art, Washington, D.C. (Ailsa Mellon Bruce Fund).

Pollock's paintings are pure abstractions that emphasize the creative process. His mural-size canvases consist of rhythmic drips, splatters, and dribbles of paint that draw viewers into a lacy spider web.

1 ft.

So dominant was Greenberg that scholars often refer to the general modernist tenets during this period as Greenbergian formalism (see "Greenbergian Formalism," above).

The Abstract Expressionist movement developed along two lines—*gestural abstraction* and *chromatic abstraction*. The gestural abstractionists relied on the expressiveness of energetically applied pigment. In contrast, the chromatic abstractionists focused on color's emotional resonance.

JACKSON POLLOCK The artist whose work best exemplifies gestural abstraction is JACKSON POLLOCK (1912–1956), who developed his signature style in the mid-1940s. By 1950, Pollock had refined his technique and was producing large-scale abstract paintings such as *Number 1, 1950* (*Lavender Mist*; FIG. **30-6**), which consist of rhythmic drips, splatters, and dribbles of paint. The mural-sized fields of energetic skeins of pigment envelop viewers, drawing them into a lacy spider web. Using sticks or brushes, Pollock flung, poured, and

ARTISTS ON ART

Jackson Pollock on Easel and Mural Painting

Jackson Pollock's canvases (FIG. 30-6) constitute a revolution in the art of painting, not only because of their purely abstract form but also in the artist's rejection of the centuries-old tradition of applying pigment to stretched canvases supported vertically on an easel. In two statements Pollock made in 1947, one as part of his application for a Guggenheim Fellowship and one in a published essay, the artist explained the motivations for his new kind of "action painting" and described the tools he used and the way he produced his monumental canvases (FIG. 30-7).

> I intend to paint large movable pictures which will function between the easel and mural. . . . I believe the easel picture to be a dying form, and the tendency of modern feeling is towards the wall picture or mural.*
>
> My painting does not come from the easel. I hardly ever stretch my canvas before painting. I prefer to tack the unstretched canvas to the hard wall or the floor. I need the resistance of a hard surface. On the floor I am more at ease. I feel nearer, more a part of the painting, since this way I can walk around it, work from the four sides and literally be *in* the painting. This is akin to the method of the Indian sand painters of the West [see page 1093]. I continue to get further away from the usual painter's tools such as easel, palette, brushes, etc. I prefer sticks, trowels, knives and dripping fluid paint or a heavy impasto with sand, broken glass and other foreign matter added. When I am *in* my painting, I'm not aware of what I'm doing. . . . [T]he painting has a life of its own. I try to let it come through. . . . The source of my painting is the unconscious.†

Indeed, art historians have linked Pollock's ideas about improvisation in the creative process to his interest in what psychiatrist Carl Jung called the collective unconscious. The improvisational nature of Pollock's work and his reliance on the subconscious also have parallels in the "psychic automatism" of Surrealism and the work of Vassily Kandinsky (FIG. 29-7), whom critics described as an Abstract Expressionist as early as 1919. In addition to Pollock's unique working methods and the expansive scale of his canvases, the lack of a well-defined compositional focus in his paintings significantly departed from conventional easel painting.

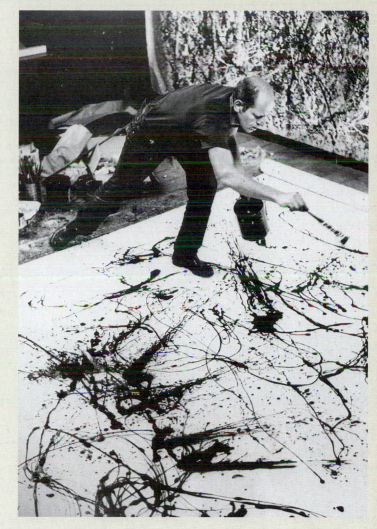

30-7 HANS NAMUTH, *Jackson Pollock painting in his studio in Springs, Long Island, New York*, 1950. Gelatin silver print, 8" × 10". Center for Creative Photography, University of Arizona, Tucson.

"Gestural abstraction" nicely describes Pollock's working technique. Using sticks or brushes, he flung, poured, and dripped paint onto a section of canvas that he simply unrolled across his studio floor.

*Quoted in Francis V. O'Connor, *Jackson Pollock* (New York: Museum of Modern Art, 1967), 39.
†Ibid., 39–40.

dripped paint (not only traditional oil paints but aluminum paints and household enamels as well) onto a section of canvas that he simply unrolled across his studio floor (see "Jackson Pollock on Easel and Mural Painting," above, and FIG. 30-7). This working method earned Pollock the derisive nickname "Jack the Dripper." Responding to the image as it developed, he created art that was spontaneous yet choreographed. Pollock's painting technique highlights the most significant aspect of gestural abstraction—its emphasis on the creative process. Indeed, Pollock literally immersed himself in the painting during its creation.

LEE KRASNER A towering figure in 20th-century art, Pollock tragically died in a car accident at age 44, cutting short the development of his innovative artistic vision. Surviving him was his wife, LEE KRASNER (1908–1984), whom art historians recognize as a major Abstract Expressionist painter (FIG. 30-7A), although overshadowed by Pollock during her lifetime.

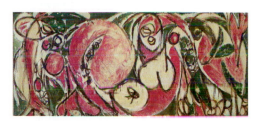

⊿**30-7A** KRASNER, *The Seasons*, 1957.

WILLEM DE KOONING Despite the public's skepticism about Pollock's art, other artists enthusiastically pursued similar avenues of expression. Dutch-born WILLEM DE KOONING (1904–1997) also developed a gestural abstractionist style. Even images such as *Woman I* (FIG. **30-8**), although rooted in figuration, display the sweeping gestural brushstrokes and energetic application of pigment typical of gestural abstraction. Out of the jumbled array of slashing lines and agitated patches of color appears a ferocious-looking woman with staring eyes and ponderous breasts. Her toothy smile, inspired by an ad for Camel cigarettes, seems to devolve into a grimace. Female models on advertising billboards partly inspired *Woman I* and de Kooning's other paintings of women. However, he did not consider the figures to be pictures of individual women but images of fertility goddesses or a satiric inversion of the traditional image of Venus, the goddess of love.

Process was important to de Kooning, as it was to Pollock. Continually working on *Woman I* for almost two years, de Kooning painted an image and then scraped it away the next day and began anew. His wife, Elaine, also an accomplished painter, estimated that he painted approximately 200 scraped-away images of women on this canvas before settling on the final one.

In addition to his *Woman* series, de Kooning created nonrepresentational works dominated by huge swaths and splashes of pigment. The images suggest rawness and intensity. His dealer, Sidney Janis (1896–1989), confirmed this impression, recalling

that de Kooning occasionally brought him paintings with ragged holes in them, the result of overly vigorous painting. Like Pollock, de Kooning was very much "in" his paintings. Vigorous physical interaction between the painter and the canvas led the critic Harold Rosenberg (1906–1978) to describe the work of the New York School as *action painting*. In his influential 1952 article, "The American Action Painters," Rosenberg described the attempts of Pollock, de Kooning, and others to get "inside the canvas," although he did not name any individual painters in his essay.

> At a certain moment the canvas began to appear to one American painter after another as an arena in which to act—rather than as a space in which to reproduce, redesign, analyze or "express" an object, actual or imagined. What was to go on the canvas was not a picture but an event. The painter no longer approached his easel with an image in his mind; he went up to it with material in his hand to do something to that other piece of material in front of him. The image would be the result of this encounter. . . . With traditional aesthetic references discarded as irrelevant, what gives the canvas its meaning is . . . the way the artist organizes his emotional and intellectual energy as if he were in a living situation. The interest lies in the kind of act taking place in the four-sided arena, a dramatic interest. Criticism must begin by recognizing in the painting the assumptions inherent in its mode of creation. Since the painter has become an actor, the spectator has to think in a vocabulary of action.[2]

JOAN MITCHELL Critics and the public at large regarded action painting as a violent, heroic, and distinctly masculine art form, but some of the most prominent Abstract Expressionists were women,

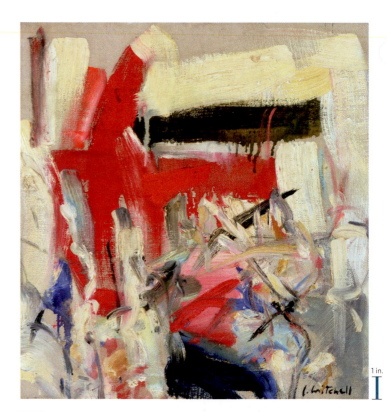

1 ft.

30-8 WILLEM DE KOONING, *Woman I*, 1950–1952. Oil on canvas, 6' 3$\frac{7}{8}$" × 4' 10". Museum of Modern Art, New York.

Although rooted in figuration, including pictures of female models on advertising billboards, de Kooning's *Woman I* displays the energetic application of pigment typical of gestural abstraction.

1 in.

30-9 JOAN MITCHELL, *Untitled*, ca. 1955. Oil on canvas, 1' 5" × 1' 4". Butler Institute of American Art, Youngstown (gift of Marilynn Meeker, 1986).

Influenced by de Kooning and Kline, Mitchell's abstract paintings of the 1950s feature asymmetrical compositions of broad intersecting bands of bright color mixed with narrower curving strokes.

notably Lee Krasner (FIG. 30-7A), Helen Frankenthaler (FIG. 30-14), and JOAN MITCHELL (1925–1992). Mitchell enjoyed a privileged childhood in a wealthy and socially prominent Chicago family. She attended Smith College and the Art Institute of Chicago before moving to New York City in 1947 and the next year to France, returning to New York in 1949, where she took up in earnest her career as a painter. She returned to France often between 1955 and 1959 and painted there exclusively from 1959 on. Gorky (FIG. 30-5) and de Kooning (FIG. 30-8) were major influences on her early work—for example, the painting illustrated here (FIG. 30-9), one of Mitchell's characteristically untitled canvases. It features the energetic application of pigment seen in the work of other gestural abstractionists, including broad intersecting bands of red, black, and white, mixed with shorter, narrower, curving brushstrokes that fill almost the entire surface of the canvas. In contrast to the central placement of the main motif in most works in the Western tradition, both figural and abstract, this composition's focus of attention is off-center at the upper left.

Once, when asked to define her style and technique, Mitchell responded:

> Abstract is not a style. I simply want to make a surface work. This is just a use of space and form: it's an ambivalence of forms and space. Style in painting has to do with labels. Lots of painters are obsessed with inventing something. When I was young, it never occurred to me to invent. All I wanted to do was paint.[3]

Among the other prominent New York School Abstract Expressionists were Pennsylvania-born FRANZ KLINE (1910–1962), whose predominantly black-and-white paintings (FIG. 30-9A) resemble Chinese and Japanese calligraphy, and ROBERT MOTHERWELL

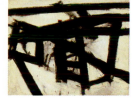

📐 **30-9A** KLINE, *Mahoning,* 1956.

(1915–1991), best known for his series of paintings inspired by the Spanish civil war (FIG. 30-9B). In the 1970s and later, a new generation of artists, including SUSAN ROTHENBERG (b. 1945; FIG. 30-9C), reinvigorated Abstract Expressionism in a movement that art historians have dubbed *Neo-Expressionism* (see page 1012).

BARNETT NEWMAN In contrast to the aggressively energetic images of the gestural abstractionists, the paintings produced by the chromatic abstractionists exude a quieter aesthetic, exemplified by the work of Barnett Newman and Mark Rothko. The emotional resonance of their canvases derives from their eloquent use of color. In his early paintings, New York native BARNETT NEWMAN (1905–1970) presented organic abstractions inspired by his study of biology and his fascination with Native American art. He soon simplified his compositions so that each canvas—for example, the enormous Latin-titled *Vir Heroicus Sublimis* (*Sublime Heroic Man*; FIG. 30-10)—consists of a single slightly modulated color field split by narrow bands that the artist called "zips," which run from one edge of the painting to the other. As Newman explained it, "The streak was always going through an atmosphere; I kept trying to create a world around it."[4] He did not intend the viewer to perceive the zips as specific entities, separate from the ground, but as accents or interruptions energizing the large color fields and giving them scale. By simplifying his compositions, Newman increased color's capacity to communicate and to express his feelings about the tragic condition of modern life and the human struggle to survive. He claimed that "the artist's problem . . . [is] the

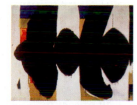

📐 **30-9B** MOTHERWELL, *Elegy to Spanish Republic,* 1953-1954.

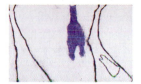

📐 **30-9C** ROTHENBERG, *Tattoo,* 1979.

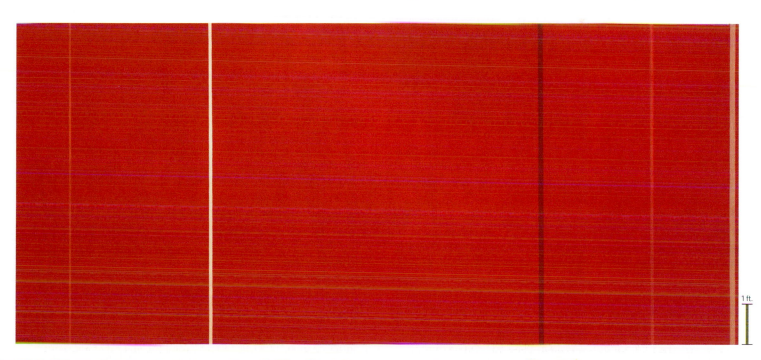

1 ft.

30-10 BARNETT NEWMAN, *Vir Heroicus Sublimis* (*Sublime Heroic Man*), 1950–1951. Oil on canvas, 7' 11$\frac{3}{8}$" × 17' 9$\frac{1}{4}$". Museum of Modern Art, New York (gift of Mr. and Mrs. Ben Heller).

Newman's canvases consist of a single slightly modulated color field split by "zips" (narrow bands) running from one edge of the painting to the other, energizing the color field and giving it scale.

Painting, Sculpture, and Photography **957**

idea-complex that makes contact with mystery—of life, of men, of nature, of the hard black chaos that is death, or the grayer, softer chaos that is tragedy."[5] Confronted by one of Newman's grandiose colored canvases, viewers truly feel as if they are in the presence of the epic.

MARK ROTHKO The work of MARK ROTHKO (1903–1970) also deals with universal themes. Born in Russia, Rothko moved with his family to the United States when he was 10. His early paintings were figural, but he soon came to believe that references to anything specific in the physical world conflicted with the sublime idea of the universal, supernatural "spirit of myth," which he saw as the core of meaning in art. In a statement cowritten with Newman and artist Adolph Gottlieb (1903–1974), Rothko expressed his beliefs about art:

> We favor the simple expression of the complex thought. We are for the large shape because it has the impact of the unequivocal. . . . We assert that . . . only that subject matter is valid which is tragic and timeless. That is why we profess spiritual kinship with primitive and archaic art.[6]

Rothko's paintings became compositionally simple, and he increasingly focused on color as the primary conveyor of meaning. In works such as *No. 14* (FIG. 30-11), Rothko created compelling visual experiences by confining his compositions to two or three large rectangles of pure color with hazy edges. The forms seem to float on the canvas surface, hovering in front of a colored background. Rothko often displayed his paintings in rows so that the several canvases together presented shimmering veils of intensely luminous colors. Although the color juxtapositions are visually captivating, Rothko intended them as more than decorative. He saw color as a doorway to another reality, and insisted that color could express "basic human emotions—tragedy, ecstasy, doom. . . . The people who weep before my pictures are having the same religious experience I had when I painted them. And if you, as you say, are moved only by their color relationships, then you miss the point."[7] Like the other Abstract Expressionists, Rothko produced highly evocative paintings reliant on formal elements rather than on specific representational content to elicit emotional responses in the viewer.

Post-Painterly Abstraction

Post-Painterly Abstraction, another postwar American art movement, developed out of Abstract Expressionism. Indeed, many of the artists associated with Post-Painterly Abstraction produced Abstract Expressionist work early in their careers. Yet Post-Painterly Abstraction, a term coined by Clement Greenberg, manifests a sensibility radically different from Abstract Expressionism. Whereas Abstract Expressionism conveys a feeling of intense passion, Post-Painterly Abstraction is characterized by a cool, detached rationality emphasizing tighter pictorial control. Greenberg saw this art as contrasting with "painterly" art, characterized by loose, visible pigment application. Evidence of the artist's hand, so prominent in gestural abstraction, is conspicuously absent in Post-Painterly Abstraction. Greenberg championed this art form because it embodied his idea of purity in art.

ELLSWORTH KELLY Attempting to arrive at pure painting, the Post-Painterly Abstractionists distilled painting down to its essential elements, producing spare, elemental images. A key figure in the Post-Painterly Abstraction movement is ELLSWORTH KELLY (b.

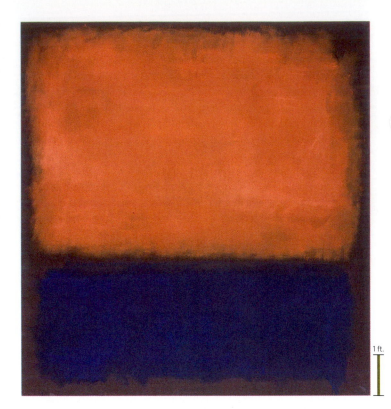

1 ft.

30-11 MARK ROTHKO, *No. 14,* 1960. Oil on canvas, 9' 6" × 8' 9". San Francisco Museum of Modern Art, San Francisco (Helen Crocker Russell Fund Purchase).

Rothko's chromatic abstractionist paintings—consisting of hazy rectangles of pure color hovering in front of a colored background—are compositionally simple but compelling visual experiences.

1923). Born in Newburgh on the Hudson River north of New York City, Kelly studied at the Pratt Institute in Brooklyn, at the School of the Museum of Fine Arts in Boston, and at the École des Beaux-Arts in Paris. Kelly's independence from any formal school was influenced by his experiences in France between 1948 and 1954. With its razor-sharp edges and clearly delineated simple abstract shapes, *Red Blue Green* (FIG. 30-12) is a characteristic example of his work from the 1960s. Since the beginning of his career, Kelly's emphasis on pure form and color and his impulse to suppress gesture in favor of creating spatial unity have played a pivotal role in the development of abstract art in America.

FRANK STELLA Another artist associated with the movement of the 1960s is Massachusetts-born FRANK STELLA (b. 1936), the leading Post-Painterly Abstraction exponent of hard-edge painting. Stella studied history at Princeton University and moved to New York City in 1958, but did not favor the rough, expressive brushwork of the Abstract Expressionists. In works such as *Mas o Menos* (*More or Less*; FIG. 30-13), Stella eliminated many of the variables associated with painting. His simplified images of thin, evenly spaced pinstripes on colored grounds have no central focus, no painterly or expressive elements, only limited surface modulation, and no tactile quality. His systematic painting illustrates Greenberg's insistence on purity in art. The artist's own famous comment on his work, "What you see is what you see," reinforces the notions that painters interested in producing advanced art must reduce their work to its essential elements and that the viewer must acknowledge that a painting is simply pigment on a flat surface.

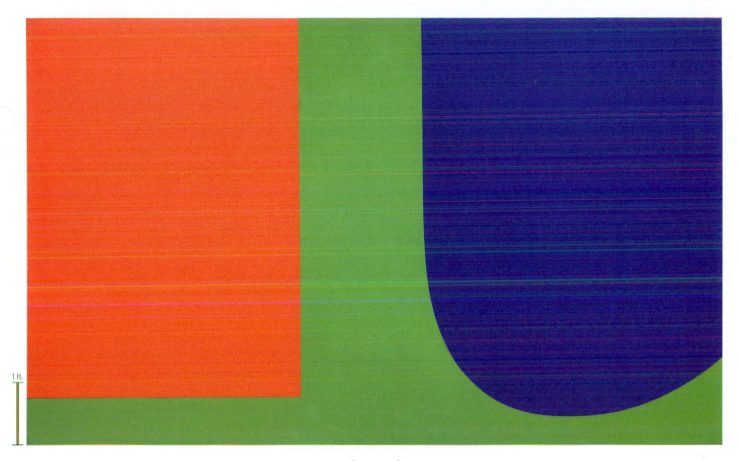

30-12 ELLSWORTH KELLY, *Red Blue Green*, 1963. Oil on canvas, 6' 11⅝" × 11' 3⅞". Museum of Contemporary Art, San Diego (gift of Dr. and Mrs. Jack M. Farris).

Suppressing gesture in favor of spatial unity, Kelly distills painting to its essential elements emphasizing pure line, form, and color.

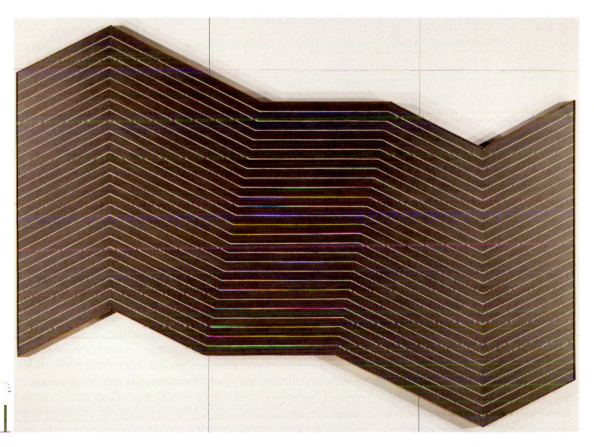

30-13 FRANK STELLA, *Mas o Menos* (*More or Less*), 1964. Metallic powder in acrylic emulsion on canvas, 9' 10" × 13' 8½". Musée National d'Art Moderne, Centre Georges Pompidou, Paris (purchase 1983 with participation of Scaler Foundation).

In his hard-edge paintings, Stella tried to achieve purity in painting using evenly spaced pinstripes on colored grounds. His canvases have no central focus, no painterly or expressive elements, and no tactile quality.

ARTISTS ON ART

Helen Frankenthaler on Color-Field Painting

Helen Frankenthaler, the daughter of a New York State Supreme Court justice, began her study of art at the Dalton School in New York City under Rufino Tamayo (FIG. 29-75A). She painted in New York for virtually her entire career, and in 1958 married fellow abstract painter Robert Motherwell (FIG. 30-9B). In 1965, the art critic Henry Geldzahler (1935–1994) interviewed Frankenthaler about her work as a color-field painter. In the following excerpt, Frankenthaler described the approach that she took to placing color on canvas in *The Bay* (FIG. 30-14) and similar abstract paintings she produced in the early 1960s, and compared her method with the way earlier modernist artists used color in their paintings.

I will sometimes start a picture feeling "What will happen if I work with three blues and another color, and maybe more or less of the other color than the combined blues?" And very often midway through the picture I have to change the basis of the experience. Or I add and add to the canvas. And if it's over-worked and beyond help I throw it away. I used to try to work from a given, made shape. But I'm less involved now with the shape as such. . . . When you first saw a Cubist or Impressionist picture there was a whole way of instructing the eye or the subconscious. Dabs of color had to stand for real things; it was an abstraction of a guitar or a hillside. The opposite is going on now. If you have bands of blue, green, and pink, the mind doesn't think sky, grass, and flesh. These are colors and the question is what are they doing with themselves and with each other. Sentiment and nuance are being squeezed out so that if something is not altogether flatly painted then there might be a hint of edge, chiaroscuro, shadow and if one wants just that pure thing these associations get in the way.*

Frankenthaler's "unsentimental" abstract canvases are very different from Matisse's emotive Fauve representations of recognizable

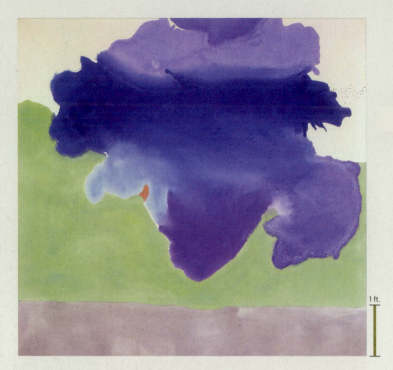

30-14 HELEN FRANKENTHALER, *The Bay*, 1963. Acrylic on canvas, 6' 8⅞" × 6' 9⅞". Detroit Institute of Arts, Detroit.

Frankenthaler and other color-field painters poured paint onto plain canvas, allowing the pigments to soak into the fabric. Their works underscore that a painting is simply pigment on a flat surface.

figures, objects, and places, but her comments on a painter's struggle to find the right combination of colors without regard to colors in nature echo those of Matisse almost 60 years before (see "Henri Matisse on Color," page 884).

*Henry Geldzahler, "Interview with Helen Frankenthaler," *Artforum* 4, no. 2 (October 1965): 36–38.

HELEN FRANKENTHALER *Color-field painting*, another variant of Post-Painterly Abstraction, also emphasized painting's basic properties. However, rather than produce sharp, unmodulated shapes as the hard-edge artists had done, the color-field painters poured diluted paint onto plain canvas and allowed the pigments to soak in. It is hard to conceive of another painting method resulting in such literal flatness. The images created, such as *The Bay* (FIG. 30-14) by HELEN FRANKENTHALER (1928–2011), appear spontaneous and almost accidental (see "Helen Frankenthaler on Color-Field Painting," above). These works differ from those by Rothko and Newman in that Frankenthaler subordinated the emotional component, so integral to Abstract Expressionism, in favor of resolving formal problems.

MORRIS LOUIS Baltimore native MORRIS LOUIS (1912–1962), who spent most of his career in Washington, D.C., also became a champion of color-field painting. Clement Greenberg, an admirer of Frankenthaler's paintings, took Louis to her studio, where she introduced him to the possibilities presented by the staining technique.

Louis used this method of pouring diluted paint onto the surface of unprimed canvas in several series of paintings. *Saraband* (FIG. 30-15) is one of the works in Louis's *Veils* series. By holding up the canvas edges and pouring diluted acrylic resin, Louis created billowy, fluid, transparent shapes running down the length of the canvas. Like Frankenthaler, Louis reduced painting to the concrete fact of the paint-impregnated material.

CLYFFORD STILL Although not a member of the New York School, another American painter whose work art historians usually classify as Post-Painterly Abstraction was CLYFFORD STILL (1904–1980), whom Clement Greenberg held in very high esteem. Born in North Dakota, Still spent most of his career on the West Coast or in Maryland. He is best known for the large series of canvases that he titled simply with their dates, underscoring his rejection of the very notion that the purpose of art is to represent places, people, or objects. Nonetheless, Still's paintings remind many viewers of vast landscapes seen from the air, even though the artist's canvases make no reference to any forms in nature. His paintings, for example,

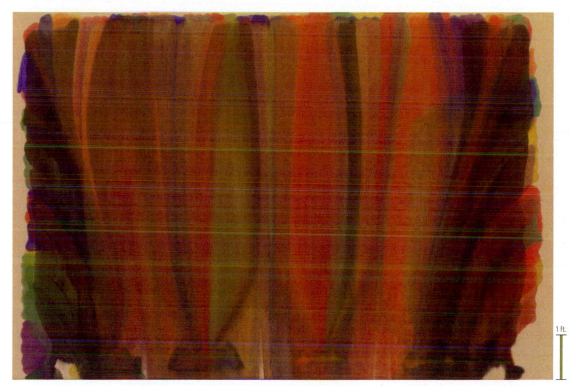

30-15 Morris Louis, *Saraband,* 1959. Acrylic resin on canvas, 8' 5$\frac{1}{8}$" × 12' 5". Solomon R. Guggenheim Foundation, New York.

Louis created his color-field paintings by holding up the canvas edges and pouring diluted acrylic resin to produce billowy, fluid, transparent shapes running down the length of the fabric.

1 ft.

1948-C (FIG. I-2), are pure exercises in the expressive use of color, shape, and texture. Said Greenberg of Still's work: "Clifford Still . . . is one of the great innovators of modernist art . . . The picture no longer divided itself into shapes or even patches, but into zones and areas and fields of color."[8]

Op Art

A major artistic movement of the 1960s was *Op Art* (short for Optical Art), in which painters sought to produce optical illusions of motion and depth using only geometric forms on two-dimensional surfaces. Among the primary sources of the movement was the work of Josef Albers, whose series of paintings called *Homage to the Square* (FIG. I-11) explored the optical effects of placing different colors next to each other. Ultimately, Op Art can be traced to 19th-century theories of color perception and the pointillism of Georges Seurat (see "Pointillism and 19th-Century Color Theory," page 855, and FIGS. 28-16 and 28-17).

BRIDGET RILEY The artist whose name is synonymous with Op Art is the British artist BRIDGET RILEY (b. 1931), who painted in a neo-pointillist manner in the 1950s before developing her signature black-and-white Op Art style. Her paintings—for example, *Fission* (FIG. **30-16**) of 1963—came to the public's attention after being featured in the December 1964 issue of *Life* magazine. The publicity unleashed a craze for Op Art designs in clothing. In 1965, the exhibition *The Responsive Eye* at the Museum of Modern Art, which also featured paintings by Ellsworth Kelly and Morris Louis, among others, bestowed an official stamp of approval on the movement.

In *Fission*, Riley filled the canvas with black dots of varied sizes and shapes, creating the illusion of a pulsating surface that caves in at the center (hence the painting's title). The effect on the viewer of Op Art paintings such as *Fission* is disorienting and sometimes disturbing, and some works can even induce motion sickness. Thoroughly modernist is the Op artist's insistence that a painting

is a two-dimensional surface covered with pigment and not a representation of any person, object, or place. Nonetheless, the Op Art movement embraced the Renaissance notion that the painter can create the illusion of depth through perspective.

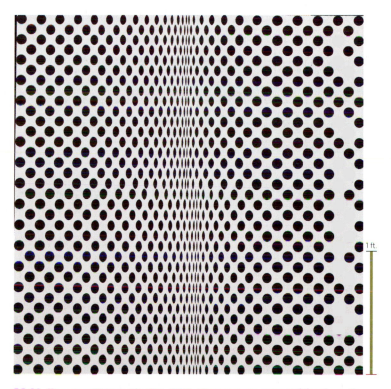

1 ft.

30-16 BRIDGET RILEY, *Fission,* 1963. Tempera on composition board, 2' 11" × 2' 10". Museum of Modern Art, New York (gift of Philip Johnson).

Op Art paintings create the illusion of motion and depth using only geometric forms. The effect can be disorienting. The pattern of black dots in Riley's *Fission* appears to cave in at the center.

ARTISTS ON ART
David Smith on Outdoor Sculpture

From ancient times, sculptors have frequently created statues for display in the open air, whether a portrait of a Roman emperor in a forum or Michelangelo's *David* (FIG. 22-13) in Florence's Piazza della Signoria. But rarely have sculptors taken into consideration the effects of sunlight in the conception of their works. American sculptor David Smith was an exception.

Smith learned to weld in an automobile plant in 1925 and later applied to his art the technical expertise in handling metals that he gained there. In addition, working on industrial-scale projects helped him visualize the possibilities for large-scale metal sculpture. Nonetheless, his works—for example, *Cubi XII* (FIG. 30-17)—differ from machine-made parts in important ways. Smith usually added gestural elements reminiscent of Abstract Expressionism by burnishing the metal with steel wool, producing swirling, random-looking patterns that draw attention to the two-dimensionality of the sculptural surface. This treatment, which captures the light hitting the artwork, activates the surface and imparts a texture to his pieces, a key element of all of his sculptures, which he designed for display outdoors. Indeed, the *Cubi* lose much of their character in the sterile lighting of a museum.

> I like outdoor sculpture and the most practical thing for outdoor sculpture is stainless steel, and I make them and I polish them in such a way that on a dull day, they take on the dull blue, or the color of the sky in the late afternoon sun, the glow, golden like the rays, the colors of nature. And in a particular sense, I have used atmosphere in a reflective way on the surfaces. They are colored by the sky and the surroundings, the green or blue of water. Some are down by the water and some are by the mountains. They reflect the colors. They are designed for the outdoors.*

*Quoted in Cleve Gray, ed., *David Smith by David Smith* (New York: Holt, Rinehart, and Winston, 1968), 133.

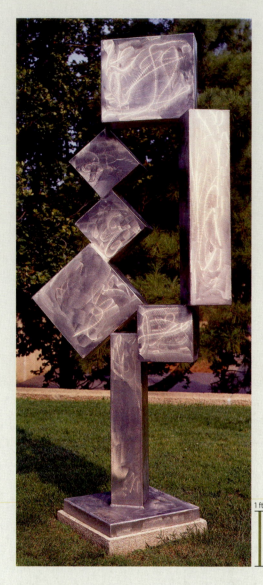

30-17 DAVID SMITH, *Cubi XII*, 1963. Stainless steel, 9' 1⅝" high. Hirshhorn Museum and Sculpture Garden, Smithsonian Institution, Washington, D.C. (gift of the Joseph H. Hirshhorn Foundation, 1972). Art © Estate of David Smith/Licensed by VAGA, New York, NY.

David Smith designed his abstract metal sculptures of simple geometric forms to reflect the natural light and color of their outdoor settings, not the sterile illumination of a museum gallery.

1 ft.

Abstraction in Sculpture

Painters were not the only artists interested in Clement Greenberg's formalist ideas (see "Greenbergian Formalism," page 954). American sculptors also strove to arrive at purity in their medium. While painters worked to emphasize flatness, sculptors, understandably, chose to focus on three-dimensionality as the essential characteristic and inherent limitation of the sculptural medium.

DAVID SMITH After experimenting with a variety of sculptural styles and materials, Indiana-born and Ohio-raised DAVID SMITH (1906–1965) produced metal sculptures that have affinities with the Abstract Expressionist movement in painting. In the 1960s, he produced a series of large-scale works called *Cubi* that he created to be seen in the open air (see "David Smith on Outdoor Sculpture," above). *Cubi XII* (FIG. 30-17), a characteristic example, consists of simple geometric forms—cubes and rectangular bars. Made of stainless-steel sections piled on top of one another, often at unstable angles, and then welded together, the *Cubi* sculptures make a striking visual statement.

TONY SMITH A predominantly sculptural movement that emerged in the 1960s among artists seeking Greenbergian purity of form was *Minimalism*. One of the leading Minimalist sculptors was New Jersey native TONY SMITH (1912–1980), who created simple volumetric sculptures such as *Die* (FIG. 30-18). Minimalist artworks generally lack identifiable subjects, colors, surface textures, and narrative elements, and are perhaps best described simply as three-dimensional objects. By rejecting illusionism and reducing sculpture to basic geometric forms, Smith and other Minimalists emphatically emphasized their art's "objecthood" and concrete tangibility. In so doing, they reduced experience to its most fundamental level, preventing viewers from drawing on assumptions or preconceptions when dealing with the art before them.

DONALD JUDD Another important Minimalist sculptor was DONALD JUDD (1928–1994), who embraced a spare, universal aesthetic corresponding to the core tenets of the movement. Born in Missouri, Judd studied philosophy and art history at Columbia University in New York City, where he produced most of his major works. Judd's determination to arrive at a visual vocabulary devoid of deception or ambiguity propelled him away from representation and toward precise and simple sculpture. For Judd, a work's power derived from its character as a whole and from the specificity of its materials (see "Donald Judd on Sculpture and Industrial Materials," page 963). *Untitled* (FIG. 30-19) presents basic geometric boxes constructed of brass and red Plexiglas, undisguised by paint or

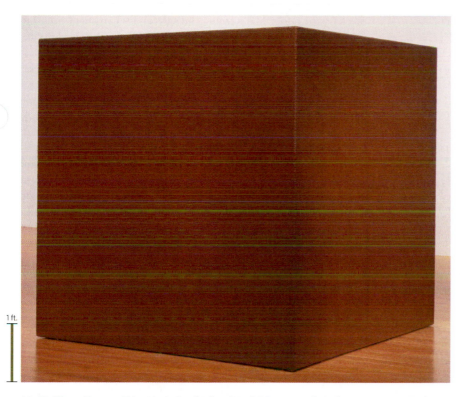

30-18 TONY SMITH, *Die*, 1962. Steel, 6' × 6' × 6'. Museum of Modern Art, New York (gift of Jane Smith in honor of Agnes Gund).

By rejecting illusionism and symbolism and reducing sculpture to basic geometric forms, Minimalist Tony Smith emphasized the "objecthood" and concrete tangibility of his sculptures.

other materials. The artist did not intend the work to be metaphorical or symbolic. It is a straightforward declaration of sculpture's objecthood. Judd used Plexiglas because its translucency enables the viewer access to the interior, thereby rendering the sculpture both open and enclosed. This aspect of the design reflects Judd's desire to banish ambiguity or falseness from his works.

Perhaps surprisingly, despite the ostensible connections between Minimalism and Greenbergian formalism, the critic did not embrace this direction in art:

> Minimal Art remains too much a feat of ideation [the mental formation of ideas], and not enough anything else. Its idea remains an idea, something deduced instead of felt and discovered. The geometrical and modular simplicity may announce and signify the artistically furthest-out, but the fact that the signals are understood for what they want to mean betrays them artistically. There is hardly any aesthetic surprise in Minimal Art. . . . Aesthetic surprise hangs on forever—it is there in Raphael as it is in Pollock—and ideas alone cannot achieve it.[9]

LOUISE NEVELSON Although Minimalism was a dominant sculptural trend in the 1960s, many sculptors, including the German artist EVA HESSE

ARTISTS ON ART
Donald Judd on Sculpture and Industrial Materials

In a 1965 essay titled "Specific Objects," the Minimalist sculptor Donald Judd described the advantages of sculpture over painting and the attractions of using industrial materials for his works, such as his 1969 Plexiglas sculpture characteristically called *Untitled* (FIG. 30-19).

> Three dimensions are real space. That gets rid of the problem of illusionism . . . one of the salient and most objectionable relics of European art. The several limits of painting are no longer present. A work can be as powerful as it can be thought to be. Actual space is intrinsically more powerful and specific than paint on a flat surface. . . . The use of three dimensions makes it possible to see all sorts of materials and colors. Most of [my] work involves new materials, either recent inventions or things not used before in art. Little was done until lately with the wide range of industrial products. . . . Materials vary greatly and are simply materials—formica, aluminum, cold-rolled steel, plexiglas, red and common brass, and so forth. They are specific. If they are used directly, they are more specific. Also, they are usually aggressive. There is an objectivity to the obdurate identity of a material. . . . The form of a work of art and its materials are closely related. In earlier work the structure and the imagery were executed in some neutral and homogeneous material.*

*Donald Judd, *Complete Writings 1959–1975* (New York: New York University Press, 1975), 181–189.

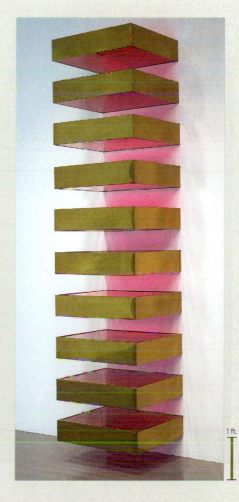

30-19 DONALD JUDD, *Untitled*, 1969. Brass and colored fluorescent Plexiglas on steel brackets, 10 units, $6\frac{1}{8}$" × 2' × 2' 3" each, with 6" intervals. Hirshhorn Museum and Sculpture Garden, Smithsonian Institution, Washington, D.C. (gift of Joseph H. Hirshhorn, 1972). © Donald Judd Estate/Licensed by VAGA, New York, NY.

Judd's Minimalist sculpture incorporates boxes fashioned from undisguised industrial materials. The artist used Plexiglas because its translucency gives the viewer access to the work's interior.

(1936–1970; FIG. **30-19A**) and Russian-born LOUISE NEVELSON (1899–1988), pursued other styles. Nevelson created sculptures combining a sense of the architectural fragment with the power of Dada and Surrealist found objects to express her personal sense of life's underlying significance. Multiplicity of meaning was important to Nevelson. She sought "the in-between place. . . . The dawns and the dusks"[10]—the transitional realm between one state of being and another.

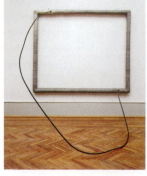

30-19A HESSE, *Hang-Up*, 1965.

Beginning in the late 1950s, Nevelson assembled sculptures of found wood objects and forms. She enclosed small sculptural compositions in boxes of varied sizes, and joined the boxes to one another to form "walls." She then painted the forms in a single hue—usually black, white, or gold. This monochromatic color scheme unifies the diverse parts of pieces such as *Tropical Garden II* (FIG. **30-20**) and creates a mysterious field of shapes and shadows. The structures suggest magical environments resembling the treasured secret hideaways dimly remembered from childhood. Yet the boxy frames and the precision of the manufactured found objects create a rough geometric structure that the eye roams over freely, lingering on some details, including occasional pieces of unmodified driftwood. The parts of a Nevelson sculpture and their interrelation recall the *Merz* constructions of Kurt Schwitters (FIG. 29-29). The effect is also rather like viewing the side of an apartment building from a moving elevated train or looking down on a city from the air.

LOUISE BOURGEOIS In contrast to the architectural nature of Nevelson's work, a sensuous organic quality recalling the evocative Biomorphic Surrealist forms of Joan Miró (FIG. 29-58) pervades the work of French-American artist LOUISE BOURGEOIS (1911–2010). *Cumul I* (FIG. **30-21**) is a collection of round-headed units huddled, with their heads protruding, within a collective cloak dotted with holes. The units differ in size, and their position within the group lends a distinctive personality to each. Although the shapes remain abstract, they refer strongly to human figures. Bourgeois used a wide variety of materials in her works, including wood, plaster, latex, and plastics, in addition to alabaster, marble, and bronze. She exploited each material's qualities to suit the expressiveness of the piece.

In *Cumul I,* the alternating high gloss and matte finish of the marble increases the sensuous distinction between the group of swelling forms and the soft folds swaddling them. Like Barbara Hepworth (FIG. 29-63), Bourgeois connected her sculpture with the body's multiple relationships to landscape: "[My pieces] are anthropomorphic and they are landscape also, since our body could be considered from a topographical point of view, as a land with mounds and valleys and caves and holes."[11] However, Bourgeois's sculptures are more personal and more openly sexual than Hepworth's. *Cumul I* perfectly represents the allusions Bourgeois sought: "There has always been sexual suggestiveness in my work. Sometimes I am totally concerned with female shapes—characters of breasts like clouds—but often I merge the activity—phallic breasts, male and female, active and passive."[12]

30-20 LOUISE NEVELSON, *Tropical Garden II*, 1957–1959. Wood painted black, 5' 11½" × 10' 11¾" × 1'. Musée National d'Art Moderne, Centre Georges Pompidou, Paris.

The monochromatic color scheme unifies the diverse sculpted forms and found objects in Nevelson's "walls" and creates a mysterious field of shapes and shadows suggesting magical environments.

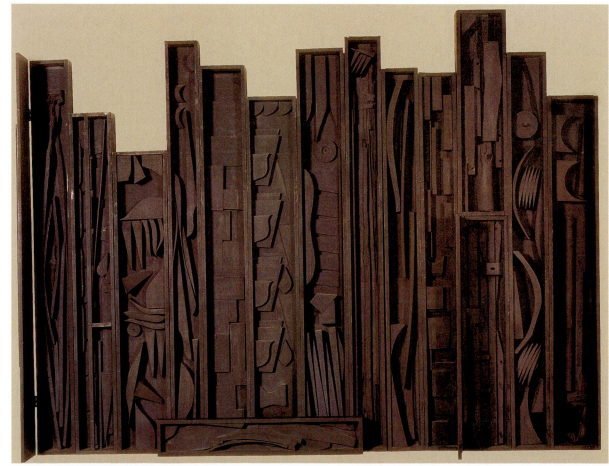

1 ft.

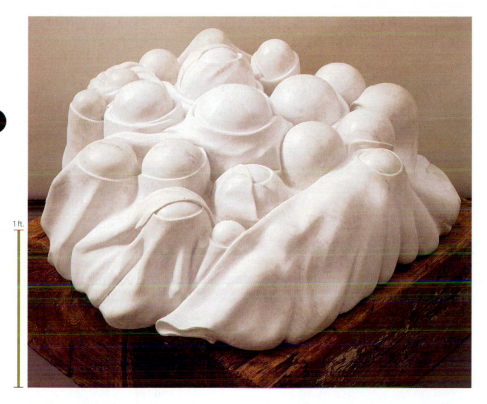

30-21 LOUISE BOURGEOIS, *Cumul I*, 1969. Marble, 1' 10 3/8" × 4' 2" × 4'. Musée National d'Art Moderne, Centre Georges Pompidou, Paris. © Louise Bourgeois/Licensed by VAGA, New York, NY.

Bourgeois's sculptures are made up of sensuous organic forms that recall the Biomorphic Surrealist forms of Miró (FIG. 29-58). Although the shapes remain abstract, they refer strongly to human figures.

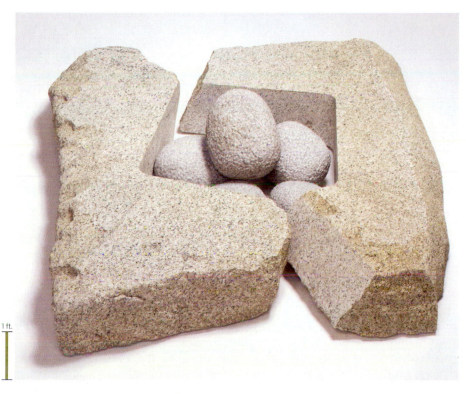

30-22 ISAMU NOGUCHI, *Shodo Shima Stone Study*, 1978. Granite, 5' 6" × 5' 9". Walker Art Center, Minneapolis (gift of the artist, 1978).

Japanese American sculptor Noguchi here created a miniature Japanese rock garden. Two irregularly shaped pieces of granite frame a trio of egglike stones suggesting birth from a primordial nest.

ISAMU NOGUCHI Another sculptor often considered a Minimalist because of pure geometric works such as *Red Cube*, which he created for the sidewalk in front of a New York City skyscraper, is ISAMU NOGUCHI (1904–1988). His work defies easy classification, however. Although born in Los Angeles, Noguchi, the son of a Japanese poet and an American writer, spent most of his childhood in Japan. In 1926 he won a Guggenheim Fellowship to study sculpture in Paris, where he worked as an apprentice to Constantin Brancusi (FIGS. 29-61A and 29-62). During his long career, Noguchi completed a wide range of commissions in the United States, Europe, and Asia in a variety of styles ranging from the abstract *Kouros* of 1944, strongly influenced by Miró's Biomorphic Surrealism (FIG. 29-58), to the Minimalist *Red Cube* of 1968. Some of his most interesting works, however, wed the traditions of the West with those of the East, especially his designs for gardens and garden sculptures, which reflect his Japanese heritage.

A little-known work of great beauty in the last category is *Shodo Shima Stone Study* (FIG. 30-22), a miniature version of a Japanese garden in which two roughly shaped pieces of granite form a rectangular frame for a trio of egglike granite stones. Shodo Shima (Magical Island) is an island off the coast of Japan and the source of the stone that Noguchi used for this work. In form it recalls the design of Zen Buddhist gardens (FIG. 34-2) and a bird's nest. Noguchi observed: "In Japan the rocks in a garden are so planted as to suggest a protuberance from the primordial mass below. Every rock gains enormous weight, and that is why the whole garden may be said to be a sculpture, whose roots are joined way below."[13] The "eggs" in Noguchi's miniature rock garden in the Walker Art Center suggest a birth out of a primordial nest.

Pop Art

Despite their differences, the Abstract Expressionists, Post-Painterly Abstractionists, Op Art painters, and Minimalist sculptors all adopted an artistic vocabulary of pure abstraction. Other artists, however, observing that the insular and introspective attitude of the avant-garde had alienated the public, sought to harness the communicative power of art to reach a wide audience. Thus was born the art movement that came to be known as Pop. Art historians trace the roots of *Pop Art* to the young British artists, architects, and writers who formed the Independent Group at the Institute of Contemporary Art in London in 1952. They sought to initiate fresh thinking in art, in part by sharing their fascination with the aesthetics and content of such facets of popular culture as advertising, comic books, and movies (see "Pop Art and Consumer Culture," page 966). In 1956, an Independent Group member, RICHARD HAMILTON (1922–2011), made

ART AND SOCIETY

Pop Art and Consumer Culture

Although the acceptance of pure abstraction as an artistic mode had gained significant momentum in the decades after the end of World War II, many artists, as well as the general public, reacted against pure formalism in painting and sculpture. In the 1950s and 1960s, the artists of the *Pop Art* movement reintroduced all the devices that the postwar abstractionists had purged from their artworks. Pop artists revived the tools traditionally used to convey meaning in art, such as signs, symbols, metaphors, allusions, illusions, and figural imagery. They not only embraced representation but also firmly grounded their art in the consumer culture and mass media of the postwar period, thereby making it much more accessible and understandable to the average person. Indeed, the name "Pop Art"—credited to the British art critic Lawrence Alloway (1926–1990)—is short for "popular art" and referred to the popular mass culture and familiar imagery of the contemporary urban environment, such as the collection of everyday objects, advertisements, and celebrity photographs featured in Richard Hamilton's collage *Just What Is It That Makes Today's Homes So Different, So Appealing?* (FIG. 30-23).

The fantasy interior in Hamilton's collage reflects the values of mid-20th-century consumer culture through figures and objects cut from glossy magazines. *Just What Is It?* includes references to mass media (the television, the theater marquee outside the window, the newspaper), to advertising (Hoover vacuum cleaners, Ford cars, Armour hams, Tootsie Pops), and to popular culture (the "girlie magazine," the body builder Charles Atlas, romance comic books). Artworks

of this sort stimulated viewers' wide-ranging speculation about society's values. This kind of intellectual toying with mass-media meaning and imagery typified Pop Art both in Europe and America.

Alloway eloquently described the intellectual basis of Pop Art in a 1958 essay:

> The definition of culture is changing as the result of the pressure of the great audience . . . [I]t is no longer sufficient to define culture solely as something that a minority guards for the few and the future . . . Our definition of culture is being stretched beyond the fine art limits imposed on it by Renaissance theory, and refers now, increasingly, to the whole complex of human activities. Within this definition, rejection of the mass produced arts is not, as critics think, a defense of culture but an attack on it.*

*Lawrence Alloway, "The Arts and the Mass Media," *Architectural Design* (February 1958): 34–35.

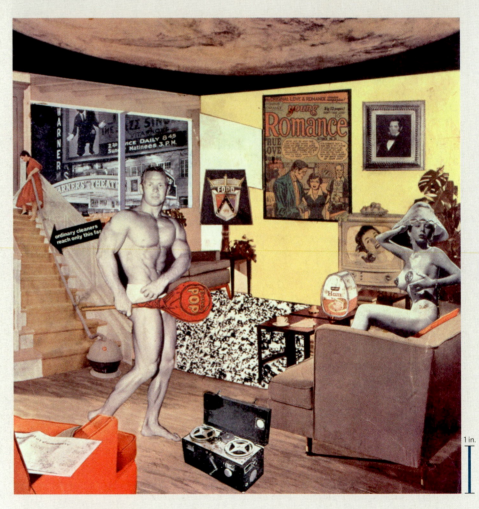

30-23 RICHARD HAMILTON, *Just What Is It That Makes Today's Homes So Different, So Appealing?* 1956. Collage, $10\frac{1}{4}'' \times 9\frac{3}{4}''$. Kunsthalle Tübingen, Tübingen.

The fantasy interior in Hamilton's collage of figures and objects cut from glossy magazines reflects the values of modern consumer culture. Toying with mass-media imagery typifies British Pop Art.

---

a small collage, *Just What Is It That Makes Today's Homes So Different, So Appealing?* (FIG. 30-23), which exemplifies British Pop Art. Trained as an engineering draftsman, exhibition designer, and painter, Hamilton studied the way that advertising shapes public attitudes. Long intrigued by Marcel Duchamp's ideas (see page 902), Hamilton consistently combined elements of popular art and fine art, seeing both as belonging to the whole world of visual communication. He created *Just What Is It?* for the poster and catalog of one section of an exhibition titled *This Is Tomorrow*, which included images from Hollywood cinema, science fiction, and the mass media.

JASPER JOHNS Although Pop Art originated in England, the movement found its greatest articulation and success in the United States, in large part because the more fully matured American consumer culture provided a fertile environment in which the movement flourished through the 1960s. Indeed, Independent Group members claimed that their inspiration came from Hollywood, Detroit, and New York's Madison Avenue, paying homage to America's predominance in the realms of mass media, mass production, and advertising.

One of the artists pivotal to the early development of American Pop Art was JASPER JOHNS (b. 1930), who grew up in South Carolina

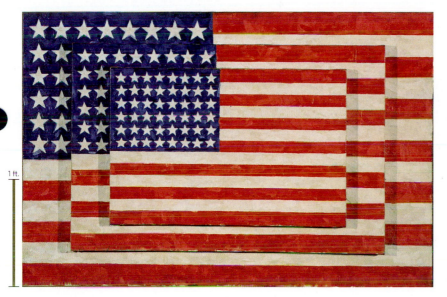

American Pop artist Jasper Johns wanted to draw attention to common objects that people view frequently but rarely scrutinize. He made many paintings of targets, flags, numbers, and alphabets.

and moved to New York City in 1952. Johns sought to draw attention to common objects in the world—what he called things "seen but not looked at."[14] To this end, he did several series of paintings of numbers, alphabets, flags, and maps of the United States—all of which are items that people view frequently but rarely scrutinize. He created his first flag painting in 1954 at the height of the Cold War. Initially labeled a Neo-Dadaist because of the kinship of his works to Marcel Duchamp's readymades (FIG. 29-26), Johns also had strong ties to the Surrealists, especially René Magritte, whose painting of a pipe labeled "This is not a pipe" (FIG. 29-56) is conceptually a forerunner of Johns's flags—for example, *Three Flags* (FIG. 30-24), which could easily carry the label "These are not flags." In fact, when asked why he chose the American flag as a subject, Johns replied that he had a dream in which he saw himself painting a flag. The world of dreams was central to Surrealism (see "André Breton's First Surrealist Manifesto," page 922).

In *Three Flags*, Johns painted a trio of overlapping American national banners of decreasing size, with the smallest closest to the viewer, reversing traditional perspective, which calls for diminution of size with distance. Johns drained meaning from the patriotic emblem by reducing it to a repetitive pattern—not the flag itself but three pictures of a flag in one. Nevertheless, the heritage of Abstract Expressionism is still apparent. Although Johns rejected the heroic, highly personalized application of pigment championed by the 1950s action painters, he painted his flags in *encaustic* (liquid wax and dissolved pigment; see "Encaustic Painting," page 217) mixed with newsprint on three overlapping canvases. His flags thus retain a pronounced surface texture, emphasizing that the viewer is looking at a handmade painting, not a machine-made fabric. The painting, like the flags, is an object, not an illusion of other objects.

ROBERT RAUSCHENBERG
A close friend of Johns's, ROBERT RAUSCHENBERG (1925–2008) began using mass-media images in his work in the 1950s. Rauschenberg set out to create works that would be open and indeterminate, and he began by making multimedia works that he called *combines*, which intersperse painted passages with sculptural elements. Rauschenberg's combines are, in a sense, his personal variation on *assemblages*, artworks constructed from already existing objects. At times, these combines seem to be sculptures with painting incorporated into certain sections. Others seem to be paintings with three-

dimensional objects attached to the surface. In the 1950s, Rauschenberg's assemblages usually contained an array of art reproductions, magazine and newspaper clippings, and passages painted in an Abstract Expressionist style. In the early 1960s, he adopted the commercial medium of *silk-screen printing*, first in black and white and then in color, and began filling entire canvases with appropriated news images and anonymous photographs of city scenes.

Canyon (FIG. 30-25) is typical of Rauschenberg's combines. Pieces of printed paper and photographs cover parts of the canvas.

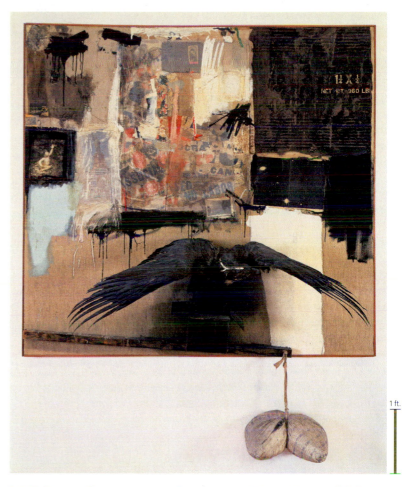

Rauschenberg's "combines" intersperse painted passages with sculptural elements. *Canyon* incorporates pigment on canvas with pieces of printed paper, photographs, a pillow, and a stuffed eagle.

In November 1963, Roy Lichtenstein was one of eight painters interviewed for a profile on Pop Art in *Art News*. Gene R. Swenson posed the questions. Some of Lichtenstein's answers follow.

[Pop Art is] the use of commercial art as a subject matter in painting . . . [Pop artists portray] what I think to be the most brazen and threatening characteristics of our culture, things we hate, but which are also so powerful in their impingement on us. . . . I paint directly . . . [without] perspective or shading. It doesn't look like a painting *of* something, it looks like the thing itself. Instead of looking like a painting *of* a billboard . . . Pop art seems to be the actual thing. It is an intensification, a stylistic intensification of the excitement which the subject matter has for me; but the style is . . . cool. One of the things a cartoon does is to express violent emotion and passion in a completely mechanized and removed style. To express this thing in a painterly style would dilute it.

Everybody has called Pop Art "American" painting, but it's actually industrial painting. America was hit by industrialism and capitalism harder and sooner . . . I think the meaning of my work is that it's industrial, it's what all the world will soon become. Europe will be the same way, soon, so it won't be American; it will be universal.*

The influence of comic books is evident in Lichtenstein's mature works—for example, his 1963 painting titled *Hopeless* (FIG. 30-26). Here, Lichtenstein excerpted an image from a comic book, a form of entertainment meant to be read and discarded, and immortalized the image on a large canvas. Aside from that modification, Lichtenstein remained remarkably faithful to the original comic-strip image. His subjects were typically the melodramatic scenes that were mainstays of romance comic books popular at the time, and included "balloons" with the words that the characters speak. Lichtenstein also used the

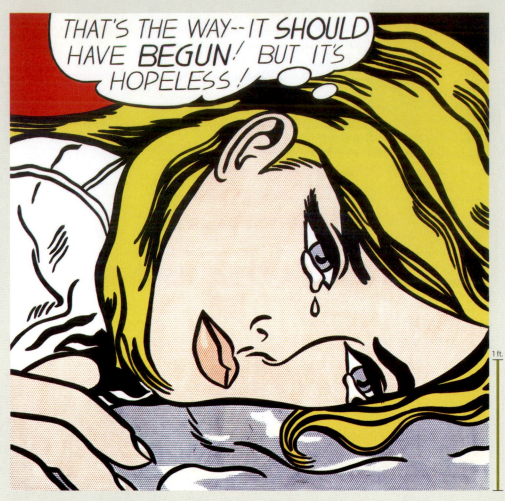

30-26 ROY LICHTENSTEIN, *Hopeless*, 1963. Oil and synthetic polymer paint on canvas, 3' 8" × 3' 8". Kunstmuseum Basel, Basel. © Estate of Roy Lichtenstein.

Comic books appealed to Lichtenstein because they were a mainstay of popular culture, meant to be read and discarded. The Pop artist immortalized their images on large canvases.

visual vocabulary of the comic strip, with its dark black outlines and unmodulated color areas, and retained the familiar square dimensions. Moreover, by emulating the printing technique called *benday dots*, he called attention to the mass-produced derivation of the image. Named after its inventor, the newspaper printer Benjamin Day (1810–1889), the benday-dot system involves the modulation of colors through the placement and size of colored dots. Lichtenstein thus transferred the visual shorthand language of the comic book to the realm of monumental painting.

*G. R. Swenson, "What Is Pop Art? Interviews with Eight Painters," *Art News* 62, no. 7 (November 1963): 25, 64.

Much of the unevenly painted surface consists of pigment roughly applied in a manner reminiscent of de Kooning's work (FIG. 30-8). A stuffed bald eagle attached to the lower part of the combine spreads its wings as if lifting off in flight toward the viewer. Completing the combine, a pillow dangles from a string attached to a wood stick below the eagle. The artist presented the work's components in a jumbled fashion. He tilted or turned some of the images sideways, and each overlays part of another image. The compositional confusion may resemble that of a Dada collage, but the parts of Rauschenberg's combines maintain their individuality more than those, for example, in a Schwitters piece (FIG. 29-29). The eye scans a Rauschenberg canvas much as it might survey the environment on a walk through a city. The various recognizable images and objects seem unrelated and defy a consistent reading, although Rauschenberg chose all the elements of his combines with specific meanings in mind. For example, Rauschenberg based *Canyon* on a Rembrandt painting of Jupiter in the form of an eagle carrying the boy Ganymede heavenward. The photo in the combine is a reference to the Greek boy, and the hanging bag is a visual pun on his buttocks.

ROY LICHTENSTEIN As the Pop Art movement matured, the images became more concrete and tightly controlled. ROY LICHTENSTEIN (1923–1997), who was born in Manhattan not far from Madison Avenue, the center of the American advertising industry, developed an interest in art in elementary school and as a teenager took weekend painting classes at the Parsons School of Design before enrolling at Ohio State University. He served in the army during World War II and was stationed in France, where he was able to visit the Musée du Louvre and Chartres Cathedral. In the late 1950s, however, he turned his attention to commercial art and especially to the comic book as a mainstay of American popular culture (see "Roy Lichtenstein on Pop Art and Comic Books," page 968, and FIG. **30-26**).

ANDY WARHOL The quintessential American Pop artist was ANDY WARHOL (1928–1987). An early successful career as a commercial artist and illustrator grounded Warhol in the sensibility and visual rhetoric of advertising and the mass media. This knowledge proved useful for his Pop artworks, which often depicted icons of mass-produced consumer culture, such as *Green Coca-Cola Bottles* (FIG. **30-27**), and Hollywood celebrities, such as Marilyn Monroe (1926–1962; FIG. **30-27A**). Warhol favored reassuringly familiar objects and people. He explained his attraction to the ubiquitous curved Coke bottle:

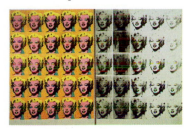

30-27A WARHOL, *Marilyn Diptych*, 1962.

What's great about this country is that America started the tradition where the richest consumers buy essentially the same things as the poorest. You can be watching TV and see Coca-Cola, and you can know that the President drinks Coke, Liz Taylor drinks Coke, and just think, you can drink Coke, too. A Coke is a Coke and no amount of money can get you a better Coke.[15]

As did other Pop artists, Warhol used a visual vocabulary and a printing method that reinforced the image's connections to consumer culture. The silk-screen technique enabled Warhol to print the image endlessly (although he varied each bottle slightly). The repetition and redundancy of the Coke bottle reflect the saturation of this product in American society—in homes, at work, literally everywhere, including gas stations, as immortalized by GEORGE SEGAL (1924–2000) in 1963 (FIG. **30-27B**). So immersed was Warhol in a culture of mass production that he not only produced numerous canvases of the same image but also named his studio "the Factory."

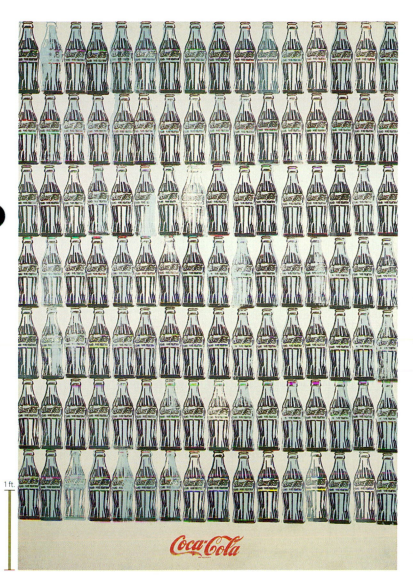

1 ft.

30-27 ANDY WARHOL, *Green Coca-Cola Bottles*, 1962. Oil on canvas, 6' 10½" × 4' 9". Whitney Museum of American Art, New York.

Warhol was the quintessential American Pop artist. Here, he selected an icon of mass-produced consumer culture and then multiplied it, reflecting Coke's omnipresence in American society.

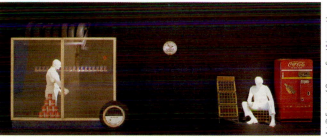

30-27B SEGAL, *Gas Station*, 1963.

JAMES ROSENQUIST Because of the close connection between Pop Art and consumer culture, many Pop artworks also incorporated social commentary. That is especially true of the work of JAMES ROSENQUIST (b. 1933). Born in Grand Forks, North Dakota, Rosenquist studied painting at the Minneapolis Art Institute and the University of Minnesota and initially supported himself by painting commercial billboards. In 1955, he moved to New York City and met several of the most innovative artists of the day, including Ellsworth Kelly, Jasper Johns, Robert Rauschenberg, and Claes Oldenburg. In addition to painting billboards in Times Square and elsewhere, Rosenquist created window displays for upscale jewelry and fashion stores Tiffany and Bonwit Teller until he established his reputation as an artist with his first (sold-out) solo exhibition in 1962.

ARTISTS ON ART

James Rosenquist on *F-111*

F-111 (FIG. 30-28) is James Rosenquist's most ambitious work. It exemplifies his singular contribution to the Pop Art movement in its grandiose scale (comparable to the billboards he painted to earn a living), its imagery drawn from America's consumer culture, and its implied social and political commentary. The F-111 was the latest technological marvel, an enormously costly fighter jet that, for Rosenquist, was emblematic of the U.S. "military-industrial complex" that produced the Vietnam War, the subject of widespread protest demonstrations at the time (1965). The gigantic aircraft fills the full length of *F-111,* but interspersed are meticulously painted motifs from daily life, including spaghetti, a lightbulb, an automobile tire, a smiling girl under a hairdryer that resembles a missile head, and an atomic explosion under a beach umbrella. Rosenquist's idea was to show the F-111, a war machine, flying through consumer society, and to suggest complicity between the two. He explained:

> [The F-111] is the newest, latest fighter-bomber . . . This first of its type cost many million dollars. People are planning their lives through work on this bomber . . . A man has a contract from the company making the bomber, and he plans his third automobile and his fifth child because he is a technician and has work for the next couple of years. Then the original idea is expanded, another thing is invented; and the plane already seems obsolete. The prime force of this thing has been to keep people working, an economic tool; but behind it, this is a war machine.

In the same interview, Rosenquist also talked about his approach to painting and about the scale of *F-111.*

> The style I use was gained by doing outdoor commercial work as hard and as fast as I could. My techniques for me are still anti-style. I have an idea what I want to do, what it will look like when I want it finished—in between is just a hell of a lot of work. When they say the Rosenquist style is very precise, maybe they just know that painting style as they know it is going out of style. . . . The *F-111* was enclosed—four walls of a room in a gallery. My idea was to make an extension of ways of showing art in a gallery, instead of showing single pictures with wall space that usually gives your eye a relief. In this picture, because it did seal up all the walls, I could set the dial and put in the stops and rests for the person's eye in the whole room instead of allowing the eye to wander and think in an empty space.*

*G. R. Swenson, "The F-111: An Interview with James Rosenquist," *Partisan Review* 32, no. 4 (Autumn 1965): 589–601.

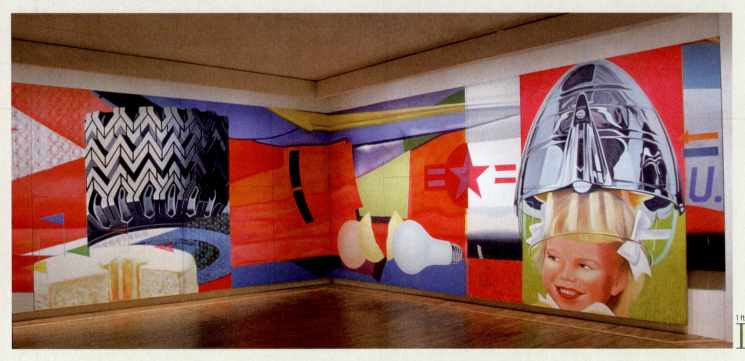

30-28 JAMES ROSENQUIST, *F-111,* 1965. Oil on canvas and aluminum, 10' × 86'. Museum of Modern Art, New York. (Gift, by exchange, of Mr. and Mrs. Alex L. Hillman and Lillie P. Bliss Bequest.) Art © James Rosenquist/Licensed by VAGA, New York, NY.

In this billboard-like Pop Art masterpiece, Rosenquist interspersed everyday images with a fighter jet to comment on the connection between the "military-industrial complex" and the American consumer.

Rosenquist's largest and most important work is *F-111* (FIG. 30-28), a 23-panel, 10-foot-high and 86-foot-long mural-like painting designed to wrap around the four walls of the main room of the Leo Castelli Gallery in Manhattan (see "James Rosenquist on *F-111,*" above).

CLAES OLDENBURG In the 1960s, CLAES OLDENBURG (b. 1929) also produced Pop artworks that incisively commented on American consumer culture, but his medium was sculpture. The son of a Swedish diplomat who moved to the United States in 1936, Oldenburg attended school in Chicago and graduated from Yale

30-29 CLAES OLDENBURG, *Lipstick (Ascending) on Caterpillar Tracks,* 1969; reworked, 1974. Painted steel, aluminum, and fiberglass, 21' high. Morse College, Yale University, New Haven (gift of Colossal Keepsake Corporation).

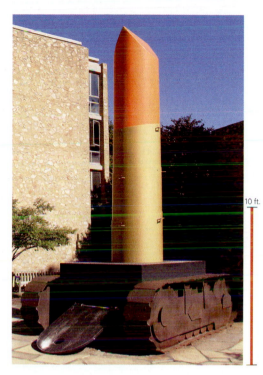

Designed as a speaker's platform for antiwar protesters, *Lipstick* humorously combines phallic and militaristic imagery. Originally, the lipstick tip was soft red vinyl and had to be inflated.

10 ft.

NIKI DE SAINT-PHALLE Also usually classified as a Pop Art sculptor was French-born NIKI DE SAINT-PHALLE (1930–2002), because her sculptures remind many viewers of dolls and folk art. Her most famous works are the series of polyester statues of women she called "Nanas" (FIG. **30-29A**), oversized, brightly colored sculptures that are feminist commentaries on popular stereotypes of female beauty.

Superrealism

Like the Pop artists, the artists associated with *Superrealism* sought a form of artistic communication more accessible to the public than the remote, unfamiliar visual language of the Abstract Expressionists, Post-Painterly Abstractionists, and Minimalists. The Superrealists expanded Pop's iconography in both painting and sculpture by making images in the late 1960s and 1970s involving scrupulous fidelity to optical fact. Because many Superrealists used photographs as sources for their imagery, art historians also refer to this postwar art movement as *Photorealism.*

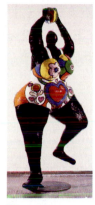

🔊 **30-29A** SAINT-PHALLE, *Black Venus,* 1965–1967.

AUDREY FLACK One of Superrealism's pioneers was lifelong New Yorker AUDREY FLACK (b. 1931), who studied the history of art at New York University's Institute of Fine Arts after graduating from Yale. Her paintings, such as *Marilyn* (FIG. **30-30**), are not simply technical exercises in recording objects in minute detail. They are also conceptual inquiries into the nature of photography and the extent to which photography constructs an understanding of reality. Flack observed: "[Photography is] my whole life, I studied art

University in 1950. His early works consisted of plaster reliefs of food and clothing items. Oldenburg constructed these sculptures of plaster layered on chicken wire and muslin, painting them with cheap commercial house enamel. In later works, focused on the same subjects, he shifted to large-scale stuffed sculptures of sewn vinyl or canvas, many of which he exhibited in a show he titled *The Store*—an appropriate comment on the function of art as a commodity in a consumer society.

Oldenburg is best known, however, for his mammoth outdoor sculptures. In 1966, a group of graduate students at the Yale School of Architecture, calling themselves the Colossal Keepsake Corporation, raised funds for materials for a giant sculpture that Oldenburg agreed to create (in secret and without a fee) as a gift to his alma mater. The work, *Lipstick (Ascending) on Caterpillar Tracks* (FIG. **30-29**), was Oldenburg's first large-scale public sculpture. He installed *Lipstick* on Ascension Day, May 15, 1969, on Beineke Plaza across from the office of the university's president, the site of many raucous protests against the Vietnam War. Oldenburg's characteristic humor emerges unmistakably in the combination of phallic and militaristic imagery, especially in the double irony of the "phallus" being a woman's cosmetic item, and the Caterpillar-type endless-loop metal tracks suggesting not a tractor-earthmover for construction work but a military tank designed for destruction in warfare. *Lipstick* was to be a speaker's platform for protesters, and originally the lipstick tip was a drooping red vinyl balloon that the speaker had to inflate, underscoring the sexual innuendo. (Oldenburg once remarked that art collectors preferred nudes, so he produced nude cars, nude telephones, and nude electric plugs to please them.)

Vandalism and exposure to the elements (the original tractor was plywood) caused so much damage to *Lipstick* that it had to be removed, and Oldenburg reconstructed it in metal and fiberglass. Yale formally accepted the controversial and unsolicited repaired gift in 1974, when the architectural historian Vincent Scully (b. 1920), then master of Yale's Morse College, offered a permanent home for *Lipstick* in the college courtyard. Oldenburg expressed mixed feelings about the recognition of what he viewed as a political statement as a "work of art."

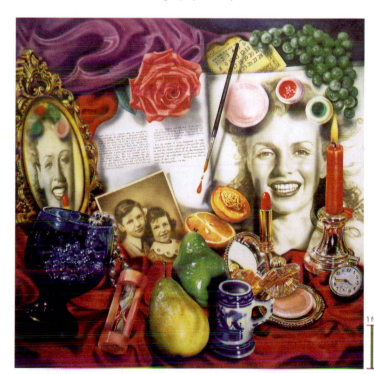

30-30 AUDREY FLACK, *Marilyn,* 1977. Oil over acrylic on canvas, 8' × 8'. University of Arizona Museum, Tucson (museum purchase with funds provided by the Edward J. Gallagher Jr. Memorial Fund).

1 ft.

Flack's pioneering Photorealist still lifes record objects with great optical fidelity. *Marilyn* alludes to Dutch vanitas paintings (FIG. 25-21) and incorporates multiple references to the transience of life.

ARTISTS ON ART
Chuck Close on Photorealist Portrait Painting

Chuck Close (FIG. 30-31) based his paintings of the late 1960s and early 1970s on photographs, and his main goal was to translate photographic information into painted information. Because he aimed simply to record visual information about his subject's appearance, Close deliberately avoided creative compositions, flattering lighting effects, and revealing facial expressions. Not interested in providing great insight into the personalities of those portrayed, Close painted anonymous and generic people, mostly friends. By reducing the variables in his paintings (even their canvas size is a constant 9 by 7 feet), he could focus on employing his methodical presentations of faces, thereby encouraging the viewer to deal with the formal aspects of his works. Indeed, because of the large scale of Close's paintings, careful scrutiny causes the images to dissolve into abstract patterns.

In a widely read 1970 interview in the journal *Artforum,* art critic Cindy Nemser (b. 1937) asked Close about the scale of his huge portraits and the relationship of his Photorealist canvases to the photographs that lie behind them. He answered in part:

> The large scale allows me to deal with information that is overlooked in an eight-by-ten inch photograph . . . My large scale forces the viewer to focus on one area at a time. In that way he is made aware of the blurred areas that are seen with peripheral vision. Normally we never take those peripheral areas into account. When we focus on an area it is sharp. As we turn our attention to adjacent areas they sharpen up too. In my work, the blurred areas don't come into focus, but they are too large to be ignored. . . . In order to . . . make [my painted] information stack up with photographic information, I tried to purge my work of as much of the baggage of traditional portrait painting as I could. To avoid a painterly brush stroke and surface, I use some pretty devious means, such as razor blades, electric drills and airbrushes. I also work as thinly as possible and I don't use white paint as it tends to build up and become chalky and opaque. In fact, in a nine-by-seven foot picture, I only use a couple of tablespoons of black paint to cover the entire canvas.*

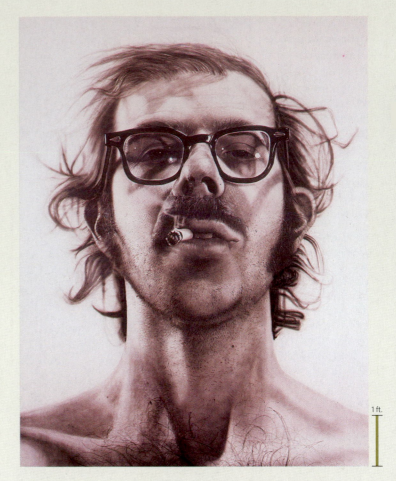

30-31 CHUCK CLOSE, *Big Self-Portrait*, 1967–1968. Acrylic on canvas, 8' 11" × 6' 11". Walker Art Center, Minneapolis (Art Center Acquisition Fund, 1969).

Close's goal was to translate photographic information into painted information. In his portraits, he deliberately avoided creative compositions, flattering lighting effects, and revealing facial expressions.

*Cindy Nemser, "Chuck Close: Interview with Cindy Nemser," *Artforum* 8, no. 5 (January 1970): 51–55.

history, it was always photographs, I never saw the paintings, they were in Europe. . . . Look at TV and at magazines and reproductions, they're all influenced by photo-vision."[16] The photograph's formal qualities also intrigued her, and she used photographic techniques by first projecting an image in slide form onto the canvas. By next using an *airbrush* (a device originally designed as a photo-retouching tool that sprays paint with compressed air), Flack could duplicate the smooth gradations of tone and color found in photographs.

Most of Flack's paintings are still lifes that present the viewer with a collection of familiar objects painted with great optical fidelity. *Marilyn* is a still life incorporating photographs of the face of famed Hollywood actress Marilyn Monroe. It is a poignant commentary on Monroe's tragic life and differs markedly from Warhol's *Marilyn Diptych* (FIG. 30-27A), which celebrates celebrity and makes no allusion to the death of the glamorous star. Flack's still life includes multiple references to death and alludes to Dutch *vanitas* paintings (FIG. 25-21). In addition to the black-and-white photo-

graphs of a youthful, smiling Monroe, Flack painted fresh fruit, an hourglass, a burning candle, a watch, and a calendar, all of which refer to the passage of time and the transience of life on earth.

CHUCK CLOSE Perhaps the most famous Superrealist is CHUCK CLOSE (b. 1940), who grew up near Seattle and attended the University of Washington and Yale University. He is best known for his large-scale portraits, such as *Big Self-Portrait* (FIG. **30-31**). However, Close felt that his connection to the Photorealists was tenuous, because for him, realism was not an end in itself but rather the result of an intellectually rigorous, systematic approach to painting (see "Chuck Close on Photorealist Portrait Painting," above).

LUCIAN FREUD Born in Berlin in 1922, LUCIAN FREUD (1922–2011) moved to London with his family in 1933 when Adolph Hitler became German chancellor. The grandson of Sigmund Freud, the painter is best known for his unflattering close-up views of faces in

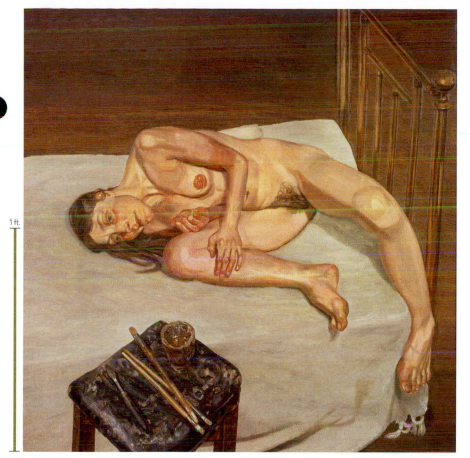

30-32 Lucian Freud, *Naked Portrait*, 1972–1973. Oil on canvas 2' × 2'. Tate Modern, London.

Freud's brutally realistic portrait of an unnamed woman lying on a bed in an awkward position gives the impression that the viewer is an intruder in a private space, but the setting is the artist's studio.

whose poses he determined, his paintings convey the impression that the artist and the viewer are intruders in a private realm.

In *Naked Portrait* (FIG. **30-32**), the viewer observes an unnamed woman lying in an uncomfortable, almost fetal, position at the foot of a bed. Freud depicted her from a sharp angle above and to the left. In the foreground is a small table with the painter's tools on it, revealing that this is not the woman's bedroom but the painter's studio and that the woman is the subject of intense scrutiny by the artist. Freud's models do not have perfect bodies. Some are overweight, and many are well beyond their prime. These are truly "naked portraits" of real people. They break sharply with the Western tradition from Greek antiquity to the Renaissance and into the modern era of depicting idealized Venuses, Eves, and courtesans in graceful and often erotic poses. Freud explained his interest in nudity: "I'm really interested in people as animals. Part of my liking to work from them naked is for that reason. Because I can see more."[17] Regarding the setting of his paintings, Freud observed: "I work from people that interest me, and that I care about and think about, in rooms that I live in and know."[18]

which the sitter seems almost unaware of the painter's presence, and for his portrayals of female and male nudes in foreshortened and often contorted poses. Although Freud always used living models

DUANE HANSON Not surprisingly, many sculptors also were Superrealists, including Minnesota-born DUANE HANSON (1925–1996), who spent much of his career in southern Florida. Hanson perfected a casting technique that enabled him to create life-size figurative sculptures that many viewers mistake at first for real people. Hanson began by making plaster molds from live models and then filled the molds with polyester resin. After the resin hardened, he removed the outer molds and cleaned, painted with an airbrush, and decorated the sculptures with wigs, clothes, and other accessories. These works, such as *Supermarket Shopper* (FIG. **30-33**), depict stereotypical average Americans, striking chords with the

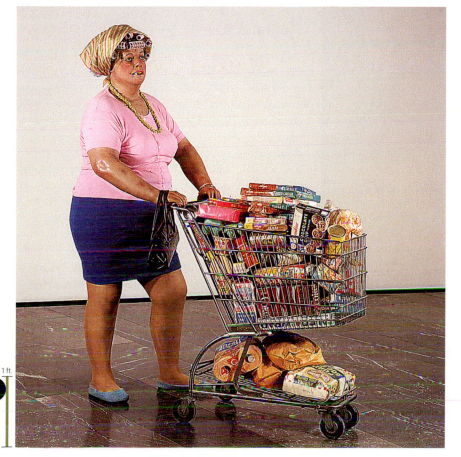

30-33 Duane Hanson, *Supermarket Shopper*, 1970. Polyester resin and fiberglass polychromed in oil, with clothing, steel cart, and groceries, life-size. Nachfolgeinstitut, Neue Galerie, Sammlung Ludwig, Aachen. Art © Estate of Duane Hanson/Licensed by VAGA, New York, NY.

Hanson used molds from live models to create his Superrealist life-size painted plaster sculptures. His aim was to capture the emptiness and loneliness of average Americans in familiar settings.

public specifically because of their familiarity. Hanson explained his choice of imagery:

> The subject matter that I like best deals with the familiar lower- and middle-class American types of today. To me, the resignation, emptiness and loneliness of their existence captures the true reality of life for these people. . . . I want to achieve a certain tough realism which speaks of the fascinating idiosyncrasies of our time.[19]

Photography

Although Superrealist artists admired the ability of photography to reproduce faithfully the appearance of people, objects, and places, photographers themselves used their medium to pursue varied ends. The photographs of Edward Weston (FIGS. 29-44 and 29-44A) and Dorothea Lange (FIG. 29-77) represent the two poles of American photography between the world wars—the art photograph (Weston), which transforms the real into the abstract, and the documentary photograph (Lange), which records people and events directly, without artifice. In the postwar period, leading photographers adopted both approaches.

One documentary photographer who achieved a prominent position in the circle of innovative photographers was Diane Arbus (1923–1971). Often described as a "photographer of freaks," Arbus

specialized in taking black-and-white photographs (not illustrated) of ordinary people with all their blemishes, both physical and psychological. Among her subjects were people with physical deformities, and people at the margins of society—transvestites, a Mexican dwarf, a man tattooed from head to foot, a young man smoking with his hair in curlers, another of enormous height ("a Jewish giant") at home with his diminutive parents, a boy in New York's Central Park menacingly holding a toy hand grenade—in short, people who were rarely the chosen subjects of professional photographers.

MINOR WHITE The other pole of mid-20th-century photography in America is perhaps best represented by the work of Minneapolis native MINOR WHITE (1908–1976), who moved to Portland, Oregon in 1938 and became a photographer for the Works Progress Administration. He served in the United States Army in World War II and then settled in New York City in 1945, where he met Alfred Stieglitz, whose *Equivalent* photographs (FIG. 29-43A) he greatly admired. Deeply influenced by Zen Buddhism (see "Zen Buddhism," page 1067), White sought to incorporate a mystical element in his own work.

His 1962 photograph (FIG. **30-34**) of a rock formation in Utah is a characteristic example. A "straight photograph" in the tradition of Stieglitz and Weston, it is also an abstract composition of jagged shapes and contrasts of light and dark reminiscent of Abstract Expressionist paintings (FIG. 30-9). Viewers of *Moencopi Strata, Capitol Reef, Utah* may recognize White's nominal subject as a detail of a landscape, but in his hands, nature becomes the springboard for meditation. As one of the founders and the longtime editor (1952–1975) of *Aperture,* the leading art photography magazine of the time, White had a profound influence on the development of the medium in the postwar period.

Feminist Art

With the renewed interest in representation that the Pop artists and Superrealists introduced in the 1960s and 1970s, artists once again began to embrace the persuasive powers of art to communicate with a wide audience. In the 1970s, many artists began to investigate the social dynamics of power and privilege, especially in relation to gender, although racial, ethnic, and sexual orientation issues have also figured prominently in the art of recent decades (see Chapter 31). Women artists played a significant role in the feminist movement, which sought equal rights for women in contemporary society and focused attention on the subservient place of women in societies throughout history. Spearheading the feminist art movement of the 1970s were Judy Chicago (FIG. **30-35**) and Miriam Schapiro

30-34 MINOR WHITE, *Moencopi Strata, Capitol Reef, Utah,* 1962. Gelatin silver print, $1'\frac{1}{8}'' \times 9\frac{1}{4}''$. Museum of Modern Art, New York. © The Minor White Archive, Princeton University.

White's "straight photograph" of a natural rock formation is also an abstract composition of jagged shapes and contrasts of light and dark reminiscent of Abstract Expressionist paintings.

1 in.

ARTISTS ON ART
Judy Chicago on *The Dinner Party*

One of the acknowledged masterpieces of feminist art is Judy Chicago's *The Dinner Party* (FIG. 30-35), which required a team of nearly 400 to create and assemble. In 1979, Chicago published a book explaining the genesis and symbolism of the work.

[By 1974] I had discarded [my original] idea of painting a hundred abstract portraits on plates, each paying tribute to a different historic female figure. . . . In my research I realized over and over again that women's achievements had been left out of history . . . My new idea was to try to symbolize this. . . . [I thought] about putting the plates on a table with silver, glasses, napkins, and tablecloths, and over the next year and a half the concept of *The Dinner Party* slowly evolved. I began to think about the piece as a reinterpretation of the Last Supper from the point of view of women, who, throughout history, had prepared the meals and set the table. In my "Last Supper," however, the women would be the honored guests. Their representation in the form of plates set on the table would express the way women had been confined, and the piece would thus reflect both women's achievements and their oppression. . . . My goal with *The Dinner Party* was . . . to forge a new kind of art expressing women's experience . . . [It] seemed appropriate to relate our history through art, particularly through techniques traditionally associated with women—china-painting and needlework.*

The Dinner Party rests on a triangular white tile floor inscribed with the names of 999 additional women of achievement to signify that the accomplishments of the 39 honored guests rest on a founda-tion that other women had laid. Among those with place settings at the table are the Egyptian pharaoh Hatshepsut (FIG. 3-21), the Minoan snake goddess (FIG. 4-13), the Byzantine empress Theodora (FIG. 9-14), the medieval nun Hildegard of Bingen (FIG. 12-25), and the painters Artemisia Gentileschi (FIG. 24-19 and 24-20) and Georgia O'Keeffe (FIGS. I-5 and 29-42). Other women artists among the 999 names include Lavinia Fontana (FIG. 22-40A), Élisabeth-Louise Vigée-Lebrun (FIGS. 26-15A and 26-16), Adélaïde Labille-Guiard (FIG. 26-17), Angelica Kauffman (FIG. 26-1), Mary Cassatt (FIG. 28-12), Berthe Morisot (FIGS. 28-13 and 28-13A), Gertrude Käsebier (FIG. 28-31), Käthe Kollwitz (FIG. 29-9), Paula Modersohn-Becker (FIG. 29-9A), Barbara Hepworth (FIG. 29-63), Dorothea Lange (FIG. 29-77), and Louise Nevelson (FIG. 30-20).

Each woman's place has identical eating utensils and a goblet, but features a unique oversized porcelain plate and a long place mat or table runner covered with imagery reflecting significant facts about that woman's life and culture. The plates range from simple concave shapes with china-painted imagery to dishes whose sculptured three-dimensional designs almost seem to struggle to free themselves. The designs on each plate incorporate both butterfly and vulval motifs—the butterfly as the ancient symbol of liberation and the vulva as the symbol of female sexuality. Each table runner combines traditional needlework techniques, including needlepoint, embroidery, crochet, beading, patchwork, and appliqué.

The Dinner Party is more than the sum of its parts, however. Of monumental size, as so many great works of public art have been throughout the ages, Chicago's 1979 masterwork provides viewers with a powerful launching point for considering broad feminist concerns.

*Judy Chicago, "The Dinner Party": A Symbol of Our Heritage (Garden City, N.Y.: Anchor Press, 1979), 11–12.

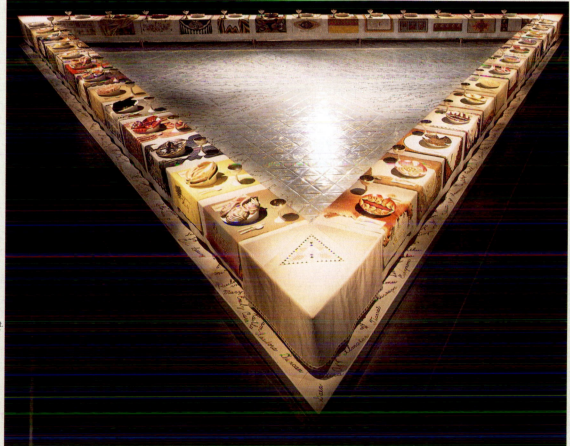

10 ft.

30-35 JUDY CHICAGO, *The Dinner Party*, 1979. Multimedia, including ceramics and stitchery, 48' × 48' × 48'. The Brooklyn Museum, Brooklyn.

Chicago's *Dinner Party* honors 39 women from antiquity to 20th-century America. The triangular form and the materials—painted china and fabric—are traditionally associated with women.

(FIG. 30-36). Chicago and a group of students at California State University in Fresno founded the Feminist Art Program, and Chicago and Schapiro coordinated it at the California Institute of the Arts in Valencia. In 1972, as part of this program, teachers and students joined to create projects such as Womanhouse, an abandoned house in Los Angeles that they completely converted into a suite of "environments," each based on a different aspect of women's lives and fantasies.

JUDY CHICAGO A major goal of Chicago native Judy Cohen, who took the name JUDY CHICAGO (b. 1939), was to educate the public about women's role in history and the fine arts and to establish a respect for women and their art. Chicago sought to forge a new kind of art expressing women's experiences and to find a way to make that art accessible to a large audience. Inspired early in her career by the work of Barbara Hepworth (FIG. 29-63), Georgia O'Keeffe (FIGS. I-5 and 29-42), and Louise Nevelson (FIG. 30-20), Chicago developed a personal painting style that consciously included abstract organic vaginal images.

In the early 1970s, Chicago began planning an ambitious piece, *The Dinner Party* (FIG. 30-35), using craft techniques (such as china painting and needlework) traditionally practiced by women, to celebrate the achievements and contributions that women had made throughout history (see "Judy Chicago on *The Dinner Party*," page 975). She originally conceived the work as a feminist *Last Supper* for 13 "honored guests," as in the biblical account of Christ's passion, but at Chicago's table, the guests are women instead of men. The number of women in a witches' coven is also 13, and the artist intended her feminist *Dinner Party* additionally to refer to witchcraft and the worship of the Mother Goddess. But because Chicago had uncovered so many worthy women in the course of her research, she tripled the number of guests and placed table settings for 39 women around a triangular table 48 feet long on each side. The triangular form refers to the ancient symbol for both woman and the Goddess. The notion of a dinner party also alludes to women's traditional role as homemakers.

MIRIAM SCHAPIRO After enjoying a thriving career as a hard-edge painter in California in the late 1960s, Toronto-born MIRIAM SCHAPIRO (b. 1923) became fascinated with the hidden metaphors for womanhood that she then saw in her abstract paintings. Intrigued by the materials she had used to create a doll's house for her part in Womanhouse, in the 1970s Schapiro began to make huge sewn collages, assembled from fabrics, quilts, buttons, sequins, lace trim, and rickrack collected at antique shows and fairs. She called these works *femmages*—from the French *femme* ("woman") and an inversion of the French *homage* ("homage") from *homme* ("man"). She wanted to make the point that women had been doing collages using these materials long before Pablo Picasso (FIG. 29-14) introduced them to the art world. *Anatomy of a Kimono* (FIG. **30-36**) is one of a series of gigantic femmages based on the patterns of Japanese kimonos, fans, and robes. This vast 10-panel composition is more than 52 feet long and almost 7 feet high and repeats the kimono shape in a rich array of fabric fragments.

CINDY SHERMAN After studying painting in Buffalo, CINDY SHERMAN (b. 1954) switched to photography as her primary means of expression. She addresses in her work the way that much of Western art presents female beauty for the enjoyment of the "male gaze," a primary focus of contemporary feminist theory, which explores gender as a socially constructed concept. Since 1977, Sherman has produced a series of more than 80 black-and-white photographs called *Untitled Film Stills*. She got the idea for the series after examining soft-core pornography magazines and noting the stereotypical ways that they depicted women. She decided to produce her own series of photographs, designing, acting in, directing, and photographing the works. In so doing, she took control of her own image and constructed her own identity, a primary feminist concern.

In works from the series, such as *Untitled Film Still #35* (FIG. **30-37**), Sherman appears, often in costume and wig, in a photograph that seems to be a film still. Most of the images in this series recall popular film genres but are sufficiently generic that the viewer cannot relate them to specific movies. Sherman often reveals the constructed nature of these images by holding in her hand the shutter release cable used to take the pictures. (The cord runs across the floor in *#35*.) Although the artist is still the object of the viewer's gaze in these images, the identity is one that she alone chose to assume by posing for the photographs.

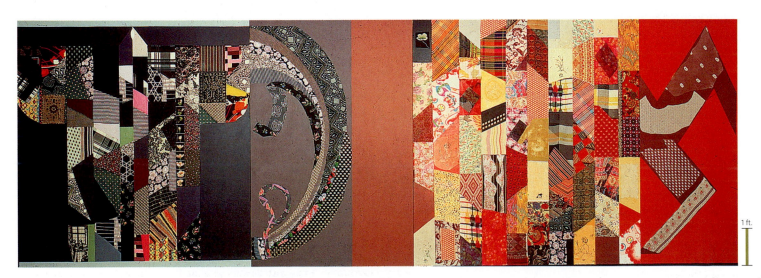

30-36 MIRIAM SCHAPIRO, *Anatomy of a Kimono* (detail of 2 panels of a 10-panel composition), 1976. Fabric and acrylic on canvas, entire work 6' 8" × 52' 2½". Collection of Bruno Bischofberger, Zurich.

Schapiro calls her huge sewn collages "femmages" to make the point that women had been doing collages of fabric long before Picasso (FIG. 29-14). This femmage incorporates patterns from Japanese kimonos.

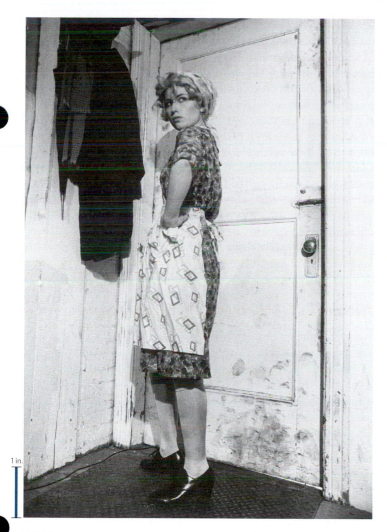

30-37 CINDY SHERMAN, *Untitled Film Still #35*, 1979. Gelatin silver-print, 10" × 8". Private collection.

Sherman here assumed a role for one of 80 photographs resembling film stills in which she addressed the way that women have traditionally been presented in Western art for the enjoyment of the "male gaze."

ANA MENDIETA Two other feminist artists who used their bodies as key components of their artworks were New Yorker HANNAH WILKE (1940–1993; FIG. **30-37A**) and Cuban-born ANA MENDIETA (1948–1985; FIG. **30-38**), who left her native land as a child when Fidel Castro came to

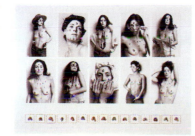

30-37A WILKE, *S.O.S.*, 1974-1982.

power. Although gender issues concerned Mendieta, her art also deals with issues of spirituality and cultural heritage. The artist's best-known series, *Silueta* (*Silhouettes*), consists of approximately 200 earth/body works completed between 1973 and 1980. These works represented Mendieta's attempt to carry on, as she described, "a dialogue between the landscape and the female body (based on my own silhouette)."[20]

Flowers on Body (FIG. 30-38) is a documentary photograph of the first of the earth/body sculptures in the *Silueta* series. In this work, Mendieta appears covered with flowers in an earthen, womb-like cavity. Executed at El Yagul, a Mexican archaeological site, the

work speaks to the issues of birth and death, the female experience of childbirth, and the human connection to the earth. Objects and locations from nature play an important role in Mendieta's art. She explained the centrality of this connection to nature:

> I believe this has been a direct result of my having been torn from my homeland during my adolescence. I am overwhelmed by the feeling of having been cast from the womb (nature). My art is the way I re-establish the bonds that unite me to the universe. It is a return to the maternal source. Through my earth/body sculptures I become one with the earth.[21]

Beyond their sensual, moving presence, Mendieta's works also generate a palpable spiritual force. In longing for her homeland, she sought the cultural understanding and acceptance of the spiritual powers inherent in nature that modern Western societies often seem to reject in favor of scientific and technological developments. Mendieta's art is lyrical and passionate and operates at the intersection of cultural, spiritual, physical, and feminist concerns.

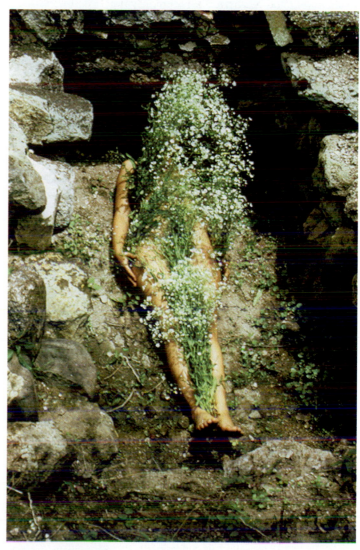

30-38 ANA MENDIETA, *Flowers on Body*, 1973. Color photograph of earth/body work with flowers, executed at El Yagul, Mexico. Courtesy of the Estate of Ana Mendieta and Galerie Lelong, New York.

In this earth/body sculpture, Mendieta appears covered with flowers in a womblike cavity to address issues of birth and death, as well as the human connection to the earth.

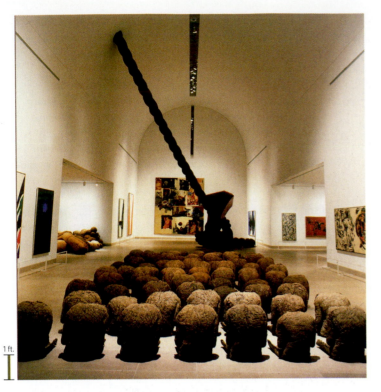

30-39 MAGDALENA ABAKANOWICZ, *80 Backs*, 1976–1980. Burlap and resin, each 2' 3" high. Museum of Modern Art, Dallas.

Polish fiber artist Abakanowicz explored the stoic, everyday toughness of the human spirit in this group of nearly identical sculptures that serve as symbols of distinctive individuals lost in the crowd.

MAGDALENA ABAKANOWICZ Not strictly feminist in subject, but created using materials traditionally associated with women, are the sculptures of Polish fiber artist MAGDALENA ABAKANOWICZ (b. 1930). A leader in the exploration of the expressive power of weaving techniques in large-scale artworks, Abakanowicz gained fame with experimental freestanding figural works expressing the stoic, everyday toughness of the human spirit. For Abakanowicz, fiber materials are deeply symbolic:

> I see fiber as the basic element constructing the organic world on our planet, as the greatest mystery of our environment. It is from fiber that all living organisms are built—the tissues of plants and ourselves. . . . Fabric is our covering and our attire. Made with our hands, it is a record of our souls.[22]

Abakanowicz's sculptures are to a great degree reflections of her early life experiences as a member of an aristocratic family disturbed by the dislocations of World War II and its aftermath. Initially attracted to weaving as a medium easily adaptable to the small studio space she had available,

Abakanowicz gradually developed huge abstract hangings that she called Abakans, which suggest organic spaces as well as giant pieces of clothing. She returned to a smaller scale with works based on human forms—*Heads, Seated Figures,* and *Backs*—multiplying each type for exhibition in groups as symbols for the individual in society lost in the crowd yet retaining some distinctiveness.

This impression is especially powerful in *80 Backs* (FIG. **30-39**). Abakanowicz made each piece by pressing layers of natural organic fibers into a plaster mold. Every sculpture depicts the slumping shoulders, back, and arms of a figure of indeterminate gender, and rests legless directly on the floor. The repeated pose of the figures in *80 Backs* suggests meditation, submission, and anticipation. Although made from a single mold, the figures achieve a touching sense of individuality because each assumed a slightly different posture as the material dried and because the artist imprinted a different pattern of fiber texture on each.

ARCHITECTURE AND SITE-SPECIFIC ART

Some of the most innovative architects of the first half of the 20th century, most notably Frank Lloyd Wright (FIGS. 29-45, 29-46, and 29-80), Ludwig Mies van der Rohe (FIG. 29-68), and Le Corbusier (FIG. 29-69), concluded their long and productive careers in the postwar period. At the same time, younger architects rose to international prominence, some working in the modernist idiom but others taking architectural design in new "postmodern" directions (see "After Modernism: Postmodernist Architecture," page 949, and "Robert Venturi and Postmodernist Complexity and Contradiction," page 982).

Modernism

In parallel with the progressive movement toward formal abstraction in painting and sculpture in the decades following World War II, modernist architects became increasingly concerned with a formalism stressing simplicity. They articulated this in buildings that retained intriguing organic sculptural qualities, as well as in buildings adhering to a more rigid geometry.

FRANK LLOYD WRIGHT The last great building that Frank Lloyd Wright designed was the Solomon R. Guggenheim Museum

30-40 FRANK LLOYD WRIGHT, Solomon R. Guggenheim Museum (looking southeast), New York, 1943–1959.

Using reinforced concrete almost as a sculptor might use resilient clay, Wright designed a snail shell–shaped museum with a winding, gently inclined interior ramp for the display of artworks.

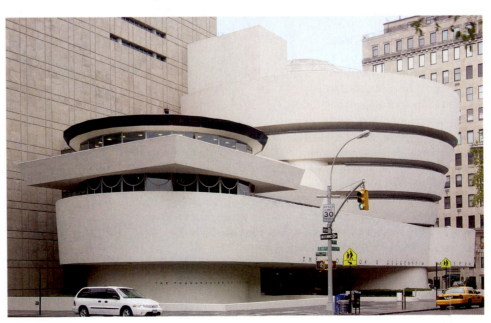

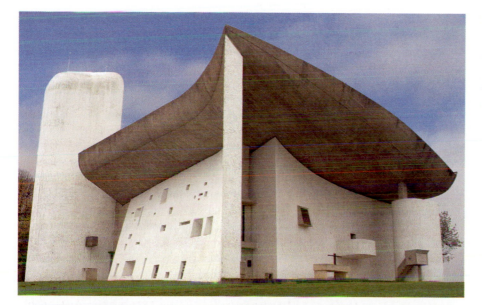

30-41 Le Corbusier, Notre-Dame-du-Haut (looking northwest), Ronchamp, France, 1950–1955.

The organic forms of Le Corbusier's mountaintop chapel present a fusion of architecture and sculpture. The architect based the shapes on praying hands, a dove's wings, and a ship's prow.

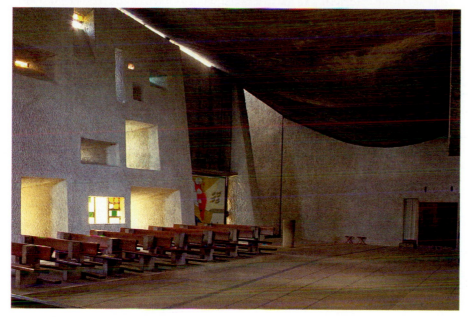

30-42 Le Corbusier, interior of Notre-Dame-du-Haut (looking southwest), Ronchamp, France, 1950–1955.

Constructed of concrete sprayed on a frame of steel and metal mesh, the heavy walls of the Ronchamp chapel enclose an intimate and mysteriously lit interior that has the aura of a sacred cave.

(FIG. 30-40) in New York City. Using reinforced concrete almost as a sculptor might use resilient clay, Wright, who often described his architecture as "organic" (see "Frank Lloyd Wright on Organic Architecture," page 917), designed a structure inspired by the spiral of a snail's shell. Wright had introduced curves and circles into some of his plans in the 1930s, and as the architectural historian Peter Blake noted, "The spiral was the next logical step; it is the circle brought into the third and fourth dimensions."[23] Inside the building (FIG. 31-34), the shape of the shell expands toward the top, and a winding interior ramp spirals to connect the gallery bays. A skylight strip embedded in the museum's outer wall provides illumination to the ramp, which visitors can stroll down at a leisurely pace after taking an elevator to the top of the building, viewing the artworks displayed along the gently sloping pathway. Thick walls and the solid organic shape give the building, outside and inside, the sense of turning in on itself, and the long interior viewing area opening onto a 90-foot central well of space creates a sheltered environment, secure from the bustling city outside.

LE CORBUSIER Compared with his pristine geometric design for Villa Savoye (FIG. 29-69), the organic forms of Le Corbusier's Notre-Dame-du-Haut (FIG. 30-41) come as a startling surprise. Completed

in 1955 at Ronchamp, France, the chapel attests to the boundless creativity of this great architect. A fusion of architecture and sculpture, the small chapel, which replaced a building destroyed in World War II, occupies a pilgrimage site in the Vosges Mountains. The monumental impression of Notre-Dame-du-Haut seen from afar is somewhat deceptive. Although one massive exterior wall (FIG. 30-41, *right*) contains a pulpit resembling a balcony that faces a spacious outdoor area for large-scale open-air services on holy days, the interior (FIG. 30-42) holds at most 200 people. The intimate scale, stark and heavy walls, and mysterious illumination (jewel tones cast from the deeply recessed stained-glass windows) give this space an aura reminiscent of a sacred cave or a medieval monastery.

Notre-Dame-du-Haut's structure may look free-form to the untrained eye, but Le Corbusier, like the designers of Romanesque and Gothic cathedrals, based it on an underlying mathematical system. The pilgrimage church has a frame of steel and metal mesh, which the builders sprayed with concrete (an engineering innovation pioneered in Italy by PIER LUIGI NERVI (1891–1979; FIG. 30-42A) and painted

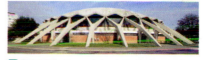

30-42A NERVI, Palazzetto dello Sport, 1958-1959.

white, except for two interior private chapel niches with colored walls and the roof, which Le Corbusier wished to have darken naturally with the passage of time. The roof appears to float freely above the worshipers in their pews (FIG. 30-42), intensifying the quality of mystery in the interior space. In reality, a series of nearly invisible blocks holds up the roof. The mystery of the roof's means of support recalls the reaction to Hagia Sophia's miraculously floating dome (FIG. 9-8) a millennium and a half before in Byzantium. Le Corbusier's preliminary sketches for the building indicate that he linked the design with the shape of praying hands, with the wings of a dove (representing both peace and the Holy Spirit), and with the prow of a ship (a reminder that the term for the central aisle in a traditional basilican church is *nave*—Latin for "ship"). Le Corbusier hoped that in the mystical interior he created and in the rolling hills around the church, men and women would reflect on the sacred and the natural. No one who has visited Notre-Dame-du-Haut, whether on a bright sunlit day or in a thundering storm, has come away unmoved.

EERO SAARINEN Dramatic, sweeping, curvilinear reinforced concrete rooflines are also characteristic features of the buildings de-

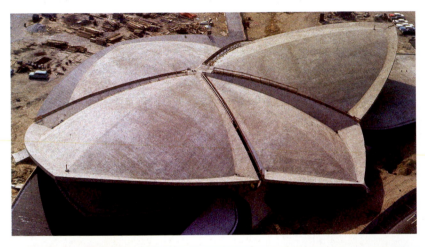

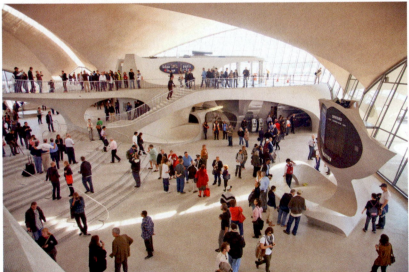

30-43 EERO SAARINEN, Terminal 5 (JetBlue Airways terminal, formerly the Trans World Airlines terminal), John F. Kennedy International Airport, New York, 1956–1962. *Top:* exterior looking southeast; *bottom:* interior.

Saarinen based his design on the theme of motion. The concrete-and-glass air terminal's dramatic, sweeping rooflines suggest expansive wings and flight. The interior features the same curvilinear vocabulary.

signed by Finnish-born architect EERO SAARINEN (1910–1961). One of his signature buildings of the late 1950s is the former Trans World Airlines terminal (now the JetBlue Airways terminal, FIG. 30-43, *top*) at New York's John F. Kennedy International Airport. The terminal, which Saarinen based on the theme of motion, consists of two immense concrete shells split down the middle and slightly rotated, giving the building a fluid curved outline that fits its corner site. The shells immediately suggest expansive wings and flight. Saarinen also designed every detail of the spacious, light-filled interior (FIG. 30-43, *bottom*), including the furniture, ventilation ducts, and signboards, with this same curvilinear vocabulary in mind. The design brilliantly combines symbolism, drama, and function.

JOERN UTZON Saarinen was responsible for selecting a kindred spirit, the Danish architect JOERN UTZON (1918–2008) to build the Sydney Opera House (FIG. 30-44) in Australia. Utzon's design is a bold composition of organic forms on a colossal scale. Utzon worked briefly with Frank Lloyd Wright at Taliesin (Wright's Wisconsin residence), and the style of the Sydney Opera House resonates distantly with the graceful curvature of New York's Guggenheim Museum. Clusters of immense concrete shells—the largest is 200 feet tall—rise from massive platforms and soar to delicate peaks. Recalling at first the *ogival* (pointed) shapes of Gothic vaults, the shells also suggest both the buoyancy of seabird wings and the billowing sails of the tall ships of the European settlers who emigrated to Australia in the 18th and 19th centuries. These architectural metaphors are appropriate to the harbor surrounding Bennelong Point, whose bedrock foundations support the building. Utzon's matching of the structure with its site and atmosphere adds to the organic nature of the design.

Although construction of the building began in 1959, completion of the opera house had to wait until 1972, primarily because Utzon's daring design required construction technology not yet developed. Today the opera house is Sydney's defining symbol, a monument of civic pride that functions as the city's cultural center. In addition to the opera auditorium, the complex houses auxiliary halls and rooms for concerts, the performing arts, motion pictures, lectures, art exhibitions, and conventions.

MIES VAN DER ROHE Sculpturesque building design was not the only manifestation of postwar modernist architecture. From the mid-1950s through the 1970s, other architects created massive, sleek, and geometrically rigid buildings. They designed most of these structures following Bauhaus architect Mies van der Rohe's contention that "less is more." Many of these more Minimalist designs are powerful, heroic presences in the urban landscape, effectively symbolizing the giant corporations that often were the skyscrapers' primary tenants.

The purest example of these corporate skyscrapers is the mid-1950s rectilinear glass-and-bronze Seagram Building (FIG. 30-45) in Manhattan, designed by Mies van der Rohe and American architect Philip Johnson (FIG. 30-48). By this time, the concrete-steel-and-glass towers pioneered by Louis Sullivan (FIGS. 28-42, 28-42A, and 28-43) and carried further by Mies van der Rohe himself (FIG. 29-68) had become a familiar sight in cities all over the world. Appealing in its structural logic and clarity, the style, easily imitated, quickly became the norm

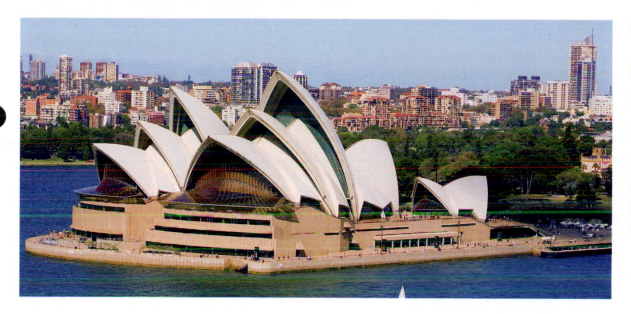

30-44 JOERN UTZON, Sydney Opera House (looking southeast), Sydney, Australia, 1959–1972.

The soaring clusters of concrete shells of Utzon's opera house on an immense platform in Sydney's harbor suggest both the buoyancy of seabird wings and the billowing sails of tall ships.

for postwar commercial high-rise buildings. The architects of the Seagram Building deliberately designed it as a thin shaft, leaving the front quarter of its midtown site as an open pedestrian plaza. The tower appears to rise from the pavement on stilts. Glass walls even surround the recessed lobby. The building's recessed structural elements make it appear to have a glass skin, interrupted only by the thin strips of bronze anchoring the windows. The bronze metal and the amber glass windows give the tower a richness found in few of its neighbors. Mies van der Rohe and Johnson carefully planned every detail of the Seagram Building, inside and out, to create an elegant whole. They even designed the interior and exterior lighting to make the edifice an impressive sight both day and night.

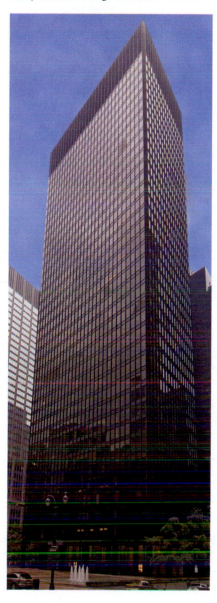

30-45 LUDWIG MIES VAN DER ROHE and PHILIP JOHNSON, Seagram Building (looking northeast), New York, 1956–1958.

Massive, sleek, and geometrically rigid, this modernist skyscraper has a bronze-and-glass skin masking its concrete-and-steel frame. The giant corporate tower appears to rise from the pavement on stilts.

SKIDMORE, OWINGS & MERRILL The architectural firm SKIDMORE, OWINGS & MERRILL (SOM), perhaps the purest proponent of Miesian-inspired structures, designed a number of these simple rectilinear glass-sheathed buildings, and SOM's success indicates the popularity of this building type. By 1970, the company comprised more than a thousand architects and had offices in New York, Chicago, San Francisco, Portland, and Washington, D.C. In 1974, the firm completed the Sears Tower (now Willis Tower; FIG. **30-46**), a mammoth corporate

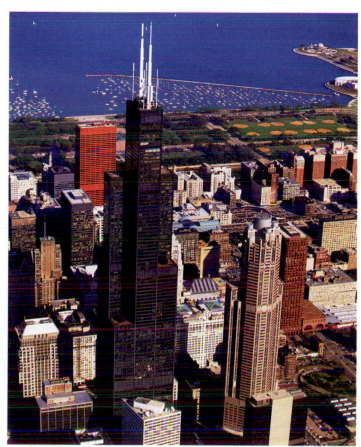

30-46 SKIDMORE, OWINGS & MERRILL, Willis Tower (formerly Sears Tower; looking east), Chicago, 1974.

Consisting of nine black aluminum and smoked glass shafts soaring to 110 stories, the Willis (Sears) Tower dominates Chicago's skyline. It was the world's tallest building at the time of its construction.

PROBLEMS AND SOLUTIONS
Robert Venturi and Postmodernist Complexity and Contradiction

The restrictiveness of modernist architecture and the impersonality and sterility of many modernist structures eventually led to a rejection of modernism's authority in architecture. But the question faced by architects dissatisfied with the modernist mode was what to put in its place. The answer was the diversity of solutions that architectural historians use the generic term *postmodernism* to describe. Postmodernist architecture is not a unified style. It is a widespread cultural phenomenon far more encompassing and accepting than the more rigid confines of modernist practice, which, critics believed, failed to respond to the unique character of the cities and neighborhoods in which modernist architects erected their buildings. In contrast to modernist architecture, which features simple shapes and little ornamentation, postmodern architecture is complex and eclectic. Whereas the modernist program was reductive, the postmodern vocabulary is expansive and inclusive.

Among the first to explore this new direction in architecture were Jane Jacobs (1916–2006) and ROBERT VENTURI (b. 1925). In their influential books *The Death and Life of Great American Cities* (Jacobs, 1961) and *Complexity and Contradiction in Architecture* (Venturi, 1966), Jacobs and Venturi argued that the uniformity and anonymity of modernist architecture (in particular, corporate skyscrapers, such as the Seagram Building [FIG. 30-45] and the Sears Tower [FIG. 30-46] that then domi-

nated many urban skylines) were unsuited to human social interaction. Jacobs and Venturi further maintained that diversity is the great advantage of urban life. Postmodern architects accepted, indeed embraced, the messy and chaotic nature of big-city life.

When designing these varied buildings, many postmodern architects consciously selected past architectural elements or references and juxtaposed them with contemporary elements or fashioned them of high-tech materials, thereby creating a dialogue between past and present, as Charles Moore did in Piazza d'Italia (FIG. 30-1). Postmodern architecture incorporates references not only to traditional architecture but also to mass culture and popular imagery. This was precisely the "complexity and contradiction" Venturi referred to in the title of his book and that he explored further in *Learning from Las Vegas* (1972), coauthored with Denise Scott Brown (b. 1931) and Steven Izenour (1940–2001).

An early example of Venturi's work is the house (FIG. 30-47) he designed in 1962 for his mother. A fundamental axiom of modernism is that a building's form must arise directly and logically from its function and structure. Against this rule, Venturi asserted that form should be separate from function and structure. Thus the Vanna Venturi house has an oversized gable roof that recalls classical temple design more than domestic architecture. However, the gable has a missing central section, which reveals the house's "chimney" (a penthouse suite). Moreover, Venturi inserted an arch motif over the doorway's lintel, and the placement of the windows violates the symmetry of both classical and modernist design.

30-47 ROBERT VENTURI, Vanna Venturi house, Chestnut Hill, Pennsylvania, 1962.

Venturi advocated complexity and contradiction in architectural design, in contrast to modernist simplicity and uniformity. An early example of the postmodern approach that he championed is his mother's house.

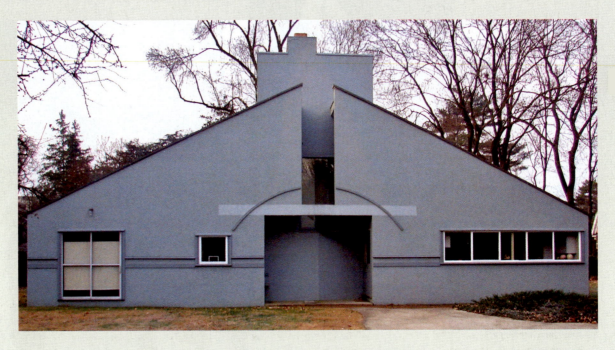

building in Chicago. Consisting of nine clustered shafts soaring vertically, this 110-floor building provides offices for more than 12,000 workers. Original plans called for 104 stories, but the architects acquiesced to Sears's insistence on making the building the tallest (measured to the structural top) in the world at the time. The tower's size, coupled with the black aluminum sheathing it and the smoked glass, establishes a dominant presence in a city of many corporate skyscrapers—exactly the image Sears executives wanted to project.

Postmodernism

Within a few years of the completion of the Seagram Building (FIG. 30-45) in the heart of New York City, some architects were already questioning the validity of the modernist approach to architectural design. Thus was born the diverse and complex style called *postmodernism* (see page 949 and "Robert Venturi and Postmodernist Complexity and Contradiction," above, and FIG. **30-47**).

ARTISTS ON ART
Philip Johnson on Postmodern Architecture

Philip Johnson, who died in 2005 at age 98, had a distinguished career spanning almost the entire 20th century, during which he transformed himself from a modernist closely associated with Mies van der Rohe (FIG. 30-45) into one of the leading postmodernists, whose AT&T (now Sony) Building (FIG. 30-48) in New York City remains an icon of 1970s postmodernism. In the following passages, Johnson commented on his early "Miesian" style and about the incorporation of various historical styles in postmodernist buildings.

> My eyes are set by the Miesian tradition . . . The continuity with my Miesian approach also shows through in my classicism. . . . [But in] 1952, about the same time that my whole generation did, I became very restless. . . . In the last decade there has been such a violent switch that it is almost embarrassing. But it isn't a switch, so much as a centrifugal splintering of architecture, to a degree that I don't think has been seen in the past few hundred years. Perfectly responsible architects build, even in one year, buildings that you cannot believe are done by the same person.*
>
> Structural honesty seems to me one of the bugaboos that we should free ourselves from very quickly. The Greeks with their marble columns imitating wood, and covering up the roofs inside! The Gothic designers with their wooden roofs above to protect their delicate vaulting. And Michelangelo, the greatest architect in history, with his Mannerist column! There is only one absolute today and this is change. There are no rules, surely no certainties in any of the arts. There is only the feeling of a wonderful freedom, of endless possibilities to investigate, of endless past years of historically great buildings to enjoy.†

*Quoted in Paul Heyer, *Architects on Architecture: New Directions in America* (New York: Van Nostrand Reinhold, 1993), 285–286.

†Ibid., 279.

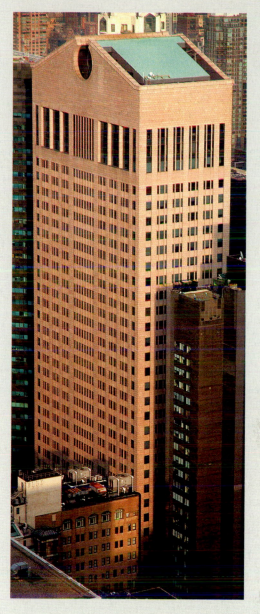

30-48 PHILIP JOHNSON and JOHN BURGEE (with SIMMONS ARCHITECTS), Sony Building (formerly AT&T Building; looking northeast), New York, 1978–1984.

In a startling shift of style, modernist Johnson (FIG. 30-45) designed this postmodern skyscraper with more granite than glass and with a variation on a classical pediment as the crowning motif.

PHILIP JOHNSON Even architects instrumental in the proliferation of the modernist idiom embraced postmodernism. Early in his career, PHILIP JOHNSON (1906–2005), for example, had been a leading proponent of modernism and worked with Mies van der Rohe on the design of the Seagram Building (FIG. 30-45). Johnson even served as director of the Department of Architecture at New York's Museum of Modern Art, the bastion of modernism, in 1930–1934 and 1946–1954. Yet he made one of the most startling shifts of style in 20th-century architecture, eventually moving away from the severe geometric formalism exemplified by the Seagram Building to a classical transformation of it in his AT&T (American Telephone and Telegraph) Building—now the Sony Building (FIG. **30-48**)—in New York City. Architect JOHN BURGEE (b. 1933) codesigned the Manhattan skyscraper with assistance from the firm SIMMONS ARCHITECTS. This structure was influential in turning architectural taste and practice away from modernism and toward postmodernism—from organic "concrete sculpture" and the rigid "glass box" to elaborate shapes, motifs, and silhouettes freely adapted from his-

torical styles (see "Philip Johnson on Postmodernist Architecture," above).

The 660-foot-high slab of the former AT&T Building is mostly granite. Johnson reduced the window space to some 30 percent of the structure, in contrast to modernist glass-sheathed skyscrapers. His design of its exterior elevation is classically tripartite, having an arcaded base and arched portal; a tall, shaftlike body segmented by slender *mullions* (vertical elements dividing a window); and a crowning pediment broken by an *orbiculum* (a disclike opening). The arrangement refers to the base, column, and entablature system of classical architecture (FIG. 5-13). More specifically, the pediment, indented by the circular space, resembles the crown of a typical 18th-century Chippendale high chest of drawers. It rises among the monotonously flat-topped glass towers of the New York skyline as an ironic rebuke to the rigid uniformity of modernist architecture.

MICHAEL GRAVES Philip Johnson at first endorsed, then disapproved of, a building that rode considerably farther on the wave

hoods on one pair of opposite facades and a frieze of stylized Baroque roundels tied by bands on the other pair. A huge painted keystone motif joins five upper levels on one facade pair, and painted surfaces further define the building's base, body, and penthouse levels.

The modernist purist surely would not welcome the ornamental wall, color painting, or symbolic references. These features, taken together, raised an even greater storm of criticism than greeted the Sydney Opera House or the AT&T Building. Various critics denounced Graves's Portland Building as "an enlarged jukebox," an "oversized Christmas package," a "marzipan monstrosity," a "histrionic masquerade," and a kind of "pop surrealism." Yet others approvingly noted its classical references as constituting a "symbolic temple" and praised the building as a courageous architectural adventure. Whatever history's verdict will be, the Portland Building, like the AT&T tower, is an early marker of postmodernist innovation that borrowed from the lively, if more-or-less garish, language of pop culture. The night-lit dazzle of entertainment sites such as Las Vegas, and the carnival colors, costumes, and fantasy of theme-park props all lie behind the Portland Building design, which many critics regard as a vindication of architectural populism against the pretension of modernist elitism.

ROGERS AND PIANO During their short-lived partnership, British architect RICHARD ROGERS (b. 1933) and Italian architect RENZO PIANO (b. 1937) used motifs and techniques from ordinary industrial buildings in their design for the Georges Pompidou National Center of Art and Culture in Paris (FIG. 30-50). The architects fully exposed the anatomy of this six-level building, which is a kind of updated version of the Crystal Palace (FIG. 27-47), and made its "metabolism" visible. They color-coded pipes, ducts, tubes, and corridors according to function (red for the movement of people, green for water, blue for air-conditioning, and yellow for electricity), much as in a sophisticated factory.

Critics who deplore the building's industrial qualities disparagingly refer to the complex as a "cultural supermarket" and point out that its exposed entrails require excessive maintenance to protect them from the elements. Nevertheless, the Pompidou Center has

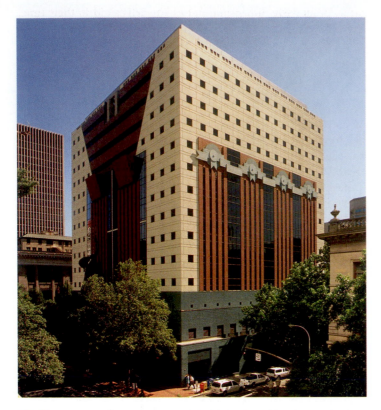

30-49 MICHAEL GRAVES, Portland Building (looking northeast), Portland, 1980.

In this early example of postmodern architecture, Graves reasserted the horizontality and solidity of the wall. He drew attention to the wall surfaces through polychromy and ornamental motifs.

of postmodernism than did his AT&T tower. The Portland Building (FIG. 30-49) by Indianapolis-born architect MICHAEL GRAVES (b. 1934) reasserts the wall's horizontality against the verticality of the tall, window-filled shaft. Graves favored the square's solidity and stability, making it the main body of his composition (echoed in the windows), which rests on a wider base and carries a set-back penthouse crown. Narrow vertical windows tying together seven stories open two paired facades. These support capital-like large

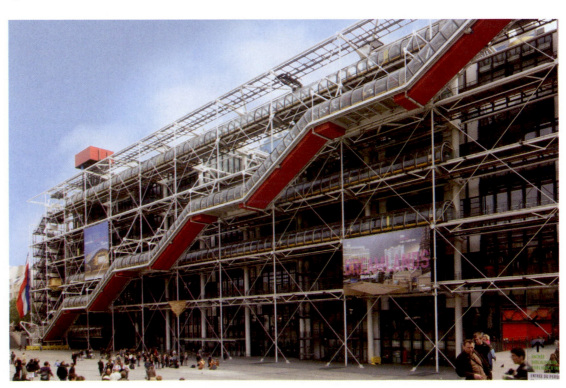

30-50 RICHARD ROGERS and RENZO PIANO, Centre Georges Pompidou (the "Beaubourg," looking northeast), Paris, France, 1977.

The architects fully exposed the anatomy of this six-level building, as in the century-earlier Crystal Palace (FIG. 27-47), and color-coded the internal parts according to function, as in a factory.

been immensely popular with visitors since it opened. The flexible interior spaces and the colorful structural body provide a festive environment for the crowds flowing through the building and enjoying its art galleries, industrial design center, library, science and music centers, conference rooms, research and archival facilities, movie theaters, rest areas, and restaurant (which looks down and through the building to the terraces outside), as well as dramatic panoramas of Paris from its terrace. The sloping plaza in front of the main entrance has become part of the local scene. Peddlers, street performers, Parisians, and tourists fill this square at almost all hours of the day and night. The kind of secular activity that once occurred in the open spaces in front of cathedral entrances now takes place next to a center for culture and popular entertainment.

Environmental and Site-Specific Art

One of the most exciting developments in postwar art and architecture has been *Environmental Art,* sometimes called *earthworks.* Environmental Art stands at the intersection of architecture and sculpture. It emerged as a major form of artistic expression in the 1960s and includes a wide range of artworks, most of which are *site-specific* (created for a unique location) and in the open air. Many artists associated with the Environmental Art movement also used natural or organic materials, including the land itself. It is no coincidence that this art form developed during a period of increased concern for the environment. The ecology movement of the 1960s and 1970s aimed to publicize and combat escalating pollution, depletion of natural resources, and the dangers of toxic waste. The problems of public aesthetics (for example, litter, urban sprawl, and compromised scenic areas) were also at issue. Widespread concern in the United States about the environment led to the passage of the National Environmental Policy Act in 1969 and the creation of the federal Environmental Protection Agency. Environmental artists used their art to call attention to the landscape and, in so doing, were part of this national dialogue.

As an innovative artistic genre challenging traditional assumptions about art making, Environmental Art clearly has an avant-garde, progressive dimension. But as Pop artists did in their time, Environmental artists insist on moving art out of the rarefied atmosphere of museums and galleries and into the public sphere. Most encourage spectator interaction with their works. Ironically, the remote locations of many earthworks have limited public access to them.

ROBERT SMITHSON One of the pioneering Environmental artists was New Jersey–born ROBERT SMITHSON (1938–1973), who used industrial construction equipment to manipulate vast quantities of earth and rock on isolated sites. Smithson's best-known project is *Spiral Jetty* (FIG. **30-51**), a mammoth 1,500-foot-long coil of black basalt, limestone rocks, and earth extending out into Utah's Great Salt Lake. As he was driving by the lake one day, Smithson came across some abandoned mining equipment, left there by a company that had tried and failed to extract oil from the site. Smithson saw this as a testament to the enduring power of nature and the inability of humans to conquer it. He decided to create an artwork in the lake that ultimately became a monumental spiral curving out from the shoreline and running 1,500 feet into the water. Smithson insisted on designing his work in response to the location itself. He wanted to avoid the arrogance of an artist merely imposing an unrelated concept on the site. The spiral idea grew from Smithson's first impression of the location. Then, while researching Great Salt Lake, Smithson discovered that the molecular structure of the salt crystals coating the rocks at the water's edge is spiral in form.

> As I looked at the site, it reverberated out to the horizons only to suggest an immobile cyclone while flickering light made the entire landscape appear to quake. A dormant earthquake spread into the fluttering stillness, into a spinning sensation without movement. The site was a rotary that enclosed itself in an immense roundness. From that gyrating space emerged the possibility of the Spiral Jetty.[24]

Smithson not only recorded *Spiral Jetty* in photographs, but also filmed its construction in a movie describing the forms and life of the whole site. The photographs and film have become increasingly important, because fluctuations in Great Salt Lake's water level often place *Spiral Jetty* underwater. Smithson tragically died at age 35 in a plane crash while surveying a site for a new earthwork at Amarillo, Texas.

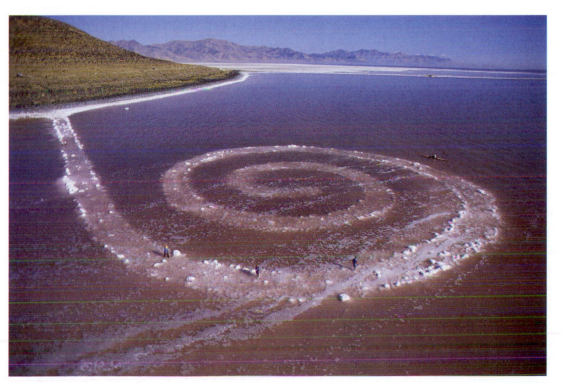

30-51 ROBERT SMITHSON, *Spiral Jetty* (looking northeast), Great Salt Lake, Utah, 1970. Art © Estate of Robert Smithson/ Licensed by VAGA, New York, NY.

Smithson used industrial equipment to create Environmental artworks by manipulating earth and rock. *Spiral Jetty* is a mammoth coil of black basalt, limestone, and earth extending into Great Salt Lake.

PERFORMANCE AND CONCEPTUAL ART AND NEW MEDIA

Environmental Art, although a singular artistic phenomenon, typifies postwar developments in the art world in redefining the nature of an "artwork" and expanding the range of works that artists and the general public consider "art." Some of the new types of artworks are the result of the invention of new media, such as computers and video cameras. But the new art forms also reflect avant-garde artists' continued questioning of the status quo.

Performance Art

An important new artistic genre that emerged in the decades following World War II was *Performance Art*. Performance artists replace traditional stationary artworks with movements, gestures, and sounds performed before an audience, whose members may or may not participate in the performance. The informal and spontaneous events that early Performance artists staged anticipated the rebellion and youthful exuberance of the 1960s and at first pushed art outside the confines of the mainstream art institutions—museums and galleries. Performance Art also served as an antidote to the pretentiousness of most traditional art objects and challenged art's function as a commodity. In the later 1960s, however, museums began to commission performances with increasing frequency, thereby neutralizing much of the subversiveness characteristic of this new art form. Unfortunately, because the earliest Performance artists created their works before the widespread availability of inexpensive handheld video cameras, the only records of their performances are the documentary photographs taken during the events. Photographs are unsatisfying, if invaluable, records because they lack the elements of sound and motion integral to Performance Art.

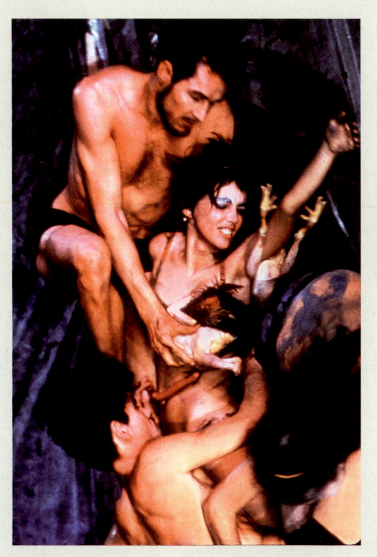

30-52 Carolee Schneemann, *Meat Joy* (performance at Judson Church, New York City), 1964.

In her performances, Schneemann transformed the nature of Performance Art by introducing a feminist dimension through the use of her body (often nude) to challenge traditional gender roles.

ARTISTS ON ART
Carolee Schneemann on Painting, Performance Art, and Art History

Born in Pennsylvania, Carolee Schneemann (FIG. 30-52) studied painting at Bard College and the University of Illinois before settling in New York City in 1962, where she became one of the pioneering Performance artists of the 1960s. In notes she wrote in 1962–1963, Schneemann reflected on the nature of art production and contrasted her kinetic works with more traditional art forms.

> Environments, happenings—concretions—are an extension of my painting-constructions which often have moving (motorized) sections. . . . [But the] steady exploration and repeated viewing which the eye is required to make with my painting-constructions is reversed in the performance situation where the spectator is overwhelmed with changing recognitions, carried emotionally by a flux of evocative actions and led or held by the specified time sequence which marks the duration of a performance. In this way the audience is actually *visually* more *passive* than when confronting a . . . "still" work . . . With paintings, constructions and sculptures the viewers are able to carry out repeated examinations of the work, to select and vary viewing positions (to walk with the eye), to touch surfaces and to freely indulge responses to areas of color and texture at their chosen speed.*

Readers of this book will also take special interest in Schneemann's 1975 essay titled "Woman in the Year 2000," in which she envisioned what introductory art history courses would be like at the beginning of the 21st century:

> By the year 2000 [every] young woman will study Art Istory [sic] courses enriched by the inclusion, discovery, and re-evaluation of works by women artists: works (and lives) until recently buried away, willfully destroyed, [or] ignored.†

A comparison between this 15th edition of *Art through the Ages* and editions published in the 1960s and 1970s will immediately reveal the accuracy of Schneemann's prediction.

*Quoted in Bruce McPherson, ed., *More Than Meat Joy: Complete Performance Works and Selected Writings* (New Paltz, N.Y.: Documentext, 1979), 10–11.
†Ibid., 198.

JOHN CAGE Many of the artists instrumental in the development of Performance Art were students or associates of the charismatic American teacher and composer John Cage (1912–1992). Cage encouraged his students at both the New School for Social Research in New York and Black Mountain College in North Carolina to link their art directly with life. He brought to music composition some of the ideas of Duchamp and of Eastern philosophy. Cage used methods such as chance to avoid the closed structures marking traditional music and, in his view, separating it from the unpredictable and multilayered qualities of daily existence. For example, the score for one of Cage's piano compositions instructs the performer to appear, sit down at the piano, raise the keyboard cover to mark the beginning of the piece, remain motionless at the instrument for 4 minutes and 33 seconds, and then close the keyboard cover, rise, and bow to signal the end of the work. The "music" would be the unplanned sounds and noises (such as coughs and whispers) emanating from the audience during the "performance."

ALLAN KAPROW One of Cage's students in the 1950s was ALLAN KAPROW (1927–2006). Schooled in art history as well as music composition, Kaprow sought to explore the intersection of art and life. He believed, for example, that Jackson Pollock's actions when producing a painting (FIG. 30-7) were more important than the finished painting. This led Kaprow to develop a type of event known as a *Happening*. He described a Happening as

> an assemblage of events performed or perceived in more than one time and place. Its material environments may be constructed, taken over directly from what is available, or altered slightly: just as its activities may be invented or commonplace. A Happening, unlike a stage play, may occur at a supermarket, driving along a highway, under a pile of rags, and in a friend's kitchen, either at once or sequentially. If sequentially, time may extend to more than a year. The Happening is performed according to plan but without rehearsal, audience, or repetition. It is art but seems closer to life.[25]

Happenings were often participatory. One Happening consisted of a constructed setting with partitions on which viewers wrote phrases, while another involved spectators walking on a pile of tires. One of Kaprow's first Happenings, titled *18 Happenings in Six Parts*, took place in 1959 in the Reuben Gallery in New York City. For the event, he divided the gallery space into three sections with translucent plastic sheets. Over the course of the 90-minute piece, performers, including Kaprow's artist friends, bounced balls, read from placards, extended their arms like wings, and played records as slides and lights switched on and off in programmed sequences.

FLUXUS Other Cage students interested in the composer's search to find aesthetic potential in the nontraditional and commonplace formed the *Fluxus* group. Eventually expanding to include European and Japanese artists, this group's performances were more theatrical than Happenings. To distinguish their performances from Happenings, the artists associated with Fluxus coined the term *Events* to describe their work. Events focused on single actions, such as turning a light on and off or watching falling snow—what Fluxus artist La Monte Young (b. 1935) called "the theater of the single event."[26] Events usually took place on a stage separating the performers from the audience but without costumes or added decor. Events were not spontaneous. They followed a compositional "score," which, given the restricted nature of these performances, was short.

CAROLEE SCHNEEMANN Some artists, notably CAROLEE SCHNEEMANN (b. 1939) in the United States and members of the Concrete Art Association (FIG. 34-19) in Japan, produced artworks integrating painting and performance (see "Carolee Schneemann on Painting, Performance Art, and Art History," page 986). Schneemann's self-described "kinetic theater" radically transformed the nature of Performance Art by introducing a feminist dimension through the use of her body (often nude) to challenge "the psychic territorial power lines by which women were admitted to the Art Stud Club."[27] In her 1964 performance, *Meat Joy* (FIG. 30-52), which was designed to be both erotic and revolting, Schneemann cavorted with male performers and reveled in the taste, smell, and feel of raw sausages, chickens, and fish.

JOSEPH BEUYS The leftist politics of the Fluxus group in the early 1960s strongly influenced German artist JOSEPH BEUYS (1921–1986; FIG. 30-53). Drawing on Happenings and Fluxus, Beuys created actions aimed at illuminating the condition of modern humanity.

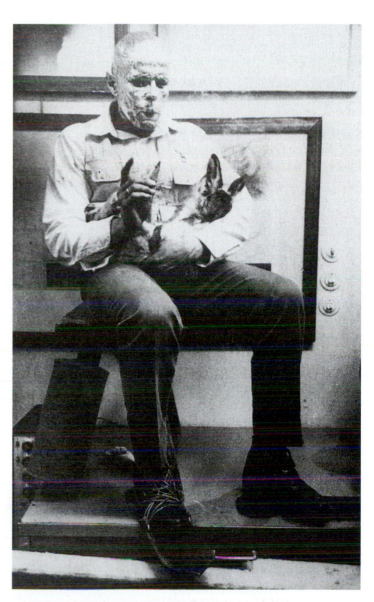

30-53 JOSEPH BEUYS, *How to Explain Pictures to a Dead Hare* (performance at Schmela Gallery, Düsseldorf), 1965.

In this one-person event, Beuys coated his head with honey and gold leaf and spoke to a dead hare. Assuming the role of a shaman, he used stylized actions to evoke a sense of mystery and sacred ritual.

He wanted to make a new kind of sculptural object that would include "Thinking Forms: how we mold our thoughts or Spoken Forms: how we shape our thoughts into words or Social Sculpture: how we mold and shape the world in which we live."[28]

Beuys's commitment to artworks stimulating thought about art and life derived in part from his experiences as a pilot during World War II. After the enemy shot down his plane over Crimea, nomadic Tatars nursed him back to health by swaddling his body in fat and felt to warm him. Fat and felt thus symbolized healing and regeneration to Beuys, and he incorporated these materials into many of his sculptures and actions, such as *How to Explain Pictures to a Dead Hare* (FIG. 30-53), in which the seated Beuys rests his left foot on soft felt and, to make a contrast with the often cold and unyielding contemporary world, rests his right foot on steel. In this one-person event, Beuys performed stylized actions evoking a sense of mystery and sacred ritual. He appeared in a room hung with his drawings, cradling a dead hare to which he spoke softly. Beuys coated his head with honey covered with gold leaf, creating a shimmering mask. In this manner, he took on the role of the shaman, an individual with special spiritual powers. As a shaman, Beuys believed he was acting to help revolutionize human thought so that each human being could become a truly free and creative person. But the impossibility of communicating with a dead hare symbolized the difficulty of achieving successful exchanges among alienated people in modern society.

JEAN TINGUELY The paradoxical notion of destruction as an act of creation surfaces in a number of kinetic artworks, most notably in the sculpture of JEAN TINGUELY (1925–1991). Trained as a painter in his native Switzerland, Tinguely gravitated to motion sculpture. In the 1950s, he made a series of motor-driven devices that he called *metamatics,* which produced instant abstract paintings. He programmed these metamatics electronically to act with an antimechanical unpredictability when someone inserted a felt-tipped marking pen into a pincer and pressed a button to initiate the pen's motion across a small sheet of paper clipped to an "easel." Participants in his metamatic demonstrations could use different-colored markers in succession and could stop and start the device to achieve some degree of control over the final image. These operations created a series of small works resembling Abstract Expressionist paintings.

In 1960, Tinguely expanded the scale of his work with a kinetic piece designed to "perform" and then destroy itself in the sculpture garden of the Museum of Modern Art in New York City. He created *Homage to New York* (FIG. **30-54**) with the aid of engineer Billy Klüver (1927–2004), who helped him scrounge wheels and other moving objects from a dump near Manhattan. The completed structure, painted white for visibility against the dark night sky, included a player piano modified into a metamatic painting machine, a weather balloon that inflated during the performance, vials of colored smoke, and a host of gears, pulleys, wheels, and other found machine parts.

Homage to New York premiered (and instantly self-destructed) on March 17, 1960, with the state's governor, Nelson Rockefeller (1908–1979), an array of other distinguished guests, and three television crews in attendance. Once Tinguely turned on the machine, smoke poured from its interior and the piano caught fire. Various

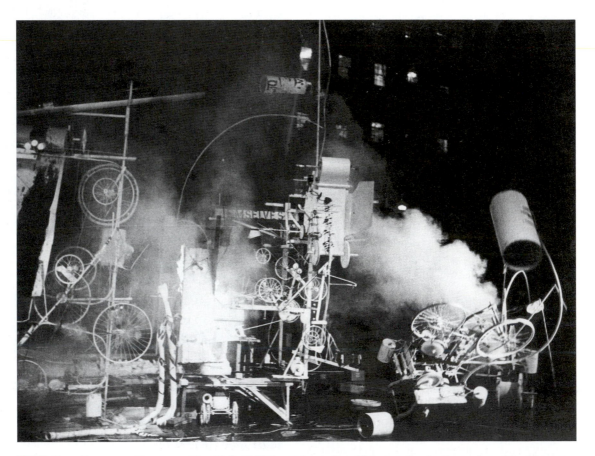

30-54 JEAN TINGUELY, *Homage to New York,* 1960, just prior to its self-destruction in the garden of the Museum of Modern Art, New York.

Tinguely produced motor-driven devices programmed to make instant abstract paintings. To explore the notion of destruction as an act of creation, he designed this one to perform and then destroy itself.

PROBLEMS AND SOLUTIONS
Rethinking "Art": Conceptual Art

In many ways, the most radical of avant-garde art movements of the postwar era was Conceptual Art, which reconsidered the very definition of what "art" is. Conceptual artists maintained that the "art-fulness" of art lay in the artist's idea, rather than in its final expression. These artists regarded the idea, or concept, as the defining component of the artwork. Indeed, in their effort to solve the problem of creating artworks that are ideas instead of tangible objects, some Conceptual artists do not create new objects at all.

One of the leading Conceptual artists and theorists was Joseph Kosuth. Born in Toledo, Ohio, and educated at the School of Visual Arts in New York City, Kosuth summarized the intellectual transformation that he and other Conceptual artists had to undergo in their effort to rethink everything they had been taught about art.

> Like everyone else I inherited the idea of art as a set of *formal* problems. So when I began to re-think my ideas of art, I had to re-think that thinking process . . . [T]he radical shift, was in changing the idea of art itself. . . . It meant you could have an art work which was that *idea* of an art work, and its formal components weren't important. I felt I had found a way to make art without formal components being confused for an expressionist composition. The expression was in the idea, not the form—the forms were only a device in the service of the idea.*

Kosuth's work operates at the intersection of language and vision, dealing with the relationship between the abstract and the concrete. For example, in *One and Three Chairs* (FIG. 30-55), Kosuth juxtaposed a real chair, a full-scale photograph of the same chair, and an enlarged reproduction of a dictionary definition of the word "chair." By so doing, the Conceptual artist asked viewers to ponder the notion of what constitutes "chairness."

Other Conceptual artists pursued the notion that the idea itself is a work of art by creating works involving invisible materials, such as inert gases, radioactive isotopes, or radio waves. In each case, viewers must base their understanding of the artwork on what they know about the properties of these materials, rather than on any visible empirical data, and must depend on the artist's linguistic description of the work. Ultimately, the Conceptual artists challenged the very premises of artistic production, pushing art's boundaries to a point where no concrete definition of art is possible.

*"Joseph Kosuth: Art as Idea as Idea," in Jeanne Siegel, ed., *Artwords: Discourse on the 60s and 70s* (Ann Arbor, Mich.: UMI Research Press, 1985), 221, 225.

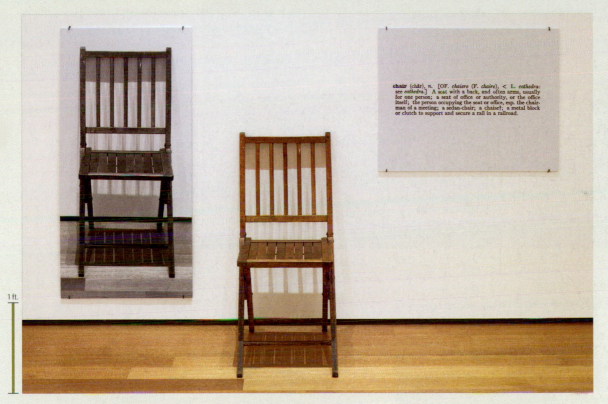

1 ft.

30-55 JOSEPH KOSUTH, *One and Three Chairs,* 1965. Wood folding chair, photographic copy of a chair, and photographic enlargement of a dictionary definition of a chair; chair, 2' 8$\frac{3}{8}$" × 1' 2$\frac{7}{8}$" × 1' 8$\frac{7}{8}$"; photo panel, 3' × 2' $\frac{1}{8}$"; text panel, 2' × 2' $\frac{1}{8}$". Museum of Modern Art, New York (Larry Aldrich Foundation Fund).

Conceptual artists regard the concept as an artwork's defining component. To portray "chairness," Kosuth juxtaposed a chair, a photograph of the chair, and a dictionary definition of "chair."

parts of the machine broke off and rambled away, while one of the metamatics tried but failed to produce an abstract painting. Finally, Tinguely summoned a firefighter to extinguish the blaze and ensure the demise of his artwork-machine with an ax. Like Tinguely's other kinetic sculptures, *Homage to New York* recalls the satiric Dadaist spirit and the droll import of Klee's *Twittering Machine* (FIG. 29-59). But Tinguely deliberately made the wacky behavior of *Homage to New York* more playful and more endearing. Having been given a freedom of eccentric behavior unprecedented in the mechanical world, Tinguely's creations often seemed to behave with the whimsical individuality of human actors.

Conceptual Art

The relentless challenges to artistic convention fundamental to the historical avant-garde reached a logical conclusion with *Conceptual Art* in the mid-1960s and the work of JOSEPH KOSUTH (b. 1945; FIG. 30-55) and others (see "Rethinking 'Art': Conceptual Art," above).

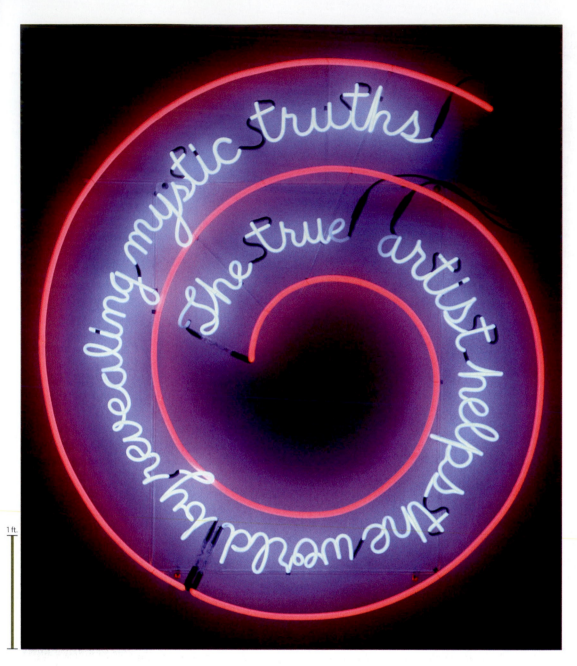

30-56 BRUCE NAUMAN, *The True Artist Helps the World by Revealing Mystic Truths*, 1967. Neon with glass tubing suspension frame, 4' 11" high. Private collection.

In his art, Nauman explores his interest in language and wordplay. He described this Conceptual neon sculpture's emphatic assertion as "a totally silly idea," but an idea he believed.

the foundation of much of his art, and in his interest in language and wordplay.

The True Artist Helps the World by Revealing Mystic Truths (FIG. 30-56) was the first of Nauman's many neon sculptures. Nauman selected neon, which Charles Moore also employed to great effect in his postmodern Piazza d'Italia (FIG. 30-1), because he wanted to find a medium that would be identified with a nonartistic function. Determined to discover a way to connect objects with words, he drew on the method outlined in *Philosophical Investigations,* in which the Austrian philosopher Ludwig Wittgenstein (1889–1951) encouraged contradictory and nonsensical arguments. Nauman's neon sculpture spins out an emphatic assertion, which is also the work's title, but as

BRUCE NAUMAN About the time that Kosuth made *One and Three Chairs* (FIG. 30-55), his slightly older contemporary, Indiana native BRUCE NAUMAN (b. 1941), made his artistic presence known in California when he abandoned painting and turned to object-making. Since then, his work, produced since 1979 in New Mexico, has been extremely varied. In addition to sculptural pieces constructed from different materials, including neon lights (FIG. 30-56), rubber, fiberglass, and cardboard, he has also produced photographs (FIG. 30-56A), films, videos, books, and large room installations, as well as Performance Art. Nauman's work of the 1960s intersected with that of the Conceptual artists, especially in terms of the philosophical exploration that was

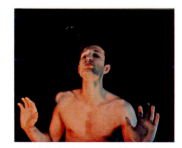

30-56A NAUMAN, *Self-Portrait as Fountain*, 1966–1967.

Nauman explained, "[The statement] was kind of a test—like when you say something out loud to see if you believe it. . . . [I]t was on the one hand a totally silly idea and yet, on the other hand, I believed it."[29]

New Media

During the 1960s and 1970s, many avant-garde artists eagerly embraced technologies previously unavailable in their attempt to find new avenues of artistic expression. Among the most popular new media were video recording and computer graphics.

VIDEO Initially, only commercial television studios possessed video equipment, but in the 1960s, with the development of relatively inexpensive portable video recorders and of electronic devices allowing manipulation of recorded video material, artists began to explore in earnest the expressive possibilities of this new technology. In its basic form, video recording involves a special motion-picture

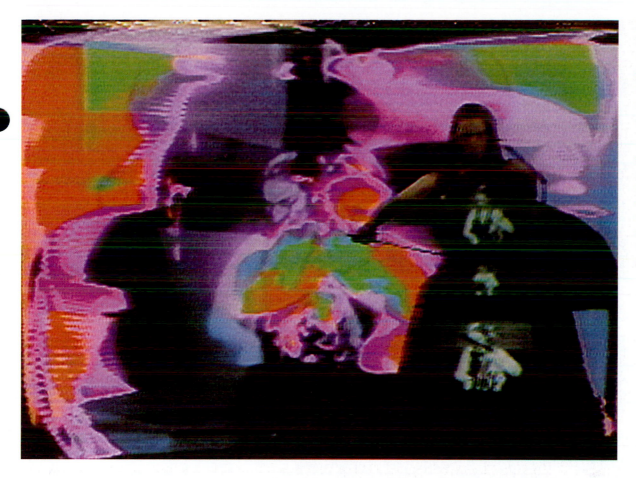

30-57 Nam June
Paik, video still from
Global Groove, 1973.
$\frac{3}{4}''$ videotape, color,
sound, 30 minutes.
Collection of the
artist.

Korean-born video
artist Paik's best-known
work is a cascade of
fragmented sequences
of performances and
commercials intended
as a sample of the rich
worldwide television
menu of the future.

camera that captures visible images and translates them into electronic data for display on a video monitor or television screen. Video pictures resemble photographs in the amount of detail they contain, but, like computer graphics, a video image consists of a series of points of light on a grid, giving the impression of soft focus. Viewers looking at television or video art are not aware of the monitor's surface. Instead, fulfilling the ideal of Renaissance artists, they concentrate on the image and look through the glass surface, as through a window, into the "space" beyond. Video images combine the optical realism of photography with the sense that the subjects move in real time in a deep space "inside" the monitor.

NAM JUNE PAIK When video introduced the possibility of manipulating subjects in real time, artists such as Korean-born NAM JUNE PAIK (1932–2006) were eager to work with the medium. After studying music performance, art history, and Eastern philosophy in Korea and Japan, Paik worked with electronic music in Germany in the late 1950s. In 1965, after relocating to New York City, Paik acquired the first inexpensive video recorder sold in Manhattan (the Sony Porta-Pak) and immediately recorded everything he saw out the window of his taxi on the return trip to his studio downtown. Experience acquired as artist-in-residence at television stations WGBH in Boston and WNET in New York enabled him to experiment with the most advanced broadcast video technology.

A grant permitted Paik to collaborate with the gifted Japanese engineer-inventor Shuya Abe (b. 1932) in developing a video synthesizer. This instrument enables artists to manipulate and change the electronic video information in various ways, causing images or parts of images to stretch, shrink, change color, or break up. With the synthesizer, artists can also layer images, inset one image into

another, or merge images from various cameras with those from video recorders to make a single visual kaleidoscopic "time-collage." This kind of compositional freedom enabled Paik to combine his interests in painting, music, Eastern philosophy, global politics for survival, humanized technology, and cybernetics. Inspired by the ideas of John Cage, Paik called his video works "physical music" and said his musical background enabled him to understand time better than could video artists trained in painting or sculpture.

Paik's best-known video work, *Global Groove* (FIG. **30-57**), was commissioned for broadcast over the United Nations satellite. The video combines in quick succession fragmented sequences of female tap dancers, poet Allen Ginsberg (1926–1997) reading his work, a performance by Fluxus artist and cellist Charlotte Moorman (1933–1991) using a man's back as her instrument, Pepsi commercials from Japanese television, Korean drummers, and a shot of the Living Theatre group performing a controversial piece called *Paradise Now*. The cascade of imagery in *Global Groove* gives viewers a glimpse of the rich worldwide television menu that Paik predicted would be available in the future—a prediction that has been fulfilled with the advent of affordable cable and satellite television service.

COMPUTER GRAPHICS Perhaps the most promising new medium for creating and manipulating illusionistic three-dimensional forms is computer graphics. This new medium uses light to make images and, like photography, can incorporate specially recorded camera images. Unlike video recording, computer graphic art enables artists to work with wholly invented forms, as painters can. Developed during the 1960s and 1970s, this technology opened up new possibilities for both abstract and figural art. It involves electronic programs dividing the surface of the computer monitor's

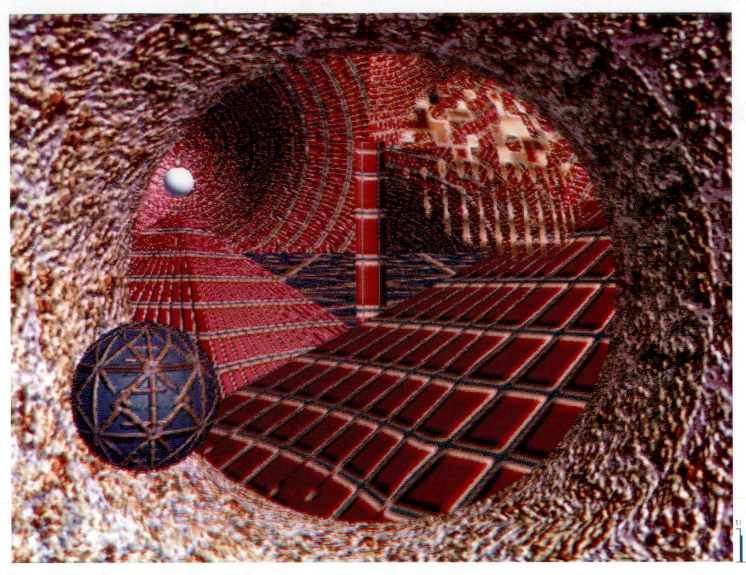

30-58 DAVID EM, *Nora*, 1979. Computer-generated color photograph, 1' 5" × 1' 11". Private collection.

Unlike video recording, computer graphic art enables the creation of wholly invented forms, as in painting. Em builds fantastic digital images of imaginary landscapes out of tiny boxes called pixels.

cathode-ray tube into a grid of tiny boxes called "picture elements," or *pixels*. Artists can electronically address pixels individually to create a design, much as knitting or weaving patterns have a grid matrix as a guide for making a design in fabric. Once created, parts of a computer graphic design can be changed quickly through an electronic program, enabling artists to revise or duplicate shapes in the design and to manipulate at will the color, texture, size, number, and position of any desired detail. Computer graphic pictures appear in luminous color on the cathode-ray tube. The effect suggests a view into a vast world existing inside the tube.

DAVID EM One of the pioneering artists working in this electronic painting mode, DAVID EM (b. 1952) uses what he terms "computer imaging" to fashion fantastic imaginary landscapes. These have an eerily believable existence within the "window" of the computer monitor. When he was artist-in-residence at the California Institute of Technology's Jet Propulsion Laboratory, Em created brilliantly colored scenes of alien worlds using the laboratory's advanced computer graphics equipment. He also had access to software programs

developed to create computer graphic simulations of NASA's missions in outer space. Creating images with the computer afforded Em great flexibility in manipulating simple geometric shapes—shrinking or enlarging them, stretching or reversing them, repeating them, adding texture to their surfaces, and creating the illusion of light and shadow. In images such as *Nora* (FIG. **30-58**), Em created futuristic geometric versions of Surrealistic dreamscapes whose forms seem familiar and strange at the same time. The illusion of space in these works is immensely vivid and seductive. It almost seems possible to wander through the tubelike foreground "frame" and up the inclined foreground plane or to hop aboard the hovering globe at the lower left for a journey through the strange patterns and textures of this mysterious labyrinthine setting.

AFTER 1980 The decades following the conclusion of World War II were unparalleled in art history for innovation in form and content and for the development of new media. Those exciting trends have continued unabated since 1980—and with an increasingly international dimension that will be explored in Chapter 31.

MODERNISM AND POSTMODERNISM IN EUROPE AND AMERICA, 1945 TO 1980

Painting, Sculpture, and Photography

- The art of the decades following World War II reflects cultural upheaval—the rejection of traditional values, the civil rights and feminist movements, and the new consumer society.

- The first major postwar avant-garde art movement was Abstract Expressionism, which championed an artwork's formal elements rather than its subject. Gestural abstractionists, such as Pollock, de Kooning, Krasner, and Mitchell, sought expressiveness through energetically applied pigment. Chromatic abstractionists, such as Rothko, struck emotional chords through large areas of pure color.

- Post-Painterly Abstraction promoted a cool rationality in contrast to Abstract Expressionism's passion. Both hard-edge painters, such as Kelly and Stella, and color-field painters, such as Frankenthaler and Louis, pursued purity in art by emphasizing the flatness of pigment on canvas.

- Pop artists, such as Johns, Lichtenstein, and Warhol, rejected abstraction to represent subjects grounded in popular culture—flags, comic strips, Coca-Cola bottles—sometimes employing commercial printing techniques. Rosenquist incorporated social and political commentary into his billboard-size paintings.

- Riley and other Op artists sought to produce optical illusions of motion and depth using only geometric forms on two-dimensional surfaces.

- Superrealists, such as Flack, Close, and Hanson—kindred spirits to Pop artists in many ways—created paintings and sculptures featuring scrupulous fidelity to optical fact.

- The leading sculptural movement of this period was Minimalism. Tony Smith and Judd created artworks consisting of simple and unadorned geometric shapes to underscore the "objecthood" of their sculptures.

- Arbus and White represent the two poles of photography in the postwar period—documentary photography and art photography.

- Many artists pursued social agendas in their work. Postwar feminist artists include Chicago, whose *Dinner Party* honors important women throughout history and features crafts traditionally associated with women; Sherman, who explored the "male gaze" in her photographs resembling film stills; and Mendieta and Wilke, whose bodies were their subjects.

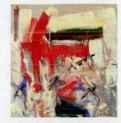

Mitchell, *Untitled*, ca. 1953–1954

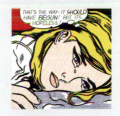

Lichtenstein, *Hopeless*, 1963

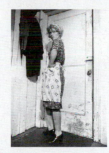

Sherman, *Untitled Film Still #35*, 1979

Architecture and Site-Specific Art

- Some of the leading early-20th-century modernist architects remained active after 1945. Wright built the snail-shell Guggenheim Museum, Le Corbusier the sculpturesque Notre-Dame-du-Haut, and Mies van der Rohe the Minimalist Seagram skyscraper. Younger architects Saarinen and Utzon designed structures with dramatic curvilinear rooflines.

- In contrast to modernist architecture, postmodernist architecture is complex and eclectic and often incorporates references to historical styles. Among the best-known postmodern projects are Moore's Piazza d'Italia and Graves's Portland Building, both of which incorporate classical motifs.

- Site-specific art stands at the intersection of architecture and sculpture. Smithson's *Spiral Jetty* is a mammoth coil of natural materials in Utah's Great Salt Lake.

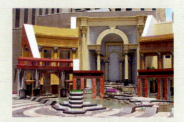

Moore, Piazza d'Italia, New Orleans, 1976–1980

Performance and Conceptual Art and New Media

- Among the most significant developments in the art world after World War II has been the expansion of the range of works considered "art."

- Performance artists, notably Schneemann and Beuys, replace traditional stationary artworks with movements and sounds performed before an audience. Performance Art often addresses the same social and political issues that contemporaneous painters and sculptors explore.

- Kosuth and other Conceptual artists believe that the "artfulness" of art is in the artist's idea, not the work resulting from the idea.

- Paik and others have embraced video recording technology to produce artworks combining images and sounds.

- Em was a pioneer in exploring computer graphics as an art form. Unlike video recording, computer art enables artists to work with wholly invented forms, as painters can.

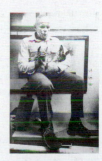

Beuys, *How to Explain Pictures to a Dead Hare*, 1965

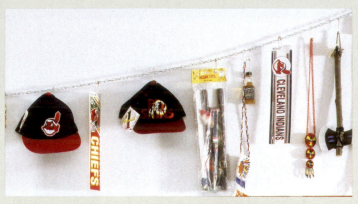

▲ **31-1a** Smith's *Trade* celebrates her Native American identity. The cheap trinkets she offers in return for confiscated land include sports team memorabilia with offensive names, such as Braves and Redskins.

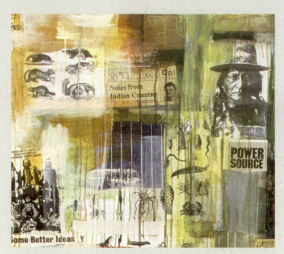

▲ **31-1b** Newspaper clippings chronicle the conquest of Native America by Europeans and include references to the problems facing those living on reservations today—poverty, alcoholism, and disease.

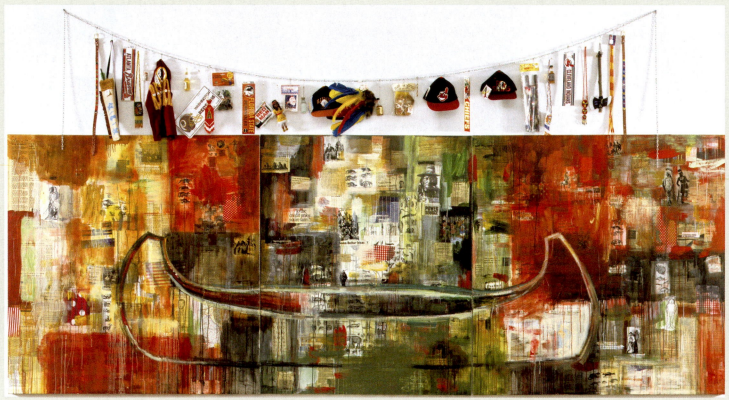

1 ft.

31-1   JAUNE QUICK-TO-SEE SMITH, *Trade (Gifts for Trading Land with White People)*, 1992. Oil and mixed media on canvas, 5' × 14' 2". Chrysler Museum of Art, Norfolk.

▶ **31-1c** Overlapping the collage and the central motif of the canoe in Smith's anti–Columbus Quincentenary Celebration is dripping red paint, symbolic of the shedding of Native American blood.

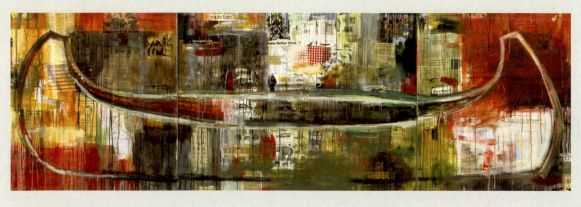

Contemporary Art Worldwide

ART AS SOCIOPOLITICAL MESSAGE

Although televisions, smartphones, and the Internet have brought people all over the world closer together than ever before in history, national, ethnic, religious, and racial conflicts are also an unfortunate and pervasive characteristic of contemporary life. Some of the most eloquent voices raised in protest about the major political and social issues of the day have been those of painters and sculptors, who can harness the power of art to amplify the power of the written and spoken word.

JAUNE QUICK-TO-SEE SMITH (b. 1940) is a Native American artist descended from the Shoshone, Salish, and Cree peoples. Raised on the Flatrock Reservation in Montana, she is steeped in the traditional culture of her ancestors, but she trained as an artist in the European American tradition at Framingham State University in Massachusetts and at the University of New Mexico. Smith's ethnic heritage has always informed her art, however, and her concern about the invisibility of Native American artists has led her to organize exhibitions of their art. Her self-identity has also been the central theme of her mature work as an artist.

In 1992, Smith created what many critics consider her masterpiece: *Trade* (FIG. 31-1), subtitled *Gifts for Trading Land with White People*. A complex multimedia work of imposing size, *Trade* is Smith's response to what she called "the Quincentenary Non-Celebration"—that is, white America's celebration of the 500th anniversary of Christopher Columbus's arrival in what Europeans called the New World. *Trade* incorporates collage elements and attached objects, reminiscent of a Rauschenberg *combine* (FIG. 30-25), with energetic brushwork recalling Willem de Kooning's Abstract Expressionist canvases (FIG. 30-8). Among the items in *Trade*'s collage are clippings from Native American newspapers featuring images chronicling the conquest of Native America by Europeans and references to the problems facing those living on reservations today—poverty, alcoholism, and disease. The dripping red paint overlaying the collage with the central motif of the canoe is symbolic of the shedding of Native American blood.

Above the painting, as if hung from a clothesline, is an array of objects. These include Native American artifacts, such as beaded belts and feather headdresses, plastic tomahawks, "Indian princess" dolls, and contemporary sports memorabilia from teams with American Indian–derived names: the Cleveland Indians, Atlanta Braves, and Washington Redskins. The inclusion of these objects reminds viewers of the vocal opposition to the use of these and similar names for high school and college as well as professional sports teams. All the cheap artifacts together also have a deeper significance. As the title indicates and Smith explained: "Why won't you consider trading the land we handed over to you for these silly trinkets that so honor us? Sound like a bad deal? Well, that's the deal you gave us."[1]

ART TODAY

This is an "incomplete" or "unfinished" chapter, because the story of the art of the present generation—that is, the history of the art and architecture of the past 35 to 40 years—is still unfolding, and the body of material to be surveyed is increasing literally daily. It is both impractical and unwise to try to impose a strict chronological development scheme on the extraordinarily diverse range of paintings, sculptures, photographs and videos, buildings and monuments, and multimedia works produced worldwide since 1980. Instead, this survey of contemporary art is organized thematically and stylistically and, to a lesser degree, by medium, under the following headings: Personal and Group Identity; Political and Social Commentary; Representation and Abstraction; New Media; Environmental and Site-Specific Art; and Architecture. It is important to note, however, that most contemporary artworks fall into more than one of these categories. For example, a painting that explores personal and group identity, such as Jaune Quick-to-See Smith's *Trade* (FIG. 31-1), can also be a work of social commentary and combine representation and abstraction and several different media. Nevertheless, these six categories constitute a useful way to approach the complex phenomenon of contemporary art and architecture.

PERSONAL AND GROUP IDENTITY

Trade is the unique product of Smith's heritage as a Native American who has sought to bridge native and European artistic traditions, but her work parallels that of many other innovative artists of the decades since 1980 in addressing contemporary life. This focus on the content and meaning of art represents, as did the earlier work of the Pop artists and Superrealists (see pages 965–973), a rejection of modernist formalist doctrine and a desire on the part of artists once again to embrace the persuasive power of art to communicate with a wide audience—an audience that, thanks to smartphones, the Internet, and other technological breakthroughs, is now instantly international in character. It also represents in many respects a return to the core principle of the 19th-century Realists, as defined by Gustave Courbet (see page 816): "[A]rt in painting should consist only of the representation of things that are visible and tangible to the artist. Every age should be represented only by its own artists, that is to say, by the artists who have lived in it."[2]

The multicultural diversity of the world today has made almost everybody keenly aware of her or his distinct national, ethnic, racial, and religious identity. Not surprisingly, many contemporary artists have made their personal and group identity the focus of their work.

African American Art

Prominent among those for whom race has been a key element of the art that they have produced during the past few decades are African Americans. This is a very significant development in the history of art because outside Africa, Africans and people of African descent have rarely been the subject of artworks produced by European and American artists except in marginal and often demeaning

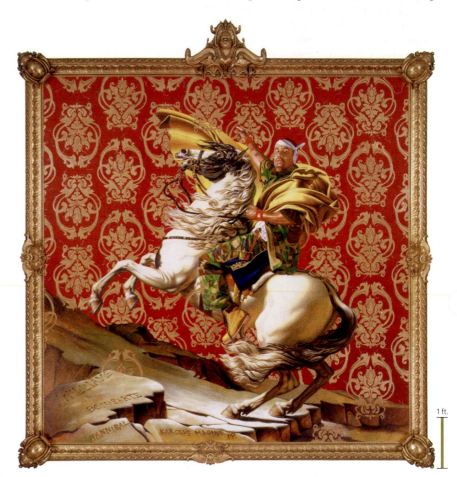

1 ft.

31-2 KEHINDE WILEY, *Napoleon Leading the Army over the Alps*, 2005. Oil on canvas, 9' × 9'. Brooklyn Museum, Brooklyn (Collection of Suzi and Andrew B. Cohen).

Wiley's trademark paintings are reworkings of famous portraits (FIG. 27-2A) in which he substitutes young African American men in contemporary dress in order to situate them in "the field of power."

roles. Black artists have also been omitted from most histories of Western art until recently.

KEHINDE WILEY One leading living African American artist who has lamented the near-total absence of blacks in Western painting and sculpture—and who has set out to correct that discriminatory imbalance—is Los Angeles native KEHINDE WILEY (b. 1977). Wiley earned his BFA at the San Francisco Art Institute and his MFA at Yale University and is currently based in New York City, where he was artist-in-residence at the Studio Museum in Harlem in 2001–2002. Wiley has achieved renown for his large-scale portraits of young urban African American men. His trademark paintings, however, are reworkings of historically important portraits in which he substitutes figures of young black men in contemporary dress in order to situate them in what he calls "the field of power."

A characteristic example is *Napoleon Leading the Army over the Alps* (FIG. **31-2**) based on Jacques-Louis David's painting (FIG. 27-2A) of the same subject. To evoke the era of the original, Wiley presented his portrait of an African American Napoleon on horseback in a gilt wood frame. Although in many details an accurate reproduction of David's canvas, Wiley's version is by no means a mechanical copy. His heroic narrative unfolds against a vibrantly colored ornate wallpaper-like background instead of a dramatic sky—a distinctly modernist reminder to the viewer that this is a painting and not a window onto an Alpine landscape.

JEAN-MICHEL BASQUIAT Among other contemporary artists whose work has focused on the experiences of American men of African descent are MELVIN EDWARDS (b. 1937; FIG. **31-2A**) and JEAN-MICHEL BASQUIAT (1960–1988), whose father was an accoun-

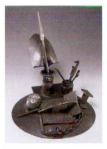

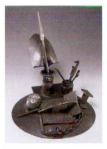

31-2A EDWARDS, *Tambo*, 1993.

tant from Haiti and whose mother was a black Puerto Rican. Basquiat grew up in a comfortable middle-class home in Brooklyn, but he rebelled against his parents' values, dropped out of school at 17, and took to the streets. He first burst onto the New York art scene as the anonymous author of witty graffiti in Lower Manhattan signed SAMO (a dual reference to the derogatory name *Sambo* for African Americans and to "same old shit"). Basquiat first drew attention as an artist in 1980 when he participated in a group show—the "Times Square Show"—in an abandoned 42nd Street building. Eight years later, after a meteoric rise to fame, he died of a heroin overdose at age 27.

Basquiat was self-taught, both as an artist and about the history of art, but he was not a "primitive." His sophisticated style owes a debt to diverse sources, including the late paintings of Pablo Picasso, Abstract Expressionism, and the "art brut" of Jean Dubuffet (FIG. 30-4). Many of Basquiat's paintings celebrate black heroes—for example, the legendary jazz musicians Charlie "Bird" Parker and Dizzy Gillespie, whom he memorialized in *Horn Players* (FIG. **31-3**). The fractured figures, the bold colors against a black background, and the deliberately scrawled, crossed-out, and misspelled graffiti

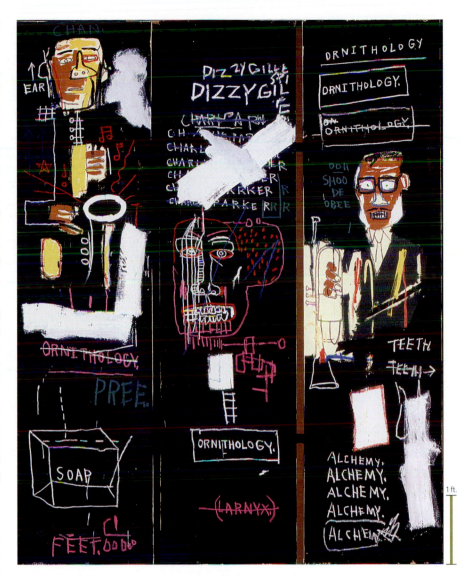

31-3 JEAN-MICHEL BASQUIAT, *Horn Players*, 1983. Acrylic and oil paintstick on three canvas panels, 8' × 6' 3". Broad Art Foundation, Santa Monica.

In this tribute to two legendary African American musicians, Basquiat combined bold colors, fractured figures, and graffiti to capture the dynamic rhythms of jazz and the excitement of New York.

("ornithology"—the study of birds—is a pun on Parker's nickname and also the title of one of Parker's musical compositions) create a dynamic composition suggesting the rhythms of jazz music and the excitement of the streets of New York, "the city that never sleeps."

FAITH RINGGOLD Just as Wiley, Basquiat, and Edwards have examined the lives of African American men in their art, several leading contemporary black women artists have made the challenges faced by African American women the subject of their artworks. One of them is Harlem native FAITH RINGGOLD (b. 1930), who studied painting at the City College of New York and taught art in the New York public schools for 18 years. In the 1960s, Ringgold produced numerous works that provided incisive commentary on the realities of racial prejudice. She increasingly incorporated references to gender as well and, in the 1970s, turned to fabric as the predominant material in her art. Using fabric enabled Ringgold to make more pointed reference to the domestic sphere, traditionally associated with women, and to collaborate with her mother, Willi Posey, a fashion designer.

After her mother's death in 1981, Ringgold created *Who's Afraid of Aunt Jemima?* (FIG. **31-4**), a quilt composed of dyed, painted, and pieced fabric. A moving tribute to her mother, this "story quilt"—Ringgold's signature art form—merges the personal and the political. Combining words with pictures, as did Basquiat (FIG. 31-3) and many other contemporary artists (FIGS. 31-6 and 31-8), Ringgold incorporates a narrative in her quilt. *Aunt Jemima* tells the witty story of the family of the stereotypical black "mammy" in the mind of the public, but here Jemima is a successful African American businesswoman. Ringgold narrates the story using black dialect interspersed with embroidered portraits and traditional patterned squares. *Aunt Jemima*, while incorporating autobiographical references, also speaks to the larger issues of the history of African American culture and the struggles of women to overcome oppression.

CARRIE MAE WEEMS Among the other contemporary feminist artists who have addressed the racial and social issues of concern to African American women are LORNA SIMPSON (b. 1960; FIG. **31-4A**) and CARRIE MAE WEEMS (b. 1953), both of whom have chosen photography as their favored medium of expression. Oregon-born Weems trained at the California Institute of the Arts in Valencia and the University of California, San Diego, and now lives in Syracuse, New York. Her critically acclaimed work as a photographer and video artist includes the *Kitchen Table* series of 20 photographs interwoven with 13 text panels and audio recordings examining the domestic life of an African American family. The *Kitchen Table* pictorial, verbal, and audio narratives resonate with a much broader audience, however.

The setting of each photo is a kitchen table, with the viewer positioned at one end and Weems seated at the other. A ceiling fixture resembling a lamp in an interrogation cell illuminates the small room. In *Man Smoking/Malcolm X* (FIG. **31-5**), Weems and a man smoking a cigarette play cards while consuming alcohol. Weems stares at her companion, attempting not only to determine the cards he holds but to size up the man's character. Behind her on the wall is a large photograph of Malcolm X (1925–1965) preaching, flanked

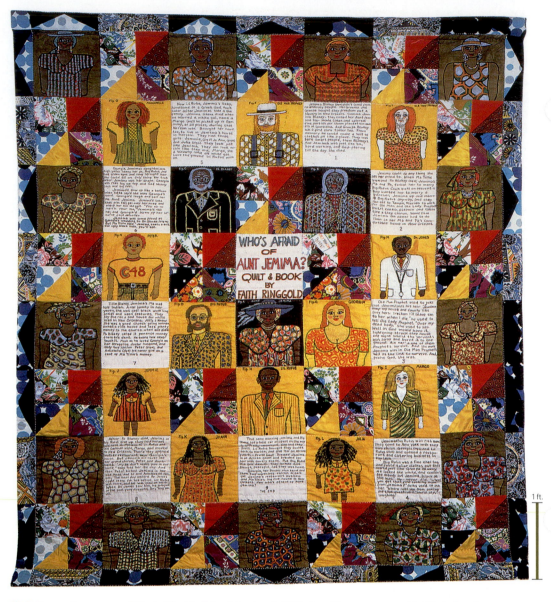

31-4 FAITH RINGGOLD, *Who's Afraid of Aunt Jemima?* 1983. Acrylic on canvas with fabric borders, quilted, 7' 6" × 6' 8". Private collection.

In this quilt, a medium associated with women, Ringgold presented a tribute to her mother that also addresses African American culture and the struggles of women to overcome oppression.

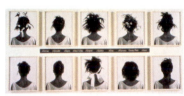

31-4A SIMPSON, *Stereo Styles*, 1988.

by smaller personal photographs revealing Weems's own character. Like the other 19 images in the *Kitchen Table* series, this photograph tells a universal story about personal relationships in addition to capturing a characteristic moment in one African American household (compare FIG. 27-38). As Weems explained,

> I'm not simply describing African-American culture. I'm really involved with other levels of description that move across several different kinds of categories. On the one hand, I might be interested in what's happening in gender with men and women, black and white and Asian, and maybe I'm interested in questions of globalism and class.[3]

Gender and Sexuality

The interest in feminist issues among African American women artists is but one aspect of a more general concern among contemporary artists of all races and nationalities with gender and sexuality

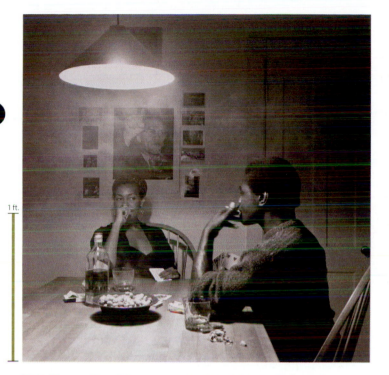

31-5 CARRIE MAE WEEMS, *Man Smoking/Malcolm X*, from the *Kitchen Table* series, 1990. Gelatin silver print, 2' 4$\frac{1}{4}$" × 2' 4$\frac{1}{4}$". Brooklyn Museum, Brooklyn (Caroline A.L. Pratt Fund).

Weems appears in each of the photographs in her *Kitchen Table* series, which records the domestic life of an African American family, but the issues addressed resonate with a much wider audience.

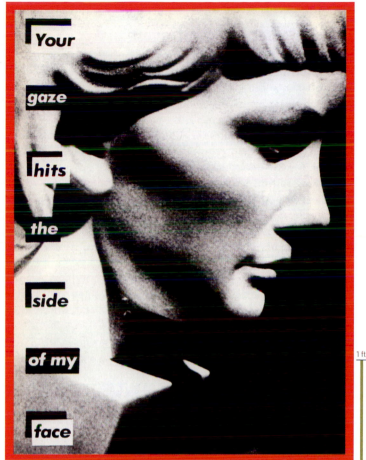

31-6 BARBARA KRUGER, *Your Gaze Hits the Side of My Face*, 1981. Photograph, red painted frame, 4' 7" × 3' 5". © Barbara Kruger/ Courtesy Mary Boone Gallery, New York.

Kruger has explored the "male gaze" in her art. Using the layout techniques of mass media, she constructed this word-and-photograph collage to challenge culturally constructed notions of gender.

as core elements of their personal identity. Feminism and homosexuality are the central themes explored by a diverse group of artists, including Barbara Kruger, Robert Mapplethorpe, and David Wojnarowicz in America and the Pakistani artist Shahzia Sikander.

BARBARA KRUGER In the 1970s, some feminist artists, chief among them Cindy Sherman (FIG. 30-37), used their art to explore the "male gaze" and the culturally constructed notion of gender. BARBARA KRUGER (b. 1945), who studied at Syracuse University and then at the Parsons School of Design in New York under Diane Arbus, examines similar issues in her photographs. The strategies and techniques of contemporary mass media have fascinated Kruger, who was a commercial graphic designer early in her career and the art director of *Mademoiselle* magazine in the late 1960s. In *Your Gaze Hits the Side of My Face* (FIG. 31-6), Kruger incorporated the layout techniques that magazine and billboard designers use to sell consumer goods. Although she chose the reassuringly familiar format and look of advertising for *Your Gaze* and similar works, Kruger's goal was to subvert the typical use of advertising imagery. She aimed to expose the deceptiveness of the media messages that viewers complacently absorb. Kruger wants to undermine the myths—particularly those about women—that the media constantly reinforce. Her large (often 4-by-6-foot) word-and-photograph collages challenge the cultural attitudes embedded in commercial advertising. She often uses T-shirts, postcards, matchbooks, and billboards to present her work to a wide public audience.

In *Your Gaze*, Kruger overlaid a photograph of a classically beautiful sculpted head of a woman (compare FIG. 5-62A) with a vertical row of text composed of eight words. The words cannot be taken in with a single glance. Reading them is a staccato exercise,

with an overlaid cumulative quality that delays understanding and intensifies the meaning (rather like a series of words painted on the pavement to be read by a driver in a moving car). Kruger's use of text in her work is significant. Many cultural theorists have asserted that language is one of the most powerful vehicles for internalizing stereotypes and conditioned roles. The combined pictorial and verbal message in this case is that the woman being viewed not only feels the viewer's gaze but can repel it, reversing the power relationship between the male observer and the observed woman. In fact, some feminist artists, most notably the GUERRILLA GIRLS (FIG. 31-6A), have created powerful artworks consisting only of words—presented in a style and format reminiscent of the same kinds of magazine ads that Kruger incorporates in her photo-collages.

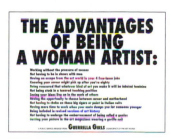

31-6A GUERRILLA GIRLS, *Advantages of Being a Woman Artist*, 1988.

ROBERT MAPPLETHORPE For many artists, their homosexuality is as important an element of their personal identity as their gender, ethnicity, or race—often more important. One brilliant

ART AND SOCIETY

Public Funding of Controversial Art

Although art can be beautiful and uplifting, throughout history art has also often challenged and offended. Since the early 1980s, a number of heated controversies about art have surfaced in the United States. There have been many calls to remove "offensive" works from public view (see "Richard Serra's *Tilted Arc*," page 1022) and, in reaction, accusations of censorship. The central questions in all cases have been whether there are limits to what art can appropriately be exhibited and whether governmental authorities have the right to monitor and pass judgment on creative endeavors. A related question is whether the acceptability of a work should be a criterion in determining the public funding of art.

Two exhibits in 1989 placed the National Endowment for the Arts (NEA), a U.S. government agency charged with distributing federal funds to support the arts, squarely in the middle of this debate. One of the exhibitions, devoted to recipients of the Awards for the Visual Arts (AVA), took place at the Southeastern Center for Contemporary Art in North Carolina. Among the award winners was Andres Serrano, whose *Piss Christ*, a photograph of a crucifix submerged in urine, sparked an uproar. Responding to this artwork, Reverend Donald Wildmon, an evangelical minister from Mississippi and head of the American Family Association, expressed outrage that this kind of work was in an exhibition funded by the NEA and the Equitable Life Assurance Society (a sponsor of the AVA). He demanded that the work be removed, and launched a letter-writing campaign that caused Equitable Life to cancel its sponsorship of the awards. To Wildmon and other staunch conservatives, this exhibition, along with *Robert Mapplethorpe: The Perfect Moment*, which included erotic homosexual images of the artist (FIG. 31-7) and others, served as evidence of cultural depravity and immorality. These critics insisted that art of an offensive character should not be funded by government agencies such as the NEA.

As a result of media furor over *The Perfect Moment*, the director of the Corcoran Museum of Art in Washington, D.C., decided to cancel the scheduled exhibition of this traveling show. But Dennis Barrie, director of the Contemporary Arts Center in Cincinnati, chose to mount the exhibition. The government indicted Barrie on charges of obscenity, but a jury acquitted him six months later.

These controversies intensified public criticism of the NEA and its funding practices. The next year, the head of the NEA, John Frohnmayer, vetoed grants for four lesbian, gay, or feminist performance artists—Karen Finley, John Fleck, Holly Hughes, and Tim Miller—who became known as the "NEA Four." Infuriated by what they perceived as governmental censorship, the artists filed suit, eventually settling the case and winning reinstatement of their grants. Congress responded by dramatically reducing the NEA's budget, and the agency no longer awards grants or fellowships to individual artists.

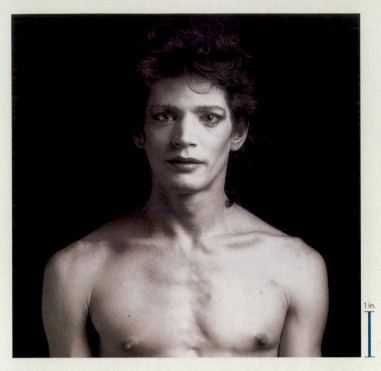

31-7 ROBERT MAPPLETHORPE, *Self-Portrait*, 1980. Gelatin silver print, $7\frac{3}{4}'' \times 7\frac{3}{4}''$. Robert Mapplethorpe Foundation, New York.

Mapplethorpe's *Perfect Moment* show led to a landmark court case on freedom of expression for artists. In this self-portrait, an androgynous Mapplethorpe confronts the viewer with a steady gaze.

Controversies have also erupted on the municipal level. In 1999, Rudolph Giuliani, then mayor of New York, joined a number of individuals and groups protesting the inclusion of several artworks in the exhibition *Sensation: Young British Artists from the Saatchi Collection* at the Brooklyn Museum. Chris Ofili's *The Holy Virgin Mary* (FIG. 31-10), a collage of Mary incorporating cutouts from pornographic magazines and shellacked clumps of elephant dung, became the flashpoint for public furor. Denouncing the show as "sick stuff," the mayor threatened to cut off all city subsidies to the museum.

Art that seeks to unsettle and challenge is critical to the cultural, political, and psychological life of a society. The regularity with which this kind of art raises controversy suggests that it operates at the intersection of two competing principles: free speech and artistic expression on the one hand, and a reluctance to impose images on an audience that finds them repugnant or offensive on the other. What these controversies do demonstrate, beyond doubt, is the enduring power of art—and artists.

---

gay artist who became the central figure in a heated debate in the halls of the U.S. Congress as well as among the public at large was ROBERT MAPPLETHORPE (1946–1989). Born in Queens, New York, Mapplethorpe studied drawing, painting, and sculpture at the Pratt Institute in Brooklyn, but after he purchased a Polaroid camera in 1970, he became increasingly interested in photography. Mapplethorpe's *The Perfect Moment* traveling exhibition, funded in part by the National Endowment for the Arts, featured an extensive series

of his photographs, including many of people, often nude, some depicting children, some openly homoerotic and sadomasochistic in nature. The show led to a landmark court case in Cincinnati on freedom of expression for artists and prompted new legislation establishing restrictions on government funding of the arts (see "Public Funding of Controversial Art," above).

Never at issue was Mapplethorpe's technical mastery of the photographic medium. His gelatin silver prints have glowing tex-

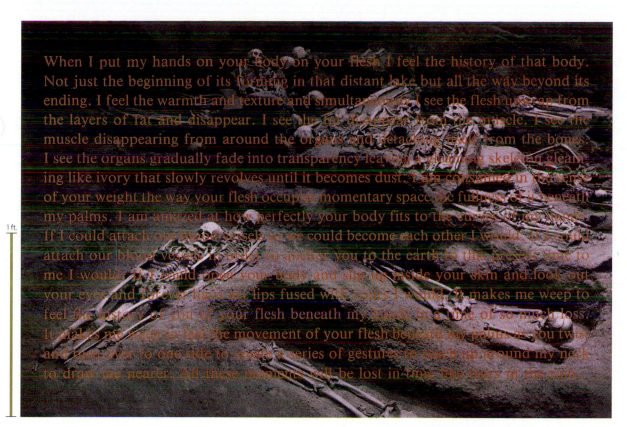

When I put my hands on your body on your flesh I feel the history of that body. Not just the beginning of its forming in that distant lake but all the way beyond its ending. I feel the warmth and texture and simultaneously I see the flesh unwrap from the layers of fat and disappear. I see the fat disappear from the muscle. I see the muscle disappearing from around the organs and detaching itself from the bones. I see the organs gradually fade into transparency leaving a gleaming skeleton gleaming like ivory that slowly revolves until it becomes dust. I am consumed in the very sight of your weight the way your flesh occupies momentary space the fullness of it beneath my palms. I am amazed at how perfectly your body fits to the curves of my hands. If I could attach our blood vessels so we could become each other I would. If I could attach our blood vessels in order to anchor you to the earth to this present time to me I would. If I could open your body and slip up inside your skin and look out your eyes and forever have my lips fused with yours I would. It makes me weep to feel the history of you of your flesh beneath my hands in a time of so much loss. It makes me weep to feel the movement of your flesh beneath my palms as you twist and turn over to one side to create a series of gestures to reach up around my neck to draw me nearer. All these moments will be lost in time like tears in the rain.

1 ft.

31-8 DAVID WOJNAROWICZ, *When I Put My Hands on Your Body,* 1990. Gelatin silver print and silk-screened text on museum board, 2' 2" × 3' 2". Private collection.

In this disturbing yet eloquent print, Wojnarowicz overlaid typed commentary on a photograph of skeletal remains. He movingly communicated his feelings about watching a loved one die of AIDS.

tures with rich tonal gradations of black, gray, and white. In many ways, Mapplethorpe was the heir of Edward Weston, whose innovative compositions of still lifes (FIG. 29-44) and nudes (FIG. 29-44A) helped establish photography as an art form on a par with painting and sculpture. What shocked the public was not nudity per se—a traditional subject with roots in antiquity, indeed at the very birth of art during the Old Stone Age (FIGS. 1-4, 1-5, and 1-5A)—but the openly gay character of many of Mapplethorpe's images. *The Perfect Moment* photographs included, in addition to some very graphic images of homosexual men, a series of self-portraits documenting Mapplethorpe's changing appearance almost up until he died from having contracted AIDS only months after the show opened in Philadelphia in December 1988. The self-portrait reproduced here (FIG. 31-7) presents Mapplethorpe as an androgynous young man with long hair and makeup, confronting the viewer with a steady gaze. Mapplethorpe's photographs, like the work of David Wojnarowicz (FIG. 31-8) and other gay and lesbian artists of the time, are inextricably bound up with the social upheavals in American society and the struggle for equal rights for women, homosexuals, minorities, and the disabled that emerged in the decades following World War II.

DAVID WOJNAROWICZ The disease that killed Mapplethorpe in 1989 and cut short the careers of many other gay artists in the 1980s and 1990s was a most unwelcome reinforcement of these artists' self-identification. Some sculptors and painters responded to the devastating impact of AIDS in the gay community by producing deeply moving works of art. DAVID WOJNAROWICZ (1955–1992) was a gay-rights activist who dropped out of high school in his hometown of Red Bank, New Jersey, and moved to New York City, where he lived on the streets before achieving success as an artist. As did so many others in the gay community, Wojnarowicz watched

his lover and many of his friends die of AIDS. He reacted by creating disturbing yet eloquent works about the tragedy of this disease, which eventually claimed his own life.

In *When I Put My Hands on Your Body* (FIG. 31-8), Wojnarowicz overlaid a photograph of a pile of skeletal remains with evenly spaced typed commentary communicating his feelings about watching a loved one dying of AIDS. Wojnarowicz movingly describes the effects of AIDS on the human body and soul:

> When I put my hands on your body on your flesh I feel the history of that body. . . . I see the flesh unwrap from the layers of fat and disappear. . . . I see the organs gradually fade into transparency. . . . It makes me weep to feel the history of you of your flesh beneath my hands.

Wojnarowicz's juxtaposition of text and imagery, as in the works by Barbara Kruger (FIG. 31-6) and the Guerrilla Girls (FIG. 31-6A), paralleled the use of both words and images in advertising. The public's familiarity with this format ensured greater receptivity to these artists' messages.

SHAHZIA SIKANDER The struggle for recognition and equal rights has never been confined to the United States, least of all in the present era of instant global communication. In the Muslim world, women and homosexuals face especially difficult challenges, which SHAHZIA SIKANDER (b. 1969) brilliantly addresses in her work. Born in Lahore, Pakistan, and trained at the National College of Arts in the demanding South Asian/Persian art of miniature painting (see "Indian Miniature Painting," page 1037), Sikander earned an MFA from the Rhode Island School of Design and now lives in New York City. So thoroughly immersed in the methods of miniature painting that she makes her own paper, pigments, and squirrel-hair brushes, Sikander nonetheless imbues this traditional art form with

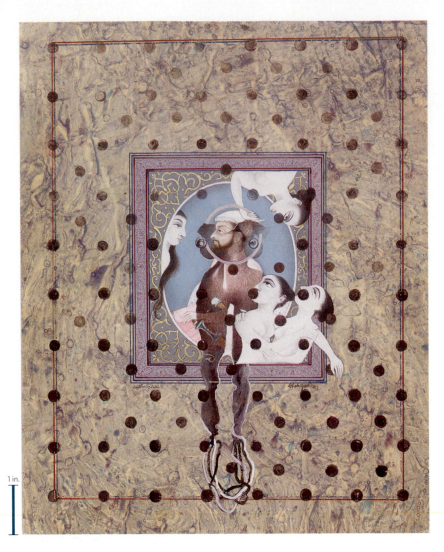

Imbuing miniature painting with a contemporary message about hypocrisy and intolerance, Sikander portrayed a gay friend as a homosexual Mughal emperor who enforced Muslim orthodoxy.

ial homeland figures prominently in his art. One of the major themes Ofili has addressed is religion, as interpreted through the eyes of an artist with his racial and national background. His *The Holy Virgin Mary* (FIG. **31-10**) depicts Mary in a manner that departs radically from conventional Renaissance representations. Ofili's work presents the Virgin in simplified form, and she appears to float in an indeterminate space. The artist employed brightly colored pigments applied to the canvas in multiple layers of beadlike dots (inspired by images from ancient caves in Zimbabwe). Surrounding the Virgin, whose face is that of an African woman, are tiny images of genitalia and buttocks cut out from pornographic magazines, which, to the artist, parallel the putti often surrounding Mary in Renaissance paintings. Another reference to Ofili's African heritage surfaces in the clumps of elephant dung—one forming the Virgin's breast, and two more serving as supports for the canvas. The dung enabled Ofili to incorporate Africa into his work in a literal way. Still, he wants the viewer to move beyond the cultural associations of the materials and see them in new ways.

Not surprisingly, *The Holy Virgin Mary* elicited strong reactions, as Ofili clearly intended it to do when he decided to merge the sacred and the vile. The paint-

contemporary meaning. In *Perilous Order* (FIG. **31-9**), she addresses homosexuality, intolerance, and hypocrisy by portraying a gay friend in the guise of the Mughal emperor Aurangzeb (r. 1658–1707), who was a strict enforcer of Islamic orthodoxy although reputed to be a homosexual. Sikander depicted him framed against a magnificent marbleized background ringed by voluptuous nude Hindu nymphs and behind the shadow of a veiled Hindu goddess. *Perilous Order* thus also incorporates a reference to the tensions between the Muslim and Hindu populations of Pakistan and India today.

National Identity

As in the case of Shahzia Sikander, a person's birthplace is often a central component of personal identity, even if the artist has migrated to another country. National identity looms large in the work of many contemporary artists.

CHRIS OFILI A British-born Catholic of Nigerian descent, CHRIS OFILI (b. 1968) is one of the leading European artists whose famil-

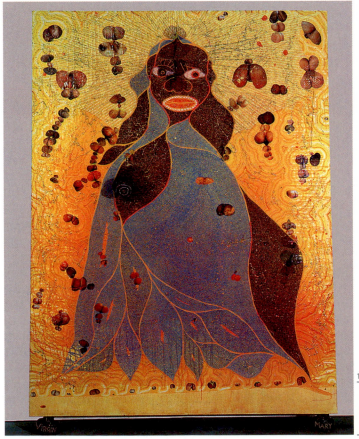

31-10 CHRIS OFILI, *The Holy Virgin Mary*, 1996. Paper collage, oil paint, glitter, polyester resin, map pins, elephant dung on linen, 7' 11" × 5' 11 $\frac{5}{16}$". Museum of Old and New Art, Hobart.

Ofili, a British-born Catholic of Nigerian descent, represented the Virgin Mary with African elephant dung as a breast and with genitalia and buttocks surrounding her. The painting produced a public outcry.

ARTISTS ON ART
Shirin Neshat on Iran after the Revolution

In an interview with Arthur C. Danto in 2000, expatriate Iranian artist Shirin Neshat discussed how the Islamic Revolution of 1979 affected her work as an artist.

[I]n 1993 . . . I began to seriously make artworks again. . . . I thought photography was the most appropriate medium for my subject as it had the realism that I needed. In the 1990s I finally began going back to Iran. I had been away for over ten years—since the Islamic Revolution. As I traveled back and forth a lot of things started to go through my mind, which eventually led me to develop the work that I have. My focus from the beginning was the subject of women in relation to the Iranian society and the revolution, so I produced a series of photographic images that explored that topic. . . . The first group of photographic work I produced in 1993 certainly reflected the point of view of an Iranian living abroad, looking back in time and trying to analyze and comprehend the changes that had taken place in Iran since the revolution. It was the approach of an artist who had been away for a long time, and it was an important turning point for me artistically and personally, as it became more than art making but a type of journey back to my native country. I was deeply invested in understanding the ideological and philosophical ideas behind contemporary Islam, most of all the origin of the revolution and how it had transformed my country. I knew the subject was very complex and broad so I minimized my focus to something tangible and specific. I chose to concentrate on the meanings behind "martyrdom," a concept which became the heart of the Islamic government's mission at the time, particularly during the Iran/Iraq War. It promoted faith, self-sacrifice, rejection of the material world, and ultimately, life after death. Mostly, I was interested in how their ideas of spirituality, politics and violence were and still are so interconnected and inseparable from one another.*

Neshat often poses for her photographs wearing a veil—which is for her a symbol both of ethnic pride and of the repression of Muslim women—and with her face and exposed parts of her body covered with Farsi (Persian) messages. Unlike the words in the photographs and posters of Simpson (FIG. 31-4A), Kruger (FIG. 31-6), the Guerrilla Girls (FIG. 31-6A), and Wojnarowicz (FIG. 31-8), which evoke commercial typography, Neshat's handwritten additions to her photographs remind the viewer of the long tradition of calligraphy in Persian art (see page 297). A rifle also often figures prominently in Neshat's photographs as an emblem of militant feminism, a notion foreign to the Muslim faith.

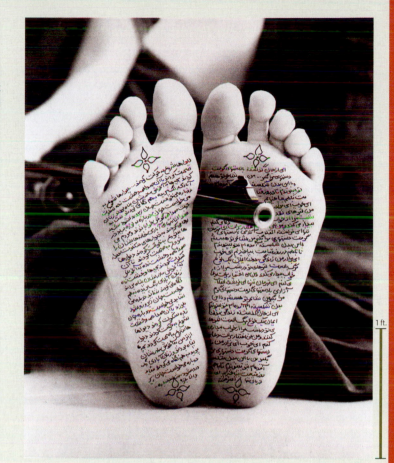

1 ft.

31-11 SHIRIN NESHAT, *Allegiance and Wakefulness*, 1994. Offset print with ink calligraphy, 3' 5$\frac{1}{4}$" × 2' 9". Israel Museum, Jerusalem (anonymous gift, New York, to American Friends of the Israel Museum).

Neshat's photographs address the repression of women in postrevolutionary Iran. She poses in traditional veiled garb but wields a rifle and displays militant Farsi poetry on her exposed body parts.

In *Allegiance and Wakefulness* (FIG. **31-11**) from her *Women of Allah* series, Neshat omitted her face and most of her body, and focused on her feet covered with verses of militant Farsi poetry and on the barrel of a rifle she points menacingly toward the viewer.

*Kristine Stiles and Peter Selz, *Theories and Documents of Contemporary Art: A Sourcebook of Artists' Writings*, 2d ed. (Berkeley: University of California Press, 2012), 547–548.

ing's inclusion in the *Sensation* exhibition at the Brooklyn Museum in 1999 with other "sensational" works by young British artists prompted indignant (but unsuccessful) demands for cancellation of the show and countercharges of censorship (see "Public Funding of Controversial Art," page 1000).

SHIRIN NESHAT Born in Iran, SHIRIN NESHAT (b. 1957) grew up in a Westernized home and attended a Catholic boarding school in Tehran before leaving her homeland to study art in California, where she earned undergraduate and graduate degrees from the University of California, Berkeley. Today she lives in New York City and produces films, videos, and photographs critical of the funda-

mentalist Islamic regime in Iran, especially its treatment of women (see "Shirin Neshat on Iran after the Revolution," above).

Not every artist who has achieved an international reputation has migrated to the West to pursue a career. CLIFF WHITING (TE WHANAU-A-APANUI, b. 1936) of New Zealand, for example, continues the Maori tradition of woodcarving, but in a distinctly modern style in works such as *Tawhiri-Matea* (FIG. **31-11A**).

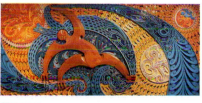

31-11A WHITING, *Tawhiri-Matea*, 1984.

POLITICAL AND SOCIAL COMMENTARY

Although almost all of the works discussed thus far are commentaries on contemporary society (seen through the lens of the artists' personal experiences), they do not incorporate references to specific events, nor do they address conditions affecting all people regardless of their race, national origin, gender, or sexual orientation—for example, homelessness, industrial pollution, and street violence. Other artists, however, have confronted precisely those aspects of late 20th- and early 21st-century life in their work.

KRZYSZTOF WODICZKO Polish-born KRZYSZTOF WODICZKO (b. 1943) is one of many living artists who focus on some of these more universal concerns in his art. When working in Canada in 1980, he developed artworks involving the outdoor display of enormous slide images. He projected photographs on specific buildings to expose how civic buildings embody, legitimize, and perpetuate power. When Wodiczko moved to New York City in 1983, he became troubled by the pervasive homelessness in a city that is the financial capital of the world and home to many of America's wealthiest families. He resolved to use his art to publicize this problem, and got the opportunity in 1987, albeit in Boston instead of New York. On Boston Common, as part of the city's New Year's celebration, Wodiczko produced *The Homeless Projection* (FIG. **31-12**), a temporary artwork consisting of images of homeless people projected on all four sides of the Civil War Soldiers and Sailors Monument. In these photos, the homeless appear flanked by plastic bags filled with their few possessions. At the top of the monument, Wodiczko projected a local condominium construction site, which helped viewers make a connection between urban development and homelessness.

EDWARD BURTYNSKY The destructive effects of industrial plants and mines on the environment have been the motivation for the photographs of "manufactured landscapes" by Canadian EDWARD BURTYNSKY (b. 1955). The son of a Ukrainian immigrant who worked in the General Motors plant in St. Catharines, Ontario, Burtynsky studied photography and graphic design at Ryerson University and Niagara College. He uses a large-format field camera to produce high-resolution negatives of industrial landscapes littered with tires, scrap metal, and industrial refuse. His choice of subjects is itself an unambiguous negative commentary on modern manufacturing processes, but Burtynsky transforms ugliness into beauty in his color prints. For example, his photograph (FIG. **31-13**) of a Toronto recycling plant from his *Urban Mines* series converts bundles of compressed scrap metal into a striking abstract composition of multicolored rectangles. Burtynsky's work thus merges documentary and fine-art photography and bears comparison with the photographs of Margaret Bourke-White (FIG. 29-78) and Minor White (FIG. 30-34).

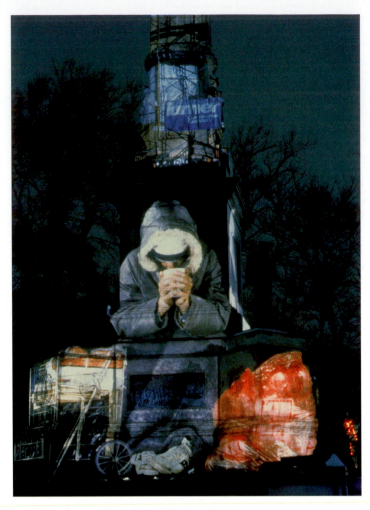

31-12 KRZYSZTOF WODICZKO, *The Homeless Projection,* 1986. Outdoor slide projection at the Civil War Soldiers and Sailors Monument, Boston Common, Boston.

To publicize the plight of the homeless, Wodiczko projected on the walls of a monument on Boston Common images of them with their plastic bags containing their few possessions.

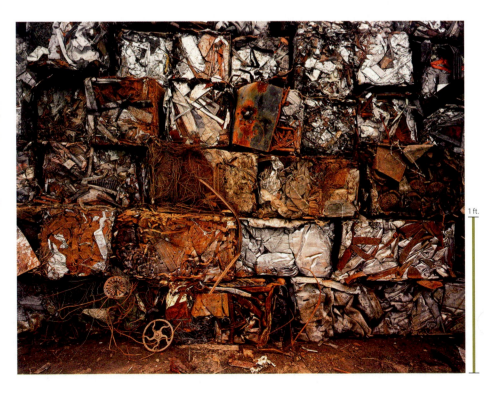

31-13 EDWARD BURTYNSKY, *Densified Scrap Metal #3A, Toronto, Ontario,* 1997. Dye coupler print, 2' 2$\frac{3}{4}$" × 2' 10$\frac{3}{8}$". National Gallery of Canada, Ottawa (gift of the artist, 1998).

Burtynsky's "manufactured landscapes" are commentaries on the destructive effects on the environment of industrial plants and mines, but his photographs transform ugliness into beauty.

1 ft.

ARTISTS ON ART
Leon Golub on *Mercenaries*

Mercenaries IV (FIG. 31-14), which rivals the huge history paintings of the 19th century in size, presents a mysterious tableau of five tough freelance military professionals willing, for a price, to fight for anyone willing to pay. The three clustering at the right side of the canvas react with tense physical gestures to something one of the two other mercenaries standing at the far left is saying. The dark uniforms and skin tones of the four black fighters flatten their figures and make them stand out against the searing dark red background. The slightly modulated background seems to push their forms forward up against the picture plane and becomes an echoing void in the space between the two groups. Golub painted the mercenaries so that the viewer's eye is level with the menacing figures' knees. He placed the men so close to the front plane of the work that the lower edge of the painting cuts off their feet, thereby trapping the viewer in the painting's compressed space. The feeling of peril confronts viewers mercilessly. They become one with all the victims caught in today's political battles.

Golub emphasized both the scarred light tones of the white mercenary's skin and the weapons. Modeled with shadow and gleaming highlights, the guns contrast with the harshly scraped, flattened surfaces of the figures. The rawness of the canvas reinforces the rawness of the imagery. Indeed, Golub's working method is, appropriately, itself violent, as he explained in a 1981 interview with Matthew Baigell:

> [My *Mercenaries* paintings] arise out of the contemporary world as given to us by the media: the uses of mercenaries or irregulars . . . to enforce political ends. The mercenary is not a common subject

of art, but is a near-universal means of establishing or maintaining control under volatile or up-for-grabs political circumstances.

> I do not have the total conceptual framework for a painting in mind until the later stages. I orient the figures, their gestures, their glances, their intentions. I reinterpret these on the basis of changing body stances. For example, I intend a figure to act out a certain gesture. As I work, the psychic dimensions of that individual and what he portends might shift. The figure gets more or less menacing, more or less active. My original intentions shift considerably in the balancing of energies which move across the canvas. I may use drawings or parts of photographs enlarged through an opaque projector onto the vertical hanging canvas. A figure might develop from two or three or half a dozen photographs or drawings. Other figures are then located in stressed tension to the first. I then evolve the drawing to precise military dress, weapons, and, most important, intention. . . . The particular individual has to both typify and illustrate mercenaries and to appear to possess an idiosyncratic, singular experience. The figures are outlined and partially shaded in black paint. Then a coat of white paint is put on for highlights and lighter areas. I then apply layers of local colors to define skin, metal, wood, cloth, etc. The painting is then laid on the floor. Areas are partially dissolved with solvents and scraped with sculpture tools, more recently, a meat cleaver, to erode the paint skin. . . . I continue to reconstruct and erode until I get to the point where . . . the different figures, their gestures, grins and leers, etc., are in some sort of achieved tension.*

*Kristine Stiles and Peter Selz, *Theories and Documents of Contemporary Art: A Sourcebook of Artists' Writings*, 2d ed. (Berkeley: University of California Press, 2012), 266–268.

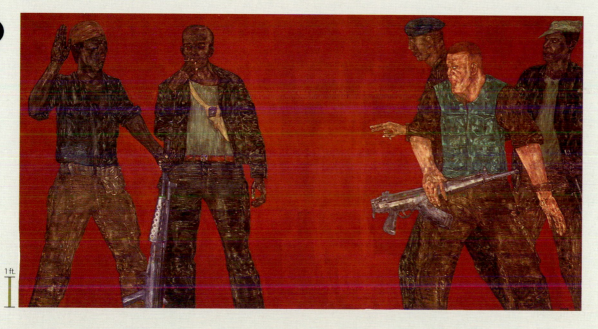

1 ft.

31-14 LEON GOLUB, *Mercenaries IV*, 1980. Acrylic on linen, 10' × 19' 2". Courtesy Ronald Feldman Fine Arts, New York. Art © Estate of Leon Golub/ Licensed by VAGA, New York, NY.

The violence of contemporary life is the subject of Golub's huge paintings. Here, five mercenaries loom over the viewer, instilling a feeling of peril. The rough textures reinforce the raw imagery.

LEON GOLUB The brutality of urban life and warfare was the focus of painter LEON GOLUB (1922–2004) during his long career. Born in Chicago and trained at the University of Chicago and the Art Institute of Chicago, Golub is best known for his two series of paintings titled *Assassins* and *Mercenaries* (FIG. 31-14). In these large-scale works, anonymous characters inspired by newspaper and magazine photographs of urban gangs and Latin American death squads participate in atrocious street violence and military operations (see "Leon Golub on *Mercenaries*," above). The paintings have a universal impact because they suggest not specific stories but a condition of being. This impression is fostered in large part by Golub's removal of the figures from time and space by placing them against a featureless red background, which, although inspired by and modeled freely on ancient Roman mural paintings (compare FIG. 7-18), also is the color of the blood shed by the victims of Golub's assassins.

MARTHA ROSLER Street violence and armed combat are themes that have also been explored in depth by SANDOW BIRK (b. 1962) in paintings such as *Death of Manuel* (FIG. 31-14A) and by MARTHA ROSLER (b. 1943), especially in a series of photomontages called *Bringing the War Home: House Beautiful.* Born in Brooklyn, Rosler graduated from Brooklyn College and earned an MFA at the University of California, San Diego. A professor at Rutgers University for three decades and a prolific writer, Rosler has produced a diverse body of artistic work, including videos and performance art as well as photography. Throughout her career, Rosler has focused on social and political commentary, primarily issues concerning women, housing and homelessness, and war and its depiction in the media.

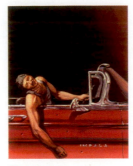

⬈ **31-14A** BIRK, *Death of Manuel*, 1992.

Gladiators (FIG. 31-15) is one of the recent additions to the *House Beautiful* series, originally created between 1967 and 1972 as a critical commentary on the Vietnam War but expanded in 2004 in reaction to the war in Iraq. Like the other photomontages in the series, *Gladiators* brings disturbing images of combat into the domestic sphere by inserting armed soldiers (modern "gladiators") into the tranquil living rooms of upscale houses, literally "bringing the war home" to those whose sons and daughters, unlike those of working-class families, rarely enlist in the armed forces and fight for their country.

FERNANDO BOTERO Perhaps the most emotionally wrenching recent artworks to express outrage against war in general and specifically the inhumane treatment of prisoners is the large series of paintings and drawings by Colombian artist FERNANDO BOTERO (b. 1932). Still active in his 80s, Botero, who has lived and worked in Paris for decades, reacted with horror to the news reports and photographs of the humiliation and torture of Iraqi prisoners at the hands of American military personnel at Abu Ghraib prison. The paintings—for example, *Abu Ghraib 46* (FIG. 31-16)—are peopled by Botero's trademark larger-than-life inflated bodies, but they differ markedly from his usually tranquil domestic subjects. As in the published photographs from Abu Ghraib, the men

31-15 MARTHA ROSLER, *Gladiators,* 2004, from *Bringing the War Home: House Beautiful.* Photomontage, 1' 8" × 2'. Mitchell-Innes & Nash Gallery, New York.

Rosler's *House Beautiful* photomontages disturbingly insert images of armed soldiers (modern "gladiators") into the tranquil living rooms of upscale houses, literally "bringing the war home."

in Botero's paintings are stripped of their clothes, blindfolded, bound, beaten, and bloodied, and are often threatened by ferocious dogs or forced to wear women's underwear. Critics have compared these graphic depictions of physical and mental torture to the passion of Christ and the martyrdom of saints. Botero has insisted that the paintings are not intended as anti-American but as a broad condemnation of cruelty in violation of the Geneva Convention. He has refused to profit from sales of the Abu Ghraib paintings and has donated them to museums—many, including the illustrated example, are gifts to the University of California's Berkeley Art Museum—on the condition that they forever remain on display.

WILLIE BESTER The use of their craft by artists such as Botero, Golub, and Rosler to express outrage at violence, warfare, and social and political injustices of all kinds is indeed a global phenomenon in the late 20th and early 21st centuries, but it is not new in the history of art. Beckmann's *Night* (FIG. 29-49), Picasso's *Guernica* (FIG. 29-16), Goya's *Third of May, 1808* (FIG. 27-12), Géricault's *Raft of the Medusa* (FIG. 27-1), and Turner's *Slave Ship* (FIG. 27-22) are but a few notable examples. In South Africa, many artists became vocal critics of apartheid (government-sponsored racial separation) and used painting as a potent means of protesting the oppression of blacks by the minority white government.

WILLIE BESTER (b. 1956) is probably the most prominent South African artist to take up that cause. His 1992 *Homage to Steve Biko* (FIG. 31-17) is a tribute to the gentle and heroic leader of the South African Black Consciousness Movement whom the authorities killed while he was in detention. The exoneration of the two white doctors in charge of him sparked protests around the world. Bester packed his picture with references to death and injustice. Biko's portrait, at the center, is near another of the police minister, James Kruger, who had him transported 1,100 kilometers (almost 700 miles) to Pretoria in the yellow Land Rover ambulance seen left of center and again beneath Biko's portrait. Bester portrayed Biko with his chained fists raised in the classic worldwide protest gesture. This portrait memorializes both Biko and the many other antiapartheid activists, as indicated by the white graveyard crosses above a blue sea of skulls

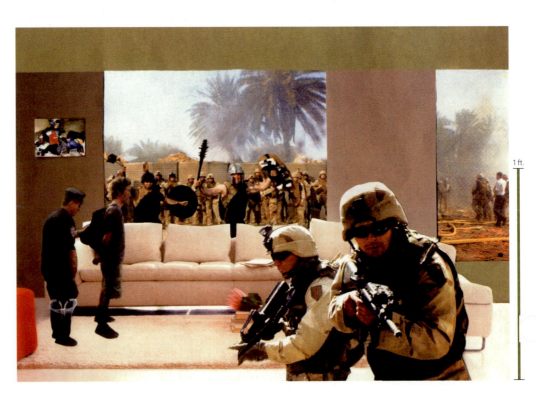

1 ft.

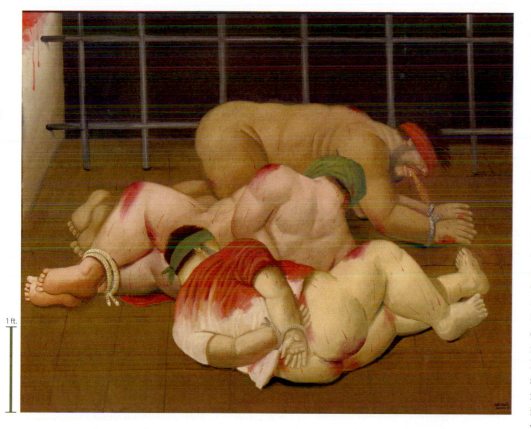

1 ft.

31-16 Fernando Botero, *Abu Ghraib 46*, 2005. Oil on canvas, 4' 9½" × 5' 9⅝". Berkeley Art Museum, Berkeley (gift of the artist).

Botero's *Abu Ghraib* series is a condemnation of the humiliation and torture of Iraqi prisoners by American military personnel. Critics have compared the paintings to scenes of martyrdom.

The red crosses on this vehicle's door and on Kruger's reflective dark glasses repeat, with sad irony, the graveyard crosses.

Blood-red and ambulance-yellow are in fact unifying colors dripped or painted on many parts of the canvas. Writing and numbers, found fragments, and stenciled and painted signs—favorite Cubist motifs (FIGS. 29-13 and 29-14; compare FIG. 31-3)—also appear throughout the composition. Numbers refer to the dehumanized life of blacks under apartheid. Found objects—wire, sticks, cardboard, sheet metal, cans, and other discards—from which the poor construct fragile, impermanent township dwellings, remind viewers of the degraded lives of most South

beside Biko's head. The crosses stand out against a red background, recalling the inferno of burned townships. The stop sign (lower left) seems to mean "stop Kruger," or perhaps "stop apartheid." The tagged foot, as if in a morgue, above the ambulance also refers to Biko's death.

African people of color. The oilcan guitar (bottom center), another recurrent Bester symbol, refers both to the social harmony and joy provided by music and to the control imposed by apartheid policies. The whole composition is rich in texture and dense in its collage combinations of objects, photographs, signs, symbols, and pigment. *Homage to Steve Biko* is a powerful critique of an oppressive sociopolitical system, and it exemplifies the extent to which art can be invoked in the political process.

Protests against apartheid have taken many forms, however—for example, opposition to corporate investment in South Africa, the approach taken by German artist HANS HAACKE (b. 1936) in *MetroMobiltan* (FIG. **31-17A**).

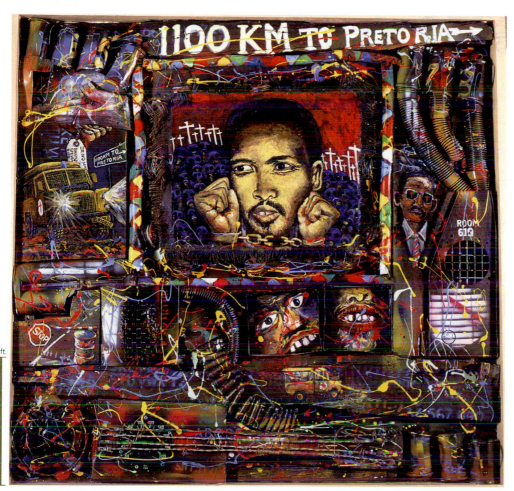

1 ft.

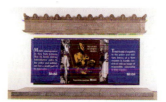

31-17A Haacke, *MetroMobiltan*, 1985.

31-17 Willie Bester, *Homage to Steve Biko*, 1992. Mixed media, 3' 7⅚" × 3' 7⅚". Collection of the artist.

Homage to Steve Biko is a tribute to a leader of the Black Consciousness Movement, which protested apartheid in South Africa. References to the injustice of Biko's death fill this complex painting.

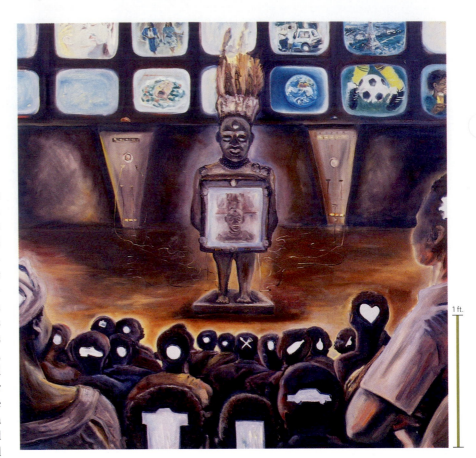

Ta Tele is a commentary on contemporary life showing Congolese citizens transfixed by television pictures of the world outside Africa. Even the traditional power figure at the center has a TV screen for a chest.

TRIGO PIULA The Democratic Republic of Congo's TRIGO PIULA (b. ca. 1950) is a painter trained in Western artistic techniques and styles who creates works that fuse Western and Congolese images and objects in a pictorial blend providing social commentary on present-day Congolese culture. *Ta Tele* (FIG. 31-18) depicts a group of Congolese citizens staring transfixed at colorful pictures of life beyond Africa displayed on 14 television screens. The TV images include references to travel to exotic places (such as Paris, symbolized by the Eiffel Tower, FIG. 28-40), sports events, love, the earth seen from a satellite, and Western worldly goods. A traditional Kongo power figure (compare FIG. 37-5) associated with warfare and divination stands at the composition's center as a visual mediator between the anonymous foreground viewers and the multiple TV images. In traditional Kongo contexts, this figure's feather headdress links it to supernatural and magical powers from the sky, such as lightning and storms. In Piula's rendition, the headdress perhaps refers to the power of airborne televised pictures. In the stomach area, where Kongo power figures often have glass in front of a medicine packet, Piula painted a television screen showing a second power figure, as if to double the figure's power. The artist shows most of the television viewers with a small white image of a foreign object—for example, a car, shoe, or bottle—on the backs of their heads.

One meaning of this picture appears to be that television messages have deadened the minds of Congolese people to anything but modern Western thoughts or commodities. Two speaker cabinets set against the back wall beneath the TV screens have wires leading to the power figure, implying that even this ancient symbol of native power has been subjected to the greater power of modern television. Clearly, Piula suggests, the contemporary world's new television-induced consumerism is poisoning the minds and souls of Congolese people as if by magic or sorcery.

ZHANG XIAOGANG Political and social commentary is also the principal interest of Chinese painter ZHANG XIAOGANG (b. 1958). Zhang is best known for his *Bloodline* portraits—for example, *Big Family*

31-19 ZHANG XIAOGANG, *Bloodline: Big Family No. 2,* 1995. Oil on canvas, 5' 11" × 7' 6 5/8". Private collection.

Ironically titled *Big Family* in reaction to the government's one-child policy, Zhang's generic, personality-less portraits intentionally recall black-and-white family photographs of the Mao era in China.

No. 2 (FIG. 31-19). Based on the black-and-white photographs of Chinese families popular during the Cultural Revolution, the *Bloodline* paintings are not really portraits. Instead, they depict generic, personality-less fathers, mothers, and children wearing the approved plain clothes of the Mao era in China. Ironically titled *Big Family,* these somber three-figure groups are also commentaries on the longstanding, though recently eased, government policy of restricting most married couples to having only a single child, a policy that has led many families to seek abortions, often in order to raise a boy instead of a girl. The *Bloodline* series takes its name from

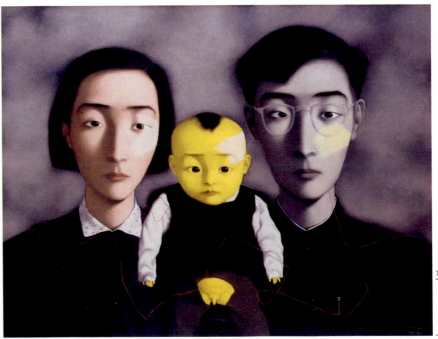

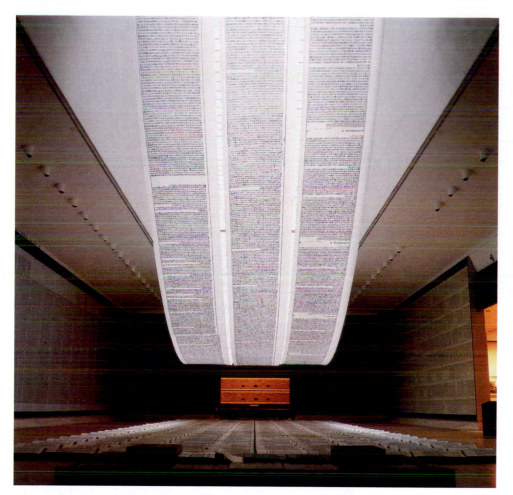

31-20 Xu Bing, *A Book from the Sky*, 1987. Installation of woodblock printed books at the Elvehjem (now Chazen) Museum of Art, University of Wisconsin, Madison, 1991.

Xu trained as a printmaker in Beijing. *A Book from the Sky,* with its invented Chinese woodblock characters, may be a stinging critique of the meaninglessness of contemporary political language.

of the meaninglessness of contemporary political language and as a commentary on the illegibility of the past. Xu himself has characterized the work as intentionally ambiguous:

People have so many perspectives on *Book from the Sky* because the work is empty. The work does not present any clear message. . . . I used every possible method to force people to believe in the legitimacy of this work, while at the same time extracting all content completely. . . . The artwork itself is a contradiction because it makes a parody of culture while also placing culture in a temple to be taken very seriously. *Book from the Sky* invites your desire to understand it and pushes you away at the same time. It treats everyone as equal—educated or uneducated, Chinese or non-Chinese—because no one can "read" it.[4]

Like many postmodern artists, who, like postmodern architects, reject pure formalism and emphasize content and historical references (see "After Modernism: Postmodern Architecture," page 949), Xu created *A Book from the Sky* to be read on many levels.

REPRESENTATION AND ABSTRACTION

Despite the high visibility of contemporary artists whose work deals with the pressing social and political issues of the world, some critically acclaimed living or recently deceased artists have produced innovative modernist art during the postmodern era. Abstraction remains a valid and compelling approach to painting and sculpture in the 21st century, as does more traditional representational art, both figural and landscape.

Figural Art and Landscape

Recent decades have brought a revival of interest in figural art, both in painting and sculpture, a trend best exemplified in the earlier postwar period by Lucian Freud (FIG. 30-32), who remained an active and influential painter until his death in July 2011.

JENNY SAVILLE Fellow Briton JENNY SAVILLE (b. 1970) is the leading figure painter in the Freud mold of the younger generation of European and American artists. Born in Cambridge, England, and trained at the Glasgow School of Art in Scotland, Saville lives and paints in an old palace in Palermo, Italy. Her best-known works are over-life-size self-portraits in which she exaggerates the girth of her body and delights in depicting heavy folds of flesh with visible veins in minute detail and from a sharply foreshortened angle, which further distorts the body's proportions. Her nude self-portraits deserve comparison not only with those of Freud but also of Egon Schiele (FIG. 29-10), despite the vivid contrast between Schiele's emaciated body and Saville's (false) obesity.

the faint red lines connecting the figures—a device used earlier by Frida Kahlo (FIG. 29-76). The red bloodlines are the only touches of color in Zhang's otherwise intentionally subdued palette, save for, in the illustrated example, the yellow that draws attention to the highly desirable male child.

XU BING A different kind of commentary on Chinese culture has been the hallmark of the work of XU BING (b. 1955), a Chongqing, China, native who was forced to work in the countryside with peasants during the Cultural Revolution of 1966 to 1976 under Mao Tse-tung (1893–1976). Xu later studied printmaking in Beijing at the Central Academy of Fine Arts, where he is now professor and vice president. In 1990, however, Xu moved to the United States at the invitation of the University of Wisconsin, where two years earlier he had exhibited his most famous work, a large *installation* (an assemblage that creates an artistic environment in a room or gallery) called *A Book from the Sky* (FIG. **31-20**). First exhibited in China before being installed at Wisconsin's Elvehjem (now Chazen) Museum of Art, the work presents an enormous number of *woodblock*-printed texts in *characters* evocative of Chinese writing but invented by the artist. Producing them required both an intimate knowledge of genuine Chinese characters and extensive training in woodblock carving. Xu's work, however, is no hymn to tradition. Critics have interpreted it both as a stinging critique

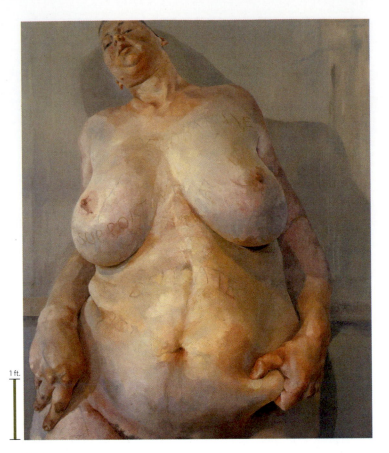

31-21 JENNY SAVILLE, *Branded,* 1992. Oil on canvas, 7' × 6'. Saatchi Gallery, London.

Saville's unflattering foreshortened self-portrait "branded" with words such as "delicate" and "petite" underscores the dichotomy between the perfect bodies of fashion models and those of most people.

Saville's paintings are a commentary on the contemporary obsession with the lithe bodies of fashion models. In *Branded* (FIG. **31-21**), she underscores the dichotomy between the popular notion of a beautiful body and the imperfect bodies of most people by "branding" her body with words inscribed in her flesh—"delicate," "decorative," "petite." Art critic Michelle Meagher has described Saville's paintings as embodying a "feminist aesthetics of disgust."[5]

KIKI SMITH A distinctly unflattering approach to the representation of the human body is also the hallmark of New York–based KIKI SMITH (b. 1954), the daughter of Minimalist sculptor Tony Smith (FIG. 30-18). In her work, Smith has explored the question of who controls the human body, an interest that grew out of her training as an emergency medical service technician. Her studies of bodies afflicted by illnesses deserve comparison with other artists' works addressing the physical devastation brought on by AIDS (see page 1001), but Smith's goals are different. She wants to reveal the socially constructed nature of the body, and she encourages the viewer to consider how external forces shape people's perceptions of their bodies. In works such as *Untitled* (FIG. **31-22**), the artist dramatically departed from conventional representations of the body, both in art and in the media. She suspended two life-size wax figures, one male and one female, both nude, from metal stands. Smith marked each of the sculptures with long white drips—body fluids running from the woman's breasts and down the man's leg. She commented:

> Most of the functions of the body are hidden . . . from society. . . . [W]e separate our bodies from our lives. But, when people are dying, they are

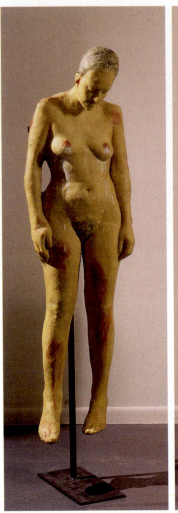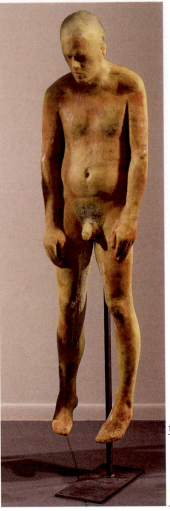

31-22 KIKI SMITH, *Untitled,* 1990. Beeswax and microcrystalline wax figures on metal stands, female figure installed height 6' 1½" and male figure installed height 6' 4 15/16". Whitney Museum of American Art, New York (purchased with funds from the Painting and Sculpture Committee).

Asking "Who controls the body?" Kiki Smith sculpted two life-size wax figures of a nude man and woman with body fluids running from the woman's breasts and down the man's leg.

losing control of their bodies. That loss of function can seem humiliating and frightening. But, on the other hand, you can look at it as a kind of liberation of the body. It seems like a nice metaphor—a way to think about the social—that people lose control despite the many agendas of different ideologies in society, which are trying to control the body(ies) . . . medicine, religion, law, etc. Just thinking about control—who has control of the body? . . . Does the mind have control of the body? Does the social?[6]

Underscoring the diversity of contemporary art, not all recent figure painters have worked in a realistic mode. It is hard to imagine a more vivid contrast with the figures portrayed by Saville and Smith than the exuberantly animated, joyful cartoon-like figures in the paintings of KEITH HARING (1958–1990; FIG. **31-22A**), who, like Jean-Michel Basquiat (FIG. 31-3), began his career as a street artist in New York City.

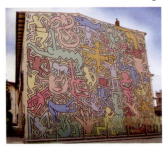

⬀ 31-22A HARING, *Tuttomondo,* 1989.

JEFF KOONS Haring's painted figures are firmly rooted in popular culture, as are the sculptures of JEFF KOONS (b. 1955). Trained at the Maryland Institute College of Art in Baltimore, Koons worked early in his career as a commodities broker. He first became prominent in the art world for a series of works in the early 1980s involving the exhibition of everyday commercial products such as vacuum cleaners. Clearly following in the footsteps of Marcel Duchamp (FIG. 29-26), Koons made no attempt to manipulate or alter the machine-made objects. More recently, he, like Californian ROBERT ARNESON (1930–1992; FIG. **31-22B**), turned to ceramic sculpture. In *Pink Panther* (FIG. **31-23**), Koons, who divides his time between his hometown of York, Pennsylvania, and New York City, playfully intertwined a pin-up nude with a famous cartoon character. He reinforced the trite and kitschy nature of this imagery by titling the exhibition of which this work was a part *The Banality Show*. Koons intends his work to draw attention to everything that he believes is wrong with contemporary American society. His prominence in the art world is based on his acute understanding of the dynamics of consumer culture. Haring too enjoyed great commercial success owing to his sensitivity to popular taste and his shrewd marketing of his trademark motifs to the general public.

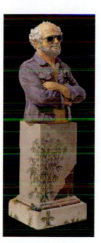

☑ **31-22B** ARNESON, *California Artist*, 1982.

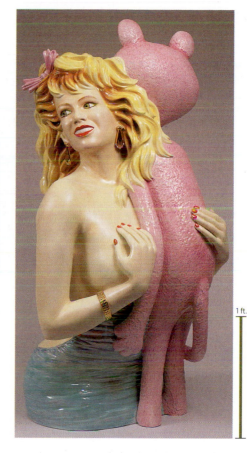

MARISOL Known simply by her first name, MARISOL ESCOBAR (b. 1930) grew up in a wealthy, widely traveled Venezuelan family. Born in Paris and educated there, in Los Angeles, and in New York City, Marisol first studied painting and drawing, but after discovering Pre-Columbian art in 1951, she pursued a career as a sculptor. Marisol also spent time in Italy, where she developed a deep admiration for Renaissance art.

In the 1960s, Marisol was one of the inner circle of New York Pop artists, and she appeared in two of Andy Warhol's films. Some of her works at that time portrayed prominent public figures, including the Hollywood actor John Wayne and the family of U.S.

president John F. Kennedy. Her subjects were always people, however, not the commercial products of consumer culture that fascinated most leading Pop artists and still are prominent in the art of Jeff Koons and others.

Marisol retained her interest in figural sculpture long after Pop Art gave way to other movements. One of her most ambitious works (FIG. **31-24**) is a multimedia three-dimensional version of Leonardo da Vinci's *Last Supper* (FIG. 22-4), including the walls and windows of the dining room in order to replicate the Renaissance master's application of linear perspective. By reproducing the fresco in three dimensions, Marisol transformed it into an object. The figures in her version of Leonardo's composition are painted wood, with the exception of Christ, whose stone body is the physical and emotional anchor of the composition. In many of her sculptures, the female figures have Marisol's features, and in this tableau she added a

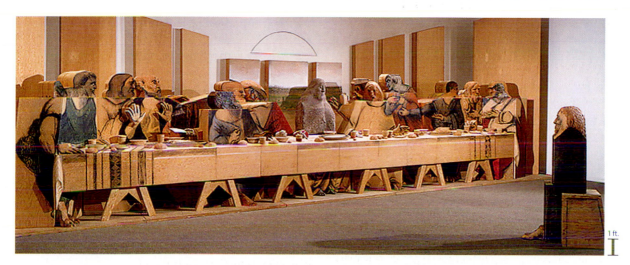

31-24 MARISOL, *Self-Portrait Looking at the Last Supper*, 1982–1984. Painted wood, stone, plaster, and aluminum, $10' 1\frac{1}{2}" \times 29' 10" \times 5' 1"$. Metropolitan Museum of Art, New York (gift of Mr. and Mrs. Roberto C. Polo, 1986). Art © Marisol Escobar/Licensed by VAGA, New York, NY.

In a tribute to the Renaissance master, Marisol created a sculptural replica of Leonardo da Vinci's *Last Supper* (FIG. 22-4), transforming the fresco into an object. She is the seated viewer as well as the artist.

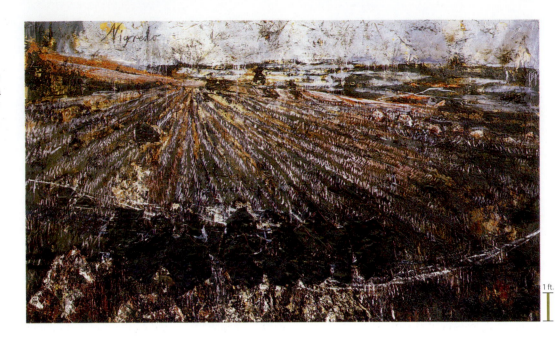

31-25 ANSELM KIEFER, *Nigredo*, 1984. Oil paint on photosensitized fabric, acrylic emulsion, straw, shellac, relief paint on paper pulled from painted wood, 11' × 18'. Philadelphia Museum of Art, Philadelphia (gift of Friends of the Philadelphia Museum of Art).

Kiefer's paintings have thickly encrusted surfaces incorporating materials such as straw. Here, the German artist used perspective to pull the viewer into an incinerated landscape alluding to the Holocaust.

seated armless portrait of herself looking at the *Last Supper.* Catholic and deeply religious—as a teenager she emulated martyr saints by inflicting physical harm on herself—Marisol may have wanted to show herself as a witness to Christ's last meal. But more likely her presence here is a tribute to the 16th-century painter. (She also made a sculptural replica of Leonardo's *Madonna and Child with Saint Anne* [FIG. 22-3].)

Marisol's *Self-Portrait Looking at the Last Supper* is a commentary on the artist not only as a creator but also as a viewer of the works of earlier artists, a link in an artistic chain extending back to antiquity. One pervasive element in the work of contemporary artists is a self-consciousness of the postmodern painter's or sculptor's position in the continuum of art history, as noted earlier in the discussions of Kehinde Wiley's *Napoleon* (FIG. 31-2) and Sandow Birk's *Manuel* (FIG. 31-14A). However, no one better exemplifies that aspect of contemporary art than MARK TANSEY (b. 1949; FIG. 31-24A).

⊿ **31-24A** TANSEY, *A Short History of Modernist Painting*, 1982.

ANSELM KIEFER Traditional realistic landscape painting remains a popular mode of artistic expression in the early 21st century, but some of the most innovative landscapes of the past few decades have verged on abstraction. German artist ANSELM KIEFER (b. 1945) studied art in Düsseldorf with Joseph Beuys (FIG. 30-53) in the early 1970s, and has lived and worked in Barjac, France, since 1992. His canvases, such as *Nigredo* (FIG. **31-25**), are large in scale and feature highly textured surfaces of pigment mixed with nontraditional materials such as straw and lead. It is not merely the impressive physicality of Kiefer's paintings that accounts for the impact of his work, however. His images function on a mythological or metaphorical level as well as on a historically specific one. Many of Kiefer's works involve a reexamination of German history, particularly the painful Nazi era of 1933–1945, and evoke a feeling of despair. Kiefer believes that Germany's participation in World War II and the Holocaust left permanent scars on the souls of the German people and on the souls of all humanity.

Nigredo ("blackening") pulls the viewer into an expansive landscape depicted using Renaissance perspective principles. This landscape, however, is far from pastoral or carefully cultivated. Rather, it appears bleak and charred. Although it does not make specific reference to the Holocaust, this incinerated landscape indirectly alludes to the horrors of that tragic event. More generally, the blackness of the landscape may refer to the notion of alchemical change or transformation, a concept of great interest to Kiefer. Black is one of the four symbolic colors of the alchemist—a color referencing both death and the molten, chaotic state of substances broken down by fire. Because the alchemist focuses on the transformation of substances, the emphasis on blackness is not absolute, but can also be perceived as part of a process of renewal and redemption. Kiefer thus imbued his work with a deep symbolic meaning that, when combined with the intriguing visual quality of his parched, congealed surfaces, results in paintings of enduring power.

Abstract Painting and Sculpture

In the 1970s, Susan Rothenberg (FIG. 30-9C) had produced large-scale "Neo-Expressionist" paintings inspired by German Expressionism and American Abstract Expressionism. Today, many artists continue to explore this dynamic style, including some who, like Anselm Kiefer, have produced works with landscape as the central theme—for example, *Summer Trees* (FIG. 31-25A) by Korean painter SONG SU-NAM (b. 1938) and *Wild Vines with Flowers Like Pearls* (FIG. **31-25B**) by the recently deceased Chinese painter WU GUANZHONG (1919–2010).

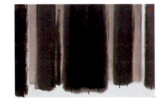

⊿ **31-25A** SONG, *Summer Trees*, 1983.

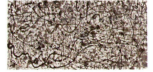

⊿ **31-25B** WU, *Wild Vines*, 1997.

JULIAN SCHNABEL In the United States, New Yorker JULIAN SCHNABEL (b. 1951), who wrote and directed a 1996 film about fellow artist Jean-Michel Basquiat (FIG. 31-3), has, like Anselm Kiefer (FIG. 31-25), experimented widely with media and materials

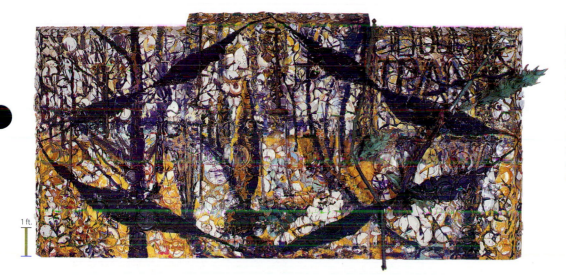

31-26 JULIAN SCHNABEL, *The Walk Home*, 1984–1985. Oil, plates, copper, bronze, fiberglass, and Bondo on six wood panels, 9' 4" × 19' 4". Broad Art Foundation, Santa Monica.

Schnabel's paintings recall the work of the midcentury American gestural abstractionists, but he employs an amalgamation of media, bringing together painting, mosaic, and low-relief sculpture.

1 ft.

in his forceful restatements of the premises of Abstract Expressionism. Schnabel's Neo-Expressionist works range from paint on velvet and tarpaulin to a mixture of pigment and fragmented china plates bonded to wood. He has a special interest in the physicality of objects, and by combining broken crockery and paint, as in *The Walk Home* (FIG. 31-26), he has found an extension of what paint can do. Superficially, Schnabel's paintings recall the work of the gestural abstractionists, especially the spontaneous drips of Jackson Pollock (FIG. 30-6) and the energetic brushstrokes of Willem de Kooning (FIG. 30-8), but their Abstract Expressionist works lack the thick, mosaic-like texture of Schnabel's canvases. The amalgamation

of media brings together painting, mosaic, and low-relief sculpture, and considerably amplifies the expressive impact of his paintings.

ELIZABETH MURRAY AND HELEN OJI One of the few things that paintings as diverse as those examined so far have in common is that they share the standard rectilinear format that has characterized paintings on wood, canvas, or silk from antiquity to the present day. Two contemporary artists who have experimented with alternate shapes are ELIZABETH MURRAY (1940–2007)—see "Rethinking the Shape of Painting," below, and FIG. 31-27)—and HELEN OJI (b. 1950).

PROBLEMS AND SOLUTIONS
Rethinking the Shape of Painting

Rectangular frames for paintings have been since antiquity the norm worldwide for decorated vases, wood panels, frescoed walls, oil-on-canvas, manuscript illustrations, and silk scrolls alike. Even during the past century, when artists have rethought almost every traditional tenet of the art of painting, the vertically or horizontally oriented rectilinear painting surface has with few exceptions (for example, FIG. 30-13) reigned supreme, even among artists who have abandoned easel painting in favor of applying pigment to unstretched canvas spread out on the floor (FIG. 30-7). Recently, however, some artists have experimented not merely with other geometric shapes but with highly irregular formats.

Chief among them is Elizabeth Murray. Born in Chicago, Murray graduated from that city's famed Art Institute and then earned an MFA at Mills College. She moved to New York City in 1967 and painted there until her death in 2007, the year after a major retrospective exhibition of her work was mounted at the Museum of Modern Art—a rare honor accorded to few women before her.

Can You Hear Me? (FIG. 31-27) is typical of Murray's innovative approach to abstract painting. It is an irregularly shaped composite of several small canvas-on-wood panels that bear comparison not only to Abstract Expressionist works but to the Biomorphic Surrealist paintings of Joan Miró (FIG. 29-58) and also to cartoon art. The central—although almost unnoticed at first—motif of *Can You Hear Me?* is a face with a wide-open mouth out of which emerges a shape resembling an elongated comic-strip balloon but without words—the reason the

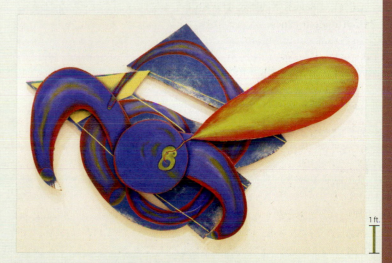

1 ft.

31-27 ELIZABETH MURRAY, *Can You Hear Me?* 1984. Oil on canvas on wood, 8' 10" × 13' 3" × 1'. Dallas Museum of Art, Dallas (Foundation for the Arts Collection).

Elizabeth Murray is the most prominent contemporary artist who rejected the traditional rectilinear format for painting in favor of a multilayered composite of canvas-on-wood panels.

viewer cannot hear what the face is saying. Murray has acknowledged that Edvard Munch's *Scream* (FIG. 28-29) was the source of inspiration for her painting, but in *Can You Hear Me?* emotional frenzy is expressed by purely abstract means, most notably through the centrifugal force of the propeller-like shape of the painting itself.

Representation and Abstraction **1013**

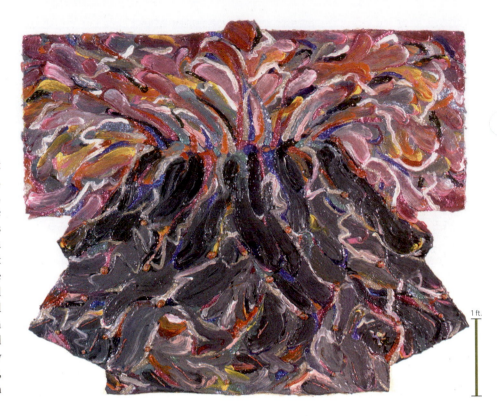

31-28 HELEN OJI, *Mount St. Helens*, 1980. Acrylic, Rhoplex, and glitter on paper, 5' × 6'. Home Insurance Company, New York.

Shaped like a kimono in acknowledgment of the artist's Japanese heritage, Oji's *Mount St. Helens* is a highly textured abstract landscape celebrating the eruptive power of Washington State's active volcano.

Born in Sacramento, California, and trained at California State University's Sacramento campus, where she earned both BA and MA degrees in art, Oji has lived and worked in New York City since 1976. *Mount St. Helens* (FIG. **31-28**) is one of a series of acrylic and glitter paintings in the shape of a kimono (compare FIG. 30-36) in acknowledgment of Oji's Japanese heritage. But the decoration of the "garment" bears little resemblance to traditional textile design. Oji's kimono is a highly textured abstract landscape that has much in common with the canvases of Kiefer (FIG. 31-25) and Schnabel (FIG. 31-26). It captures and celebrates the raw power of Washington State's Mount St. Helens, one of the world's few still-active volcanoes, which erupted in 1980, inspiring this painting.

YAYOI KUSAMA One of the most successful—and certainly one of the most market-savvy—abstract artists active today is YAYOI KUSAMA (b. 1929) of Japan. Now in her 80s, during her long career Kusama has worked in many artistic genres, including painting, sculpture, film, and performance art, and has written poems and novels. She is best known for her brightly colored compositions ("psychedelic" is a common adjective used to describe her paintings) that recall in some ways the Biomorphic Surrealist canvases of Joan Miró (FIG. 29-58) reinterpreted in a mode that draws on both Pop Art and Abstract Expressionism. Kusama's signature motif is the polka dot, and in the illustrated photograph (FIG. **31-29**), taken in 2012 at a retrospective exhibition of her abstract paintings at the Whitney Museum of American Art in New York, she wears a dress of her own design, one item in a complete line of clothing, shoes, watches, jewelry, and leather goods distributed worldwide by Louis Vuitton. Kusama personifies the conjunction of art, popular culture, advertising, and marketing that increasingly characterizes the art world of the 21st century but has its roots in the launching of a line of clothing based on Bridget Riley's Op Art paintings of the 1960s (see page 961 and FIG. 30-16).

31-29 YAYOI KUSAMA seated in a wheelchair in front of a selection of her acrylic-on-canvas paintings at the Whitney Museum of American Art in New York City, July 9, 2012.

Multifaceted octogenarian Japanese artist Yayoi Kusama is best known for her psychedelically colored paintings that draw on Biomorphic Surrealism, Pop Art, and Abstraction Expressionism.

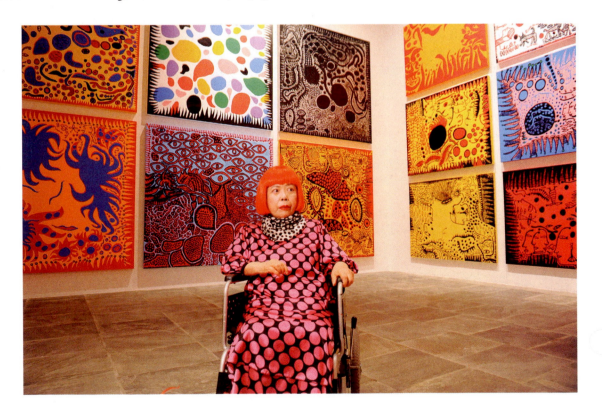

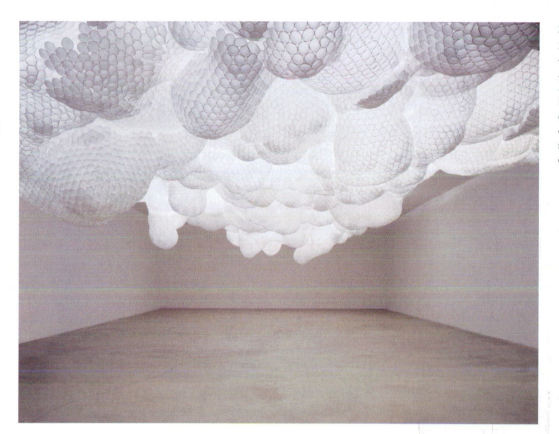

31-30 Tara Donovan, *Untitled*, 2003. Styrofoam cups and hot glue, variable dimensions. Installation at the Ace Gallery, Los Angeles, 2005.

Donovan's sculptures consist of everyday components, such as straws, plastic cups, toothpicks, and wire. The abstract shapes suggest rolling landscapes, clouds, fungus, and other natural forms.

TARA DONOVAN For sculptors as well as painters, abstraction remains a compelling mode of artistic expression today. Brooklynite TARA DONOVAN (b. 1969) is one of the leading contemporary sculptors producing abstract work. The first recipient (in 2005) of the Alexander Calder Foundation's Calder Prize for sculpture, Donovan studied at the School of Visual Arts in New York City, the Corcoran College of Art and Design in Washington, D.C., and Virginia Commonwealth University in Richmond. She has earned an international reputation for her installations, such as *Untitled* (FIG. 31-30), composed of thousands of small everyday objects—for example, toothpicks, straws, pins, paper plates, plastic cups, and electrical wire. Her large-scale abstract sculptures often suggest rolling landscapes, clouds, fungus, and other natural forms, although she seeks in her work not to mimic those forms but to capture nature's dynamic growth. Some of Donovan's installations are unstable and can change shape during the course of an exhibition.

KIMIO TSUCHIYA Unlike the paintings of Yayoi Kusama (FIG. 31-29), which are firmly in the Western tradition in style, content, and technique, the works produced by some contemporary Japanese artists are rooted in traditions integral to and distinctive of native Japanese culture. For example, the Shinto beliefs in the generative forces in nature and in humankind's position as part of the totality of nature (see "Shinto," page 495) hold great appeal for KIMIO TSUCHIYA (b. 1955), who studied sculpture in London and Tokyo. Tsuchiya is best known for his large-scale sculptures (FIG. 31-31) constructed of branches or driftwood. Despite their abstract nature, his works assert the life forces found in natural materials, thereby engaging viewers in a consideration of their own relationship to nature. Tsuchiya does not specifically invoke Shinto when speaking about his art, but it is clear that he has internalized Shinto principles. He identifies as his goal "to bring out and present the life of nature emanating from this energy of trees. . . . It is as though the wood is part of myself, as though the wood has the same kind of life force."[7]

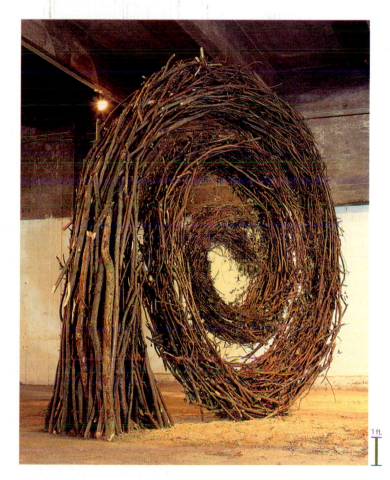

1 ft.

31-31 KIMIO TSUCHIYA, *Symptom*, 1987. Branches, 13' 1½" × 14' 9⅛" × 3' 11¼". Installation at the exhibition *Jeune Sculpture '87*, Paris 1987.

Tsuchiya's sculptures consist of branches or driftwood, and despite their abstract nature, they assert the life forces found in natural materials. His approach to sculpture reflects ancient Shinto beliefs.

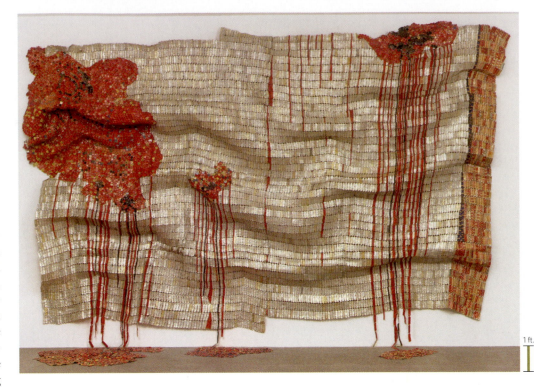

31-32 EL ANATSUI, *Bleeding Takari II*, 2007. Aluminum bottle tops and copper wire, 12' 11" × 18' 11". Museum of Modern Art, New York (gift of Donald L. Bryant Jr., and Jerry Speyer, 2008).

Anatsui's unique "metal hangings" are a cross between abstract sculptures and textiles. They are assemblages of thousands of crushed and pierced bottle caps and aluminum cans stitched together with copper wire.

EL ANATSUI Probably the most unusual abstract artworks being created today are those of Ghana-born and -educated EL ANATSUI (b. 1944), who, unique among African artists, established his international reputation without moving his studio to Europe or America. Anatsui has spent his entire adult life in Nigeria and, even more remarkably, did not begin producing the art that has made him famous until his 60s. *Bleeding Takari II* (FIG. 31-32) is a characteristic example of the artistic genre that Anatsui invented, a kind of artwork that is so different from all others that art historians have yet to agree on a label for it. A cross between sculpture and textile design, Anatsui's "metal hangings" (as they are often called) are labor-intensive constructions of crushed bottle caps and lids of aluminum cans pierced and stitched together using copper wire. The colors (primarily red, gold, and black) that Anatsui uses have close parallels in Asante *kente* cloth (FIG. 37-24), and his works can be rolled and folded like fabric. When displayed on museum walls or hanging from a ceiling—or even draped on a building's facade—the metal sheets undulate with any breeze. Anatsui's artworks-in-motion deserve comparison with Alexander Calder's pioneering *mobiles* (FIG. 29-79). They are, however, thoroughly in tune with 21st-century concerns in being assembled (by a large team of assistants) almost entirely from recycled materials.

NEW MEDIA

In addition to taking the ancient arts of painting and sculpture in new directions, contemporary artists have continued to explore the expressive possibilities of the various new media developed in the postwar period, especially digital photography, computer graphics, and video.

31-33 ANDREAS GURSKY, *Chicago Board of Trade II,* 1999. C-print, 6' 9$\frac{1}{2}$" × 11' 5$\frac{5}{8}$". Matthew Marks Gallery, New York.

Gursky manipulates digital photographs to produce vast tableaus depicting places that are characteristic of the modern global economy. The size of his prints rivals that of 19th-century history paintings.

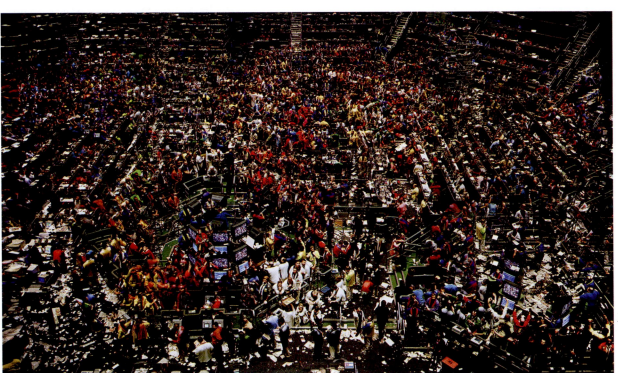

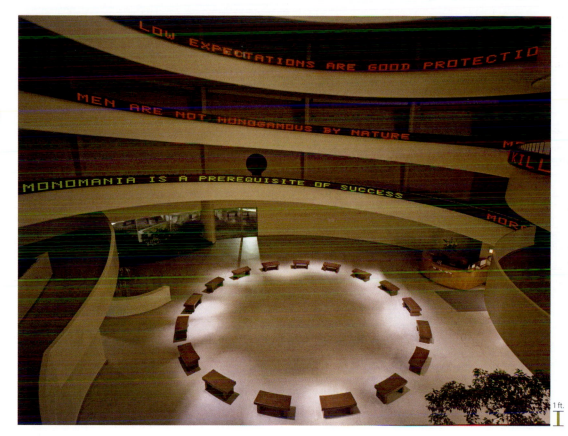

31-34 Jenny Holzer, *Untitled* (selections from *Truisms, Inflammatory Essays, The Living Series, The Survival Series, Under a Rock, Laments,* and *Child Text*), 1989. Extended helical tricolor LED electronic display signboard, 16' × 162' × 6'. Installation at the Solomon R. Guggenheim Museum, New York, December 1989–February 1990 (partial gift of the artist, 1989).

Holzer's 1989 installation consisted of electronic signs created using LED technology. The continuous display of texts wound around the Guggenheim Museum's spiral interior ramp.

1 ft.

ANDREAS GURSKY German photographer Andreas Gursky (b. 1955) grew up in Düsseldorf, where his father was a commercial photographer. Andreas studied photography at Düsseldorf's Kunstakademie (Academy of Art) and since the mid-1990s has used computer and digital technology to produce gigantic color prints in which he combines and manipulates photographs taken with a wide-angle lens, usually from a high vantage point. The size of his photographs, sometimes almost a dozen feet wide, intentionally rivals 19th-century history paintings. But as was true of Gustave Courbet (FIGS. 27-26 and 27-27) in his day, Gursky chooses his subjects from everyday life. He records the mundane world of the modern global economy—vast industrial plants, major department stores, hotel lobbies, and stock and commodity exchanges—and transforms the commonplace into striking, almost abstract, compositions. (Compare the photographs of Edward Burtynsky, FIG. 31-13.)

Gursky's nearly 12-foot-wide 1999 print (FIG. **31-33**) documenting the frenzied activity on the main floor of the Chicago Board of Trade is a characteristic example of his work. He took a series of photographs from a gallery, creating a panoramic view of the traders in their brightly colored jackets. He then combined several digital images using commercial photo-editing software to produce a blurred tableau of bodies, desks, computer terminals, and strewn paper in which both mass and color are so evenly distributed as to negate the traditional Renaissance notion of perspective. In using the computer to modify the "objective truth" and spatial recession of "straight photography," Gursky blurs the distinction between painting and photography.

JENNY HOLZER Gallipolis, Ohio, native Jenny Holzer (b. 1950) studied art at Ohio University and the Rhode Island School of Design. In 1990, she became the first woman to represent the United States at the prestigious Venice Biennale art exhibition. Holzer has won renown for several series of artworks using electronic signs, most involving light-emitting diode (LED) technology, and has created light-projection shows worldwide. In 1989, she assembled a major installation at the Solomon R. Guggenheim Museum in New York that included elements from her previous series and consisted of a large continuous LED display spiraling around the interior ramp (FIG. **31-34**) of Frank Lloyd Wright's landmark building (FIG. 30-40). Holzer believes in the communicative power of language, and her installation focused specifically on text. She invented sayings with an authoritative tone for her LED displays—for example, "Protect me from what I want," "Abuse of power comes as no surprise," and "Romantic love was invented to manipulate women." The statements, which people could read from a distance, were intentionally vague and, in some cases, contradictory.

BILL VIOLA The successors of pioneering video artist Nam June Paik (FIG. 30-57) include Adrian Piper (b. 1948; FIG. **31-34A**) and Bill Viola (b. 1951), who have explored the capabilities of digitized imagery, producing many and varied video installations. Viola often focuses on sensory perception. His pieces not only heighten viewer awareness of

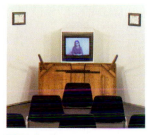

31-34A Piper, *Cornered*, 1988.

the senses but also suggest an exploration into the spiritual realm. After majoring in art and music at Syracuse University, Viola spent years seriously studying Buddhist, Christian, Sufi, and Zen mysticism. Because he fervently believes in art's transformative power and in a spiritual view of human nature, Viola designs works encouraging spectator introspection. His video projects make use of contrasts in scale, shifts in focus, mirrored reflections, extreme slow motion, staccato editing, and multiple or layered screens to achieve dramatic effects.

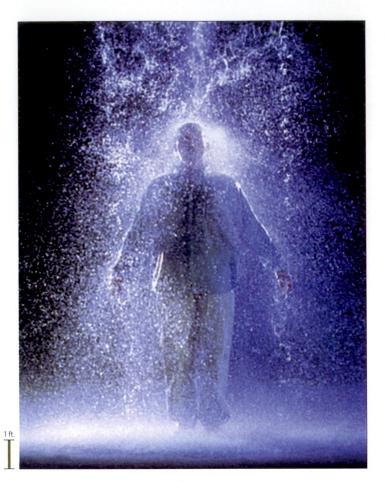

31-35 Bill Viola, *The Crossing,* 1996. Video/sound installation with two channels of color video projection onto screens 16' high.

Viola's video projects use contrasts in scale, shifts in focus, mirrored reflections, extreme slow motion, and staccato editing to create dramatic sensory experiences rooted in tangible reality.

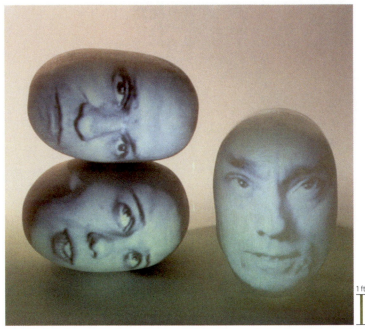

31-36 Tony Oursler, *Mansheshe,* 1997. Ceramic, glass, video player, videocassette, CPJ-200 video projector, sound, 11" × 7" × 8" each. Courtesy of the artist and Metro Pictures, New York.

Video artist Oursler projects his digital images onto sculptural objects, insinuating them into the "real" world. Here, he projected talking heads onto egg-shaped forms suspended from poles.

The power of Viola's work is evident in *The Crossing* (FIG. **31-35**), an installation piece involving two color video channels projected on 16-foot-high screens. The artist either shows the two projections on the front and back of the same screen or on two separate screens in the same installation. In these two companion videos, shown simultaneously on the two screens, a man surrounded in darkness appears, moving closer until he fills the screen. On one screen, drops of water fall from above onto the man's head, while on the other screen, a small fire breaks out at the man's feet. Over the next few minutes, the water and fire increase in intensity until the man disappears in a torrent of water on one screen (FIG. 31-35) and flames consume the man on the other screen. The deafening roar of a raging fire and a torrential downpour accompany these visual images. Eventually, everything subsides and fades into darkness. This installation's elemental nature and its presentation in a dark space immerse viewers in a pure sensory experience very much rooted in tangible reality.

TONY OURSLER Whereas Viola, Piper, and other artists present video and digital imagery to their audiences on familiar flat screens, thus reproducing the format in which we most often come into contact with electronic images, New Yorker TONY OURSLER (b. 1957), who studied art at the California Institute of the Arts, manipulates his images, projecting them onto sculptural objects. This has the effect of taking the images out of the digital world and insinuating them into the "real" world. Accompanied by sound tapes, Oursler's

installations, such as *Mansheshe* (FIG. **31-36**), not only engage but often challenge the viewer. In this example, Oursler projected talking heads onto egg-shaped forms suspended from poles. Because the projected images of people look directly at the viewer, the statements they make about religious beliefs, sexual identity, and interpersonal relationships cannot be easily dismissed.

MATTHEW BARNEY A major trend in the art world today is the relaxation of the traditional boundaries between artistic media—and not just those between painting, photography, sculpture, and textile art. Many contemporary artists are combining new and traditional media to create vast and complex multimedia installations. One of these artists is MATTHEW BARNEY (b. 1967), who studied art at Yale University. The 2003 installation (FIG. **31-37**) of his epic *Cremaster* cycle (1994–2002) at the Solomon R. Guggenheim Museum in New York typifies the expansive scale of many contemporary works. A multimedia extravaganza involving drawings, photographs, sculptures, videos, films, and performances (presented in videos), the *Cremaster* cycle is a lengthy narrative set in a self-enclosed universe that Barney created. The title of the work refers to the cremaster muscle, which controls testicular contractions in response to external stimuli. Barney uses the development of this muscle in the embryonic process of sexual differentiation as the conceptual springboard for the entire *Cremaster* project, in which he explores the notion of creation in expansive and complicated ways.

The cycle's narrative, revealed in the five 35-millimeter feature-length films and the artworks, makes reference to, among other things, a musical revue in Boise, Idaho (where San Francisco–born Barney grew up), the life cycle of bees, the execution of convicted murderer Gary Gilmore, the construction of the Chrysler Building (FIG. 29-47), Celtic mythology, Masonic rituals, a motorcycle race, and a lyric opera set in late-19th-century Budapest. In the installation, Barney tied the artworks together conceptually with a five-channel video piece projected on screens hanging in the Guggenheim's rotunda. Immersion in Barney's constructed world is disorienting and overwhelming and has a force that competes with the immense scale and often frenzied pace of contemporary life.

ENVIRONMENTAL AND SITE-SPECIFIC ART

When Robert Smithson created *Spiral Jetty* (FIG. 30-51) in Utah's Great Salt Lake in 1970, he was a trailblazer in the new genre of Environmental Art, or earthworks. In recent decades, earthworks and other site-specific artworks that bridge the gap between architecture and sculpture have become an established mode of artistic expression. As is true of all other media in the postmodern era, these artworks take a dazzling variety of forms—and some of them have engendered heated controversies.

CHRISTO AND JEANNE-CLAUDE The most prominent heir today to Smithson's earthworks movement is Canadian ANDY GOLDS-

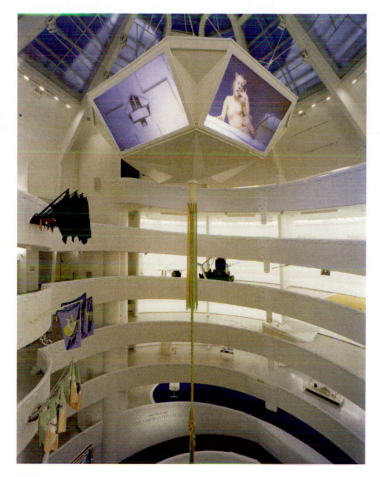

31-37 MATTHEW BARNEY, *Cremaster* cycle, installation at the Solomon R. Guggenheim Museum, New York, 2003.

Barney's vast multimedia installations of drawings, photographs, sculptures, and videos typify the relaxation at the opening of the 21st century of the traditional boundaries among artistic media.

WORTHY (b. 1956; FIG. **31-37A**), but the most famous Environmental artists of the past few decades are CHRISTO (b. 1935) and JEANNE-CLAUDE (1935–2009). In their works, the couple sought to intensify the viewer's awareness of the space and features of rural and urban sites. However, rather than physically alter the land itself, as Smithson often did, Christo and Jeanne-Claude prompted this awareness by temporarily modifying the landscape with cloth.

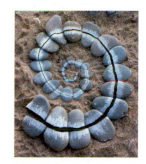

⤴ **31-37A** GOLDSWORTHY, *Cracked Rock Spiral*, 1985.

Christo studied art in his native Bulgaria and in Austria. After moving from Vienna to Paris, he began to encase objects in clumsy wrappings, thereby appropriating bits of the real world into the mysterious world of the unopened package whose contents can be dimly seen in silhouette under the wrap. Starting in 1961, a year before their marriage, Christo and Jeanne-Claude began to collaborate on large-scale projects normally dealing with the environment itself. For example, in 1969 they wrapped more than a million square feet of Australian coastline and in 1972 hung a vast curtain across a valley at Rifle Gap, Colorado. Their projects require years of preparation and research, and scores of meetings with local authorities and interested groups of local citizens. These temporary artworks are usually on view for only a few weeks.

Surrounded Islands 1980–83 (FIG. **31-38**), created in Biscayne Bay in Miami, Florida, for

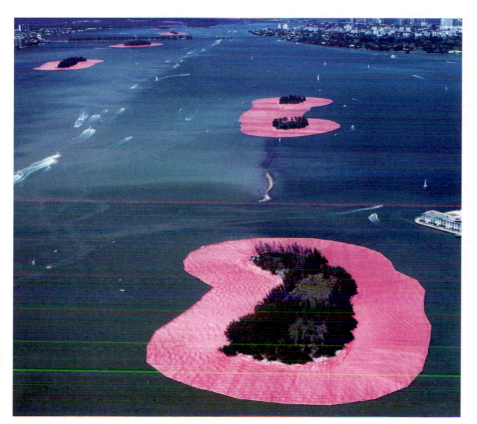

31-38 CHRISTO AND JEANNE-CLAUDE, *Surrounded Islands, Biscayne Bay, Greater Miami, Florida, 1980–83*, 1980–1983.

Christo and Jeanne-Claude created this Environmental artwork by surrounding 11 small islands with 6.5 million square feet of pink fabric. Characteristically, the work existed for only two weeks.

ART AND SOCIETY

Maya Lin's Vietnam Veterans Memorial

Maya Lin's design for the Vietnam Veterans Memorial (FIG. 31-39) is, like Minimalist sculptures (FIGS. 30-18 and 30-19), an unadorned geometric form. Yet the monument, despite its serene simplicity, actively engages viewers in a psychological dialogue, rather than standing mute. This dialogue gives visitors the opportunity to explore their feelings about the Vietnam War and perhaps arrive at some sense of closure.

The history of the Vietnam Veterans Memorial provides dramatic testimony to this monument's power. In 1981, a jury of architects, sculptors, and landscape architects selected Lin's design from among 1,400 entries in a blind competition for a memorial to be placed in Constitution Gardens in Washington, D.C. Conceivably, the jury not only found her design compelling but also thought that its simplicity would be the least likely to provoke controversy. But when the jury made its selection public, heated debate ensued. Even the wall's color came under attack. One veteran charged that black is "the universal color of shame, sorrow and degradation in all races, all societies worldwide."* But the sharpest protests concerned the form and siting of the monument. Because of the stark contrast between the massive white memorials (the Washington Monument and the Lincoln Memorial) bracketing Lin's sunken wall, some people interpreted her Minimalist design as minimizing the Vietnam War and, by extension, the efforts of those who fought in the conflict. Lin herself, however, described the wall as follows:

> The Vietnam Veterans Memorial is not an object inserted into the earth but a work formed from the act of cutting open the earth and polishing the earth's surface—dematerializing the stone to pure surface, creating an interface between the world of the light and the quieter world beyond the names.[†]

Because of the vocal opposition, a compromise was necessary to ensure the memorial's completion. The Commission of Fine Arts, the federal group overseeing the project, commissioned an additional memorial from artist Frederick Hart (1943–1999) in 1983. This larger-than-life-size realistic bronze sculpture of three soldiers, armed and uniformed, now stands approximately 120 feet from Lin's wall. Several years later, a group of nurses, organized as the Vietnam Women's Memorial Project, received approval for a sculpture honoring women's service in the Vietnam War. The 7-foot-tall bronze statue by Glenna Goodacre (b. 1939) depicts three female figures, one cradling a wounded soldier in her arms. Unveiled in 1993, the work occupies a site about 300 feet south of the Lin memorial.

Whether celebrated or condemned, Lin's Vietnam Veterans Memorial generates dramatic responses. Commonly, visitors react very emotionally, even those who knew none of the soldiers named on the monument. The polished granite surface prompts individual soul-searching—viewers see themselves reflected among the names. Many visitors leave mementos at the foot of the wall in memory of loved ones whom they lost in the Vietnam War or make rubbings from the incised names. It can be argued that much of this memorial's power derives from its Minimalist simplicity. Like Minimalist sculpture, it does not dictate response and therefore successfully encourages personal exploration.

*Elizabeth Hess, "A Tale of Two Memorials," *Art in America* 71, no. 4 (April 1983): 122.

[†]Excerpt from an unpublished 1995 lecture, quoted in Kristine Stiles and Peter Selz, *Theories and Documents of Contemporary Art: A Sourcebook of Artists' Writings* (Berkeley and Los Angeles: University of California Press, 1996), 525.

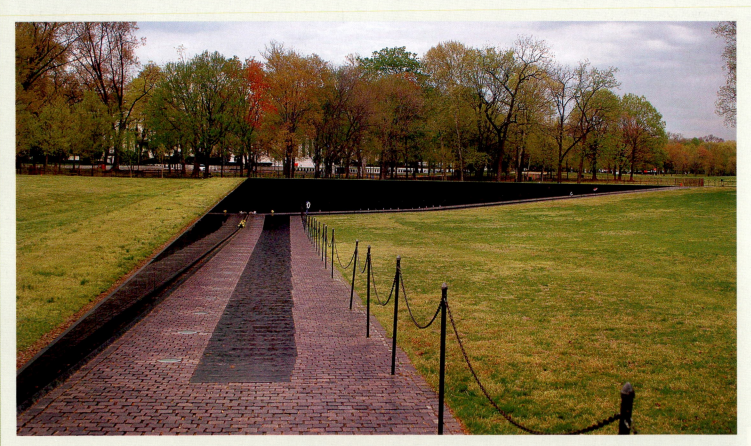

31-39 MAYA LIN, Vietnam Veterans Memorial (looking north), Washington, D.C., 1981–1983.

Like Minimalist sculpture, Lin's memorial to veterans of the Vietnam War is a simple geometric form. Its inscribed polished walls actively engage viewers in a psychological dialogue about the war.

two weeks in May 1983, typifies Christo and Jeanne-Claude's work. For this project, they surrounded 11 small artificial islands in the bay (created from a dredging project) with 6.5 million square feet of specially fabricated pink polypropylene floating fabric. This Environmental artwork required three years of preparation to obtain the required permits, assemble the labor force, and obtain the $3.2 million needed to complete the project. The artists raised the money by selling preparatory drawings, collages, and models of works they created in the 1950s and 1960s. Huge crowds watched as crews removed accumulated trash from the 11 islands (to assure maximum contrast between their dark colors, the pink of the cloth, and the blue of the bay) and then unfurled the fabric "cocoons" to form magical floating "skirts" around each tiny bit of land. Despite the brevity of its existence, *Surrounded Islands 1980–83* lives on in the host of photographs, films, and books documenting the project.

MAYA LIN Often classified as either a work of Minimalist sculpture or as an architectural monument, the Vietnam Veterans Memorial (FIG. **31-39**) in Washington, D.C., is perhaps best considered under the heading of site-specific art. The now-acclaimed war memorial was designed in 1981 by MAYA YING LIN (b. 1960) when she was a 21-year-old student at the Yale School of Architecture. Austere and simple, the Vietnam memorial takes the form of a V-shaped wall constructed of polished black granite panels. The two 246-foot-long wings of the wall begin at ground level at each end and gradually ascend to a height of 10 feet at the center of the V. Lin set the memorial into the landscape, enhancing visitors' awareness of descent as they walk along the wall toward the center. The names of the Vietnam War's 57,939 American casualties (and those missing in action) inscribed on the two wings (in the order of their deaths) contribute to the memorial's dramatic effect.

When Lin designed this pristinely simple monument, she gave a great deal of thought to the purpose of war memorials. She was determined to create a memorial that would

> be honest about the reality of war and be for the people who gave their lives. . . . [I] didn't want a static object that people would just look at, but something they could relate to as on a journey, or passage, that would bring each to his own conclusions. . . . I wanted to work with the land and not dominate it. I had an impulse to cut open the earth . . .

an initial violence that in time would heal. The grass would grow back, but the cut would remain.[8]

In light of the tragedy of the war, this unpretentious memorial's allusion to a wound and long-lasting scar contributes to its visual and psychological impact (see "Maya Lin's Vietnam Veterans Memorial," page 1020).

RACHEL WHITEREAD Another controversial memorial commissioned for a specific historical setting is the Viennese Holocaust Memorial (FIG. **31-40**) by British sculptor RACHEL WHITEREAD (b. 1963). In 1996, the city of Vienna chose Whiteread as the winner of the competition to design a commemorative monument to the 65,000 Austrian Jews who perished at the hands of the Nazis during World War II. The decision to focus attention on a past that most Austrians wished to forget unleashed a controversy that delayed construction of the monument until 2000. Also controversial was the Minimalist severity of Whiteread's massive block of concrete planted in a Baroque square at the heart of the Austrian capital—as was, at least initially, the understated form of Lin's Vietnam monument (FIG. **31-39**) juxtaposed with the Washington and Lincoln Monuments in Washington, D.C.

Whiteread modulated the surface of the Holocaust memorial only slightly by depicting in low relief the shapes of two doors and hundreds of identical books on shelves, with the edges of the covers and the pages rather than the spines facing outward. The book motif was a reference both to Jews as "People of the Book" and to the book burnings that accompanied Jewish persecutions throughout the centuries and under the Nazis. Around the base, Whiteread inscribed the names of Nazi concentration camps in German, Hebrew, and English. The setting for the memorial is Judenplatz (Jewish Square), the site of a synagogue destroyed in 1421. The brutality of the tomblike monument—it cannot be entered, and its shape suggests a prison block—is a visual as well as psychological shock in that beautiful Viennese square. Whiteread's purpose, however, was not to please but to create a memorial that met the jury's charge to "combine dignity with reserve and spark an aesthetic dialogue with the past in a place that is replete with history."

Whiteread had gained fame in 1992 for her monument commemorating the demolition of a working-class neighborhood in East London. *House* took the form of a concrete cast of the space inside the last standing Victorian house on the site. She had also made sculptures of "negative spaces"—for example, the space beneath a chair or mattress or sink. In Vienna, she represented the space behind the shelves of a library. In drawing viewers' attention to the voids between and inside objects and buildings, Whiteread pursued in a different way the same goal as Pop Art innovator Jasper Johns (FIG. 30-24), who painted things "seen but not looked at."

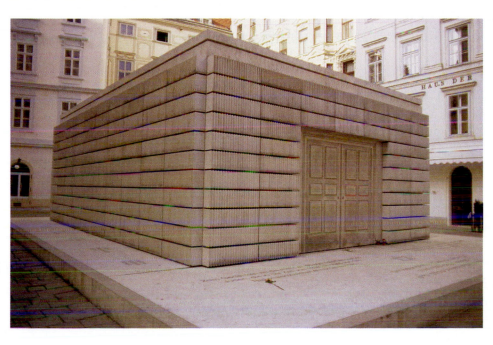

31-40 RACHEL WHITEREAD, Holocaust Memorial (looking northwest), Judenplatz, Vienna, Austria, 2000.

Whiteread's monument to the 65,000 Austrian Jews who perished in the Holocaust is a tomblike concrete block with doors that cannot be opened and library books seen from behind.

ART AND SOCIETY
Richard Serra's *Tilted Arc*

When Richard Serra installed *Tilted Arc* (FIG. 31-41) in the plaza in front of the Javits Federal Building in New York City in 1981, much of the public immediately responded with hostile criticism. Prompting the chorus of complaints was the uncompromising presence of a Minimalist sculpture bisecting the plaza. Many argued that *Tilted Arc* was ugly, attracted graffiti, interfered with the view across the plaza, and prevented use of the plaza for performances or concerts. Because of the sustained barrage of protests and petitions demanding the removal of *Tilted Arc*, the General Services Administration, which had commissioned the sculpture, held a series of public hearings. Afterward, the agency decided to remove Serra's sculpture despite its prior approval of the artist's model. Understandably, this infuriated Serra, who had a legally binding contract acknowledging the site-specific nature of *Tilted Arc*. "To remove the work is to destroy the work," the artist stated.*

This episode raised intriguing issues about the nature of public art, including the public reception of experimental art, the artist's responsibilities and rights when executing public commissions, censorship in the arts, and the purpose of public art. If an artwork is on display in a public space outside the relatively private confines of a museum or gallery, do different guidelines apply? As one participant in the *Tilted Arc* saga asked, "Should an artist have the right to impose his values and taste on a public that now rejects his taste and values?"† Historically,

one of the express functions of the artistic avant-garde was to challenge convention by rejecting tradition and disrupting the complacency of the viewer. Will placing experimental art in a public place always cause controversy? From Serra's statements, it is clear that he intended the sculpture to challenge the public.

Another issue that *Tilted Arc* presented involved the rights of the artist, who in this case accused the GSA of censorship. Serra filed a lawsuit against the federal government for infringement of his First Amendment rights and insisted that "the artist's work must be uncensored, respected, and tolerated, although deemed abhorrent, or perceived as challenging, or experienced as threatening."‡ Did removal of the work constitute censorship? A U.S. district court held that it did not.

Ultimately, who should decide what artworks are appropriate for the public arena? One artist argued, "We cannot have public art by plebiscite [popular vote]."§ But to avoid recurrences of the *Tilted Arc* controversy, the GSA changed its procedures and now solicits input from a wide range of civic and neighborhood groups before commissioning public artworks. Despite the removal of *Tilted Arc* (now languishing in storage), the sculpture maintains a powerful presence in all discussions of the aesthetics, politics, and dynamics of public art.

*Grace Glueck, "What Part Should the Public Play in Choosing Public Art?" *New York Times,* February 3, 1985, 27.

†Calvin Tomkins, "The Art World: Tilted Arc," *New Yorker,* May 20, 1985, 98.

‡Ibid., 98–99.

§Ibid., 98.

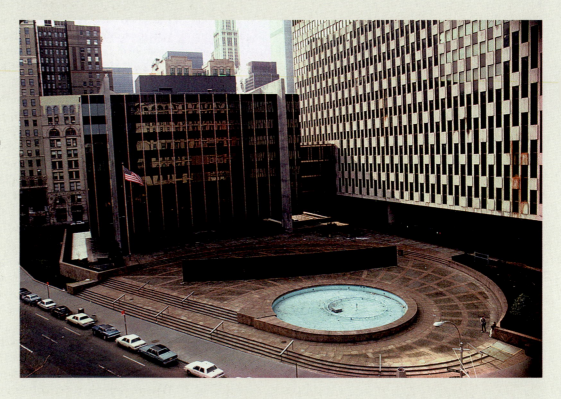

31-41 RICHARD SERRA, *Tilted Arc,* as installed before its removal from Jacob K. Javits Federal Plaza (looking southwest), New York City, 1981.

Serra intended his Minimalist *Tilted Arc* to alter the character of an existing public space. He succeeded, but unleashed a storm of protest that caused the government to remove the work.

RICHARD SERRA Also unleashing an emotional public debate, but for different reasons and with a decidedly different outcome, was *Tilted Arc* (FIG. **31-41**) by San Franciscan RICHARD SERRA (b. 1939), who worked in steel mills in California before studying art at Yale University. He now lives in New York, where he received a commission in 1979 from the General Services Administration (GSA), the federal agency responsible for overseeing the selection and installa-

tion of artworks for government buildings, to install a 120-foot-long, 12-foot-high curved wall of Cor-Ten steel in the plaza in front of the Jacob K. Javits Federal Building in lower Manhattan. He completed the project in 1981. Serra wished *Tilted Arc* to "dislocate or alter the decorative function of the plaza and actively bring people into the sculpture's context."⁹ In pursuit of that goal, Serra situated the sculpture so that it bisected and consequently significantly altered the space

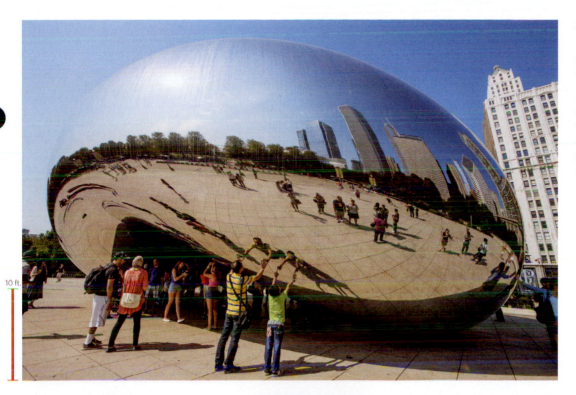

Kapoor's enormous polished stainless steel sculpture has delighted visitors to Chicago's Millennium Park, who enjoy seeing distorted views of themselves and the city's skyline in *Cloud Gate*'s curving mirrored surface.

10 ft.

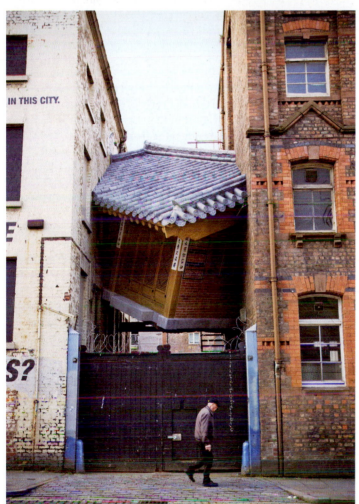

31-43 DO-HO SUH, *Bridging Home*, 2010. Korean house installation in Duke Street, Liverpool, England.

Bridging Home is an empty Korean house wedged between two buildings in Liverpool. It effectively communicates Suh's sense of displacement as a nomad dividing his life between Seoul and New York.

of the open plaza and interrupted the traffic flow across the square. By creating such an intrusive presence in this large public space, Serra forced viewers to reconsider the plaza's physical space as a sculptural form—but only temporarily, because the public succeeded in having the sculpture removed (see "Richard Serra's *Tilted Arc*," page 1022).

ANISH KAPOOR The public reacted very differently to the installation in 2004 in Chicago's Millennium Park of *Cloud Gate* (FIG. **31-42**), a 33-foot-tall and 66-foot-long polished stainless steel abstract sculpture by the recently knighted Mumbai-born British sculptor ANISH KAPOOR (b. 1954). Affectionately known to Chicagoans as the Bean, Kapoor's gigantic, gently curving sculpture is large enough that people can walk under its swelling arched form, hence its title *Cloud Gate*. Rather than disrupting activity in the park, as Serra's *Tilted Arc* (FIG. 31-41) did in Manhattan, Kapoor's *Cloud Gate* encourages viewers to interact with it. Indeed, most people delight in seeing their reflection (with the backdrop of the panorama of Chicago's skyline) in the mirrorlike surface. On many days, *Cloud Gate* also reflects clouds of similar bean shape. The reflections of people, buildings, and clouds, however, are distorted by the Bean's curved surface, as Kapoor intended them to be, adding another dimension to the pleasure of looking at the work.

DO-HO SUH Some of the most interesting site-specific artworks being created today are the work of Korean DO-HO SUH (b. 1962), who studied at Seoul National University, the Rhode Island School of Design, and Yale University. Suh maintains a studio in Seoul, but his installations are designed for display on several continents. His pieces are to a large extent autobiographical in that they often are based on the modest houses and apartments in which he has lived. An outstanding example is *Bridging Home* (FIG. 31-43), which Suh wedged between two buildings on Duke Street in Liverpool, England, for the 2010 International Festival of Contemporary Arts. The title—*Bridging Home*—is a reference to Suh's dividing his personal and professional life between Seoul and New York City. The insertion of an empty Korean home into a Liverpool street effectively communicated Suh's sense of rootlessness and displacement as a nomadic citizen of the world.

31-44 David Hammons, *Public Enemy*, installation at Museum of Modern Art, New York, 1991. Photographs, balloons, sandbags, guns, and other mixed media.

Hammons intended this multimedia installation, with Theodore Roosevelt flanked by an African American and a Native American as servants, to reveal the racism embedded in America's cultural heritage.

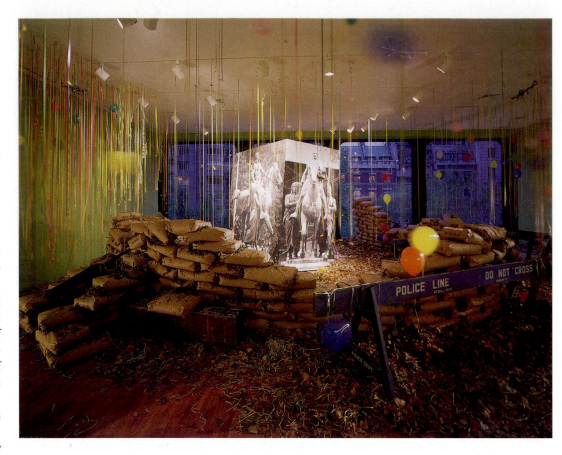

DAVID HAMMONS Suh's works have been exhibited in many museums as well as outdoors. In fact, museums throughout the world have in recent decades increasingly allocated more of their limited exhibition space to installation art. One example of this kind of indoor site-specific art that encourages viewer interaction at the same time that it makes a powerful statement about racism in America is *Public Enemy* (FIG. **31-44**) by DAVID HAMMONS (b. 1943), which he created for an exhibition at the Museum of Modern Art in New York in 1991. Born in Springfield, Illinois, Hammons, an African American, moved to Los Angeles in 1962, where he studied art at the Chouinard and Otis Art Institutes before settling in Harlem in 1974. In his installations, Hammons combines sharp social commentary with beguiling sensory elements.

In *Public Enemy,* he enticed viewers to interact with the installation by scattering fragrant autumn leaves on the floor and positioning helium-filled balloons throughout the gallery. The leaves crunched underfoot, and the dangling strings of the balloons gently brushed spectators walking around the installation. Once drawn into the environment, viewers encountered the centerpiece of *Public Enemy*—large black-and-white photographs of a public monument in front of the American Museum of Natural History in New York City depicting President Theodore Roosevelt (1858–1919) triumphantly seated on a horse, flanked by an African American man and a Native American man, both men appearing in the role of servant. Around the edge of the installation, circling the photographs of the monument, were piles of sandbags with both real and toy guns propped on top, aimed at the statue. By selecting evocative found objects and presenting them in a dynamic manner, encouraging viewer interaction, Hammons attracted an audience and then revealed the racism embedded in received cultural heritage and prompted reexamination of American values and cultural emblems.

ARCHITECTURE

The work of architects today is as varied as that of contemporary painters, sculptors, and new-media artists, but the common denominator in the diversity of contemporary architectural design is the breaking down of national boundaries, with leading practitioners working in several countries and even on several continents, often simultaneously. In the late 20th and early 21st centuries, one of the by-products of the globalization of the world's economy has been that in the rapidly developing emerging markets of Asia, the Middle East, Africa, Latin America, and elsewhere, virtually every architect with an international reputation can list on his or her résumé a recent building in a bustling new urban center. In this brief survey of contemporary architecture, the projects of eight internationally acclaimed architects are considered under three major headings: Postmodernism, Deconstructivism, and High-Tech and Green architecture.

Postmodernism

The decades following the conclusion of World War II witnessed the rejection of the unadorned modernist aesthetic in architecture, exemplified by the Seagram Building (FIG. 30-45) in New York City, even by that building's codesigner, in favor of a more complex architectural vocabulary incorporating references to historical styles (see "After Modernism: Postmodern Architecture" and "Philip Johnson on Postmodern Architecture," pages 949 and 983). Architectural postmodernism remains a major stylistic trend today. Two internationally renowned architects who have produced significant postmodern buildings are I. M. Pei and James Stirling.

I. M. PEI The latest chapter in the long architectural history of the Louvre—the former French royal residence (FIGS. 20-16, 23-23, and 25-25), now one of the world's greatest art museums—is a monumental glass-and-steel pyramid erected in the palace's main courtyard in 1988. Designed by the Chinese American architect I. M. (IEOH MING) PEI (b. 1917), the Grand Louvre Pyramide (FIG. **31-45**) is the dramatic glass-and-steel entryway to the museum's priceless

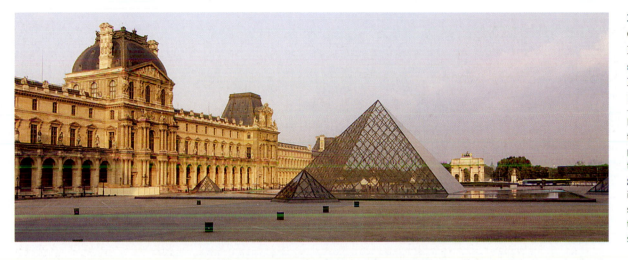

31-45 I. M. PEI, Grand Louvre Pyramide (looking southwest), Musée du Louvre, Paris, France, 1988.

Egyptian stone architecture inspired Pei's postmodern entryway to the Louvre, but his glass-and-steel pyramid is a transparent tent serving as a skylight for the underground extension of the old museum.

collections. Although initially controversial because conservative critics considered it a jarring, dissonant intrusion in a hallowed public space left untouched for centuries, Pei's pyramid, like Rogers and Piano's Pompidou Center (FIG. 30-50) a decade before, quickly captured the French public's imagination and admiration.

In fact, Pei erected four glass pyramids in the Louvre courtyard: the grand central pyramid plus the three small echoes of it bordering the large fountain-filled pool surrounding the dominating glass entryway. Consistent with postmodern aesthetics, Pei turned to the past for inspiration, choosing the quintessential emblem of ancient Egypt (FIG. 3-8), an appropriate choice given the Louvre's rich collection of Egyptian art. But Pei transformed his ancient solid stone models (see "Building the Great Pyramids," page 62) into a transparent "tent," simultaneously permitting an almost uninterrupted view of the wings of the royal palace courtyard and serving as a skylight for the new underground network of ticket booths, offices, shops, restaurants, and conference rooms that he also designed.

JAMES STIRLING In England, the leading postmodern architect was JAMES STIRLING (1926–1994). Like other architects who achieved critical acclaim, Stirling received commissions for buildings throughout Europe and North America. His masterpiece may be the Neue Staatsgalerie (FIG. 31-46) in Stuttgart, a brilliant solution to a challenging commission calling for an addition to a Renaissance Revival museum on a difficult hillside site wedged between existing terraced buildings and an eight-lane traffic-clogged thoroughfare. Stirling's sprawling design—which is impossible to encompass in a single photograph other than an aerial view and cannot be fully appreciated except from the ground—intentionally recalls Karl Friedrich Schinkel's Altes Museum (FIG. 27-42) in Berlin in having a central rotunda. But at Stuttgart, the rotunda (FIG. 31-46, *bottom*) is an open

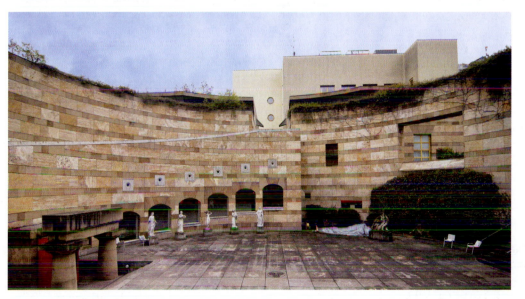

31-46 JAMES STIRLING, Neue Staatsgalerie, Stuttgart, Germany, 1977–1983. *Top:* facade (looking north); *bottom:* courtyard (looking northwest).

Stirling's postmodern design for Stuttgart's new museum complex incorporates Egyptian and Greco-Roman architectural references as well as contemporary High-Tech design elements.

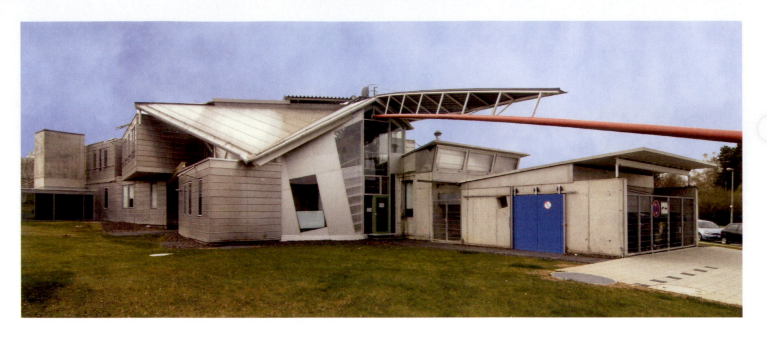

31-47 GÜNTER BEHNISCH, Hysolar Institute (looking south), University of Stuttgart, Stuttgart, Germany, 1987.

The roof, walls, and windows of the Deconstructivist Hysolar Institute seem to explode, avoiding any suggestion of stable masses and frustrating viewers' expectations of how a building should look.

courtyard that forms the centerpiece of an asymmetrical plan that breaks sharply from the rules of classical architectural design.

Like most art museums today—which are income-producing cultural supermarkets with restaurants, shops, theaters, and reception areas for gala events, in addition to exhibition halls with related curatorial offices and workshops—the Staatsgalerie is a multifaceted, multifunctional building. It also incorporates multiple historical references, which are unexpectedly revealed to visitors as they move from one part of the architectural complex to another. The sandstone ramps and pylonlike walls of the facade facing the roadway (FIG. 31-46, *top*) owe their inspiration to ancient Egyptian temples (FIGS. 3-20, 3-24, 3-24A, and 3-39), but Stirling also included an undulating glass wall based on the shape of a grand piano, a red-and-blue steel glass-roofed taxi stand, and, in the courtyard (FIG. 31-46, *bottom*), Greco-Roman columns and architraves scattered like abandoned ruins. The historical eclecticism of Stirling's Staatsgalerie is quintessentially postmodern.

Deconstructivism

Perhaps the most radical development in architectural design during the closing decades of the 20th century was *Deconstructivism*. Deconstructivist architects attempt to disrupt the conventional categories of architecture and to rupture the viewer's expectations based on them. Destabilization plays a major role in Deconstructivist architecture. Disorder, dissonance, imbalance, asymmetry, irregularity, and confusion replace their opposites—order, harmony, balance, symmetry, regularity, and clarity. The seemingly haphazardly presented volumes, masses, planes, borders, lighting, locations, directions, and spatial relations, as well as the disguised structural facts of Deconstructivist design, challenge the viewer's assumptions about architectural form as it relates to function. According to Deconstructivist principles, the very absence of the stability of traditional categories of architecture in a structure announces a "deconstructed" building.

GÜNTER BEHNISCH An early example of this audacious architectural mode is the Hysolar Institute (FIG. **31-47**) at the University of Stuttgart, Germany, by GÜNTER BEHNISCH (1922–2010). Behnisch, who gained international attention as the architect of the Olympic Park in Munich for the 1972 Olympic Games, designed the institute as part of a joint German–Saudi Arabian research project on the technology of solar energy. In the Hysolar Institute, Behnisch intended to deny the possibility of spatial enclosure altogether, and his apparently chaotic arrangement of the structural units defies easy analysis. The shapes of the roof, walls, and windows seem to explode, avoiding any suggestion of clear, stable masses. Behnisch aggressively played with the traditional concepts of architectural design, frustrating the viewer's expectations of how a building should look. The disordered architectural elements appear precarious, seemingly prevented from collapsing only by a curved red steel cable running through the building and anchored to the ground on each end.

FRANK GEHRY The architect most closely identified with Deconstructivist architecture is Canadian-born American FRANK GEHRY (b. 1929). Trained in sculpture, and at different times a collaborator with Donald Judd (FIG. 30-19) and Claes Oldenburg (FIG. 30-29), Gehry works up his designs by constructing models and then cutting them up and arranging the parts until he has a satisfying composition. Among Gehry's most notable projects is the Guggenheim Museum (FIGS. 31-48 and 31-49) in Bilbao, Spain, one of several art museum projects of the past few decades—including the Grand Louvre Pyramid (FIG. 31-45), the Neue Staatsgalerie (FIG. 31-46), and the Denver Art Museum (FIG. **31-47A**) by DANIEL LIBESKIND (b. 1946)—that are as notable for their innovative architectural designs as for the important art collections they house.

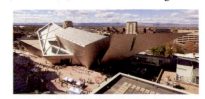

⬈31-47A LIBESKIND, Denver Art Museum, 2006.

ARTISTS ON ART

Frank Gehry on Architectural Design and Materials

Frank Gehry has been designing buildings since the 1950s, but only in the 1970s did he begin to break away from the rectilinearity of modernist architecture and develop the dramatic sculptural style seen in buildings such as the Guggenheim Museum (FIGS. **31-48** and **31-49**) in Bilbao. In 1999, the Deconstructivist architect reflected on his career and his many projects in a book simply titled *Gehry Talks*.

> My early work was rectilinear because you take baby steps. I guess the work has become a kind of sculpture as architecture. . . . I'm a strict modernist in the sense of believing in purity, that you shouldn't decorate. And yet buildings need decoration, because they need scaling elements. They need to be human scale, in my opinion. They can't just be faceless things. That's how some modernism failed.*

They teach materials and methods in architecture school, as a separate course. I'm a craftsman. . . . It seems to me that when you're doing architecture, you're building something out of something. There are social issues, there's context, and then there's how do you make the enclosure and what do you make it with? . . . I explored metal: how it dealt with the light . . . It does beautiful things with light. . . . Flat was a fetish, and everybody was doing that. I found out that I could use metal if I didn't worry about it being flat; I could do it cheaper. It was intuitive. I just went with it. I liked it. Then when I saw it on the building, I loved it. . . . Bilbao . . . [is] titanium. . . . [I] prefer titanium because it's stronger; it's an element, a pure element, and it doesn't oxidize. It stays the same forever. They give a hundred-year guarantee![†]

*Milton Friedman, ed., *Gehry Talks: Architecture + Process,* rev. ed. (New York: Universe, 2002), 47–48.

[†]Ibid., 44, 47.

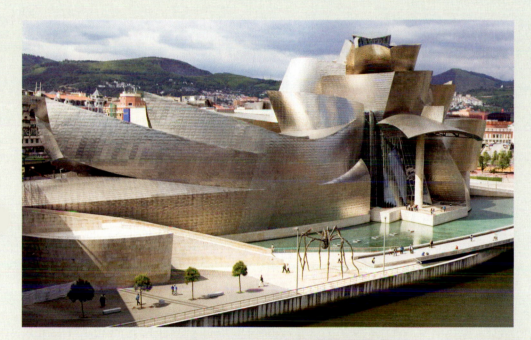

31-48 FRANK GEHRY, Guggenheim Bilbao Museo (looking southwest), Bilbao, Spain, 1997.

Gehry's limestone-and-titanium Bilbao museum is an immensely dramatic building. Its disorder and seeming randomness of design epitomize Deconstructivist architectural principles.

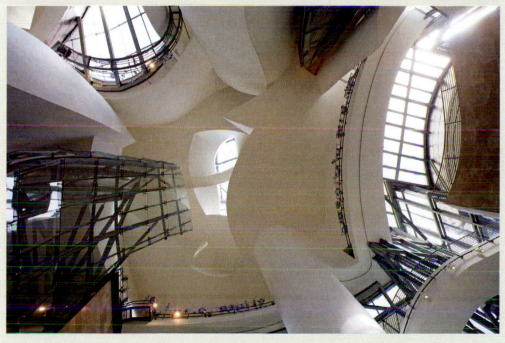

31-49 FRANK GEHRY, atrium of the Guggenheim Bilbao Museo (view looking up), Bilbao, Spain, 1997.

The glass-walled atrium of the Guggenheim Bilbao Museum soars skyward 165 feet. The asymmetrical and imbalanced screens and vaults flow into one another, creating a sense of disequilibrium.

Gehry's Bilbao museum appears to be a collapsed or collapsing aggregate of units. Visitors approaching the building see a mass of irregular asymmetrical and imbalanced forms whose profiles change dramatically with every shift of the viewer's position. The limestone- and titanium-clad exterior lends a space-age character to the structure, and highlights further the unique cluster effect of the many forms (see "Frank Gehry on Architectural Design and Materials," page 1027). A group of organic forms that Gehry refers to as a "metallic flower" tops the museum. In the center of the building, an enormous glass-walled atrium (FIG. 31-49) soars 165 feet above the ground, serving as the focal point for the three levels of galleries radiating from it. The seemingly weightless screens, vaults, and volumes of the interior float and flow into one another, guided only by light and dark cues. The Guggenheim Museum in Bilbao is a profoundly compelling structure. Its disorder, its deceptive randomness of design, and the disequilibrium it prompts in viewers exemplify Deconstructivist principles.

31-50 ZAHA HADID, proposal for Signature Towers, Dubai, United Arab Emirates, designed 2006; not yet constructed.

Originally dubbed the Dancing Towers, Hadid's triad of corporate skyscrapers in Dubai features two towers that seem to be in motion. They bend to merge halfway up, enabling passage between them.

ZAHA HADID One of the most innovative living architects is Iraqi Deconstructivist ZAHA HADID (b. 1950), the first woman to win the Pritzker Architecture Prize (in 2004), the architectural equivalent of the Nobel Prize in literature. The first recipient was Philip Johnson in 1979. Other previous winners include Norman Foster (FIGS. 31-51 and 31-53), Frank Gehry, I. M. Pei, Renzo Piano, James Stirling, Joern Utzon, and Robert Venturi. Born in Baghdad, Hadid studied mathematics in Beirut, Lebanon, and architecture in London, and has designed buildings in England, Germany, Austria, France, Italy, Spain, the United States, and elsewhere. Deeply influenced by the Suprematist theories and paintings of Kazimir Malevich (FIG. 29-30), who championed the use of pure colors and abstract geometric shapes to express "the supremacy of pure feeling in creative art," Hadid employs unadorned surfaces (the antithesis of typical postmodernist design) in dynamic arrangements that have an emotional effect on the viewer.

One of her most ambitious projects is a triad of skyscrapers in Dubai, the capital of the oil-rich United Arab Emirates, where many interesting buildings by major architects are being erected today. Originally dubbed the Dancing Towers and now called the Signature Towers (FIG. **31-50**), the three skyscrapers that will house offices, a hotel, a restaurant with a panoramic view, and luxurious private apartments deviate sharply from traditional skyscraper design because Hadid proposes to give the impression that two of the towers "dance." The undulating motion is, of course, illusory. But the towers do bend in order to merge about halfway up to enable people to move from tower to tower without descending to the ground and exiting. The more traditional tower, which also bends, connects to the central tower, but at ground level.

High-Tech and Green Architecture

From its beginnings in the late 19th century (see "The First Skyscrapers," page 876), skyscraper design has always required the collaboration of engineers to provide heating, plumbing, lighting, elevators, and all the other necessities of modern life for the hundreds or thousands of people who work or live in these urban towers. Today, engineering concerns are most readily apparent in the work of technologically savvy architects and especially in the design of buildings that conserve natural resources.

NORMAN FOSTER Pritzker award–winning architect NORMAN FOSTER (b. 1935) began his study of architectural design at the University of Manchester, England. After graduating, he won a fellowship to attend the master's degree program at the Yale School of Architecture, where he met Richard Rogers (FIG. 30-50). The two decided to open a joint architectural firm when they returned to London in 1962, but they established separate practices several years later. Their designs still have much in common, however, because they share a similar outlook. Foster and Rogers are the leading proponents of what critics call *High-Tech architecture*, the roots of which can be traced to Joseph Paxton's mid-19th-century Crystal Palace (FIG. 27-47) in London. High-Tech architects design buildings incorporating the latest innovations in engineering and technology and exposing the structures' component parts. High-Tech architecture, like Deconstructivist architecture, is distinct from other postmodern architectural movements in dispensing with all historical references.

Foster's design for the headquarters (FIG. **31-51**) of the Hong Kong and Shanghai Bank Corporation (HSBC), which even a quarter century ago cost $1 billion to build, exemplifies the High-Tech approach to architecture. The banking tower is as different from Philip Johnson's postmodern AT&T Building (FIG. 30-48) as it is from the modernist glass-and-steel Seagram Building (FIG. 30-45)

and Sears Tower (FIG. 30-46). The 47-story Hong Kong skyscraper has an exposed steel skeleton with the elevators and other service elements located in giant piers at the short ends of the building, a design that provides uninterrupted communal working spaces on each cantilevered floor. Foster divided the tower into five horizontal units of six to nine floors each that he calls "villages," suspended from steel girders resembling bridges. Escalators connect the floors in each village—the floors are related by function—but the elevators stop at only one floor in each community of floors. At the base of the building is a plaza opening onto the neighboring streets. Visitors ascend on escalators from the plaza to a spectacular 10-story, 170-foot-tall atrium bordered by balconies with additional workspaces. What Foster calls "sun scoops"—computerized mirrors on the south side of the building—track the movement of the sun across the Hong Kong sky and reflect the sunlight into the atrium and plaza, flooding the dramatic spaces with light at all hours of the day. Not surprisingly, the roof of this High-Tech skyscraper serves as a landing pad for corporate helicopters.

RENZO PIANO The harnessing of solar energy as a power source is one of the key features of what critics commonly refer to as *Green architecture*—ecologically friendly buildings that use "clean energy" and sustain the natural environment. Green architecture is the most important trend in architectural design in the early 21st century. A pioneer in this field is Renzo Piano, the codesigner with Richard Rogers of the Pompidou Center (FIG. 30-50) in Paris. Piano won an international competition to design the Tjibaou Cultural Centre (FIG. **31-52**) in Noumea, New Caledonia. Named in honor of the assassinated political leader Jean-Marie Tjibaou (1936–1989), the center consists of 10 beehive-shaped bamboo "huts" nestled in pine trees on a narrow island peninsula in the Pacific Ocean. Rooted in the village architecture of the Kanak people of New Caledonia (see MAP 36-1), each unit of Piano's complex has an adjustable skylight as a roof to provide natural—sustainable—climate control. The curved profile of the Tjibaou pavilions also helps the structures withstand the pressure of the hurricane-force winds common in the South Pacific.

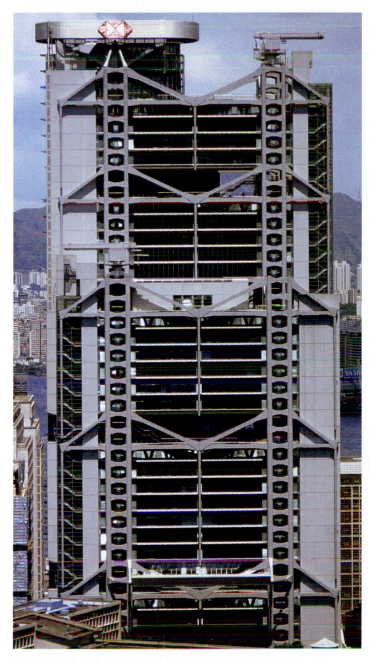

31-51 NORMAN FOSTER, Hong Kong and Shanghai Bank (looking southwest), Hong Kong, China, 1979–1986.

Foster's High-Tech tower has an exposed steel skeleton featuring floors with uninterrupted working spaces. At the base is a 10-story atrium illuminated by computerized mirrors that reflect sunlight.

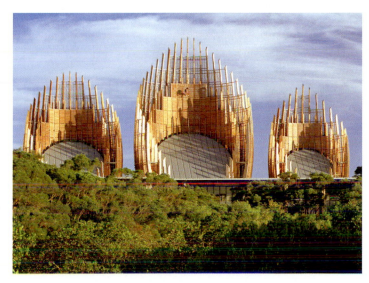

31-52 RENZO PIANO, Tjibaou Cultural Centre (looking southeast), Noumea, New Caledonia, 1998.

A pioneering example of Green architecture, Piano's complex of 10 bamboo units, based on traditional New Caledonian village huts, has adjustable skylights in the roofs for natural climate control.

PROBLEMS AND SOLUTIONS
Norman Foster, the Gherkin, and Green Architectural Design

One of the major recent additions to the skyline of London is Norman Foster's corporate tower officially called 30 St Mary Axe, formerly named after the global reinsurance company Swiss Re, which commissioned the skyscraper as its U.K. headquarters. However, the building is popularly known as the Gherkin because of its distinctive swelling shape resembling a cucumber. The 590-foot-tall, 40-story tower, the sixth-tallest building in London at the time of its construction, stands in the midst of mostly low-rise buildings in the Canary Wharf district and replaced a 1903 structure damaged in a 1992 bombing by the Irish Republican Army. The Gherkin has consequently figured prominently in debates about the intrusion of gigantic skyscrapers in old historical neighborhoods.

Far more attention, however, has been devoted to its award-winning high-tech design and innovative "green" solution to the problem of constructing massive buildings housing thousands of workers in the heart of a densely populated city, where the conservation of resources such as fossil fuel and electricity are high priorities. For example, the tower's ventilated double skin greatly reduces the need to heat the building in the winter and cool it in the summer. The cavity of the two-layer exterior of the Gherkin traps air and provides natural insulation, and panels installed in the same space capture the sun's rays to produce heat or deflect it to reduce the need for air conditioning. The glass panes that make up most of the building's exterior also provide abundant natural light to the offices within, reducing the need for electrical lighting. Energy consumption is further reduced by light controls throughout the building, which respond to motion and automatically turn off when a space is unoccupied. The building has consequently become the "poster child" for Green architecture in England and, more generally, in the world at large. The Gherkin is pointing the way toward the fully sustainable urban environments of the future.

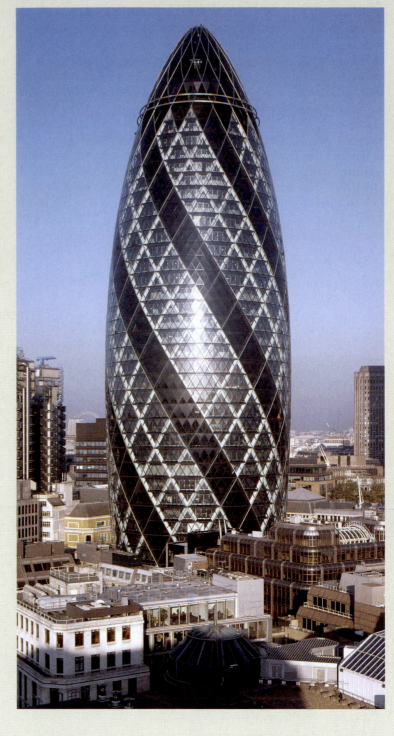

31-53 Norman Foster, 30 St Mary Axe ("the Gherkin," looking southwest), London, England, erected 2001–2003, opened 2004.

Foster's cucumber-shaped skyscraper, originally built as the headquarters of Swiss Re, is a High-Tech marvel that incorporates the latest innovations in Green design to conserve natural resources.

GHERKIN, LONDON Buildings that conserve energy and provide sustainable living and working environments are especially desirable in densely populated areas, where the demands on the earth's natural resources are greatest. A recent triumph of Green architectural design is the corporate tower in London popularly known as the Gherkin (see "Norman Foster, the Gherkin, and Green Architectural Design," above, and FIG. **31-53**).

WHAT NEXT? No one knows what the next years and decades will bring, but given the expansive scope of postmodern art and

architecture, it is certain that no single approach or style will dominate.

New technologies will undoubtedly continue to redefine what constitutes a "work of art" or "a building." The universally expanding presence of computers, digital technology, and the Internet may well erode what few conceptual and geographical boundaries remain, and make art and information about art available to virtually everyone, thereby creating a truly global artistic community. As this chapter has revealed, substantial progress has already been made in that direction.

CONTEMPORARY ART WORLDWIDE

Personal and Group Identity

- The vast number of artworks created since 1980 worldwide are extraordinarily diverse in style, format, content, and technique, but can be classified under a few major themes, including personal and group identity. Many artists of African descent, including Wiley, Basquiat, Edwards, Ringgold, Simpson, and Weems, have produced important works addressing issues of concern to black Americans. Quick-to-See Smith has focused on her Native American heritage. Gender and sexuality are central themes in the work of Kruger, the Guerrilla Girls, Mapplethorpe, Wojnarowicz, and Sikander. National identity looms large in the art created by Neshat (Iran), Ofili (Nigeria), and Whiting (New Zealand).

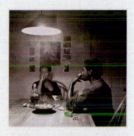

Weems, *Man Smoking/ Malcolm X*, 1990

Political and Social Commentary

- Other contemporary artists have treated political and economic issues that affect society at large. Polish-born Krystof Wodiczko has used gigantic slide projections to publicize the plight of the homeless. Canadian Edward Burtynsky's photographs of "manufactured landscapes" highlight the destructive effects of industrial pollution.

- The violence of contemporary life has been addressed in America by Golub (urban gangs and Latin American death squads), by Martha Rosler (the effects of war on the home front), and in Paris by Colombian Fernando Botero (torture at Abu Ghraib).

- Willie Bester has protested apartheid in South Africa and Zhang Xiaogang has produced biting commentaries on the Cultural Revolution in China.

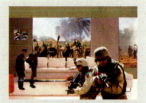

Rosler, *Gladiators*, 2004

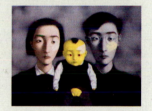

Zhang, *Big Family No. 2*, 1995

Representation, Abstraction, and New Media

- Contemporary art, both in America and worldwide, encompasses a phenomenal variety of styles ranging from abstraction to brutal realism.

- Among today's best-known figural painters and sculptors are Kiki Smith, Koons, and Venezuelan Marisol in the United States, and expatriate Englishwoman Saville in Italy.

- Leading abstract painters and sculptors include Schnabel, Murray, Oji, and Donovan in the United States, Kusama and Tsuchiya in Japan, Wu Guanzhong in China, and Anatsui in Nigeria.

- Many contemporary artists have harnessed new technologies for their art: Gursky, digital photography; Holzer, LED displays; Piper, Viola, and Oursler, video; and Barney, multimedia installations.

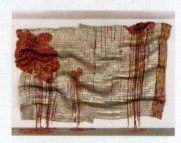

Anatsui, *Bleeding Takari II*, 2007

Site-Specific Art and Architecture

- The site-specific works of Lin, Whiteread, Serra, Kapoor, and Suh bridge the gap between architecture and sculpture, as do the Environmental artworks of Christo and Jean-Claude and of Goldsworthy.

- Postmodern architecture is as diverse as contemporary painting and sculpture. Pei and Stirling incorporate historical references in their buildings. Among the major champions of Deconstructivism are Behnisch, Gehry, Libeskind, and Hadid. Leading Hi-Tech and Green architects include Foster and Piano.

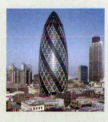

Foster, *Gherkin, London*, 2001–2003

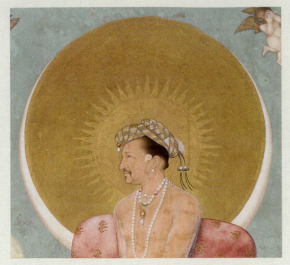

▲ **32-1a** Jahangir sits on an hourglass throne, symbolically seated above time. The radiant halo of sun and moon behind his head indicates that the Mughal emperor is the center of the universe and its light source.

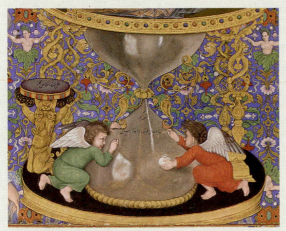

▲ **32-1b** As the sands of time run out, two cupids (clothed, unlike Bichitr's European prototypes) inscribe Jahangir's hourglass throne with a wish for the Mughal emperor to live a thousand years.

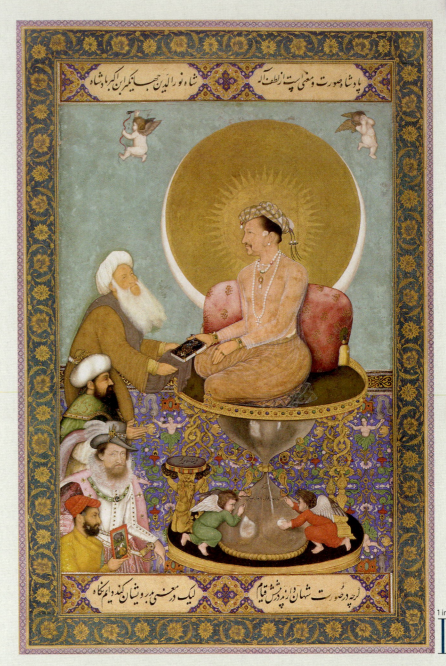

32-1 BICHITR, *Jahangir Preferring a Sufi Shaykh to Kings*, ca. 1615–1618. Opaque watercolor on paper, 1' 6 $\frac{7}{8}$" × 1' 1". Freer Gallery of Art, Washington, D.C.

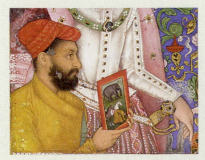

◀ **32-1c** The Hindu artist not only signed this painting but inserted a self-portrait. Bichitr bows before Jahangir and holds a painting of two horses and an elephant, costly gifts to the painter from the emperor.

South and Southeast Asia, 1200 to 1980

PAINTING AT THE MUGHAL IMPERIAL COURT

From the 16th to the 19th century, the most powerful rulers in South Asia were the Mughal emperors. *Mughal*, originally a Western term, means "descended from the Mongols," although the Mughals considered themselves descendants of Timur (r. 1370–1405), the Muslim conqueror whose capital was at Samarkand in Uzbekistan. The Mughal dynasty presided over a cosmopolitan court with refined tastes. British ambassadors, European merchants, and Jesuit priests were frequent visitors, and the Mughal emperors acquired many European luxury goods. They were also great admirers of Persian art and maintained an imperial workshop of painters who, in sharp contrast to pre-Mughal artists in India, often signed their works.

The influence of European as well as Persian styles on Mughal painting is evident in an allegorical portrait (FIG. **32-1**) of Jahangir (r. 1605–1627), the great-grandson of the founder of the Mughal Empire. The Hindu painter BICHITR represented the emperor seated on an hourglass throne. As the sands of time run out, two cupids (clothed, unlike their European models more closely copied at the top of the painting) inscribe the throne with the wish that Jahangir would live a thousand years. Bichitr portrayed his patron as an emperor above time and placed behind Jahangir's head a radiant halo combining a golden sun and a white crescent moon, indicating that Jahangir is the center of the universe and its light source. One of the inscriptions in the upper and lower borders gives the emperor's title as "Light of the Faith."

At the left are four figures. The lowest, both spatially and in the social hierarchy, is Bichitr, who wears a red turban and holds a painting representing two horses and an elephant, costly gifts to him from Jahangir. In the painting-within-the-painting, Bichitr bows deeply before the emperor. In the larger painting, the artist signed his name across the top of the footstool Jahangir uses to step up to his hourglass throne. Thus the ruler steps on Bichitr's name, further indicating the painter's inferior status.

Above Bichitr is a portrait in full European style (compare FIGS. 23-11, 23-11A, and 23-21) of King James I of England (r. 1603–1625), copied from a painting by John de Critz (ca. 1552–1642) that was a gift the English ambassador to the Mughal court had presented to Jahangir. Above the king is a Turkish sultan, a convincing portrayal but probably not a specific likeness. The highest member of the foursome is an elderly Muslim Sufi *shaykh* (mystic saint). Jahangir's father, Akbar, had gone to the mystic to pray for an heir. The current emperor, the answer to Akbar's prayers, presents the holy man with a sumptuous book as a gift. An inscription explains that "although to all appearances kings stand before him, Jahangir looks inwardly toward the *Dervishes* [Islamic *ascetic* holy men]" for guidance. Bichitr's allegorical painting portrays his emperor in both words and pictures as favoring spiritual over worldly power.

INDIA

Arab armies first appeared in South Asia (MAP 32-1)—at Sindh in present-day Pakistan—in 712, more than 800 years before the founding of the Mughal Empire. With the Arabs came Islam, the new religion that had already spread with astonishing speed from the Arabian peninsula to Syria, Iraq, Iran, Egypt, North Africa, and even southern Spain (see page 285). At first, the *Muslims* (see "Muhammad and Islam," page 288) established trading settlements in South Asia but did not press deeper into the subcontinent. But in 1192, at the Battle of Tarain in what is today Afghanistan, Muhammad of Ghor (d. 1206) defeated the armies of a confederation of independent states. The Ghorids and other Islamic rulers gradually transformed South Asian society, religion, art, and architecture.

Sultanate of Delhi

In 1206, Qutb al-Din Aybak (d. 1210), Muhammad of Ghor's general, established the Sultanate of Delhi (1206–1526). The *sultan* passed power to his former slave and son-in-law, Iltutmish (r. 1211–1236), who extended Ghorid rule across northern India.

QUTB MINAR To mark the triumph of Islam, Qutb al-Din Aybak built a great *congregational mosque* (see "The Mosque," page 291) at Delhi, in part with pillars and other building materials taken from 27 local Hindu and other temples. He named Delhi's first mosque the Quwwat al-Islam (Might of Islam) Mosque. During the course of the next century, as the Islamic population of Delhi grew, the sultans enlarged the mosque to more than triple its original size.

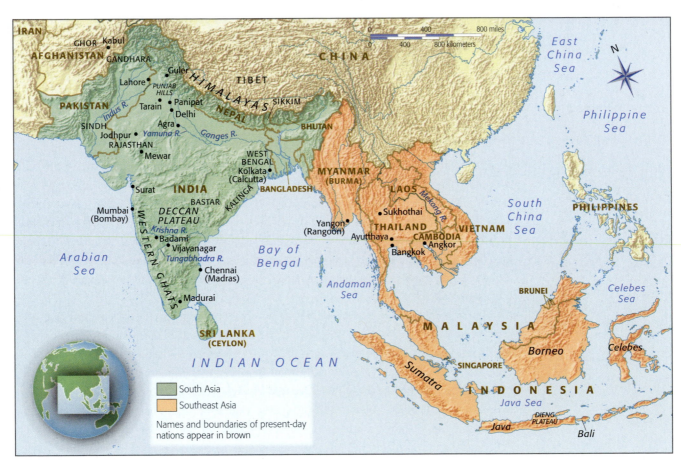

MAP 32-1 South and Southeast Asia, 1200 to 1980.

SOUTH AND SOUTHEAST ASIA, 1200 TO 1980

1206–1526
- Arabs establish the Muslim Sultanate of Delhi (1206–1526) and introduce Islamic art and architecture to northern India
- In the south, Hindu kings rule the Vijayanagar Empire (1336–1565) and construct buildings mixing elements of both Hindu and Islamic architecture

1526–1877
- Miniature painting flourishes in the Mughal Empire (1526–1857)
- Muslim builders construct the Taj Mahal
- Rajput painters in northwestern India produce vividly colored miniature paintings with Hindu subjects
- The southern Nayak dynasty (1529–1736) builds towering Hindu temple precinct gateways decorated with painted stucco sculptures
- Buddhism and Buddhist art and architecture dominate Southeast Asia

1877–1980
- Queen Victoria I of England becomes Empress of India in 1877. European-inspired art and architecture accompany colonial rule
- India and Pakistan achieve independence in 1947. Post-World War II art in South and Southeast Asia is a mix of traditional and Western modernist styles

THE PATRON'S VOICE
The Qutb Minar and the Triumph of Islam

The 238-foot tapering sandstone Qutb Minar (FIG. 32-2, *left*) at Delhi is the tallest extant mosque tower in the world and the largest stone tower of any kind in India. It is too tall, in fact, to serve the principal function of a minaret—to provide a platform from which to call the Islamic faithful to prayer. Rather, it is a soaring monument to the victory of Islam, engraved with inscriptions in Arabic and Persian that, together with those of the mosque proper, express the Delhi sultans' pride in conquering the former Hindu city and bringing Islam to India. The minaret's inscriptions refer to the tower variously as a "pillar of fame" and a "pillar of victory" and celebrate the conqueror Muhammad of Ghor, who defeated the Hindu king, Prithviraj Chauhan, in 1192, and Muhammad's successors in Delhi.

The following selection of inscriptions on the mosque and the minaret, respectively, underscores the triumphal character of these two religious monuments.

> This fortress was conquered and this Masjid Jami [*congregational, or Friday, mosque*] was built during the months of the year 587 [1192] by the great and mighty commander-in-chief Qutb al-Din Aybak, the pivot of the kingdom and the faith, commander of commanders . . . Materials from 27 idol temples . . . have been used in this Masjid. May Almighty God send mercy on him, who prays for the rest of the builder.*

> The very revered sultan [Iltutmish], the great emperor, the master of mankind, the first of the kings of Arabia and Ajam [Afghanistan], the shadow of God on earth, the sun of the world and the faith, the refuge of Islam and Muslims, the crown of the kings and sultans, the extender of the scope of equity in the world, the glory of the mighty kingdom, the splendor of the supreme nation, helped with the heavenly grace, giver of victory over the enemies, the shining star of the heaven of khilafat, the diffuser of justice and kindness, the conqueror of the kingdom of the world, the divulger of the high word of God . . . ; may God make his reign and rule eternal and give supremacy to his government.†

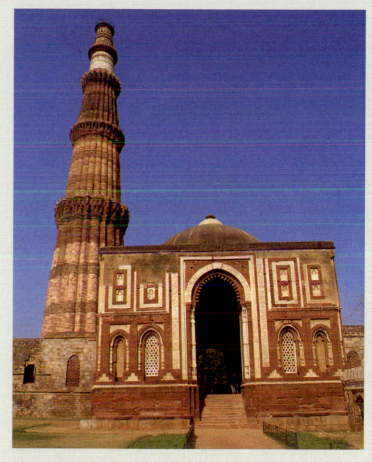

32-2 Qutb Minar (*left*, looking north), begun early 13th century, and Alai Darvaza (*right*), 1311, Delhi, India.

Qutb al-Din Aybak established the Sultanate of Delhi in 1206 and built the city's first mosque to mark the triumph of Islam in northern India. The 238-foot-high Qutb Minar is the world's tallest minaret.

*Rustamji Nasarvanji Munshi, *The History of the Kutb Minar* (Mumbai: Fort Printing Press, 1911), 20–21.
†Munshi, 45.

Iltutmish erected the mosque's gigantic *minaret*, the Qutb Minar (see "The Qutb Minar and the Triumph of Islam," above, and FIG. **32-2**, *left*). Added in 1311, the Alai Darvaza, the entrance pavilion (FIG. 32-2, *right*), is a mix of architectural traditions, combining Islamic pointed arches, decorative grills over the windows, and a hemispherical dome, with a crowning *finial* recalling the motifs at the top of many Hindu temple towers (see "Hindu Temples," page 452).

Vijayanagar Empire

While Muslim sultans from Central Asia ruled much of northern India from Delhi, Hindu kings controlled most of central and southern India. The most powerful Hindu dynasty of the era was the Vijayanagar. Established in 1336 by Harihara, a local king, the Vijayanagar Empire (1336–1565) takes its name from Vijayanagara (City of Victory) on the Tungabhadra River. Under the patronage of the royal family, Vijayanagara, located at the junction of several trade routes through Asia, became one of the most magnificent cities in the East.

Although today the capital lies in ruins, at its peak, ambassadors and travelers from as far away as Italy and Portugal marveled at Vijayanagara's riches. Under its greatest king, Krishnadevaraya (r. 1509–1529), who was also a renowned poet, the Vijayanagar kingdom was a magnet for the learned and cultured from all corners of India.

LOTUS MAHAL Vijayanagara's sacred center, built up over two centuries, boasts imposing temples to the Hindu gods in the style of southern India, with tall pyramidal *vimanas* (towers) over the *garbha griha*, the inner sanctuary (see "Hindu Temples," page 452). The buildings of the so-called Royal Enclave are more eclectic in character. One example in this prosperous royal city is the two-story monument of uncertain function known as the Lotus Mahal

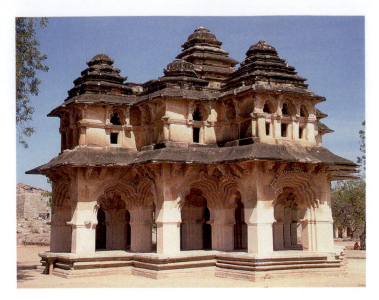

32-3 Lotus Mahal (looking southwest), Vijayanagara, India, 15th or early 16th century.

The Vijayanagar Empire was the most powerful Hindu kingdom in southern India during the 14th to 16th centuries. The Lotus Mahal's design mixes Hindu and Islamic architectural elements.

(FIG. 32-3). The stepped towers crowning the vaulted second-story rooms resemble the pyramidal roofs of southern Indian temple vimanas (FIG. 15-27). But the windows of the upper level as well as the arches of the ground-floor piers have the distinctive multi-lobed contours of Islamic architecture (FIGS. 10-12 and 10-13). The Lotus Mahal, like the entrance pavilion of Delhi's first mosque (FIG. 32-2, *right*), exemplifies the stylistic crosscurrents typical of much of South Asian art and architecture of the second millennium.

Mughal Empire

The 16th century was a time of upheaval in South Asia. In 1565, only a generation after Krishnadevaraya, a confederacy of sultanates in the Deccan plateau of central India brought the Vijayanagar Empire of the south to an end. Even earlier, a Muslim prince named Babur (1483–1530) had defeated the last of the Ghorid sultans of northern India at the Battle of Panipat. Declaring himself the ruler of India, Babur established the Mughal Empire (1526–1857) at Delhi. In 1527, Babur vanquished the Rajput Hindu kings of Mewar (see page 1039). By the time of his death in 1530, Babur headed a vast new empire in India.

HUMAYUN The emperor who succeeded Babur was Humayun (r. 1530–1556), but in 1543 the sultan of Gujarat temporarily wrested control of the Mughal Empire. Humayun sought sanctuary in Iran at the court of the Safavid ruler Shah Tahmasp (r. 1524–1576; FIG. 32-5) and remained in exile until 1555. During his years at the Safavid court, the Mughal emperor acquired a taste for Persian illustrated books. On his return to power, Humayun brought with him to Delhi two Safavid master painters. Pupils of the renowned Bihzad (FIG. 10-33), they in turn trained a generation of Mughal artists.

AKBAR THE GREAT The first great flowering of Mughal art and architecture occurred during the long reign of Humayun's son, Akbar (r. 1556–1605), called the Great, who ascended the throne at age 14. Like his father, Akbar greatly admired the narrative paintings (FIG. 10-33) produced at the Safavid court, and he resolved to establish

his capital as a great art center. To achieve that goal, the young ruler enlarged the number of painters in Humayun's imperial workshop to about a hundred and kept them busy working on a series of ambitious projects. One of these was to illustrate the text of the *Hamzanama*—the story of Hamza, Muhammad's uncle—in some 1,400 large paintings on cloth. The assignment took 15 years to complete.

The illustrated books and engravings that traders, diplomats, and Christian missionaries brought from Europe to India also fascinated Akbar. In 1580, Portuguese Jesuits brought one particularly important source, the eight-volume *Royal Polyglot Bible,* as a gift to Akbar. This massive set of books, printed in Antwerp, contained engravings by several Flemish artists. Akbar immediately set his painters to copying the illustrations.

AKBARNAMA Akbar also commissioned Abul Fazl (1551–1602), a member of his court and close friend, to chronicle his life in a great biography, the *Akbarnama* (*History of Akbar*), which the emperor asked

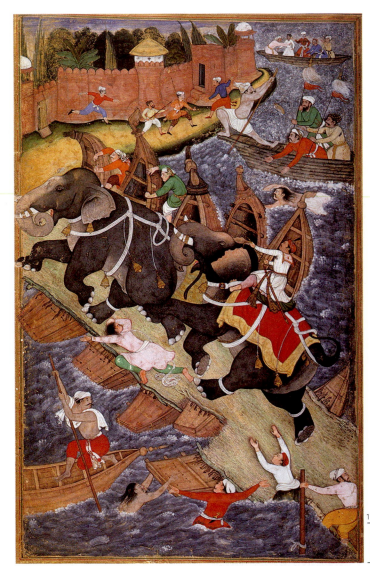

32-4 BASAWAN and CHATAR MUNI, *Akbar and the Elephant Hawai,* folio 22 from the *Akbarnama* (*History of Akbar*) by Abul Fazl, ca. 1590. Opaque watercolor on paper, $1' 1\frac{7}{8}'' \times 8\frac{3}{4}''$. Victoria & Albert Museum, London.

For this miniature portraying the young emperor Akbar bringing an elephant under control, Basawan chose the moment of maximum danger. The episode is an allegory of Akbar's ability to rule.

his painters to illustrate. One of the full-page illustrations, or so-called *miniatures* (see "Indian Miniature Painting," below), in the emperor's personal copy of the *Akbarnama* was a collaborative effort between the painter BASAWAN, who designed and drew the composition, and CHATAR MUNI, who colored it. The painting (FIG. **32-4**) depicts the episode of Akbar and Hawai, a wild elephant that the 19-year-old ruler had mounted and pitted against another ferocious elephant. When the second animal fled in defeat, Hawai, still carrying Akbar, chased it to a pontoon bridge. The enormous weight of the elephants capsized the boats, but Akbar managed to bring Hawai under control and dismount safely. The young ruler viewed the episode as an allegory of his ability to govern—that is, to take charge of an unruly state.

For his pictorial record of that frightening day, Basawan chose the moment of maximum chaos and danger—when the elephants crossed the pontoon bridge, sending boatmen flying into the water. The composition is a bold one, with a very high horizon and two strong diagonal lines formed by the bridge and the shore. Together these devices tend to flatten out the vista, yet at the same time, Basawan created a sense of

depth by diminishing the size of the figures in the background. He was also a master of vivid gestures and anecdotal detail. Note especially the bare-chested figure in the foreground clinging to the end of a boat; the figure near the lower right corner with outstretched arms, sliding into the water as the bridge sinks; and the oarsman just beyond the bridge who strains to steady his vessel while his three passengers stand up or lean overboard in reaction to the surrounding commotion.

SAHIFA BANU Another Mughal miniaturist whose name is known is SAHIFA BANU (active early 17th century), a princess in the court of Jahangir (FIGS. 32-1 and **32-4A**) and the most renowned female artist of the Mughal Empire. In one of her miniatures (FIG. **32-5**), she paid tribute to Shah Tahmasp

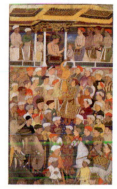

32-4A ABDUL HASAN and MANOHAR, *Darbar of Jahangir,* ca. 1620.

MATERIALS AND TECHNIQUES
Indian Miniature Painting

Although India had a tradition of mural painting going back to ancient times (see "The Painted Caves of Ajanta," page 447, and FIG. 15-17), the most popular form of painting under the Mughal emperors (FIGS. 32-1, 32-4, 32-4A, and 32-5) and Rajput kings (FIGS. 32-8 and 32-8A) was miniature painting. Art historians usually call these paintings *miniatures* because of their small size (about the size of a page in this book) compared with paintings on walls, wood panels, or canvas, but the original terminology derives from the red lead (*miniatum*) used as a pigment. The artists who painted the Indian miniatures designed them to be held in the hands, either as illustrations in books or as loose-leaf pages in albums. Owners did not place Indian miniatures in frames and only very rarely hung them on walls.

Indian artists used opaque watercolors and paper (occasionally cotton cloth) to produce their miniatures. The manufacturing and painting of miniatures was a complicated process and required years of training as an apprentice in a workshop. The painters' assistants created pigments by grinding natural materials—minerals such as malachite for green and lapis lazuli for blue; earth ochers for red and yellow; and metallic foil for gold, silver, and copper. They fashioned brushes from bird quills and kitten or baby squirrel hairs. For minute details, the painters used brushes with a single hair.

The artist began the painting process by making a full-size sketch of the composition. The next step was to transfer the sketch onto paper by *pouncing*, or tracing, using thin, transparent gazelle skin placed on top of the drawing and pricking the contours of the design with a pin. Then, with the skin laid on a fresh sheet of fine paper, the painter forced black pigment through the tiny holes, reproducing the outlines of the composition.

Painting proper started with the darkening of the outlines with black or reddish-brown ink. Painters of miniatures sat on the ground, resting their painting boards on one raised knee. Each pigment color was in a separate half seashell. The paintings usually required several layers of color, with gold always applied last. The final step was to burnish the painted surface. The artists accomplished this by placing the miniature, painted side down, on a hard, smooth surface and stroking the paper with polished agate or crystal.

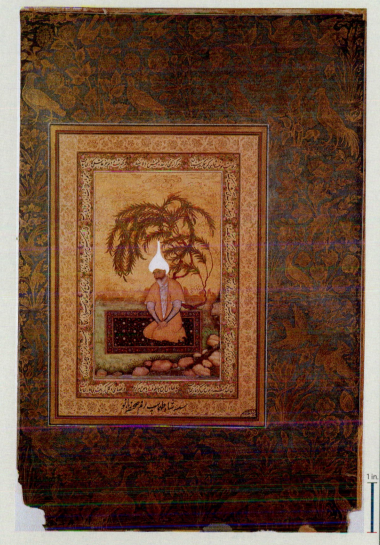

32-5 SAHIFA BANU, *Shah Tahmasp,* early 17th century. Opaque watercolor on paper, figure panel 6" × 3⅝". Victoria & Albert Museum, London.

This miniature by one of the few known Mughal women artists depicts the Persian emperor Shah Tahmasp. Two of his court painters went to India to train Mughal imperial book illustrators.

WRITTEN SOURCES
Abd al-Hamid Lahori on the Taj Mahal

Abd al-Hamid Lahori (d. 1654), Shah Jahan's court historian, witnessed the construction of the Taj Mahal (FIG. 32-6) and wrote an extensive account of the building campaign in his *Padshahnama* (*Chronicle of the Emperor*). The historian's account includes such details as the cost of construction, the dimensions of all features, and the number of stonemasons and other artisans employed, and also comments on the symbolism of the mausoleum and its gardens.

The walls bear long inscriptions quoting passages from the Koran, and it appears that the architect conceived the mausoleum as the throne of God perched above the gardens of Paradise. The tomb's minarets hold up the canopy of that throne. In Islam, the most revered place of burial is beneath the throne of God.

Some excerpts of Lahori's account follow.

> In the middle of [the] platform plinth—which ranks [in magnificence] with the heavenly Throne of God—there was constructed another solid and level platform . . . In the center of the second platform [is the] heaven-lofty and Paradise-like mausoleum. . . . In the center of the tomb lies the divinely graced grave of [Mumtaz Mahal] who occupies the reclining couch of the highest heaven and the chief seat in the loftiest mansions [of Paradise]. . . . At the corners of the white marble platform . . . stand four minarets . . . appearing like ladders reaching toward the Heavens. . . . All over the interior and exterior of [this Paradise-like] mausoleum, wonder-working and magic-making artisans have inlaid carnelian and other kinds of colored and precious stones [FIG. 32-7]. . . . Below the red stone terrace is the Paradise-like garden . . . abounding in aromatic herbs and different kinds of trees. Within the four walkways laid out in the middle of the garden . . . there runs a water-channel . . . in which fountains jet up spouts of water.*

Especially interesting is Lahori's description of Shah Jahan's personal involvement in his building projects:

> [T]he superintendents of construction of royal buildings, in company with the wonder-working architects, lay before the critical royal eye plans of proposed edifices. The royal mind . . . pays full attention to the planning and construction of these lofty and substantial buildings . . . For the majority of buildings, he himself draws the plans. And on the plans prepared by the skillful architects . . . he makes appropriate alterations and emendations.†

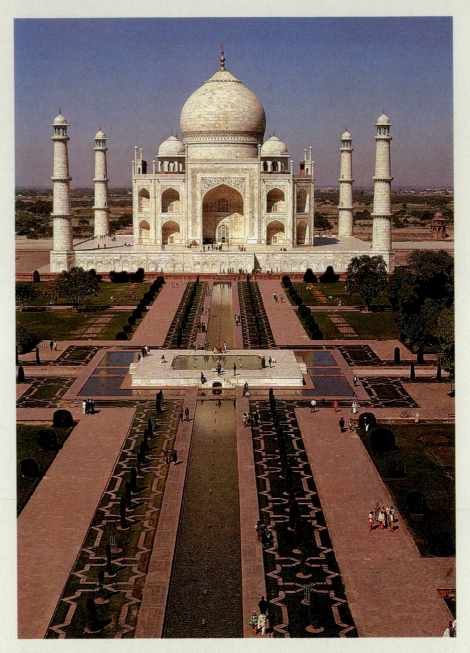

32-6 USTAD AHMAD LAHORI(?), Taj Mahal and gardens (looking north), Agra, India, 1632–1647.

The mausoleum for Shah Jahan's favorite wife seems to float magically over reflecting pools in a vast garden. The tomb may have been conceived as the throne of God perched above the gardens of Paradise.

*Lahori I, 322–328. Translated by W. E. Begley and Z. A. Desai, *Taj Mahal: The Illumined Tomb. An Anthology of Seventeenth-Century Mughal and European Documentary Sources* (Cambridge, Mass.: Aga Khan Program for Islamic Architecture, 1989), 66–67, 74.

†Lahori I, 148. Begley and Desai, 9–10.

of Iran, the great patron of Safavid painting who sent two of his masters to Delhi to train the early Mughal miniaturists at the court of Humayun. The Safavid ruler sits on a magnificent Persian carpet at the edge of a stream underneath the windblown branches of a tree. As in other Mughal paintings (FIGS. 32-1, 32-4, and 32-4A)—in sharp contrast to the almost obsessive interest in linear perspective in contemporaneous European painting—the Indian artist combined different viewpoints in the same frame, depicting

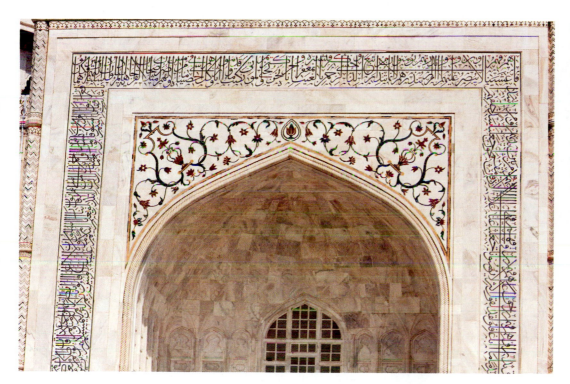

32-7 Detail of the pietra dura stonework of the area above the central niche of the facade of the Taj Mahal (FIG. 32-6), Agra, India, 1632–1647.

Set into the light-reflecting marble walls of the Taj Mahal are inlaid precious and semiprecious stones. This pietra dura stonework enhances the impression that the huge structure is weightless.

the shah and the tree seen from eye level, and the carpet, ground, and stream seen from above. This composition enabled the princess to reproduce the intricate design of the woven carpet (compare FIG. 10-31) with pristine clarity and without the distortion that would have resulted from foreshortening the textile patterns. In fact, the miniature itself, with its decorative border, has a textilelike quality and resembles Tahmasp's carpet in both format and proportions. The frame around Banu's portrait of Tahmasp also features elegant calligraphy (compare FIG. 32-1). Although female Mughal painters were rare, many court women were accomplished calligraphers.

TAJ MAHAL Monumental tombs were not part of either the Hindu or Buddhist traditions but had a long history in Islamic architecture. The Delhi sultans had erected tombs in India, but none could compare in grandeur to the fabled Taj Mahal (FIG. **32-6**) at Agra. Shah Jahan (r. 1628–1658), Jahangir's son, built the immense *mausoleum* as a memorial to his favorite wife, whose official title was Mumtaz Mahal (1593–1631), or "Chosen of the Palace." Taj Mahal means "Crown Palace," and the mausoleum eventually became the ruler's tomb as well. It figures prominently in official histories of Shah Jahan's reign (see "Abd al-Hamid Lahori on the Taj Mahal," page 1038).

The dome-on-cube shape of the central block has antecedents in earlier Islamic mausoleums (FIGS. 10-10 and 10-25) and other Islamic buildings, such as the Alai Darvaza (FIG. 32-2, *right*) at Delhi, but modifications and refinements in the design of the Agra tomb converted the earlier massive structures into an almost weightless vision of glistening white marble. The Agra mausoleum seems to float magically above the broad water channels and tree-lined reflecting pools punctuating the fountain-filled garden leading to it. Reinforcing the illusion of the marble tomb being suspended above water is the absence of any visible means of ascent to the upper platform. A stairway does exist, but the architect intentionally hid it from the view of anyone who approaches the memorial.

The Taj Mahal follows the traditional *char-bagh* ("four-plot") plan of Iranian garden pavilions, which symbolized the Koranic Garden of Paradise. Today, however, the mausoleum appears to stand at the northern end of the garden on the edge of the Yamuna River,

rather than in the center of the formal garden, as it should in a char-bagh plan. Originally, the gardens extended to the other side of the river, and the Taj Mahal did, in fact, occupy a central position. The tomb itself is octagonal in plan and has typically Iranian arcuated niches (FIG. 10-28) on each side. The interplay of shadowy voids with light-reflecting marble walls that seem paper-thin creates an impression of translucency, further enhanced by the *pietra dura* inlay (FIG. **32-7**) of precious and semiprecious stones in the stone walls. The pointed arches lead the eye in a sweeping upward movement toward the climactic dome, shaped like a crown (*taj*). Four carefully related minarets and two flanking triple-domed pavilions enhance and stabilize the soaring form of the mausoleum. The designer—probably USTAD AHMAD LAHORI (d. 1649), Shah Jahan's chief court architect—achieved this delicate balance between verticality and horizontality by strictly applying an all-encompassing system of proportions. The Taj Mahal (excluding the minarets) is as wide as it is tall, and the height of its dome is equal to the height of the facade. The mausoleum is a unique and brilliant fusion of Islamic, Hindu, and Byzantine elements.

Hindu Rajput Kingdoms

The Mughal emperors ruled vast territories, but much of northwestern India (present-day Rajasthan) remained under the control of Hindu Rajput (Sons of Kings) rulers. These small kingdoms, some claiming to have originated well before 1500, had stubbornly resisted Mughal expansion, but even the strongest of them—Mewar—eventually submitted to the Mughal emperors. When Jahangir defeated the Mewari forces in 1615, the Mewari maharana ("great king"), like the other Rajput rulers, maintained a degree of independence but had to pay tribute to the Mughal treasury until the demise of the Mughal Empire in 1857.

Rajput painting resembles Mughal (and Persian) painting in format and material, but it differs sharply in other respects. Most Rajput artists, for example, worked in anonymity, never inserting self-portraits into their paintings as the Mughal painter Bichitr did in his miniature (FIG. 32-1) of Jahangir sitting on an hourglass throne.

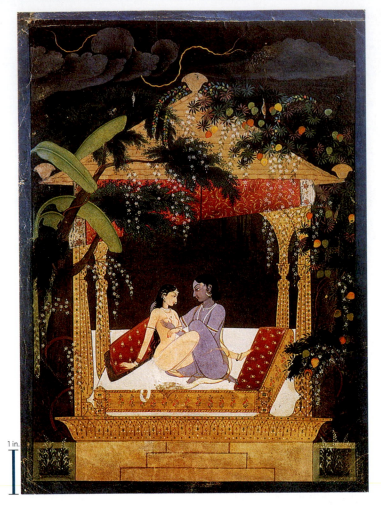

32-8 *Krishna and Radha in a Pavilion*, ca. 1760. Opaque watercolor on paper, $11\frac{1}{8}" \times 7\frac{3}{4}"$. National Museum, New Delhi.

The love of Krishna, the "Blue God," for Radha is the subject of this colorful, lyrical, and sensual Pahari watercolor. Their love was a model of the devotion paid to the Hindu god Vishnu.

KRISHNA AND RADHA One of the most popular subjects for Rajput paintings was the amorous adventures of Krishna, the "Blue God," the most popular of the *avatars,* or incarnations, of the Hindu god Vishnu, who descends to earth to aid mortals (see "Hinduism and Hindu Iconography," page 448). Krishna was a herdsman who spent an idyllic existence tending his cows, playing the flute, and sporting with beautiful herdswomen. His favorite lover was Radha. The 12th-century poet Jayadeva related the story of Krishna and Radha in the *Gita Govinda* (*Song of the Cow-herd*). Their love was a model of the devotion, or *bhakti,* paid to Vishnu. Jayadeva's poem was the source for hundreds of later paintings, including *Krishna and Radha in a Pavilion* (FIG. 32-8) and *Krishna and the Gopis* (FIG. 32-8A).

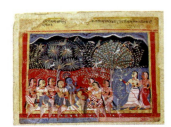

⤴ 32-8A *Krishna and the Gopis,* ca. 1550.

Krishna and Radha in a Pavil-ion was the work of an artist in the Punjab Hills, probably in the employ of Raja Govardhan Chand of Guler (r. 1741–1773). The artists producing paintings for the rulers of the Punjab Hill states—

referred to collectively as the Pahari School—had a distinctive style. Although Pahari painting owed much to Mughal drawing style, its coloration, lyricism, and sensuality are readily recognizable. In the Krishna and Radha miniature, the lovers sit naked on a bed beneath a jeweled pavilion in a lush garden of ripe mangoes and flowering shrubs. Krishna gently touches Radha's breast while looking directly into her face. Radha shyly averts her gaze. It is night, the time of lovemaking, and the dark monsoon sky momentarily lights up with a lightning flash indicating the moment's electric passion. Lightning is one of the standard symbols used in Rajput and Pahari miniatures to represent sexual excitement.

Nayak Dynasty

The Nayakas, governors under the Vijayanagar kings, declared their independence in 1529, and after their former overlords' defeat in 1565 at the hands of the Deccan sultanates, they continued Hindu rule in the far south of India for two centuries (1529–1736).

GREAT TEMPLE, MADURAI Construction of some of the largest temple complexes in India occurred under Nayak patronage. The most striking features of these huge complexes are their gateway towers called *gopuras* (FIG. 32-9), decorated from top to bottom with painted sculptures. After erecting the gopuras, the builders constructed walls to connect them and then built more gopuras, always expanding outward from the center. Each set of gopuras was taller than those of the previous wall circuit. The outermost towers reached colossal size, dwarfing the temples at the heart of the complexes. The tallest gopuras of the Great Temple at Madurai, dedicated to Shiva (under his local name, Sundareshvara, the Handsome One) and his consort Minakshi (the Fish-eyed One), stand about 150 feet tall. Rising in a series of tiers of diminishing size, they culminate in a *barrel-vaulted* roof with finials.

The ornamentation of the Madurai gopuras is extremely rich, consisting of row after row of brightly painted stucco sculptures (FIG. 32-10) representing the vast pantheon of Hindu deities and a host of attendant figures. Reconsecration of the temple occurs at 12-year intervals, at which time the gopura sculptures receive a new coat of paint, which accounts for the vibrancy of their colors today. The Madurai Nayak temple complex also contains large and numerous *mandapas*, as well as great water tanks that worshipers use for ritual bathing. These temples were, and continue to be, almost independent cities, with thousands of pilgrims, merchants, and priests flocking from near and far to the many yearly festivals hosted by the temples.

The British in India

English merchants first arrived in India toward the end of the 16th century, attracted by the land's spices, gems, and other riches. On December 31, 1599, Queen Elizabeth I (r. 1558–1603) granted a charter to the East India Company, which sought to compete with the Portuguese and Dutch in the lucrative trade with South Asia. The company established a "factory" (trading post) at the port of Surat, approximately 150 miles from Mumbai (Bombay) in western India in 1613. After securing trade privileges with the Mughal emperor Jahangir (FIG. 32-1), the British expanded their factories to Chennai (Madras), Kolkata (Calcutta), and Mumbai by 1661. These outposts gradually spread throughout India, especially after the British defeat of the ruler of Bengal in 1757. By the opening

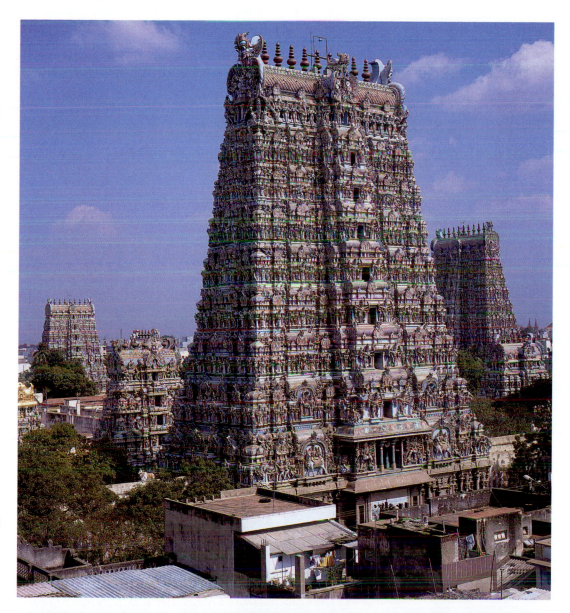

32-9 Outermost gopuras of the Great Temple (looking southeast), Madurai, India, completed 17th century.

The Great Temple at Madurai lies within a huge complex enclosed by a series of walls connecting colossal gateway towers, or gopuras. Each ring of gopuras is taller than those of the previous wall circuit.

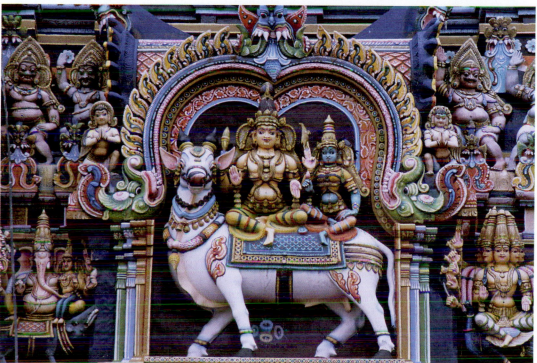

32-10 Shiva and Parvati riding Nandi, detail of one of the inner gopuras of the Great Temple, Madurai, India, remodeled in the 17th century.

The gigantic gopuras erected during the Nayak dynasty at the Great Temple at Madurai feature stucco sculptures representing the vast pantheon of Hindu deities. They are repainted every 12 years.

PROBLEMS AND SOLUTIONS
Victoria Terminus as Cathedral of Modernization

Construction of the immense railway station (FIG. 32-11) in Mumbai named in honor of Victoria, Queen of England and Empress of India, began in 1878 and took a decade to complete. The architect selected to build this modern transportation hub, not surprisingly, was British—FREDERICK W. STEVENS (1847–1900). The challenge Stevens faced was how to design a vast terminal serving thousands of travelers daily that exemplified European modernity but incorporated references to local architectural traditions.

Stevens's solution was to work within the currently fashionable European *Gothic Revival* style (see page 828) but to construct the building of the same South Asian sandstone used for temples and statues throughout India's long history and to incorporate domes, multilobed arches, and motifs recalling minarets. These features constitute the distinctively British colonial interpretation of Islamic architecture called *Indo-Saracen*. Despite the references to local traditions, Victoria Terminus is a European transplant to the subcontinent. The Indo-Saracen style is, in fact, the architectural counterpart of colonial rule.

Conceived as a cathedral to modernization, Victoria Terminus fittingly has an allegorical statue of Progress crowning its tallest dome. Statues personifying Commerce, Agriculture, and Science also decorate the railway station. Ironically, Progress here stands atop a structure that in stylistic terms looks backward, not forward. Inside, passengers gaze up at *Neo-Gothic groin-vaulted* ceilings and *stained-glass* windows, and the exterior of the station resembles an English Gothic church with a gabled facade and flanking towers (compare FIG. 13-39). For other aspects of Victoria Terminus, especially its tiers of screened windows, Stevens took as his primary models the elegant buildings of 14th- and 15th-century Venice (FIGS. 14-23 and 21-38).

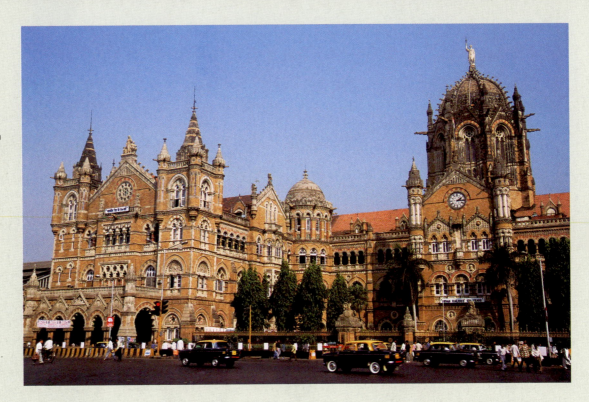

32-11 FREDERICK W. STEVENS, Victoria Terminus (now Chhatrapati Shivaji Terminus; looking northeast), Mumbai (Bombay), India, 1878–1887.

Victoria Terminus is a monument to colonial rule celebrating modern technology. Designed by a British architect, it is a European transplant to India, but incorporates traditional South Asian motifs.

of the 19th century, the East India Company effectively ruled large portions of the subcontinent, and in 1835, the British declared English India's official language. A great rebellion in 1857 persuaded the British Parliament that the East India Company could no longer be the agent of British rule. The next year, Parliament abolished the company and replaced its governor-general with a viceroy of the crown. Two decades later, in 1877, Queen Victoria (r. 1837–1901) assumed the title Empress of India with sovereignty over all the former Indian states.

VICTORIA TERMINUS The British brought the Industrial Revolution and railways to India. One of the most enduring monuments of British rule, still used by millions of travelers, is Victoria Terminus (see "Victoria Terminus as Cathedral of Modernization," above, and FIG. 32-11) in Mumbai, named at the time of its construction for the first British empress of India (but now called Chhatrapati Shivaji Terminus).

JASWANT SINGH With British rulers and modern railways also came British or, more generally, European ideas, but Western culture and religion never supplanted India's own rich traditions. Many Indians, however, readily took on the trappings of European society. When Maharaja Jaswant Singh, the ruler of Jodhpur (r. 1873–1895) in Rajasthan, sat for his portrait (FIG. 32-12) around 1880, he chose to sit in an ordinary chair, rather than on a throne, with his arm resting on a simple table with a bouquet and a book on it. In other words, he posed as if he were an ordinary British gentleman in his sitting room. Nevertheless, the painter, an anonymous local artist

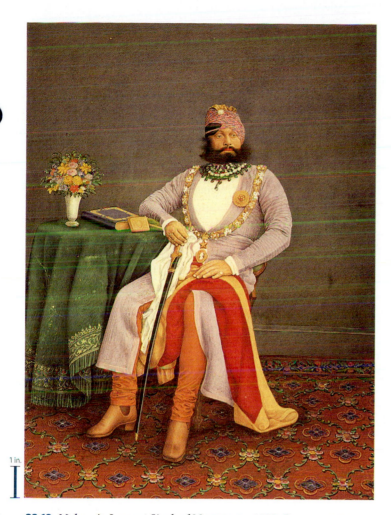

32-12 *Maharaja Jaswant Singh of Marwar*, ca. 1880. Opaque watercolor on paper, 1' 3½" × 11⅝". Brooklyn Museum, Brooklyn (gift of Mr. and Mrs. Robert L. Poster).

1 in.

Maharaja Jaswant Singh, the ruler of Jodhpur, had himself portrayed as a British gentleman in his sitting room, but the artist employed the same materials that Indian miniature painters had used for centuries.

Indian artists readily adopted the new medium, not just to produce portraits but also to record landscapes and monuments.

In 19th-century India, however, admiration of Western art and culture was by no means universal. At the end of the century, ABANINDRANATH TAGORE (1871–1951; FIG. **32-12A**) founded a nationalistic art movement, and the opening decades of the 20th century brought ever-louder calls for Indian self-government. Under the leadership of Mahatma Gandhi (1869–1948) and others, India achieved independence in 1947—not, however, as a unified state but as the predominantly Hindu and Muslim nations of India and Pakistan, respectively.

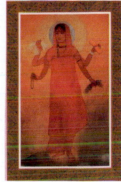

↗ 32-12A TAGORE, *Bharat Mata*, 1905.

who had embraced Western style, left no question about Jaswant Singh's regal presence and pride. The maharaja wears a turban made of rich fabric and fastened with a large jeweled brooch, a marker of kingship and more generally of power. The ruler's powerful chest and arms, along with the sword and his leather riding boots, indicate his abilities as a warrior and hunter. The curled beard signified fierceness to Indians of that time. The unflinching gaze records the ruler's confidence. Perhaps the two necklaces Jaswant Singh wears best exemplify the combination of his two worlds. One necklace is a bib of huge emeralds and diamonds, the heritage of the wealth and splendor of his family's rule. The other, a wide gold band with a cameo, is the Order of the Star of India, a high honor bestowed on him by his British overlords.

The painter of this portrait worked on the same scale and employed the same materials—opaque watercolor on paper—that Indian miniature painters had used for centuries, but the artist copied the ruler's likeness from a photograph. This accounts in large part for the realism of the portrait. Indian artists sometimes even painted directly on top of photographs. Photography arrived in India at an early date. In 1840, just one year after its invention in Paris, the *daguerreotype* (FIG. 27-48) was introduced in Kolkata.

20th Century

Modern art in India is as multifaceted a phenomenon as modern art is elsewhere in the world. Many traditional artists work at the village level, making images of deities for local use out of inexpensive materials, such as clay, plaster, and papier-mâché. Some urban artists use these same materials to produce elaborate religious scenes, such as depictions of the goddess Durga killing the buffalo demon—the central motif of the annual 10-day Durga Festival in Kolkata. Participants in the festival often ornament the scenes with thousands of colored electric lights. The most popular art form for religious imagery, however, is the brightly colored print, sold for only a few rupees each.

Many contemporary artists, in contrast, create works for the international market. Although many of them received their training in South or Southeast Asia or Japan, others attended schools in Europe or the United States, and some—for example, Pakistani Shahzia Sikander (FIG. 31-9) and Mumbai-born Anish Kapoor (FIG. 31-42), now work outside their home countries. They face one of the fundamental quandaries of many contemporary Asian artists: how to identify themselves and situate their work between local and international, traditional and modern, and non-Western and Western cultures.

MEERA MUKHERJEE One Indian artist who successfully bridged these two poles of modern Asian art was MEERA MUKHERJEE (1923–1998). Mukherjee studied with European masters in Germany, but when she returned to India, she rejected much of what she had learned in favor of the techniques long employed by traditional sculptors of the Bastar tribe in central India. Mukherjee went to live with Bastar bronze-casters, who had perfected a variation on the classic *lost-wax process* (see "Hollow-Casting Life-Size Bronze Statues," page 127). Beginning with a rough core of clay, the Bastar sculptors build up what will be the final shape of the statue by placing long threads of beeswax over the core. Then they apply a coat of clay paste to the beeswax and tie up the mold with metal wire. After heating the mold over a charcoal fire, which melts the wax away, they pour liquid bronze into the space once occupied by the wax threads. Large sculptures require many separate molds. The Bastar artists complete their statues by welding together the separately cast sections, usually leaving the seams visible.

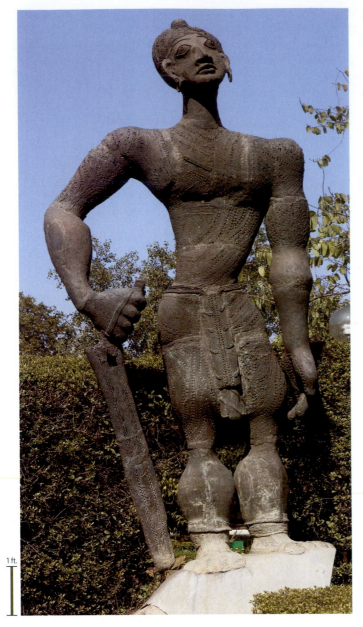

1 ft.

32-13 Meera Mukherjee, *Ashoka at Kalinga,* 1972. Bronze, 11' 6¾" high. Maurya Sheraton Hotel, New Delhi.

Mukherjee combined the Bastar tribe's traditional bronze-casting techniques with the swelling forms of 20th-century European sculpture in this statue of King Ashoka—a pacifist's protest against violence.

Many scholars regard *Ashoka at Kalinga* (FIG. **32-13**) as Mukherjee's greatest work. Twice life-size and assembled from 26 cast-bronze sections, the towering statue combines the intricate surface textures of traditional Bastar work with the expressively swelling abstract forms of some 20th-century European sculpture (FIG. 29-63). Mukherjee chose as her subject the third-century BCE Maurya emperor Ashoka standing on the battlefield at Kalinga. There, Ashoka witnessed more than 100,000 deaths and, shocked by the horrors of the war he had unleashed, rejected violence and adopted Buddhism as the official religion of his empire (see "Ashoka's Sponsorship of Buddhism," page 440). Mukherjee conceived her statue as a pacifist protest against the political violence unleashed by the 1971 conflict between India and Pakistan over the creation of the new independent nation of Bangladesh, formerly part of Pakistan. By reaching into India's remote history to make a contemporary political statement and by employ-

ing the bronze-casting methods of tribal sculptors while molding her forms in a modern idiom, she united her native land's past and present in a single work of great emotive power.

SOUTHEAST ASIA

India was not alone in experiencing major shifts in political power and religious preferences during the past 800 years. The Khmer of Angkor (see page 456), after reaching the height of their power at the beginning of the 13th century, lost one of their outposts in northern Thailand to their Thai vassals at midcentury. The newly founded Thai kingdoms quickly replaced Angkor as the region's major power, while Theravada Buddhism (see "The Buddha, Buddhism, and Buddhist Iconography," page 439) became the religion of the entire mainland except Vietnam. The Vietnamese, restricted to the northern region of present-day Vietnam, gained independence in the 10th century after a thousand years of Chinese political and cultural domination. They pushed to the south, ultimately destroying the indigenous Cham culture, which had dominated there for more than a millennium. A similar Burmese drive southward in Myanmar matched the Thai and Vietnamese expansions. All these movements resulted in demographic changes during the second millennium that led to the cultural, political, and artistic transformation of mainland Southeast Asia. A religious shift also occurred in Indonesia. With Islam growing in importance, all of Indonesia except the island of Bali became predominantly Muslim by the 16th century.

Thailand

Southeast Asians practiced both Buddhism and Hinduism, but by the 13th century, in contrast to developments in India, Hinduism was in decline and Buddhism dominated much of the mainland. Two prominent Buddhist kingdoms came to power in Thailand during the 13th and early 14th centuries. Historians date the beginning of the Sukhothai kingdom to 1292, the year King Ramkhamhaeng (r. 1279–1299) erected a four-sided stele bearing the first inscription written in the Thai language. Sukhothai's political dominance proved to be short-lived, however. Ayuthaya, a city founded in central Thailand in 1350, quickly became the more powerful kingdom and warred sporadically with other states in Southeast Asia until the mid-18th century. Scholars nonetheless regard the Sukhothai period as the golden age of Thai art. In the inscription on his stele, Ramkhamhaeng (Rama the Strong) described Sukhothai as a city of monasteries and many images of the Buddha.

WALKING BUDDHA Theravada Buddhism came to Sukhothai from Sri Lanka (see page 439). At the center of the city stood Wat Mahathat, Sukhothai's most important Buddhist monastery. Its *stupa* (mound-shaped Buddhist shrine; see "The Stupa," page 435) housed a *relic* of the Buddha (Wat Mahathat means "Monastery of the Great Relic") and attracted large crowds of pilgrims. Sukhothai's crowning artistic achievement was the development of a type of walking-Buddha statue (FIG. **32-14**) displaying a distinctively Thai approach to body form. The bronze Buddha has broad shoulders and a narrow waist and wears a clinging monk's robe. He strides forward, his right heel off the ground and his left arm raised with the hand held in the do-not-fear *mudra* (gesture) that encourages worshipers to come forward in reverence (see "Buddhist Iconography," page 439). A flame leaps from the top of the Buddha's head, and a sharp nose projects from his rounded face. The right arm hangs loosely, seemingly without muscles or joints, and resembles an elephant's trunk.

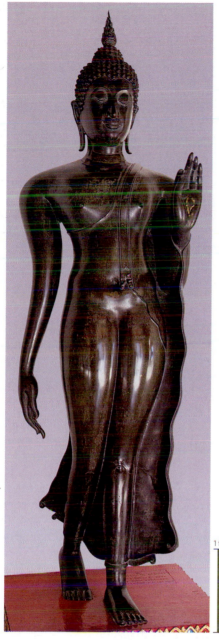

32-14 Walking Buddha, from Sukhothai, Thailand, 14th century. Bronze, 7' 2½" high. Wat Bechamabopit, Bangkok.

Walking-Buddha statues are unique to Thailand and display a distinctive approach to human anatomy. The Buddha's body is soft and elastic, and the right arm hangs loosely, like an elephant's trunk.

The Sukhothai artists intended the body type to suggest a supernatural being—broad shoulders traditionally connote power—and to express the Buddha's beauty and perfection through his supple body and polished skin. Although images in stone exist, the Sukhothai artists handled bronze best, a material well suited to their conception of the Buddha's body as elastic and glowing. The Sukhothai walking-Buddha statuary type is unique in Buddhist art, but it may reflect the ancient Buddhist iconographic tradition of representing the Buddha only by his footprints (see page 443).

EMERALD BUDDHA A second distinctive Buddha image from northern Thailand is the *Emerald Buddha* (FIG. **32-15**), housed in the Emerald Temple on the royal palace grounds in Bangkok. The sculpture is small, only 30 inches tall, and conforms to the ancient type of the Buddha seated in meditation in a yogic posture with his legs crossed and his hands in his lap, palms upward (FIG. 15-13). It first appears in historical records in 1434 in northern Thailand, where Buddhist chronicles record its story. The chronicles describe the Buddha image as plaster encased, and thus no one knew the statue was green stone. A lightning bolt caused some of the plaster to flake off, disclosing its gemlike nature. According to tradition, the statue was taken by various rulers to a series of cities in northern Thailand and in Laos over the course of more than 300 years and finally reached Bangkok in 1778 in the possession of the founder of the present Thai royal dynasty.

The *Emerald Buddha* is not, in fact, emerald but probably green jade. Nonetheless, its nature as a gemstone gives it a special aura.

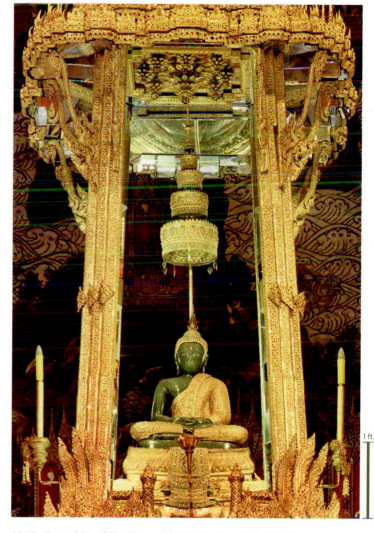

32-15 *Emerald Buddha*, Emerald Temple, Bangkok, Thailand, 15th century. Jade or jasper, 2' 6" high.

The Thai king dresses the *Emerald Buddha*, carved from green jade or jasper, in a monk's robe and a king's robe at different times of the year, underscoring the image's symbolic role as both Buddha and king.

The Thai believe that the gem enables the *chakravartin* ("universal king") who possesses the statue to bring the rains. The historical Buddha renounced his secular destiny for the spiritual life, yet his likeness carved from the gem of a universal king enables fulfillment of the Buddha's royal destiny as well. The Buddha is also the universal king. Thus the combination of the sacred and the secular in the small image explains its symbolic power. The Thai king dresses the *Emerald Buddha* at different times of the year in a monk's robe and a king's robe (in FIG. 32-15, the Buddha wears the royal garment), reflecting the image's dual nature and accentuating its symbolic role as both Buddha and king. The Thai king possessing the image therefore has both religious and secular authority.

Myanmar

Myanmar, like Thailand, is overwhelmingly a Theravada Buddhist country today. Important Buddhist monasteries and monuments dot the countryside.

SCHWEDAGON PAGODA In Rangoon, an enormous complex of buildings, including shrines filled with Buddha images, has as its

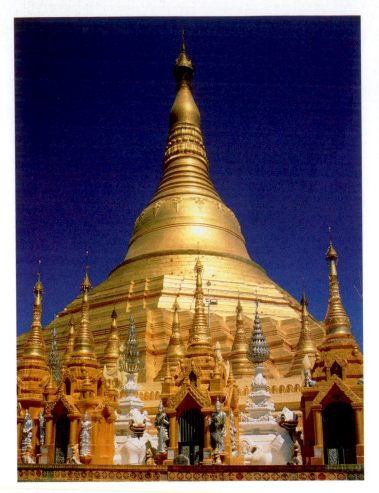

32-16 Schwedagon Pagoda (looking northeast), Rangoon (Yangon), Myanmar (Burma), 14th century or earlier (rebuilt several times).

The 344-foot-tall Schwedagon Pagoda houses some of the Buddha's hairs. Silver and jewels and 13,153 gold plates sheathe its exterior. The gold ball at the top is inlaid with 4,351 diamonds.

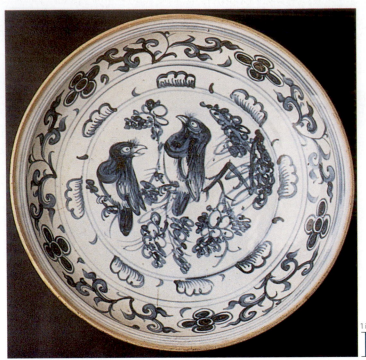

32-17 Dish with two mynah birds on flowering branch, from Vietnam, 16th century. Stoneware painted with underglaze-cobalt, 1' 2½" in diameter. Pacific Asia Museum, Pasadena.

Vietnamese ceramists exported underglaze pottery throughout Southeast Asia and beyond. The spontaneous depiction of mynah birds on this dish contrasts with the formality of Chinese porcelains.

centerpiece one of the largest stupas in the world, the Schwedagon Pagoda (FIG. 32-16). (*Pagoda* derives from the Portuguese version of a word for "stupa.") The Rangoon pagoda houses some of the Buddha's hairs, traditionally said to have been brought to Myanmar by merchants who received them from the Buddha himself. Rebuilt several times, this highly revered stupa is famous for the gold, silver, and jewels encrusting its surface. The Schwedagon Pagoda stands 344 feet high. Covering its upper part are 13,153 plates of gold, each about a foot square. At the very top is a seven-tiered umbrella crowned with a gold ball inlaid with 4,351 diamonds, one of which weighs 76 carats. This great wealth was a gift to the Buddha from the laypeople of Myanmar to earn merit on their path to enlightenment. As with the *Emerald Buddha,* the lavish materials associate the pagoda with royalty, lending added prestige to the religious shrine.

Vietnam

The history of Vietnam is particularly complex, as it reveals both an Indian-related art and culture, broadly similar to those of the rest of Southeast Asia, and a unique and intense relationship with China's art and culture. Vietnam's tradition of fine ceramics is of special interest. The oldest Vietnamese ceramics date to the Han period (206 BCE–220 CE), when the Chinese began to govern the northern area of Vietnam. China directly controlled Vietnam for a thousand

years, and early Vietnamese ceramics closely reflected Chinese wares. But during the Ly (1009–1225) and Tran (1225–1400) dynasties, when Vietnam had regained its independence, Vietnamese potters developed an array of ceramic shapes, designs, and *glazes* that brought their wares to the highest levels of quality and creativity.

UNDERGLAZE CERAMICS In the 14th century, the Vietnamese began exporting *underglaze* wares modeled on the blue-and-white ceramics first produced in China (see "Chinese Porcelain," page 1053). During the 15th and 16th centuries, the ceramic industry in Vietnam had become the supplier of pottery of varied shapes to an international market extending throughout Southeast Asia and to the Middle East. A 16th-century Vietnamese dish (FIG. 32-17) with two mynah birds on a flowering branch reveals both the potter's debt to China and how the spontaneity, power, and playfulness of Vietnamese painting contrast with the formality of Chinese wares (FIG. 33-5). The artist suggested the foliage with curving and looped lines executed in almost one continuous movement of the brush over the surface. This technique—very different from the more deliberate Chinese habit of lifting the brush after painting a single motif in order to separate the shapes more sharply—facilitated rapid production. Combined with the painter's control, it allowed a fresh and unique design, making Vietnamese pottery attractive to a wide export market.

CONTEMPORARY ART In the Buddhist countries of Southeast Asia, some artists continue to produce traditional images of the Buddha, primarily in bronze, for worship in homes, businesses, and temples. But, as in South Asia, many contemporary artists work in an international modernist idiom.

SOUTH AND SOUTHEAST ASIA, 1200 TO 1980

Sultanate of Delhi

- After defeating a confederation of South Asian states, Qutb al-Din Aybak (r. 1206–1211) established the Sultanate of Delhi (1206–1526), bringing Muslim rule to northern India and transforming South Asian society, religion, art, and architecture.
- To mark the triumph of Islam, the sultans built Delhi's first mosque—the Might of Islam Mosque—and its 238-foot Qutb Minar, the tallest minaret in the world.

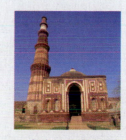

Qutb Minar, Delhi, begun early 13th century

Vijayanagar Empire

- The most powerful Hindu kingdom in southern India when Muslim sultans ruled the north was the Vijayanagar Empire (1336–1565).
- Vijayanagar buildings—for example, the Lotus Mahal—display a distinctive mix of Islamic multilobed arches and crowning elements resembling Hindu temple vimanas.

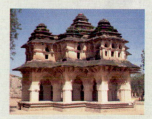

Lotus Mahal, Vijayanagara, 15th or early 16th century

Mughal Empire

- Babur (r. 1526–1530) defeated the Delhi sultans in 1526 and established the Mughal Empire (1526–1857).
- The first great flowering of Mughal art and architecture occurred under Akbar the Great (r. 1556–1605). The imperial painting workshop continued to produce magnificent illustrated books under his son Jahangir (r. 1605–1627) and his successors. The names of many Mughal miniature painters are known.
- Shah Jahan (r. 1628–1658) built the Taj Mahal as a memorial to his favorite wife. The mausoleum may symbolize the throne of God above the gardens of Paradise.

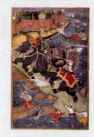

Basawan and Chatar Muni, *Akbar and the Elephant Hawai*, ca. 1590

Other South and Southeast Asian Kingdoms

- During the Mughal Empire, Hindu Rajput kings ruled much of northwestern India. The coloration and sensuality of Rajput painting distinguish it from the contemporaneous Mughal style.
- Between 1529 and 1736, the Hindu Nayak dynasty controlled southern India and erected temple complexes with immense gateway towers (gopuras) decorated with painted stucco sculptures.
- In Thailand, Theravada Buddhism was the dominant religion. The Sukhothai walking-Buddha statuary type displays a unique approach to body form, as seen, for example, in the Buddha's trunklike right arm.
- Myanmar's Schwedagon Pagoda in Rangoon, one of the largest stupas in the world, is encrusted with gold, silver, and jewels.

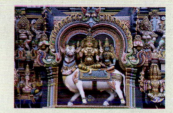

Great Temple, Madurai, 17th century

British Colonial Period to 1980

- Queen Elizabeth I (r. 1558–1603) authorized the establishment of the East India Company, which eventually effectively ruled large portions of the subcontinent. In 1877, Queen Victoria I (r. 1837–1901) assumed the title Empress of India. British colonial rule lasted from 1600 to 1947, and Victoria Terminus is its architectural symbol—a European transplant to India capped by an allegorical statue of Progress.
- Under the leadership of Mahatma Gandhi (1869–1948), India and Pakistan achieved independence from England in 1947. Post–World War II South and Southeast Asian art ranges from the traditional to the modern and embraces both native and Western styles.

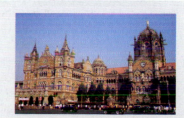

Stevens, Victoria Terminus, Mumbai, 1878–1887

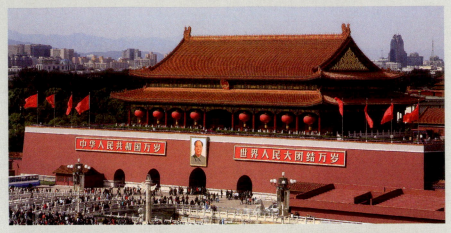

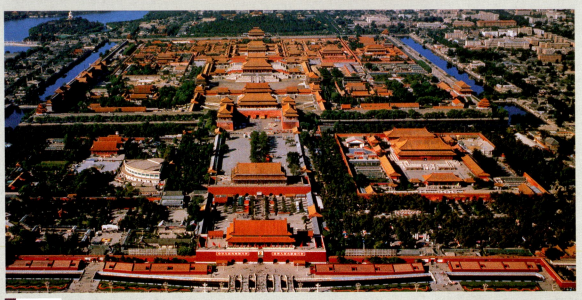

33-1a The southern entrance to the Forbidden City was the Noon Gate. Only the emperor could walk through the central portal. Those of decreasing rank used the lateral passageways.

33-1 **Aerial view (looking north) of the Forbidden City, Beijing, China, Ming dynasty, 15th century and later.**

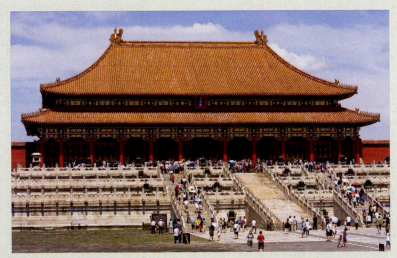

▲ **33-1b** The Hall of Supreme Harmony is the climax of the imperial palace complex's long north-south axis. It is the largest wood building in China and has 72 gigantic columns carved from Sichuan trees.

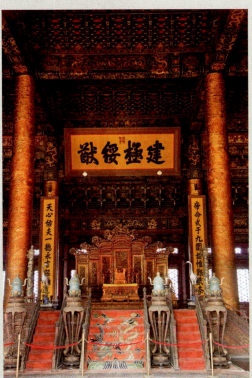

▲ **33-1c** Inside the Hall of Supreme Harmony is the emperor's opulently appointed throne room. Here, the Ming Son of Heaven, elevated on a stepped platform, received important visitors.

33

FRAMING THE ERA

China and Korea, 1279 to 1980

THE FORBIDDEN CITY

In 1368, Zhu Yuanzhong led a popular uprising that drove the last Mongol emperor from Beijing. After expelling the foreigners from China, he founded the native Chinese Ming dynasty (r. 1368–1644) and assumed the official name of the Hongwu (Abundantly Martial) emperor (r. 1368–1398). Zhu built his capital at Nanjing (Southern Capital), but the third Ming ruler, the Yongle (Perpetual Happiness) emperor (r. 1403–1424), moved the imperial seat back to Beijing (Northern Capital). Although Beijing had been home to the Yuan dynasty, Ming architects designed much of the city as well as the imperial palace at its core, which, with the Great Wall, is the enduring emblem of China.

The Ming builders laid out Beijing as three nested walled cities. The outer perimeter wall was 15 miles long and enclosed the walled Imperial City, with a perimeter of 6 miles, and, within the city, the vast imperial palace compound (FIG. 33-1) surrounded by a 50-yard-wide moat. The strict symmetry of the palace's plan symbolized the order that the Ming emperor, the Son of Heaven, brought to the world. Appropriately, his throne room was situated at the center of that world. Known since 1576 as the Forbidden City because of the highly restricted access to the inner compound, the palace provided the perfect setting for the elaborate ritual of the Ming court. For example, the entrance gateway to the complex, the Noon Gate, has five portals. Only the emperor could walk through the central doorway. The two entrances to its left and right were reserved for the imperial family and high officials. Others had to use the outermost passageways. Entrance to the Forbidden City proper was through the nearly 40-yard-tall triple-passageway Meridian Gate, through which only the Son of Heaven and his retinue and foreign ambassadors who had been granted an official audience could pass.

Within the Forbidden City, more gates and a series of courtyards, gardens, temples, and other buildings lead eventually to a series of marble staircases and the Hall of Supreme Harmony, which is the climax of a long north-south axis. The fill of the immense platform supporting the Hall of Supreme Harmony consists of the soil and rocks that the Ming engineers collected from the excavation of the great moat around the imperial complex. The hall is the largest wood building in China. For its 72 columns, the Ming builders had to transport gigantic tree trunks down the Yangtze River from Sichuan Province. Inside the hall sat the emperor on his dragon throne on a high stepped platform.

Beyond the Hall of Supreme Harmony is the even more restricted Inner Court and the Palace of Heavenly Purity—the private living quarters of the emperor and his extended family of wives, concubines, and children. At the northern end of the central axis of the Forbidden City is the Gate of Divine Prowess, through which the palace servants gained access to the complex.

CHINA

In 1210, the Mongols invaded northern China from Central Asia (MAP 33-1), opening a new chapter in the history and art of that ancient land. Under the dynamic leadership of Genghis Khan (1167–1230), the Mongol armies pushed into China with extraordinary speed. By 1215, the Mongols had destroyed the Jin dynasty's capital at Beijing and taken control of northern China. Two decades later, they attacked the Song dynasty in southern China. It was not until 1279, however, that the last Song emperor fell at the hands of Genghis Khan's grandson, Kublai Khan (1215–1294). Kublai proclaimed himself emperor (r. 1279–1294) of the new Yuan dynasty.

Yuan Dynasty

During the relatively brief tenure of the Yuan (r. 1279–1368), trade between Europe and Asia increased dramatically. It was no coincidence that Marco Polo (1254–1324), the most famous early European visitor to China, arrived during the reign of Kublai Khan. Part fact and part fable, Marco Polo's chronicle of his travels to and within China was the only eyewitness description of East Asia available in Europe for several centuries. The Venetian's account makes clear that he profoundly admired Yuan China. He marveled not only at Kublai Khan's luxurious lifestyle and sumptuous palaces but also at the volume of commercial traffic on the Yangtze River; the splendors

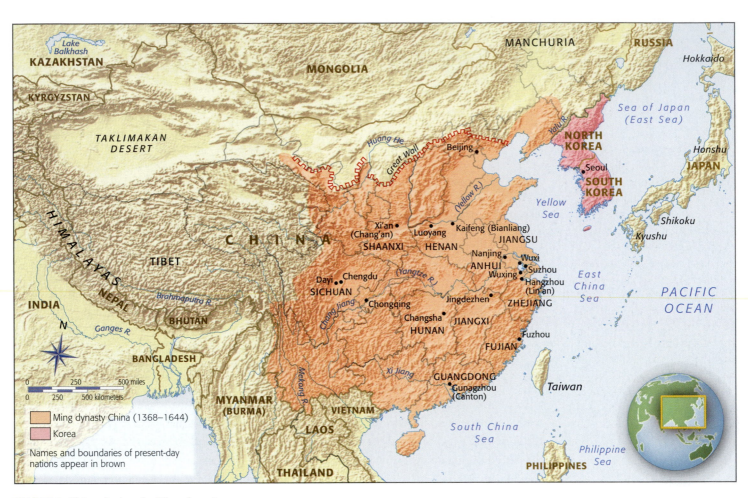

MAP 33-1 China during the Ming dynasty.

CHINA AND KOREA, 1279 TO 1980

1279–1368
Yuan Dynasty

- Mongol invaders establish the Yuan dynasty
- Huang Gongwang, Ni Zan, Wang Meng, and Wu Zhen achieve fame as the Four Great Masters of Yuan landscape painting
- The Jingdezhen kilns produce porcelain pottery with cobalt-blue underglaze decoration

1368–1644
Ming Dynasty

- The third Ming emperor begins construction of the Forbidden City in Beijing
- The Orchard Factory creates luxurious carved lacquer-covered wood furniture
- Landscape architects design uncultivated scenic gardens at Suzhou
- The Joseon dynasty (r. 1392–1910) in Korea erects the Namdaemun gate in Seoul

1644–1911
Qing Dynasty

- The Manchus overthrow the native Ming emperors and rule China as the Qing dynasty
- Shitao experiments with bold new approaches to traditional literati landscape painting
- Jesuit missionaries introduce Western painting styles

1912–1980
Modern China

- Marxist themes dominate the state-sponsored art of the People's Republic of China
- With the unwinding of Mao Zedong's Cultural Revolution, Chinese artists begin to rise to prominence in the international art world

of Hangzhou; the use of paper currency, porcelain, and coal; the efficiency of the Chinese postal system; and the hygiene of the Chinese people. In the early second millennium, China was richer and technologically more advanced than late medieval Europe.

ZHAO MENGFU The Mongols were distrustful of the Chinese and very selective in admitting former Southern Song subjects into their administration. In addition, many Chinese loyal to the former emperors refused to collaborate with their new foreign overlords, whom they considered barbarian usurpers. Indeed, most of the great art created during the Yuan dynasty was the work of men and women who refused to play any role in the Mongol court. One artist who did accept an official post under Kublai Khan was ZHAO MENGFU (1254–1322), a descendant of the first Song emperor. A learned man, skilled in both calligraphy and poetry, he won renown as a painter of horses and of landscapes, but he also painted other subjects (for example, FIG. 33-1A).

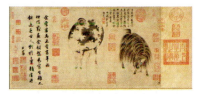

33-1A ZHAO MENGFU, *Sheep and Goat*, ca. 1300.

MATERIALS AND TECHNIQUES
Calligraphy and Inscriptions on Chinese Paintings

Many Chinese paintings (FIGS. 16-13, 16-18, 16-23, 16-26, 33-1A, 33-3, 33-4A, and 33-12 to 33-14) bear inscriptions, texts written on the same surface as the picture, or *colophons*, texts written on attached pieces of paper or silk. Throughout history, the Chinese have held *calligraphy* (Greek, "beautiful writing") in high esteem—higher, in fact, than painting. Inscriptions appear almost everywhere in China—on buildings and in gardens, on furniture and sculpture. Chinese calligraphy and painting have always been closely connected. Even the primary implements and materials for writing and painting are the same: a round tapered brush, soot-based ink, and paper or silk. Calligraphy depends for its effects on the controlled vitality of individual brushstrokes and on the dynamic relationships of strokes within a *character* (an elaborate Chinese sign that by itself can represent several words) and even among the characters themselves. Training in calligraphy was a fundamental part of the education and self-cultivation of Chinese scholars and officials, and inscriptions are especially common on *literati* paintings. Many stylistic variations exist in Chinese calligraphy. At the most formal extreme, each character consists of distinct straight and angular strokes and is separate from the next character. At the other extreme, the characters flow together as cursive abbreviations with many rounded forms.

A long tradition in China links pictures and poetry. Famous poems frequently provided subjects for paintings, and poets composed poems inspired by paintings. Either practice might prompt inscriptions on art, some addressing painted subjects, some praising the painting's quality or the character of the painter or another individual. The Ming painter Shen Zhou added a long poem in beautiful Chinese characters to his painting of Mount Lu (FIG. 33-12). The poem praises a beloved teacher. Sometimes inscriptions explain the circumstances of the work. The Yuan painter Guan Daosheng's *Bamboo Groves in Mist and Rain* has two inscriptions (not included in the detail reproduced in FIG. 33-2). One is a dedication to another noblewoman. The other states that Guan painted the handscroll "in a boat on the green waves of the lake." Later admirers and owners of paintings frequently inscribed their own appreciative words. The inscriptions are often quite prominent and sometimes compete for the viewer's attention with the painted motifs (FIGS. 33-1A and 33-3).

Painters, inscribers, and even owners usually also added *seal* impressions in red ink (FIGS. 33-2 to 33-4A and 33-12 to 33-16) to identify themselves. With all these textual additions, some paintings that have passed through many collections may seem cluttered to Western viewers. However, the historical importance given to these inscriptions and to the works' ownership history has been and remains a critical aspect of painting appreciation in China.

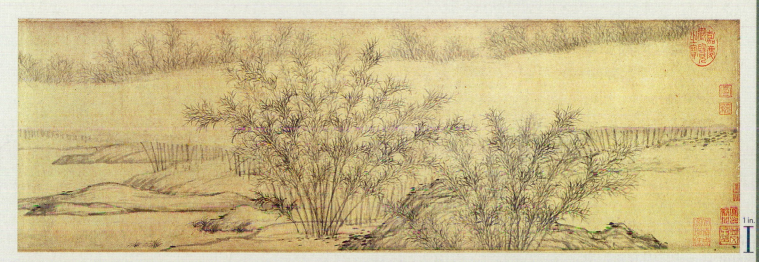

33-2 GUAN DAOSHENG, *Bamboo Groves in Mist and Rain* (detail), Yuan dynasty, 1308. Section of a handscroll, ink on paper, full scroll $9\frac{1}{8}$" × 3' $8\frac{7}{8}$". National Palace Museum, Tabei.

Guan Daosheng was a calligrapher, poet, and painter. She achieved the misty atmosphere in this landscape by using a narrow range of ink tones and by blurring the bamboo thickets in the distance.

33-3 Wu Zhen, *Stalks of Bamboo by a Rock,* Yuan dynasty, 1347. Hanging scroll, ink on paper, 2' 11½" × 1' 4⅝". National Palace Museum, Tabei.

Wu Zhen was one of the leading Yuan literati (scholar-artists). The bamboo plants in his hanging scroll are perfect complements to the prominently featured black Chinese calligraphic characters.

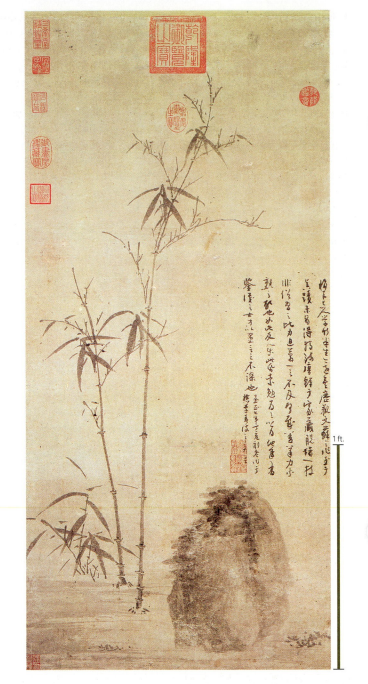

GUAN DAOSHENG Zhao's wife, GUAN DAOSHENG (1262–1319), was also a successful painter, calligrapher, and poet. Female artists were at least as rare in China at this time as they were in the West, and not only because of women's similarly restricted roles in society. In China, because calligraphy was so closely allied with painting, and so few women could read or write, the barriers to becoming an artist were even greater. As a general rule, only an educated woman from a well-to-do family could succeed as an artist. Guan Daosheng is, in fact, the first woman artist in Chinese history to win widespread fame. She enjoyed the admiration even of the emperor himself.

Guan painted a variety of subjects, including Buddhist murals in Yuan temples—an even more unusual pursuit for a woman—but she became famous for her paintings of bamboo. The plant was a popular subject because it was a symbol of the ideal Chinese gentleman, who bends in adversity but does not break, and because depicting bamboo branches and leaves approximated the cherished art of calligraphy (see "Calligraphy and Inscriptions on Chinese Paintings," page 1051). *Bamboo Groves in Mist and Rain* (FIG. 33-2), a *handscroll* (see "Chinese Painting Materials and Formats," page 479), is one of Guan's best paintings. The hallmark of her landscapes is the misty atmosphere she achieved by restricting the ink tones to a narrow range and by blurring the bamboo thickets in the distance, suggesting not only the receding terrain but fog as well.

WU ZHEN The Yuan painter WU ZHEN (1280–1354), in stark contrast to Zhao Mengfu and Guan Daosheng, shunned the Mongol court and lived as a hermit, far from the luxurious milieu of the Yuan emperors. He was one of the *literati,* or scholar-artists, who emerged during the Song dynasty. The literati were men and women from prominent families who painted primarily for a small audience of their social peers. Highly educated and steeped in traditional Chinese culture, they cultivated calligraphy, poetry, painting, and other arts as a sign of social status and refined taste. Literati art is usually personal in nature and often shows nostalgia for the past.

Wu Zhen's treatment of the bamboo theme, *Stalks of Bamboo by a Rock* (FIG. 33-3), differs sharply from Guan's. The artist clearly differentiated the individual bamboo plants and reveled in the abstract patterns formed by the stalks and leaves. The bamboo stalks in his *hanging scroll* (see "Chinese

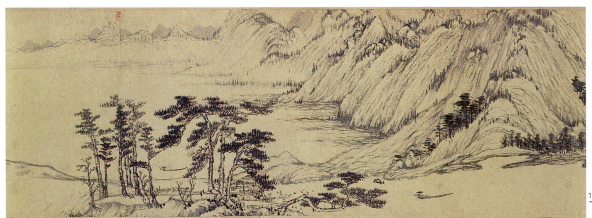

33-4 HUANG GONGWANG, *Dwelling in the Fuchun Mountains,* Yuan dynasty, 1347–1350. Section of a handscroll, ink on paper, full scroll 1' ⅞" × 20' 9". National Palace Museum, Tabei.

In this Yuan handscroll, Huang built up the textured mountains with richly layered wet and dry brushstrokes and ink-wash accents, capturing the landscape's inner structure and momentum.

Painting Materials and Formats," page 479) are perfect complements to the calligraphic beauty of the Chinese black characters and red seals so prominently featured on the scroll (see "Calligraphy and Inscriptions," page 1051). Both the bamboo and the inscriptions gave Wu Zhen the opportunity to display his proficiency with the brush.

HUANG GONGWANG Later artists and critics revered Wu Zhen as one of the Four Great Masters of Yuan painting. The eldest was HUANG GONGWANG (1269–1354), a former civil servant and a teacher of Daoist philosophy. His *Dwelling in the Fuchun Mountains* (FIG. 33-4) is one of the great works of Yuan literati painting. According to the artist's explanatory inscription at the end of the long handscroll, Huang sketched the full composition in one burst of inspiration, but then added to and modified his painting whenever he felt moved to do so over a period of years. In the detail shown in FIG. 33-4, the painter built up the textured mountains with richly layered brushstrokes, at times interweaving dry brushstrokes and at other times placing dry strokes over wet ones and darker strokes over lighter ones, often with ink-wash accents. The rhythmic play of brush and ink captures the landscape's inner structure and momentum. In fact, the purpose of landscape painting in China was rarely to record the features of a specific setting. Instead, Chinese artists sought to represent the essential beauty of the natural world through the artful depiction of mountains, trees, and streams.

Huang summarized his approach to painting nature in a treatise titled *Secrets of Landscape Painting*, in which he also noted the kinship of ink painting and the art of calligraphy.

> In painting each furrow and rock, one should give free rein to the ink allowing it to run unrestrained. . . . [T]oo much detail description will make it look like craftsmanship. . . . For the most part, just as in calligraphy, practicing diligently will make mastery perfect.[1]

NI ZAN Completing the quartet of renowned Yuan masters were two younger artists born in the early 14th century—NI ZAN (1301- or 1306–1374) and Wang Meng (ca. 1308–1385). Both were still active during the early years of the Ming dynasty, when Ni painted his most famous work, *Rongxi Studio* (FIG. 33-4A), a literati landscape of unsurpassed quality.

JINGDEZHEN PORCELAIN By the Yuan period, Chinese potters had extended their mastery to fully developed *porcelains*, a technically demanding medium (see "Chinese Porcelain," below). Two tall temple vases, known as the *David Vases* (FIG. 33-5) after the

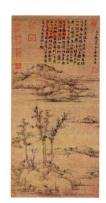

33-4A NI ZAN, *Rongxi Studio*, 1372.

MATERIALS AND TECHNIQUES
Chinese Porcelain

No other Chinese art form has achieved such worldwide admiration, inspired such imitation, or penetrated so deeply into everyday life as *porcelain* (FIGS. 33-5 and 33-17). Long imported by China's Asian neighbors as luxury goods and treasures, Chinese porcelains later captured great attention in the West, where potters did not succeed in mastering the production process until the early 18th century.

In China, primitive porcelains emerged during the Tang dynasty (618–907), and mature forms developed in the Song (960–1279). Like *stoneware* (see "Chinese Earthenwares and Stonewares," page 463), porcelain objects are fired in a kiln at an extremely high temperature (well over 2,000° F) until the clay fully fuses into a dense, hard substance resembling stone or glass. Unlike stoneware, however, ceramists create porcelain from a fine white clay called kaolin mixed with ground petuntse (a type of feldspar). True porcelain is translucent and rings when struck. Its rich, shiny surface resembles jade, a luxurious natural material that the Chinese treasured from very early times (see "Chinese Jade," page 466).

Chinese ceramists often decorate porcelains with colored designs or pictures, working with finely ground minerals suspended in water and a binding agent (such as glue). The minerals change color dramatically in the kiln. The painters apply some mineral colors to the clay surface before the main firing and then apply a clear *glaze* over them. This *underglaze* decoration fully bonds to the piece in the kiln, but because the raw materials must withstand intense heat, Yuan dynasty potters could fire only a few colors. The most stable and widely used coloring agents for porcelains are cobalt compounds, which emerge from the kiln as an intense blue (FIG. 33-5). Rarely, ceramists use copper compounds to produce stunning reds by carefully manipulating the kiln's temperature and oxygen content.

To obtain a wider palette, an artist must paint on top of the glaze after firing the work (FIG. 33-17). These *overglaze* colors, or *enamels*,

then fuse to the glazed surface in an additional firing at a much lower temperature. Enamels also offer ceramic painters a much brighter palette, with colors ranging from deep browns to brilliant reds and greens, but they do not have the durability of underglaze decoration.

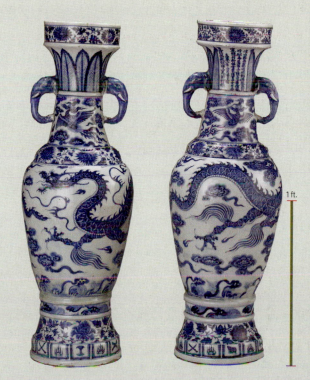

33-5 *David Vases*, Yuan dynasty, 1351. Pair of white porcelain vases with cobalt-blue underglaze, each 2' 1" tall. British Museum, London (Sir Percival David Foundation of Chinese Art).

The *David Vases* are early examples of porcelain with cobalt-blue underglaze decoration. Dragons and phoenixes are the major painted motifs. They may be symbols of male and female energy, respectively.

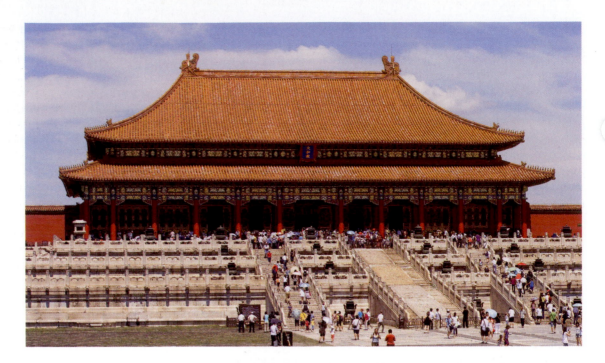

33-6 Hall of Supreme Harmony (looking north), Forbidden City, Beijing, China, Ming dynasty, 15th century and later.

The Hall of Supreme Harmony is the largest wood building in China. For its gigantic columns, the Ming builders had to transport huge tree trunks down the Yangtze River from Sichuan Province.

collector who acquired them, are the best surviving examples from the Jingdezhen kilns, which during the Ming dynasty became the official source of porcelains for the court. The pair can be dated exactly by the inscription citing the emperor's regnal year, equivalent to 1351 in the Western calendar. The inscription also says that the vases, together with an incense burner, composed an altar set donated to a Buddhist temple as a prayer for peace, protection, and prosperity for the donor's family. The *David Vases* are among the earliest dated examples of fine porcelain with cobalt-blue *underglaze* decoration. The painted decoration consists of bands of floral motifs between broader zones containing auspicious symbols, including phoenixes in the lower part of the neck and dragons (compare FIG. 16-6) on the main body of the vessel, both among clouds. These motifs may suggest the donor's high status or invoke prosperity blessings. Because of their vast power and associations with nobility and prosperity, the dragon and phoenix also symbolize the emperor and empress, respectively, and often appear on objects made for the imperial household. The dragon also may represent *yang,* the Chinese principle of active masculine energy, while the phoenix may represent *yin,* the principle of passive feminine energy.

Ming Dynasty

The Ming emperors who succeeded the Yuan as rulers of China (see page 1049) were, like many other powerful dynasts throughout history, great builders. The grandest Ming architectural project was the Forbidden City (FIGS. 33-1, **33-6**, and **33-7**), discussed briefly in the introduction to this chapter. The new imperial palace complex in Beijing was strictly organized along a north-south axis as a series of courtyards and traditional wood buildings featuring curved rooflines (see "Chinese Wood Construction," page 470). At the heart of the Forbidden City, then as today, is the Hall of Supreme Harmony (FIG. 33-6), where the Son of Heaven received official visitors in the opulently furnished room (FIG. 33-7) that housed his throne atop a flight of stairs. The hall's columns, walls, and ceiling are richly decorated with gold lacquer and imperial dragon motifs. In front of the hall are bronze statues of a turtle and a crane, symbols of longevity.

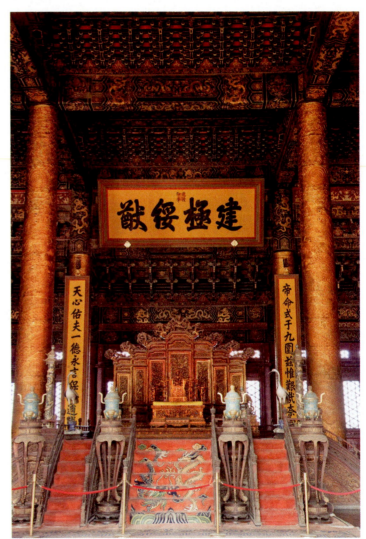

33-7 Throne room, Hall of Supreme Harmony, Forbidden City, Beijing, China, Ming dynasty, 15th century and later.

The Ming emperors held official audiences in the opulently appointed throne room in the Hall of Supreme Harmony. Beyond was the Inner Court, where the emperor and his extended family resided.

PROBLEMS AND SOLUTIONS
Planning an Unplanned Garden

The Ming gardens at Suzhou are among the most precious examples of landscape architecture anywhere in the world. Several have been meticulously restored, and in each one, the designers grappled with the problem of how to design a garden that appears not to have been designed—that is, a planned garden that seems unplanned, like nature itself. Laying out a Ming garden was not a matter of cultivating plants in rows or of laying out terraces, flower beds, and avenues in geometric fashion, as was the case in many other cultures (compare, for example, the 17th-century French gardens at Versailles, FIG. 25-26). Instead, Ming gardens, such as the huge (almost 54,000-square-foot) Wangshi Yuan (Garden of the Master of the Fishing Nets; FIG. **33-8**), are often scenic arrangements of natural and artificial elements intended to reproduce the irregularities of uncultivated nature. Verandas and pavilions rise on pillars above the water, and stone bridges, paths, and causeways encourage wandering through ever-changing vistas of trees, flowers, rocks, and their reflections in the ponds. The typical design is a sequence of carefully contrived visual surprises, the polar opposite of the predictable formality of Ming palace architecture (FIG. 33-1).

A favorite garden element, fantastic rockwork, is a prominent feature of Liu Yuan (Lingering Garden; FIG. **33-9**) in Suzhou. Workmen dredged the stones from nearby Lake Tai, and then sculptors shaped them to create an even more natural look. The one at the center of FIG. 33-9, called the Guanyun (Cloud Crowned) Peak, is about 20 feet tall and weighs approximately 5 tons. The Ming gardens of Suzhou were the pleasure retreats of high officials and the landed gentry, sanctuaries where the wealthy could commune with nature in all its representative forms and as an ever-changing and boundless presence. Chinese poets never cease to sing of the restorative effect of gardens on mind and spirit.

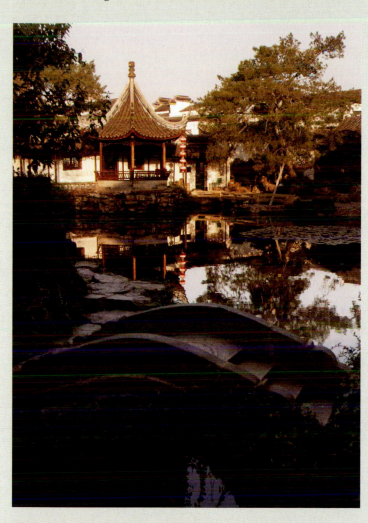

33-8 Wangshi Yuan (Garden of the Master of the Fishing Nets), Suzhou, China, Ming dynasty, 16th century and later.

Ming gardens are arrangements of natural and artificial elements intended to reproduce the irregularities of nature. This approach to design is the opposite of the formality and axiality of the Ming palace (FIG. 33-1).

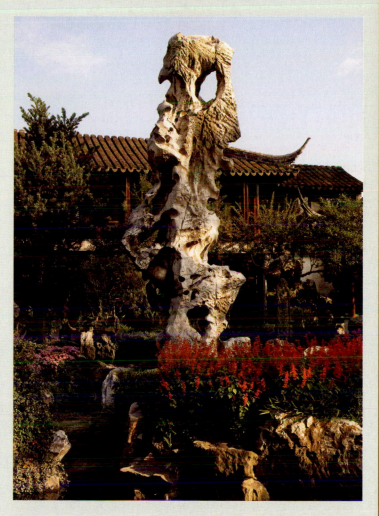

33-9 Guanyun (Cloud Crowned) Peak, rock formation in the Liu Yuan (Lingering Garden), Suzhou, China, Ming dynasty, 16th century and later.

A favorite element of Chinese gardens was fantastic rockwork. For the Lingering Garden, workmen dredged the stones from a nearby lake, and sculptors shaped them to produce an even more natural look.

SUZHOU GARDENS In the Forbidden City in Beijing, everything, even the gardens, is tightly organized, reflecting the order that the emperor, the Son of Heaven, brings to the world. At the opposite pole of architectural design are the Ming gardens of Suzhou. Indeed, there can hardly be a greater contrast than that between the formality and rigid axiality of the Forbidden City and the seemingly unplanned Suzhou pleasure gardens (see "Planning an Unplanned Garden," above).

MATERIALS AND TECHNIQUES
Lacquered Wood

From ancient times, the Chinese used *lacquer* to cover wood, whether small objects, furniture, or huge columns, such as those in the throne room (FIG. 33-7) of the Forbidden City.

Artisans produced lacquer from the sap of the Asiatic sumac tree, native to central and southern China. When it dries, lacquer cures to great hardness and prevents the wood from decaying. Often colored with mineral pigments, lacquered objects have a lustrous surface that transforms the appearance of natural wood. The earliest examples of lacquered wood to survive in quantity date to the Eastern Zhou period (770–256 BCE).

The first step in producing a lacquered object is to heat and purify the sap. Then the lacquer worker mixes the minerals—carbon black and cinnabar red are the most common—into the sap. To apply the lacquer, the artisan uses a hair brush similar to a calligrapher's or painter's brush, building up the coating one layer at a time. Each coat must dry and be sanded before another layer can be applied. If the artisan builds up a sufficient number of layers, the lacquer can be carved as if it were the wood itself. The lacquer workers in the Orchard Factory in Beijing were master carvers and counted the Ming emperors as major clients for luxurious lacquered furniture. Examples such as the illustrated table (FIG. 33-10) boast elaborate carving in many layers of lacquer and took a great deal of time as well as skill to produce.

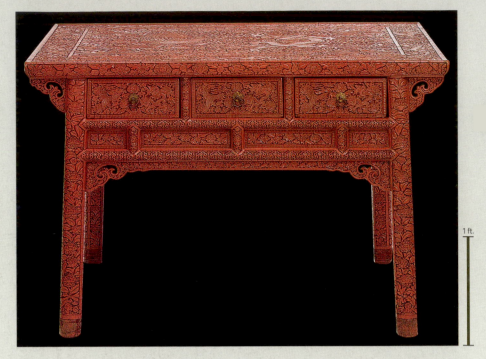

33-10 Table with drawers, Ming dynasty, ca. 1426–1435. Carved red lacquer on a wood core, 3' 11" long. Victoria & Albert Museum, London.

The Orchard Factory was the leading Ming workshop for lacquered wood furniture. The lacquer on this table was thick enough to be carved with floral motifs and the imperial dragon and phoenix.

Other techniques for decorating lacquer include inlaying metals and lustrous materials, such as mother-of-pearl, and sprinkling gold powder into the still-wet lacquer. Korean and Japanese (FIG. 34-11) artists also employed these techniques to produce masterful lacquered objects.

ORCHARD FACTORY The Ming court's lavish appetite for luxury goods to use and display in the imperial palace gave new impetus to brilliant technical achievement in the decorative arts. As did the Yuan emperors, the Ming dynasty turned to the Jingdezhen kilns for fine porcelains. For objects in lacquer-covered wood (see "Lacquered Wood," above), their patronage went to a large workshop in Beijing known today as the Orchard Factory. A table with drawers (FIG. 33-10), made between 1426 and 1435, is one of the workshop's masterpieces. The artist carved floral motifs, along with the dragon and phoenix imperial emblems,

33-11 SHANG XI, *Guan Yu Captures General Pang De*, Ming dynasty, ca. 1430. Hanging scroll, ink and colors on silk, 6' 5" × 7' 7". Palace Museum, Beijing.

The official painters of the Ming court lived in the Forbidden City and specialized in portraiture and history painting. This very large hanging scroll celebrates a famed general of the third century.

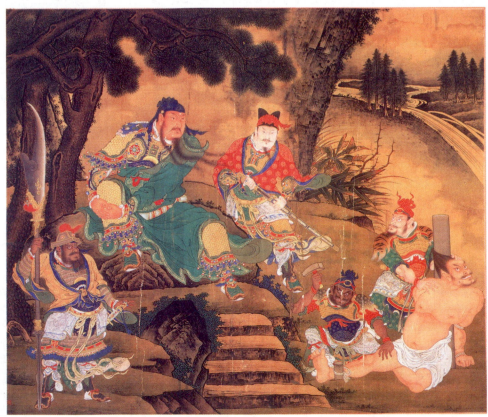

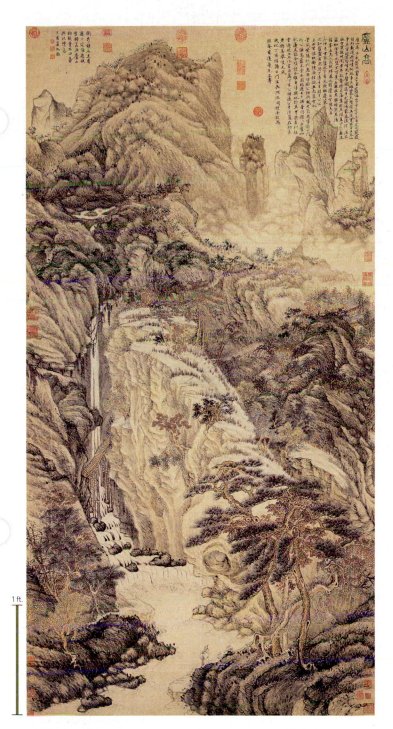

33-12 SHEN ZHOU, *Lofty Mount Lu*, Ming dynasty, 1467. Hanging scroll, ink and colors on paper, 6' 4$\frac{1}{4}$" × 3' 2$\frac{5}{8}$". National Palace Museum, Tabei.

Inscriptions and seals are essential elements in this hanging scroll, in which Shen used the lofty peaks of Mount Lu to express visually the grandeur of a beloved teacher's virtue and character.

1 ft.

into the thick cinnabar-colored lacquer, which had to be built up in numerous layers.

SHANG XI At the Ming court, the official painters lived in the Forbidden City itself, and portraiture of the imperial family was their major subject. The court artists also depicted historical figures as exemplars of virtue, wisdom, or heroism (compare FIG. 16-18). An exceptionally large example of Ming history painting is a hanging scroll painted by SHANG XI (active ca. 1425–1440) around 1430.

Guan Yu Captures General Pang De (FIG. **33-11**) represents an episode from China's tumultuous third century (Period of Disunity; see page 471), whose wars inspired one of the first great Chinese novels, *The Romance of the Three Kingdoms*. Guan Yu was a famed general of the Wei dynasty (220–280) and a fictional hero in the novel. Shang's painting depicts the historical Guan, renowned for his loyalty to his emperor and for his military valor, being presented with the captured enemy general Pang De. In the painting, Shang used color to focus attention on Guan and his attendants, who stand out sharply from the ink landscape. He also contrasted the victors' armor and bright garments with the vulnerability of the captive, who has been stripped almost naked, further heightening his humiliation.

SHEN ZHOU Just as the formality of Ming official architecture contrasts with the informality of the gardens of Suzhou, the work of Shang Xi and other professional court painters, designed to promote the official Ming ideology, differs sharply in both form and content from the venerable tradition of literati painting, which also flourished during the Ming dynasty. As under the Yuan emperors, Ming literati practiced their art largely independently of court patronage. One of the leading figures was SHEN ZHOU (1427–1509), a master of the Wu School of painting, so called because of the ancient name (Wu) of the city of Suzhou. Shen came from a well-to-do family of scholars and painters and declined an offer to serve in the Ming bureaucracy in order to concentrate on poetry and painting. *Lofty Mount Lu* (FIG. 33-12), perhaps his finest hanging scroll, was a birthday gift to one of his teachers. It bears a long poem that the artist composed in the teacher's honor (see "Calligraphy and Inscriptions on Chinese Paintings," page 1051). Shen had never seen Mount Lu, but he stated that he chose the subject because he wished the lofty mountain peaks to express the grandeur of his teacher's virtue and character. Shen suggested the immense scale of Mount Lu by placing a tiny figure at the bottom center of the painting, sketched in lightly and partly obscured by a rocky outcropping. The composition owes a great deal to Fan Kuan (FIG. 16-22) and other early masters. But, characteristic of literati painting in general, the scroll is in the end a very personal conversation—in pictures and words—between the artist and the teacher it honors. In a later painting (FIG. 33-12A), Shen depicted himself as a poet on a mountaintop and included a poem that he wrote, in this case reflecting on the beauty of music and landscape.

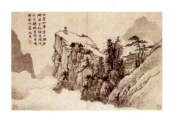

33-12A SHEN ZHOU, *Poet on a Mountaintop*, ca. 1490-1500.

DONG QICHANG One of the most intriguing and influential literati of the late Ming dynasty was DONG QICHANG (1555–1636), a wealthy landowner and high official who was a poet, calligrapher, and painter. He also amassed a vast collection of Chinese art and achieved great fame as an art critic. In Dong's view, most Chinese landscape painters could be classified as belonging to either the Northern School of precise, academic painting or the Southern School of more subjective, freer painting. "Northern" and "Southern" were not geographic but stylistic labels. Dong chose these names for the two schools because he determined that their characteristic styles had parallels in the northern and southern schools of *Chan* Buddhism (see "Chan Buddhism," page 485). Northern Chan Buddhists were "gradualists" and believed that enlightenment could

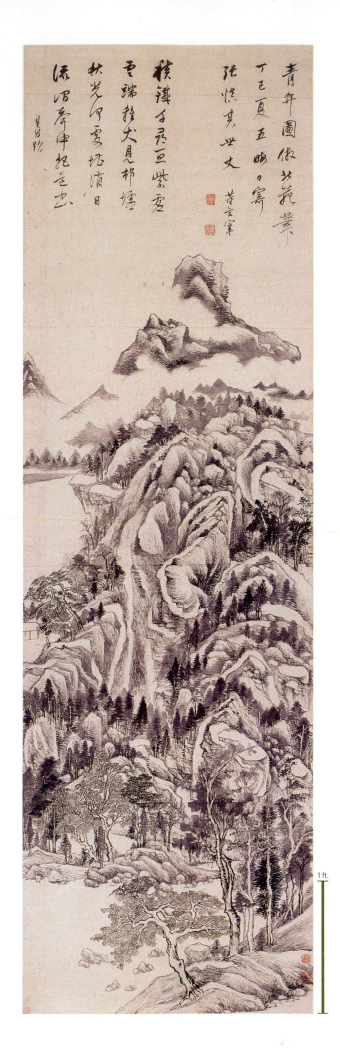

青年圖倣北苑筆
丁巳夏五明。寄
張惶其世文
積謹子尚豆紫雲
雲端推尖見郊墟
秋光日雲坏頂日
溪河亭申起老忠
其昌識

1 ft.

33-13 DONG QICHANG, *Dwelling in the Qingbian Mountains,* Ming dynasty, 1617. Hanging scroll, ink on paper, 7' 3$\frac{1}{2}$" × 2' 2$\frac{1}{2}$". Cleveland Museum of Art, Cleveland (Leonard C. Hanna Jr. bequest).

Dong Qichang, "the first modernist painter," conceived his landscapes as shaded masses of rocks alternating with blank bands, flattening the composition and creating expressive, abstract patterns.

be achieved only after long training. The Southern Chan Buddhists believed that enlightenment could come suddenly. Dong's Northern School therefore comprised professional, highly trained court painters. The leading painters of the Southern School were the literati, whose freer and more expressive style Dong judged to be far superior.

Dong's own work—for example, *Dwelling in the Qingbian Mountains* (FIG. **33-13**), painted in 1617—belongs, not surprisingly, to the Southern School that he admired so much. The scroll's subject and style, as well as the incorporation of a long inscription at the top, immediately reveal the artist's debt to earlier literati painters. But Dong was also an innovator, especially in his treatment of the towering mountains, where shaded masses of rocks alternate with flat, blank bands, flattening the composition and creating highly expressive and abstract patterns. Some critics have called Dong Qichang the first *modernist* painter, because his work foreshadows developments in 19th-century European landscape painting (FIG. 28-22).

WEN SHU Landscape painting was the most prestigious artistic subject in Ming China, but artists also painted other subjects—for example, flowers. WEN SHU (1595–1634), the daughter of an aristocratic Suzhou family and the wife of Zhao Jun (d. 1640), descended from Zhao Mengfu and the Song imperial house, was probably the finest flower painter of the Ming era. Her *Carnations and Garden Rock* (FIG. **33-14**) is also an example of Chinese arc-shaped fan painting, a format imported from Japan. In this genre, the artist paints on flat paper, but then folds the completed painting and mounts it on sticks to form a fan. The best fan paintings were probably never used as fans. Collectors purchased them to store in albums. As in her other flower paintings, Wen focused on a few essential elements—in this instance, a central rock formation and three sprays of flowers—and presented them against a plain background. Using delicate brushstrokes and a restricted palette, she brilliantly communicated the fragility of the red flowers, contrasting them with the solidity of the brown rock. The spare composition creates a quiet mood of contemplation.

Qing Dynasty

The Ming bureaucracy's internal decay enabled another group of invaders, the Manchus of Manchuria, to overrun China in the 17th century and establish the Qing dynasty (r. 1644–1911). The Manchus quickly restored effective imperial rule in the north, but southern China remained rebellious until the second Qing ruler, the Kangxi (Lasting Prosperity) emperor (r. 1662–1722), succeeded in pacifying all of China. The Manchurian rulers adapted themselves to Chinese life and cultivated knowledge of China's arts, including literati painting, which under the Yuan emperors was primarily the preferred style of artists who shunned the court.

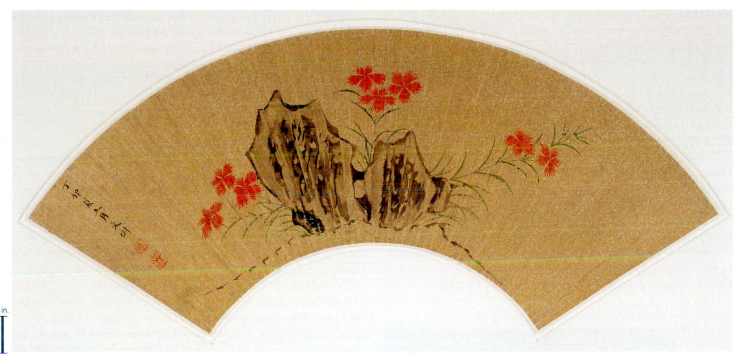

33-14 WEN SHU, *Carnations and Garden Rock,* Ming dynasty, 1627. Fan, ink and colors on gold paper, $6\frac{3}{8}$" × 1' $9\frac{1}{4}$".
Honolulu Academy of Arts, Honolulu (gift of Mr. Robert Allerton).

Wen was probably the finest flower painter of the Ming era. Her depiction of a rock formation and three flower sprays is also an example
of fan painting, a format imported from Japan.

SHITAO One Qing artist who took traditional landscape painting in a new direction was Shitao (Daoji, 1642–1707), a descendant of the Ming imperial family who became a Chan Buddhist monk at age 20, which protected him from prosecution as a Ming loyalist. (Most of his family had been murdered and he was orphaned as an infant.) Shitao's theoretical writings, most notably his *Sayings on Painting from Monk Bitter Gourd* (his adopted name), called for use of the "single brushstroke" or "primordial line" as the root of all phenomena and representation. Although he carefully studied earlier masterpieces, Shitao opposed mimicking those works and believed that he could not learn anything from the paintings of others unless he changed them.

Riding the Clouds (FIG. 33-15) is one album leaf (see "Chinese Painting Materials and Formats," page 479) in a series of twelve that Shitao produced during the last year of his life. Each of the paintings encapsulates his personal feelings, some happy, some sad, about his reclusive life in Nanjing. Here, the solitary rider scaling a steep mountain path expresses the themes of loneliness and perseverance. The sharp angle Shitao used to record the landscape and the massing of thick ink alternating with sinuous lines and large blank areas are characteristic features of this innovative artist's distinctive style. Unlike traditional literati, Shitao did not so much depict the landscape's appearance as animate it, applying ink with unprecedented expressive force.

33-15 SHITAO, *Reminiscences of Nanjing: Riding the Coulds,* Qing dynasty, 1707. Album leaf, ink and colors on paper, 1'$\frac{1}{4}$" × $8\frac{7}{8}$". Arthur M. Sackler Gallery, Smithsonian Institution, Washington, D.C.

Shitao experimented with unusual compositions and extreme effects of massed ink. In this album leaf, the solitary rider scaling a steep mountain expresses loneliness and perseverance.

GIUSEPPE CASTIGLIONE During the Qing dynasty, European Jesuit missionaries were familiar figures at the imperial court. Many of the missionaries were also artists, and they were instrumental in introducing modern European (that is, High Renaissance and Baroque; see Chapters 22 to 25) painting styles to China. The Chinese, while admiring the Europeans' technical virtuosity, found Western style unsatisfactory. Those Jesuit painters who were successful in China adapted their styles to Chinese tastes. The most prominent European artist at the Qing court was GIUSEPPE CASTIGLIONE (1688–1768), who went by the name LANG SHINING in China. *Auspicious Objects* (FIG. 33-16), which Castiglione painted in 1724 in honor of the birthday of the third Qing ruler, the Yongzheng (Concord and Rectitude) emperor (r. 1723–1735), exemplifies his hybrid Italian-Chinese painting style. The Jesuit painter's emphasis on a single source of light, consistently cast shadows, and three-dimensional volume are unmistakably European stylistic concerns. But the impact of Chinese literati painting on the Italian artist is equally evident, especially in the composition of the branches and leaves of the overhanging pine tree and the rock formations in the lower half of the scroll. Above all, the subject is purely Chinese. The white eagle, the pine tree, the rocks, and the red mushroomlike plants (lingzhi) are traditional Chinese symbols. The eagle connotes imperial status, courage, and military achievement. The evergreen pines and the rocks connote long life, which, according to Chinese belief, eating lingzhi will promote. All are fitting motifs for a painting celebrating the birthday of an emperor.

QING PORCELAIN Qing potters at the imperial kilns at Jingdezhen continued to expand on Yuan and Ming achievements in developing fine porcelain pieces with underglaze and overglaze decoration—a ceramic technology that gained wide admiration in Europe. The dish with a lobed rim reproduced here (FIG. 33-17) exemplifies the overglaze technique. All of the colors—black, green, brown, yellow, and even blue—come from applying enamels after the first firing and then firing the dish again at a lower temperature (see "Chinese Porcelain," page 1053).

The decoration of the dish reflects important social changes in China. Economic prosperity and the possibility of advancement through success on civil service examinations made it realistic for many more families to hope that their sons could achieve wealth and higher social standing. In the center of this dish, painted for one of these upwardly mobile families, are Fu, Lu, and Shou, the three star gods of happiness, success, and longevity. The cranes and spotted deer, believed to live to advanced ages, and the pine trees around the rim are all symbols of long life. Artists represented similar themes in the woodblock prints produced in great quantities during the Qing era. The porcelain dish and especially the inexpensive prints were the commoners' equivalent of Castiglione's imperial painting of auspicious symbols (FIG. 33-16).

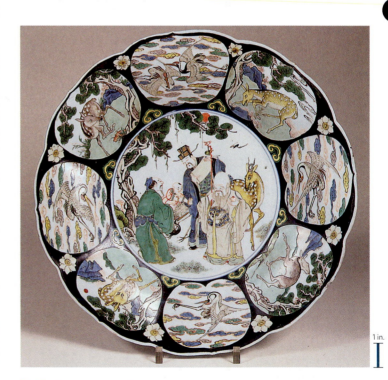

33-16 GIUSEPPE CASTIGLIONE (LANG SHINING), *Auspicious Objects,* Qing dynasty, 1724. Hanging scroll, ink and colors on silk, 7' 11¾" × 5' 1⅞". Palace Museum, Beijing.

Castiglione was a Jesuit painter in Qing China who successfully combined European lighting techniques and three-dimensional volume with traditional Chinese literati subjects and compositions.

33-17 Dish with lobed rim, Qing dynasty, ca. 1700. White porcelain with multicolored overglaze, 1' 1⅝" diameter. Percival David Foundation of Chinese Art, London.

This dish depicting the three star gods of happiness, success, and longevity exemplifies the overglaze porcelain technique in which all the colors come from applying enamels on top of the glaze surface.

People's Republic

The overthrow of the Qing dynasty and the establishment of the Republic of China under the Nationalist Party in 1912 did not bring an end to the traditional themes and modes of Chinese art. But the triumph of Marxism in 1949, when the Communists took control of China and founded the People's Republic, inspired a social realism that broke drastically with the past. The intended purpose of Communist state-sponsored art was to promote Marxist ideas and official government propaganda.

YE YUSHAN *Rent Collection Courtyard* (FIG. **33-18**) is a 1965 tableau 100 yards long and incorporating 114 life-size figures created by YE YUSHAN (b. 1935) and a team of sculptors for the Communist government in Dayi. The purpose of the commission was to depict the grim times in Sichuan Province before the establishment of the People's Republic. Peasants, worn and bent by toil, bring their taxes (in produce) to the courtyard of their merciless, plundering landlord. (The group was first displayed in the actual courtyard of the former home of the pre-Communist rural landlord Liu Wencai.) The official 1968 publication of the Dayi group by the Foreign Languages Press in Beijing is titled *Rent Collection Courtyard: Sculptures of Oppression and Revolt*. The message of the statues and of the book is clear—this kind of thing must not happen again, and the Communist government will ensure that it does not.

Initially, the authorities who commissioned the work did not reveal the artists' names. The anonymity of those who depicted the event is significant and consistent with the Communist ethic. By withholding the identities of the artists, the state underscored that in the People's Republic, collective action, not individual initiative, was the best means to transform society for the better.

CHINA TODAY In the second decade of the 21st century, China is one of the world's great economic powers, and the unwinding of the Cultural Revolution initiated by Mao Zedong (1893–1976) has led to a fruitful artistic exchange between China and the West, with artists such as Zhang Xiaogang (FIG. 31-19), Xu Bing (FIG. 31-20), and Wu Guanzhong (FIG. 31-25B) achieving international reputations. Their works, which can be found in the collections of major museums in Europe and America as well as China, are treated in Chapter 31 in the context of contemporary art worldwide.

KOREA

The great political, social, religious, and artistic changes that took place in China from the Mongol era to the time of the People's Republic find parallels elsewhere in East Asia, especially in Korea. From the medieval period through the early 20th century, Korea was ruled by two long-lived dynasties, the Goryeo and Joseon, but unlike China, whose emperors were overthrown by an internal revolution, Korea became absorbed into another nation—Japan—before regaining its independence after World War II.

Joseon Dynasty

At the time the Yuan overthrew the Song dynasty, the Goryeo dynasty (918–1392), which had ruled Korea since the downfall of China's Tang dynasty, was still in power (see page 488). The Goryeo kings outlasted the Yuan as well. Toward the end of the Goryeo dynasty, however, the Ming emperors of China attempted to take control of northeastern Korea. General Yi Seong-gye (1335–1408) repelled them and founded the last Korean dynasty, the Joseon, in 1392. The long rule of the Joseon kings ended only in 1910, when Japan annexed Korea.

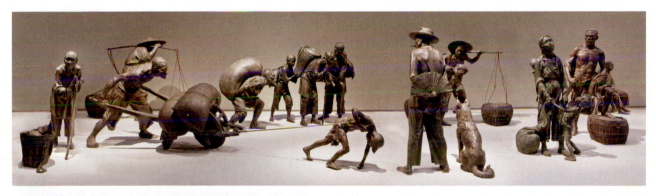

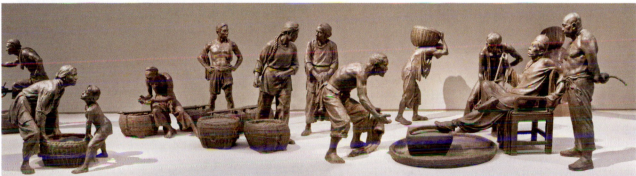

33-18 YE YUSHAN and others, *Rent Collection Courtyard* (two details of a larger tableau), Dayi, China, 1965. Clay, 100 yards long with life-size figures.

In this propagandistic tableau incorporating 114 figures, sculptors depicted the exploitation of peasants by their merciless landlords during the grim times before the Communist takeover of China.

The new Joseon dynasty rulers constructed the south gate to their new capital of Seoul as a symbol of their authority. Namdaemun combines stone foundations with Chinese-style bracketed wood construction.

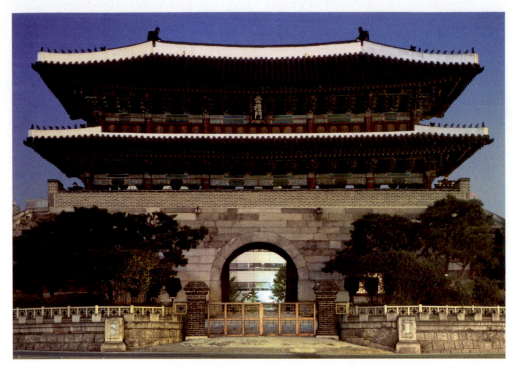

NAMDAEMUN, SEOUL Public building projects helped give the new Korean state an image of dignity and power. One impressive early monument, built for the new Joseon capital of Seoul, is the city's south gate, or Namdaemun (FIG. **33-19**). It combines the imposing strength of its impressive stone foundations with the sophistication of its intricately bracketed wood superstructure—the latter regrettably severely damaged by an arson fire in 2008. In East Asia, elaborate gateways, often in a processional series, are a standard element in city designs as well as royal and sacred compounds, all usually surrounded by walls, as in Beijing's Forbidden City (FIG. 33-1). These gateways served as magnificent symbols of the ruler's authority, as did the triumphal arches of imperial Rome (FIGS. 7-40, 7-44A, and 7-73).

JEONG SEON Over the long course of the Joseon dynasty, Korean painters worked in many different modes and treated the same wide range of subjects seen in Ming and Qing China. One of Korea's most renowned painters was JEONG SEON (1676–1759), a great admirer of Chinese Southern School painting who brought a unique vision to the traditional theme of the mountainous landscape. In *Geumgangsan* (*Diamond*) *Mountains* (FIG. 33-20), a view of the 1,638-meter-high mountain peak in North Korea near the border with South Korea, Jeong evoked a specific scene, an approach known in Korea as "true view" painting. Using sharper, darker versions of the fibrous brushstrokes that most Chinese literati favored, he was able to represent the bright crystalline appearance of the mountains and to emphasize their spiky forms.

Modern Korea

After its annexation in 1910, Korea remained part of Japan until 1945, when the Western Allies and the Soviet Union took control of the peninsula nation at the end of World War II. Korea was divided into the Democratic People's Republic of Korea (North Korea) and the Republic of Korea (South Korea) in 1948. South Korea soon emerged as a fully industrialized nation, and its artists have had a wide exposure to art styles from around the globe. While some Korean artists continue to work in a traditional East Asian manner, others—for example, Song Su-nam (FIG. 31-25A) and Do-Ho Suh (FIG. 31-43)—have embraced developments in Europe and America, but modified their Western models to produce distinctively Korean artworks. Contemporary Korean art is examined in Chapter 31.

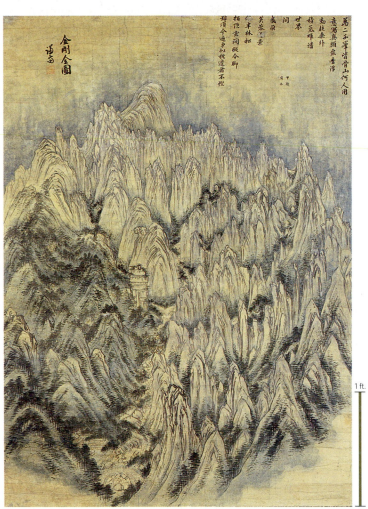

1 ft.

33-20 JEONG SEON, *Geumgangsan Mountains*, Joseon dynasty, 1734. Hanging scroll, ink and colors on paper, 4' 3$\frac{1}{2}$" × 1' 11$\frac{1}{4}$". Hoam Art Museum, Kyunggi-Do.

In a variation on Chinese literati painting, Jeong Seon used sharp, dark brushstrokes to represent the bright crystalline appearance and spiky forms of the towering Diamond Mountains in North Korea.

CHINA AND KOREA, 1279 TO 1980

Yuan Dynasty 1279–1368

- The Mongols invaded northern China in 1210 and defeated the last Song emperor in 1279. Under the first Yuan emperor, Kublai Khan, and his successors, China was richer and technologically more advanced than Europe.
- Most Chinese artists refused to serve in the Mongol administration, but traditional landscape painting and calligraphy continued to flourish in literati circles during the century of Yuan rule.
- The Jingdezhen kilns gained renown for porcelain pottery with cobalt-blue underglaze decoration.

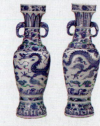

David Vases, Yuan dynasty, 1351

Ming Dynasty 1368–1644

- A popular uprising in 1368 drove the last Mongol emperor from Beijing. The new native Ming dynasty expanded the capital and constructed a vast new imperial palace compound, the Forbidden City. Surrounded by a moat and featuring an axial plan, it was the ideal setting for court ritual.
- At the opposite architectural pole are the gardens of Suzhou. The Ming designers employed pavilions, bridges, ponds, winding paths, and sculpted rocks to reproduce the irregularities of uncultivated nature.
- Ming painting is also diverse, ranging from formal official portrait and history painting to landscape painting. Another subject that artists explored was flowers, sometimes painted on fans.
- The workshop known as the Orchard Factory satisfied the Ming court's appetite for luxury goods with furniture and other objects in lacquered wood.

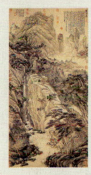

Shen Zhou, *Lofty Mount Lu*, 1467

Qing Dynasty 1644–1911

- In 1644, the Ming dynasty fell to the Manchus, northern invaders who, unlike the Yuan, embraced Chinese art and culture.
- Traditional painting styles remained fashionable, but the Qing painter Shitao experimented with extreme effects of massed ink and free brushwork patterns.
- Increased contact with Europe brought many Jesuit missionaries to the Qing court. The most prominent Jesuit artist was Guiseppe Castiglione, who developed a hybrid Italian-Chinese painting style.
- The Jingdezhen imperial potters developed multicolor porcelains using the overglaze enamel technique.

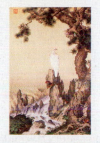

Castiglione, *Auspicious Objects*, 1724

Modern China 1912–1980

- The overthrow of the Qing dynasty did not bring a dramatic change in Chinese art, but after the Communists gained control in 1949, state art focused on promoting Marxist ideals. Teams of sculptors produced vast propaganda pieces, such as *Rent Collection Courtyard*.

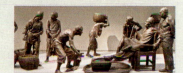

Ye Yushan, *Rent Collection Courtyard*, 1965

Korea 1392–1980

- The last Korean dynasty was the Joseon (r. 1392–1910), which established its capital at Seoul and erected impressive public monuments, such as the Namdaemun gate, to serve as symbols of imperial authority.
- After the division of Korea into two republics following World War II, South Korea emerged as a modern industrial nation. Some of its artists have brilliantly combined native and international traditions.

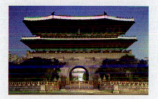

Namdaemun, Seoul, 1398

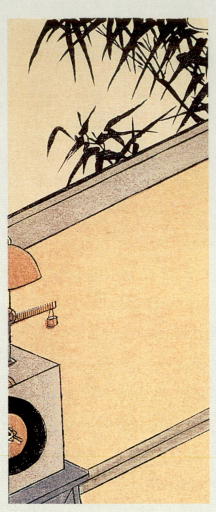

◄ **34-1a** From a sharply elevated viewpoint, Harunobu depicted two beautiful women in an intimate setting. The Edo artist's nishiki-e (brocade pictures) took their name from their costly pigments and paper.

▶ **34-1b** The maid who attends her mistress turns her head toward a chiming clock. Harunobu based his print on a Chinese series featuring temple bells, but substituted a Japanese clock for the Chinese bells.

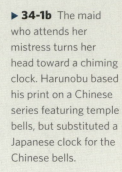

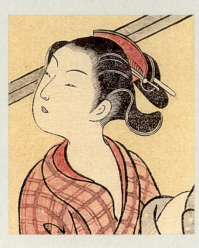

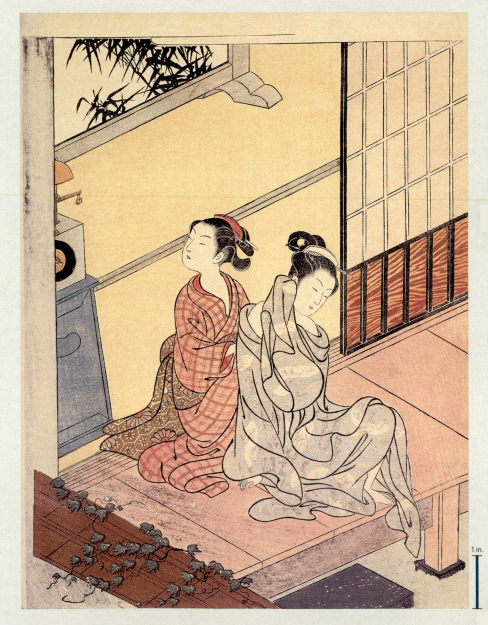

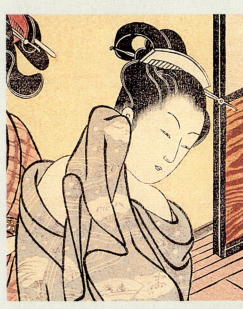

▲ **34-1c** Harunobu's prints focus on the daily lives of Japanese women, a subject he pioneered. Erotic themes are quite common in ukiyo-e. Here, a beautiful woman dries herself on her veranda after bathing.

1 in.

34-1 **SUZUKI HARUNOBU,** *Evening Bell at the Clock,* **from** *Eight Views of the Parlor* **series, Edo period, 1765. Woodblock print, 11$\frac{1}{4}$" × 8$\frac{1}{2}$". Art Institute of Chicago, Chicago (Clarence Buckingham Collection).**

FRAMING THE ERA

Japan, 1333 to 1980

THE FLOATING WORLD OF EDO

In 1185, the Japanese emperor in Kyoto appointed the first *shogun* (head of the military government) in Kamakura in eastern Japan (MAP 34-1). In theory, the shogun managed the country on the emperor's behalf, but in reality the emperor lost most of his governing authority. The Japanese *shogunate* was a political and economic arrangement in which feudal lords called *daimyo* (Japanese, "great names"), the leaders of powerful warrior bands composed of *samurai* (Japanese, "guards"), pledged allegiance to the shogun but retained ownership of and control over their own domains. In 1615, the shogun set up his headquarters in Edo (modern Tokyo), initiating the Edo period (1615–1868) of Japanese history and art.

The ensuing rapid urbanization of Edo led to an increase in the pursuit of sensual pleasure and entertainment in the city's brash popular theaters and brothels of its Yoshiwara district, which the prosperous merchant class and samurai frequented. Those of lesser means could partake in these pleasures and amusements vicariously. Rapid developments in the printing industry led to the availability of inexpensive *prints* (see "Japanese Woodblock Prints," page 1077), and these *ukiyo-e* ("pictures of the floating world") conveyed the city's delights for a fraction of the cost of direct participation.

One of the most admired ukiyo-e printmakers was SUZUKI HARUNOBU (ca. 1725–1770), who played a key role in developing polychrome prints. Called *nishiki-e* ("brocade pictures") because of their sumptuous and brilliant color, these prints, in contrast to most Edo prints, employed the highest-quality paper and costly pigments.

The sophistication of Harunobu's work is evident in *Evening Bell at the Clock* (FIG. 34-1), from a series called *Eight Views of the Parlor.* This series drew upon a Chinese series, *Eight Views of the Xiao and Xiang Rivers,* in which each image focuses on a particular time of day or year. In Harunobu's adaptation, beautiful young women and the activities occupying their daily lives became the subject of each image. These themes were new to the ukiyo-e repertoire, but after Harunobu introduced them, they became common. In *Evening Bell at the Clock,* two young women seen from the typically Japanese elevated viewpoint sit on a veranda. One is drying herself after a bath. The viewer gets a privileged glimpse of a private moment. (Erotic themes, including explicit depictions of lovemaking, are quite common in ukiyo-e.) The bather's companion—her maid—turns to face the chiming clock. Here, the artist playfully transformed the great temple bell ringing over the waters in the Chinese series into a modern Japanese clock. In Harunobu's nishiki-e prints, the flatness of the depicted objects and the rich color recall the traditions of court painting, but in a much more affordable medium. This was especially true of the more ordinary prints sold in small shops and on the street, which went for the price of a bowl of noodles.

MUROMACHI

The Kamakura shogunate (see page 502) ruled Japan for more than a century, but collapsed in 1332. Several years of civil war followed, ending only when Ashikaga Takauji (1305–1358) succeeded in establishing domination of his clan over all of Japan and became the new imperially recognized shogun.

The civil war leading to the rise of the Ashikaga clan marked the beginning of the Muromachi period (1333–1573), named after the district in Kyoto in which the Ashikaga shogunate maintained its headquarters. During the Muromachi period, *Zen* Buddhism (see "Zen Buddhism," page 1067) rose to prominence alongside the older traditions, such as Pure Land and Esoteric Buddhism. Unlike the Pure Land faith, which focused on death and the saving power of Amida, the Buddha of the West, Zen emphasized rigorous discipline and personal responsibility. For this reason, Zen held a special attraction for the upper echelons of samurai, whose behavioral codes placed high values on loyalty, courage, and self-control. Further, familiarity with Chinese Zen culture (see "Chan Buddhism," page 485) carried implications of superior knowledge and refinement, thereby legitimizing the elevated status of the warrior elite.

Zen, however, was not exclusively the religion of Zen monks and highly placed warriors. Aristocrats, merchants, and others studied at and supported Zen temples. Furthermore, those who embraced Zen, including samurai, also generally accepted other Buddhist teachings, especially the ideas of the Pure Land sects. Zen temples functioned not only as religious institutions but also as centers of secular culture, where people could study Chinese art, literature, and learning, which the Japanese imported along with Zen Buddhism. Some Zen monasteries accumulated considerable wealth overseeing trade missions to China.

KARESANSUI GARDENS Gardens played a major role in Zen Buddhist monasteries, providing the monks with an austere and serene place where they could walk and meditate, far removed from the noise and distractions of daily life. One early example is the Kokedera (Moss Temple; FIG. **34-1A**) of the lower garden of Kyoto's Saihoji temple. Even more severe is the *karesansui* (Japanese, "dry-landscape") rock garden (FIG. **34-2**) of Ryoanji (Temple of the Peaceful Dragon) in northwestern Kyoto. The land belonged to the Muromachi shogun Hosokawa Katsumoto (1430–1473), who left his estate to the Rinzai Zen sect, which erected the temple on the site around 1488. The Ryoanji karesansui garden probably dates to that time as well, although many scholars believe that its present form is the result of a later remodeling. Unlike the sprawling Saihoji moss garden, the Ryoanji karesansui is surrounded by low walls. Situated

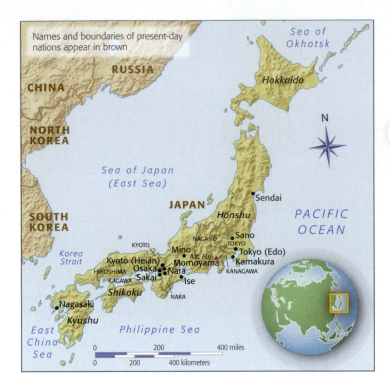

MAP 34-1 Modern Japan.

adjacent to the abbot's quarters, the garden measures only about 30 by 10 yards. Continuously tended by the monks, who rake it daily and remove any weeds that may have emerged, the garden consists of 15 artfully placed, irregularly shaped rocks of varying sizes set in a bed of white gravel with green moss growing on and around the stones. The unknown designer intended the monks to view the garden from a stationary position, but from any vantage point it is possible to see only 14 rocks at one time—symbolizing the sense of incompleteness a monk experiences before achieving enlightenment. Although the arrangement of rocks and raked lines (circular around the stones, parallel lines everywhere else) is an abstract composition, striking in its severity and emptiness especially in contrast to the dense and colorful foliage that forms a backdrop to the enclosed garden, many observers have variously compared the Ryoanji garden to islands in a calm lake, to mountain peaks projecting through the clouds (compare FIG. 34-10A), or to a cherry tree with branches. The purpose of the garden, however, is to inspire meditation and to direct the attention of the monks inward, not to the natural world.

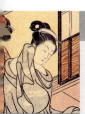

JAPAN, 1333 TO 1980

1333-1573
Muromachi

- Zen Buddhist temples feature dry-landscape (karesansui) gardens
- Sesshu Toyo produces paintings in the splashed-ink (haboku) style
- Kano Motonobu helps establish the Kano School as a virtual Japanese national painting academy

1573-1615
Momoyama

- Japanese warlords decorate their palatial residences inside huge fortress-castles with painted folding screens featuring lavish use of gold leaf
- Sen no Rikyu becomes the most renowned master of the Japanese tea ceremony and designs teahouses that foster humility
- Ceramics from the Mino kilns exemplify the aesthetic principles of wabi and sabi

1615-1868
Edo

- The Katsura Imperial Villa at Kyoto sets the standard for Japanese domestic architecture
- The Rinpa School emerges as the major alternative style of painting to the Kano School
- Japanese woodblock prints depicting the sensual pleasures of Edo's "floating world" reach a wide audience

1868-1989
Meiji and Showa

- European styles and techniques, including oil painting, influence Japanese art after Japan opens its doors to the West
- Ceramic master Hamada Shoji receives official recognition as a Living National Treasure
- Kenzo Tange designs the modernist stadiums for the 1964 Olympics in Tokyo

RELIGION AND MYTHOLOGY
Zen Buddhism

Zen (*Chan* in Chinese), as a fully developed Buddhist tradition, began filtering into Japan in the late 12th century during the Kamakura shogunate and had its most pervasive influence on Japanese culture starting in the 14th century during the Muromachi period. The first Zen sect introduced into Japan was the Rinzai school, brought from the mainland in 1191 by the monk Eisai (1141–1215). Later, the monk Dogen (1200–1253) introduced the Soto school of Zen Buddhism. As in other forms of Buddhism, Zen followers hoped to achieve enlightenment. Zen teachings assert that everyone has the potential for enlightenment, but worldly knowledge and mundane thought patterns are barriers to achieving it. Thus followers must succeed in breaking through the boundaries of everyday perception and logic. This is most often accomplished through meditation. Indeed, the Japanese word *zen* means "meditation."

Some Zen schools stress meditation as a long-term practice eventually leading to enlightenment, whereas others stress the benefits of sudden shocks to the worldly mind. One of these shocks is the subject of Kano Motonobu's *Zen Patriarch Xiangyen Zhixian Sweeping with a Broom* (FIG. 34-4), in which the shattering of a fallen roof tile opens the monk's mind. Beyond personal commitment, the guidance of an enlightened Zen teacher is essential to arriving at enlightenment. Years of strict training involving manual labor under the tutelage of this master, coupled with meditation, provide the foundation for a receptive mind. According to Zen beliefs, by cultivating discipline and intense concentration, Buddhists can transcend their ego and release themselves from the shackles of the mundane world. Although Zen is not primarily devotional, followers do pray to specific Buddhas, bodhisattvas, and guardian figures. In general, Zen teachings view mental calm, lack of fear, and spontaneity as signs of a person's advancement on the path to enlightenment.

Zen training for monks takes place at temples, some of which have gardens designed in accord with Zen principles, such as Kyoto's Saihogi moss garden (FIG. 34-1A) and Ryoanji dry-landscape garden (FIG. 34-2). Zen temples also sometimes served as centers of Chinese learning and conducted funeral rites. These temples even embraced many traditional Buddhist observances, such as devotional rituals before images, which had little to do with meditation per se.

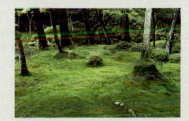

⬈ **34-1A** Moss garden, Saihoji, Kyoto, 14th century.

As Zen teachings spread, they reverberated throughout Japanese culture. Lay followers as well as Zen monks painted pictures and produced other artworks that appear to reach toward Zen ideals through their subjects and their means of expression. Other cultural practices reflected the widespread appeal of Zen Buddhism. For example, the tea ceremony (see "The Japanese Tea Ceremony," page 1072), or ritual drinking of tea, as it developed in the 15th and 16th centuries, offered a temporary respite from everyday concerns, especially when the ceremony took place in a quiet setting with a meditative atmosphere, such as the Taian teahouse (FIG. 34-8).

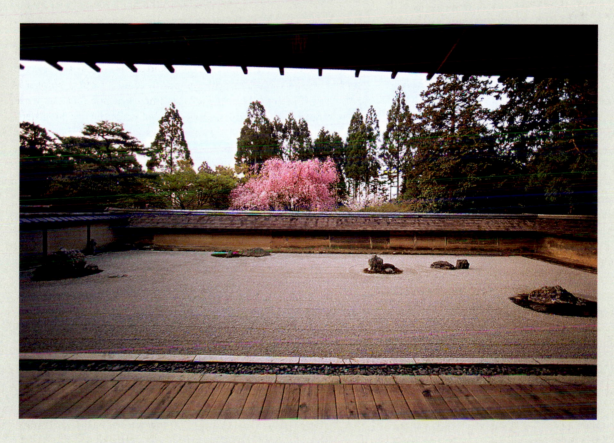

34-2 Karesansui (dry-landscape) garden, Ryoanji, Kyoto, Japan, Muromachi period, ca. 1488.

Perfectly suited for meditation by Zen Buddhist monks, the karesansui garden of the Peaceful Dragon Temple features artfully placed, irregularly shaped rocks in a bed of raked white gravel.

SESSHU TOYO As was common in earlier eras of Japanese history, Muromachi painters usually closely followed Chinese precedents (often arriving by way of Korea), which artists throughout East Asia regarded as part of a shared cultural heritage. Muromachi painting nonetheless displays great variety in both style and subject matter. Indeed, individual masters often worked in different styles, as

WRITTEN SOURCES
Sesshu Toyo

Despite the prestige of Chinese art in Japan, few Japanese artists had the opportunity to travel to the mainland to study Chinese art or architecture firsthand. One who did was the renowned Muromachi painter Sesshu Toyo (FIG. 34-3), who traveled to China with a trading mission between 1467 and 1469 and visited Buddhist monasteries, major cities, and famous scenic sites. Accompanying Sesshu on his journey to China was the priest and poet Genryu Shuko (d. 1491), who left an invaluable personal account of Sesshu's travels and the artist's philosophy of painting.

> When the venerable Sesshu went to China, I was on the same boat. He saw, one after another, all the famous cities, the prosperity and beauty of the capitals and the provinces . . . Art took him to far places . . . The Emperor looked at his paintings and considered them rare treasures [and awarded him] the First Seat in the famous Tendo temple in order to show appreciation for his art. Upon his return to Japan, his reputation increased tenfold. Sesshu said, "Within the great country of China, there are no painting masters. That is not to say that there are no paintings, but no painting teachers there except as there are mountains . . . and as there are rivers . . . strange plants, trees, birds, and beasts, different men and their manners and customs. Such are the real paintings of China. In regard to the techniques of using ink and the art of handling the brush these must be mastered first in the mind and then translated by the hand . . . That is what I mean by saying that there are no teachers in China" . . . Truly [Sesshu] is one man in a thousand years. . . . Those of the upper classes such as princes and others of the nobility, and those of the lower classes such as businessmen and merchants—all beg for a few strokes from his brush or any fragments that may be left about. Many come and go, and it is said that the crowds are held back from entering [Sesshu's] studio by an iron gate . . . Through the open door [one can see in] every direction paints and brushes lie disordered among large and small paintings. Some are on finely woven silk and others on coarse paper. There are rolls of finished and unfinished paintings rising to the ridge of the roof, while mounted paintings hang on the walls. At the end of the day, when weary in body and spirit from studying colors and painting the seasons, [Sesshu] rests by the railing, loosens his robes at the neck, and lets the wind caress his skin. Often he draws deep breaths and expands his lungs, meditating on the meaning of painting.*

*Translated by Jon C. Covell. Quoted in Stephen Addiss, Gerald Groemer, and J. Thomas Rimer, *Traditional Japanese Arts and Culture: An Illustrated Sourcebook* (Honolulu: University of Hawaii Press, 2006), 103–104.

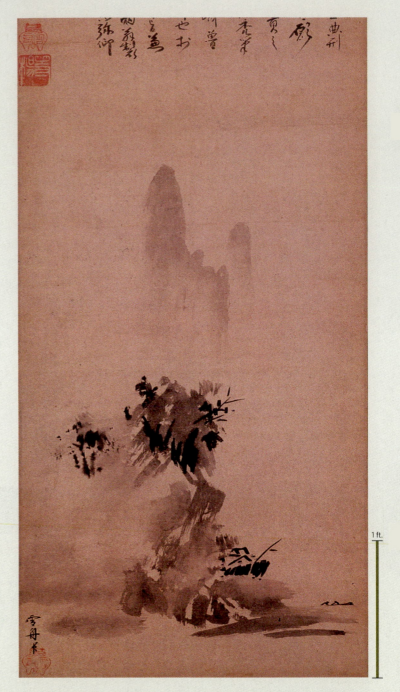

1 ft.

34-3 SESSHU TOYO, splashed-ink (haboku) landscape, detail of the lower part of a hanging scroll, Muromachi period, 1495. Ink on paper, full scroll 4' 10$\frac{1}{4}$" × 1' $\frac{7}{8}$", detail 4$\frac{1}{2}$" high. Tokyo National Museum, Tokyo.

In this haboku landscape, the artist applied primarily broad, rapid strokes, sometimes dripping the ink on the paper. The result hovers at the edge of legibility, without dissolving into abstraction.

did the most celebrated Muromachi priest-painter, SESSHU TOYO (1420–1506), one of the few Japanese painters who traveled to China and studied contemporaneous Ming painting (see "Sesshu Toyo," above). His most dramatic works are in the *splashed-ink (haboku)* style, a technique with Chinese roots. The painter of a haboku picture pauses to visualize the image, loads the brush with ink, and then applies primarily broad, rapid strokes, sometimes even dripping the ink onto the paper. The result often hovers at the edge of legibility, without dissolving into sheer abstraction. This balance between spontaneity and a thorough knowledge of the painting tradition gives the pictures their artistic strength. The haboku landscape illustrated here (FIG. 34-3) is a detail of the lower part of a hanging scroll, or *kakemono*, that Sesshu presented as a gift to a favorite pupil on the completion of his studies. Images of mountains, trees, and buildings

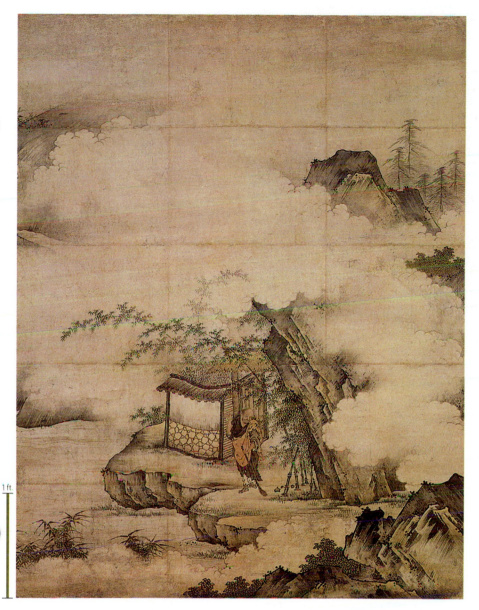

34-4 KANO MOTONOBU, *Zen Patriarch Xiangyen Zhixian Sweeping with a Broom*, from Daitokuji, Kyoto, Japan, Muromachi period, ca. 1513. Hanging scroll, ink and color on paper, 5' 7$\frac{3}{8}$" × 2' 10$\frac{3}{4}$". Tokyo National Museum, Tokyo.

The Kano School and splashed-ink painting represent opposite poles of Muromachi style. In this Kano scroll depicting a Zen patriarch experiencing enlightenment, bold outlines define the forms.

splashed-ink painting, Motonobu's work displays exacting precision in applying ink in bold outlines by holding the brush perpendicular to the paper. Thick clouds obscure the mountainous setting and focus the viewer's attention on the sharp, angular rocks, bamboo branches, and modest hut framing the patriarch. Lightly applied colors also draw attention to Xiangyen Zhixian, whom Motonobu showed as having dropped his broom with his right hand as he recoils in astonishment. Although very different in style, the Japanese painting recalls the subject of Liang Kai's Song hanging scroll (FIG. 16-28) representing the Sixth Chan Patriarch's "Chan moment" while chopping bamboo.

MOMOYAMA

Despite the hierarchical nature of Japanese society during the Muromachi period, the control that the Ashikaga shogunate exerted was tenuous and precarious. Ambitious daimyo often seized opportunities to expand their power, sometimes aspiring to become shogun themselves. By the late 15th century, Japan was experiencing violent confrontations over territory and dominance. In fact, scholars refer to the last century of the Muromachi period as the Era of Warring States, intentionally borrowing the terminology used to describe a much earlier tumultuous period in Chinese history (see page 466). Finally, three successive warlords seized power during the short-lived Momoyama period (1573–1615). In 1573, Oda Nobunaga (1534–1582) overthrew the Ashikaga shogunate in Kyoto but was later killed by one of his generals. Toyotomi Hideyoshi (1536–1598) took control of the government after Nobunaga's assassination and held on to power until he died of natural causes in 1598. In the struggle following Hideyoshi's death, Tokugawa Ieyasu (1542–1616) emerged victorious, and the emperor granted him the title of shogun in 1603. Ieyasu continued to face challenges, but by 1615 he had eliminated his last rival and established his clan as the de facto rulers of Japan for two-and-a-half centuries during the Edo period (see page 1073).

HIMEJI CASTLE To reinforce their power and to defend themselves against possible attack, the Momoyama warlords constructed immense fortified castles to serve as their palatial residences. These castles also housed within their protective circuit walls the warlords' families, retainers, garrisons of loyal warriors, horses, and arms. After 1558, the Momoyama warlords' weaponry included Western firearms and cannons that dramatically changed the nature of

emerge from the ink-washed surface. Two figures appear in a boat (to the lower right), and the two swift strokes nearby represent the pole and banner of a wine shop.

KANO MOTONOBU Representing the opposite pole of Muromachi painting style is the Kano School, founded by Kano Masanobu (1434–1530), who became the shogunate's official painter in 1481. But it was his son, KANO MOTONOBU (1476–1559), who was largely responsible for establishing the Kano style as the preeminent style of the Muromachi period. By the 17th century, the Kano School had become virtually a national painting academy. The school flourished until the late 19th century.

Zen Patriarch Xiangyen Zhixian Sweeping with a Broom (FIG. 34-4) is one of six panels that Kano Motonobu designed as *fusuma* (sliding door paintings) for the abbot's room in the Zen temple complex of Daitokuji in Kyoto. Each panel depicted a different Zen patriarch. The illustrated example, later refashioned as a hanging scroll, represents Xiangyen Zhixian (d. 898) at the moment he achieved enlightenment. Motonobu portrayed the patriarch sweeping the ground near his rustic retreat as a roof tile falls at his feet and shatters. His Zen training is so deep that the resonant sound propels the patriarch into an awakening. In contrast to Muromachi

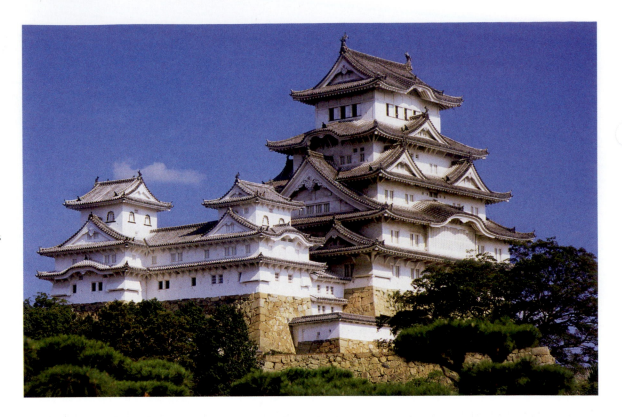

34-5 White Heron Castle, Himeji, Japan, constructed in 1346 and enlarged during the Momoyama period in 1581 and again in 1601–1609.

Called White Heron Castle because of its white plastered wood walls, Himeji Castle, despite its militaristic aspects, exudes a sense of weightlessness because of the winglike profiles of its elegant tile roofs.

Japanese warfare. The most impressive extant Momoyama castle is at Himeji (FIG. **34-5**), west of Osaka, constructed in 1346 and enlarged in 1581 by Hideyoshi and again between 1601 and 1609 by the son-in-law of Ieyasu. Known as Shirasagi—the White Heron Castle—because of the white plaster fire-resistant coating of its wood walls, the Momoyama residential complex rises several stories above high masonry walls that have a steep incline designed to make them impossible for an enemy to scale. Ringing the complex is a moat, and, to provide further protection, the builders laid out the castle grounds with a succession of interior gates and narrow passageways. The uppermost level of the warlord's private apartment complex, which commands a view of the surrounding countryside from narrow windows on all four sides, could be reached only by a ladder. Despite its militaristic aspects, the Himeji castle exudes a sense of weightlessness, achieved in part by means of its bright white walls, which reflect sunlight, but primarily by the winglike profiles of the curving tiled roofs, which lead the viewer's eye in pyramid fashion to the narrow top story silhouetted against the sky.

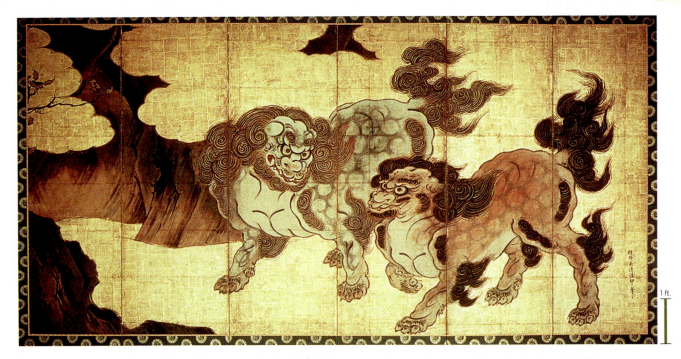

34-6 KANO EITOKU, *Chinese Lions*, Momoyama period, late 16th century. Six-panel screen, ink, colors, and gold-leaf on paper, 7' 4" × 14' 10". Museum of the Imperial Collections, Tokyo.

Chinese lions were fitting imagery for the castle of a Momoyama warlord because they exemplified power and bravery. Eitoku's huge screen features boldly outlined forms on a gold ground.

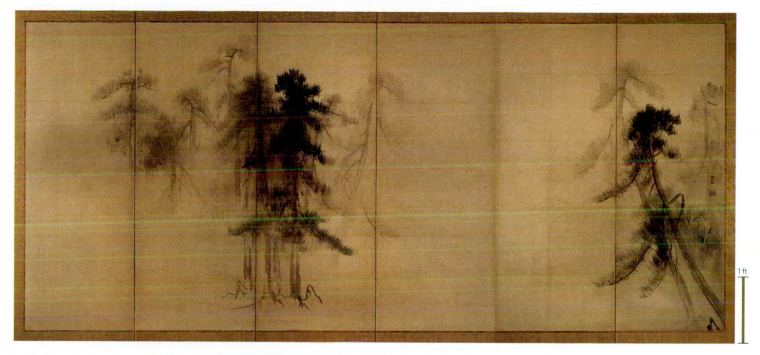

1 ft

34-7 HASEGAWA TOHAKU, *Pine Forest,* Momoyama period, late 16th century. One of a pair of six-panel screens, ink on paper, 5' 1\frac{3}{8}" × 11' 4". Tokyo National Museum, Tokyo.

Tohaku used wet brushstrokes to paint a grove of great pines shrouded in mist. In Zen terms, the six-panel screen suggests the illusory nature of mundane reality while evoking a meditative mood.

The castles of the Momoyama period were so numerous and so symptomatic of these turbulent times that historians have named the era after one of Hideyoshi's castles southeast of Kyoto—Momoyama (Peach Blossom Hill).

KANO EITOKU Although the Momoyama period was only a brief interlude between two major shogunates, the artists of this era produced many outstanding artworks. Each Momoyama warlord commissioned lavish decorations for the interior of his castle, including paintings, fusuma, and *byobu* (folding screens) in ink, color, and gold leaf. Gold screens had been known since Muromachi times, but Momoyama painters made them even bolder, reducing the number of motifs and often greatly enlarging them against flat, shimmering fields of gold leaf.

The grandson of Kano Motonobu, KANO EITOKU (1543–1590), was the leading painter of murals and screens and received numerous commissions from the powerful Momoyama warlords. So extensive were these commissions (in both scale and number) that Eitoku adopted a painting system developed by his grandfather, which depended on a team of specialized painters to assist him. Unfortunately, little of Eitoku's elaborate work remains because of the subsequent destruction of the ostentatious castles he helped decorate—not surprising in an era marked by power struggles. However, still extant is a six-panel screen (FIG. 34-6), originally one of a pair that Eitoku created for Toyotomi Hideyoshi as a gift to another feudal lord. The subject—two ancient Chinese mythological beasts, a lion and a lioness—was appropriate for a warlord's castle. Appearing in both religious and secular contexts, lions were associated with power and bravery. Indeed, Chinese lions became an important symbolic motif during the Momoyama period. In Eitoku's painting, the colorful beasts' powerfully muscled bodies, defined and flattened by the characteristic Kano School heavy black outlines, stride forward in a schematic landscape of brown rocks

and gold clouds. The dramatic effect of this work derives in part from its scale—it is more than 7 feet tall and nearly 15 feet long.

HASEGAWA TOHAKU Momoyama painters did not work exclusively in the colorful style exemplified by Eitoku's *Chinese Lions.* HASEGAWA TOHAKU (1539–1610) was a leading painter who became familiar with the aesthetics and techniques of Chinese Chan and Japanese Zen painters such as Sesshu Toyo (FIG. 34-3) by studying the art collections of the Daitokuji temple in Kyoto. Tohaku sometimes painted in ink monochrome, using loose brushwork with brilliant success, as seen in *Pine Forest* (FIG. **34-7**), one of a pair of six-panel byobu. His wet brushstrokes—long and slow, short and quick, dark and pale—present a grove of great pines shrouded in mist. His trees emerge from and recede into the heavy atmosphere, as if the landscape hovers at the edge of formlessness. In Zen terms, the picture suggests the illusory nature of mundane reality while evoking a calm, meditative mood.

SEN NO RIKYU A favorite exercise of cultivation and refinement in the Momoyama period was the tea ceremony (see "The Japanese Tea Ceremony," page 1072). In Japan, this important practice eventually came to carry political and ideological implications, and provided a means for those relatively new to political or economic power to assert authority in the cultural realm. For example, on returning from a major military campaign, Toyotomi Hideyoshi held an immense tea ceremony lasting 10 days and open to everyone in Kyoto. The ceremony's political connotations became so important that warlords reserved the right to grant or withhold permission for their vassals to host these rituals.

The most venerated tea master of the Momoyama period was SEN NO RIKYU (1522–1591), who was instrumental in establishing the aesthetics and rituals of the tea ceremony—for example, the exclusive use of natural construction materials of modest cost

ART AND SOCIETY

The Japanese Tea Ceremony

The Japanese tea ceremony (*chanoyu*) involves the ritual preparation, serving, and drinking of powdered green tea. The fundamental practices began in China. It was not until the ninth century that a monk named Eichu brought tea to Japan from China. Eventually, however, the Japanese ritual of serving tea, although based on Chinese practice, developed to a much higher degree of sophistication, peaking in the Momoyama period. Simple forms of the tea ceremony started in Japan in Zen temples as a symbolic withdrawal from the ordinary world to cultivate the mind and spirit. The practices spread to other social groups, especially samurai and, by the late 16th century, wealthy merchants. Until the late Muromachi period, grand tea ceremonies in warrior residences served primarily as an excuse to display treasured collections of Chinese objects, especially porcelains, lacquers, and paintings.

Initially, the Japanese held tea ceremonies in a room or section of a house. As the popularity of tea ceremonies increased, freestanding teahouses (FIG. 34-8) became common. The

ceremony involves a sequence of rituals in which both host and guests participate. The host's responsibilities include serving the guests; selecting special utensils, such as water jars (FIG. 34-9) and tea bowls; and determining the tearoom's decoration, which changes according to occasion and season. Acknowledged as having superior aesthetic sensibilities, individuals recognized as master tea-ceremony practitioners (tea masters) advise patrons on the ceremony and acquire students. Tea masters even influence the design of teahouses and tearooms within larger structures (including interiors and gardens), as well as the design of tea utensils. They often make simple bamboo implements and occasionally even ceramic vessels.

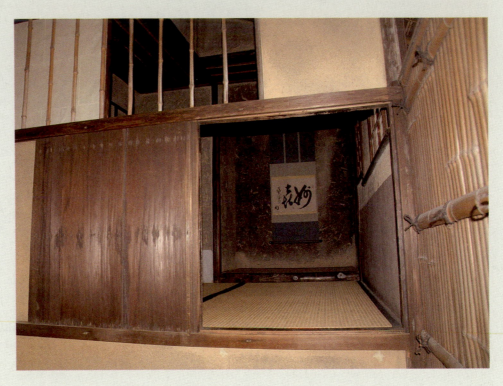

34-8 SEN NO RIKYU, interior of the Taian teahouse, Myokian temple, Kyoto, Japan, Momoyama period, ca. 1582.

The dimness and tiny size of the Taian tearoom and its alcove produce a cavelike feeling and encourage intimacy among the host and guests, who must crawl through a small door to enter.

(wood, mud, stone, and straw) and the manner of entry into a teahouse (crawling on one's hands and knees). Rikyu believed that crawling fostered humility and created the impression, however unrealistic, that there was no rank in a teahouse. Rikyu was the designer of the first Japanese teahouse, or *chashitsu*, built as an independent structure as opposed to being part of a house. The Taian teahouse (FIG. 34-8) at the Myokian temple in Kyoto, also attributed to Rikyu, is the oldest in Japan. The interior displays two standard features of Japanese residential architecture of the late Muromachi period—very thick, rigid straw mats called *tatami* (a Heian innovation) and an alcove called a *tokonoma*. The tatami accommodate the traditional Japanese customs of not wearing shoes indoors and of sitting on the floor. They are still features of Japanese homes today. Less common in contemporary houses are tokonoma, which developed as places to hang scrolls of painting or calligraphy and to display other prized objects.

The Taian tokonoma and the tearoom as a whole have unusually dark walls, with earthen plaster covering even some of the square corner posts. The room's dimness and tiny size (about 6 feet square, the size of two tatami mats) produce a cavelike feel and encourage intimacy among the tea host and guests. The guests enter from the garden outside by crawling through a small sliding door. The means

of entrance emphasizes a guest's passage into a ceremonial space set apart from the ordinary world.

WABI AND SABI Sen no Rikyu also was influential in determining the aesthetics of tea-ceremony utensils. In his view, value and refinement lay in character and ability, not in bloodline or rank, and he therefore encouraged the use of tea items whose value was their inherent beauty rather than their monetary worth. Even before Rikyu, in the late 15th century during the Muromachi period, admiration of the technical brilliance of Chinese objects had begun to give way to ever-greater appreciation of the virtues of rustic Korean and Japanese wares. This new aesthetic of refined rusticity, or *wabi*, promoted especially by the Buddhist priest and influential tea master Murata Juko (1423–1502), was consistent with Zen concepts. Wabi suggests austerity and simplicity. Related to wabi and also important as a philosophical and aesthetic principle was *sabi*—the value found in the old and weathered, suggesting the tranquility reached in old age.

Wabi and sabi aesthetics underlie the ceramic vessels produced for the tea ceremony, such as the Shino water jar named *Kogan* (FIG. 34-9). The name, which means "ancient stream bank," comes from the brown-and-black painted design—marsh grass—on the jar's surface as well as from its coarse texture and rough form, both

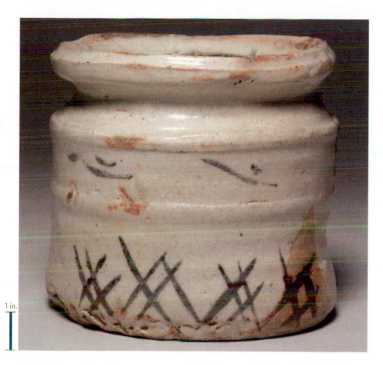

34-9 Kogan (tea-ceremony water jar), Momoyama period, late 16th century. Shino glazed stoneware with underglaze iron slip decoration, $7\frac{3}{4}"$ high. Cleveland Museum of Art, Cleveland (John L. Severance Fund).

The vessels used in the Japanese tea ceremony reflect the concepts of wabi, the aesthetic of refined rusticity, and sabi, the value found in weathered objects, suggesting the tranquility of old age.

reminiscent of earth cut by water. The term *Shino* generally refers to ceramic wares produced during the late 16th and early 17th centuries in kilns at Mino, northeast of Kyoto. Shino vessels typically have rough surfaces and feature heavy glazes containing feldspar. These glazes are predominantly white when fired, but pinkish-red or "mouse-gray" (*nezumi*) hues were also popular. The illustrated water jar is of the white variety. Its coarse stoneware body and seemingly casual decoration offer the same sorts of aesthetic and interpretive challenges and opportunities as dry-landscape gardens (FIG. 34-2). This Kogan, for example, has surface cracks, an irregular rim, and sagging contours (all intentional)

to suggest the accidental and natural, qualities essential to the values of wabi and sabi.

EDO

When Tokugawa Ieyasu consolidated his power in 1615, he abandoned Kyoto, the official capital, for Edo (see page 1065). The new regime instituted many policies designed to severely limit the pace of social and cultural change in Japan. Christianity, for example, had gained its initial foothold in Japan when the Portuguese Jesuit Francis Xavier (1506–1552) led the first mission to the islands in 1549. Later in the century, Christian missionaries began to build the first churches in Japan. As the popularity of the Western religion grew, the Tokugawa shogunate began to fear the same kind of colonization that had occurred in New Spain (see page 1084), and banned Christianity and expelled all Western foreigners except the Dutch. The Edo period marks the beginning of a long-lasting policy of government-imposed isolation for Japan.

The Tokugawa were also concerned about destabilization of the social order, and instituted Confucian ideas of social stratification and civic responsibility as public policy. They made a concerted effort to control the social influence of urban merchants, some of whom had accumulated wealth far outstripping that of most warrior leaders. However, the population's great expansion in urban centers, the spread of literacy in the cities and beyond, and a growing thirst for knowledge and diversion made for a very lively popular culture not easily subject to tight control.

KATSURA IMPERIAL VILLA In the Edo period, the power of the Japanese court remained as it had been for centuries—symbolic and ceremonial—but the imperial family continued to wield influence in matters of taste and culture, which the shogunate encouraged as far preferable to the emperor's seeking to reassert governing authority.

In 1620, Prince Toshihito (1579–1629) began to develop a modest country retreat into a villa that became the standard for domestic Japanese architecture. His son, Prince Noritada (b. 1619), continued the project, which required almost half a century to complete and eventually boasted five teahouses in addition to the residential units. Since the early 20th century, the Katsura Imperial Villa (FIG. 34-10) has inspired architects worldwide (FIG. 29-45), even as ordinary

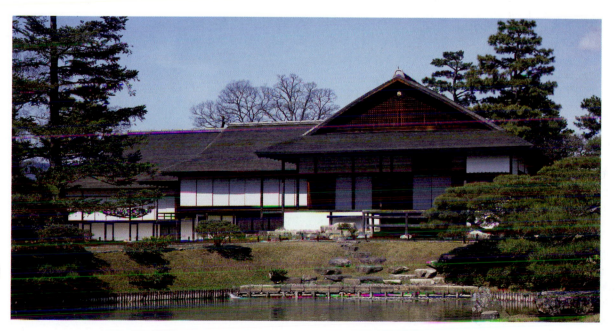

34-10 East facade of the Katsura Imperial Villa, Kyoto, Japan, Edo period, 1620–1663.

The Katsura Imperial Villa became the standard for Japanese residential architecture. The design relies on subtleties of proportion, color, and texture instead of ornamentation for its aesthetic appeal.

living environments in Japan became increasingly Westernized in structure and decor. The villa takes its name from its location on the Katsura River southwest of Kyoto. The design incorporates many features derived from earlier teahouses, such as Rikyu's Taian (FIG. 34-8), but by the Edo period, tea-ceremony aesthetics had retreated from Rikyu's wabi extremes, and the Katsura Villa's builders incorporated elements of courtly gracefulness as well.

Unlike in the castles of the Momoyama warlords, ornamentation that advertises the owner's wealth and disguises structural forms has little place in this architecture's appeal, which relies instead on subtleties of proportion, color, and texture. A variety of textures (stone, wood, tile, plaster) and subdued colors and tonal values enrich the villa's lines, planes, and volumes. Artisans painstakingly rubbed and burnished all surfaces to bring out the natural beauty of their grains and textures. The rooms are not large, but parting or removing the sliding doors between them creates broad rectangular spaces. Perhaps most important, the residents can open the doors to the outside to achieve a harmonious integration of building and garden—one of the primary ideals of Japanese residential architecture.

RINPA In painting, the Kano School enjoyed official governmental sponsorship during the Edo period, and its workshops provided paintings to the Tokugawa shogunate and its major vassals. By the mid-18th century, Kano masters also served as the primary painting teachers for nearly everyone aspiring to a career in the field. Even so, individualist painters and other schools emerged and flourished, working in quite distinct styles.

The earliest major alternative school to emerge in the Edo period, Rinpa, was quite different in nature from the Kano School. The Rinpa School did not have a similar continuity of lineage and training through father and son, master and pupil. Instead, over time, Rinpa aesthetics and principles attracted a variety of individuals as practitioners and champions. Stylistically, Rinpa works feature vivid color and extensive use of gold and silver and often incorporate decorative patterns. The roots of the Rinpa School can be traced to TAWARAYA SOTATSU (d. 1643), an artist who emerged as an important figure during the late Momoyama period, and whose *Waves at Matsushima* (FIG. 34-10A) is one of the early masterworks of Edo painting. Rinpa, however, takes its name from the last syllable in the name of OGATA KORIN (1658–1716; FIG. I-12)

and *pa* ("school"). Both Sotatsu and Korin were scions of wealthy merchant families with close connections to the Japanese court. Many Rinpa works incorporate literary themes that the nobility favored.

HONAMI KOETSU One of the earliest Rinpa masters was HONAMI KOETSU (1558–1637), the heir of a family of swordsmiths in the ancient capital of Kyoto. Koetsu was a greatly admired (and apparently self-trained) calligrapher who was related to both Sotatsu and Korin by marriage and who also participated in and produced ceramics for the tea ceremony. Many scholars credit him with overseeing the design of wood objects with lacquer decoration (see "Lacquered Wood," page 1056), perhaps with the aid of Sotatsu, who was the proprietor of a fan-painting shop. Scholars do know that the two drew on ancient traditions of painting and craft decoration to develop a style that collapsed boundaries between the two arts. Paintings, the lacquered surfaces of writing boxes, and ceramics shared motifs and compositions.

In typical Rinpa fashion, Koetsu's *Boat Bridge* writing box (FIG. 34-11) exhibits motifs drawn from a 10th-century poem about the boat bridge at Sano, north of Edo. The lid presents a subtle, gold-on-gold scene of small boats lined up side by side in the water to support the planks of a temporary bridge. The bridge itself, a lead overlay, forms a band across the lid's convex surface. The raised metallic lines on the water, boats, and bridge are a few Japanese characters from the poem, which describes the experience of crossing a bridge as evoking reflection on life's insecurities. The box also shows the dramatic contrasts of form, texture, and color typifying Rinpa aesthetics, especially the juxtaposition of the bridge's dark metal and the box's brilliant gold surface. The gold decoration comes from careful sprinkling of gold dust in wet lacquer. Whatever Koetsu's contribution to the design process, specialists well versed in the demanding techniques of metalworking and lacquering produced the writing box.

LITERATI PAINTING In the 17th and 18th centuries, Japan's increasingly urban, educated population spurred a cultural and social restlessness among commoners and samurai of lesser rank that the policies of the restrictive Tokugawa could not suppress. People eagerly sought new ideas and images, directing their attention

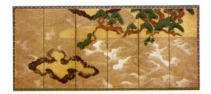

34-10A SOTATSU, *Waves at Matsushima*, ca. 1630.

34-11 HONAMI KOETSU, *Boat Bridge*, writing box, Edo period, early 17th century. Lacquered wood with sprinkled gold and lead overlay, $9\frac{1}{2}" \times 9" \times 4\frac{3}{8}"$. Tokyo National Museum, Tokyo.

Koetsu's writing box is an early work of the Rinpa School, which drew on ancient traditions of painting and craft decoration to develop a style that collapsed boundaries between the two arts.

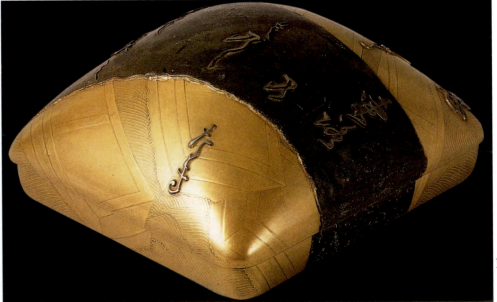

primarily to China, as had happened throughout Japanese history, but also to the West. From each direction, dramatically new ideas about painting emerged.

Starting in the late 17th century, emigrant Chinese monks and merchants, illustrations in woodblock-printed painting manuals, and imported paintings of lesser quality brought limited knowledge of Chinese literati painting (see page 1052) into Japan. Korea, however, was the essential link at this time between Japan and China, as it was so often in the past. Edo Japan had no official ties with Qing China, but welcomed ambassadors and scholars from Korea. Because of this exposure to Chinese painting, some Edo artists began to emulate Chinese models, although the difference in context resulted in variations. In China, literati were cultured intellectuals whose education and upbringing as landed gentry afforded them positions in the country's governmental bureaucracy. Chinese literati artists were predominantly amateurs and pursued painting as one of the proper functions of an educated and cultivated person. In contrast, although Japanese literati artists acquired a familiarity with and appreciation for Chinese literature, they were mostly professionals, painting to earn a living. Among them, however, were many women, who could more easily work in this painting genre because of its traditional association with amateurism and private intellectual pursuits. Because of the diffused infiltration of Chinese literati painting into Japan, the resulting character of Japanese literati painting was less narrowly defined stylistically than in China. Despite the inevitable changes as Chinese ideas disseminated throughout Japan, the newly seen Chinese models were valuable in supporting emerging ideals of self-expression in painting by offering a worthy alternative to the Kano School's standardized repertoire.

YOSA BUSON One of the outstanding early representatives of Japanese literati painting was YOSA BUSON (1716–1783). A master writer of *haiku* (the 17-syllable Japanese poetic form very popular from the 17th century on), Buson had a command of literati painting that extended beyond knowledge of Chinese models. His poetic abilities gave rise to a lyricism that pervaded both his haiku and his painting. *Cuckoo Flying over New Verdure* (FIG. **34-12**) exemplifies his fully mature style. In this hanging scroll, he incorporated basic elements of Chinese literati painting by rounding the landscape forms and rendering their soft texture in fine fibrous brushstrokes, and by including dense foliage patterns. The cuckoo, however, is a motif specific to Japanese poetry and literati painting. Moreover, although Buson imitated the vocabulary of brushstrokes associated with the Chinese literati, his touch was bolder and more abstract, and the gentle palette of pale colors was very much his own.

UKIYO-E Although the Tokugawa shogunate tried to hold in check the pursuit of sensual pleasure in the rapidly growing cities of Osaka, Kyoto, and Edo, their efforts were largely in vain, in part because of demographics. The population of Edo during this period included significant numbers of merchants and samurai and their families, and both groups were eager to enjoy secular city life. Taking part in the emerging urban culture involved more than simple physical satisfactions and rowdy entertainments. Many who participated were also admirers of literature, music, and art. The best-known products of this sophisticated counterculture are known as *ukiyo-e* (see "The Floating World of Edo," page 1065), a term suggesting the transience of human life and the ephemerality of the material world. The subjects of these paintings and especially prints (see "Japanese Woodblock Prints," page 1077) came mainly from the realms of pleasure, such as the Yoshiwara brothels and the popular theater.

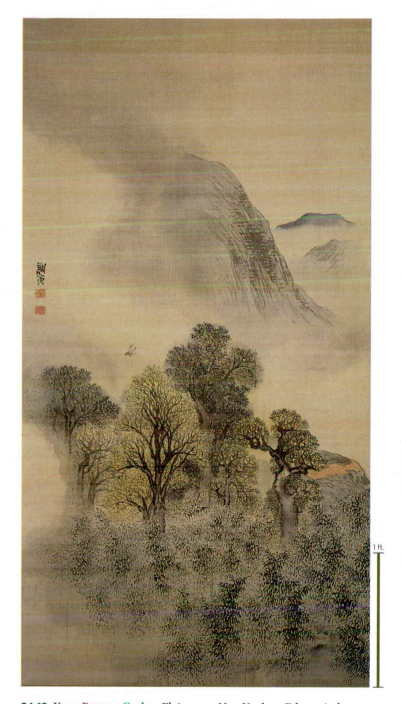

34-12 YOSA BUSON, *Cuckoo Flying over New Verdure*, Edo period, late 18th century. Hanging scroll, ink and colors on silk, 5' $\frac{1}{2}$" × 2' 7 $\frac{1}{4}$". Hiraki Ukiyo-e Museum, Yokohama.

A master of haiku poetry, Yosa Buson was a leading Japanese literati painter. Although inspired by Chinese works, he used a distinctive palette of pale colors and bolder, more abstract brushstrokes.

However, Edo printmakers also frequently depicted beautiful young women in both domestic (FIG. 34-1) and public settings (FIG. **34-12A**, by KITAGAWA UTAMARO [1753–1806]), as well as sea- and landscapes (FIGS. 34-13 and 34-14).

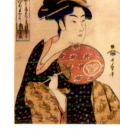

34-12A UTAMARO, *Ohisa of the Takashima Tea Shop*, 1792–1793.

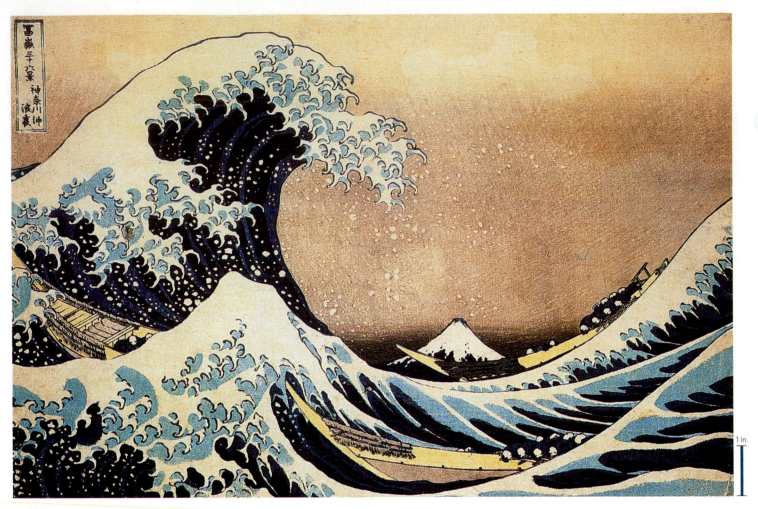

34-13 KATSUSHIKA HOKUSAI, *The Great Wave off Kanagawa,* from *Thirty-six Views of Mount Fuji* series, Edo period, ca. 1826–1833. Woodblock print, ink and colors on paper, $9\frac{7}{8}$" × 1' $2\frac{3}{4}$". Museum of Fine Arts, Boston (Bigelow Collection).

Adopting the low horizon line of Western painting, master woodblock printmaker Hokussai used the flat and powerful graphic forms of Japanese art to depict the threatening wave in the foreground.

KATSUSHIKA HOKUSAI Landscape painting—long revered as a major genre of Chinese and Korean painting—emerged in the 18th century in Japan as an immensely popular subject with the proliferation of inexpensive multicolor woodblock prints. Although inspired in part by Dutch landscape engravings imported into Japan at a time when the ruling Tokugawa government was pursuing its isolationist policy, Japanese printmakers radically transformed the compositions and coloration of their Western models. One of the most famous Japanese landscape artists was KATSUSHIKA HOKUSAI (1760–1849), who was the son of a peasant family from a village east of Edo. In *The Great Wave off Kanagawa* (FIG. **34-13**), part of a woodblock series called *Thirty-six Views of Mount Fuji,* the huge foreground wave dwarfs the artist's representation of the distant mountain. This contrast and the whitecaps' ominous fingers magnify the wave's threatening aspect, enhanced by the fact that Japanese viewers knew Mount Fuji was an active volcano that had last erupted in 1707. The men in the trading boats bend low to dig their oars against the rough sea and drive their long, low vessels past the danger. Although Hokusai's print draws on Western techniques and incorporates the distinctive European color called Prussian blue, it also engages the Japanese pictorial tradition. Against a background with the low horizon typical of Western painting, Hokusai placed in the foreground the wave's more traditionally flat and powerfully graphic forms, mainly curved triangles.

ANDO HIROSHIGE The leading landscape printmaker of the mid-19th century was ANDO HIROSHIGE (1797–1858). Born into a wealthy family, Hiroshige decided early on to pursue a career as an artist rather than follow in his father's footsteps as chief of a fire brigade. In August 1832, he traveled on an official government mission to the emperor in Kyoto and the following year published a series of prints based on sketches he made on that journey—*Fifty-three Stations of the Tokaido Highway.* That collection of views of the countryside along the major roadway on Japan's east coast was an instant success. Many other editions followed, including views of Kyoto (1834) and his last and most ambitious series, published shortly before his death, *One Hundred Famous Views of Edo.*

Plum Estate, Kameido (FIG. **34-14**), dated "11th Month, 1857," comes from the *Edo* series. The "famous views" are not monuments and buildings but places of leisure and natural beauty where the Japanese sought to escape from the noise and pressures of city life. Many of the sites are Shinto shrines (see "Shinto," page 495) and Buddhist temples. Others, including the plum orchard of Kameido, were favorite spots to visit at particular times of the year, when their natural beauty was at its peak. The main attraction of the Kameido estate was the Sleeping Dragon Plum, the most famous tree in Edo, celebrated for its large white blossoms and aromatic fragrance. Hiroshige's print shows only a partial view of the venerable tree, with its branches spreading out to touch all sides of the print and

MATERIALS AND TECHNIQUES
Japanese Woodblock Prints

During the Edo period, woodblock prints with ukiyo-e themes became enormously popular. People with very modest incomes could therefore collect prints in albums or paste them on their walls. A highly efficient production system made this wide distribution of Japanese graphic art possible.

Ukiyo-e artists were generally painters who did not themselves manufacture the prints that made them so famous both in their own time and today. As the designers, they sold drawings to publishers, who in turn oversaw their printing. The publishers also played a role in creating ukiyo-e prints by commissioning specific designs or adapting them before printing. Consequently, the names of both designer and publisher often appeared on the final prints.

Unacknowledged in nearly all cases, however, were the individuals who produced the prints, the block carvers and printers. Using skills honed since childhood, they worked with both speed and precision for relatively low wages and thus made ukiyo-e prints affordable. The master print designers were primarily men. Women, especially wives and daughters, often assisted painters and other artists, but few gained separate recognition. Among the exceptions was the daughter of Katsushika Hokusai (FIG. 34-13), Katsushika Oi (1818–1854), who became well known as a painter and probably helped her father with his print designs.

Japanese prints during the Edo period tend to have black outlines separating distinct color areas (FIGS. 34-1, 34-13, and 34-14). This format is a result of the printing process. A master carver pasted the linear designs face down on a wood block. Wetting and gently scraping the thin paper revealed the reversed image to guide the cutting of the block. After the carving, only the outlines of the forms and other elements that would be black in the final print remained raised in relief. The master printer then coated the block with black ink and printed several initial outline prints. These master prints became the guides for carving the other blocks, one for each color used. On each color block, the carver left in relief only the areas to be printed in that color. Even ordinary prints sometimes required up to 20 colors and thus 20 blocks, although to reduce costs, Edo printmakers often cut designs into both sides of each block used. Most prints were 10 to 15 inches high and 8 to 10 inches wide. To print a color, a printer applied the appropriate pigment to a block's raised surface, laid a sheet of paper on it, and rubbed the back of the paper with a smooth flat object. Then another printer would print a different color on the same sheet of paper. Perfect alignment of the paper in each step was critical to prevent overlapping of colors, so the carvers included printing guides in their blocks—an L-shaped ridge in one corner and a straight ridge on one side. The printers could cover small alignment errors with a final printing of the black outlines from the last block.

The materials used in printing varied over time, but by the mid-18th century had reached a high level of standardization. The blocks were planks of fine-grained hardwood, usually cherry. The best paper came from the white layer beneath the bark of mulberry trees, because its long fibers helped the paper stand up to repeated rubbing on the blocks. The printers used a few mineral pigments, but tended to favor inexpensive dyes made from plants for most colors. As a result, the

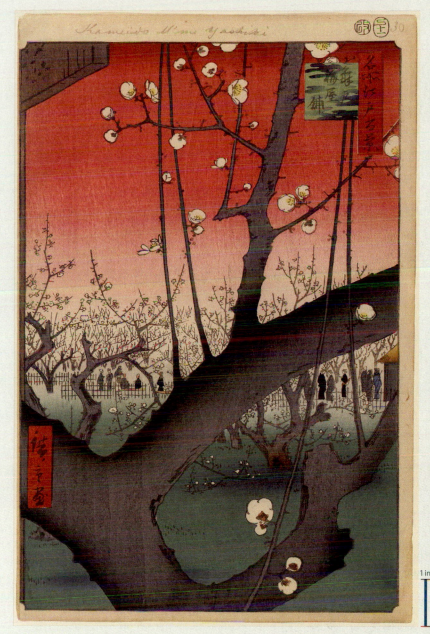

34-14 ANDO HIROSHIGE, *Plum Estate, Kameido*, from *One Hundred Famous Views of Edo*, Edo period, 1857. Woodblock print, ink and colors on paper, 1' $1\frac{1}{4}$" × $8\frac{5}{8}$". Brooklyn Museum, Brooklyn (gift of Anna Ferris).

Hiroshige's multicolor woodblock print shows only a partial view of the Kameido Sleeping Dragon Plum, whose branches spread out in abstract patterns resembling the beloved Japanese art of calligraphy.

colors of ukiyo-e prints were and are highly susceptible to fading, especially when exposed to strong light. In the early 19th century, more permanent European synthetic dyes began to enter Japan. The first such color, Prussian blue, appears in Hokusai's *The Great Wave off Kanagawa* (FIG. 34-13).

The popularity of ukiyo-e prints extended to the Western world as well. Their affordability and the ease with which they could be transported facilitated dissemination of the prints, especially throughout Europe. Ukiyo-e prints appear in the backgrounds of a number of Impressionist and Post-Impressionist paintings, attesting to the appeal that these works held for Westerners. Some Japanese prints—for example, Ando Hiroshige's *Plum Estate, Kameido* (FIG. 34-14)—inspired 19th-century European artists to produce near-copies (see "Japonisme," page 850, and FIG. 28-17B).

forming a bold abstract pattern resembling the beloved art of calligraphy. The pattern of the tree's limbs so dominates the print that the viewer hardly notices the crowd of onlookers behind a fence in the background. The unnatural coloration of the red sky enhances the abstract effect, flattening the pictorial space in a manner completely foreign to the Western notion of perspective. It was precisely this quality that fascinated 19th-century European painters who were trying to break free of the Renaissance ideals perpetuated by the official painting academies. One of those artists was Vincent van Gogh, who paid tribute to Hiroshige by painting his own version of the Kameido woodblock print (FIG. 28-17B).

MEIJI AND SHOWA

The Edo period and the rule of the shoguns ended in 1868, when rebellious samurai from provinces far removed from Edo toppled the Tokugawa. Facilitating this revolution was the shogunate's inability to handle the increasing pressure from Western nations for Japan to throw open its doors to the outside world. Although the rebellion restored direct sovereignty to the imperial throne, real power rested with the emperor's cabinet. As a symbol of imperial authority, however, the official name of this new period was Meiji (Enlightened Rule; 1868–1912), after the emperor's chosen regnal name.

TAKAHASHI YUICHI Oil painting became a major genre in Japan in the late 19th century. Ambitious students studied with Westerners at government schools and during trips abroad. One oil painting highlighting the cultural ferment of the early Meiji period is *Oiran* (*Grand Courtesan*; FIG. **34-15**), painted by TAKAHASHI YUICHI (1828–1894), who opened a school to teach young Japanese artists how to paint in the Western manner. Ironically, Takahashi created *Oiran* for a patron nostalgic for vanishing elements of Japanese culture. He asked the artist to make an accurate record of a geisha who still wore her hair in the distinctive, out-of-fashion Japanese style. Ukiyo-e printmakers frequently represented similar grand courtesans of the pleasure quarters. In the painting, however, Takahashi did not portray the courtesan's features in the idealizing manner of ukiyo-e artists but in the more analytical manner of Western portraiture and, in accord with the portrait's purpose, meticulously reproduced the geisha's hairpin-filled coiffure. Yet the painter's more abstract rendering of the garments reflects a very old practice in East Asian portraiture.

KANO HOGAI Unbridled enthusiasm for Westernization in some quarters led to resistance and concern over a loss of distinctive Japanese identity in other quarters. Ironically, one of those most eager to preserve "Japaneseness" in the arts was Ernest Fenollosa (1853–1908), an American professor of philosophy and political economy at Tokyo Imperial University. He and a former student named Okakura Kakuzo (1862–1913) joined with others in a movement that eventually led to the founding under Okakura's direction of a new academy, the Tokyo School of Fine Arts, dedicated to Japanese arts. Their goal was to make Japanese painting viable in the modern age rather than preserve it as a relic. To this end, they encouraged students to incorporate some Western techniques, such as chiaroscuro, perspective, and bright hues, in Japanese-style paintings. The name given to the resulting style was *nihonga* (Japanese painting), as opposed to *yoga* (Western painting). One of the first professors appointed by Okakura (although he died before he could take up the position) was KANO HOGAI (1828–1888), who studied

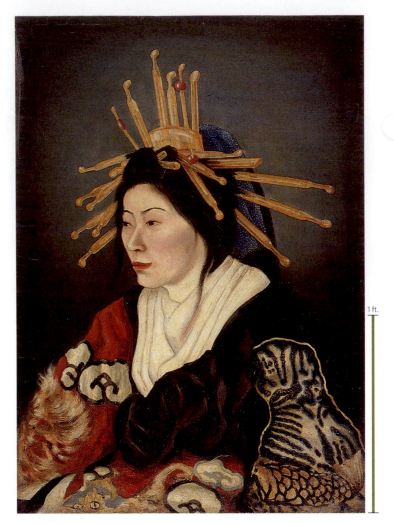

34-15 TAKAHASHI YUICHI, *Oiran* (*Grand Courtesan*), Meiji period, 1872. Oil on canvas, 2′ 6½″ × 1′ 9⅝″. Tokyo National University of Fine Arts and Music, Tokyo.

The subject and abstract rendering of this courtesan's garment derive from ukiyo-e and traditional Japanese art, but the oil technique and the meticulous recording of the coiffure follow Western norms.

painting in Tokyo under the tutelage of a master of the venerable Kano School. Hogai had met Fenellosa in 1883, and the American promoted his career and purchased several of his paintings, including *Bodhisattva Kannon* (FIG. **34-16**), later acquired by the American industrialist and art collector Charles Lang Freer (1854–1919). The painting depicts Kannon (Chinese Guanyin; compare FIGS. 16-17A and 16-24A), the mustached but effeminate bodhisattva of infinite compassion. Kannon stands on a cloud and pours drops of the water of wisdom from a small flask upon a newborn suspended in a transparent globe. Fenellosa called the painting *The Creation of Man*. In composition, theme, medium, and format, this ink-and-color silk hanging scroll exemplifies the nihonga style.

SHOWA During the Showa period (1926–1989), Japan became increasingly prominent on the world stage in economics, politics, and culture, and played a leading role in World War II. The most tragic consequences of that conflict for Japan were the widespread devastation and loss of life resulting from the atomic bombings of Hiroshima and Nagasaki in 1945. During the succeeding occupation period, the United States imposed new democratic institutions on Japan, with the emperor serving as a ceremonial

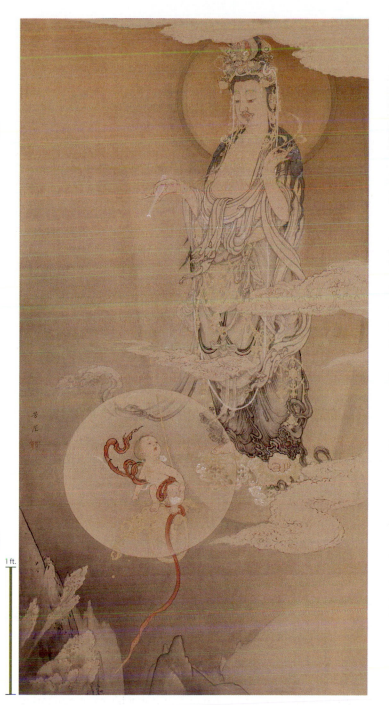

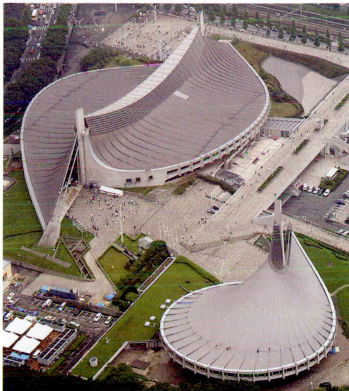

34-17 KENZO TANGE, national indoor Olympic stadiums, Tokyo, Japan, Showa period, 1961–1964.

Tange was one of the most daring architects of postwar Japan. His Olympic stadiums employ a cable suspension system that enabled him to shape steel and concrete into remarkably graceful structures.

1 ft.

34-16 KANO HOGAI, *Bodhisattva Kannon*, Meiji period, 1883. Hanging scroll, ink, colors, and gold on silk, 5' 4$\frac{3}{8}$" × 2' 9$\frac{3}{8}$". Freer Gallery of Art, Smithsonian Institution, Washington, D.C. (gift of Charles Lang Freer).

In composition, theme, medium, and format, this ink-and-color hanging silk scroll exemplifies the nihonga revival of Japanese subject matter and style, a sharp break from Westernized yoga.

head of state. Japan's economy rebounded with remarkable speed, and its gross national product became one of the largest in the world. During the past several decades, Japanese artists have also made a mark in the international art world. As they did in earlier times with the art and culture of China and Korea, many Japanese painters, sculptors, and architects internalized Western styles and techniques and incorporated them as a part of Japan's own vital culture. Others, however, shunned Western art forms and worked in more traditional modes.

KENZO TANGE In the 20th century, Japanese architecture, especially public buildings, underwent rapid transformation along Western lines. In fact, architecture may be the most influential Japanese art form on the world stage today. Japanese architects have made major contributions to both modern and postmodern developments. One of the most daringly experimental architects of the post–World War II period was KENZO TANGE (1913–2005). In his design of the stadiums (FIG. **34-17**) for the 1964 Olympics, he employed a cable suspension system that enabled him to shape steel and concrete into remarkably graceful structures. His attention to both the sculptural qualities of each building's raw concrete form and the fluidity of its spaces allied him with architects worldwide who carried on the legacy of the late style of Le Corbusier (FIG. 30-41) in France. His stadiums thus bear comparison with the JetBlue terminal and the Sydney Opera House (FIGS. 30-43 and 30-44).

HAMADA SHOJI One modern Japanese art form with ancient roots is ceramics. Many contemporary admirers of folk art (*mingei*) are avid collectors of traditional Japanese pottery. A formative figure in Japan's folk art movement, the philosopher Yanagi Soetsu (1889–1961), promoted an ideal of beauty inspired by the Japanese tea ceremony. He argued that true beauty could be achieved only in functional objects made of natural materials by anonymous craftspeople, such as the Shino water jar (FIG. 34-9) discussed earlier. Among the ceramists who produced this type of folk pottery was HAMADA SHOJI (1894–1978). Although Hamada espoused Yanagi's selfless ideals, he still gained international fame and in 1955 received official recognition in Japan as a Living National

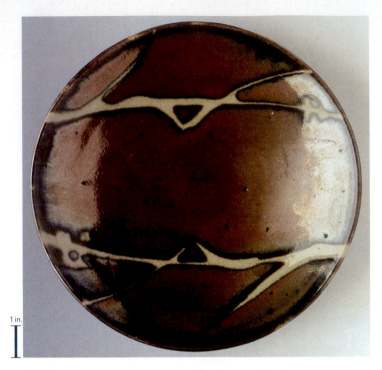

1 in.

34-18 HAMADA SHOJI, large plate, Showa period, 1958. Stoneware with porcelain enamel glaze, 10¾" diameter. Private collection.

A leading figure in the modern folk art movement in Japan, Hamada Shoji gained international fame. His unsigned stoneware features casual slip designs and a coarser, darker texture than porcelain.

artistic influence extended beyond the production of pots. He traveled to England in 1920 and, along with English potter Bernard Leach (1887–1978), established a community of ceramists committed to the mingei aesthetic. Together, Hamada and Leach expanded international knowledge of Japanese ceramics, and even now, the "Hamada-Leach aesthetic" is part of potters' education worldwide.

GUTAI One of the most significant developments in 20th-century art was the emergence of *Performance Art* as a major genre (see page 986), and Japanese artists played a seminal role. Gutai Bijutsu Kyokai (Concrete Art Association) was a group of 18 Japanese artists in Osaka who expanded the principles of *action painting* into the realm of performance—in a sense, taking Jackson Pollock's painting methods (see "Jackson Pollock on Easel and Mural Painting," page 955, and FIG. 30-7) into a public arena. Led by Jiro Yoshihara (1905–1972), Gutai, founded in 1954, devoted itself to art that combined Japanese traditional practices such as Zen (see "Zen Buddhism," page 1067) with a renewed appreciation for materials. In the *Gutai Art Manifesto,* Yoshihara explained: "Gutai does not alter the material. Gutai imparts life to the material. . . . [T]he human spirit and the material shake hands with each other, but keep their distance."[1] Accordingly, the Gutai group's performances—for example, *Making a Work with His Own Body* (FIG. 34-19), by KAZUO SHIRAGA (1924–2008)—involved actions such as throwing paint balls at blank canvases or wallowing in mud as a means of shaping it. In *Making a Work,* Shiraga used his body to "paint" with mud. The Gutai group disbanded upon Yoshihara's death in 1972, but their work was an important influence on Western Performance artists such as Carolee Schneemann (FIG. 30-52).

Treasure. Works such as his plate (FIG. 34-18) with casual slip designs are unsigned, but connoisseurs easily recognize them as his. This kind of stoneware is coarser, darker, and heavier than porcelain and lacks the latter's fine decoration. To those who appreciate simpler, earthier beauty, however, this dish holds great attraction. Hamada's

CONTEMPORARY ART In the interconnected community that the world has become over the past few decades, some Japanese artists have also achieved international renown. The work of Tsuchiya Kimio (FIG. 31-31) and other contemporary Asian sculptors and painters is treated in its worldwide context in Chapter 31.

34-19 KAZUO SHIRAGA, *Making a Work with His Own Body,* Showa period, 1955. Mud.

The members of the Gutai Bijutsu Kyokai (Concrete Art Association) expanded postwar action painting into the realm of Performance Art. Shiraga used his body to "paint" with mud.

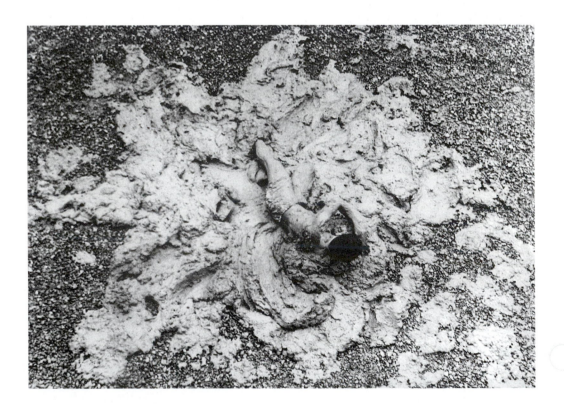

JAPAN, 1333 TO 1980

Muromachi 1333-1573

- The Muromachi period takes its name from the Kyoto district in which the Ashikaga shogunate maintained its headquarters.

- At this time, Zen Buddhism rose to prominence in Japan. Zen temples often featured gardens of the karesansui (dry-landscape) type, which facilitated meditation.

- Muromachi painting displays great variety in both subject and style. One characteristic technique is the haboku (splashed-ink) style, which has Chinese roots. An early haboku master was Sesshu Toyo.

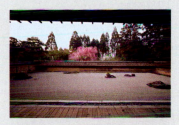

Karesansui garden, Ryoanji, ca. 1488

Momoyama 1573-1615

- Three successive warlords dominated this brief but artistically rich interlude between two long-lasting shogunates. The period takes its name from one of the warlord's castles (Momoyama, Peach Blossom Hill) outside Kyoto. The best preserved Momoyama castle is the White Heron Castle at Himeji.

- Many of the finest works of this period were commissions from those warlords, including *Chinese Lions* by Kano Eitoku, a six-part folding screen featuring animals considered to be symbols of power and bravery.

- During the Momoyama period, the Japanese tea ceremony became an important social ritual. The tea master Sen no Rikyu designed the first teahouse built as an independent structure. The favored tea utensils were rustic wares from the Mino kilns.

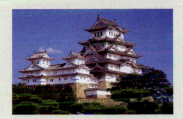

White Heron Castle, Himeji, 1581-1609

Edo 1615-1868

- The Edo period began when the shogun Tokugawa Ieyasu (1542-1616) moved his headquarters from Kyoto to Edo (modern Tokyo).

- The Katsura Imperial Villa, which relies for its aesthetic appeal on subtleties of proportion, color, and texture instead of ornamentation, set the standard for later Japanese domestic architecture.

- The Rinpa School, named for Ogata Korin, emerged as a major alternative school of painting to the Kano School, which had become a virtual national art academy. Rinpa paintings and crafts feature vivid colors and extensive use of gold, as in the *Boat Bridge* writing box by Honami Koetsu.

- Growing urbanization in major Japanese cities fostered a lively popular culture focused on sensual pleasure and theatrical entertainment. The best-known products of this sophisticated counterculture are the ukiyo-e woodblock prints of Edo's "floating world" by Suzuki Harunobu and others. The prints feature scenes from brothels and the theater as well as beautiful women in domestic settings.

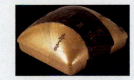

Koetsu, *Boat Bridge*, early 17th century

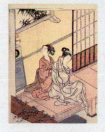

Harunobu, *Evening Bell at the Clock*, 1765

Meiji and Showa 1868-1989

- The Tokugawa shogunate toppled in 1868, opening the modern era of Japanese history. In art, Western styles and techniques had a great influence, and many Japanese artists, including Takahashi Yuichi, incorporated shading and perspective in their works and even produced oil paintings.

- In the post–World War II period, many Japanese artists and architects achieved worldwide reputations. Kenzo Tange was a master of creating dramatic shapes using a cable suspension system for his concrete-and-steel buildings. Kazuo Shiraga played a seminal role in the development of Performance Art as a major modern genre.

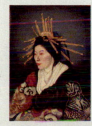

Takahashi, *Oiran*, 1872

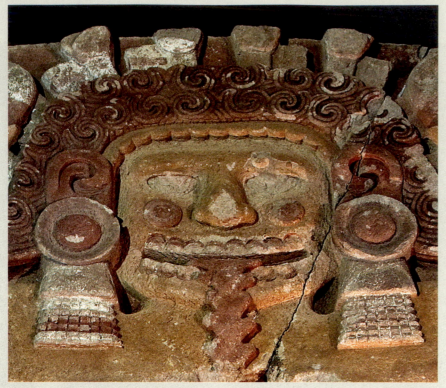

▲ **35-1a** This colossal relief depicting Tlaltecuhtli weighs 12 tons in its fragmentary state. The slab covered a treasure-filled shaft probably associated with the grave of Emperor Ahuitzotl, who died in 1502.

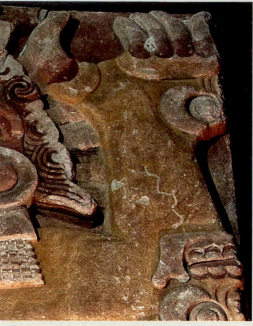

▲ **35-1b** Tlaltecuhtli is the Aztec earth goddess, whom the sculptor represented facing the viewer with arms raised and drinking her own blood. She has claws instead of hands and feet.

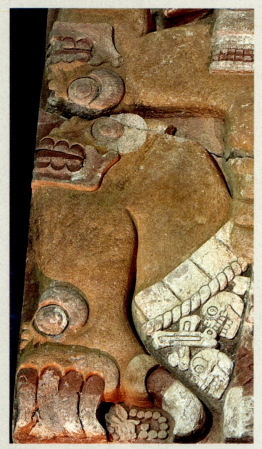

▲ **35-1c** In this relief, Tlaltecuhtli is shown squatting to give birth. In place of kneecaps, the earth goddess has skulls. The mineral colors—ocher, red, blue, white, and black—are well preserved.

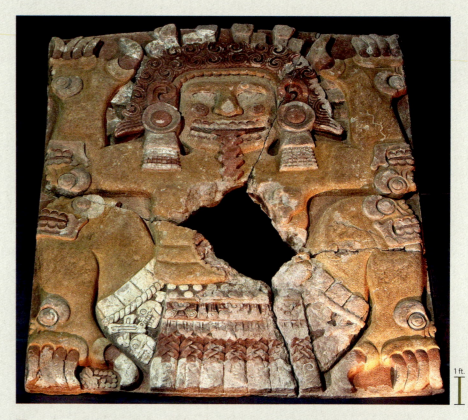

35-1 **Tlaltecuhtli, from the Great Temple of Tenochtitlán, Mexico City, Mexico, Aztec, 1502. Andesite, painted with mineral colors, 13' 9" × 11' 10½". Museo del Templo Mayor, Mexico City.**

1 ft.

Native American Cultures, 1300 to 1980

TLALTECUHTLI, THE AZTEC EARTH GODDESS

When their insatiable quest for gold brought the Spaniards, led by Hernán Cortés, into contact in 1519 with the Aztec Empire in what is today Mexico, they encountered the latest in a long line of highly sophisticated indigenous *Mesoamerican* art-producing cultures in what the Spaniards called the "New World." Known as the Mexica—from which the modern nation's name derives—the Aztecs, like their predecessors, practiced bloodletting and human sacrifice to please the gods and sustain the great cycles of the universe. The Aztecs, however, engaged in human sacrifice on a greater scale than any earlier culture, even waging special battles, called the "flowery wars," expressly to obtain captives for future sacrifice.

Contemporaneous European accounts record at length how shocked the Spanish conquistadors were by what they saw in the Aztec capital of Tenochtitlán. For example, Bernal Díaz del Castillo (ca. 1495–1585), a solder in Cortés's army, described the amazement of the Spaniards when they discovered a group of foul-smelling men with uncut fingernails, long hair matted with blood, black body paint, and ears covered in cuts. The Europeans did not realize that these men were priests who were performing rites in honor of the deities they served, including piercing their skin with cactus spines to draw blood. The Aztec priests were the opposite of the "barbarians" that the "Old World" conquistadors considered them to be. They were, in fact, the most highly educated men in Mesoamerica.

The rites conducted by the Aztec priests, and the gods and goddesses in whose honor those rites were performed, figured prominently in Aztec art. Fortunately, despite the attempts of the Spaniards to eradicate all of the Aztecs' despised "idols," several masterful examples of Aztec sculpture are preserved. One, which Mexican archaeologists uncovered in 2006, is a gigantic *monolithic* (one-piece) pink andesite relief (FIG. 35-1) painted in ocher, red, blue, white, and black depicting the earth goddess Tlaltecuhtli. The Aztec sculptor depicted the goddess facing the viewer with arms raised, wearing elaborate headgear, and posed in a squatting position to give birth while drinking her own blood. She has claws instead of hands and feet, and skulls in place of knees.

The relief weighs nearly 12 tons even in its fragmentary state and required at least 200 men to transport the huge stone from the quarry at Lake Texcoco to Tenochtitlán. The carved and painted slab covered a deep shaft at the foot of the north side of the Templo Mayor pyramid, the most important Aztec temple. Below, the excavators discovered sacrificial knives, gold bells, two eagles with jade and gold ornaments, and a dog or wolf with a jade necklace and turquoise ear ornaments, as well as 62 species of marine creatures from both the Atlantic and Pacific Oceans—that is, from every corner of the Aztec world. The relief and the treasure-filled shaft are probably associated with the as-yet-unlocated grave of the Aztec emperor Ahuitzotl (r. 1486–1502).

MESOAMERICA

In the years following the arrival of Christopher Columbus (1451–1506) in the New World in 1492, Spain poured money into expeditions probing the coasts of North and South America, but the Spaniards had little luck finding the wealth they sought. When brief stops on the coast of Yucatán, Mexico, yielded a small but still impressive amount of gold and other precious artifacts, the Spanish governor of Cuba outfitted yet another expedition. Headed by Hernán Cortés (1485–1547), this contingent of explorers was the first to make contact with the great Aztec emperor Moctezuma II (r. 1502–1521) at Tenochtitlán (MAP 35-1). In only two years, with the help of guns, horses, native allies revolting against their Aztec overlords, and perhaps also a smallpox epidemic that had swept across the Caribbean and already thinned the Aztec ranks, Cortés managed to overthrow the vast and rich Aztec Empire. His victory in 1521 opened the door to hordes of Spanish conquistadors seeking their fortunes and to missionaries eager for new converts to Christianity. The ensuing clash of cultures led to a century of turmoil throughout New Spain.

The Aztec Empire of the early 16th century succeeded several other great Mesoamerican civilizations. After the fall and destruction of the important central Mexican city of Teotihuacán (FIG. 18-5) in the eighth century and the abandonment of the southern Maya sites around 900, new cities arose to take their places during the period that scholars call the early Postclassic (ca. 900–1200). Notable were the Maya city of Chichén Itzá (FIGS. 18-15 to 18-17) in Yucatán and the Toltec capital of Tula (FIG. 18-19), not far from the later seat of Aztec power in Tenochtitlán. Their dominance was relatively short-lived, however.

Mixteca-Puebla

One of the most impressive art-producing peoples of the late Postclassic period (ca. 1200–1521) in Mesoamerica was the Mixtecs, who succeeded the Zapotecs at Monte Albán in southern Mexico after 700. They extended their political sway in Oaxaca by dynastic intermarriage as well as by warfare. The treasures found in the tombs at Monte Albán bear witness to Mixtec wealth, and the quality of these works demonstrates the culture's high level of artistic achievement. The Mixtecs were highly skilled goldsmiths and won renown for their work in *mosaic* using turquoise obtained from far-off regions such as present-day New Mexico.

BORGIA CODEX The peoples of Mesoamerica prized illustrated books, and the Postclassic Maya were preeminent in the art of writing. Their books—almost all destroyed by the Spanish conquistadors—were precious vehicles for recording history, rituals, astronomical tables, calendar calculations, maps, and trade and trib-

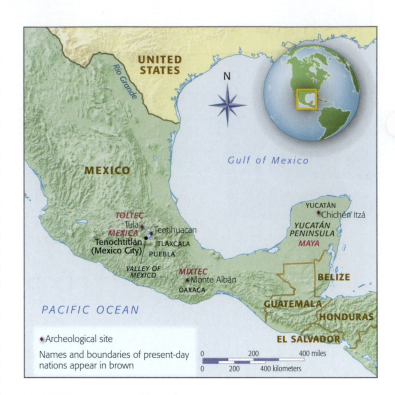

MAP 35-1 Mixteca-Puebla and Aztec sites in Mesoamerica.

ute accounts. The texts consisted of *hieroglyphic* columns read from left to right and top to bottom. Miraculously, three preconquest Maya books survived the depredations of the Europeans. Bishop Diego de Landa (1524–1579), the author of an invaluable treatise on the Maya of Yucatán, described how the Maya made their books and why so few remain:

> They wrote their books on a long sheet doubled in folds, which was then enclosed between two boards finely ornamented; the writing was on one side and the other, according to the folds. . . . We found a great number of books in these [Mayan] letters and, since they contained nothing but superstitions and falsehoods of the devil, we burned them all, which they took most grievously, and which gave them great pain.[1]

In contrast, 10 non-Maya Postclassic books survive, five from Mixtec Oaxaca and five from the Puebla region. Art historians have named the style that they represent Mixteca-Puebla, an interesting example of a Mesoamerican style crossing both ethnic and regional boundaries. The Mixteca-Puebla artists painted on long sheets of deerskin, which they first coated with fine white lime plaster and folded into accordion-like pleats to form *codices* (sing. *codex*) with covers of wood, mosaic, or feathers.

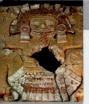

NATIVE AMERICAN CULTURES, 1300 TO 1980

1300–1532
- Mixteca-Puebla artists produce illustrated codices
- Aztecs build the Templo Mayor at Tenochtitlán and place monumental statues and reliefs in the sacred precinct
- Inka construct more than 20,000 miles of roads in the Andes and build Machu Picchu and the Temple of the Sun in Cuzco

1532–1800

1800–1900
- Kwakwaka'wakw and Tlingit artists carve transformation and war masks
- Great Plains artists fashion elaborate robes and regalia for the elite
- During the reservation period, Native American artists record traditional lifestyles in ledger books

1900–1980
- Many Native American artists continue to practice traditional crafts
- Southwest ceramists develop black-on-black glazed pottery
- Bill Reid carves monumental wood sculptures illustrating traditional Haida themes

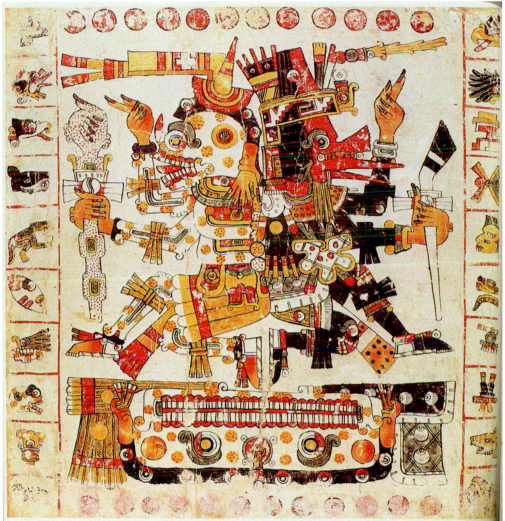

1 in.

35-2 Mictlantecuhtli and Quetzalcoatl, folio 56 of the *Borgia Codex,* from Puebla or Tlaxcala, Mexico, Mixteca-Puebla, ca. 1400–1500. Mineral and vegetable pigments on deerskin, $10\frac{5}{8}" \times 10\frac{3}{8}"$. Facsimile, Biblioteca Apostolica Vaticana, Rome.

One of the rare surviving Mesoamerican books, the Mixteca-Puebla *Borgia Codex* includes this painting depicting the gods of life and death above an inverted skull symbolizing the Underworld.

Aztec

The Aztecs were a Nahuatl-speaking people who left behind, in the *Codex Mendoza* and elsewhere, a history of their rise to power. Scholars have begun to question the accuracy of that Aztec account, however, and some think it is a mythic construct. According to the traditional history, the destruction of Toltec Tula about 1200 (see page 524) brought a century of anarchy to the Valley of Mexico, the vast highland valley 7,000 feet above sea level that is now home to sprawling Mexico City. Waves of northern invaders established warring city-states and wrought destruction in the valley. The Aztecs were the last of these conquerors. With astonishing rapidity, they transformed themselves within a few generations from migratory outcasts and serfs to mercenaries for local rulers and then to masters in their own right of the Valley of Mexico's small kingdoms. They began to call themselves Mexica, and, fulfilling a legendary prophecy that they would build a city where they saw an eagle perched on a cactus with a serpent in its mouth, they settled on an island in Lake Texcoco. Their settlement grew into the magnificent city of Tenochtitlán, which in 1519 so amazed the Spaniards.

Recognized by those they subdued as fierce in war and cruel in peace, the Aztecs indeed seemed to glory in battle and in military prowess. They radically changed the social and political situation in Mesoamerica. Subservient groups not only had to submit to Aztec military power but also had to provide victims to be sacrificed to Huitzilopochtli, the hummingbird god of war, and to other Aztec deities (see "Aztec Religion," page 1088).

TENOCHTITLÁN In the 16th century, the total population of the area of present-day Mexico that the Aztecs dominated was approximately 11 million. Their capital, Tenochtitlán, was home to more than 150,000 people. Tenochtitlán's ruins lie directly beneath the center of densely populated Mexico City in the Zócalo, the modern city's main square. The Aztecs constructed broad causeways to connect Tenochtitlán to the mainland and laid out the city on a grid plan, dividing it into quarters (FIG. 35-3) and wards, reminiscent of Teotihuacán (FIG. 18-5), which, long abandoned, had become a pilgrimage site for the Aztecs. Many of the Spaniards thought of

One extensively illustrated book that escaped the Spanish destruction is the *Borgia Codex,* from somewhere in central highland Mexico (either the state of Puebla or Tlaxcala). It is the largest and most elaborate of several manuscripts known as the Borgia Group. The page reproduced here (FIG. **35-2**) shows two richly attired and vividly gesticulating gods rendered predominantly in reds and yellows with black outlines. The god of life, the black Quetzalcoatl (depicted here as a masked human rather than in the usual form of a feathered serpent), sits back-to-back with the god of death, the white Mictlantecuhtli. Below them is an inverted skull with a double keyboard of teeth, a symbol of the Underworld (Mictlan), which could be entered through the mouth of a great earth monster. Both figures hold scepters in one hand and gesticulate with the other. The image conveys the inevitable relationship of life and death, an important theme in Mesoamerican art. Some scholars believe that the image may also be a kind of writing conveying a specific divinatory meaning. Symbols of the 13 divisions of 20 days in the 260-day Mesoamerican ritual calendar appear in panels in the margins (compare FIG. 35-3). The origins of this calendar, used even today in remote parts of Mexico and Central America, are unknown. Save for the Mixtec genealogical codices, most books painted before and immediately after the Spanish conquest deal with astronomy, calendars, divination, and ritual—with the notable exception of the *Codex Mendoza* (FIG. 35-3), which records the history of the Aztecs, the greatest Mesoamerican culture at the time that Cortés and his compatriots arrived in Mexico.

35-3 The founding of Tenochtitlán, folio 2 recto of the *Codex Mendoza*, from Mexico City, Mexico, Aztec, ca. 1540–1542. Ink and colors on paper, $1'\frac{7}{8}'' \times 8\frac{5}{8}''$. Bodleian Library, Oxford University, Oxford.

Produced for Charles V, the *Codex Mendoza* recounts the history of the Aztec Empire. The frontispiece represents the legendary landing of the eagle on a cactus and the founding of Tenochtitlán in 1325.

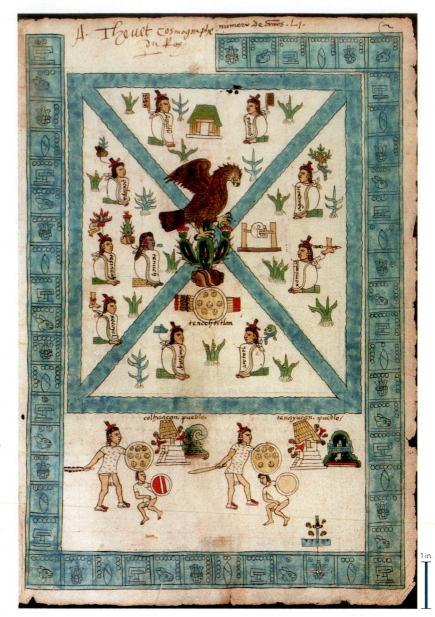

Venice when they saw Tenochtitlán rising from its canals like a radiant vision. Crowded with buildings, plazas, and courtyards, the Aztec capital also boasted a vast and bustling marketplace. In the words of Díaz del Castillo, who accompanied Cortés when he first entered Tenochtitlán on August 13, 1521: "Some of the soldiers among us who had been in many parts of the world, in Constantinople, and all over Italy, and in Rome, said that so large a marketplace and so full of people, and so well regulated and arranged, they had never beheld before."[2]

CODEX MENDOZA After Cortés's defeat of the Aztecs, New Spain was overseen by a Spanish viceroy. The first, Antonio de Mendoza (1495–1552), held that post from 1535 to 1550. Sometime between 1540 and 1542, Mendoza commissioned native scribes and painters to produce a remarkable illustrated manuscript (on European paper) recounting the history of the empire that Cortés had vanquished. The *Codex Mendoza* also included a description of the customs of the people who called themselves Mexica. The intended audience for the book was Charles V of Spain, but the king never saw the manuscript because French pirates intercepted the Spanish ship at sea. Although produced for a Spanish patron, the *Codex Mendoza* closely reflects the format and style of contemporaneous Aztec illustrated manuscripts.

The opening 16 pages of the 71-page codex—a bound volume resembling a modern book, in contrast to earlier books in the form of a scroll (*rotulus*)—summarize the 196-year history of the Mexica through the Spanish conquest of 1521. The frontispiece (FIG. **35-3**), with explanatory labels in Aztec hieroglyphs and Spanish, represents the founding of the capital city of Tenochtitlán in 1325 on an island in Lake Texcoco (Lake of the Moon). There, according to legend, an eagle landed on a prickly pear cactus growing out of a stone, marking the spot where the chief Aztec deity, Huitzilopochtli, instructed the nomadic warriors to settle. The artist depicted the eagle on the cactus (now the central motif on the Mexican flag) at the intersection of two canals, referring to the division of Tenochtitlán into four quarters. At the center of the city—considered the center of the universe—was the sacred precinct that archaeologists call the Templo Mayor (Great Temple, FIG. 35-4), represented in abbreviated form above the eagle as a single temple—one of two surmounting a great pyramid. To the right of the cactus is the rack of skulls of the sacrificial victims whose bodies the Aztec priests threw down the pyramid's steps after cutting out their hearts. The labeled figures seated on reed mats in Tenochtitlán's four quarters are the legendary founders of the city. Below, the painter represented two historical events in stereotypical form. Aztec warriors with clubs and shields conquer two cities, Colhuacán and Tenayuca, shown as temple-pyramids set ablaze. The border contains the hieroglyphs for 51 of the 52 years of one of the recurring cycles of the Aztec calendar system.

HUETEOCALLI In the 1970s, Mexican archaeologists identified the exact location of many of the most important structures within Tenochtitlán's sacred precinct. The excavations in the Zócalo near the city's cathedral (FIG. 24-33) have already uncovered impressive remains of architecture and sculpture, most recently the 12-ton image of Tlaltecuhtli (FIG. 35-1) discussed in the introduction to this chapter. Additional extraordinary artworks are likely to come to light in the years ahead as excavations continue. The principal building of Tenochtitlán's religious center was the Hueteocalli—now called the Templo Mayor (FIG. **35-4**)—a temple-pyramid honoring the Aztec god Huitzilopochtli and the local rain god Tlaloc (see "Aztec Religion," page 1088). Two great staircases originally swept upward from the plaza level to the two sanctuaries at the summit.

The Hueteocalli is a remarkable example of *superimposition*, a common trait in Mesoamerican architecture. The excavated structure, composed of seven shells, indicates how earlier walls nested within later ones. (Today, only two of the inner structures remain. The Spaniards destroyed the later ones in the 16th century.) The sacred precinct also contained the temples of other deities, a ball court (see "The Mesoamerican Ball Game," page 517), a skull rack for the exhibition of the heads of victims killed in sacrificial rites (compare FIG. 35-3, *center right*), and a school for children of the nobility.

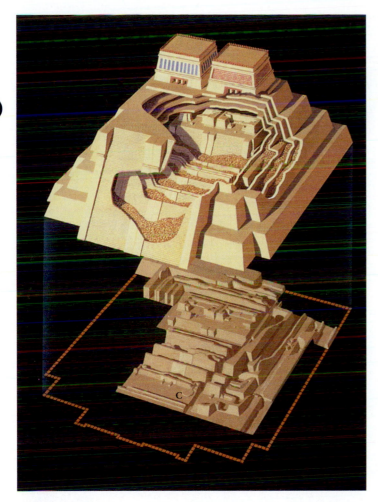

35-4 Reconstruction drawing with cutaway view of various rebuildings of the Great Temple, Tenochtitlán, Mexico City, Mexico, Aztec, ca. 1400–1500. C = Coyolxauhqui disk (FIG. 35-5).

The Great Temple in the Aztec capital encases successive earlier structures. The latest temple honored the gods Huitzilopochtli and Tlaloc, whose sanctuaries were at the top of a stepped pyramid.

swiftly appropriated the best artworks and most talented artists in the conquered territories, bringing both back to Tenochtitlán. Thus craftspeople from other areas, such as the Mixtecs of Oaxaca, may have created much of the exquisite pottery, goldwork, and turquoise mosaics used by the Aztec elite. Gulf Coast artists probably made the life-size terracotta sculptures of eagle warriors found at the Great Temple. Nonetheless, the Aztecs' sculptural style, developed at the height of their power in the later 15th and early 16th centuries, is unique.

COYOLXAUHQUI The Temple of Huitzilopochtli at Tenochtitlán commemorated the god's victory over his sister and 400 brothers, who had plotted to kill their mother, Coatlicue (see "Aztec Religion," page 1088, and FIG. 35-6). The myth signifies the birth of the sun at dawn, a role that Huitzilopochtli sometimes assumed, and the sun's battle with the forces of darkness, the stars and moon. Huitzilopochtli killed or chased away his brothers and dismembered the body of his sister, the moon goddess Coyolxauhqui, at Coatepec Mountain near Tula (symbolized by the pyramid itself). The mythical event is the subject of a huge stone disk (FIG. 35-5), whose discovery in 1971 set off the ongoing archaeological investigations in the Zócalo. The Aztecs placed the relief at the foot of the staircase leading up to one of Huitzilopochtli's earlier temples on the site. (Cortés and his army never saw the disk because it lay within the outermost shell of the Great Temple.) The relief presents the image of the murdered and segmented body of Coyolxauhqui.

AZTEC SCULPTURE Given the Aztecs' almost meteoric rise from obscurity to their role as the dominant culture of Mesoamerica, the quality of the art they sponsored is astonishing. Granted, they

The mythological theme also carried a contemporary political message. The Aztecs sacrificed their conquered enemies at the top of the Great Temple and then hurled their bodies down the temple stairs to land on this stone. The victors thus forced their foes to reenact the horrible fate of the dismembered goddess.

The Coyolxauhqui disk is a superb example of art in the service of state ideology. The unforgettable image of the fragmented goddess proclaimed the power of the Mexica over their enemies and the inevitable fate that must befall their foes when defeated. Marvelously composed, the relief has a kind of dreadful beauty. Within the circular space, the design's carefully balanced, richly detailed components have a slow turning rhythm reminiscent of a revolving galaxy. The carving is in low relief, a smoothly even, flat surface raised from a flat ground. It is the sculptural equivalent of the line and flat tone, the figure and neutral ground, characteristic of Mesoamerican painting.

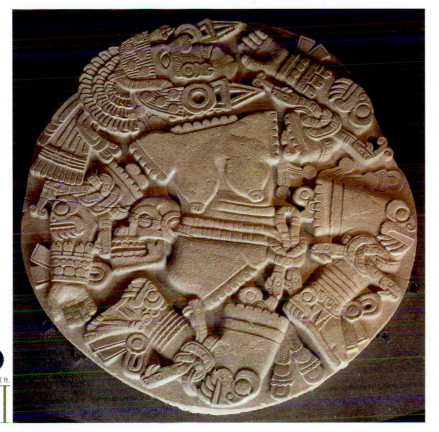

35-5 Coyolxauhqui, from the Great Temple of Tenochtitlán, Mexico City, Mexico, Aztec, ca. 1469. Stone, diameter 10' 10". Museo del Templo Mayor, Mexico City.

The sacrificed foes' bodies that the Aztecs hurled down the Great Temple's stairs landed on this disk, which depicts the segmented body of the moon goddess, Coyolxauhqui, Huitzilopochtli's sister.

1 ft.

RELIGION AND MYTHOLOGY
Aztec Religion

The Aztecs saw their world as a flat disk resting on the back of a monstrous earth deity. Tenochtitlán, their capital, was at its center. Hueteocalli, the Great Temple (FIG. 35-4) at the heart of the city, represented the Hill of Coatepec, the sacred Serpent Mountain and reputed birthplace of Huitzilopochtli, and formed the axis passing up to the heavens and down through the Underworld—a concept with parallels in other cultures (see, for example, "The Stupa," page 435). Each of the four cardinal points had its own god, color, tree, and calendar symbol. The sky consisted of 13 layers, whereas the Underworld had 9. The Aztec Underworld was an unpleasant place where the dead gradually ceased to exist.

Because the Aztecs often adopted the gods of conquered peoples, their pantheon was complex and varied. When the Aztecs arrived in the Valley of Mexico, their own chief god, **Huitzilopochtli** (Hummingbird of the South), a war and sun/fire deity, joined such well-established Mesoamerican gods as the rain and fertility god **Tlaloc** and the feathered serpent **Quetzalcoatl**, who was a benevolent god of life, wind, and learning and culture, as well as the patron of priests. Huitzilopochtli was the son of **Coatlicue** (She of the Serpent Skirt, FIG. 35-6). Coatlicue was also the mother of **Coyolxauhqui** (She of the Golden Bells, FIG. 35-5) and 400 sons, the **Centzon Huitznahua** (Four Hundred Southerners), who, jealous that their mother was pregnant with Huitzilopochtli, banded together to murder her. At the moment of Coatlicue's death, she gave birth to Huitzilopochtli, who slaughtered Coyolxauhqui and most of his brothers, then cut his sister's body into pieces and threw them down Coatepec Mountain.

Other important Aztec deities were **Mictlantecuhtli** (Lord of the Underworld) and **Tlaltecuhtli** (Lord of the Earth, FIG. 35-1), the earth goddess with a masculine name. As the Aztecs went on to conquer much of Mesoamerica, they appropriated the gods of their subjects, such as **Xipe Totec**, a god of spring fertility and patron of gold workers that they imported from the Gulf Coast and Oaxaca. Freestanding images of the various gods—made of stone (FIG. 35-6), terracotta, wood, and even dough (eaten at the end of rituals)—stood in and around their temples. Reliefs (FIGS. 35-1 and 35-5) depicting Aztec deities also adorned the temple complexes.

The Aztecs' ritual cycle was very full, because they celebrated events in two calendars—a sacred calendar of 260 days and a solar calendar of 360 days plus 5 unlucky and nameless days. The Spanish friars of the 16th century noted that the solar calendar dealt largely with agricultural matters. The two Mesoamerican calendars functioned simultaneously, requiring 52 years for the same date to recur in both. A ritual called the New Fire Ceremony commemorated this rare event. The Aztecs broke pots and made new ones for the next period, hid their pregnant women, and extinguished all fires. At midnight on a mountaintop, fire priests took out the heart of a sacrificial victim and with a fire drill renewed the flame in the exposed cavity. Then they set ablaze bundles of sticks representing the 52 years just passed, ensuring that the sun would rise in the morning and another cycle would begin. The Aztecs celebrated the last New Fire Ceremony in 1507.

Thousands of priests and priestesses served in the Aztecs' temples, with the women primarily stationed in shrines dedicated to various earth mother cults. Most Aztec ceremonies involved the

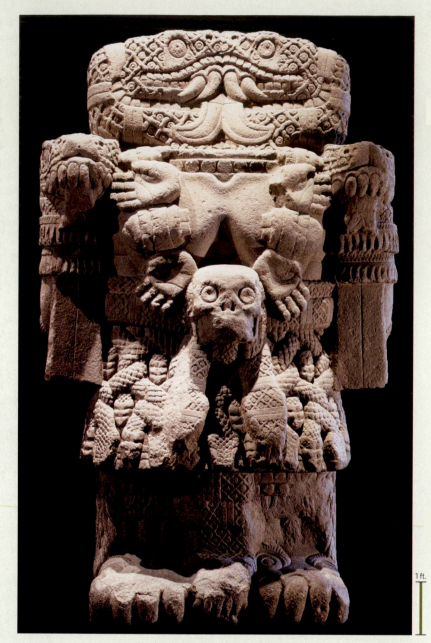

35-6 Coatlicue, from Tenochtitlán, Mexico City, Mexico, Aztec, ca. 1487–1520. Andesite, 11′ 6″ high. Museo Nacional de Antropología, Mexico City.

This colossal statue may have stood near the Great Temple. The beheaded goddess wears a necklace of human hands and hearts. Entwined snakes form her skirt. All her attributes symbolize sacrificial death.

1 ft.

burning of incense. Colorfully attired dancers and actors performed, and musicians played conch-shell trumpets, drums, rattles, rasps, bells, and whistles. Almost every Aztec festival also included human sacrifice. To Tlaloc, the priests offered small children because their tears brought the rains.

Rituals also marked the completion of important religious structures. The dedication of the last major rebuilding of Hueteocalli at Tenochtitlán in 1487, for example, reportedly involved the sacrifice of thousands of captives from recent wars in the Gulf Coast region. Varied offerings have been found within earlier layers of the temple, many representing tribute from subjugated peoples. These include blue-painted stone and ceramic vessels, conch shells, a jaguar skeleton, flint and obsidian knives, and even Mesoamerican "antiques"—carved stone Olmec and Teotihuacán masks made hundreds of years before the Aztec ascendancy.

COATLICUE In addition to relief carving, the Aztecs produced freestanding statuary. The most impressive surviving example is the colossal statue (FIG. 35-6) of the beheaded Coatlicue discovered in 1790 near Mexico City's cathedral. The sculpture's original setting is unknown, but some scholars believe that it was one of a group set up at the Great Temple. The main forms are in high relief, the details executed either in low relief or by incising. The overall aspect is of an enormous blocky mass, its ponderous weight looming over awestruck viewers. From the beheaded goddess's neck writhe two serpents whose heads meet to form a tusked mask. Coatlicue wears a necklace of severed human hands and excised human hearts. The pendant of the necklace is a skull. Entwined snakes form her skirt. From between her legs emerges another serpent, symbolic perhaps of both menses and the male member. Like most Aztec deities, Coatlicue has both masculine and feminine traits. Her hands and feet have great claws. All her attributes symbolize sacrificial death. Yet, in Aztec thought, this mother of the gods combined savagery and tenderness, for out of destruction arose new life, a theme seen earlier at Teotihuacán (FIG. 18-7).

AZTECS AND SPANIARDS Unfortunately, despite the occasional spectacular find, such as the Tlaltecuhtli monolith (FIG. 35-1), most Aztec and Aztec-sponsored art did not survive the Spanish conquest and the subsequent period of evangelization. The conquerors took Aztec gold artifacts back to Spain and melted them down, zealous friars destroyed "idols" and illustrated books, and perishable materials such as textiles and wood largely disappeared. Aztec artisans also fashioned beautifully worked feathered objects and even created mosaic-like images with feathers, an art that they put to service for the Catholic Church for a brief time after the Spanish conquest, creating religious pictures and decorating ecclesiastical clothing with the bright feathers of tropical birds.

The Spanish conquerors found it impossible to reconcile the beauty of the great city of Tenochtitlán with what they regarded as its hideous cults. They admired its splendid buildings ablaze with color, its luxuriant and spacious gardens, its sparkling waterways, its teeming markets, and its grandees resplendent in exotic bird feathers. But when Moctezuma II brought Cortés and his entourage into the shrine of Huitzilopochtli's temple, the newcomers started back in horror, recoiling in disgust at the huge statues clotted with dried blood. Cortés was furious. Denouncing Huitzilopochtli as a devil, he proposed to put a high cross above the pyramid and a statue of the Virgin in the sanctuary to exorcise its evil. This proposal came to symbolize the Spanish conquest of Mesoamerica. The conquistadors venerated the cross and the Virgin, triumphant, in new shrines built on the ruins of the plundered temples of the ancient American gods. In turn, the banner of the Most Catholic King of Spain waved over new atrocities of a European kind.

SOUTH AMERICA

Late Horizon is the name of the period in the Andes Mountains of Peru and Bolivia (MAP 35-2) corresponding to the end of the late Postclassic period in Mesoamerica. The dominant power in the region at that time was the Inka.

Inka

The Inka were a small highland group who established themselves in the Cuzco Valley around 1000. In the 15th century, however, they rapidly extended their power until their empire stretched from

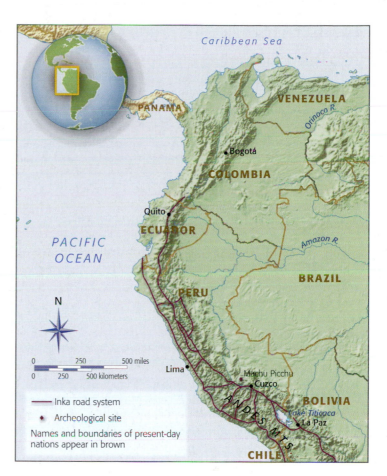

MAP 35-2 Inka sites in Andean South America.

modern Quito, Ecuador, to central Chile. At the time of the Spanish conquest, the Inka Empire, although barely a century old, was the largest in the world. Expertise in mining and metalwork enabled the Inka to accumulate enormous wealth and to amass the fabled troves of gold and silver that the Spanish coveted. An empire as vast and rich as the Inka's required skillful organizational and administrative control. The Inka had rare talent for both.

During the century preceding the Spanish conquest, the Inka population probably reached or exceeded 12 million men, women, and children living as much as 3,000 miles apart. The Inka rulers divided their Andean empire, which they called Tawantinsuyu (Land of the Four Quarters), into sections and subsections, provinces and communities, whose boundaries all converged on, or radiated from, the capital city of Cuzco. To feed their far-flung subjects, the Inka employed expert terracing and irrigation to overcome the difficult problems of agriculture in a mountainous region. They knitted together their extensive territories with networks of highways and bridges, upgrading or constructing more than 20,000 miles of roads, one main highway running through the highlands and another along the coast, with connecting roads linking the two regions. Instead of using wheeled vehicles and horses, they efficiently moved goods on their highways by llama herds. They also established a remarkably swift communication system of relay runners who carried messages the length of the empire. The Inka emperor in Cuzco could get fresh fish from the coast in only three days. Where the terrain was too steep for a paved flat surface, the Inka built stone steps, and their rope bridges crossed canyons high over impassable rivers. They placed small settlements along the roads no more than a day apart, where travelers could rest and obtain supplies for the journey.

PROBLEMS AND SOLUTIONS
Inka Record-Keeping and the Khipu

Unlike the Maya (see page 516), the Inka never developed a writing system, but they were still able to maintain highly accurate accounts using a device known as the *khipu,* which enabled them to record calendar and astronomical information, census and tribute totals, and inventories. For example, the Spaniards noted admiringly that Inka officials always knew exactly how much maize or cloth was in any storeroom in their empire.

Not a book or a tablet, the khipu consisted of a main fiber cord and other knotted threads hanging perpendicularly off it. The color and position of each thread, as well as the kind of knot and its location, signified numbers and categories of things, whether people, llamas, or crops. Studies of khipus have demonstrated that the Inka used the decimal system, were familiar with the concept of zero, and could record numbers up to five digits. The Inka census taker or tax collector could easily roll up and carry the khipu, one of the most lightweight and portable "computers" ever invented.

Illustrated here is a page (FIG. **35-7**) from the *Codex Murúa* showing a kneeling Inka man working with a khipu at the direction of an Inka official. The codex is named after the Spanish missionary Martín de Murúa (ca. 1525–ca. 1618), who volunteered to serve in Peru, where he lived from 1595 until his return to Spain in 1611. Murúa was the author of the indispensable *Historia general del Piru: Origen y descendencia de los Incas* (1611), a chronicle of Inka and colonial history based on firsthand familiarity with the region and its culture. Two versions of his manuscript exist today. The one reproduced here is the later one, dating to 1615–1616, and is in the J. Paul Getty Museum in Los Angeles.

The illustrations in the Getty *Codex Murúa* seem to be the result of a collaboration between a Spanish and an Inka artist, or at least between a Spanish illustrator and a native knowledgeable about Inka customs and costumes. For example, the two main figures on the codex page reproduced here look more European than Inka, and they stand in a plaza whose paving stones recede into the background according to the principles of Renaissance *linear perspective* (compare FIGS. 21-9, 21-41, 22-7, and 22-9).

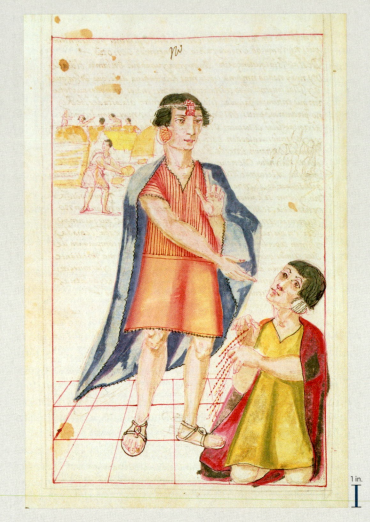

35-7 Inka man working with a khipu, illustration in the *Codex Murúa*, 1615–1616. Ink and colors on vellum, 1' 11¼" × 1' 3¼". J. Paul Getty Museum, Los Angeles.

The illustrations in the *Codex Murúa* provide invaluable evidence of Inka customs. This one shows a kneeling Inka man working with a khipu, a highly sophisticated record-keeping device.

The Inka genius for managing their vast territories is reflected also in their development of a remarkably sophisticated record-keeping system (see "Inka Record-Keeping and the Khipu," above).

The Inka aimed at imposing not only political and economic control but also their art style throughout their realm, subjugating local traditions to those of the empire. Control extended even to clothing, which communicated the social status of the person wearing the garment. The Inka wove bands of small squares of various repeated abstract designs into their fabrics. Scholars believe that the patterns had political meaning, connoting membership in particular social groups. The Inka ruler's tunics displayed a full range of abstract motifs, perhaps to indicate his control over all groups. Those the Inka conquered had to wear their characteristic local dress at all times, a practice reflected in the distinctive and varied clothing of today's indigenous Andean peoples.

MACHU PICCHU The engineering prowess of the Inka matched their talent for governing, and they were gifted architects as well.

Although they also worked with adobe, the Inka were supreme masters of shaping and fitting stone. As a militant people, they selected breathtaking, naturally fortified sites and further strengthened them by building various defensive structures. Inka settlement planning reveals an almost instinctive grasp of the harmonious relationship of architecture to site.

One of the world's most awe-inspiring sights is the terraced Inka settlement near Cuzco called Machu Picchu (FIG. **35-8**), which perches on a ridge between two jagged peaks 9,000 feet above sea level. Invisible from the Urubamba River Valley some 1,600 feet below, Machu Picchu remained unknown to the outside world until Hiram Bingham (1875–1956), an American explorer, discovered it in 1911. In the very heart of the Andes, Machu Picchu is about 50 miles north of Cuzco and, like some of the region's other sites, was the estate of a powerful mid-15th-century Inka ruler, probably the emperor Pachacuti (r. 1438–1472). Though relatively small and insignificant compared to its neighbors (its resident population was a little more than a thousand), Machu Picchu is of great archaeological importance as a rare undisturbed Inka settlement. The accommodation of its architecture to the landscape is so complete that the buildings seem a natural part of the mountain ranges surrounding the site on all sides. The Inka even cut large stones to echo the shapes of the mountain beyond. Terraces spill down the mountainsides and extend even up to the very peak of Huayna Picchu, the great hill just beyond the settlement's main plaza. The Inka carefully sited buildings so that windows and doors framed spectacular views of sacred peaks and facilitated the recording of important astronomical events. Machu Picchu is among the architectural and engineering wonders of the premodern world.

CUZCO In the 16th century, the Spanish conquistadors largely destroyed the Inka capital at Cuzco. Consequently, architectural historians have gleaned most of their information about the city from often-contradictory Spanish sources rather than from archaeology. Some accounts describe Cuzco's plan as having the shape of a puma—a symbol of Inka royal power—with a great shrine-fortress on a hill above the city representing its head and the southeastern convergence of two rivers forming its tail. Cuzco residents still refer to the river area as "the puma's tail." A great plaza, still the hub of the modern city, is nestled below the animal's stomach.

One Inka building at Cuzco that survives in small part is the Temple of the Sun (FIG. **35-9**), built of *ashlar masonry* (stone blocks fit together without mortar), an ancient construction technique that the Inka had mastered. Cuzco masons laid the stones with perfectly joined faces. Remarkably, the Inka produced the close joints of their masonry by abrasion alone, grinding the surfaces to a perfect fit. The stonemasons usually laid the blocks in regular horizontal *courses* (FIG. 35-9, *right*). Inka builders were so skilled that they could fashion walls with

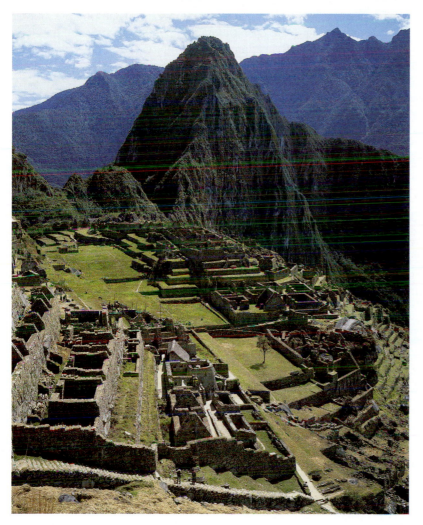

35-8 Machu Picchu (looking northwest), Peru, Inka, 15th century.

Machu Picchu was probably the estate of the Inka emperor Pachacuti. Large upright stones echo the contours of sacred peaks. Precisely placed windows and doors facilitated astronomical observations.

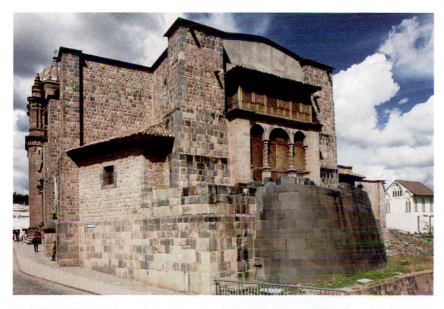
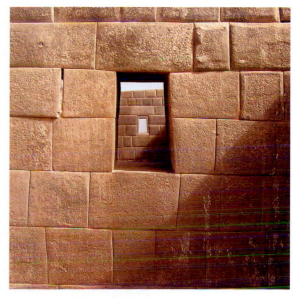

35-9 Remains of the Temple of the Sun (surmounted by the church of Santo Domingo), Cuzco, Peru, Inka, 15th century. General view of the exterior (*left*; looking southeast) and detail of the interior masonry (*right*).

Perfectly constructed ashlar masonry walls are all that remain of the Temple of the Sun, the most important shrine in the Inka capital. Gold, silver, and emeralds covered the temple's interior walls.

curved surfaces (FIG. 35-9, *left*), their planes as level and continuous as if they were a single form. The surviving walls of the Temple of the Sun are a prime example of this single-form effect. On the exterior, for example, the stones, precisely fitted and polished, form a curving semiparabola. The Inka set the ashlar blocks for flexibility during earthquakes, allowing for a temporary dislocation of the courses, which then return to their original position.

Known to the Spanish as Coricancha (Golden Enclosure), the Temple of the Sun was the most magnificent of all Inka shrines. The 16th-century Spanish chroniclers wrote in awe of Coricancha's splendor, its interior veneered with sheets of gold, silver, and emeralds and housing life-size statues of silver and gold. Nothing survives, but some preserved Inka statuettes (FIG. **35-9A**) may suggest the appearance of the lost large-scale statues. Built on the site of the home of Manco Capac, son of the sun god and founder of the Inka dynasty, the Temple of the Sun housed mummies of some of the early rulers. Dedicated to the worship of several Inka deities, including the creator god Viracocha and the gods of the sun, moon, stars, and the elements, the temple was the center point of a network of radiating sight lines leading to some 350 shrines, which had both calendar and astronomical significance.

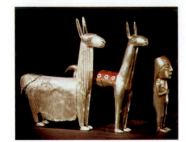

35-9A Inka llama, alpaca, and woman, ca. 1475–1532.

END OF THE INKA Smallpox spreading south from Spanish-occupied Mesoamerica killed the last Inka emperor and his heir before they ever laid eyes on a Spaniard. The deaths of the emperor and his named successor unleashed a struggle among competing elite families and aided the Europeans in their conquest. In 1532, Francisco Pizarro (1471–1541), the Spanish explorer of the Andes, ambushed the would-be emperor Atawalpa on his way to be crowned at Cuzco after vanquishing his rival half-brother. Although Atawalpa paid a huge ransom of gold and silver, the Spaniards killed him and took control of his vast domain, only a decade after

Cortés had defeated the Aztecs in Mexico. Following the murder of Atawalpa, the Spanish erected the church of Santo Domingo (FIG. 35-9, *left*), in an imported European style, on what remained of the Golden Enclosure. A curved section of Inka wall serves to this day as the foundation for Santo Domingo's *apse*. A violent earthquake in 1950 seriously damaged the colonial building, but the Peruvians rebuilt the church. The two contrasting structures remain standing one atop the other. The Coricancha is therefore of more than architectural and archaeological interest. It is a symbol of the Spanish conquest of the Americas and serves as a composite monument to it.

NORTH AMERICA

In North America during the centuries preceding the arrival of Europeans, power was much more widely dispersed and the native art and architecture more varied than in Mesoamerica and Andean South America. Three major regions of the United States and Canada are of special interest: the American Southwest, Alaska and the Northwest Coast (British Columbia and the northwestern United States from Washington to northern California), and the Great Plains (MAP 35-3).

Southwest

The dominant culture of the American Southwest between 1300 and 1500 was the Ancestral Puebloan (formerly called the Anasazi), the builders of great architectural complexes such as Chaco Canyon (FIG. 18-34) and Cliff Palace (FIG. 18-35). The spiritual center of Puebloan life (*pueblo* is Spanish for "urban settlement") was the *kiva,* or male council house, usually decorated with elaborate mural paintings representing deities associated with agricultural fertility. According to their descendants, the present-day Hopi and Zuni, the detail of the Kuaua Pueblo mural shown here (FIG. 35-10) depicts a "lightning man" on the left side. Fish and eagle images (associated with rain) appear on the right side. Seeds, a lightning bolt, and a rainbow stream from the eagle's mouth. All these figures are associated with the fertility of the earth and the life-giving properties of

35-10 Detail of a kiva mural from Kuaua Pueblo (Coronado State Monument), New Mexico, Ancestral Puebloan, late 15th to early 16th century. Interior of the kiva, 18' × 18'. Museum of New Mexico, Santa Fe.

The kiva, or male council house, was the spiritual center of Puebloan life. Kivas were decorated with mural paintings associated with agricultural fertility. This one depicts a lightning man, fish, birds, and seeds.

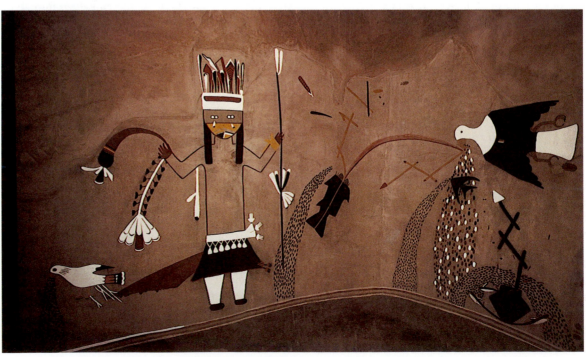

1 ft.

Every thumbnail illustration has a corresponding full-size Bonus Image and accompanying Bonus Essay online.

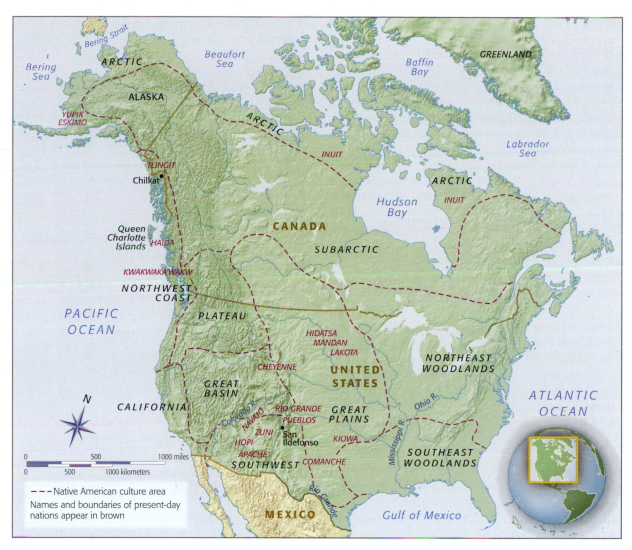

MAP 35-3 Later Native American sites in North America.

the seasonal rains, a constant preoccupation of Southwest farmers. The Ancestral Puebloan painter depicted the figures with great economy, using thick black lines, dots, and a restricted palette of black, brown, yellow, and white. The frontal figure of the lightning man seen against a neutral ground makes an immediate visual impact.

NAVAJO PAINTING When the first Europeans came into contact with the ancient peoples of the Southwest, they called them "Pueblo Indians." The successors of the Ancestral Puebloan and other Southwest groups, the Pueblo Indians include linguistically diverse but culturally similar peoples such as the Hopi of northern Arizona and the Rio Grande Pueblos of New Mexico. Living among them are the descendants of nomadic hunters who arrived in the Southwest from their homelands in northwestern Canada sometime between 1200 and 1500. These are the Apache and Navajo, who, although culturally quite distinct from the original inhabitants of the Southwest, adopted many features of Pueblo life.

Among these borrowed elements is *sand painting*, which the Navajo learned from the Pueblos but transformed into an extraordinarily complex ritual art form. The temporary sand paintings (also known as *dry paintings*), constructed to the accompaniment of prayers and chants, are an essential part of ceremonies for curing disease. In the healing ceremony, the patient sits in the painting's center to absorb the life-giving powers of the gods and their

representations. The Navajo perform similar rites to assure success in hunting and to promote fertility in human beings and nature alike. The artists who supervise the making of these complex images are religious leaders or "medicine men" (rarely women), thought to have direct contact with the powers of the supernatural world, which they use to help both individuals and the community. Because of the sacred nature of the sand paintings, the Navajo do not permit their reproduction.

The natural materials used—sand, varicolored powdered stones, corn pollen, and charcoal—play a symbolic role reflecting the Native Americans' preoccupation with the forces of nature. The paintings depict the gods and mythological heroes whose help the Navajo seek. As part of the ritual, the participants destroy the sand paintings, so no models exist. However, the traditional prototypes, passed on from artist to artist but never publicly displayed, must be adhered to as closely as possible. Mistakes can render the ceremony ineffective. Navajo dry painting is therefore highly stylized. Simple curves, straight lines, right angles, and serial repetition characterize most sand paintings.

NAVAJO TEXTILES By the mid-17th century, the Navajo had learned how to weave from their Hopi and other Pueblo neighbors, quickly adapting to new materials such as sheep's wool and synthetic dyes introduced by Spanish settlers and, later, by Anglo-Americans.

ART AND SOCIETY
Gender Roles in Native American Art

Although both Native American women and men have created art objects for centuries, they have traditionally worked in different media or at different tasks. Among the Navajo, for example, weavers tend to be women, whereas among the neighboring Hopi, the men weave. According to Navajo myth, long ago Spider Woman's husband built her a loom for weaving. In turn, she taught Changing Woman, who in turn taught Navajo women how to spin and weave so that they might have clothing to wear. Today, young girls learn from their mothers how to work the loom (FIG. 35-11), just as Changing Woman instructed their ancestors, passing along the techniques and designs from one generation to the next.

Among the Pueblos, pottery making normally has been the domain of women. The most famous Pueblo ceramic artist is MARÍA MONTOYA MARTÍNEZ (1887–1980), of San Ildefonso Pueblo in New Mexico. María coiled, slipped, and burnished her pots, but in response to heavy demand for her wares, her husband, Julian, painted the designs. Although they worked in many styles, some based on prehistoric ceramics, around 1918 the couple invented the black-on-black ware (FIG. 35-13) that made María, and indeed the whole pueblo, famous. The elegant shapes of the pots, as well as the traditional but abstract designs, had affinities with the contemporaneous Art Deco style in architecture (FIG. 29-47) and interior design, and collectors avidly sought (and continue to seek) them. When nonnative buyers suggested that she sign her pots to increase their value, María obliged, but in the communal spirit typical of the Pueblos, she also signed her neighbors' names so that they might share in her good fortune. María died in 1980, but her descendants continue to garner awards as outstanding potters.

Women also produced the elaborately decorated animal-skin and, later, the trade-cloth clothing of the Woodlands and Plains, using moose hair, dyed porcupine quills, and imported beads. Among the Cheyenne, quillworking was a sacred art, and young women worked at learning both proper ritual and correct techniques to obtain membership in the prestigious quillworkers' guild. Women gained the same honor and dignity from creating finely worked utilitarian objects that men earned from warfare. Both women and men painted on *tipis* (Native American tent dwellings) and clothing (FIGS. 35-18A, 35-19, and 35-20), with women creating abstract designs (FIG. 35-19) and men working in a more realistic narrative style, often celebrating their exploits in war (FIG. 35-18A) or recording the cultural changes that the transfer to reservations brought about.

In the far north, women tended to work with soft materials such as animal skins, whereas men were sculptors of wood masks (FIG. 35-15) among the Alaskan Yupik Eskimos and of walrus ivory pieces (FIG. 18-29) throughout the Arctic. The introduction of printmaking, a foreign medium with no established gender associations, to

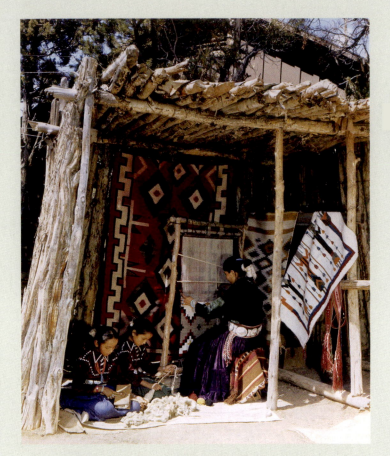

35-11 Photograph taken on January 9, 1948, in Mesa Verde National Park (FIG. 18-35) of a Navajo mother weaving a blanket on a loom while her daughters assist her by preparing wool for the loom.

Navajo textiles are famous throughout the world. Unlike the Hopi, Navajo weavers are traditionally women, who teach their daughters how to work the loom, passing down their expertise to the next generation.

some Canadian Inuit communities in the 1950s provided both native women and men with a new creative outlet. Printmaking became an important source of economic independence vital to these isolated and once-impoverished settlements. Today, both Inuit women and men make prints, but men still dominate in carving stone sculpture, another new medium also produced for and sold to outsiders.

Throughout North America, indigenous artists continue to work in traditional media, such as ceramics, beadwork, and basketry, marketing their wares through museum shops, galleries, regional art fairs, and, most recently, the Internet. Many also obtain degrees in art and express themselves in European media such as oil painting, often using their art to comment on political, social, and economic issues of central concern to Native Americans (FIG. 31-1).

They rapidly transformed their wearing blankets into handsome rugs in response to the new market created by the arrival of the railroad and early tourists in the 1880s. Other tribes, including those of the Great Plains, also purchased Navajo textiles, which became famous for their quality (the thread count in a typical Navajo rug is extraordinarily high) as well as the sophistication of their designs. Navajo rugs often incorporate vivid abstract motifs known as "eye

dazzlers" and patterns derived from sand paintings (altered to preserve the sacred quality of the impermanent ritual images).

Navajo weaving is a highly sophisticated art form that still flourishes today, practiced almost exclusively by women, who often enlist their daughters in their work (FIG. 35-11) and train them to be weavers themselves (see "Gender Roles in Native American Art," above).

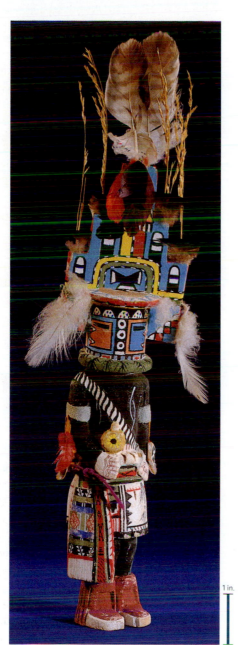

35-12 Отто Pentewa, Katsina figurine, New Oraibi, Arizona, Hopi, carved before 1959. Cottonwood root and feathers, 1' high. Arizona State Museum, University of Arizona, Tucson.

Katsinas are benevolent spirits living in mountains and water sources. This Hopi katsina represents a rain-bringing deity wearing a mask with geometric patterns symbolic of water and agricultural fertility.

HOPI KATSINAS Another art form from the Southwest, the *katsina* figurine, also has deep roots in the area. Katsinas are benevolent supernatural spirits personifying ancestors and natural elements living in mountains and water sources. Humans join their world after death. Among contemporary Pueblo groups, masked dancers ritually impersonate katsinas during yearly festivals dedicated to rain, fertility, and good hunting. To educate young girls in ritual lore, the Hopi traditionally give them miniature representations of the masked dancers. The Hopi katsina illustrated here (FIG. 35-12), carved in cottonwood root with added feathers, is the work of Отто Pentewa (d. 1963). It represents a rain-bringing deity who wears a mask painted in geometric patterns symbolic of water and agricultural fertility. Topping the mask are a stepped shape signifying thunderclouds, and feathers to carry the Hopis' airborne prayers. The origins of the katsina figurines have been lost in time (they even may have developed from carved saints that the Spanish introduced during the colonial period). However, the cult is probably very ancient.

NAGPRA Otto Pentewa's katsina, like countless other Native American objects, is an artwork that also has sacred significance. Often, Native Americans do not permit anyone to photograph their sacred objects. Indeed, the study of Native American art presents special problems for art historians, especially since the passage in November 1990 of the Native American Graves Protection and Repatriation Act (NAGPRA), which, among other provisions, requires any museum receiving federal funding to repatriate sacred Native American objects when requested by a descendant. Native

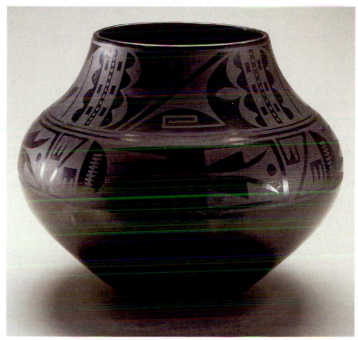

35-13 María Montoya Martínez, jar, San Ildefonso Pueblo, New Mexico, ca. 1939. Blackware, $11\frac{1}{8}$" × 1' 1". National Museum of Women in the Arts, Washington, D.C. (gift of Wallace and Wilhelmina Hollachy).

Pottery is traditionally a Native American woman's art form. María Montoya Martínez won renown for her black-on-black vessels of striking shapes with matte designs on highly polished surfaces.

views about what is sacred and what should not be illustrated in textbooks may lead to the removal in future editions of *Art through the Ages* of some works reproduced in the 15th and earlier editions.

PUEBLO POTTERY The Southwest has also provided the finest examples of North American pottery. Originally producing utilitarian forms, Southwest potters traditionally work without the potter's wheel and instead coil shapes of clay that they then slip, polish, and fire. Decorative motifs, often abstract and conventionalized, deal largely with forces of nature—clouds, wind, and rain. The efforts of San Ildefonso Pueblo potter María Montoya Martínez and her husband, Julian Martínez (see "Gender Roles," page 1094), in the early decades of the 20th century revived old techniques to produce forms of striking shape, proportion, and texture. Her black-on-black pieces (FIG. 35-13) feature matte designs on highly polished surfaces specially fired in an oxygen-poor atmosphere.

Northwest Coast and Alaska

The Native Americans of the coasts and islands of northern Washington state, the province of British Columbia in Canada, and southern Alaska have long enjoyed a rich and reliable environment. Traditionally, they fished, hunted sea mammals and game, gathered edible plants, and made their homes, utensils, ritual objects, and even clothing from the region's great cedar forests. Among the numerous groups who make up the Northwest Coast area are the Kwakwaka'wakw of southern British Columbia; the Haida, who live on the Queen Charlotte Islands off the coast of the province; and the Tlingit of southern Alaska (MAP 35-3).

ART AND SOCIETY
Kwakwaka'wakw Transformation Masks

Like so many objects produced by Native Americans through the centuries, the masks fashioned by Northwest Coast artists were not created as display pieces but for use in sacred rituals, especially those concerned with healing. Kwakwaka'wakw religious specialists, for example, wore masks in dramatic public performances during the winter ceremonial season. The animals and mythological creatures represented in masks and a host of other carvings derive from the Northwest Coast's rich oral tradition and celebrate the mythological origins and inherited privileges of high-ranking families, who trace their lineage to mythic animals or composite human-animals.

The artist who made the Kwakwaka'wakw mask illustrated here (FIG. 35-14) meant it to be seen in flickering firelight, and ingeniously constructed it to open and close rapidly when the wearer manipulated hidden strings. He could thus magically transform himself from human to eagle and back again as he danced. The transformation theme, in myriad forms, is a central aspect of the art and religion of the Americas.

The Kwakwaka'wakw mask's human aspect also owes its dramatic character to the exaggeration and distortion of facial parts—such as the hooked beaklike nose and flat, flaring nostrils—and to the deeply undercut curvilinear depressions, which form strong shadows. In contrast to the carved human face, but painted in the same colors, is the two-dimensional abstract image of the eagle painted on the inside of the outer mask.

35-14 Eagle transformation mask, closed (*top*) and open (*bottom*) views, Alert Bay, Canada, Kwakwaka'wakw, late 19th century. Wood, feathers, and string, 1' 10" × 11". American Museum of Natural History, New York.

The wearer of this Kwakwaka'wakw mask could open and close it rapidly by manipulating hidden strings, magically transforming himself from human to eagle and back again as he danced.

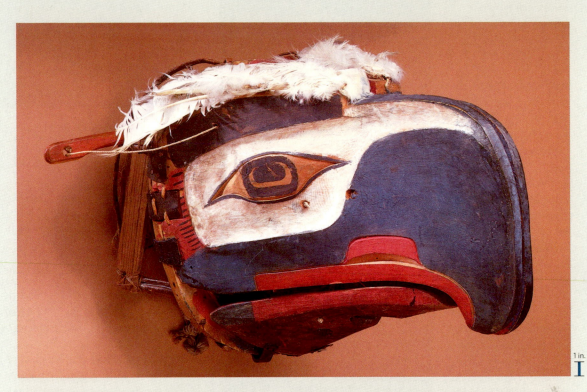

1 in.

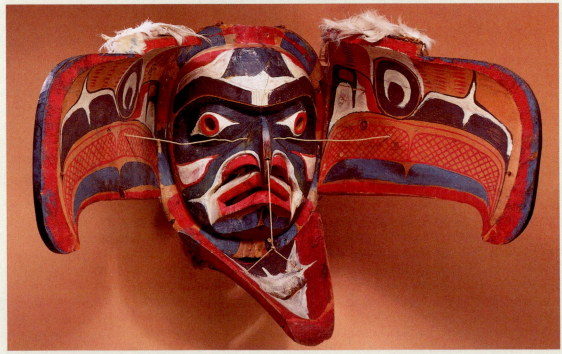

1 in.

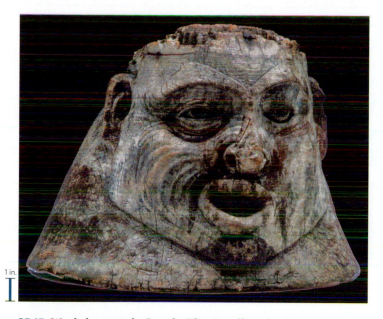

35-15 War helmet mask, Canada, Tlingit, collected 1888–1893. Wood, 1' high. American Museum of Natural History, New York.

This war helmet mask may be a naturalistic portrait of a Tlingit warrior or a representation of a supernatural being. The carver intended the face's grimacing expression to intimidate enemies.

NORTHWEST MASKS In the Northwest, a class of professional artists developed, in contrast to the more typical Native American pattern, in which artists pursued a variety of activities and produced art only part of the time. Working in a highly formalized, subtle style, Northwest Coast artists have produced a wide variety of art objects for centuries: masks, *totem poles* (carved tree trunks featuring a vertical row of stylized heads; FIG. 35-16), rattles, chests, bowls, clothing, charms, and decorated houses and canoes. Some artistic traditions originated as early as 500 BCE, although others developed only after the arrival of Europeans in North America. Of special interest are the masks of the Kwakwaka'wakw (formerly

transliterated as Kwakiutl; see "Kwakwaka'wakw Transformation Masks," page 1096, and FIG. **35-14**) and the Tlingit.

Unlike the highly stylized Kwakwaka'wakw masks, those of the Tlingit are more naturalistic. The carved-wood Tlingit war helmet (FIG. **35-15**) shown here may be a portrait, but it also might represent a supernatural being whose powers enhance the wearer's strength. In either case, the artist surely created its grimacing expression to intimidate the enemy.

HAIDA TOTEM POLES Although Northwest Coast arts have a spiritual dimension, they are often more important as expressions of social status. For example, the Haida set up poles in front of their houses that display totemic emblems of clan groups—a striking expression of the Haida interest in prestige and family history. Totem poles emerged as a major art form about 300 years ago. The examples in FIG. **35-16** date to the 19th century. They stand today in a reconstructed Haida village that BILL REID (1920–1998, Haida) and his assistant DOUG CRANMER (1927–2006, Namgis) completed in 1962. Reid was a master woodcarver who also made monumental sculptures featuring Haida themes—for example, *The Raven and the First Men* (FIG. **35-16A**). Each of the superimposed forms carved on the Haida totem poles represents a crest, an animal, or a supernat-

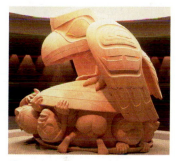

35-16A REID, *The Raven and the First Men*, 1978–1980.

ural being who figures in the clan's origin story. Additional crests could also be obtained through marriage and trade. The Haida so jealously guarded the right to own and display crests that even warfare could break out over the disputed ownership of a valued crest. In the poles shown, the crests represented include an upsidedown dogfish (a small shark), an eagle with a downturned beak, and a killer whale with a crouching human between its snout and its upturned tail flukes. During the 19th century, the Haida erected

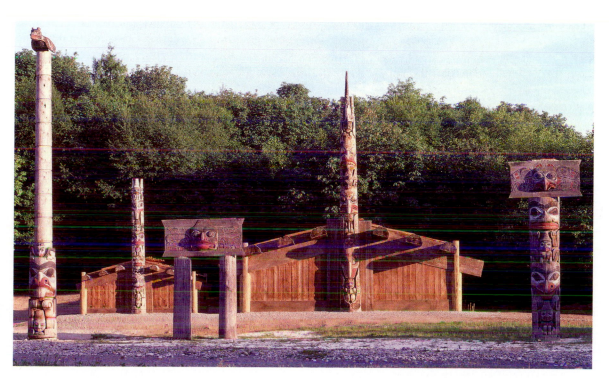

35-16 BILL REID (Haida), assisted by DOUG CRANMER (Namgis), re-creation of a 19th-century Haida village with totem poles, Queen Charlotte Island, Canada, 1962.

Each of the superimposed forms carved on Haida totem poles represents a crest, an animal, or a supernatural being who figures in the clan's origin story. Some Haida poles are 60 feet tall.

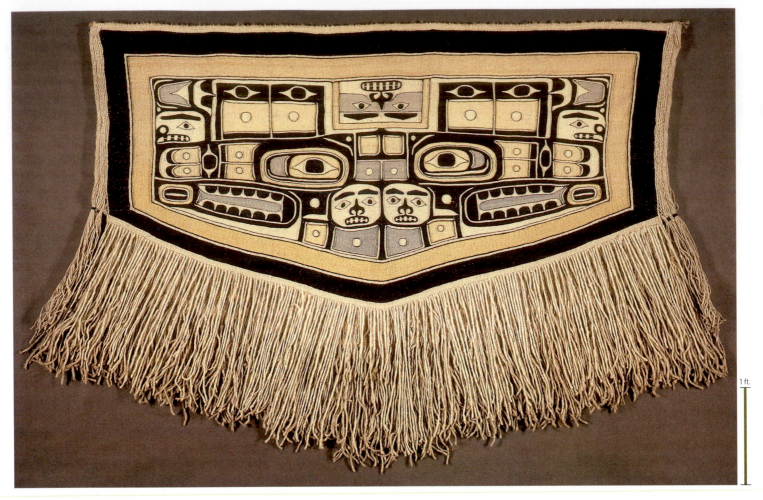

1 ft.

35-17 Chilkat blanket with stylized animal motifs, Canada, Tlingit, early 20th century. Mountain goat wool and cedar bark, 6' × 2' 11". Southwest Museum of the American Indian, Los Angeles.

Chilkat blankets were collaborations between male designers and female weavers. Decorated with animal and abstract motifs, they were worn over the shoulder and were items of ceremonial dress.

more poles and made them larger in response to greater competitiveness and the availability of metal tools. The artists carved poles up to 60 feet tall from the trunks of single cedar trees.

CHILKAT BLANKETS Another characteristic Northwest Coast art form is the Chilkat blanket (FIG. **35-17**), named for an Alaskan Tlingit village. Male designers provided the templates for these blankets in the form of wood pattern boards for female weavers. Woven of shredded cedar bark and mountain goat wool suspended from a single bar instead of on a loom, the Tlingit blankets took at least six months to complete. These blankets, which served as robes worn over the shoulders, became widespread prestige items of ceremonial dress during the 19th century. They display several characteristics of the Northwest Coast style recurrent in all media: symmetry and rhythmic repetition, schematic abstraction of animal motifs (a bear in the illustrated robe), eye designs, a regularly swelling and thinning line, and a tendency to round off corners.

YUPIK MASKS Farther north, the 19th-century Yupik Eskimos living around the Bering Strait of Alaska had a highly developed ceremonial life focused on game animals, particularly seal. Their religious specialists wore highly imaginative masks with moving parts. The Yupik generally made these masks for single occasions and then abandoned them. Consequently, many masks have ended up in museums and private collections. The example shown here (FIG. **35-18**) represents the spirit of the north wind, its face surrounded by a hoop signifying the universe, its voice mimicked by the rattling appendages. The paired human hands commonly found on these masks refer to the wearer's power to attract animals for hunting. The painted white spots represent snowflakes.

The devastating effects of 19th-century epidemics, coupled with government and missionary repression of Native American ritual and social activities, threatened to wipe out the traditional arts of the Northwest Coast and the Eskimos. The past half century, however, has brought an impressive revival of traditional art forms (some created for collectors and the tourist trade) as well as the development of new ones, such as printmaking. In recent years, for example, Canadian Eskimos, known as the Inuit, have set up cooperatives to produce and market stone carvings and prints. With these new media, artists generally depict themes from the rapidly vanishing, traditional Inuit way of life.

Great Plains

After colonial governments disrupted settled indigenous communities on the East Coast and the Europeans introduced the horse to North America, a new mobile Native American culture flourished on the Great Plains for a short time. Great Plains artists worked in

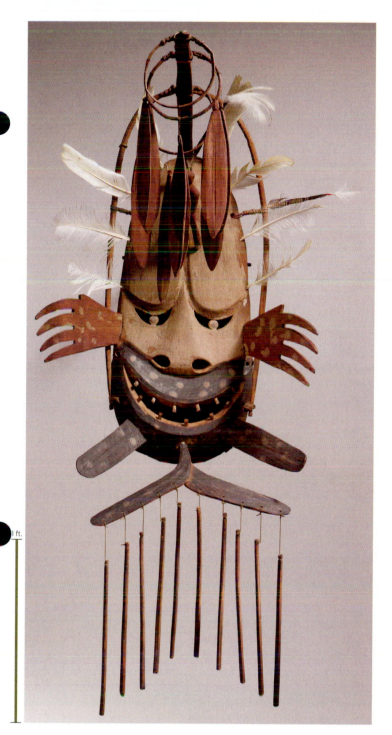

35-18 North Wind mask, Alaska, Yupik Eskimo, early 20th century. Wood and feathers, 3' 9" high. Metropolitan Museum of Art, New York (Michael C. Rockefeller Memorial Collection, gift of Nelson Rockefeller).

This Yupik mask represents the spirit of the north wind, its face surrounded by a hoop signifying the universe, its voice mimicked by the rattling appendages. The white spots represent snowflakes.

for example, on a Mandan buffalo-hide robe; FIG. **35-18A**), sometimes in styles adapted from those of visiting European artists.

HIDATSA REGALIA During the 18th and 19th centuries, most Plains peoples abandoned their permanent agricultural communities and adapted a nomadic lifestyle. Consequently, they focused their aesthetic

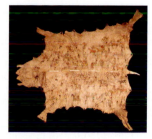

35-18A Mandan buffalo-hide robe, ca. 1800.

attention largely on their clothing and bodies and on other portable objects, such as shields, clubs, pipes, tomahawks, and various containers. Transient but important Plains art forms can sometimes be found in the paintings and drawings of American and European artists, who recorded Native American costumes as anthropological curiosities, relics of a soon-to-be-lost era as the descendants of Europeans pursued their Manifest Destiny to take over the continent (see page 814). KARL BODMER (1809–1893) of Switzerland, for example, portrayed the personal decoration of Pehriska-Ruhpa (Two Ravens), a Hidatsa warrior, in an 1833 watercolor (FIG. **35-19**). The painting depicts his pipe, painted buffalo-hide robe, bear-claw necklace, and feather decorations, all symbolic of his affiliations and

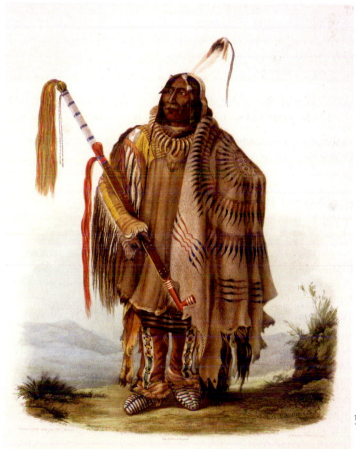

35-19 KARL BODMER, *Hidatsa Warrior Pehriska-Ruhpa* (*Two Ravens*), 1833. Engraving by PAUL LEGRAND after the original watercolor in the Joslyn Art Museum, Omaha, 1' 3$\frac{7}{8}$" × 11$\frac{1}{2}$". Engraving: Buffalo Bill Historical Center, Cody.

The personal regalia of a Hidatsa warrior included his pipe, painted buffalo-hide robe, bear-claw necklace, and feather decorations, all symbols of his affiliations and military accomplishments.

materials and styles quite different from those of the Northwest Coast and Eskimo/Inuit peoples. Much artistic energy went into the decoration of leather garments, pouches, and horse trappings, first with compactly sewn quill designs and later with beadwork patterns. Artists painted tipis, tipi linings, and buffalo-skin robes with geometric and stiff figural designs prior to about 1800. Later, they gradually introduced naturalistic scenes, often of war exploits (as,

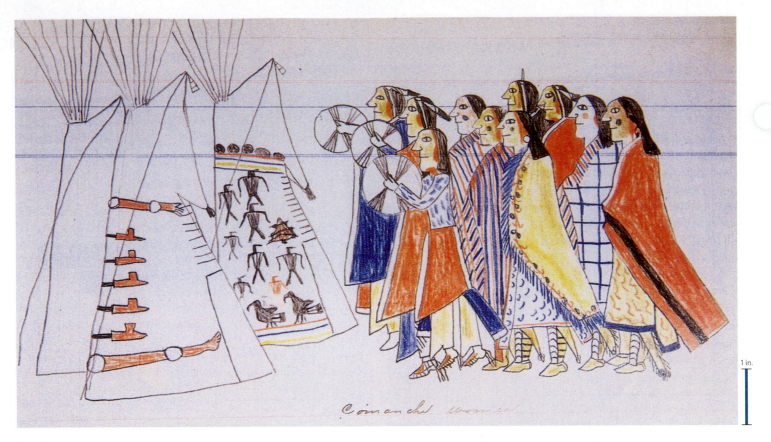

35-20 Honoring song at painted tipi, in Julian Scott Ledger, Kiowa, 1880. Pencil, ink, and colored pencil, $7\frac{1}{2}$" × 1'. Charles and Valerie Diker Collection.

During the reservation period, some Plains artists recorded their traditional lifestyle in ledger books. This one depicts men and women dancing an honoring song in front of three painted tipis.

military accomplishments. These items represent his life story—a composite artistic statement in several media immediately intelligible to other Native Americans. The concentric circle design over his left shoulder, for example, is an abstract rendering of an eagle-feather war bonnet.

Plains peoples also made shields and shield covers that were both artworks and symbols of power. Shield paintings often derived from personal religious visions. The owners believed that the symbolism, the pigments themselves, and added materials, such as feathers, provided them with magical protection and supernatural power.

LEDGER PAINTINGS Plains warriors battled incursions into their territory throughout the 19th century. The pursuit of Plains natives culminated in the 1890 slaughter of Lakota participants who had gathered for a ritual known as the Ghost Dance at Wounded Knee Creek, South Dakota. Indeed, from the 1830s on, U.S. troops forcibly removed Native Americans from their homelands and resettled them in other parts of the country. Toward the end of the century, governments confined them to reservations in both the United States and Canada.

During the reservation period, some Plains arts continued to flourish, notably beadwork (produced by women) and painting in ledger books (a men's art form). Traders, the army, and Indian agents had for years provided Plains peoples with pencils and new or discarded ledger books. They, in turn, used them to draw their personal exploits for themselves or for interested Anglo buyers. Sometimes warriors carried them into battle, where U.S. Army opponents retook the ledgers. After confinement to reservations,

Plains artists began to record not only their heroic past and vanished lifestyle but also their reactions to their new surroundings, frequently in a place far from home. These images, often poignant and sometimes humorous, are important native documents of a time of great turmoil and change.

In the example shown here (FIG. **35-20**), the work of an unknown Kiowa artist, a group of men and women, possibly Comanches (allies of the Kiowa), appear to dance an honoring song before three tipis, the left forward one painted with red stone pipes and a dismembered leg and arm. The women (in the middle and rear rows) wear the mixture of clothing typical of the late 19th century among the Plains Indians—traditional high leather moccasins, dresses made from calico trade cloth, and (at the far right) a red Hudson's Bay blanket with a black stripe. Although the Plains peoples no longer paint ledger books, beadwork has never completely died out. The ancient art of creating quilled, beaded, and painted clothing has evolved into the elaborate costumes displayed today at competitive dances called *powwows*.

Whether secular and decorative or spiritual and highly symbolic, the diverse styles and forms of Native American art in the United States and Canada have traditionally reflected the indigenous peoples' reliance on and reverence toward the environment they considered it their privilege to inhabit. Today, some Native American artists work in media and styles indistinguishable from those of other contemporary artists worldwide, but in the work of others—for example, Jaune Quick-to-See Smith (FIG. 31-1)—the Native American experience remains central to their artistic identity.

NATIVE AMERICAN CULTURES, 1300 TO 1980

Mesoamerica

- When the first Europeans arrived in the New World, they encountered native peoples with sophisticated civilizations and a long history of art production, including illustrated books. The few surviving preconquest books, the *Borgia Codex* among them, provide precious insight into Mesoamerican rituals, science, mythology, and painting style.

- The Aztec Empire was the dominant power in Mesoamerica in the centuries before Hernán Cortés overthrew it. Tenochtitlán (Mexico City), the Aztec capital with a population of more than 150,000, was a magnificent island city laid out on a grid plan.

- The Great Temple at Tenochtitlán was a towering pyramid encasing several earlier pyramids. Dedicated to the worship of Huitzilopochtli and Tlaloc, it was also the place where the Aztecs sacrificed their enemies and threw their battered bodies down the stone staircase to land on a huge disk with a representation in relief of the dismembered body of the goddess Coyolxauhqui.

- In addition to relief carving, Aztec sculptors produced stone statues, some of colossal size—for example, the 11′ 6″ image from Tenochtitlán of the beheaded Coatlicue, who wears a necklace of severed human hands and excised human hearts.

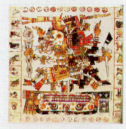

Borgia Codex, ca. 1400–1500

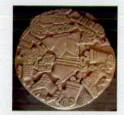

Coyolxauhqui, ca. 1469

South America

- In the 15th century, the Inka Empire, with its capital at Cuzco in present-day Peru, extended from Ecuador to Chile. The Inka were superb engineers and constructed 20,000 miles of roads to exert control over their vast empire. They kept track of inventories, census and tribute totals, and astronomical information using a "computer of strings" called a khipu.

- Master architects, the Inka were experts in ashlar masonry construction. The most impressive preserved Inka site is Machu Picchu, probably the estate of the Inka emperor Pachacuti. Stone terraces spill down the mountainsides, and the buildings have windows and doors designed to frame views of sacred peaks and facilitate the recording of important astronomical events.

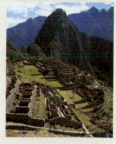

Machu Picchu, 15th century

North America

- In North America, power was much more widely dispersed and the native art and architecture more varied than in Mesoamerica and Andean South America.

- In the American Southwest, the Ancestral Puebloans built urban settlements (pueblos) and decorated their council houses (kivas) with mural paintings. The Navajo produced magnificent textiles and created temporary sand paintings as part of complex rituals. The Hopi carved katsina figurines representing benevolent supernatural spirits. The Pueblo Indian pottery produced by artists such as María Montoya Martínez is among the finest in the world.

- On the Northwest Coast, masks played an important role in religious rituals. Some examples can open and close rapidly so that the wearer can magically transform himself from human to animal and back again. Haida totem poles sometimes reach 60 feet in height and are carved with superimposed forms representing clan crests, animals, and supernatural beings. Chilkat blankets are the result of a fruitful collaboration between male designers and female weavers.

- The peoples of the Great Plains won renown for their magnificent painted buffalo-hide robes, bead necklaces, feather headdresses, and shields. Native American art lived on even after the U.S. government forcibly removed the Plains peoples to reservations. Painted ledger books record their vanished lifestyle, but the production of fine crafts continues to the present day.

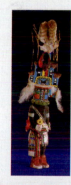

Pentewa, katsina figurine, Hopi, before 1959

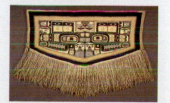

Chilkat blanket, Tlingit, early 20th century

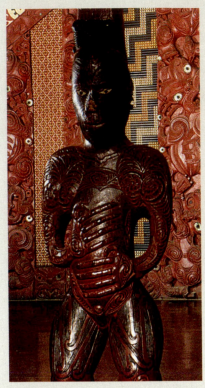

▲ **36-1a** Maori meeting houses symbolically represent an ancestor's body. Freestanding figures (pou tokomanawa) literally support the ridgepole that is the symbolic spine of the meeting house.

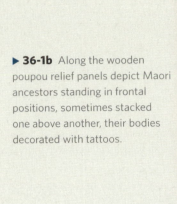

▶ **36-1b** Along the wooden poupou relief panels depict Maori ancestors standing in frontal positions, sometimes stacked one above another, their bodies decorated with tattoos.

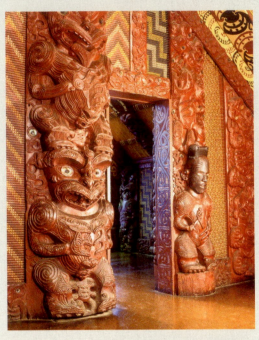

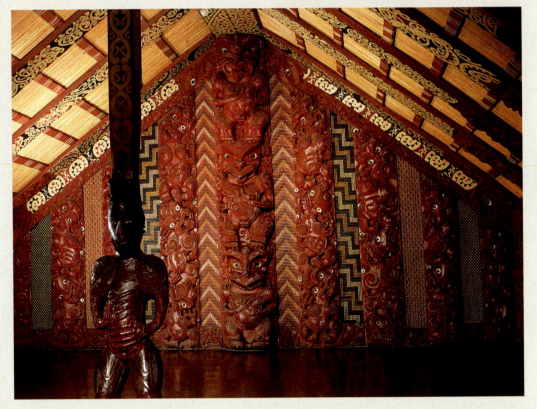

| 36-1 | **RAHARUHI RUKUPO and others, interior of the Te Hau-ki-Turanga wharenui (meeting house), Poverty Bay, New Zealand, Polynesia, 1842–1845. Reconstructed in Te Papa Tongarewa, Museum of New Zealand, Wellington.** |

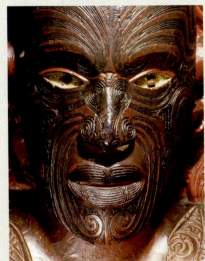

◀ **36-1c** The lead sculptor, Raharuhi Rukupo, who was also chief of the Rongowhakaata tribe, included a self-portrait among the ancestor portraits. His face features an elaborate Maori moko tattoo.

Oceania before 1980

MAORI MEN'S MEETING HOUSES

The number and variety of preserved artworks from the South Pacific are extraordinary, especially in light of the relatively sparse population of this vast region encompassing some 25,000 islands. But in Oceania—the name often given to the Pacific islands—as in many cultures worldwide, artists did not create "artworks" purely for display as aesthetic objects. The art objects Pacific Islanders have produced over the centuries always played important functional roles in religious and communal life. Oceanic art thus cannot be understood apart from its cultural context.

One of the major venues for the display of art in many Oceanic societies was the men's communal house, which itself should be considered a "work of art." A premier example is the Te Hau-ki-Turanga (Spirit of Turanga) meeting house (FIG. 36-1) of the Rongowhakaata tribe at Poverty Bay in New Zealand. RAHARUHI RUKUPO (ca. 1800–1873) and a team of 18 Maori woodcarvers constructed and decorated the building between 1842 and 1845. The Turanga meeting house was a place for the male members of the community to assemble in the benevolent presence of their ancestors. The very structure of the building symbolized the body of an ancestor or of the ultimate ancestor, the sky father, with the exterior *barge boards* (the angled boards outlining the house gables) representing his outstretched arms, the *ridgepole* his spine, and the rafters his ribs. Along the walls, relief panels (*poupou*) depict ancestors standing in frontal positions, sometimes stacked one above another, their bodies decorated with *tattoos*. Freestanding figures (*pou tokomanawa*) comparable to classical caryatids (FIGS. 5-17 and 5-54) literally support the symbolic spine of the ancestral body that is the meeting house. The *tukutuku* (stitched lattice panels) between the poupou are the work of female fabric artists, but because women could not enter the meeting house, they installed the panels from the outside.

Raharuhi Rukupo was not only a master carver. He was a priest, warrior, and, after the death of his older brother, the chief of the Rongowhakaata. He dedicated the Turanga meeting house in honor of his late brother and, as chief, included a self-portrait holding a woodcutter's adze among the ancestor portraits of the poupou. His face features an elaborate *moko* tattoo (see "Tattoo in Polynesia," page 1115).

Working in the long-established Maori tradition of woodcarving but using modern metal tools in place of the stone tools their predecessors employed, Rukupo and his assistants were able to complete the meeting house in only three years. The house remains the property of the Rongowhakaata tribe, but in 1935 was restored and reerected in the Museum of New Zealand at Wellington.

ISLAND CULTURES OF THE SOUTH PACIFIC

When people think of the South Pacific (MAP 36-1), images of balmy tropical islands usually come to mind. But the islands of the Pacific Ocean encompass a wide range of habitats. Environments range from the arid deserts of the Australian outback to the tropical rainforests of inland New Guinea and the coral atolls of the Marshall Islands. The region is not only geographically varied but also politically, linguistically, culturally, and artistically diverse.

In 1831, the French explorer Jules Sébastien César Dumont d'Urville (1790–1842) proposed dividing the Pacific islands into major regions based on general geographical, racial, and linguistic distinctions. Despite its limitations, his division of Oceania into the areas of Melanesia ("black islands"), Micronesia ("small islands"), and Polynesia ("many islands") continues in use today. Melanesia includes the islands of New Guinea, New Ireland, New Britain, New Caledonia, the Admiralty Islands, and the Solomon Islands, along with other smaller island groups. Micronesia consists primarily of the Caroline, Mariana, Gilbert, and Marshall Islands in the western Pacific. Polynesia covers much of the eastern Pacific and consists of a triangular area defined by the Hawaiian Islands in the north, Rapa Nui (Easter Island) in the east, and Aotearoa (New Zealand) in the southwest.

Although documentary evidence is lacking about Oceanic cultures before the arrival of seafaring Europeans in the early 16th century, archaeologists have determined that humans have inhabited the islands for tens of thousands of years. The archaeological evidence indicates that different parts of the Pacific experienced distinct migratory waves. The first group arrived during the last Ice Age, at least 40,000 and perhaps as many as 75,000 years ago, when a large continental shelf extended from Southeast Asia and enabled land access to Australia and New Guinea. After the end of the Ice

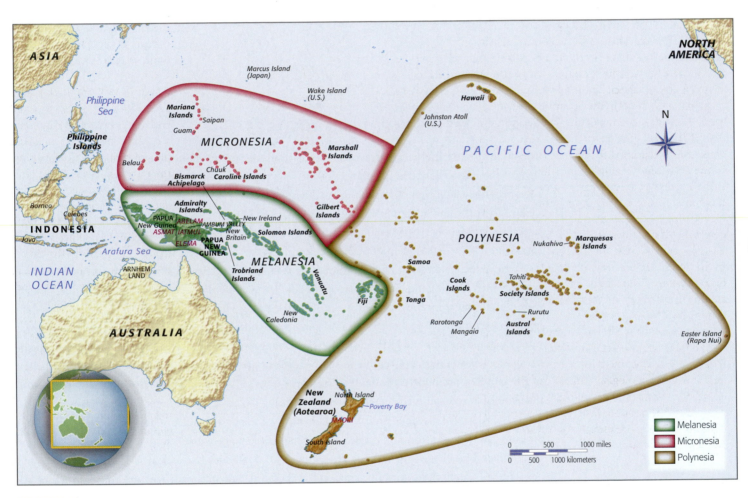

MAP 36-1 Oceania.

OCEANIA BEFORE 1980

1500–0 BCE	0–1200 CE	1200–1500 CE	1500–1800	1800–1900	1900–1980
▪ The earliest Oceanic artworks, datable around 1500 BCE, are composite human-animal stone figurines from Papua New Guinea.		▪ The largest Oceanic sculptures are also among the oldest: the moai of Rapa Nui, some of which are 50 feet tall.		▪ The traditional 19th-century Oceanic art forms in Melanesia, Micronesia, and Polynesia include sculptures and masks of ancestors and deities, painted wood prow ornaments, and communal men's houses.	▪ Oceanic artworks produced during the past century take a great variety of forms, ranging from the painted bark-cloth produced by Tongan women to the sculpted Dilukai figures of Belau men's ceremonial houses.

Age, descendants of these first settlers dispersed to other islands in Melanesia. The most recent migratory wave took place sometime after 3000 BCE and involved peoples of Asian ancestry moving to areas of Micronesia and Polynesia. The last Pacific islands to be settled were those of Polynesia, but habitation of its most far-flung islands—Hawaii, New Zealand, and Easter Island—began no later than 500 to 1000 CE. Because of the expansive chronological span of these migrations, Pacific cultures vary widely. For example, the Aboriginal peoples of Australia speak a language unrelated to any of those of New Guinea, whose languages fall into a distinct but diverse group. In contrast, most of the rest of the Pacific Islanders speak languages derived from the Austronesian language family.

These island groups came to Western attention as a result of the extensive exploration and colonization that began in the 16th century and reached its peak in the 19th century. Virtually all of the major Western nations—including Great Britain, France, Spain, Holland, Germany, and the United States—established a presence in the Pacific. Much of the history of Oceania in the 20th century revolved around indigenous peoples' struggles for independence from these colonial powers. Yet colonialism also facilitated an exchange of ideas—not solely the transfer of Western cultural values and technology to the Pacific. Oceanic art, for example, had a strong influence on many Western artists, especially the late-19th-century French painter Paul Gauguin (FIG. 28-21). The "primitive" art of Oceania also inspired many early-20th-century artists (see "Primitivism," page 891).

This chapter focuses on Oceanic art from the European discovery of the islands in the 16th century until 1980, although the earliest preserved sculptures—for example, the *Ambum Stone* (FIG. 36-1A) from Papua New Guinea—date to around 1500 BCE. The colossal stone statues of Easter Island (FIG. 36-13)—probably the most famous artworks in the South Pacific—also predate the arrival of Europeans. Knowledge of early Oceanic art and the history of the Pacific islands in general is unfortunately very incomplete. Tra-

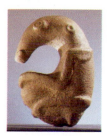

🔗 **36-1A** *Ambum Stone*, Papua New Guinea, ca. 1500 BCE.

ditionally, the transmission of information from one generation to the next in Pacific societies was largely oral, rather than written, and little archival documentation exists. Nonetheless, archaeologists, linguists, anthropologists, ethnologists, and art historians continue to make progress in illuminating the Oceanic past.

Given the pronounced regional variations among the Pacific island groups, the organization of this chapter is geographical rather than chronological.

AUSTRALIA AND MELANESIA

The westernmost Oceanic islands are the continent-nation of Australia and New Guinea in Melanesia. Together they dwarf the area of all the other Pacific islands combined.

Australia

Over the past 40,000 years, the Aboriginal peoples of Australia spread out over the entire continent and adapted to a variety of ecological conditions, ranging from those of tropical and subtropical areas in the north to desert regions in the continent's interior and more temperate locales in the south. European explorers reaching the region in the late 18th and early 19th centuries found that the Aborigines had a special relationship with the land on which they lived. Many

contemporary aboriginal artists still retain close ties to the land and the spirits that inhabit it. The Aboriginal perception of the world centers on a concept known as the Dreamings—ancestral beings whose spirits pervade the present. All Aborigines identify certain Dreamings as totemic ancestors, and those who share the same Dreamings have social links. The Aborigines call the spiritual domain that the Dreamings occupy Dreamtime, which is both a physical space within which the ancestral beings moved in creating the landscape and a psychic space providing Aborigines with cultural, religious, and moral direction. Because of the importance of Dreamings to all aspects of Aboriginal life, native Australian art symbolically links Aborigines with these ancestral spirits. The Aborigines recite creation myths in concert with songs and dances, and many art forms—body painting, carved figures, sacred objects, decorated stones, and rock and bark painting—serve as essential props in these dramatic re-creations.

Most Aboriginal art is relatively small and portable. As hunters and gatherers in difficult terrain, the Aborigines were generally nomadic peoples, rendering large-scale art impractical.

BARK PAINTING Bark, widely available in Australia, is portable and lightweight, and bark painting thus became a mainstay of Aboriginal art. Dreamings, mythic narratives (often tracing the movement of various ancestral spirits through the landscape), and sacred places were common subjects. Ancestral spirits pervade the lives of the Aborigines, and these paintings served to give visual form to that presence. Traditionally, because knowledge of Dreamings was sacred and restricted, an Aborigine could depict only a Dreaming with which the artist had a connection. Thus specific Aboriginal lineages, clans, or regional groups "owned" individual designs, and it is often difficult for outsiders to interpret the representations. The bark painting illustrated here (FIG. 36-2) depicts a Dreaming

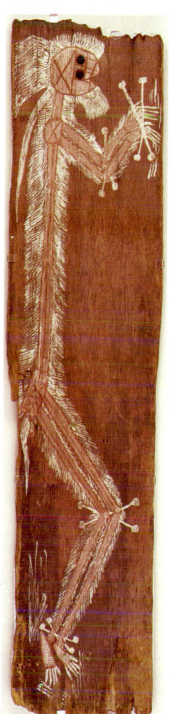

1 ft.

36-2 Ancestor figure, male, East Alligator Rivers, Northern Territory, 1913. Ocher on bark, 4' 10⅝" × 1' 1". Museum Victoria, Melbourne.

Aboriginal painters frequently depicted Dreamings, ancestral beings whose spirits pervade the present, using the X-ray style that shows both the figure's internal organs and its external appearance.

known as Auuenau and comes from Arnhem Land in northern Australia. The artist represented the elongated figure in a style known as "X-ray," which Aboriginal painters used to depict both animal and human forms. In this style, the artist simultaneously depicts the subject's internal organs and exterior appearance. The painting possesses a fluid and dynamic quality, with the X-ray-like figure clearly defined against a solid background.

New Guinea

Because of its sheer size, New Guinea, the third-largest island in the world, dominates Melanesia. This 309,000-square-mile island consists today of parts of two countries—the provinces of Papua and West Papua of nearby Indonesia, on the island's western end, and Papua New Guinea on the eastern end. New Guinea's inhabitants together speak more than 800 different languages, almost one-quarter of the world's known tongues. Among the Melanesian cultures discussed in this chapter, the Asmat, Iatmul, Elema, and Abelam peoples of New Guinea all speak Papuan-derived languages. Scholars believe they are descendants of the early settlers who came to the island in the remote past. In contrast, the people of New Ireland and the Trobriand Islands are Austronesian speakers and probably descendants of a later wave of Pacific migrants.

Typical Melanesian societies are fairly democratic and relatively unstratified. What political power exists belongs to groups of elder men and, in some areas, elder women. The elders handle the people's affairs in a communal fashion. Within some of these groups, persons of local distinction, known as "Big Men," renowned for their political, economic, and, historically, warrior skills, have accrued power. Because power and position in Melanesia can be earned (within limits), many cultural practices (such as rituals and cults) revolve around the acquisition of knowledge that enables advancement in society. To represent and acknowledge this advancement in rank, Melanesian societies mount elaborate festivals, construct communal meeting houses, and produce art objects. These cultural products serve to reinforce the social order and maintain social stability. Given the wide diversity in environments and languages, it should come as no surprise that hundreds of art styles flourished on New Guinea alone. Only a sample can be presented here.

ASMAT Living along the southwestern coast of New Guinea, the Asmat of Papua province eke out their existence by hunting and gathering the varied flora and fauna found in the mangrove swamps, rivers, and tropical forests. Each Asmat community is in constant competition for limited resources. Historically, the Asmat extended this competitive spirit beyond food and materials to energy and power as well. To increase one's personal energy or spiritual power, one had to take it forcibly from someone else. As a result, warfare and headhunting became central to Asmat culture and art. The Asmat did not believe that any death was natural. Death could result only from a direct assault (headhunting or warfare) or sorcery, and it diminished ancestral power. Thus, to restore a balance of spirit power, an enemy's head had to be taken to avenge a death and to add to one's communal spirit power. Headhunting was still common in the 1930s when Europeans established an administrative and missionary presence among the Asmat. As a result of European efforts, headhunting ceased by the 1960s, and many traditional beliefs about life and death have yielded to modern ideas.

When they still practiced headhunting, the Asmat erected *bisj* poles (FIG. **36-3**) that served as a pledge to avenge a relative's death. A man would set up a bisj pole when he could command the sup-

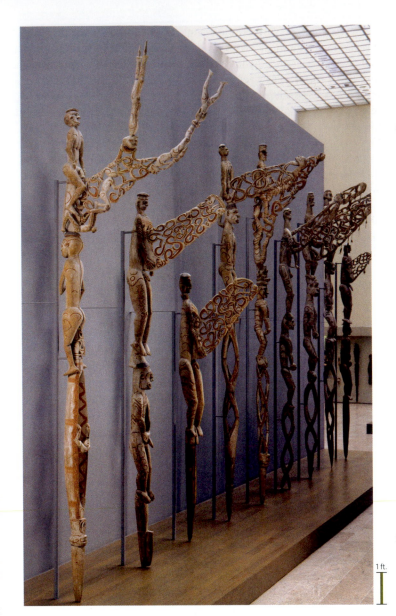

36-3 Asmat bisj poles, from Omadesep village, Faretsj River, Papua province, Melanesia, mid-20th century. Mangrove wood, paint, and fiber, 18' high. Metropolitan Museum of Art, New York (Michael C. Rockefeller Collection, bequest of Nelson A. Rockefeller, 1979).

The Asmat carved bisj poles from mangrove tree trunks and erected them before undertaking a headhunting raid. The carved figures represent the relatives whose deaths the hunters must avenge.

port of enough men to undertake a headhunting raid. Carved in one piece from the trunk of a single mangrove tree, bisj poles include superimposed figures of deceased individuals. At the top, extending winglike from the abdomen of the uppermost figure on the bisj pole, is the *cemen*, one of the tree's buttress roots carved into an openwork pattern.

All of the decorative elements on the bisj pole relate to headhunting and foretell a successful raid. The many animals carved on the mangrove poles (and in Asmat art in general) are symbols of headhunting. The Asmat saw the human body as a tree—the feet and legs as the roots, the torso as the trunk, the arms and hands as the branches, and the head as the fruit. Thus any fruit-eating animal (such as the black king cockatoo, the hornbill, or the flying fox) symbolized the headhunter, and consequently they appear frequently on bisj poles.

Traditional Asmat art also often includes representations of the praying mantis. The Asmat consider the female praying mantis's practice of beheading her mate after copulation and then eating him as another form of headhunting. The curvilinear or spiral patterns filling the pierced openwork at the top of the bisj poles can be related to the characteristic curved tail of the cuscus (a fruit-eating mammal) or the tusk of a boar (related to hunting and virility). Once the Asmat sculptors carved the mangrove poles, they placed them on a rack near the community's men's house. After the success of the headhunting expedition, the men discarded the bisj poles and allowed them to rot, because they had served their purpose.

IATMUL The Iatmul live along the middle Sepik River in Papua New Guinea in communities based on kinship. Villages include extended families as well as different clans. The social center of every Iatmul village is a massive saddle-shaped men's ceremonial house (FIG. 36-4). In terms of both function and form, the men's house reveals the primacy of the kinship network. The meeting house reinforces kinship links by serving as the locale for the initiation of local youths to advance in rank, for men's discussions of community issues, and for ceremonies linked to the Iatmul's ancestors. Because only men can advance in Iatmul society, women and uninitiated boys cannot enter the men's house. In this manner, the Iatmul men control access to knowledge and therefore to power. Given its important political and cultural role, the men's house is appropriately monumental, physically dominating Iatmul villages and dwarfing family houses. Although men's houses are common in New Guinea, those of the Iatmul are among the most lavishly decorated.

Traditionally, the house symbolizes the protective mantle of the ancestors and represents an enormous female ancestor. The facade is her face and the rest of the house her body. The Iatmul house and its female ancestral figures symbolize a reenacted death and rebirth when a clan member enters and exits the second story of the building. The gable ends of men's houses are usually covered and sometimes include a giant female gable mask, making the ancestral symbolism visible. The interior carvings, however, are normally hidden from view. The Iatmul placed carved images of clan ancestors on the central ridge-support posts and on the roof-support posts on both sides of the house. They topped each roof-support post with large faces representing mythical spirits of the clans. At the top of the two raised spires at each end, birds symbolizing the war spirit of the village men sit above carvings of headhunting victims (or, on occasion, of male ancestors).

The subdivision of the house's interior into parts for each clan reflects the social demographic of the village. Many meeting houses have three parts—a front, middle, and end—representing the three major clans who built it. These parts have additional subclan divisions, which also have support posts carved with images of mythical male and female ancestors. Beneath the house, each clan keeps large carved *slit-gongs* to serve as both instruments of communication (for sending drum messages within and between villages) and the voices of ancestral spirits. On the second level of the house, above the horizontal crossbeam beneath the gable, the Iatmul place carved wood figures symbolizing female clan ancestors, depicted in a birthing position (compare FIGS. 36-11 and 36-12). The Iatmul also keep various types of portable art in their ceremonial houses. These include ancestors' skulls covered with clay modeled to form a likeness of the deceased (a practice similar to one documented thousands of years before in Neolithic Jericho, FIG. 1-13), ceremonial chairs, sacred flutes, hooks for hanging sacred items and food, and several types of masks.

ELEMA Central to the culture of the Elema people of Orokolo Bay in the Papuan Gulf was *Hevehe*, an elaborate cycle of ceremonial activities. Conceptualized as the mythical visitation of the water spirits (*ma-hevehe*), the Hevehe cycle involved the production and presentation of large, ornate masks (also called hevehe). The Elema last practiced Hevehe in the 1930s. Primarily organized by the male elders of the village, the cycle was a communal undertaking, and normally took from 10 to 20 years to complete. The duration of the Hevehe and the resources and human labor required reinforced cultural and economic relations and maintained the social structure in which elder male authority dominated.

Throughout the cycle, the Elema held ceremonies to initiate male youths into higher ranks. These ceremonies involved the exchange of wealth (such as pigs and shell ornaments), thereby also serving an economic purpose. The cycle culminated in the display of the finished hevehe

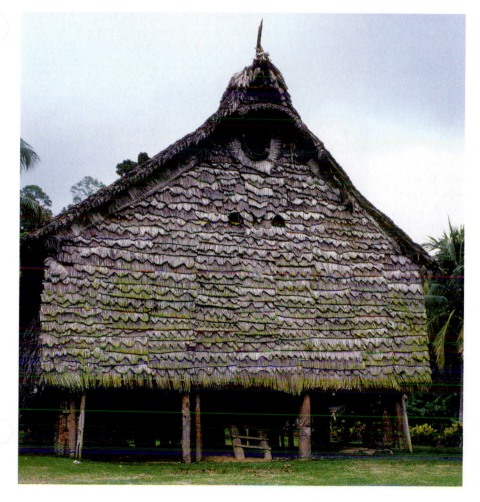

36-4 Iatmul ceremonial men's house, East Sepik, Papua New Guinea, Melanesia, mid- to late 20th century.

The men's house is the center of Iatmul life. Its distinctive saddle-shaped roof symbolizes the protective mantle of ancestors. The carved decoration often includes female ancestors in the birthing position.

The Hevehe was a cycle of ceremonial activities spanning 10 to 20 years, culminating in the dramatic appearance of hevehe masks from the Elema men's house. The masks represent female sea spirits.

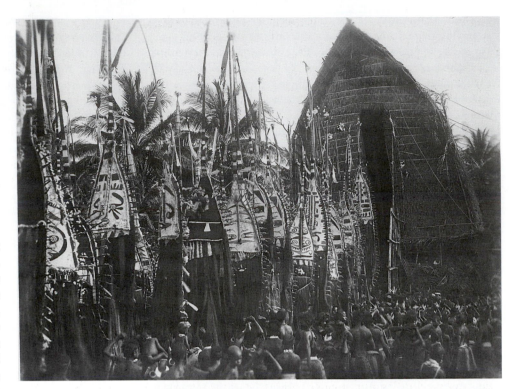

masks (FIG. 36-5). Each mask consisted of painted barkcloth (see "Barkcloth," page 1114) stretched around a cane-and-wood frame fitted over the wearer's body. A hevehe mask was normally 9 to 10 feet in height, although extensions often raised the height to as much as 25 feet. Because of their size and intricate designs, hevehe masks required great skill to construct, and only trained men would participate in mask making. Designs were specific to particular clans, and elder men passed them down to the next generation from memory. Each mask represented a female sea spirit, but the decoration of the mask often incorporated designs from local flora and fauna as well.

The final stage of the cycle focused on the dramatic appearance of the masks from the *eravo* (men's house). After a procession, the masks were brought back into the eravo (FIG. 36-5), and the men wearing the hevehe mingled with relatives. Upon conclusion of related dancing (often lasting about a month), the Elema ritually killed and then dumped the masks in piles and burned them. This destruction allowed the sea spirits to return to their mythic domain and provided a pretext for commencing the cycle again.

ABELAM The eravo that forms the backdrop of the hevehe festival in FIG. 36-5 resembles Iatmul ceremonial houses (FIG. 36-4) and the *tamberan* (FIG. **36-5A**) of the Abelam people, whose architecture and portable artworks illustrate how Oceanic art often includes references both to fundamental spiritual beliefs and to basic subsistence. The Abelam are agriculturists living in the hilly regions north of the Sepik River. Relatively isolated, the Abelam received only sporadic visits from foreigners until the 1930s, so little is known about early Abelam history.

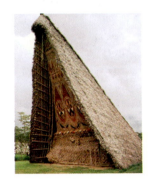

36-5A Abelam tamberan, Maprik, photographed 1974.

The principal Abelam crop is the yam. Because of the importance of yams to the survival of Abelam society, those who can grow the largest yams achieve power and prestige. Indeed, the Abelam developed a complex yam cult, which involves a series of rites and activities intended to promote the growth of the tubers. Special plantations focus on yam cultivation. Only initiated men who observe strict rules of conduct, including sexual abstinence, can work these fields. The Abelam believe that ancestors aid in the growth of yams, and they hold ceremonies to honor these ancestors. Special long yams (distinct from the short yams cultivated for consumption) are on display during these festivities, and the largest (9 to 10 feet long) bear the names of important ancestors. Yam masks (FIG. 36-6) with

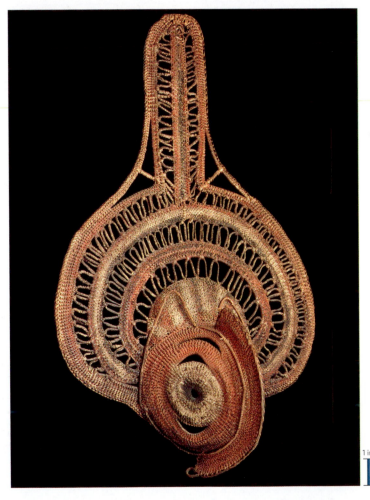

1 in.

36-6 Abelam yam mask, from Maprik district, Papua New Guinea, Melanesia, early to mid-20th century. Painted cane, 1' 6$\frac{9}{10}$" high. Musée Barbier-Mueller, Geneva.

The Abelam believe that their ancestors aid in the growth of their principal crop, the yam. Painted cane yam masks are an important part of the elaborate ceremonies honoring these ancestors.

cane or wood frames, usually painted red, white, yellow, and black, are an integral part of the ceremonies. The most elaborate masks also incorporate sculpted faces, cassowary feathers, and shell ornaments. They covered the "heads" of the long yams. Humans never wear the yam masks, but the Abelam use the same designs to decorate their bodies for dances, revealing how closely they identify with their principal food source.

New Ireland and the Trobriand Islands

East of New Guinea but part of the modern nation of Papua New Guinea are New Ireland and the Trobriand Islands, two important Melanesian art centers.

NEW IRELAND Mortuary rites and memorial festivals are a central concern of the Austronesian-speaking peoples who live in the northern section of New Ireland. The term *malanggan* refers to both the festivals held in honor of the deceased and the carvings and objects produced for these festivals. Malanggan rites are part of an ancestor cult and are critical in facilitating the transition of the soul from the world of the living to the realm of the dead and the rechanneling of energy from the deceased into the community of the living. In addition to the religious function of malanggan, the extended ceremonies also promote social solidarity and stimulate the economy through the investment necessary to mount impressive festivities. To educate the younger generation about these practices, malanggan also includes the initiation of young men.

Of the wide range of malanggan carvings that New Irelanders have produced—masks, figures, poles, friezes, and ornaments—probably the most extraordinary are their wooden *uli* figures (FIG. **36-7**). Sculptors created these statues for use in malanggan rituals in which the skulls of illustrious ancestors were dug up and then reburied with new sacred plants. During the ceremony, which is no longer practiced and in which only men could participate, New Ireland religious leaders coaxed the deceased chief to enter the uli. Afterward, the uli would be displayed in the community's men's house until reused (after repainting) in a subsequent malanggan. The uli illustrated here is of exceptionally high quality but is typical of the series. The ferocious-looking figure stands upright with raised arms. Most notable is the uli's bisexuality, featuring the genitals of a man and the breasts of a woman, symbolizing the chief's strength and ability to lead as well as his benevolent nurturing of his people.

Also created for the malanggan are tatanua masks (FIG. **36-8**). *Tatanua* represent the spirits of specific deceased people. The materials used to make New Ireland tatanua masks are primarily soft wood, vegetable fiber, and rattan. The crested hair, made of fiber, duplicates a hairstyle formerly common among the men (compare FIG. 36-7). For the eyes, the mask makers insert sea-snail shells. Traditionally, artists paint the masks black, white, yellow, and red—colors that the people of New Ireland associate with warfare, magic spells, and violence. Although some masks are display pieces, dancers wear most of them. As with the uli figures, rather than destroying

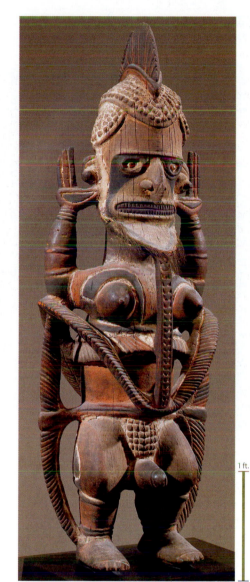

36-7 Uli statue, from New Ireland, Papua New Guinea, 18th or early 19th century. Wood, ocher, and charcoal, 4' 11$\frac{1}{8}$" high. Musée du quai Branly, Paris.

Uli figures, used in malanggan rites, have ferocious expressions on their faces and are bisexual with male genitals and female breasts, symbolizing the deceased chief's strength and his nurturing of his people.

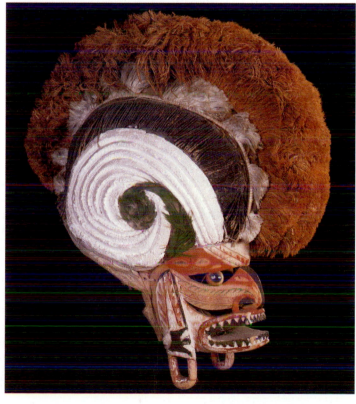

36-8 Tatanua mask, from New Ireland, Papua New Guinea, Melanesia, 19th to 20th centuries. Wood, fiber, shell, lime, and feathers, 1' 5$\frac{1}{2}$" high. Otago Museum, Dunedin.

In New Ireland, malanggan rites facilitate the transition of the soul from this world to the land of the dead. Dancers wearing tatanua masks representing the deceased play a key role in these ceremonies.

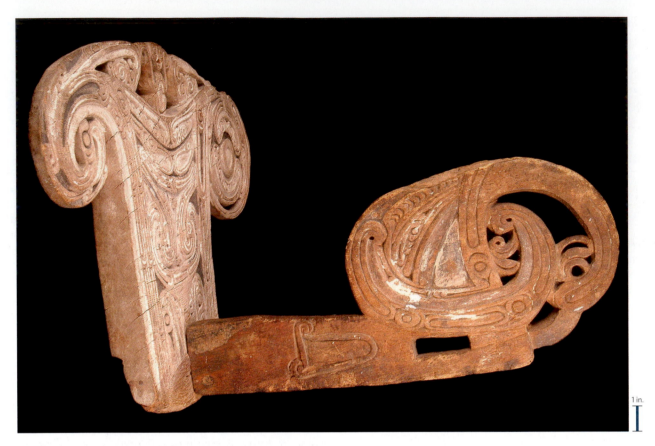

36-9 Canoe prow and splashboard, from Trobriand Islands, Papua New Guinea, Melanesia, 19th to 20th centuries. Painted wood, 1' 3½" high, 1' 11" long. Musée du quai Branly, Paris.

To participate in kula exchanges, the Trobriand Islanders had to undertake dangerous sea voyages. They decorated their canoes with abstract human, bird, and serpent motifs referring to sea spirits.

their ritual masks after the conclusion of the ceremonies, as some other cultures do, the New Irelanders store them for future use.

TROBRIAND ISLANDS The various rituals of Oceanic cultures discussed thus far often involve exchanges intended to cement social relationships and reinforce or stimulate the economy. Further, these rituals usually have a spiritual dimension. All of these aspects apply to the practices of the Trobriand Islanders, who live off the coast of the southeastern corner of New Guinea. *Kula*—an exchange of white conus-shell arm ornaments for red chama-shell necklaces—is a characteristic practice of the Trobriand Islanders. Kula exchanges may have originated some 500 years ago. They can be complex, and there is great competition for valuable shell ornaments (determined by aesthetic appeal and exchange history). Because of the isolation imposed by their island existence, the Trobriand Islanders had to undertake potentially dangerous voyages to participate in kula trading. Appropriately, the Trobrianders lavish a great deal of effort on decorating their large and elaborately carved canoes, which feature ornate prows and splashboards (FIG. **36-9**). To ensure a successful kula expedition, the Trobrianders invoke spells when attaching these prows to the canoes. Human, bird, and serpent motifs—references to sea spirits, ancestors, and totemic animals—appear on the prows and splashboards. Because the sculptors use highly stylized motifs in intricate intertwined curvilinear designs, identification of the specific representations is difficult. In recent decades, the Trobrianders have adapted kula to modern circumstances, largely abandoning canoes for motorboats. The exchanges now facilitate business and political networking.

MICRONESIA

Some 2,500 islands, most of them tiny, scattered over nearly three million square miles of ocean make up Micronesia, home to about 200,000 people today. The Austronesian-speaking cultures of Micronesia tend to be more socially stratified than those found in New Guinea and other Melanesian areas. Micronesian cultures frequently center on chieftainships with craft and ritual specializations, and their religions honor named deities as well as ancestors. Life in virtually all Micronesian cultures focuses on seafaring activities—fishing, trading, and long-distance travel in large oceangoing vessels. For this reason, much of the artistic imagery of Micronesia relates to the sea.

Caroline Islands

The Caroline Islands are the largest island group in Micronesia. The arts of the Caroline Islands include the carving of canoes and the fashioning of charms and images of spirits to protect travelers at sea and for fishing and fertility magic.

CHUUK Given the importance of seafaring, it is not surprising that many of the most highly skilled artists in the Caroline Islands were master canoe builders. The canoe ornament illustrated here (FIG. **36-10**) comes from Chuuk. Carved from a single plank of wood and fastened to the prow of a large, paddled war canoe, the ornament served a decorative purpose but also provided protection on arduous or long voyages. That this and similar ornaments

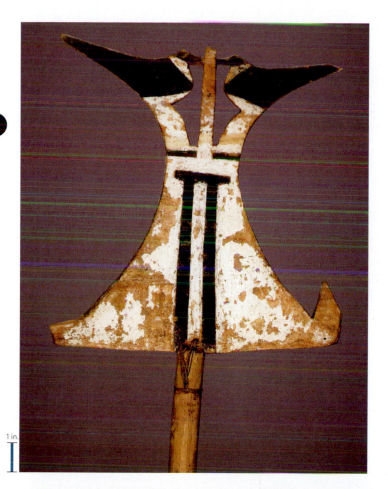

36-10 Canoe prow ornament, from Chuuk, Caroline Islands, Micronesia, late 19th century. Painted wood, birds $11'' \times 10\frac{5}{8}''$. British Museum, London.

Prow ornaments protected canoe paddlers and could be lowered to signal a peaceful voyage. This Micronesian example may represent facing sea swallows or perhaps a stylized human figure.

1 in.

are not permanent parts of the canoes reflects their function. When approaching another vessel, the Micronesian seafarers lowered these ornaments as a signal that their voyage was a peaceful one. The Chuuk prow seems at first to be an abstract design but may represent, at the top, two facing sea swallows—creatures capable of navigating long distances. Some scholars, however, think that the entire piece represents a stylized human figure, with the "swallows" constituting the arms.

BELAU On Belau (formerly Palau) in the Caroline Islands, the islanders put much effort into creating and maintaining elaborately painted men's ceremonial clubhouses called *bai*. Whereas the Iatmul and Abelam make their ceremonial houses (FIGS. 36-4 and 36-5A) by tying, lashing, and weaving different-size posts, trees, saplings, and grasses, the Belau people make the main structure of the bai entirely of worked, fitted, joined, and pegged wood pieces, which enables them to assemble it easily. Belau bai, such as the one illustrated here (FIG. **36-11**), have steep overhanging roofs decorated with geometric patterns along the roof boards. Skilled artists carve the gable in low relief and paint it with narrative scenes, as well as with various abstracted forms of the shell money used traditionally on Belau as currency. These decorated storyboards illustrate important historical events and myths related to the clan that built the bai. Similar carved and painted crossbeams are inside the house. The rooster images along the base of the facade symbolize the rising sun, while the multiple frontal human faces carved and painted above the entrance and on the vertical elements above the rooster images represent a deity called Blellek. He warns women to stay away from the ocean and the bai or he will molest them.

Although the bai was the domain of men, women figured prominently in the clubhouse's imagery, consistent with the important symbolic and social positions women held in Belau culture (see "Women's Roles in Oceania," page 1112). A common element surmounting the main bai entrance was a simple, symmetrical wood sculpture (on occasion, a painting) of a splayed female figure, known as *Dilukai*

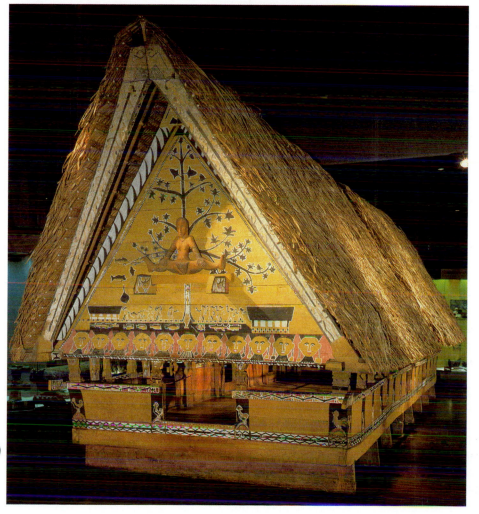

36-11 Model of a men's ceremonial house (bai) at 75 percent scale, from Belau (Palau), Micronesia, 20th century. Ethnologisches Museum, Staatliche Museen zu Berlin, Berlin.

The Belau men's clubhouses (bai) have extensive carved and painted decorations illustrating important events and myths related to the clan that built the bai. The central motif is a Dilukai (FIG. 36-12).

ART AND SOCIETY
Women's Roles in Oceania

Given the prominence of men's houses and the importance of male initiation in so many Oceanic societies, women might appear to be peripheral members of these cultures. Much of the extant material culture—ancestor masks, shields, clubs—seems to corroborate this. In reality, however, women play crucial roles in most Pacific cultures. In addition to their significant contributions through exchange and ritual activities to the maintenance and perpetuation of the social network on which the stability of village life depends, women are important producers of art.

Historically, women's artistic production has been restricted mainly to forms such as barkcloth, weaving, and pottery. In some cultures in New Guinea, potters were primarily female. Throughout much of Polynesia, women produced barkcloth (see "Tongan Barkcloth," page 1114), which they often dyed and stenciled, and sometimes even perfumed. Women in the Trobriand Islands still make brilliantly dyed skirts of shredded banana fiber that not only are aesthetically beautiful but also serve as a form of wealth, presented symbolically during mortuary rituals.

In most Oceanic cultures, women usually do not use the same adzes and axes that male sculptors employ, and they do not work in hard materials, such as wood, stone, bone, or ivory. Further, they do not produce images having religious or spiritual powers or that confer status on their users. Scholars investigating the role of the artist in Oceania have concluded that the reason for these restrictions is a perceived difference in innate power. Because women have the natural power to create and control life, male-dominated societies developed elaborate ritual practices to counteract this female power. By excluding women from participating in these rituals and denying them access to knowledge about specific practices, men derived a political authority that could be perpetuated. It is important to note, however, that even in rituals or activities restricted to men, women often participate. For example, in the now-defunct Hevehe ceremonial cycle (FIG. 36-5) in Papua New Guinea, women made the fiber skirts for the hevehe masks but feigned ignorance about these sacred objects, because such knowledge was the exclusive privilege of initiated men.

Pacific cultures often acknowledged women's innate power in the depictions of women in Oceanic art. For example, the splayed Dilukai female sculpture (FIG. 36-12) that appears regularly on Palauan bai (men's houses; FIG. 36-11) celebrates women's procreative powers. Often flanked by figures of sexually aroused men, these female figures were surrounded by images of sun disks, trees, and birds. They faced east toward the rising sun and symbolized the sun's gifts to earth as

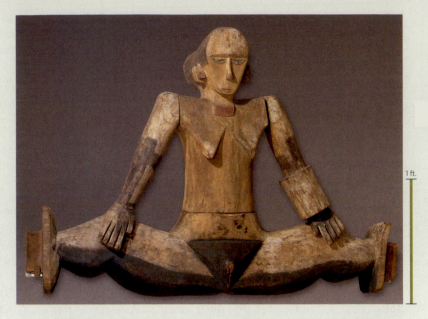

1 ft.

36-12 Dilukai, from Belau (Palau), Micronesia, late 19th or early 20th century. Wood, paint, and kaolin, 2' 1⅝" high. Metropolitan Museum of Art, New York (Michael C. Rockefeller Collection, bequest of Nelson A. Rockefeller, 1979).

Sculpted wood figures of a splayed female, or Dilukai, commonly appear over the entrance to a Belau bai (FIG. 36-11). The figures served as symbols of fertility and protected the men's house.

well as human fertility. The Dilukai figure also confers protection on visitors to the bai, another symbolic acknowledgment of female power. Similar concepts underlie the design of the Iatmul men's house (FIG. 36-4). Conceived as a giant female ancestor, the men's house incorporates women's natural power into the conceptualization of what is normally the most important architectural structure in an Iatmul village. In addition, the Iatmul associate entrance and departure from the men's house with death and rebirth, thereby reinforcing the primacy of fertility and the perception of the men's house as representing a woman's body.

One reason that scholars have tended to overlook the active participation of women in all aspects of Oceanic life is that until recently, the objects that visitors to the Pacific collected were primarily those suggesting aggressive, warring societies. That the majority of these Western travelers were men and therefore had contact predominantly with men no doubt accounts for this pattern of collecting. Recent scholarship has done a great deal to correct this misperception, thereby revealing the richness of social, artistic, and political activity in the Pacific.

(FIGS. 36-11 and 36-12). She wears jewelry and an armband, emblems of wealth and power, and serves as a symbol of both protection and fertility.

POLYNESIA

Polynesia was one of the last areas in the world to be settled. Habitation in the western Polynesian islands did not begin until about the end of the first millennium BCE, and in the south not until the first millennium CE. The settlers brought complex sociopolitical and religious institutions with them. Whereas Melanesian societies are fairly egalitarian and advancement in rank is possible, Polynesian societies typically are highly stratified, with power determined by heredity. Indeed, rulers often trace their genealogies directly to the gods of creation. Most Polynesian societies possess elaborate political organizations headed by chiefs and ritual specialists. By the 1800s, some Polynesian cultures (Hawaii and the Society Islands, for example) had evolved into kingdoms. Because of this social hierarchy, historically most Polynesian art belonged to persons of noble or high religious background and served to reinforce their power and prestige. These objects, like their chieftain owners, often possessed *mana*, or spiritual power.

Rapa Nui (Easter Island)

Some of the earliest datable artworks in Oceania are also the largest. This is especially true of the colossal sculptures of Rapa Nui.

MOAI The *moai* (FIG. **36-13**) of Rapa Nui are monumental sculptures as much as 50 feet tall and weighing up to 100 tons. They stand as silent sentinels on stone platforms (*ahu*) marking burial or sacred sites used for religious ceremonies. Most of the moai consist of huge, blocky figures with fairly planar facial features—large staring eyes, strong jaws, straight noses with carefully articulated nostrils, and elongated earlobes. A number of the moai have *pukao*—small red scoria (a local volcanic stone) cylinders that serve as a sort of top-knot or hat—atop their heads. Although debate continues, many scholars believe that lineage chiefs or their sons erected the moai and that the sculptures depict ancestral chiefs. The moai, however, are not individual portraits but generic images that the Easter Islanders believed had the ability to accommodate spirits or gods. The statues thus mediate between chiefs and gods, and between the natural and cosmic worlds.

Archaeological surveys have documented nearly 1,000 moai erected on some 250 ahu. Most of the stones are soft volcanic tuff and came from the same quarry at Rano Raraku. Some of the sculptures are red scoria, basalt, or trachyte. After quarrying, the Easter Islanders dragged the moai to the ahu sites and then positioned them vertically. Given the extraordinary size of these *monoliths,* their production and placement serve as testaments to the achievements of this Polynesian culture. According to one scholar, it would have taken 30 men one year to carve a moai, 90 men two months to transport it from the quarry to the ahu site (often several miles away), and 90 men three months to position it vertically on the platform.

Tonga

Tonga is the westernmost island group in Polynesia. One of its most distinctive products is barkcloth, which women have traditionally produced throughout Polynesia.

BARKCLOTH Artists produce barkcloth from the inner bark of the paper mulberry tree. The finished product goes by various names in Polynesia, but during the 19th century, when the production of barkcloth reached its zenith, *tapa* became the most widely used term. Although the primary use of tapa in Polynesia was for clothing and bedding, in Tonga, large sheets (FIG. 36-14) were (and still are) produced for exchange (see "Tongan Barkcloth," page 1114). Barkcloth can also have a spiritual dimension and can serve to confer sanctity on the object wrapped in it. Appropriately, the Polynesians traditionally wrapped the bodies of high-ranking deceased chiefs in barkcloth.

The uses and decoration of tapa have varied over the years. In the 19th century, everyday tapa clothing was normally unadorned, whereas tapa used for ceremonial or ritual purposes was dyed, painted, stenciled, and sometimes perfumed. The designs applied to the tapa differed depending on the particular island group producing it and the function of the cloth. The production process was complex and time-consuming. Indeed, some Pacific cultures, such as those of Tahiti and Hawaii, constructed buildings specifically for the beating stage in the production of barkcloth.

Tapa production reached its peak in the early 19th century, partly as a result of the interest expressed by Western whalers and missionaries. By the late 19th century, the use of tapa for cloth had been abandoned throughout much of eastern Polynesia, although its use in rituals (for example, as a wrap for corpses of deceased chiefs or as a marker of tabooed sites) continued. Today, tapa exchanges are still an integral part of funerals and marriage ceremonies, and even the coronation of kings.

The decorated *ngatu* (barkcloth) shown in FIG. 36-14 clearly demonstrates the richness of pattern, subtlety of theme, and variation of geometric forms characteristic of Tongan royal barkcloths. MELE SITANI made this ngatu for the accession ceremony of King Tupou IV (r. 1965–2006) of Tonga. She kneels in the middle of the ngatu, which features triangular patterns known as *manulua*. This pattern results from the intersection of three or four pointed triangles. *Manulua* means "two birds," and the design gives the illusion of two birds flying together. The motif symbolizes chieftain status derived from both parents.

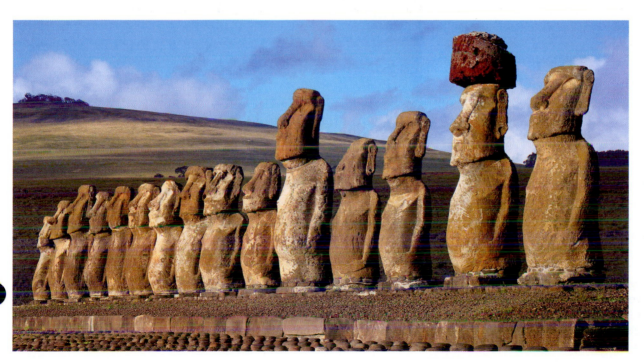

36-13 Row of moai on a stone platform, Ahu Tongariki, Rapa Nui (Easter Island), Polynesia, ca. 1200–1500. Volcanic tuff and red scoria.

The moai of Rapa Nui are monoliths as much as 50 feet tall. Most scholars believe that they portray ancestral chiefs. They stand on platforms marking burials or sites for religious ceremonies.

MATERIALS AND TECHNIQUES
Tongan Barkcloth

Tongan barkcloth (FIG. 36-14) provides an instructive example of the labor-intensive process of tapa production. At the time of early contact between Europeans and Polynesians in the late 18th and early 19th centuries, ranking women in Tonga made decorated barkcloth (*ngatu*). Today, women's organizations called *kautaha*, sponsored by Tongan women of high rank, produce ngatu.

In Tonga, men plant the paper mulberry tree and harvest it in two to three years. They cut the trees into about 10-foot lengths and dry them for several days. Then the women strip off the outer bark and soak the inner bark in water to prepare it for further processing. They place these soaked inner bark strips over a wood anvil and repeatedly strike them with a wood beater until they spread out and flatten. Folding and layering the strips while beating them, a felting process, results in a wider piece of ngatu than the original strips. Afterward, the beaten barkcloth dries and bleaches in the sun.

The next stage of ngatu production involves the placement of the thin, beaten sheets over semicircular boards. The women then fasten embroidered design tablets (*kupesi*—usually produced by men) of coconut-leaf midribs and string patterns to the boards. They transfer the patterns on the design tablets to the outer barkcloth by rubbing.

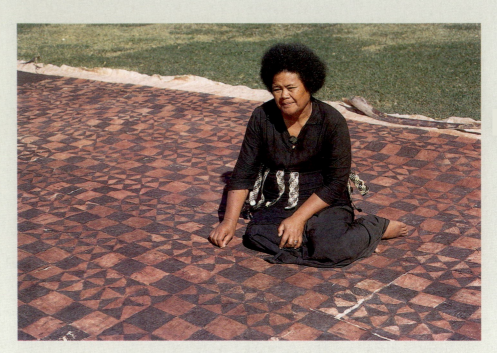

36-14 MELE SITANI, ngatu with manulua designs, Tonga, Polynesia, 1967. Barkcloth.

In Tonga, the production of decorated barkcloth, or ngatu, involves dyeing, painting, stenciling, and perfuming. Mele Sitani made this one with a two-bird design for the coronation of Tupou IV.

Then the women fill in the lines and patterns by painting, covering the large white spaces with colored figures.

The Tongans use brown, red, and black pigments derived from various types of bark, clay, fruits, and soot to create the colored patterns on ngatu. Sheets, rolls, and strips of ngatu play an important role in weddings, funerals, and ceremonial presentations for ranking persons.

Marquesas, Austral, and Cook Islands

Even though the Polynesians were skillful navigators, various island groups remained isolated from one another for centuries by the vast distances they would have had to cover in open outriggers. This geographical separation explains the development of distinct regional styles within a recognizable general Polynesian style.

MARQUESAS ISLANDS Although Marquesan chiefs trace their right to rule by descent from earlier rulers, the political system before European contact allowed for the acquisition of power by force. As a result, warfare was widespread through the late 19th century. Among the items produced by Marquesan artists were ornaments that often adorned the hair of warriors. The hollow, cylindrical bone or ivory ornaments (*ivi p'o*; FIG. 36-15) functioned as protective amulets. Warriors wore them until they avenged the death of a kinsman. The ornaments are in the form of *tiki*—carvings of exalted, deified ancestor figures. The large, rounded eyes and wide mouths of the tiki are typically Marquesan, as is the use of a continuous line to outline both the nose, with its wide nostrils, and the oversized eyes.

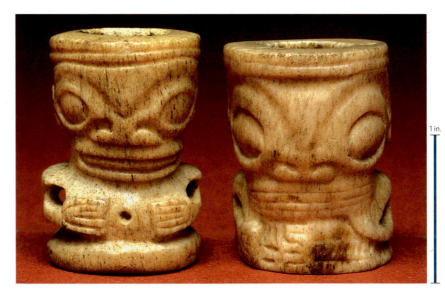

1 in.

36-15 Hair ornaments, from the Marquesas Islands, Polynesia, early to mid-19th century. Bone, 1½" high (*left*), 1⅖" high (*right*). University of Pennsylvania Museum of Archaeology and Anthropology, Philadelphia.

These hollow cylindrical bone ornaments representing deified ancestors adorned the hair of Marquesan warriors during the 19th century. The warriors wore them until they avenged the death of a kinsman.

ART AND SOCIETY
Tattoo in Polynesia

Throughout Pacific societies, as in Africa (see page 1137), body decoration was an important means of representing cultural and personal identity. In addition to clothing and ornaments, body adornment most often took the form of tattoo. Although tattooing was a common practice in Micronesia, it was more pervasive in Polynesia. Indeed, the English term *tattoo* is Polynesian in origin, related to the Tahitian, Samoan, and Tongan word *tatau* or *tatu*. In New Zealand, the markings are called *moko*. Within Polynesian cultures, tattoo reached its zenith in the highly stratified societies of New Zealand, the Marquesas Islands, Tahiti, Tonga, Samoa, and Hawaii. Both sexes displayed tattoos. In general, men had more tattoos than women, and the location of tattoos on the body differed. For instance, in New Zealand, the face and buttocks were the primary areas of male tattoo, whereas tattoos appeared on the lips and chin of women.

Historically, tattooing served a variety of functions in Polynesia beyond personal beautification. It indicated status, because the quantity and quality of tattoos often reflected rank. In the Marquesas Islands, for example, tattoos completely covered the bodies of men of high status (FIG. 36-16). Certain patterns could be applied only to ranking individuals, but commoners also had tattoos, generally on a less extensive scale than elite individuals. For identification purposes, slaves had tattoos on their foreheads in Hawaii and on their backs in New Zealand. According to some accounts, victors placed tattoos on defeated warriors. In Polynesia, tattoos often identified clan or familial connections. Tattoos could also serve a protective function by in essence wrapping the body in a spiritual armor. On occasion, tattoos marked significant events. In Hawaii, for example, a tattooed tongue was a sign of grief. The pain that the tattooed person endured was a sign of respect for the deceased.

Priests who were specially trained in the art form usually applied the tattoos. Rituals, chants, or ceremonies often accompanied the procedure, which took place in a special structure. Tattooing involves the introduction of black, carbon-based pigment under the skin with the use of a bird-bone tattooing comb or chisel and a mallet. In New Zealand, a distinctive technique emerged for tattooing the face. In a manner similar to Maori woodcarving, a serrated chisel created a groove in the skin to receive pigment, thereby producing a colored line.

Polynesian tattoo designs were predominantly geometric, and affinities with other forms of Polynesian art are evident. For example, the curvilinear patterns found on decorated wall panels (*poupou*) in Maori meeting houses (FIGS. 36-1 and 36-21A) resemble and make reference to the patterns that predominate in Maori facial moko. Depending on their specific purpose, many tattoos could be "read" or deciphered. For facial tattoos, the Maori generally divided the face into four major, symmetrical zones: the left and right forehead down to

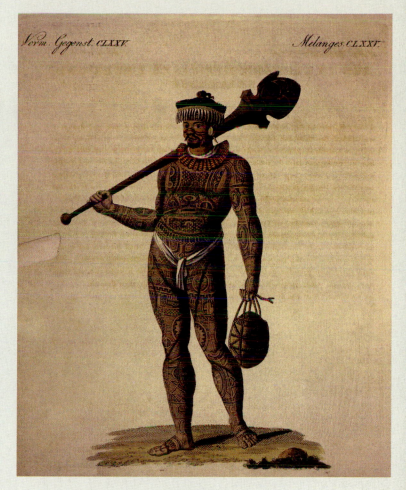

36-16 Tattooed warrior with war club, Nukahiva, Marquesas Islands, Polynesia, early 19th century. Color engraving in Carl Bertuch, *Bilderbuch für Kinder* (Weimar, 1813).

In Polynesia, with its hierarchical social structure, noblemen and warriors accumulated tattoo patterns to enhance their status and beauty. Tattoos wrapped a warrior's body in spiritual armor.

the eyes, the left lower face, and the right lower face. The right-hand side conveyed information on the father's rank, tribal affiliations, and social position, whereas the left-hand side provided matrilineal information. Smaller secondary facial zones provided information about the tattooed individual's profession and position in society. Te Pehi Kupe (FIG. I-19) was the chief of the Ngati Toa tribe in the early 19th century. The upward and downward *koru* (unrolled spirals) in the middle of his forehead connote his descent from two paramount tribes. The small design in the center of his forehead documents the extent of his domain—north, south, east, and west. The five double koru in front of his left ear indicate that the supreme chief (the highest rank in Maori society) was part of his matrilineal line. The designs on his lower jaw and the anchor-shaped koru nearby reveal that Te Pehi Kupe was not only a master carver but descended from master carvers as well.

Another important art form for Marquesan warriors during the 19th century was *tattoo*, which protected the individual, serving in essence as a form of spiritual armor, as did the hair ornaments. Body decoration in general is among the most pervasive art forms found throughout Oceania. Polynesians developed the painful but prestigious art of tattoo more fully than many other Oceanic peoples (see "Tattoo in Polynesia," above), although tattooing also occurred in various parts of Micronesia. In Polynesia, with its hierarchical social structure, nobles and warriors in particular accumulated various tattoo patterns over the years to enhance their status, mana, and personal beauty. Largely as a result of missionary pressure in the 19th century, tattooing virtually disappeared in many Oceanic societies, but some Pacific peoples have revived tattooing as an expression of cultural pride.

An 1813 engraving (FIG. 36-16) depicts a Marquesan warrior from Nukahiva Island covered with elaborate tattoo patterns. The warrior holds a large wood war club over his right shoulder and carries a decorated water gourd in his left hand. The various tattoo patterns marking his entire body seem to subdivide his body parts into zones on both sides of a line down the center. Some tattoos accentuate joint areas, whereas others separate muscle masses into horizontal and vertical geometric shapes. The warrior also covered his face, hands, and feet with tattoos.

RURUTU Deity images with multiple figures attached to their bodies are characteristic of Rurutu (FIG. 36-17) in the Austral Islands as well as Rarotonga (FIG. 36-18) and Mangaia in the Cook Islands. These carvings probably represented clan and district ancestors, honored for their protective and procreative powers. Ultimately, the images refer to the creator deities that the Polynesians revere for their central role in human fertility.

Rurutu is the northernmost of the Austral Islands in French Polynesia. In August 1821, following an edict of its leaders, the entire population converted to Christianity. As a symbol of their embrace of the new monotheistic religion, the inhabitants presented statues of their gods to the British missionaries stationed on a neighboring island. The wood statue illustrated here (FIG. **36-17**), representing the god A'a, was one of those gifts to the London Missionary Society. A'a was the original inhabitant of Rurutu, the ancestor of all its people. He was deified after his death. Distributed over the front and back of the god's body—and forming the eyes, nose, mouth, and ears of the disk-shaped head—are tiny relief figures of the gods and men whom A'a created. The sculptor depicted them in a variety of positions, including head

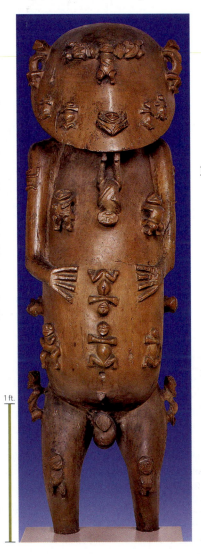

36-17 A'a, from Rurutu, Austral Islands, Polynesia, ca. 1800. Wood, 3' 8" high. British Museum, London.

A'a is the chief Rurutu ancestor god. Covering his body—and forming the features of his head—are relief figures of his progeny. A large cavity at the back of the statue held 24 more figures.

downward. At the back of the figure is a large cavity that once contained 24 additional miniature figures and perhaps also ancestral bones. The god places his hands on his belly, a gesture that calls attention to the interior compartment holding his progeny.

RAROTONGA Although closely related thematically to the Rurutu statues of A'a, the wood sculptures representing Rarotonga gods are very different in style and format. The inhabitants of that central Polynesian island used various types of carved deity figures well into the early decades of the 19th century, when Christians converted the islanders and destroyed their "idols" as part of the conversion process. These included carved wood fishermen's gods, large naturalistic deity images, and at least three types of staff gods (also called district gods), some more than 20 feet tall.

The example illustrated here (FIG. **36-18**) is one of the smaller but best-preserved examples. It may represent the Polynesian creator god Tangaroa. His head, with its enormous eyes, is about a third of the height of the sculpture. The "body" of the god resembles a spinal column and consists of seven figures with alternating frontal and profile heads. They probably represent the successive generations of humans whom Tangaroa created. The imagery suggests that these humans come from the body of the god. Several of the figures have erect penises, an unmistakable reference to sexual reproduction and the continuation of the race for many generations to come.

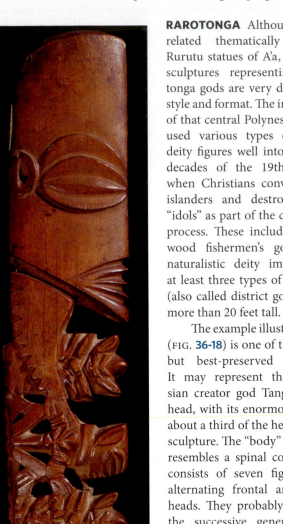

36-18 Staff god (Tangaroa?), from Rarotonga, Cook Islands, Polynesia, ca. 1900. Wood, 2' 4½" high. Cambridge University Museum of Archaeology and Anthropology, Cambridge.

The "body" of the Polynesian god Tangaroa consists of seven figures that probably represent generations of his human offspring. Several of the figures have erect penises, a reference to procreation.

Hawaii

The Hawaiians developed the most highly stratified social structure in the Pacific. By 1795, the chief Kamehameha unified the major islands of the Hawaiian archipelago and ascended to the pinnacle of power as King Kamehameha I (r. 1810–1819). The kingdom he established did not endure, however, and Hawaii soon came under American control. The United States annexed Hawaii as a territory in 1898 and eventually conferred statehood on the island group in 1959.

KUKA'ILIMOKU As elsewhere in the Pacific, the gods were a pervasive presence in Hawaiian society and were part of every person's life, regardless of status. Chiefs in particular invoked them regularly and publicized their ancestral links to the gods to reinforce their right to rule. One of the more prominent Hawaiian deities was Kuka'ilimoku, the war god. As chiefs in the prekingdom years struggled to maintain and expand their control, warfare was constant—hence the god's importance. Indeed, Kuka'ilimoku served as Kamehameha's special tutelary deity, and the Kuka'ilimoku sculpture illustrated here (FIG. 36-19) stood in a *heiau* (temple) on the island of Hawaii (Big Island), where Kamehameha I originally ruled before expanding his authority to the entire Hawaiian chain.

This late-18th- or early-19th-century Hawaiian wood temple image, which is more than 4 feet tall, confronts its audience with a ferocious expression. The war god's head comprises nearly a third of his entire body. His enlarged, angled eyes and prominent teeth in his wide-open figure-eight-shaped mouth convey aggression and defiance. Kuka'ilimoku's muscular body appears to stand slightly flexed, as if ready to attack. The artist realized this Hawaiian war god's overall athleticism through the full-volumed,

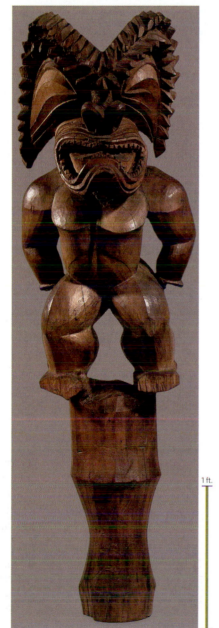

36-19 Kuka'ilimoku, from Hawaii, Polynesia, ca. 1790–1810. Wood, 4' 3¼" high. British Museum, London.

This wood statue of the Hawaiian war god comes from a temple. His muscular body is flexed to attack, and his wide mouth with bared teeth set in a large head conveys aggression and defiance.

faceted treatment of his arms, legs, and chest. In addition to sculptures of deities such as this, Hawaiians placed smaller versions of lesser deities and ancestral images in the heiau. Differing styles surface in the various islands of the Hawaiian chain, but the sculpted figures share a tendency toward athleticism and expressive defiance.

LONO Hawaiian artists also fashioned images of their gods from rare bird feathers and other natural materials placed over a wickerwork armature. The head illustrated here (FIG. 36-20), which incorporates pearl shells for eyes as well as human hair and dog's teeth, is one of five heads in the British Museum that Captain James Cook (1728–1779) took back to England after his third voyage to the South Pacific from 1776 to 1779. The Hawaiian feather heads were sacred objects and costly to produce because they incorporated feathers from thousands of birds. The Hawaiians believed that their gods had feathers covering their flesh. Feathers therefore connoted prestige, and the feather heads were also thought to be faithful reproductions of the deities' appearance. The Hawaiians mounted the gods' heads on poles, displayed them in religious processions, and carried them as standards into battle. When not

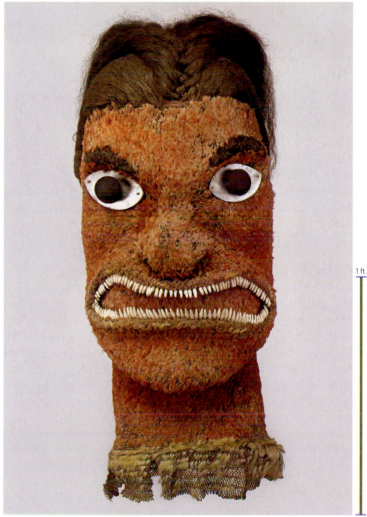

36-20 Head of Lono, from Hawaii, Polynesia, ca. 1775–1780. Feathers over wickerwork, human hair, dog's teeth, and pearl shells, 2' ¾" high. British Museum, London.

Feather heads of the Hawaiian gods with grimacing mouths, such as this one of Lono with human hair, pearl-shell eyes, and dog's teeth, were mounted on poles and carried in processions and into battle.

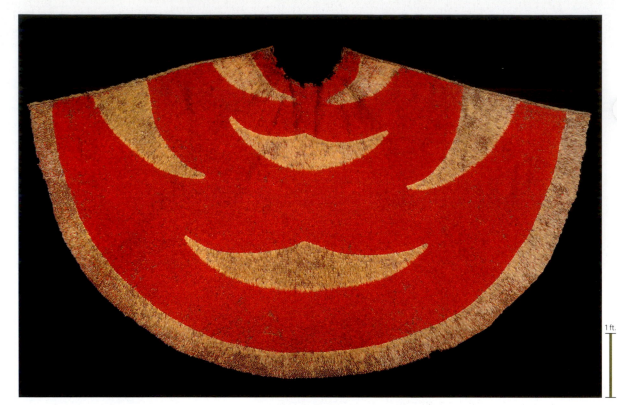

36-21 Feather cloak, from Hawaii, Polynesia, ca. 1824–1843. Feathers and fiber netting, 4' 8⅓" × 8'. Bishop Pauahi Museum, Honolulu.

Costly Hawaiian feather cloaks ('ahu 'ula) such as this one, which belonged to King Kamehameha III, provided the wearer with the gods' protection. Each cloak required the feathers of thousands of birds.

1 ft.

in use, they were on exhibit in temples under the care of religious officials.

Although very different in material and overall character, the feather heads of the gods share many iconographical and stylistic traits with Hawaiian full-length wood statues (FIG. 36-19) of gods, especially the larger-than-life grimacing mouths. Scholars believe that the heads with large central crests of feathers represent the war god Kuka'ilimoku. The head in the British Museum instead has a crown of parted human hair and probably depicts Lono, the god of agriculture, fertility, and peace.

FEATHER CLOAKS Because perpetuation of the social structure was crucial to social stability, chiefs' regalia, which visualized and reinforced the hierarchy of Hawaiian society, were a prominent part of artistic production. For example, elegant feather cloaks ('ahu 'ula) such as the early-19th-century example shown here (FIG. **36-21**) belonged to men of high rank. Every aspect of the 'ahu 'ula reflected the status of its wearer. The materials were exceedingly precious, particularly the red and yellow feathers from the 'i 'iwi, 'apapane, 'o 'o, and (now extinct) mamo birds. Some of these birds yield only six or seven suitable feathers, and because a full-length cloak could require up to 500,000 feathers, the resources and labor required to produce a cloak were extraordinary. The cloak also linked its owner to the gods. The Polynesians associated the plaited fiber base for the feathers with deities. Not only did these cloaks confer the protection of the gods on their wearers, but their dense fiber base and feather matting also provided physical protection. The artists who fashioned the cloaks chanted as they worked, believing that the power of the sacred chants permeated the fabric lining. The cloak in FIG. 36-21 originally belonged to King Kamehameha III (r. 1824–1854), who gave it to Commodore Lawrence Kearny of the U.S. frigate *Constellation* in 1843 in gratitude for Kearny's assistance during a temporary occupation of Hawaii.

New Zealand

The Maori of Aotearoa (New Zealand) share many cultural practices with other Polynesian societies. Ancestors and lineage traditionally played an important role, as is evident in the form and decoration of Maori meeting houses, such as those at Poverty Bay (FIG. 36-1) and at Whakatane (WEPIHA APANUI, lead sculptor; FIG. **36-21A**) and in the design of Maori facial moko (see "Tattoo in Polynesia," page 1115, and FIG. I-19). But as in many other Oceanic cultures, in New Zealand, largely as a result of colonial and missionary intervention in the early 19th through 20th centuries, traditional artistic methods, such as those used in carving, were modified with the introduction of contemporary methods and tools. Demand for traditional arts such as weaving and carving from international and local

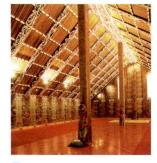

36-21A Mataatua wharenui (meeting house), Maori, 1871-1875.

museums, as well as from collectors and tourists, has ensured the continued development of traditional artistic methods alongside contemporary forms.

CLIFF WHITING In New Zealand, CLIFF WHITING (TE WHANAU-A-APANUI, b. 1936) and others have carried on the historical Maori woodcarving craft. Whiting has achieved renown for his stunning "carved murals" (FIG. 31-11A). He and other artists throughout the Pacific islands have championed not only the renewal of native cultural life and its continuity in art but also the education of the young in the values that made the Pacific cultures great. The preservation of native identity will depend on the success of the next generation in making the traditional Oceanic cultures once again their own.

OCEANIA BEFORE 1980

Australia and Melanesia

- The westernmost Oceanic islands have been populated for at least 40,000 years, but most of the preserved art dates to the last several centuries.

- The Aboriginal art of Australia focuses on ancestral spirits called Dreamings, whom artists represented in an X-ray style showing the internal organs.

- The Asmat of New Guinea avenged a relative's death by headhunting. Before embarking on a raid, they erected bisj poles with carved and painted figures of ancestors and animals.

- The center of every Iatmul village was a saddle-shaped ceremonial men's house representing a woman. Images of clan ancestors decorated the interior.

- Masks figured prominently in many Melanesian cultures. The Elerna celebrated water spirits in the festive cycle called Hevehe, which involved ornate masks up to 25 feet tall. The Abelam fashioned yam masks for rituals revolving around their principal crop. In New Ireland, dancers wore tatanua masks representing the spirits of the deceased.

- Artworks frequently played important roles in religious and funerary rituals. The bisexual uli figures of New Ireland symbolize a deceased chief's strength and his nurturing of his people.

- Seafaring was also a major theme of much Melanesian art. The Trobriand Islanders decorated their canoes with elaborately carved prows and splashboards.

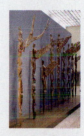

Asmat bisj poles, Papua province, mid-20th century

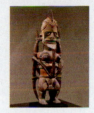

Uli, New Ireland, 18th or early 19th century

Micronesia

- The major themes of Melanesian art are also found in Micronesia. For example, in the Caroline Islands, many of the most skilled artists carved and painted wood prow ornaments for their canoes.

- The Micronesian peoples also erected ceremonial men's houses. The bai of Belau are distinctive in having Dilukai figures in the gable of the eastern entrance. The Dilukai is a woman with splayed legs who faces the sun and serves as a symbol of procreation and as a guardian of the house.

Men's ceremonial house, Belau, 20th century

Polynesia

- Polynesia was one of the last areas of the world to be settled, but the oldest large-scale art of Oceania is the series of moai on Rapa Nui (Easter Island). These colossal monolithic sculptures, which stood in rows on stone platforms, probably represent ancestors.

- Barkcloth is an important art form in Polynesia even today. The decorated barkcloth, or ngatu, of Tonga was used to wrap the corpses of deceased chiefs and for other ritual purposes, including the coronation of kings.

- Body adornment in the form of tattooing was widespread in Polynesia, especially in the Marquesas Islands and New Zealand. Beyond personal beautification, tattoos served to distinguish rank and provided warriors with a kind of spiritual armor.

- Meeting houses played an important role in Polynesian societies, as elsewhere in the Pacific islands. The meeting houses of the Maori of Aotearoa (New Zealand) are notable for their elaborate ornamentation featuring carved relief panels depicting ancestors.

- Images of named gods are common in Polynesia. Wood sculptures from Rurutu represent the chief ancestor god A'a. The Hawaiians erected statues of the war god Kuka'ilimoku in their temples and fashioned images of Lono and other deities from rare bird feathers. Hawaiian artists also produced elite regalia using feathers—for example, in cloaks worn exclusively by kings and other men of high rank.

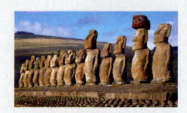

Moai, Rapa Nui, ca. 1200–1500

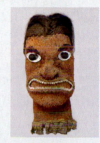

Lono, Hawaii, ca. 1775–1780

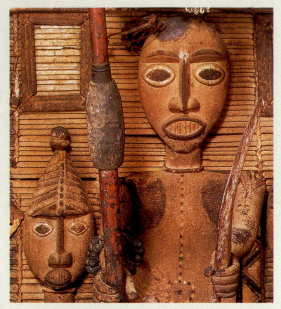

▲ **37-1a** Kalabari Ijaw ancestral screens are memorials to the chiefs of trading companies called canoe houses. The deceased, the central figure holding a long staff and curved knife, is also the largest.

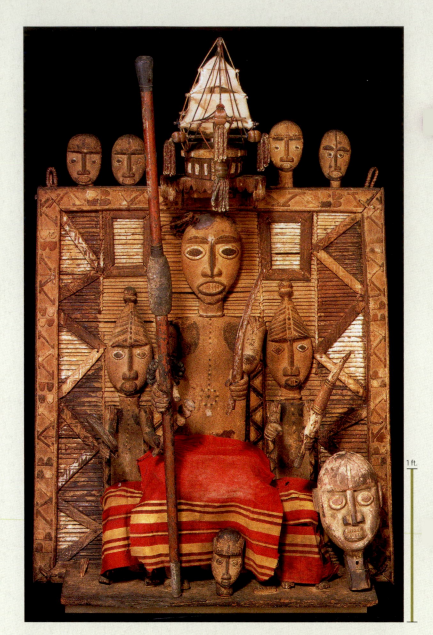

1 ft.

| 37-1 | **Ancestral screen (nduen fobara), Kalabari Ijaw, Nigeria, late 19th century. Wood, fiber, and cloth, 3' 9½" high. British Museum, London.** |

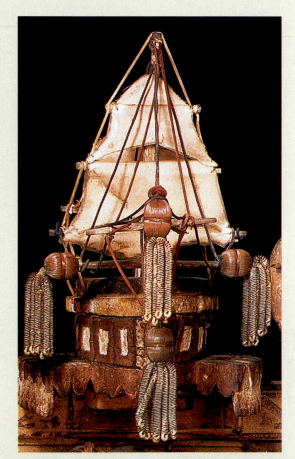

▲ **37-1b** The name for these screens is nduen fobara ("foreheads of the deceased"). The chief's headdress is in the form of a 19th-century European sailing ship, a reference to the deceased's trading business.

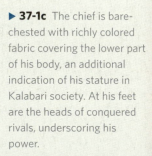
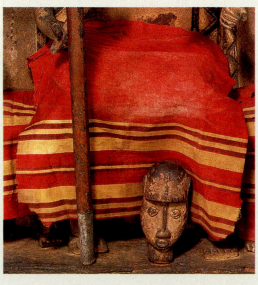

▶ **37-1c** The chief is bare-chested with richly colored fabric covering the lower part of his body, an additional indication of his stature in Kalabari society. At his feet are the heads of conquered rivals, underscoring his power.

Africa, 1800 to 1980

HONORING CHIEFS AND ANCESTORS

Throughout the continent, Africans create artworks for a variety of purposes. Among those explored in detail in this chapter are artworks honoring leaders and ancestors. Virtually all societies worldwide from ancient times to the present have enlisted artists to celebrate rulers and other leaders, both secular and religious, but Africans have traditionally lavished special attention on ancestors. Africans venerate their forebears for the continuing aid that they believe they provide the living, including help in maintaining the productivity of the earth for bountiful crop production and ensuring successful hunts.

In some African societies—for example the Fang and Kota—people place the bones of their ancestors in containers guarded by sculpted figures (FIGS. 37-2 and 37-3) in order to protect these treasured *relics* from theft or harm. In highly stratified societies headed by a monarch—for example, the Benin kingdom—the royal family maintains altars (FIG. 37-4) at which the current king offers animal sacrifices to honor his ancestors and enlist their help in protecting the living and assuring prosperity.

The Kalabari Ijaw peoples have hunted and fished in the eastern delta of the Niger River in present-day Nigeria for several centuries. The memorials that the Kalabari set up in honor of their ancestors are of unique form because a cornerstone of their economy has long been trade, and trading organizations known locally as "canoe houses" play a central role in Kalabari society. Kalabari ancestor shrines are screens of wood, fiber, textiles, and other materials.

An especially elaborate example (FIG. 37-1) is the almost 4-foot-tall *nduen fobara* ("foreheads of the deceased") honoring a former chief of a trading company. The chief's family usually commissioned these memorial screens on or about the one-year anniversary of his death. Displayed in the house in which the chief lived, the screens represent the deceased himself at the center. In this case, he holds a long, silver-tipped staff in his right hand and a curved knife in his left hand. His chest is bare, but covering the lower part of his body is a richly colored fabric, an emblem of his elevated stature in Kalabari society. His impressive headdress is in the form of a 19th-century European sailing ship, a reference to the chief's successful trading business, and another indication of the important role that costume plays in Africa. Flanking the chief are his attendants, smaller in size as is appropriate for their lower rank. The heads of his slaves are at the top of the screen and those of his conquered rivals are at the bottom. The hierarchical composition and the stylized rendition of human anatomy and facial features are common in African art, but the richness and complexity of this shrine are exceptional.

AFRICA, 1800 TO 1980

Africa (MAP 37-1) was one of the first art-producing regions of the world (see pages 16 and 541), but its early history remains largely undocumented. In fact, a generation ago, scholars still often presented African art as if it had no history. For the period treated in this chapter, however, art historians are on firmer ground. Archaeology and field research in Africa (mainly interviews with local people) have provided much more detail on the function and meaning of art objects produced during the past two centuries than for the period before 1800. As in earlier eras, the arts in Africa are integral to a great variety of human situations, and knowledge of these contexts is essential for understanding the artworks. In Africa, art is nearly always an active agent in the lives of its diverse peoples. This chapter presents a selection of important works from different regions of the continent from the early 19th century to 1980, organized thematically rather than chronologically or geographically in order to highlight characteristic continent-wide features of modern African art. Chapter 31 treats African art and artists of the past few decades in a worldwide context.

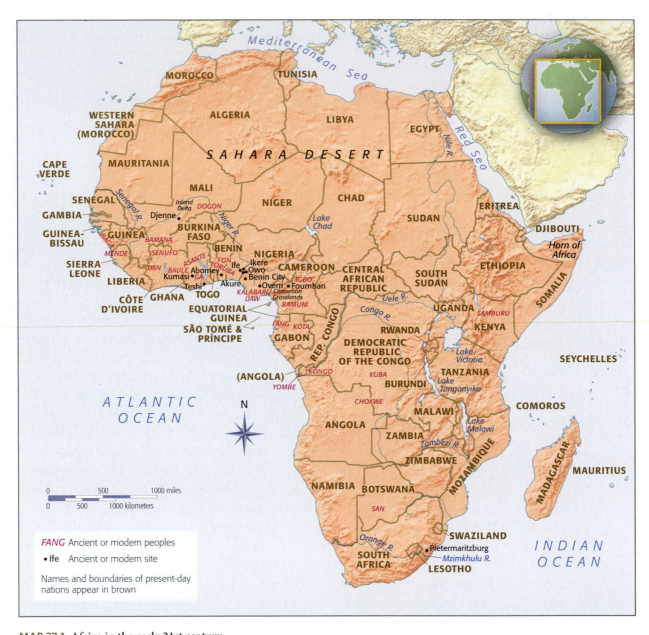

MAP 37-1 Africa in the early 21st century.

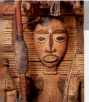

AFRICA, 1800 TO 1980

1800–1900
- San rock paintings record contemporaneous events
- Fang, Kota, and Kalabari Ijaw artists produce reliquary guardian figures and memorial screens to venerate ancestors
- Royal arts include the throne of Bamum king Ngansu and Fon king Glele's *bocio* of the god Gu
- Yombe, Dogon, and Baule sculptors carve wood groups of mother and child or man and woman

1900–1980
- Royal arts continue to flourish in highly stratified societies, such as the Benin kingdom
- The recording of artists' names becomes more common; Osei Bonsu and Olowe of Ise achieve wide renown as sculptors
- Throughout the continent, African peoples produce elaborate masks to be danced at masquerades
- Personal adornment is a major art form, including body painting, complex coiffures, rich textiles, and the lavish regalia of kings

ANCESTORS AND SPIRITS

The Kalabari Ijaw screen (FIG. 37-1) already discussed is typical of many of the artworks examined in this chapter in illustrating multiple themes of African art—in that case, honoring ancestors and leaders, and the important role of costume in African societies. This section treats works whose main function is to celebrate ancestors and honor the world of spirits.

Reliquaries

Outstanding examples of ancestral artworks are the *reliquary* guardian figures of the Fang and Kota peoples just south of the equator in Gabon and Cameroon. Both the Fang and Kota collected relics (cranial and other bones) of the deceased and deposited them in special containers for use in ancestor worship.

FANG BIERI Stylized wood human figures (FIG. 37-2), or in some cases simply heads, protected the Fang relic containers. The sculptors of these Fang guardian figures, or *bieri,* designed them to sit on the edge of cylindrical bark boxes of ancestral bones, ensuring that no harm would befall the ancestral spirits. The sculpted figures are symmetrical, with proportions greatly emphasizing the head, and they feature a rhythmic buildup of forms suggestive of contained power. Particularly striking are the proportions of the bodies of the bieri, which resemble those of an infant, although the muscularity of the figures implies an adult. Scholars believe that the Fang sculptors chose this combination of traits to suggest the cycle of life, appropriate for an art form connected with the cult of ancestors.

37-2 Reliquary guardian figure (bieri), Fang, Gabon, late 19th century. Wood, 1' 8 3/8" high. Philadelphia Museum of Art, Philadelphia.

Bieri guard cylindrical bark boxes of Fang ancestor bones (reliquaries). The figures have the bodies of infants and the muscularity of adults, a combination of traits suggesting the cycle of life.

KOTA MBULU NGULU The Kota of Gabon also produced reliquary guardian figures, called *mbulu ngulu* (FIG. 37-3), but they differ markedly from the Fang bieri. The Kota figures have severely stylized bodies in the form of an open diamond below a wood head. The sculptors of these reliquary guardians covered both the head and the abstract body with strips and sheets of polished copper and brass. The Kota believed that the gleaming surfaces repelled evil. The simplified heads have hairstyles flattened out laterally above and beside the face. Geometric ridges, borders, and subdivisions add a textured elegance to the shiny forms. The copper alloy on most of these images is reworked sheet brass (or copper wire) taken from brass basins originating in Europe and traded into this area of equatorial Africa in the 18th and 19th centuries. The Kota inserted the lower portion of the image into a basket or box of ancestral relics.

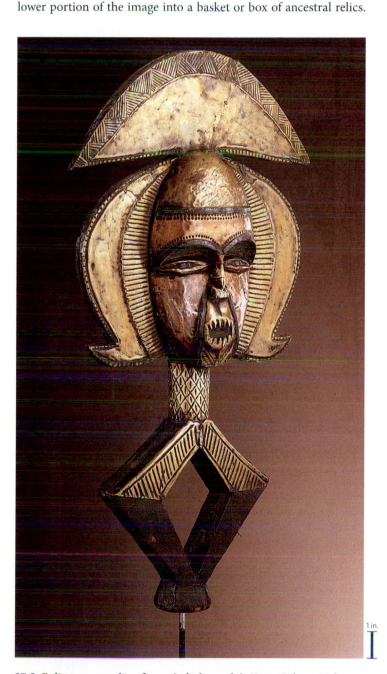

1 in.

37-3 Reliquary guardian figure (mbulu ngulu), Kota, Gabon, 19th or early 20th century. Wood, copper, iron, and brass, 1' 9 1/16" high. Musée Barbier-Mueller, Geneva.

Kota guardian figures have large heads and bodies in the form of an open diamond. Polished copper and brass sheets cover the wood forms. The Kota believe that gleaming surfaces repel evil.

1 in.

Altars

Some of the most important 20th-century African artworks come from areas with strong earlier artistic traditions—for example, the kingdom of Benin (FIGS. I-15, 19-1, 19-14, and 19-14A) in present-day Nigeria. Ancestor worship in Benin focused primarily on royalty (see "The Royal Arts of Benin," page 539), another major theme of African art (see page 1127).

SHRINE OF EWEKA II In 1897, when the British sacked Benin City, there were still 17 shrines to ancestors in the Benin royal palace. Today, only one 20th-century altar (FIG. **37-4**) remains. According to oral history, it is similar to centuries-earlier versions. With a base of sacred riverbank clay, it is an assemblage of varied materials, objects, and symbols: a central copper-alloy altarpiece depicting a sacred king flanked by members of his entourage, plus copper-alloy heads, each fitted on top with an ivory tusk carved in relief. Behind are wood staffs and metal bells. The heads represent both the kings themselves and, through the durability of the material, the enduring nature of kingship. Their glistening surfaces, seen as red and signaling danger, repel evil forces that might adversely affect the shrine and thus the king and kingdom. Elephant-tusk relief carvings atop the heads commemorate important events and personages in Benin history. Their bleached white color signifies purity and goodness (probably of royal ancestors), and the tusks themselves represent male physical power. The bamboolike, segmented forms of the carved wood rattle-staffs standing at the back refer to generations of dynastic ancestors. The rattle-staffs and the pyramidal copper-alloy bells serve the important function of calling royal ancestral spirits to rituals performed at the altar.

The Benin king's head stands for wisdom, good judgment, and divine guidance for the kingdom. The several heads of royal ancestors on the altar multiply these qualities. By means of animal sacrifices at this site, the living king annually purifies his own head (and being) by invoking the collective strength of his ancestors, whose presence is made manifest by their heads. Thus the varied objects, symbols, colors, and materials of this shrine contribute both visually and ritually to the imaging of royal power, as well as to its history, renewal, and perpetuation. The composition of the shrine, like that of the altar at its center and the mid-18th-century Altar to the Hand (FIG. I-15), is hierarchical. At the center of all Benin hierarchies stands the king (FIG. 19-1).

Statuary

As in the case of the reliquary guardian figures (FIGS. 37-2 and 37-3) of the Fang and Kota, wood statues, often enhanced by the addition of metals, shells, beads, and other materials, play a key role in the veneration of ancestors and spirits in many African societies.

KONGO NKISI N'KONDI Among the most distinctive African sculptures of the 19th century are the Kongo power figures called *nkisi n'kondi,* such as the standing statue illustrated here (FIG. **37-5**), which depicts a man bristling with nails and blades. These images, consecrated by trained priests using precise ritual formulas, embodied spirits believed to heal and give life, or sometimes to inflict harm, disease, or even death. Each figure had its specific role, just as it wore particular medicines—here protruding from the abdomen, which features a large cowrie shell. The Kongo also activated every image differently. Owners appealed to a figure's forces every

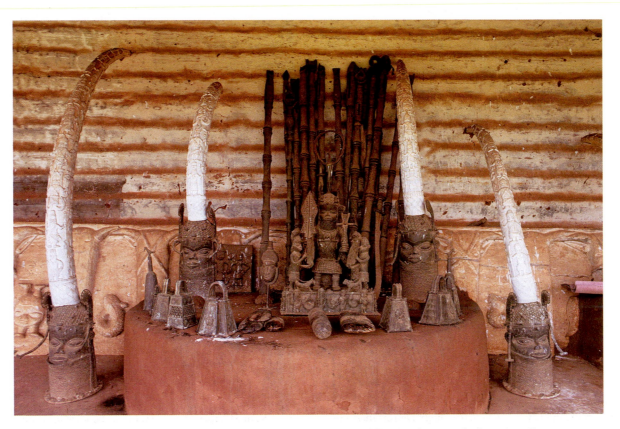

37-4 Royal ancestral altar of King Eweka II, in the palace in Benin City, Nigeria, photographed in 1970. Clay, copper alloy, wood, and ivory. Photo: National Museum of African Art, Washington, D.C.

This shrine to the heads of royal ancestors is an assemblage of materials, objects, and symbols. By sacrificing animals at this altar, the Benin king annually invokes the collective strength of his ancestors.

time they inserted a nail or blade, as if to prod the spirit to do its work. People invoked other spirits by repeating specific chants, rubbing the images, or applying special powders. The roles of power figures varied enormously, from curing minor ailments to stimulating crop growth, from punishing thieves to weakening enemies. Very large Kongo figures, such as this one, which is nearly 4 feet tall, had exceptional ascribed powers and aided entire communities. Although benevolent for their owners, the figures stood at the boundary between life and death, and most villagers held them in awe. Compared with the sculptures of other African peoples, this Kongo figure is relatively naturalistic, although the carver simplified the facial features and magnified the size of the head for emphasis.

DOGON LINKED COUPLE The Dogon live in the Bandiagara escarpment south of the inland delta region of the great Niger River in what is today Mali. Numbering around 800,000, spread among hundreds of small villages, the Dogon practice farming as their principal occupation. The Dogon statuette illustrated here (FIG. 37-6) depicts a human couple, one of the most common themes in African art. This Dogon example is, however, of exceptional quality. It dates to the early 19th century and may have served as a portable shrine or altar, although contextual information is lacking. Interpretations vary, but the image vividly documents primary gender roles in

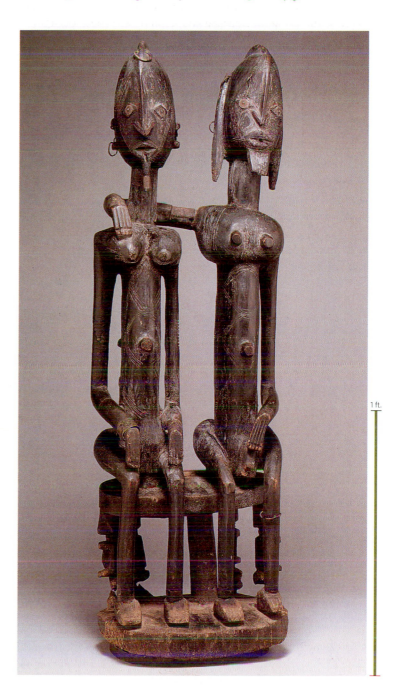

37-5 Nail figure (*nkisi n'kondi*), Kongo, from Shiloango River area, Democratic Republic of Congo, ca. 1875–1900. Wood, nails, blades, medicinal materials, and cowrie shell, 3' 10¾" high. Detroit Institute of Arts, Detroit.

Only priests using ritual formulas could consecrate Kongo power figures, which embody spirits that can heal or inflict harm. This statue has simplified anatomical forms and an oversize head.

37-6 Seated couple, Dogon, Mali, ca. 1800–1850. Wood, 2' 4" high. Metropolitan Museum of Art, New York (gift of Lester Wunderman).

This Dogon carving of a linked man and woman documents gender roles in traditional African society. The protective man wears a quiver on his back. The nurturing woman carries a child on hers.

traditional African society. The man wears a quiver on his back. The woman carries a child on hers. Thus the man assumes a protective role as hunter or warrior, the woman a nurturing role. The slightly larger man reaches behind his mate's neck and touches her breast, as if to protect her. His left hand points to his genitalia. Four stylized figures support the stool on which they sit. They are probably either spirits or ancestors, but the identity of the larger figures is uncertain.

The strong stylization of Dogon sculptures contrasts sharply with the organic, relatively realistic treatment of the human body in Kongo art (FIG. 37-5). The artist who carved the Dogon couple based the forms more on the idea or concept of the human body than on observation of individual heads, torsos, and limbs. The linked body parts are tubes and columns articulated inorganically. The carver reinforced the almost abstract geometry of the overall composition by incising rectilinear and diagonal patterns on the surfaces. The Dogon artist also understood the importance of space, and charged the voids, as well as the sculptural forms, with rhythm and tension.

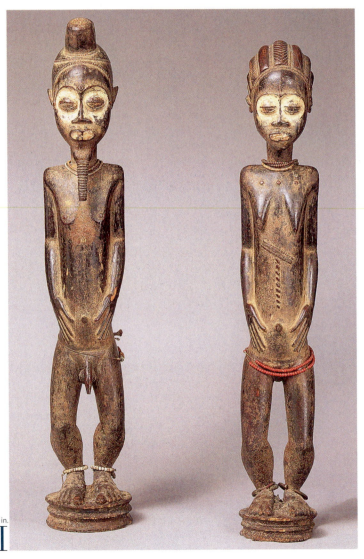

37-7 Male and female figures, probably bush spirits (asye usu), Baule, Côte d'Ivoire, late 19th or early 20th century. Wood, beads, and kaolin, man 1' 9¾" high, woman 1' 8⅝" high. Metropolitan Museum of Art, New York (Michael C. Rockefeller Memorial Collection, gift of Nelson A. Rockefeller).

In contrast to the Dogon couple (FIG. 37-6), this pair includes many naturalistic aspects of human anatomy, but the sculptor enlarged the necks, calves, and heads, a form of idealization in Baule culture.

BAULE BUSH SPIRITS The Baule of present-day Côte d'Ivoire do not have kings, and their societies are relatively egalitarian, especially compared with other highly stratified African population groups, but Baule art encompasses many of the same basic themes seen elsewhere on the continent. The Baule statues of a man and woman illustrated here (FIG. 37-7) probably portray bush spirits (asye usu). The sculptor most likely carved the pair of wood figures for a trance diviner, a religious specialist who consulted the spirits symbolized by the statues on behalf of clients who were either sick or in some way troubled. In Baule thought, bush spirits are short, horrible-looking, and sometimes deformed creatures, yet Baule sculptors represent them in the form of beautiful, ideal human beings, because ugly figures would offend the spirits, who would then refuse to work for the diviner. Among the Baule, as among many West African peoples, bush or wilderness spirits not only cause difficulties in life but, if properly addressed and placated, also may solve problems or cure sickness. In dance and trance performances—with wood figures and other objects displayed nearby—the diviner can divine, or understand, the will of unseen spirits as well as their needs or prophecies, which the diviner passes on to clients. When not set up outdoors for a performance, the figures and other objects remain in the diviner's house or shrine, where more private consultations take place. In striking contrast to the Dogon sculptor of the seated man and woman (FIG. 37-6), the artist who created this matched pair of Baule male and female images recorded many naturalistic aspects of human anatomy, skillfully translating them into finished sculptural form. At the same time, the sculptor

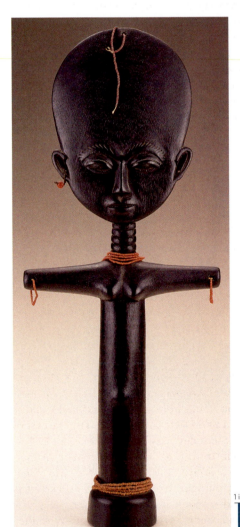

37-8 OSEI BONSU, akua'ba ("Akua's child"), Asante, Ghana, ca. 1960. Wood and glass beads, 1' 2½" high. National Museum of African Art, Washington, D.C. (gift of Herbert C. Madison).

Osei Bonsu was one of Africa's leading sculptors. This figure, carried by women hoping to conceive a child, has a flattened face and crosshatched eyebrows, typical features of the artist's style.

ART AND SOCIETY

African Artists and Apprentices

Like European art before the Renaissance, most African art is anonymous, primarily because early researchers rarely asked for artists' names (see "Dating African Art and Identifying African Artists," page 542). Nonetheless, connoisseurs can recognize many individual hands or styles even when an artist's name has not been recorded. And, as art historians regularly do with unsigned European artworks, they will assign names to the artists who produced them—for example, the Master of the Symbolic Execution (FIG. 19-16), an anonymous 16th-century sculptor from Sierra Leone. During the past century, art historians and anthropologists have been systematically noting the names and life histories of specific individual artists, many of whom have strong regional reputations. One of the earliest recorded names is that of the mid-19th-century Fon sculptor and metalsmith Akati Akpele Kendo (FIG. 37-13). Two 20th-century artists, renowned even beyond their homelands, were Osei Bonsu (FIGS. 37-8 and 37-9), based in the Asante capital of Kumasi, and the Yoruba sculptor called Olowe of Ise (FIGS. 37-11 and 37-11A) because he came from the town of Ise. Both artists were master carvers, producing sculptures for kings and commoners alike.

Like other great artists throughout history, both Bonsu and Olowe had apprentices to assist them for several years while learning their trade. Although there are various kinds of apprenticeship in Africa, novices typically lived with their masters and were household servants as well as assistant carvers. They helped fell trees, carry logs, and rough out basic shapes, which the master later transformed into finished work. African sculptors typically worked on commission. Sometimes, as in Bonsu's case, patrons traveled to the home of the artist. But other times, Bonsu moved to the home of a patron for weeks or months while working on a commission. Masters, and in some instances also apprentices, lived and ate in the patron's compound. Olowe, for example, resided with different kings for many months at a time while he carved doors (FIG. 37-11), veranda posts (FIG. 37-11A), and other works for royal families.

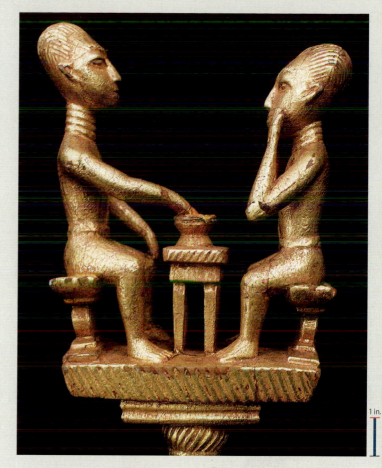

1 in.

37-9 OSEI BONSU, two men sitting at a table of food (linguist's staff), Asante, Ghana, mid-20th century. Wood and gold leaf, section shown 10" high. Collection of the Paramount Chief of Offinso, Asante.

Bonsu carved this gold-covered wood linguist's staff for someone who could speak for the Asante king. At the top are two men sitting at a table of food—a metaphor for the office of the king.

was well aware of creating *waka sran* ("people of wood") rather than living beings. Thus the artist freely exaggerated the length of the figures' necks and the size of their heads and calf muscles, all of which are forms of idealization in Baule culture.

ASANTE AKUA'BA The Asante of modern Ghana formed a strong confederacy around 1700. They are one of several peoples, including the Baule of Côte d'Ivoire, who speak an Akan dialect. A common stylistic characteristic of Asante figural art is the preference for conventionalized, flattened heads. Many Akan peoples considered long, slightly flattened foreheads to be emblems of beauty, and mothers gently molded their children's cranial bones to reflect this value. These anatomical features occur in a wood statuette (FIG. **37-8**) representing a young girl, or *akua'ba* ("Akua's child"), carved by one of the 20th century's leading African sculptors, OSEI BONSU (1900–1976). After consecrating a simplified wood akua'ba sculpture at a shrine, a young woman hoping to conceive carried it with her. Once pregnant, she continued to carry the figure to ensure the safe delivery of a healthy and handsome child—among these matrilineal people, preferably a girl. Compared with traditional sculptures of this type, the more naturalistic rendering of the face and crosshatched eyebrows in

Osei Bonsu's sculpture are distinctive features of his personal style (see "African Artists and Apprentices," above).

LEADERSHIP AND ROYALTY

In addition to power and prestige, African kings, chiefs, and other leaders possessed considerable wealth, which they used to commission artworks fashioned by the finest artists employing the costliest materials (see "Art and Leadership in Africa," page 545). Not surprisingly, some of the greatest works of African art of every era were made to honor or to be used by African leaders, whether secular or religious.

Emblems of Leadership

Among the African masters who fashioned royal emblems for kings and their entourage was Osei Bonsu.

LINGUIST'S STAFF One of Bonsu's masterworks is a gold-covered wood sculpture (FIG. **37-9**) depicting two men sitting at a table of food. This object, commonly called a *linguist's staff* because its carrier often speaks for a king or chief, has a related proverb: "Food is for its rightful owner, not for the one who happens to be hungry." Food is a metaphor for the office that the king or chief rightfully holds. The "hungry" man lusts for the office. The linguist, who is an important counselor and adviser to the king, might carry this staff to a meeting at which a rival contests the king's title to the stool (his throne, the office). Many hundreds of sculptures from the Akan region have proverbs or other sayings associated with them, which has created a rich verbal tradition relating to the visual arts of the Akan peoples.

DAN CEREMONIAL SPOONS African sculptors also carved emblems of power and prestige for women. Notable examples are the ceremonial spoons or ladles (FIG. **37-9A**) of the Dan of Côte d'Ivoire.

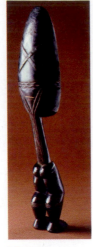

🔼 **37-9A** Ceremonial spoon, Dan, 19th–20th century.

THRONE OF NSANGU Perhaps the most widely recognized emblem of kingship in Africa is the throne. One of the best surviving examples comes from the kingdom of Bamum in present-day Cameroon, where a long line of kings lived in a palace compound at the capital city of Foumban until its destruction in 1910. The royal arts of Bamum make extensive use of richly colored textiles and luminous materials, such as glass beads and cowrie shells. The Bamum throne illustrated here (FIG. **37-10**) belonged to King Nsangu (r. 1865–1872 and 1885–1887). Intertwining blue and black serpents decorate the cylindrical seat. Above are the figures of two of the king's retainers, perpetually at his service. One, a man, holds the royal drinking horn. The other, a woman holding a serving bowl in her hands. Below are two of the king's bodyguards wielding European rifles. Dancing figures decorate the rectangular footstool. When the king sat on this throne (compare FIG. 37-23), his rich garments complemented the bright colors of his seat, advertising his wealth and power to all who were admitted to his palace.

Palace Architecture

African artists were also called on to decorate the living quarters of kings and chiefs. One of these artists was OLOWE OF ISE (ca. 1873–1938), a Yoruba sculptor who achieved international recognition.

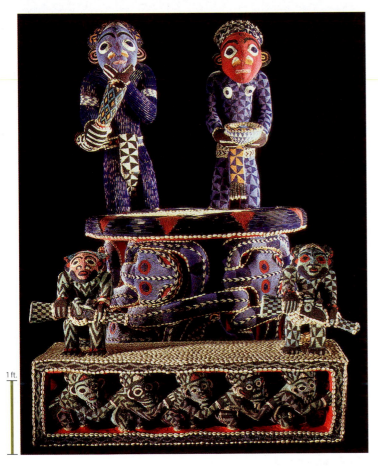

37-10 Throne and footstool of King Nsangu, Bamum, Cameroon, ca. 1870. Wood, textile, glass beads, and cowrie shells, 5' 9" high. Museum für Völkerkunde, Staatliche Museen zu Berlin, Berlin.

King Nsangu's throne features luminous beads and shells and richly colored textiles. The decoration includes intertwining serpents, male and female retainers, and bodyguards with European rifles.

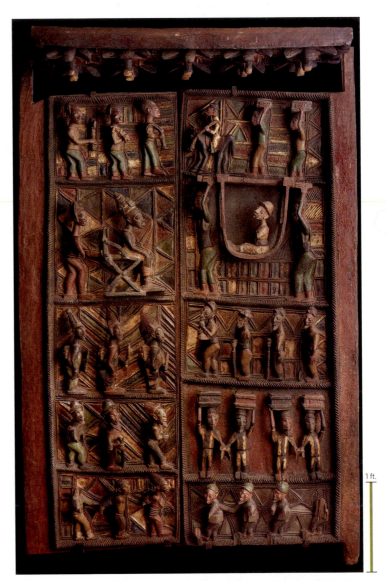

37-11 OLOWE OF ISE, doors from the shrine of the king's head in the royal palace, Ikere, Yoruba, Nigeria, 1910–1914. Painted wood, 6' high. British Museum, London.

These masterfully carved and painted doors to the shrine of the king's head in the Ikere palace are the work of Olowe of Ise, one of the few African artists whose name and career have been recorded.

OLOWE OF ISE The Yoruba have a long history in southwestern Nigeria and the southern Republic of Benin, going back to the founding of Ile-Ife in the 11th century (see page 546). In 1925, the British Museum acquired directly from the Yoruba *ogoga* (king) of Ikere (in exchange for a British throne) the elaborately carved and painted doors (FIG. 37-11) of the shrine of the king's head in his palace in northeastern Yorubaland. At the time, the museum did not inquire about the artist's name. Not until after World War II, when art historians began to document the careers of individual African artists (see "African Artists and Apprentices," page 1127), did the British curators learn that the master carver was Olowe of Ise, the most famous Yoruba sculptor of the early 20th century. Kings and aristocrats throughout Yorubaland employed Olowe to carve reliefs, masks, bowls, veranda posts (FIG. 37-11A), and other works for them, and he traveled widely in his homeland to execute those commissions. Between 1910 and 1914, he resided at Ikere while working for the ogoga. The palace shrine doors date from that time.

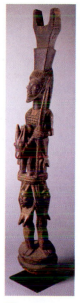

37-11A OLOWE OF ISE, veranda post, Akure, 1920s.

Departing from convention, Olowe made the two doors of unequal width to accommodate a rare historical narrative (compare FIGS. 37-26 and 37-27) in ten panels in five registers. The reliefs recount the 1897 visit of the representative of the British Empire, Major W. R. Reeve-Tucker, the first traveling commissioner of Ondo province. Litter-bearers carry Reeve-Tucker into the palace compound, where the enthroned king (far larger than the British emissary) and his principal wife receive him. The other panels on each door depict the entourage of the two protagonists, including, at the left, the king's bodyguards and other wives and, on the right door, shackled slaves carrying chests. Characteristically for Olowe, the relief is so high that some of the figures project as much as 6 inches from the surface, which has a vividly colored patterned background. Olowe also carved the veranda posts of the courtyard in front of the shrine.

Statuary

Wood sculptures representing gods, heroes, kings, and queens are among the most common surviving examples of African royal art.

CHIBINDA ILUNGA The Chokwe occupy the area of west-central Africa corresponding to parts of northeastern Angola and southwestern Democratic Republic of Congo. Local legend claims that the Chokwe are the descendants of the widely traveled Chibinda Ilunga, who won fame as a hunter. He married a princess named Lueji, who was a hereditary ruler of one of the kingdoms of the Lunda Empire, an important regional power during the 16th through 19th centuries. Lueji gave Chibinda a sacred bracelet, the basis and symbol of her rule, which established his authority. Chibinda taught the Lunda to be great hunters, enriched the kingdom, and extended its territory. The Chokwe, one of the population groups resulting from that territorial expansion, became skilled elephant hunters and ivory traders. They eventually revolted against the Lunda kings and brought about the collapse of the Lunda Empire in the mid-19th century.

The Chokwe revere Chibinda Ilunga as founder, hunter, and civilizing hero, and he figures prominently in their royal arts. The

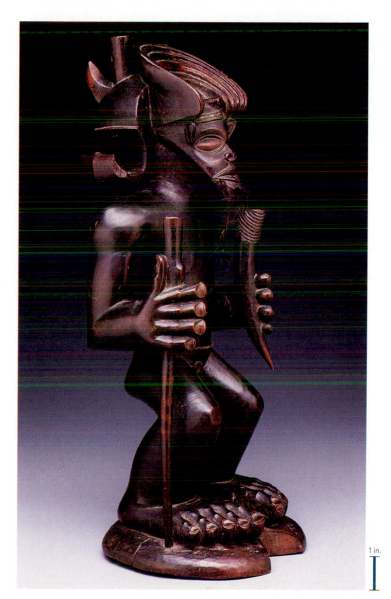

37-12 Chibinda Ilunga, Chokwe, from Angola or Democratic Republic of Congo, late 19th to 20th century. Wood and human hair, 1' 4" high. Kimbell Art Museum, Fort Worth.

The Chokwe claim descent from the legendary hunter Chibinda Ilunga, portrayed in art as a muscular man with a chief's headdress, oversized hands and feet, and a beard of human hair.

statue illustrated here (FIG. 37-12) is one of the finest examples. It shows the legendary hunter-king wearing a chief's barkcloth-and-rattan headdress and holding a staff in his right hand and, in his left hand, a medicine horn containing powerful substances to aid hunters. The unknown master sculptor portrayed Chibinda with a muscular body and oversized arms and feet to underscore the hunter's manual dexterity and ability to undertake long journeys. A rare feature of this and other Chokwe figures is the use of human hair for Chibinda's beard.

KING GLELE The founding of the Fon kingdom in the present-day Republic of Benin dates to around 1600. Under King Guezo (r. 1818–1858), the Fon became a regional power with an economy based largely on trade in palm oil. In 1900, the French dismantled the kingdom.

ART AND SOCIETY

Gender Roles in African Art Production

Until recently, art production in Africa has been quite rigidly gender-specific. Men have been, and largely still are, ironsmiths and gold and copper-alloy casters. Men were architects, builders, and carvers of both wood and ivory. Women were, and for the most part remain, wall and body painters, calabash decorators, potters, and often clay sculptors, although men make clay figures in some areas. Both men and women work with beads and weave baskets and textiles, with men executing narrow strips (later sewn together) on horizontal looms and women working wider pieces of cloth on vertical looms.

Much African art, however, is collaborative. Men may build a clay wall, for example, but women will normally decorate it. The Igbo people build *mbari* houses (FIG. 37-14A)—for ceremonies to honor the earth goddess—that are truly collaborative despite the fact that professional male artists model the figures displayed in the houses. Festivals, invoking virtually all the arts, are also collaborative. Masquerades (see "African Masquerades," page 1131) are largely the province of men, yet in some cases women contribute costume elements such as skirts, wrappers, and scarves. Even though women dance and wear the masks in the masquerades of the Mende and related peoples (see "Mende Women as Maskers," page 1135), men have always carved the masks themselves.

In late colonial and especially in postcolonial times, earlier gender distinctions in art production began breaking down. Today, women as well as men weave *kente* cloth (FIG. 37-24), and a number of women are now sculptors in wood, metal, stone, and composite materials. Men are making pottery, once the exclusive prerogative of women. Both women and men make international art forms in urban and university settings, although male artists are more numerous. One well-known Nigerian woman artist, Sokari Douglas Camp (b. 1958), produces welded metal sculptures,

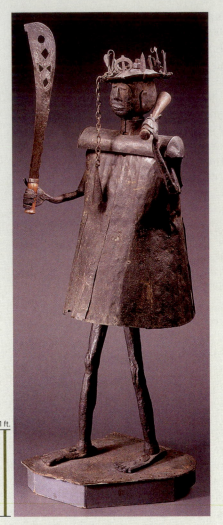

37-13 AKATI AKPELE KENDO, Warrior figure (Gu?), from the palace of King Glele, Abomey, Fon, Republic of Benin, 1858–1859. Iron, 5' 5" high. Musée du quai Branly, Paris.

This bocio, or empowerment figure, probably representing the war god Gu, was the centerpiece of a circle of iron swords. The Fon believed that it protected their king, and they set it up on the battlefield.

sometimes of masqueraders. Douglas Camp is thus doubly unusual as a metal sculptor and mask maker. She might find it difficult to pursue either role in her traditional home in the Niger River delta, but because she lives and works in London, she encounters no adverse response. In the future, there will undoubtedly be a further breaking down of restrictive barriers and greater mobility for artists.

After his first military victory, Guezo's son Glele (r. 1858–1889) commissioned a prisoner of war, AKATI AKPELE KENDO, to make a life-size iron statue (FIG. 37-13) of a warrior, probably Gu, the Fon god of war and iron, for a battle shrine in Glele's palace at Abomey. This *bocio*, or empowerment figure, was the centerpiece of a circle of iron swords and other weapons set vertically into the ground. The warrior strides forward with weapons in both hands, ready to do battle. He wears a crown of miniature swords and tools on his head. The form of the crown echoes the circle of swords around the statue. The Fon believed that the bocio protected their king, and they transported it to the battlefield whenever they set out to fight an enemy force. King Glele's iron warrior is remarkable for its size and for the fact that not only the patron's name is known but also the artist's—a rare instance in Africa before the 20th century (see "African Artists," page 1127).

It is no coincidence that the iron sculptor who worked for King Glele was a man, but women as well as men have long been active in African art production—usually, however, specializing in different types of objects (see "Gender Roles in African Art Production," above).

YOMBE PFEMBA The Congo River formed the principal transportation route for the peoples of central Africa during the 19th century, fostering cultural exchanges as well as trade, both among Africans and with Europeans. One of the region's major art-producing societies was the Yombe in the Democratic Republic

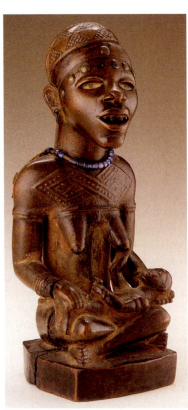

37-14 Yombe mother and child (pfemba), Kongo, Democratic Republic of Congo, late 19th century. Wood, glass, glass beads, brass tacks, and pigment, $10\frac{1}{8}$" high. National Museum of African Art, Washington, D.C.

The mother in this Yombe group wears a royal cap and jewelry and displays her chest scarification. The image may commemorate an ancestor or, more likely, a legendary founding clan mother.

of Congo, perhaps best known for their mother-and-child groups (*pfemba*), which some scholars believe may reflect the influence of Christian Madonna-and-Child imagery. The Yombe pfemba are not deities, however, but images of Kongo royalty. One masterful 19th-century example (FIG. 37-14) represents a woman with a royal cap, chest scarification, and jewelry (see Costume and Body Art, page 1136). The image may commemorate an ancestor or, more likely, a legendary founding clan mother. The Kongo call some of these figures "white chalk," a reference to the medicinal power of white kaolin clay. Diviners own some of them, and others have been used by women's organizations to treat infertility, but the function of this 19th-century pfemba is uncertain.

RITUALS AND MASQUERADES

As noted, the Yombe pfemba may have been used to overcome infertility, and many of the artworks that Africans have produced from very early times to today have been made specifically for use

in religious rituals and entertainments, most notably in masquerades, but also for display in shrines (FIG. 37-14A).

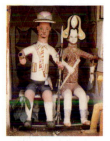

SENUFO MASQUERADES The Senufo of the western Sudan region in what is now northern Côte d'Ivoire have a population today of more than a million. They speak several different languages, sometimes even in the same village. Not surprisingly, there are many different Senufo art forms, including woodcarving (FIG. 37-14B) and mask making (FIGS. 37-15 and 37-16), all closely tied to community life.

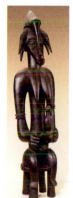

🔗 **37-14A** Ala and Amadioha, Igbo, photographed 1966.

🔗 **37-14B** Ancient Mother, Senufo, early 20th century.

African Masquerades

The art of masquerade, in which performers, almost always men, dance after donning masks, has long been a quintessential African expressive form, laden with meaning and of the highest importance culturally. This is true today, but was even more so in colonial times and earlier, when African masking societies boasted extensive regulatory and judicial powers. In stateless societies, such as those of the Senufo (FIGS. 37-15 and 37-16), Dogon (FIG. 37-17), and Mende (FIG. 37-22), masks sometimes became so influential that they had their own priests and served as power sources or as oracles. Societies empowered maskers to levy fines and to apprehend witches (usually defined as socially destructive people) and criminals, and to judge and punish them. Normally, however—especially today—masks are less threatening and more secular and educational and serve as diversions from the humdrum of daily life. Masked dancers usually embody either ancestors, seen as briefly returning to the human realm, or various nature spirits called on for their special powers.

The mask, a costume ensemble's focal point, combines with held objects, music, and dance gestures to invoke a specific named character, almost always considered a spirit. A few masked spirits appear by themselves, but more often several characters come out together or in turn. Maskers enact a broad range of human, animal, and fantastic otherworldly behavior that is usually both stimulating and didactic. Masquerades, in fact, vary in function or effect along a continuum from weak spirit power and strong entertainment value to those rarely seen but possessing vast executive powers backed by powerful shrines. Most operate between these extremes, crystallizing varieties of human and animal behavior—caricatured, ordinary, comic, bizarre, serious, or threatening. Such actions inform and affect audience members because of their dramatic staging. It is the purpose of most masquerades to move people, to affect them, and to effect change.

Thus masks and masquerades are mediators—between men and women, youths and elders, initiated and uninitiated, powers of nature and those of human agency, and even life and death. For many groups in West and Central Africa, masking plays (or once played) an

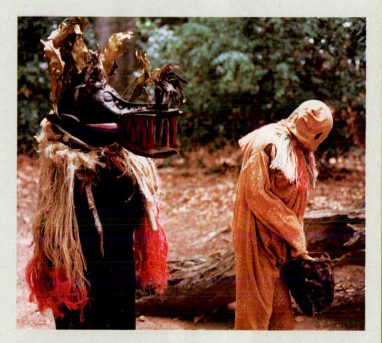

37-15 Senufo masquerader, Côte d'Ivoire, photographed ca. 1980–1990.

Senufo masqueraders are always men. Their masks often represent composite creatures incarnating both ancestors and bush powers. They fight malevolent spirits with their aggressively powerful forms.

active role in the socialization process, especially for men, who control most masks. Maskers carry boys (and, more rarely, girls) away from their mothers to bush initiation camps, put them through ordeals and schooling, and welcome them back to society as men months or even years later. A second major role is in aiding the transformation of important deceased persons into productive ancestors who, in their new roles, can bring benefits to the living community. Because most masking cultures are agricultural, it is not surprising that Africans often invoke masquerades to increase the productivity of the fields, to stimulate the growth of crops, and later to celebrate the harvest.

Senufo men dance many masks (see "African Masquerades," page 1131), mostly in the context of Poro, the main association for socialization and initiation—a protracted process taking nearly 20 years for men to complete. Maskers also perform at funerals and other public spectacles. Large Senufo masks (for example, FIG. 37-15) are composite creatures, combining characteristics of antelope, crocodile, warthog, hyena, and human: sweeping horns, a head, and an open-jawed snout with sharp teeth. These masks incarnate both ancestors and bush powers that combat witchcraft and sorcery, malevolent spirits, and the wandering dead. They are protectors who fight evil with their aggressively powerful forms and their medicines.

At funerals, Senufo maskers attend the corpse and, by dancing the masks, they help expel the deceased from the village. This is the deceased individual's final transition, a rite of passage parallel to that undergone by all men during their years of Poro socialization, in which masks also play a role. When an important person dies, the convergence of several masking groups, as well as the music, dancing, costuming, and feasting of many people, constitute a festive and complex work of art that transcends any one mask or character.

Some Senufo men also dance female masks. The most recurrent type has a small face with fine features, several extensions, and varied motifs—a hornbill bird in the illustrated example (FIG. **37-16**)—rising from the forehead. The men who dance these feminine characters also wear knitted body suits or trade-cloth costumes to indicate their beauty and their ties with the order and civilization of the village. They may be called "pretty young girl," "beautiful lady," or "wife" of one of the heavy, terrorizing masculine masks (FIG. 37-15) appearing before or after them.

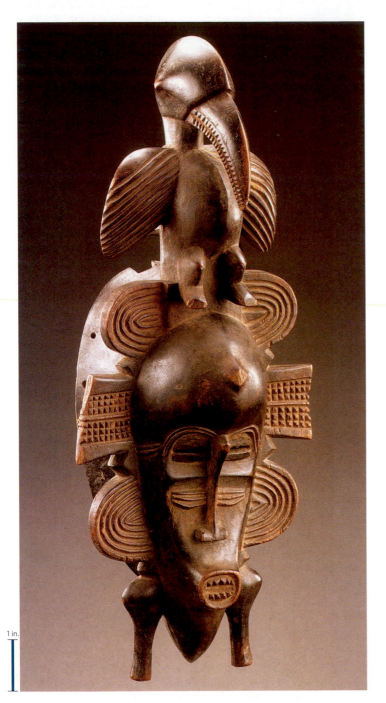

37-16 "Beautiful Lady" dance mask, Senufo, Côte d'Ivoire, late 20th century. Wood, 1' $\frac{1}{2}$" high. Musée Barbier-Mueller, Geneva.

Some Senufo men dance female masks such as this one with a hornbill bird rising from the forehead. The female characters are sometimes the wives of the terrorizing male masks (FIG. 37-15).

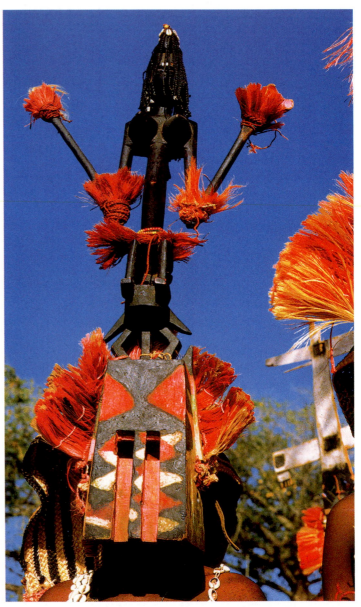

37-17 Satimbe masquerader, Dogon, Mali, mid- to late 20th century.

Satimbe ("sister on the head") masks commemorate the legend describing women as the first masqueraders. The mask's crown is a woman with large breasts and sticklike bent arms.

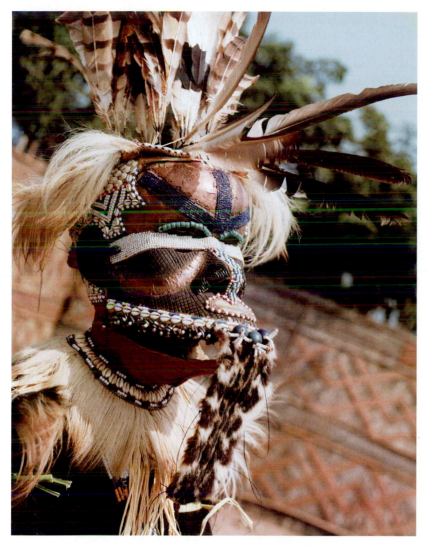

At Kuba festivals, masqueraders reenact creation legends involving Bwoom, Mwashamboy, and Ngady Amwaash. The first two characters are males who vie for the attention of Ngady, the first female ancestor.

DOGON SATIMBE MASKS Dogon masquerades dramatize creation legends. These stories say that women were the first ancestors to imitate spirit maskers and thus the first human masqueraders. Men later took over the masks, forever barring women from direct involvement with masking processes. A mask called *Satimbe* (FIG. **37-17**)—that is, "sister on the head"—seems to represent all women and commemorates this legend. Satimbe masks consist of a roughly rectangular covering for the head with narrow rectangular openings for the eyes and a crowning element, much larger than the mask proper, depicting a schematic woman with large protruding breasts and sticklike bent arms. In ceremonies called Dama, held every several years to honor the lives of people who have died since the last Dama, Satimbe is among the dozens of different masked spirit characters escorting dead souls away from the village. In recent times, gunfire accompanying the masquerade aids in chasing the souls of the deceased out of the village. The souls are sent off to the land of the dead, where, as ancestors, they will be enjoined to benefit their living descendants and stimulate agricultural productivity.

KUBA MASQUERADES The Kuba have been well established in the Democratic Republic of Congo since at least the 16th century. They represent almost 20 different ethnic groups, but they all recognize the authority of a single king. At the court of Kuba kings, three masks, known as Mwashamboy, Bwoom, and Ngady Amwaash, represent legendary royal ancestors. Mwashamboy symbolizes the founding ancestor, Woot, and embodies the king's supernatural and political powers. Bwoom (FIG. **37-18**), with its bulging forehead, represents a legendary dwarf or pygmy who signifies the indigenous peoples on whom kingship was imposed. Bwoom also vies with Mwashamboy for the attention of the beautiful ancestress, Ngady Amwaash (FIG. **37-19**), who symbolizes both the first woman and all women. On her cheeks are striped tears. They symbolize the pain of childbirth as well as Ngady's sorrow at having been forced to commit incest with her father, Woot, in order to procreate. These three characters reenact creation stories during royal initiation ceremonies. The masks and their costumes, with elaborate beads, feathers, animal pelts, cowrie shells, cut-pile cloth, and ornamental trappings, make for a sumptuous display at Kuba festivals.

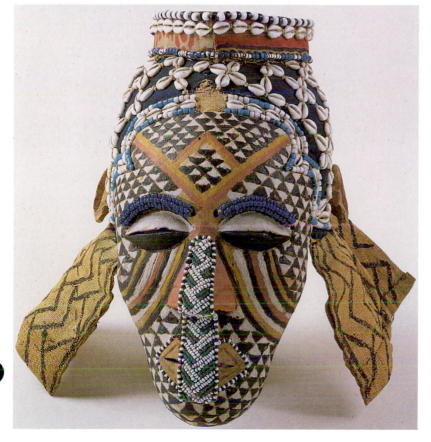

37-19 Ngady Amwaash mask, Kuba, Democratic Republic of Congo, late 19th or early 20th century. Peabody Museum of Archaeology and Ethnology, Harvard University, Cambridge.

Ngady's mask incorporates beads, shells, and feathers in geometric patterns. The stripes on her cheeks are tears from the pain of childbirth after incest with her father, represented by the Mwashamboy mask.

BAMANA CI WARA Among the most striking African sculptures are the *Ci Wara* antelope headdresses (FIG. **37-20**) of the Bamana of southern Mali. Raffia-clad young dancers wore these stylized antelope figures on their heads, which they also covered with fabric, in the Ci Wara rituals that prepared boys for their future roles as husbands and farmers. Ci Wara is the legendary primordial wild antelope that taught the Bamana the secrets of agriculture. In the annual Ci Wara masquerade, two boys dress as Ci Wara and his female consort and perform a dance in which they hold staffs and bend over, as if hoeing the fields. The piercing of the antelope's body and the sweeping arc of the horns of the Ci Wara headdresses form abstract patterns that greatly appealed to early-20th-century European painters and sculptors seeking a new formal vocabulary (see "Primitivism and Colonialism," page 891).

BAGA D'MBA Until the early 20th century, when Muslim missionaries suppressed the custom, the Baga of northern Guinea danced a masquerade in honor of the Mother of Fertility to protect pregnant

1 ft.

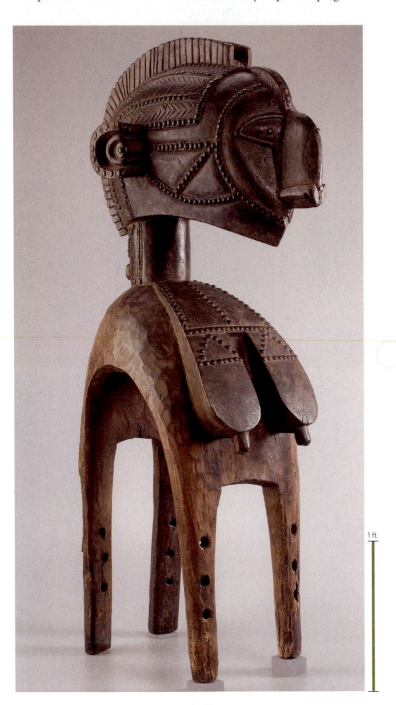

37-20 Ci Wara headdress, Bamana, from the Bamako region of Mali, late 19th or early 20th century. Wood, metal bands, and thread, 2' 11" high. Metropolitan Museum of Art, New York (Michael C. Rockefeller Collection, gift of Nelson A. Rockefeller).

Bamana boys wear Ci Wara headdresses at festivals that prepare them for their future roles as husbands and farmers. Ci Wara is the legendary wild antelope that taught the Bamana the secrets of agriculture.

1 ft.

37-21 D'mba mask, Baga, Guinea, late 19th or early 20th century. Wood and brass, 4' 4" high. Yale University Art Gallery, New Haven (Charles B. Benenson Collection).

Baga men wear d'mba masks on their shoulders with raffia skirts concealing their bodies. The masks portray the Mother of Fertility with flattened breasts. She is the ideal woman who has suckled countless babies.

ART AND SOCIETY

Mende Women as Maskers

The Mende and neighboring peoples of Sierra Leone, Liberia, and Guinea are distinctive in Africa because the women perform masquerades. However, the masks and costumes that the women wear conceal their bodies from the audience attending their performance.

The Sande society of the Mende controls the initiation, education, and acculturation of Mende girls. Women leaders who dance the Sande masks serve as priestesses and judges during the three years that the women's society controls the ritual calendar (alternating with the men's society in this role), thus serving the community as a whole. Women maskers, who function as initiators, teachers, and mentors, help girl novices with their transformation into educated and marriageable women. Sande women associate their Sowie masks with water spirits and the color black, which the society, in turn, connects with human skin color and the civilized world. The women wear these helmet masks on top of their heads as headdresses, with black raffia and cloth costumes to hide the wearers' individual identities while personifying the spirits during public performances. Elaborate coiffures, shiny black color, dainty triangular-shaped faces with slit eyes, rolls around the neck, and real and carved versions of amulets and various emblems on the top commonly characterize Sowie masks (FIG. 37-22). These symbolize the adult women's roles as wives, mothers, providers for the family, and keepers of medicines for use within the Sande association and the society at large.

Sande members commission the masks from male carvers, with the carver and patron together determining the type of mask needed for a particular societal purpose. The Mende often keep, repair, and reuse masks for many decades, thereby preserving them as models for subsequent generations of carvers.

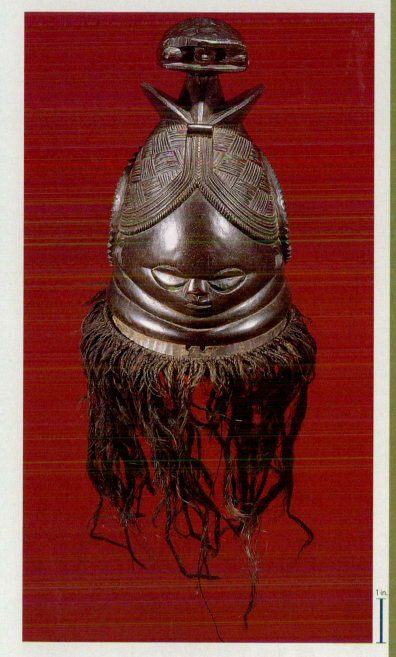

37-22 Female mask, Mende, Sierra Leone, mid- to late 20th century. Painted wood, 1' 2$\frac{1}{2}$" high. Fowler Museum of Cultural History, University of California, Los Angeles (gift of the Wellcome Trust).

This Mende mask refers to ideals of female beauty, morality, and behavior. The large forehead signifies wisdom, the neck design beauty and health, and the plaited hair the order of ideal households.

1 in.

women and promote abundant harvests. (The government restored the practice in 1984.) The masks that the Baga dancers wear, one of which was in the collection of Pablo Picasso (FIG. 29-12), are called *d'mba* and take the form of the head and torso of a woman (FIG. 37-21). Carved from a single piece of wood, the masks have four "legs" so that Baga men can rest them on their shoulders. The dancer thus appears about 8 feet tall and towers over all others in the community. The d'mba's legs provide stability for the heavy masks, which often weigh as much as 80 pounds. The legs are hidden beneath a long raffia skirt, which also disguises the dancer's identity. Holes between the mask's prominent breasts enable the wearer to see. The breasts themselves are flattened because they are the breasts of an ideal woman who has suckled countless babies. The face has a large nose, and the forehead and cheeks as well as the breasts feature scarification patterns. The Mother of Fertility masks are danced at weddings, funerals, and harvest festivals exclusively by men, despite the identity of the d'mba.

MENDE FEMALE MASKERS The Mende have long been farmers whose homeland is on the Atlantic coast of Africa in Sierra Leone. Although men own and perform most masks in Africa, in Mende society, women control and dance Sande society masks (see "Mende Women as Maskers," above), while Mende men perform the Poro society masks.

The glistening black surface of Mende Sowie masks (FIG. 37-22) evokes female spirits newly emergent from their underwater homes (also symbolized by the turtle on top). The mask and its parts refer to ideals of female beauty, morality, and behavior. A high, broad forehead signifies wisdom and success. The neck ridges have multiple meanings. They are signs of beauty, good health, and prosperity and also reference the ripples in the water from which the water spirits emerge. Intricately woven or plaited hair is the essence of harmony and order found in ideal households. A small, closed mouth and downcast eyes indicate the silent, serious demeanor expected of recent initiates.

COSTUME AND BODY ART

Masquerade is, of course, costume art as well as ritual dancing, but the costumes are not those worn in contemporary society. Clothing, however, also plays an important role in the daily life of Africans. Throughout history, African costumes have been laden with meaning and have projected messages that all members of the society could read.

KOT A-MBWEEKY III A photograph (FIG. **37-23**) taken in 1970 shows the Kuba king Kot a-Mbweeky III (r. 1969–) seated in state before his court, bedecked in a dazzling multimedia costume with many symbolic elements. The king commissioned the costume that he wears. Eagle feathers, leopard skin, cowrie shells, imported beads, raffia, and other materials combine to overload and expand the image of the man, making him larger than life and truly a work of art. He is a *collage*, an assemblage. He holds not one but two weapons, symbolic of his military might and underscoring his wealth, dignity, and grandeur. The man, with his regalia, embodies the office of sacred kingship. He is a superior being, in fact and figuratively,

raised on a dais, flanked by ornate drums, with a treasure basket of sacred relics by his left foot. The geometric patterns on the king's costume and nearby objects, and the abundance and redundancy of rich materials, exemplify the opulent style of Kuba court arts.

KENTE *Kente* cloth, the distinctive textile of the Akan area, has, until recently, been woven exclusively by men since the 16th century. The brightly colored patterns famous today date to the 18th century. The name derives from *kenten* (basket), but the material used is cotton, except for the costliest examples, which are silk. Weavers produced the earliest silk examples, reserved for Asante kings, by unraveling imported fabrics and reusing the silk threads. The Asante produce kente cloth on horizontal looms in long strips 2 to 4 inches wide and then sew the strips together to create larger fabrics. Kente robes (FIG. **37-24**) are typically 6 or 7 feet by 12 or 13 feet. Men wear them like Roman *togas*, unbelted and draped over the left shoulder and arm with the right shoulder bare. Women also wear kente garments, usually consisting of a separate skirt and bodice. Researchers have documented more than 300 distinct colored warp and weft patterns, some associated with specific kings,

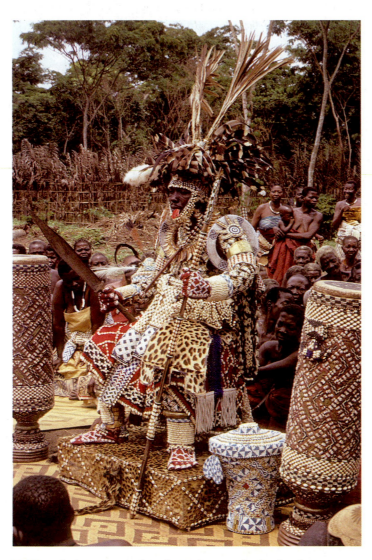

37-23 Kuba king Kot a-Mbweeky III during a display for photographer and filmmaker Eliot Elisofon in 1970, Mushenge, Democratic Republic of Congo.

Eagle feathers, leopard skin, cowrie shells, imported beads, raffia, and other materials combine to make the Kuba king larger than life. He is a collage of wealth, dignity, and military might.

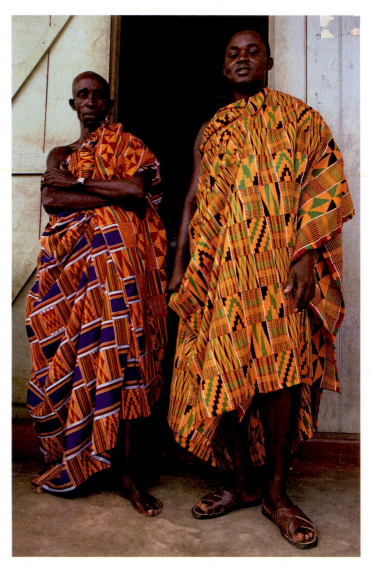

37-24 Two Asante noblemen wearing kente cloth robes, Kumasi, Ghana, photographed in January 1972.

Originally reserved for Asante kings, kente cloth is traditionally woven on horizontal looms exclusively by men. It is produced in long strips and then sewn together to form robes worn draped over the left shoulder.

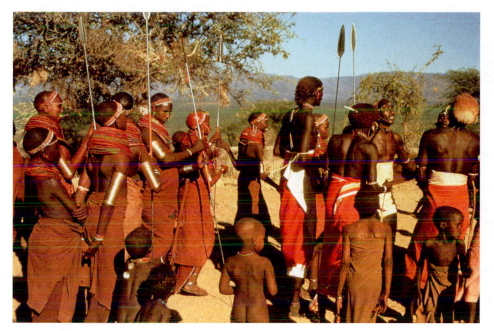

Men and women in many rural areas of Africa paint their bodies and wear elaborate hairstyles and beaded jewelry. This personal adornment reveals their age, marital status, and parentage.

each having a name variously derived from proverbs, historical events, or people.

After the first president of Ghana, Kwame Nkrumah (r. 1957–1966), wore a kente robe during his official visit to the United States in 1958, kente cloth became synonymous with native African dress. Kente garments have become a symbol of African American pride, highlighted by the 1998 traveling exhibition *Wrapped in Pride: Ghanaian Kente and African American Identity*.

BODY ADORNMENT In addition to wearing masks and costumes on special occasions, people in many rural areas of eastern Africa, including the Samburu in northern Kenya, continue to embellish their own bodies. The Samburu men and women shown in FIG. 37-25 at a spontaneous dance have distinct styles of personal decoration. Men, particularly warriors who are not yet married, expend hours creating elaborate hairstyles for one another. They paint their bodies with red ocher and wear bracelets, necklaces, and other bands of beaded jewelry made for them by young women. For themselves, women fashion more lavish constellations of beaded collars, which they mass around their necks. As if to help separate the genders, women shave their heads and adorn them with beaded headbands. Personal decoration begins in childhood, increasing to become lavish and highly self-conscious in young adulthood and diminishing as people age. Much of the decoration contains coded information—age, marital or initiation status, parentage of a warrior son—that can be read by those who know the codes. Dress ensembles have evolved over time. Different colors and sizes of beads became available, as did plastics and aluminum, and specific fashions have changed, but the overall concept of fine personal adornment—that is, dress raised to the level of art—remains much the same today as it was centuries ago.

HISTORICAL NARRATIVE

Historical narratives are much rarer in traditional African art than in Europe, America, and Asia, but are not unknown. Olowe of Ise, for example, on commission from the ogoga of Ikere, commemorated the 1897 visit of a British emissary to the Ikere palace in the reliefs he carved for a pair of large wood doors (FIG. 37-11). Interestingly, many examples of historical narrative appear in the oldest art form in Africa—rock paintings (FIGS. 1-2 and 19-2).

SAN ROCK PAINTINGS The latest examples of African rock painting date as recently as the 19th century, and some of these, like Olowe's Ikere doors, depict events involving Europeans. Many examples have been found in South Africa. Some of the finest are those produced by the peoples whom scholars refer to as the San, who occupied parts of southwestern Africa in present-day Namibia and Botswana at the time of the earliest European colonization. The San were hunters and gatherers, and their art often centered on the animals they pursued.

One of the most impressive preserved San rock paintings (FIGS. 37-26 and 37-27), originally about 8 feet long but now regrettably in fragments, comes from near the source of the Mzimkhulu River at Bamboo Mountain and dates to the mid-19th century. At that time, the increasing development of colonial ranches and the settlements of African agriculturists had greatly affected the lifestyle and movement patterns of San hunters and gatherers, often displacing them from their ancestral lands. In some regions, the San began to raid local ranches for livestock and horses as an alternate food source. The Bamboo Mountain rock painting probably depicts one of a series of stock raids carried out between about 1838 and 1848. Various South African military and police forces unsuccessfully

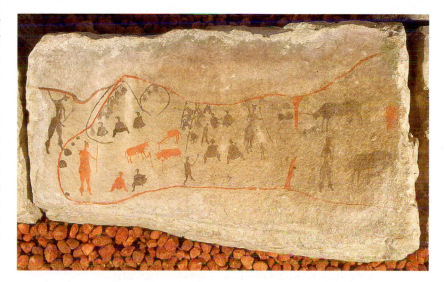

37-26 Stock raid with cattle, horses, and encampment, rock painting, San, from Bamboo Mountain, South Africa, mid-19th century. Natal Museum, Pietermaritzburg.

Rock paintings are among the most ancient arts in Africa, and the tradition continued into the 19th century. This example depicts the 1838–1848 stock raids by San hunters.

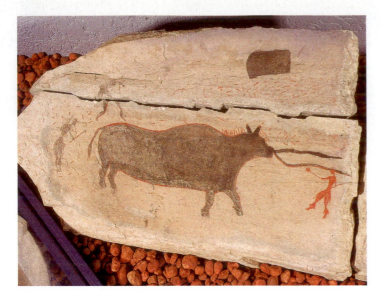

37-27 Magical "rain animal," rock painting, San, from Bamboo Mountain, South Africa, mid-19th century. Natal Museum, Pietermaritzburg.

Another fragment of the 8-foot-long rock painting from Bamboo Mountain depicts a man, possibly a diviner in a trance, leading an eland, an animal believed to facilitate rainmaking.

CONTEMPORARY ART

The art forms of contemporary Africa vary immensely and defy easy classification. Those of distinctly modern or postmodern character that have garnered international attention are discussed in Chapter 31. Others—for example, the Dogon men's house treated here—testify to the continuing vitality of traditional African art in the 21st century.

DOGON TOGU NA Traditionalism and modernism unite in the Dogon *togu na,* or "men's house of words." The togu na is so called because men's deliberations vital to community welfare take place under its sheltering roof. The Dogon consider it the "head" and the most important part of the community, and they characterize the togu na with human attributes. The Dogon build the men's houses over time. Earlier posts, such as the central one in the illustrated togu na (FIG. **37-28**), show schematic renderings of legendary female ancestors, similar to stylized ancestral couples (FIG. 37-6) or masked figures (FIG. 37-17). Recent replacement posts display narrative and topical scenes of varied subjects, such as horsemen or hunters or women preparing food, and feature abundant descriptive detail, bright polychrome painting in enamels, and even some writing. Unlike earlier traditional sculptors, the contemporary artists who made these posts want to be recognized, and they are eager to sell their work (other than these posts) to tourists.

During the past two centuries and especially in recent decades, the encroachments of Christianity, Islam, Western education, and market economies have led to increasing secularization in all the arts of Africa. Many figures and masks earlier commissioned for shrines or as incarnations of ancestors or spirits are now made mostly for sale to outsiders, essentially as tourist arts. They are also sold in art galleries abroad as collector's items for display. In towns and cities, painted murals and cement sculptures appear frequently, often making implicit comments about modern life. Nonetheless, despite the growing importance of urbanism, most African people still live in rural communities. Traditional values, although under pressure, hold considerable force in villages especially, and some people adhere to spiritual beliefs that uphold traditional art forms. African art remains as varied as the vast continent itself and continues to evolve.

pursued the San raiders. Poor weather, including frequent rains and fog, added to the difficulty of capturing a people who had lived in the region for many generations and knew its terrain intimately.

Reproduced here are two details of the larger, fragmentary composition. On the right side (not illustrated), two San riders on horses laden with meat drive a large herd of cattle and horses toward a San encampment located left of center (FIG. 37-26) and encircled by an outline. Within the camp are various women and children. To the far left (FIG. **37-27**), a single figure (perhaps a diviner or rainmaker) leads an eland, an animal that the San considered effective in rainmaking and ancestor rituals, toward the encampment. The similarity of this scene to other rock paintings with spiritual interpretations (a human leading an animal) suggests that this may represent a ritual leader in a trance state. The leader calls on rain—brought by the intervention of the sacred eland—to foil the attempts of the government soldiers and police to locate and punish the San raiders. The close correspondence between the painting's imagery and the raids of 1838–1848 adds to the likelihood that San painters created this work to record contemporaneous events as well as to facilitate rainmaking.

37-28 Togu na ("men's house of words"), Dogon, Mali, photographed in 1989.

Dogon men hold their communal deliberations in a togu na. The posts of this one are of varied date. The oldest have traditional carvings, and the newest feature polychrome narrative or topical paintings.

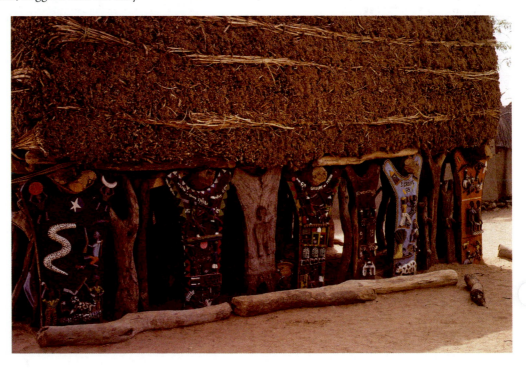

AFRICA, 1800 TO 1980

Ancestors and Spirits

- Most of the traditional forms of African art continued to play dominant roles during the past 200 years. Among these are sculptures and shrines connected with the veneration of ancestors. Wood or metal-covered wood figures guarded Fang and Kota reliquaries. Especially elaborate are some Kalabari Ijaw screens with figures of a deceased chief, his retainers, and the heads of his slaves and conquered rivals.

- Kongo nkisi n'kondi (power figures) represent men bristling with nails and blades and are believed to embody spirits that can heal and give life. Baule bush spirits are thought to be ugly and deformed, but artists portrayed them as ideal human beings.

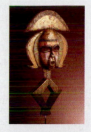

Kota reliquary guardian,
19th or early 20th century

Leadership and Royalty

- The arts associated with African kings, chiefs, and other leaders include emblems of status—for example, thrones, the decoration of royal palaces, and statues representing local gods and heroes, as well as images of the leaders themselves. Royalty could afford to hire the finest artists using the costliest materials.

- The throne of King Nsangu of Bamum, for example, incorporates richly colored textiles and glass beads, cowrie shells, and other luminous materials. Fon king Glele commissioned Akati Akpele Kendo—one of the first recorded names of an African artist—to make an iron statue of the war god Gu. The ogoga of Ikere commissioned the renowned sculptor Olowe of Ise to carve doors and veranda posts for his palace compound.

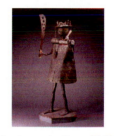

Kendo, warrior figure (Gu?),
1858–1859

Rituals and Masquerades

- In Africa, art is nearly always an active agent in the lives of its peoples. A major African art form is the fashioning of masks for festive performances. Masqueraders are almost always men—even when the masks they dance are female, as among the Senufo, Dogon, and Kuba—but in Mende society, women are maskers too.

- African masks take many forms. Some cover the dancer's face. Others, such as the d'mba of the Baga, have "legs" designed to sit on the wearer's shoulders, making the dancer 8 feet tall. Other "masks" are more accurately described as headdresses, worn above the dancer's head, such as the antelope headdresses of the Bamana, which depict in abstract form Ci Wara, the primordial creature that taught humans the secrets of agriculture.

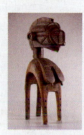

Baga d'mba mask,
late 19th or early 20th century

Costume and Body Art

- Africans have also traditionally lavished attention on costume and jewelry and other forms of body adornment, such as elaborate coiffures and body painting. The decoration often contains coded information about age, status, and parentage. Royal costumes consist of animal skins, feathers, shells, beads, and raffia, and symbols of power such as crowns, swords, and scepters. They make men, such as the Kuba king Kot a-Mbweeky III, seem larger than life.

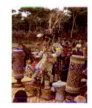

Kuba king Kot a-Mbweeky III, 1970

Historical Narrative

- Historical narratives are much rarer in traditional African art than in Europe, America, and Asia, but are not unknown. Important early examples are the San rock paintings from Bamboo Mountain in southern Africa, which depict a series of stock raids carried out between about 1838 and 1848 as well as rainmaking rituals.

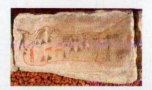

Bamboo Mountain stock raid,
mid-19th century

Notes

INTRODUCTION

1. Quoted in George Heard Hamilton, *Painting and Sculpture in Europe, 1880–1940,* 6th ed. (New Haven, Conn.: Yale University Press, 1993), 345.
2. Quoted in *Josef Albers: Homage to the Square* (New York: Museum of Modern Art, 1964), n.p.

CHAPTER 20

1. Francisco de Hollanda, *De pintura antigua* (1548), quoted in Robert Klein and Henri Zerner, *Italian Art, 1500–1600: Sources and Documents* (Englewood Cliffs, N.J.: Prentice Hall, 1966), 33.

CHAPTER 21

1. Translated by Catherine Enggass, in Howard Saalman, ed., *Antonio Manetti, Life of Brunelleschi* (University Park: Pennsylvania State University Press, 1970), 42.
2. Giorgio Vasari, "Life of Lorenzo Ghiberti." Translated by Gaston du C. de Vere, ed., *Giorgio Vasari, Lives of the Painters, Sculptors and Architects* (New York: Knopf, 1996), 1:304.
3. Ghiberti, *Commentarii,* 2.22. Quoted in Elizabeth Gilmore Holt, ed., *A Documentary History of Art, I: The Middle Ages and the Renaissance* (Princeton, N.J.: Princeton University Press, 1981), 161.
4. Stephen J. Campbell and Michael W. Cole, *Italian Renaissance Art* (New York: Thames & Hudson, 2011), 151.
5. Quoted in H. W. Janson, *The Sculpture of Donatello* (Princeton, N.J.: Princeton University Press, 1965), 154.
6. Vasari, "Life of Masaccio." Translated by Gaston du C. de Vere, 1:318.
7. Martial, *Epigrams,* 10.32.

CHAPTER 22

1. Plato, *Ion,* 534. Translated by Benjamin Jowett, *The Dialogues of Plato,* 4th ed. (Oxford: Clarendon Press, 1953), 1:107–108.
2. Leonardo da Vinci to Ludovico Sforza, ca. 1480–1481. Elizabeth Gilmore Holt, ed., *A Documentary History of Art* (Princeton: Princeton University Press, 1981), 1:274–275.
3. Quoted in Anthony Blunt, *Artistic Theory in Italy, 1450–1600* (London: Oxford University Press, 1964), 34.
4. James M. Saslow, *The Poetry of Michelangelo: An Annotated Translation* (New Haven, Conn.: Yale University Press, 1991), 407.
5. Giorgio Vasari, *Lives of the Painters, Sculptors and Architects.* Translated by Gaston du C. de Vere (New York: Knopf, 1996), 2:736.
6. Quoted in A. Richard Turner, *Renaissance Florence: The Invention of a New Art* (New York: Abrams, 1997), 163.
7. Quoted in Bruce Boucher, *Andrea Palladio: The Architect in His Time* (New York: Abbeville Press, 1998), 229.
8. Quoted in Robert J. Clements, *Michelangelo's Theory of Art* (New York: New York University Press, 1961), 320.
9. Giorgio Vasari, *The Lives of the Artists.* Translated by Julia Conaway Bondanella and Peter Bondanella (New York: Oxford University Press, 1991), 489.

CHAPTER 23

1. Translated by Erwin Panofsky, in Wolfgang Stechow, *Northern Renaissance Art 1400–1600: Sources and Documents* (Evanston, Ill.: Northwestern University Press, 1989), 123.
2. Translated by Bernhard Erling, in Stechow, 129–130.
3. Translated by Fred S. Kleiner. Giorgio Vasari, *De' più eccellenti pittori scultori ed architettori* (Gaetano Milanesi, ed.; Florence: Sansoni, 1881), 7:584.

CHAPTER 24

1. Filippo Baldinucci, *Vita del Cavaliere Giovanni Lorenzo Bernini* (1681). Translated by Robert Enggass, in Enggass and Jonathan Brown, *Italian and Spanish Art 1600–1750: Sources and Documents* (Evanston, Ill.: Northwestern University Press, 1992), 116.

CHAPTER 25

1. Albert Blankert, *Johannes Vermeer van Delft 1632–1675* (Utrecht: Spectrum, 1975), 133, no. 51. Translated by Bob Haak, *The Golden Age: Dutch Painters of the Seventeenth Century* (New York: Abrams, 1984), 450.
2. Translated by Kristin Lohse Belkin, *Rubens* (London: Phaidon, 1998), 47.

CHAPTER 26

1. Quoted in Thomas A. Bailey, *The American Pageant: A History of the Republic,* 2d ed. (Boston: Heath, 1961), 280.

CHAPTER 27

1. Théophile Gautier, *Histoire de Romantisme* (Paris: Charpentier, 1874), 204.
2. Quoted in Helmut Borsch-Supan, *Caspar David Friedrich* (New York: Braziller, 1974), 7.
3. Ibid., 7–8.
4. Quoted in Frederick Merk, *Manifest Destiny and Mission in American History: A Reinterpretation* (New York: Knopf, 1963), 32.
5. Quoted in Linda Nochlin, *Realism and Tradition in Art 1848–1900* (Upper Saddle River, N.J.: Prentice Hall, 1966), 42.
6. Quoted in George Heard Hamilton, *Manet and His Critics* (New Haven, Conn.: Yale University Press, 1954), 45.
7. Quoted in Charles Harrison, Paul Wood, and Jason Gaiger, eds., *Art in Theory 1815–1900: An Anthology of Changing Ideas* (Oxford: Blackwell, 1998), 515.
8. Ibid., 518.
9. *New York Weekly Tribune,* September 30, 1865.
10. Quoted in Nikolai Cikovsky Jr. and Franklin Kelly, *Winslow Homer* (Washington, D.C.: National Gallery of Art, 1995), 26.
11. Quoted in Lloyd Goodrich, *Thomas Eakins, His Life and Work* (New York: Whitney Museum of American Art, 1933), 51–52.
12. Quoted in Nicholas Pevsner, *An Outline of European Architecture* (Baltimore: Penguin, 1960), 627.
13. Letter from Delaroche to François Arao, quoted in Helmut Gernsheim, *Creative Photography* (New York: Bonanza Books, 1962), 24.
14. Quoted in Naomi Rosenblum, *A World History of Photography,* 4th ed. (New York: Abbeville Press, 2007), 69.
15. Quoted in Kenneth MacGowan, *Behind the Screen* (New York: Delta, 1965), 49.

CHAPTER 28

1. Charles Baudelaire, *Le peintre de la vie moderne* (1863). Translated by Jonathan Mayne, ed., *The Painter of Modern Life and Other Essays by Charles Baudelaire,* 2d ed. (New York: Phaidon, 1995), 12.
2. Clement Greenberg, "Modernist Painting," *Art and Literature,* no. 4 (Spring 1965): 193–194.
3. Translated by Carola Hicks, in Charles Harrison, Paul Wood, and Jason Gaiger, eds., *Art in Theory 1815–1900: An Anthology of Changing Ideas* (Oxford: Blackwell, 1998), 595.
4. Quoted in John McCoubrey, *American Art 1700–1960: Sources and Documents* (Englewood Cliffs, N.J.: Prentice Hall, 1965), 184.
5. Quoted in Robert Goldwater and Marco Treves, eds., *Artists on Art, from the XIV to the XX Century* (New York: Pantheon, 1945), 322.

6. Vincent van Gogh to Theo van Gogh, September 1888, in J. van Gogh-Bonger and V. W. van Gogh, eds., *The Complete Letters of Vincent van Gogh* (Greenwich, Conn.: New York Graphic Society, 1979), 3:534.

7. Vincent van Gogh to Theo van Gogh, July 16, 1888, in W. H. Auden, ed., *Van Gogh: A Self-Portrait. Letters Revealing His Life as a Painter* (New York: Dutton, 1963), 299.

8. Reported by Joachim Gasquet (1873–1921). Quoted in Michael Doran, ed., *Conversations with Cézanne* (Berkeley: University of California Press, 2000), 122.

9. Translated by Akane Kawakami, in Harrison, Wood, and Gaiger, 1066.

10. Quoted in V. Frisch and J. T. Shipley, *Auguste Rodin* (New York: Stokes, 1939), 203.

CHAPTER 29

1. Quoted in John Elderfield, *The "Wild Beasts": Fauvism and Its Affinities* (New York: Museum of Modern Art, 1976), 29.

2. Translated by Charles Harrison and Paul Wood, eds., *Art in Theory 1900–2000: An Anthology of Changing Ideas* (Oxford: Blackwell, 2003), 65.

3. Quoted in Frederick S. Levine, *The Apocalyptic Vision: The Art of Franz Marc as German Expressionism* (New York: Harper & Row, 1979), 57.

4. Quoted in Sam Hunter, John Jacobus, and Daniel Wheeler, *Modern Art,* rev. 3d. ed. (Upper Saddle River, N.J.: Prentice Hall, 2004), 121.

5. Quoted in George Heard Hamilton, *Painting and Sculpture in Europe, 1880–1940,* 6th ed. (New Haven: Yale University Press, 1993), 246.

6. Ibid., 238.

7. Quoted in Edward Fry, ed., *Cubism* (London: Thames & Hudson, 1966), 112–113.

8. Quoted in Françoise Gilot and Carlton Lake, *Life with Picasso* (New York: McGraw-Hill, 1964), 77.

9. Pablo Picasso, "Statement to Simone Téry," in Harrison and Wood, 649.

10. Quoted in Roland Penrose, *Picasso: His Life and Work,* rev. ed. (New York: Harper & Row, 1971), 311.

11. Filippo Tommaso Marinetti, *The Foundation and Manifesto of Futurism* (*Le Figaro,* February 20, 1909). Translated by Joshua C. Taylor, in Herschel B. Chipp, *Theories of Modern Art: A Source Book by Artists and Critics* (Berkeley and Los Angeles: University of California Press, 1968), 284.

12. Ibid., 286.

13. Quoted in Robert Short, *Dada and Surrealism* (London: Octopus Books, 1980), 18.

14. Quoted in Robert Motherwell, ed., *The Dada Painters and Poets: An Anthology,* 2d ed. (Cambridge, Mass.: Belknap Press, 1989).

15. Hans Richter, *Dada: Art and Anti-Art* (London: Thames & Hudson, 1961), 64–65.

16. Ibid., 57.

17. Quoted in Arturo Schwarz, *The Complete Works of Marcel Duchamp* (London: Thames & Hudson, 1965), 466.

18. Translated by Howard Dearstyne, in Robert L. Herbert, *Modern Artists on Art,* 2d ed. (Mineola, N.Y.: Dover, 2000), 117.

19. Ibid., 124.

20. Translated by Herbert Read and Leslie Martin, quoted in Chipp, 325–330.

21. Quoted in Sam Hunter, *American Art of the 20th Century* (New York: Abrams, 1972), 30.

22. Ibid., 37.

23. Charles C. Eldredge, "The Arrival of European Modernism," *Art in America* 61 (July–August 1973): 35.

24. Quoted in Gail Stavitsky, "Reordering Reality: Precisionist Directions in American Art, 1915–1941," in *Precisionism in America 1915–1941: Reordering Reality* (New York: Abrams, 1994), 12.

25. Quoted in Karen Tsujimoto, *Images of America: Precisionist Painting and Modern Photography* (Seattle: University of Washington Press, 1982), 70.

26. Quoted in Matthias Eberle, *World War I and the Weimar Artists: Dix, Grosz, Beckmann, Schlemmer* (New Haven: Yale University Press, 1985), 54.

27. Ibid., 22.

28. Ibid., 42.

29. Quoted in Hamilton, 392.

30. Quoted in Richter, 155.

31. Ibid., 159.

32. Quoted in William S. Rubin, *Dada, Surrealism, and Their Heritage* (New York: Museum of Modern Art, 1968), 111.

33. Quoted in Hunter, Jacobus, and Wheeler, 179.

34. Quoted in William S. Rubin, *Miró in the Collection of the Museum of Modern Art* (New York: Museum of Modern Art, 1973), 32.

35. Translated by Norbert Guterman, quoted in Chipp, 182–186.

36. Translated by Nicholas Bullock, quoted in Harrison and Wood, 281.

37. Quoted in Kenneth Frampton, *Modern Architecture: A Critical History,* 4th ed. (New York: Thames & Hudson, 2007), 147.

38. Quoted in H. H. Arnason and Peter Kalb, *History of Modern Art,* 5th ed. (Upper Saddle River, N.J.: Prentice Hall, 2004), 154.

39. Quoted in Robert L. Herbert, *Modern Artists on Art,* 2d ed. (Mineola, N.Y.: Dover, 2000), 173.

40. Ibid., 177.

41. Quoted in Hans L. C. Jaffé, ed., *De Stijl* (New York: Abrams, 1971), 185–188.

42. Piet Mondrian, *Dialogue on the New Plastic* (1919). Translated by Harry Holzman and Martin S. James, in Harrison and Wood, 285.

43. Quoted in Vivian Endicott Barnett, "Banned German Art: Reception and Institutional Support of Modern German Art in the United States, 1933–45," in Stephanie Barron, *Exiles and Emigrés: The Flight of European Artists from Hitler* (Los Angeles: Los Angeles County Museum of Art, 1997), 283.

44. Quoted in Frances K. Pohl, *Ben Shahn: New Deal Artist in a Cold War Climate, 1947–1954* (Austin: University of Texas Press, 1989), 159.

45. Wanda M. Corn, *Grant Wood: The Regionalist Vision* (New Haven: Yale University Press, 1983), 131.

46. Quoted in Matthew Baigell, *A Concise History of American Painting and Sculpture* (New York: Harper & Row, 1984), 264.

47. Quoted in Milton Meltzer, *Dorothea Lange: A Photographer's Life* (New York: Farrar, Strauss & Giroux, 1978), 133, 220.

48. Quoted in Philip Johnson, *Mies van der Rohe,* rev. ed. (New York: Museum of Modern Art, 1954), 200–201.

CHAPTER 30

1. Dawn Ades and Andrew Forge, *Francis Bacon* (London: Thames & Hudson, 1985), 8; and David Sylvester, *The Brutality of Fact: Interviews with Francis Bacon,* 3d ed. (London: Thames & Hudson, 1987), 182.

2. Harold Rosenberg, "The American Action Painters," *Art News* 51 (December 1952): 22–29; reprinted in Rosenberg, *The Tradition of the New* (New York: Horizon Press, 1959), 23–39.

3. Quoted in an interview by Yves Michaud in *Joan Mitchell: New Paintings* (New York: Xavier Fourcade, 1986), n.p.

4. Quoted in Thomas Hess, *Barnett Newman* (New York: Walker and Company, 1969), 51.

5. Quoted in John P. O'Neill, ed., *Barnett Newman: Selected Writings and Interviews* (New York: Knopf, 1990), 108.

6. Marcus Rothko and Adolph Gottlieb, quoted in Edward Alden Jewell, "The Realm of Art: A New Platform and Other Matters: 'Globalism' Pops into View," *New York Times,* June 13, 1943, 9.

7. Quoted in Selden Rodman, *Conversations with Artists* (New York: Devin-Adair, 1957), 93–94.

8. Clement Greenberg, "After Abstract Expressionism," *Art International* 7, no. 8 (October 1962): 24–32.

9. Clement Greenberg, "Recentness of Sculpture," in Gregory Battcock, ed., *Minimal Art: A Critical Anthology* (New York: Dutton, 1968), 183–184.

10. Louise Nevelson, quoted in John Gordon, *Louise Nevelson* (New York: Praeger, 1967), 12.

11. Quoted in Deborah Wye, *Louise Bourgeois* (New York: Museum of Modern Art, 1982), 22.

12. Ibid., 25.

13. Isamu Noguchi, *A Sculptor's World* (New York: Harper & Row, 1968), 40.

14. Quoted in Richard Francis, *Jasper Johns* (New York: Abbeville Press, 1984), 21.

15. Andy Warhol, *The Philosophy of Andy Warhol* (New York: Harcourt Brace Jovanovich, 1975), 100.

16. Quoted in Christine Lindey, *Superrealist Painting and Sculpture* (London: Orbis, 1980), 50.

17. Quoted in Sebastian Smee, *Lucian Freud: Beholding the Animal* (Cologne: Taschen, 2009), 61.

18. Ibid., 7.

19. Quoted in Lindey, 130.

20. Quoted in Susanna Torruella Leval, "Recapturing History: The (Un)official Story in Contemporary Latin American Art," *Art Journal* 51, no. 4 (Winter 1992): 74.

21. Ibid.

22. Quoted in Mary Jane Jacob, *Magdalena Abakanowicz* (New York: Abbeville, 1982), 94.

23. Peter Blake, *Frank Lloyd Wright* (Harmondsworth: Penguin, 1960), 115.

24. Quoted in Nancy Holt, ed., *The Writings of Robert Smithson* (New York: New York University Press, 1975), 111.

25. Quoted in H. H. Arnason and Peter Kalb, *History of Modern Art,* 5th ed. (Upper Saddle River, N.J.: Prentice Hall, 2004), 489.

26. Quoted in Barbara Haskell, *Blam! The Explosion of Pop, Minimalism, and Performance 1958–1964* (New York: Whitney Museum of American Art), 53.

27. Quoted in Bruce McPherson, ed., *More Than Meat Joy: Complete Performance Works and Selected Writings* (New Paltz, N.Y.: Documentext, 1979), 52.

28. Quoted in Caroline Tisdall, *Joseph Beuys* (New York: Thames & Hudson, 1979), 6.

29. Quoted in Brenda Richardson, *Bruce Nauman: Neons* (Baltimore: Baltimore Museum of Art, 1982), 20.

CHAPTER 31

1. Quoted in Arlene Hirschfelder, *Artists and Craftspeople* (New York: Facts on File, 1994), 115.

2. Translated by Petra ten-Doesschate Chu, *Letters of Gustave Courbet* (Chicago: University of Chicago Press, 1992), 203–204.

3. Interview by Susan Sollins, in Marybeth Sollins, ed., *Art:21 (Art in the Twenty-First Century)* (New York: Abrams, 2009), 5:55.

4. Jerome Silbergeld and Dora C.Y. Ching, eds., *Persistence/Transformation: Text as Image in the Art of Xu Bing* (Princeton, N.J.: Princeton University Press, 2006), 99–101.

5. Michelle Meagher, "Jenny Saville and a Feminist Aesthetics of Disgust," *Hypatia* 18, no. 4 (2003): 23–41.

6. Quoted in Donald Hall, *Corporal Politics* (Cambridge: MIT List Visual Arts Center, 1993), 46.

7. Quoted in Junichi Shiota, *Kimio Tsuchiya, Sculpture 1984–1988* (Tokyo: Morris Gallery, 1988), 3.

8. Quoted in "Vietnam Memorial: America Remembers," *National Geographic* 167, no. 5 (May 1985): 557.

9. Quoted in Calvin Tomkins, "The Art World: *Tilted Arc,*" *New Yorker,* May 20, 1985, 100.

CHAPTER 33

1. Translated by Wang Youfen. Quoted by Wen C. Fong, in Ouyang Zhongshi, Wen C. Fong, et al., *Chinese Calligraphy* (New Haven, Conn.: Yale University Press, 2008), 26.

CHAPTER 34

1. Jiro Yoshihara, "Gutai Art Manifesto" (1956). Translated by Reiko Tomii, in Alexandra Monroe, ed., *Japanese Art after 1945: Scream against the Sky* (Yokohama: Yokohama Museum of Art, 1994), 370.

CHAPTER 35

1. Diego de Landa, *Yucatan before and after the Conquest,* translated by William Gates (Mineola, N.Y.: Dover, 1978), 13, 82.

2. Bernal Díaz del Castillo, *The Discovery and Conquest of Mexico.* Translated by A. P. Maudslay (New York: Farrar, Straus, Giroux, 1956), 218–219.

Glossary

a secco—Italian, "dry." See *fresco*. (627)

abstract—Nonrepresentational; forms and colors arranged without reference to the depiction of an object. (5)

Abstract Expressionism—The first major American avant-garde movement, Abstract Expressionism emerged in New York City in the 1940s. The artists produced *abstract* paintings that expressed their state of mind and that they hoped would strike emotional chords in viewers. The movement developed along two lines: *gestural abstraction* and *chromatic abstraction*. (953)

action painting—Also called *gestural abstraction*. The kind of *Abstract Expressionism* practiced by Jackson Pollock, in which the emphasis was on the creation process, the artist's gesture in making art. Pollock poured liquid paint in linear webs on his canvases, which he laid out on the floor, thereby physically surrounding himself in the painting during its creation. (956, 1080)

additive light—Natural light, or sunlight, the sum of all the wavelengths of the visible *spectrum*. See also *subtractive light*. (7)

additive sculpture—A kind of sculpture *technique* in which materials (for example, clay) are built up or "added" to create form. (11)

aerial perspective—See *perspective*. (586)

agone—Italian, "foot race." (701)

ahu—A stone platform on which the *moai* of Easter Island stand. Ahu marked burial sites or served ceremonial purposes. (1113)

'ahu 'ula—A Hawaiian feather cloak. (1118)

airbrush—A tool that uses compressed air to spray paint onto a surface. (972)

aisle—The portion of a *basilica* flanking the *nave* and separated from it by a row of *columns* or *piers*. (12)

akua'ba—"Akua's child." A Ghanaian image of a young girl. (1127)

album leaf—A painting on a single sheet of paper for a collection stored in an album. (1059)

alchemy—The study of seemingly magical changes, especially chemical changes. (687)

altarpiece—A panel, painted or sculpted, situated above and behind an altar. See also *retable*. (415, 558)

amphitheater—Greek, "double theater." A Roman building type resembling two Greek theaters put together. The Roman amphitheater featured a continuous elliptical cavea around a central arena. (411)

Analytic Cubism—The first phase of *Cubism*, developed jointly by Pablo Picasso and Georges Braque, in which the artists analyzed form from every possible vantage point to combine the various views into one pictorial whole. (892)

anamorphic image—A distorted image that must be viewed by some special means (such as a mirror) to be recognized. (685)

ancien régime—French, "old order." The term used to describe the political, social, and religious order in France before the Revolution at the end of the 18th century. (773)

aphros—Greek, "foam." (581)

apostle—Greek, "messenger." One of the 12 disciples of Jesus. (417)

apse—A recess, usually semicircular, in the wall of a building, commonly found at the east end of a *church*. (424, 1092)

aqueduct—A channel for carrying water, often elevated on *arches*. (774)

arcade—A series of *arches* supported by *piers* or *columns*. (424)

Arcadian (adj.)—In Renaissance and later art, depictions of an idyllic place of rural peace and simplicity. Derived from Arcadia, an ancient district of the central Peloponnesos in southern Greece. (650)

arch—A curved structural member that spans an opening and is generally composed of wedge-shaped blocks (*voussoirs*) that transmit the downward pressure laterally. See also *thrust*. (412)

architrave—The *lintel* or lowest division of the *entablature*; also called the epistyle. (669)

arcuated—*Arch*-shaped. (14-9A, 20-6A)

armature—The crossed, or diagonal, *arches* that form the skeletal framework of a *Gothic rib vault*. In sculpture, the framework for a clay form. (11)

arriccio—In *fresco* painting, the first layer of rough lime plaster applied to the wall. (419)

Art Brut—French, "Crude Art." The mid-20th-century art movement led by Jean Dubuffet that rejected the conventions of traditional art in favor of the untaught art of children and the mentally ill. (952)

Art Deco—Descended from *Art Nouveau*, this movement of the 1920s and 1930s sought to upgrade industrial design as a "fine art" and to work new materials into decorative patterns that could be either machined or handcrafted. Characterized by streamlined, elongated, and symmetrical design. (916)

Art Nouveau—French, "new art." A late-19th- and early-20th-century art movement whose proponents tried to synthesize all the arts in an effort to create art based on natural forms that could be mass produced by technologies of the industrial age. The movement had other names in other countries: Jugendstil in Austria and Germany, Modernismo in Spain, and Stile Floreale in Italy. (873)

ascetic—One who follows a path of self-denial. (1033)

asceticism—Self-discipline and self-denial. (1033)

ashlar masonry—Carefully cut and regularly shaped blocks of stone used in construction, fitted together without mortar. (607, 1091)

assemblage—An artwork constructed from already existing objects. (967)

asye usu—Baule (Côte d'Ivoire) bush spirits. (1126)

atmospheric perspective—See *perspective*. (586, 20-11A, 20-11B)

atrium (pl. **atria**)—The central reception room of a Roman domus that is partly open to the sky. Also, the open, *colonnaded* court in front of and attached to a Christian *basilica*. (704)

attribute—(n.) The distinctive identifying aspect of a person—for example, an object held, an associated animal, or a mark on the body. (v.) To make an *attribution*. (5)

attribution—Assignment of a work to a maker or makers. (6)

automatism—In painting, the process of yielding oneself to instinctive motions of the hands after establishing a set of conditions (such as size of paper or *medium*) within which a work is to be created. (921)

avant-garde—French, "advance guard" (in a platoon). Late-19th- and 20th-century artists who emphasized innovation and challenged established convention in their work. Also used as an adjective. (883)

avatar—A manifestation of a deity incarnated in some visible form in which the deity performs a sacred function on earth. In Hinduism, an incarnation of a god. (1040)

bacchanal—An orgiastic revel in which the followers of the Greco-Roman god Bacchus take part. (654, 28-32A)

bai—An elaborately painted men's ceremonial house on Belau (formerly Palau) in the Caroline Islands of Micronesia. (1111)

baldacchino—A canopy on *columns*, frequently built over an altar. The term derives from *baldacco*. (704)

baldacco—Italian, "silk from Baghdad." See *baldacchino*. (704)

baldric—A sashlike belt worn over one shoulder and across the chest to support a sword. (24-30A)

barge boards—The angled boards that outline the exterior gables of a Maori meeting house. (1103)

Baroque/baroque—The traditional blanket designation for European art from 1600 to 1750. Uppercase *Baroque* refers to the art of this period, which features dramatic theatricality and elaborate ornamentation in contrast to the simplicity and orderly rationality of *Renaissance* art, and is most appropriately applied to Italian art. Lowercase *baroque* describes similar stylistic features found in the art of other periods—for example, the Hellenistic period in ancient Greece. The term derives from *barroco*. (702)

barrel vault—See *vault*. (606, 1040)

barroco—Portuguese, "irregularly shaped pearl." See *Baroque*. (702)

basilica (adj. **basilican**)—In Roman architecture, a public building for legal and other civic proceedings, rectangular in plan, with an entrance usually on a long side. In Christian architecture, a *church* somewhat resembling the Roman basilica, usually entered from one end and with an *apse* at the other. (424, 604)

bas-relief—See *relief*. (12, 862)

battlement—A low parapet at the top of a circuit wall in a fortification. (427, 26-28A)

Bauhaus—A *school* of architecture in Germany in the 1920s under the aegis of Walter Gropius, who emphasized the unity of art, architecture, and design. (932)

bay—The space between two *columns*, or one unit in the *nave arcade* of a *church*; also, the passageway in an *arcuated* gate. (424)

Beaux-Arts—An architectural *style* of the late 19th and early 20th centuries in France. Based on ideas taught at the École des Beaux-Arts in Paris, the Beaux-Arts style incorporated *classical* principles, such as symmetry in design, and included extensive exterior ornamentation. (831)

belvedere—Italian, "beautiful view." A building or other structure with a view of a *landscape* or seascape. (648)

benday dots—Named after the newspaper printer Benjamin Day, the benday dot system involves the modulation of *colors* through the placement and size of colored dots. (968)

bhakti—In Buddhist thought, the adoration of a personalized deity as a means of achieving unity with it; love felt by the devotee for the deity. In Hinduism, the devout, selfless direction of all tasks and activities of life to the service of one god. (1040)

Bharat Mata—Mother India; the female personification of India. (32-12A)

bibliophile—Lover of books. (572)

bieri—The wood *reliquary* guardian figures of the Fang in Gabon and Cameroon. (1123)

Biomorphic Surrealism—See *Surrealism*. (921)

bisj pole—An elaborately carved pole constructed from the trunk of the mangrove tree. The Asmat people of southwestern New Guinea created bisj poles to indicate their intent to avenge a relative's death. (1106)

bocio—A Fon (Republic of Benin) empowerment figure. (1130)

Book of Hours—A Christian religious book for private devotion containing prayers to be read at specified times of the day. (571)

bosquet—French, "grove." One of the subdivisions within the gardens of the palace at Versailles. (25-28A)

bottega—An artist's studio-shop. (590)

braccia—Italian, "arm." A unit of measurement; 1 braccia equals 23 inches. (604)

breakfast piece—A Dutch *still life* that includes bread and fruit. (736)

breviary—A Christian religious book of selected daily prayers and Psalms. (571)

bucranium (pl. **bucrania**)—Latin, "bovine skull." A common motif in classical architectural ornament. (688)

buon fresco—See *fresco*. (419, 627)

burgher—A middle-class citizen. (28-33A)

burgomeister—Chief magistrate (mayor) of a Flemish city. (561)

burin—A pointed tool used for *engraving* or *incising*. (578)

bust—A freestanding sculpture of the head, shoulders, and chest of a person. (11)

buttress—An exterior masonry structure that opposes the lateral *thrust* of an *arch* or a *vault*. A pier buttress is a solid mass of masonry. A flying buttress consists typically of an inclined member carried on an arch or a series of arches and a solid buttress to which it transmits lateral thrust. (21-29A, 21-29B)

byobu—Japanese painted folding screens. (1071)

Byzantine—The art, territory, history, and culture of the Eastern Christian Empire and its capital of Constantinople (ancient Byzantium). (411)

caduceus—See *kerykeion*. (602)

calligraphy—Greek, "beautiful writing." Handwriting or penmanship, especially elegant writing as a decorative art. (1051)

calotype—From the Greek *kalos*, "beautiful." A photographic process in which a positive image is made by shining light through a negative image onto a sheet of sensitized paper. (834, 835)

camera lucida—Latin, "lighted room." A device in which a small lens projects the image of an object downward onto a sheet of paper. (835)

camera obscura—Latin, "dark room." An ancestor of the modern camera in which a tiny pinhole, acting as a lens, projects an image on a screen, the wall of a room, or the ground-glass wall of a box; used by artists in the 17th, 18th, and early 19th centuries as an aid in drawing from nature. (747, 781)

campanile—A bell tower of a *church*, usually, but not always, freestanding. (427)

campo—Italian, "field." (421)

canon—A rule (for example, of proportion). The ancient Greeks considered beauty to be a matter of "correct" proportion and sought a canon of proportion, for the human figure and for buildings. The fifth-century BCE sculptor Polykleitos wrote the *Canon*, a treatise incorporating his formula for the perfectly proportioned *statue*. Also, a *church* official who preaches, teaches, administers sacraments, and tends to pilgrims and the sick. (10)

canonization (adj. **canonized**)—The declaration by the Catholic Church of a person as a *saint* after his or her death, often as a *martyr*. (14-5A)

capital—The uppermost member of a *column*, serving as a transition from the shaft to the *lintel*. In *classical* architecture, the form of the capital varies with the *order*. (412)

capriccio—Italian, "originality." One of several terms used in Italian *Renaissance* literature to praise the originality and talent of artists. (628)

cartoon—In painting, a full-size preliminary drawing from which a painting is made. (419, 626)

carving—A sculptural *technique* in which the artist cuts away material (for example, from a stone block) in order to create a *statue* or a *relief*. (11)

cassone (pl. **cassoni**)—A carved chest, often painted or gilded, popular in *Renaissance* Italy for the storing of household clothing. (655)

casting—A sculptural *technique* in which the artist pours liquid metal, plaster, clay, or another material into a *mold*. When the material dries, the sculptor removes the cast piece from the mold. (11)

cathedral—A bishop's *church*. The word derives from *cathedra*, referring to the bishop's chair. (423)

cella—The chamber at the center of an ancient temple; in a *classical* temple, the room (Greek, *naos*) in which the a diety statue usually stood. (643, 688)

cemen—The winglike openwork projection at the top of an Asmat *bisj pole*. (1106)

central plan—See *plan*. (606)

chacmool—A *Mesoamerican* statuary type depicting a fallen warrior on his back with a receptacle on his chest for sacrificial offerings. (930)

chakravartin—In South Asia, the ideal king, the Universal Lord who ruled through goodness. (1045)

Chan—See *Zen*. (1057, 1067)

chancel arch—The arch separating the chancel (the *apse* or *choir*) or the *transept* from the *nave* of a basilica or *church*. (424)

chanoyu—Japanese, "tea ceremony." (1072)

chapter house—The meeting hall in a *monastery*. (605)

characters—In Chinese writing, signs that record spoken words. (1009, 1051)

char-bagh—The "four-plot" plan of Iranian gardens. (1039)

chartreuse—A Carthusian *monastery*. (557)

chashitsu—Japanese, "teahouse." (1072)

chasing—The *engraving* or embossing of metal. (705)

chasseur—French cavalry officer. (805)

château (pl. **châteaux**)—French, "castle." A luxurious country residence for French royalty, developed from medieval castles. (694)

cherub—A chubby winged child angel. (573)

chiaroscuro—In drawing or painting, the treatment and use of light and dark, especially the gradations of light that produce the effect of *modeling*. (420, 626)

chiaroscuro woodcut—A *woodcut technique* using two blocks of wood instead of one. The printmaker carves and inks one block in the usual way in order to produce a traditional black-and-white print. Then the artist cuts a second block consisting of broad highlights that can be inked in gray or color and printed over the first block's impression. (684)

choir—The space reserved for the clergy and singers in the *church*, usually east of the *transept* but, in some instances, extending into the *nave*. (12)

Christophoros—Greek, "he who carries Christ"—that is, Saint Christopher. (20-21A)

chromatic abstraction—A kind of *Abstract Expressionism* that focuses on the emotional resonance of color, as exemplified by the work of Barnett Newman and Mark Rothko. (954)

chronology—In art history, the dating of art objects and buildings. (2)

church—Christian house of worship.

Ci Wara—The legendary wild antelope that taught humans the secrets of agriculture, portrayed in *abstract* Bamana headdresses used in masquerades. (1134)

Cinquecento—Italian, "500"—that is, the 16th century (the 1500s) in Italy. (623)

circus—An ancient Roman chariot racecourse. (701)

city-state—An independent, self-governing city. (417)

Classical/classical—The art and culture of ancient Greece between 480 and 323 BCE. Lowercase *classical* refers more generally to Greco-Roman art and culture. (412)

clerestory—The windowed part of a building that rises above the roofs of the other parts. The oldest known clerestories are Egyptian. In Roman *basilicas* and medieval *churches*, clerestories are the windows that form the *nave*'s uppermost level below the timber ceiling or the *vaults*. (424, 20-6A)

cloisonné—A decorative metalwork *technique* employing cloisons; also, decorative brickwork in later Byzantine architecture. (858)

cloister—A *monastery* courtyard, usually with covered walks along its sides. (597)

codex (pl. **codices**)—Separate pages of *vellum* or *parchment* bound together at one side; the predecessor of the modern book. The codex

superseded the *rotulus*. In *Mesoamerica*, a painted and inscribed book on long sheets of bark paper or deerskin coated with fine white plaster and folded into accordion-like pleats. (1084)

collage—A composition made by combining on a flat surface various materials, such as newspaper, wallpaper, printed text and illustrations, photographs, and cloth. (8, 894, 1136)

coller—French, "to stick." (894)

colonnade—A series or row of *columns*, usually spanned by *lintels*.

colophon—An inscription, usually on the last page, giving information about a book's manufacture. In Chinese painting, written texts on attached pieces of paper or silk. (1051)

color—The value, or tonality, of a color is the degree of its lightness or darkness. The intensity, or saturation, of a color is its purity, its brightness or dullness. See also *primary colors, secondary colors,* and *complementary colors*. (7)

color-field painting—A variant of *Post-Painterly Abstraction* in which artists sought to reduce painting to its physical essence by pouring diluted paint onto unprimed canvas and letting these pigments soak into the fabric, as exemplified by the work of Helen Frankenthaler and Morris Louis. (960)

colorito—Italian, "colored" or "painted." A term used to describe the application of paint. Characteristic of the work of 16th-century Venetian artists who emphasized the application of paint as an important element of the creative process. Central Italian artists, in contrast, largely emphasized *disegno*—careful design preparation based on preliminary drawing. (651)

colossal order—An architectural design in which the *columns* or *pilasters* are two or more stories tall. Also called a giant order. (618)

column—A vertical, weight-carrying architectural member, circular in cross-*section* and consisting of a base (sometimes omitted), a shaft, and a *capital*. (10, 412, 609)

combines—The name that American artist Robert Rauschenberg gave to his *assemblages* of painted passages and sculptural elements. (967, 995)

commedia dell'arte—A traditional Italian comic play performed by actors and musicians. (29-17A)

complementary colors—Those pairs of *colors*, such as red and green, that together embrace the entire *spectrum*. The complement of one of the three *primary colors* is a mixture of the other two. (7, 855)

compline—The last prayer of the day in a *Book of Hours*. (571)

compose—See *composition*. (7)

Composite capital—A capital combining *Ionic* volutes and *Corinthian* acanthus leaves, first used by the ancient Romans. (21-34A)

composition—The way in which an artist organizes *forms* in an artwork, either by placing shapes on a flat surface or arranging forms in space. (7)

compound pier—A *pier* with a group, or cluster, of attached shafts, especially characteristic of *Gothic* architecture. (14-13A)

Conceptual Art—An American *avant-garde* art movement of the 1960s whose premise was that the "artfulness" of art lay in the artist's idea rather than its final expression. (989)

condottiere (pl. **condottieri**)—An Italian mercenary general. (582)

confraternity—In Late Antiquity, an association of Christian families pooling funds to purchase property for burial. In late medieval Europe, an organization founded by laypersons who dedicated themselves to strict religious observances. (415)

congregational mosque—A city's main *mosque*, designed to accommodate the entire *Muslim* population for the Friday noonday prayer. Also called the great mosque or Friday mosque. (1034, 1035)

connoisseur—An expert in *attributing* artworks to one artist rather than another. More generally, an expert on artistic *style*. (6)

Constructivism—An early-20th-century Russian art movement formulated by Naum Gabo, who built up his sculptures piece by piece in space instead of carving or *modeling* them. In this way, the sculptor worked with "volume of mass" and "volume of space" as different materials. (906)

continuous narration—The depiction of the same figure more than once in the same space at different stages of a story. (20-11A)

contour line—In art, a continuous *line* defining the outer shape of an object. (7)

contrapposto—The disposition of the human figure in which one part is turned in opposition to another part (usually hips and legs one way, shoulders and chest another), creating a counterpositioning of the body about its central axis. Sometimes called "weight shift" because the weight of the body tends to be thrown to one foot, creating tension on one side and relaxation on the other. (586)

corbel—A projecting wall member used as a support for some element in the superstructure. Also, *courses* of stone or brick in which each course projects beyond the one beneath it. Two such walls, meeting at the topmost course, create a *corbeled arch* or *corbeled vault*. (427, 671)

Corinthian capital—A more ornate form than *Doric* or *Ionic*; it consists of a double row of acanthus leaves from which tendrils and flowers grow, wrapped around a bell-shaped echinus. Although this *capital* is often cited as the distinguishing feature of the Corinthian *order*, in strict terms no such order exists. The Corinthian capital is a substitute for the standard capital used in the Ionic order. (412, 600)

cornice—The projecting, crowning member of the *entablature* framing the *pediment*; also, any crowning projection. (607)

corona civica—Latin, "civic crown." A Roman honorary wreath worn on the head. (7)

course—In masonry construction, a horizontal row of stone blocks. (1091)

crenellation—Alternating solid merlons and open crenels in the notched tops of walls, as in *battlements*. (26-28A)

cross-hatching—See *hatching*. (578)

crossing—The space in a *cruciform church* formed by the intersection of the *nave* and the *transept*. (14-19A)

crossing square—The area in a *church* formed by the intersection (*crossing*) of a *nave* and a *transept* of equal width, often used as a standard *module* of interior proportion. (21-31A)

cruciform—Cross-shaped. (21-31B)

Crude Art—See *Art Brut*. (951)

crypt—A *vaulted* space under part of a building, wholly or partly underground; in *churches*, normally the portion under an *apse*. (14-5A)

Cubism—An early-20th-century art movement that rejected *naturalistic* depictions, preferring *compositions* of shapes and *forms* *abstracted* from the conventionally perceived world. See also *Analytic Cubism* and *Synthetic Cubism*. (892)

cupola—An exterior architectural feature composed of a drum with a shallow cap; a *dome*. (665)

cura animarum—Latin, "care of souls," the duty of a Catholic priest. (642)

Curia—The papal court in the Vatican. (644)

cutaway—An architectural drawing that combines an exterior view with an interior view of part of a building. (12, 629, 896)

Dada—An early-20th-century art movement prompted by a revulsion against the horror of World War I. Dada embraced political anarchy, the irrational, and the intuitive. A disdain for convention, often enlivened by humor or whimsy, is characteristic of the art the Dadaists produced. (900)

daguerreotype—A photograph made by an early method on a plate of chemically treated metal; developed by Louis J. M. Daguerre. (834, 835, 1043)

daimyo—Local lords who controlled small regions and owed obeisance to the *shogun* in the Japanese *shogunate* system. (1065)

darbar—The official audience of a *Mughal* emperor. (32-4A)

De Stijl—Dutch, "the style." An early-20th-century art movement (and magazine), founded by Piet Mondrian and Theo van Doesburg, whose members promoted utopian ideals and developed a simplified geometric style. (928)

Deconstructivism—A late-20th-century architectural *style*. Deconstructivist architects attempt to disorient the observer by disrupting the conventional categories of architecture. The haphazard presentation of *volumes, masses, planes*, lighting, and so forth challenges the viewer's assumptions about *form* as it relates to function. (1026)

Der Blaue Reiter—German, "the blue rider." An early-20th-century *German Expressionist* art movement founded by Vassily Kandinsky and Franz Marc. The artists selected the whimsical name because of their mutual interest in the color blue and horses. (885)

Dervish—A *Muslim* ascetic holy man. (1033)

di sotto in sù—Italian, "from below upward." A *perspective* view seen from below. (619, 664)

dictator perpetuo—Dictator for life. (790)

Die Brücke—German, "the bridge." An early-20th-century *German Expressionist* art movement under the leadership of Ernst Ludwig Kirchner. The group thought of itself as the bridge between the old age and the new. (885)

Dilukai—A female figure with splayed legs, a common motif over the entrance to a Belau *bai*, serving as both guardian and fertility symbol. (1111)

diptych—A two-paneled painting or *altarpiece*; also, an ancient Roman, Early Christian, or Byzantine hinged writing tablet, often of ivory and carved on the external sides. (562)

disegno—Italian, "drawing" and "design." *Renaissance* artists considered drawing to be the external physical manifestation (*disegno esterno*) of an internal intellectual idea of design (*disegno interno*). (628, 651, 713)

divine right—The belief in a king's absolute power as God's will. (750)

divisionism—See *pointillism*. (854)

d'mba—A Baga mask of the Mother of Fertility in the form of the head and breasts of a woman, worn over the shoulders and with a raffia skirt concealing the dancer's identity. (1135)

documentary evidence—In art history, the examination of written sources in order to determine the date of an artwork, the circumstances of its creation, or the identity of the artist(s) who made it. (2)

doge—Italian (Venetian dialect), "duke." (432, 609)

dome—A hemispherical *vault*; theoretically, an *arch* rotated on its vertical axis. In Mycenaean architecture, domes are beehive-shaped. (14-19A)

donor portrait—A portrait of the individual(s) who commissioned (donated) a religious work (for example, an *altarpiece*) as evidence of devotion. (561)

Doric—One of the two systems (or *orders*) invented in ancient Greece for articulating the three units of the *elevation* of a *classical* building—the platform, the *colonnade*, and the superstructure (*entablature*). The Doric order is characterized by, among other features, *capitals* with funnel-shaped echinuses, *columns* without bases, and a *frieze* of *triglyphs* and metopes. See also *Ionic*. (609, 669)

dormer—A projecting gable-capped window. (694)

dressed masonry—Stone blocks shaped to the exact dimensions required, with smooth faces for a perfect fit. (607)

dry painting—See *sand painting*. (1093)

drypoint—An *engraving* in which the design, instead of being cut into the plate with a *burin*, is scratched into the surface with a hard steel "pencil." See also *etching, intaglio*. (578)

Duecento—Italian, "200"—that is, the 13th century (the 1200s) in Italy. (412)

duomo—Italian, "cathedral." (428)

earthworks—See *Environmental Art*. (985)

edition—A set of impressions taken from a single *incised* metal plate or carved woodblock. (577)

elevation—In architecture, a head-on view of an external or internal wall, showing its features and often other elements that would be visible beyond or before the wall. (12, 424)

empiricism—The search for knowledge based on observation and direct experience. (815)

en plein air—See *plein air*. (843, 845)

enamel—A decorative coating, usually colored, fused onto the surface of metal, glass, or ceramics. (666, 1053, 28-25A)

encaustic—A painting *technique* in which pigment is mixed with melted wax and applied to the surface while the mixture is hot. (967)

engaged column—A half-round *column* attached to a wall. See also *pilaster*. (609)

engraving—The process of *incising* a design in hard material, often a metal plate (usually copper); also, the *print* or impression made from such a plate. (576, 578)

Enlightenment—The 18th-century Western philosophy based on empirical evidence. The Enlightenment was a new way of thinking critically about the world and about humankind, independently of religion, myth, or tradition. (763)

entablature—The part of a building above the *columns* and below the roof. The entablature has three parts: *architrave, frieze,* and *pediment*. (31-17A)

Environmental Art—An American art form that emerged in the 1960s. Often using the land itself as their material, Environmental artists construct monuments of great scale and minimal form. Permanent or impermanent, these works transform some section of the environment, calling attention both to the land itself and to the hand of the artist. Sometimes referred to as earthworks. (985)

eravo—A ceremonial men's meeting house constructed by the Elema people in New Guinea. (1108)

escutcheon—An emblem bearing a coat of arms. (654)

etching—A kind of *engraving* in which the design is *incised* in a layer of wax or varnish on a metal plate. The parts of the plate left exposed are then etched (slightly eaten away) by the acid in which the plate is immersed after incising. See also *drypoint, intaglio*. (578)

Eucharist—In Christianity, the partaking of the bread and wine, which believers hold to be either Christ himself or symbolic of him. (558)

Event—See *Fluxus*. (987)

exedra—Recessed area, usually semicircular. (949)

exemplum virtutis—Latin, "example or model of virtue." (763)

existentialism—A philosophy asserting the absurdity of human existence and the improbability of achieving certitude. (951)

Expressionism—Twentieth-century art that is the result of the artist's unique inner or personal vision and that often has an emotional dimension. Expressionism contrasts with art focused on visually describing the empirical world. (885)

facade—Usually, the front of a building; also, the other sides when they are emphasized architecturally. (424)

fan vault—See *vault*. (26-28A)

fantasia—Italian, "imagination." One of several terms used in Italian *Renaissance* literature to praise the originality and talent of artists. (628)

fasces—A bundle of rods with an ax attached, an emblem of authority in ancient Rome. (790)

Fauves—French, "wild beasts." See *Fauvism*. (883)

Fauvism—An early-20th-century art movement led by Henri Matisse. For the Fauves, *color* became the formal element most responsible for pictorial coherence and the primary conveyor of meaning. (883)

Favrile—A type of leaded stained glass patented by Louis Comfort Tiffany in the late 19th century. (28-38B)

femmages—The name that American artist Miriam Schapiro gave to her sewn *collages,* assembled from fabrics, quilts, buttons, sequins, lace trim, and rickrack collected at antique shows and fairs. (976)

femme fatale—French, "fatal woman." A destructive temptress of men. (863)

femme savante—French, "learned woman." The term used to describe the cultured hostesses of *Rococo* salons. (765)

fenestra coeli—Latin, "window to Heaven." (721)

ferroconcrete—Concrete strengthened by a skeleton of iron bars; also called reinforced concrete. (935)

fête galante—French, "amorous festival." A type of *Rococo* painting depicting the outdoor amusements of French upper-class society. (768)

feudalism—The medieval political, social, and economic system held together by the relationship between landholding liege lords and the vassals who were granted tenure of a portion of their land and in turn swore allegiance to the liege lord. (556)

fidere—Latin, "to trust." (562)

fin-de-siècle—French, "end of the century." A period in Western cultural history from the end of the 19th century until just before World War I, when decadence and indulgence masked anxiety about an uncertain future. (866)

finial—A crowning ornament. (562, 1035)

fleur-de-lis—A three-petaled iris flower; the royal flower of France. (735)

florin—The denomination of gold coin of *Renaissance* Florence that became an international currency for trade. (428)

Fluxus—A group of American, European, and Japanese artists of the 1960s who created *Performance Art*. Their performances, or Events, often focused on single actions, such as turning a light on and off or watching falling snow, and were more theatrical than *Happenings*. (987)

flying buttress—See *buttress*. (12, 949, 20-6A)

fons vitae—Latin, "fountain of life." A symbolic fountain of everlasting life. (558)

foreshortening (adj. **foreshortened**)—The use of *perspective* to represent in art the apparent visual contraction of an object that extends back in space at an angle to the perpendicular plane of sight. (9, 411)

form—In art, an object's shape and structure, either in two dimensions (for example, a figure painted on a surface) or in three dimensions (such as a *statue*). (7)

formal analysis—The visual analysis of artistic *form*. (7)

formalism—Strict adherence to, or dependence on, stylized shapes and methods of *composition*. An emphasis on an artwork's visual elements rather than its subject. (953)

freestanding sculpture—See *sculpture in the round*. (11)

fresco—Painting on lime plaster, either dry (dry fresco, or fresco secco) or wet (true, or buon, fresco). In the latter method, the pigments are mixed with water and become chemically bound to the freshly laid lime plaster. Also, a painting executed in either method. (419)

fresco secco—See *fresco*. (419, 627)

frieze—The part of the *entablature* between the *architrave* and the *cornice*; also, any sculptured or painted band. (669)

fusuma—Japanese painted sliding-door panels. (1069)

Futurism—An early-20th-century Italian art movement that championed war as a cleansing agent and that celebrated the speed and dynamism of modern technology. (898)

garbha griha—Hindi, "womb chamber." In Hindu temples, the *cella,* the holy inner sanctum often housing the god's image or *symbol*. (1035)

genius—Latin, "spirit." In art, the personified spirit of a person or place. (22-52A)

genre—A *style* or category of art; also, a kind of painting that realistically depicts scenes from everyday life. (5, 572, 688)

German Expressionism—An early-20th-century regional *Expressionist* movement. (885)

gesso—Plaster mixed with a binding material, used as the base coat for paintings on wood panels. (566, 872, 21-28A)

gestural abstraction—Also known as *action painting*. A kind of *abstract* painting in which the gesture, or act of painting, is seen as the subject of art. Its most renowned proponent was Jackson Pollock. See also *Abstract Expressionism*. (954)

giant order—See *colossal order*. (618)

gigantomachy—In ancient Greek mythology, the battle between gods and giants. (670)

giornata (pl. **giornate**)—Italian, "day." The section of plaster that a *fresco* painter expects to complete in one session. (419)

glaze—A vitreous coating applied to pottery to seal and decorate the surface; it may be colored, transparent, or opaque, and glossy or *matte*. In *oil painting*, a thin, transparent, or semitransparent layer applied over a *color* to alter it slightly. (559, 606, 1046, 1053)

glazing—The application of successive layers of *glaze* in *oil painting*. (559)

gleaning—The collection by peasants of wheat scraps left in the field after a harvest. (818)

Gobelin tapestry—A *tapestry* produced on a vertical loom using a weaving *technique* in which no horizontal (weft) threads extend the full width of the fabric. (29-67B)

gold leaf—Gold beaten into tissue-paper-thin sheets that then can be applied to surfaces. (416)

gopi—South Asian herdswoman. (32-8A)

gopuras—The massive, ornamented entrance gateway towers of southern Indian temple compounds. (1040)

Gothic—Originally a derogatory term named after the Goths, used to describe the history, culture, and art of western Europe in the 12th to 14th centuries. Typically divided into periods designated Early (1140–1194), High (1194–1300), and Late (1300–1500). (412, 558)

Gothic Revival—See *Neo-Gothic*. (1042, 26-28A)

gouache—A painting *medium* consisting of watercolor mixed with gum. (889)

Grand Manner portraiture—A type of 18th-century portrait painting designed to communicate a person's grace and class through certain standardized conventions, such as the large scale of the figure relative to the canvas, the controlled pose, the *landscape* setting, and the low *horizon line*. (779)

Greek cross—A cross with four arms of equal length. (646, 709)

green architecture—Ecologically friendly architectural design using clean energy to sustain the natural environment. (1029)

grisaille—A *monochrome* painting done mainly in neutral grays to simulate sculpture. (420, 640, 20-9A)

groin vault—See *vault*. (1042, 14-13A)

guild—An association of merchants, craftspersons, or scholars in medieval and *Renaissance* Europe. (422, 555)

haboku—In Japanese art, a loose and rapidly executed painting *style* in which the ink seems to have been applied by flinging or splashing it onto the paper. (1068)

haiku—A 17-syllable Japanese poetic form. (1075)

halo—An aureole appearing around the head of a holy figure to signify divinity. (416)

handscroll—In Asian art, a horizontal painted scroll that is unrolled right to left, section by section, and often used to present illustrated religious texts or *landscapes*. (1052)

hanging scroll—In Asian art, a vertical scroll hung on a wall with pictures mounted or painted directly on it. (1052)

Happenings—A term coined by American artist Allan Kaprow in the 1960s to describe loosely structured performances, whose creators were trying to suggest the aesthetic and dynamic qualities of everyday life; as actions, rather than objects, Happenings incorporate the fourth dimension (time). (987)

hard-edge painting—A variant of *Post-Painterly Abstraction* that rigidly excluded all reference to gesture and incorporated smooth knife-edge geometric forms to express the notion that painting should be reduced to its visual components. (958)

harpies—Mythological creatures of the underworld. (22-8A)

hatching—A series of closely spaced drawn or *engraved* parallel *lines*. Cross-hatching employs sets of lines placed at right angles. (578, 20-21A)

hay wain—A hay-filled wagon. (811)

heiau—A Hawaiian temple. (1117)

Hevehe—An elaborate cycle of ceremonial activities performed by the Elema people of the Papuan Gulf region of New Guinea. Also,

the large, ornate masks produced for and presented during these ceremonies. (1107)

hierarchy of scale—An artistic convention in which greater size indicates greater importance. (11, 14-16A)

hieroglyph—A *symbol* or picture used to confer meaning in *hieroglyphic* writing. (1084)

hieroglyphic (n., adj.)—A system of writing using *hieroglyphs*. (1084)

high relief—See *relief*. (12)

High-Tech—A contemporary architectural *style* calling for buildings that incorporate the latest innovations in engineering and technology and expose the structures' component parts. (1028)

hokkyo—Japanese, "bridge of the law." The third-highest rank among Buddhist monks. (34-10A)

hookah—A Moroccan water pipe. (808)

horizon line—See *perspective*. (567, 587)

hôtel—French, "town house." (764)

hue—The name of a *color*. See also *primary colors, secondary colors,* and *complementary colors*. (7, 855)

humanism—In the *Renaissance*, an emphasis on education and on expanding knowledge (especially of *classical* antiquity), the exploration of individual potential and a desire to excel, and a commitment to civic responsibility and moral duty. (418)

icon—A portrait or image; especially in *Byzantine churches*, a panel with a painting of sacred personages that are objects of veneration. In the visual arts, a painting, a piece of sculpture, or even a building regarded as an object of veneration. (416)

iconoclasm—The destruction of religious or sacred images. In Byzantium, the period from 726 to 843 when there was an imperial ban on such images. The destroyers of images were known as iconoclasts. Those who opposed such a ban were known as iconophiles. (564, 681)

iconography—Greek, the "writing of images." The term refers both to the content, or subject, of an artwork and to the study of content in art. It also includes the study of the symbolic, often religious, meaning of objects, persons, or events depicted in works of art. (5)

ikegobo—A Benin royal shrine. (10)

Il Magnifico—Italian, "the magnificent one," the epithet of Lorenzo de' Medici. (581)

illuminated manuscript—A luxurious handmade book with painted illustrations and decorations. (416)

illusionism (adj. **illusionistic**)—The representation of the three-dimensional world on a two-dimensional surface in a manner that creates the illusion that the person, object, or place represented is three-dimensional. See also *perspective*. (8, 419)

impasto—A layer of thickly applied pigment. (658, 952)

impost block—The uppermost block of a wall or *pier* beneath the springing of an *arch*. (605)

Impressionism—A late-19th-century art movement that sought to capture a fleeting moment, thereby conveying the elusiveness and impermanence of images and conditions. (841, 842)

incise—To cut into a surface with a sharp instrument, especially to decorate metal and pottery. (578)

incubus—A demon believed in medieval times to prey, often sexually, on sleeping women. (802)

Indo-Saracen—The distinctive hybrid architectural style, based on Indian and Islamic architecture but mixed with European motifs, that was in vogue in India under British colonial rule. (1042)

indulgence—A religious pardon for a sin committed. (641, 680)

ingegno—Italian, "innate talent." One of several terms used in Italian *Renaissance* literature to praise the originality and talent of artists. (628)

installation—An artwork that creates an artistic environment in a room or gallery. (1009, 30-27B)

intaglio—A graphic *technique* in which the design is *incised*, or scratched, on a metal plate, either manually (*engraving, drypoint*) or chemically (*etching*). The incised lines of the design take the ink, making this the reverse of the *woodcut technique*. (578)

intensity—See *color*. (7)

internal evidence—In art history, the examination of what an artwork represents (people, clothing, hairstyles, and so on) in order to determine its date. Also, the examination of the *style* of an artwork to identify the artist who created it. (3)

International Gothic—A *style* of 14th- and 15th-century painting begun by Simone Martini, who fused the French *Gothic* manner with Sienese art. This style appealed to the aristocracy because of its brilliant *color*, lavish costumes, intricate ornamentation, and themes involving splendid processions of knights and ladies. (424, 593)

International style—A *style* of 20th-century architecture associated with Le Corbusier, whose elegance of design came to influence the look of modern office buildings and skyscrapers. (934)

intonaco—In *fresco* painting, the last layer of smooth lime plaster applied to the wall; the painting layer. (419)

invenzione—Italian, "invention." One of several terms used in Italian *Renaissance* literature to praise the originality and talent of artists. (628, 713)

Ionic—One of the two systems (or *orders*) invented in ancient Greece for articulating the three units of the elevation of a classical building: the platform, the colonnade, and the superstructure (*entablature*). The Ionic order is characterized by, among other features, *volutes, capitals, columns* with bases, and an uninterrupted *frieze*.

ivi p'o—Hollow, cylindrical bone or ivory ornaments produced in the Marquesas Islands (Polynesia). (1114)

Japonisme—The French fascination with all things Japanese. Japonisme emerged in the second half of the 19th century. (850)

jouer—French, "to play." (893)

jouir—French, "to enjoy." (893)

journaux—French, "newspapers." (893)

Jugendstil—See *Art Nouveau*. (873)

kakemono—Japanese, "hanging scroll." (1068)

karesansui—A Japanese dry-*landscape* (rock) garden. (1066)

katsina—An art form of Native Americans of the Southwest, the katsina doll represents benevolent supernatural spirits (katsinas) living in mountains and water sources. (1095)

kautaha—Women's organizations in Tonga (Polynesia) that produce barkcloth. (1114)

kente—Brightly colored patterned cloth woven by Asante men on horizontal looms in long, narrow strips sewn together to form *toga*-like robes. (1016, 1130, 1136)

kerykeion—In ancient Greek mythology, a serpent-entwined herald's rod (Latin, *caduceus*), the attribute of Hermes (Roman Mercury), the messenger of the gods. (602)

key block—In the production of *chiaroscuro woodcuts*, the block that carries the linear design. (684)

keystone—See *voussoir*. (669)

khipu—Andean record-keeping device consisting of numerous knotted strings hanging from a main cord; the strings signified, by position and *color*, numbers and categories of things. (1090)

king's gallery—The band of *statues* running the full width of the *facade* of a *Gothic cathedral* directly above the *rose window*. (424)

kiva—A square or circular underground structure that is the spiritual and ceremonial center of *Pueblo* Indian life. (1092)

Kogan—The name of a distinctive type of *Shino* water jar. (1072)

Kommerzbank—German, "commerce bank." (904)

koru—An unrolled spiral design used by the Maori of New Zealand in their *tattoos*. (1115)

kouros (pl. **kouroi**)—Greek, "young man." An Archaic Greek *statue* of a young man. (892)

kula—An exchange of white conus-shell arm ornaments and red chama-shell necklaces that takes place among the Trobriand Islanders of Papua New Guinea. (1110)

kupesi—Embroidered design tablets used by Tonga (Polynesia) women in the production of barkcloth. (1114)

lacquer—A varnishlike substance made from the sap of the Asiatic sumac tree, used to decorate wood and other organic materials. Often colored with mineral pigments, lacquer cures to great hardness and has a lustrous surface. (1056)

lancet—In *Gothic* architecture, a tall narrow window ending in a *pointed arch*. (558, 939, 14-5A, 27-43A)

landscape—A picture showing natural scenery, without narrative content. (5, 428)

Landschaft—German, "landscape." (691)

lantern—A small towerlike structure, usually with windows, capping the top of a *dome* to stabilize the dome and admit light to the interior. (711, 21-29A, 21-29B)

lateral section—See *section*. (12)

laudatio—Latin, "essay of praise." (591)

line—The extension of a point along a path, made concrete in art by drawing on or chiseling into a *plane*. (7)

linear perspective—See *perspective*. (567, 587, 588, 1090)

linguist's staff—In Africa, a staff carried by a person authorized to speak for a king or chief. (1127)

lintel—A horizontal beam used to span an opening.

literati—In China, talented amateur painters and scholars from the landed gentry. (1051, 1052, 31-25A, 33-1A)

lithograph—See *lithography*. (818)

lithography—A printmaking *technique* in which the artist uses an oil-based crayon to draw directly on a stone plate and then wipes water onto the stone. When ink is rolled onto the plate, it adheres only to the drawing. The *print* produced by this method is a lithograph. (818, 819)

local color—An object's true *color* in white light. (843)

loggia—A gallery with an open *arcade* or a *colonnade* on one or both sides. (597, 14-20A)

longitudinal plan—See *plan*. (606)

longitudinal section—See *section*. (12)

lost-wax process—A bronze-*casting* method in which a figure is modeled in wax and covered with clay; the whole is fired, melting away the wax (French, *cire perdue*) and hardening the clay, which then becomes a *mold* for molten metal. Also called the cire perdue process. (705, 1043)

low relief—See *relief*. (12)

lunette—A semicircular area (with the flat side down) in a wall over a door, niche, or window; also, a painting or *relief* with a semicircular frame. (571)

machicolated gallery—A gallery in a defensive tower with holes in the floor to allow stones or hot liquids to be dumped on enemies below. (427)

magus (pl. **magi**)—One of the three wise men from the East who presented gifts to the infant Jesus. (594)

ma-hevehe—Mythical Oceanic water spirits. The Elema people of New Guinea believed that these spirits visited their villages. (1107)

malanggan—Festivals held in honor of the deceased in New Ireland (Papua New Guinea). Also, the carvings and objects produced for these festivals. (1109)

mana—In Polynesia, spiritual power. (1112)

mandapa—Pillared hall of a Hindu temple. (1040)

maniera—Italian, "style" or "manner." See *Mannerism*. (659, 713)

maniera greca—Italian, "Greek manner." The Italo-*Byzantine* painting *style* of the 13th century. (415, 636)

Mannerism—A *style* of later *Renaissance* art that emphasized "artifice," often involving contrived imagery not derived directly from nature. Such artworks showed a self-conscious stylization involving complexity, caprice, fantasy, and polish. Mannerist architecture tended to flout the *classical* rules of order, stability, and symmetry, sometimes to the point of parody. (624, 658)

mano—Italian, "hand." (658)

manulua—Triangular patterns based on the form of two birds, common in Tongan *tapa* designs. (1113)

martyr—A person who chooses to die rather than deny his or her religious belief. See also *saint*.

martyrium (pl. **martyria**)—A shrine to a Christian *martyr*. (645)

mass—The bulk, density, and weight of matter in *space*. (8)

Mass—The Catholic and Orthodox ritual in which believers understand that Christ's redeeming sacrifice on the cross is repeated when the priest consecrates the bread and wine in the *Eucharist*. (558)

matins—In Christianity, early morning prayers. (571)

matte—In painting, pottery, and photography, a dull finish. (558)

maulstick—A stick used to steady the hand while painting. (689)

mausoleum (pl. **mausolea**)—A monumental tomb. The name derives from the mid-fourth-century BCE tomb of Mausolos at Halikarnassos, one of the Seven Wonders of the ancient world. (557, 1039)

mbari—A ceremonial Igbo (Nigeria) house built about every 50 years in honor of the earth goddess Ala. (1130, 37-14A)

mbulu ngulu—The wood-and-metal *reliquary* guardian figures of the Kota of Gabon. (1123)

medium (pl. **media**)—The material (for example, marble, bronze, clay, *fresco*) in which an artist works; also, in painting, the vehicle (usually liquid) that carries the pigment. (7)

mela medica—Italian, "medicinal apples" (oranges). The emblem of the Medici family of *Renaissance* Florence. (601)

memento mori—Latin, "reminder of death." In painting, a reminder of human mortality, usually represented by a skull. (748, 26-7B, 30-27B)

mendicants—In medieval Europe, friars belonging to the Franciscan and Dominican orders, who renounced all worldly goods, lived by contributions of laypersons (the word *mendicant* means "beggar"), and devoted themselves to preaching, teaching, and doing good works. (415)

Mesoamerica—The region that comprises Mexico, Guatemala, Belize, Honduras, and the Pacific coast of El Salvador. (1083)

metamatics—The name that Swiss artist Jean Tinguely gave to the motor-driven devices he constructed to produce instant *abstract* paintings. (988)

minaret—A distinctive feature of *mosque* architecture, a tower from which the faithful are called to worship. (1035)

mingei—A type of modern Japanese folk pottery. (1079)

miniatures—Small individual Indian paintings intended to be held in the hand and viewed by one or two individuals at one time. (1037, 28-25A, 32-4A)

Minimalism—A predominantly sculptural American trend of the 1960s characterized by works featuring a severe reduction of *form*, often to single, homogeneous units. (962)

moai—Large, blocky figural stone sculptures found on Rapa Nui (Easter Island) in Polynesia. (1113)

mobile—A kind of sculpture, invented by Alexander Calder, combining nonobjective organic forms and motion in balanced structures hanging from rods, wires, and colored, organically shaped plates. (944, 1016)

modeling—The shaping or fashioning of three-dimensional forms in a soft material, such as clay; also, the gradations of light and shade reflected from the surfaces of matter in space, or the illusion of such gradations produced by alterations of *value* in a drawing, painting, or *print*.

modernism—A movement in Western art that developed in the second half of the 19th century and sought to capture the images and sensibilities of the age. Modernist art goes beyond simply dealing with the present and involves the artist's critical examination of the premises of art itself. (841, 842, 1058)

Modernismo—See *Art Nouveau*. (873)

module (adj. **modular**)—A basic unit of which the dimensions of the major parts of a work are multiples. The principle is used in sculpture and other art forms, but it is most often employed in architecture, where the module may be the dimensions of an important part of a building, such as the diameter of a *column*. (10, 604)

moko—The form of tattooing practiced by the Maori of New Zealand. (1103, 1115)

mold—A hollow form for *casting*. (11)

monastery—A group of buildings in which monks live together, set apart from the secular community of a town.

monastic order—An organization of monks living according to the same rules. For example, the Benedictine, Franciscan, and Dominican orders. (415)

monochrome (adj. **monochromatic**)—One *color*. (741)

monolith (adj. **monolithic**)—A stone *column* shaft that is all in one piece (not composed of drums); a large, single block or piece of stone used in *megalithic* structures. Also, a colossal *statue* carved from a single piece of stone. (1083, 1113)

mosaic—Patterns or pictures made by embedding small pieces (tesserae) of stone or glass in cement on surfaces such as walls and floors; also, the *technique* of making such works. (1084, 28-25A)

mosque—The Islamic building for collective worship. From the Arabic word *masjid*, meaning a "place for bowing down."

mudra—In Buddhist and Hindu *iconography*, a stylized and symbolic hand gesture. The dhyana (meditation) mudra consists of the right hand over the left, palms upward, in the lap. In the bhumisparsha (earth-touching) mudra, the right hand reaches down to the ground, calling the earth to witness the Buddha's enlightenment. The dharmachakra (Wheel of the Law, or teaching) mudra is a two-handed gesture with right thumb and index finger forming a circle. The abhaya (do not fear) mudra, with the right hand up, palm outward, is a gesture of protection or blessing. (1044)

Mughal—"Descended from the Mongols." The *Muslim* rulers of India, 1526–1857. (1033)

mullion—A vertical member that divides a window or that separates one window from another. (983)

mural—A wall painting. (418)

Muslim—A believer in Islam. (1034)

mystery play—A dramatic enactment of the holy mysteries of the Christian faith, performed at *church* portals and in city squares. (420, 558)

mystic marriage—A spiritual marriage of a woman with Christ. (569)

Nabis—Hebrew, "prophet." A group of *Symbolist* painters influenced by Paul Gauguin. (863)

naturalism (adj. **naturalistic**)—The *style* of painted or sculpted representation based on close observation of the natural world that was at the core of the *classical* tradition. (411)

Naturalistic Surrealism—See *Surrealism*. (921)

nave—The central area of an ancient Roman *basilica* or of a *church*, demarcated from *aisles* by *piers* or *columns*. (424, 980)

nave arcade—In *basilica* architecture, the series of *arches* supported by *piers* or *columns* separating the *nave* from the *aisles*. (20-6A)

nduen fobara—A Kalabari Ijaw (Nigeria) ancestral screen in honor of a deceased chief of a trading house. (1121)

Neo-Baroque—The revival of *Baroque style* in later, especially 19th-century, architecture. (830)

Neoclassicism—A *style* of art and architecture that emerged in the late 18th century as part of a general revival of interest in *classical* cultures. Neoclassical artists adopted themes and *styles* from ancient Greece and Rome. (763)

Neo-Expressionism—An art movement that emerged in the 1970s and that reflects artists' interest in the expressive capability of art, seen earlier in *German Expressionism* and *Abstract Expressionism*. (957, 30-9C)

Neo-Gothic—The revival of the *Gothic style* in architecture, especially in the 19th century. (829, 1042, 26-28A)

Neoplasticism—The Dutch artist Piet Mondrian's theory of "pure plastic art," an ideal balance between the universal and the individual using an *abstract* formal vocabulary. (928)

Neo-Platonism—An ancient school of philosophy based on the ideas of Plato, revived during the *Renaissance* and modified by the teachings of Christianity. (581)

Neue Sachlichkeit—German, "new objectivity." An art movement that grew directly out of the World War I experiences of a group of German artists who sought to show the horrors of the war and its effects. (918)

nezumi—Japanese, "mouse-gray" (ceramics). (1073)

ngatu—Decorated *tapa* made by women in Tonga. (1113, 1114)

nihonga—A 19th-century Japanese painting *style* that incorporated some Western *techniques* in Japanese-style painting, as opposed to *yoga* (Western painting). (1078)

nipote—Italian, "nephew." (21-40A)

nirvana—In Buddhism and Hinduism, a blissful state brought about by absorption of the individual soul or consciousness into the supreme spirit. Also called moksha. (28-35A)

nishiki-e—Japanese, "brocade pictures." Japanese polychrome *woodcut prints* valued for their sumptuous *colors*. (1065)

nkisi n'kondi—A power figure carved by the Kongo people of the Democratic Republic of Congo. Such images embodied spirits believed to heal and give life or to be capable of inflicting harm or death. (1124)

nymphs—In *classical* mythology, female divinities of springs, caves, and woods. (581)

obelisk—A tall four-sided *monolithic pillar* with a pyramidal top—symbolic of the Egyptian sun god Re. (701)

oculus (pl. **oculi**)—Latin, "eye." The round central opening of a *dome*. Also, a small round window in a *Gothic cathedral*. (605, 619, 14-5B)

odalisque—A woman in a Turkish harem. (801)

ogee arch—An *arch* composed of two double-curving lines meeting at a point. (432)

ogive (adj. **ogival**)—The diagonal *rib* of a *Gothic vault*; a pointed, or Gothic, *arch*. (413, 980, 21-29A, 21-29B)

Ogoga—A Yoruba king. (1129)

oil painting—A painting *technique* using oil-based pigments that rose to prominence in northern Europe in the 15th century and is now the standard medium for painting on canvas. (558)

Op Art—An artistic movement of the 1960s in which painters sought to produce optical illusions of motion and depth using only geometric forms on two-dimensional surfaces. (961)

optical mixture—The visual effect of juxtaposed *complementary colors*. (855)

orbiculum—A disklike opening. (983)

order—In classical architecture, a style represented by a characteristic design of the *columns* and *entablature*. See also *superimposed orders*.

Orientalism—The fascination on the part of Westerners with Oriental cultures, especially characteristic of the *Romanticism* movement in 19th-century European painting. (798)

Orphism—A form of *Cubism* developed by the French painter Robert Delaunay in which color plays an important role. (897)

orrery—A mechanical model of the solar system demonstrating how the planets revolve around the sun. (772)

orthogonal—A line imagined to be behind and perpendicular to the picture *plane*; the orthogonals in a painting appear to recede toward a *vanishing point* on the horizon. (567, 587)

overglaze—In *porcelain* decoration, the *technique* of applying mineral *colors* over the *glaze* after the work has been fired. The overglaze colors, or *enamels*, fuse to the glazed surface in a second firing at a much lower temperature than the main firing. See also *underglaze*. (1053)

pa—Japanese, "school." (1074)

pagoda—An East Asian tower, usually associated with a Buddhist temple, having a multiplicity of winged eaves; thought to be derived from the Indian *stupa*. (1046)

paintrix—Latin, "woman painter." (690)

palazzo (pl. **palazzi**)—Italian, "palace." (606, 832)

palazzo pubblico—Italian, "public palace." City hall. (426)

palette knife—A flat tool used to scrape paint off the palette. Artists sometimes also use the palette knife in place of a brush to apply paint directly to the canvas. (817)

palmette—A *classical* decorative motif in the form of stylized palm leaves. (609)

papier collé—French, "stuck paper." See *collage*. (894)

parallel hatching—See *hatching*. (578)

parapet—A low, protective wall along the edge of a balcony, roof, or bastion. (427)

parchment—Lambskin prepared as a surface for painting or writing. (628)

pastel—A powdery paste of pigment and gum used for making crayons; also, the pastel crayons themselves.

patrician—A Roman freeborn landowner. (790)

pediment—In *classical* architecture, the triangular space (gable) at the end of a building, formed by the ends of the sloping roof above the *colonnade*; also, an ornamental feature having this shape. (604)

pendentive—A concave, triangular section of a hemisphere, four of which provide the transition from a square area to the circular base of a covering *dome*. Although pendentives appear to be hanging (pendant) from the dome, they in fact support it. (606)

Performance Art—An American *avant-garde* art trend of the 1960s that made time an integral element of art. It produced works in which movements, gestures, and sounds of persons communicating with an audience replace physical objects. Documentary photographs are generally the only evidence remaining after these events. See also *Happenings*. (986, 1080)

period style—See *style*. (3)

Perpendicular—An English Late *Gothic style* of architecture distinguished by the pronounced verticality of its decorative details. (26-28A)

personal style—See *style*. (4)

personification—An *abstract* idea represented in bodily form. (5, 428)

perspective—A method of presenting an illusion of the three-dimensional world on a two-dimensional surface. In linear perspective, the most common type, all parallel lines or surface edges converge on one, two, or three vanishing points located with reference to the eye level of the viewer (the horizon line of the picture), and associated objects are rendered smaller the farther from the viewer they are intended to seem. Atmospheric, or aerial, perspective creates the illusion of distance by the greater diminution of *color* intensity, the shift in color toward an almost neutral blue, and the blurring of contours as the intended distance between eye and object increases. (8, 417, 587)

pfemba—A Yombe (Democratic Republic of Congo) mother-and-child group. (1131)

philosophe—French, "thinker, philosopher." The term applied to French intellectuals of the *Enlightenment*. (771)

photomontage—A *composition* made by pasting together pictures or parts of pictures, especially photographs. See also *collage*. (903)

Photorealism—See *Superrealism*. (971)

physical evidence—In art history, the examination of the materials used to produce an artwork in order to determine its date. (2)

piano nobile—Italian, "noble floor." The main (second) floor of a building. (610)

piazza—Italian, "plaza." (421)

picturesque—see *Picturesque garden*. (25-28A)

Picturesque garden—An "unordered" garden designed in accord with the *Enlightenment* taste for the natural. (787)

pier—A vertical, freestanding masonry support. (12)

Pietà—A painted or sculpted representation of the Virgin Mary mourning over the body of the dead Christ. (565, 889)

pietra dura—Stonework inlaid with precious and semiprecious stones. (1039)

pilaster—A flat, rectangular, vertical member projecting from a wall of which it forms a part. It usually has a base and a *capital* and is often fluted. (564, 592)

pillar—Usually a weight-carrying member, such as a *pier* or a *column*; sometimes an isolated, freestanding structure used for commemorative purposes.

pinnacle—In *Gothic churches*, a sharply pointed ornament capping the *piers* or flying *buttresses*; also used on *church façades*. (421, 424, 27-43A)

pittura—Italian, "painting. (717)

Pittura Metafisica—Italian, "metaphysical painting." An early-20th-century Italian art movement led by Giorgio de Chirico, whose work conveys an eerie mood and visionary quality. (922)

pixels—Shortened form of "picture elements." The tiny boxes that make up digital images displayed on a computer monitor. (992)

plan—The horizontal arrangement of the parts of a building or of the buildings and streets of a city or town, or a drawing or diagram showing such an arrangement. In an axial plan, the parts of a building are organized longitudinally, or along a given axis; in a central plan, the parts of the structure are of equal or almost equal dimensions around the center. (12)

plane—A flat surface. (7)

Plateresque—A *style* of Spanish architecture characterized by elaborate decoration based on *Gothic, Italian Renaissance,* and Islamic sources; derived from the Spanish word *platero,* meaning "silversmith." (695)

platero—See *Plateresque.* (695)

plein air—An approach to painting very popular among the *Impressionists,* in which an artist sketches outdoors to achieve a quick impression of light, air, and *color.* (843, 845)

poesia—A term describing "poetic" art, notably Venetian *Renaissance* painting, which emphasizes the lyrical and sensual. (652)

pointed arch—A narrow *arch* of pointed profile, in contrast to a semicircular arch. (3, 432, 26-28A)

pointillism—A system of painting devised by the 19th-century French painter Georges Seurat. The artist separates *color* into its component parts and then applies the component colors to the canvas in tiny dots (points). The image becomes comprehensible only from a distance, when the viewer's eyes optically blend the pigment dots. Sometimes referred to as divisionism. (854, 855)

polychrome—Multicolored. (722)

polyptych—An *altarpiece* composed of more than three sections. (558)

Pop Art—A term coined by British art critic Lawrence Alloway to refer to art, first appearing in the 1950s, that incorporated elements from consumer culture, the mass media, and popular culture, such as images from motion pictures and advertising. (965, 966)

porcelain—Extremely fine, hard, white ceramic. Unlike *stoneware,* porcelain is made from a fine white clay called kaolin mixed with ground petuntse, a type of feldspar. True porcelain is translucent and rings when struck. (1053)

portico—A roofed *colonnade;* also an entrance porch. (597)

positivism—A Western philosophical model that promoted science as the mind's highest achievement. (815)

Post-Impressionism—The term used to describe the stylistically heterogeneous work of the group of late-19th-century painters in France, including van Gogh, Gauguin, Seurat, and Cézanne, who more systematically examined the properties and expressive qualities of *line,* pattern, *form,* and *color* than the *Impressionists* did. (852)

postmodernism—A reaction against *modernist formalism,* which was seen as elitist. Far more encompassing and accepting than the more rigid confines of modernist practice, postmodernism offers something for everyone by accommodating a wide range of *styles,* subjects, and formats, from traditional easel painting to *installation* and from *abstraction* to *illusionistic* scenes. Postmodern art often includes irony or reveals a self-conscious awareness of the position of the artist in the history of art. (876, 949, 982)

Post-Painterly Abstraction—An American art movement that emerged in the 1960s and was characterized by a cool, detached rationality emphasizing tighter pictorial control. See also *color-field painting* and *hard-edge painting.* (958)

pou tokomanawa—A sculpture of an ancestor that supports the *ridgepole* of a Maori (New Zealand) meeting house. (1103)

pouncing—The method of transferring a sketch onto paper or a wall by tracing, using thin paper or transparent gazelle skin placed on top of the sketch, pricking the contours of the design into the skin or paper with a pin, placing the skin or paper on the surface to be painted, and forcing black pigment through the holes. (1037, 32-4A)

poupou—A decorated wall panel in a Maori (New Zealand) meeting house. (1103, 1115)

Poussiniste—A member of the French Royal Academy of Painting and Sculpture during the early 18th century who followed Nicolas Poussin in insisting that *form* was the most important element of painting. See also *Rubéniste.* (768)

powwow—A traditional Native American ceremony featuring dancing in quilled, beaded, and painted costumes. (1100)

Precisionism—An American art movement of the 1920s and 1930s. The Precisionists concentrated on portraying manmade environments in a clear and concise manner to express the beauty of perfect and precise machine forms. (912)

predella—The narrow ledge on which an *altarpiece* rests on an altar. (421)

prefabricated architecture—Construction using structural elements manufactured in advance and transported to the building site ready for assembly. (833)

prefiguration—In Early Christian art, the depiction of Old Testament persons and events as prophetic forerunners of Christ and New Testament events. (569, 583)

Pre-Raphaelite art—A 19th-century English art movement whose members wished to create art free from what they considered the artificial manner propagated in the academies by the successors of Raphael. (827)

primary colors—Red, yellow, and blue—the *colors* from which all other colors may be derived. (7, 855)

primitivism—The incorporation in early-20th-century Western art of stylistic elements from the artifacts of Africa, Oceania, and the native peoples of the Americas. (891)

print—An artwork on paper, usually produced in multiple impressions. (577, 1065)

proportion—The relationship in size of the parts of persons, buildings, or objects, often based on a *module.* (10)

proscenium—The part of a theatrical stage in front of the curtain. (707)

provenance—Origin or source; findspot. (3)

psalter—A book containing the Psalms. (571)

pueblo—A communal multistoried dwelling made of stone or adobe brick by the Native Americans of the Southwest. Uppercase *Pueblo* refers to various groups that occupied such dwellings. (1092)

pukao—A small red scoria cylinder serving as a topknot or hat on Easter Island *moai.* (1113)

pulpit—A raised platform in a *church* or *mosque* on which a priest or *imam* stands while leading the religious service. (412)

punchwork—Tooled decorative work in *gold leaf.* (423)

Purism—An early-20th-century art movement that embraced the "machine aesthetic" and sought purity of *form* in the clean functional lines of industrial machinery. (898)

putto (pl. **putti**)—A cherubic young boy. (592, 28-32A)

quadrifrons—Latin, "four-fronted." An *arch* with four equal *facades* and four *arcuated bays.* (23-23A)

quadro riportato—A ceiling design in which painted scenes are arranged in panels that resemble framed pictures transferred to the surface of a shallow, curved *vault.* (712)

quatrefoil—A shape or *plan* in which the parts assume the form of a cloverleaf. (430)

Quattrocento—Italian, "400"—that is, the 15th century (the 1400s) in Italy. (581)

quoins—The large, sometimes *rusticated,* usually slightly projecting stones that often form the corners of the exterior walls of masonry buildings. (646)

Rayograph—A photograph produced without a camera by placing objects on photographic paper and then exposing the paper to light; named for the American artist Man Ray. (910)

Realism (adj. **Realist**)—A movement that emerged in mid-19th-century France. Realist artists represented the subject matter of everyday life (especially subjects that previously had been considered inappropriate for depiction) in a relatively *naturalistic* mode. (815, 816)

refectory—The dining hall of a Christian *monastery*. (597)

regional style—See *style*. (3)

Regionalism—A 20th-century American art movement that portrayed American rural life in a clearly readable, *Realist* style. Major Regionalists include Grant Wood and Thomas Hart Benton. (938)

relics—The body parts, clothing, or objects associated with a holy figure, such as the Buddha or Christ or a Christian *saint*. Also, in Africa, the bones of ancestors. (1044, 1121)

relief—In sculpture, figures projecting from a background of which they are part. The degree of relief is designated high, low (bas), or sunken. In the last, the artist cuts the design into the surface so that the highest projecting parts of the image are no higher than the surface itself. (12, 577)

relief sculpture—See *relief*. (11)

reliquary—A container for holding *relics*. (1123)

Renaissance—French, "rebirth." The term used to describe the history, culture, and art of 14th- through 16th-century western Europe during which artists consciously revived the *classical* style. (411, 418)

renovatio—Latin, "renewal." During the *Carolingian* period, Charlemagne sought to revive the culture of ancient Rome (*renovatio imperii Romani*). (412)

renovatio imperii Romani—See *renovatio*. (412)

retable—An architectural screen or wall above and behind an altar, usually containing painting, sculpture, or other decorations. See also *altarpiece*. (558)

retablo—Spanish, "altarpiece." (723)

revetment—In architecture, a wall covering or facing. (420)

rib—A relatively slender, molded masonry arch that projects from a surface. In *Gothic* architecture, the ribs form the framework of the vaulting. A diagonal rib is one of the ribs that form the X of a *groin vault*. A transverse rib crosses the nave or aisle at a 90-degree angle.

rib vault—A *vault* in which the diagonal and transverse *ribs* compose a structural skeleton that partially supports the masonry web between them. (14-5A)

ridgepole—The beam running the length of a building below the peak of the gabled roof. (1103)

rocaille—See *Rococo*. (764)

Rococo—A style, primarily of interior design, that appeared in France around 1700. Rococo interiors featured lavish decoration, including small sculptures, ornamental mirrors, easel paintings, *tapestries, reliefs*, wall paintings, and elegant furniture. The term Rococo derived from the French word *rocaille* (pebble) and referred to the small stones and shells used to decorate grotto interiors. (764)

Romanesque—"Roman-like." A term used to describe the history, culture, and art of medieval western Europe from ca. 1050 to ca. 1200. (424, 558, 21-36A)

Romanticism—A Western cultural phenomenon, beginning around 1750 and ending about 1850, that gave precedence to feeling and imagination over reason and thought. More narrowly, the art movement that flourished from about 1800 to 1840. (790, 793)

rose window—A circular *stained-glass* window. (424)

rostrum—A speaker's platform. (949)

rotulus (pl. **rotuli**)—The manuscript scroll used by Egyptians, Greeks, Etruscans, and Romans; predecessor of the *codex*. (1086)

rotunda—The circular area under a *dome*; also, a domed round building. (558)

roundel—See *tondo*. (606)

Rubéniste—A member of the French Royal Academy of Painting and Sculpture during the early 18th century who followed Peter Paul Rubens in insisting that *color* was the most important element of painting. See also *Poussiniste*. (768)

rustication (adj. **rusticated**)—To give a rustic appearance by roughening the surfaces and beveling the edges of stone blocks to emphasize the joints between them. Rustication is a *technique* employed in ancient Roman architecture, and was also popular during the *Renaissance*, especially for stone *courses* at the ground-floor level. (607, 14-9B)

sabi—Japanese; the value found in the old and weathered, suggesting the tranquility reached in old age. (1072)

sacra conversazione—Italian, "holy conversation." A style of *altarpiece* painting popular after the middle of the 15th century, in which *saints* from different epochs are joined in a unified space and seem to be conversing either with one another or with the audience. (650)

sacra rappresentazione (pl. **sacre rappresentazioni**)—Italian, "holy representation." A more elaborate version of a *mystery play* performed for a lay audience by a *confraternity*. (420)

saint—From the Latin word *sanctus*, meaning "made holy by God." Applied to persons who suffered and died for their Christian faith or who merited reverence for their Christian devotion while alive. In the Roman Catholic Church, a worthy deceased Catholic who is canonized by the pope. (412)

Saint-Simonianism—An early-19th-century utopian movement that emphasized the education and enfranchisement of women. (820)

saltimbanque—An itinerant circus performer. (29-10A)

samurai—Medieval Japanese warriors. (1065)

sand painting—A temporary painting *technique* using sand, varicolored powdered stones, corn pollen, and charcoal. Sand paintings, also called dry paintings, are integral parts of sacred Navajo rituals. (1093)

sapienza—Italian, "knowledge" or "wisdom." (710)

sarcophagus (pl. **sarcophagi**)—Greek, "consumer of flesh." A coffin, usually of stone. (413)

Satimbe—"Sister on the head." A Dogon (Mali) mask representing all women. (1133)

saturation—See *color*. (7, 855)

satyr—A Greek mythological follower of Dionysos having a man's upper body, a goat's hindquarters and horns, and a horse's ears and tail. (27-33A, 28-32A)

school—A chronological and stylistic classification of works of art with a stipulation of place. (6)

scriptorium (pl. **scriptoria**)—The writing studio of a *monastery*. (577, 20-21A)

scudo (pl. **scudi**)—Italian, "shield." A coin denomination in 17th-century Italy. (716)

sculpture in the round—Freestanding figures, *carved* or *modeled* in three dimensions. (11)

seal—In Asian painting, a stamp affixed to a painting to identify the artist, the *calligrapher*, or the owner. (1051)

secco—Italian, "dry." See also *fresco*. (419, 627)

secondary colors—Orange, green, and purple, obtained by mixing pairs of *primary colors* (red, yellow, blue). (7, 855)

section—In architecture, a diagram or representation of a part of a structure or building along an imaginary *plane* that passes through it vertically. Drawings showing a theoretical slice across a structure's width are lateral sections. Those cutting through a building's length are longitudinal sections. See also *elevation* and *cutaway*. (12)

segmental pediment—A *pediment* with a curved instead of a triangular *cornice*. (646)

sfumato—Italian, "smoky." A smokelike haziness that subtly softens outlines in painting; particularly applied to the paintings of Leonardo da Vinci and Correggio. (559, 629)

shaykh—An Islamic mystic *saint*. (1033)

Shino—Japanese ceramic wares produced during the late 16th and early 17th centuries in kilns in Mino. (1073)

shogun—In 12th- through 19th-century Japan, a military governor who managed the country on behalf of a figurehead emperor. (1065)

shogunate—The Japanese military government of the 12th through 19th centuries. (1065)

sibyl—A Greco-Roman mythological prophetess. (562, 639, 22-18A)

signoria—Italian, "lordship." The governing body of medieval and *Renaissance* Florence. (14-9B)

silk-screen printing—An industrial printing *technique* that creates a sharp-edged image by pressing ink through a design on silk or a similar tightly woven porous fabric stretched tight on a frame. (967)

silverpoint—A *stylus* made of silver, used in drawing in the 14th and 15th centuries because of the fine *line* it produced and the sharp point it maintained. (555)

Simultanéisme—Robert Delaunay's version of *Cubism* in which he created spatial effects and kaleidoscopic movement solely through *color* contrasts; also known as *Orphism*. (897)

simultaneous contrasts—The phenomenon of juxtaposed *colors* affecting the eye's reception of each, as when a painter places dark green next to light green, making the former appear even darker and the latter even lighter. See also *successive contrasts*. (855)

sinopia—A burnt-orange pigment used in *fresco* painting to transfer a *cartoon* to the *arriccio* before the artist paints the plaster. (419)

site-specific art—Art created for a specific location. See also *Environmental Art*. (985)

slit-gong—A hollow, usually cylindrical, bamboo or wood percussion instrument. (1107)

space—In art history, both the actual area that an object occupies or a building encloses and the *illusionistic* representation of space in painting and sculpture. (8)

spectrum—The range or band of visible *colors* in natural light. (7)

sphinx—A mythical Egyptian beast with the body of a lion and the head of a human. (783)

splashed-ink painting—See *haboku*. (1068)

stadium—An ancient Roman long and narrow theater-like structure for footraces and other athletic contests. (701)

stained glass—In *Gothic* architecture, the colored glass used for windows. (12, 858, 1042, 14-5A, 20-6A)

stanza (pl. **stanze**)—Italian, "room." (630)

statue—A three-dimensional sculpture. (11)

stigmata—In Christian art, the wounds Christ received at his crucifixion that miraculously appear on the body of a *saint*. (416, 612)

Stile Floreale—See *Art Nouveau*. (873)

still life—A picture depicting an arrangement of inanimate objects. (5, 721)

stoa—In ancient Greek architecture, an open building with a roof supported by a row of *columns* parallel to the back wall. A covered *colonnade* or *portico*. (829)

stoneware—Pottery fired at high temperatures to produce a stonelike hardness and density. (1053)

stretcher bar—One of a set of wood bars used to stretch canvas to provide a taut surface for painting. (564)

stringcourse—A raised horizontal *molding*, or band, in masonry. Its principal use is ornamental, but it usually reflects interior structure. (607)

stupa—A large, mound-shaped Buddhist shrine. (1044)

style—A distinctive artistic manner. Period style is the characteristic style of a specific time. Regional style is the style of a particular geographical area. Personal style is an individual artist's unique manner. (3, 658)

stylistic evidence—In art history, the examination of the *style* of an artwork in order to determine its date or the identity of the artist. (3)

stylobate—The uppermost course of the platform of a *classical* Greek temple, which supports the *columns*. (643)

stylus—A needlelike tool used in *engraving* and *incising*; also, an ancient writing instrument used to inscribe clay or wax tablets. (555, 578)

subtractive light—The painter's light in art; the light reflected from pigments and objects. See also *additive light*. (7)

subtractive sculpture—A kind of sculpture *technique* in which materials are taken away from the original mass; *carving*. (11)

successive contrasts—The phenomenon of colored afterimages. When a person looks intently at a *color* (green, for example) and then shifts to a white area, the fatigued eye momentarily perceives the *complementary color* (red). See also *simultaneous contrasts*. (855)

sultan—A *Muslim* ruler. (1034)

superimposed orders—*Orders* of architecture that are placed one above another in an *arcaded* or *colonnaded* building, usually in the following sequence: Doric or Tuscan (the first story), *Ionic*, and *Corinthian*. Superimposed orders are found in later Greek architecture and were used widely by Roman and *Renaissance* builders. (696)

superimposition—In *Mesoamerican* architecture, the erection of a new structure on top of, and incorporating, an earlier structure; the nesting of a series of buildings inside each other. (1086)

Superrealism—A painting and sculpture movement of the 1960s and 1970s that emphasized producing artworks based on scrupulous fidelity to optical fact. The Superrealist painters were also called Photorealists because many used photographs as sources for their imagery. (971)

Suprematism—A type of art formulated by Kazimir Malevich to convey his belief that the supreme reality in the world is pure feeling, which attaches to no object and thus calls for new, nonobjective *forms* in art—shapes not related to objects in the visible world. (904)

Surrealism—A successor to *Dada*, Surrealism incorporated the improvisational nature of its predecessor into its exploration of the ways to express in art the world of dreams and the unconscious. Biomorphic Surrealists, such as Joan Miró, produced largely *abstract compositions*. Naturalistic Surrealists, notably Salvador Dalí, presented recognizable scenes transformed into a dream or nightmare image. (921)

symbol—An image that stands for another image or encapsulates an idea. (5)

Symbolism—A late-19th-century movement based on the idea that the artist was not an imitator of nature but a creator who transformed the facts of nature into a *symbol* of the inner experience of that fact. (863)

Synthetic Cubism—A later phase of *Cubism*, in which paintings and drawings were constructed from objects and shapes cut from paper or other materials to represent parts of a subject, in order to engage the viewer with pictorial issues, such as figuration, realism, and abstraction. (893)

taj—Arabic and Persian, "crown." (1039)

tamberan—An Abelam (New Guinea) ceremonial house. (1108, 36-5A)

tapa—Barkcloth made particularly in Polynesia. Tapa is often dyed, painted, stenciled, and sometimes perfumed. (1113)

tapestry—A weaving *technique* in which the horizontal (weft) threads are packed densely over the vertical (warp) threads so that the designs are woven directly into the fabric. (764)

tatami—The traditional woven straw mat used for floor covering in Japanese architecture. (1072)

tatanua—In New Ireland (Papua New Guinea), the spirits of the dead. (1109)

tatau—See *tattoo*. (1115)

tattoo—A permanent design on the skin produced using indelible dyes. The term derives from the Tahitian, Samoan, and Tongan word *tatau* or *tatu*. (1103, 1115)

tatu—See *tattoo*. (1115)

technique—The processes artists employ to create *form*, as well as the distinctive, personal ways in which they handle their materials and tools. (7)

tempera—A *technique* of painting using pigment mixed with egg yolk, glue, or casein; also, the *medium* itself. (415, 558, 559)

tenebrism—Painting in the "shadowy manner," using violent contrasts of light and dark, as in the work of Caravaggio. The term derives from *tenebroso*. (715)

tenebroso—Italian, "shadowy." See *tenebrism*. (715)

terminus ante quem—Latin, "point [date] before which." (2)

terminus post quem—Latin, "point [date] after which." (2)

terracotta—Hard-baked clay, used for sculpture and as a building material. It may be *glazed* or painted. (426, 606)

terribilità—Italian, "the sublime shadowed by the fearful." A term used to describe Michelangelo Buonarroti. (623)

texture—The quality of a surface (rough, smooth, hard, soft, shiny, dull) as revealed by light. In represented texture, a painter depicts an object as having a certain texture even though the pigment is the real texture. (8)

tholos (pl. **tholoi**)—A temple with a circular plan. Also, the burial chamber of a tholos tomb. (643)

thrust—The outward force exerted by an *arch* or a *vault* that must be counterbalanced by a *buttress*. (21-29A, 21-29B)

tiki—A Marquesas Islands (Polynesia) three-dimensional carving of an exalted, deified ancestor figure. (1114)

tipi—A Native American tent dwelling. (1094)

toga—The garment worn by an ancient Roman male citizen. (1136)

togu na—"House of words." A Dogon (Mali) men's house, where deliberations vital to community welfare take place. (1138)

tokonoma—A shallow alcove in a Japanese room, which is used for decoration, such as a painting or stylized flower arrangement. (1072)

tonality—See *color*. (7)

tondo (pl. **tondi**)—A circular painting or *relief* sculpture. (592)

tone block—In the production of *chiaroscuro woodcuts*, the block that carries the coloring. (684)

totem pole—A Native American carved tree trunk featuring a vertical row of stylized heads. (1096)

tracery—Ornamental stonework for holding *stained glass* in place, characteristic of *Gothic cathedrals*. In plate tracery, the glass fills only the "punched holes" in the heavy ornamental stonework. In bar tracery, the stained-glass windows fill almost the entire opening, and the stonework is unobtrusive. (425, 558, 26-28A)

tramezzo—A screen placed across the *nave* of a *church* to separate the clergy from the lay audience. (14-5B)

transept—The part of a *church* with an axis that crosses the *nave* at a right angle. (586, 14-5A)

transubstantiation—The transformation of the Eucharistic bread and wine into the body and blood of Christ. (24-18B)

Trecento—Italian, "300"—that is, the 14th century (the 1300s) in Italy. (417)

trefoil arch—A triple-lobed arch. (412)

trident—The three-pronged pitchfork associated with the ancient Greek sea god Poseidon (Roman Neptune). (688)

triforium—In a *Gothic cathedral*, the blind arcaded gallery below the *clerestory*; occasionally, the *arcades* are filled with *stained glass*. (20-6A)

triglyph—A triple projecting, grooved member of a *Doric frieze* that alternates with metopes. (669)

tripod—An ancient Greek deep bowl on a tall three-legged stand. (783)

triptych—A three-paneled painting, ivory plaque, or *altarpiece*. Also, a small, portable shrine with hinged wings used for private devotion. (425, 886)

triumphal arch—In Roman architecture, a freestanding *arch* commemorating an important event, such as a military victory or the opening of a new road. (596)

trompe l'oeil—French, "fools the eye." A form of *illusionistic* painting that aims to deceive viewers into believing that they are seeing real objects rather than a representation of those objects. (619, 669, 24-14A, 26-6A)

true fresco—See *fresco*. (419)

trumeau—In *church* architecture, the *pillar* or center post supporting the *lintel* in the middle of the doorway. (20-2A)

tukutuku—A stitched lattice panel found in a Maori (New Zealand) meeting house. (1103)

Tuscan column—The standard type of Etruscan *column*. It resembles ancient Greek *Doric* columns but is made of wood, is unfluted, and has a base. Also a popular motif in *Renaissance* and *Baroque* architecture. (609, 643, 704)

tympanum (pl. **tympana**)—The space enclosed by a *lintel* and an *arch* over a doorway. (614, 14-13A, 22-52A)

ukiyo-e—Japanese, "pictures of the floating world." During the Edo period, *woodcut prints* depicting brothels, popular entertainment, and beautiful women. (1065, 1075, 28-17B)

uli—A New Ireland statuary type of a standing figure with male genitals and female breasts, used in *malanggan* rituals. (1109)

underglaze—In *porcelain* decoration, the *technique* of applying mineral *colors* to the surface before the main firing, followed by an application of clear *glaze*. See also *overglaze*. (1046, 1053)

Usonian—Frank Lloyd Wright's term for the inexpensive houses he designed for ordinary people. *Usonian* derives from "United States of North America." (946)

value—See *color*. (7, 855)

vanishing point—See *perspective*. (567, 587)

vanitas—Latin, "vanity." A term describing paintings (particularly 17th-century Dutch *still lifes*) that include references to death. (683, 748, 835, 972, 26-7B)

vault (adj. **vaulted**)—A masonry roof or ceiling constructed on the *arch* principle, or a concrete roof of the same shape. A barrel (or tunnel) vault, semicylindrical in cross-*section*, is in effect a deep arch or an uninterrupted series of arches, one behind the other, over an oblong space. A quadrant vault is a half-barrel vault. A groin (or cross) vault is formed at the point at which two barrel vaults intersect at right angles. In a ribbed vault, there is a framework of *ribs* or arches under the intersections of the vaulting sections. A sexpartite vault is one whose ribs divide the vault into six compartments. A fan vault is a vault characteristic of English *Perpendicular Gothic* architecture, in which radiating ribs form a fanlike pattern. (12)

veduta (pl. **vedute**)—Italian, "scenic view." (780, 781)

vellum—Calfskin prepared as a surface for writing or painting. (628)

vimana—A pyramidal tower over the *garbha griha* of a Hindu temple of the southern style. (1035)

vita—Italian, "life." Also, the title of a biography. (713)

volume—The *space* that *mass* organizes, divides, or encloses. (8)

voussoir—A wedge-shaped stone block used in the construction of a true *arch*. The central voussoir, which sets the arch, is called the *keystone*. (669)

wabi—A 16th-century Japanese art *style* characterized by refined rusticity and an appreciation of simplicity and austerity. (1072)

wainscoting—Paneling on the lower part of interior walls. (872)

waka sran—"People of wood." Baule (Côte d'Ivoire) wood figural sculptures. (1127)

weld—To join metal parts by heating, as in assembling the separate parts of a *statue* made by *casting*. (11)

wet-plate photography—An early photographic process in which the photographic plate is exposed, developed, and fixed while wet. (834)

woodblock—See *woodcut*. (849, 1009)

woodcut—A wood block on the surface of which those parts not intended to *print* are cut away to a slight depth, leaving the design raised; also, the printed impression made with such a block. (576, 577, 885)

yang—In Chinese cosmology, the principle of active masculine energy, which permeates the universe in varying proportions with *yin*, the principle of passive feminine energy. (1054)

yin—See *yang*. (1054)

yoga—A method for controlling the body and relaxing the mind used in later Indian religions to yoke, or unite, the practitioner to the divine. (1078)

Zen—A Japanese Buddhist sect and its doctrine, emphasizing enlightenment through intuition and introspection rather than the study of scripture. In Chinese, Chan. (1066, 1067)

zoopraxiscope—A device invented by Eadweard Muybridge in the 19th century to project sequences of still photographic images; a predecessor of the modern motion-picture projector. (838)

Bibliography

This list of books is very selective, but comprehensive enough to satisfy the reading interests of the beginning art history student and general reader. Significantly expanded from the previous edition, the 15th edition bibliography can also serve as the basis for undergraduate research papers. The resources listed range from works that are valuable primarily for their reproductions to those that are scholarly surveys of schools and periods or monographs on individual artists. The emphasis is on recent in-print books and on books likely to be found in college and municipal libraries. No entries for periodical articles appear, but the bibliography begins with a list of some of the major journals that publish art historical scholarship in English.

Selected Periodicals

African Arts
American Art
American Indian Art
American Journal of Archaeology
Antiquity
Archaeology
Archives of American Art
Archives of Asian Art
Ars Orientalis
Art Bulletin
Art History
Art in America
Art Journal
Artforum International
Artnews
Burlington Magazine
Gesta
History of Photography
Journal of Egyptian Archaeology
Journal of Roman Archaeology
Journal of the Society of Architectural Historians
Journal of the Warburg and Courtauld Institutes
Latin American Antiquity
October
Oxford Art Journal
Women's Art Journal

General Studies

Baxandall, Michael. *Patterns of Intention: On the Historical Explanation of Pictures*. New Haven, Conn.: Yale University Press, 1985.

Bindman, David, ed. *The Thames & Hudson Encyclopedia of British Art*. London: Thames & Hudson, 1988.

Boström, Antonia. *The Encyclopedia of Sculpture*. 3 vols. London: Routledge, 2003.

Broude, Norma, and Mary D. Garrard, eds. *The Expanding Discourse: Feminism and Art History*. New York: Harper Collins, 1992.

Bryson, Norman. *Vision and Painting: The Logic of the Gaze*. New Haven, Conn.: Yale University Press, 1983.

Bryson, Norman, Michael Ann Holly, and Keith Moxey. *Visual Theory: Painting and Interpretation*. New York: Cambridge University Press, 1991.

Burden, Ernest. *Illustrated Dictionary of Architecture*. 2d ed. New York: McGraw-Hill, 2002.

Büttner, Nils. *Landscape Painting: A History*. New York: Abbeville, 2006.

Carrier, David. *A World Art History and Its Objects*. University Park: Pennsylvania State University Press, 2012.

Chadwick, Whitney. *Women, Art, and Society*. 5th ed. New York: Thames & Hudson, 2012.

Cheetham, Mark A., Michael Ann Holly, and Keith Moxey, eds. *The Subjects of Art History: Historical Objects in Contemporary Perspective*. New York: Cambridge University Press, 1998.

Chilvers, Ian, and Harold Osborne, eds. *The Oxford Dictionary of Art*. 3d ed. New York: Oxford University Press, 2004.

Ching, Francis D. K., Mark Jarzombek, and Vikramaditya Prakash. *A Global History of Architecture*. 2d ed. Hoboken, NJ: Wiely, 2010.

Corbin, George A. *Native Arts of North America, Africa, and the South Pacific: An Introduction*. New York: Harper Collins, 1988.

Crouch, Dora P., and June G. Johnson. *Traditions in Architecture: Africa, America, Asia, and Oceania*. New York: Oxford University Press, 2000.

Curl, James Stevens. *Oxford Dictionary of Architecture and Landscape Architecture*. 2d ed. New York: Oxford University Press, 2006.

Davis, Whitney. *A General Theory of Visual Culture*. Princeton, N.J.: Princeton University Press, 2011.

Duby, Georges, ed. *Sculpture: From Antiquity to the Present*. 2 vols. Cologne: Taschen, 1999.

Encyclopedia of World Art. 17 vols. New York: McGraw-Hill, 1959–1987.

Evers, Bernd, and Christof Thoenes. *Architectural Theory from the Renaissance to the Present*. Cologne: Taschen, 2011.

Fielding, Mantle. *Dictionary of American Painters, Sculptors, and Engravers*. 2d ed. Poughkeepsie, N.Y.: Apollo, 1986.

Fine, Sylvia Honig. *Women and Art: A History of Women Painters and Sculptors from the Renaissance to the 20th Century*. Rev. ed. Montclair, N.J.: Alanheld & Schram, 1978.

Fleming, John, Hugh Honour, and Nikolaus Pevsner. *The Penguin Dictionary of Architecture and Landscape Architecture*. 5th ed. New York: Penguin, 2000.

Frazier, Nancy. *The Penguin Concise Dictionary of Art History*. New York: Penguin, 2000.

Freedberg, David. *The Power of Images: Studies in the History and Theory of Response*. Chicago: University of Chicago Press, 1989.

Gaze, Delia, ed. *Dictionary of Women Artists*. 2 vols. London: Routledge, 1997.

Hall, James. *Dictionary of Subjects and Symbols in Art*. 2d ed. Boulder, Colo.: Westview, 2008.

Harris, Anne Sutherland, and Linda Nochlin. *Women Artists: 1550–1950*. Los Angeles: Los Angeles County Museum of Art; New York: Knopf, 1977.

Hauser, Arnold. *The Sociology of Art*. Chicago: University of Chicago Press, 1982.

Hults, Linda C. *The Print in the Western World: An Introductory History*. Madison: University of Wisconsin Press, 1996.

Ingersoll, Richard, and Spiro Kostof. *World Architecture: A Cross-Cultural History*. New York: Oxford University Press, 2012.

Kemp, Martin. *The Science of Art: Optical Themes in Western Art from Brunelleschi to Seurat*. New Haven, Conn.: Yale University Press, 1990.

Kirkham, Pat, and Susan Weber, eds. *History of Design: Decorative Arts and Material Culture, 1400–2000*. New Haven, Conn.: Yale University Press, 2013.

Kostof, Spiro, and Gregory Castillo. *A History of Architecture: Settings and Rituals*. 2d ed. Oxford: Oxford University Press, 1995.

Kultermann, Udo. *The History of Art History*. New York: Abaris, 1993.

Le Fur, Yves, ed. *Musée du Quai Branly: The Collection. Art from Africa, Asia, Oceania, and the Americas*. Paris: Flammarion, 2009.

Lucie-Smith, Edward. *The Thames & Hudson Dictionary of Art Terms*. 2d ed. New York: Thames & Hudson, 2004.

Moffett, Marian, Michael Fazio, and Lawrence Wadehouse. 3d ed. *A World History of Architecture*. London: Laurence King, 2013.

Morgan, Anne Lee. *Oxford Dictionary of American Art and Artists*. New York: Oxford University Press, 2008.

Murray, Peter, and Linda Murray. *The Penguin Dictionary of Art and Artists*. 7th ed. New York: Penguin, 1998.

Nelson, Robert S., and Richard Shiff, eds. *Critical Terms for Art History*. Chicago: University of Chicago Press, 1996.

Pazanelli, Roberta, ed. *The Color of Life: Polychromy in Sculpture from Antiquity to the Present*. Los Angeles: J. Paul Getty Museum, 2008.

Penny, Nicholas. *The Materials of Sculpture*. New Haven, Conn.: Yale University Press, 1993.

Pevsner, Nikolaus. *A History of Building Types*. London: Thames & Hudson, 1987. Reprint of 1979 ed.

———. *An Outline of European Architecture*. 8th ed. Baltimore: Penguin, 1974.

Pierce, James Smith. *From Abacus to Zeus: A Handbook of Art History*. 7th ed. Upper Saddle River, N.J.: Pearson Prentice Hall, 1998.

Placzek, Adolf K., ed. *Macmillan Encyclopedia of Architects*. 4 vols. New York: Macmillan, 1982.

Podro, Michael. *The Critical Historians of Art*. New Haven, Conn.: Yale University Press, 1982.

Pollock, Griselda. *Vision and Difference: Femininity, Feminism, and Histories of Art*. London: Routledge, 1988.

Pregill, Philip, and Nancy Volkman. *Landscapes in History Design and Planning in the Eastern and Western Traditions*. 2d ed. Hoboken, N.J.: Wiley, 1999.

Preziosi, Donald, ed. *The Art of Art History: A Critical Anthology*. New York: Oxford University Press, 1998.

Read, Herbert. *The Thames & Hudson Dictionary of Art and Artists*. Rev. ed. New York: Thames & Hudson, 1994.

Reid, Jane D. *The Oxford Guide to Classical Mythology in the Arts 1300–1990s*. 2 vols. New York: Oxford University Press, 1993.

Rogers, Elizabeth Barlow. *Landscape Design: A Cultural and Architectural History*. New York: Abrams, 2001.

Roth, Leland M. *Understanding Architecture: Its Elements, History, and Meaning*. 2d ed. Boulder, Colo.: Westview, 2006.

Schama, Simon. *The Power of Art*. New York: Ecco, 2006.

Slatkin, Wendy. *Women Artists in History: From Antiquity to the 20th Century*. 4th ed. Upper Saddle River, N.J.: Prentice Hall, 2000.

Squire, Michael. *The Art of the Body: Antiquity and Its Legacy*. New York: Oxford University Press, 2011.

Steer, John, and Antony White. *Atlas of Western Art History: Artists, Sites, and Monuments from Ancient Greece to the Modern Age*. New York: Facts on File, 1994.

Stratton, Arthur. *The Orders of Architecture: Greek, Roman, and Renaissance*. London: Studio, 1986.

Summers, David. *Real Spaces: World Art History and the Rise of Western Modernism*. London: Phaidon, 2003.

Sutcliffe, Antony. *Paris: An Architectural History*. New Haven, Conn.: Yale University Press, 1996.

Sutton, Ian. *Western Architecture: From Ancient Greece to the Present*. New York: Thames & Hudson, 1999.

Trachtenberg, Marvin, and Isabelle Hyman. *Architecture, from Prehistory to Post-Modernism*. 2d ed. Upper Saddle River, N.J.: Prentice Hall, 2003.

Turner, Jane, ed. *The Dictionary of Art*. 34 vols. New ed. New York: Oxford University Press, 2003.

Watkin, David. *A History of Western Architecture*. 5th ed. London: Laurence King, 2011.

Wescoat, Bonna D., and Robert G. Ousterhout, eds. *Architecture of the Sacred: Space, Ritual, and Experience from Classical Greece to Byzantium*. New York: Cambridge University Press, 2012.

West, Shearer. *Portraiture*. New York: Oxford University Press, 2004.

Wittkower, Rudolf. *Sculpture Processes and Principles*. New York: Harper & Row, 1977.

Wren, Linnea H., and Janine M. Carter, eds. *Perspectives on Western Art: Source Documents and Readings from the Ancient Near East through the Middle Ages*. New York: Harper & Row, 1987.

Zijlmans, Kitty, and Wilfried van Damme, eds. *World Art Studies: Exploring Concepts and Approaches*. Amsterdam: Valiz, 2008.

Medieval Art, General

Alexander, Jonathan J. G. *Medieval Illuminators and Their Methods of Work*. New Haven, Conn.: Yale University Press, 1992.

The Art of Medieval Spain, AD 500–1200. New York: Metropolitan Museum of Art, 1993.

Benton, Janetta Rebold. *Art of the Middle Ages*. New York: Thames & Hudson, 2002.

Binski, Paul. *Painters (Medieval Craftsmen)*. Toronto: University of Toronto Press, 1991.

Calkins, Robert G. *Illuminated Books of the Middle Ages*. Ithaca, N.Y.: Cornell University Press, 1983.

———. *Medieval Architecture in Western Europe: From AD 300 to 1500*. New York: Oxford University Press, 1998.

Coldstream, Nicola. *Masons and Sculptors (Medieval Craftsmen)*. Toronto: University of Toronto Press, 1991.

———. *Medieval Architecture*. New York: Oxford University Press, 2002.

Cross, Frank L., and Livingstone, Elizabeth A., eds. *The Oxford Dictionary of the Christian Church*. 3d ed. New York: Oxford University Press, 1997.

De Hamel, Christopher. *A History of Illuminated Manuscripts*. Oxford: Phaidon, 1986.

———. *Scribes and Illuminators (Medieval Craftsmen)*. Toronto: University of Toronto Press, 1992.

Doig, Allan. *Liturgy and Architecture: From the Early Church to the Middle Ages*. New York: Ashgate, 2008.

Heller, Ena Giurescu, and Patricia C. Pongracz. *Perspectives on Medieval Art: Learning through Looking*. New York: Museum of Biblical Art, 2010.

Holcomb, Melanie, ed. *Pen and Parchment: Drawing in the Middle Ages*. New York: Metropolitan Museum of Art, 2009.

Hourihane, Colum, ed. *The Grove Encyclopedia of Medieval Art and Architecture*. New York: Oxford University Press, 2012.

Kessler, Herbert L. *Seeing Medieval Art*. Toronto: Broadview, 2004.

———. *Spiritual Seeing: Picturing God's Invisibility in Medieval Art*. Philadelphia: University of Pennsylvania Press, 2000.

Lasko, Peter. *Ars Sacra, 800–1200*. 2d ed. New Haven, Conn.: Yale University Press, 1994.

Murray, Peter, and Linda Murray. *The Oxford Companion to Christian Art and Architecture*. New York: Oxford University Press, 1996.

Pelikan, Jaroslav. *Mary through the Centuries: Her Place in the History of Culture*. New Haven, Conn.: Yale University Press, 1996.

Prache, Anne. *Cathedrals of Europe*. Ithaca, N.Y.: Cornell University Press, 1999.

Raguin, Virginia Chieffo. *Stained Glass from Its Origins to the Present*. New York: Abrams, 2003.

Ross, Leslie. *Medieval Art: A Topical Dictionary*. Westport, Conn.: Greenwood, 1996.

Schütz, Bernard. *Great Cathedrals*. New York: Abrams, 2002.

Sekules, Veronica. *Medieval Art*. New York: Oxford University Press, 2001.

Snyder, James, Henry Luttikhuizen, and Dorothy Verkerk. *Art of the Middle Ages*. 2d ed. Upper Saddle River, N.J.: Prentice Hall, 2006.

Stokstad, Marilyn. *Medieval Art*. 2d ed. Boulder, Colo.: Westview, 2004.

Tasker, Edward G. *Encyclopedia of Medieval Church Art*. London: Batsford, 1993.

CHAPTER 14
Late Medieval Italy

Bomford, David. *Art in the Making: Italian Painting before 1400*. London: National Gallery, 1989.

Borsook, Eve, and Fiorelli Superbi Gioffredi. *Italian Altarpieces 1250–1550: Function and Design*. Oxford: Clarendon, 1994.

Bourdua, Louise. *The Franciscans and Art Patronage in Late Medieval Italy*. New York: Cambridge University Press, 2004.

Cole, Bruce. *Sienese Painting: From Its Origins to the Fifteenth Century*. New York: Harper Collins, 1987.

Derbes, Anne. *Picturing the Passion in Late Medieval Italy: Narrative Painting, Franciscan Ideologies, and the Levant*. New York: Cambridge University Press, 1996.

Derbes, Anne, and Mark Sandona, eds. *The Cambridge Companion to Giotto*. New York: Cambridge University Press, 2004.

Flores d'Arcais, Francesca. *Giotto*. 2d ed. New York: Abbeville, 2012.

Hills, Paul. *The Light of Early Italian Painting*. New Haven, Conn.: Yale University Press, 1987.

Maginnis, Hayden B. J. *Painting in the Age of Giotto: A Historical Reevaluation*. University Park: Pennsylvania State University Press, 1997.

———. *The World of the Early Sienese Painter*. University Park: Pennsylvania State University Press, 2001.

Meiss, Millard. *Painting in Florence and Siena after the Black Death*. Princeton, N.J.: Princeton University Press, 1976.

Moskowitz, Anita Fiderer. *Italian Gothic Sculpture, c. 1250–c. 1400*. New York: Cambridge University Press, 2001.

———. *Nicola & Giovanni Pisano: The Pulpits: Pious Devotion, Pious Diversion*. London: Harvey Miller, 2005.

Norman, Diana, ed. *Siena, Florence, and Padua: Art, Society, and Religion 1280–1400*. New Haven, Conn.: Yale University Press, 1995.

Poeschke, Joachim. *Italian Frescoes: The Age of Giotto, 1280–1400*. New York: Abbeville, 2005.

Pope-Hennessy, John. *Italian Gothic Sculpture*. 3d ed. Oxford: Phaidon, 1986.

Stubblebine, James H. *Duccio di Buoninsegna and His School*. Princeton, N.J.: Princeton University Press, 1979.

White, John. *Art and Architecture in Italy: 1250–1400*. 3d ed. New Haven, Conn.: Yale University Press, 1993.

———. *Duccio: Tuscan Art and the Medieval Workshop.* London: Thames & Hudson, 1979.

Renaissance Art, General

Adams, Laurie Schneider. *Italian Renaissance Art.* Boulder, Colo.: Westview, 2001.

Ames-Lewis, Francis, ed. *Florence.* Artistic Centers of the Italian Renaissance. New York: Cambridge University Press, 2011.

Anderson, Christy. *Renaissance Architecture.* New York: Oxford University Press, 2013.

Andrés, Glenn M., John M. Hunisak, and Richard Turner. *The Art of Florence.* 2 vols. New York: Abbeville, 1988.

Campbell, Gordon. *The Grove Encyclopedia of Northern Renaissance Art.* New York: Oxford University Press, 2009.

———. *Renaissance Art and Architecture.* New York: Oxford University Press, 2005.

Campbell, Lorne. *Renaissance Portraits: European Portrait-Painting in the Fourteenth, Fifteenth, and Sixteenth Centuries.* New Haven, Conn.: Yale University Press, 1990.

Campbell, Stephen J., and Michael W. Cole. *Italian Renaissance Art.* New York: Thames & Hudson, 2011.

Christian, Kathleen, and David J. Drogin, eds. *Patronage and Italian Renaissance Sculpture.* Burlington, Vt.: Ashgate, 2010.

Christiansen, Keith, and Stefan Weppelmann, eds. *The Renaissance Portrait from Donatello to Bellini.* New York: Metropolitan Museum of Art, 2011.

Cole, Bruce. *Italian Art, 1250–1550: The Relation of Renaissance Art to Life and Society.* New York: Harper & Row, 1987.

———. *The Renaissance Artist at Work: From Pisano to Titian.* New York: Harper Collins, 1983.

Cranston, Jodi. *The Poetics of Portraiture in the Italian Renaissance.* New York: Cambridge University Press, 2000.

Freedman, Luba. *The Revival of the Olympian Gods in Renaissance Art.* New York: Cambridge University Press, 2003.

Frommel, Christoph Luitpold. *The Architecture of the Italian Renaissance.* London: Thames & Hudson, 2007.

Furlotti, Barbara, and Guido Rebecchini. *The Art of Mantua: Power and Patronage in the Renaissance.* Los Angeles: J. Paul Getty Museum, 2008.

Hall, Marcia B. *Color and Meaning: Practice and Theory in Renaissance Painting.* Cambridge: Cambridge University Press, 1992.

———, ed. *Rome.* Artistic Centers of the Italian Renaissance. New York: Cambridge University Press, 2005.

Hartt, Frederick, and David G. Wilkins. *History of Italian Renaissance Art.* 7th ed. Upper Saddle River, N.J.: Prentice Hall, 2010.

Haskell, Francis, and Nicholas Penny. *Taste and the Antique: The Lure of Classical Sculpture 1500–1900.* New Haven, Conn.: Yale University Press, 1981.

Humfrey, Peter, ed. *Venice and the Veneto.* Artistic Centers of the Italian Renaissance. New York: Cambridge University Press, 2008.

Joost-Gaugier, Christiane L. *Italian Renaissance Art: Understanding Its Meaning.* Malden, Mass.: Wiley-Blackwell, 2013.

Kent, F. W., and Patricia Simons, eds. *Patronage, Art, and Society in Renaissance Italy.* Canberra: Humanities Research Centre and Clarendon Press, 1987.

King, Catherine E. *Renaissance Women Patrons: Wives and Widows in Italy, c. 1300–1550.* Manchester: Manchester University Press, 1998.

Landau, David, and Peter Parshall. *The Renaissance Print, 1470–1550.* New Haven, Conn.: Yale University Press, 1996.

Levey, Michael. *Florence: A Portrait.* Cambridge, Mass.: Harvard University Press, 1998.

Lubbock, Jules. *Storytelling in Christian Art from Giotto to Donatello.* New Haven, Conn.: Yale University Press, 2006.

Paoletti, John T., and Gary M. Radke. *Art, Power, and Patronage in Renaissance Italy.* Upper Saddle River, N.J.: Prentice Hall, 2005.

Partridge, Loren. *Art of Renaissance Florence, 1400–1600.* Berkeley and Los Angeles: University of California Press, 2009.

Pope-Hennessy, John. *Introduction to Italian Sculpture.* 3d ed. 3 vols. New York: Phaidon, 1986.

Richardson, Carol M., Kim W. Woods, and Michael W. Franklin, eds. *Renaissance Art Reconsidered: An Anthology of Primary Sources.* Malden, Mass.: Blackwell, 2007.

Romanelli, Giandomencio, ed., *Venice: Art & Architecture.* Cologne: Könemann, 2005.

Rosenberg, Charles M., ed. *The Court Cities of Northern Italy: Milan, Parma, Piacenza, Mantua, Ferrara, Bologna, Urbino, Pesaro, and Rimini.* Artistic Centers of the Italian Renaissance. New York: Cambridge University Press, 2010.

Servida, Sonia. *The Story of Renaissance Architecture.* New York: Prestel, 2011.

Smith, Jeffrey Chipps. *The Northern Renaissance.* New York: Phaidon, 2004.

Snyder, James, Larry Silver, and Henry Luttikhuizen. *Northern Renaissance Art: Painting, Sculpture, the Graphic Arts from 1350 to 1575.* 2d ed. Upper Saddle River, N.J.: Prentice Hall, 2005.

Strinati, Claudio, and Pomeroy, Jordana. *Italian Women Artists from Renaissance to Baroque.* Milan: Skira, 2007.

Thomson, David. *Renaissance Architecture: Critics, Patrons, and Luxury.* Manchester: Manchester University Press, 1993.

Tinagli, Paola. *Women in Italian Renaissance Art: Gender, Representation, Identity.* Manchester: Manchester University Press, 1997.

Wittkower, Rudolf. *Architectural Principles in the Age of Humanism.* 4th ed. London: Academy, 1988.

Woods, Kim W. *Making Renaissance Art.* New Haven, Conn.: Yale University Press, 2007.

———. *Viewing Renaissance Art.* New Haven, Conn.: Yale University Press, 2007.

Woods-Marsden, Joanna. *Renaissance Self-Portraiture: The Visual Construction of Identity and the Social Status of the Artist.* New Haven, Conn.: Yale University Press, 1998.

CHAPTER 20
Late Medieval and Early Renaissance Northern Europe

Ainsworth, Maryan W., and Maximiliaan P. J. Martens. *Petrus Christus, Renaissance Master of Bruges.* New York: Metropolitan Museum of Art, 1994.

Art from the Court of Burgundy: The Patronage of Philip the Bold and John the Fearless 1364–1419. Cleveland: Cleveland Museum of Art, 2004.

Baxandall, Michael. *The Limewood Sculptors of Renaissance Germany.* New Haven, Conn.: Yale University Press, 1980.

Borchert, Till-Holger. *Age of Van Eyck: The Mediterranean World and Early Netherlandish Painting, 1430–1530.* New York: Thames & Hudson, 2002.

Brinkmann, Bodo. *Konrad Witz.* Ostfildern: Hatje Cantz, 2011.

Campbell, Lorne. *The Fifteenth-Century Netherlandish Schools.* London: National Gallery Publications, 1998.

———. *Van der Weyden.* London: Chaucer, 2004.

Chapuis, Julien. *Stefan Lochner: Image Making in Fifteenth-Century Cologne.* Turnhout, Belgium: Brepols, 2004.

———, ed. *Tilman Riemenschneider, c. 1460–1531.* Washington, D.C.: National Gallery of Art, 2004.

Châtelet, Albert. *Early Dutch Painting.* New York: Konecky, 1988.

Friedlander, Max J. *Early Netherlandish Painting.* 14 vols. New York: Praeger/Phaidon, 1967–1976.

———. *From Van Eyck to Bruegel.* 3d ed. Ithaca, N.Y.: Cornell University Press, 1981.

Harbison, Craig. *The Mirror of the Artist: Northern Renaissance Art in Its Historical Context.* New York: Abrams, 1995.

Jacobs, Lynn F. *Early Netherlandish Carved Altarpieces, 1380–1550: Medieval Tastes and Mass Marketing.* Cambridge: Cambridge University Press, 1998.

Kemperdick, Stephan. *Rogier van der Weyden.* Cologne: H. F. Ullmann, 2007.

Kemperdick, Stephan, and Jocen Sander, eds. *The Master of Flémalle and Rogier van der Weyden.* Ostfildern: Hatje Cantz, 2009.

Lane, Barbara G. *The Altar and the Altarpiece: Sacramental Themes in Early Netherlandish Painting.* New York: Harper & Row, 1984.

Lehrs, Max, Joram Meron, and Anja Eichelberg. *Martin Schongauer: The Complete Engravings: A Catalogue Raisonné.* San Francisco: Alan Wofsy, 2005.

Meiss, Millard. *French Painting in the Time of Jean de Berry: The Limbourgs and Their Contemporaries.* New York: Braziller, 1974.

Michiels, Alfred. *Hans Memling.* London: Parkstone, 2008.

Morand, Kathleen. *Claus Sluter: Artist at the Court of Burgundy.* Austin: University of Texas Press, 1991.

Müller, Theodor. *Sculpture in the Netherlands, Germany, France, and Spain: 1400–1500.* New Haven, Conn.: Yale University Press, 1986.

Nash, Susie. *Northern Renaissance Art.* New York: Oxford University Press, 2008.

Os, Henk van. *The Art of Devotion in the Late Middle Ages in Europe, 1300–1500.* Princeton, N.J.: Princeton University Press, 1995.

Pächt, Otto. *Early Netherlandish Painting from Rogier van der Wayden to Gerard David.* New York: Harvey Miller, 1997.

Panofsky, Erwin. *Early Netherlandish Painting: Its Origins and Character.* 2 vols. Cambridge, Mass.: Harvard University Press, 1966.

Parshall, Peter, ed. *The Woodcut in Fifteenth-Century Europe.* New Haven, Conn.: Yale University Press, 2009.

Parshall, Peter, and Rainer Schoch. *Origins of European Printmaking: Fifteenth-Century Woodcuts and Their Public.* New Haven, Conn.: Yale University Press, 2005.

Périer-d'Ieteren, Catherine. *Dieric Bouts: The Complete Works.* London: Thames & Hudson, 2006.

Prevenier, Walter, and Wim Blockmans. *The Burgundian Netherlands*. Cambridge: Cambridge University Press, 1986.

Tomlinson, Amanda. *Van Eyck*. London: Chaucer, 2007.

Wilson, Jean C. *Painting in Bruges at the Close of the Middle Ages: Studies in Society and Visual Culture*. University Park: Pennsylvania State University Press, 1998.

Wolfthal, Diane. *The Beginnings of Netherlandish Canvas Painting, 1400–1530*. New York: Cambridge University Press, 1989.

CHAPTER 21
The Renaissance in Quattrocento Italy

Ahl, Diane Cole. *Fra Angelico*. New York: Phaidon, 2008.

——, ed. *The Cambridge Companion to Masaccio*. New York: Cambridge University Press, 2002.

Ames-Lewis, Francis. *Drawing in Early Renaissance Italy*. 2d ed. New Haven, Conn.: Yale University Press, 2000.

——. *The Intellectual Life of the Early Renaissance Artist*. New Haven, Conn.: Yale University Press, 2000.

Baxandall, Michael. *Painting and Experience in Fifteenth-Century Italy: A Primer in the Social History of Pictorial Style*. 2d ed. New York: Oxford University Press, 1988.

Bober, Phyllis Pray, and Ruth Rubinstein. *Renaissance Artists and Antique Sculpture: A Handbook of Sources*. Oxford: Oxford University Press, 1986.

Borsook, Eve. *The Mural Painters of Tuscany*. New York: Oxford University Press, 1981.

Cole, Alison. *Virtue and Magnificence: Art of the Italian Renaissance Courts*. New York: Abrams, 1995.

Cole, Bruce. *Masaccio and the Art of Early Renaissance Florence*. Bloomington: Indiana University Press, 1980.

Dempsey, Charles. *The Portrayal of Love: Botticelli's* Primavera *and Humanist Culture at the Time of Lorenzo the Magnificent*. Princeton, N.J.: Princeton University Press, 1992.

Edgerton, Samuel Y., Jr. *The Heritage of Giotto's Geometry: Art and Science on the Eve of the Scientific Revolution*. Ithaca, N.Y.: Cornell University Press, 1991.

——. *The Renaissance Rediscovery of Linear Perspective*. New York: Harper & Row, 1976.

Gilbert, Creighton, ed. *Italian Art 1400–1500: Sources and Documents*. Evanston, Ill.: Northwestern University Press, 1992.

Goldthwaite, Richard A. *The Building of Renaissance Florence: An Economic and Social History*. Baltimore: Johns Hopkins University Press, 1980.

Goy, Richard J. *Building Renaissance Venice: Patrons, Architects, and Builders c. 1430–1500*. New Haven, Conn.: Yale University Press, 2006.

Grafton, Anthony. *Leon Battista Alberti: Master Builder of the Italian Renaissance*. Cambridge, Mass.: Harvard University Press, 2002.

Henry, Tom. *The Life and Art of Luca Signorelli*. New Haven, Conn.: Yale University Press, 2012.

Heydenreich, Ludwig H. *Architecture in Italy, 1400–1500*. 2d ed. New Haven, Conn.: Yale University Press, 1996.

Hollingsworth, Mary. *Patronage in Renaissance Italy: From 1400 to the Early Sixteenth Century*. Baltimore: Johns Hopkins University Press, 1994.

Holmes, Megan. *Fra Filippo Lippi: The Carmelite Painter*. New Haven, Conn.: Yale University Press, 1999.

Kemp, Martin. *Behind the Picture: Art and Evidence in the Italian Renaissance*. New Haven, Conn.: Yale University Press, 1997.

Kempers, Bram. *Painting, Power, and Patronage: The Rise of the Professional Artist in the Italian Renaissance*. London: Penguin, 1992.

Kent, Dale. *Cosimo de' Medici and the Florentine Renaissance: The Patron's Oeuvre*. New Haven, Conn.: Yale University Press, 2000.

Lieberman, Ralph. *Renaissance Architecture in Venice*. New York: Abbeville, 1982.

Lindow, James R. *The Renaissance Palace in Florence: Magnificence and Splendour in Fifteenth-Century Italy*. Burlington Vt.: Ashgate, 2007.

Manca, Joseph. *Andrea Mantegna and the Italian Renaissance*. New York: Parkstone, 2006.

McAndrew, John. *Venetian Architecture of the Early Renaissance*. Cambridge, Mass.: MIT Press, 1980.

Murray, Peter. *Renaissance Architecture*. New York: Electa/Rizzoli, 1985.

Musacchio, Jacqueline Marie. *Art, Marriage, and Family in the Florentine Renaissance Palace*. New Haven, Conn.: Yale University Press, 2009.

Olson, Roberta J. M. *Italian Renaissance Sculpture*. London: Thames & Hudson, 1992.

Osborne, June. *Urbino: The Story of a Renaissance City*. Chicago: University of Chicago Press, 2003.

Payne, Alina A. *The Architectural Treatise in the Italian Renaissance: Architectural Invention, Ornament and Literary Culture*. New York: Cambridge University Press, 1999.

Poeschke, Joachim. *Donatello and His World: Sculpture of the Italian Renaissance*. New York: Abrams, 1993.

Radke, Gary M., ed. *The Gates of Paradise: Lorenzo Ghiberti's Renaissance Masterpiece*. New Haven, Conn.: Yale University Press, 2007.

Seymour, Charles. *Sculpture in Italy: 1400–1500*. New Haven, Conn.: Yale University Press, 1992.

Tavernor, Robert. *On Alberti and the Art of Building*. New Haven, Conn.: Yale University Press, 1999.

Turner, A. Richard. *Renaissance Florence: The Invention of a New Art*. New York: Abrams, 1997.

Wackernagel, Martin. *The World of the Florentine Renaissance Artist: Projects and Patrons, Workshops and Art Market*. Princeton, N.J.: Princeton University Press, 1981.

Welch, Evelyn. *Art and Society in Italy 1350–1500*. Oxford: Oxford University Press, 1997.

White, John. *The Birth and Rebirth of Pictorial Space*. 3d ed. Boston: Faber & Faber, 1987.

Wright, Alison. *The Pollaiuolo Brothers: The Arts of Florence and Rome*. New Haven, Conn.: Yale University Press, 2005.

Zöllner, Frank. *Sandro Botticelli*. New ed. New York: Prestel, 2009.

CHAPTER 22
Renaissance and Mannerism in Cinquecento Italy

Bazzotti, Ugo. *Palazzo Te: Giulio Romano's Masterwork*. London: Thames & Hudson, 2012.

Beltramini, Guido, and Howard Burns. *Palladio*. London: Royal Academy, 2008.

Blunt, Anthony. *Artistic Theory in Italy, 1450–1600*. London: Oxford University Press, 1975.

Brambilla Barcilon, Pinnin. *Leonardo: The Last Supper*. Chicago: University of Chicago Press, 2001.

Brock, Maurice. *Bronzino*. Paris: Flammarion, 2002.

Brown, David Alan, and Sylvia Ferino-Pagden, eds. *Bellini, Giorgione, Titian, and the Renaissance of Venetian Painting*. New Haven, Conn.: Yale University Press, 2006.

Brown, Patricia Fortini. *Art and Life in Renaissance Venice*. New York: Abrams, 1997.

Cole, Bruce. *Titian and Venetian Painting, 1450–1590*. Boulder, Colo.: Westview, 2000.

Cooper, Tracy E. *Palladio's Venice: Architecture and Society in a Renaissance Republic*. New Haven, Conn.: Yale University Press, 2005.

Cranston, Jodi. *The Muddled Mirror: Materiality and Figuration in Titian's Later Paintings*. University Park, Pa.: Pennsylvania State University Press, 2010.

Dal Pozzolo, Enrico. *Giorgione*. Milan: Motta, 2010.

De Vecchi, Pierluigi. *Raphael*. New York: Abbeville, 2002.

Ekserdjian, David. *Correggio*. New Haven, Conn.: Yale University Press, 1997.

——. *Parmigianino*. New Haven, Conn.: Yale University Press, 2006.

Falomir, Miguel, ed. *Tintoretto*. Madrid: Museo Nacional del Prado, 2007.

Ferino-Pagden, Sylvia, and Giovanna Nepi Scirè. *Giorgione: Myth and Enigma*. Milan: Skira, 2004.

Franklin, David. *Painting in Renaissance Florence, 1500–1550*. New Haven, Conn.: Yale University Press, 2001.

Freedberg, Sydney J. *Painting in Italy: 1500–1600*. 3d ed. New Haven, Conn.: Yale University Press, 1993.

Goffen, Rona. *Piety and Patronage in Renaissance Venice: Bellini, Titian, and the Franciscans*. New Haven, Conn.: Yale University Press, 1986.

——. *Renaissance Rivals: Michelangelo, Leonardo, Raphael, Titian*. New Haven, Conn.: Yale University Press, 2002.

Hall, Marcia B. *After Raphael: Painting in Central Italy in the Sixteenth Century*. New York: Cambridge University Press, 1999.

——. *The Sacred Image in the Age of Art: Titian, Tintoretto, Barocci, El Greco, Caravaggio*. New Haven, Conn.: Yale University Press, 2011.

——, ed. *The Cambridge Companion to Raphael*. New York: Cambridge University Press, 2005.

Hollingsworth, Mary. *Patronage in Sixteenth Century Italy*. London: John Murray, 1996.

Holt, Elizabeth Gilmore, ed. *A Documentary History of Art. Vol. 2, Michelangelo and the Mannerists*. Rev. ed. Princeton, N.J.: Princeton University Press, 1982.

Humfrey, Peter. *Painting in Renaissance Venice*. New Haven, Conn.: Yale University Press, 1995.

——. *Titian*. London: Phaidon, 2007.

Huse, Norbert, and Wolfgang Wolters. *The Art of Renaissance Venice: Architecture, Sculpture, and Painting*. Chicago: University of Chicago Press, 1990.

Ilchman, Frederick, ed. *Titian, Tintoretto, Veronese: Rivals in Renaissance Venice*. Boston: Museum of Fine Arts, 2009.

Kliemann, Julian-Matthias, and Michael Rohlmann. *Italian Frescoes: High Renaissance and Mannerism, 1510–1600*. New York: Abbeville, 2004.

Levey, Michael. *High Renaissance*. New York: Viking Penguin, 1978.

Lotz, Wolfgang. *Architecture in Italy, 1500–1600*. 2d ed. New Haven, Conn.: Yale University Press, 1995.

Meilman, Patricia, ed. *The Cambridge Companion to Titian*. New York: Cambridge University Press, 2004.

Natali, Antonio. *Andrea del Sarto*. New York: Abbeville, 1999.

Nichols, Tom. *Tintoretto: Tradition and Identity*. London: Reaktion, 2004.

Partridge, Loren. *The Art of Renaissance Rome*. New York: Abrams, 1996.

Pietrangeli, Carlo, André Chastel, John Shearman, John O'Malley, S.J., Pierluigi de Vecchi, Michael Hirst, Fabrizio Mancinelli, Gianluigi Colalucci, and Franco Bernbei. *The Sistine Chapel: The Art, the History, and the Restoration*. New York: Harmony, 1986.

Pilliod, Elizabeth. *Pontormo, Bronzino, Allori: A Genealogy of Florentine Art*. New Haven, Conn.: Yale University Press, 2001.

Pope-Hennessy, John. *Italian High Renaissance and Baroque Sculpture*. 3d ed. 3 vols. Oxford: Phaidon, 1986.

Rosand, David. *Painting in Cinquecento Venice: Titian, Veronese, Tintoretto*. New Haven, Conn.: Yale University Press, 1982.

Rowe, Colin, and Leon Satkowski. *Italian Architecture of the 16th Century*. New York: Princeton Architectural Press, 2002.

Rubin, Patricia Lee. *Giorgio Vasari: Art and History*. New Haven, Conn.: Yale University Press, 1995.

Shearman, John K. G. *Mannerism*. Baltimore: Penguin, 1978.

———. *Only Connect . . . Art and the Spectator in the Italian Renaissance*. Princeton, N.J.: Princeton University Press, 1990.

Summers, David. *Michelangelo and the Language of Art*. Princeton, N.J.: Princeton University Press, 1981.

Talvacchia, Bette. *Raphael*. London: Phaidon, 2007.

Tronzo, William, ed. *St. Peter's in the Vatican*. New York: Cambridge University Press, 2005.

Wallace, William. *Michelangelo: The Artist, the Man, and His Times*. New York: Cambridge University Press, 2009.

Wilde, Johannes. *Venetian Art from Bellini to Titian*. Oxford: Clarendon, 1981.

Williams, Robert. *Art, Theory, and Culture in Sixteenth-Century Italy: From Techne to Metatechne*. New York: Cambridge University Press, 1997.

Zöllner, Frank. *Leonardo da Vinci: The Complete Paintings and Drawings*. Cologne: Taschen, 2007.

CHAPTER 23
High Renaissance and Mannerism in Northern Europe and Spain

Ainsworth, Maryan W. *Man, Myth, and Sensual Pleasures: Jan Gossart's Renaissance. The Complete Works*. New York: Metropolitan Museum of Art, 2010.

Bartrum, Giulia, ed. *Albrecht Dürer and His Legacy: The Graphic Work of a Renaissance Artist*. Princeton, N. J.: Princeton University Press, 2003.

Bätschmann, Oskar, and Pascal Griener. *Hans Holbein*. Princeton, N. J.: Princeton University Press, 1997.

Blunt, Anthony. *Art and Architecture in France, 1500–1700*. Rev. ed. New Haven, Conn.: Yale University Press, 1999.

Brinkmann, Bodo, ed. *Cranach*. London: Royal Academy of Arts, 2008.

Buck, Stephanie, and Jochen Sander. *Hans Holbein the Younger: Painter at the Court of Henry VIII*. New York: Thames & Hudson, 2004.

Chapius, Julien. *Tilman Riemenschneider: Master Sculptor of the Late Middle Ages*. Washington, D.C.: National Gallery of Art, 1999.

Chastel, André. *French Art: The Renaissance, 1430–1620*. Paris: Flammarion, 1995.

Cox-Rearick, Janet. *The Collection of Francis I: Royal Treasures*. New York: Abrams, 1996.

Davies, David, and John H. Elliott. *El Greco*. London: National Gallery, 2003.

Dixon, Laurinda. *Bosch*. New York: Phaidon, 2003.

Farago, Claire, ed. *Reframing the Renaissance: Visual Culture in Europe and Latin America, 1450–1650*. New Haven, Conn.: Yale University Press, 1995.

Foister, Susan. *Holbein and England*. New Haven, Conn.: Paul Mellon Centre for British Art, 2005.

Gibson, W. S. *"Mirror of the Earth": The World Landscape in Sixteenth-Century Flemish Painting*. Princeton, N.J.: Princeton University Press, 1989.

Harbison, Craig. *The Mirror of the Artist: Northern Renaissance Art in Its Historical Context*. New York: Abrams, 1995.

Jollet, Etienne. *Jean and François Clouet*. London: Thames & Hudson, 1997.

Knecht, Robert J. *Renaissance Warrior and Patron: The Reign of Francis I*. New York: Cambridge University Press, 1994.

Koerner, Joseph Leo. *The Reformation of the Image*. Chicago: University of Chicago Press, 2004.

Landau, David, and Peter Parshall. *The Renaissance Print: 1470–1550*. New Haven, Conn.: Yale University Press, 1994.

Marías, Fernando. *El Greco: Life and Work—A New History*. London: Thames & Hudson, 2013.

Price, David Hotchkiss. *Albrecht Dürer's Renaissance: Humanism, Reformation, and the Art of Faith*. Ann Arbor: University of Michigan Press, 2003.

Roberts-Jones, Philippe, and Françoise Roberts-Jones. *Pieter Bruegel*. New York: Abrams, 2002.

Silver, Larry. *Hieronymous Bosch*. New York: Abbeville, 2006.

———. *Pieter Bruegel*. New York: Abbeville, 2011.

Smith, Jeffrey Chipps. *Dürer*. London: Phaidon: 2012.

———. *German Sculpture of the Later Renaissance, c. 1520–1580: Art in an Age of Uncertainty*. Princeton, N.J.: Princeton University Press, 1993.

Stechow, Wolfgang. *Northern Renaissance Art, 1400–1600: Sources and Documents*. Evanston, Ill.: Northwestern University Press, 1989.

Thomson, David. *Renaissance Paris: Architecture and Growth, 1475–1600*. Los Angeles and Berkeley: University of California Press, 1984.

Wood, Christopher S. *Albrecht Altdorfer and the Origins of Landscape*. Chicago: University of Chicago Press, 1993.

Zerner, Henri. *Renaissance Art in France: The Invention of Classicism*. Paris: Flammarion, 2003.

Baroque Art, General

Blunt, Anthony, ed. *Baroque and Rococo: Architecture and Decoration*. Cambridge: Harper & Row, 1982.

Harris, Ann Sutherland. *Seventeenth-Century Art & Architecture*. 2d ed. Upper Saddle River, N.J.: Prentice Hall, 2008.

Harrison, Charles, Paul Wood, and Jason Gaiger, eds. *Art in Theory, 1648–1815: An Anthology of Changing Ideas*. Oxford: Blackwell, 2000.

Held, Julius, and Donald Posner. *17th- and 18th-Century Art: Baroque Painting, Sculpture, Architecture*. New York: Abrams, 1971.

Lagerlöf, Margaretha R. *Ideal Landscape: Annibale Carracci, Nicolas Poussin, and Claude Lorrain*. New Haven, Conn.: Yale University Press, 1990.

Lawrence, Cynthia, ed. *Women and Art in Early Modern Europe: Patrons, Collectors, and Connoisseurs*. University Park: Pennsylvania State University Press, 1997.

Lemerle, Frédérique, and Yves Pauwels. *Baroque Architecture, 1600–1750*. Paris: Flammarion, 2008.

Minor, Vernon Hyde. *Baroque & Rococo: Art & Culture*. New York, Abrams, 1999.

Norberg-Schulz, Christian. *Baroque Architecture*. New York: Rizzoli, 1986.

———. *Late Baroque and Rococo Architecture*. New York: Electa/Rizzoli, 1985.

Tarabra, Daniela, and Claudia Zanlungo. *The Story of Baroque Architecture*. New York: Prestel, 2012.

Toman, Rolf. *Baroque: Architecture, Sculpture, Painting*. Cologne: Könemann, 1998.

CHAPTER 24
The Baroque in Italy and Spain

Bailey, Gauvin Alexander. *Baroque & Rococo*. London: Phaidon, 2012.

Bissel, R. Ward. *Artemisia Gentileschi and the Authority of Art*. University Park: Pennsylvania State University Press, 1999.

Brown, Jonathan. *The Golden Age of Painting in Spain*. New Haven, Conn.: Yale University Press, 1991.

———. *Velázquez: Painter and Courtier*. New Haven, Conn.: Yale University Press, 1988.

Christiansen, Keith, and Judith W. Mann. *Orazio and Artemisia Gentileschi*. New York: Metropolitan Museum of Art, 2001.

Contini, Roberto, and Francesco Solinas. *Artemisia Gentileschi: The Story of a Passion*. Milan: 24 Ore Cultura, 2011.

Enggass, Robert, and Jonathan Brown. *Italy and Spain, 1600–1750: Sources and Documents*. Upper Saddle River, N.J.: Prentice Hall, 1970.

Freedberg, Sydney J. *Circa 1600: A Revolution of Style in Italian Painting*. Cambridge, Mass.: Harvard University Press, 1983.

Fried, Michael. *The Moment of Caravaggio*. Princeton, N.J.: Princeton University Press, 2010.

Haskell, Francis. *Patrons and Painters: A Study in the Relations between Italian Art and Society in the Age of the Baroque*. Rev. ed. New Haven, Conn.: Yale University Press, 1980.

Krautheimer, Richard. *The Rome of Alexander VII, 1655–1677*. Princeton, N.J.: Princeton University Press, 1985.

Montagu, Jennifer. *Roman Baroque Sculpture: The Industry of Art*. New Haven, Conn.: Yale University Press, 1989.

O'Malley, John W., and Gauvin Alexander Bailey. *The Jesuits and the Arts, 1540–1773*. Philadelphia: Saint Joseph's University Press, 2005.

Puglisi, Catherine. *Caravaggio*. London: Phaidon, 2000.

Schroth, Sarah, and Ronni Baer. *El Greco to Velazquez: Art during the Reign of Philip III*. Boston: Museum of Fine Arts, 2008.

Spear, Richard E., and Philip Sohm, eds. *Painting for Profit: The Economic Lives of Seventeenth-Century Italian Painters*. New Haven, Conn.: Yale University Press, 2010.

Strinati, Claudio, and Pomeroy, Jordana. *Italian Women Artists from Renaissance to Baroque*. Milan: Skira, 2007.

Tomlinson, Janis. *From El Greco to Goya: Painting in Spain 1561–1828*. Upper Saddle Ridge, N.J.: Prentice Hall, 1997.

Tronzo, William, ed. *St. Peter's in the Vatican*. New York: Cambridge University Press, 2005.

Trusted, Marjorie. *The Arts of Spain: Iberia and Latin America 1450–1700*. University Park: Pennsylvania State University Press, 2007.

Varriano, John. *Caravaggio: The Art of Realism*. University Park: Pennsylvania State University Press, 2006.

——. *Italian Baroque and Rococo Architecture*. New York: Oxford University Press, 1986.

Wittkower, Rudolf. *Art and Architecture in Italy 1600–1750*. 6th ed. 3 vols. Revised by Joseph Connors and Jennifer Montagu. New Haven, Conn.: Yale University Press, 1999.

CHAPTER 25
The Baroque in Northern Europe

Alpers, Svetlana. *The Art of Describing: Dutch Art in the Seventeenth Century*. Chicago: University of Chicago Press, 1984.

——. *The Making of Rubens*. New Haven, Conn.: Yale University Press, 1995.

——. *Rembrandt's Enterprise: The Studio and the Market*. Chicago: University of Chicago Press, 1988.

Bajou, Valérie. *Versailles*. New York: Abrams, 2012.

Belkin, Kristin Lohse. *Rubens*. London: Phaidon, 1998.

Biesboer, Pieter, Martina Brunner-Bulst, Henry D. Gregory, and Christian Klemm. *Pieter Claesz: Master of Haarlem Still Life*. Zwolle: Waanders, 2005.

Blunt, Anthony. *Art and Architecture in France, 1500–1700*. Rev. ed. New Haven, Conn.: Yale University Press, 1999.

Brown, Christopher. *Scenes of Everyday Life: Dutch Genre Painting of the Seventeenth Century*. London: Faber & Faber, 1984.

Bryson, Norman. *Word and Image: French Painting of the Ancien Régime*. Cambridge: Cambridge University Press, 1981.

Carr, Dawson W., ed. *Velázquez*. London: National Gallery, 2006.

Chapman, Perry. *Rembrandt's Self-Portraits: A Study in 17th-Century Identity*. Princeton, N.J.: Princeton University Press, 1990.

Chastel, André. *French Art: The Ancien Régime, 1620–1775*. New York: Flammarion, 1996.

Chong, Alan, and Wouter Kloek. *Still-Life Paintings from the Netherlands, 1550–1720*. Zwolle: Waanders, 1999.

Franits, Wayne. *Dutch Seventeenth-Century Genre Painting: Its Stylistic and Thematic Evolution*. New Haven, Conn.: Yale University Press, 2008.

——. *Looking at Seventeenth-Century Dutch Art: Realism Reconsidered*. Cambridge: Cambridge University Press, 1997.

——, ed. *The Cambridge Companion to Vermeer*. New York: Cambridge University Press, 2001.

Haak, Bob. *The Golden Age: Dutch Painters of the Seventeenth Century*. New York: Abrams, 1984.

Hochstrasser, Julie Berger. *Still Life and Trade in the Dutch Golden Age*. New Haven, Conn.: Yale University Press, 2007.

Keazor, Henry. *Nicholas Poussin, 1594–1665*. Cologne: Taschen, 2007.

Kiers, Judikje, and Fieke Tissink. *Golden Age of Dutch Art: Painting, Sculpture, Decorative Art*. New York: Thames & Hudson, 2000.

Liedtke, Walter. *Vermeer: The Complete Paintings*. Antwerp: Ludion, 2008.

——. *A View of Delft: Vermeer and His Contemporaries*. Zwolle: Wanders, 2000.

Mérot, Alain. *French Painting in the Seventeenth Century*. New Haven, Conn.: Yale University Press, 1995.

Muller, Sheila D., ed. *Dutch Art: An Encyclopedia*. New York: Garland, 1997.

North, Michael. *Art and Commerce in the Dutch Golden Age*. New Haven, Conn.: Yale University Press, 1997.

Olson, Todd P. *Poussin and France*. New Haven, Conn.: Yale University Press, 2000.

Rosenberg, Jakob, Seymour Slive, and E. H. ter Kuile. *Dutch Art and Architecture, 1600–1800*. New Haven, Conn.: Yale University Press, 1979.

Schama, Simon. *The Embarrassment of Riches: An Interpretation of Dutch Culture in the Golden Age*. Berkeley: University of California Press, 1988.

Schroth, Sarah, and Ronni Baer, eds. *El Greco to Velázquez: Art during the Reign of Philip III*. Boston: Museum of Fine Arts, 2008.

Slatkes, Leonard J., and Wayne Franits. *The Paintings of Hendrick ter Brugghen 1588–1629: Catalogue Raisonné*. Philadelphia: John Benjamins, 2007.

Stechow, Wolfgang. *Dutch Landscape Painting of the 17th Century*. 3d ed. Oxford: Phaidon, 1981.

Summerson, John. *Inigo Jones*. New Haven, Conn.: Yale University Press, 2000.

Sutton, Peter C. *Masters of 17th Century Dutch Landscape Painting*. Boston: Museum of Fine Arts, 1988.

Thompson, Ian. *The Sun King's Garden: Louis XIV, André Le Nôtre and the Creation of the Gardens of Versailles*. London: Bloomsbury, 2006.

Vlieghe, Hans. *Flemish Art and Architecture, 1585–1700*. New Haven, Conn.: Yale University Press, 1998.

Westermann, Mariët. *Rembrandt*. London: Phaidon, 2000.

——. *A Worldly Art: The Dutch Republic 1585–1718*. New Haven, Conn.: Yale University Press, 1996.

Zega, Andres, and Bernd H. Dams. *Palaces of the Sun King: Versailles, Trianon, Marly: The Châteaux of Louis XIV*. New York: Rizzoli, 2002.

Zell, Michael. *Reframing Rembrandt: Jews and the Christian Image in Seventeenth-Century Amsterdam*. Berkeley: University of California Press, 2002.

CHAPTER 26
Rococo to Neoclassicism: The 18th Century in Europe and America

Beddington, Charles. *Venice: Canaletto and His Rivals*. London: National Gallery, 2010.

Bermingham, Ann. *Landscape and Ideology: The English Rustic Tradition, 1740–1850*. Berkeley: University of California Press, 1986.

Boime, Albert. *Art in the Age of Revolution, 1750–1800*. Chicago: University of Chicago Press, 1987.

Bowron, Edgar Peters, and Joseph J. Rishel, eds. *Art in Rome in the Eighteenth Century*. Philadelphia: Philadelphia Museum of Art, 2000.

Bowron, Edgar Peters, and Peter Björn Kerber. *Pompeo Batoni: Prince of Painters in Eighteenth-Century Rome*. New Haven, Conn.: Yale University Press, 2007.

Braham, Allan. *The Architecture of the French Enlightenment*. Berkeley: University of California Press, 1980.

Conisbee, Philip. *Painting in Eighteenth-Century France*. Ithaca, N.Y.: Phaidon/Cornell University Press, 1981.

Craske, Matthew. *Art in Europe, 1700–1830: A History of the Visual Arts in an Era of Unprecedented Urban Economic Growth*. New York: Oxford University Press, 1997.

Crow, Thomas E. *Painters and Public Life in Eighteenth-Century Paris*. New Haven, Conn.: Yale University Press, 1985.

Goodman, Elise, ed. *Art and Culture in the Eighteenth Century: New Dimensions and Multiple Perspectives*. Newark: University of Delaware Press, 2001.

Harrison, Charles, Paul Wood, and Jason Gaiger, eds. *Art in Theory, 1648–1815: An Anthology of Changing Ideas*. Oxford: Blackwell, 2000.

Hedley, Jo. *François Boucher: Seductive Visions*. London: Wallace Collection, 2004.

Herrmann, Luke. *British Landscape Painting of the Eighteenth Century*. New York: Oxford University Press, 1974.

Honour, Hugh. *Neo-Classicism*. Harmondsworth: Penguin, 1968.

Irwin, David. *Neoclassicism*. London: Phaidon, 1997.

Jarrassé, Dominique. *18th-Century French Painting*. Paris: Terrail, 1999.

Lee, Simon. *David*. London: Phaidon, 1999.

Levey, Michael. *Rococo to Revolution: Major Trends in Eighteenth-Century Painting*. London: Thames & Hudson, 1966.

Plax, Julie-Ann. *Watteau and the Cultural Politics of Eighteenth-Century France*. New York: Cambridge University Press, 2000.

Rosenblum, Robert. *Transformations in Late Eighteenth-Century Art*. Princeton, N.J.: Princeton University Press, 1970.

Roworth, Wendy Wassyng. *Angelica Kauffman: A Continental Artist in Georgian England*. London: Reaktion, 1992.

Rykwert, Joseph. *The First Moderns: Architects of the Eighteenth Century*. Cambridge, Mass.: MIT Press, 1983.

Sheriff, Mary D. *The Exceptional Woman: Elisabeth Vigée-Lebrun and the Cultural Politics of Art*. Chicago: University of Chicago Press, 1996.

Solkin, David. *Painting for Money: The Visual Arts and the Public Sphere in Eighteenth-Century England*. New Haven, Conn.: Paul Mellon Centre for British Art, 1993.

Stillman, Damie. *English Neo-Classical Architecture*. 2 vols. London: Zwemmer, 1988.

Waterhouse, Ellis Kirkham. *Painting in Britain: 1530–1790*. 4th ed. New Haven, Conn.: Yale University Press, 1979.

Wendorf, Richard. *Sir Joshua Reynolds: The Painter in Society*. Cambridge, Mass.: Harvard University Press, 1996.

Wilton, Andrew. *The Swagger Portrait: Grand Manner Portraiture in Britain from Van Dyck to Augustus John, 1630–1930*. London: Tate Gallery, 1992.

19th and 20th Centuries, General

Arnason, H. H., and Peter Kalb. *History of Modern Art: Painting, Sculpture, Architecture, Photography*. 6th ed. Upper Saddle River, N.J.: Prentice Hall, 2009.

Ashton, Dore. *Twentieth-Century Artists on Art*. New York: Pantheon Books, 1985.

Barnitz, Jacueline. *Twentieth-Century Art of Latin America*. Austin: University of Texas Press, 2001.

Brettell, Richard R. *Modern Art, 1851–1929: Capitalism and Representation*. New York: Oxford University Press, 1999.

Brown, Milton, Sam Hunter, and John Jacobus. *American Art: Painting, Sculpture, Architecture, Decorative Arts, Photography*. New York: Abrams, 1979.

Burnham, Jack. *Beyond Modern Sculpture: The Effects of Science and Technology on the Sculpture of This Century*. New York: Braziller, 1968.

Butler, Cornelia, and Alexandra Schwartz, eds. *Modern Women: Women Artists at the Museum of Modern Art*. New York: Museum of Modern Art, 2010.

Chipp, Herschel B. *Theories of Modern Art*. Berkeley: University of California Press, 1968.

Chu, Petra ten-Doesschate. *Nineteenth-Century European Art*. 3d ed. Upper Saddle River, N.J.: Prentice Hall, 2011.

Coke, Van Deren. *The Painter and the Photograph from Delacroix to Warhol*. Rev. ed. Albuquerque: University of New Mexico Press, 1972.

Colquhoun, Alan. *Modern Architecture*. New York: Oxford University Press, 2002.

Craven, Wayne. *American Art: History and Culture*. Rev. ed. New York: McGraw-Hill, 2002.

Dennis, Rafael Cardoso, and Colin Trodd, eds. *Art and the Academy in the Nineteenth Century*. New Brunswick, N.J.: Rutgers University Press, 2000.

Doordan, Dennis P. *Twentieth-Century Architecture*. New York: Abrams, 2002.

Doss, Erika. *Twentieth-Century American Art*. New York: Oxford University Press, 2002.

Driskell, David C. *Two Centuries of Black American Art*. Los Angeles: Los Angeles County Museum of Art; New York: Knopf, 1976.

Eisenmann, Stephen F., ed. *Nineteenth-Century Art: A Critical History*. 4th ed. New York: Thames & Hudson, 2011.

Elsen, Albert. *Origins of Modern Sculpture*. New York: Braziller, 1974.

Facos, Michelle. *An Introduction to Nineteenth-Century Art*. New York: Routledge, 2011.

Foster, Hal, Rosalind Krauss, Yve-Alain Bois, and Benjamin H. D. Buchloh. *Art since 1900: Modernism, Antimodernism, Postmodernism*. 2d ed. New York: Thames & Hudson, 2011.

Frampton, Kenneth. *Modern Architecture: A Critical History*. 4th ed. New York: Thames & Hudson, 2007.

Frascina, Francis, and Charles Harrison, eds. *Modern Art and Modernism: A Critical Anthology*. New York: Harper & Row, 1982.

Giedion, Siegfried. *Space, Time, and Architecture: The Growth of a New Tradition*. 4th ed. Cambridge, Mass.: Harvard University Press, 1965.

Goldwater, Robert, and Marco Treves, eds. *Artists on Art*. 3d ed. New York: Pantheon, 1958.

Greenough, Sarah, Joel Snyder, David Travis, and Colin Westerbeck. *On the Art of Fixing a Shadow: One Hundred and Fifty Years of Photography*. Washington, D.C.: National Gallery of Art; Chicago: Art Institute of Chicago, 1989.

Hamilton, George H. *Painting and Sculpture in Europe, 1880–1940*. 6th ed. New Haven, Conn.: Yale University Press, 1993.

Harrison, Charles, and Paul Wood. *Art in Theory, 1900–2000: An Anthology of Changing Ideas*. Oxford: Blackwell, 2003.

Herbert, Robert L., ed. *Modern Artists on Art*. Upper Saddle River, N.J.: Prentice Hall, 1971.

Hertz, Richard, and Norman M. Klein, eds. *Twentieth-Century Art Theory: Urbanism, Politics, and Mass Culture*. Englewood Cliffs, N.J.: Prentice Hall, 1990.

Heyer, Paul. *Architects on Architecture: New Directions in America*. New York: Van Nostrand Reinhold, 1993.

Hills, Patricia. *Modern Art in the USA: Issues and Controversies of the 20th Century*. Upper Saddle River, N.J.: Prentice Hall, 2000.

Hitchcock, Henry-Russell. *Architecture: Nineteenth and Twentieth Centuries*. 4th ed. New Haven, Conn.: Yale University Press, 1977.

Hunter, Sam, John Jacobus, and Daniel Wheeler. *Modern Art: Painting, Sculpture, Architecture, Photography*. Rev. 3d ed. Upper Saddle River, N.J.: Prentice Hall, 2004.

Janson, Horst W. *19th-Century Sculpture*. New York: Abrams, 1985.

Jencks, Charles. *Modern Movements in Architecture*. Garden City, N.Y.: Anchor; Doubleday, 1973.

Kaufmann, Edgar, Jr., ed. *The Rise of an American Architecture*. New York: Metropolitan Museum of Art; Praeger, 1970.

Krauss, Rosalind E. *The Originality of the Avant-Garde and Other Modernist Myths*. Cambridge, Mass.: MIT Press, 1985.

———. *Passages in Modern Sculpture*. Cambridge, Mass.: MIT Press, 1981.

Lewis, Samella S. *African American Art and Artists*. Rev. ed. Berkeley: University of California Press, 1994.

Licht, Fred. *Sculpture, Nineteenth and Twentieth Centuries*. Greenwich, Conn.: New York Graphic Society, 1967.

Marien, Mary Warner. *Photography: A Cultural History*. 3d ed. Upper Saddle River, N.J.: Prentice Hall, 2011.

Mason, Jerry, ed. *International Center of Photography Encyclopedia of Photography*. New York: Crown, 1984.

McCoubrey, John W. *American Art, 1700–1960: Sources and Documents*. Englewood Cliffs, N.J.: Prentice Hall, 1965.

Newhall, Beaumont. *The History of Photography*. New York: Museum of Modern Art, 1982.

Osborne, Harold. *The Oxford Companion to Twentieth-Century Art*. New York: Oxford University Press, 1981.

Pohl, Frances K. *Framing America: A Social History of American Art*. 3d ed. New York: Thames & Hudson, 2012.

Rose, Barbara. *American Art since 1900*. Rev. ed. New York: Praeger, 1975.

Rosenblum, Naomi. *A World History of Photography*. 4th ed. New York: Abbeville, 2007.

Rosenblum, Robert. *Modern Painting and the Northern Romantic Tradition: Friedrich to Rothko*. New York: Harper & Row, 1975.

Rosenblum, Robert, and Horst W. Janson. *19th-Century Art*. Rev. ed. Upper Saddle River, N.J.: Prentice Hall, 2005.

Ross, Stephen David, ed. *Art and Its Significance: An Anthology of Aesthetic Theory*. Albany: State University of New York Press, 1987.

Russell, John. *The Meanings of Modern Art*. New York: Museum of Modern Art; Thames & Hudson, 1981.

Scully, Vincent. *Modern Architecture*. Rev. ed. New York: Braziller, 1974.

Spalding, Francis. *British Art since 1900*. London: Thames & Hudson, 1986.

Spencer, Harold. *American Art: Readings from the Colonial Era to the Present*. New York: Scribner, 1980.

Steinberg, Leo. *Other Criteria: Confrontations with 20th-Century Art*. New York: Oxford University Press, 1972.

Szarkowski, John. *Photography until Now*. New York: Museum of Modern Art, 1989.

Upton, Dell. *Architecture in the United States*. Oxford: Oxford University Press, 1998.

Weaver, Mike. *The Art of Photography: 1839–1989*. New Haven, Conn.: Yale University Press, 1989.

Whiffen, Marcus, and Frederick Koeper. *American Architecture, 1607–1976*. Cambridge, Mass.: MIT Press, 1983.

Wilmerding, John. *American Art*. Harmondsworth: Penguin, 1976.

Wilson, Simon. *Holbein to Hockney: A History of British Art*. London: Tate Gallery & Bodley Head, 1979.

CHAPTER 27
Romanticism, Realism, Photography: Europe and America, 1800 to 1870

Amic, Sylvain, et al. *Gustave Courbet*. Ostfildern: Hatje Cantz, 2008.

Athanassaglou-Kallmyer, Nina. *Théodore Géricault*. London: Phaidon, 2008.

Barringer, Tim, Jason Rosenfeld, and Alison Smith, eds. *Pre-Raphaelites: Victorian Art and Design*. New Haven, Conn.: Yale University Press, 2013.

Bartoli, Damien, and Frederick C. Ross. *William Bouguereau*. 2 vols. New York: Antique Collectors' Club, 2010.

Bellenger, Sylvain. *Girodet, 1767–1824*. Paris: Gallimard, 2005.

Bergdoll, Barry. *European Architecture 1750–1890*. New York: Oxford University Press, 2000.

Boime, Albert. *The Academy and French Painting in the 19th Century*. London: Phaidon, 1971.

———. *Art and the French Commune: Imagining Paris after War and Revolution*. Princeton, N.J.: Princeton University Press, 1995.

———. *Art in the Age of Bonapartism, 1800–1815*. Chicago: University of Chicago Press, 1990.

Bordes, Philippe. *Jacques-Louis David: Empire to Exile*. New Haven, Conn.: Yale University Press, 2007.

Brown, David Blayney. *Romanticism*. New York: Phaidon, 2001.

Bryson, Norman. *Tradition and Desire: From David to Delacroix*. New York: Cambridge University Press, 1984.

Burns, Sarah, and John Davis. *American Art to 1900: A Documentary History*. Berkeley and Los Angeles: University of California Press, 2009.

Chu, Petra ten-Doesschate. *The Most Arrogant Man in France: Gustave Courbet and the Nineteenth-Century Media Culture*. Princeton, N.J.: Princeton University Press, 2007.

Clark, T. J. *The Absolute Bourgeois: Artists and Politics in France, 1848–1851*. London: Thames & Hudson, 1973.

———. *Image of the People: Gustave Courbet and the 1848 Revolution*. London: Thames & Hudson, 1973.

———. *The Painting of Modern Life: Paris in the Art of Manet and His Followers*. Princeton, N.J.: Princeton University Press, 1984.

Clay, Jean. *Romanticism*. New York: Phaidon, 1981.

Eitner, Lorenz. *Neoclassicism and Romanticism, 1750–1850: An Anthology of Sources and Documents*. New York: Harper & Row, 1989.

Fried, Michael. *Courbet's Realism*. Chicago: University of Chicago Press, 1982.

———. *Manet's Modernism, or, The Face of Painting in the 1860s*. Chicago: University of Chicago Press, 1996.

Grave, Johannes. *Caspar David Friedrich*. New York: Prestel, 2012.

Harvey, Eleanor Jones. *The Civil War and American Art*. New Haven, Conn.: Yale University Press, 2012.

Hilton, Timothy. *The Pre-Raphaelites*. New York: Oxford University Press, 1970.

Hofmann, Werner. *Caspar David Friedrich*. New York: Thames & Hudson, 2001.

———. *Goya*. New York: Thames & Hudson, 2003.

Holt, Elizabeth Gilmore, ed. *From the Classicists to the Impressionists: A Documentary History of Art and Architecture in the Nineteenth Century*. Garden City, N.J.: Anchor Books; Doubleday, 1966.

Honour, Hugh. *Romanticism*. New York: Harper & Row, 1979.

Koerner, Joseph Leo. *Caspar David Friedrich and the Subject of Landscape*. 2d ed. London: Reaktion, 2009.

Krämer, Felix. *Dark Romanticism: From Goya to Max Ernst*. Ostfildern: Hatje Cantz, 2013.

Krell, Alain. *Manet and the Painters of Contemporary Life*. London: Thames & Hudson, 1996.

Kroeber, Karl. *British Romantic Art*. Berkeley: University of California Press, 1986.

Lampert, Catherine, ed. *Daumier: Visions of Paris*. London: Royal Academy of Arts, 2013.

Le Men, Ségolène. *Courbet*. New York: Abbeville, 2008.

Lewis, Michael J. *The Gothic Revival*. New York: Thames & Hudson, 2002.

Licht, Fred. *Goya*. New York: Abbeville, 2001.

Mainardi, Patricia. *Art and Politics of the Second Empire: The Universal Expositions of 1855 and 1867*. New Haven, Conn.: Yale University Press, 1987.

———. *The End of the Salon: Art and the State in the Early Third Republic*. Cambridge: Cambridge University Press, 1993.

Middleton, Robin. *Architecture of the Nineteenth Century*. London: Phaidon, 2003.

Middleton, Robin, and David Watkin. *Neoclassical and 19th-Century Architecture*. 2 vols. New York: Electa/Rizzoli, 1987.

Needham, Gerald. *19th-Century Realist Art*. New York: Harper & Row, 1988.

Nochlin, Linda. *Realism and Tradition in Art, 1848–1900: Sources and Documents*. Upper Saddle River, N.J.: Prentice Hall, 1966.

Novak, Barbara. *American Painting of the Nineteenth Century: Realism and the American Experience*. New York: Harper & Row, 1979.

Novak, Barbara. *Nature and Culture: American Landscape and Painting, 1825–1875*. 3d ed. New York: Oxford University Press, 2007.

Novotny, Fritz. *Painting and Sculpture in Europe, 1780–1880*. 3d ed. New Haven, Conn.: Yale University Press, 1988.

Porterfield, Todd. *The Allure of Empire: Art in the Service of French Imperialism 1798–1836*. Princeton, N.J.: Princeton University Press, 1998.

Porterfield, Todd, and Susan L. Siegfried. *Staging Empire: Napoleon, Ingres, and David*. University Park: Pennsylvania State University Press, 2006.

Rosen, Charles, and Henri Zerner. *Romanticism and Realism: The Mythology of Nineteenth-Century Art*. New York: Viking, 1984.

Rubin, James Henry. *Courbet*. London: Phaidon, 1997.

———. *Manet: Initial M, Hand and Eye*. Paris: Flammarion, 2010.

Shelton, Andrew Carrington. *Ingres*. London: Phaidon, 2008.

Sloane, Joseph C. *French Painting between the Past and the Present: Artists, Critics, and Traditions from 1848 to 1870*. Princeton, N.J.: Princeton University Press, 1973.

Symmons, Sarah. *Goya*. London: Phaidon, 1998.

Taylor, Joshua, ed. *Nineteenth-Century Theories of Art*. Berkeley: University of California Press, 1987.

Tillier, Betrand, et al. *Gustave Courbet*. New York: Metropolitan Museum of Art, 2008.

Toman, Rolf, ed. *Neoclassicism and Romanticism: Architecture, Sculpture, Painting, Drawings, 1750–1848*. Cologne: Könemann, 2006.

Vaughn, William. *German Romantic Painting*. New Haven, Conn.: Yale University Press, 1980.

Wolf, Bryan Jay. *Romantic Revision: Culture and Consciousness in Nineteenth-Century American Painting and Literature*. Chicago: University of Chicago Press, 1986.

Wood, Christopher. *The Pre-Raphaelites*. New York: Viking, 1981.

CHAPTER 28

Impressionism, Post-Impressionism, Symbolism: Europe and America, 1870 to 1900

Baal-Teshuva, Jacob. *Louis Comfort Tiffany*. Cologne: Taschen, 2008.

Bergdoll, Barry. *European Architecture 1750–1890*. New York: Oxford University Press, 2000.

Breuer, Karin. *Japanesque: The Japanese Print in the Era of Impressionism*. New York: Prestel, 2010.

Bryson, Norman. *Tradition and Desire: From David to Delacroix*. New York: Cambridge University Press, 1984.

Burnham, Helen, ed. *Looking East: Western Artists and the Allure of Japan*. Boston: Museum of Fine Arts, 2014.

Calloway, Stephen. *Aubrey Beardsley*. New York: Harry N. Abrams, 1998.

Clark, T. J. *The Painting of Modern Life: Paris in the Art of Manet and His Followers*. Princeton, N.J.: Princeton University Press, 1984.

Cogeval, Guy, ed. *Claude Monet, 1840–1926*. Paris: Réunion des Musées Nationaux, 2010.

Distel, Anne. *Renoir*. New York: Abbeville, 2010.

Dorra, Henri, ed. *Symbolist Art Theories: A Critical Anthology*. Berkeley and Los Angeles: University of California Press, 1995.

Eitner, Lorenz. *Neoclassicism and Romanticism, 1750–1850: An Anthology of Sources and Documents*. New York: Harper & Row, 1989.

Facos, Michelle. *Symbolism in Context*. Berkeley: University of California Press, 2009.

Hauptmann, Jodi. *Beyond the Visible: The Art of Odilon Redon*. New York: Museum of Modern Art, 2005.

Herbert, Robert L. *Impressionism: Art, Leisure, and Parisian Society*. New Haven, Conn.: Yale University Press, 1988.

Kendall, Richard, and Jill Devonyar. *Degas and the Ballet: Picturing Movement*. London: Royal Academy of Arts, 2011.

Lewis, Mary Tompkins, ed. *Critical Readings in Impressionism and Post-Impressionism: An Anthology*. Berkeley and Los Angeles: University of California Press, 2007.

Loyrette, Henri, Sebastien Allard, and Laurence Des Cars. *Nineteenth Century French Art: From Romanticism to Impressionism, Post-Impressionism, and Art Nouveau*. Paris: Flammarion, 2007.

Masson, Raphaël, and Véronique Mattiussi. *Rodin*. Paris: Flammarion, 2004.

McShine, Kynaston, ed. *Edvard Munch: The Modern Life of the Soul*. New York: Museum of Modern Art, 2006.

Middleton, Robin. *Architecture of the Nineteenth Century*. London: Phaidon, 2003.

Middleton, Robin, and David Watkin. *Neoclassical and 19th-Century Architecture*. 2 vols. New York: Electa/Rizzoli, 1987.

Pfeiffer, Ingrid, et al. *Women Impressionists*. Ostfildern: Hatje Cantz, 2008.

Rey, Jean-Dominique. *Berthe Morisot*. Paris: Flammarion, 2011.

Swinbourne, Anna. *James Ensor*. New York: Museum of Modern Art, 2009.

Thomson, Belinda, ed. *Gauguin: Maker of Myth*. London: Tate, 2010.

Walther, Ingo F., ed. *Impressionist Art 1860–1920*. 2 vols. Cologne: Taschen, 2010.

Zerbst, Rainer. *Gaudí: The Complete Buildings*. Cologne: Taschen, 2005.

CHAPTER 29

Modernism in Europe and America, 1900 to 1945

Antliff, Mark. *Cultural Politics and the Parisian Avant-Garde*. Princeton, N.J.: Princeton University Press, 1993.

Antliff, Mark, and Patricia Leighten. *Cubism and Culture*. New York: Thames & Hudson, 2001.

Arnaldo, Javier, and Max Hollein. *Kirchner*. Ostfildern: Hatje Cantz, 2010.

Baigell, Matthew. *The American Scene: American Painting of the 1930s*. New York: Praeger, 1974.

Barr, Alfred H., Jr. *Cubism and Abstract Art: Painting, Sculpture, Construc-tions, Photography, Architecture, Industrial Arts, Theatre, Films, Posters, Typography.* Cambridge, Mass.: Belknap, 1986.

Barron, Stephanie. *Exiles and Emigrés: The Flight of European Artists from Hitler.* Los Angeles: Los Angeles County Museum of Art, 1997.

———, ed. *"Degenerate Art": The Fate of the Avant-Garde in Nazi Germany.* Los Angeles: Los Angeles County Museum of Art, 1991.

Bayer, Herbert, Walter Gropius, and Ise Gropius. *Bauhaus, 1919–1928.* New York: Museum of Modern Art, 1975.

Bearden, Romare, and Harry Henderson. *A History of African-American Artists from 1792 to the Present.* New York: Pantheon, 1993.

Bergdoll, Barry. *Bauhaus 1919–1933.* New York: Museum of Modern Art, 2009.

Bouvet, Vincent, and Gérard Durozoi. *Paris between the Wars 1919–1939: Art, Life & Culture.* New York: Vendome, 2010.

Breton, André. *Surrealism and Painting.* New York: Harper & Row, 1972.

Brown, Milton. *Story of the Armory Show: The 1913 Exhibition That Changed American Art.* 2d ed. New York: Abbeville, 1988.

Campbell, Mary Schmidt, David C. Driskell, David Lewis Levering, and Deb-orah Willis Ryan. *Harlem Renaissance: Art of Black America.* New York: Studio Museum in Harlem; Abrams, 1987.

Clark, T. J. *Picasso and Truth: From Cubism to Guernica.* Princeton, N.J.: Princeton University Press, 2013.

Cowling, Elizabeth, ed. *Picasso: Challenging the Past.* London: National Gallery, 2011.

Cox, Neil. *Cubism.* London: Phaidon, 2000.

Curtis, Penelope. *Sculpture 1900–1945.* New York: Oxford University Press, 1999.

Curtis, William J. R. *Modern Architecture since 1900.* Upper Saddle River, N.J.: Prentice Hall, 1996.

D'Alessandro, Stephanie, ed. *Magritte: The Mystery of the Ordinary, 1926–1938.* New York: Museum of Modern Art, 2013.

Davidson, Abraham A. *Early American Modernist Painting, 1910–1935.* New York: Harper & Row, 1981.

Dickerman, Leah, ed. *Inventing Abstraction, 1910–1925.* New York: Museum of Modern Art, 2013.

Dietrich, Dorothea, ed. *Dada: Zurich, Berlin, Hannover, Cologne, New York, Paris.* Washington, D.C.: National Gallery, 2008.

Du Pont, Diana C. *Tamayo: A Modern Icon Reinterpreted.* Santa Barbara, Calif.: Santa Barbara Museum of Art, 2007.

Eberle, Matthias. *World War I and the Weimar Artists: Dix, Grosz, Beckmann, Schlemmer.* New Haven, Conn.: Yale University Press, 1985.

Edwards, Steve, and Paul Wood, eds. *Art of the Avant-Gardes.* New Haven, Conn.: Yale University Press, 2004.

Elderfield, John. *The "Wild Beasts": Fauvism and Its Affinities.* New York: Museum of Modern Art, 1976.

Favole, Paolo. *The Story of Modern Architecture.* New York: Prestel, 2012.

Fer, Briony, David Batchelor, and Paul Wood. *Realism, Rationalism, Surreal-ism: Art between the Wars.* New Haven, Conn.: Yale University Press, 1993.

Friedman, Mildred, ed. *De Stijl, 1917–1931: Visions of Utopia.* Minneapolis: Walker Art Center; New York: Abbeville, 1982.

Gale, Matthew. *Dada and Surrealism.* London: Phaidon, 1997.

Gale, Matthew, ed. *Paul Klee: Making Visible.* London: Tate Modern and Thames & Hudson, 2013.

Goldberg, Rose Lee. *Performance: Live Art 1909 to the Present.* New York: Abrams, 1979.

Golding, John. *Cubism: A History and an Analysis, 1907–1914.* Cambridge, Mass.: Belknap, 1988.

Gordon, Donald E. *Expressionism: Art and Idea.* New Haven, Conn.: Yale University Press, 1987.

Harrison, Charles, Francis Frascina, and Gil Perry. *Primitivism, Cubism, Abstraction: The Early Twentieth Century.* New Haven, Conn.: Yale University Press, 1993.

Herbert, James D. *Fauve Painting: The Making of Cultural Politics.* New Haven, Conn.: Yale University Press, 1992.

Herrera, Hayden, ed. *Frida Kahlo.* Minneapolis: Walker Art Center, 2007.

Hills, Patricia. *Painting Harlem Modern: The Art of Jacob Lawrence.* Berkeley and Los Angeles: University of California Press, 2009.

Hitchcock, Henry-Russell, and Philip Johnson. *The International Style.* New York: Norton, 1995.

Hurlburt, Laurance P. *The Mexican Muralists in the United States.* Albuquer-que: University of New Mexico Press, 1989.

Jaffé, Hans L. C. *De Stijl, 1917–1931: The Dutch Contribution to Modern Art.* Cambridge, Mass.: Belknap, 1986.

Krauss, Rosalind. *The Originality of the Avant-Garde and Other Modernist Myths.* Cambridge, Mass.: MIT Press, 1986.

Kushner, Marilyn Satin, Kimberly Orcutt, and Casey Nelson Blake, eds. *The Armory Show at 100: Modernism and Revolution.* New York: New York Historical Society, 2013.

Kuspit, Donald. *The Cult of the Avant-Garde Artist.* Cambridge: Cambridge University Press, 1993.

Lloyd, Jill. *German Expressionism: Primitivism and Modernity.* New Haven, Conn.: Yale University Press, 1991.

Lodder, Christina. *Russian Constructivism.* New Haven, Conn.: Yale Univer-sity Press, 1983.

Lozano, Luis Martin, and Juan Coronel Rivera. *Diego Rivera: The Complete Murals.* Cologne: Taschen, 2008.

Martin, Marianne W. *Futurist Art and Theory.* Oxford: Clarendon, 1968.

McCully, Marilyn. *Picasso in Paris, 1900–1907.* New York: Vendome, 2011.

Messinger, Lisa Mintz, ed. *Stieglitz and His Artists: Matisse to O'Keeffe.* New York: Metropolitan Museum of Art, 2011.

Motherwell, Robert, ed. *The Dada Painters and Poets: An Anthology.* 2d ed. Boston: Hall, 1981.

Mundy, Jennifer. *Duchamp, Man Ray, Picabia.* London: Tate, 2008.

Oles, James. *Art and Architecture in Mexico.* New York: Thames & Hudson, 2013.

Orvell, Miles. *American Photography.* New York: Oxford University Press, 2003.

Peters, Olaf. *Otto Dix.* New York: Prestel, 2010.

Poggi, Christine. *Inventing Futurism: The Art and Politics of Artificial Optimism.* Princeton, N.J.: Princeton University Press, 2009.

Rhodes, Colin. *Primitivism and Modern Art.* New York: Thames & Hudson, 1994.

Richter, Hans. *Dada: Art and Anti-Art.* London: Thames & Hudson, 1961.

Rochfort, Desmond. *Mexican Muralists: Orozco, Rivera, Siqueiros.* San Francisco: Chronicle, 1998.

Rosenblum, Robert. *Cubism and Twentieth-Century Art.* Rev. ed. New York: Abrams, 1984.

Rubin, William S. *Dada and Surrealist Art.* New York: Abrams, 1968.

———, ed. *Pablo Picasso: A Retrospective.* New York: Museum of Modern Art; Boston: New York Graphic Society, 1980.

———. *"Primitivism" in 20th-Century Art: Affinity of the Tribal and the Modern.* 2 vols. New York: Museum of Modern Art, 1984.

Selz, Peter. *German Expressionist Painting.* Berkeley: University of California Press, 1974. Reprint of 1957 edition.

Silver, Kenneth E. *Esprit de Corps: The Art of the Parisian Avant-Garde and the First World War, 1914–1925.* Princeton, N.J.: Princeton University Press, 1989.

Smith, Terry. *Making the Modern: Industry, Art, and Design in America.* Chicago: University of Chicago Press, 1993.

Spieler, Reinhard. *Max Beckmann 1884–1950: The Path to Myth.* Cologne: Taschen, 2011.

Stott, William. *Documentary Expression and Thirties America.* New York: Oxford University Press, 1973.

Taylor, Joshua C. *Futurism.* New York: Museum of Modern Art, 1961.

Taylor, Michael R., ed. *Arshile Gorky: A Retrospective.* New Haven, Conn.: Yale University Press, 2009.

Terraroli, Valerio, ed. *Art of the Twentieth Century, 1900–1919: The Avant-Garde Movements.* Milan: Skira, 2006.

———. *Art of the Twentieth Century, 1920–1945: The Artistic Culture between the Wars.* Milan: Skira, 2006.

Tisdall, Caroline, and Angelo Bozzolla. *Futurism.* New York: Oxford Univer-sity Press, 1978.

Trachtenberg, Alan. *Reading American Photographs: Images as History—Mathew Brady to Walker Evans.* New York: Hill and Wang, 1989.

Troyen, Carol, ed. *Edward Hopper.* Boston: Museum of Fine Arts, 2007.

Tsujimoto, Karen. *Images of America: Precisionist Painting and Modern Pho-tography.* Seattle: University of Washington Press, 1982.

Tucker, William. *Early Modern Sculpture.* New York: Oxford University Press, 1974.

Vogt, Paul. *Expressionism: German Painting, 1905–1920.* New York: Abrams, 1980.

Weiss, Jeffrey S. *The Popular Culture of Modern Art: Picasso, Duchamp, and Avant-Gardism.* New Haven, Conn.: Yale University Press, 1994.

Whitford, Frank. *Bauhaus.* New York: Thames & Hudson, 1984.

CHAPTER 30
Modernism and Postmodernism in Europe and America, 1945 to 1980

Adamson, Glenn, and Jane Pavitt, eds. *Postmodernism: Style and Subversion, 1970–1990.* London: Victoria & Albert Museum, 2011.

Alloway, Lawrence. *American Pop Art.* New York: Whitney Museum of Amer-ican Art; Macmillan, 1974.

———. *Topics in American Art since 1945.* New York: Norton, 1975.

Altshuler, Bruce. *Isamu Noguchi*. New York: Abbeville, 1994.

Anfam, David. *Abstract Expressionism*. New York: Thames & Hudson, 1990.

Anreus, Alejandro, Robin Adèle Greeley, and Leonard Folgarait, eds. *Mexican Muralism: A Critical History*. Berkeley and Los Angeles: University of California Press, 2012.

Archer, Michael. *Art since 1960*. New ed. New York: Thames & Hudson, 2002.

Ashton, Dore. *American Art since 1945*. New York: Oxford University Press, 1983.

———. *The New York School: A Cultural Reckoning*. Harmondsworth: Penguin, 1979.

Ballantyne, Andrew, ed. *Architectures: Modernism and After*. Malden, Mass: Blackwell, 2004.

Battcock, Gregory, ed. *Idea Art: A Critical Anthology*. New York: Dutton, 1973.

———. *Minimal Art: A Critical Anthology*. New York: Studio Vista, 1969.

———. *The New Art: A Critical Anthology*. New York: Dutton, 1973.

———. *New Artists Video: A Critical Anthology*. New York: Dutton, 1978.

Battcock, Gregory, and Robert Nickas, eds. *The Art of Performance: A Critical Anthology*. New York: Dutton, 1984.

Beardsley, John, and Jane Livingston. *Hispanic Art in the United States: Thirty Contemporary Painters and Sculptors*. Houston: Museum of Fine Arts; New York: Abbeville, 1987.

Beardsley, Richard. *Earthworks and Beyond: Contemporary Art in the Landscape*. New York: Abbeville, 1984.

Broude, Norma, and Mary D. Garrard. *The Power of Feminist Art: The American Movement of the 1970s, History and Impact*. New York: Abrams, 1994.

Bürger, Peter. *Theory of the Avant-Garde*. Minneapolis: University of Minnesota Press, 1984.

Butler, Cornelia H., ed. *WACK! Art and the Feminist Revolution*. Cambridge, Mass.: MIT Press, 2007.

Causey, Andrew. *Sculpture since 1945*. New York: Oxford University Press, 1998.

Caws, Mary Ann. *Robert Motherwell*. New York: Columbia University Press, 1996.

Celant, Germano, ed. *Louise Nevelson*. Turin: Skira, 2012.

Cockcroft, Eva, John Weber, and James Cockcroft. *Toward a People's Art*. New York: Dutton, 1977.

Cohn, Marjorie, and Eliza Rathbone. *Mark Rothko*. Ostfildern: Hatje Cantz, 2001.

Collins, Bradford R. *Pop Art*. London: Phaidon, 2012.

Crow, Thomas. *The Rise of the Sixties: American and European Art in the Era of Dissent*. New Haven, Conn.: Yale University Press, 2005.

Finch, Christopher. *Chuck Close: Work*. New York: Prestel, 2010.

Fineberg, Jonathan. *Art since 1940: Strategies of Being*. 3d ed. Upper Saddle River, N.J.: Prentice Hall, 2010.

Foster, Hal. *The First Pop Age: Painting and Subjectivity in the Art of Hamilton, Lichtenstein, Warhol, Richter, and Ruscha*. Princeton, N.J.: Princeton University Press, 2011.

Frascina, Francis, ed. *Pollock and After: The Critical Debate*. New York: Harper & Row, 1985.

Gale, Matthew, ed. *Francis Bacon*. New York: Rizzoli, 2009.

Gaugh, Harry F. *Franz Kline*. New York: Abbeville, 1994.

Geldzahler, Henry. *New York Painting and Sculpture, 1940–1970*. New York: Dutton, 1969.

Godfrey, Mark, and Nicholas Serota, eds. *Gerhard Richter: Panorama. A Retrospective*. London: Tate, 2011.

Godfrey, Tony. *Conceptual Art*. London: Phaidon, 1998.

Goldberg, Rose Lee. *Performance Art: From Futurism to the Present*. Rev. ed. New York: Abrams, 1988.

Goldhagen, Sarah Williams, and Réjean Legault. *Anxious Modernisms: Experimentation in Postwar Architectural Culture*. Cambridge, Mass.: MIT Press, 2002.

Goodman, Cynthia. *Digital Visions: Computers and Art*. New York: Abrams, 1987.

Goodyear, Frank H., Jr. *Contemporary American Realism since 1960*. Boston: New York Graphic Society, 1981.

Gouma-Peterson, Thalia. *Miriam Schapiro: Shaping the Fragments of Art and Life*. New York: Abrams, 2000.

Green, Jonathan. *American Photography: A Critical History 1945 to the Present*. New York: Abrams, 1984.

Greenberg, Clement. *Clement Greenberg: The Collected Essays and Criticism*. Edited by J. O'Brien. 4 vols. Chicago: University of Chicago Press, 1986–1993.

Grundberg, Andy. *Photography and Art: Interactions since 1945*. New York: Abbeville, 1987.

Guilbaut, Serge. *How New York Stole the Idea of Modern Art*. Chicago: University of Chicago Press, 1983.

Hays, K. Michael, and Carol Burns, eds. *Thinking the Present: Recent American Architecture*. New York: Princeton Architectural, 1990.

Henri, Adrian. *Total Art: Environments, Happenings, and Performance*. New York: Oxford University Press, 1974.

Hobbs, Robert. *Lee Krasner*. New York: Abbeville, 1993.

Hoffman, Katherine. *Explorations: The Visual Arts since 1945*. New York: Harper Collins, 1991.

Hopkins, David. *After Modern Art, 1945–2000*. New York: Oxford University Press, 2000.

Hughes, Robert. *The Shock of the New*. New York: Knopf, 1981.

Hunter, Sam. *An American Renaissance: Painting and Sculpture since 1940*. New York: Abbeville, 1986.

Jacobs, Jane. *The Death and Life of Great American Cities*. New York: Random House, 1961.

Jacobus, John. *Twentieth-Century Architecture: The Middle Years, 1940–1964*. New York: Praeger, 1966.

Jencks, Charles. *The Language of Post-Modern Architecture*. 6th ed. New York: Rizzoli, 1991.

———. *What Is Post-Modernism?* 3d ed. London: Academy Editions, 1989.

Johnson, Ellen H., ed. *American Artists on Art from 1940 to 1980*. Boulder, Colo.: Westview, 1982.

Joselit, David. *American Art since 1945*. New York: Thames & Hudson, 2003.

Kaprow, Allan. *Assemblage, Environments, and Happenings*. New York: Abrams, 1966.

Kirby, Michael. *Happenings*. New York: Dutton, 1966.

Kotz, Mary Lynn. *Rauschenberg: Art and Life*. New York: Abrams, 2004.

Kramer, Hilton. *The Age of the Avant-Garde: An Art Chronicle of 1956–1972*. New York: Farrar, Straus & Giroux, 1973.

Leja, Michael. *Reframing Abstract Expressionism: Subjectivity and Painting in the 1940s*. New Haven, Conn.: Yale University Press, 1993.

Lippard, Lucy R. *Mixed Blessings: New Art in a Multicultural America*. New York: Pantheon, 1990.

———. *Pop Art*. New York: Praeger, 1966.

———, ed. *From the Center: Feminist Essays on Women's Art*. New York: Dutton, 1976.

———. *Six Years: The Dematerialization of the Art Object from 1966 to 1972*. New York: Praeger, 1973.

Livingston, Jane, ed. *The Paintings of Joan Mitchell*. New York: Whitney Museum of American Art, 2002.

Lobel, Michael. *James Rosenquist: Pop Art, Politics, and History in the 1960s*. Berkeley and Los Angeles: University of California Press, 2009.

Lovejoy, Margot. *Postmodern Currents: Art and Artists in the Age of the Electronic Media*. Ann Arbor, Mich.: UMI Research Press, 1989.

Lucie-Smith, Edward. *Art Now*. Edison, N.J.: Wellfleet, 1989.

———. *Movements in Art since 1945*. New ed. New York: Thames & Hudson, 2001.

Mamiya, Christin J. *Pop Art and Consumer Culture: American Super Market*. Austin: University of Texas Press, 1992.

Marder, Tod A. *The Critical Edge: Controversy in Recent American Architecture*. New Brunswick, N.J.: Rutgers University Press, 1980.

———. *An International Survey of Recent Painting and Sculpture*. New York: Museum of Modern Art, 1984.

Mercurio, Gianni. *Lichtenstein: Meditations on Art*. Milan: Skira, 2010.

Mesch, Claudia. *Art and Politics: A Small History of Art for Social Change since 1945*. New York: I. B. Tauris, 2013.

Meyer, Ursula. *Conceptual Art*. New York: Dutton, 1972.

Mitchell, William J. *The Reconfigured Eye: Visual Truth in the Post-Photographic Era*. Cambridge, Mass.: MIT Press, 1992.

Morris, Francis, ed. *Louise Bourgeois*. New York: Rizzoli, 2008.

Osborne, Peter, ed. *Conceptual Art*. London: Phaidon, 2002.

Polcari, Stephen. *Abstract Expressionism and the Modern Experience*. Cambridge: Cambridge University Press, 1991.

Popper, Frank. *Origins and Development of Kinetic Art*. Translated by Stephen Bann. Greenwich, Conn.: New York Graphic Society, 1968.

Price, Jonathan. *Video Visions: A Medium Discovers Itself*. New York: New American Library, 1977.

Reichardt, Jasia, ed. *Cybernetics, Art, and Ideas*. Greenwich, Conn.: New York Graphics Society, 1971.

Robbins, Corinne. *The Pluralist Era: American Art, 1968–1981*. New York: Harper & Row, 1984.

Rondeau, James, and Sheena Wagstaff, eds. *Roy Lichtenstein: A Retrospective*. Chicago: Art Institute of Chicago, 2012.

Rorimer, Anne. *New Art in the 60s and 70s: Redefining Reality*. New York: Thames & Hudson, 2001.

Rosen, Randy, and Catherine C. Brawer, eds. *Making Their Mark: Women Artists Move into the Mainstream, 1970–1985*. New York: Abbeville, 1989.

Rosenberg, Harold. *The Tradition of the New.* New York: Horizon, 1959.

Rush, Michael. *New Media in Art.* 2d ed. New York: Thames & Hudson, 2005.

Russell, John, and Suzi Gablik. *Pop Art Redefined.* New York: Praeger, 1969.

Sackler, Elizabeth A., ed. *Judy Chicago.* New York: Watson-Guptill, 2002.

Sandford, Mariellen R., ed. *Happenings and Other Acts.* New York: Routledge, 1995.

Sandler, Irving. *Art of the Postmodern Era.* New York: Harper Collins, 1996.

———. *The Triumph of American Painting: A History of Abstract Expressionism.* New York: Praeger, 1970.

Sayre, Henry M. *The Object of Performance: The American Avant-Garde since 1970.* Chicago: University of Chicago Press, 1989.

Schimmel, Paul, ed. *Destroy the Picture: Painting the Void, 1949–1962.* Los Angeles: Museum of Contemporary Art, 2012.

Schneider, Ira, and Beryl Korot. *Video Art: An Anthology.* New York: Harcourt Brace Jovanovich, 1976.

Shapiro, David, and Cecile Shapiro. *Abstract Expressionism: A Critical Record.* New York: Cambridge University Press, 1990.

Shiff, Richard. *Barnett Newman: A Catalogue Raisonné.* New Haven, Conn.: Yale University Press, 2004.

Siegel, Katy. *Since '45: America and the Making of Contemporary Art.* London: Reaktion, 2011.

———, ed. *Abstract Expressionism.* New York: Phaidon, 2011.

Sims, Lowery Stokes. *Wifredo Lam and the International Avant-Garde, 1923–1982.* Austin, Tex.: University of Texas Press, 2002.

Smagula, Howard. *Currents: Contemporary Directions in the Visual Arts.* 2d ed. Upper Saddle River, N.J.: Prentice Hall, 1989.

Smee, Sebastian. *Lucian Freud: Beholding the Animal.* Cologne: Taschen, 2009.

Sonfist, Alan, ed. *Art in the Landscape: A Critical Anthology of Environmental Art.* New York: Dutton, 1983.

Sontag, Susan. *On Photography.* New York: Farrar, Straus & Giroux, 1973.

Stiles, Kristine, and Peter Selz. *Theories and Documents of Contemporary Art: A Sourcebook of Artists' Writings.* Berkeley and Los Angeles: University of California Press, 1996.

Taylor, Brendon. *Contemporary Art: Art since 1970.* Upper Saddle River, N.J.: Prentice Hall, 2005.

Terraroli, Valerio, ed. *Art of the Twentieth Century, 1946–1968: The Birth of Contemporary Art.* Milan: Skira, 2007.

Theriault, Kim S. *Rethinking Arshile Gorky.* University Park: Pennsylvania State University Press, 2009.

Tuchman, Maurice. *American Sculpture of the Sixties.* Los Angeles: Los Angeles County Museum of Art, 1967.

Ursprung, Philip. *Allan Kaprow, Robert Smithson, and the Limits to Art.* Berkeley and Los Angeles: University of California Press, 2013.

Varnedoe, Kirk. *Pictures of Nothing: Abstract Art since Pollock.* Princeton: Princeton University Press, 2006.

Venturi, Robert. *Complexity and Contradiction in Architecture.* New York: Museum of Modern Art, 1966.

Venturi, Robert, Denise Scott-Brown, and Steven Isehour. *Learning from Las Vegas.* Cambridge, Mass.: MIT Press, 1972.

Waldman, Diane. *Collage, Assemblage, and the Found Object.* New York: Abrams, 1992.

Wallis, Brian, ed. *Art after Modernism: Rethinking Representation.* New York: New Museum of Contemporary Art in association with David R. Godine, 1984.

Wheeler, Daniel. *Art since Mid-Century: 1945 to the Present.* Upper Saddle River, N.J.: Prentice Hall, 1991.

Wood, Paul. *Modernism in Dispute: Art since the Forties.* New Haven, Conn.: Yale University Press, 1993.

CHAPTER 31
Contemporary Art Worldwide

Andrews, Julia F., and Kuiyi Shen. *The Art of Modern China.* Berkeley and Los Angeles: University of California Press, 2012.

Anfam, David, ed. *Anish Kapoor.* New York: Phaidon, 2009.

Buchhart, Dieter, et al. *Jean-Michel Basquiat.* Ostfildern: Hatje Cantz, 2010.

Butler, Cornelia H., and Lisa Gabrielle Mark. *WACK!: Art and the Feminist Revolution.* Cambridge, Mass.: MIT Press, 2007.

Celent, Germano. *Anselm Kiefer.* Milan: Skira, 2007.

Chilvers, Ian, and John Glaves-Smith. *Oxford Dictionary of Modern and Contemporary Art.* 2d ed. New York: Oxford University Press, 2009.

Chiu, Melissa, and Benjamin Genocchio. *Asian Art Now.* New York: Monacelli, 2010.

Cook, Peter. *New Spirit in Architecture.* New York: Rizzoli, 1990.

Cummings, P. *Dictionary of Contemporary American Artists.* 6th ed. New York: St. Martin's, 1994.

Dadi, Iftikhar. *Modernism and the Art of Muslim South Asia.* Chapel Hill: University of North Carolina Press, 2010.

Danto, Arthur C., and Marina Abramovic. *Shirin Neshat.* New York: Rizzoli, 2010.

Deepwell, K., ed. *New Feminist Art.* Manchester: Manchester University Press, 1994.

Enwezor, Okwui, and Chika Okeke-Agulu. *Contemporary African Art since 1980.* Bologna: Damiani, 2009.

Favole, Paolo. *The Story of Contemporary Architecture.* New York: Prestel, 2011.

Ferguson, Russell, ed. *Discourses: Conversations in Postmodern Art and Culture.* Cambridge, Mass.: MIT Press, 1990.

Fineberg, Jonathan. *Art since 1940: Strategies of Being.* 3d ed. Upper Saddle River, N.J.: Prentice Hall, 2011.

Galassi, Peter. *Andreas Gursky.* New York: Museum of Modern Art, 2001.

Ghirardo, Diane. *Architecture after Modernism.* New York: Thames & Hudson, 1996.

Goldsworthy, Andy. *Andy Goldsworthy: A Collaboration with Nature.* New York: Abrams, 1990.

Heartney, Eleanor. *Art & Today.* New York: Phaidon, 2008.

Heartney, Eleanor, Helaine Posner, Nancy Princenthal, and Sue Scott. *After the Revolution: Women Who Transformed Contemporary Art.* New York: Prestel, 2007.

Hertz, Richard, ed. *Theories of Contemporary Art.* 2d ed. Upper Saddle River, N.J.: Prentice Hall, 1993.

Hopkins, David. *After Modern Art, 1945–2000.* New York: Oxford University Press, 2000.

Jencks, Charles. *The New Paradigm in Architecture: The Language of Post-Modernism.* New Haven, Conn.: Yale University Press, 2002.

Jodidio, Philip. *100 Contemporary Architects.* Cologne: Taschen, 2008.

Joselit, David. *After Art.* Princeton, N.J.: Princeton University Press, 2013.

Kasfir, Sidney Littlefield. *Contemporary African Art.* New York: Thames & Hudson, 1999.

Kolossa, Alexandra. *Keith Haring 1958–1990: A Life for Art.* Cologne: Taschen, 2009.

Kotz, Mary Lunn. *Rauschenberg: Art and Life.* New York: Abrams, 2004.

Lippard, Lucy R. *Mixed Blessings: New Art in a Multicultural America.* New York: Pantheon, 1990.

Mesch, Claudia. *Art and Politics: A Small History of Art for Social Change since 1945.* New York: I. B. Tauris, 2013.

Moszynska, Anna. *Sculpture Now.* New York: Thames & Hudson, 2013.

Mullins, Charlotte. *Painting People: Figure Painting Today.* New York: Thames & Hudson, 2008.

Neri, Louise, and Takaya Goto, eds. *Yayoi Kusama.* New York: Rizzoli, 2012.

Nesbitt, Judith, ed. *Chris Ofili.* London: Tate, 2010.

Norris, Christopher, and Andrew Benjamin. *What Is Deconstruction?* New York: St. Martin's, 1988.

O'Brien, Elaine, Everlyn Nicodemus, Melissa Chiu, Benjamin Genocchio, Mary K. Coffey, and Roberto Tejada, eds. *Modern Art in Africa, Asia, and Latin America: An Introduction to Global Modernisms.* Malden, Mass.: Wiley-Blackwell, 2013.

Paul, Christiane. *Digital Art.* 2d ed. New York: Thames & Hudson, 2008.

Pauli, Lori, ed. *Manufactured Landscapes: The Photographs of Edward Burtynsky.* New Haven, Conn.: Yale University Press, 2003.

Perry, Gill, and Paul Wood. *Themes in Contemporary Art.* New Haven, Conn.: Yale University Press, 2004.

Raskin, David. *Donald Judd.* New Haven, Conn.: Yale University Press, 2010.

Risatti, Howard, ed. *Postmodern Perspectives: Issues in Contemporary Art.* Upper Saddle River, N.J.: Prentice Hall, 1990.

Sandler, Irving. *Art of the Postmodern Era.* New York: Harper Collins, 1996.

Smith, Terry. *What Is Contemporary Art?* Chicago: University of Chicago Press, 2009.

Sollins, Susan, ed. *Art: 21 (Art in the Twenty-first Century).* 5 vols. New York: Abrams, 2001–2009.

Stiles, Kristine, and Peter Selz. *Theories and Documents of Contemporary Art: A Sourcebook of Artists' Writings.* 2d ed. Berkeley and Los Angeles: University of California Press, 2012.

Storr, Robert. *Elizabeth Murray.* New York: Museum of Modern Art, 2005.

Taylor, Brendon. *Contemporary Art: Art since 1970.* Upper Saddle River, N.J.: Prentice Hall, 2005.

Terraroli, Valerio, ed. *Art of the Twentieth Century, 1969–1999: Neo-avant-gardes, Postmodern and Global Art.* Milan: Skira, 2009.

Vogel, Susan Mullin. *El Anatsui: Art and Life.* New York: Prestel, 2012.

Wands, Bruce. *Art of the Digital Age.* New York: Thames & Hudson, 2007.

Warren, Lynne. *Jeff Koons.* New Haven, Conn.: Yale University Press, 2008.

Wines, James. *Green Architecture.* Cologne: Taschen, 2008.

Asian Art, General

Brown, Rebecca M., and Deborah S. Hutton. *Asian Art (Blackwell Anthologies in Art History)*. Malden, Mass.: Blackwell, 2006.

Clark, John. *Modern Asian Art*. Honolulu: University of Hawaii Press, 1998.

McArthur, Meher. *The Arts of Asia: Materials, Techniques, Styles*. New York: Thames & Hudson, 2005.

CHAPTER 32
South and Southeast Asia, 1200 to 1980

Asher, Catherine B. *Architecture of Mughal India*. New York: Cambridge University Press, 1992.

Beach, Milo Cleveland. *Mughal and Rajput Painting*. Cambridge: Cambridge University Press, 1992.

Beach, Milo Cleveland, Eberhard Fischer, and B. N. Goswamy, eds. *Masters of Indian Painting, 1100–1900*. 2 vols. Zurich: Artibus Asiae, 2011.

Blurton, T. Richard. *Hindu Art*. Cambridge, Mass.: Harvard University Press, 1993.

Chakraverty, Anjan. *Indian Miniature Painting*. New Delhi: Roli & Janssen, 2005.

Chaturachinda, Gwyneth, Sunanda Krishnamurty, and Pauline W. Tabtiang. *Dictionary of South and Southeast Asian Art*. Chiang Mai, Thailand: Silkworm Books, 2000.

Craven, Roy C. *Indian Art: A Concise History*. Rev. ed. London: Thames & Hudson, 1997.

Dallapiccola, Anna Libera, ed. *Vijayanagara: City and Empire*. 2 vols. Stuttgart: Steiner, 1985.

Dehejia, Vidya. *Indian Art*. London: Phaidon, 1997.

Encyclopedia of Indian Temple Architecture. 8 vols. New Delhi: American Institute of Indian Studies; Philadelphia: University of Pennsylvania Press, 1983–1996.

Girard-Geslan, Maud, ed. *Art of Southeast Asia*. New York: Abrams, 1998.

Guy, John, and Jorrit Britschgi. *Wonder of the Age: Master Painters of India, 1100–1900*. New York: Metropolitan Museum of Art, 2011.

Harle, James C. *The Art and Architecture of the Indian Subcontinent*. 2d ed. New Haven, Conn.: Yale University Press, 1994.

Huntington, Susan L., and John C. Huntington. *The Art of Ancient India: Buddhist, Hindu, Jain*. New York: Weatherhill, 1985.

Koch, Ebba. *The Complete Taj Mahal and the Riverfront Gardens of Agra*. London: Thames & Hudson, 2006.

Lambah, Abha Narian, and Alka Patel, eds. *The Architecture of the Indian Sultanates*. Mumbai: Marg, 2006.

Michell, George. *Architecture and Art of Southern India: Vijayanagara and the Successor States, 1350–1750*. Cambridge: Cambridge University Press, 1995.

———. *Hindu Art and Architecture*. New York: Thames & Hudson, 2000.

———. *The Hindu Temple: An Introduction to Its Meaning and Forms*. Chicago: University of Chicago Press, 1988.

———. *Mughal Architecture & Gardens*. New York: Antique Collectors Club, 2011.

Mitter, Partha. *Indian Art*. New York: Oxford University Press, 2001.

Pal, Pratapaditya, ed. *Master Artists of the Imperial Mughal Court*. Mumbai: Marg, 1991.

Rawson, Phillip. *The Art of Southeast Asia*. New York: Thames & Hudson, 1990.

Schimmel, Annemarie. *The Empire of the Great Mughals: History, Art, and Culture*. London: Reaktion, 2006.

Stadtner, Donald M. *The Art of Burma: New Studies*. Mumbai: Marg, 1999.

Stevenson, John, and John Guy, eds. *Vietnamese Ceramics: A Separate Tradition*. Chicago: Art Media Resources, 1997.

Stierlin, Henri. *Hindu India from Khajuraho to the Temple City of Madurai*. Cologne: Taschen, 1998.

Stronge, Susan. *Painting for the Mughal Emperor: The Art of the Book, 1560–1660*. London: Victoria & Albert Museum, 2002.

Tingley, Nancy, ed. *Arts of Ancient Viet Nam: From River Plain to Open Sea*. Houston: Museum of Fine Arts, 2009.

Topsfield, Andrew. *In the Realm of Gods and Kings: Arts of India*. London: Philip Wilson, 2004.

Verna, Som Prakash. *Painting the Mughal Experience*. New York: Oxford University Press, 2005.

Welch, Stuart Cary. *Imperial Mughal Painting*. New York: Braziller, 1978.

———. *India: Art and Culture 1300–1900*. New York: Metropolitan Museum of Art, 1985.

Zimmer, Heinrich, and Joseph Campbell. *The Art of Indian Asia: Its Mythology and Transformation*. 2 vols. New Delhi: Motilal Banarsidass, 2001.

CHAPTER 33
China and Korea, 1279 to 1980

Andrews, Julia Frances, and Kuiyi Shen. *A Century in Crisis: Modernity and Tradition in the Art of Twentieth-Century China*. New York: Guggenheim Museum, 1998.

Barnhart, Richard M. *Painters of the Great Ming: The Imperial Court and the Zhe School*. Dallas: Dallas Museum of Art, 1993.

Cahill, James. *The Painter's Practice: How Artists Lived and Worked in Traditional China*. New York: Columbia University Press, 1994.

Clunas, Craig. *Art in China*. 2d ed. New York: Oxford University Press, 2009.

———. *Empire of Great Brightness: Visual and Material Cultures of Ming China, 1369–1644*. London: Reaktion, 2007.

———. *Pictures and Visuality in Early Modern China*. Princeton: Princeton University Press, 1997.

Fahr-Becker, Gabriele, ed. *The Art of East Asia*. Cologne: Könemann, 1999.

Fisher, Robert E. *Buddhist Art and Architecture*. New York: Thames & Hudson, 1993.

Fong, Wen C., and James C. Y. Watt. *Preserving the Past: Treasures from the National Palace Museum, Taipei*. New York: Metropolitan Museum of Art, 1996.

Hearn, Maxwell K. *How to Read Chinese Paintings*. New York: Metropolitan Museum of Art, 2008.

Howard, Angela Falco, Li Song, Wu Hong, and Yang Hong. *Chinese Sculpture*. New Haven, Conn.: Yale University Press, 2006.

Laing, Ellen Johnston. *The Winking Owl: Art in the People's Republic of China*. Berkeley: University of California Press, 1989.

Li, Chu-tsing, ed. *Artists and Patrons: Some Social and Economic Aspects of Chinese Painting*. Lawrence, Kans.: Kress Department of Art History in cooperation with Indiana University Press, 1989.

Li, He, and Michael Knight. *Power and Glory: Court Arts of China's Ming Dynasty*. San Francisco: Asian Art Museum, 2008.

Nakata, Yujiro, ed. *Chinese Calligraphy*. New York: Weatherhill, 1983.

Portal, Jane. *Korea: Art and Archaeology*. New York: Thames & Hudson, 2000.

Rawson, Jessica, ed. *The British Museum Book of Chinese Art*. New York: Thames & Hudson, 1992.

Sickman, Laurence, and Alexander C. Soper. *The Art and Architecture of China*. 3d ed. New Haven, Conn.: Yale University Press, 1992.

Silbergeld, Jerome. *Chinese Painting Style: Media, Methods, and Principles of Form*. Seattle: University of Washington Press, 1982.

Steinhardt, Nancy S., ed. *Chinese Architecture*. New Haven, Conn.: Yale University Press, 2002.

Sullivan, Michael. *Art and Artists of Twentieth-Century China*. Berkeley: University of California Press, 1996.

———. *The Arts of China*. 5th ed. Berkeley: University of California Press, 2009.

Thorp, Robert L. *Son of Heaven: Imperial Arts of China*. Seattle: Son of Heaven, 1988.

Thorp, Robert L., and Richard Ellis Vinograd. *Chinese Art and Culture*. New York: Abrams, 2001.

Vainker, S. J. *Chinese Pottery and Porcelain: From Prehistory to the Present*. London: Braziller, 1991.

Watson, William. *The Arts of China 900–1260*. New Haven, Conn.: Yale University Press, 2000.

———. *The Arts of China after 1260*. New Haven, Conn.: Yale University Press, 2007.

Watt, James C. Y., ed. *The World of Khubiliai Khan: Chinese Art in the Yuan Dynasty*. New York: Metropolitan Museum of Art, 2010.

Weidner, Marsha, ed. *Flowering in the Shadows: Women in the History of Chinese and Japanese Painting*. Honolulu: University of Hawaii Press, 1990.

———. *Views from Jade Terrace: Chinese Women Artists 1300–1912*. Indianapolis: Indianapolis Museum of Art, 1988.

Xin, Yang, Nie Chongzheng, Lang Shaojun, Richard M. Barnhart, James Cahill, and Wu Hung. *Three Thousand Years of Chinese Painting*. New Haven, Conn.: Yale University Press, 1997.

Zheng, Xinmiao, Hongxing Zhang, Jingjing Shao, Guang Guo, Bo Zhang, Peng Jiang, and Lin Li. *Masterpieces of Classical Chinese Painting*. New York: Abbeville, 2011.

Zhiyan, Li, Virginia L. Bower, and He Li. *Chinese Ceramics: From the Paleolithic Period through the Qing Dyansty*. New Haven, Conn.: Yale University Press, 2010.

Zhongshi, Ouyang, Wen C. Fong, et al. *Chinese Calligraphy*. New Haven, Conn.: Yale University Press, 2008.

CHAPTER 34
Japan, 1333 to 1980

Addiss, Stephen. *The Art of Zen.* New York: Abrams, 1989.

Addiss, Stephen, Gerald Groemer, and J. Thomas Rimer, eds. *Traditional Japanese Arts and Culture: An Illustrated Sourcebook.* Honolulu: University of Hawaii Press, 2006.

Baekeland, Frederick. *Imperial Japan: The Art of the Meiji Era (1868–1912).* Ithaca, N.Y.: Herbert F. Johnson Museum of Art, 1980.

Brown, Kendall. *The Politics of Reclusion: Painting and Power in Muromachi Japan.* Honolulu: University of Hawaii Press, 1997.

Cahill, James. *Scholar Painters of Japan.* New York: Asia Society, 1972.

Calza, Gian Carlo. *Ukiyo-e.* New York: Phaidon, 2005.

Coaldrake, William H. *Architecture and Authority in Japan.* London: Routledge, 1996.

Fontein, Jan, and Money L. Hickman. *Zen Painting and Calligraphy.* Greenwich, Conn.: New York Graphic Society, 1970.

Guth, Christine. *Art of Edo Japan: The Artist and the City, 1615–1868.* New Haven, Conn.: Yale University Press, 1996.

Hickman, Money L., John T. Carpenter, Bruce A. Coats, Christine Guth, Andrew J. Pekarik, John M. Rosenfield, and Nicole C. Rousmaniere. *Japan's Golden Age: Momoyama.* New Haven, Conn.: Yale University Press, 1996.

Kawakita, Michiaki. *Modern Currents in Japanese Art.* Translated by Charles E. Terry. New York: Weather-hill, 1974.

Kidder, J. Edward, Jr. *The Art of Japan.* New York: Park Lane, 1985.

Lane, Richard. *Images from the Floating World: The Japanese Print.* New York: Dorset, 1978.

Lippit, Yukio. *Painting of the Realm: The Kano House of Painters in Seventeenth-Century Japan.* Seattle: University of Washington Press, 2012.

Marks, Andreas. *Japanese Woodblock Prints: Artists, Publishers, and Masterworks: 1680–1900.* North Clarendon, Vt.: Tuttle, 2010.

Mason, Penelope. *History of Japanese Art.* 2d ed. New York: Abrams, 2004.

Meech, Julia, and Jane Oliver. *Designed for Pleasure: The World of Edo Japan in Prints and Drawings, 1680–1860.* Seattle: University of Washington Press, 2008.

Munroe, Alexandra. *Japanese Art after 1945: Scream against the Sky.* New York: Abrams, 1994.

Nishi, Kazuo, and Kazuo Hozumi. *What Is Japanese Architecture?* Translated by H. Mack Horton. New York: Kodansha International, 1985.

Ohki, Sadak. *Tea Culture of Japan.* New Haven, Conn.: Yale University Press, 2009.

Paine, Robert Treat, and Alexander Soper. *The Art and Architecture of Japan.* 3d ed. New Haven, Conn.: Yale University Press, 1992.

Phillips, Quitman E. *The Practices of Painting in Japan, 1475–1500.* Stanford, Calif.: Stanford University Press, 2000.

Sadao, Tsnukeo S., and Stephanie Wada. *Discovering the Arts of Japan: A Historical Overview.* New York: Abbeville, 2010.

Sanford, James H., William R. LaFleur, and Masatoshi Nagatomi. *Flowing Traces: Buddhism in the Literary and Visual Arts of Japan.* Princeton, N.J.: Princeton University Press, 1992.

Shimizu, Yoshiaki, ed. *Japan: The Shaping of Daimyo Culture, 1185–1868.* Washington, D.C.: National Gallery of Art, 1988.

Singer, Robert T. *Edo: Art in Japan 1615–1868.* Washington, D.C.: National Gallery of Art, 1998.

Stanley-Baker, Joan. *Japanese Art.* Rev. ed. New York: Thames & Hudson, 2000.

Stewart, David B. *The Making of a Modern Japanese Architecture, 1868 to the Present.* New York: Kodansha International, 1988.

Tiampo, Ming. *Gutai: Decentering Modernism.* Chicago: University of Chicago Press, 2011.

CHAPTER 35
Native American Cultures, 1300 to 1980

Bawden, Garth. *Moche.* Oxford: Blackwell, 1999.

Berlo, Janet Catherine, ed. *Plains Indian Drawings 1865–1935.* New York: Abrams, 1996.

Berlo, Janet Catherine, and Ruth B. Phillips. *Native North American Art.* New York: Oxford University Press, 1998.

Boone, Elizabeth. *The Aztec World.* Washington, D.C.: Smithsonian Institution Press, 1994.

Bruhns, Karen O. *Ancient South America.* New York: Cambridge University Press, 1994.

Burger, Richard L., and Lucy C. Salaza, eds. *Machu Picchu: Unveiling the Mystery of the Incas.* New Haven, Conn.: Yale University Press, 2004.

Coe, Michael D. *The Maya.* 7th ed. New York: Thames & Hudson, 2011.

Coe, Michael D., and Rex Koontz. *Mexico: From the Olmecs to the Aztecs.* 7th ed. New York: Thames & Hudson, 2013.

D'Altroy, Terence N. *The Incas.* New ed. Oxford: Blackwell, 2003.

Davies, Nigel. *The Ancient Kingdoms of Peru.* New York: Penguin, 1997.

Feest, Christian F. *Native Arts of North America.* 2d ed. New York: Thames & Hudson, 1992.

Fienup-Riordan, Ann. *The Living Tradition of Yup'ik Masks.* Seattle: University of Washington Press, 1996.

Fitzhugh, William W., and Aron Crowell, eds. *Crossroads of Continents: Cultures of Siberia and Alaska.* Washington, D.C.: Smithsonian Institution Press, 1988.

Gasparini, Graziano, and Luise Margolies. *Inca Architecture.* Bloomington: Indiana University Press, 1980.

Hill, Tom, and Richard W. Hill, Sr., eds. *Creation's Journey: Native American Identity and Belief.* Washington, D.C.: Smithsonian Institution Press, 1994.

Jonaitis, Aldona. *Art of the Northwest Coast.* Seattle: University of Washington Press, 2006.

Kolata, Alan L. *Ancient Inca.* New York: Cambridge University Press, 2013.

Kubler, George. *The Art and Architecture of Ancient America: The Mexican, Maya, and Andean Peoples.* 3d ed. New Haven, Conn.: Yale University Press, 1992.

Malpass, Michael A. *Daily Life in the Inca Empire.* Westport, Conn.: Greenwood, 1996.

Mathews, Zena, and Aldona Jonaitis, eds. *Native North American Art History.* Palo Alto, Calif.: Peek, 1982.

Matos, Eduardo M. *The Great Temple of the Aztecs: Treasures of Tenochtitlan.* New York: Thames & Hudson, 1988.

Maurer, Evan M. *Visions of the People: A Pictorial History of Plains Indian Life.* Seattle: University of Washington Press, 1992.

McEwan, Gordon F. *The Incas: New Perspectives.* Santa Barbara, Calif.: ABC-CLIO, 2006.

Miller, Mary Ellen. *The Art of Mesoamerica, from Olmec to Aztec.* 5th ed. New York: Thames & Hudson, 2012.

Miller, Mary, and Karl Taube. *An Illustrated Dictionary of the Gods and Symbols of Ancient Mexico and the Maya.* New York: Thames & Hudson, 1993.

Minelli, Laura Laurencich. *The Inca World.* Norman: University of Oklahoma Press, 2000.

Morris, Craig, and Adriana von Hagen. *The Incas.* New York: Thames & Hudson, 2011.

———. *The Inka Empire and Its Andean Origins.* New York: Abbeville, 1993.

Moseley, Michael E. *The Incas and Their Ancestors: The Archaeology of Peru.* Rev. ed. New York: Thames & Hudson, 2001.

Nabokov, Peter, and Robert Easton. *Native American Architecture.* New York: Oxford University Press, 1989.

Pasztory, Esther. *Aztec Art.* New York: Abrams, 1983.

———. *Pre-Columbian Art.* New York: Cambridge University Press, 1998.

Penney, David W. *North American Indian Art.* New York: Thames & Hudson, 2004.

Phillips, Ruth B. *Trading Identities: The Souvenir in Native North American Art.* Seattle: University of Washington Press, 1998.

Samuel, Cheryl. *The Chilkat Dancing Blanket.* Norman: University of Oklahoma Press, 1982.

Schaafsma, Polly, ed. *Kachinas in the Pueblo World.* Albuquerque: University of New Mexico Press, 1994.

Silverman, Helaine. *The Nasca.* Oxford: Blackwell, 2002.

———, ed. *Andean Archaeology.* Oxford: Blackwell, 2004.

Smith, Michael Ernest. *The Aztecs.* 2d ed. Oxford: Blackwell, 2003.

Stewart, Hilary. *Looking at Totem Poles.* Seattle: University of Washington Press, 1993.

Stone, Rebecca R. *Art of the Andes from Chavín to Inca.* 3d ed. New York: Thames & Hudson, 2012.

Townsend, Richard F. *The Aztecs.* 2d ed. New York: Thames & Hudson, 2000.

Von Hagen, Adriana, and Craig Morris. *The Cities of the Ancient Andes.* New York: Thames & Hudson, 1998.

Wardwell, Allen. *Tangible Visions: Northwest Coast Indian Shamanism and Its Art.* New York: Monacelli, 1996.

Washburn, Dorothy. *Living in Balance: The Universe of the Hopi, Zuni, Navajo, and Apache.* Philadelphia: University Museum, 1995.

Weaver, Muriel Porter. *The Aztecs, Mayas, and Their Predecessors.* 3d ed. San Diego: Academic, 1993.

Wright, Robin K. *Northern Haida Master Carvers.* Seattle: University of Washington Press, 2001.

Wyman, Leland C. *Southwest Indian Drypainting.* Albuquerque: University of New Mexico Press, 1983.

CHAPTER 36
Oceania before 1980

Brunt, Peter, and Nicholas Thomas, eds. *Art in Oceania: A New History*. New Haven, Conn.: Yale University Press, 2012.

Caruana, Wally. *Aboriginal Art*. 2d ed. New York: Thames & Hudson, 2003.

Cox, J. Halley, and William H. Davenport. *Hawaiian Sculpture*. Rev. ed. Honolulu: University of Hawaii Press, 1988.

D'Alleva, Anne. *Arts of the Pacific Islands*. New York: Abrams, 1998.

Ellis, Juniper. *Tattooing the World. Pacific Designs in Print & Skin*. New York: Columbia University Press, 2008.

Feldman, Jerome, and Donald H. Rubinstein. *The Art of Micronesia*. Honolulu: University of Hawaii Art Gallery, 1986.

Greub, Suzanne, ed. *Authority and Ornament: Art of the Sepik River, Papua New Guinea*. Basel: Tribal Art Centre, 1985.

Hanson, Allan, and Louise Hanson, eds. *Art and Identity in Oceania*. Honolulu: University of Hawaii Press, 1990.

Kaeppler, Adrienne L. *The Pacific Arts of Polynesia & Micronesia*. New York: Oxford University Press, 2008.

Kaeppler, Adrienne L., Christian Kaufmann, and Douglas Newton. *Oceanic Art*. New York: Abrams, 1997.

Kjellgren, Eric. *Oceania: Art of the Pacific Islands in the Metropolitan Museum of Art*. New York: Metropolitan Museum of Art, 2007.

Kjellgren, Eric, and Carol Ivory. *Adorning the World: Art of the Marquesas Islands*. New York: Metropolitan Museum of Art, 2005.

Kooijman, Simon. *Tapa in Polynesia*. Honolulu: Bishop Museum Press, 1972.

Lilley, Ian, ed. *Archaeology of Oceania: Australia and the Pacific Islands*. Malden, Mass: Blackwell, 2006.

Mead, Sidney Moko, ed. *Te Maori: Maori Art from New Zealand Collections*. New York: Abrams in association with the American Federation of Arts, 1984.

Morphy, Howard. *Aboriginal Art*. London: Phaidon, 1998.

Rainbird, Paul. *The Archaeology of Micronesia*. New York: Cambridge University Press, 2004.

Sayers, Andrew. *Australian Art*. New York: Oxford University Press, 2001.

Schneebaum, Tobias. *Embodied Spirits: Ritual Carvings of the Asmat*. Salem, Mass.: Peabody Museum of Salem, 1990.

Smidt, Dirk, ed. *Asmat Art: Woodcarvings of Southwest New Guinea*. New York: Braziller in association with Rijksmuseum voor Volkenkunde, Leiden, 1993.

Starzecka, Dorota, ed. *Maori Art and Culture*. Chicago: Art Media Resources, 1996.

Sutton, Peter, ed. *Dreamings: The Art of Aboriginal Australia*. New York: Braziller in association with the Asia Society Galleries, 1988.

Thomas, Nicholas. *Oceanic Art*. London: Thames & Hudson, 1995.

CHAPTER 37
Africa, 1800 to 1980

Abiodun, Roland, Henry J. Drewal, and John Pemberton III, eds. *The Yoruba Artist: New Theoretical Perspectives on African Arts*. Washington, D.C.: Smithsonian Institution Press, 1994.

Bassani, Ezio. *Arts of Africa: 7,000 Years of African Art*. Milan: Skira, 2005.

Binkley, David A., and Patricia Darish. *Kuba*. Milan: 5 Continents, 2009.

Blier, Suzanne P. *The Royal Arts of Africa*. New York: Abrams, 1998.

Boyer, Alain-Michel. *Baule*. Milan: 5 Continents, 2007.

Cole, Herbert M. *Icons: Ideals and Power in the Art of Africa*. Washington, D.C.: National Museum of African Art, Smithsonian Institution, 1989.

——. *Igbo*. Milan: 5 Continents, 2013.

——, ed. *I Am Not Myself: The Art of African Masquerade*. Los Angeles: UCLA Fowler Museum of Cultural History, 1985.

Cole, Herbert M., and Chike C. Aniakor. *Igbo Art: Community and Cosmos*. Los Angeles: UCLA Fowler Museum of Cultural History, 1984.

Fraser, Douglas F., and Herbert M. Cole, eds. *African Art and Leadership*. Madison: University of Wisconsin Press, 1972.

Geary, Christraud M. *Bamum*. Milan: 5 Continents, 2011.

——. *Things of the Palace: A Catalogue of the Bamum Palace Museum in Foumban (Cameroon)*. Weisbaden: Franz Steiner Verlag, 1983.

Glaze, Anita J. *Art and Death in a Senufo Village*. Bloomington: Indiana University Press, 1981.

Kasfir, Sidney L. *Contemporary African Art*. London: Thames & Hudson, 1999.

——. *West African Masks and Cultural Systems*. Tervuren: Musée Royal de l'Afrique Centrale, 1988.

LaGamma, Alisa. *Eternal Ancestors: The Art of the Central African Reliquary*. New York: Metropolitan Museum of Art, 2007.

——. *Heroic Africans: Legendary Leaders, Iconic Sculptures*. New York: Metropolitan Museum of Art, 2011.

Lawal, Babatunde, and Constantine Petridis. *Yoruba*. Milan: 5 Continents, 2012.

Magnin, Andre, with Jacques Soulillou. *Contemporary Art of Africa*. New York: Abrams, 1996.

Meyer, Laure. *African Forms: Art and Ritual*. New York: Assouline, 2001.

Nooter, Mary H. *Secrecy: African Art That Conceals and Reveals*. New York: Museum for African Art, 1993.

Oguibe, Olu, and Okwui Enwezor, eds. *Reading the Contemporary: African Art from Theory to the Marketplace*. London: Institute of International Visual Arts, 1999.

Perani, Judith, and Fred T. Smith. *The Visual Arts of Africa: Gender, Power, and Life Cycle Rituals*. Upper Saddle River, N.J.: Prentice Hall, 1998.

Perrois, Louis. *Fang*. Milan: 5 Continents, 2006.

——. *Kota*. Milan: 5 Continents, 2012.

Phillips, Ruth B. *Representing Women: Sande Masquerades of the Mende of Sierra Leone*. Los Angeles: UCLA Fowler Museum of Cultural History, 1995.

Plankensteiner, Barbara. *Benin*. Milan: 5 Continents, 2010.

——, ed. *Benin Kings and Rituals: Court Arts from Nigeria*. Antwerp: Snoeck, 2007.

Sieber, Roy, and Roslyn A. Walker. *African Art in the Cycle of Life*. Washington, D.C.: Smithsonian Institution Press, 1987.

Stepan, Peter. *Spirits Speak: A Celebration of African Masks*. Munich: Prestel, 2005.

Thompson, Robert F., and Joseph Cornet. *The Four Moments of the Sun: Kongo Art in Two Worlds*. Washington, D.C.: National Gallery of Art, 1981.

Vinnicombe, Patricia. *People of the Eland: Rock Paintings of the Drakensberg Bushmen as a Reflection of Their Life and Thought*. Pietermaritzburg: University of Natal Press, 1976.

Visonà, Monica B., ed. *A History of Art in Africa*. 2d ed. Englewood Cliffs, N.J.: Prentice Hall, 2007.

Vogel, Susan M. *Baule: African Art, Western Eyes*. New Haven, Conn.: Yale University Press, 1997.

——, ed. *Africa Explores: Twentieth-Century African Art*. New York: Te Neues, 1990.

Walker, Roslyn A. *Olowe of Ise: A Yoruba Sculptor to Kings*. Washington, D.C.: National Museum of African Art, 1998.

Wastiau, Boris. *Chokwe*. Milan: 5 Continents, 2008.

Credits

NOTE: *All references in the following credits are to figure numbers unless otherwise indicated.*

Before 1300—p. xxi: John Burge/Cengage Learning; **p. xxiii:** (t) © 2008 Fred S. Kleiner, (bl) © 2013 Fred S. Kleiner, (br) © 2011 Fred S. Kleiner; **p. xxiv:** John Burge/Cengage Learning; **p. xxv:** (tl) Jonathan Poore/Cengage Learning, (tr) Scala/Art Resource, NY, (bl) Jonathan Poore/Cengage Learning, (br) Copyright Photo Henri Stierlin, Geneve; **p. xxvi:** (l) John Burge/Cengage Learning, (r) Jonathan Poore/Cengage Learning; **p. xxvii:** (tl) John Burge/Cengage Learning, (tr) Jonathan Poore/Cengage Learning, (bl) John Burge/Cengage Learning, (br) Jonathan Poore/Cengage Learning; **p. xxviii:** (tl) David Pearson/Alamy, (tr) Alinari/Art Resource, (b) John Burge/Cengage Learning; **p. xxix:** (l) Royal Ontario Museum, (cl) The Art Archive/Olympia Museum Greece/Gianni Dagli Orti/Picture Desk, (cr) Scala/Art Resource, NY, (r) Scala/Art Resource, NY; **p. xxx:** (l) The Metropolitan Museum of Art, The Cloisters Collection, 1954 (54.1.2). Image © The Metropolitan Museum (r) Scala/Art Resource, NY; **p. xxxi:** (l) The Trustees of The British Museum/Art Resource, NY, (r) Firenze, Biblioteca Medicea Laurenziana, Ms. Laur. Plut. 1.56, c. 13v; **p. xxxii:** (l) akg-images/Bildarchiv Monheim (r) Scala/Art Resource, NY; **p. xxxiii:** (l) Giraudon/Art Resource, NY, (r) Scala/Art Resource, NY; **p. xxxiv:** Freer Gallery of Art, Smithsonian Institution, Washington, DC. Purchase, F1949.9a-d; **p. xxxv:** (l) © Dinodia/AGE Fotostock.com, (r) Saskia Ltd.

Introduction—Opener: National Gallery, London/Art Resource, NY; **I-2:** Hirshhorn Museum and Culture Garden, Smithsonian Institution, Washington, DC, Joseph H. Hirshhorn Purchase Fund, 1992 © City and county of Denver, courtesy the Clyfford Still Museum. Photo: akg images; **I-3:** Interior view of the choir, begun after 1284 (photo), French School, (13th century)/Beauvais Cathedral, Beauvais, France/© Paul Maeyaert/The Bridgeman Art Library; **I-4:** akg-images/Rabatti-Dominigie; **I-5:** National Gallery of Art, Alfred Stieglitz Collection, Bequest of Georgia O'Keeffe 1987.58.3; **I-6:** Art © Estate of Ben Shahn/Licensed by VAGA, New York, NY. Photo: Whitney Museum of American Art, New York (gift of Edith and Milton Lowenthal in memory of Juliana Force); **I-7:** © Jonathan Poore/Cengage Learning; **I-8:** akg-images; **I-9:** The Metropolitan Museum of Art/Art Resource, NY; **I-10:** Courtesy Saskia Ltd., © Dr. Ron Wiedenhoeft; **I-11:** © 2011 The Josef and Anni Albers Foundation/Artists Rights Society (ARS), New York. Photo: © Whitney Museum of American Art; **I-12:** Photograph © 2011 Museum of Fine Arts, Boston. 11.4584; **I-13:** bpk, Berlin/Staatsgemaeldesammlungen, Munich, Germany/Art Resource, NY; **I-14:** Jürgen Liepe, Berlin; **I-15:** The Trustees of the British Museum/Art Resource, NY; **I-16:** Nimatallah/Art Resource, NY; **I-17:** Scala/Art Resource, NY; **I-18:** Cengage Learning; **I-19 left:** Portrait of Te Pehi Kupe wearing European clothes, c.1826 (w/c), Sylvester, John (fl.1826)/© National Library of Australia, Canberra, Australia/The Bridgeman Art Library; **I-19 right:** Public Domain.

Chapter 14—Opener: Scala/Art Resource, NY; **14-2:** © Jonathan Poore/Cengage Learning; **14-3:** © Jonathan Poore/Cengage Learning; **14-4:** © Jonathan Poore/Cengage Learning; **14-5:** Scala/Art Resource, NY; **14-5A:** Alinari/Art Resource, NY; **14-5B:** Photo by Ralph Lieberman; **14-5C:** Erich Lessing/Art Resource, NY; **14-6:** Scala/Ministero per i Beni e le Attività culturali/Art Resource, NY; **14-7:** Art Resource/The Art Archive; **14-8:** Summerfield Press/Corbis/Art Corbis/Corbis; **14-9:** Scala/Art Resource, NY; **14-9A:** akg images; **14-9B:** Alinari/Art Resource, NY; **14-10:** Scala/Art Resource, NY; **14-11:** Scala/Art Resource, NY; **14-11A:** Scala/Art Resource, NY; **14-12:** Scala/Art Resource, NY; **14-13:** © Jonathan Poore/Cengage Learning; **14-13A:** © Jonathan Poore/Cengage Learning; **14-14:** Canali Photobank; **14-15:** Scala/Art Resource, NY; **14-16:** © Jonathan Poore/Cengage Learning; **14-16A:** Scala/Art Resource, NY; **14-17:** Scala/Art Resource, NY; **14-18:** Scala/Art Resource, NY; **14-19:** Alinari/Art Resource, NY; **14-19A:** Scala/Art Resource, NY; **14-19B:** © Jonathan Poore/Cengage Learning; **14-20:** South Door of the Baptistry of San Giovanni, 1336 (bronze), Pisano, Andrea (1270–1349)/Baptistery, Florence, Italy/The Bridgeman Art Library; **14-2A:** Scala/Art Resource, NY; **14-21:** © Jonathan Poore/Cengage Learning; **14-22:** © Jonathan Poore/Cengage Learning; **14-23:** © Fred S. Kleiner, 2012.

Chapter 20—Opener: Photograph © 2011 Museum of Fine Arts, Boston. 93.153; **20-1a:** Photograph © 2011 Museum of Fine Arts, Boston. 93.153; **20-1b:** Photograph © 2011 Museum of Fine Arts, Boston. 93.153; **20-1c:** Photograph © 2011 Museum of Fine Arts, Boston. 93.153; **20-2:** Erich Lessing/Art Resource, NY; **20-2A:** © Jonathan Poore/Cengage Learning; **20-3:** Erich Lessing/Art Resource, NY; **20-4:** Image copyright © The Metropolitan Museum of Art. Image source: Art Resource, NY; **20-5:** Scala/Art Resource, NY; **20-6:** Erich Lessing/Art Resource, NY; **20-6A:** Bildarchiv Preussischer Kulturbesitz/Art Resource, NY; **20-7:** Erich Lessing/Art Resource, NY; **20-8:** © National Gallery, London/Art Resource, NY; **20-8A:** Copyright © 1999 Board of Trustees, National Gallery of Art, Washington, DC; **20-9:** Erich Lessing/Art Resource, NY; **20-9A:** © Jonathan Poore/Cengage Learning; **20-10:** Image copyright © The Metropolitan Museum of Art. Image source: Art Resource, NY; **20-11:** The Art Archive/St Peters Church Louvain/Picture Desk; **20-11A:** Giraudon/Art Resource, NY; **20-11B:** Scala/Art Resource, NY; **20-12:** Scala/Art Resource, NY; **20-13:** Erich Lessing/Art Resource, NY; **20-14:** Erich Lessing/Art Resource, NY; **20-14A:** Image copyright © The Metropolitan Museum of Art/Art Resource, NY; **20-15:** Musée Condé/Grand Palais/Art Resource, NY; **20-16:** Musée Condé/Grand Palais/Art Resource, NY; **20-17:** The Art Archive/Osterreichisches National Bibliothek Vienna/Eileen Tweedy/Picture Desk; **20-18:** bpk, Berlin/Gemaeldegalerie, Staatliche Museen/Art Resource, NY; **20-19:** Musée d'Art et d'Histoire, Geneva; **20-19A:** Erich Lessing/Art Resource, NY; **20-20:** Erich Lessing/Art Resource, NY; **20-21:** AKG Images; **20-21A:** Buxheim Saint Christopher, 1423. Hand-colored woodcut, 11 3/8" × 8 1/8". John Rylands University Library, University of Manchester, Manchester; **20-22:** Historical Picture Archive/CORBIS; **20-23:** Scala/Art Resource, NY.

Chapter 21—Opener: Summerfield Press Ltd.; **21-2:** Erich Lessing/Art Resource, NY; **21-3:** Erich Lessing/Art Resource, NY; **21-4:** © Jonathan Poore/Cengage Learning; **21-5:** © Jonathan Poore/Cengage Learning; **21-6:** © Jonathan Poore/Cengage Learning; **21-7:** © Jonathan Poore/Cengage Learning; **21-8:** © Jonathan Poore/Cengage Learning; **21-9:** © Jonathan Poore/Cengage Learning; **21-10:** Scala/Art Resource, NY; **21-11:** Erich Lessing/Art Resource; **21-11A:** akg-images/Rabatti-Domingie; **21-12:** Erich Lessing/Art Resource, NY; **21-13:** Scala/Art Resource, NY; **21-14:** © Jonathan Poore/Cengage Learning; **21-15:** © 2013 Fred S. Kleiner; **21-16:** © 2010 Fred Kleiner; **21-17:** Erich Lessing/Art Resource, NY; **21-18:** Scala/Art Resource, NY; **21-19:** Canali Photobank, Italy; **21-20:** Erich Lessing/Art Resource, NY; **21-21:** Canali Photobank, Italy; **21-22:** Scala/Art Resource, NY; **21-23:** National Gallery, London/Art Resource, NY; **21-24:** Canali Photobank, Italy; **21-25:** Scala/Art Resource, NY; **21-25A:** Nicolo Orsi Battaglini/Art Resource, NY; **21-26:** Scala/Art Resource; **21-27:** Giovanna Tornabuoni, nee Albizzi, 1488, detail (oil on panel), Ghirlandaio, Domenico (Domenico Bigordi) (1449–94)/Thyssen-Bornemisza Collection, Madrid, Spain/The Bridgeman Art Library; **21-28:** Scala/Art Resource, NY; **21-28A:** Rabatti-Domingie/Galleria degli Uffizi/akg-images; **21-29:** Image copyright © The Metropolitan Museum of Art/Art Resource, NY; **21-29A:** © Jonathan Poore/Cengage Learning; **21-29B:** © Jonathan Poore/Cengage Learning; **21-30:** © Jonathan Poore/Cengage Learning; **21-31:** View of the Nave, 1425–46 (photo), Brunelleschi, Filippo (1377–1446)/San Lorenzo, Florence, Italy/The Bridgeman Art Library; **21-31A:** Alinari/Art Resource, NY; **21-31B:** Cengage Learning; **21-32:** © Jonathan Poore/Cengage Learning; **21-33:** Cengage Learning; **21-34:** © Jonathan Poore/Cengage Learning; **21-34A:** © Jonathan Poore/Cengage Learning; **21-35:** © Jonathan Poore/Cengage Learning; **21-36:** © Jonathan Poore/Cengage Learning; **21-36A:** © Jonathan Poore/Cengage Learning; **21-37:** © Jonathan Poore/Cengage Learning; **21-38:** © 2010 Fred Kleiner; **21-39:** Cameraphoto Arte, Venice/Art Resource, NY; **21-40:** © The Frick Collection, NY. 1915.1.03; **21-4A:** Scala/Art Resource, Inc.; **21-41:** Scala/Art Resource, Inc.; **21-42:** Scala/Art Resource, NY; **21-43:** Scala/Ministero per i Beni e le Attività culturali/Art Resource, NY; **21-44:** Scala/Art Resource, NY; **21-44A:** Scala/Ministero per i Beni e le Attività culturali/Art Resource, NY; **21-45:** Alinari/Art Resource, NY; **21-46:** Cengage Learning; **21-47:** Canali Photobank, Italy; **21-48:** Scala/Art Resource, NY; **21-49:** Scala/Art Resource, NY; **21-49A bottom:** © Jonathan Poore/Cengage Learning; **21-49A top:** St. James the Great on his Way to Execution (fresco) (b/w photo) (detail), Mantegna, Andrea (1431–1506)/Ovetari Chapel, Eremitani Church, Padua, Italy/Alinari/The Bridgeman Art Library; **21-50:** Erich Lessing/Art Resource, NY.

Chapter 22—Opener: Canali Photobank; **22-1a:** © Bracchietti-Zigrosi/Vatican Museums; **22-1b:** Vatican Museums and Galleries, Vatican City, Italy/The Bridgeman Art Library International; **22-1c:** akg-images/Electa; **22-2:** Erich Lessing/Art Resource, NY; **22-3:** The Art Archive/National Gallery London/Eileen Tweedy/Picture Desk; **22-4:** Alinari/Art Resource, NY; **22-5:** RMN-Grand Palais/Art

Resource, NY; **22-5A:** Scala/Art Resource, NY; **22-6:** The Royal Collection © 2011 Her Majesty Queen Elizabeth II; **22-6A:** Réunion des Musées Nationaux/Art Resource, NY; **22-7:** Erich Lessing/Art Resource, NY; **22-8:** Erich Lessing/Art Resource, NY; **22-8A:** Scala/Art Resource, NY; **22-9:** © M. Sarri 1983/Photo Vatican Museums; **22-10:** Scala/Ministero per i Beni e le Attività culturali/Art Resource, NY; **22-10A:** Erich Lessing/Art Resource, NY; **22-11:** Scala/Art Resource, NY; **22-12:** Araldo de Luca/CORBIS; **22-13:** Arte & Immagini srl/CORBIS; **22-14:** Scala/Art Resource, NY; **22-15:** Scala/Art Resource, NY; **22-16:** Scala/Art Resource, NY; **22-17:** Photo Vatican Museums; **22-18:** © Bracchietti-Zigrosi/Vatican Museums; **22-18A:** Vatican Museums and Galleries, Vatican City, Italy/The Bridgeman Art Library International; **22-18B:** Sistine Chapel Ceiling: Libyan Sibyl, c. 1508–10 (fresco), Buonarroti, Michelangelo (1475–1564)/Vatican Museums and Galleries, Vatican City/Alinari/Bridgeman Images; **22-19:** akg-images/Electa; **22-20:** Erich Lessing/Art Resource, NY; **22-21:** © Jonathan Poore/Cengage Learning; **22-22:** Cengage Learning; **22-23:** © The Trustees of the British Museum/Art Resource, NY; **22-23A:** Tips Images/SuperStock; **22-24:** Cengage Learning; **22-25:** Tips Images/SuperStock; **22-26:** © Jonathan Poore/Cengage Learning; **22-27:** Alinari Archives/CORBIS; **22-28:** Marka/SuperStock; **22-29:** Cengage Learning; **22-30:** © 2010 Fred S. Kleiner; **22-31:** L.Hammel/A.van der Voort/akg-images; **22-31A:** Scala/Art Resource, NY; **22-32:** Scala/Art Resource, NY; **22-33:** © 1999 Board of Trustees, National Gallery of Art, Washington, DC; **22-34:** Cameraphoto Arte, Venice/Art Resource, NY; **22-35:** Erich Lessing/Art Resource, NY; **22-36:** Scala/Art Resource, NY; **22-37:** Scala/Art Resource, NY; **22-38:** Erich Lessing/Art Resource, NY; **22-39:** Scala/Ministero per i Beni e le Attività culturali/Art Resource, NY; **22-40:** Erich Lessing/Art Resource, NY; **22-4A:** Lavinia Fontana (Italian, 1552–1614) Portrait of a Noblewoman ca. 1580 Oil on canvas, 45 1/4 × 35 1/4 in. Gift of Wallace and Wilhelmina Holladay. National Museum of Women in the Arts; **22-41:** Scala/Art Resource, NY; **22-42:** Scala/Art Resource, NY; **22-42A:** The Art Archive/Pinacoteca Nazionale di Siena/Alfredo Dagli Orti/Picture Desk; **22-43:** Erich Lessing/Art Resource, NY; **22-44:** Scala/Ministero per i Beni e le Attività culturali/Art Resource, NY; **22-45:** National Gallery, London/Art Resource, NY; **22-46:** Portrait of Eleanor of Toledo and her Son, Giovanni de Medici, c. 1544–45 (tempera on panel), Bronzino, Agnolo (1503–72)/Galleria degli Uffizi, Florence, Italy/The Bridgeman Art Library; **22-46A:** Image copyright © The Metropolitan Museum of Art/Art Resource, NY; **22-47:** The Bridgeman Art Library International; **22-48:** Scala/Art Resource, NY; **22-49:** Scala/Art Resource, NY; **22-50:** Canali Photobank, Italy; **22-51:** Alinari/Art Resource, NY; **22-52:** Erich Lessing/Art Resource, NY; **22-52A:** The Nymph of Fontainebleau, 1542 (bronze), Cellini, Benvenuto (1500–71)/Louvre, Paris, France/Lauros/Giraudon/The Bridgeman Art Library; **22-53:** © 2006 Fred S. Kleiner; **22-54:** SuperStock/SuperStock; **22-55:** Scala/Art Resource, NY; **22-56:** © Jonathan Poore/Cengage Learning; **22-57:** © Jonathan Poore/Cengage Learning; **22-58:** Cengage Learning.

Chapter 23—Opener: V&A Images, London/Art Resource, NY; **23-1a:** The Metropolitan Museum of Art. Image source: Art Resource, NY; **23-1b:** The Metropolitan Museum of Art. Image source: Art Resource, NY; **23-1c:** Foto Marburg/Art Resource, NY; **23-2a and b:** O. Zimmermann/Musée d'Unterlinden, Colmar; **23-3:** akg-images; **23-3A:** The Great Piece of Turf, 1503 (bodycolours, heightened with opaque white on vellum), Dürer or Duerer, Albrecht (1471–1528)/Graphische Sammlung Albertina, Vienna, Austria/Giraudon/The Bridgeman Art Library; **23-4:** Photograph © 2011 Museum of Fine Arts, Boston. 68.187; **23-4A:** The Trustees of The British Museum/Art Resource, NY; **23-5:** Bildarchiv Preussischer Kulturbesitz/Art Resource, NY; **23-6:** The British Museum; **23-7:** LUCAS CRANACH THE ELDER, Judgment of Paris, 1530. Oil on wood, 1' 1-1/2" × 9-1/2". Staatliche Kunsthalle, Karlsruhe. **23-8:** The Trustees of the British Museum/Art Resource, NY; **23-9:** Erich Lessing/Art Resource, NY; **23-10:** Bildarchiv Preussischer Kulturbesitz/Art Resource, NY; **23-11:** Heritage Image Partnership Ltd/Alamy; **23-11A:** Scala/Art Resource, NY; **23-12:** The Garden of Earthly Delights, c. 1500 (oil on panel), Bosch, Hieronymus (c. 1450–1516)/Prado, Madrid, Spain/The Bridgeman Art Library; **23-13:** RMN-Grand Palais/Art Resource, NY; **23-14:** Bildarchiv Preussischer Kulturbesitz/Art Resource, NY; **23-14A:** Erich Lessing/Art Resource, NY; **23-15:** Uppsala University Art Collection; **23-16:** Oeffentliche Kunstsammlung Basel, photo Martin Bühler; **23-17:** The Royal Collection © 2011 Her Majesty Queen Elizabeth II; **23-18:** Erich Lessing/Art Resource, NY; **23-19:** bpk, Berlin/Gemaeldegalerie, Staatliche Museen/Joerg P. Anders/Art Resource, NY; **23-20:** Kunsthistorisches Museum, Vienna; **23-2A:** Scala/Art Resource, NY; **23-21:** RMN-Grand Palais/Art Resource, NY; **23-22:** © Jonathan Poore/Cengage Learning; **23-23:** © Jonathan Poore/Cengage Learning; **23-23A:** © 2009 Fred. S. Kleiner; **23-24A:** John Elk III; **23-25:** Adam Woolfitt/Robert Harding/Getty Images; **23-26:** Image copyright © The Metropolitan Museum of Art/Art Resource, NY; **23-27:** Scala/Art Resource, NY.

Chapter 24—Opener, 24-1a, 24-1b, 24-1c: Jonathan Poore/Cengage Learning; **24-2:** © Jonathan Poore/Cengage Learning; **24-3:** © Jonathan Poore/Cengage Learning; **24-4:** Alinari Archives/Corbis; **24-4A:** Canali Photobank, Italy; **24-5:** akg-images/Joseph Martin; **24-6:** Scala/Art Resource, NY; **24-6A:** Araldo de Luca/Corbis; **24-7:** akg-images/Pirozzi; **24-8:** Araldo de Luca; **24-9A:** Scala/Art Resource, NY; **24-9 left:** © Jonathan Poore/Cengage Learning; **24-9 right:** Vladimir Khirman/Alamy; **24-10:** © Jonathan Poore/Cengage Learning; **24-11:** © Jonathan Poore/Cengage Learning; **24-12:** © Jonathan Poore/Cengage Learning; **24-13:** Cengage Learning 2016; **24-14:** © Jonathan Poore/Cengage Learning; **24-14A:** Dome of the Chapel of the Holy Shroud, 1668–94 (photo), Guarini, Guarino (1624–83)/Turin Cathedral, Turin, Italy/Alinari/The Bridgeman Art Library; **24-15:** Alinari/Art Resource, NY; **24-16:** Scala/Art Resource, NY; **24-17:** Image copyright © The Metropolitan Museum of Art/Art Resource, NY; **24-18:** Scala/Art Resource, NY; **24-18A:** Scala/Art Resource, NY; **24-18B:** Scala/Art Resource, NY; **24-19:** Alinari/Art Resource, NY; **24-20:** The Royal Collection © 2011 Her Majesty Queen Elizabeth II; **24-21:** Nimatallah/Art Resource, NY; **24-22:** Glorification of the Reign of Pope Urban VIII (1568–1644) ceiling painting in the Great Hall, 1633–39 (fresco), Cortona, Pietro da (Berrettini) (1596–1669)/Palazzo Barberini, Rome, Italy/The Bridgeman Art Library; **24-23:** © Jonathan Poore/Cengage Learning; **24-24:** © Jonathan Poore/Cengage Learning; **24-25:** Erich Lessing/Art Resource, NY; **24-26:** Erich Lessing/Art Resource, NY; **24-27:** Wadsworth Atheneum Museum of Art/Art Resource, NY; **24-28:** Album/Art Resource, NY; **24-29:** Erich Lessing/Art Resource, NY; **24-29A:** Scala/Art Resource, NY; **24-30:** Scala/Art Resource, NY; **24-3A:** The Frick Collection, NY; **24-31:** Erich Lessing/Art Resource, NY; **24-32:** Erich Lessing/Art Resource, NY; **24-33:** Angelo Hornak/Alamy; **24-34:** © Beren Patterson/Alamy.

Chapter 25—Opener: Erich Lessing/Art Resource, NY; **25-1A:** Erich Lessing/Art Resource, NY; **25-2:** IRPA-KIK, Brussels, www.kikirpa.be; **25-2A:** Erich Lessing/Art Resource, NY; **25-3:** Scala/Art Resource, NY; **25-4:** Erich Lessing/Art Resource, NY; **25-5:** RMN-Grand Palais/Art Resource, NY; **25-6:** Scala/Art Resource, NY; **25-7:** Centraal Museum, Utrecht, photo Ernst Moritz, The Hague; **25-8:** Supper with the Minstrel and his Lute, c. 1617 (oil on canvas), Honthorst, Gerrit van (1590–1656)/Galleria degli Uffizi, Florence, Italy/Alinari/The Bridgeman Art Library; **25-9:** Universal Images Group/SuperStock; **25-10:** age fotostock/Alamy; **25-11:** National Gallery of Art; **25-12:** Erich Lessing/Art Resource, NY; **25-13:** The Nightwatch, c. 1642 (oil on canvas), Rembrandt Harmenszoon van Rijn (1606–69)/Rijksmuseum, Amsterdam, The Netherlands/Artothek/The Bridgeman Art Library; **25-13A:** akg-images; **25-14:** Return of the Prodigal Son, c. 1668–69 (oil on canvas) by Rembrandt Harmensz. van Rijn (1606–69) Hermitage, St. Petersburg, Russia/The Bridgeman Art Library; **25-15:** © English Heritage Photo Library/The Bridgeman Art Library International; **25-15A:** Rembrandt Harmensz van Rijn (1606–1669) Self-Portrait, 1658. oil on canvas. 52-5/8 in. × 40-7/8 in. (133.67 cm × 103.82 cm) Henry Clay Frick Bequest. Accession number: 1906.1.97; **25-16:** The Pierpont Morgan Library/Art Resource, NY; **25-17:** National Gallery, London/Art Resource, NY; **25-18:** Mauritshuis, The Hague; **25-18A:** Erich Lessing/Art Resource, NY; **25-18B:** View of Delft, c. 1660–61 (oil on canvas), Vermeer, Jan (1632–75)/Mauritshuis, The Hague, The Netherlands/Giraudon/The Bridgeman Art Library; **25-18C:** akg-images; **25-19:** National Gallery of Art; **25-20:** Rijksmuseum, Amsterdam; **25-21:** akg-images; **25-22:** The Bridgeman Art Library International; **25-23:** The Toledo Museum of Art, OH. Purchased with funds from the Libbey Endowment, Gift of Edward Drummond Libbey, 1956.57; **25-24:** © RMN-Grand Palais/Art Resource, NY; **25-25:** © Jonathan Poore/Cengage Learning; **25-26:** © Yann Arthus-Bertrand/Altitude; **25-27:** Massimo Listri/Corbis; **25-28:** © Fred S. Kleiner 2012; **25-28A:** © Fred S. Kleiner 2012; **25-29:** akg-images/Paul M. R. Maeyaert; **25-30:** © Jonathan Poore/Cengage Learning; **25-31:** Erich Lessing/Art Resource, NY; **25-32:** Nicolas Poussin, French, 1594–1665, Landscape with Saint John on Patmos, 1640, oil on canvas, 100.3 × 136.4 cm, A. A. Munger Collection, 1930.500 post-treatment. Reproduction, The Art Institute of Chicago. **25-32A:** Scala/Art Resource, NY; **25-33:** Photo copyright © Philadelphia Museum of Art, E1950-2-1; **25-34:** Réunion des Musées Nationaux/Art Resource, NY; **25-35:** Erich Lessing/Art Resource, NY; **25-36:** Erich Lessing/Art Resource, NY; **25-37:** Angelo Hornak/Corbis; **25-38:** Angelo Hornak/Corbis.

Chapter 26—Opener: Photo: Katherine Wetzel © Virginia Museum of Fine Arts; **26-1A:** Jason Hawkes/Terra/Corbis; **26-2:** Bildarchiv Monheim/akg-images; **26-3:** Erich Lessing/Art Resource, NY; **26-3A:** Hervé Champollion/akg-images; **26-4:** © Jonathan Poore; **26-5:** John Burge; **26-6:** © Jonathan Poore; **26-6A:** Bildarchiv Monheim/akg-images; **26-6B:** Erich Lessing/Art Resource, NY; **26-7:** Scala/Art Resource, NY; **26-7A:** Musée du Louvre Paris/Gianni Dagli Orti/The Art Archive/Picture Desk; **26-7B:** Bildarchiv Preussischer Kulturbesitz/Art Resource, NY; **26-8:** By kind permission of the Trustees of the Wallace Collection, London. **26-9:** © Wallace Collection, London, UK/The Bridgeman Art Library; **26-10:** Image copyright © The Metropolitan Museum of Art/Art Resource, NY; **26-11:** Scala/Ministero per i Beni e le Attività culturali/Art Resource, NY; **26-11A:** © National Gallery, London/Art Resource, NY; **26-12:** Bridgeman-Giraudon/Art Resource, NY; **26-13:** John Meek/The Art Archive/Picture Desk; **26-14:** Réunion des Musées Nationaux/Art Resource, NY; **26-15:** Musée du Louvre Paris/Gianni Dagli Orti/The Art Archive/Picture Desk; **26-15A:** Erich Lessing/Art Resource, NY; **26-16:** Summerfield Press, Ltd.; **26-17:** The Metropolitan Museum of Art/Art Resource, NY; **26-18:** National Gallery, London//Art Resource, NY; **26-19:** The National Gallery of Art; **26-20:** National Gallery, London, UK/The Bridgeman Art Library; **26-21:** National Gallery of Canada; **26-22:** Photograph © 2011 Museum of Fine Arts, Boston, 30.781; **26-23:** Scala/Art Resource, NY; **26-24:** Portrait of Charles John Crowle (1738–1811) of Crowle Park, c. 1761–62 (oil on canvas), Batoni, Pompeo Girolamo (1708–87)/Louvre, Paris, France/Giraudon/The Bridgeman Art Library; **26-25:** Peter Aprahamian/Corbis; **26-25A:** Electa/akg-images; **26-26:** Réunion des Musées Nationaux/Art Resource, Inc.; **26-27:** Scala/Art Resource, NY; **26-28:** © Jonathan Poore/Cengage Learning; **26-28A:** Bildarchiv Monheim/akg-images; **26-29:** Eric Crichton/Encyclopedia/Corbis; **26-29A:** Bildarchiv Monheim/akg-images; **26-30:** ART on FILE/Corbis Art/Corbis; **26-31:** Thomas Jefferson Foundation; **26-32:** Michael Freeman/Value Art/Corbis; **26-33:** Photo © The Library of Virginia; **26-34:** Smithsonian American Art Museum, Washington, DC/Art Resource, NY.

Chapter 27—Opener: Erich Lessing/Art Resource, NY; **27-2:** © Jonathan Poore/Cengage Learning; **27-2A:** Erich Lessing/Art Resource, NY; **27-3:** RMN-Grand Palais/Art Resource, NY; **27-3A:** RMN-Grand Palais/Art Resource, NY; **27-3B:** Erich Lessing/Art Resource, NY; **27-4:** Scala/Ministero per i Beni e le Attività culturali/Art Resource, NY; **27-5:** RMN-Grand Palais/Art Resource,

NY; **27-6:** RMN-Grand Palais/Art Resource, NY; **27-6A:** RMN-Grand Palais/Art Resource, NY; **27-7:** RMN-Grand Palais/Art Resource, NY; **27-8:** Réunion des Musées Nationaux/Art Resource, NY; **27-9:** The Nightmare, 1781 (oil on canvas), Fuseli, Henry (Fussli, Johann Heinrich) (1741–1825)/Detroit Institute of Arts, USA/Founders Society purchase with Mr. and Mrs. Bert L. Smokler/and Mr. and Mrs. Lawrence A. Fleischman funds/The Bridgeman Art Library; **27-10:** The Pierpont Morgan Library/Art Resource, NY; **27-11:** The Metropolitan Museum of Art/Art Resource, NY; **27-11A:** Erich Lessing/Art Resource, NY; **27-12:** The Art Archive/Museo del Prado Madrid/Gianni Dagli Orti; **27-13:** Erich Lessing/Art Resource, NY; **27-13A:** Bridgeman-Giraudon/Art Resource, NY; **27-14:** RMN-Grand Palais/Art Resource, NY; **27-15:** RMN-Grand Palais/Art Resource, NY; **27-15A:** Erich Lessing/Art Resource, NY; **27-16:** RMN-Grand Palais/Art Resource, NY; **27-16A:** The Art Archive/Musée d'Orsay Paris/Gianni Dagli Orti/Picture Desk; **27-17:** Erich Lessing/Art Resource, NY; **27-18:** © Jonathan Poore/Cengage Learning; **27-18A:** Sharon Adams Poore; **27-19:** Bildarchiv Preussischer Kulturbesitz/Art Resource, NY; **27-20:** Friedrich, Caspar David (1774–1840), Der Wanderer über dem Nebelmeer, ca. 1817. Oil on canvas. Bildarchiv Preussischer Kulturbesitz/Art Resource, NY; **27-21:** National Gallery, London/Art Resource, NY; **27-22:** Photography © 2011 Museum of Fine Arts, Boston, 99.22; **27-23:** The Metropolitan Museum of Art/Art Resource, NY; **27-24:** Smithsonian American Art Museum, Washington, DC/Art Resource, NY; **27-25:** Image © The Cleveland Museum of Art Frederic Edwin Church (American, 1826–1900). Twilight in the Wilderness, 1860. Oil on canvas, 101.6 × 162.6 cm. © The Cleveland Museum of Art. Mr. and Mrs. William H. Marlatt Fund, 1965.233; **27-26:** The Stone Breakers, 1849 (oil on canvas) (destroyed in 1945), Courbet, Gustave (1819–77)/Galerie Neue Meister, Dresden, Germany/© Staatliche Kunstsammlungen Dresden/The Bridgeman Art Library; **27-27:** Erich Lessing/Art Resource, NY; **27-28:** RMN-Grand Palais/Art Resource, NY; **27-29:** Yale University Art Gallery/Art Resource, NY; **27-30:** The Metropolitan Museum of Art/Art Resource, NY; **27-31:** The Metropolitan Museum of Art/Art Resource, NY; **27-32:** Erich Lessing/Art Resource, NY; **27-33:** Scala/Art Resource, NY; **27-33A:** Nymphs and Satyr, 1873 (oil on canvas), Bouguereau, William-Adolphe (1825–1905)/Sterling & Francine Clark Art Institute, Williamstown, Massachusetts, USA/The Bridgeman Art Library; **27-34:** bpk, Berlin/Hamburger Kunsthalle, Hamburg, Germany/Elke Walford/Art Resource, NY; **27-35:** The Metropolitan Museum of Art/Art Resource, NY; **27-36:** The Philadelphia Museum of Art/Art Resource, NY; **27-37:** Photograph © 2014 Museum of Fine Arts, Boston, 19.124; **27-38:** Art Resource, NY; **27-39:** The Granger Collection, NYC. All rights reserved; **27-40:** Tate, London/Art Resource, NY; **27-41:** Tate, London/Art Resource, NY; **27-41A:** © Jonathan Poore; **27-42:** © Jonathan Poore; **27-43:** Andrew Aitchison/Alamy; **27-43A:** Leo Sorel; **27-44:** Roger Antrobus/Terra/Corbis; **27-45:** © Jonathan Poore/Cengage Learning; **27-46:** LOOK-foto/SuperStock; **27-46A:** Dennis Hallinan/Alamy; **27-47:** Crystal Palace, Sydenham, c. 1862 (colour litho), Martinet, Achille-Louis (1806–77)/Private Collection/The Stapleton Collection/The Bridgeman Art Library; **27-48:** Louis Daguerre/Time & Life Pictures/Getty Images; **27-49:** Massachusetts General Hospital Archives and Special Collections, Boston; **27-49A:** Nadar (1820–1910) elevating Photography to the height of Art, published 1862 (litho), Daumier, Honore (1808–79)/Private Collection/The Stapleton Collection/The Bridgeman Art Library; **27-50:** Nadar/Bettmann/Corbis; **27-51:** Courtesy George Eastman House; **27-52:** New York Public Library/Art Resource, NY; **27-53:** Courtesy George Eastman House; **28-2:** Erich Lessing/Art Resource, NY.

Chapter 28—Opener: A Bar at the Folies-Bergere, 1881–82 (oil on canvas), Manet, Edouard (1832–83)/© Samuel Courtauld Trust, The Courtauld Gallery, London, UK/The Bridgeman Art Library; **28-2A:** Claude Monet, French, 1840–1926, On the Bank of the Seine, Bennecourt, 1868, oil on canvas, 32 1/16 × 39 5/8 in. (81.5 × 100.7 cm), Potter Palmer Collection, 1922.427 Reproduction, The Art Institute of Chicago. **28-2B:** Neue Pinakothek/Bayerische Staatsgemaeldesammlungen/Art Resource, NY; **28-3:** The Metropolitan Museum of Art/Art Resource, NY; **28-4:** Erich Lessing/Art Resource, NY; **28-5:** Photography © The Art Institute of Chicago, 1964.336; **28-6:** Digital Image © 2009 Museum Associates/LACMA/Art Resource, NY; **28-7:** RMN-Grand Palais/Art Resource, NY; **28-8:** © Culture and Sport Glasgow (Museums); **28-9:** RMN-Grand Palais/Art Resource, NY; **28-10:** RMN-Grand Palais/Art Resource, NY; **28-11:** Nocturne in Black and Gold, the Falling Rocket, 1875 (oil on panel), Whistler, James Abbott McNeill (1834–1903)/Detroit Institute of Arts, USA/Gift of Dexter M. Ferry Jr./The Bridgeman Art Library; **28-12:** Photography © The Art Institute of Chicago, 1910.2; **28-13:** Summer's Day, 1879 (oil on canvas), Morisot, Berthe (1841–95)/National Gallery, London, UK/The Bridgeman Art Library; **28-13A:** Photo © The Norton Simon Art Foundation; **28-14:** Photography © The Art Institute of Chicago, 1928.610; **28-15:** Jane Avril, 1893 (litho), Toulouse-Lautrec, Henri de (1864–1901)/San Diego Museum of Art, USA/Gift of the Baldwin M. Baldwin Foundation/The Bridgeman Art Library; **28-16:** The Art Institute of Chicago; **28-17:** Helen Birch Bartlett Memorial Collection, 1926.224, The Art Institute of Chicago. Photography © The Art Institute of Chicago; **28-17A:** The Potato Eaters, 1885 (oil on canvas), Gogh, Vincent van (1853–90)/Van Gogh Museum, Amsterdam, The Netherlands/De Agostini Picture Library/The Bridgeman Art Library; **28-17B:** Hermann Buresch/bpk, Berlin/Van Gogh Museum/Art Resource, NY; **28-18:** Yale University Art Gallery/Art Resource, NY; **28-19:** Digital Image © The Museum of Modern Art/Licensed by SCALA/Art Resource, NY; **28-20:** National Galleries of Scotland, Dist./RMN-Grand Palais/Art Resource, NY; **28-21:** Photograph © 2011 Museum of Fine Arts, Boston, 36.270; **28-22:** Photograph © Philadelphia Museum of Art, E1936-1-1; **28-23:** Photography © The Art Institute of Chicago, 1926.252; **28-23A:** The Philadelphia Museum of Art/Art Resource, NY; **28-24:** Photography © The Art Institute of Chicago, 1922.445; **28-25:** akg-images; **28-25A:** RMN-Grand Palais/Art Resource, NY; **28-26:** © The Kröller-Müller Foundation, Otterlo; **28-27:** Digital Image © The Museum of Modern Art/Licensed by SCALA/Art Resource, NY; **28-27A:** The Museum of Modern Art/SCALA/Art Resource, NY; **28-28:** Christ's Triumphant Entry into Brussels, 1888 (oil on canvas), Ensor, James (1860–1949)/J. Paul Getty Museum, Los Angeles, USA/© DACS/Giraudon/The Bridgeman Art Library; **28-28A:** Victoria & Albert Museum, London/Art Resource, NY; **28-29:** © 2011 The Munch Museum/The Munch-Ellingsen Group/Artists Rights Society (ARS), NY. Photo: © Erich Lessing/Art Resource, NY; **28-30:** Erich Lessing/Art Resource, NY; **28-31:** The Metropolitan Museum of Art/Art Resource, NY; **28-32:** The Metropolitan Museum of Art/Art Resource, NY; **28-32A:** The Dance, 1868 (stone), Carpeaux, Jean-Baptiste (1827–75)/Musee d'Orsay, Paris, France/Giraudon/The Bridgeman Art Library; **28-33:** © RMN-Grand Palais/Art Resource, NY; **28-33A:** © Vanni Archive/Art Resource, NY; **28-34:** The Gates of Hell, 1880–90 (bronze), Rodin, Auguste (1840–1917)/Musee Rodin, Paris, France/Peter Willi/The Bridgeman Art Library; **28-35:** Erich Lessing/Art Resource, NY; **28-35A:** Smithsonian American Art Museum, Washington, DC/Art Resource, NY; **28-36:** Massimo Listri/Fine Art/Corbis; **28-37:** © Culture and Sport Glasgow (Museums); **28-38:** SOFAM; **28-38A:** © 2009 SOFAM Architect V. Horta, Photo Bastin and Evrard sprl.; **28-38B:** The Metropolitan Museum of Art/Art Resource, NY; **28-39:** Pixtal/SuperStock; **28-40:** © Jonathan Poore/Cengage Learning; **28-41:** Chicago Architectural Photographing Company; **28-42:** Thomas A. Heinz/Fine Art/Corbis; **28-42A:** ART on FILE/Terra/Corbis; **28-43:** Hedrich Blessing Collection/Archive Photos/Chicago History Museum/Getty Images.

Chapter 29—Opener: © 2014 Estate of Pablo Picasso/Artists Rights Society (ARS), New York, Digital Image © The Museum of Modern Art/Licensed by SCALA/Art Resource; **29-2:** © 2014 Succession H. Matisse, Paris/Artists Rights Society (ARS), NY. Photo © San Francisco Museum of Modern Art; **29-2A:** © 2014 Succession H. Matisse/Artists Rights Society (ARS), New York. Photograph: © The Bridgeman Art Library; **29-3:** © 2014 Succession H. Matisse/Artists Rights Society (ARS). Photograph © Succession H. Matisse; **29-4:** © 2011 Artists Rights Society (ARS), NY/ADAGP, Paris. Photo: National Gallery of Art, Washington, John Hay Whitney Collection 1982.76.4; **29-5:** Erich Lessing/Art Resource, NY; **29-6:** Digital Image © The Museum of Modern Art/Licensed by SCALA/Art Resource, NY; **29-7:** © 2011 Artists Rights Society (ARS), New York/ADAGP, Paris. Photo: © Solomon R. Guggenheim Museum; **29-8:** Oeffentliche Kunstsammlung Basel, photo Martin Bühler; **29-9:** © 2011 Artist's Rights Society (ARS), New York/VG Bild-Kunst, Bonn. Photo: © Erich Lessing/Art Resource, NY; **29-9A:** akg-images; **29-9B:** © Burstein Collection/Corbis Art/Corbis; **29-10:** © Art Resource, NY; **29-10A:** © 2012 Estate of Pablo Picasso/Artists Rights Society (ARS), New York; **29-11:** Pablo Picasso, Gertrude Stein, 1906, Oil on canvas, H. 39-3/8 × W. 32 in. (100 × 81.3 cm). Image copyright © The Metropolitan Museum of Art/Art Resource, NY. Art © 2011 Estate of Pablo Picasso/Artists Rights Society (ARS), New York; **29-12:** © 2011 Licensed by Artist's Rights Society (ARS), NY. Photo: © Réunion des Musées Nationaux/Art Resource, NY; **29-13:** © 2011 Artists Rights Society (ARS), NY/ADAGP, Paris. Photo: © Bridgeman-Giraudon/Art Resource, NY; **29-14:** © 2011 Estate of Pablo Picasso. Licensed by Artist's Rights Society (ARS), NY. Photo: © Réunion des Musées Nationaux/Art Resource, NY; **29-15:** © 2011 Artists Rights Society (ARS), NY/ADAGP, Paris. Bottle, Newspaper Pipe and Glass, 1913 (charcoal and collage on paper), Braque, Georges (1882–1963)/Private Collection/The Bridgeman Art Library; **29-16:** © 2011 Estate of Pablo Picasso/Artists Rights Society (ARS), NY. Photo: © Erich Lessing/Art Resource, NY; **29-17:** © 2011 Estate of Pablo Picasso/Artists Rights Society (ARS), NY. Photo: © The Museum of Modern Art/Licensed by SCALA/Art Resource, NY; **29-17A:** © 2011 Estate of Pablo Picasso/Artists Rights Society (ARS), NY. Digital Image © The Museum of Modern Art/Licensed by SCALA/Art Resource, NY; **29-18:** © 2011 Estate of Aleksandr Archipenko/Artists Rights Society (ARS), NY. Photo: The Museum of Modern Art/Licensed by SCALA/Art Resource, NY; **29-18A:** © The Estate of Jacques Lipchitz, courtesy Marlborough Gallery, New York. Photo: Jamison Miller, The Nelson-Atkins Museum of Art; **29-19:** © 2011 Artists Rights Society (ARS), NY/ADAGP, Paris. Photo © The Museum of Modern Art/Licensed by SCALA/Art Resource, NY; **29-20:** © Kunstmuseum Basel, Basel (Emanuel Hoffman Foundation); **29-20A:** © The Art Institute of Chicago; **29-21:** © 2011 Artists Rights Society (ARS), New York/ADAGP, Paris. Photo: © The Philadelphia Museum of Art/Art Resource, NY; **29-21A:** © 2011 Artists Rights Society (ARS), New York/The Museum of Modern Art/Licensed by SCALA/Art Resource, NY; **29-22:** © 2011 Artist's Rights Society (ARS), NY. © DACS/The Bridgeman Art Library; **29-23:** Digital Image © The Museum of Modern Art/Licensed by SCALA/Art Resource, NY; **29-24:** © 2011 Artist's Rights Society (ARS), New York/ADAGP, Paris. Photo: © Richard S. Zeisler Collection, New York/The Bridgeman Art Library; **29-25:** © 2011 Artists Rights Society (ARS), NY Photo Credit: Digital Image © The Museum of Modern Art/Licensed by SCALA/Art Resource, NY; **29-26:** © 2011 Artists Rights Society (ARS), New York/ADAGP, Paris/Succession Marcel Duchamp. Photo: © Philadelphia Museum of Art, 1998-74-1; **29-26A:** © 2011 Artists Rights Society/ADAGP, Paris/Succession Marcel Duchamp. Photo: © Philadelphia Museum of Art. 1950-134-934; **29-27:** © 2011 Artists Rights Society (ARS), New York/ADAGP, Paris/Succession Marcel Duchamp. Photo: © Philadelphia Museum of Art, 1952-98-1; **29-28:** © 2014 Artists Rights Society (ARS), New York/VG Bild-Kunst, Bonn. Digital image: bpk, Berlin/Nationalgalerie, Staatliche Museen, Berlin, Germany/Jörg P. Anders/Art Resource, NY; **29-29:** © 2011 Artists Rights Society, (ARS), NY/VG Bild-Kunst, Bonn. Photo © Yale University Art Gallery/Art Resource, NY;

29-30: Digital Image © The Museum of Modern Art/Licensed by SCALA/Art Resource, NY; **29-30A:** Painterly Architectonics, 1916–17, Popova, Lyubov Sergeevna (1889–1924)/Tretyakov Gallery, Moscow, Russia/The Bridgeman Art Library; **29-31:** The Work of Naum Gabo © Nina & Graham Williams. Photograph by David Heald © The Solomon R. Guggenheim Foundation, NY, 55.1429; **29-32:** Photo © akg-images, © Estate of Vladimir Tatlin; **29-33:** Peter Eberts/Bildarchiv Monheim GmbH/Alamy; **29-34:** © 2011 Artists Rights Society (ARS), NY. Photo: © The Philadelphia Museum of Art/Art Resource, NY; **29-35:** Photo © Philadelphia Museum of Art, 1950-134-59, © 2008 Artists Rights Society (ARS), New York/ADAGP, Paris/Succession Marcel Duchamp; **29-36:** © The Estate of Arthur G. Dove, c/o Terry Dintenfass, Inc. Photograph: The Art Institute of Chicago; **29-37:** © 2012 Man Ray Trust/Artists Rights Society (ARS), NY/ADAGP, Paris. Digital Image © The Museum of Modern Art/Licensed by SCALA/Art Resource, NY; **29-38:** © The Metropolitan Museum of Art Resource, NY; **29-39:** Art © Estate of Stuart Davis/Licensed by VAGA, NY. Digital Image © The Museum of Modern Art/Licensed by SCALA/Art Resource, NY; **29-40:** Fisk University Galleries, University of Tennessee, Nashville; **29-40A:** Aaron Douglas/Art and Artifacts Division, Schomburg Center for Research in Black Culture, The New York Public Library/Art Resource, NY; **29-41:** © 2003 Whitney Museum of American Art; **29-42:** © 2011 Georgia O'Keeffe Museum/Artists Rights Society (ARS), NY. Sheldon Museum of Art. **29-43:** Digital Image © The Museum of Modern Art/Licensed by SCALA/Art Resource, NY; **29-43A:** © 2011 Georgia O'Keeffe Museum/Artist Rights Society (ARS), New York. Reproduction, The Art Institute of Chicago; **29-44:** Photograph by Edward Weston. Collection Center for Creative Photography ©1981 Arizona Board of Regents; **29-44A:** Photograph by Edward Weston. Collection Center for Creative Photography ©1981 Arizona Board of Regents; **29-45:** © 2011 Frank Lloyd Wright Foundation, Scottsdale, AZ/Artists Rights Society (ARS), NY. Photo © Dennis Light/Light Photographic; **29-46:** © 2008 Frank Lloyd Wright Foundation, Scottsdale, AZ/Artists Rights Society (ARS), NY; **29-47:** © Jonathan Poore/Cengage Learning; **29-47A:** Art © Estate of George Grosz/Licensed by VAGA, New York, NY Digital Image © The Museum of Modern Art/Licensed by Scala/Art Resource, NY; **29-48:** Art © Estate of George Grosz. Licensed by VAGA, NY. Photo © The Heckscher Museum of Art, Huntington, NY; **29-49:** © 2011 Artists Rights Society (ARS), NY/VG Bild-Kunst, Bonn. Photo © Erich Lessing/Art Resource, NY; **29-50:** 2010 Artists Rights Society (ARS), New York/VG Bild-Kunst, Bonn/Staatliche Kunstsammlungen, Dresden, Germany//Digital image Erich Lessing/Art Resource, NY; **29-51:** © Ernst Barlach Lizenzverwaltung, GmbH & Co. KG. Photo: akg-images/ullstein bild; **29-52:** © 2011 Estate of Giorgio de Chirico, Licensed by Artist's Rights Society (ARS), NY. Photo: © The Museum of Modern Art/Licensed by SCALA/Art Resource, NY; **29-53:** © 2011 Artists Rights Society (ARS), NY/ADAGP, Paris. Digital Image © The Museum of Modern Art/Licensed by Scala/Art Resource, NY, 00256.37; **29-54:** Staatliche Museen zu Berlin; **29-55:** © 2012 Salvador Dali, Gala-Salvador Dali Foundation/Artists Rights Society (ARS), NY. Digital Image © The Museum of Modern Art/Licensed by Scala/Art Resource, NY, 162.1934; **29-56:** Digital Image © 2009 Museum Associates/LACMA/Art Resource, NY; **29-56A:** The Museum of Modern Art/Licensed by SCALA/Art Resource, NY; **29-57:** © 2011 Artist's Right's Society (ARS), NY/ProLitteris, Zürich. Digital Image © The Museum of Modern Art/Licensed by SCALA/Art Resource, NY; **29-58:** © 2011 Successió Miró/Artists Rights Society (ARS), NY/ADAGP, Paris. Digital Image © The Museum of Modern Art/Licensed by Scala/Art Resource, NY, 229.1937; **29-59:** © 2011 Artists Rights Society (ARS), NY/VG-Bild Kunst, Bonn. Digital Image © The Museum of Modern Art/Licensed by Scala/Art Resource, NY, 564.1939; **29-60:** © 2011 Artists Rights Society (ARS), New York; Photo: Digital Image © The Museum of Modern Art/Licensed by SCALA/Art Resource, NY; **29-61:** © 2011 Mondrian/Holtzman Trust c/o HCR International, VA, USA; **29-61A:** The Philadelphia Museum of Art/Art Resource, NY; **29-62:** © 2012 Artists Rights Society (ARS), NY/ADAGP, Paris. © Philadelphia Museum of Art/Corbis, 1950-134-14, 15; **29-63:** © Bowness, Hepworth Estate. Photo © Tate, London/Art Resource, NY; **29-64:** Photograph © 1985 The Detroit Institute of Arts, © Reproduced by permission of The Henry Moore Foundation; **29-65:** Art © Estate of Vera Mukhina/RAO, Moscow/VAGA, NY Photo © Gregor Schmid/Corbis; **29-66:** Florian Monheim/Bildarchiv Monheim GmbH/Alamy; **29-67:** © Jonathan Poore/Cengage Learning; **29-67A:** Digital Image © The Museum of Modern Art/Licensed by Scala/Art Resource, NY; **29-67B:** © 2011 Artists Rights Society (ARS), New York/PICTORIGHT, Amsterdam. Photograph: © Bauhaus-Archiv Museum für Gestaltung, Berlin; **29-68:** © 2011 Artists Rights Society (ARS), NY/VG Bild-Kunst, Bonn. Digital Image © The Museum of Modern Art/Licensed by Scala/Art Resource, NY; **29-69:** © Jonathan Poore/Cengage Learning; **29-70:** Photography © The Art Institute of Chicago, 1942.51, Estate of Edward Hopper © The Whitney Museum of American Art; **29-71:** © 2011 The Jacob and Gwendolyn Lawrence Foundation, Seattle/Artists Rights Society (ARS), NY. Photo: The Phillips Collection, Washington, DC; **29-72:** Art © Figge Art Museum, successors to the Estate of Nan Wood Graham/Licensed by VAGA, New York, NY Photography © The Art Institute of Chicago,1930.934; **29-73:** Art © T. H. Benton and R. P. Benton Testamentary Trusts/UMB Bank Trustee/Licensed by VAGA, New York, NY. Photo © Lloyd Grotjan/Full Spectrum Photo, Jefferson City; **29-74:** © 2011 Orozco Valladares Family/SOMAAP, Mexico. Artists Rights Society (ARS). Photograph: Hood Museum of Art, Dartmouth College; **29-75:** © 2011 Banco de México Trust. Licensed by Artist's Rights Society (ARS), NY. Dirk Bakker, photographer for the Detroit Institute of Arts/The Bridgeman Art Library; **29-75A:** © D. R. Rufino Tamayo/Herederos/Mexico/2011. Fundacion Olga y Rufino Tamayo A.C. Photo: © 2009 Museum Associates/LACMA/Art Resource, NY; **29-76:** © 2011 Banco de México Trust. Licensed by Artists Rights Society (ARS), NY. Photo © Schalkwijk/Art Resource, NY; **29-77:** Courtesy The Dorothea Lange Collection, The Oakland Museum of California; **29-78:** Margaret Bourke-White/Time & Life Pictures/Getty Images; **29-79:** © 2011 Estate of Alexander Calder/Artists Rights Society (ARS), NY. Digital Image © The Museum of Modern Art/Licensed by Scala/Art Resource, NY, 590.1939 a-d; **29-80:** Peter Cook/VIEW View Pictures/Newscom.

Chapter 30—Opener: © Fred S. Kleiner; **30-2:** © 2011 Artists Rights Society (ARS), NY/ADAGP, Paris. Photo: © Des Moines Art Center; **30-3:** © 2011 The Estate of Francis Bacon/ARS, NY/DACS, London. Digital Image © The Museum of Modern Art/Licensed by Scala/Art Resource, NY, 229.1948; **30-3A:** © 2011 The Estate of Francis Bacon. All rights reserved/ARS, New York/DACS, London. Photograph by Bob Hashimoto. Reproduction, The Art Institute of Chicago; **30-4:** © 2011 Artists Rights Society (ARS), NY/ADAGP, Paris. Photo © Tate Gallery, London/Art Resource, NY; **30-4A:** Gerhard Richter Studio; **30-5:** © 2014 The Arshile Gorky Foundation/The Artists Rights Society (ARS), New York. Photograph: © The Museum of Modern Art/Licensed by SCALA/Art Resource, NY; **30-6:** © 2011 The Pollock-Krasner Foundation/Artists Rights Society (ARS), NY. Photo © National Gallery of Art, 1976.37.1; **30-7:** Courtesy Center for Creative Photography, University of Arizona © 1991 Hans Namuth Estate; **30-7A:** © 2011 Pollock-Krasner Foundation/Artists Rights Society (ARS), New York. Photograph: © The Whitney Museum of American Art; **30-8:** © 2011 The Willem de Kooning Foundation/Artists Rights Society (ARS), NY. Digital Image © The Museum of Modern Art/Licensed by Scala/Art Resource, NY, 478.1953; **30-9:** © Estate of Joan Mitchell Photograph: © Butler Institute of American Art, Youngstown, OH, USA/Gift of Marilynn Meeker, 1986 Courtesy of the Joan Mitchell Foundation, NYC/The Bridgeman Art Library International; **30-9A:** © 2011 The Franz Kline Estate/Artists Rights Society (ARS), New York. Photograph: Whitney Museum of American Art, New York; **30-9B:** Albright-Knox Art Gallery/Art Resource, NY. Art © Dedalus Foundation/Licensed by VAGA, New York, NY; **30-9C:** © 2011 Susan Rothenberg/Artists Rights Society (ARS), NY. Photo: Susan Rothenberg, Tattoo, 1979. Acrylic paint on canvas, 5' 7" × 8' 7". Collection Walker Art Center, Minneapolis. Purchased with the aid of funds from Mr. and Mrs. Edmond R. Ruben, Mr. and Mrs. Julius E. Davis, the Art Center Acquisition Fund, and the National Endowment for the Arts, 1979; **30-10:** Digital Image © The Museum of Modern Art/Licensed by Scala/Art Resource, NY, 240.1969, © 2008 Barnett Newman Foundation/Artists Rights Society (ARS), NY; **30-11:** © 2011 Kate Rothko Prizel & Christopher Rothko. Licensed by Artists Rights Society (ARS), NY. Photo: © San Francisco Museum of Modern Art; **30-12:** © Ellsworth Kelly, photo Philipp Scholz Rittermann; **30-13:** © 2011 Frank Stella/Artists Rights Society (ARS), NY. Photo © CNAC/MNAM/Dist. Réunion des Musées Nationaux/Art Resource, NY; **30-14:** Helen Frankenthaler, The Bay, 1963 (acrylic on canvas), 205.1 × 207.7 cm, Detroit Institute of Arts, USA/© DACS/Founders Society Purchase, Dr. & Mrs. Hilbert H. DeLawter Fund/The Bridgeman Art Library International. Art © 2011 Helen Frankenthaler/Artists Rights Society (ARS), New York; **30-15:** Solomon R. Guggenheim Museum, NY, 64.1685; **30-16:** The Museum of Modern Art/Licensed by SCALA/Art Resource, NY. © Bridget Riley 2014. All rights reserved, courtesy Karsten Schubert, London; **30-17:** Hirshhorn Museum and Sculpture Garden, Smithsonian Institution. Photo: Lee Stalsworth. Art: Estate of David Smith/Licensed by VAGA, New York, NY; **30-18:** © 2011 Estate of Tony Smith/Artists Rights Society (ARS), NY. Digital Image © The Museum of Modern Art/Licensed by Scala/Art Resource, NY, 333.1998; **30-19:** Art © Judd Foundation/Licensed by VAGA, NY Hirshhorn Museum and Sculpture Garden, Smithsonian Institution, photo Lee Stalsworth, 72.154; **30-19A:** Photography © The Art Institute of Chicago, © 2008 The Estate of Eva Hesse/Galerie Hauser & Wirth, Zürich; **30-20:** © 2012 Estate of Louise Nevelson/Artists Rights Society (ARS), NY. Photo © CNAC/MNAM/Dist. Réunion des Musées Nationaux/Art Resource, NY; **30-21:** Art © Louise Bourgeois Trust/Licensed by VAGA, New York, NY Photo © CNAC/MNAM/Dist. Réunion des Musées Nationaux/Art Resource, NY; **30-22:** © 2011 ISAMU NOGUCHI Licensed by Artist's Rights Society (ARS), New York. Collection Walker Art Center, Minneapolis (gift of the artist, 1978); **30-23:** © 2011 Artists Rights Society (ARS), NY/DACS, London. Photo © The Bridgeman Art Library; **30-24:** Art © Jasper Johns/Licensed by VAGA, New York, NY Photo:Whitney Museum of American Art, New York, USA/© DACS/The Bridgeman Art Library; **30-25:** Art © Estate of Robert Rauschenberg/Licensed by VAGA, New York, NY. Digital Image © The Museum of Modern Art/Licensed by SCALA/Art Resource, NY; **30-26:** © Estate of Roy Lichtenstein; **30-27:** © The Whitney Museum of American Art, New York, Photograph by Geoffrey Clements, © 2012 The Andy Warhol Foundation for the Visual Arts, Inc./Artists Rights Society (ARS), New York; **30-27A:** © 2012 The Andy Warhol Foundation for the Visual Arts, Inc./Artists Rights Society (ARS), New York Photo: © Tate Gallery, London/Art Resource, NY; **30-27B:** Art © Estate of George Segal/Licensed by VAGA, New York, NY Photo:National Gallery of Canada, Ottawa; **30-28:** Digital Image © The Museum of Modern Art/Licensed by SCALA/Art Resource, NY; **30-29:** Art © Copyright 1969 Claes Oldenburg. Photo: © 2009 Fred S. Kleiner; **30-29A:** © 2011 Niki Charitable Art Foundation. All rights reserved/ARS, NY/ADAGP, Paris. Photograph: © Whitney Museum of American Art, New York; **30-30:** © Audrey Flack, Collection of The University of Arizona Museum of Art & Archive of Visual Arts, Tucson; Museum Purchase with Funds Provided By the Edward J. Gallagher, Jr. Memorial Fund; **30-31:** Close, Chuck Big Self Portrait 1967–68, acrylic on canvas. Collection Walker Art Center Minneapolis. Art Center Acquisition Fund, 1969; **30-32:** © Lucian Freud. Licensed by Goodman Derrick, LLP. Photo: © Tate, London/Art Resource, NY; **30-33:** Art © Estate of Duane Hanson/Licensed by VAGA, New York, NY Photo by Anne Gold; **30-34:** Reproduced with permission of the Minor White Archive,

Princeton University Art Museum. © Trustees of Princeton University. Digital Image © The Museum of Modern Art/Licensed by SCALA/Art Resource, NY; **30-35:** © 2011 Judy Chicago. Licensed by Artists Rights Society (ARS), NY. Photo: © The Brooklyn Museum; **30-36:** Miriam Schapiro, courtesy Flomenhaft Gallery, NY; **30-37:** Cindy Sherman, courtesy the artist and Metro Pictures; **30-37A:** © Marsie, Emanuelle, Damon and Andrew Scharlatt/Licensed by VAGA, New York, NY. Digital file Courtesy Ron Feldman Fine Arts, New York; **30-38:** © The Estate of Ana Mendieta Collection Courtesy Galerie Lelong, New York; **30-39:** Magdalena Abakanowicz, courtesy Marlborough Gallery, NY; **30-40:** © Jonathan Poore/Cengage Learning; **30-41:** © 2012 Artists Rights Society (ARS), New York/ADAGP, Paris/F.L.C./Photo by Jonathan Poore/Cengage Learning; **30-42:** © 2012 Artists Rights Society (ARS), New York/ADAGP, Paris/F.L.C. Photo: © Francis G. Mayer/CORBIS; **30-42A:** © Jonathan Poore; **30-43 bottom:** © Randy Duchaine/Alamy; **30-43 top:** Photo © Dmitri Kessel/Time & Life Pictures/Getty Images; **30-44:** age fotostock/SuperStock; **30-45:** © Jonathan Poore/Cengage Learning; **30-46:** Alan Schein Photography/Surf/Corbis; **30-47:** Smallbones/Wikimedia Commons; **30-48:** Ambient Images Inc./Alamy; **30-49:** dk/Alamy; **30-50:** © Jonathan Poore/Cengage Learning; **30-51:** Art © Estate of Robert Smithson/Licensed by VAGA, New York, NY//Photo © George Steinmetz/Corbis; **30-52:** © 2011 Carolee Schneemann/Artists Rights Society (ARS), NY. Photo © Al Geise, Courtesy PPOW Gallery; **30-53:** Photo: © Ute Klophaus. ARS; **30-54:** © 2011 Artists Rights Society (ARS), NY/ADAGP, Paris Photo Credit: Digital Image © The Museum of Modern Art/Licensed by SCALA/Art Resource, NY; **30-55:** Digital Image © The Museum of Modern Art/Licensed by SCALA/Art Resource, NY; **30-56:** Jean Baptiste Lacroix/WireImage; **30-56A:** Ted Thai/Time & Life Pictures/Getty Images; **30-57:** Courtesy Nam June Paik Studios, Inc.; **30-58:** 1979 David Em.

Chapter 31—Opener: Courtesy artist Jaune Quick-to-See Smith (Salish member of the Confederated Salish and Kootenai Nation, MT, and The Accola Griefen Gallery, New York). Digital Photo: Chrysler Museum of Art; **31-2:** Napoleon Leading the Army Over the Alps © Kehinde Wiley Studio. Used by Permission; **31-2A:** Smithsonian American Art Museum, Washington, DC/Art Resource, NY; **31-3:** The Broad Art Foundation, Santa Monica Photography credit: Douglas M. Parker Studio, Los Angeles; **31-4:** © 1983 Faith Ringgold; **31-4A:** Lorna Simpson; **31-5:** Art: Courtesy of the artist and Jack Shainman Gallery, NY. Photo: Brooklyn Museum of Art, New York, USA/Caroline A.L. Pratt Fund/The Bridgeman Art Library International; **31-6:** COPYRIGHT: BARBARA KRUGER. COURTESY: MARY BOONE GALLERY, NEW YORK; **31-6A:** Copyright © 1988 Guerrilla Girls, courtesy www.guerrillagirls.com; **31-7:** Self-Portrait, 1980 © Copyright The Robert Mapplethorpe Foundation. Courtesy Art + Commerce; **31-8:** Courtesy of the Estate of David Wojnarowicz and P.P.O.W. Gallery, NY; **31-9:** © Shahzia Sikander. Photograph: Sheldan C. Collins, courtesy Whitney Museum of American Art; **31-10:** © Chris Ofili, courtesy Chris Ofili-Afroco and Victoria Miro Gallery, photo by Stephen White; **31-11:** Allegiance with Wakefulness, 1994 (offset print), Neshat, Shirin (b. 1957)/84 × 105 cm/The Israel Museum, Jerusalem, Israel/Anonymous gift, New York/to American Friends of the Israel Museum/The Bridgeman Art Library; **31-11A:** Meteorological Service of New Zealand Ltd. Collection, Wellington; **31-12:** © Krzysztof Wodcizko Courtesy Galerie Lelong, New York; **31-13:** © Edward Burtynsky, courtesy Nicholas Metivier, Toronto/Howard Greenberg & Bryce Wolkowitz, New York; **31-14:** Art © Estate of Leon Golub/Licensed by VAGA, New York, NY Courtesy Ronald Feldman Gallery; **31-14A:** Courtesy of Koplin Del Rio Gallery, Culver City, CA; **31-15:** Photograph by Martha Rosler, Represented by Mitchell-Innes & Nash, NYC; **31-16:** Marlborough Gallery in NY; **31-17:** Willie Bester; **31-17A:** © CNAC/MNAM/Dist. RMN-Grand Palais/Art Resource, NY; **31-18:** Trigo Piula; **31-19:** Bloodline: Big Family, No. 2, 1995 (oil on canvas), Zhang Xiaogang (b. 1958)/Private Collection/Photo © Christie's Images/The Bridgeman Art Library; **31-20:** Copyright © Xu Bing, courtesy Chazen Museum of Art (formerly Elvehjem Museum of Art), University of Wisconsin; **31-21:** Artwork © Jenny Saville; **31-22:** Photo © Whitney Museum of American Art, © Kiki Smith; **31-22A:** Art © The Keith Haring Foundation. Photo © Jonathan Poore/Cengage Learning; **31-22B:** Art © Estate of Robert Arneson/Licensed by VAGA, NY Photo: San Francisco Museum of Modern Art; **31-23:** Museum of Contemporary Art, Chicago © Jeff Koons; **31-24:** Art © Marisol Escobar/Licensed by VAGA, New York, NY; **31-24A:** Mark Tansey, courtesy Gagosian Gallery, NY; **31-25:** © Anselm Kiefer. Courtesy Gagosian Gallery. Photography by Robert McKeever. © Philadelphia Museum of Art, 1985-5-1; **31-25A:** Heritage Images, © The British Museum; **31-25B:** Collection of National Heritage Board, Singapore Art Museum; **31-26:** The Broad Art Foundation, Santa Monica; **31-27:** Dallas Museum of Art, Dallas; **31-28:** Collection of Home Insurance Company, New York. Courtesy of the artist; **31-29:** © Fairchild Photo Service/Condé Nast/Corbis; **31-30:** © Tara Donovan. Ace Gallery, Los Angeles, **31-31:** Association de la Jeune Sculpture 1987/2 photo © Serge Goldberg; **31-32:** Digital Image © The Museum of Modern Art/Licensed by SCALA/Art Resource, NY; **31-33:** © 2011 Andreas Gursky/Artists Rights Society (ARS), New York/VG Bild-Kunst, Bonn. Photo, Courtesy Sprüth Magers Berlin London; **31-34:** © 2011 Jenny Holzer/Artists Rights Society (ARS), NY. photograph by David Heald © The Solomon R. Guggenheim Foundation; **31-34A:** Adrian Piper Research Archive; **31-35:** Bill Viola, photo: Kira Perov; **31-36:** Tony Oursler, courtesy of the artist and Metro Pictures, NY; **31-37:** Photograph by David Heald © The Solomon R. Guggenheim Foundation, NY; **31-37A:** © Andy Goldsworthy Courtesy Galerie Lelong, New York; **31-38:** Wolfgang Volz © 1983 Christo; **31-39:** Kokyat Choong/The Image Works; **31-40:** Robert O'Dea/akg-images; **31-41:** © 2011 Richard Serra/Artists Rights Society (ARS), NY. Photo © Burt Roberts, courtesy of Harriet Senie; **31-42:** © Richard T. Nowitz/Corbis; **31-43:** © Colin McPherson/Corbis; **31-44:** Scott Frances/OTTO/Esto; **31-45:** © Jonathan Poore/Cengage Learning; **31-46:** © Jonathan Poore/Cengage Learning; **31-47:** © Jonathan Poore/Cengage Learning; **31-47A:** The Denver Art Museum; **31-48:** 2006 © Joe Sohm/The Image Works; **31-49:** © F1ONLINE digitale Bildagentur GmbH/Alamy; **31-50:** Zaha Hadid Architects; **31-51:** Martin Jones/Ecoscene/Encyclopedia/Corbis; **31-52:** John Gollings/Arcaid/Architecture (RM)/Corbis; **31-53:** View Pictures/Getty Images.

Chapter 32—Opener: Freer Gallery of Art, Smithsonian Institution, Washington, DC, Purchase, F1942.15a; **32-2:** Robert Harding Productions; **32-3:** IndiaPictures/UIG/Getty Images; **32-4:** V&A Images, London/Art Resource, NY; **32-4A:** Museum of Fine Arts, Boston, Francis Bartlett Donation of 1912 and Picture Fund, 14.654. Photograph © 2011 Museum of Fine Arts, Boston; **32-5:** V&A Images, London/Art Resource, NY; **32-6:** Kevin R. Morris/Documentary Value/Corbis; **32-7:** Charles O. Cecil/Alamy; **32-8:** National Museum, New Delhi; **32-8A:** Courtesy of the Trustees of the Chhatrapati Shivaji Maharaj Vastu Sangrahalaya formerly Prince of Wales Museum of Western India, Mumbai. Not to be reproduced without prior permission of the Trustees; **32-9:** F1ONLINE/SuperStock; **32-10:** akg-images; **32-11:** Tony Waltham/Robert Harding Picture Library; **32-12:** The Brooklyn Museum of Art, 87.234.6; **32-12A:** ABANINDRANATH TAGORE, Public Domain; **32-13:** Dr. Ronald V. Wiedenhoeft/Saskia, Ltd.; **32-14:** Stuart Westmorland; **32-15:** Robert Harding Picture Library Ltd/Alamy; **32-16:** Ladislav Janicek/Flame/Corbis; **32-17:** The Metropolitan Museum of Art/Art Resource, NY.

Chapter 33—Opener: Photos12.com; **33-1a:** Best View Stock/Photolibrary; **33-1A:** Freer Gallery of Art, Smithsonian Institution, Washington, DC; **33-1b:** Best View Stock/Getty Images; **33-1c:** Vidler Steve/Prisma Bildagentur AG/Alamy; **33-2:** Collection of the National Palace Museum, Taiwan, Republic of China; **33-3:** Collection of the National Palace Museum, Taiwan, Republic of China; **33-4:** Collection of the National Palace Museum, Taiwan, Republic of China; **33-4A:** Collection of the National Palace Museum, Taiwan, Republic of China; **33-5:** © The Trustees of the British Museum; **33-6:** Best View Stock/Getty Images; **33-7:** Vidler Steve/Prisma Bildagentur AG/Alamy; **33-8:** Michael Snell/Alamy; **33-9:** Best View Stock/Alamy; **33-10:** Victoria & Albert Museum/Art Resource, NY; **33-11:** Cultural Relics Publishing House, Beijing; **33-12:** Collection of the National Palace Museum, Taiwan, Republic of China; **33-12A:** William Rockhill Nelson Trust (46-51/2); **33-13:** Image © Cleveland Museum of Art, Cleveland; **33-14:** Gift of Mr. Robert Allerton, 1957 (2306.1), photo copyright © Honolulu Academy of Arts; **33-15:** Freer and Sackler Galleries of Art: Smithsonian's Museums of Asian Art. Gift of Arthur M. Sackler S1987.204.10; **33-16:** Cultural Relics Publishing House, Beijing; **33-17:** Percival David Foundation of Chinese Art, A821; **33-18:** Photograph by Norbert Miguletz. Exhibited at Schirn Kunsthalle, Frankfurt; **33-19:** Yoshio Tomii/SuperStock; **33-20:** Leeum, Samsung Museum of Art.

Chapter 34—Opener: 1925.2043, Photography © The Art Institute of Chicago; **34-2:** Michael S. Yamashita/Documentary Value/Corbis; **34-3:** TNM Image Archives, Source: http//TNMArchives.jp/; **34-4:** TNM Image Archives, Source: http//TNMArchives.jp/; **34-5:** Steve Vidler/SuperStock; **34-6:** Sakamoto Photo Research Laboratory/Corbis; **34-7:** TNM Image Archives, Source: http//TNMArchives.jp/; **34-8:** Photograph by Oyamazaki Town Office. Haga Library/Lebrecht Music and Arts Photo Library; **34-9:** The AMICA Library at The Cleveland Museum of Art; **34-10:** Lebrecht Music and Arts Photo Library; **34-10A:** Smithsonian Freer Gallery of Art and Arthur M. Sackler Gallery; **34-11:** TNM Image Archives, Source: http//TNMArchives.jp/; **34-12:** custodial by Japanese Agency for Cultural Affairs; **34-12A:** Erich Lessing/Art Resource, NY; **34-13:** Photograph © 2011 Museum of Fine Arts, Boston. 11.17652; **34-14:** Brooklyn Museum 30.1478.30 Gift of Anna Ferris. Museum photograph © 2006 The Brooklyn Museum; **34-15:** Tokyo National University of Fine Arts and Music; **34-16:** Freer Gallery of Art, Smithsonian Institution, Washington, DC, Purchase, F1902.225; **34-17:** AP Photo/Kyodo News; **34-18:** © DEA PICTURE LIBRARY; **34-19:** Copyright: Fujiko Shiraga and the former members of the Gutai Art Association Courtesy: Ashiya City Museum of Art and History.

Chapter 35—Opener: Ronaldo Schemidt/AFP/Getty Images; **35-2:** Facsimile copy of a page of the Borgia codex depicting Death and Life gods placed side by side (colour lithograph), Mixtec (c. 1300–1521) (after)/Private Collection/Jean-Pierre Courau/The Bridgeman Art Library; **35-3:** The Bodleian Libraries, University of Oxford. Shelfmark: MS. Arch. Selden. A.1, fol. 2r; **35-4:** Adapted from an image by Ned Seidler/National Geographic Society; **35-5:** Gianni Dagli Orti/Fine Art/Corbis; **35-6:** Gianni Dagli Orti/Fine Art/Corbis; **35-7:** Illustration of a Quipu, from "Historia y Genealogia Real de los Reyes Incas del Peru, de sus hechos, costumbres, trajes y manera de Gobierno," known as the Codice Murua (vellum), Spanish School, (16th century)/Private Collection/The Bridgeman Art Library; **35-8:** De Agostini Picture Library/Getty Images; **35-9A:** Llama, alpaca and woman, from Lake Titicaca, Bolivia, c. 1475–1532 (silver), Incan/American Museum of Natural History, New York, USA/The Bridgeman Art Library; **35-9 left:** Michael Freeman/Encyclopedia/Corbis; **35-9 right:** © Milton Keiles; **35-10:** Ira Block/National Geographic/Getty Images; **35-11:** The Art Archive/Willard Culver/NGS Image Collection; **35-12:** Arizona State Museum, University of Arizona, photo W. McLennan; **35-13:** Photo © National Museum of Women in the Arts; **35-14 bottom:** Image # 4481, American Museum of Natural History, Library; **35-14 top:** Image # 4480, American Museum of Natural History, Library; **35-15:** Image # PP-10-P0007-35-13, American Museum of Natural History, Library; **35-16:** Museum of Anthropology at the University of British Columbia, photo W. McLennan; **35-16A:** The Art Archive/Neil Setchfield; **35-17:** Southwest Museum of the American Indian Collection, Autry National Center; 761.G.33; **35-18:** The Metropolitan Museum of Art/Art Resource, NY; **35-18A:** Buffalo hide robe with battle scene, Mandan, from the upper Missouri River, North Dakota, ca. 1800. Buffalo hide with deerskin fringe, porcupine quills, and mineral pigments, 8' 6" × 7' 10". Peabody Museum of Archaeology, Harvard University, Cambridge; **35-19:** The Art Archive/Gift of Clara S Peck/Buffalo Bill Center of the West, Cody, Wyoming/Buffalo Bill Center of the West/21.69.37; **35-20:** Collection of Mr. and Mrs. Charles Diker.

Chapter 36—Opener: The National Museum of New Zealand, Wellington; **36-1A:** Werner Forman/Art Resource, NY; **36-2:** Reproduced courtesy Museum of Victoria; **36-3:** Image copyright © The Metropolitan Museum of Art. Image source: Art Resource, NY; **36-4:** NHPA/Photoshot; **36-5:** AA353/3/22 Vyse Collection. F. E. Williams, photographer, South Australian Museum Archives; **36-5A:** Robert Harding Picture Library/SuperStock; **36-6:** abm-Archives Barbier-Mueller, photographer Wolfgang Pulfer; **36-7:** Erich Lessing/Art Resource, NY; **36-8:** Copyright © Otago Museum, Dunedin, New Zealand, D45.179; **36-9:** Musée du Quai Branly/Scala/Art Resource, NY; **36-10:** © Trustees of the British Museum/Art Resource, NY; **36-11:** Bildarchiv Preussischer Kulturbesitz/Art Resource, NY; **36-12:** © The Metropolitan Museum of Art/Art Resource, NY; **36-13:** Stephen Tapply/Alamy; **36-14:** Adrienne Kaeppler; **36-15:** Photo © University of Pennsylvania Museum/153195; **36-16:** akg-images; **36-17:** The Trustees of The British Museum/Art Resource, NY; **36-18:** Reproduced by permission of the University of Cambridge Museum of Archaeology & Anthropology, E 1895.158; **36-19:** Heritage Images/The British Museum; **36-20:** The Trustees of The British Museum/Art Resource, NY; **36-21:** Photo by Seth Joel, Bernice Pauahi Bishop Museum, Honolulu; **36-21A:** The Ngati Awa.

Chapter 37—Opener: The Trustees of the British Museum/Art Resource, NY; **37-2:** The Philadelphia Museum of Art/Art Resource, NY; **37-3:** abm-Archives Barbier-Mueller; **37-4:** Photo by Eliot Elisofon, 1970. Image no. EEPA EECL 7590. Eliot Elisofon Photographic Archives. National Museum of African Art, Smithsonian Institution; **37-5:** Nail figure (nkisi n'kondi) Yombe, Congo (mixed media), African School, (19th Century)/Detroit Institute of Arts, USA/Founders Society Purchase/Eleanor Clay Ford Fund for African Art/The Bridgeman Art Library; **37-6:** © The Metropolitan Museum of Art/Art Resource, NY; **37-7:** The Metropolitan Museum of Art/Art Resource, NY; **37-8:** Photograph by Franko Khoury. National Museum of African Art, Smithsonian Institution; **37-9:** Herbert M. Cole; **37-9A:** Aldo Tutino/Art Resource, NY; **37-10:** Bildarchiv Preussischer Kulturbesitz/Art Resource, NY; **37-11:** © Trustees of the British Museum, London; **37-11A:** Denver Art Museum Collection: Funds from 1996 Collectors' Choice and partial gift of Valerie Franklin; **37-12:** Werner Forman/Art Resource, NY; **37-13:** Musée du Quai Branly/Scala/Art Resource, NY; **37-14:** Photograph by Franko Khoury. National Museum of African Art, Smithsonian Institution; **37-14A:** Herbert M. Cole; **37-15:** Fulvio Roiter/Documentary Value/Corbis; **37-15B:** Photograph by Franko Khoury. National Museum of African Art, Smithsonian Institution; **37-16:** Musée Barbier-Mueller, Geneva; **37-17:** Charles & Josette Lenars/Documentary Value/Corbis; **37-18:** Otto Lang/CORBIS; **37-19:** 2007 Peabody Museum, Harvard University 17-41-50/B1908 T762.1; **37-20:** The Metropolitan Museum of Art. Image source: Art Resource, NY; **37-21:** Yale University Art Gallery/Art Resource, NY; **37-22:** Fowler Museum at UCLA, photo: Don Cole; **37-23:** Photograph by Eliot Elisofon, 1971, EEPA EECL 2139, Eliot Elisofon Photographic Archives, National Museum of African Art, Smithsonian Institution; **37-24:** Owen Franken/Encyclopedia/Corbis; **37-25:** Herbert M. Cole; **37-26:** Natal Museum, Pietermaritzburg, South Africa; **37-27:** Natal Museum, Pietermaritzburg, South Africa; **37-28:** photograph by Philip L. Ravenhill, 1989, EEPA 1989-060346, Eliot Elisofon Photographic Archives, National Museum of African Art, Smithsonian Institution.

Index